Equity and Fixed Income

VEL I
007

CFA® PROGRAM CURRICULUM • VOLUME 5

Cover photograph courtesy of Veer Inc.

Printed in the United States of America

10 9 8 7 6 5 4

ISBN 0-536-16727-3

2005160773

BK/JS

Please visit our web site at *www.pearsoncustom.com*

PEARSON CUSTOM PUBLISHING
75 Arlington Street, Suite 300, Boston, MA 02116
A Pearson Education Company

CONTENTS

$4\frac{5}{8}$ $4\frac{11}{16}$ — $\frac{3}{8}$

$5\frac{1}{2}$ $5\frac{1}{2}$ — $\frac{3}{8}$

$5\frac{1}{2}$ $21\frac{3}{16}$ — $\frac{1}{16}$

$20\frac{5}{8}$ $21\frac{3}{16}$ — $\frac{7}{8}$

$17\frac{3}{8}$ $18\frac{1}{8}$ + $\frac{7}{8}$

$13\frac{1}{2}$ $6\frac{1}{2}$ — $\frac{1}{2}$

$6\frac{1}{2}$ $6\frac{1}{2}$ — $\frac{1}{8}$

$7\frac{1}{4}$ $31\frac{1}{32}$ — $\frac{1}{8}$

$15\frac{1}{16}$

1 $9\frac{1}{16}$ $9\frac{1}{16}$

$9\frac{1}{16}$

$1\frac{9}{32}$

$7\frac{15}{16}$ $7\frac{13}{16}$ $7\frac{15}{16}$

$7\frac{15}{16}$

$2\frac{5}{8}$ $2\frac{11}{32}$ $2\frac{1}{2}$ +

546 $2\frac{3}{4}$ $2\frac{1}{4}$ $2\frac{1}{4}$

327 $2\frac{3}{4}$ $2\frac{1}{4}$ $2\frac{1}{4}$

$51\frac{6}{5}$ $11\frac{3}{8}$ $11\frac{3}{4}$ +

$12\frac{1}{16}$ $11\frac{3}{8}$ $11\frac{3}{4}$ +

87 $33\frac{3}{4}$ 33 $33\frac{1}{8}$ —

602 $25\frac{5}{8}$ $24\frac{9}{16}$ $25\frac{5}{8}$ +

833 12 $11\frac{5}{8}$ $11\frac{7}{8}$ +

16 $10\frac{1}{2}$ $10\frac{1}{2}$ $10\frac{1}{2}$ —

78 $15\frac{7}{8}$ $15\frac{13}{16}$ $15\frac{7}{8}$ —

4608 $9\frac{1}{16}$ $8\frac{1}{4}$ $8\frac{7}{8}$ +

430 $11\frac{1}{4}$ $10\frac{1}{8}$ $10\frac{3}{4}$

HOW TO USE THE CFA PROGRAM CURRICULUM

Congratulations on your decision to enter the Chartered Financial Analyst (CFA®) Program. This exciting and rewarding program of study reflects your desire to become a serious investment professional. You are embarking on a program noted for its requirement of ethics and breadth of knowledge, skills, and abilities.

The credential you seek is respected around the world as a mark of accomplishment and dedication, and each level of the program represents a distinct achievement in professional development. Successful completion of the program is rewarded with membership in a prestigious global community of investment professionals. CFA charterholders are dedicated to life-long learning and maintaining currency with the ever-changing dynamics of a challenging profession.

Curriculum Development

The CFA Program curriculum is grounded in the practice of the investment profession. CFA Institute regularly conducts a practice analysis survey of investment professionals around the world to determine the knowledge, skills, and abilities that are relevant to the profession. The survey results define the Candidate Body of Knowledge (CBOK™), an inventory of knowledge and responsibilities expected of the investment management professional at the level of a new CFA charterholder. The survey also determines how much emphasis each of the major topic areas receives on the CFA examinations.

A committee made up of practicing charterholders, in conjunction with CFA Institute staff, designs the CFA Program curriculum to deliver the CBOK to candidates. The examinations, also written by practicing charterholders, are designed for you to demonstrate mastery of the CBOK as set forth in the CFA Program curriculum. As you structure your personal study program, you should emphasize mastery of the CBOK and the practical application of that knowledge. For more information on the practice analysis, CBOK, and development of the CFA Program curriculum, please visit www.cfainstitute.org/course.

Organization

The 2007 Level I CFA Program curriculum is organized into 10 topic areas. Each topic area begins with a topic level learning outcome that summarizes the broad objective of the material to follow and indicates the depth of knowledge expected. Each topic area is then divided into one or more study sessions, each devoted to a sub-topic (or group of sub-topics) within that topic area. The 2007 Level I curriculum is organized into 18 study sessions. Each study session begins with a purpose statement defining the content structure and objective of that session. Finally, each study session is further divided into reading assignments. *The outline on the inside front cover of each volume should further illustrate this important hierarchy.*

The reading assignments are the basis for all examination questions. The readings are selected or developed specifically to teach candidates the CBOK. Readings are drawn from textbook chapters, professional journal articles, research analyst reports, CFA Program-commissioned content, and cases. Many readings include problems and solutions as well as appendices to help you learn.

Reading-specific Learning Outcome Statements (LOS) are listed in the study session opener page as well as prior to each reading. Reading-specific LOS indicate what you should be able to accomplish after studying the reading. It is important, however, not to interpret LOS narrowly by focusing on a few key sentences in a reading. Readings, particularly CFA Program-commissioned readings, provide context for the learning outcome and enable you to apply a principle or concept in a variety of scenarios. Thus, you should use the LOS to guide and focus your study, as each examination question is based explicitly on one or more LOS. We encourage you to thoroughly review how to properly use LOS and the list and descriptions of commonly used LOS command words at www.cfainstitute.org/toolkit. The command words signal the depth of learning you are expected to achieve from the reading.

Features for 2007

▶ **Required vs. Optional segments** - Several reading assignments use only a portion of the original source textbook chapter or journal article. In order to allow you to read the assignment within its full context, however, we have reprinted the entire chapter or article in the curriculum. When an optional segment begins, you will see an icon. A vertical solid bar in the outside margin will continue until the optional segment ends, symbolized by another icon. Unless the material is specifically noted as optional, you should assume it is required. Keep in mind that the optional material is provided strictly for your convenience and will not be tested. *You should rely on the required segments and the reading-specific LOS in preparing for the examination.*

▶ **Problems/Solutions** - When appropriate, we have developed and assigned problems after readings to demonstrate practical application and reinforce understanding of the concepts presented. The solutions to the problems are provided in an appendix at the back of each volume. Candidates should consider all problems and solutions required material as your ability to solve these problems will prepare you for exam questions.

▶ **Margins** - We have inserted wide margins throughout each volume to allow for easier note taking.

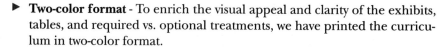

▶ **Two-color format** - To enrich the visual appeal and clarity of the exhibits, tables, and required vs. optional treatments, we have printed the curriculum in two-color format.

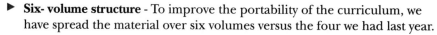

▶ **Six- volume structure** - To improve the portability of the curriculum, we have spread the material over six volumes versus the four we had last year.

▶ **Glossary and Index** - For your convenience, we have printed a comprehensive glossary and index in each volume. Throughout the curriculum, a **bolded blue** word in a reading denotes a glossary term.

Designing your personal study program:

Create a schedule - An orderly, systematic approach to preparation is critical to successful completion of the examination. You should dedicate a consistent block of time every week to reading and studying. Complete all reading assignments and the associated problems and solutions in each study session. Review the LOS both before and after you study each reading to ensure that you have mastered the applicable content and can complete the action(s) specified. Upon completion of each study session, review the session's purpose statement and confirm that you thoroughly understand the subject matter. When you complete a topic area, review the topic level learning outcome and verify that you have mastered the objectives.

CFA Institute estimates that you will need to devote a minimum of 10-15 hours per week for 18 weeks to study the assigned readings. Allow a minimum of one week for each study session spread over several days, with completion scheduled for at least 30-45 days prior to the examination. This schedule will allow you to spend the final four to six weeks before the examination reviewing the assigned material and taking multiple on-line sample examinations. At CFA Institute, we believe that candidates need to commit to a *minimum* of 250 hours reading and reviewing the curriculum and taking online sample exams to master the material. This recommendation, however, may substantially underestimate the hours needed for appropriate exam preparation depending on individual circumstances and academic background.

You will undoubtedly adjust your study time to conform to your own strengths and weaknesses and academic background, and you will probably spend more time on some study sessions than on others. You should allow ample time for both in-depth study of all topic areas and additional concentration on those topic areas for which you feel least prepared.

Preliminary Readings - The reading assignments in Economics and Financial Statement Analysis assume candidates already have a basic mastery of the concepts typically presented in introductory university-level economics and accounting courses. Information on suggested readings to improve your knowledge of these topics precedes these study sessions.

Candidate Preparation Toolkit - We have created the online toolkit to provide a single comprehensive location for resources and guidance for candidate preparation. In addition to in-depth information on study program planning, the CFA Program curriculum, and the online sample exams, the toolkit also contains curriculum errata, printable study session outlines, sample exam questions, and more. We encourage you to use the toolkit as your central preparation resource during your tenure as a candidate. Visit the toolkit at www.cfainstitute.org/toolkit.

Online Sample Exams - After completing your study of the assigned curriculum, use the CFA Institute online sample exams to measure your knowledge of the topics and improve your exam-taking skills. After each question, you will receive immediate feedback noting the correct response and indicating the assigned curriculum for further study. The sample exams are designed by the same people who create the actual CFA exams, and reflect the question formats, topics, and level of difficulty of the actual CFA examinations, in a timed environment. Aggregate data indicate that the CFA examination pass rate was higher among candidates who took one or more online sample examinations than for candidates who did not take the online sample exams. For more information on the online sample exams, please visit www.cfainstitute.org/toolkit.

Review Programs - After you enroll in the CFA Program, you may receive numerous solicitations for preparatory courses and review materials. Although preparatory courses and notes may be helpful to some candidates, you should view these resources as *supplements to the assigned CFA Program curriculum.* The CFA exams reference *only* the 2007 CFA Institute assigned curriculum; no preparatory course or review course materials are consulted or referenced.

Furthermore, CFA Institute does not endorse, promote, review, or warrant the accuracy of the products or services offered by preparatory organizations. CFA Institute does not verify or endorse the pass rates or other claims made by these organizations.

Feedback

At CFA Institute, we are committed to delivering a comprehensive and rigorous curriculum for the development of competent, ethically grounded investment professionals. We rely on candidate and member feedback as we work to incorporate content, design, and packaging improvements. You can be assured that we will continue to listen to your suggestions. Please send any comments or feedback to curriculum@cfainstitute.org. Ongoing improvements in the curriculum will help you prepare for success on the upcoming examinations, and for a lifetime of learning as a serious investment professional.

ANALYSIS OF EQUITY INVESTMENTS

TOPIC LEVEL LEARNING OUTCOME

The candidate should be able to demonstrate a working knowledge of the analysis of equity investments, including securities markets, efficient market theory, the analysis of equity risk and return (for industries and companies), and technical analysis.

4⅝ 4¹¹/₁₆ — ⅜
5½ 5½ — ⅜
5½ 21³/₁₆ — ¼
20⅝ 21³/₁₆ — ⅞
17⅜ 18⅛ + ⅞
13½ 17⅜
6½ 6½ — ½
7¼ 6½ 31/32 — ⅛
15/16
1 9/16 9/16
1⅗/₃₂
7¹⁵/₁₆ 7¹³/₁₆ 7¹⁵/₁₆
2⅝ 2¹¹/₃₂ 2½ +
2¾ 2¼ 2¼
6½ 12¹/₁₆ 11⅜ 11¾ +
87 33¾ 33 33⅛ —
692 25⅝ 24⁹/₁₆ 25⅝ +
833 12 11⅝ 11⅞ +
16 10½ 10½ 10½ —
78 15⅞ 15¹³/₁₆ 15⅞ —
4808 9¹/₁₆ 8¼ 8⅞ +
430 11¼ 10⅛

STUDY SESSION 13
ANALYSIS OF EQUITY INVESTMENTS:
Securities Markets

READING ASSIGNMENTS

This study session addresses how securities are bought and sold and what constitutes a well-functioning securities market. The reading on market indexes offers a solid understanding of how these indexes are constructed and calculated and, therefore, the biases inherent in each of the weighting schemes used.

Some of the most interesting and important work in the investment field during the past several decades revolves around the efficient market hypothesis (EMH) and its implications for active versus passive equity portfolio management. The readings on this subject provide an understanding of the EMH and the seemingly persistent anomalies to the theory, an understanding that is necessary to judge the value of fundamental or technical security analysis.

LEARNING OUTCOMES

Reading 55: Organization and Functioning of Securities Markets

The candidate should be able to:

a. describe the characteristics of a well-functioning securities market;

b. distinguish between competitive bids, negotiated sales, and private placements for issuing bonds;

c. distinguish between primary and secondary capital markets, and explain how secondary markets support primary markets;

d. distinguish between call and continuous markets;

e. compare and contrast the structural differences among national stock exchanges, regional stock exchanges, and the over-the-counter (OTC) markets;

f. compare and contrast major characteristics of exchange markets, including exchange membership, types of orders, and market makers;

g. describe the process of selling a stock short and discuss an investor's likely motivation for selling short;

h. describe the process of buying a stock on margin, compute the rate of return on a margin transaction, define maintenance margin and determine the stock price at which the investor would receive a margin call;

i. discuss major effects of the institutionalization of securities markets.

Reading 56: Security-Market Indexes

The candidate should be able to:

a. discuss the source and direction of bias exhibited by each of the three predominant weighting schemes, and compute a price-weighted, a market-weighted, and an unweighted index series for three stocks;

b. compare and contrast major structural features of domestic and global stock indexes, bond indexes, and composite stock-bond indexes.

Reading 57: Efficient Capital Markets

The candidate should be able to:

a. define an efficient capital market, discuss arguments supporting the concept of efficient capital markets, describe and contrast the forms of the efficient market hypothesis (EMH): weak, semistrong, and strong, and describe the tests used to examine the weak form, the semistrong form, and the strong form of the EMH;

b. identify various market anomalies and explain their implications for the EMH, and explain the overall conclusions about each form of the EMH;

c. explain the implications of stock market efficiency for technical analysis and fundamental analysis, discuss the implications of efficient markets for the portfolio management process and the role of the portfolio manager, and explain the rationale for investing in index funds.

Reading 58: "Market Efficiency and Anomalies"

The candidate should be able to:

a. explain limitations to fully efficient markets;

b. describe the limits of arbitrage to correct anomalies;

c. illustrate why investors should be skeptical of anomalies.

ORGANIZATION AND FUNCTIONING OF SECURITIES MARKETS*

by Frank K. Reilly and Keith C. Brown

LEARNING OUTCOMES

The candidate should be able to:

a. describe the characteristics of a well-functioning securities market;

b. distinguish between competitive bids, negotiated sales, and private placements for issuing bonds;

c. distinguish between primary and secondary capital markets, and explain how secondary markets support primary markets;

d. distinguish between call and continuous markets;

e. compare and contrast the structural differences among national stock exchanges, regional stock exchanges, and the over-the-counter (OTC) markets;

f. compare and contrast major characteristics of exchange markets, including exchange membership, types of orders, and market makers;

g. describe the process of selling a stock short and discuss an investor's likely motivation for selling short;

h. describe the process of buying a stock on margin, compute the rate of return on a margin transaction, define maintenance margin and determine the stock price at which the investor would receive a margin call;

i. discuss major effects of the institutionalization of securities markets.

INTRODUCTION   1

The stock market, the Dow Jones Industrials, and the bond market are part of our everyday experience. Each evening on television news broadcasts we find out how stocks and bonds fared; each morning we read in our daily newspapers about expectations for a market rally or decline. Yet most people have an

---

* The authors acknowledge helpful comments on this reading from Robert Battalio and Paul Schultz of the University of Notre Dame.

Investment Analysis and Portfolio Management, Eighth Edition, by Frank K. Reilly and Keith C. Brown, Copyright © 2005. Reprinted with permission of South-Western, a division of Thomson Learning.

imperfect understanding of how domestic and world capital markets actually function. To be a successful investor in a global environment, you must know what financial markets are available around the world and how they operate.

In this reading we take a broad view of securities markets and provide a detailed discussion of how major stock markets function. We conclude with a consideration of how global securities markets have changed during recent years and probably will change in the near future.

We begin with a discussion of securities markets and the characteristics of a good market. We describe two components of the capital markets primary and secondary. Our main emphasis is on the secondary stock market. We consider the national stock exchanges around the world and how these markets, separated by geography and by time zones, are becoming linked into a 24-hour market. We also consider regional stock markets and the Nasdaq market and provide a detailed analysis of how alternative exchange markets operate, including the Electronic Communication Networks (ECNs). In the final section we consider numerous historical changes in financial markets, additional current changes, and significant future changes expected. These numerous changes in our securities markets will have a profound effect on what investments are available from around the world and how we buy and sell them.

2   WHAT IS A MARKET?

A **market** is the means through which buyers and sellers are brought together to aid in the transfer of goods and/or services. Several aspects of this general definition seem worthy of emphasis. First, a market need not have a physical location. It is only necessary that the buyers and sellers can communicate regarding the relevant aspects of the transaction.

Second, the market does not necessarily own the goods or services involved. For a good market, ownership is not involved; the important criterion is the smooth, cheap transfer of goods and services. In most financial markets, those who establish and administer the market do not own the assets but simply provide a physical location or an electronic system that allows potential buyers and sellers to interact. They help the market function by providing information and facilities to aid in the transfer of ownership.

Finally, a market can deal in any variety of goods and services. For any commodity or service with a diverse clientele, a market should evolve to aid in the transfer of that commodity or service. Both buyers and sellers benefit from the existence of a market.

Characteristics of a Good Market

We will discuss markets for different investments such as stocks, bonds, options, and futures in the United States and throughout the world. We will refer to these markets using various terms of quality such as *strong, active, liquid,* or *illiquid.* There are many financial markets, but they are not all equal—some are active and liquid, others are relatively illiquid and inefficient in their operations. To appreciate these discussions, you should be aware of the following characteristics that investors look for when evaluating the quality of a market.

One enters a market to buy or sell a good or service quickly at a price justified by the prevailing supply and demand. To determine the appropriate price, participants must have timely and accurate information on the volume and prices of past transactions and all currently outstanding bids and offers. Therefore, one attribute of a good market is **timely and accurate information**.

Another prime requirement is **liquidity**, the ability to buy or sell an asset quickly and at a known price—that is, a price not substantially different from the prices for prior transactions, assuming no new information is available. An asset's likelihood of being sold quickly, sometimes referred to as its *marketability,* is a necessary, but not a sufficient, condition for liquidity. The expected price should also be fairly certain, based on the recent history of transaction prices and current bid-ask quotes. For a formal discussion of liquidity, see Handa and Schwartz (1996) and AIMR's articles on *Best Execution and Portfolio Performance* (Jost, 2001).

A component of liquidity is **price continuity**, which means that prices do not change much from one transaction to the next unless substantial new information becomes available. Suppose no new information is forthcoming, and the last transaction was at a price of $20; if the next trade were at $20.10, the market would be considered reasonably continuous.[1] A **continuous market** without large price changes between trades is a characteristic of a liquid market.

A market with price continuity requires *depth,* which means that there are numerous potential buyers and sellers willing to trade at prices above and below the current market price. These buyers and sellers enter the market in response to changes in supply, demand, or both and thereby prevent drastic price changes. In summary, liquidity requires marketability and price continuity, which, in turn, requires depth.

Another factor contributing to a good market is the transaction cost. Lower costs (as a percent of the value of the trade) make for a more efficient market. An individual comparing the cost of a transaction between markets would choose a market that charges 2 percent of the value of the trade compared with one that charges 5 percent. Most microeconomic textbooks define an efficient market as one in which the cost of the transaction is minimal. This attribute is referred to as *internal efficiency.*

Finally, a buyer or seller wants the prevailing market price to adequately reflect all the information available regarding supply and demand factors in the market. If such conditions change as a result of new information, the price should change accordingly. Therefore, participants want prices to adjust quickly to new information regarding supply or demand, which means that prevailing market prices reflect all available information about the asset. This attribute is referred to as external, or informational, efficiency. We discuss this attribute extensively in Reading 57.

In summary, a good market for goods and services has the following characteristics:

1. Timely and accurate information on the price and volume of past transactions.

2. Liquidity, meaning an asset can be bought or sold quickly at a price close to the prices for previous transactions (has price continuity), assuming no new information has been received. In turn, price continuity requires depth.

---

[1] You should be aware that common stocks are currently sold in decimals (dollars and cents), which is a significant change from the pre-2000 period when they were priced in eighths and sixteenths. This change to decimals is discussed at the end of this subsection.

3. Low transaction costs, including the cost of reaching the market, the actual brokerage costs, and the cost of transferring the asset.

4. Prices that rapidly adjust to new information, so the prevailing price is fair since it reflects all available information regarding the asset.

Decimal Pricing

Prior to the initiation of changes in late 2000 that were completed in early 2001, common stocks in the United States were always quoted in fractions. Specifically, prior to 1997 they were quoted in eighths (e.g., $\frac{1}{8}$, $\frac{2}{8}$, ..., $\frac{7}{8}$), with each eighth equal to $0.125. This was modified in 1997 when the fractions for most stocks went to sixteenths (e.g., $\frac{1}{16}$, $\frac{2}{16}$, ..., $\frac{15}{16}$), equal to $0.0625. Now U.S. equities are priced in decimals (cents), so the minimum spread can be in cents (e.g., $30.10–$30.12).

The espoused reasons for the change to decimal pricing are threefold. First is the ease with which investors can understand the prices and compare them. Second, decimal pricing should save investors money since it reduces the size of the bid-ask spread from a minimum of 6.25 cents (when prices are quoted in sixteenths) to 1 cent (when prices are in decimals). (Of course, this is also why many brokers and investment firms were against the change—the spread is the price of liquidity for the investor and the compensation to the dealer.) Third, the change should make U.S. markets more competitive on a global basis since other countries price on a comparable basis. Thus, transaction costs should be lower.

The effect of decimalization has been substantial. Because it reduced spread size, there has been a decline in transaction costs. This has led to a decline in transaction size and a corresponding increase in the number of transactions—for example, the number of transactions on the NYSE went from a daily average of 877,000 in 2000 to 3,702,000 in 2004, while the average trade size went from 1,187 shares in 2000 to 393 shares in 2004.

Organization of the Securities Market

Before we discuss the specific operation of the securities market, we need to understand its overall organization. The principal distinction is between **primary markets**, where new securities are sold, and **secondary markets**, where outstanding securities are bought and sold. Each of these markets is further divided based on the economic unit that issued the security. We will consider each of these major segments of the securities market, with an emphasis on the individuals involved and the functions they perform.

3   PRIMARY CAPITAL MARKETS

The primary market is where new issues of bonds, preferred stock, or common stock are sold by government units, municipalities, or companies to acquire new capital. For a review of studies on the primary market, see Jensen and Smith (1986).

Government Bond Issues

All U.S. government bond issues are subdivided into three segments based on their original maturities. **Treasury bills** are negotiable, non-interest-bearing securities with original maturities of one year or less. **Treasury notes** have original maturities of 2 to 10 years. Finally, **Treasury bonds** have original maturities of more than 10 years.

To sell bills, notes, and bonds, the Treasury relies on Federal Reserve System auctions.

Municipal Bond Issues

New municipal bond issues are sold by one of three methods: competitive bid, negotiation, or private placement. **Competitive bid** sales typically involve sealed bids. The bond issue is sold to the bidding syndicate of underwriters that submits the bid with the lowest interest cost in accordance with the stipulations set forth by the issuer. **Negotiated sales** involve contractual arrangements between underwriters and issuers wherein the underwriter helps the issuer prepare the bond issue and set the price and has the exclusive right to sell the issue. **Private placements** involve the sale of a bond issue by the issuer directly to an investor or a small group of investors (usually institutions).

Note that two of the three methods require an *underwriting* function. Specifically, in a competitive bid or a negotiated transaction, the investment banker typically underwrites the issue, which means the investment firm purchases the entire issue at a specified price, relieving the issuer from the risk and responsibility of selling and distributing the bonds. Subsequently, the underwriter sells the issue to the investing public. For municipal bonds, this underwriting function is performed by both investment banking firms and commercial banks.

The underwriting function can involve three services: origination, risk-bearing, and distribution. Origination involves the design of the bond issue and initial planning. To fulfill the risk-bearing function, the underwriter acquires the total issue at a price dictated by the competitive bid or through negotiation and accepts the responsibility and risk of reselling it for more than the purchase price. Distribution means selling it to investors, typically with the help of a selling syndicate that includes other investment banking firms and/or commercial banks.

In a negotiated bid, the underwriter will carry out all three services. In a competitive bid, the issuer specifies the amount, maturities, coupons, and call features of the issue and the competing syndicates submit a bid for the entire issue that reflects the yields they estimate for the bonds. The issuer may have received advice from an investment firm on the desirable characteristics for a forthcoming issue, but this advice would have been on a fee basis and would not necessarily involve the ultimate underwriter who is responsible for risk-bearing and distribution. Finally, a private placement involves no risk-bearing, but an investment banker would typically assist in locating potential buyers and negotiating the characteristics of the issue.

Corporate Bond Issues

Corporate bond issues are almost always sold through a negotiated arrangement with an investment banking firm that maintains a relationship with the issuing firm. In a global capital market that involves an explosion of new instruments, the origination function, which involves the design of the security in terms of characteristics and currency, is becoming more important because the corporate chief financial officer (CFO) will probably not be completely familiar with the availability and issuing requirements of many new instruments and the alternative capital markets around the world. Investment banking firms compete for underwriting business by creating new instruments that appeal to existing investors and by advising issuers regarding desirable countries and currencies. As a result, the expertise of the investment banker can help reduce the issuer's cost of new capital.

Once a stock or bond issue is specified, the underwriter will put together an underwriting syndicate of other major underwriters and a selling group of smaller firms for its distribution, as shown in Exhibit 55-1.

Corporate Stock Issues

In addition to the ability to issue fixed-income securities to get new capital, corporations can also issue equity securities—generally common stock. For corporations, new stock issues are typically divided into two groups (1) seasoned equity issues and (2) initial public offerings (IPOs).

Seasoned equity issues are new shares offered by firms that already have stock outstanding. An example would be General Electric, which is a large, well-regarded firm that has had public stock trading on the NYSE for over 50 years. If General Electric needed additional capital, it could sell additional shares of its common stock to the public at a price very close to the current price of the firm's stock.

Initial public offerings (IPOs) involve a firm selling its common stock to the public for the first time. At the time of an IPO offering, there is no existing public market for the stock; that is, the company has been closely held. An example was an IPO by Polo Ralph Lauren at $26 per share. At the time, the company was a leading manufacturer and distributor of men's clothing. The purpose of the offering was to get additional capital to expand its operations.

New issues (seasoned or IPOs) are typically underwritten by investment bankers, who acquire the total issue from the company and sell the securities to interested investors. The underwriter gives advice to the corporation on the general characteristics of the issue, its pricing, and the timing of the offering. The underwriter also accepts the risk of selling the new issue after acquiring it from the corporation. For further discussion, see Brealey and Myers (2004, Chapter 15).

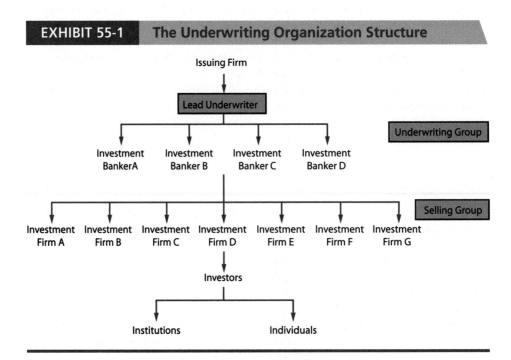

EXHIBIT 55-1   The Underwriting Organization Structure

Relationships with Investment Bankers   The underwriting of corporate issues typically takes one of three forms negotiated, competitive bids, or best-efforts arrangements. As noted, negotiated underwritings are the most common, and the procedure is the same as for municipal issues.

A corporation may also specify the type of securities to be offered (common stock, preferred stock, or bonds) and then solicit competitive bids from investment banking firms. This is rare for industrial firms but is typical for utilities, which may be required by law to sell the issue via a competitive bid. Although a competitive bid typically reduces the cost of an issue, it also means that the investment banker gives less advice but still accepts the risk-bearing function by underwriting the issue and fulfills the distribution function.

Alternatively, an investment banker can agree to sell an issue on a *best-efforts basis*. This is usually done with speculative new issues. In this arrangement the investment banker does not underwrite the issue because it does not buy any securities. The stock is owned by the company, and the investment banker acts as a *broker* to sell whatever it can at a stipulated price. Because it bears no risk, the investment banker earns a lower commission on such an issue than on an underwritten issue.

Introduction of Rule 415   The typical practice of negotiated arrangements involving numerous investment banking firms in syndicates and selling groups has changed with the introduction of Rule 415, which allows large firms to register security issues and sell them piecemeal during the following two years. These issues are referred to as *shelf registrations* because, after they are registered, the issues lie on the shelf and can be taken down and sold on short notice whenever it suits the issuing firm. As an example, General Electric could register an issue of 5 million shares of common stock during 2006 and sell a million shares in early 2006, another million shares late in 2006. 2 million shares in early 2007, and the rest in late 2007.

Each offering can be made with little notice or paperwork by one underwriter or several. In fact, because relatively few shares may be involved, the lead underwriter often handles the whole deal without a syndicate or uses only one or two other firms. This arrangement has benefited large corporations because it provides great flexibility, reduces registration fees and expenses, and allows firms issuing securities to request competitive bids from several investment banking firms.

On the other hand, some observers fear that shelf registrations do not allow investors enough time to examine the current status of the firm issuing the securities. Also, the follow-up offerings reduce the participation of small underwriters because the underwriting syndicates are smaller and selling groups are almost nonexistent. Shelf registrations have typically been used for the sale of straight debentures rather than common stock or convertible issues. For further discussion of Rule 415, see Rogowski and Sorensen (1985).

Private Placements and Rule 144A

Rather than a public sale using one of these arrangements, primary offerings can be sold privately. In such an arrangement, referred to as a *private placement*, the firm designs an issue with the assistance of an investment banker and sells it to a small group of institutions. The firm enjoys lower issuing costs because it does not need to prepare the extensive registration statement required for a public offering. The institution that buys the issue typically benefits because the issuing firm passes some of these cost savings on to the investor as a higher return. In fact, the institution should require a higher return because of the absence of any secondary market for these securities, which implies higher liquidity risk.

The private placement market changed dramatically when Rule 144A was introduced by the SEC. This rule allows corporations—including non-U.S. firms—to place securities privately with large, sophisticated institutional investors without extensive registration documents. It also allows these securities to be subsequently traded among these large sophisticated investors (those with assets in excess of $100 million). The SEC intends to provide more financing alternatives for U.S. and non-U.S. firms and possibly increase the number, size, and liquidity of private placements, as discussed by Milligan (1990) and Hanks (1990). Presently, over 80 percent of high-yield bonds are issued as 144A issues.

4   SECONDARY FINANCIAL MARKETS

In this section we first consider the purpose and importance of secondary markets and provide an overview of the secondary markets for bonds, financial futures, and stocks. Next, we consider national stock markets around the world. Finally, we discuss other primary listing markets, regional exchanges, third markets, and the rapidly growing electronic communication networks (ECNs) and provide a detailed presentation on the functioning of stock exchanges.

Secondary markets permit trading in outstanding issues; that is, stocks or bonds already sold to the public are traded between current and potential owners. The proceeds from a sale in the secondary market do not go to the issuing unit (the government, municipality, or company), but rather to the current owner of the security.

Why Secondary Markets Are Important

Before discussing the various segments of the secondary market, we must consider its overall importance. Because the secondary market involves the trading of securities initially sold in the primary market, *it provides liquidity to the individuals who acquired these securities.* After acquiring securities in the primary market, investors may want to sell them again to acquire other securities, buy a house, or go on a vacation. The primary market benefits greatly from the liquidity provided by the secondary market because investors would hesitate to acquire securities in the primary market if they thought they could not subsequently sell them in the secondary market. That is, without an active secondary market, potential issuers of stocks or bonds in the primary market would have to provide a much higher rate of return to compensate investors for the substantial liquidity risk.

Secondary markets are also important to those selling seasoned securities because the prevailing market price of the securities (*price discovery*) is determined by transactions in the secondary market. New issues of outstanding stocks or bonds to be sold in the primary market are based on prices and yields in the secondary market. Notably, the secondary market also has an effect on market efficiency and price volatility, as discussed by Foster and Viswanathan (1993) and Jones, Kaul, and Lipson (1994). Even forthcoming IPOs are priced based on the prices and values of comparable stocks or bonds in the public secondary market.

Secondary Bond Markets

The secondary market for bonds distinguishes among those issued by the federal government, municipalities, or corporations.

Secondary Markets for U.S. Government and Municipal Bonds   U.S. government bonds are traded by bond dealers that specialize in either Treasury bonds or agency bonds. Treasury issues are bought or sold through a set of 35 primary dealers, including large banks in New York and Chicago and some of the large investment banking firms (for example, Merrill Lynch, Goldman Sachs, Morgan Stanley). These institutions and other firms also make markets for government agency issues, but there is no formal set of dealers for agency securities.

The major market makers in the secondary municipal bond market are banks and investment firms. Banks are active in municipal bond trading and underwriting of general obligation issues since they invest heavily in these securities. Also, many large investment firms have municipal bond departments that underwrite and trade these issues.

Secondary Corporate Bond Markets   Currently, all corporate bonds are traded over the counter by dealers who buy and sell for their own accounts. The major bond dealers are the large investment banking firms that underwrite the issues: firms such as Merrill Lynch, Goldman Sachs, Salomon Brothers, Lehman Brothers, and Morgan Stanley. Because of the limited trading in corporate bonds compared to the fairly active trading in government bonds, corporate bond dealers do not carry extensive inventories of specific issues. Instead, they hold a limited number of bonds desired by their clients, and when someone wants to do a trade, they work more like brokers than dealers.

Notably, there is a movement toward a widespread transaction-reporting service as with stocks, especially for some large, actively traded bond issues. For example, *The Wall Street Journal* publishes a table entitled "Corporate Bonds" that contains daily trading information on forty active bonds. Also, as of July 2005, dealers are required to report trades within 15 minutes of the transaction on 17,000 corporate bonds.

Financial Futures

In addition to the market for the bonds, a market has developed for futures contracts related to these bonds. These contracts allow the holder to buy or sell a specified amount of a given bond issue at a stipulated price. The two major futures exchanges are the Chicago Board of Trade (CBOT) and the Chicago Mercantile Exchange (CME).

Secondary Equity Markets

Before 2000, the secondary equity markets in the United States and around the world were divided into three segments: national stock exchanges, regional stock exchanges, regional stock exchanges, and over-the-counter (OTC) markets for stocks not on an exchange. Because of numerous changes over the past decade, a better classification has been suggested by Harris (2003), as presented in Exhibit 55-2. Following our background discussions on alternative trading systsems and call versus continuous markets, we will describe the market types listed in Exhibit 55-2 and discuss how they complement and compete against each other to provide price discovery and liquidity to individual and institutional investors.

Basic Trading Systems   Although stock exchanges are similar in that only qualified stocks can be traded by individuals who are members of the exchange, they can differ in their *trading systems*. There are two major trading systems, and an exchange can use one or a combination of them. One is a *pure auction*

EXHIBIT 55-2	U.S. Secondary Equity Markets: Classification and Examples
Market Type	**Examples**
Primary listing markets	New York Stock Exchange American Stock Exchange Nasdaq National Market System (NMS) Nasdaq Small-Cap Market (SCM) Nasdaq OTC Electronic Bulletin Board National Quotation Bureau (NQB) Pink Sheets
Regional markets	Boston Stock Exchange Chicago Stock Exchange Cincinnati Stock Exchange Pacific Exchange Philadelphia Stock Exchange
Third-market dealers/brokers	Madoff Investment Securities Knight Trading Group Jefferies Group ITG Nasdaq InterMarket

Alternative Trading Systems (ATSs)
    Electronic Communications
    Networks (ECNs)
	Archipelago
	BRUT
	Instinet
	Island
	REDIBook

Electronic Crossing Systems (ECSs)	POSIT Global Instinet Crossing Arizona Stock Exchange

Source: Adapted from Larry Harris, *Trading and Exchanges* (Oxford University Press, 2003), p. 49.

market (also referred to as an *order-driven market*), in which interested buyers and sellers submit bid-and-ask prices for a given stock to a central location where the orders are matched by a broker who does not own the stock but acts as a facilitating agent. Participants also refer to this system as *price-driven* because shares of stock are sold to the investor with the highest bid price and bought from the seller with the lowest offering price. Advocates of an auction market argue for a very centralized market that ideally will include all the buyers and sellers of the stock.

The other major trading system is a *dealer market* (also referred to as a *quote-driven* market) where individual dealers provide liquidity for investors by buying and selling the shares of stock for themselves. Ideally, with this system there will be numerous dealers who will compete against each other to provide the highest bid prices when you are selling and the lowest asking price when you are buying stock. Clearly, this is a very decentralized system that derives its benefit from the competition among the dealers to provide the best price for the buyer and seller. When we discuss the various equity markets, we will indicate the trading system used.

Call versus Continuous Markets   Beyond the different trading systems for equities, the operation of exchanges can differ in terms of when and how the stocks are traded.

In **call markets**, the intent is to gather all the bids and asks for the stock at a point in time and attempt to arrive at a single price where the quantity demanded is as close as possible to the quantity supplied. Call markets are generally used during the early stages of development of an exchange when there are few stocks listed or a small number of active investors-traders. For an exchange that is strictly a call market with a few listed stocks and traders, a designated market maker would call the roll of stocks and ask for interest in one stock at a time. After determining the available buy and sell orders, exchange officials specify a single price that will satisfy *most* of the orders, and all orders are transacted at this price.

Notably, call markets also are used at the opening for stocks on a large exchange if there is an overnight buildup of buy and/or sell orders, in which case the opening price can differ from the prior day's closing price. Also, this concept is used if trading is suspended during the day because of some significant new information. In either case, the specialist or market maker would attempt to derive a new equilibrium price using a call-market approach that would reflect the imbalance and take care of most of the orders. For example, assume a stock has been trading at about $42 per share and some significant, new, positive information was released overnight or during the day. If it happened overnight it would affect the opening price; if it happened during the day, trading would be temporarily suspended and a call-market process would be used to determine a new equilibrium price that reflects the supply and demand due to the new information. If the buy orders were three or four times as numerous as the sell orders, the price based on the call market might be $44. For an analysis of price movements surrounding trading halts, see Hopewell and Schwartz (1978) and Fabozzi and Ma (1988). Several studies have shown that using the call-market mechanism contributes to a more orderly market and less volatility in such instances.

In a **continuous market**, trades occur at any time the market is open wherein stocks are priced either by auction or by dealers. In a dealer market, dealers make a market in the stock, which means that they are willing to buy or sell for their own account at a specified bid-and-ask price. In an auction market, enough buyers and sellers are trading to allow the market to be continuous; that is, when one investor comes to buy stock, there is another investor available and willing to sell stock. A compromise between a pure dealer market and a pure auction market is a combination structure wherein the market is basically an auction market, but there exists an intermediary who is willing to act as a dealer if the pure auction market does not have enough activity. These intermediaries who act as both brokers and dealers provide temporary liquidity to ensure the market will be liquid and continuous.

CLASSIFICATION OF U.S. SECONDARY EQUITY MARKETS

Now let's delve into the different secondary equity markets that currently exist in the United States, as listed in Exhibit 55-2.

Primary Listing Markets

Primary listing markets are formal exchanges or markets where a corporate stock is primarily or formally listed. This category includes the two traditional national exchanges (New York Stock Exchange and American Stock Exchange) and the Nasdaq markets that previously were considered over-the-counter markets but are now recognized as equity markets that simply differ in how they trade securities (as will be discussed).

New York Stock Exchange (NYSE)   The New York Stock Exchange (NYSE), the largest organized securities market in the United States, was established in 1817 as the New York Stock and Exchange Board. The Exchange dates its founding to when the famous Buttonwood Agreement was signed in May 1792 by 24 brokers.[2] The name was changed to the New York Stock Exchange in 1863.

At the end of 2004, approximately 2,747 companies had their stock listed on the NYSE, for a total of about 3,000 stock issues (common and preferred) with a total market value of more than $12.5 trillion. The specific listing requirements for the NYSE appear in Exhibit 55-3.

The average number of shares traded daily on the NYSE has increased steadily and substantially, as shown in Exhibit 55-4. Prior to the 1960s, the daily share trading volume averaged less than 3 million shares, compared with the 2004 average daily volume of about 1.46 billion shares.

The NYSE has dominated the other exchanges in the United States in trading volume. Given its stringent listing requirements and its prestige, most of the largest and best known U.S. companies are listed on the NYSE. Historically, about 80 percent of the trading volume for these stocks takes place on the NYSE.

EXHIBIT 55-3	Listing Requirements for Stocks on the NYSE
Pretax income last year	$2,500,000
Pretax income last two years	$2,000,000
Shares publicly held	1,100,000
Market value of publicly held shares[a]	$100,000,000
Minimum number of holders of round lots (100 shares or more)	2,000

[a] This minimum required market value is $60 million for spin-offs, carve-outs, or IPOs and it varies over time, depending on the value of the NYSE Common Stock Index. For specifics, see the *2004 NYSE Fact Book*, 37.

Source: NYSE Fact Book (New York: NYSE, 2004): 37.

---

[2] The NYSE considers the signing of this agreement the birth of the Exchange and celebrated its 200th birthday during 1992.

EXHIBIT 55-4	Average Daily Reported Share Volume Traded on Selected Stock Markets (× 1,000)				
Year	NYSE	Nasdaq	Year	NYSE	Nasdaq
1955	2,578	N.A.	1996	411,953	543,700
1960	3,042	N.A.	1997	526,925	650,324
1965	6,176	N.A.	1998	673,590	801,747
1970	11,564	N.A.	1999	809,183	1,077,500
1975	18,551	5,500	2000	1,041,578	1,759,900
1980	44,871	26,500	2001	1,239,957	1,900,068
1985	109,169	82,100	2002	1,441,015	1,752,643
1990	156,777	131,900	2003	1,398,400	1,449,000
1995	346,101	401,400	2004	1,457,000	1,259,000

N.A. = not available.

Sources: NYSE Fact Book (various issues); Nasdaq Research Department.

The volume of trading and relative stature of the NYSE is reflected in the price of a membership on the exchange (referred to as a *seat*). As shown in Exhibit 55-5, the price of membership has fluctuated in line with trading volume and other factors that influence the profitability of membership, as discussed by Ip (1998a).

American Stock Exchange (AMEX)   The American Stock Exchange (AMEX) was begun by a group who traded unlisted shares at the corner of Wall and Hanover Streets in New York. It was originally called the Outdoor Curb Market. In 1910, it established formal trading rules and changed its name to the New York Curb Market Association. The members moved inside a building in 1921 and

EXHIBIT 55-5	Membership Prices on the NYSE ($000)				
Year	High	Low	Year	High	Low
1925	$150	$99	1995	$1,050	$785
1935	140	65	1996	1,450	1,225
1945	95	49	1997	1,750	1,175
1955	90	49	1998	2,000	1,225
1960	162	135	1999	2,650	2,000
1965	250	190	2000	2,000	1,650
1970	320	130	2001	2,300	2,000
1975	138	55	2002	2,550	2,000
1980	275	175	2003	2,000	1,500
1985	480	310	2004	1,515	975
1990	430	250			

Source: NYSE Fact Book (New York: NYSE, 2005): 110. Reprinted by permission of the New York Stock Exchange.

continued to trade mainly in unlisted stocks (stocks not listed on one of the registered exchanges) until 1946, when its volume in listed stocks finally outnumbered that in unlisted stocks. The current name was adopted in 1953.

The AMEX is a national exchange, distinct from the NYSE because, except for a short period in the late 1970s, no stocks have been listed on both the NYSE and AMEX at the same time. Historically, the AMEX emphasized foreign securities and warrants.

The AMEX became a major stock options exchange in January 1975 and subsequently has added options on interest rates and stock indexes. In addition, exchange-traded funds (ETFs) that have grown in number and popularity are almost all listed on the AMEX.

The AMEX and the Nasdaq merged in 1998, although they continued to operate as separate markets. In 2005 Nasdaq sold the AMEX back to its members (see Horowirtz and Kelly, 2005).

An Aside on Global Stock Exchanges   The equity-market environment outside the United States is similar in that each country typically will have one relatively large exchange that dominates the market. Examples include the Tokyo Stock Exchange, the London Stock Exchange, the Frankfurt Stock Exchange, and the Paris Bourse.

In a few instances there may also be regional exchanges, but these are rare. Notably, even in small or emerging economies, stock exchanges have been created because of the liquidity that secondary equity markets provide, as discussed earlier.

Three points about these international exchanges: first, there has been a trend toward consolidations or affiliations that will provide more liquidity and greater economies of scale to support the technology required by investors. Second, many of the larger companies in these countries that can qualify for listing on a U.S. exchange become dual-listed. As a result, about 20 percent of the stocks listed on the NYSE are non-U.S. firms. Third, the existence of these strong international exchanges has made possible a global equity market wherein stocks that have a global constituency can be traded around the world continuously, as discussed in the following section. There is intense competition between the various exchanges, as discussed by Ewing and Ascarelli (2000) and Cherney and Beal (2000).

The Global 24-Hour Market   Our discussion of the global securities market will emphasize the markets in New York, London, and Tokyo because of their relative size and importance, and because they represent the major segments of a worldwide 24-hour stock market. You will often hear about a continuous market where investment firms "pass the book" around the world. This means the major active market in securities moves around the globe as trading hours for these three markets begin and end.

Consider the individual trading hours for each of the three exchanges, translated into a 24-hour eastern standard time (EST) clock:

	Local Time (24-hr. notations)	24-Hour EST
New York Stock Exchange (NYSE)	0930–1600	0930–1600
Tokyo Stock Exchange (TSE)	0900–1100	2300–0100
	1300–1500	0300–0500
London Stock Exchange (LSE)	0815–1615	0215–1015

Imagine trading starting in New York at 0930 and going until 1600 in the afternoon, being picked up by Tokyo late in the evening and going until 0500 in the morning, and continuing in London (with some overlap) until it begins in New York again (with some overlap) at 0930. Alternatively, it is possible to envision trading as beginning in Tokyo at 2300 hours and continuing until 0500, when it moves to London, then ends the day in New York. This latter model seems the most relevant, because the first question a London trader asks in the morning is, "What happened in Tokyo?" The U.S. trader asks, "What happened in Tokyo and what *is* happening in London?" The point is, the markets operate almost continuously and are related in their response to economic events. Therefore, investors are not dealing with three separate and distinct exchanges, but with one interrelated world market. Clearly, this interrelationship is growing daily because of numerous multiple listings where stocks are listed on several exchanges around the world (such as the NYSE and TSE) and the availability of sophisticated telecommunications. Examples of stocks that are part of this global market are General Electric, Pfizer, Johnson and Johnson, and McDonald's.

Nasdaq National Market System (NMS)[3] This system has historically been known as the over-the-counter (OTC) market, which included stocks not formally listed on the two major exchanges (NYSE and AMEX). This description has changed since it has been recognized that this is an equity market similar to the major exchanges with several differences that are not relevant to the purpose of this market. The first difference is that it is a *dealer market,* in contrast to a broker/dealer (specialists) market as is the NYSE. Second, exchange trading takes place electronically rather than on a trading floor as in the other exchanges. What Nasdaq has in common with the other exchanges is a set of requirements for a stock to be traded on the Nasdaq NMS. Also, while Nasdaq dealers do not have to pay for a seat (membership) on the exchange, they are required to be members of the National Association of Security Dealers (NASD) and abide by its rules.

Size of the Nasdaq NMS The Nasdaq NMS market is the largest segment of the U.S. secondary market in terms of the number of issues traded. As noted earlier, there are about 3,000 issues traded on the NYSE and about 600 issues on the AMEX. In contrast, more than 2,800 issues are actively traded on the Nasdaq NMS and almost 700 on the Nasdaq Small-Cap Market (SCM). The Nasdaq market is also the most diverse secondary market component in terms of quality because it has multiple minimum requirements. Stocks that trade on the total Nasdaq market (NMS and SCM) range from those of small, unprofitable companies to large, extremely profitable firms such as Microsoft and Intel.

Nasdaq's growth in average daily trading is shown in Exhibit 55-4 relative to that of the NYSE. At the end of 2004 almost 650 issues of Nasdaq were either foreign stocks or **American Depository Receipts (ADRs)**, representing over 8 percent of total Nasdaq share volume. About 300 of these issues trade on both Nasdaq and a foreign exchange such as Toronto. Nasdaq has developed a link with the Singapore Stock Exchange that allows 24-hour trading from Nasdaq in New York to Singapore to a Nasdaq/London link and back to New York.

Although the Nasdaq market has the greatest number of issues, the NYSE has a larger total value of trading. In 2004 the approximate value of average daily

---

[3] Nasdaq is an acronym for National Association of Securities Dealers Automated Quotations. The system is discussed in detail in a later section. To be traded on the NMS, a firm must have a certain size and trading activity and at least four market makers. A specification of requirements for various components of the Nasdaq system is contained in Exhibit 55-6.

equity trading on the NYSE was about $46 billion and on Nasdaq was about $27 billion.

Operation of the Nasdaq Market   As noted, stocks can be traded on the Nasdaq market as long as there are dealers who indicate a willingness to make a market by buying or selling for their own account.[4]

The Nasdaq System   The *National Association of Securities Dealers Automated Quotation (Nasdaq) system* is an automated, electronic quotation system. Any number of dealers can elect to make markets in a Nasdaq stock. The actual number depends on the activity in the stock. In 2004, the average number of market makers for all stocks on the Nasdaq NMS was about eight.

Nasdaq makes all dealer quotes available immediately. The broker can check the quotation machine and call the dealer with the best market, verify that the quote has not changed, and make the sale or purchase. The Nasdaq quotation system has three levels to serve firms with different needs and interests.

Level 1 provides a single median representative quote for the stocks on Nasdaq. This quotation system is for firms that want current quotes on Nasdaq stocks but do not consistently buy or sell these stocks for their customers and are not market makers. This representative quote changes constantly to adjust for any changes by individual market makers.

Level 2 provides instantaneous current quotations on Nasdaq stocks by all market makers in a stock. This quotation system is for firms that consistently trade Nasdaq stocks. Given an order to buy or sell, brokers check the quotation machine, call the market maker with the best market for their purposes (highest bid if they are selling, lowest offer if buying), and consummate the deal.

Level 3 is for Nasdaq market makers. Such firms want Level 2, but they also need the capability to change their own quotations, which Level 3 provides.

Listing Requirements for Nasdaq   Quotes and trading volume for the Nasdaq market are reported in two lists a National Market System (NMS) list and a regular Nasdaq list. Exhibit 55-6 contains the alternative standards for initial listing and continued listing on the Nasdaq NMS as of late 2004. A company must meet all of the requirements under at least one of the three listing standards for initial listing and then meet at least one continued listing standard to maintain its listing on the NMS. For stocks on this system, reports include up-to-the-minute volume and last-sale information for the competing market makers as well as end-of-the-day information on total volume and high, low, and closing prices.

A Sample Trade   Assume you are considering the purchase of 100 shares of Intel. Although Intel is large enough and profitable enough to be listed on the NYSE, the company has never applied for listing because it enjoys an active market on Nasdaq. (It is one of the volume leaders, with daily volume typically above 25 million shares and often in excess of 50 million shares.) When you contact your broker, she will consult the Nasdaq electronic quotation machine to determine the current dealer quotations for INTC, the trading symbol for Intel.[5] The quote machine will show

---

[4] *Dealer* and *market maker* are synonymous.

[5] Trading symbols are one- to four-letter codes used to designate stocks. Whenever a trade is reported on a stock ticker, the trading symbol appears with the figures. Many symbols are obvious, such as GM (General Motors), F (Ford Motors), GE (General Electric), GS (Goldman Sachs), HD (Home Depot), AMGN (Amgen), and DELL (Dell).

| **EXHIBIT 55-6** | **Nasdaq National Market Listing Requirements** |

A company must meet all of the requirements under at least one of three listing standards for initial listing on The Nasdaq National Market®. A company must continue to meet at least one continued listing standard to maintain its listing.

| Requirements | Initial Listing | | | Continued Listing | |
	Standard 1 Marketplace Rule 4420(a)	Standard 2 Marketplace Rule 4420(b)	Standard 3 Marketplace Rule 4420(c)	Standard 1 Marketplace Rule 4450(a)	Standard 2 Marketplace Rule 4450(b)
Stockholders' equity	$15 million	$30 million	N/A	$10 million	N/A
Market value of listed securities	N/A	N/A	$75 million[1,2]	N/A	$50 million
or			or		or
Total assets			$75 million		$50 million
and			and		and
Total revenue			$75 million		$50 million
Income from continuing operations before income taxes (in latest fiscal year or 2 of last 3 fiscal years)	$1 million	N/A	N/A	N/A	N/A
Publicly held shares[3]	1.1 million	1.1 million	1.1 million	750,000	1.1 million
Market value of publicly held shares	$8 million	$18 million	$20 million	$5 million	$15 million
Minimum bid price	$5	$5	$5[2]	$1	$1
Shareholders (round lot holders)[4]	400	400	400	400	400
Market makers[5]	3	3	4	2	4
Operating history	N/A	2 years	N/A	N/A	N/A
Corporate governance[6]	Yes	Yes	Yes	Yes	Yes

[1] For initial listing under Standard 3, a company must satisfy one of the following: the market value of listed securities requirement or the total assets and the total revenue requirement. Under Marketplace Rule 4200(a)(20), listed securities is defined as "securities quoted on Nasdaq or listed on a national securities exchange."

[2] Seasoned companies (those companies already listed or quoted on another market place) qualifying only under the market value of listed securities requirement of Standard 3 must meet the market value of listed securities and the bid price requirements for 90 consecutive trading days prior to applying for listing.

[3] Publicly held shares is defined as total shares outstanding less any shares held by officers, directors, or beneficial owners of 10 percent or more.

[4] Round lot holders are shareholders of 100 shares or more.

[5] An Electronic Communications Network (ECN) is not considered a market maker for the purpose of these rules.

[6] Marketplace Rules 4350 and 4351.

Source: www.Nasdaq.com (accessed September 2004).

that about 35 dealers are making a market in INTC. An example of differing quotations might be as follows:

Dealer	Bid	Ask
1	30.60	30.75
2	30.55	30.65
3	30.50	30.65
4	30.55	30.70

Assuming these are the best markets available from the total group, your broker would call either dealer 2 or dealer 3 because they have the lowest offering prices. After verifying the quote, your broker would give one of these dealers an order to buy 100 shares of INTC at $30.65 a share. Because your firm was not a market maker in the stock, the firm would act as a broker and charge you $3,065 plus a commission for the trade. If your firm had been a market maker in INTC, with an asking price of $30.65 the firm would have sold the stock to you at $30.65 net (without commission). If you had been interested in selling 100 shares of Intel instead of buying, the broker would have contacted dealer 1, who made the highest bid ($30.60).

Changing Dealer Inventory   Let's consider the price quotations by a Nasdaq dealer who wants to change his inventory on a given stock. For example, assume dealer 4, with a current quote of 30.55 bid–30.70 ask, decides to increase his holdings of INTC. The Nasdaq quotes indicate that the highest bid is currently 30.60. Increasing the bid to 30.60 would bring some of the business currently going to dealer 1. Taking a more aggressive action, dealer 4 might raise the bid to 30.63 and buy all the stock offered, because he has the highest bid. In this example, the dealer raises the bid price but does not change the ask price, which was above those of dealers 2 and 3. This dealer will buy stock but probably will not sell any. A dealer who had excess stock would keep the bid below the market (lower than 30.60) and reduce the ask price to 30.65 or less. Dealers constantly change their bid-and-ask prices, depending on their current inventories or changes in the outlook based on new information for the stock.

Other Nasdaq Market Segments   Now that we are familiar with the Nasdaq system and its operation, we can easily describe the other segments of this market since the major differences relate to the size and liquidity of the stocks involved.

▶ **The Nasdaq Small-Cap Market (SCM)** has initial listing requirements that consider the same factors as the NMS but are generally about one-half to one-third of the values required for the NMS. As of May 31, 2004, there were 683 stocks listed in the Nasdaq small-cap segment. This compares to about 600 stocks listed in the section entitled "Nasdaq NM Issues Under $100 Million Market Cap" and about 2,200 in the section entitled "Nasdaq National Market Issues." In total, the Nasdaq NMS contained 2,819 issues as of May 31, 2004. Therefore, the total Nasdaq market includes 3,502 issues (2,819 NMS and 683 issues on the SCM).

▶ **The Nasdaq OTC Electronic Bulletin Board (OTCBB)** reports indications for smaller stocks sponsored by NASD dealers. As of May 31, 2004, there were 3,305 stocks included on the OTCBB.

▶ **The National Quotation Bureau (NQB) Pink Sheets** reports order indications for the smallest publicly traded stocks in the United States. Pre-1970, these pink sheets (actually printed on pink sheets of paper) were the primary daily source of OTC stock quotes. With the creation of the Nasdaq electronic quotation system, the sheets were superseded. Currently, the NQB publishes a weekly edition on paper and distributes a daily edition electronically with these small-stock quotes.

Regional Stock Exchanges

The second category in Harris's classification of U.S. secondary markets (Exhibit 55-2) is the regional market. Regional exchanges typically have the same operating procedures as national exchanges in the same countries, but they differ in their listing requirements and the geographic distributions of the listed firms. Regional stock exchanges exist for two main reasons: First, they provide trading facilities for local companies not large enough to qualify for listing on one of the national exchanges. Their listing requirements are typically less stringent than those of the national exchanges.

Second, regional exchanges in some countries list firms that also list on one of the national exchanges to give local brokers who are not members of a national exchange access to these securities. As an example, Wal-Mart and General Motors are listed on both the NYSE and several regional exchanges. This dual listing allows a local brokerage firm that is not large enough to purchase a membership on the NYSE to buy and sell shares of the dual-listed stock without going through the NYSE and giving up part of the commission. In addition, regional exchanges can trade some stocks on the Nasdaq market under *unlisted trading privileges* (UTP) granted by the SEC. The majority of trading on regional exchanges is due to dual-listed and UTP stocks.

The regional exchanges in the United States are shown in Exhibit 55-2. The Chicago, Pacific, and PBW exchanges account for about 90 percent of all regional exchange volume. In turn, total regional exchange volume is 9 to 10 percent of total exchange volume in the United States.

The Third Market

Harris's third category is called the **third market.** The term third market involves dealers and brokers who trade shares that are listed on an exchange away from the exchange. Although most transactions in listed stocks do take place on an exchange, an investment firm that is not a member of an exchange can make a market in a listed stock away from the exchange. Most of the trading on the third market is in well-known stocks such as General Electric, IBM, and Ford. The success or failure of the third market depends on whether the non-exchange market in these stocks is as good as the exchange market and whether the relative cost of the transaction compares favorably with the cost on the exchange. This market is critical during the relatively few periods when trading is not available on the NYSE either because trading is suspended or the exchange is closed. This market has also grown because of the quality and cost factors mentioned. Third market dealers typically display their quotes on the *Nasdaq InterMarket* system. For articles that discuss the impact of regional exchanges and the practice of purchasing order flow, see Battalio (1997); Battalio, Greene, and Jennings (1997); and Easley, Kiefer, and O'Hara (1996).

Alternative Trading Systems (ATSs)

The final category in Exhibit 55-2 is alternative trading systems. This is the facet of the equity market where the biggest changes have occurred during the last decade. *Alternative trading systems (ATSs)* are nontraditional, computerized trading systems that compete with or supplement dealer markets and traditional exchanges. These trading systems facilitate the exchange of millions of shares every day through electronic means. Notably, they do not provide listing services. The most well-known ATSs are the Electronic Communication Networks (ECNs) and the Electronic Crossing Systems (ECSs).

▶ *Electronic Communication Networks (ECNs)* are electronic facilities that match buy and sell orders directly via computer, mainly for retail and small institutional trading. ECNs do *not* buy or sell from their own account but act as very cheap, efficient electronic brokers. As shown in Exhibit 55-2, the major ECNs are Archipelago, BRUT, Instinet, Island, and REDIBook.

▶ *Electronic Crossing Systems (ECSs)* are electronic facilities that act as brokers to match *large* buy and sell orders. The most well-known ECSs are POSIT, Global Instinet Crossing, and Arizona Stock Exchange.

The trading of exchange-listed stocks using one of these ATSs has become the *fourth market.*

6   DETAILED ANALYSIS OF EXCHANGE MARKETS

The importance of listed exchange markets requires that we discuss them at some length. In this section, we discuss alternative members on the exchanges, the major types of orders, and exchange market makers—a critical component of a good exchange market.

Exchange Membership

Stock exchanges typically have four major categories of membership (1) specialist, (2) commission broker, (3) floor broker, and (4) registered trader. We will discuss specialists (or exchange market makers), who constitute about 25 percent of the total membership on exchanges, after our description of types of orders.

Commission brokers are employees of a member firm who buy or sell for the customers of the firm. When an investment firm receives an order to buy or sell a stock, it transmits it to a commission broker, who takes it to the appropriate trading post on the floor and completes the transaction.

Floor brokers are independent members of an exchange who act as brokers for other members. As an example, when commission brokers for Merrill Lynch become too busy to handle all of their orders, they will ask one of the floor brokers to help them. For a discussion of unwanted notoriety for these brokers, read Starkman and McGeehan (1998) and McGee (1998).

Registered traders use their memberships to buy and sell for their own accounts. While they save commissions on their trading, observers believe they provide the market with added liquidity, even though regulations limit how they trade and how many registered traders can be in a trading crowd around a specialist's booth at any time. Today they often are called **registered competitive**

market makers (RCMMs) and have specific trading obligations set by the exchange. Their activity is reported as part of the specialist group.[6]

Types of Orders

It is important to understand the different types of orders available to investors and the specialist as a dealer.

Market Orders The most frequent type of order is a **market order**, an order to buy or sell a stock at the best current price. An investor who enters a market sell order indicates a willingness to sell immediately at the highest bid available at the time the order reaches a specialist on an exchange, a Nasdaq dealer, or an ECN. A market buy order indicates the investor is willing to pay the lowest offering price available at the time on the exchange, Nasdaq, or an ECN. Market orders provide immediate liquidity for an investor willing to accept the prevailing market price.

Assume you are interested in General Electric (GE) and you call your broker to find out the current "market" on the stock. The quotation machine indicates that the prevailing market is 35 bid–35.10 ask. This means that the highest current bid on the books of the specialist is 35; that is, $35 is the most that anyone has offered to pay for GE. The lowest offer is 35.10; that is, this is the lowest price anyone is willing to accept to sell the stock. If you placed a market buy order for 100 shares, you would buy 100 shares at $35.10 a share (the lowest ask price) for a total cost of $3,510 plus commission. If you submitted a market sell order for 100 shares, you would sell the shares at $35 each and receive $3,500 less commission.

Limit Orders The individual placing a **limit order** specifies the buy or sell price. You might submit a limit-order bid to purchase 100 shares of Coca-Cola (KO) stock at $50 a share when the current market is 60 bid-60.10 ask, with the expectation that the stock will decline to $50 in the near future.

You must also indicate how long the limit order will be outstanding. Alternative time specifications are basically boundless. A limit order can be instantaneous ("fill or kill," meaning fill the order instantly or cancel it). It can also be good for part of a day, a full day, several days, a week, or a month. It can also be open-ended, or good until canceled (GTC).

Rather than wait for a given price on a stock, because KO is listed on the NYSE your broker will give the limit order to the specialist, who will put it in a limit-order book and act as the broker's representative. When and if the market price for KO reaches the limit-order price, the specialist will execute the order and inform your broker. The specialist receives a small part of the commission for rendering this service.

Short Sales Most investors purchase stock ("go long") expecting to derive their return from an increase in value. If you believe that a stock is overpriced, however, and want to take advantage of an expected decline in the price, you can sell the stock short. A **short sale** is the sale of stock that you do not own with the intent of purchasing it back later at a lower price. Specifically, you would *borrow* the stock from another investor through your broker, sell it in the market, and subsequently replace it at (you hope) a price lower than the price at which you sold it. The investor who lent the stock has the proceeds of the sale as collateral

---

[6] Prior to the 1980s, there also were odd-lot dealers who bought and sold to individuals with orders for less than round lots (usually 100 shares). Currently, this function is handled by either the specialist or some large brokerage firm.

and can invest these funds in short-term, risk-free securities. Although a short sale has no time limit, the lender of the shares can decide to sell the shares, in which case your broker must find another investor willing to lend the shares. For discussions of both good and bad experiences with short-selling, see Power (1993), Loomis (1996), Weiss (1996), Beard (2001), and McKay (2005).

Three technical points affect short sales. First, a short sale can be made only on an *uptick trade,* meaning the price of the short sale must be higher than the last trade price. This is because the exchanges do not want traders to force a profit on a short sale by pushing the price down through continually selling short. Therefore, the transaction price for a short sale must be an uptick or, without any change in price, the previous price must have been higher than its previous price (a zero uptick). For an example of a zero uptick, consider the following set of transaction prices 42, 42.25, 42.25. You could sell short at 42.25 even though it is no change from the previous trade at 42.25 because that previous trade was an uptick trade.

The second technical point concerns dividends. The short seller must pay any dividends due to the investor who lent the stock. The purchaser of the short-sale stock receives the dividend from the corporation, so the short seller must pay a similar dividend to the lender.

Finally, short sellers must post the same margin as an investor who had acquired stock. This margin can be in any unrestricted securities owned by the short seller.

Special Orders   In addition to these general orders, there are several special types of orders. A *stop loss order* is a conditional market order whereby the investor directs the sale of a stock if it drops to a given price. Assume you buy a stock at 50 and expect it to go up. If you are wrong, you want to limit your losses. To protect yourself, you could put in a stop loss order at 45. In this case, if the stock dropped to 45, your stop loss order would become a market sell order, and the stock would be sold at the prevailing market price. The stop loss order does not guarantee that you will get the $45; you can get a little bit more or a little bit less. Because of the possibility of market disruption caused by a large number of stop loss orders, exchanges have, on occasion, canceled all such orders on certain stocks and not allowed brokers to accept further stop loss orders on those issues.

A related stop loss tactic for an investor who has entered into a short sale is a *stop buy order.* Such an investor who wants to minimize loss if the stock begins to increase in value would enter this conditional buy order at a price above the short-sale price. Assume you sold a stock short at 50, expecting it to decline to 40. To protect yourself from an increase, you could put in a stop buy order to purchase the stock using a market buy order if it reached a price of 55. This conditional buy order would hopefully limit any loss on the short sale to approximately $5 a share.

Margin Transactions   When investors buy stock, they can pay for the stock with cash or borrow part of the cost, leveraging the transaction. Leverage is accomplished by buying on margin, which means the investor pays for the stock with some cash and borrows the rest through the broker, putting up the stock for collateral.

As shown in Exhibit 55-7, the dollar amount of margin credit extended by NYSE members increased consistently since 1993, hitting a peak in early 2000 followed by a decline into 2003 and a subsequent increase in dollar terms but not as a percent of market capitalization. The interest rate charged on these loans by the investment firms is typically 1.50 percent above the rate charged by the bank making the loan. The bank rate, referred to as the *call money rate,* is generally about 1 percent below the prime rate. For example, in May 2005 the prime rate was 6.00 percent, and the call money rate was 4.75 percent.

EXHIBIT 55-7	NYSE Member Firm Customers' Margin Debt in Dollars and as a Percentage of U.S. Market Capitalization: 1993–2004

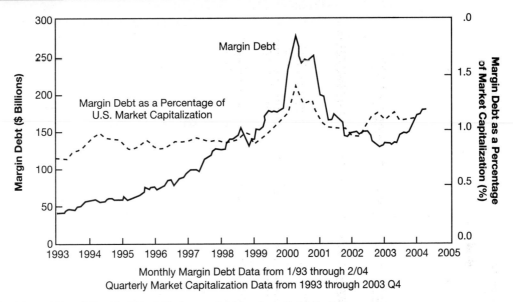

Monthly Margin Debt Data from 1/93 through 2/04
Quarterly Market Capitalization Data from 1993 through 2003 Q4

Sources: Federal Reserve Board; New York Stock Exchange; Goldman Sachs Portfolio Strategy.

Federal Reserve Board Regulations T and U determine the maximum proportion of any transaction that can be borrowed. This *margin requirement* (the proportion of total transaction value that must be paid in cash) has varied over time from 40 percent (allowing loans of 60 percent of the value) to 100 percent (allowing no borrowing). As of May 2005, the initial margin requirement specified by the Federal Reserve was 50 percent, although individual investment firms can require higher percents.

After the initial purchase, changes in the market price of the stock will cause changes in the *investor's equity,* which is equal to the market value of the collateral stock minus the amount borrowed. Obviously, if the stock price increases, the investor's equity as a proportion of the total market value of the stock increases, that is, the investor's margin will exceed the **initial margin requirement**.

Assume you acquired 200 shares of a $50 stock for a total cost of $10,000. A 50 percent initial margin requirement allowed you to borrow $5,000, making your initial equity $5,000. If the stock price increases by 20 percent to $60 a share, the total market value of your position is $12,000, and your equity is now $7,000, or 58 percent ($7,000/$12,000). In contrast, if the stock price declines by 20 percent to $40 a share, the total market value would be $8,000, and your investor's equity would be $3,000, or 37.5 percent ($3,000/$8,000).

This example demonstrates that buying on margin provides all the advantages and the disadvantages of leverage. Lower margin requirements allow you to borrow more, increasing the percentage of gain or loss on your investment when the stock price increases or decreases. The leverage factor equals 1/percent margin. Thus, as in the example, if the margin is 50 percent, the leverage factor is 2, that is, 1/0.50. Therefore, when the rate of return on the stock is plus or minus 10 percent, the return on your equity is plus or minus 20 percent. If the margin requirement declines to 33 percent, you can borrow more (67 percent), and the leverage factor is 3(1/0.33). As discussed by Ip (2000), when you acquire stock or other investments on margin, you are increasing the financial risk of the investment beyond the risk inherent in the security itself. You should increase your required rate of return accordingly.

The following example shows how borrowing by using margin affects the distribution of your returns before commissions and interest on the loan. If the stock increased by 20 percent, your return on the investment would be as follows:

1. The market value of the stock is $12,000, which leaves you with $7,000 after you pay off the loan.

2. The return on your $5,000 investment is

$$\frac{7,000}{5,000} - 1 = 1.40 - 1$$
$$= 0.40 = 40\%$$

In contrast, if the stock declined by 20 percent to $40 a share, your return would be as follows:

1. The market value of the stock is $8,000, which leaves you with $3,000 after you pay off the loan.

2. The negative return on your $5,000 investment is

$$\frac{3,000}{5,000} - 1 = 0.60 - 1$$
$$= -0.40 = -40\%$$

Notably, this symmetrical increase in gains and losses is only true prior to commissions and interest. Obviously, if we assume a 6 percent interest on the borrowed funds (which would be $5,000 \times 0.06 = \$300$) and a $100 commission on the transaction, the results would indicate a lower increase and a larger negative return as follows:

$$20\% \text{ increase: } \frac{\$12,000 - \$5,000 - \$300 - \$100}{5,000} - 1 = \frac{6,600}{5,000} - 1$$
$$= 0.32 = 32\%$$

$$20\% \text{ decline: } \frac{\$8,000 - \$5,000 - \$300 - \$100}{5,000} - 1 = \frac{2,600}{5,000} - 1$$
$$= -0.48 = -48\%$$

In addition to the initial margin requirement, another important concept is the maintenance margin, which is the required proportion of your equity to the total value of the stock; the maintenance margin protects the broker if the stock price declines. At present, the minimum **maintenance margin** specified by the Federal Reserve is 25 percent, but, again, individual brokerage firms can dictate higher margins for their customers. If the stock price declines to the point where your investor's equity drops below 25 percent of the total value of the position, the account is considered undermargined, and you will receive a **margin call** to provide more equity. If you do not respond with the required funds in time, the stock will be sold to pay off the loan. The time allowed to meet a margin call varies between investment firms and is affected by market conditions. Under volatile conditions, the time allowed to respond to a margin call can be shortened drastically.

Given a maintenance margin of 25 percent, when you buy on margin you must consider how far the stock price can fall before you receive a margin call. The computation for our example is as follows If the price of the stock is P and you own 200 shares, the value of the position is 200P and the equity in the account is 200P − $5,000. The percentage margin is (200P − $5,000)/200P. To determine the price, P, that is equal to 25 percent (0.25), we use the following equation:

$$\frac{200P - \$5,000}{200P} = 0.25$$

$$200P - \$5,000 = 50P$$

$$150P = \$5,000$$

$$P = \$33.33$$

Therefore, when the stock is at $33.33, the equity value is exactly 25 percent; so if the stock declines from $50 to below $33.33, you will receive a margin call.

To continue the previous example, if the stock declines to $30 a share, its total market value would be $6,000 and your equity would be $1,000, which is only about 17 percent of the total value ($1,000/$6,000). You would receive a margin call for approximately $667, which would give you equity of $1,667, or 25 percent of the total value of the account ($1,667/$6,667). If the stock declined further, you would receive additional margin calls.

Exchange Market Makers

Now that we have discussed the overall structure of the exchange markets and the orders that are used to buy and sell stocks, we can discuss the role and function of the market makers on the exchange. These people and the role they play differ among exchanges. For example, on U.S. exchanges these people are called **specialists.** Most exchanges do not have a single market maker but have competing dealers. On exchanges that have central market makers, these individuals are critical to the smooth and efficient functioning of these markets.

As noted, a major requirement for a good market is liquidity, which depends on how the market makers do their job. Our initial discussion centers on the specialist's role in U.S. markets, followed by a consideration of comparable roles on exchanges in other countries.

U.S. Markets　　The specialist is a member of the exchange who applies to the exchange to be assigned stocks to handle. The typical specialist will handle 10 to 15 stocks. The minimum capital requirement for specialists is currently $1 million or the value of 15,000 shares of each stock assigned, whichever is greater.

Functions of the Specialist　　Specialists have two major functions. First, they serve as *brokers* to match buy and sell orders and to handle special limit orders placed with member brokers. As noted earlier, an individual broker who receives a limit order (or stop loss or stop buy order) leaves it with the specialist, who executes it when the specified price occurs.

The second major function of a specialist is to act as a *dealer* to maintain a fair and orderly market by providing liquidity when the normal flow of orders is not adequate. As a dealer, the specialist must buy and sell for his or her own account (like a Nasdaq dealer) when public supply or demand is insufficient to provide a continuous, liquid market.

Consider the following example. If a stock is currently selling for about $40 per share, assume that the current bid and ask in an auction market (without the intervention of the specialist) was 40 bid–41 ask. Under such conditions, random market buy and sell orders might cause the stock price to fluctuate between 40 and 41 constantly—a movement of 2.5 percent between trades. Most investors would probably consider such a price pattern too volatile; the market would not be considered liquid. Under such conditions, the specialist is expected to provide "bridge liquidity" by entering alternative bids and asks or both to narrow the spread and improve the stock's price continuity. In this example, the specialist could enter a bid of 40.25 or 40.50 or an ask of 40.50 or 40.75 to narrow the spread to one-half or one-quarter point.

Specialists can enter either side of the market, depending on several factors, including the trend of the market. Notably, they are expected to buy or sell against the market when prices are clearly moving in one direction. Specifically, they are required to buy stock for their own inventories when there is a clear excess of sell orders and the market is definitely declining. Alternatively, they must sell stock from their inventories or sell it short (i.e., borrow shares) to accommodate an excess of buy orders when the market is rising. Specialists are not expected to prevent prices from rising or declining, but only to ensure that *prices change in an orderly fashion* (that is, to maintain price continuity). Evidence that they have fulfilled this requirement is that during recent years NYSE stocks traded unchanged from, or within 10 cents of, the price of the previous trade about 95 percent of the time.

Assuming that there is not a clear trend in the market, several factors will affect how specialists close the bid-ask spread. One factor is their current inventory position in the stock. For example, if they have large inventories of a given stock, all other factors being equal, they would probably enter on the ask (sell) side to reduce these heavy inventories. In contrast, specialists who have little or no inventory of shares because they had been selling from their inventories, or selling short, would tend toward the bid (buy) side of the market to rebuild their inventories or close out their short positions.

Second, the position of the limit-order book will influence how they narrow the spread. Numerous limit buy orders (bids) close to the current market and few limit sell orders (asks) might indicate a tendency toward higher prices because demand is apparently heavy and supply is limited. Under such conditions, a specialist who is not bound by one of the other factors would probably opt to accumulate stock in anticipation of a price increase. The specialists on the NYSE have historically participated as dealers in about 15 percent of the trades, but this percent has been increasing in recent years—from about 18 percent in 1996 to about 27 percent in 2000, as discussed by Ip (2001a).

Specialist Income   The specialist derives income from the broker and dealer functions. The actual breakdown between the two sources depends on the specific stock. In an actively traded stock such as IBM or GE, a specialist has little need to act as a dealer because the substantial public interest in the stock creates a tight market (that is, a narrow bid-ask spread). In such a case, the main source of income would come from maintaining the limit orders for the stock. The broker income derived from a high-volume stock such as IBM is substantial and without risk.

In contrast, a stock with low trading volume and substantial price volatility would probably have a fairly wide bid-ask spread, and the specialist would have to be an active dealer. The specialist's income from such a stock would depend on his or her ability to trade it profitably. Specialists have a major advantage when trading because of their limit-order books. Officially, only specialists are supposed to see the limit-order book, which means that they would have a monopoly on very important information regarding the current supply and demand for a stock. The fact is, most specialists routinely share the limit-order book with other brokers, so it is not a competitive advantage.

Most specialists attempt to balance their portfolios between strong broker stocks that provide steady, riskless income and stocks that require active dealer roles. It has been noted that the increase in dealer activity has been matched with an increase in return on capital for specialists. For further analysis of specialists, see Madhaven and Sofianos (1998) and Benveniste, Marcus, and Wilhelm (1992).

New Trading Systems

As daily trading volume has gone from about 5 million shares to more than a billion shares on both the NYSE and Nasdaq, it has become necessary to introduce new technology into the trading process. Following are some technological innovations that assist in the trading process.

On the NYSE:

▶ **Super Dot**. Super Dot is an electronic order-routing system through which member firms transmit market and limit orders in NYSE-listed securities directly to the posts where securities are traded or to the member firm's booth. After the order has been executed, a report of execution is returned directly to the member firm office over the same electronic circuit, and the execution is submitted directly to the comparison systems. Member firms can enter market orders up to 2,099 shares and limit orders in round or odd lots up to 30,099 shares. An estimated 85 percent of all market orders enter the NYSE through the Super Dot system.

▶ **The Display Book**. The Display Book is an electronic workstation that keeps track of all limit orders and incoming market orders. This includes incoming Super Dot limit orders.

▶ **Opening Automated Report Service (OARS)**. OARS, the opening feature of the Super Dot system, accepts member firms' preopening market orders up to 30,099 shares. OARS automatically and continuously pairs buy and sell orders and presents the imbalance to the specialist prior to the opening of a stock. This system helps the specialist determine the opening price and the potential need for a preopening call market, as discussed earlier.

▶ **Market-Order Processing**. Super Dot's postopening market-order system is designed to accept member firms' postopening market orders up to 30,099 shares. The system provides rapid execution and reporting of market orders. During 2004, 94.5 percent of market orders were executed and reported in less than thirty seconds.

▶ **Limit-Order Processing**. The limit-order processing system electronically files orders to be executed when and if a specific price is reached. The system accepts limit orders up to 99.999 shares and electronically updates the Specialists' Display Book. Good-until-canceled orders that are not executed on the day of submission are automatically stored until executed or canceled.

On Nasdaq:

▶ *Small-Order Execution System (SOES)*. **SOES** was introduced in 1984. Market makers receiving SOES orders must honor their bids for automatic executions up to 1,000 shares. SOES became compulsory following the October 1987 crash, when many small investors could not trade and suffered significant losses.

▶ *SelectNet.* Introduced in 1990, **SelectNet** is an order-routing and execution service for institutional investors that allows brokers and dealers to communicate through Nasdaq terminals instead of the phone. Once two parties agree to a trade on SelectNet, the execution is automatic.

Innovations for Competition

By this time you should realize that the U.S. secondary equity market is being served by two competing models. As mentioned early in this chapter, the first is the *order-driven* stock exchange market where buy and sell orders interact directly with the specialist market maker acting as both a broker and a dealer when necessary. This model is ideal for a secondary market when there is a concentration of participants and all orders come to one central location (either physically or electronically).

The second model is a *quote-driven* market, also referred to as a dealer market, where numerous dealers compete against each other by providing bid-ask quotations and commit to buy and sell given securities at these quoted prices. Generally, in this model buy and sell orders never interact directly, but the best prices are derived due to the competition among dealers who are independent and separated—it is a fragmented market.

Given these two models, the Securities and Exchange Commission has encouraged competition between the two market models by encouraging three innovations: the CQS, the ITS, and the CAES.

The *Consolidated Quotation System (CQS)* is an electronic service that provides quotations on issues listed on the NYSE, the AMEX, and regional exchanges, and issues traded by market makers in the Nasdaq InterMarket (the third market). Provided to subscribers by the Composite Quotation Service, the CQS makes it possible for subscribers to see all competing dealer and exchange quotes for a stock listed on any exchange. The volume of trading for stocks on the consolidated tape has grown dramatically and is now over 400 billion shares annually.

The *Intermarket Trading System (ITS)* is a centralized quotation and routing system developed by the American, Boston, Chicago, New York, Pacific, and Philadelphia Stock Exchanges and the NASD. ITS consists of a central computer facility with interconnected terminals in the participating market centers. As shown in Exhibit 55-8, the number of issues included, the volume of trading, and the size of trades have all grown substantially. There were over 5,000 issues included on the system in 2004.

With ITS, brokers and market makers in each market center indicate specific buying and selling commitments through a composite quotation display that shows the current quotes for each stock in every market center. A broker is expected to go to the best market to execute a customer's order by sending a message committing to a buy or sell at the price quoted. When this commitment is accepted, a message reports the transaction. The following example illustrates how ITS works.

A broker on the NYSE has a **market order** to sell 100 shares of GE stock. Assuming the quotation display at the NYSE shows that the best current bid for GE is on the Pacific Stock Exchange (PSE), the broker will enter an order to sell 100 shares at the bid on the PSE. Within seconds, the commitment flashes on the computer screen and is printed out at the PSE specialist's post, where it is executed against the PSE bid. The transaction is reported back to New York and on the consolidated tape. Both brokers receive immediate confirmation and the results are transmitted at the end of each day. Thereafter, each broker completes his or her own clearance and settlement procedure.

EXHIBIT 55-8	Intermarket Trading System (ITS) Activity

DAILY AVERAGE

Year	Issues Eligible	Share Volume	Executed Trades	Average Size of Trade
1980	884	1,565,900	2,868	546
1985	1,288	5,669,400	5,867	966
1990	2,126	9,387,114	8,744	1,075
1995	3,542	12,185,064	10,911	1,117
1996	4,001	12,721,968	11,426	1,113
1997	4,535	15,429,377	14,057	1,098
1998	4,844	18,136,472	17,056	1,063
1999	5,056	21,617,723	19,315	1,119
2000	4,664	28,176,178	23,972	1,175
2001	4,575	34,029,513	29,728	1,145
2002	4,718	50,036,437	37,694	1,327
2003	4,808	64,077,468	46,582	1,376
2004	5,041	70,924,190	53,331	1,330

Source: NYSE Fact Book (New York: NYSE, 2005): 28. Reprinted by permission of the New York Stock Exchange.

The ITS system currently provides centralized quotations for stocks listed on the NYSE and specifies whether a bid or ask *away* from the NYSE market is superior to that *on* the NYSE. Note, however, that the system lacks several characteristics. It does not automatically execute at the best market. Instead, an investor must contact the market maker and indicate that he wants to buy or sell, at which time the bid or ask may be withdrawn. Also, it is not mandatory that a broker go to the best market. Although the best price may be at another market center, a broker might consider it inconvenient to trade on that exchange if the price difference is not substantial. Still, even with these shortcomings, substantial technical and operational progress has occurred through this central quotation and routing system.

The *Computer-Assisted Execution System (CAES)* is a service created by Nasdaq that automates order routing and transaction execution for securities listed on domestic exchanges that are part of the ITS. This system makes it possible for market makers who are involved with ITS to execute trades with specialists on the exchanges using CAES.

Where Do We Go from Here?

One cannot help but be struck by the significant changes that have taken place in both the U.S. and global equity markets during the new millenium. The technological advances and the decimalization of prices have contributed to significant reductions in trading costs for institutional and retail investors. Although we have two different trading models (order-driven and quote-driven), it appears that they can survive together. But both are challenged by the ECNs that can match orders electronically and provide faster, cheaper transactions. Based on the percent of Nasdaq transactions completed on the ECNs (about 25 to 30 percent), it appears that the ECNs are very good at finding, matching, and executing trades for dealer stocks (as brokers) and when they cannot broker the trade they send the orders to the Nasdaq market. The unknown factor with ECNs is "best price."

In response to challenge from the ECNs, the order-driven exchanges (mainly the NYSE) have attempted regulations to protect the exchange from competition. The first was Rule 390, which was motivated by the concept that the best auction market is one where *all* participants are *centralized* in one location so that the market benefits from having all bids and offers available to interact and provide the very best prices. To help create and protect this centralized auction market, the NYSE introduced Rule 390, which required members to obtain the exchange's permission to carry out a transaction in a listed stock off the exchange. The NYSE argued that without such a rule, the market would become fragmented and many orders would be internalized (members would match orders between customers) rather than exposed to the public. After several years of debate, in late 1999 the SEC ruled that this regulation was clearly anti-competitive and Rule 390 was rescinded (the final order was dated May 5, 2000).

The second regulation that constrains the ECNs from competing with the NYSE is the *trade-through rule*. Specifically, this rule dictates that markets *not* ignore superior prices that are available in competing markets. Put another way, traders are not allowed to "trade through" superior prices—for example, if the best bid is at $30, a dealer cannot fill the order at $29.95. Notably, this rule almost always works to the advantage of the NYSE for stocks listed on the exchange because the bulk of trading in these listed stocks (about 70 to 80 percent) is done on the exchange, so one would expect it to have the best price. The problem is that the search for the best price and the ensuing order transfer can slow the trade by about 30 seconds, which is a long time on the exchange, and prices can change in the interim. Thus the debate is over *speed of execution* versus *best price*. The discussion between the SEC, the NYSE, and the several advocates of electronic trading heated up during 2004 and 2005. Some earlier discussions on the controversy included Solomon and Kelly (2003), Kelly (2004a, b), Craig and Kelly (2004), and Kelly and Solomon (2004). As the votes approached, the NYSE actively lobbied the SEC as discussed by Lucchetti (2005a).

The speed-of-execution contingent (ECNs and other ATSs) want some flexibility on the price: either allow the customer to specify a price range of one to three cents a share from the best price or have a general band whereby the order can be consummated if the electronic price is within one or two cents of the best price. The NYSE is considering such price bands but contend that block traders need to have the benefit of specialists who can ensure the best price for the total block. There is also a greater need for specialists for very small illiquid shares. The point is, relatively small transactions (e.g., under 5,000 shares) for large, liquid stocks (e.g., GE, IBM, 3M, and Johnson and Johnson) can be handled quickly and at very low cost via electronic trading and will typically be at the best price. But very large block trades for liquid stocks and most trades for very small illiquid stocks usually need human intervention.

So, where *do* we go from here? Most likely, further technological advances and the Internet will greatly influence the answer. But it is also likely that human financial experts will always be needed to exercise judgment in the investment process. Coincident with the debate on how stocks should be traded is a related question on the basic future of the NYSE as a public entity, as discussed in Der Hovanesian (2004), Anderson (2005), and Ascarelli and McKay (2005). This question was answered in late April 2005 when the NYSE announced plans to acquire Archipelago (a public firm) and thereby enter the electronic trading business and become public as discussed by Lucchetti (2005b). Shortly thereafter, the NASDAQ market announced plans to acquire Instinet.

THE INTERNET

Investments Online

Many Internet sites deal with different aspects of investing. Earlier site suggestions led you to information and prices of securities traded both in the U.S. and around the globe. Here are some additional sites of interest:

finance.yahoo.com One of the best sites for a variety of investment information including market quotes, commentary, and research, both domestic and international.

finance.lycos.com This site offers substantial market information, including price quotes on stocks, selected bonds, and options. Price charts are available.

www.sec.gov The Web site of the SEC (Securities and Exchange Commission) offers news and information, investor assistance and complaint handling, SEC rules, enforcement, and data.

www.nyse.com, www.amex.com, www.nasdaq.com The Web sites of the New York Stock Exchange, the American Stock Exchange, and the Nasdaq Exchange system offer information about the relevant market, price quotes, listings of firms, and investor services. The AMEX site includes price quotes for SPDRs (S&P Depository Receipts, which represent ownership in the S&P 500 index or the S&P Midcap 400 index) and iShares MSCI Index Funds, which track the Morgan Stanley Capital International (MSCI) indexes of over 20 countries and regions.

www.etrade.com, www.schwab.com, www.ml.com Many brokerage houses have Web pages. These are three examples of such sites. E*Trade Securities is an example of an on-line brokerage firm that allows investors to trade securities over the Internet. Schwab is a discount broker, whereas Merrill Lynch is a full-service broker with a reputation for good research.

www.fibv.com The Web site of the World Federation of Exchanges contains links and data on virtually every public exchange (including stock, bond, and derivatives exchanges) on the globe.

Links to country stock and other financial markets are available at www.internationalist.com/business/stocks/, biz.yahoo.com/ifc/, and www.wall-street.com/foreign.html.

SUMMARY

▶ The securities market is divided into primary and secondary markets. While primary markets are important sources of new capital for the issuers of securities, the secondary markets provide the liquidity that is critical to the primary markets.

▶ The composition of the secondary bond market has experienced small changes over the past 20 years. In sharp contrast, the secondary equity market has experienced significant change and is continuing to evolve due to new technology and consolidation. In addition to several primary listing markets that include exchanges and several Nasdaq components, the secondary market includes several robust regional exchanges, a viable third market, and most recently, the creation, growth, and consolidation of numerous alternative trading systems that provide automatic electronic transactions for stocks on both exchanges and dealer markets.

▶ The components of a good exchange market include several types of membership as well as various types of orders. In addition, market makers play a critical role in maintaining the liquidity of the market.

▶ It appears that changes, especially those due to these technological innovations, have only just begun. Therefore, it is important for investors who will be involved in this market to understand how this market has evolved, what is its current structure, and how it can develop in the future. As an investor, you will need to understand how to analyze securities to find the best securities for your portfolio, but also you need to know the best way to buy/sell the security, that is, how and where to complete the transaction. Our discussion in this chapter should provide the background you need to make that trading decision.

PROBLEMS FOR READING 55

1. Lauren has a **margin account** and deposits $50,000. Assuming the prevailing margin requirement is 40 percent, commissions are ignored, and the Gentry Shoe Corporation is selling at $35 per share.

 A. How many shares can Lauren purchase using the maximum allowable margin?

 B. What is Lauren's profit (loss) if the price of Gentry's stock

  i. rises to $45?

  ii. falls to $25?

 C. If the maintenance margin is 30 percent, to what price can Gentry Shoe fall before Lauren will receive a margin call?

2. Suppose you buy a round lot of Maginn Industries stock on 55 percent margin when the stock is selling at $20 a share. The broker charges a 10 percent annual interest rate, and commissions are 3 percent of the total stock value on both the purchase and sale. A year later you receive a $0.50 per share dividend and sell the stock for 27. What is your rate of return on the investment?

3. You decide to sell short 100 shares of Charlotte Horse Farms when it is selling at its yearly high of 56. Your broker tells you that your margin requirement is 45 percent and that the commission on the purchase is $155. While you are short the stock, Charlotte pays a $2.50 per share dividend. At the end of one year, you buy 100 shares of Charlotte at 45 to close out your position and are charged a commission of $145 and 8 percent interest on the money borrowed. What is your rate of return on the investment?

4⅝ 4¹¹/₁₆

5½ 5½ − ⅜

5½ 21³/₁₆ − ¹/₁₆

20⅝ 18⅛ + ⅞

17⅜ 18⅛ +

18½ 6½ − ½

7¼ 6½

15/₁₆ 31/₃₂ − ¹/₁₆

1 9/₁₆ 9/₁₆

9/₁₆

1⁹/₃₂ 7¹⁵/₁₆

7¹⁵/₁₆ 7¹³/₁₆ 7¹⁵/₁₆

2⅝ 2¹¹/₃₂ 2½ +

327 2¾ 2¼ 2¼

516 12¹/₁₆ 11⅜ 11¾ +

87 33¾ 33 33¹/₁₆ −

802 25⅝ 24⁹/₁₆ 25⅝ +

833 12 11⅝ 11⅞ +

16 10½ 10½ 10⅞ −

78 15⅝ 15¹³/₁₆ 15⅞ −

4508 9¹/₁₆ 8¼ 8⅞ +

430 11¼ 10⅞

SECURITY-MARKET INDEXES

by Frank K. Reilly and Keith C. Brown

LEARNING OUTCOMES

The candidate should be able to:

a. discuss the source and direction of bias exhibited by each of the three predominant weighting schemes, and compute a price-weighted, a market-weighted, and an unweighted index series for three stocks;

b. compare and contrast major structural features of domestic and global stock indexes, bond indexes, and composite stock-bond indexes.

INTRODUCTION   1

A fair statement regarding **security-market indexes**—especially those outside the United States—is that everybody talks about them but few people understand them. Even those investors familiar with widely publicized stock-market series, such as the Dow Jones Industrial Average (DJIA), usually know little about indexes for the U.S. bond market or for non-U.S. stock markets such as Tokyo or London.

Although portfolios are obviously composed of many different individual stocks, investors typically ask, "What happened to the market today?" The reason for this question is that if an investor owns more than a few stocks or bonds, it is cumbersome to follow each stock or bond individually to determine the composite performance of the portfolio. Also, there is an intuitive notion that most individual stocks or bonds move with the aggregate market. Therefore, if the overall market rose, an individual's portfolio probably also increased in value. To supply investors with a composite report on market performance, some financial publications or investment firms have developed stock-market and bond-market indexes.

Investment Analysis and Portfolio Management, Eighth Edition, by Frank K. Reilly and Keith C. Brown, Copyright © 2005. Reprinted with permission of South-Western, a division of Thomson Learning.

In Section 2 of this reading we discuss several ways that investors use market indexes. An awareness of these significant functions should provide an incentive for becoming familiar with these series and indicates why we present a full reading on this topic. In Section 3 we consider what characteristics cause various indexes to differ. Investors need to understand these differences and why one index is preferable for a given task because of its characteristics. In Section 4 we present the most well-known U.S. and global stock-market indexes, separated into groups based on the weighting scheme used. Then, in the fifth section, we consider bond-market indexes—a relatively new topic because the creation and maintenance of total return bond indexes are new. Again, we consider international bond indexes following the domestic indexes. In the fifth section we consider composite stock market-bond market series. In our final section we examine how alternative indexes relate to each other over monthly intervals. This comparison demonstrates the important factors that cause high or low correlation among series. With this background, you should be able to make an intelligent choice of the index that is best for you based on how you want to use it.

2   USES OF SECURITY-MARKET INDEXES

Security-market indexes have at least five specific uses. A primary application is to use the index values to compute total returns and risk for an aggregate market or some component of a market over a specified time period and use the computed return as a *benchmark* to judge the performance of individual portfolios. A basic assumption when evaluating portfolio performance is that any investor should be able to experience a risk-adjusted rate of return comparable to the market by randomly selecting a large number of stocks or bonds from the total market; hence, a superior portfolio manager should consistently do better than the market. Therefore, *an aggregate stock- or bond-market index can be used as a benchmark to judge the performance of professional money managers.*

An obvious use of indexes is to develop an index portfolio. As we have discussed, it is difficult for most money managers to consistently outperform specified market indexes on a risk-adjusted basis over time.[1] If this is true, an obvious alternative is to invest in a portfolio that will emulate this market portfolio. This notion led to the creation of *index funds* and *exchange-traded funds* (ETFs), whose purpose is to track the performance of the specified market series (index) over time. The original index funds were common-stock funds as discussed in Malkiel (2000), Reading 62, and Mossavar-Rahmani (2005). The development of comprehensive, well-specified bond-market indexes and bond-portfolio managers' inability to outperform these indexes has led to a similar phenomenon in the fixed-income area (bond-index funds), as noted by Hawthorne (1986) and Dialynas (2005).

Securities analysts, portfolio managers, and academicians doing research use security-market indexes to examine the factors that influence aggregate security price movements (that is, the indexes are used to measure aggregate market movements) and to compare the risk-adjusted performance of alternative asset classes (e.g., stocks versus bonds versus real estate).

---

[1] Throughout this reading we will use *indicator series* and *indexes* interchangeably, although *indicator series* is the more correct specification because it refers to a broad class of series; one popular type of series is an index, but there can be other types and many different indexes.

Another group interested in an aggregate market index is composed of "technicians," who believe past price changes can be used to predict future price movements. For example, to project future stock price movements, technicians would plot and analyze price and volume changes for a stock-market series like the Dow Jones Industrial Average.

Finally, work in portfolio and capital market theory has implied that the relevant risk for an individual risky asset is its *systematic risk*, which is the relationship between the rates of return for a risky asset and the rates of return for a market portfolio of risky assets.[2] Therefore, in this case an aggregate market index is used as a proxy for the market portfolio of risky assets.

DIFFERENTIATING FACTORS IN CONSTRUCTING MARKET INDEXES

3

Because the indexes are intended to reflect the overall movements of a group of securities, we need to consider three factors that are important when constructing an index intended to represent a total population.

The Sample

The first factor is the sample used to construct an index. The size, the breadth, and the source of the sample are all important.

A small percentage of the total population will provide valid indications of the behavior of the total population *if* the sample is properly selected. In some cases, because of the economics of computers, virtually all the stocks on an exchange or market are included, with a few deletions of unusual securities. The sample should be *representative* of the total population; otherwise, its size will be meaningless. A large biased sample is no better than a small biased sample. The sample can be generated by completely random selection or by a nonrandom selection technique designed to incorporate the important characteristics of the desired population. Finally, the *source* of the sample is important if there are any differences between segments of the population, in which case samples from each segment are required.

Weighting Sample Members

The second factor is the weight given to each member in the sample. Three principal weighting schemes are used for security-market indexes: (1) a price-weighted index, (2) a market-value-weighted index, and (3) an unweighted index, or what would be described as an equal-weighted index. We will discuss each of these in detail shortly.

Computational Procedure

The final consideration is the computational procedure used. One alternative is to take a simple arithmetic mean of the various members in the index. Another is to compute an index and have all changes, whether in price or value, reported in terms of the basic index. Finally, some prefer using a geometric mean of the components rather than an arithmetic mean.

---

[2] This concept and its justification are discussed in Readings 53 and 54.

4   STOCK-MARKET INDEXES

As mentioned previously, we hear a lot about what happens to the Dow Jones Industrial Average (DJIA) each day. You might also hear about other stock indexes, such as the S&P 500 index, the Nasdaq composite, or even the Nikkei Average. If you listen carefully, you will realize that these indexes experience different percentage changes (which is the way that the changes should be reported). Reasons for some differences are obvious, such as the DJIA versus the Nikkei Average, but others are not. In this section we briefly review how the major series differ in terms of the characteristics discussed in the prior section, which will help you understand why the percent changes over time for alternative indexes *should* differ.

We have organized the discussion of the indexes by the weighting of the sample of stocks. We begin with the price-weighted index because some of the most popular indexes are in this category. The next group is the value-weighted index, which is the technique currently used for most indexes. Finally, we will examine the unweighted indexes.

Price-Weighted Index

A **price-weighted index** is an arithmetic mean of current prices, which means that index movements are influenced by the differential prices of the components.

Dow Jones Industrial Average   The best-known price-weighted index is also the oldest and certainly the most popular stock-market index, the Dow Jones Industrial Average (DJIA). The DJIA is a price-weighted average of thirty large, well-known industrial stocks that are generally the leaders in their industry (blue chips). The DJIA is computed by totaling the current prices of the 30 stocks and dividing the sum by a divisor that has been adjusted to take account of stock splits and changes in the sample over time.[3] The divisor is adjusted so the index value will be the same before and after the split. An adjustment of the divisor is demonstrated in Exhibit 56-1. The equation is

$$DJIA_t = \sum_{i=1}^{30} \frac{P_{it}}{D_{adj}}$$

where:

$DJIA_t$ = the value of the DJIA on day t
P_{it} = the closing price of stock i on day t
D_{adj} = the adjusted divisor on day t

In Exhibit 56-1, we employ three stocks to demonstrate the procedure used to derive a new divisor for the DJIA when a stock splits. When stocks split, the divisor becomes smaller, as shown. The cumulative effect of splits can be derived from the fact that the divisor was originally 30.0, but as of May 2005, it was 0.13532775.

The adjusted divisor ensures that the new value for the index is the same as it would have been without the split. In this case, the presplit index value was 20. Therefore, after the split, given the new sum of prices, the divisor is adjusted downward to maintain this value of 20. The divisor is also changed when there is a change in the sample makeup of the index.

---

[3] A complete list of all events that have caused a change in the divisor since the DJIA went to 30 stocks on October 1, 1928, is contained in Phyllis S. Pierce, ed., *The Business One Irwin Investor's Handbook* (Burr Ridge, IL: Dow Jones Books, annual).

EXHIBIT 56-1	Example of Change in DJIA Divisor When a Sample Stock Splits		

Stock	Before Split	After Three-for-One Split by Stock A	
	Prices	Prices	
A	30	10	
B	20	20	
C	$\dfrac{10}{60} \div 3 = 20$	$\dfrac{10}{40} \div X = 20$	$X = 2$ (New Divisor)

Because the index is price weighted, a high-priced stock carries more weight than a low-priced stock. As shown in Exhibit 56-2, a 10 percent change in a $100 stock ($10) will cause a larger change in the index than a 10 percent change in a $30 stock ($3). For Case A, when the $100 stock increases by 10 percent, the average rises by 5.5 percent; for Case B, when the $30 stock increases by 10 percent, the average rises by only 1.7 percent.

The DJIA has been criticized on several counts. First, the sample used for the index is limited to 30 nonrandomly selected blue-chip stocks that cannot be representative of the thousands of U.S. stocks. Further, the stocks included are large, mature, blue-chip firms rather than typical companies. Several studies have shown that the DJIA has not been as volatile as other market indexes, and its long-run returns are not comparable to other NYSE stock indexes.

In addition, because the DJIA is price weighted, when companies have a stock split, their prices decline and therefore their weight in the DJIA is reduced—even though they may be large and important. Therefore, the weighting scheme causes a downward bias in the DJIA; because high-growth stocks will have higher prices and because such stocks tend to split, they will consistently lose weight within the index. For a discussion of specific differences between indexes, see Ip (1998b). Dow Jones also publishes a price-weighted index of 20 stocks in the transportation industry and 15 utility stocks. Detailed reports of the averages are contained daily in *The Wall Street Journal* and weekly in *Barron's*, including hourly figures.

EXHIBIT 56-2	Demonstration of the Impact of Differently Priced Shares on a Price-Weighted Index		

Stock	Period T	Period T + 1	
		Case A	Case B
A	100	110	100
B	50	50	50
C	30	30	33
Sum	180	190	183
Divisor	3	3	3
Average	60	63.3	61
Percentage change		5.5	1.7

Nikkei–Dow Jones Average   Also referred to as the Nikkei Stock Average Index, the Nikkei-Dow Jones Average is an arithmetic mean of prices for 225 stocks on the First Section of the Tokyo Stock Exchange (TSE). This best-known series in Japan shows stock price trends since the reopening of the TSE. Notably, it was formulated by Dow Jones and Company, and, similar to the DJIA, it is a price-weighted index. It is also criticized because the 225 stocks only comprise about 15 percent of all stocks on the First Section. It is reported daily in *The Wall Street Journal* and the *Financial Times* and weekly in *Barron's*.

Value-Weighted Index

A **value-weighted index** is generated by deriving the initial total market value of all stocks used in the index (Market Value = Number of Shares Outstanding (or freely floating shares) × Current Market Price). Prior to 2004, the tradition was to consider all outstanding shares. In mid-2004, Standard & Poor's began only considering "freely floating shares" that exclude shares held by insiders. This initial figure is typically established as the base and assigned an index value (the most popular beginning index value is 100, but it can vary—say, 10, 50). Subsequently, a new market value is computed for all securities in the index, and the current market value is compared to the initial "base" market value to determine the percentage of change, which in turn is applied to the beginning index value.

$$\text{Index}_t = \frac{\Sigma P_t Q_t}{\Sigma P_b Q_b} \times \text{Beginning Index Value}$$

where:

Index_t = index value on day t
P_t = ending prices for stocks on day t
Q_t = number of outstanding or freely floating shares on day t
P_b = ending price for stocks on base day
Q_b = number of outstanding or freely floating shares on base day

A simple example for a three-stock index in Exhibit 56-3 indicates that there is an *automatic adjustment* for stock splits and other capital changes with a value-weighted index because the decrease in the stock price is offset by an increase in the number of shares outstanding. In a value-weighted index, the importance of individual stocks in the sample depends on the market value of the stocks. Therefore, a specified percentage change in the value of a large company has a greater impact than a comparable percentage change for a small company. As shown in Exhibit 56-4, if we assume that the only change is a 20 percent increase in the value of stock A, which has a beginning value of $10 million, the ending index value would be $202 million, or an index of 101. In contrast, if only stock C increases by 20 percent from $100 million, the ending value will be $220 million or an index value of 110. The point is, price changes for the large market value stocks in a value-weighted index will dominate changes in the index value over time. Therefore, it is important to be aware of the large-value stocks in the index.

Unweighted Index

In an **unweighted index**, all stocks carry equal weight regardless of their price or market value. A $20 stock is as important as a $40 stock, and the total market value of the company is unimportant. Such an index can be used by individuals who randomly select stock for their portfolio and invest the same dollar amount in

| EXHIBIT 56-3 | Example of a Computation of a Value-Weighted Index |

Stock	Share Price	Number of Shares	Market Value
December 31, 2005			
A	$10.00	1,000,000	$ 10,000,000
B	15.00	6,000,000	90,000,000
C	20.00	5,000,000	100,000,000
Total			$200,000,000
			Base Value Equal to an Index of 100
December 31, 2006			
A	$12.00	1,000,000	$ 12,000,000
B	10.00	12,000,000[a]	120,000,000
C	20.00	5,500,000[b]	110,000,000
Total			$242,000,000

$$\text{New Index Value} = \frac{\text{Current Market Value}}{\text{Base Value}} \times \text{Beginning Index Value}$$

$$= \frac{\$242,000,000}{\$200,000,000} \times 100$$

$$= 1.21 \times 100$$

$$= 121$$

[a] Stock split two-for-one during the year.

[b] Company paid a 10 percent stock dividend during the year.

| EXHIBIT 56-4 | Demonstration of the Impact of Different Values on a Market-Value-Weighted Stock Index |

| | December 31, 2005 | | | December 31, 2006 | | | | |
| | | | | Case A | | Case B | | |
Stock	Number of Shares	Price	Value	Price	Value	Price	Value
A	1,000,000	$10.00	$ 10,000,000	$12.00	$ 12,000,000	$10.00	$ 10,000,000
B	6,000,000	15.00	90,000,000	15.00	90,000,000	15.00	90,000,000
C	5,000,000	20.00	100,000,000	20.00	100,000,000	24.00	120,000,000
			$200,000,000		$202,000,000		$220,000,000
Index Value			100.00		101.00		110.00

each stock. One way to visualize an unweighted index is to assume that equal dollar amounts are invested in each stock in the portfolio (for example, an equal $1,000 investment in each stock would work out to 50 shares of a $20 stock, 100 shares of a $10 stock, and 10 shares of a $100 stock). In fact, the actual movements in the index are typically based on *the arithmetic mean of the percent changes in price or value for the stocks in the index.* The use of percentage price changes means that the price level or the market value of the stock does not make a difference—each percentage change has equal weight. This arithmetic mean of percent changes procedure is used in academic studies when the authors specify equal weighting.

In contrast to computing an arithmetic mean of percentage changes, both Value Line and the *Financial Times* Ordinary Share Index compute a *geometric* mean of the holding period returns and derive the holding period yield from this calculation. Exhibit 56-5, which contains an example of an arithmetic and a geometric mean, demonstrates the downward bias of the geometric calculation. Specifically, the geometric mean of holding period yields (HPY) shows an average change of only 5.3 percent versus the actual change in wealth of 6 percent.

Style Indexes

Financial service firms such as Dow Jones, Moody's, Standard & Poor's, Russell, and Wilshire Associates are generally very fast in responding to changes in investment practices. One example is the growth in popularity of small-cap stocks following academic research in the 1980s that suggested that over long-term periods, small-cap stocks outperformed large-cap stocks on a risk-adjusted basis. In response to this, Ibbotson Associates created the first small-cap stock index, and this was followed by small-cap indexes by Frank Russell Associates (the Russell 2000 index), the Standard & Poor's 600, the Wilshire 1750, and the Dow Jones Small-Cap Index. For a comparative analysis of these indexes, see Reilly and Wright (2002). This led to sets of size indexes, including large-cap, midcap, small-cap, and micro-cap. These new size indexes were used to evaluate the performance of money managers who concentrated in those size sectors.

The next innovation was for money managers to concentrate in *types* of stocks—that is, *growth* stocks or *value* stocks. We included a designation of these stocks in Reading 52 in terms of what they are and how they are identified. As this money management innovation evolved, the financial services firms again responded by creating indexes of growth stocks and value stocks based on relative

EXHIBIT 56-5	Example of an Arithmetic and Geometric Mean of Percentage Changes

	Share Price			
Stock	**T**	**T + 1**	**HPR**	**HPY**
X	10	12	1.20	0.20
Y	22	20	.91	−0.09
Z	44	47	1.07	0.07

$$\Pi = 1.20 \times .91 \times 1.07 \qquad \Sigma = 0.18$$
$$= 1.168 \qquad 0.18/3 = 0.06$$
$$1.168^{1/3} = 1.0531 \qquad = 6\%$$

Index Value (T) × 1.0531 = Index Value (T + 1)

Index Value (T) × 1.06 = Index Value (T + 1)

P/E, price-book value, price-cash flow ratios, and other metrics such as return on equity (ROE) and revenue growth rates.

Eventually, these two styles (size and type) were combined into six categories:

Small-cap growth	Small-cap value
Midcap growth	Midcap value
Large-cap growth	Large-cap value

Currently, most money managers identify their investment style as one of these, and consultants generally use these categories to identify money managers.

The most recent addition to style indexes are those created to track ethical funds referred to as *socially responsible investment* (SRI) funds. These SRI indexes are further broken down by country and include a global ethical stock index.

The best source for style stock indexes (both size and type of stock) is *Barron's*.

Exhibit 56-6 shows the "Stock-Market Data Bank" from *The Wall Street Journal* of February 2, 2005, which contains values for many of the U.S. stock indexes we have discussed. Exhibit 56-7 shows a table for numerous international stock indexes contained in *The Wall Street Journal*.

EXHIBIT 56-6   **Stock-Market Data Bank**

Major Stock Indexes

	DAILY					52-WEEK			YTD
Dow Jones Averages	HIGH	LOW	CLOSE	NET CHG	% CHG	HIGH	LOW	% CHG	% CHG
30 Industrials	10570.26	10489.64	10551.94	+62.00	+0.59	10854.54	9749.99	+ 0.45	-2.14
20 Transportations	3614.84	3597.14	3605.73	+ 7.25	+0.20	3811.62	2750.80	+26.46	-5.06
15 Utilities	345.84	342.88	345.40	+ 1.94	+0.56	345.40	261.89	+26.64	+3.12
65 Composite	3331.17	3310.86	3326.83	+15.65	+0.47	3412.44	2852.12	+11.66	-2.03
Dow Jones Indexes									
Wilshire 5000	11729.47	11639.56	11721.58	+79.01	+0.68	11987.82	10293.52	+ 5.98	-2.08
US Total Market	283.77	281.56	283.55	+ 1.91	+0.68	289.74	250.37	+ 5.52	-2.01
US Large-Cap	255.24	253.22	255.00	+ 1.71	+0.68	260.21	229.69	+ 3.49	-1.82
US Mid-Cap	362.10	359.27	361.86	+ 2.31	+0.64	370.71	301.79	+12.47	-2.37
US Small-Cap	402.01	398.63	401.79	+ 3.01	+0.75	415.01	335.75	+ 8.92	-3.03
US Growth	1066.78	1058.83	1065.66	+ 5.80	+0.55	1092.49	944.85	+ 1.61	-2.30
US Value	1494.46	1481.78	1493.51	+11.61	+0.78	1523.39	1308.11	+ 8.49	-1.85
Global Titans 50	192.19	190.56	191.94	+ 1.24	+0.65	195.41	176.36	+ 2.01	-1.57
Asian Titans 50	117.59	116.76	116.77	- 0.51	-0.43	120.26	98.30	+ 7.56	-2.90
DJ STOXX 50	2844.20	2815.80	2844.20	+25.01	+0.89	2844.20	2541.84	+ 5.53	+2.50
Nasdaq Stock Market									
Nasdaq Comp	2071.52	2058.66	2068.70	+ 6.29	+0.30	2178.34	1752.49	+ 0.12	-4.91
Nasdaq 100	1527.91	1517.30	1523.66	+ 4.03	+0.27	1627.46	1304.43	+ 2.13	-6.01
Biotech	731.22	723.96	729.59	+ 4.32	+0.60	845.11	622.19	- 7.73	-5.07
Computer	930.18	923.04	928.44	+ 3.09	+0.33	973.84	768.60	- 3.01	-3.82
Standard & Poor's Indexes									
500 Index	1190.39	1180.95	1189.41	+ 8.14	+0.69	1213.55	1063.23	+ 4.70	-1.86
MidCap 400	651.15	645.66	650.82	+ 4.85	+0.75	664.50	549.51	+10.80	-1.88
SmallCap 600	323.85	321.11	323.82	+ 2.71	+0.84	329.58	263.47	+16.52	-1.51
SuperComp 1500	267.13	265.02	266.93	+ 1.85	+0.70	272.32	236.65	+ 5.63	-1.85
New York Stock Exchange and Others									
NYSE Comp	7149.52	7089.83	7146.21	+56.38	+0.80	7253.56	6217.06	+ 8.69	-1.43
NYSE Financial	7354.18	7275.66	7343.47	+67.80	+0.93	7493.92	6322.00	+ 6.74	-2.01
Russell 2000	628.61	623.43	628.14	+ 4.12	+0.66	654.57	517.10	+ 8.46	-3.60
Value Line	391.34	388.47	391.34	+ 2.56	+0.66	404.84	332.98	+ 5.00	-3.24
Amex Comp	1435.58	1424.45	1433.16	+ 4.77	+0.33	1434.34	1160.18	+18.10	-0.08

Source: Reuters

Source: From *The Wall Street Journal*, February 2, 2005, p. C2. Copyright © 2005 Dow Jones. Reprinted by permission of Copyright Clearance Center.

EXHIBIT 56-7	International Stock-Market Indexes

International Stock Market Indexes

COUNTRY	INDEX	2/1/05 CLOSE	NET CHG	% CHG	YTD NET CHG	YTD % CHG	P/E
World	DJ World Index	210.33	+0.91	+0.43	-3.67	-1.71	17
Argentina	Merval	1373.41	-0.38	-0.03	-1.96	-0.14	...
Australia	S&P/ASX 200	4127.70	+20.40	+0.50	+77.10	+1.90	17
Belgium	Bel-20	3010.57	+12.97	+0.43	+77.95	+2.66	12
Brazil	Sao Paulo Bovespa	24149.46	-201.16	-0.83	-2046.79	-7.81	11
Canada	S&P/TSX Composite	9270.13	+66.08	+0.72	+23.48	+0.25	17
Chile	Santiago IPSA	1803.58	-6.30	-0.35	+2.34	+0.13	17
China	Dow Jones CBN China 600	9605.95	-20.56	-0.21	-566.94	-5.57	19
China	Dow Jones China 88	107.36	+0.34	+0.32	-3.52	-3.17	18
Europe	DJ STOXX 600	258.86	+2.01	+0.78	+7.84	+3.12	21
Europe	DJ STOXX 50	2844.20	+25.01	+0.89	+69.43	+2.50	20
Euro Zone	DJ Euro STOXX	274.52	+1.96	+0.72	+7.14	+2.67	21
Euro Zone	DJ Euro STOXX 50	3008.85	+24.26	+0.81	+57.61	+1.95	18
France	Paris CAC 40	3939.18	+25.49	+0.65	+118.02	+3.09	16
Germany	Frankfurt Xetra DAX	4279.97	+25.12	+0.59	+23.89	+0.56	14
Hong Kong	Hang Seng	13578.26	-143.43	-1.05	-651.88	-4.58	16
India	Bombay Sensex	6552.47	-3.47	-0.05	-50.22	-0.76	16
Israel	Tel Aviv 25	635.32	+0.02	...	+17.38	+2.81	...
Italy	S&P/MIB	31515	+181	+0.58	+612	+1.98	19
Japan	Tokyo Nikkei Stock Average	11384.40	-3.19	-0.03	-104.36	-0.91	...
Japan	Tokyo Nikkei 300	219.16	+0.09	+0.04	-2.91	-1.31	...
Japan	Tokyo Topix Index	1146.49	+0.35	+0.03	-3.14	-0.27	115
Mexico	I.P.C. All-Share	13340.52	+243.40	+1.86	+422.64	+3.27	16
Netherlands	Amsterdam AEX	364.41	+3.99	+1.11	+16.33	+4.69	11
Russia	DJ Russia Titans 10	2058.30	+12.38	+0.61	+83.02	+4.20	32
Singapore	Straits Times	2094.65	-1.67	-0.08	+28.51	+1.38	14
South Africa	Johannesburg All Share	12957.44	+158.89	+1.24	+300.58	+2.37	15
South Korea	KOSPI	923.69	-9.01	-0.97	+27.77	+3.10	16
Spain	IBEX 35	9257.00	+33.10	+0.36	+176.20	+1.94	17
Sweden	SX All Share	232.25	+2.29	+1.00	+3.84	+1.68	22
Switzerland	Zurich Swiss Market	5797.90	+26.50	+0.46	+104.70	+1.84	16
Taiwan	Weighted	5981.54	-12.69	-0.21	-158.15	-2.58	12
Turkey	Istanbul National 100	27849.79	+519.44	+1.90	+2878.11	+11.53	26
U.K.	London FTSE 100-share	4906.20	+53.90	+1.11	+91.90	+1.91	16
U.K.	London FTSE 250-share	7225.40	+59.20	+0.83	+288.60	+4.16	18

Source: From *The Wall Street Journal,* February 2, 2005, p. C18. Copyright 2005 DOW JONES & CO INC. Reproduced with permission of DOW JONES & CO INC in the format Other Book via Copyright Clearance Center.

Global Equity Indexes

As shown in Exhibit 56-7, there are stock-market indexes available for most individual foreign markets. While these local indexes are closely followed within each country, a problem arises in comparing the results implied by these indexes to one another because of a lack of consistency among them in sample selection, weighting, or computational procedure. To solve these comparability problems, several investment data firms have computed a set of consistent country stock indexes. As a result, these indexes can be directly compared and combined to create various regional indexes (for example, Pacific Basin). We will describe the three major sets of global equity indexes.

FT/S&P-Actuaries World Indexes The FT/S&P-Actuaries World Indexes are jointly compiled by the Financial Times Limited, Goldman Sachs & Company, and Standard & Poor's (the "compilers") in conjunction with the Institute of Actuaries and the Faculty of Actuaries. Approximately 2,500 equity securities in 30 countries are measured, covering at least 70 percent of the total value of all listed companies in each country. All securities included must allow direct holdings of shares by foreign nationals.

The indexes are market value weighted and have a base date of December 31, 1986 = 100. The index results are typically reported in U.S. dollars, but, on occasion, have been reported in U.K. pound sterling, Japanese yen, euros, and the local currency of the country. In addition to the individual countries and the world index, there are several geographic subgroups, as shown in Exhibit 56-8.

Morgan Stanley Capital International (MSCI) Indexes The Morgan Stanley Capital International Indexes consist of three international, 19 national, and 38 international industry indexes. The indexes consider some 1,673 companies listed on stock exchanges in 19 countries, with a combined market capitalization that represents approximately 60 percent of the aggregate market value of the stock exchanges of these countries. All the indexes are market value weighted. Exhibit 56-9 contains the countries included, the number of stocks, and market values for stocks in the various countries and groups.

EXHIBIT 56-8   **Financial Times Global Equity Index Series**

FTSE GLOBAL EQUITY INDEX SERIES

Feb 04

Countries & regions	No of stocks	US $ index	Day %	Mth %	YTD %	Total retn	YTD %	Gross Div Yield	FTSE All-World Industry Sectors	No of stocks	US $ index	Day %	Mth %	YTD %	Total retn	YTD %	Gross Div Yield
FTSE Global All-Cap	7581	303.67	0.9	1.2	-0.7	317.09	-0.6	2.0	Resources	157	288.50	0.8	8.4	4.7	325.98	4.8	2.5
FTSE Global Large Cap	1085	286.10	0.9	0.6	-1.1	299.51	-0.9	2.1	Mining	48	484.36	-0.1	7.2	2.4	544.80	2.4	2.0
FTSE Global Mid Cap	1907	346.13	1.0	2.4	0.1	359.56	0.2	1.7	Oil & Gas	109	271.14	0.9	8.6	5.1	306.68	5.3	2.5
FTSE Global Small Cap	4589	360.75	0.9	3.0	0.3	373.68	0.4	1.5	Basic Industries	340	309.13	1.2	3.0	0.9	345.16	1.0	2.0
FTSE All-World (Large/Mid Cap)	2992	181.58	0.9	1.0	-0.8	198.19	-0.7	2.0	Chemicals	117	280.65	1.0	1.9	-0.3	313.26	-0.2	2.0
FTSE World (Large/Mid Cap)	2564	323.46	0.9	1.0	-0.9	473.65	-0.8	2.0	Construction & Building Materials	119	338.94	1.7	6.6	5.2	377.71	5.3	1.8
FTSE Global All-Cap ex UK	7082	303.40	0.9	1.1	-0.9	315.88	-0.8	1.8	Forestry & Paper	32	274.28	1.8	-3.3	-5.7	311.95	-5.5	2.9
FTSE Global All-Cap ex USA	5129	330.80	0.7	0.9	-0.6	348.90	-0.5	2.3	Steel & Other Metals	72	363.72	0.6	3.5	0.4	400.91	0.8	1.9
FTSE Global All-Cap ex Japan	6246	303.13	0.9	1.3	-0.6	317.14	-0.5	2.1	General Industrials	287	186.13	0.8	1.0	-0.9	202.03	-0.7	1.7
FTSE Global All-Cap ex Eurobloc	6829	298.91	0.9	1.3	-0.7	311.36	-0.5	1.9	Aerospace & Defence	24	210.85	0.7	4.6	1.3	230.07	1.4	1.8
FTSE All-World Developed	2107	293.45	0.9	0.9	-0.9	306.50	-0.8	2.0	Diversified Industrials	62	178.73	0.6	0.3	-0.7	196.29	-0.6	2.1
FTSE Developed All-Cap	6076	300.35	0.9	1.1	-0.8	313.39	-0.7	1.9	Electronic & Electrical Equipment	106	168.33	0.9	-0.4	-2.5	179.41	-2.2	1.3
FTSE Developed Large Cap	769	281.89	0.9	0.5	-1.2	294.90	-1.1	2.1	Engineering & Machinery	95	291.11	0.9	1.6	-0.5	317.71	-0.4	1.5
									Cyclical Consumer Goods	173	202.82	0.6	-1.4	-2.5	220.91	-2.4	1.8
FTSE Developed Europe Large Cap	189	305.63	0.8	0.1	-1.3	325.27	-1.1	2.8	Automobiles & Parts	80	211.60	0.8	-1.4	-2.1	231.91	-2.1	2.0
FTSE Developed Europe Mid Cap	325	355.96	0.8	1.9	0.8	377.21	1.0	2.3	Household Goods & Textiles	93	185.04	0.4	-1.4	-3.2	198.89	-3.1	1.4
FTSE Developed Europe Small Cap	1026	409.65	0.6	4.3	3.1	433.16	3.2	2.2	Non-Cyclical Consumer Goods	354	202.85	0.8	0.7	-0.8	220.22	-0.7	1.9
FTSE All-World Developed Europe	514	195.60	0.8	0.4	-0.9	220.53	-0.7	2.7	Beverages	50	221.11	1.3	1.8	0.7	241.46	0.8	2.2
									Food Producers & Processors	92	275.43	0.2	1.6	0.2	305.30	0.3	2.3
FTSE North America Large Cap	281	265.12	1.0	1.0	-0.9	275.42	-0.7	1.8	Health	77	263.24	0.8	5.6	3.5	273.20	3.6	0.4
FTSE North America Mid Cap	539	328.79	1.3	2.7	-0.4	338.61	-0.3	1.3	Personal Care & Household Products	27	256.73	-0.3	2.0	0.6	278.47	0.9	1.8
FTSE North America Small Cap	1875	338.61	1.2	2.0	-1.6	347.93	-1.5	1.3	Pharmaceuticals	93	153.31	0.8	-2.6	-4.2	165.20	-4.1	2.0
FTSE All-World North America	820	170.75	1.1	1.4	-0.8	183.64	-0.6	1.7	Tobacco	15	402.61	3.3	6.4	5.6	497.83	5.9	4.0
FTSE All-World Dev ex North Am	1287	190.11	0.8	0.2	-1.1	211.34	-1.0	2.4	Cyclical Services	491	196.07	0.7	-0.2	-1.8	208.91	-1.8	1.2
									General Retailers	114	260.15	0.6	-1.0	-2.4	272.67	-2.3	1.1
FTSE Japan Large Cap	177	288.83	0.6	-2.0	-3.5	294.96	-3.5	1.0	Leisure & Hotels	62	197.06	1.0	-0.2	-1.6	208.09	-1.6	1.5
FTSE Japan Mid Cap	303	358.77	0.6	2.8	1.5	366.51	1.5	0.9	Media & Entertainment	128	149.60	0.7	-0.1	-1.6	157.62	-1.6	0.9
FTSE Japan Small Cap	855	393.52	0.5	5.4	4.1	404.30	4.1	1.1	Support Services	67	167.82	0.8	-1.0	-3.0	178.14	-2.9	1.3
FTSE Japan (Large/Mid Cap)	480	115.40	0.6	-1.0	-2.5	133.33	-2.5	1.0	Transport	120	271.21	0.9	2.4	0.4	292.67	0.5	1.6
FTSE Asia Pacific Large Cap ex Japan	302	343.43	0.4	2.3	1.0	366.75	1.2	2.9	Non-Cyclical Services	150	129.19	0.9	-0.9	-2.2	141.62	-2.0	2.4
FTSE Asia Pacific Mid Cap ex Japan	563	361.67	0.2	0.9	-0.4	382.98	-0.1	2.5	Food & Drug Retailers	38	177.40	0.3	3.9	2.9	190.05	3.0	1.4
FTSE Asia Pacific Small Cap ex Japan	714	345.91	0.3	3.1	2.6	365.61	2.7	2.6	Telecommunication Services	112	121.93	1.0	-1.8	-3.2	134.30	-2.9	2.6
FTSE All-World Asia Pacific ex Japan	865	260.43	0.3	2.0	0.7	296.84	0.9	2.8	Utilities	145	214.26	1.0	4.1	2.2	252.98	2.4	3.4
FTSE All Emerging All-Cap	1505	374.09	0.5	2.9	1.0	396.17	1.3	2.6	Electricity	94	232.83	0.9	4.1	2.2	276.69	2.5	3.5
FTSE All Emerging Large Cap	316	370.06	0.5	3.1	1.1	392.02	1.5	2.7	Utilities Other	51	228.32	1.3	4.2	2.1	268.92	2.3	3.1
FTSE All Emerging Mid Cap	569	371.74	0.5	1.4	-0.5	391.41	-0.2	2.4	Financials	638	222.03	0.8	-0.1	-1.5	248.53	-1.3	2.6
FTSE All Emerging Small Cap	620	356.43	0.5	3.8	3.0	375.60	3.2	2.3	Banks	259	253.62	0.7	-0.2	-1.3	290.92	-1.1	3.1
FTSE All-World All Emerging Europe	57	343.43	0.8	5.0	4.2	374.50	4.2	1.6	Insurance	74	169.21	1.2	-0.2	-0.6	180.55	-0.6	1.6
FTSE Latin Americas All-Cap	175	481.90	1.8	7.0	2.5	517.30	2.7	3.5	Life Assurance	35	174.80	0.7	0.7	-0.7	196.01	-0.7	2.3
FTSE Middle East Africa All-Cap	173	399.85	0.4	-2.9	-5.5	427.62	-5.2	2.6	Investment Companies	21	227.31	0.3	2.0	0.6	252.88	0.8	2.4
									Real Estate	102	267.63	1.1	-1.1	-3.2	312.95	-3.1	3.3
FTSE UK All-Cap	499	306.35	0.9	2.5	1.2	328.55	1.3	3.0	Speciality & Other Finance	147	195.70	1.0	-0.5	-2.3	209.40	-2.2	1.4
FTSE USA All-Cap	2452	281.58	1.1	1.5	-0.8	291.61	-0.6	1.6	Information Technology	257	83.96	1.6	-1.2	-3.6	86.11	-3.6	0.7
FTSE Europe All-Cap	1624	325.61	0.8	0.9	-0.4	346.04	-0.3	2.6	Information Technology Hardware	174	72.28	1.9	-0.8	-3.7	74.28	-3.6	0.8
FTSE Eurobloc All-Cap	752	336.59	0.8	0.3	-1.0	357.35	-0.8	2.6	Software & Computer Services	83	119.45	1.1	-1.8	-3.6	121.99	-3.6	0.7

www.ftse.com. On September 22 2003, FTSE launched the FTSE Global Equity Index Series. The family contains the new FTSE Global Small Cap Indices and broader FTSE Global All Cap Indices (large/mid/small cap) as well as the enhanced FTSE All-World Index Series (large/mid cap). This table has been updated to reflect the additional indices. The FTSE Industry Sectors table relates to the FTSE All-World Index Series Sectors (large/mid cap). To learn more about the enhancement and new indices, please visit www.ftse.com/geis. © FTSE International Limited 2005. All rights reserved. 'FTSE', 'FT-SE' and 'Footsie' are trade marks of the London Stock Exchange and The Financial Times and are used by FTSE International under license. Latest prices were unavailable for this edition.

Source: Financial Times, February 8, 2005, p. 27. Reprinted by permission of The Financial Times Limited.

EXHIBIT 56-9	Market Coverage of Morgan Stanley Capital International Indexes as of November 30, 2004

	GDP Weights[a]			Weight as Percent of Index	
	Percent EAFE	Companies in Index	Market Cap. U.S. $ Billion	EAFE	World
Austria	1.8	13	69.6	0.3	0.1
Belgium	2.3	20	239.5	1.3	0.5
Denmark	3.4	20	137.8	0.8	0.3
Finland	2.0	19	198.2	1.8	0.6
France	10.7	57	1,412.7	9.4	3.9
Germany	14.8	47	1,056.1	6.8	2.8
Greece	1.1	20	109.9	0.5	0.2
Ireland	1.0	15	93.9	0.8	0.3
Italy	9.6	41	606.7	4.0	1.6
The Netherlands	3.2	26	508.9	4.8	1.9
Norway	1.6	14	133.0	0.6	0.2
Portugal	0.9	10	67.2	0.4	0.1
Spain	5.3	31	774.7	3.8	1.5
Sweden	1.9	44	353.6	2.5	1.0
Switzerland	1.8	35	707.0	6.9	2.8
United Kingdom	10.8	121	2,560.0	25.2	10.3
Europe	69.1	563	9,118.0	69.5	28.5
Australia	3.5	72	675.0	5.4	2.2
Hong Kong	1.0	37	402.5	1.7	0.7
Japan	25.4	344	3,492.2	22.3	9.1
New Zealand	0.5	16	25.8	0.2	0.1
Singapore	0.6	35	169.0	0.6	0.3
Pacific	30.9	504	4,764.4	30.5	12.5
Pacific ex Japan	5.6	160	1,272.2	6.2	3.4
EAFE	100.0	1,067	13,002.4	100.0	40.9
Canada	—	90	1,083.7	—	2.9
United States	—	51.6	14,816.4	—	51.3
The World Index	—	1,673	29,782.5	—	100.0
EMU	51.5	299	5,217.8	—	13.6
Europe ex UK	58.2	412	6,549.2	—	18.1
Far East	27.0	416	4,062.7	24.8	10.2
North America	—	606	15,900.1	—	54.1
Kokusai Index (World ex Japan)	—	1,329	29,453.7	—	90.9

[a] GDP weight figures represent the initial weights applicable for the first month. They are used exclusively in the MSCI "GDP weighted" indexes.

Source: MSCI. Reprinted with permission.

EXHIBIT 56-10	Listing of Morgan Stanley Capital International Stock Index Values

MSCI Indexes

	JAN 31	JAN 28	% CHG FROM 12/03
U.S.	1108.2	1099.1	+6.0
Britain	1467.7	1461.8	+8.8
Canada	1132.2	1123.8	+11.0
Japan	689.4	686.8	+8.2
France	1290.1	1276.5	+10.6
Germany	522.0	515.5	+6.1
Hong Kong	7375.7	7338.0	+16.3
Switzerland	756.7	754.1	+5.9
Australia	813.0	811.1	+24.0
World Index	1142.3	1133.4	+10.2
MSCI EAFE	1487.0	1476.2	+15.4

As calculated by Morgan Stanley Capital International Perspective, Geneva. Each index, calculated in local currencies, is based on the close of 1969 equaling 100.

Source: From *The Wall Street Journal,* February 2, 2005, p. C14. Copyright 2005 by DOW JONES & CO INC. Reproduced with permission of DOW JONES & CO INC in the format Other Book via Copyright Clearance Center.

In addition to reporting the indexes in U.S. dollars and the country's local currency, the following valuation information is available: (1) price-to-book value (P/BV) ratio, (2) price-to-cash earnings (earnings plus depreciation) (P/CE) ratio, (3) price-to-earnings (P/E) ratio, and (4) dividend yield (YLD). These ratios help in analyzing different valuation levels among countries and over time for specific countries.

Notably, the Morgan Stanley group index for Europe, Australia, and the Far East (EAFE) is the basis for futures and options contracts on the Chicago Mercantile Exchange and the Chicago Board Options Exchange. Several of the MSCI country indexes, the EAFE index, and a world index are reported daily in *The Wall Street Journal* as shown in Exhibit 56-10.

Dow Jones World Stock Index   In January 1993, Dow Jones introduced its World Stock Index. Composed of more than 2,200 companies worldwide and organized into 120 industry groups, the index includes 28 countries representing more than 80 percent of the combined capitalization of these countries. In addition to the 34 individual countries shown in Exhibit 56-11, the countries are grouped into three regions: Asia/Pacific, Europe/Africa, and the Americas. Finally, each country's index is calculated in its own currency as well as in U.S. dollars, British pounds, euros, and Japanese yen. The index for the individual countries is reported daily in *The Wall Street Journal* (domestic), in *The Wall Street Journal Europe,* and in *The Asian Wall Street Journal.* It is published weekly in *Barron's.*

Comparison of World Stock Indexes   As shown in Exhibit 56-12, the correlations between the three series since December 31, 1991, when the DJ series became available, indicate that the results with the various world stock indexes are quite comparable.

EXHIBIT 56-11	Dow Jones Country Indexes

Dow Jones Country Indexes

Feb. 1, 2005 5:15 p.m. ET

In U.S. dollar terms

COUNTRY	INDEX	CHG	% CHG	YTD % CHG	COUNTRY	INDEX	CHG	% CHG	YTD % CHG
Australia	282.84	+0.40	+0.14	+0.78	Mexico	265.33	+5.47	+2.10	+3.14
Austria	272.71	+1.82	+0.67	-1.72	Netherlands	281.22	+3.18	+1.14	+0.64
Belgium	307.19	+1.57	+0.51	-1.19	New Zealand	232.64	+0.96	+0.41	-1.04
Brazil	494.46	+1.83	+0.37	-2.70	Norway	223.53	+2.28	+1.03	-2.04
Canada	281.74	+1.66	+0.59	-3.24	Philippines	92.05	-1.32	-1.41	+9.35
Chile	253.14	-2.09	-0.82	-6.80	Portugal	200.14	+1.16	+0.58	+1.68
Denmark	301.92	+2.13	+0.71	-1.90	Singapore	161.05	-1.01	-0.62	+1.53
Finland	813.07	+6.79	+0.84	-2.51	South Africa	204.01	-2.74	-1.33	-6.73
France	248.12	+1.01	+0.41	-0.94	South Korea	139.17	-1.54	-1.09	+5.45
Germany	199.36	+0.66	+0.33	-3.58	Spain	273.56	+0.37	+0.14	-2.19
Greece	193.15	-1.28	-0.66	-0.51	Sweden	335.42	+3.54	+1.07	-3.86
Hong Kong	242.98	-2.58	-1.05	-5.01	Switzerland	382.19	-0.34	-0.09	-2.95
Indonesia	77.95	-0.17	-0.22	+7.50	Taiwan	121.06	-0.05	-0.04	-2.91
Ireland	469.28	+5.79	+1.25	-0.33	Thailand	78.01	+0.76	+0.98	+6.93
Italy	213.50	+0.78	+0.37	-2.12	U.K.	207.44	+1.53	+0.74	+0.08
Japan	88.81	-0.49	-0.55	-1.98	U.S.	283.55	+1.91	+0.68	-2.02
Malaysia	122.13	Closed	...	+1.19	Venezuela	41.04	+2.17	+5.58	-7.15

Source: From *The Wall Street Journal*, February 2, 2005, p. C18. Copyright 2005 by DOW JONES & CO INC. Reproduced with permission of DOW JONES & CO INC in the format Other Book via Copyright Clearance Center.

EXHIBIT 56-12	Correlations of Percentage Price Changes of Alternative World Stock Indexes 12/31/91–12/31/03

	U.S. Dollars
FT-MS:	.997
FT-DJ:	.996
MS-DJ:	.994

5   BOND-MARKET INDEXES[4]

Investors know little about the several bond-market indexes because these indexes are relatively new and not widely published. Knowledge regarding these indexes is becoming more important because of the growth of fixed-income mutual funds and the consequent need to have a reliable set of benchmarks to use in evaluating their performance. Also, because the performance of many fixed-income money managers has been unable to match that of the aggregate bond market, interest has been growing in bond-index funds, which requires the development of an index to emulate as discussed by Dialynas (2005) and Volpert (2005).

Notably, it is more difficult to create and compute a bond-market index than a stock-market index for several reasons. First, the universe of bonds is much broader than that of stocks, ranging from U.S. Treasury securities to bonds in default. Second, the universe of bonds is changing constantly because of new issues, bond maturities, calls, and bond sinking funds. Third, the volatility of prices for

---

[4] The discussion in this section draws heavily from Reilly and Wright (2005).

individual bonds and bond portfolios changes because **bond price volatility** is affected by duration, which is likewise changing constantly because of changes in maturity, coupon, and market yield. Finally, significant problems can arise in correctly pricing the individual bond issues in an index (especially corporate and **mortgage bonds**) compared to the current and continuous transactions prices available for most stocks used in stock indexes.

Our subsequent discussion will be divided into the following three subsections: (1) U.S. investment-grade bond indexes, including Treasuries; (2) U.S. high-yield bond indexes; and (3) global government bond indexes. All of these indexes indicate total rates of return for the portfolio of bonds and the indexes are market value weighted. Exhibit 56-13 is a summary of the characteristics for the indexes available for these three segments of the bond market.

U.S. Investment-Grade Bond Indexes

As shown in Exhibit 56-13, four investment firms have created and maintain indexes for Treasury bonds and other bonds considered investment grade, that is, the bonds are rated Bbb or higher. As demonstrated in a subsequent section, the relationship among the returns for these investment-grade bonds is strong (that is, correlations average about 0.95), regardless of the segment of the market.

High-Yield Bond Indexes

One of the fastest-growing segments of the U.S. bond market during the past 20 years has been the high-yield bond market, which includes bonds that are not investment grade—that is, they are rated Bb, B, Ccc, Cc, and C. Because of this growth, four investment firms created indexes related to this market. A summary of the characteristics for these indexes is included in Exhibit 56-13. For an analysis of the alternative high-yield bond benchmarks, see Reilly and Wright (1994); for an analysis of this whole market, see Reilly and Wright (2001).

Global Government Bond Indexes

The global bond market has experienced significant growth in size and importance during the past fifteen years. Unlike the high-yield bond market, the global segment is completely dominated by government bonds because few non-U.S. countries have a corporate bond market. Once again, several major investment firms have created indexes that reflect the performance for the global bond market. As shown in Exhibit 56-13, the various indexes have similar characteristics. At the same time, the total sample sizes and the numbers of countries included differ.

COMPOSITE STOCK-BOND INDEXES   6

Beyond separate stock indexes and bond indexes for individual countries, a natural step is the development of a composite index that measures the performance of all securities in a given country. With a composite index investors can examine the benefits of diversifying with a combination of asset classes such as stocks and bonds in addition to diversifying within the asset classes of stocks on bonds. There are two such indexes available.

First, a market-value-weighted index called Merrill Lynch-Wilshire Capital Markets Index (ML-WCMI) measures the total return performance of the combined U.S. taxable fixed-income and equity markets. It is basically a combination of the Merrill Lynch fixed-income indexes and the Dow Jones Wilshire 5000

EXHIBIT 56-13 Summary of Bond-Market Indexes

Name of Index	Number of Issues	Maturity	Size of Issues	Weighting	Pricing	Reinvestment Assumption	Subindexes Available
U.S. Investment-Grade Bond Indexes							
Lehman Brothers	5,000+	Over 1 year	Over $100 million	Market value	Trader priced and model priced	No	Government, gov./corp., corporate mortgage-backed, asset-backed
Merrill Lynch	5,000+	Over 1 year	Over $50 million	Market value	Trader priced and model priced	In specific bonds	Government, gov./corp., corporate, mortgage
Ryan Treasury	300+	Over 1 year	All Treasury	Market value and equal	Market priced	In specific bonds	Treasury
Smith Barney	5,000+	Over 1 year	Over $50 million	Market value	Trader priced	In one-month T-bill	Broad inv. grade, Treas.-agency, corporate, mortgage
U.S. High-Yield Bond Indexes							
C. S. First Boston	423	All maturities	Over $75 million	Market value	Trader priced	Yes	Composite and by rating
Lehman Brothers	624	Over 1 year	Over $100 million	Market value	Trader priced	No	Composite and by rating
Merrill Lynch	735	Over 1 year	Over $25 million	Market value	Trader priced	Yes	Composite and by rating
Smith Barney	299	Over 7 years	Over $50 million	Market value	Trader priced	Yes	Composite and by rating

(Exhibit continued on next page ....)

EXHIBIT 56-13   Summary of Bond-Market Indexes (continued)

Global Government Bond Indexes

Name of Index	Number of Issues	Maturity	Size of Issues	Weighting	Pricing	Reinvestment Assumption	Subindexes Available
Lehman Brothers	800	Over 1 year	Over $200 million	Market value	Trader priced	Yes	Composite and 13 countries, local and U.S. dollars
Merrill Lynch	9,736	Over 1 year	Over $50 million	Market value	Trader priced	Yes	Composite and 9 countries, local and U.S. dollars
J. P. Morgan	445	Over 1 year	Over $100 million	Market value	Trader priced	Yes in index	Composite and 11 countries, local and U.S. dollars
Smith Barney	400	Over 1 year	Over $250 million	Market value	Trader priced	Yes at local short-term rate	Composite and 14 countries, local and U.S. dollars

Source: Frank K. Reilly, Wenchi Kao, and David J. Wright, "Alternative Bond Market Indexes," *Financial Analysts Journal* 48, no. 3 (May–June, 1992): 14–58; Frank K. Reilly and David J. Wright, "An Analysis of High-Yield Bond Benchmarks," *Journal of Fixed Income* 3, no. 4 (March 1994): 6–24; and Frank K. Reilly and David J. Wright, "Global Bond Markets: Alternative Benchmarks and Risk-Return Performance," presented at Midwest Finance Association Meeting, Chicago, IL., March 2000.

common-stock index. As such, it tracks more than 10,000 U.S. stocks and bonds and, as of March 2005, the relative weights are about 33 percent bonds and 67 percent stocks.

The second composite index is the Brinson Partner Global Security Market Index (GSMI), which contains U.S. stocks and bonds as well as non-U.S. equities and nondollar bonds along with an allocation to cash. The specific breakdown as of February 2005 was U.S. equities, 40 percent; non-U.S. equities, 25 percent; U.S. bonds, 24 percent; and non-U.S. bonds, 11 percent.

Although related to the relative market values of these asset classes, the weights specified were derived using optimization techniques to identify the portfolio mix of available global asset classes that matches the risk level of a typical U.S. pension plan. The index is balanced to the policy weights monthly.

Because the GSMI contains both U.S. and international stocks and bonds, it is clearly the most diversified benchmark available with a weighting scheme that approaches market values. As such, it is closest to the theoretically specified "market portfolio of risky assets" referred to in the CAPM literature. It is used in Reilly and Akhtar (1995) to demonstrate the impact of alternative benchmarks when evaluating portfolio performance.

7   COMPARISON OF INDEXES OVER TIME

We now look at price movements in the different indexes for monthly intervals.

Correlations between Monthly Equity Price Changes

Exhibit 56-14 contains a listing of the correlation coefficients of the monthly percentage of price changes for a set of U.S. and non-U.S. equity-market indexes with the S&P 500 index during the 22-year period from 1980 to 2001. Most of the correlation differences are attributable to the different sample of firms listed on the different stock exchanges. Most of the major indexes—except the Nikkei Stock Average—are market-value-weighted indexes that include a large number of stocks. Therefore, the computational procedure is generally similar and the sample sizes are large or all-encompassing. Thus, the major difference between the indexes is that the sample of stocks are from different segments of the U.S. stock market or from different countries.

There is a high positive correlation (0.98-0.99) between the S&P 500 and the several comprehensive U.S. equity indexes, Wilshire, NYSE, and Russell 3000. In contrast, there are lower correlations between these comprehensive indexes and various style indexes such as the Russell Large-Cap 1000 (0.886) or the Russell 2000 Small-Cap index (0.783).

The correlations between the S&P 500 and indexes from Canada, the United Kingdom, Germany, and Japan support the case for global investing. Specifically, the U.S.–Toronto correlation was about 0.75, the U.S.–*Financial Times* correlation was about 0.67, and the U.S.–Japan correlations (the Nikkei and the Tokyo S.E.) averaged about 0.38. These diversification results were confirmed with the composite international series—with the MSCI EAFE and the IFC Emerging Market the correlations were about 0.54 and 0.39, respectively. These results confirm the benefits of global diversification because such low correlations would reduce the variance of a pure U.S. stock portfolio.

Correlations between Monthly Bond Indexes

The correlations with the monthly Lehman Bros. Govt. bond return index in Exhibit 56-14 consider a variety of bond indexes. The correlations between the longer-term U.S. investment-grade bond indexes ranged from about 0.94 to 0.98, confirming that although the *level* of interest rates differs due to the risk premium, the overriding factors that determine the rates of return for investment-grade bonds over time are *systematic* interest rate variables.

The correlations among investment-grade bonds and high-yield bonds indicate significantly lower correlations (about 0.49) caused by definite equity characteristics of high-yield bonds as shown in Reilly and Wright (2001). Finally, the low and diverse relationships among U.S. investment-grade bonds and world government bonds without the United States (about 0.35) reflect different interest rate movements and exchange rate effects (these non-U.S. government results are presented as U.S. dollar returns). Again, these results support global diversification of bond portfolios.

EXHIBIT 56-14 Correlation Coefficients between Montly Percentage Price Changes in Various Stock and Bond Indexes, 1980–2001

Stock Indexes	S&P 500	Bond Indexes	Lehman Brothers Govt. Bonds
Wilshire 5000	0.983	LB Aggregate Bonds	0.981
NYSE Composite	0.993	LB Corporate Bonds	0.945
Russell 3000	0.992	LB High-Yield Bonds	0.489
Russell 1000	0.886	ML World Govt Bonds[a]	0.596
Russell 2000	0.783	ML World Govt Bonds	0.345
MSCI EAFE	0.538	w/o U.S.[a]	
Toronto S.E. 300	0.753	Treasury Bill—30-day	0.186
Financial Times	0.667	Treasury Bill—6-month[b]	0.561
All-Share		Treasury Bill—2-year[b]	0.917
Frankfurt (FAZ) Index	0.536		
Nikkei Index	0.418		
Tokyo S.E. Index	0.328		
IFC Emerging Mkt.	0.392		
M.S. World Index	0.604		
Brinson GSMI	0.915		

[a] Based on 1986–2001 data only

[b] Based on 1981–2001 data only

Source: Frank K. Reilly and David J. Wright, "An Analysis of Risk-Adjusted Performance for Global Market Assets," *Journal of Portfolio Management* 30, no. 3 (Spring, 2004), pp. 63–77. This copyrighted material is reprinted with permission from *Journal of Portfolio Management*, a publication of Institutional Investor, Inc.

Mean Annual Security Returns and Risk

The use of security indexes to measure returns and risk was demonstrated in Exhibit 3-14, which showed the average annual price change, or rate of return, and risk measure for a large set of asset indexes. As one would expect, there were clear differences between the indexes due to the different asset classes (e.g., stocks versus bonds) and the different samples within asset classes (e.g., the results for NYSE stocks versus Nasdaq stocks). Equally important, the results were generally consistent with what one should expect in a risk-averse world—that is, there was a positive relationship between the average rate of return for an asset and its measure of risk (e.g., the return-risk results for T-Bills versus the results for the S&P 500 stocks).

THE INTERNET

Investments Online

We've seen several previous Web sites which offer online users a look at current market conditions in the form of a time-delayed market index (some sites offer real-time stock and index prices, but only at a cost to their customers). Here are a few others:

www.bloomberg.com The site is somewhat of an Internet version of the "Bloomberg machine," which is prevalent in many brokerage house offices. It offers both news and current data on a wide variety of global market securities and indexes, including historical charts. The site contains information on interest rates, commodities, and currencies.

www.barra.com Barra offers downloadable historical data on several S&P/Barra equity indexes, including S&P 500, midcap, and small cap indexes as well as Canadian equity indexes. Also included is information about the characteristics of the indexes.

www.msci.com Morgan Stanley Capital International contains links to sites which offer downloadable data on several of its international equity indexes. Information and graphics on several fixed income indexes are available, too.

ecommerce.barcap.com/indices/ and the home page of Barclays Capital, www.barcap.com, offer information on European bond market indexes.

Additional global bond index performance information can be found on this page of the Thomson Financial Web site: www.thomson.com/financial/financial_products_az.jsp.

Information on Japanese bond indexes is available at a Daiwa Institute of Research site, www.dir.co.jp/InforManage/dbi/menu.html.

SUMMARY

▶ Given the several uses of security-market indexes, it is important to know how they are constructed and the differences between them. To use one of the many indexes to learn how the market is doing, you need to be aware of what market you are dealing with so you can select the appropriate index. As an example, are you only interested in the NYSE or do you also want to consider Nasdaq? Beyond the U.S. market, are you interested in Japanese or U.K. stocks, or do you want to examine the total world market? This choice is discussed in Merjos (1990).

▶ Indexes are also used as benchmarks to evaluate portfolio performance. In this case, you must be sure the index (benchmark) is consistent with your investing universe. If you are investing worldwide, you should not judge your performance relative to the DJIA, which is limited to 30 U.S. blue-chip stocks. For a bond portfolio, the index should match your investment philosophy. Finally, if your portfolio contains both stocks and bonds, you must evaluate your performance against an appropriate combination of indexes.

▶ Investors need to examine numerous market indexes to evaluate the performance of their investments. The selection of the appropriate indexes for information or evaluation will depend on how knowledgeable you are regarding the various indexes. The background from this chapter should help you understand what to look for and how to make the right decision in this area.

PROBLEMS FOR READING 56

1. You are given the following information regarding prices for a sample of stocks.

		Price	
Stock	**Number of Shares**	**T**	**T + 1**
A	1,000,000	60	80
B	10,000,000	20	35
C	30,000,000	18	25

A. Construct a *price-weighted* index for these three stocks, and compute the percentage change in the index for the period from T to T + 1.

B. Construct a *value-weighted* index for these three stocks, and compute the percentage change in the index for the period from T to T + 1.

C. Briefly discuss the difference in the results for the two indexes.

2. A. Given the data in Problem 1, construct an equal-weighted index by assuming $1,000 is invested in each stock. What is the percentage change in wealth for this portfolio?

B. Compute the percentage of price change for each of the stocks in Problem 1. Compute the arithmetic mean of these percentage changes. Discuss how this answer compares to the answer in Part a.

C. Compute the geometric mean of the percentage changes in Part b. Discuss how this result compares to the answer in Part b.

EFFICIENT CAPITAL MARKETS
by Frank K. Reilly and Keith C. Brown

LEARNING OUTCOMES

The candidate should be able to:

a. define an efficient capital market, discuss arguments supporting the concept of efficient capital markets, describe and contrast the forms of the efficient market hypothesis (EMH): weak, semistrong, and strong, and describe the tests used to examine the weak form, the semistrong form, and the strong form of the EMH;

b. identify various market anomalies and explain their implications for the EMH, and explain the overall conclusions about each form of the EMH;

c. explain the implications of stock market efficiency for technical analysis and fundamental analysis, discuss the implications of efficient markets for the portfolio management process and the role of the portfolio manager, and explain the rationale for investing in index funds.

INTRODUCTION
1

An **efficient capital market** is one in which security prices adjust rapidly to the arrival of new information and, therefore, the current prices of securities reflect all information about the security. Some of the most interesting and important academic research during the past 20 years has analyzed whether our capital markets are efficient. This extensive research is important because its results have significant real-world implications for investors and portfolio managers. In addition, the question of whether capital markets are efficient is one of the most controversial areas in investment research. Recently, a new dimension has been added to the controversy because of the rapidly expanding research in **behavioral finance** that likewise has major implications regarding the concept of efficient capital markets.

Because of its importance and controversy, you need to understand the meaning of the terms *efficient capital markets* and the *efficient market hypothesis (EMH)*. You should understand the analysis performed to test the EMH and the results of studies that either support or contradict the hypothesis. Finally, you should be aware of the implications of these results when you analyze alternative investments and work to construct a portfolio.

We are considering the topic of efficient capital markets at this point for two reasons. First, the prior discussion indicated how the capital markets function, so now it seems natural to consider the efficiency of the market in terms of how security prices react to new information. Second, the overall evidence on capital market efficiency is best described as mixed; some studies support the hypothesis, and others do not. The implications of these diverse results are important for you as an investor involved in analyzing securities and building a portfolio.

This reading contains five major sections. Section 2 discusses why we would expect capital markets to be efficient and the factors that contribute to an efficient market where the prices of securities reflect available information.

The efficient market hypothesis has been divided into three subhypotheses to facilitate testing. Section 3 describes these three subhypotheses and the implications of each of them.

Section 4 is the largest section because it contains a discussion of the results of numerous studies. This review of the research reveals that a large body of evidence supports the EMH, but a growing number of other studies do not support the hypotheses.

In Section 5, we discuss the concept of behavioral finance, the studies that have been done in this area related to efficient markets, and the conclusions as they relate to the EMH.

The final section discusses what these results imply for an investor who uses either technical analysis or fundamental analysis or what they mean for a portfolio manager who has access to superior or inferior analysts. We conclude with a brief discussion of the evidence for markets in foreign countries.

2 WHY SHOULD CAPITAL MARKETS BE EFFICIENT?

As noted earlier, in an efficient capital market, security prices adjust rapidly to the infusion of new information, and, therefore, current security prices fully reflect all available information. To be absolutely correct, this is referred to as an **informationally efficient market**. Although the idea of an efficient capital market is relatively straightforward, we often fail to consider *why* capital markets *should* be efficient. What set of assumptions imply an efficient capital market?

An initial and important premise of an efficient market requires that *a large number of profit-maximizing participants analyze and value securities,* each independently of the others.

A second assumption is that *new information regarding securities comes to the market in a random fashion,* and the timing of one announcement is generally independent of others.[1]

The third assumption is especially crucial: *profit-maximizing investors adjust security prices rapidly to reflect the effect of new information.* Although the price adjustment may be imperfect, it is unbiased. This means that sometimes the market will overadjust and other times it will underadjust, but you cannot predict which will occur at any given time. Security prices adjust rapidly because of the many profit-maximizing investors competing against one another.

The combined effect of (1) information coming in a random, independent, unpredictable fashion and (2) numerous competing investors adjusting stock prices rapidly to reflect this new information means that one would expect price changes to be independent and random. You can see that the adjustment process requires a large number of investors following the movements of the security, analyzing the impact of new information on its value, and buying or selling the security until its price adjusts to reflect the new information. This scenario implies that informationally efficient markets require some minimum amount of trading and that more trading by numerous competing investors should cause a faster price adjustment, making the market more efficient. We will return to this need for trading and investor attention when we discuss some anomalies of the EMH.

Finally, because security prices adjust to all new information, these security prices should reflect all information that is publicly available at any point in time. Therefore, the security prices that prevail at any time should be an unbiased reflection of all currently available information, including the risk involved in owning the security. Therefore, in an efficient market, *the expected returns implicit in the current price of the security should reflect its risk,* which means that investors who buy at these informationally efficient prices should receive a rate of return that is consistent with the perceived risk of the stock. Put another way, in terms of the CAPM, all stocks should lie on the SML such that their expected rates of return are consistent with their perceived risk.

ALTERNATIVE EFFICIENT MARKET HYPOTHESES   3

Most of the early work related to efficient capital markets was based on the *random walk hypothesis,* which contended that changes in stock prices occurred randomly. This early academic work contained extensive empirical analysis without much theory behind it. An article by Fama (1970) attempted to formalize the theory and organize the growing empirical evidence. Fama presented the efficient market theory in terms of a *fair game model,* contending that investors can be confident that a current market price fully reflects all available information about a security and the expected return based upon this price is consistent with its risk.

In his original article, Fama divided the overall efficient market hypothesis (EMH) and the empirical tests of the hypothesis into three subhypotheses

---

[1] New information, by definition, must be information that was not known before, and it is not predictable. If it were predictable, it would have been impounded in the security price.

depending on the information set involved: (1) weak-form EMH, (2) semistrong-form EMH, and (3) strong-form EMH.

In a subsequent review article, Fama (1991a) again divided the empirical results into three groups but shifted empirical results between the prior categories. Therefore, the following discussion uses the original categories but organizes the presentation of results using the new categories.

In the remainder of this section, we describe the three subhypotheses and the implications of each of them. As will be noted, the three subhypotheses are based on alternative information sets. In the following section, we briefly describe how researchers have tested these hypotheses and summarize the results of these tests.

Weak-Form Efficient Market Hypothesis

The **weak-form EMH** assumes that current stock prices fully reflect *all security market information,* including the historical sequence of prices, rates of return, trading volume data, and other market-generated information, such as odd-lot transactions, block trades, and transactions by exchange specialists. Because it assumes that current market prices already reflect all past returns and any other security market information, this hypothesis implies that past rates of return and other historical market data should have no relationship with future rates of return (that is, rates of return should be independent). Therefore, this hypothesis contends that you should gain little from using any **trading rule** that decides whether to buy or sell a security based on past rates of return or any other past security market data.

Semistrong-Form Efficient Market Hypothesis

The **semistrong-form EMH** asserts that security prices adjust rapidly to the release of *all public information;* that is, current security prices fully reflect all public information. The semistrong hypothesis encompasses the weak-form hypothesis, because all the market information considered by the weak-form hypothesis, such as stock prices, rates of return, and trading volume, is public. Public information also includes all nonmarket information, such as earnings and dividend announcements, price-to-earnings (P/E) ratios, dividend-yield (D/P) ratios, price-book value (P/BV) ratios, stock splits, news about the economy, and political news. This hypothesis implies that investors who base their decisions on any important new information *after it is public* should not derive above-average risk-adjusted profits from their transactions, considering the cost of trading because the security price already reflects all such new public information.

Strong-Form Efficient Market Hypothesis

The **strong-form EMH** contends that stock prices fully reflect *all information from public and private sources.* This means that no group of investors has monopolistic access to information relevant to the formation of prices. Therefore, this hypothesis contends that no group of investors should be able to consistently derive above-average risk-adjusted rates of return. The strong-form EMH encompasses both the weak-form and the semistrong-form EMH. Further, the strong-form EMH extends the assumption of efficient markets, in which prices adjust rapidly to the release of new public information, to assume perfect markets, in which all information is cost-free and available to everyone at the same time.

TESTS AND RESULTS OF EFFICIENT MARKET HYPOTHESES

4

Now that you understand the three components of the EMH and what each of them implies regarding the effect on security prices of different sets of information, we can consider the tests used to see whether the data support the hypotheses. Therefore, in this section we discuss the specific tests and summarize the results of these tests.

Like most hypotheses in finance and economics, the evidence on the EMH is mixed. Some studies have supported the hypotheses and indicate that capital markets are efficient. Results of other studies have revealed some **anomalies** related to these hypotheses, indicating results that do not support the hypotheses.

Weak-Form Hypothesis: Tests and Results

Researchers have formulated two groups of tests of the weak-form EMH. The first category involves statistical tests of independence between rates of return. The second set of tests entails a comparison of risk–return results for trading rules that make investment decisions based on past market information relative to the results from a simple buy-and-hold policy, which assumes that you buy stock at the beginning of a test period and hold it to the end.

Statistical Tests of Independence   As discussed earlier, the EMH contends that security returns over time should be independent of one another because new information comes to the market in a random, independent fashion and security prices adjust rapidly to this new information. Two major statistical tests have been employed to verify this independence.

First, **autocorrelation tests** of independence measure the significance of positive or negative correlation in returns over time. Does the rate of return on day t correlate with the rate of return on day $t - 1$, $t - 2$, or $t - 3$?[2] Those who believe that capital markets are efficient would expect insignificant correlations for all such combinations.

Several researchers have examined the serial correlations among stock returns for several relatively short time horizons including 1 day, 4 days, 9 days, and 16 days. The results typically indicated insignificant correlation in stock returns over time. Some recent studies that considered portfolios of stocks of different market size have indicated that the autocorrelation is stronger for portfolios of small market size stocks. Therefore, although the older results tend to support the hypothesis, the more recent studies cast doubt on it for portfolios of small firms, although these results could be affected by transaction costs of small-cap stocks and non-synchronous trading for small-cap stocks.

The second statistical test of independence as discussed by DeFusco et al. (2004), is the runs test. Given a series of price changes, each price change is either designated a plus (+) if it is an increase in price or a minus (−) if it is a decrease in price. The result is a set of pluses and minuses as follows: $+++-+--++-++$. A run occurs when two consecutive changes are the same; two or more consecutive positive or negative price changes constitute one run. When the price changes in a different direction, such as when a negative

---

[2] For a discussion of tests of time series independence, see DeFusco, McLeavey, Pinto, and Runkle (2004), Chapter 10.

price change is followed by a positive price change, the run ends and a new run may begin. To test for independence, you would compare the number of runs for a given series to the number in a table of expected values for the number of runs that should occur in a random series.

Studies that have examined stock price runs have confirmed the independence of stock price changes over time. The actual number of runs for stock price series consistently fell into the range expected for a random series. Therefore, these statistical tests of stocks on the NYSE and on the Nasdaq market have likewise confirmed the independence of stock price changes over time.

Although short-horizon stock returns have generally supported the weak-form EMH, several studies that examined price changes for individual *transactions* on the NYSE found significant serial correlations. Notably, none of these studies attempted to show that the dependence of transaction price movements could be used to earn above-average risk-adjusted returns after considering the trading rule's substantial transaction costs.

Tests of Trading Rules   The second group of tests of the weak-form EMH were developed in response to the assertion that the prior statistical tests of independence were too rigid to identify the intricate price patterns examined by technical analysts. As we will discuss in Reading 63, technical analysts do not expect a set number of positive or negative price changes as a signal of a move to a new equilibrium in the market. They typically look for a general consistency in the price trends over time. Such a trend might include both positive and negative changes. For this reason, technical analysts believed that their trading rules were too sophisticated and complicated to be properly tested by rigid statistical tests.

In response to this objection, investigators attempted to examine alternative technical trading rules through simulation. Advocates of an efficient market hypothesized that investors could not derive abnormal profits above a buy-and-hold policy using any trading rule that depended solely on past market information.

The trading rule studies compared the risk–return results derived from trading-rule simulations, including transaction costs, to the results from a simple buy-and-hold policy. Three major pitfalls can negate the results of a trading-rule study:

1. The investigator should *use only publicly available data* when implementing the trading rule. As an example, the trading activities of specialists as of December 31 may not be publicly available until February 1, so you should not factor in information about specialist trading activity until the information is public.

2. When computing the returns from a trading rule, you should *include all transaction costs* involved in implementing the trading strategy because most trading rules involve many more transactions than a simple buy-and-hold policy.

3. You must *adjust the results for risk* because a trading rule might simply select a portfolio of high-risk securities that should experience higher returns.

Researchers have encountered two operational problems in carrying out these tests of specific trading rules. First, some trading rules require too much subjective interpretation of data to simulate mechanically. Second, the almost infinite number of potential trading rules makes it impossible to test all of them. As a result, only the better-known technical trading rules have been examined.

Another factor that should be recognized is that the simulation studies have typically been restricted to relatively simple trading rules, which many technicians contend are rather naïve. In addition, many of these studies employed readily available data from the NYSE, which is biased toward well-known, heavily traded stocks that certainly should trade in efficient markets. Recall that markets should be more efficient when there are numerous aggressive, profit-maximizing investors attempting to adjust stock prices to reflect new information, so market efficiency will be related to trading volume. Specifically, *more trading in a security should promote market efficiency.* Alternatively, for securities with relatively few stockholders and little trading activity, the market could be inefficient simply because fewer investors would be analyzing the effect of new information, and this limited interest would result in insufficient trading activity to move the price of the security quickly to a new equilibrium value that reflects the new information. Therefore, using only active, heavily traded stocks when testing a trading rule could bias the results toward finding efficiency.

Results of Simulations of Specific Trading Rules   In the most popular trading technique, **filter rule**, an investor trades a stock when the price change exceeds a filter value set for it. As an example, an investor using a 5 percent filter would envision a positive breakout if the stock were to rise 5 percent from some base, suggesting that the stock price would continue to rise. A technician would acquire the stock to take advantage of the expected continued rise. In contrast, a 5 percent decline from some peak price would be considered a breakout on the downside, and the technician would expect a further price decline and would sell any holdings of the stock and possibly even sell the stock short.

Studies of this trading rule have used a range of filters from 0.5 percent to 50 percent. The results indicated that small filters would yield above-average profits *before* taking account of trading commissions. However, small filters generate numerous trades and, therefore, substantial trading costs. When these trading costs were considered, all the trading profits turned to losses. Alternatively, trading using larger filters did not yield returns above those of a simple buy-and-hold policy.

Researchers have simulated other trading rules that used past market data other than stock prices. Trading rules have been devised that consider advanced-decline ratios, short sales, short positions, and specialist activities.[3] These simulation tests have generated mixed results. Most of the early studies suggested that these trading rules generally would not outperform a buy-and-hold policy on a risk-adjusted basis after commissions, although several recent studies have indicated support for specific trading rules. Therefore, most evidence from simulations of specific trading rules indicates that most trading rules tested have not been able to beat a buy-and-hold policy. Therefore, these test results generally support the weak-form EMH, but the results are not unanimous.

Semistrong-Form Hypothesis Tests and Results

Recall that the semistrong-form EMH asserts that security prices adjust rapidly to the release of all public information; that is, security prices fully reflect all public information. Studies that have tested the semistrong-form EMH can be divided into the following sets of studies:

1. *Studies to predict future rates of return using available public information beyond pure market information such as prices and trading volume considered in the weak-form tests.* These studies can involve either *time-series analysis* of returns or the *cross-section distribution* of returns for individual stocks. Advocates of the EMH contend that it would not be possible to predict *future* returns using

---

[3] Many of these trading rules are discussed in Reading 63, which deals with technical analysis.

past returns or to predict the distribution of future returns (e.g., the top quartile or decile of returns) using public information.

2. *Event studies that examine how fast stock prices adjust to specific significant economic events.* A corollary approach would be to test whether it is possible to invest in a security after the public announcement of a significant event and experience significant abnormal rates of return. Again, advocates of the EMH would expect security prices to adjust rapidly, such that it would not be possible for investors to experience superior risk-adjusted returns by investing after the public announcement and paying normal transaction costs.

Adjustment for Market Effects   For any of these tests, you need to adjust the security's rates of return for the rates of return of the overall market during the period considered. The point is, a 5 percent return in a stock during the period surrounding an announcement is meaningless until you know what the aggregate stock market did during the same period and how this stock normally acts under such conditions. If the market had experienced a 10 percent return during this announcement period, the 5 percent return for the stock may be lower than expected.

Authors of pre-1970 studies generally recognized the need to make such adjustments for market movements. They typically assumed that the individual stocks should experience returns equal to the aggregate stock market. This assumption meant that the market-adjustment process simply entailed subtracting the market return from the return for the individual security to derive its **abnormal rate of return**, as follows:

$$AR_{it} = R_{it} - R_{mt} \qquad \textbf{(57-1)}$$

where:

AR_{it} = abnormal rate of return on security i during period t
R_{it} = rate of return on security i during period t
R_{mt} = rate of return on a market index during period t

In the example where the stock experienced a 5 percent increase while the market increased 10 percent, the stock's abnormal return would be minus 5 percent.

Since the 1970s, many authors have adjusted the rates of return for securities by an amount different from the market rate of return because they recognize that, based on work with the CAPM, all stocks do not change by the same amount as the market. That is, as we discuss in Reading 54, some stocks are more volatile than the market, and some are less volatile. These possibilities mean that you must determine an **expected rate of return** for the stock based on the market rate of return *and* the stock's relationship with the market (its beta). As an example, suppose a stock is generally 20 percent more volatile than the market (that is, it has a beta of 1.20). In such a case, if the market experiences a 10 percent rate of return, you would expect this stock to experience a 12 percent rate of return. Therefore, you would determine the abnormal rate of return by computing the difference between the stock's actual rate of return and its *expected rate of return* as follows:

$$AR_{it} = R_{it} - E(R_{it}) \qquad \textbf{(57-2)}$$

where:

$E(R_{it})$ = the expected rate of return for stock i during period t based on the market rate of return and the stock's normal relationship with the market (its beta)

Continuing with the example, if the stock that was expected to have a 12 percent return (based on a market return of 10 percent and a stock beta of 1.20) had only a 5 percent return, its abnormal rate of return during the period would be minus 7 percent. Over the normal long-run period, you would expect the abnormal returns for a stock to sum to zero. Specifically, during one period the returns may exceed expectations and the next period they may fall short of expectations.

To summarize, there are two sets of tests of the semistrong-form EMH. The first set of studies are referred to as **return prediction studies**. For this set of studies, investigators attempt to predict the time series of future rates of return for individual stocks or the aggregate market using public information. For example, is it possible to predict abnormal returns over time for the market based on public information such as specified values or changes in the aggregate dividend yield or the risk premium spread for bonds? Another example would be **event studies** that examine abnormal rates of return for a period immediately after an announcement of a significant economic event, such as a stock split, a proposed merger, or a stock or bond issue, to determine whether an investor can derive above-average risk-adjusted rates of return by investing after the release of public information.

The second set of studies are those that predict cross-sectional returns. In these studies, investigators look for public information regarding individual stocks that will allow them to predict the cross-sectional distribution of future risk-adjusted rates of return. For example, they test whether it is possible to use variables such as the price-earnings ratio, market value size, the price/book-value ratio, the P/E/growth rate (PEG) ratio, or the dividend yield to predict which stocks will experience above-average (e.g., top quartile) or below-average risk-adjusted rates of return in the future.

In both sets of tests, the emphasis is on the analysis of abnormal rates of return that deviate from long-term expectations or returns that are adjusted for a stock's specific risk characteristics and overall market rates of return during the period.

Results of Return Prediction Studies   The **time-series analysis** assumes that in an efficient market the best estimate of *future* rates of return will be the long-run *historical* rates of return. The point of the tests is to determine whether any public information will provide superior estimates of returns for a short-run horizon (one to six months) or a long-run horizon (one to five years).

The results of these studies have indicated limited success in predicting short-horizon returns, but the analysis of long-horizon returns has been quite successful. A prime example is dividend yield studies. After postulating that the aggregate dividend yield (D/P) was a proxy for the risk premium on stocks, they found a positive relationship between the D/P and future long-run stock market returns.

In addition, several studies have considered two variables related to the term structure of interest rates: (1) a *default spread,* which is the difference between the yields on lower-grade and Aaa-rated long-term corporate bonds (this spread has been used in earlier readings of this book as a proxy for a market risk premium), and (2) the *term structure spread,* which is the difference between the long-term Treasury bond yield and the yield on one-month Treasury bills. These variables have been used to predict stock returns and bond returns. Similar variables in foreign countries have also been useful for predicting returns for foreign common stocks.

The reasoning for these empirical results is as follows: When the two most significant variables—the dividend yield (D/P) and the bond default spread—are high, it implies that investors are expecting or requiring a high return on stocks and bonds. Notably, this occurs during poor economic environments, as reflected in the growth rate of output. A poor economic environment also implies a low-wealth environment wherein investors perceive higher risk for investments. As a result, for investors to invest and shift consumption from the present to the future, they will require a high rate of return. It is suggested that, if you invest during this risk-averse period, your subsequent returns will be above normal. In contrast, when these values are small, it implies that investors have reduced their risk premium and required rates of return and, therefore, your future returns will be below normal.

Quarterly Earnings Reports   Studies that address quarterly reports are considered part of the times-series analysis. Specifically, these studies question whether it is possible to predict future returns for a stock based on publicly available quarterly earnings reports. The typical test examined firms that experienced changes in quarterly earnings that differed from expectations. The results generally indicated abnormal returns during the 13 or 26 weeks *following* the announcement of a large *unanticipated* earnings change—referred to as an **earnings surprise**. These results suggest that an earnings surprise is *not* instantaneously reflected in security prices.

An extensive analysis by Rendleman, Jones, and Latané (1982) and a follow-up by Jones, Rendleman, and Latané (1985) using a large sample and daily data from 20 days before a quarterly earnings announcement to 90 days after the announcement indicated that 31 percent of the total response in stock returns came before the earnings announcement, 18 percent on the day of the announcement, and 51 percent *afterward.*

Several studies examined reasons for the earnings drift following earnings announcements and found that unexpected earnings explained more than 80 percent of the subsequent stock price drift for the total time period. Authors who reviewed the prior studies such as Benesh and Peterson (1986). Bernard and Thomas (1989), and Baruch (1989), contended that the reason for the stock price drift was the *earnings revisions* that followed the earnings surprises and contributed to the positive correlations of prices.

In summary, these results indicate that the market has not adjusted stock prices to reflect the release of quarterly earnings surprises as fast as expected by the semistrong EMH, which implies that earnings surprises and earnings revisions can be used to predict returns for individual stocks. These results are evidence against the EMH.[4]

The final set of calendar studies questioned whether some regularities in the rates of return during the calendar year would allow investors to predict returns on stocks. These studies include numerous studies on "the January anomaly" and studies that consider a variety of other daily and weekly regularities.

The January Anomaly   Several years ago, Branch (1977) and Branch and Chang (1985) proposed a unique trading rule for those interested in taking advantage of tax selling. Investors (including institutions) tend to engage in tax selling toward the end of the year to establish losses on stocks that have declined. After the new year, the tendency is to reacquire these stocks or to buy other stocks that look attractive. This scenario would produce downward pressure on stock prices in late November and December and positive pressure in early January. Such a seasonal pattern is inconsistent with the EMH since it should be eliminated by arbitrageurs who would buy in December and sell in early January.

A supporter of the hypothesis found that December trading volume was abnormally high for stocks that had declined during the previous year and that

---

[4] Academic studies such as these, which have indicated the importance of earnings surprises, have led *The Wall Street Journal* to publish a section on earnings surprises in connection with regular quarterly earnings reports.

significant abnormal returns occurred during January for stocks that had experienced losses during the prior year. It was concluded that, because of transaction costs, arbitrageurs must not be eliminating the January tax-selling anomaly. Subsequent analysis showed that most of the **January effect** was concentrated in the first week of trading, particularly on the first day of the year.

Several studies provided support for a January effect inconsistent with the tax-selling hypothesis by examining what happened in foreign countries that did not have our tax laws or a December year-end. They found abnormal returns in January, but the results could not be explained by tax laws. It has also been shown that the classic relationship between risk and return is strongest during January and there is a year-end trading volume bulge in late December–early January.

As pointed out by Keim (1986), despite numerous studies, the January anomaly poses as many questions as it answers.

Other Calendar Effects   Several other "calendar" effects have been examined, including a monthly effect, a weekend/day-of-the-week effect, and an intraday effect. One study found a significant monthly effect wherein all the market's cumulative advance occurred during the first half of trading months.

An analysis of the weekend effect found that the mean return for Monday was significantly negative during five-year subperiods and a total period. In contrast, the average return for the other four days was positive.

A study decomposed the Monday effect that is typically measured from Friday close to Monday close into a *weekend effect* (from Friday close to Monday open), and a *Monday trading effect* (from Monday open to the Monday close). It was shown that the negative Monday effect found in prior studies actually occurs from the Friday close to the Monday open (it is really a weekend effect). After adjusting for the weekend effect, the Monday trading effect was positive. Subsequently, it was shown that the Monday effect was on average positive in January and negative for all other months.

Finally, for *large firms*, the negative Monday effect occurred before the market opened (it was a weekend effect), whereas for *smaller firms* most of the negative Monday effect occurred during the day on Monday (it was a Monday trading effect).

Predicting Cross-Sectional Returns   Assuming an efficient market, *all securities should have equal risk-adjusted returns* because security prices should reflect all public information that would influence the security's risk. Therefore, studies in this category attempt to determine if you can use public information to predict what stocks will enjoy above-average or below-average risk-adjusted returns.

These studies typically examine the usefulness of alternative measures of size or quality to rank stocks in terms of risk-adjusted returns. Notably, all of these tests involve *a joint hypothesis* because they not only consider the efficiency of the market but are dependent on the asset pricing model that provides the measure of risk used in the test. Specifically, if a test determines that it is possible to predict risk-adjusted returns, these results could occur because the market is not efficient, *or* they could be because the measure of risk is faulty and, therefore, the measures of risk-adjusted returns are wrong.

Price-Earnings Ratios   Several studies beginning with Basu (1977) have examined the relationship between the historical **price-earnings (P/E) ratios** for stocks and the returns on the stocks. Some have suggested that low P/E stocks will outperform high P/E stocks because growth companies enjoy high P/E ratios, but the market tends to overestimate the growth potential and thus overvalues these growth companies, while undervaluing low-growth firms with low P/E ratios. A relationship between the historical P/E ratios and subsequent risk-adjusted market performance would constitute evidence against the semistrong EMH, because it would imply that investors could use publicly available information regarding P/E ratios to predict future abnormal returns.

Performance measures that consider both return and risk indicated that low P/E ratio stocks experienced superior risk-adjusted results relative to the market, whereas high P/E ratio stocks had significantly inferior risk-adjusted results. Subsequent analysis concluded that publicly available P/E ratios possess valuable information regarding future returns, which is inconsistent with semistrong efficiency.

Peavy and Goodman (1983) examined P/E ratios with adjustments for firm size, industry effects, and infrequent trading and likewise found that the risk-adjusted returns for stocks in the lowest P/E ratio quintile were superior to those in the highest P/E ratio quintile.

Price-Earnings/Growth Rate (PEG) Ratios   During the past decade, there has been a significant increase in the use of the ratio of a stock's price-earnings ratio divided by the firm's expected growth rate of earnings (referred to as the PEG ratio) as a relative valuation tool, especially for stocks of growth companies that have P/E ratios substantially above average. Advocates of the PEG ratio hypothesize an inverse relationship between the PEG ratio and subsequent rates of return—that is, they expect that stocks with relatively low PEG ratios (i.e., less than one) will experience above-average rates of return while stocks with relatively high PEG ratios (i.e., in excess of three or four) will have below-average rates of return. A study by Peters (1991) using quarterly rebalancing supported the hypothesis of an inverse relationship. These results would constitute an anomaly and would not support the EMH. A subsequent study by Reilly and Marshall (1999) assumed annual rebalancing and divided the sample on the basis of a risk measure (beta), market value size, and by expected growth rate. Except for stocks with low betas and very low expected growth rates, the results were not consistent with the hypothesis of an inverse relationship between the PEG ratio and subsequent rates of return.

In summary, the results related to using the PEG ratio to select stocks are mixed—several studies that assume either monthly or quarterly rebalancing indicate an anomaly because the authors use public information and derive above-average rates of return. In contrast, a study with more realistic annual rebalancing indicated that no consistent relationship exists between the PEG ratio and subsequent rates of return.

The Size Effect   Banz (1981) examined the impact of size (measured by total market value) on the risk-adjusted rates of return. The risk-adjusted returns for extended periods (20 to 35 years) indicated that the small firms consistently experienced significantly larger risk-adjusted returns than the larger firms. Reinganum (1981) contended that it was the size, not the P/E ratio, that caused the results discussed in the prior subsection, but this contention was disputed by Basu (1983).

Recall that abnormal returns may occur because the markets are inefficient or because the market model provides incorrect estimates of risk and expected returns.

It was suggested that the riskiness of the small firms was improperly measured because small firms are traded less frequently. An alternative risk measure technique confirmed that the small firms had much higher risk, but the difference in beta did not account for the large difference in rates of return.

A study by Stoll and Whaley (1983) that examined the impact of transaction costs confirmed the size effect but also found that firms with small market value have low stock prices. Because transaction costs vary inversely with price per share, these costs must be considered when examining the small-firm effect. It was shown that there was a significant difference in the percentage total transaction cost for large firms (2.71 percent) versus small firms (6.77 percent). This differential in transaction costs, with frequent trading, can have a significant impact on the results. Assuming daily transactions, the original small-firm effects are reversed. The point is, size-effect studies must consider realistic transaction costs and specify holding period assumptions. A study by Reinganum (1983) that considered both factors over long periods demonstrated that infrequent rebalancing (about once a year) is almost ideal—the results are better than long-run buy-and-hold and avoids frequent rebalancing that experiences excess costs. In summary, the small firms outperformed the large firms after considering risk and transaction costs, assuming annual rebalancing.

Most studies on the size effect employed large databases and long time periods (over 50 years) to show that this phenomenon has existed for many years. In contrast, a study that examined the performance over various intervals of time concluded that *the small-firm effect is not stable.* During most periods they found the negative relationship between size and return; but, during others (such as 1967 to 1975), they found that large firms outperformed the small firms. Notably, this positive relationship held during the following recent periods: 1984–87; 1989–90: and 1995–99. A study by Reinganum (1992) acknowledges this instability but contends that the small-firm effect is still a long-run phenomenon.

In summary, firm size is a major efficient market anomaly. Numerous attempts to explain the size anomaly indicate that the two strongest explanations are the risk measurements and the higher transaction costs. Depending on the frequency of trading, these two factors may account for much of the differential. Keim (1983) also related it to seasonality. These results indicate that the size effect must be considered in any **event study** that considers long time periods and contains a sample of firms with significantly different market values.

Neglected Firms and Trading Activity   Arbel and Strebel (1983) considered an additional influence beyond size—attention or neglect. They measured attention in terms of the number of analysts who regularly follow a stock and divided the stocks into three groups: (1) highly followed, (2) moderately followed, and (3) neglected. They confirmed the small-firm effect but also found a neglected-firm effect caused by the lack of information and limited institutional interest. The neglected-firm concept applied across size classes. Contrary results are reported by Beard and Sias (1997) who found no evidence of a neglected firm premium after controlling for capitalization.

James and Edmister (1983) examined the impact of trading volume by considering the relationship between returns, market value, and trading activity. The results confirmed the relationship between size and rates of return, but the results indicated no significant difference between the mean returns of the highest and lowest trading activity portfolios. A subsequent study hypothesized that firms with less information require higher returns. Using the period of listing as a proxy for information, they found a negative relationship between returns and the period of listing after adjusting for firm size and the January effect.

Book Value–Market Value Ratio   This ratio relates the book value (BV) of a firm's equity to the market value (MV) of its equity. Rosenberg, Reid, and Lanstein (1985) found a significant positive relationship between current values for this ratio and future stock returns and contended that such a relationship between available public information on the BV/MV ratio and future returns was evidence against the EMH.[5]

---

[5] Many studies define this ratio as "book-to-market value" (BV/MV) because it implies a positive relationship, but most practitioners refer to it as the "price-to-book value" (P/B) ratio. Obviously the concept is the same, but the sign changes.

Strong support for this ratio was provided by Fama and French (1992) who evaluated the joint effects of market beta, size, E/P ratio, leverage, and the BV/MV ratio (referred to as BE/ME) on a cross section of average returns. They analyzed the hypothesized positive relationship between beta and expected returns and found that this positive relationship held pre-1969 but disappeared during the period 1963 to 1990. In contrast, the negative relationship between size and average return was significant by itself and significant after inclusion of other variables.

In addition, they found a significant positive relationship between the BV/MV ratio and average return that persisted even when other variables are included. Most importantly, *both* size and the BV/MV ratio are significant when included together and they dominate other ratios. Specifically, although leverage and the E/P ratio were significant by themselves or with size, they become insignificant when *both* size and the BV/MV ratio are considered.

The results in Exhibit 57-1 show the separate and combined effect of the two variables. As shown, going across the Small-ME (small size) row, BV/MV captures strong variation in average returns (0.70 to 1.92 percent). Alternatively, controlling for the BV/MV ratio leaves a size effect in average returns (the high BV/MV results decline from 1.92 to 1.18 percent when going from small to large). These positive results for the BV/MV ratio were replicated for returns on Japanese stocks.

In summary, studies that have used publicly available ratios to predict the cross section of expected returns for stocks have provided substantial evidence in conflict with the semistrong-form EMH. Significant results were found for P/E ratios, market value size, neglected firms, and BV/MV ratios. Although the research by Fama and French indicated that the optimal combination appears to be size and the BV/MV ratio, a study by Jensen, Johnson, and Mercer (1997) indicates that this combination only works during periods of expansive monetary policy.

Results of Event Studies   Recall that the intent of event studies is to examine abnormal rates of return surrounding significant economic information. Those who advocate the EMH would expect returns to adjust quickly to announcements of new information such that investors cannot experience positive abnormal rates of return by acting after the announcement. Because of space constraints, we can only summarize the results for some of the more popular events considered.

The discussion of results is organized by event or item of public information. Specifically, we will examine the price movements and profit potential surrounding stock splits, the sale of initial public offerings, exchange listings, unexpected world or economic events, and the announcements of significant accounting changes. Notably, the results for most of these studies have supported the semistrong-form EMH.

Stock Split Studies   Many investors believe that the prices of stocks that split will increase in value because the shares are priced lower, which increases demand for them. In contrast, advocates of efficient markets would not expect a change in value because the firm has simply issued additional stock and nothing fundamentally affecting the value of the firm has occurred.

The classic study by Fama, Fisher, Jensen, and Roll (1969), referred to hereafter as FFJR, hypothesized no significant price change following a stock split, because any relevant information (such as earnings growth) that caused the split would have already been discounted. The FFJR study analyzed abnormal price movements surrounding the time of the split and divided the stock split sample into those stocks that did or did not raise their dividends. Both groups experienced positive abnormal price changes prior to the split. Stocks that split but did

EXHIBIT 57-1	Average Monthly Returns on Portfolios Formed on Size and Book-to-Market Equity; Stocks Sorted by ME (Down) and Then BE/ME (Across); July 1963 to December 1990

In June of each year t, the NYSE, AMEX, and Nasdaq stocks that meet the CRSP-COMPUSTAT data requirements are allocated to 10 size portfolios using the NYSE size (ME) breakpoints. The NYSE, AMEX, and Nasdaq stocks in each size decile are then sorted into 10 BE/ME portfolios using the book-to-market ratios for year $t - 1$. BE/ME is the book value of common equity plus balance-sheet deferred taxes for fiscal year t 1, over market equity for December of year $t - 1$. The equal-weighted monthly portfolio returns are then calculated for July of year t to June of year $t + 1$.

Average monthly return is the time-series average of the monthly equal-weighted portfolio returns (in percent).

The All column shows average returns for equal-weighted size decile portfolios. The All row shows average returns for equal-weighted portfolios of the stocks in each BE/ME group.

					Book-to-Market Portfolios						
	All	**Low**	**2**	**3**	**4**	**5**	**6**	**7**	**8**	**9**	**High**
All	1.23	0.64	0.98	1.06	1.17	1.24	1.26	1.39	1.40	1.50	1.63
Small-ME	1.47	0.70	1.14	1.20	1.43	1.56	1.51	1.70	1.71	1.82	1.92
ME-2	1.22	0.43	1.05	0.96	1.19	1.33	1.19	1.58	1.28	1.43	1.79
ME-3	1.22	0.56	0.88	1.23	0.95	1.36	1.30	1.30	1.40	1.54	1.60
ME-4	1.19	0.39	0.72	1.06	1.36	1.13	1.21	1.34	1.59	1.51	1.47
ME-5	1.24	0.88	0.65	1.08	1.47	1.13	1.43	1.44	1.26	1.52	1.49
ME-6	1.15	0.70	0.98	1.14	1.23	0.94	1.27	1.19	1.19	1.24	1.50
ME-7	1.07	0.95	1.00	0.99	0.83	0.99	1.13	0.99	1.16	1.10	1.47
ME-8	1.08	0.66	1.13	0.91	0.95	0.99	1.01	1.15	1.05	1.29	1.55
ME-9	0.95	0.44	0.89	0.92	1.00	1.05	0.93	0.82	1.11	1.04	1.22
Large-ME	0.89	0.93	0.88	0.84	0.71	0.79	0.83	0.81	0.96	0.97	1.18

Source: Eugene F. Fama and Kenneth French, "The Cross Section of Expected Stock Returns," *Journal of Finance* 47, no. 2 (June 1992): 446. Reprinted with permission of Blackwell Publishing.

not increase their dividend experienced abnormal price *declines* following the split and within 12 months lost all their accumulated abnormal gains. In contrast, stocks that split and increased their dividend experienced no abnormal returns after the split.

These results support the semistrong EMH because they indicate that investors cannot gain from the information on a stock split after the public announcement. These results were confirmed by most (but not all) subsequent studies. In summary, most studies found no short-run or long-run positive impact on security returns because of a stock split, although the results are not unanimous.

Initial Public Offerings (IPOs)   During the past 20 years, a number of closely held companies have gone public by selling some of their common stock. Because of uncertainty about the appropriate offering price and the risk involved in underwriting such issues, it has been hypothesized that the underwriters would tend to underprice these new issues.

Given this general expectation of underpricing, the studies in this area have generally considered three sets of questions: (1) How great is the underpricing on average? Does the underpricing vary over time? If so, why? (2) What factors cause different amounts of underpricing for alternative issues? (3) How fast does the market adjust the price for the underpricing?

The answer to the first question is an average underpricing of almost 18 percent, but it varies over time as shown by the results in Exhibit 57-2. The major variables that cause differential underpricing seem to be: various risk measures, the size of the firm, the prestige of the underwriter, and the status of the firm's accounting firms. On the question of direct interest to the EMH, results in Miller and Reilly (1987) and Ibbotson, Sindelar, and Ritter (1994) indicate that the price adjustment to the underpricing takes place within one day after the offering. Therefore, it appears that some underpricing occurs based on the original offering price, but the only ones who benefit from this underpricing are investors who receive allocations of the original issue. More specifically, institutional investors captured most (70 percent) of the short-term profits. This rapid adjustment of the initial underpricing would support the semistrong EMH. Finally, studies by Ritter (1991); Carter, Dark, and Singh (1998); and Loughran and Ritter (1995) that examined the long-run returns on IPOs indicate that investors who acquire the stock after the initial adjustment do *not* experience positive long-run abnormal returns.

Exchange Listing   A significant economic event for a firm is its stock's being listed on a national exchange, especially the NYSE. Such a listing is expected to increase the market liquidity of the stock and add to its prestige. An important question is, can an investor derive abnormal returns from investing in the stock when a new listing is announced or around the time of the actual listing? The results regarding abnormal returns from such investing were mixed. All the studies agreed that (1) the stocks' prices increased before any listing announcements, and (2) stock prices consistently declined after the actual listing. The crucial question is, what happens between the announcement of the application for listing and the actual listing (a period of four to six weeks)? A study by McConnell and Sanger (1989) points toward profit opportunities immediately after the announcement that a firm is applying for listing and there is the possibility of excess returns from price declines after the actual listing. Finally, studies that have examined the impact of listing on the risk of the securities found no significant change in systematic risk or the firm's cost of equity.

In summary, listing studies that provide some evidence of short-run profit opportunities for investors using public information would not support the semistrong-form EMH.

Unexpected World Events and Economic News   The results of several studies that examined the response of security prices to world or economic news have supported the semistrong-form EMH. An analysis of the reaction of stock prices to unexpected world events, such as the Eisenhower heart attack, the Kennedy assassination, and military events, found that prices adjusted to the news before the market opened or before it reopened after the announcement (generally, as with the World Trade Center attack, the Exchanges are closed immediately for various time periods—e.g., one to four days). A study by Pierce and Roley (1985) that examined the response to announcements about money supply, inflation, real economic activity, and the discount rate found an impact that did not persist beyond the announcement day. Finally, Jain (1988) did an analysis of hourly stock returns and trading volume response to surprise announcements and found that

EXHIBIT 57-2	Numbers of Offerings, Average First-Day Returns, and Gross Proceeds of Initial Public Offerings in 1975–2000		
Year	Number of Offerings[a]	Average First-Day Return, %[b]	Gross Proceeds, $ Millions[c]
1975	14	−1.9	264
1976	35	2.9	237
1977	35	21.0	151
1978	50	25.7	247
1979	81	24.6	429
1980	238	49.4	1,404
1981	438	16.8	3,200
1982	198	20.3	1,334
1983	848	20.8	13,168
1984	516	11.5	3,932
1985	507	12.4	10,450
1986	953	10.0	17,571
1987	630	10.4	13,841
1988	223	9.8	4,514
1989	210	12.6	5,721
1990	172	14.5	4,749
1991	365	14.7	16,202
1992	513	12.5	22,989
1993	665	15.2	30,587
1994	567	13.4	19,039
1995	571	20.5	29,422
1996	831	17.0	43,150
1997	603	13.2	34,010
1998	357	20.2	35,052
1999	543	66.7	65,653
2000	449	55.5	66,480
1975–79	215	14.5	1,328
1980–89	4,761	15.3	75,139
1990–99	5,187	20.6	300,853
2000	449	55.5	66,480
Total	14,698	18.6	443,800

[a] The number of offerings excludes IPOs with an offer price of less than $5.00, ADRs, best efforts offers, unit offers, Regulation A offerings (small issues, raising less than $1.5 million during the 1980s), real estate investment trusts (REITs), partnerships, and closed-end funds.

[b] First-day returns are computed as the percentage return from the offering price to the first closing market price.

[c] Gross proceeds data are from Securities Data Co. and exclude overallotment options but include the international tranche, if any. No adjustments for inflation have been made.

Source: Jay R. Ritter. "Summary Statistics on 1975–2000 Initial Public Offerings with an Offer Price of $5.00 or More" (University of Florida, January 29, 2001).

unexpected information about money supply impacted stock prices within one hour. For a review of studies that considered the impact of news on individual stocks, see Chan (2003).

Announcements of Accounting Changes   Numerous studies have analyzed the impact of announcements of accounting changes on stock prices. In efficient markets, security prices should react quickly and predictably to announcements of accounting changes. An announcement of an accounting change that affects the economic value of the firm should cause a rapid change in stock prices. An accounting change that affects reported earnings but has no economic significance should not affect stock prices. For example, when a firm changes its depreciation accounting method for reporting purposes from accelerated to straight line, the firm should experience an increase in reported earnings, but there is no economic consequence. An analysis of stock price movements surrounding this accounting change supported the EMH because there were no positive price changes following the change, and there were some negative price changes because firms making such an accounting change are typically performing poorly.

During periods of high inflation, many firms will change their inventory method from first-in, first-out (FIFO) to last-in, first-out (LIFO), which causes a decline in reported earnings but benefits the firm because it reduces its taxable earnings and, therefore, tax expenses. Advocates of efficient markets would expect positive price changes because of the tax savings, and study results confirmed this expectation.

Therefore, studies such as those by Bernard and Thomas (1990) and Ou and Penman (1989) indicate that the securities markets react quite rapidly to accounting changes and adjust security prices as expected on the basis of changes in true value (that is, analysts pierce the accounting veil and value securities on the basis of economic events).

Corporate Events   Corporate finance events such as mergers and acquisitions, reorganization, and various security offerings (common stock, straight bonds, convertible bonds) have been examined, relative to two general questions: (1) What is the market impact of these alternative events? (2) How fast does the market adjust the security prices?

Regarding the reaction to corporate events, the answer is very consistent—stock prices react as one would expect based on the underlying economic impact of the action. For example, the reaction to mergers is that the stock of the firm being acquired increases in line with the premium offered by the acquiring firm, whereas the stock of the acquiring firm typically declines because of the concern that they overpaid for the firm. On the question of speed of reaction, the evidence indicates fairly rapid adjustment—that is, the adjustment period declines as shorter interval data is analyzed (using daily data, most studies find that the price adjustment is completed in about three days). Studies related to financing decisions are reviewed by Smith (1986). Studies on corporate control that consider mergers and reorganizations are reviewed by Jensen and Warner (1988). Numerous corporate spin-offs have generated interesting stock performance as shown by Desai and Jain (1999) and Chemmanur and Yan (2004).

Summary on the Semistrong-Form EMH   Clearly, the evidence from tests of the semi-strong EMH is mixed. The hypothesis receives almost unanimous support from the numerous event studies on a range of events including stock splits, initial public offerings, world events and economic news, accounting changes, and a variety of corporate finance events. About the only mixed results come from exchange listing studies.

In sharp contrast, the numerous studies on predicting rates of return over time or for a cross section of stocks presented evidence counter to semistrong efficiency. This included time-series studies on risk premiums, calender patterns, and quarterly earnings surprises. Similarly, the results for cross-sectional predictors such as size, the BV/MV ratio (when there is expansive monetary policy), P/E ratios, and some neglected firm studies indicated nonefficiencies.

Strong-Form Hypothesis: Tests and Results

The strong-form EMH contends that stock prices fully reflect *all information,* public and private. This implies that no group of investors has access to *private information* that will allow them to consistently experience above-average profits. This extremely rigid hypothesis requires not only that stock prices must adjust rapidly to new public information but also that no group has access to private information.

Tests of the strong-form EMH have analyzed returns over time for different identifiable investment groups to determine whether any group consistently received above-average risk-adjusted returns. Such a group must have access to and act upon important private information or an ability to act on public information before other investors, which would indicate that security prices were not adjusting rapidly to *all* new information.

Investigators have tested this form of the EMH by analyzing the performance of the following four major groups of investors: (1) *corporate insiders,* (2) *stock exchange specialists,* (3) *security analysts* at Value Line and elsewhere, and (4) *professional money managers.*

Corporate Insider Trading   Corporate insiders are required to report monthly to the SEC on their transactions (purchases or sales) in the stock of the firm for which they are insiders. Insiders include major corporate officers, members of the board of directors, and owners of 10 percent or more of any equity class of securities. About six weeks after the reporting period, this insider trading information is made public by the SEC. These insider trading data have been used to identify how corporate insiders have traded and determine whether they bought on balance before abnormally good price movements and sold on balance before poor market periods for their stock. The results of studies including Chowdhury, Howe, and Lin (1993) and Pettit and Venkatesh (1995) have generally indicated that corporate insiders consistently enjoyed above-average profits, heavily dependent on selling prior to low returns and not selling before strong returns. This implies that many insiders had private information from which they derived above-average returns on their company stock.

In addition, an earlier study found that *public* investors who consistently traded with the insiders based on announced insider transactions would have enjoyed excess risk-adjusted returns (after commissions), although a subsequent study concluded that the market had eliminated this inefficiency after considering total transaction costs.

Overall, these results provide mixed support for the EMH because several studies indicate that insiders experience abnormal profits, while subsequent studies indicate it is no longer possible for noninsiders to use this information to generate excess returns. Notably, because of investor interest in these data as a result of academic research, the *Wall Street Journal* currently publishes a monthly column entitled "Inside Track" that discusses the largest insider transactions.

Stock Exchange Specialists   Several studies have determined that specialists have monopolistic access to certain important information about unfilled limit orders, and they should be able to derive above-average returns from this information.

This expectation is generally supported by the data. First, specialists generally make money because they typically sell shares at higher prices than their purchased price. Also, they apparently make money when they buy or sell after unexpected announcements and when they trade in large blocks of stock. An article by Ip (2001b) supported this belief; it contended that specialists are doing more trading as dealers and the return on their capital during 2000 was 26 percent.

Security Analysts   Several tests have considered whether it is possible to identify a set of analysts who have the ability to select undervalued stocks. The analysis involves determining whether, after a stock selection by an analyst is made known, a significant abnormal return is available to those who follow these recommendations. These studies and those that discuss performance by money managers are more realistic and relevant than those that considered corporate insiders and stock exchange specialists because these analysts and money managers are full-time investment professionals with no obvious advantage except emphasis and training. If anyone should be able to select undervalued stocks, it should be these "pros." We initially examine Value Line rankings and then analyze the usefulness of recommendations by individual analysts.

The Value Line Enigma   Value Line (VL) is a large well-known advisory service that publishes financial information on approximately 1,700 stocks. Included in its report is a timing rank, which indicates Value Line's expectation regarding a firm's common stock performance over the coming 12 months. A rank of 1 is the most favorable performance and 5 the worst. This ranking system, initiated in April 1965, assigns numbers based on four factors:

1. An earnings and price rank of each security relative to all others
2. A price momentum factor
3. Year-to-year relative changes in quarterly earnings
4. A quarterly earnings "surprise" factor (actual quarterly earnings compared with VL estimated earnings)

The firms are ranked based on a composite score for each firm. The top and bottom 100 are ranked 1 and 5, respectively; the next 300 from the top and bottom are ranked 2 and 4; and the rest (approximately 900) are ranked 3. Rankings are assigned every week based on the latest data. Notably, all the data used to derive the four factors are public information.

Several years after the ranking was started, Value Line contended that the stocks rated 1 substantially outperformed the market and the stocks rated 5 seriously underperformed the market (the performance figures did not include dividend income but also did not charge commissions).

Studies on the Value Line enigma indicate that there is information in the VL rankings (especially either rank 1 or 5) and in changes in the rankings (especially going from 2 to 1). Further, recent evidence indicates that the market is fairly efficient, because the abnormal adjustments appear to be complete by Day + 2. An analysis of study results over time indicates a faster adjustment to the rankings during recent years. Also, despite statistically significant price changes, mounting evidence indicates that it is not possible to derive abnormal returns from these announcements after considering realistic transaction costs. The strongest evidence regarding not being able to use this information is that Value Line's Centurion Fund, which concentrates on investing in rank-1 stocks, has consistently underperformed the market over the past decade.

Analysts' Recommendations   There is evidence in favor of the existence of superior analysts who apparently possess private information. A study by Womack (1996) found that analysts appear to have both market timing and stock-picking ability, especially in connection with relatively rare sell recommendations. Jegadeesh et al. (2004) found that consensus recommendations do not contain incremental information for most stocks beyond other available signals (momentum and volume), but *changes* in consensus recommendations are useful. Alternatively, research by Ivkovic and Jegadeesh (2004) indicated that the most useful information consisted of upward earning revisions in the week prior to earnings announcements.

Performance of Professional Money Managers   The studies of professional money managers are more realistic and widely applicable than the analysis of insiders and specialists because money managers typically do not have monopolistic access to important new information but are highly trained professionals who work full time at investment management. Therefore, if any "normal" set of investors should be able to derive above-average profits, it should be this group. Also, if any noninsider should be able to derive inside information, professional money managers should, because they conduct extensive management interviews.

Most studies on the performance of money managers have examined mutual funds because performance data is readily available for them. Recently, data have become available for bank trust departments, insurance companies, and investment advisers. The original mutual fund studies indicated that most funds did not match the performance of a buy-and-hold policy. When risk-adjusted returns were examined *without* considering commission costs, slightly more than half of the money managers did better than the overall market. When commission costs, load fees, and management costs were considered, approximately two-thirds of the mutual funds did *not* match aggregate market performance. It was also found that successful funds during individual years were inconsistent in their performance.

Now that it is possible to get performance data for pension plans and endowment funds, several studies have documented that the performances of pension plans and endowments did not match that of the aggregate market.

The figures in Exhibit 57-3 provide a rough demonstration of these results for recent periods. These data are collected by Russell/Mellon Analytical Services as part of its performance evaluation service. Exhibit 57-3 contains the median rates of return for several investment groups compared to a set of Russell indexes, including the very broad Russell 3000 index.[6] These results show that all but one equity universe always beat the Russell 3000 universe in all periods. In contrast, the Russell 3000 index beat the mutual fund universes for periods of five years and longer, but not for periods of three years or less. Therefore, for these periods, the money manager results are mixed related to the strong-form EMH.

Conclusions Regarding the Strong-Form EMH   The tests of the strong-form EMH have generated mixed results. The result for two unique groups of investors (corporate insiders and stock exchange specialists) did not support the hypothesis because both groups apparently have monopolistic access to important information and use it to derive above-average returns.

Tests to determine whether there are any analysts with private information concentrated on the Value Line rankings and publications of analysts' recommendations. The results for Value Line rankings have changed over time and

---

[6] The results for these individual accounts have an upward bias because they consider only accounts retained (for example, if a firm or bank does a poor job on an account and the client leaves, those results would not be included).

EXHIBIT 57-3	Annualized Rates of Return for Russell/Mellon U.S. Equity Universes and for Benchmark Indexes during Alternative Periods ending December 31, 2003

	1 Year	2 Years	3 Years	4 Years	5 Years	8 Years	10 Years
U.S. Equity Universe-Medians							
Equity accounts	30.0	1.0	−2.3	−2.2	2.2	10.6	11.8
Equity oriented accounts	30.3	1.0	−2.4	−2.5	2.7	10.7	11.8
Equity pooled	29.6	0.9	−2.3	−2.2	1.2	10.1	11.5
Special equity pooled	47.0	11.3	13.0	14.0	13.6	13.5	14.1
Value equity accounts	31.1	5.0	3.7	6.0	5.8	11.3	12.6
Market oriented accounts	29.3	0.7	−2.7	−3.0	1.2	10.5	11.7
Midcap equity accounts	38.6	6.5	4.6	7.4	9.4	13.1	13.8
Growth equity accounts	29.1	−2.8	−9.0	−9.9	−1.6	9.9	10.6
Small cap accounts	45.7	10.4	10.8	11.6	13.3	13.4	13.9
Mutual Fund Universe-Medians							
Balanced mutual funds	18.6	2.6	0.3	0.6	2.6	7.3	7.8
Equity mutual funds	−1.7	−8.4	−6.6	−3.3	−0.3	8.4	8.9
Benchmark Indexes							
Russell 1000 Growth Index	29.75	−3.27	−9.36	−12.82	−5.11	6.97	9.21
Russell 1000 Index	29.89	0.88	−3.78	−4.79	−0.13	9.41	11.00
Russell 1000 Value Index	30.03	4.81	1.22	2.64	3.56	10.76	11.88
Russell 2000 Growth Index	48.54	1.78	−2.03	−7.59	0.86	3.61	5.43
Russell 2000 Index	47.25	8.21	6.27	3.86	7.13	8.78	9.47
Russell 2000 Value Index	46.03	13.73	13.83	16.01	12.28	13.06	12.70
Russell 2500 Index	45.51	9.37	6.58	6.00	9.40	11.15	11.74
Russell 3000 Index	31.06	1.40	−3.08	−4.19	0.37	9.25	10.77
Russell Midcap Index	40.06	8.35	3.47	4.65	7.23	11.54	12.18

Source: "US Equity Universe-Medians" and "Mutual Fund Universe-Medians" reprinted with permission of Russell/Mellon Analytical Services. "Benchmark Indexes" reprinted with permission of Russell Investment Group.

currently tend toward support for the EMH. Specifically, the adjustment to rankings and ranking changes is fairly rapid, and it appears that trading is not profitable after transaction costs. Alternatively, individual analysts' recommendations and overall consensus changes seem to contain significant information.

Finally, recent performance by professional money managers provided mixed support for the strong-form EMH. Most money manager performance studies before 2002 have indicated that these highly trained, full-time investors could not consistently outperform a simple buy-and-hold policy on a risk-adjusted basis. In contrast, the recent results shown in Exhibit 57-3 show that about half the non-mutual fund universe beat the broad Russell 3000 index, while the equity mutual fund results supported the EMH for long-term periods. Because money managers are similar to most investors who do not have access to inside information, these latter results are considered more relevant to the hypothesis. Therefore, it appears that there is mixed support for the strong-form EMH as applied to most investors.

BEHAVIORAL FINANCE   5

Our discussion up to this point has dealt with standard finance theory, how this theory assumes that capital markets function, and how to test within this theoretical context whether capital markets are informationally efficient. However, in the 1990s, a new branch of financial economics has been added to the mix. **Behavioral finance** considers how various psychological traits affect the ways that individuals or groups act as investors, analysts, and portfolio managers. As noted by Olsen (1998), behavioral finance advocates recognize that the standard model of rational behavior and profit maximization can be true within specific boundaries but assert that it is an *incomplete* model since it does not consider individual behavior. Specifically, according to Olsen (1998), behavioral finance

> seeks to understand and predict systematic financial market implications of psychological decisions processes . . . behavioral finance is focused on the implication of psychological and economic principles for the improvement of financial decision-making. (p. 11)

While it is acknowledged that currently there is no unified theory of behavioral finance, the emphasis has been on identifying portfolio anomalies that can be explained by various psychological traits in individuals or groups or pinpointing instances when it is possible to experience above-normal rates of return by exploiting the biases of investors, analysts, or portfolio managers.

Explaining Biases

Over time it has been noted that investors have a number of biases that negatively affect their investment performance. Advocates of behavioral finance have been able to explain a number of these biases based on psychological characteristics. One major bias documented by Scott, Stumpp, and Xu (1999) is the propensity of investors to hold on to "losers" too long and sell "winners" too soon. Apparently, investors fear losses much more than they value gains. This is explained by *prospect theory*, which contends that utility depends on deviations from moving reference points rather than absolute wealth.

Another bias documented by Solt and Statman (1989) and Shefrin and Statman (1996) for growth companies is *overconfidence* in forecasts, which causes analysts to overestimate growth rates for growth companies and overemphasize good news and ignore negative news for these firms. Analysts and many investors generally believe that the stocks of growth companies will be "good" stocks. This bias is also referred to as *confirmation bias*, whereby investors look for information that supports their prior opinions and decisions. As a result, they will misvalue the stocks of these generally popular companies.

A study by Brown (1999) examined the effect of *noise traders* (nonprofessionals with no special information) on the volatility of closed-end mutual funds. When there is a shift in sentiment, these traders move together, which increases the prices and the volatility of these securities during trading hours. Also, Clark and Statman (1998) find that noise traders tend to follow newsletter writers, who in turn tend to "follow the herd." These writers and "the herd" are almost always wrong, which contributes to excess volatility.

Shefrin (2001) describes *escalation bias,* which causes investors to put more money into a failure that they feel responsible for rather than into a success. This leads to the relatively popular investor practice of "averaging down" on an investment that has declined in value since the initial purchase rather than consider selling the stock if it was a mistake. The thinking is that if it was a buy at $40, it is a screaming bargain at $30. Obviously, an alternative solution is to reevaluate the stock to see if some important bad news was missed in the initial valuation (therefore, sell it and accept the loss), or to confirm the initial valuation and acquire more of the "bargain." The difficult psychological factor noted by Shefrin (1999) is to seriously look for the bad news and consider the negative effects of that on the valuation.

Fusion Investing

According to Charles M. C. Lee (2003), *fusion investing* is the integration of two elements of investment valuation—fundamental value and investor sentiment. In Robert Shiller's (1984) formal model, the market price of securities is the expected dividends discounted to infinity (its fundamental value) plus a term that indicates the demand from noise traders who reflect investor sentiment. It is contended that when noise traders are bullish, stock prices will be higher than normal or higher than what is justified by fundamentals. Under this combination pricing model of fusion investing, investors will engage in fundamental analysis but also should consider investor sentiment in terms of fads and fashions. During some periods, investor sentiment is rather muted and noise traders are inactive, so that fundamental valuation dominates market returns. In other periods, when investor sentiment is strong, noise traders are very active and market returns are more heavily impacted by investor sentiments. Both investors and analysts should be cognizant of these dual effects on the aggregate market, various economic sectors, and individual stocks.

Beyond advocating awareness of the dual components of fusion investing, results from other studies have documented that fundamental valuation may be the dominant factor but takes much longer to assert itself—about three years. To derive some estimate of changing investor sentiment, Lee proposes several measures of investor sentiment, most notably analysts' recommendations, **price momentum**, and high trading turnover. Significant changes in these variables for a stock will indicate a movement from a glamour stock to a neglected stock or vice versa.

6   IMPLICATIONS OF EFFICIENT CAPITAL MARKETS

Having reviewed the results of numerous studies related to different facets of the EMH, the important question is, What does this mean to individual investors, financial analysts, portfolio managers, and institutions? Overall, the results of many studies indicate that the capital markets are efficient as related to numerous sets of information. At the same time, research has uncovered a substantial number of instances where the market fails to adjust prices rapidly to public information. Given these mixed results regarding the existence of efficient capital markets, it is important to consider the implications of this contrasting evidence of market efficiency.

The following discussion considers the implications of both sets of evidence. Specifically given results that support the EMH, we consider what techniques will not work and what you should do if you cannot beat the market. In contrast, because of the evidence that fails to support the EMH, we discuss what information and psychological biases should be considered when attempting to derive superior investment results through active security valuation and portfolio management.

Efficient Markets and Technical Analysis

The assumptions of technical analysis directly oppose the notion of efficient markets. A basic premise of technical analysis is that stock prices move in trends that persist.[7] Technicians believe that when new information comes to the market, it is not immediately available to everyone but is typically disseminated from the informed professional to the aggressive investing public and then to the great bulk of investors. Also, technicians contend that investors do not analyze information and act immediately. This process takes time. Therefore, they hypothesize that stock prices move to a new equilibrium after the release of new information in a gradual manner, which causes trends in stock price movements that persist.

Technical analysts believe that nimble traders can develop systems to detect the beginning of a movement to a new equilibrium (called a "breakout"). Hence, they hope to buy or sell the stock immediately after its breakout to take advantage of the subsequent, gradual price adjustment.

The belief in this pattern of price adjustment directly contradicts advocates of the EMH who believe that security prices adjust to new information very rapidly. These EMH advocates do not contend, however, that prices adjust perfectly, which implies a chance of overadjustment or underadjustment. Still, because it is uncertain whether the market will over- or under-adjust at any time, you cannot derive abnormal profits from adjustment errors.

If the capital market is weak-form efficient as indicated by most of the results, then prices fully reflect all relevant market information so technical trading systems that depend only on past trading data *cannot* have any value. By the time the information is public, the price adjustment has taken place. Therefore, a purchase or sale using a technical trading rule should not generate abnormal returns after taking account of risk and transaction costs.

Efficient Markets and Fundamental Analysis

As you know from our prior discussion, fundamental analysts believe that, at any time, there is a basic intrinsic value for the aggregate stock market, various industries, or individual securities and that these values depend on underlying economic factors. Therefore, investors should determine the intrinsic value of an investment asset at a point in time by examining the variables that determine value such as current and future earnings or cash flows, interest rates, and risk variables. If the prevailing market price differs from the estimated intrinsic value by enough to cover transaction costs, you should take appropriate action: You buy if the market price is substantially below intrinsic value and do not buy, or you sell, if the market price is above the intrinsic value. Investors who are engaged in fundamental analysis believe that, occasionally, market price and intrinsic value differ but eventually investors recognize the discrepancy and correct it.

---

[7] Reading 63 contains an extensive discussion of technical analysis.

An investor who can do a superior job of *estimating* intrinsic value can consistently make superior market timing (asset allocation) decisions or acquire undervalued securities and generate above-average returns. Fundamental analysis involves aggregate market analysis, industry analysis, company analysis, and portfolio management. The divergent results from the EMH research have important implications for all of these components.

Aggregate Market Analysis with Efficient Capital Markets   Reading 59 makes a strong case that intrinsic value analysis should begin with aggregate market analysis. Still, the EMH implies that if you examine only *past* economic events, it is unlikely that you will be able to outperform a buy-and-hold policy because the market rapidly adjusts to known economic events. Evidence suggests that the market experiences long-run price movements; but, to take advantage of these movements in an efficient market, you must do a superior job of *estimating* the relevant variables that cause these long-run movements. Put another way, if you only use *historical* data to estimate future values and invest on the basis of these estimates, you will *not* experience superior, risk-adjusted returns.

Industry and Company Analysis with Efficient Capital Markets   As we will discuss in Reading 60, the wide distribution of returns from different industries and companies clearly justifies industry and company analysis. Again, the EMH does not contradict the potential value of such analysis but implies that you need to (1) understand the relevant variables that affect rates of return and (2) do a superior job of *estimating future* values for these relevant valuation variables. To demonstrate this, Malkiel and Cragg (1970) developed a model that did an excellent job of explaining past stock price movements using historical data. When this valuation model was employed to project *future* stock price changes using *past* company data, however, the results were consistently inferior to a buy-and-hold policy. This implies that, even with a good valuation model, you *cannot* select stocks that will provide superior future returns using only past data as inputs. The point is, most analysts are aware of the several well-specified valuation models, so the factor that differentiates superior from inferior analysts is the ability to *provide more accurate estimates* of the critical inputs to the valuation models.

A study by Benesh and Peterson (1986) showed that the crucial difference between the stocks that enjoyed the best and worst price performance during a given year was the relationship between expected earnings of professional analysts and actual earnings (that is, it was *earnings surprises*). Specifically, stock prices increased if actual earnings substantially exceeded expected earnings and stock prices fell if actual earnings did not reach expected levels. As suggested by Fogler (1993), if you can do a superior job of projecting earnings and your expectations *differ from the consensus* (i.e., you project earnings surprises), you will have a superior stock selection record. Put another way, there are two factors that are required to be superior: (1) you must be *correct* in your estimates, and (2) you must be *different* from the consensus. Remember, if you are only correct and not different, that assumes you were predicting the consensus and the consensus was correct, which implies no surprise and no abnormal price movement.

The quest to be a superior analyst holds some good news and some suggestions. The good news is related to the strong-form tests that indicated the likely existence of superior analysts. It was shown that the rankings by Value Line contained information value, even though it might not be possible to profit from the work of these analysts after transaction costs. Also, the price adjustments to the publication of analyst recommendations also point to the existence of superior analysts. The point is, there are some superior analysts, but only a limited number, and it is *not* an easy task to be among this select group. Most notably, to be a superior analyst you must do a superior job of *estimating* the relevant valuation variables and *predicting earnings surprises.*

The suggestions for those involved in fundamental analysis are based on the studies that considered the cross section of future returns. As noted, these studies indicated that P/E ratios, size, and the BV/MV ratios were able to differentiate future return patterns with size and the BV/MV ratio appearing to be the optimal combination. Therefore, these factors should be considered when selecting a universe or analyzing firms. In addition, the evidence suggests that neglected firms should be given extra consideration. Although these ratios and characteristics have been shown to be useful in isolating superior stocks from a large sample, it is our suggestion that they are best used to derive a viable sample to analyze from the total universe (e.g., select 200 stocks to analyze from a universe of 3,000). Then the 200 stocks should be rigorously valued using the techniques discussed in this text.

How to Evaluate Analysts or Investors   If you want to determine if an individual is a superior analyst or investor, you should examine the performance of numerous securities that this analyst or investor recommends over time in relation to the performance of a set of randomly selected stocks of the same risk class. The stock selections of a superior analyst or investor should *consistently* outperform the randomly selected stocks. The consistency requirement is crucial because you would expect a portfolio developed by random selection to outperform the market about half the time.

Conclusions about Fundamental Analysis   A text on investments can indicate the relevant variables that you should analyze and describe the important analysis techniques, but actually estimating the relevant variables is as much an art and a product of hard work as it is a science. If the estimates could be done on the basis of some mechanical formula, you could program a computer to do it, and there would be no need for analysts. Therefore, the superior analyst or successful investor must understand what variables are relevant to the valuation process and have the ability and work ethic to do a superior job of *estimating* these important valuation variables. Alternatively, one can be superior if he or she has the ability to interpret the impact or estimate the effect of some public information better than others.

Efficient Markets and Portfolio Management

As noted, studies have indicated that the majority of professional money managers cannot beat a buy-and-hold policy on a risk-adjusted basis. One explanation for this generally inferior performance is that there are no superior analysts and the cost of research and trading forces the results of merely adequate analysis into the inferior category. Another explanation, which is favored by the authors and has some empirical support from the Value Line and analyst recommendation results, is that money management firms employ both superior and inferior analysts and the gains from the recommendations by the few superior analysts are offset by the costs and the poor results derived from the recommendations of the inferior analysts.

This raises the question, Should a portfolio be managed actively or passively? The following discussion indicates that the decision of how to manage the portfolio (actively or passively) should depend on whether the manager has access to superior analysts. A portfolio manager with superior analysts or an investor who believes that he or she has the time and expertise to be a superior investor can manage a portfolio actively by looking for undervalued or overvalued or overvalued securities and trading accordingly. In contrast, without access to superior analysts or the time and ability to be a superior investor, you should manage passively and assume that all securities are properly priced based on their levels of risk.

Portfolio Management with Superior Analysts   A portfolio manager with access to superior analysts who have unique insights and analytical ability should follow their recommendations. The superior analysts should make investment recommendations for a certain proportion of the portfolio, and the portfolio manager should ensure that the risk preferences of the client are maintained.

Also, the superior analysts should be encouraged to concentrate their efforts in mid-cap and small-cap stocks that possess the liquidity required by institutional portfolio managers. But because these stocks typically do not receive the attention given the top-tier stocks, the markets for these neglected stocks may be less efficient than the market for large well-known stocks.

Recall that capital markets are expected to be efficient because many receive new information and analyze its effect on security values. If the number of analysts following a stock differ, one could conceive of differences in the efficiency of the markets. New information on top-tier stocks is well publicized and rigorously analyzed so the price of these securities should adjust rapidly to reflect the new information. In contrast, middle-tier firms receive less publicity and fewer analysts follow these firms, so prices might be expected to adjust less rapidly to new information. Therefore, the possibility of finding temporarily undervalued securities among these neglected stocks is greater. Again, in line with the cross-section study results, these superior analysts should pay particular attention to the BV/MV ratio, to the size of stocks being analyzed, and to the monetary policy environment.

Portfolio Management without Superior Analysts   A portfolio manager who does not have access to superior analysts should proceed as follows. First, he or she should *measure the risk preferences* of his or her clients, then build a portfolio to match this risk level by investing a certain proportion of the portfolio in risky assets and the rest in a risk-free asset, as discussed in Reading 54.

The risky asset portfolio must be *completely diversified* on a global basis so it moves consistently with the world market. In this context, proper diversification means eliminating all unsystematic (unique) variability. In our prior discussion, it was estimated that it required about 20 securities to gain most of the benefits (more than 90 percent) of a completely diversified portfolio. More than 100 stocks are required for complete diversification. To decide how many securities to actually include in your global portfolio, you must balance the added benefits of complete worldwide diversification against the costs of research for the additional stocks.

Finally, you should *minimize transaction costs*. Assuming that the portfolio is completely diversified and is structured for the desired risk level, excessive transaction costs that do not generate added returns will detract from your expected rate of return. Three factors are involved in minimizing total transaction costs:

1. *Minimize taxes.* Methods of accomplishing this objective vary, but it should receive prime consideration.

2. *Reduce trading turnover.* Trade only to liquidate part of the portfolio or to maintain a given risk level.

3. *When you trade, minimize liquidity costs by trading relatively liquid stocks.* To accomplish this, submit limit orders to buy or sell several stocks at prices that approximate the specialist's quote. That is, you would put in limit orders to buy stock at the bid price or sell at the ask price. The stock bought or sold first is the most liquid one; all other orders should be withdrawn.

In summary, if you lack access to superior analysts, you should do the following:

1. Determine and quantify your risk preferences.
2. Construct the appropriate risk portfolio by dividing the total portfolio between risk-free assets and a risky asset portfolio.
3. Diversify completely on a global basis to eliminate all unsystematic risk.
4. Maintain the specified risk level by rebalancing when necessary.
5. Minimize total transaction costs.

The Rationale and Use of Index Funds and Exchange-Traded Funds   As the preceding discussion indicates, efficient capital markets and a lack of superior analysts imply that many portfolios should be managed *passively* so that their performance matches that of the aggregate market, minimizing the costs of research and trading. In response to this demand, several institutions have introduced *market funds*, also referred to as *index funds*, which are security portfolios designed to duplicate the composition, and therefore the performance, of a selected market index series.

Notably, this concept of stock-market index funds has been extended to other areas of investments and, as discussed by Gastineau (2001) and Kostovetsky (2003), has been enhanced by the introduction of exchange-traded funds (ETFs). Index bond funds attempt to emulate the bond-market indexes discussed in Reading 56. Also, some index funds focus on specific segments of the market such as international bond-index funds, international stock-index funds that target specific countries, and index funds that target small-cap stocks in the United States and Japan. When financial planners decide that they want a given asset class in their portfolios, they often look for index funds or to ETFs to fulfill this need. Index funds or ETFs are less costly in terms of research and commissions, and during almost all time periods they can provide the same or better performance than what is available from the majority of active portfolio managers.

Insights from Behavioral Finance   As noted earlier, the major contributions of behavioral finance researchers are explanations for some of the anomalies discovered by prior academic research and opportunities to derive abnormal rates of return by acting on some of the deeply ingrained biases of investors. Clearly, their findings support the notion that the stocks of growth companies typically will not actually be growth stocks because analysts become overconfident in their ability to predict future growth rates and eventually derive valuations that either fully value or overvalue future growth. Behavioral finance research also supports the notion of contrary investing, confirming the notion of the herd mentality of analysts in stock recommendations or quarterly earning estimates and the recommendations by newsletter writers. Also, it is important to recall the loss aversion and escalation bias that causes investors to ignore bad news and hold losers too long and in some cases acquire additional shares of losers to average down the cost. Before averaging down, be sure you reevaluate the stock and consider all the potential bad news we tend to ignore. Finally, recognize that valuation is a combination of fundamental value and investor sentiment.

THE INTERNET

Investments Online

Capital market prices reflect current news items fairly quickly. On the other hand, a portfolio manager should not ignore news just because prices adjust quickly. News provides information he/she can use to structure portfolios and allows the managers to update potential future scenarios.

A number of news sources are available on the Internet. Some of them, such as www.bloomberg.com, news.ft.com, and online.wsj.com, were listed in previous chapters. Other sites include:

finance.yahoo.com contains links to a number of news, information, commentary, and finance-related sites.

money.cnn.com The financial network site for the Cable News Network and Money magazine. The CNN Web site is www.cnn.com.

www.foxnews.com, www.abcnews.go.com, www.cbsnews.com and www.msnbc.msn.com are the URLs for news from Fox, ABC, CBS, and NBC. Meir Statman (lsb.scu.edu/finance/faculty/Statman) and Richard Thaler (gsbwww.uchicago.edu/fac/richard.thaler/research) are two leading researchers in the area of behavioral finance. These pages contain links to their research.

SUMMARY

▶ The efficiency of capital markets has implications for the investment analysis and management of your portfolio. Capital markets should be efficient because numerous rational, profit-maximizing investors react quickly to the release of new information. Assuming prices reflect new information, they are unbiased estimates of the securities' true, intrinsic value, and there should be a consistent relationship between the return on an investment and its risk.

▶ The voluminous research on the EMH has been divided into three segments that have been tested separately. The weak-form EMH states that stock prices fully reflect all market information, so any trading rule that uses past market data to predict future returns should have no value. The results of most studies consistently supported this hypothesis.

▶ The semistrong-form EMH asserts that security prices adjust rapidly to the release of all public information. The tests of this hypothesis either examine the opportunities to predict future rates of return (either a time series or a cross section) or they involve event studies in which investigators analyzed whether investors could derive above-average returns from trading on the basis of public information. The test results for this hypothesis were clearly mixed. On the one hand, the results for almost all the event studies related to economic events such as stock splits, initial public offerings, and accounting changes consistently supported the semistrong hypothesis. In contrast, several studies that examined the ability to predict rates of return on the basis of unexpected quarterly earnings, P/E ratios, size, neglected stocks, and the BV/MV ratio, as well as several calendar effects, generally did not support the hypothesis.

▶ The strong-form EMH states that security prices reflect all information. This implies that nobody has private information, so no group should be able to derive above-average returns consistently. Studies that examined the results for corporate insiders and stock exchange specialists do not support the strong-form hypothesis. An analysis of individual analysts as represented by Value Line or by recommendations published in *The Wall Street Journal* give mixed results. The results indicated that the Value Line rankings have significant information but it may not be possible to profit from it, whereas the recommendations by analysts indicated the existence of private information. In contrast, the performance by professional money managers supported the EMH because their risk-adjusted investment performance (whether mutual funds, pension funds, or endowment funds) was typically inferior to results achieved with buy-and-hold policies.

▶ During the past decade, there has been significant research in behavioral finance by investigators who contend that the standard finance theory model is incomplete since it does not consider implications of psychological decisions made by individuals that both help explain many anomalies and the existence of several biases and provide opportunities for excess returns. It is important to be aware of a number of bias for two reasons: first, they can lead to inferior performance as an analyst and portfolio manager; second, it is possible to exploit them for excess returns.

▶ Given the mixed results, it is important to consider the implications of all of this for technical or fundamental analysts and for portfolio managers. The EMH indicates that technical analysis should be of no value. All forms of fundamental analysis are useful, but they are difficult to implement because they require the ability *to estimate future values* for relevant economic variables. Superior analysis is possible but difficult because it requires superior projections. Those who manage portfolios should constantly evaluate investment advice to determine whether it is superior.

▶ Without access to superior analytical advice, you should run your portfolio like an index fund or an ETF. In contrast, those with superior analytical ability should be allowed to make decisions, but they should concentrate their efforts on mid-cap firms and neglected firms where there is a higher probability of discovering misvalued stocks. The analysis should be particularly concerned with a firm's BV/MV ratio, its size, and the monetary environment.

▶ This reading contains some good news and some bad news. The good news is that the practice of investment analysis and portfolio management is not an art that has been lost to the great computer in the sky. Viable professions still await those willing to extend the effort and able to accept the pressures. The bad news is that many bright, hardworking people with extensive resources make the game tough. In fact, those competitors have created a fairly efficient capital market in which it is extremely difficult for most analysts and portfolio managers to achieve superior results.

PROBLEMS FOR READING 57

1. Discuss the rationale for expecting an efficient capital market. What factor would you look for to differentiate the market efficiency for two alternative stocks?

2. Define and discuss the weak-form EMH. Describe the two sets of tests used to examine the weak-form EMH.

3. Define and discuss the semistrong-form EMH. Describe the two sets of tests used to examine the semistrong-form EMH.

4. Define and discuss the strong-form EMH. Why do some observers contend that the strong-form hypothesis really requires a perfect market in addition to an efficient market? Be specific.

5. *CFA Examination Level III*

   A. Briefly explain the concept of the *efficient market hypothesis* (EMH) and each of its three forms—*weak, semistrong, and strong*—and briefly discuss the degree to which existing empirical evidence supports each of the three forms of the EMH. [8 minutes]

   B. Briefly discuss the implications of the efficient market hypothesis for investment policy as it applies to:

   (i) technical analysis in the form of charting, and

   (ii) fundamental analysis. [4 minutes]

   C. Briefly explain *two* major roles or responsibilities of portfolio managers in an efficient market environment. [4 minutes]

   D. Briefly discuss whether active asset allocation among countries could consistently outperform a world market index. Include a discussion of the implications of *integration versus segmentation* of international financial markets as it pertains to portfolio diversification, but ignore the issue of stock selection. [6 minutes]

$4\frac{5}{8}$ $4\frac{11}{16}$ $-\frac{3}{8}$

$5\frac{1}{2}$ $5\frac{1}{2}$ $-\frac{3}{8}$

$20\frac{5}{8}$ $21\frac{3}{16}$ $-\frac{1}{16}$

$17\frac{3}{8}$ $18\frac{1}{8}$ $+\frac{7}{8}$

$6\frac{1}{2}$ $6\frac{1}{2}$ $-\frac{1}{2}$

$7\frac{1}{4}$ $6\frac{1}{2}$

$\frac{15}{16}$ $31\frac{1}{32}$ $-\frac{1}{8}$

$9\frac{9}{16}$

$9\frac{9}{16}$

$1\frac{1}{32}$

$7\frac{15}{16}$ $7\frac{13}{16}$ $7\frac{15}{16}$

$2\frac{5}{8}$ $2\frac{11}{32}$ $2\frac{1}{2}$ $+$

$2\frac{3}{4}$ $2\frac{1}{4}$ $2\frac{1}{4}$

$6\frac{1}{8}$ $12\frac{1}{16}$ $11\frac{3}{8}$ $11\frac{3}{4}$ $+$

87 $33\frac{3}{4}$ 33 $33\frac{1}{8}$ $-$

602 $25\frac{5}{8}$ $24\frac{9}{16}$ $25\frac{3}{8}$ $+$

833 12 $11\frac{5}{8}$ $11\frac{7}{8}$ $+$

16 $10\frac{1}{2}$ $10\frac{1}{2}$ $10\frac{1}{2}$ $-$

78 $15\frac{5}{8}$ $15\frac{13}{16}$ $15\frac{7}{8}$ $-$

4808 $9\frac{1}{16}$ $8\frac{1}{4}$ $8\frac{7}{8}$ $+$

430 $11\frac{1}{4}$ $10\frac{1}{8}$

MARKET EFFICIENCY AND ANOMALIES

by Vijay Singal

LEARNING OUTCOMES

The candidate should be able to:

a. explain limitations to fully efficient markets;

b. describe the limits of arbitrage to correct anomalies;

c. illustrate why investors should be skeptical of anomalies.

INTRODUCTION · 1

This reading addresses common questions related to market efficiency and anomalies. If prices properly reflect available information, then markets are said to be efficient. Although markets are known to be broadly efficient, there may be pockets of inefficiency that lead to mispricings or anomalies.

In general, claims of anomalous pricing must be viewed with skepticism. The discussion describes reasons for skepticism as well as causes for persistence of some anomalies. Moreover, even when profits can't be made by trading on anomalous prices, it may be possible to alter trading behavior to avoid losses due to these anomalies.

WHAT IS MARKET EFFICIENCY? · 2

Market efficiency refers to the informational efficiency of markets as opposed to structural efficiency, administrative efficiency, or operational efficiency. That is, this reading focuses on the efficiency with which information is reflected in prices. If new information becomes available about a stock (change in earnings), an industry (change in demand), or the economy (change in expected growth), an efficient market will reflect that information in a few minutes, even a few seconds. However, if only half of that information is reflected in the stock price immediately and the remaining half takes several days, then the market is less than fully efficient. Markets that are less than fully efficient open an opportunity for making profits because the inefficiency causes a mispricing in stocks. If a stock is slow to react and takes several days to fully reflect new information, then buying the stock immediately after good news and holding it for a few days would generate extra profit. However, if many people know about this inefficiency, they will all act the same way. As a result, the price will reflect the new information more quickly and the inefficiency will eventually disappear.

The idea behind efficient capital markets is quite simple but compelling. If you know that a stock is undervalued, then you will buy the stock until it is fairly valued. Or if the stock is overvalued, then you will sell the stock until it is fairly valued. Thus, market participants will ensure that prices are always accurate based on publicly available information.[1] The implicit assumption here is that trading based on nonpublic information, that is, insider trading, is illegal. Markets are said to be "semi-strong" form efficient if the prices are unbiased based on all publicly available information. If prices are unbiased based on all information (public and private), then markets are "strong" form efficient. Empirical evidence suggests that markets in the United States and other developed countries are essentially informationally efficient in the semi-strong form, though pockets of inefficiency may exist.

3 WHO CARES ABOUT MARKET EFFICIENCY?

Market efficiency is important for everyone because markets set prices. In particular, stock markets set prices for shares of stock. Currency markets set exchange rates. Commodity markets set prices of commodities such as wheat and corn. Setting correct prices is important because prices determine how available resources are allocated among different uses. If the price of a product is low relative to its cost, the investment in that product will fall. On the other hand, high prices encourage a greater allocation of resources. Thus, correct prices are important for resource allocation and, consequently, for economic growth. Unfortunately, correct prices are impossible to achieve because they require perfect foresight and information. The best a market can do is to form prices that reflect all available information.

Now, consider market efficiency for each constituent in turn: investors, companies, the government, and consumers. Investors are suppliers of capital that companies need for investment and operations. The investors earn a return on the capital they supply. If investors find that prices are predictable, then smart investors can earn extra return at the expense of naive or unsophisticated investors. This implies that unsophisticated investors earn a return that is less than the return that they should receive. In such an environment, unsophisticated investors will be reluctant to supply capital. The reduction in the availability of capital means that companies must pay a higher return for the capital due to restricted supply. However, the investors' capital does not disappear from the market altogether. The money not invested in corporate securities may be deposited with financial institutions, which may then lend that money to corporations. However, the cost of that money will be higher than if the companies could borrow directly from investors.

---

[1] Correct prices are difficult to obtain because it is impossible to predict the future. However, market efficiency requires only that prices be based on all *available* information.

Besides the cost implication, companies care about market efficiency in another way. If markets are efficient aggregators of information, then companies can learn from the stock price reaction. For example, when AT&T bid for NCR in December 1990, AT&T's stock price promptly fell more than 6 percent, while NCR's price jumped 44 percent. Robert Allen, AT&T chairman, chided the markets for not appreciating the long-term benefits that would accrue to AT&T as a result of this combination. It took five years, but the market was proven right. AT&T bought NCR for $7.48 billion in 1991 but, after losses totaling $3.85 billion over the next five years, it was forced to spin off NCR in 1996 at less than half the purchase price, about $3.5 billion. Most companies, however, listen to the market's verdict on big decisions. Some mergers are aborted because of tepid reception by the market.

In addition to investors and companies, the government and the public are concerned about market efficiency because of the effect on economic growth. If the markets do not set prices based on all available information, then allocation of resources based on market prices will be flawed. Industries that deserve more capital will not get that capital, while industries that are not deserving of greater investment will. For example, if technology companies are overvalued by the market, then too many resources will be invested in technology companies, resulting in a misallocation. Also, market inefficiency in the form of speculative bubbles can affect the financial institutions and, through them, the entire economy. For example, Japan's stock market and real estate bubble in the 1980s has left the Japanese banking sector with nonperforming assets, affecting the country's economy.[2] Improper utilization of limited capital means suboptimal use of funds and underachievement in terms of growth and social welfare. Under such conditions, it is the government's responsibility and duty to intervene in financial markets to ensure optimal resource allocation. Whether the government can achieve the desired effect is an open question.

Thus, market efficiency is important so that optimal investment ensures optimal growth and maximizes social welfare.

CAN CAPITAL MARKETS BE FULLY EFFICIENT?   4

While market efficiency is desirable, there are three limitations in achieving that ideal: the cost of information, the cost of trading, and the limits of arbitrage. Strictly speaking, *arbitrage* refers to a profit earned with zero risk and zero investment. However, in this book the term is used in its more popular interpretation, that is, a superior risk-return trade-off that probably requires both risk and investment.

Limitation 1: Cost of Information

In an article aptly titled "On the Impossibility of Informationally Efficient Markets," Sandy Grossman and Joe Stiglitz go about proving just that. The concept behind the impossibility of informationally efficient markets is straightforward. Let us assume that markets are fully efficient, that is, they

---

[2] The government must recognize and respond to the market's signals. Heizo Takenaka, Japan's financial services minister appointed in mid-2002, is the first "Japanese bank czar who seems sympathetic to the market's dim view of the [Japanese] financial system's health. Mr. Takenaka's predecessors all claimed there was nothing wrong with the quality of big banks' capital—a claim disputed by the rating agencies. But Mr. Takenaka admits there are problems. 'Technically, it's OK,' he said in an interview last week. 'But the market doesn't think so.'" Quoted in Phred Dvorak, "Japan's Financial Crisis Makes a Comeback," *Wall Street Journal*, November 22, 2002.

instantaneously reflect new information in prices. If that is the case, then no investor or market participant has any incentive to generate or report new information because the value of that information is zero. That is, when a company announces its earnings, no one wastes time trying to analyze that information because the price already reflects it. There is no value in even reading the corporate announcement. But if no one has any incentive to react to new information, then it is impossible to reflect new information in prices.

The implication of this is that markets can't be fully efficient because no one has the incentive to make them so. Market participants must be compensated in some way for making the market more efficient. Arbitrageurs and speculators must get something in return. Thus, instead of achieving instantaneous adjustment to new information, prices can adjust to new information only with a time lag. This time lag allows market participants to earn a reasonable return on their cost of obtaining and processing the information. If the return is abnormally high, it will attract more information processors, leading to a reduction in time lag. The net result is that prices take time to reflect new information because obtaining and processing that information is costly. However, if the delay is short enough (a few minutes), the markets are still considered efficient. But if they take several hours or several days, then the markets are not efficient.

Limitation 2: Cost of Trading

Like the cost of information, traders incur costs while trading: their time, brokerage costs, and other related costs. When the cost of trading is high, financial assets are likely to remain mispriced for longer periods than when the cost of trading is low. In essence, like with the cost of information, the arbitrageurs or other traders must get an adequate return after accounting for costs to engage in an activity that makes the market more efficient. To the extent that trading activity is limited, prices will not reflect all available information. One factor that can have a large influence on prices is the difficulty in short selling. If short selling (that is, selling a stock that you do not own) is more difficult than buying long (that is, buying a stock that you do not own), then prices are likely to be biased upward. And if certain stocks are more difficult (and therefore more costly) to short-sell, the upward bias in prices is likely to be greater for those stocks. Thus, the greater the cost of trading, the greater the mispricing.

Limitation 3: Limits of Arbitrage

The above discussion on why markets should be efficient suggests the presence of investors who would trade if they see a price that is inconsistent with their information, and would continue to trade until the price reflects the information they have available. On a simpler scale, consider two financial assets (say, stocks X and Y) that are equally risky but generate different returns. Obviously, one of the two assets is mispriced. If asset X generates the higher return and has a lower price, while asset Y generates the lower return and has a higher price, then to take advantage of the mispricing, arbitrageurs would buy asset X while at the same time short-selling Y. With the activities of like-minded arbitrageurs, the prices will converge and make them reflect the fundamental value associated with each asset.

There are four problems with this ideal scenario, however. First, it is not clear when, if ever, the prices will return to equilibrium levels or when the mispricing will disappear. If uninformed traders can continue to influence prices, then the prices of X and Y may actually diverge even more before eventually converging. If the divergence is significant, arbitrageurs may be forced to close their positions prematurely. Arbitrageurs who took short positions in Internet stocks in 1998 or

1999 on the belief that the stocks were overvalued would have been wiped out before the prices eventually fell. In fact, many short sellers went bankrupt in the late 1990s due to the ascent of the stock market. Even Warren Buffett, whom many regard as a smart investor, proclaimed that he had misread the new economy by not riding the technology wave. Today we know that he was correct to be skeptical of high Internet stock valuations, but at the time the prolonged period over which the mispricing seemed to persist caused him to accept defeat.

Second, it is rare to find two assets with exactly the same risk. Assume that X gives a higher return because it has a slightly higher risk than Y. However, smart investors believe that X's return is much higher than it should be based on differences in risk. Accordingly, they would like to implement a strategy of buying X while short-selling Y. But the risk inherent in such a strategy may deter them from arbitraging the mispricing. Thus, in cases where no close substitutes are available, the mispricing of a security may continue indefinitely.

Third and probably more important, we implicitly assumed that arbitrageurs have an unlimited amount of capital to take advantage of mispriced assets. That is not true. Just like everyone else, arbitrageurs have a limited amount of capital, which they devote to the most profitable strategies or to the most egregious mispricings while ignoring the remaining mispricings. The problem of limited capital becomes more severe in a bull market. Though there are potentially more mispricings in a bull market, the arbitrage capital is even more limited because most investors want to ride the market rather than find nebulous mispricings that generate relatively small returns.

Finally, most arbitrageurs act as agents because they manage other people's money. As agents, arbitrageurs must abide by the constraints imposed on them by the owners of capital (the principals). The principals are unwilling to give the agents a free hand in the pursuit of extra returns because the principals are concerned that the agents may not actually earn those extra returns and that the risk associated with those returns may be unacceptably high. Therefore, the typical mandate given to an agent will specify permitted strategies, the amount of capital at risk including the effects of leverage, and the maximum possible loss. For example, an arbitrageur may be allowed to invest only in merger arbitrage securities or only in distressed securities, with loss limited to 10 percent of the capital invested. While these constraints protect the owners of capital, they also limit the operation of arbitrage activities in the market. In addition, an arbitrageur's ability to attract more capital can be severely constrained when opportunities become more attractive if principals use an arbitrageur's past performance to judge his ability. Assume that an arbitrageur believes that a stock is undervalued by 10 percent and buys that stock. Assume further that the mispricing gets worse over the next few weeks and the stock becomes undervalued by 20 percent. The arbitrageur should probably increase his stake in the stock. However, in the meantime, due to the worsening mispricing, the arbitrageur has lost 10 percent of the capital. Principals observe the loss of 10 percent and may not believe that the arbitrageur has any superior skills. Instead of giving him or her more capital, they may ask the arbitrageur to immediately sell that stock, further depressing the stock price and making the mispricing even more acute. It is easy to see that there are serious limits of arbitrage activity that may cause mispricings to persist.

What about the small investor? Why can't the millions of small investors seek out and trade on these mispricings, especially the small mispricings that are ignored by professional arbitrageurs or where arbitrage activity is limited by constraints imposed on the arbitrageur? In general, the small investors do not have the expertise and knowledge to identify and profitably trade mispricings. If this book is able to educate investors so that they trade away the mispricings or trade in a more rational manner, the markets will become more efficient aggregators of information, with concurrent improvement in social welfare.

5   WHAT IS A PRICING ANOMALY?

A mispricing is any *predictable* deviation from a normal or expected return. For example, assume that IBM's stock is expected to earn a normal return of 15 percent a year. If the current stock price is $100, then the price should increase to $115 after one year, assuming that IBM does not distribute any dividends. If a market timer *predicts* that IBM will actually appreciate by 20 percent or more this year, and IBM does earn more than the normal return repeatedly and consistently in a predictable manner, then it is a mispricing. Similarly, a *predictable* deviation on the downside (less than 15 percent) is also a mispricing. On the other hand, an unpredictable movement in price is not a mispricing. For example, if the actual price after a year is $90 or $130, that is not a mispricing even though the actual return is different from the expected return. Deviations from the normal return are expected and, by definition, must occur for risky securities. On average, however, the deviation must be close to zero.

If a mispricing is well known and persistent, then it is referred to as an anomaly. In their article on anomalies in the *Review of Financial Studies,* Michael Brennan of UCLA and Yihong Xia of the University of Pennsylvania define an anomaly as "a statistically significant difference between the realized average returns . . . and the returns that are predicted by a particular asset pricing model." Thus, persistent realization of abnormal returns (actual return minus the expected return) is referred to as an anomaly. The persistence in abnormal returns results in predictability of returns.

6   WHEN IS A MISPRICING NOT A MISPRICING?

Investment professionals, academics, and novice traders spend a great deal of time and effort to discover mispricings because these phenomena have the potential to make someone very rich. Therefore, mispricings are frequently touted by market timers, brokers, and other investment professionals. It is important to know how to judge the validity of a mispricing. In this section, the limitations and biases in the process of discovering mispricings are discussed along with simple tests to detect whether the mispricings can be attributed to such limitations. An understanding of these biases can be used to test other mispricings. Moreover, it will be natural to become more skeptical of mispricings or anomalies that are frequently cited as evidence against market efficiency. The intent here is not to actually check for limitations of the mispricing, but to judge whether flaws in the discovery process may have caused the observed mispricing.

Measurement of Abnormal Return

If markets are efficient, then the expected *abnormal* return is zero. On the other hand, if the abnormal return is nonzero *and* it is possible to predict the direction of the deviation, then the pricing constitutes an anomaly. Since abnormal return is the actual return minus the normal return, a problem arises in defining the normal return (the term is used interchangeably with *expected return*). How do you define or measure normal return?

In the IBM example, it was assumed that the normal return is 15 percent. Is the 15 percent assumption correct? Who can say? Unfortunately, there is no accepted method for estimating a stock's normal return. Theoretical models include Nobel laureate William Sharpe's capital asset pricing model (CAPM) and Steve Ross's arbitrage pricing theory (APT). APT cannot be applied in a practical way because there are too many unknowns. CAPM is deterministic, but the CAPM does not have much empirical support. In the words of Eugene Fama, "[I]nferences about market efficiency can be sensitive to the assumed model for expected returns" (Fama 1998, 288).

Other models exist using alternate measures of risk derived from statistical methods and historical returns. Researchers have also discovered that stock return depends on such factors as size, the ratio of market value to book value, beta, momentum, and so on. However, these are empirical returns that do not necessarily have strong theoretical support. Further, there is no guarantee that these factors will continue to have explanatory power in the future. So, the question remains: what is IBM's normal return? There is no exact and generally accepted measure of expected return. However, it is possible to say that a particular return is too high or too low. For example, a normal return of 50 percent for IBM is too high and a return of 0 percent is probably too low. One way of getting a reasonable estimate is to estimate its relative return—relative to another firm with similar characteristics. The idea is to identify a similar (or control) firm—similar on several dimensions known to explain the cross section of returns, such as size, market-to-book ratio, and so on. Then measure the abnormal return for the sample firm as the difference between the sample firm's return and the control firm's return. Coke and Pepsi are good examples. If Coke and Pepsi are considered similar firms, then to find Coke's abnormal return, Pepsi's return would be used as the normal return. The difference between Coke's actual return and Pepsi's return is the abnormal return earned by Coke. Generally, it is better to use a group of firms as a control instead of using a single control firm so that one firm's chaotic price movements don't significantly influence the abnormal return calculation.

How critical is it to estimate IBM's normal return accurately for detecting a mispricing? Should it be 15 percent or 25 percent per year? The normal return becomes crucial only in long-term mispricings. Consider that IBM's return based on a particular mispricing is 25 percent over one year. The return is abnormal if the normal annual return is assumed to be 15 percent, but not if the normal annual return is 25 percent. On the other hand, if the mispricing occurs over short periods of time, then the normal return becomes essentially inconsequential. If IBM's stock earns 1 percent in a *day*, then the normal return does not really matter—whether it is 0.06 percent per day (15 percent per year based on 250 trading days per year) or 0.1 percent per day (25 percent per year). In either case, the mispricing is large: 0.94 percent or 0.90 percent for a day. This means that, holding the magnitude of mispricing constant, long-term mispricings should generally be subject to a much greater degree of skepticism than short-term mispricings.

As Fama states, "[A]n advantage of this approach [short-period event studies] is that because daily expected returns are close to zero, the model for expected returns does not have a big effect on inferences about abnormal returns" (Fama 1998, 283). He continues to stress the problem with long-term normal returns: "the bad-model problem is ubiquitous, but it is more serious in long-term returns. The reason is that bad-model errors in expected returns grow faster with the return horizon than the volatility of returns" (Fama 1998, 285).

Data Mining

If you look hard enough at almost any bunch of numbers, you can find a pattern. Since anomalies are predictable patterns in returns, a person who studies hundreds of different relationships and millions of different observations is likely to find a pattern; this is called data mining. For example, try to find a relationship between the stock return and any number of different variables, such as the weather in New York, the number of sunspots, the height of ocean waves, growth in world population, or the number of birds in San Francisco. Given a large enough number of possible relationships and enough tries, it is possible to find a statistically significant relationship between a stock return and another variable. That relationship does not really exist: it is there just by chance. Further, as Fama states, "splashy results get more attention, and this creates an incentive to find them" (Fama 1998, 287). Fischer Black once said, "[M]ost of the so-called anomalies that have plagued the literature on investments seem likely the result of data-mining" (Fischer Black 1993, 9).

An example of data mining is illustrative. Take a researcher who believes that Nasdaq 100 returns are predictable on an intraday basis. He is determined to find this predictability to impress his boss. He can generate and test for thousands of different relationships to discover a pattern. He begins by calculating the six one-hour returns for each day: 10 A.M.-11 A.M. return, 11 A.M.-12 noon return, and so on. He analyzes the hourly returns to see whether the return during the first hour is related to the return during the second hour, whether the second-hour return is related to the return during the third hour, and so on. Then he tries to find significant correlations among 13 half-hour returns, and among 26 quarter-hour returns, and among 78 five-minute returns, and among 390 one-minute returns. Unsuccessful but persistent, he introduces filters, that is, selects only those observations where the Nasdaq 100 return is more than two standard deviations away from the mean. Again he fails to discover anything interesting. Next he introduces volume as a variable. Only those observations that have trading volume in the top 10 percent are selected. He continues this process until he discovers a pattern. Finally he finds that on high-volume days, a negative Nasdaq 100 return in the 3:00–3:30 P.M. period is followed by a negative return in the 3:30–4:00 P.M. period with a 90 percent probability. This is data mining at its best, but the boss is not impressed, and I hope you are not either.

Artificial anomalies need to be separated from real anomalies. Perhaps the most important thing is to assess the intuitiveness of the relationship discovered by researchers. Does it make sense? Can the number of birds in San Francisco really mean anything for stock returns? If it doesn't make intuitive and economic sense, then it is probably a case of data mining. Another way to check for data mining is to use an out-of-sample test, which is testing the same relationship using data from a different country or for an entirely different period. If data mining worked in this case, it may not work for a different sample. If it is not possible to get another data set, then test the relationship over subperiods of the data. The results must hold for subperiods as well as for the whole period unless there is a valid reason for a change in the observed relationship.

Survivorship Bias

Another source of unreliability of an anomaly is survivorship bias, which exists whenever results are based on existing entities. For example, a simple study of existing mutual funds will find that mutual funds, on average, outperform their benchmarks. The problem with such a sample is survivorship. Only well-performing funds continue to survive, while the underperformers die. Thus, a sample of existing mutual funds will not contain funds that underperformed and died. If all funds, dead and alive, are included in the sample, then the funds, on average, do not outperform their benchmarks. The sample of existing mutual funds has a survivorship bias and will result in an overestimation of fund performance.

Survivorship is important in market timing studies, as market timing newsletters or services use many strategies and frequently add new strategies and discontinue others. Which ones does the market timer add? The ones that have shown great promise based on past trends. Which ones are discontinued? The ones that no longer show continuing profitability. The record displayed by the market timer shows only the successful strategies and not the unsuccessful strategies, giving readers the false impression of market timing prowess where none exists.

Survivorship bias is widespread in many spheres of the investment world. People with a good investment record are retained, while others are dumped. It seems as if all the investment firms have analysts who can predict the market. What about the guests on CNBC? Are they really good stock pickers, or are they simply lucky?

Small Sample Bias

Mispricings may be caused by a small sample bias. Usually the small sample refers to the period of observation. For example, riskier stocks should earn higher returns than other stocks. Since stocks with small market capitalization (size) are considered riskier than large-size stocks, small-size stocks are expected to earn higher returns. However, during the 1995–99 period, the large-size stocks outperformed the small-size stocks. Looking at this limited time period, one may conclude that a mispricing exists. However, over long periods (1926–2002 or 1962–2002) small-size stocks did earn higher returns than large-size stocks. The small sample bias is especially relevant to anomalies that do not have a reasonable explanation, especially if it appears that the mispricing has occurred just by chance.

Selection Bias

Another bias that may creep into the discovery of mispricings is selection bias, that is, the sample may be biased in favor of finding the desired result. Assume you want to measure the ownership of cell phones in the general American population. If you polled only people working in Manhattan, your estimate will be biased upward because the sample is biased and the result is falsely attributed to the entire American population, including rural and less urban areas.

In the case of stock market studies, a selection bias can creep in when the results arise from a certain part of the sample but seem to be representative of the entire market. For example, consider the January effect. According to the January effect, firms gain abnormally in the first few days of January. However, the effect is not broad-based; rather, it is due to firms that are small in size. Once the small firms are removed, the January effect disappears. The discovery of the small-firm effect is important, because it is necessary to attribute the effect to only the small firms and not to the entire stock market.

Nonsynchronous Trading

Stocks trade with different frequencies. Some stocks may trade continuously, that is, several times a minute, such as Pfizer, Intel, and Cisco. Other stocks may not trade for several hours or even several days. If a stock trades only once every day, at 10 A.M., the return based on that day's 10 A.M. trade will capture market movements that took place over the last twenty-four hours. The closing price at 4:00 P.M. will reflect the price of the last trade, which actually took place at 10 A.M., without accounting for any market movements that have taken place since 10 A.M. If the market jumped after 10 A.M., then the next day's return (but not today's return) of this stock will reflect the increase in price. If you construct a portfolio of such inactively traded stocks, then it will seem that these stocks have predictable returns—that is, the stock price will change in accordance with the market, but with a delay. Since you can predict returns, a natural strategy is to buy this portfolio whenever the market goes up after 10 A.M. and sell this portfolio if the market goes down after 10 A.M. The problem with returns caused by nonsynchronous trading is that those returns are not actually tradable. The 10 A.M. price is not a price at which a trade can be executed. As soon as any trader tries to trade, the price will move to reflect market movements, and the excess returns will disappear.

There is a way to take advantage of stocks that trade infrequently or at different times: trade mutual funds, where a buy does not necessarily trigger a trade in the underlying stock.

Risk

Most investors demand a higher return for a riskier position than for a less risky position. That is why bank deposits give a lower return than stocks, because stocks are riskier than bank deposits. Small-size stocks have higher returns than large stocks because small stocks are riskier than large stocks. This means that a riskier strategy must also generate a higher return. Therefore, it is important to control for risk when comparing trading strategies designed to take advantage of mispricings. Further, historical risk estimates may not be appropriate if the mispricing is around certain corporate or market events, because volatility, and hence risk, generally increases around those events. Thus, anomalies that are event-driven must generate higher returns to compensate for the risk associated with those events. However, risk is probably not important if only a short holding period is required.

In any case, the abnormal returns computed for any mispricing must account for the level of risk inherent in exploiting that anomaly. Inaccurate estimates of risk are more likely to affect anomalies that require long holding periods or anomalies that have very small abnormal returns even with short holding periods. Therefore, care must be taken to ensure that adequate compensation is provided for risk.

Explanation for the Mispricing

It is necessary to reiterate the importance of a reasonable and intuitive explanation as a basis for the anomaly. Anomalies that are based on reasonable explanations are less likely to be the figment of someone's imagination or data mining and are more credible. Some anomalies exist because of government regulations or arise from institutional constraints. For example, the January effect is best explained by capital gains taxes. That is not to say that all anomalies must have rational explanations. However, an anomaly with a rational explanation is more believable than one without.

7   CAN NEW MISPRICINGS BE DISCOVERED?

Until now, the discussion has focused on known anomalies. But investors, academics, and practitioners are constantly trying to discover new mispricings. Any new mispricing can potentially result in large profits to the explorer. While one must be skeptical of new mispricings—whether it is predicting when a stock split will be announced or which firm will be acquired—one must acknowledge the possibility of discovering new mispricings. Just because a pattern can't be discovered may not mean that it doesn't exist. At the same time, one must be wary of new mispricings and ensure that they meet the tests listed above.

WHY DOES A MISPRICING PERSIST?　　　8

If a mispricing exists, then smart investors and arbitrageurs should take advantage of it to earn abnormal returns. As more and more arbitrageurs participate, the mispricing should disappear. In general, persistence of an anomaly is a cause for concern. However, there could be a number of reasons for an anomaly's continuation, as discussed below.

The Mispricing Is Not Well Understood

It is possible that a mispricing is well known but not well understood. For example, the weekend effect is well known. According to the weekend effect, first discovered in the 1970s, the return on the last trading day of the week is highly positive. On the other hand, the return on the first trading day of the week is usually negative. Until recently the weekend effect did not have a good explanation. Without a satisfactory and intuitive explanation, the mispricing does not meet one of the key conditions for acceptance. Though there is overwhelming evidence of its existence based on past data, investors are wary of trading on it because the mispricing may cease to exist at any time or may not occur during the current period. As Gabriel Hawawini and Donald Keim remark, "[that] effects have persisted for nearly 100 years in no way guarantees their persistence in the future" (Hawawini and Keim, 2000, 35).

Further, without knowledge of a reason, it is difficult to identify stocks that will exhibit the mispricing. Is it only among small stocks? Is it among large stocks? Is it among stocks that have listed options? Or maybe among stocks that just issued new equity? It becomes very risky for an arbitrageur to try to profit from a mispricing without knowing why it exists. As a consequence, the mispricing may not be arbitraged by risk-averse investors.

Arbitrage Is Too Costly

Sometimes the anomaly is known and understood but the arbitrage is too costly to transact. These costs have three components. The first component is the bid-ask spread, which is the difference between the highest price that any buyer is willing to pay (the bid price) and the lowest price that a seller wants (the asking price). As all arbitrage strategies require a buy and a sell, the spread contributes to the total cost of transacting. Second, brokerage fees must be paid. Finally, each large trade can have a market impact. Even an actively traded stock such as General Electric may find it difficult to absorb a million-share order without moving the price. A large buy will cause the price to rise, meaning you pay more than the price indicated by the quotes. Similarly, a large sell will cause the price to decline. In both cases, the market impact of the order has the effect of increasing the trading costs.

Anomalies with high transactions costs may persist because large institutions or arbitrageurs may be reluctant to trade if large dollar positions cannot be taken without moving the price or if the bid-ask spreads are large. For example, the January effect has been known for decades and is caused by tax-loss selling of small-size stocks. Nonetheless, the January effect persists because it is necessary to trade hundreds of small-size stocks. Small stocks have high bid-ask spreads and low liquidity, making the potential benefit insufficient to offset the transaction costs.

Profit Potential Is Insufficient

Certain anomalies may generate small profits that cannot be multiplied easily. In those cases, institutions may not be interested because there is a limited profit potential. Imagine a $1 billion mutual fund trying to make a profit of $10,000 on a few trades. The return is only 0.001 percent. The fund manager could probably spend time more profitably on other pursuits. This is especially true of trading in small-cap stocks, where the institutions can't take large positions for fear of moving the price. Such mispricings are ideally suited to individual trading.

Arbitrage Is Not Possible Due to Trading Restrictions

A known mispricing may persist if institutional features limit trading. This is especially true for restrictions on short selling. For example, it is not possible to short-sell initial public offerings (IPOs) for a few days after the issue because shares are not available to borrow. The mispricing, if any, may persist for a few days, until short selling becomes possible. Again in the case of IPOs, the under-writers engage in price stabilization activities that can, in some cases, keep the price at an inflated level for almost a month.

A case in point is the spin-off of Palm by 3Com. 3Com sold a fraction of Palm as an IPO in March 2000 but retained 95 percent of its shares. At that time it announced that it would spin off the remaining shares to 3Com shareholders at the rate of 1.5 Palm shares for every 3Com share. Even assuming that 3Com was worth-less without Palm, 3Com's share price should have been approximately 1.5 times Palm's share price because a single 3Com share gave the right to own 1.5 Palm shares. On the first trading day after the IPO, Palm's price was $95. Using the ratio of 1.5:1, 3Com's price should have been about $142.50. However, 3Com's price was only $82. A simple strategy to earn an arbitrage profit would have been to buy 1 share of 3Com and short-sell 1.5 shares of Palm. But arbitrageurs could not employ this strategy because shares of Palm were not available to short-sell. In this case, the mispricing existed, and persisted for several days, because of trading restrictions.

Behavioral Biases May Affect Investment Decisions

If investors are reluctant to realize losses, are quick to take profits, do not diversify enough, and suffer from other instances of irrational behavior, then mispricings may occur. They may persist because investors do not change their behavior even in light of new information.

Underreaction to earnings news can be explained by behavioral biases. If the earnings announcement is positive, the stock price rises. But the rise is stymied by the premature selling initiated by individual investors who sell to realize gains. As the selling pressure abates, the stock price slowly rises to the correct level. On the other hand, if the earnings announcement is negative, the stock price falls. But it does not fall sufficiently because individual investors continue to hold on to the stock hoping to recoup their losses. The stock eventually reaches the correct price but with a delay due to the behavioral biases of the investors.

However, irrational investor behavioral can explain persistence only in conjuction with other explanations. Even if some investors are irrational, arbitrageurs should take advantage of that irrationality and in the process cause the mispricing to disappear.

Until investors learn to think and act rationally and minimize emotional trades, mispricings are also likely to be caused by irrational behavior.

Limits of Arbitrage Revisited

One reason for persistence of mispricings is the limits of arbitrage. As discussed in "Can Capital Markets Be Fully Efficient?" earlier in this reading, arbitrageurs may not have the capital or the freedom to pursue the mispricings as aggressively as they would otherwise. However, the limits placed on arbitrageurs allow individual investors to gain from their knowledge. If individual investors begin to target mispricings effectively, there will be one less reason for the persistence of mispricings in financial markets.

CAN VALID ANOMALIES BE UNPROFITABLE?   9

Besides analyzing anomalies, this book contains suggestions for implementing trading strategies designed to take advantage of mispricings. Many anomalies are especially suited to individual investors because the profit potential is small by institutional standards, the mispricing appears infrequently, or the trading costs are high. Where trading costs are high, individual investors, like institutional investors, cannot make arbitrage profits. However, individual investors can alter the timing of their trades so that they are not negatively affected by known mispricings. For example, based on the weekend effect, if an investor wants to sell a stock, he should sell it on a Friday instead of the following Monday.

At the same time, readers must recognize the limitations of this reading and factors that may make these anomalies disappear or appear not to exist.

Documented Anomalies Are Based on Averages

Just because an anomaly exists does not mean that all trades will be profitable. For example, in the case of changes to the S&P 500, stocks deleted from the S&P 500 index lose value and will usually recoup their losses within a few weeks. This statement is based on an analysis of over three hundred deletions between 1962 and 2002. Does it imply that the next stock deleted from the index is *likely* to appreciate? Yes. But *will* it appreciate? Maybe not. Similarly, the results do not imply that the next twenty stocks deleted from the index will necessarily appreciate, though they are likely to. But the results do imply that if you follow this strategy for the next two to three years *and no significant changes take place in how the market reacts to these deletions,* then you will earn risk-adjusted returns that are larger than the normal return. However, an unsuccessful run of any mispricing can cost the investor a significant loss of capital.

Positive Abnormal Returns Do Not Mean Positive Returns

The anomalous evidence presented generally focuses on abnormal returns. Since an abnormal return is the actual return minus the normal return, the actual return could be negative even though the abnormal return is positive. Consider implementing a trading strategy with a 10 percent annual abnormal return. If the market drops 23 percent during a year, as it did in 2002, then the actual return is only −13 percent. Though −13 percent is much better than −23 percent, it is still a loss. Therefore, the anomalies discussed do not suggest absolute profitability, only profitability relative to the normal return.

Conditions Governing Anomalies May Change

An anomaly may disappear because of a change in conditions. In many cases the anomalies exist because of individual or institutional reasons. For example, the

January and December effects are related to taxes. If the government reduces the capital gains tax (as in 2003), then the January and December effects are likely to slightly weaken. Similarly, it is possible to time mutual funds that hold foreign stocks because they use stale prices in computing net asset values. If the fund companies revise their rules for pricing, then the gains due to timing will disappear.

The foregoing discussion assumes that a valid explanation exists for each anomaly. That is not always the case. There are anomalies, such as the home bias, for which no reasonable explanation exists. Home bias is the tendency of investors to underweight foreign stocks compared to an optimally diversified portfolio. In other cases, the explanation, though supported by empirical evidence, may be incorrect. Whenever explanations are either false or unavailable, the anomaly is likely to disappear without any warning.

Anomalies May Be Arbitraged Away by Trading

If markets are efficient and investors are rational, then the greater the chance that people will trade on these anomalies until they are no longer profitable. To profit from this knowledge, however, it is not necessary to trade on the anomalies listed. The primary objective is to ensure an understanding of these anomalies so that investors can sidestep unprofitable situations or marginally alter their trading patterns in beneficial ways.

10   ROLE OF INDIVIDUAL INVESTORS

The fact that the market cannot be fully efficient in spite of the personal profit motive and the presence of arbitrageurs and other smart investors provides the basis for this book. As noted above, constraints placed on arbitrageurs allow many mispricings to continue. On the other hand, individual investors are free to invest and trade in any way they want, with few constraints. Unlike professional arbitrageurs, individuals can continually change the strategy they use. Trades of individual investors will not have a significant effect on price. A profit of $5,000 on a few trades is sufficient to compensate individuals for their time and effort. Individuals can design and implement an exit strategy by using limit orders and stop limit orders. Arbitrageurs are loath to take on very risky positions. They prefer small margins but work with very high volume. As a result, currency markets and bond markets attract significantly more arbitrage activity than stock markets. Stock markets can be more effectively tapped by individual investors.

Why aren't individual investors more active in arbitraging mispricings? The primary reason is that their knowledge of anomalies is limited. The purpose of this book is to identify anomalies and make them accessible to investors, professionals, and academics.[3] I hope that trading based on these anomalies will improve market efficiency with the associated benefits of superior resource allocation and enhanced social welfare.

---

[3] Many academics in finance routinely use their knowledge and research to manage hedge funds or other investment portfolios. For example, Dimensional Fund Advisors, which manages more than $30 billion in assets, is associated with Eugene Fama of the University of Chicago, Ken French of Dartmouth College, and two of their former students, David Booth and Rex Sinquefield. LSV Asset Management, which manages about $8 billion, is owned by Josef Lakonishok of the University of Illinois, Andrei Shleifer of Harvard, and Robert Vishny of the University of Chicago. Long Term Capital Management, whose failure shook world financial markets in 1998 and which had to be rescued by a group of large banks prodded on by the Federal Reserve, was advised by Nobel laureates Robert Merton and Myron Scholes.

SUMMARY

▶ Markets are said to be efficient if publicly available information is reflected in prices in an unbiased manner.

▶ Efficient markets are desirable for the society because prices determine allocation of resources.

▶ Markets cannot be fully efficient because of the cost of collecting and analyzing information, cost of trading, and limits on the capital available to arbitrageurs.

▶ All anomalies must be viewed with caution and skepticism, as spurious mispricings can surface for a variety of reasons, such as errors in defining normal return, data mining, survivorship bias, small sample bias, selection bias, nonsynchronous trading, and misestimation of risk.

▶ Though anomalies should disappear in an efficient market, they may persist because they are not well understood, arbitrage is too costly, the profit potential is insufficient, trading restrictions exist, and behavioral biases exist.

▶ Documented and valid anomalies may still be unprofitable because the evidence is based on averages (and may include a large fraction of losers), conditions responsible for the anomaly may change, and trading by informed investors may cause the anomaly to disappear.

4⅝ 4⅞ 5/8

5½ 5½ —

5½ 5½ —

20⅝ 21¹³/₁₆ — 1/₁₆

21⅛ 17⅜ 18⅛ + 7/₈

18½ 17⅜ 18⅛ +

6½ 6½ 6½ — ½

7¼ 6½ 6½ — 1/₈

31/₃₂ — 1/₈

15/₁₆

1 9/₁₆ 9/₁₆

9/₁₆ 9/₁₆

11/₃₂ 7¹⁵/₁₆

7¹⁵/₁₆ 7¹³/₁₆ 7¹⁵/₁₆

25⅝ 2¹¹/₃₂ 2½ +

546 25⅝ 2¹¹/₃₂ 2½ +

2¾ 2¼ 2¼

127 2¾ 2¼ 2¼

12¹/₁₆ 11⅜ 11¾ +

616 12¹/₁₆ 11⅜ 11¾ +

33¾ 33 33¹/₁₆ —

87 33¾ 33 33¹/₁₆ —

25⅝ 24⁹/₁₆ 25⅝ +

602 25⅝ 24⁹/₁₆ 25⅝ +

12 11⅝ 11⅞ +

833 12 11⅝ 11⅞ +

16 10½ 10½ 10½ —

78 15⅞ 15¹³/₁₆ 15⅞ —

4608 9¹/₁₆ 8¼ 8⅞ +

430 11¼ 10⅛ 10

STUDY SESSION 14
ANALYSIS OF EQUITY INVESTMENTS:
Industry and Company Analysis

READING ASSIGNMENTS

This study session focuses on industry and company analysis and describes the tools used in forming an opinion about investing in a particular stock or group of stocks.

This study session begins with the essential tools of equity valuation: the discounted cash flow technique and the relative valuation approach. These techniques provide the means to estimate what a reasonable price for a stock should be. The readings on industry analysis are an important element in the valuation process, providing the top-down context crucial to estimating a company's potential. Also addressed is estimating a company's earnings per share by forecasting sales and profit margins.

The reading on technical analysis introduces the basic philosophy and underlying assumptions relied on by technicians to forecast trends in individual stocks as well as the entire stock market. The most widely used technical indicators, trading rules, and charts are described, and their application illustrated.

The last reading in this study session focuses on price multiples, one of the most familiar and widely used tools in estimating the value of a company, and introduces the application of four commonly used price multiples to valuation.

LEARNING OUTCOMES

Reading 59: An Introduction to Security Valuation

The candidate should be able to:

a. explain the top-down approach, and its underlying logic, to the security valuation process;

b. explain the various forms of investment returns;

c. calculate and interpret the value of a preferred stock, or of a common stock, using the dividend discount model (DDM);

d. show how to use the DDM to develop an earnings multiplier model, and explain the factors in the DDM that affect a stock's price-to-earnings (P/E) ratio;

e. explain the components of an investor's required rate of return (i.e., the real risk-free rate, the expected rate of inflation, and a risk premium) and discuss the risk factors to be assessed in determining a country risk premium for use in estimating the required return for foreign securities;

f. estimate the implied dividend growth rate, given the components of the required return on equity and incorporating the earnings retention rate and current stock price;

g. describe a process for developing estimated inputs to be used in the DDM, including the required rate of return and expected growth rate of dividends.

Reading 60: Industry Analysis

The candidate should be able to describe how structural economic changes (e.g., demographics, technology, politics, and regulation) may affect industries.

Reading 61: Equity: Concepts and Techniques

The candidate should be able to:

a. classify business cycle stages and identify, for each stage, attractive investment opportunities;

b. discuss, with respect to global industry analysis, the key elements related to return expectations;

c. describe the industry life cycle and identify an industry's stage in its life cycle;

d. interpret and explain the significance of a concentration ratio and a Herfindahl index;

e. discuss, with respect to global industry analysis, the elements related to risk, and describe the basic forces that determine industry competition.

Reading 62: Company Analysis and Stock Valuation

The candidate should be able to:

a. differentiate between 1) a growth company and a growth stock, 2) a defensive company and a defensive stock, 3) a cyclical company and a cyclical stock, 4) a speculative company and a speculative stock and 5) a value stock and a growth stock;

b. describe and estimate the expected earnings per share (EPS) and earnings multiplier for a company;

c. calculate and compare the expected rate of return (based on the estimate of intrinsic value) to the required rate of return.

Reading 63: Technical Analysis

The candidate should be able to:

a. explain the underlying assumptions of technical analysis and explain how technical analysis differs from fundamental analysis;

b. discuss the advantages and challenges of technical analysis;

c. identify examples of each of the major categories of technical indicators.

Reading 64: Introduction to Price Multiples

The candidate should be able to:

a. discuss the rationales for the use of price to earnings (P/E), price to book value (P/BV), price to sales (P/S), and price to cash flow (P/CF) in equity valuation and discuss the possible drawbacks to the use of each price multiple;

b. calculate and interpret P/E, P/BV, P/S, and P/CF.

$4\frac{5}{8}$ $4\frac{11}{16}$ — $\frac{3}{8}$

$5\frac{1}{2}$ $5\frac{1}{2}$ — $\frac{3}{8}$

$5\frac{1}{2}$ $21\frac{3}{16}$ — $\frac{1}{16}$

$20\frac{5}{8}$ $21\frac{3}{16}$ — $\frac{7}{8}$

$17\frac{3}{8}$ $18\frac{1}{8}$ + $\frac{7}{8}$

$5\frac{1}{2}$ $6\frac{1}{2}$ — $\frac{1}{2}$

$6\frac{1}{2}$ $6\frac{1}{2}$ — $\frac{1}{2}$

$7\frac{1}{4}$ $3\frac{1}{32}$ — $\frac{1}{8}$

$\frac{15}{16}$

$\frac{9}{16}$ $\frac{9}{16}$

$1\frac{1}{32}$ $9\frac{1}{16}$

$7\frac{13}{16}$ $7\frac{15}{16}$

$7\frac{15}{16}$ $7\frac{13}{16}$ $7\frac{15}{16}$

$2\frac{5}{8}$ $2\frac{11}{32}$ $2\frac{1}{2}$ +

$2\frac{3}{4}$ $2\frac{1}{4}$ $2\frac{1}{4}$

$6\frac{1}{8}$ $12\frac{1}{16}$ $11\frac{3}{8}$ $11\frac{3}{4}$ +

87 $33\frac{3}{4}$ 33 $33\frac{1}{16}$ —

602 $25\frac{5}{8}$ $24\frac{9}{16}$ $25\frac{3}{8}$ +

833 12 $11\frac{5}{8}$ $11\frac{7}{8}$ +

16 $10\frac{1}{2}$ $10\frac{1}{2}$ $10\frac{1}{2}$ —

78 $15\frac{7}{8}$ $15\frac{13}{16}$ $15\frac{7}{8}$ —

4608 $9\frac{1}{16}$ $8\frac{1}{4}$ $8\frac{7}{8}$ +

430 $11\frac{1}{4}$ $10\frac{1}{8}$ $4\frac{7}{8}$

AN INTRODUCTION TO SECURITY VALUATION

by Frank K. Reilly and Keith C. Brown

LEARNING OUTCOMES

The candidate should be able to:

a. explain the top-down approach, and its underlying logic, to the security valuation process;

b. explain the various forms of investment returns;

c. calculate and interpret the value of a preferred stock, or of a common stock, using the dividend discount model (DDM);

d. show how to use the DDM to develop an earnings multiplier model, and explain the factors in the DDM that affect a stock's price-to-earnings (P/E) ratio;

e. explain the components of an investor's required rate of return (i.e., the real risk-free rate, the expected rate of inflation, and a risk premium) and discuss the risk factors to be assessed in determining a country risk premium for use in estimating the required return for foreign securities;

f. estimate the implied dividend growth rate, given the components of the required return on equity and incorporating the earnings retention rate and current stock price;

g. describe a process for developing estimated inputs to be used in the DDM, including the required rate of return and expected growth rate of dividends.

INTRODUCTION · 1

An investment is a commitment of funds for a period of time to derive a rate of return that would compensate the investor for the time during which the funds are invested, for the expected rate of inflation during the investment horizon, and for the uncertainty involved. From this definition, we know that the first step in making an investment is determining your required rate of return.

Once you have determined this rate, some investment alternatives, such as savings accounts and T-bills, are fairly easy to evaluate because they provide stated cash flows. Most investments have expected cash flows and a stated market price (for example, common stock), and you must estimate a value for the investment to determine if its current market price is consistent with your estimated intrinsic value. To do this, you must estimate the value of the security based on its expected cash flows and your required rate of return. This is the process of estimating the intrinsic value of an asset. After you have completed estimating a security's intrinsic value, you compare this estimated intrinsic value to the prevailing market price to decide whether you want to buy the security or not.

This **investment decision process** is similar to the process you follow when deciding on a corporate investment or when shopping for clothes, a stereo, or a car. In each case, you examine the item and decide how much it is worth to you (its value). If the price equals its estimated value or is less, you would buy it. The same technique applies to securities except that the determination of a security's value is more formal.

We start our investigation of security valuation by discussing the **valuation process**. There are two general approaches to the valuation process: (1) the top-down, three-step approach; or (2) the bottom-up, stock valuation, stock-picking approach. Both of these approaches can be implemented by either fundamentalists or technicians. The difference between the two approaches is the perceived importance of the economy and a firm's industry on the valuation of a firm and its stock.

Advocates of the top-down, three-step approach believe that both the economy/market and the industry effect have a significant impact on the total returns for individual stocks. In contrast, those who employ the bottom-up, stockpicking approach contend that it is possible to find stocks that are undervalued relative to their market price, and these stocks will provide superior returns *regardless* of the market and industry outlook.

Both of these approaches have numerous supporters, and advocates of both approaches have been quite successful.[1] We advocate and present the top-down, three-step approach because of its logic and empirical support. Although we believe that a portfolio manager or an investor can be successful using the bottom-up approach, we believe that it is more difficult to be successful because these stock-pickers are ignoring substantial information from the market and the firm's industry.

Although we know that the value of a security is determined by its quality and profit potential, we also believe that the economic environment and the

---

[1] For the history and selection process of a legendary stockpicker, see Hagstrom (2001) or Lowenstein (1995).

performance of a firm's industry influence the value of a security and its rate of return. Because of the importance of these economic and industry factors, we present an overview of the valuation process that describes these influences and explains how they can be incorporated into the analysis of security value. Subsequently, we describe the theory of value and emphasize the factors that affect the value of individual securities.

Next, we apply these valuation concepts to the valuation of different assets—bonds, preferred stock, and common stock. In this section, we show how the valuation models help investors calculate how much they should pay for these assets. In the final section, we emphasize the estimation of the variables that affect value (the required rate of return and the expected growth rate of cash flows). We conclude with a discussion of additional factors that must be considered when we consider the valuation of international securities.

AN OVERVIEW OF THE VALUATION PROCESS   2

Psychologists suggest that the success or failure of an individual can be caused as much by his or her social, economic, and family environment as by genetic gifts. Extending this idea to the valuation of securities means we should consider a firm's economic and industry environment during the valuation process. Regardless of the qualities or capabilities of a firm and its management, the economic and industry environment will have a major influence on the success of a firm and the realized rate of return on its stock.

As an example, assume you own shares of the strongest and most successful firm producing home furnishings. If you own the shares during a strong economic expansion, the sales and earnings of the firm will increase and your rate of return on the stock should be quite high. In contrast, if you own the same stock during a major economic recession, the sales and earnings of this firm (and probably most or all of the firms in the industry) would likely experience a decline and the price of its stock would be stable or decline. Therefore, when assessing the future value of a security, it is necessary to analyze the outlook for the aggregate economy and the firm's specific industry.

The valuation process is like the chicken-and-egg dilemma. Do you start by analyzing the macroeconomy and various industries before individual stocks, or do you begin with individual securities and gradually combine these firms into industries and the industries into the entire economy? For reasons discussed in the next section, we contend that the discussion should begin with an analysis of aggregate economies and overall securities markets and progress to different industries with a global perspective. Only after a thorough analysis of a global industry are you in a position to properly evaluate the securities issued by individual firms within the better industries. Thus, we recommend a three-step, top-down valuation process in which you first examine the influence of the general economy on all firms and the security markets, then analyze the prospects for various global industries with the best outlooks in this economic environment, and finally turn to the analysis of individual firms in the preferred industries and to the common stock of these firms. Exhibit 59-1 indicates the procedure recommended.

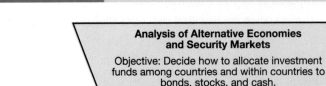

EXHIBIT 59-1   Overview of the Investment Process

Analysis of Alternative Economies and Security Markets

Objective: Decide how to allocate investment funds among countries and within countries to bonds, stocks, and cash.

Analysis of Alternative Industries

Objective: Based upon the economic and market analysis, determine which industries will prosper and which industries will suffer on a global basis and within countries.

Analysis of Individual Companies and Stocks

Objective: Following the selection of the best industries, determine which companies within these industries will prosper and which stocks are undervalued.

3   WHY A THREE-STEP VALUATION PROCESS?

General Economic Influences

Monetary and fiscal policy measures enacted by various agencies of national governments influence the aggregate economies of those countries. The resulting economic conditions influence all industries and companies within the economies.

Fiscal policy initiatives, such as tax credits or tax cuts, can encourage spending, whereas additional taxes on income, gasoline, cigarettes, and liquor can discourage spending. Increases or decreases in government spending on defense, on unemployment insurance or retraining programs, or on highways also influence the general economy. All such policies influence the business environment for firms that rely directly on such government expenditures. In addition, we know that government spending has a strong *multiplier effect*. For example, increases in road building increase the demand for earthmoving equipment and concrete materials. As a result, in addition to construction workers, the employees in those industries that supply the equipment and materials have more to spend on consumer goods, which raises the demand for consumer goods, which affects another set of suppliers.

Monetary policy produces similar economic changes. A restrictive monetary policy that reduces the growth rate of the money supply reduces the supply of funds for working capital and expansion for all businesses. Alternatively, a restrictive monetary policy that targets interest rates would raise market interest rates and therefore firms' costs and make it more expensive for individuals to finance home mortgages and the purchase of other durable goods, such as autos and appliances. Monetary policy therefore affects all segments of an economy and that economy's relationship with other economies.

Any economic analysis requires the consideration of inflation. As we have discussed, inflation causes differences between real and nominal interest rates and changes the spending and savings behavior of consumers and corporations. In addition, unexpected changes in the rate of inflation make it difficult for firms to plan, which inhibits growth and innovation. Beyond the impact on the domestic economy, differential inflation and interest rates influence the trade balance between countries and the exchange rate for currencies.

In addition to monetary and fiscal policy actions, such events as war, political upheavals in foreign countries, or international monetary devaluations produce changes in the business environment that add to the uncertainty of sales and earnings expectations and therefore the risk premium required by investors. For example, the political uncertainty in Russia during 1995–1999 caused a significant increase in the risk premium for investors in Russia and a subsequent reduction in investment and spending in Russia. In contrast, the end of apartheid in South Africa and its open election in 1994 were viewed as positive events and led to a significant increase in economic activity in the country. Similarly, the peace accord in Northern Ireland in the late 1990s caused a major influx of investment and tourist dollars.

In short, it is difficult to conceive of any industry or company that can avoid the impact of macroeconomic developments that affect the total economy. Because aggregate economic events have a profound effect on all industries and companies within these industries, these macroeconomic factors should be considered before industries are analyzed.

Taking a global portfolio perspective, the asset allocation for a country within a global portfolio will be affected by its economic outlook. If a recession is imminent in a country, you would expect a negative impact on its security prices. Because of these economic expectations, investors would be apprehensive about investing in most industries in the country. Given these expectations, the country will be **underweighted** in portfolios relative to its weight based on its market value. Further, given these pessimistic expectations, any funds invested in the country would be directed to low-risk sectors of the economy.

In contrast, optimistic economic and stock market outlooks for a given country should lead an investor to increase the overall allocation to this country (**overweight** the country compared to its weights determined by its relative market value). After allocating funds among countries, the investor looks for outstanding industries in each country. This search for the best industries is enhanced by the economic analysis because the future performance of an industry depends on the country's economic outlook *and* the industry's expected relationship to the economy during the particular phase of the business cycle.

Industry Influences

The second step in the valuation process is to identify global industries that will prosper or suffer in the long run or during the expected near-term economic environment. Examples of conditions that affect specific industries are strikes within a major producing country, import or export quotas or taxes, a worldwide shortage or an excess supply of a resource, or government-imposed regulations on an industry.

You should remember that alternative industries react to economic changes at different points in the business cycle. For example, firms typically increase capital expenditures when they are operating at full capacity at the peak of the economic cycle. Therefore, industries that provide plant and equipment will typically be affected toward the end of a cycle. In addition, alternative industries have different responses to the business cycle. As an example, cyclical industries, such as steel or autos, typically do much better than the aggregate economy during expansions, but they suffer more during contractions. In contrast, non-cyclical industries, such as retail food, would not experience a significant decline during a recession but also would not experience a strong increase during an economic expansion.

Another factor that will have a differential effect on industries is demographics. For example, it is widely recognized that the U.S. population is weighted toward "baby boomers" entering their late 50s and that there has been a large surge in the number of citizens over age 65. These two groups have heavy demand for second homes and medical care and the industries related to these segments (e.g., home furnishings and pharmaceuticals).

Firms that sell in international markets can benefit or suffer as foreign economies shift. An industry with a substantial worldwide market might experience low demand in its domestic market but benefit from growing demand in its international market. As an example, much of the growth for Coca-Cola and Pepsi and the fast-food chains, such as McDonald's and Burger King, has come from international expansion in Europe and the Far East.

In general, an industry's prospects within the global business environment will determine how well or poorly an individual firm will fare, so industry analysis should precede company analysis. Few companies perform well in a poor industry, so even the best company in a poor industry is a bad prospect for investment. For example, poor sales and earnings in the farm equipment industry during the late 1980s had a negative impact on Deere and Co., a well-managed firm and probably the best firm in its industry. Though Deere performed better than other firms in the industry (some went bankrupt), its earnings and stock performance still fell far short of its past performance, and the company did poorly compared to firms in most other industries.

Notably, even money managers who are essentially "stockpickers" consider industry analysis important because it determines a firm's business risk due to sales volatility and operating leverage, and its profitability is impacted by the competitive environment in the industry.

Company Analysis

After determining that an industry's outlook is good, an investor can analyze and compare individual firms' performance within the entire industry using financial ratios and cash flow values. Many financial ratios for firms are valid only when they are compared to the performance of their industries.

You undertake company analysis to identify the best company in a promising industry. This involves examining a firm's past performance, but more important, its future prospects. After you understand the firm and its outlook, you can determine its value using one of several valuation models. An important point that will be emphasized is that it is your estimated inputs to the valuation models that are critical, and the quality of these inputs depends on your prior market-industry-company analysis. In the final step, you compare your estimated intrinsic value to the price of the firm's stock and decide whether its stock or bonds are good investments.

Your final goal is to select the best stock or bonds within a desirable industry and include it in your portfolio based on its relationship (correlation) with all other assets in your portfolio. As we discuss in more detail in Reading 62, the best stock for investment purposes may not necessarily be issued by the best company because the stock of the finest company in an industry may be overpriced, which would cause it to be a poor investment. You cannot know whether a security is undervalued or overvalued until you have analyzed the company, estimated its intrinsic value, and compared your estimated intrinsic value to the market price of the firm's stock.

Does the Three-Step Process Work?

Although you might agree with the logic of the three-step investment process, you might wonder how well this process works in selecting investments. The results of several academic studies have supported this technique. First, studies indicated that most changes in an individual firm's *earnings* could be attributed to changes in aggregate corporate earnings and changes in the firm's industry, with the aggregate earnings changes being more important. Although the relative influence of the general economy and the industry on a firm's earnings varied among individual firms, the results consistently demonstrated that the economic environment had a significant effect on firm earnings.

Second, studies by Moore and Cullity (1988) and Siegel (1991) found a relationship between aggregate stock prices and various economic series, such as employment, income, or production. These results supported the view that a relationship exists between stock prices and economic expansions and contractions.

Third, an analysis of the relationship between *rates of return* for the aggregate stock market, alternative industries, and individual stocks showed that most of the changes in rates of return for individual stocks could be explained by changes in the rates of return for the aggregate stock market and the stock's industry. As shown by Meyers (1973), although the importance of the market effect tended to decline over time and the significance of the industry effect varied among industries, the combined market-industry effect on an individual stock's rate of return was still important.

These results from academic studies support the use of the three-step investment process. The most important decision is the asset allocation decision.[2] The asset allocation specifies: (1) what proportion of your portfolio will be invested in various nations' economies; (2) within each country, how you will divide your assets among stocks, bonds, or other assets; and (3) your industry selections, based on which industries are expected to prosper in the projected economic environment.

Now that we have described and justified the three-step process, we need to consider the theory of valuation. The application of this theory allows us to compute estimated intrinsic values for the market, for alternative industries, and for individual firms and stocks. Finally, we compare these estimated intrinsic values to current market prices and decide whether we want to make particular investments.

THEORY OF VALUATION   4

You may recall from your studies in accounting, economics, or corporate finance that the value of an asset is the present value of its expected returns. Specifically, you expect an asset to provide a stream of returns during the period of time you own it. To convert this estimated stream of returns to a value for the security, you

---

[2] The classic studies that established the importance of asset allocation are Brinson, Hood, and Beebower (1986), followed by Brinson, Singer, and Beebower (1991). A subsequent well-regarded application of these concepts is contained in Cohen (1996).

must discount this stream at your required rate of return. This process of valuation requires estimates of (1) the stream of expected returns and (2) the required rate of return on the investment.

Stream of Expected Returns (Cash Flows)

An estimate of the expected returns from an investment encompasses not only the size but also the form, time pattern, and the uncertainty of returns, which affect the required rate of return.

Form of Returns   The returns from an investment can take many forms, including earnings, cash flows, dividends, interest payments, or capital gains (increases in value) during a period. We will consider several alternative valuation techniques that use different forms of returns. As an example, one common stock valuation model applies a multiplier to a firm's earnings, whereas another valuation model computes the present value of a firm's operating cash flows, and a third model estimates the present value of dividend payments. Returns or cash flows can come in many forms, and you must consider all of them to evaluate an investment accurately.

Time Pattern and Growth Rate of Returns   You cannot calculate an accurate value for a security unless you can estimate when you will receive the returns or cash flows. Because money has a time value, you must know the time pattern and growth rate of returns from an investment. This knowledge will make it possible to properly value the stream of returns relative to alternative investments with a different time pattern and growth rate of returns or cash flows.

Required Rate of Return

Uncertainty of Returns (Cash Flows)   The required rate of return on an investment is determined by (1) the economy's real risk-free rate of return, plus (2) the expected rate of inflation during the holding period, plus (3) a risk premium that is determined by the uncertainty of returns. All investments are affected by the risk-free rate and the expected rate of inflation because these two variables determine the nominal risk-free rate. Therefore, the factor that causes a difference in required rates of return is the risk premium for alternative investments. In turn, this risk premium depends on the uncertainty of returns or cash flows from an investment.

We can identify the sources of the uncertainty of returns by the internal characteristics of assets or by market-determined factors. Earlier, we subdivided the internal characteristics for a firm into business risk (BR), financial risk (FR), liquidity risk (LR), exchange rate risk (ERR), and country risk (CR). The market-determined risk measures are the systematic risk of the asset (its beta), or a set of multiple risk factors.

Investment Decision Process: A Comparison of Estimated Values and Market Prices

To ensure that you receive your required return on an investment, you must estimate the intrinsic value of the investment at your required rate of return and then compare this estimated intrinsic value to the prevailing market price. You should not buy an investment if its market price exceeds your estimated value because the difference will prevent you from receiving your required rate of return on the investment. In contrast, if the estimated intrinsic value of the investment exceeds the market price, you should buy the investment. In summary:

> If Estimated Intrinsic Value > Market Price, Buy
> If Estimated Intrinsic Value < Market Price, Don't Buy or Sell If You Own It.

For example, assume you read about a firm that produces athletic shoes and its stock is listed on the NYSE. Using one of the valuation models we will discuss and making estimates of earnings, or cash flows, and the growth of these variables based on the company's annual report and other information, you estimate the company's intrinsic stock value using your required rate of return as $20 a share. After estimating this value, you look in the paper and see that the stock is currently being traded at $15 a share. You would want to buy this stock because you think it is worth $20 a share and you can buy it for $15 a share. In contrast, if the current market price were $25 a share, you would not want to buy the stock because, based upon your valuation, it is overvalued.

The theory of value provides a common framework for the valuation of all investments. Different applications of this theory generate different estimated values for alternative investments because of the different payment streams and characteristics of the securities. The interest and principal payments on a bond differ substantially from the expected dividends and future selling price for a common stock. The initial discussion that follows applies the discounted cash flow method to bonds, preferred stock, and common stock. This presentation demonstrates that the same basic model is useful across a range of investments. Subsequently, because of the difficulty in estimating the value of common stock, we consider two general approaches and numerous techniques for the valuation of stock.

VALUATION OF ALTERNATIVE INVESTMENTS 5

Valuation of Bonds

Calculating the value of bonds is relatively easy because the size and time pattern of cash flows from the bond over its life are known. A bond typically promises

1. Interest payments every six months equal to one-half the coupon rate times the face value of the bond
2. The payment of the principal on the bond's maturity date

As an example, in 2006, a $10,000 bond due in 2021 with a 10 percent coupon will pay $500 every six months for its 15-year life. In addition, the bond issuer promises to pay the $10,000 principal at maturity in 2021. Therefore, assuming the bond issuer does not default, the investor knows what payments (cash flows) will be made and when they will be made.

Applying the valuation theory, which states that the value of any asset is the present value of its cash flows, the value of the bond is the present value of the interest payments, which we can think of as an annuity of $500 every six months for 15 years, and the present value of the principal payment, which in this case is the present value of $10,000 to be paid at the end of 15 years. The only unknown for this asset (assuming the borrower does not default) is the required rate of return that should be used to discount the expected stream of returns (cash flows). If the prevailing nominal risk-free rate is 7 percent and the investor requires a 3 percent risk premium on this bond because there is some probability of default, the required rate of return would be 10 percent.

The present value of the interest payments is an annuity for 30 periods (15 years every six months) at one-half the required return (5 percent):

$$\$500 \times 15.3725 = \$7,686$$
(Present Value of Interest Payments at 10 Percent)

The present value of the principal is likewise discounted at 5 percent for 30 periods.[3]

$$\$10,000 \times 0.2314 = \$2,314$$
(Present Value of the Principal Payment at 10 Percent)

This can be summarized as follows:

Present Value of Interest Payments $500 × 15.3725   = $ 7,686
Present Value of Principal Payment $10,000 × 0.2314 =   2,314
Total Value of Bond at 10 Percent   = $10,000

This is the amount that an investor should be willing to pay for this bond, assuming that the required rate of return on a bond of this risk class is 10 percent. If the market price of the bond is above this value, the investor should not buy it because the promised yield to maturity at this higher price will be less than the investor's required rate of return.

Alternatively, assuming an investor requires a 12 percent return on this bond, its value would be:

$$\$500 \times 13.7648 = \$6,882$$
$$\$10,00 \times 0.1741 = \underline{1,741}$$
$$\text{Total Value of Bond at 12 Percent} = \$8,623$$

This example shows that if you want a higher rate of return, you will not pay as much for an asset; that is, a given stream of cash flows has a lower value to you. It is this characteristic that leads to the often used phrase that the prices of bonds move in an opposite direction of yields. As before, you would compare this computed value to the market price of the bond to determine whether you should invest in it.[4]

Valuation of Preferred Stock

The owner of a preferred stock receives a promise to pay a stated dividend, usually each quarter, for an infinite period. Preferred stock is a **perpetuity** because it has no maturity. As was true with a bond, stated payments are made on specified dates although the issuer of this stock does not have the same legal obligation to pay investors as do issuers of bonds. Payments are made only after the firm meets its bond interest payments. Because this reduced legal obligation increases the uncertainty of returns, investors should require a higher rate of return on a firm's preferred stock than on its bonds. Although this differential in required return

---

[3] If we used annual compounding, this would be 0.239 rather than 0.2314. We use semiannual compounding because it is consistent with the interest payments and is used in practice.

[4] To test your mastery of bond valuation, check that if the required rate of return were 8 percent, the value of this bond would be $11,729.

should exist in theory, it generally does not exist in practice because of the tax treatment accorded dividends paid to corporations. Eighty percent of intercompany preferred dividends are tax-exempt, making the effective tax rate on preferred dividends about 6.8 percent, assuming a corporate tax rate of 34 percent. This tax advantage stimulates the demand for preferred stocks by corporations; and, because of this demand, the yield on preferred stocks has generally been below that on the highest-grade corporate bonds.

Because preferred stock is a perpetuity, its value is simply the stated annual dividend divided by the required rate of return on preferred stock (k_p) as follows:

$$V = \frac{\text{Dividend}}{k_p}$$

Consider a preferred stock has a \$100 par value and a dividend of \$8 a year. Because of the expected rate of inflation, the uncertainty of the dividend payment, and the tax advantage to you as a corporate investor, assume that your required rate of return on this stock is 9 percent. Therefore, the value of this preferred stock to you is

$$V = \frac{\$8}{0.09}$$
$$= \$88.89$$

Given this estimated value, you would inquire about the current market price to decide whether you would want to buy this preferred stock. If the current market price is \$95, you would decide against a purchase, whereas if it is \$80, you would buy the stock. Also, given the market price of preferred stock, you can derive its promised yield. Assuming a current market price of \$85, the promised yield would be

$$k_p = \frac{\text{Dividend}}{\text{Price}} = \frac{\$8}{\$85.00} = 0.0941$$

Approaches to the Valuation of Common Stock

Because of the complexity and importance of valuing common stock, various techniques for accomplishing this task have been devised over time. These techniques fall into one of two general approaches: (1) the discounted cash flow valuation techniques, where the value of the stock is estimated based upon the present value of some measure of cash flow, including dividends, operating cash flow, and free cash flow; and (2) the relative valuation techniques, where the value of a stock is estimated based upon its current price relative to variables considered to be significant to valuation, such as earnings, cash flow, book value, or sales. Exhibit 59-2 provides a visual presentation of the alternative approaches and specific techniques.

An important point is that *both of these approaches and all of these valuation techniques have several common factors*. First, all of them are significantly affected by the investor's *required rate of return* on the stock because this rate becomes the discount rate or is a major component of the discount rate. Second, all valuation approaches are affected by *the estimated growth rate of the variable* used in the valuation technique—for example, dividends, earnings, cash flow, or sales. As noted in the efficient market discussion, both of these critical variables must be *estimated*. As a result, different analysts using the same valuation techniques will derive

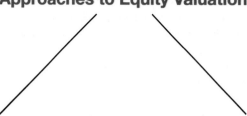

EXHIBIT 59-2   Common Stock Valuation Approaches and Specific Techniques

Approaches to Equity Valuation

Discounted Cash Flow Techniques

- **Present Value of Dividends (DDM)**
- **Present Value of Operating Free Cash Flow**
- **Present Value of Free Cash Flow to Equity**

Relative Valuation Techniques

- **Price/Earning Ratio (*P/E*)**
- **Price/Cash Flow Ratio (*P/CF*)**
- **Price/Book Value Ratio (*P/BV*)**
- **Price/Sales Ratio (*P/S*)**

different estimates of value for a stock because they have different estimates for these critical variable inputs. Put another way, you should assume that most investors are aware of the valuation models and it is the *inputs* to the models that make a difference—that is, your estimates of the discount rate and the growth rate of earnings and cash flows. If you are better at estimating these inputs, you will be a superior analyst.

The following discussion of equity valuation techniques considers the specific models and the theoretical and practical strengths and weaknesses of each of them. Notably, the authors' intent is to present these two approaches as complementary, *not* competitive, approaches—that is, you should learn and use both of them.

Why and When to Use the Discounted Cash Flow Valuation Approach

These discounted cash flow valuation techniques are obvious choices for valuation because they are the epitome of how we describe value—that is, the present value of expected cash flows. The major difference between the alternative techniques is how one specifies cash flow—that is, the measure of cash flow used.

The cleanest and most straightforward measure of cash flow is *dividends* because these are clearly cash flows that go directly to the investor, which implies that you should use *the cost of equity* as the discount rate. However, this dividend technique is difficult to apply to firms that do not pay dividends during periods of high growth, or that currently pay very limited dividends because they have high rate of return investment alternatives available. On the other hand, an advantage is that the reduced form of the **dividend discount model (DDM)** is very useful when discussing valuation for a stable, mature entity where the assumption of relatively constant growth for the long term is appropriate (a good example is the aggregate stock market).

The second specification of cash flow is the *operating free cash flow,* which is generally described as cash flows after direct costs (cost of goods and S, G & A expenses) and after allowing for cash flows to support working capital outlays and capital expenditures required for future growth, but before any payments to capital suppliers. Because we are dealing with the cash flows available for all capital suppliers, the discount rate employed is the firm's *weighted average cost of capital* (WACC). This is a very useful model when comparing firms with diverse capital structures because you determine the value of the total firm and then subtract the value of the firm's debt obligations to arrive at a value for the firm's equity.

The third cash flow measure is *free cash flow to equity*, which is a measure of cash flows similar to the operating free cash flow described above, but after payments to debt holders, which means that these are cash flows available to equity owners. Therefore, the appropriate discount rate is the firm's *cost of equity*.

Beyond being theoretically correct, these models allow a substantial amount of flexibility in terms of changes in sales and expenses that implies changing growth rates over time. Once you understand how to compute each measure of cash flow, you can estimate cash flow for each year by constructing a pro forma statement for each year or you can estimate overall growth rates for the alternative cash flow values as we will demonstrate with the DDM.

A potential difficulty with these cash flow techniques is that they are very dependent on the two significant inputs—(1) the growth rates of cash flows (both the *rate* of growth and the *duration* of growth) and (2) the estimate of the discount rate. As we will show in several instances, a small change in either of these values can have a significant impact on the estimated value. As noted earlier, everyone knows and uses a similar valuation model, but it is the *inputs* that are critical—GIGO: garbage in, garbage out! This is similar to the discussion in Reading 57 regarding being a superior analyst in a world with an efficient market.

Why and When to Use the Relative Valuation Techniques

As noted, a benefit, but also a potential problem with the discounted cash flow valuation models is that it is possible to derive intrinsic values that are substantially above or below prevailing prices depending on how you adjust your estimated inputs to the prevailing environment. An advantage of the relative valuation techniques is that they provide information about how the market is *currently* valuing stock at several levels—that is, the aggregate market, alternative industries, and individual stocks within industries. Following this reading, which provides the background for these two approaches, we will demonstrate the alternative relative valuation ratios for the aggregate market, for an industry relative to the market, and for an individual company relative to the aggregate market, to its industry, and to other stocks in its industry.

The good news is that this relative valuation approach provides information on how the market is currently valuing securities. The bad news is that it is providing information on current valuation. The point is, the relative valuation approach provides this information on current valuation, but it does not provide guidance on whether these current valuations are appropriate—that is, *all* valuations at a point in time could be too high or too low. For example, assume that the market becomes significantly overvalued. For example, if you compare the value for an industry to the very overvalued market, you might contend based on such a comparison that an industry is undervalued relative to the market. Unfortunately, your judgment may be wrong because of the benchmark you are using—that is, you might be comparing a fully valued industry to a *very* overvalued market. Alternatively, if you compare an undervalued industry to an aggregate market that is *grossly* undervalued, the industry will appear overvalued by comparison.

Put another way, the relative valuation techniques are appropriate to consider under two conditions:

1. You have a good set of comparable entities—that is, comparable companies that are similar in terms of industry, size, and, it is hoped, risk.

2. The aggregate market and the company's industry are not at a valuation extreme—that is, they are not either seriously undervalued or overvalued.

Discounted Cash Flow Valuation Techniques

All of these valuation techniques are based on the basic valuation model, which asserts that the value of an asset is the present value of its expected future cash flows as follows:

$$V_j = \sum_{t=1}^{n} \frac{CF_t}{(1 + k)^t}$$

where:

V_j = value of Stock j
n = life of the asset
CF_t = cash flow in Period t
k = the discount rate that is equal to the investors' required rate of return for Asset j, which is determined by the uncertainty (risk) of the asset's cash flows

As noted, the specific cash flows used will differ between techniques. They range from dividends (the best-known model) to operating free cash flow and free cash flow to equity. We begin with a fairly detailed presentation of the present-value-of-dividend model, referred to as the dividend discount model (DDM), because it is intuitively appealing and is the best-known model. Also, its general approach is similar to the other discounted cash flow models.

The Dividend Discount Model (DDM)   The **dividend discount model** assumes that the value of a share of common stock is the present value of all future dividends as follows:[5]

$$V_j = \frac{D_1}{(1 + k)} + \frac{D_2}{(1 + k)^2} + \frac{D_3}{(1 + k)^3} + \cdots + \frac{D_\infty}{(1 + k)^\infty}$$
$$= \sum_{t=1}^{n} \frac{D_t}{(1 + k)^t}$$

where:

V_j = value of common Stock j
D_t = dividend during Period t
k = required rate of return on Stock j

An obvious question is: What happens when the stock is not held for an infinite period? A sale of the stock at the end of Year 2 would imply the following formula:

$$V_j = \frac{D_1}{(1 + k)} + \frac{D_2}{(1 + k)^2} + \frac{SP_{j2}}{(1 + k)^2}$$

---

[5] This model was initially set forth in Williams (1938) and subsequently reintroduced and expanded by Gordon (1962).

The value is equal to the two dividend payments during Years 1 and 2 plus the sale price (*SP*) for stock *j* at the end of Year 2. The expected selling price of stock *j* at the end of Year 2 (*SP_{j2}*) is simply the value of all remaining dividend payments.

$$SP_{j2} = \frac{D_3}{(1 + k)} + \frac{D_4}{(1 + k)^2} + \cdots + \frac{D_\infty}{(1 + k)^\infty}$$

If *SP_{j2}* is discounted back to the present by $1/(1 + k)^2$, this equation becomes

$$PV(SP_{j2}) = \frac{\dfrac{D_3}{(1 + k)} + \dfrac{D_4}{(1 + k)^2} + \cdots + \dfrac{D_\infty}{(1 + k)^\infty}}{(1 + k)^2}$$

$$= \frac{D_3}{(1 + k)^3} + \frac{D_4}{(1 + k)^2} + \cdots + \frac{D_\infty}{(1 + k)^\infty}$$

which is simply an extension of the original equation. Whenever the stock is sold, its value (that is, the sale price at that time) will be the present value of all future dividends. When this ending value is discounted back to the present, you are back to the original dividend discount model.

What about stocks that pay no dividends? Again, the concept is the same, except that some of the early dividend payments are zero. Notably, there are expectations that *at some point* the firm will start paying dividends. If investors lacked such an expectation, nobody would be willing to buy the security. It would have zero value. A firm with a non-dividend-paying stock is reinvesting its capital in very profitable projects rather than paying current dividends so that its earnings and dividend stream will be larger and grow faster in the future. In this case, we would apply the DDM as:

$$V_j = \frac{D_1}{(1 + k)} + \frac{D_2}{(1 + k)^2} + \frac{D_3}{(1 + k)^3} + \cdots + \frac{D_\infty}{(1 + k)^\infty}$$

where:

$$D_1 = 0; D_2 = 0$$

The investor expects that when the firm starts paying dividends in Period 3, it will be a large initial amount and dividends will grow faster than those of a comparable stock that had paid out dividends. The stock has value because of these *future* dividends. We will apply this model to several cases having different holding periods that will show you how it works.

One-Year Holding Period Assume an investor wants to buy the stock, hold it for one year, and then sell it. To determine the value of the stock—that is, how much the investor should be willing to pay for it—using the DDM, we must estimate the dividend to be received during the period, the expected sale price at the end of the holding period, and the investor's required rate of return.

To estimate the dividend for the coming year, adjust the current dividend for expectations regarding the change in the dividend during the year. Assume the company we are analyzing earned $2.50 a share last year and paid a dividend of $1 a share. Assume further that the firm has been fairly consistent in maintaining this 40 percent payout over time. The consensus of financial analysts is that the firm will earn about $2.75 during the coming year and will raise its dividend to $1.10 per share.

A crucial estimate is the expected selling price for the stock a year from now. You can estimate this expected selling price by one or more of three alternative procedures. In the first, you can apply the dividend discount model where you estimate the specific dividend payments for a number of years into the future and calculate the value of the stock from these estimates. In the second procedure, the **earnings multiplier model** you multiply the future expected earnings for the stock by an earnings multiple, which you likewise estimate, to find an expected sale price. We will discuss the earnings multiple model in a later section of the reading.

In the third method you estimate the firm's future earnings and its dividend payout ratio to arrive at an estimate of its expected dividend at your sale date. Given this dividend and an estimate of the dividend yield on stocks, you can derive a price estimate.

Given the estimated earnings and dividend above (earnings of $2.75, and dividend of $1.10), we can use the earnings multiplier and the dividend yield procedures as follows:

The long-run **forward P/E** of stocks is between 12 and 16. Using the midpoint of 14, we get an estimated price of:

$$14 \times \$2.75 = \$35.50$$

The long-run dividend yield on stocks has been between 1.50 percent and 5.00 percent, but in recent years (since 1980) it has been 1.50 to 4.00 percent, which implies a midpoint of 2.75 percent. Using this estimate with the $1.10 dividend gives an estimated price of:

$$\frac{\$1.10}{.0275} = \$40.00$$

The average of these two estimates is $37.75, which is rounded to $38.

Finally, you must determine the required rate of return. As discussed before, the nominal risk-free rate is determined by the real risk-free rate and the expected rate of inflation. A widely used proxy for this rate is the promised yield on ten-year government bonds because the typical investment horizon (expected holding period) is 5 to 10 years. You estimate the stock's risk premium by comparing its risk level to the risk of other potential investments. In later chapters, we discuss how you can estimate this risk. For the moment, assume that ten-year government bonds are yielding 7 percent, and you believe that a 3 percent risk premium over the yield of these bonds is appropriate for this stock. Thus, you specify a required rate of return of 10 percent.

In summary, you have estimated the dividend at $1.10 (payable at year end), an ending sale price of $38, and a required rate of return of 10 percent. Given these inputs, you would estimate the value of this stock as follows:

$$
\begin{aligned}
V_1 &= \frac{\$1.10}{(1 + 0.10)} + \frac{\$38.00}{(1 + 0.10)} \\
&= \frac{\$1.10}{1.10} + \frac{\$38.00}{1.10} \\
&= \$1.00 + 34.55 \\
&= \$35.55
\end{aligned}
$$

Note that we have not mentioned the current market price of the stock. This is because the market price is not relevant to you as an investor except as a comparison to the independently derived value based on your estimates of the relevant variables. Once we have calculated the stock's value as $35.55 we can compare it to the market price and apply the investment decision rule: If the stock's market price is more than $35.55, do not buy; if it is equal to or less than $35.55, buy.

Multiple-Year Holding Period   If you anticipate holding the stock for several years and then selling it, the valuation estimate is harder. You must forecast several future dividend payments and estimate the sale price of the stock several years in the future.

The difficulty with estimating future dividend payments is that the future stream can have numerous forms. The exact estimate of the future dividends depends on two projections. The first is your outlook for earnings growth because earnings are the source of dividends. The second projection is the firm's dividend policy, which can take several forms. A firm can have a constant percent payout of earnings each year, which implies a change in dividend each year, or the firm could follow a step pattern in which it increases the dividend rate by a constant dollar amount each year or every two or three years. The easiest dividend policy is to assume that the firm enjoys a constant growth rate in earnings and maintains a constant dividend payout. This set of assumptions implies that the dividend stream will experience a constant growth rate that is equal to the earnings growth rate. Clearly, the important estimate by the analyst is the growth rate of earnings, which will provide the dividend estimates and ending estimates for earnings and the dividends that are used to derive the ending price estimate as above. As before, the estimated intrinsic value is simply the discounted value of these cash flows at your required cost of equity. Finally, compare this estimated intrinsic value for the stock to its current market price to determine whether you should buy it.

At this point, you should recognize that the valuation procedure discussed here is similar to that used in corporate finance when making investment decisions, except that the cash flows are from dividends instead of returns to an investment project. Also, rather than estimating the scrap value or salvage value of a corporate asset, we are estimating the ending sale price for the stock. Finally, rather than discounting cash flows using the firm's cost of capital, we use the individual's required rate of return on the company's equity. In both cases, we are looking for excess present value, which means that the present value of expected cash inflows—that is, the estimated intrinsic value of the asset—exceeds the present value of cash outflows, which is the market price of the asset.

Infinite Period Model   We can extend the multiperiod model by extending our estimates of dividends but the benefits derived from these extensions would be minimal. Instead, we will move to the infinite period dividend discount model, which assumes that investors estimate future dividend payments for an infinite number of periods.

Needless to say, this is a formidable task. We must make some simplifying assumptions about this future stream of dividends to make the task viable. The easiest assumptions is that *the future dividend stream will grow at a constant rate for an infinite period*. This is a rather heroic assumption in many instances, but where it does hold, we can use the model to value individual stocks as well as the aggregate market and alternative industries. This model is generalized as follows:

$$V_j = \frac{D_0(1 + g)}{(1 + k)} + \frac{D_0(1 + g)^2}{(1 + k)^2} + \cdots + \frac{D_0(1 + g)^n}{(1 + k)^n}$$

where:

V_j = the value of Stock j
D_0 = the dividend payment in the current period
g = the constant growth rate of dividends
k = the required rate of return on Stock j
n = the number of periods, which we assume to be infinite

With certain assumptions, this infinite period constant growth rate model can be simplified to the following expression (referred to as the reduced form DDM):

$$V_j = \frac{D_1}{k - g}$$

You will probably recognize this formula as one that is widely used in corporate finance to estimate the cost of equity capital for the firm—that is, $k = D/V + g$.

To use this model for valuation, you must estimate (1) the required rate of return (k) and (2) the expected constant growth rate of dividends (g). After estimating g, it is a simple matter to estimate D_1, because it is the current dividend (D_0) times ($1 + g$).

Consider the example of a stock with a current dividend of $1 a share. You believe that, over the long run, this company's earnings and dividends will grow at 7 percent; your estimate of g is 0.07, which implies that you expect the dividend next year (D_1) to be $1.07. For the long run, you expect a nominal risk-free rate of about 8 percent and a risk premium for this stock of 3 percent. Therefore, you set your long-run required rate of return on this stock at 11 percent; your estimate of k is 0.11. To summarize the relevant estimates:

$$g = 0.07$$
$$k = 0.11$$
$$D_1 = \$1.07\,(\$1.00 \times 1.07)$$
$$V = \frac{\$1.07}{0.11 - 0.07}$$
$$= \frac{\$1.07}{0.04}$$
$$= \$26.75$$

A small change in any of the original estimates will have a large impact on V, as shown by the following examples:

1. $g = 0.07$; $k = 0.12$; $D_1 = \$1.07$. (We assume an increase in k.)

$$V = \frac{\$1.07}{0.12 - 0.07}$$
$$= \frac{\$1.07}{0.05}$$
$$= \$21.40$$

2. $g = 0.08$; $k = 0.11$; $D_1 = \$1.08$ (We assume an increase in g.)

$$V = \frac{\$1.08}{0.11 - 0.08}$$
$$= \frac{\$1.08}{0.03}$$
$$= \$36.00$$

These examples show that as small a change as 1 percent in either g or k produces a large difference in the estimated value of the stock. The crucial relationship that determines the value of the stock is the *spread between the required rate of return* (k) *and the expected growth rate of dividends* (g). Anything that causes a decline in the spread will cause an increase in the computed value, whereas any increase in the spread will decrease the computed value of the stock.

Infinite Period DDM and Growth Companies

The infinite period DDM has the following assumptions:

1. Dividends grow at a constant rate.

2. The constant growth rate will continue for an infinite period.

3. The required rate of return (k) *is greater than the infinite growth rate* (g). If it is not, the model gives meaningless results because the denominator becomes negative.

What is the effect of these assumptions if you want to use this model to value the stock of growth companies, such as Intel, Pfizer, Microsoft, McDonald's, and Wal-Mart? **Growth companies** are firms that have the opportunities and abilities to earn rates of return on investments that are consistently above their required rates of return.[6] You will recall from corporate finance that the required rate of return for a corporation is its weighted average cost of capital (WACC). An example might be Intel, which has a WACC of about 12 percent, but is currently earning about 20 percent on its invested capital. Therefore, we would consider Intel a growth company. To exploit these outstanding investment opportunities, these growth firms generally retain a high percentage of earnings for reinvestment, and their earnings will grow faster than those of the typical firm. A firm's sustainable growth is a function of its retention rate and its return on equity (ROE). Notably, as discussed subsequently, the earnings growth pattern for these growth companies is inconsistent with the assumptions of the infinite period DDM.

First, the infinite period DDM assumes dividends will grow at a constant rate for an infinite period. This assumption seldom holds for companies currently growing at above average rates. As an example, both Intel and Wal-Mart have grown at rates in excess of 20 percent a year for several years. It is unlikely that they can maintain such extreme rates of growth because of the inability to continue earning the ROEs implied by this growth for an infinite period in an economy where other firms will compete with them for these high rates of return.

Second, during the periods when these firms experience abnormally high rates of growth, their rates of growth probably exceed their required rates of return. There is *no* automatic relationship between growth and risk; a high-growth company is not necessarily a high-risk company. In fact, a firm growing at a high *constant rate* would have lower risk (less uncertainty) than a low-growth firm with an unstable earnings pattern.

In summary, some firms experience periods of abnormally high rates of growth for some finite periods of time. The infinite period DDM cannot be used to value these true growth firms because these high-growth conditions are temporary and therefore inconsistent with the assumptions of the DDM. In the following section, we discuss how to adjust the DDM to value a firm with

---

[6] Growth companies are discussed in Salomon (1963) and Miller and Modigliani (1961). Models to value growth companies are discussed in Reading 62.

temporary supernormal growth. In Reading 62 we will discuss additional models used for estimating the stock value of growth companies.

Valuation with Temporary Supernormal Growth

Thus far, we have considered how to value a firm with different growth rates for short periods of time (one to three years) and how to value a stock using a model that assumes a constant growth rate for an infinite period. As noted, the assumptions of the model make it impossible to use the infinite period constant growth model to value true growth companies. The point is, in a competitive free enterprise economy, it is not reasonable to expect that a company can permanently maintain a growth rate higher than its required rate of return because competition will eventually enter this apparently lucrative business, which will reduce the firm's profit margins and therefore its ROE and growth rate. Therefore, after a few years of exceptional growth—that is, a period of temporary supernormal growth—a firm's growth rate is expected to decline. Eventually its growth rate is expected to stabilize at a constant level consistent with the assumptions of the infinite period DDM.

To determine the value of a temporary supernormal growth company, you must combine the previous models. In analyzing the initial years of exceptional growth, you examine each year individually. If the company is expected to have two or three stages of supernormal growth, you must examine each year during these stages of growth. When the firm's growth rate stabilizes at a rate below the required rate of return, you can compute the remaining value of the firm assuming constant growth using the DDM and discount this lump-sum constant growth value back to the present. The technique should become clear as you work through the following example.

The Bourke Company has a current dividend (D_0) of $2 a share. The following are the expected annual growth rates for dividends.

Year	Dividend Growth Rate
1–3	25%
4–6	20
7–9	15
10 on	9

The required rate of return for the stock (the company's cost of equity) is 14 percent. Therefore, the value equation becomes (Exhibit 59-3 presents it in a table):

$$V_j = \frac{2.00(1.25)}{1.14} + \frac{2.00(1.25)^2}{(1.14)^2} + \frac{2.00(1.25)^3}{(1.14)^3}$$

$$+ \frac{2.00(1.25)^3(1.20)}{(1.14)^4} + \frac{2.00(1.25)^3(1.20)^2}{(1.14)^5}$$

$$+ \frac{2.00(1.25)^3(1.20)^3}{(1.14)^6} + \frac{2.00(1.25)^3(1.20)^3(1.15)}{(1.14)^7}$$

$$+ \frac{2.00(1.25)^3(1.20)^3(1.15)^2}{(1.14)^8} + \frac{2.00(1.25)^3(1.20)^3(1.15)^3}{(1.14)^9}$$

$$+ \frac{\dfrac{2.00(1.25)^3(1.20)^3(1.15)^3(1.09)}{(0.14 - 0.09)}}{(1.14)^9}$$

		Discount Factor	
Year	Dividend	(14 percent)	Present Value
1	$ 2.50	0.8772	$ 2.193
2	3.12	0.7695	2.401
3	3.91	0.6750	2.639
4	4.69	0.5921	2.777
5	5.63	0.5194	2.924
6	6.76	0.4556	3.080
7	7.77	0.3996	3.105
8	8.94	0.3506	3.134
9	10.28	0.3075[b]	3.161
10	11.21		
	$224.20[a]	0.3075[b]	68.941
		Total value =	$94.355

EXHIBIT 59-3 — Computation of Value for the Stock of a Company with Temporary Supernormal Growth

[a] Value of dividend stream for Year 10 and all future dividends (that is, $11.21/(0.14 − 0.09) = $224.20).

[b] The discount factor is the ninth-year factor because the valuation of the remaining stream is made at the end of Year 9 to reflect the dividend in Year 10 and all future dividends.

The computations in Exhibit 59-3 indicate that the total value of the stock is $94.36. As before, you would compare this estimate of intrinsic value to the market price of the stock when deciding whether to purchase the stock. The difficult part of the valuation is estimating the supernormal growth rates and determining *how long* each of the growth rates will last.

To summarize this section, the initial present value of cash flow stock valuation model considered was the dividend discount model (DDM). After explaining the basic model and the derivation of its reduced form, we noted that the infinite period DDM cannot be applied to the valuation of stock for growth companies because the abnormally high growth rate of earnings for the growth company is inconsistent with the assumptions of the infinite period constant growth DDM model. Subsequently we modified the DDM model to evaluate companies with temporary supernormal growth. In the following sections, we discuss the other present value of cash flow techniques assuming a similar set of scenarios.

Present Value of Operating Free Cash Flows

In this model, you are deriving the value of the total firm because you are discounting the operating free cash flows prior to the payment of interest to the debt holders but after deducting funds needed to maintain the firm's asset base (capital expenditures). Also, because you are discounting the total firm's operating free cash flow, you would use the firm's weighted average cost of capital (*WACC*) as your discount rate. Therefore, once you estimate the value of the total firm, you subtract the value of debt, assuming your goal is to estimate the value of the firm's equity. The total value of the firm is equal to:

$$V_j = \sum_{t=1}^{n} \frac{OFCF_t}{(1 + WACC_j)^t}$$

where:

V_j = value of Firm j

n = number of periods assumed to be infinite

$OFCF_t$ = the firm's operating free cash flow in Period t. The detailed specification of operating free cash flow will be discussed in Reading 62.

$WACC_j$ = Firm j's weighted average cost of capital. The computation of the firm's $WACC$ will be discussed in Reading 62.

Similar to the process with the DDM, it is possible to envision this as a model that requires estimates for an infinite period. Alternatively, if you are dealing with a mature firm whereby its operating cash flows have reached a stage of stable growth, you can adapt the infinite period constant growth DDM model as follows:

$$V_j = \frac{OFCF_1}{WACC_j - g_{OFCF}}$$

where:

$OFCF_1$ = operating free cash flow in Period 1 equal to $OFCF_0(1 + g_{OFCF})$

g_{OFCF} = long-term constant growth rate of operating free cash flow

Alternatively, assuming that the firm is expected to experience several different rates of growth for $OFCF$, these estimates can be divided into three or four stages, as demonstrated with the temporary supernormal dividend growth model. Similar to the dividend model, the analyst must estimate the *rate* of growth and the *duration* of growth for each of these periods of supernormal growth as follows:

Year	OFCF Growth Rate
1–4	20%
5–7	16
8–10	12
11 on	7

Therefore, the calculations would estimate the specific $OFCF$s for each year through Year 10 based on the expected growth rates, but you would use the infinite growth model estimate when the growth rate reached stability after Year 10. As noted, after determining the value of the total firm V_j, you must subtract the value of all nonequity items, including accounts payable, total interest-bearing debt, deferred taxes, and preferred stock, to arrive at the estimated value of the firm's equity. This calculation will be demonstrated in Reading 62.

Present Value of Free Cash Flows to Equity

The third discounted cash flow technique deals with "free" cash flows to equity, which would be derived *after* operating free cash flows have been adjusted for debt payments (interest and principal). Also, these cash flows precede dividend payments to the common stockholder. Such cash flows are referred to as free because they are what is left after providing the funds needed to maintain the firm's asset base (similar to operating free cash flow). They are free cash flows to equity because they also adjust for payments to debt holders and any payments to preferred stockholders.

Notably, because these are cash flows available to equity owners, the discount rate used is the firm's cost of equity (k) rather than the firm's *WACC*.

$$V_j = \sum_{t=1}^{n} \frac{FCFE_t}{(1 + k_j)^t}$$

where:

V_j = value of the stock of Firm j
n = number of periods assumed to be infinite
$FCFE_t$ = the firm's free cash flow to equity in Period t. The detailed specification of free cash flow to equity will be discussed in Reading 62.

Again, how an analyst would implement this general model depends upon the firm's position in its life cycle. That is, if the firm is expected to experience stable growth, analysts can use the infinite growth model. In contrast, if the firm is expected to experience a period of temporary supernormal growth, analysts should use the multistage growth model similar to the process used with dividends and for operating free cash flow.

RELATIVE VALUATION TECHNIQUES 　　6

In contrast to the various discounted cash flow techniques that attempt to estimate a specific value for a stock based on its estimated growth rates and its discount rate, the relative valuation techniques implicitly contend that it is possible to determine the value of an economic entity (i.e., the market, an industry, or a company) by comparing it to similar entities on the basis of several relative ratios that compare its stock price to relevant variables that affect a stock's value, such as earnings, cash flow, book value, and sales. Therefore, in this section, we discuss the following relative valuation ratios: (1) price/earnings (P/E), (2) price/cash flow (P/CF), (3) price/book value (P/BV), and price/sales (P/S). We begin with the P/E ratio, also referred to as the earnings multiplier model, because it is the most popular relative valuation ratio. In addition, we will show that the P/E ratio can be directly related to the DDM in a manner that indicates the variables that affect the P/E ratio.

Earnings Multiplier Model

As noted, many investors prefer to estimate the value of common stock using an **earnings multiplier model**. The reasoning for this approach recalls the basic concept that the value of any investment is the present value of future returns. In the case of common stocks, the returns that investors are entitled to receive are the net earnings of the firm. Therefore, one way investors can estimate value is by determining how many dollars they are willing to pay for a dollar of expected earnings (typically represented by the estimated earnings during the following 12-month period or an estimate of "normalized earnings"). For example, if investors are willing to pay 10 times expected or "normal" earnings, they would value a stock they expect to earn $2 a share during the following year at $20. You can compute the prevailing earnings multiplier, also referred to as the **price/earnings (P/E) ratio**, as follows:

$$\text{Earnings Multiplier} = \text{Price/Earnings Ratio} = \frac{\text{Current Market Price}}{\text{Expected 12-Month Earnings}}$$

This computation of the current earnings multiplier (*P/E* ratio) indicates the prevailing attitude of investors toward a stock's value. Investors must decide if they agree with the prevailing *P/E* ratio (that is, is the earnings multiplier too high or too low?) based upon how it compares to the *P/E* ratio for the aggregate market, for the firm's industry, and for similar firms and stocks.

To answer this question in a defensible manner, we must consider what influences the earnings multiplier (*P/E* ratio) over time. For example, over time the aggregate stock market *P/E* ratio, as represented by the S&P Industrials Index, has varied from about 6 times earnings to about 30 times earnings.[7] The infinite period dividend discount model can be used to indicate the variables that should determine the value of the *P/E* ratio as follows:[8]

$$P_i = \frac{D_1}{k - g}$$

If we divide both sides of the equation by E_1 (expected earnings during the next 12 months), the result is

$$\frac{P_i}{E_1} = \frac{D_1/E_1}{k - g}$$

Thus, this model implies that the *P/E* ratio is determined by

1. The *expected* dividend payout ratio (dividends divided by earnings)
2. The *estimated* required rate of return on the stock (*k*)
3. The *expected* growth rate of dividends for the stock (*g*)

As an example, if we assume a stock has an expected dividend payout of 50 percent, a required rate of return of 12 percent, and an expected growth

[7] When computing historical *P/E* ratios, the practice is to use earnings for the past 12 months rather than expected earnings. Although this practice of using historical earnings will influence the level, it demonstrates the changes in the *P/E* ratio over time. Although it may be appropriate to use historical *P/E* ratios for past comparison, we strongly believe that investment decisions should emphasize future or forward *P/E* ratios that use expected earnings.

[8] In this formulation of the model we use *P* rather than *V* (that is, the value is stated as the estimated price of the stock). Although the factors that determine the *P/E* are the same for growth companies, this formula cannot be used to estimate a specific value because these firms often do not have dividends, the infinite growth rate assumption is not valid, and the (*k* − *g*) assumptions don't apply.

rate for dividends of 8 percent, this would imply that the stock's P/E ratio should be:

$$D/E = 0.50; k = 0.12; g = 0.08$$
$$P/E = \frac{0.50}{0.12 - 0.08}$$
$$= 0.50/0.04$$
$$= 12.5$$

Again, a small difference in either k or g or both will have a large impact on the earnings multiplier, as shown in the following three examples.

1. $D/E = 0.50; k = 0.13; g = 0.08$. (In this example, we assume a higher k for the stock.)

$$P/E = \frac{0.50}{0.13 - 0.08}$$
$$= \frac{0.50}{0.05}$$
$$= 10$$

2. $D/E = 0.50; k = 0.12; g = 0.09$. (In this example, we assume a higher g for the stock and the original k.)

$$P/E = \frac{0.50}{0.12 - 0.09}$$
$$= \frac{0.50}{0.03}$$
$$= 16.7$$

3. $D/E = 0.50; k = 0.11; g = 0.09$. (In this example, we assume a fairly optimistic scenario where the k for the stock is only 11 percent and there is a higher expected growth rate of dividends of 9 percent.)

$$P/E = \frac{0.50}{0.11 - 0.09}$$
$$= \frac{0.50}{0.02}$$
$$= 25$$

As before, *the spread between k and g is the main determinant of the size of the P/E ratio.* Although the dividend payout ratio has an impact, we are generally referring to a firm's long-run target payout, which is typically rather stable with little effect on year-to-year changes in the P/E ratio (earnings multiplier).

After estimating the earnings multiple, you would apply it to your estimate of earnings for the next year (E_1) to arrive at an estimated value. In turn, E_1 is based on the earnings for the current year (E_0) and your expected growth rate of earnings. Using these two estimates, you would compute an estimated value of the stock and compare this estimated value to its market price.

Consider the following estimates for an example firm:

$$D/E = 0.50$$
$$k = 0.12$$
$$g = 0.09$$
$$E_0 = \$2.00$$

Using these estimates, you would compute an earnings multiple of:

$$P/E = \frac{0.50}{0.12 - 0.09} = \frac{0.50}{0.03} = 16.7$$

Given current earnings (E_0) of $2.00 and a g of 9 percent, you would expect E_1 to be $2.18. Therefore, you would estimate the value (price) of the stock as

$$V = 16.7 \times \$2.18$$
$$= \$36.41$$

As before, you would compare this estimated value of the stock to its current market price to decide whether you should invest in it. This estimate of value is referred to as a two-step process because it requires you to estimate future earnings (E_1) and a P/E ratio based on expectations of k and g. These two estimates are discussed in Reading 62.

The Price/Cash Flow Ratio

The growth in popularity of the relative price/cash flow valuation ratio can be traced to concern over the propensity of some firms to manipulate earnings per share, whereas cash flow values are generally less prone to manipulation. Also, as noted, cash flow values are important in fundamental valuation (when computing the present value of cash flow), and they are critical when doing credit analysis where "cash is king." The price to cash flow ratio is computed as follows:

$$P/CF_j = \frac{P_t}{CF_{t+1}}$$

where:
P/CF_j = the price/cash flow ratio for Firm j
P_t = the price of the stock in Period t
CF_{t+1} = the expected cash flow per share for Firm j

Regarding what variables affect this valuation ratio, the factors are similar to the P/E ratio. Specifically, the main variables should be: (1) the expected growth rate of the cash flow variable used, and (2) the risk of the stock as indicated by the uncertainty or variability of the cash flow series over time. The specific cash flow measure used will vary depending upon the nature of the company and industry and which cash flow specification (for example, operating cash flow or free cash flow) is the best measure of performance for this industry.[9] An appropriate ratio can also be affected by the firm's capital structure.

The Price/Book Value Ratio

The price/book value (P/BV) ratio has been widely used for many years by analysts in the banking industry as a measure of relative value. The book value of a bank is typically considered a good indicator of intrinsic value because most bank

---

[9] While there has been a tendency to employ EBITDA as the proxy for cash flow, we do not recommend or encourage this because of the strong upward bias of this series compared to other cash flow measures.

assets, such as bonds and commercial loans, have a value equal to book value. This ratio gained in popularity and credibility as a relative valuation technique for all types of firms based upon a study by Fama and French (1992) that indicated a significant inverse relationship between P/BV ratios and excess rates of return for a cross section of stocks. The P/BV ratio is specified as follows:

$$P/BV_j = \frac{P_t}{BV_{t+1}}$$

where:

P/BV_j = the price/book value ratio for Firm j
P_t = the price of the stock in Period t
BV_{t+1} = the estimated end-of-year book value per share for Firm j

As with other relative valuation ratios, it is important to match the current price with the future book value that is expected to prevail at the end of the year. The difficulty is that this future book value is not generally available. One can derive an estimate of the end-of-year book value based upon an estimate of net earnings minus the expected dividends (which is added to retained earnings). The growth rate for the series can be estimated using the growth rate implied by the sustainable growth formula: $g = $ (ROE) (Retention Rate).

Regarding what factors determine the size of the P/BV ratio, it is a function of the firm's ROE relative to its cost of equity since the ratio would be one if they were equal—that is, if the firm earned its required return on equity. In contrast, if the firm's ROE is much larger than its cost of equity, it is a growth company and investors should be willing to pay a premium over book value for the stock.

The Price/Sales Ratio

The price/sales (P/S) ratio has a volatile history. It was a favorite of Philip Fisher (1984), a well-known money manager in the late 1950s; his son Kenneth Fisher (1984); and Sanchek and Martin (1987). Recently, the P/S ratio has been suggested as useful by Martin Leibowitz (1997), a widely admired stock and bond portfolio manager. These advocates consider this ratio meaningful and useful for two reasons. First, they believe that strong and consistent sales growth is a requirement for a growth company. Although they note the importance of an above-average profit margin, they contend that *the growth process must begin with sales.* Second, given all the data in the balance sheet and income statement, sales information is subject to less manipulation than any other data item. The specific P/S ratio is:

$$P/S_j = \frac{P_t}{S_{t+1}}$$

where:

P/S_j = the price to sales ratio for Firm j
P_t = the price of the stock in Period t
S_{t+1} = the expected sales per share for Firm j

Again, it is important to match the current stock price with the firm's *expected* sales per share, which may be difficult to derive for a large cross section of stocks. Two caveats are relevant to the price to sales ratio. First, this particular relative valuation ratio varies dramatically by industry. For example, the sales per share for retail firms, such as Kroger or Wal-Mart, are typically much higher than sales per share for computer or microchip firms. The second consideration is the profit margin on sales. The point is, retail food stores have high sales per share, which will cause a low *P/S* ratio, which is considered good until one realizes that these firms have low net profit margins. Therefore, your relative valuation analysis using the *P/S* ratio should be between firms in the same or similar industries.

Implementing the Relative Valuation Technique

As noted, the relative valuation technique considers several valuation ratios—such as *P/E, P/BV*—to derive a value for a stock. To properly implement this technique, it is essential to compare the various ratios but also to recognize that the analysis needs to go beyond simply comparing the ratios—it is necessary to understand what factors affect each of the valuation ratios and, therefore, know why they should differ. The first step is to compare the valuation ratio (e.g., the *P/E* ratio) for a company to the comparable ratio for the market, for the stock's industry, and to other stocks in the industry to determine how it compares—that is, is it similar to these other *P/E*s, or is it consistently at a premium or discount? Beyond knowing the overall relationship to the market, industry, and competitors, the real analysis is involved in understanding *why* the ratio has this relationship or why it should *not* have this relationship and the implications of this mismatch. Specifically, the second step is to explain the relationship. To do this, you need to understand what factors determine the specific valuation ratio and then compare these factors for the stock versus the same factors for the market, industry, and other stocks.

To illustrate this process, consider the following example wherein you want to value the stock of a pharmaceutical company and, you decide to employ the *P/E* relative valuation technique. As part of this analysis, you compare the *P/E* ratios for this firm over time (e.g., the last 15 years) to similar ratios for the S&P Industrials, the pharmaceutical industry, and specific competitors. This comparison indicates that the company *P/E* ratios are consistently above all the other sets. Following this initial observation, the second part of the analysis considers whether the fundamental factors that affect the *P/E* ratio (i.e., the firm's growth rate and its required rate of return) justify the higher *P/E*. A positive scenario would be that the firm had a historical and expected growth rate that was substantially above all the comparables and it should have a lower required rate of return. This would indicate that the higher *P/E* ratio is justified; the only question that needs to be considered is, how much higher should the *P/E* ratio be? Alternatively, the negative scenario for this stock with a *P/E* ratio above most comparables would be if the company's expected growth rate was equal to or lower than the industry and competitors' while its required *k* was higher than for the industry and competitors. This set of conditions would signal a stock that is apparently overpriced based on the fundamental factors that determine a stock's *P/E* ratio.

In subsequent sections, we discuss how an analyst arrives at estimates for *g* and *k*, and we demonstrate the process in subsequent chapters. At this point, the idea is for the reader to understand the overall process required by the relative valuation technique.

ESTIMATING THE INPUTS: THE REQUIRED RATE OF RETURN AND THE EXPECTED GROWTH RATE OF VALUATION VARIABLES

This section deals with estimating two inputs that are critical to the valuation process irrespective of which approach or technique is being used: the required rate of return (k) and the expected growth rate of earnings and other valuation variables—that is, book value, cash flow, sales, and dividends.

We will review these factors and discuss how the estimation of these variables differs for domestic versus foreign securities. Although the valuation procedure is the same for securities around the world, k and g differ among countries. Therefore, we will review the components of the required rate of return for U.S. securities and then consider the components for foreign securities. Subsequently, we consider the estimation of the growth rate of earnings, cash flow, and dividends for domestic stocks and then for foreign stocks.

Required Rate of Return (k)

This discussion reviews the determinants of the nominal required rate of return on an investment, including a consideration of factors for non-U.S. markets. This required rate of return will be the discount rate for most cash flow models and affects all the relative valuation techniques. The only difference in the discount rate is between the present value of dividends and the present value of free cash flow to equity techniques, which use the required rate of return on equity (k), versus the present value of operating free cash flow technique, which uses the weighted average cost of capital ($WACC$). Notably, the cost of equity is a critical input to estimating the firm's $WACC$.

Recall that three factors influence an equity investor's required rate of return (k):

1. The economy's **real risk-free rate ($RRFR$)**
2. The expected rate of inflation (I)
3. A risk premium (RP)

The Economy's Real Risk-Free Rate   This is the absolute minimum rate that an investor should require. It depends on the real growth rate of the investor's home economy because capital invested should grow at least as fast as the economy. As noted previously, this rate can be affected for short periods of time by temporary tightness or ease in the capital markets.

The Expected Rate of Inflation   Investors are interested in real rates of return that will allow them to increase their rate of consumption. Therefore, if investors expect a given rate of inflation, they should increase their required *nominal* risk-free rate of return ($NRFR$) to reflect any expected inflation as follows:

$$NRFR = [1 + RRFR][1 + E(I)] - 1$$

where:

$E(I)$ = expected rate of inflation

The two factors that determine the $NRFR$ affect all investments, from U.S. government securities to highly speculative land deals. Investors who hope to calculate security values accurately must carefully estimate the expected rate of inflation. Not only does the *NRFR* affect all investments, but its extreme volatility makes its estimation difficult.

The Risk Premium The **risk premium (*RP*)** causes differences in the required rates of return among alternative investments that range from government bonds to corporate bonds to common stocks. The *RP* also explains the difference in the expected return among securities of the same type. For example, this is the reason corporate bonds with different ratings of Aaa, Aa, or A have different yields, and why different common stocks have widely varying earnings multipliers despite similar growth expectations.

We noted that investors demand a risk premium because of the uncertainty of returns expected from an investment. A measure of this uncertainty of returns was the dispersion of expected returns. We suggested several internal factors that influence a firm's variability of returns, such as its business risk, financial risk, and liquidity risk. We noted that securities of foreign firms or of domestic companies with significant foreign sales and earnings (e.g., Coca-Cola and McDonald's) have additional risk factors, including exchange rate risk and country (political) risk.

Changes in the Risk Premium Because different securities (e.g., government bonds and common stocks) have different patterns of returns and different guarantees to investors, we expect their risk premiums to differ. In addition, a fact that is less recognized is that the risk premiums for the same securities can *change over time*. For example, Exhibit 59-4 shows the spread between the yields to maturity for Aaa-rated corporate bonds and Baa-rated corporate bonds from 1974 through 2004. This yield spread, or difference in yield, is a measure of the risk premium for investing in higher-risk bonds (Baa) compared to low-risk bonds (Aaa). As shown, the yield spread varied from about 0.40 percent to 2.69 percent (from less than one-half of 1 percent to almost 3 percent).

EXHIBIT 59-4	Time-Series Plot of Moody's Corporate Bond Yield Spreads (Baa Yield/Aaa Yield): Monthly 1974–2004

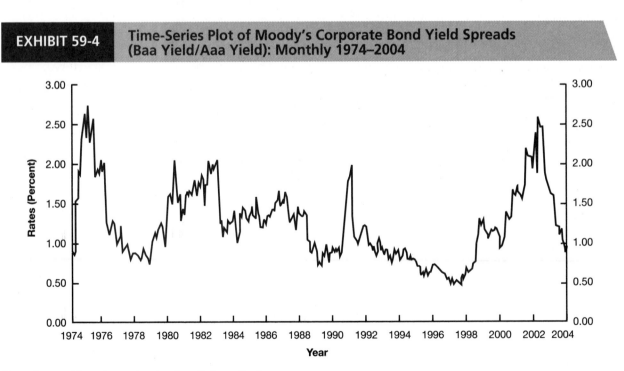

Source: Prepared by authors using data from Lehman Brothers.

| EXHIBIT 59-5 | Time-Series Plot of Corporate Bond Yield Ratio (Baa Yield/Aaa Yield): Monthly 1988–2004 |

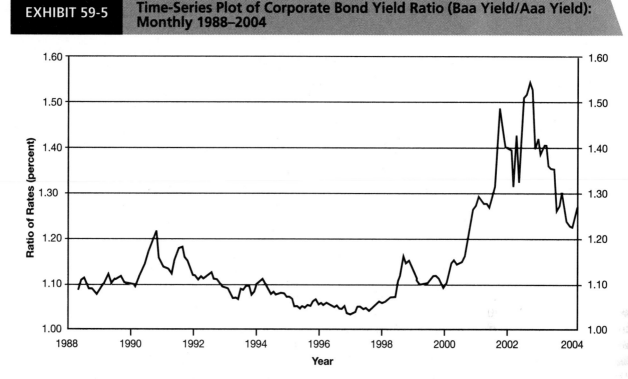

Source: Prepared by authors using data from Lehman Brothers.

Exhibit 59-5 contains a plot of the *ratio* of the yields for the same period, which indicates the percentage risk premium of Baa bonds compared to Aaa bonds. You might expect a larger difference in yield between Baa and Aaa bonds if Aaa bonds are yielding 12 percent rather than 6 percent. The yield ratio in Exhibit 59-5 adjusts for this size difference. This shows that even adjusting for the yield level difference, the risk premium ratio varies from about 1.06 to 1.56—a 6 percent premium to a 56 percent premium over the base yield on Aaa bonds. This significant change in the credit risk premium over time occurs because either investors perceive a change in the level of risk of Baa bonds compared to Aaa bonds or there is a change in the amount of return that investors require to accept the same risk differential. In either case, this change in the risk premium for a set of assets implies a change in the slope of the security market line (SML).

Estimating the Required Return for Foreign Securities

Our discussion of the required rate of return for investments has been limited to the domestic market. Although the basic valuation model and its variables are the same around the world, there are significant differences in the values for specific variables. This section points out where these differences occur.

Foreign Real RFR   Because the *RRFR* in other countries should be determined by the real growth rate within the particular economy, the estimated rate can vary substantially among countries due to differences in an economy's real growth rate. An example of differences in the real growth rate of gross domestic product (GDP) can be seen from growth expectations for 2006 real GDP contained in the

EXHIBIT 59-6	Estimates of Year 2006 Nominal RFR for Major Countries		
Country	**Real Growth in GDP**	**Expected Inflation**	**Nominal RFR**
United States	3.6%	2.4%	6.1%
Japan	1.9	0.0	1.8
Germany	1.9	1.8	3.7
Britain	2.6	2.0	4.6
Euro Area	2.3	1.7	4.0

Source: Prepared by authors using data from *IMF World Economic Outlook* (April, 2005).

IMF World Economic Outlook as shown in Exhibit 59-6. There is a range of estimates for 2006 of about 1.6 percent (that is, 1.9 percent for Germany compared to 3.6 percent for the United States with the Euro Zone estimated at about 2.3 percent). This difference in the growth rates of real GDP implies a substantial difference in the RRFR for these countries.[10]

Inflation Rate   To estimate the *NRFR* for a country, you must also estimate its expected rate of inflation and adjust the *NRFR* for this expectation. Again, this rate of inflation typically varies substantially among countries. The price change data show that the expected rate of inflation during 2006 varied from 0 percent in Japan to 2.4 percent in the United States. Assuming equal real growth, this inflation estimate implies a difference in the nominal required rate of return between Japan and the United States of 2.4 percent. Such a difference in *k* can have a substantial impact on estimated values, as demonstrated earlier. Again, you must make a separate estimate for each individual country in which you are evaluating securities.

To demonstrate the combined impact of differences in real growth and expected inflation, Exhibit 59-6 shows the results of the following computation for four countries and the Euro Area based on the year 2006 estimates:

$$NRFR = (1 + \text{Real Growth}) \times (1 + \text{Expected Inflation}) - 1$$

Given the differences between countries in the two components, the range in the *NRFR* of 4.2 percent is not surprising (6.1 percent for the United States versus 1.8 percent for Japan). As demonstrated earlier, such a difference in *k* for an investment will have a significant impact on its value.

Risk Premium   You must also derive an equity risk premium for the investments in each country. Again, the five risk components differ substantially between countries: business risk, financial risk, liquidity risk, exchange rate risk, and country risk. *Business risk* can vary because it is a function of the variability of economic activity within a country and of the operating leverage used by firms within the country. Firms in different countries assume significantly different *financial risk*

---

[10] All the estimates of real growth and inflation are from the *IMF World Economic Outlook* (April, 2005).

as well. For example, Japanese firms use substantially more financial leverage than U.S. or U.K. firms. Regarding *liquidity risk*, the U.S. capital markets are acknowledged to be the most liquid in the world, with Japan and the United Kingdom being close behind. In contrast, some emerging markets are quite illiquid and in such cases investors need to add a significant liquidity risk premium.

When investing globally, you also must estimate *exchange rate risk*, which is the additional uncertainty of returns caused by changes in the exchange rates for the currency of another country. This uncertainty can be small for a U.S. investor in a country such as Hong Kong because the currency is pegged to the U.S. dollar. In contrast, in some countries, substantial volatility in the exchange rate over time can mean significant differences in the domestic return for the country and return in U.S. dollars.[11] The level of volatility for the exchange rate differs between countries. The greater the uncertainty regarding future changes in the exchange rate, the larger the exchange rate risk for the country.[12]

Recall that country risk arises from unexpected events in a country, such as upheavals in its political or economic environment. An example of political and economic disruptions occurred in Russia during 1998 when there was substantial uncertainty about the potential devaluation of the ruble. Similarly, unrest in Indonesia during 1998 led to riots and the eventual resignation of President Suharto. Such political unrest or a change in the economic environment creates uncertainties that increase the risk of investments in these countries. Before investing in such countries, investors must evaluate the additional returns they should require to accept this increased uncertainty.

Thus, when estimating required rates of return on foreign investments, you must assign a unique risk premium for each country.

Expected Growth Rates

After arriving at a required rate of return, the investor must estimate the growth rate of cash flows, earnings, and dividends because the alternative valuation models for common stock depend heavily on good estimates of growth (g) for these variables.

Estimating Growth from Fundamentals   The growth rate of dividends is determined by the growth rate of earnings and the proportion of earnings paid out in dividends (the payout ratio). Over the short run, dividends can grow faster or slower than earnings if the firm changes its payout ratio. Specifically, if a firm's earnings grow at 6 percent a year and it pays out exactly 50 percent of earnings in dividends, then the firm's dividends will likewise grow at 6 percent a year. Alternatively, if a firm's earnings grow at 6 percent a year and the firm increases its payout, then during the period when the payout ratio increases, dividends will grow faster than earnings. In contrast, if the firm reduces its payout ratio, dividends will grow slower than earnings for a period of time. Because there is a limit to how long this difference in growth rates can continue, most investors assume that the long-run dividend payout ratio is fairly stable. Therefore, our analysis of the growth rate of dividends concentrates on an analysis of the growth rate of equity earnings. Also, as will be shown in Reading 62, equity earnings are the major factor driving the operating cash flows or the free cash flows for the firm.

---

[11] Although we generally refer to these as domestic and U.S. dollar returns, you will also see references to *hedged* returns (for example, domestic) and *unhedged* returns (returns in U.S. dollars). In some cases, the hedged returns will adjust for the cost of hedging.

[12] For a thorough analysis of exchange rate determination and forecasting models, see Rosenberg (1996).

When a firm retains earnings and acquires additional assets, if it earns some positive rate of return on these additional assets, the total earnings of the firm will increase because its asset base is larger. How rapidly a firm's earnings increase depends on (1) the proportion of earnings it retains and reinvests in new assets and (2) the rate of return it earns on these new assets. Specifically, the growth rate (g) of equity earnings (that is, earnings per share) without any external financing is equal to the percentage of net earnings retained (the retention rate, which equals $1 -$ the payout ratio) times the rate of return on equity capital.

$$g = (\text{Retention Rate}) \times (\text{Return on Equity})$$
$$= RR \times ROE$$

Therefore, a firm can increase its growth rate by increasing its retention rate (reducing its payout ratio) and investing these added funds at its historic ROE. Alternatively, the firm can maintain its retention rate but increase its ROE. For example, if a firm retains 50 percent of net earnings and consistently has an ROE of 10 percent, its net earnings will grow at the rate of 5 percent a year, as follows:

$$g = RR \times ROE$$
$$= 0.50 \times 0.10$$
$$= 0.05$$

If, however, the firm increases its retention rate to 75 percent and is able to invest these additional funds in internal projects that likewise earn 10 percent, its growth rate will increase to 7.5 percent, as follows:

$$g = 0.75 \times 0.10$$
$$= 0.075$$

If, instead, the firm continues to reinvest 50 percent of its earnings but is able to earn a higher rate of return on these investments, say 15 percent, it can likewise increase its growth rate, as follows:

$$g = 0.50 \times 0.15$$
$$= 0.075$$

Breakdown of *ROE*   Although the retention rate is a management decision, changes in the firm's *ROE* result from changes in its operating performance or its financial leverage. We can divide the *ROE* ratio into three components:

$$ROE = \frac{\text{Net Income}}{\text{Sales}} \times \frac{\text{Sales}}{\text{Total Assets}} \times \frac{\text{Total Assets}}{\text{Equity}}$$
$$= \frac{\text{Profit}}{\text{Margin}} \times \frac{\text{Total Asset}}{\text{Turnover}} \times \frac{\text{Financial}}{\text{Leverage}}$$

This breakdown allows us to consider the three factors that determine a firm's *ROE*.[13] Because it is a multiplicative relationship, an increase in any of the three ratios will cause an increase in *ROE*. The first two of the three ratios reflect operating performance, and the third one indicates a firm's financing decision.

[13] It is possible to employ an extended DuPont system that involves eight ratios. For purposes of this discussion, the three ratios indicate the significant factors and differences among countries.

The first operating ratio, net profit margin, indicates the firm's profitability on sales. This ratio changes over time for some companies and is highly sensitive to the business cycle. For growth companies, this is one of the first ratios to decline because the increased competition increases the supply of the goods or services and forces price cutting, which leads to lower profit margins. Also, during recessions, profit margins decline because of price cutting or because of higher percentages of fixed costs due to lower sales.

The second component, total asset turnover, is the ultimate indicator of operating efficiency and reflects the asset and capital requirements of the business. Although this ratio varies dramatically by industry, within an industry it is an excellent indicator of management's operating efficiency.

The product of these first two components (profit margin and total asset turnover) equals the firm's return on assets (*ROA*), which reflects the firm's operating performance before the financing impact.[14]

The final component, total assets/equity, does not measure operating performance but, rather, financial leverage. Specifically, it indicates how management has decided to finance the firm. In turn, this management decision regarding the financing of assets can contribute to a higher *ROE*, but it also has financial risk implications for the stockholder.

Knowing this breakdown of *ROE*, you must examine past results and expectations for a firm and develop *estimates* of the three components and therefore an estimate of a firm's *ROE*. This estimate of *ROE* combined with the firm's expected retention rate will indicate its future growth potential. Finally, it is important to note that when estimating growth, it is necessary to estimate, not only the *rate* of growth, but also the *duration* of growth (how long can the firm sustain this rate of growth?). Clearly, the higher the rate of growth the more significant the estimate of the duration of growth to the ultimate value of the stock. Also, a high rate of growth generally implies a high ROE, which is difficult to sustain because numerous competitors want to experience these high rates of return.

Estimating Growth Based on History   Although the authors have a strong bias in favor of using the fundamentals to estimate future growth, which involves estimating the components of *ROE*, we also believe in using all the information available to make this critical estimate. Therefore, we suggest that analysts also consider the historical growth rate of sales, earnings, cash flow, and dividends in this process.

Although we will demonstrate these computations for the market, for an industry, and for a company in subsequent readings, the following discussion considers some suggestions on alternative calculations. In terms of the relevant period to consider, one is struck by the cliché "more is better" as long as you recognize that "recent is relevant." Specifically, about 20 years of annual observations would be ideal, but it is important to consider subperiods as well as the total period—that is, 20 years, two 10-year periods, and four 5-year periods would indicate the overall growth rate but also would indicate if there were any *changes* in the growth rate in recent periods.

The specific measurement can be done using one or more of three techniques: (1) arithmetic or geometric average of annual percentage changes, (2) linear regression models, and (3) log-linear regression models. Irrespective of the measurement techniques used, we strongly encourage a time-series plot of the annual percentage changes.

---

[14] In Reading 60, we discuss a study that analyzes why and how alternative industries differ regarding the return on assets and the two components of ROA.

The arithmetic or geometric average technique involves computing the annual percentage change and then computing either the simple arithmetic average or the geometric average of these values for the alternative periods. The arithmetic average will always be a higher value than the geometric average (except when the annual values are constant) and the difference between the arithmetic and geometric average values will increase with volatility. As noted previously, we generally prefer the geometric mean because it provides the average annual compound growth rate.

The linear regression model goes well with the suggested time-series plot and is as follows:

$$EPS_t = a + bt$$

where:

EPS_t = earnings per period in Period t
t = year t where t goes from 1 to n
b = the coefficient that indicates the average absolute change in the series during the period

It would be very informative to superimpose this regression line on the time-series plot because it would provide insights on changes in absolute growth.

The log-linear model considers that the series might be better described in terms of a constant *growth rate*. This model is as follows:

$$ln(EPS_t) = a + bt$$

where:

$ln(EPS_t)$ = the natural logarithm of earnings per share in Period t
b = the coefficient that indicates *the average percentage change* in the series during the period

The analysis of these historical growth rates both visually with the **time-series graph** and the alternative calculations should provide you with significant insights into the trend of the growth rates as well as the *variability* of the growth rates over time. This could provide information on the unit's business risk with the analysis of sales and EBIT growth.

Estimating Dividend Growth for Foreign Stocks

The underlying factors that determine the growth rates for foreign stocks are similar to those for U.S. stocks, but the value of the equation's components may differ substantially from what is common in the United States. The differences in the retention rate or the components of *ROE* result from differences in accounting practices as well as alternative management performance or philosophy.

Retention Rates   The retention rates for foreign corporations differ within countries, but differences also exist among countries due to differences in the countries' investment opportunities. As an example, firms in Japan have a higher retention rate than firms in the United States, whereas the rate of retention in France is much lower. Therefore, you need to examine the retention rates for a number of firms in a country as a background for estimating the standard rate within a country.

Net Profit Margin   The net profit margin of foreign firms can differ because of different accounting conventions between countries. Foreign accounting rules allow firms to recognize revenue and allocate expenses differently from U.S. firms. For example, German firms are allowed to build up large reserves for various reasons. As a result, they report low earnings for tax purposes. Also, different foreign depreciation practices require adjustment of earnings and cash flows.

Total Asset Turnover   Total asset turnover can likewise differ among countries because of different accounting conventions on the reporting of asset values at cost or market values. For example, in Japan, a large part of the market values for some firms comes from their real estate holdings and their common stock investments in other firms. These assets are reported at cost, which typically has substantially understated their true value. This also means that the total asset turnover ratio for these firms is substantially overstated.

This ratio will also be impacted by leases that are not capitalized on the balance sheet—that is, if leases are not capitalized, both assets and liabilities are understated.

Total Asset/Equity Ratio   This ratio, a measure of financial leverage, differs among countries because of differences in economic environments, tax laws, management philosophies regarding corporate debt, and accounting conventions. In several countries, the attitude toward debt is much more liberal than in the United States. A prime example is Japan, where debt as a percentage of total assets is almost 50 percent higher than a similar ratio in the United States. Notably, most corporate debt in Japan entails borrowing from banks at fairly low rates of interest. Balance sheet debt ratios may be higher in Japan than in the United States or other countries; but, because of the lower interest rates in Japan, the fixed-charge coverage ratios, such as the times interest earned ratio, might be similar to those in other countries. The point is, it is important to consider the several cash flow financial risk ratios along with the balance sheet debt ratios.

Consequently, when analyzing a foreign stock market or an individual foreign stock that involves estimating the growth rate for earnings and dividends, you must consider the three components of the *ROE* just as you would for a U.S. stock but recognize that the financial ratios for foreign firms can differ from those of U.S. firms. Subsequent readings on valuation applied to the aggregate market, to various industries, and to companies contain examples of these differences.

THE INTERNET

Investments Online

Several sites that we discussed in earlier readings contained financial calculators. By inputting the required data, users can determine if it is better to buy or lease a car, calculate returns, and determine how much money they will have if funds are invested at a certain rate of return over time. The sites below all contain financial calculators that may be of use to investors and financial planners.

www.leadfusion.com

www.jamesko.com/FinCalc

www.numeraire.com

www.moneychimp.com

SUMMARY

▶ As an investor, you want to select investments that will provide a rate of return that compensates you for your time, the expected rate of inflation, and the risk involved. To help you find these investments, this reading considers the theory of valuation by which you derive the value of an investment using your required rate of return. We consider the two investment decision processes, which are the top-down, three-step approach and the bottom-up, stockpicking approach. Although it is recognized that either process can provide abnormal positive returns if the analyst is superior, we feel that a preferable approach is the top-down approach in which you initially consider the aggregate economy and market, then examine alternative global industries, and finally analyze individual firms and their stocks.

▶ We apply the valuation theory to a range of investments, including bonds, preferred stock, and common stock. Because the valuation of common stock is more complex and difficult, we suggest two alternative approaches (the present value of cash flows and the relative valuation approach) and several techniques for each of these approaches. Notably, these are *not* competitive approaches and we suggest that both approaches be used. Although we suggest using several different valuation models, the investment decision rule is always the same: If the estimated intrinsic value of the investment is greater than the market price, you should buy the investment; if the estimated intrinsic value of an investment is less than its market price, you should not invest in it and if you own it, you should sell it.

▶ We conclude with a review of factors that you need to consider when estimating the value of stock with either approach—your required rate of return on an investment and the growth rate of earnings, cash flow, and dividends. Finally, we consider some unique factors that affect the application of these valuation models to foreign stocks.

PROBLEMS FOR READING 59

1. The preferred stock of the Clarence Radiology Company has a par value of $100 and a $9 dividend rate. You require an 11 percent rate of return on this stock. What is the maximum price you would pay for it? Would you buy it at a market price of $96?

2. The Baron Basketball Company (BBC) earned $10 a share last year and paid a dividend of $6 a share. Next year, you expect BBC to earn $11 and continue its payout ratio. Assume that you expect to sell the stock for $132 a year from now. If you require 12 percent on this stock, how much would you be willing to pay for it?

3. Given the expected earnings and dividend payments in Problem 2, if you expected a selling price of $110 and required an 8 percent return on this investment, how much would you pay for the BBC stock?

4. Over the long run, you expect dividends for BBC in Problem 2 to grow at 8 percent and you require 11 percent on the stock. Using the infinite period DDM, how much would you pay for this stock?

5. Based on new information regarding the popularity of basketball, you revise your growth estimate for BBC to 9 percent. What is the maximum *P/E* ratio you will apply to BBC, and what is the maximum price you will pay for the stock?

6. The Shamrock Dogfood Company (SDC) has consistently paid out 40 percent of its earnings in dividends. The company's return on equity is 16 percent. What would you estimate as its dividend growth rate?

7. Given the low risk in dog food, your required rate of return on SDC is 13 percent. What *P/E* ratio would you apply to the firm's earnings?

8. What *P/E* ratio would you apply if you learned that SDC had decided to increase its payout to 50 percent? (Hint: This change in payout has multiple effects.)

9. You have been reading about the Maddy Computer Company (MCC), which currently retains 90 percent of its earnings ($5 a share this year). It earns an *ROE* of almost 30 percent. Assuming a required rate of return of 14 percent, how much would you pay for MCC on the basis of the earnings multiplier model? Discuss your answer. What would you pay for Maddy Computer if its retention rate was 60 percent and its *ROE* was 19 percent? Show your work.

10. Gentry Can Company's (GCC) latest annual dividend of $1.25 a share was paid yesterday and maintained its historic 7 percent annual rate of growth. You plan to purchase the stock today because you believe that the dividend growth rate will increase to 8 percent for the next three years and the selling price of the stock will be $40 per share at the end of that time.

    A. How much should you be willing to pay for the GCC stock if you require a 12 percent return?

    B. What is the maximum price you should be willing to pay for the GCC stock if you believe that the 8 percent growth rate can be maintained indefinitely and you require a 12 percent return?

    C. If the 8 percent rate of growth is achieved, what will the price be at the end of Year 3, assuming the conditions in Part B?

	4⅝	4¹¹/₁₆	— ⅜
	5½	5½ —	
5½	20⅝	21³/₁₆ — ¼	
	17⅜	18⅛ +	⅞
18½	6½	6½ — ½	
7¼	15/16	31/32 — ⅛	
		9/16	9/16
	1¹/₃₂		
	7¹⁵/₁₆	7¹³/₁₆	7¹⁵/₁₆
	2⅝	2¹¹/₃₂	2½ +
	2¾	2¼	2¼
6⅛	12¹/₁₆	11⅜	11¼ +
87	33¾	33	33¹/₁₆ —
602	25⅝	24⁹/₁₆	25⅜ +
833	12	11⅝	11⅞ +
16	101½	101½	10½ —
78	15⅞	15¹³/₁₆	15⅞ —
4508	9¹/₁₆	8¼	8⅛ +
430	11¼	10⅛	10

INDUSTRY ANALYSIS*

by Frank K. Reilly and Keith C. Brown

LEARNING OUTCOME

The candidate should be able to:

a. describe how structural economic changes (e.g., demographics, technology, politics, and regulation) may affect industries.

INTRODUCTION   1

When asked about his or her job, a securities analyst typically will reply that he or she is an oil analyst, a retail analyst, or a computer analyst. A widely read trade publication, *The Institutional Investor,* selects an All-American analyst team each year based on industry groups. Investment managers talk about being in or out of the metals, the autos, or the utilities. This constant reference to industry groups is because most professional investors are extremely conscious of differences among alternative industries and organize their analyses and portfolio decisions according to industry groups.

We acknowledge the importance of industry analysis as a component of the three-step fundamental analysis procedure initiated in Reading 59. Industry analysis is the second step as we progress toward selecting specific firms and stocks for our investment portfolio. In this reading, we analyze different industries to determine if the intrinsic value of an industry is equal to or greater than its market price. Based on this relationship, we decide how to weight the industry in our stock portfolio. In Reading 62, we analyze the individual companies and stocks within alternative industries.

---

* The authors acknowledge input to the discussions on "The Business Cycle and Industry Sectors" and "Structural Economic Changes" provided by Professor Edgar Norton of Illinois State University.

Investment Analysis and Portfolio Management, Eighth Edition, by Frank K. Reilly and Keith C. Brown, Copyright © 2005. Reprinted with permission of South-Western, a division of Thomson Learning.

In Section 2, we discuss the results of several studies that will help us identify the benefits and uses of industry analysis. Following that, we present and demonstrate the two approaches for valuing industries. Another section raises questions that are unique to industry analysis: we consider the impact of the competitive environment within an industry on potential industry returns. We conclude the reading with a discussion of global industry analysis, because many industries transcend U.S. borders and compete on a worldwide basis.

2   WHY DO INDUSTRY ANALYSIS?

Investment practitioners perform industry analysis because they believe it helps them isolate investment opportunities that have favorable return-risk characteristics. We likewise have recommended it as part of our three-step, top-down investment analysis approach. What exactly do we learn from an industry analysis? Can we spot trends in industries that make them good investments? Are there unique patterns in the rates of return and risk measures over time in different industries? In this section, we survey the results of studies that addressed the following set of questions designed to pinpoint the benefits and limitations of industry analysis:

▶ Is there a difference between the returns for alternative industries during specific time periods?

▶ Will an industry that performs well in one period continue to perform well in the future? That is, can we use past relationships between the market and an individual industry to predict future trends for the industry?

▶ Is the performance of firms within an industry consistent over time?

Several studies also considered questions related to risk:

▶ Is there a difference in the risk for alternative industries?

▶ Does the risk for individual industries vary, or does it remain relatively constant over time?

Based on the results of these studies, we come to some general conclusions about the value of industry analysis. In addition, this assessment helps us interpret the results of our subsequent industry valuation.

Cross-Sectional Industry Performance

To find out if the rates of return among different industries varied during a given period (e.g., during the year 2005), researchers compared the performance of alternative industries during a specific time period. Similar performance during specific time periods for different industries would indicate that industry analysis is not necessary. For example, assume that during 2005, the aggregate stock market experienced a rate of return of 10 percent and the returns for *all* industries were bunched between 9 percent and 11 percent. If this similarity in performance persisted over time, you might question whether it was worthwhile to do industry analysis to find an industry that would return 11 percent when random selection would provide a return of about 10 percent (the average return).

Studies of the annual performance by numerous industries found that different industries have consistently shown *wide dispersion in their rates of return* (e.g., a typical range of rates of return during a year will be from minus 40 percent to plus 50 percent). A specific example is the year 2004. As shown in Exhibit 60-1, although the aggregate stock market experienced a total return of almost 11 percent (the S&P 500), the industry performance ranged from 97.15 percent (general mining) to −21.65 percent (semiconductors). These results imply that *industry analysis is important and necessary* to uncover these substantial performance differences—that is, it helps identify both unprofitable and profitable opportunities.

Industry Performance over Time

Another group of researchers questioned whether individual industries that perform well in one time period would continue to perform well in subsequent time periods, or at least outperform the aggregate market in the later time period. In this case, investigators found *almost no association* in individual industry performance year to year or over sequential rising or falling markets.

EXHIBIT 60-1	How the Dow Jones U.S. Industry Groups Fared during 2004		
BEST PERFORMERS		**WORST PERFORMERS**	
% Change 12/31/2003 to 12/31/2004		**% Change 12/31/2003 to 12/31/2004**	
General mining	97.15	Semiconductors	−21.65
Consumer electronics	73.82	Aluminum	−16.82
Steel	66.21	Automobiles	−16.08
Internet	60.82	Pharmaceuticals	−10.20
Coal	57.65	Gold mining	−8.46
Hotels	44.86	Elect. components and equip.	−7.86
Trucking	44.40	Airlines	−6.61
Mobile telecommunications	43.84	Soft drinks	−5.11
Tires	40.59	Media agencies	−0.91
Oil exploration and production	40.45	Broadcasting and enter.	0.75
Transportation services	39.89	Publishing	1.24
Marine transportation	37.25	Brewers	1.29
Home construction	35.79	Food retailers and whole.	1.40
Oil equip. and services	34.51	Full line insurance	1.75
Real estate holding dev.	33.00	Waste and disposal serv.	1.78
Recreational products	33.00	Paper	2.75
Bldg. materials and fixtures	32.28	Auto parts	3.32
Gambling	31.74	Telecommunications equip.	3.58
Health care providers	30.60	Drug retailers	3.88
Footwear	30.53	Investment services	6.94

Source: The Wall Street Journal, 2 January 2005.

These time-series studies imply that past performance alone does *not* help project future industry performance. The results do *not*, however, negate the usefulness of industry analysis. They simply confirm that variables that affect industry performance change over time and each year it is necessary to estimate the current intrinsic value for individual industries on the basis of future estimates of the relevant variables and compare this to the market price.

Performance of the Companies within an Industry

Other studies were designed to determine whether there is consistency in the performance of companies *within* an industry. If all the firms within an industry performed consistently during a specified time period, investors would not need company analysis. In such a case, industry analysis alone would be enough because once you selected a profitable industry, you would know that all the stocks in that industry would do well.

These studies typically have found *wide dispersion* in the performance among companies in most industries. Studies by Meyers (1973) and Livingston (1977) have also shown evidence of an industry effect in specific industries, such as oil or autos, but most stocks showed a small industry effect that has been declining over time.

Implication of Dispersion within Industries   Some observers have contended that industry analysis is useless because all firms in an industry do not move together. Obviously, consistent firm performance in an industry would be ideal, as noted, because you would not need to do company analysis. For industries that have a strong, consistent industry influence, such as oil, gold, steel, autos, and railroads, company analysis is less critical than industry analysis.

Most analysts do not expect a strong industry influence, which means that a thorough *company* analysis is still necessary. Even for industries that do not have a strong industry influence, industry analysis is valuable because it is much easier to select a superior company from a good industry than to find a good company in a poor industry. By selecting the best stocks within a strong industry, you avoid the risk that your analysis and selection of a good company will be offset by poor industry performance.

Differences in Industry Risk

Although a number of studies have focused on industry rates of return, few studies have examined industry risk measures. The studies on industry risk investigated two questions: (1) Does risk differ among industries during a given time period? (2) Are industry risk measures stable over time? The study results regarding the dispersion of risk found *a wide range of risk* among different industries at a point in time, and the differences in industry risk typically widened during rising and falling markets. The results on the analysis of risk stability were positive—an analysis of the risk measures for individual industries over time indicated that they were *reasonably stable over time*.

These findings indicate that although risk measures for different industries showed substantial dispersion during a period of time, individual industries' risk measures are stable over time. This means that the analysis of industry risk is necessary, but this analysis of risk is useful when estimating the future risk for an industry.

Summary of Research on Industry Analysis

The conclusions of the studies dealing with industry analysis are:

▶ During any time period, the returns for different industries vary within a wide range, which means that industry analysis is an important part of the investment process.

▶ The rates of return for individual industries vary over time, so we cannot simply extrapolate past industry performance into the future.

▶ The rates of return of firms within industries also vary, so analysis of individual companies in an industry is a necessary follow-up to industry analysis.

▶ During any time period, different industries' risk levels vary within wide ranges, so we must examine and estimate the risk factors for alternative industries.

▶ Risk measures for different industries remain fairly constant over time, so the historical risk analysis is useful when estimating future risk.

Industry Analysis Process

An important question is, How should you structure your industry analysis? In our previous analysis of the economy and the aggregate equity market for the United States or any other country, we contended that it is necessary to examine the macroeconomy for two related reasons. First, although the security markets tend to move ahead of the aggregate economy, it is recognized that the markets are driven by what happens in the economy—that is, security markets reflect the strength or weakness of the economy. Second, most of the variables that determine value for the security markets are macrovariables such as interest rates, GDP, and corporate earnings. Therefore, our analysis of the aggregate equity market contained two components—one dealing with macrovariables such as **leading indicators** and monetary policy and a second being microanalysis of specific variables that affect valuation.

The point is, the industry analysis process is similar—first is a *macroanalysis* of the industry to determine how this industry relates to the business cycle and what economic variables drive this industry. This part of the process will make the second component easier and better. The second component is a microvaluation of the industry using the several valuation techniques introduced earlier. As noted, macroanalysis of the industry will make the estimation of the valuation inputs of a discount rate and expected growth for earnings and cash flows relatively easy.

The specific macroanalysis topics are:

1. The business cycle and industry sectors

2. Structural economic changes and alternative industries

3. Evaluating an industry's life cycle

4. Analysis of the competitive environment in an industry

THE BUSINESS CYCLE AND INDUSTRY SECTORS   3

Economic trends can and do affect industry performance. By identifying and monitoring key assumptions and variables, we can monitor the economy and gauge the implications of new information on our economic outlook and industry analysis. Recall that in order to beat the market on a risk-adjusted basis, we must have forecasts that differ from the market consensus *and* we must be correct more often than not.

Economic trends can take two basic forms: **cyclical changes** that arise from the ups and downs of the business cycle, and **structural changes** that occur when the economy is undergoing a major change in how it functions. For example, excess labor or capital may exist in some sectors whereas shortages of labor and capital exist elsewhere. The "downsizing" of corporate America during the 1990s, transitions from socialist to market economies in Eastern Europe, and the transition in the United States from a manufacturing to a service economy are all examples of structural change.[1] Industry analysts must examine structural economic changes for the implications they hold for the industry under review.

Most observers believe that industry performance is related to the stage of the business cycle. What makes industry analysis challenging is that every business cycle is different and those who look only at history miss the evolving trends that will determine future market performance.

Switching from one industry group to another over the course of a business cycle is known as a *rotation strategy*. When trying to determine which industry groups will benefit from the next stage of the business cycle, investors need to identify and monitor key variables related to economic trends and industry characteristics.

Exhibit 60-2 presents a stylized graphic of which industry groups typically perform well in the different stages of the business cycle. Toward the end of a recession, financial stocks rise in value because investors anticipate that banks' earnings will rise as both the economy and loan demand recover. Brokerage houses become attractive investments because their sales and earnings are expected to rise as investors trade securities, businesses sell debt and equity, and there is an increase in mergers during the economic recovery. These industry selections assume that when the recession ends there will be an increase in loan demand, housing construction, and security offerings.

EXHIBIT 60-2	The Stock Market and the Business Cycle

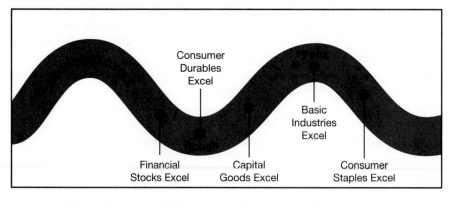

Source: Susan E. Kuhn, "Stocks Are Still Your Best Buy," *Fortune,* 21 March 1994, 140. © 1994 Time Inc. All rights reserved.

---

[1] An excellent discussion of structural changes in the U.S. economy and the implications of these changes for the business cycle, the stock market, and some specific industries is contained in Dudley and McKelvey (1997).

Once the economy begins its recovery, consumer durable firms that produce expensive consumer items, such as cars, personal computers, refrigerators, lawn tractors, and snow blowers, become attractive investments because a reviving economy will increase consumer confidence and personal income. Once businesses recognize the economy is recovering, they begin to think about modernizing, renovating, or purchasing new equipment to satisfy rising demand and reduce costs. Thus, capital goods industries such as heavy equipment manufacturers, machine tool makers, and airplane manufacturers become attractive.

Cyclical industries whose sales rise and fall along with general economic activity are attractive investments during the early stages of an economic recovery because of their high degree of operating leverage, which means that they benefit greatly from the sales increases during an economic expansion.[2] Industries with high financial leverage likewise benefit from rising sales volume.[3]

Traditionally, toward the business cycle peak, the rate of inflation increases as demand starts to outstrip supply. Basic materials industries such as oil, metals, and timber, which transform raw materials into finished products, become investor favorites. Because inflation has little influence on the cost of extracting these products and they can increase prices, these industries experience higher profit margins.

During a recession, some industries do better than others. Consumer staples, such as pharmaceuticals, food, and beverages, outperform other sectors during a recession because, although overall spending may decline, people still spend money on necessities so these "defensive" industries generally maintain their values. Similarly, if a weak domestic economy causes a weak currency, industries with large export components to growing economies may benefit because their goods become more cost competitive in overseas markets.

We have identified certain industries that typically make attractive investments over the course of the business cycle. Remember, investors should not invest based upon the current economic environment because the efficient market has already incorporated current economic news into security prices. Rather, it is necessary to *forecast* important economic variables and invest accordingly. The following subsections consider how changes in several important economic variables may affect different industries.

Inflation

Higher inflation is generally negative for the stock market, because it causes higher market interest rates, it increases uncertainty about future prices and costs, and it harms firms that cannot pass through their cost increases. Although these adverse effects are true for most industries, some industries benefit from inflation. Natural resource industries benefit *if* their production costs do not rise with inflation, because their output will likely sell at higher prices. Industries that have high operating leverage may benefit because many of their costs are fixed in nominal (current dollar) terms whereas revenues increase with inflation. Industries with high financial leverage may also gain, because their debts are repaid in cheaper dollars.

---

[2] Operating leverage arises from the existence of fixed costs in a firm's operating structure. Industries with large fixed expenses will have high degrees of operating leverage. This means a small percentage change in sales can result in a large percentage change in operating income.

[3] Financial leverage arises from fixed financial costs (that is, interest expense) in a firm's capital structure. Industries that have extensive debt financing (such as banks or utilities) will have net income that is sensitive to small changes in operating income.

Interest Rates

Financial institutions, including banks, are typically adversely impacted by higher rates because they find it difficult to pass on these higher rates to customers (i.e., lagged adjustment). High interest rates clearly harm the housing and the construction industry, but they might benefit industries that supply the do-it-yourselfer. High interest rates also benefit retirees whose income is dependent on interest income.

International Economics

Both domestic and overseas events may cause the value of the U.S. dollar to fluctuate. A weaker U.S. dollar helps U.S. industries because their exports become comparatively cheaper in overseas markets while the goods of foreign competitors become more expensive in the United States. A stronger dollar has an opposite effect. Economic growth in world regions or specific countries benefits industries that have a large presence in those areas. The creation of free trade zones, such as the European Community and the North American Free Trade Zone, assist industries that produce goods and services that previously faced quotas or tariffs in partner countries.

Consumer Sentiment

Because it comprises about two-thirds of GDP, consumption spending has a large impact on the economy. Optimistic consumers are more willing to spend and borrow money for expensive goods, such as houses, cars, new clothes, and furniture. Therefore, the performance of consumer cyclical industries will be affected by changes in consumer sentiment and by consumers' willingness and ability to borrow and spend money.

4   STRUCTURAL ECONOMIC CHANGES AND ALTERNATIVE INDUSTRIES

Influences other than the economy are part of the business environment. Demographics, changes in technology, and political and regulatory environments also can have a significant effect on the cash flow and risk prospects of different industries.

Demographics

In the past 50 years, the United States has had a baby boom and a baby bust and is now enjoying a baby boomlet as members of the baby-boom generation (those born between the end of World War II and the early 1960s) have children. The influx of the baby boom and the "graying of the baby boom" have had a large impact on U.S. consumption, from advertising strategies to house construction to concerns over social security and health care. The study of demographics includes much more than population growth and age distributions. Demographics also includes the geographical distribution of people, the changing ethnic mix in a society, and changes in income distribution. Wall Street industry analysts carefully study demographic trends and attempt to project their effect on different industries and firms.

During the period from 1990 to 2005, the fastest-growing age groups in the United States were those in their 40s and 50s, teens, and those over 70; among the declining groups were those between ages 18 and 24. As of the early 2000s, more than one in eight Americans are 65 years of age or older. The changing age profile of Americans has implications for resource availability, namely, a possible shortage of entry-level workers leading to an increase in labor costs and difficulty in finding qualified persons to replace the retiring baby boomers. The aging U.S. population also affects U.S. savings patterns, as people in the 40 to 60 age bracket usually save more than younger people. This is good for the financial services industry, which offers assistance to those who want to invest their savings. Alternatively, fewer younger workers and more "saving seniors" may have a negative impact on some industries, such as the retailing industry.

Lifestyles

Lifestyles deal with how people live, work, form households, consume, enjoy leisure, and educate themselves. Consumer behavior is affected by trends and fads. The rise and fall of designer jeans, chinos, and other styles in clothes illustrate the sensitivity of some markets to changes in consumer tastes. The increase in divorce rates, dual-career families, population shifts away from cities, and computer-based education and entertainment have influenced numerous industries, including housing, restaurants, automobiles, convenience and catalog shopping, services, and home entertainment. From an international perspective, some U.S.-brand goods—from blue jeans to movies—have a high demand overseas. They are perceived to be more in style and perhaps higher quality than items produced domestically. Sales in several industries have benefited from this exercise of consumer choice overseas.

Technology

Trends in technology can affect numerous industry factors including the product or service and how it is produced and delivered. There are literally dozens of examples of changes that have taken or are taking place due to technological innovations. For example, demand has fallen for carburetors on cars because of electronic fuel-injection technology. The engineering process has changed because of the advent of computer-aided design and computer-aided manufacturing. Perpetual improvement of designs in the semiconductor and microprocessor industry has made that industry a difficult one to evaluate. Innovations in process technology allowed steel minimills to grow at the expense of large steel producers. Advances in technology allow some plant sites and buildings to generate their own electricity, bypassing their need for power from the local electric utility. Trucks have reduced railroads' market share in the long-distance carrier industry. The information superhighway is becoming a reality and encouraging linkages between telecommunications and cable television systems. Changes in technology have spurred capital spending in technological equipment as a way for firms to gain competitive advantages. The future effect of the Internet is astronomical.

The retailing industry is a user of new technology. Some forecasters envision relationship merchandising, in which customer databases will allow closer links between retail stores and customer needs. Rather than doing market research to focus on aggregate consumer trends, specialized retailers can offer products that particular consumer segments desire in preferred locations. Technology may allow retailers to become more organizationally decentralized and geographically diversified.

Major retailers use bar-code scanning, which speeds the checkout process and allows the firm to track inventory and customer preferences. Use of customer credit cards allows firms to track customer purchases and send customized sales announcements. Electronic data interchange (EDI) allows the retailer to electronically communicate with suppliers to order new inventory and pay accounts payable. Electronic funds transfer allows retailers to move funds quickly and easily between local banks and headquarters.

Politics and Regulations

Because political change reflects social values, today's social trend may be tomorrow's law, regulation, or tax. The industry analyst needs to project and assess political changes relevant to the industry under study.

Some regulations and laws are based on economic reasoning. Due to utilities' positions as natural monopolies, their rates must be reviewed and approved by a regulatory body.[4] Some regulation involves social ends. For example, the Food and Drug Administration protects consumers by reviewing new drugs. Public and worker safety concerns spurred creation of the Consumer Product Safety Commission, the Environmental Protection Agency, and OSHA. Notably, heavy regulation of an industry can result in increasing a firm's costs but also restricting entry into the industry.

Regulatory changes have affected numerous industries. A recent example is the numerous regulations and inspections following the September 11, 2001, attacks. Changing regulations and technology are bringing participants in the financial services industry—banking, insurance, investment banking, and investment services—together.

Regulations and laws affect international commerce. International tax laws, tariffs, quotas, embargoes, and other trade barriers affect different industries and global commerce in various ways.

An interesting example is how the retail industry is affected by numerous regulatory factors. First is the minimum-wage law, which impacts many retail employees. A second factor is employer-paid health insurance, which would dramatically affect the labor costs of labor-intensive service industries, such as retailing. Third, because goods must first be delivered to the stores, regulations that affect the cost of shipping by airplane, ship, or truck will affect retailers' costs. Finally, trends toward the reduction of tariffs and quotas will allow retailers to offer imported goods at lower prices (e.g., Wal-Mart), which will expand their international production (outsourcing).

5

OPTIONAL SEGMENT BEGINS

EVALUATING THE INDUSTRY LIFE CYCLE

An insightful analysis when predicting industry sales and trends in profitability is to view the industry over time and divide its development into stages similar to those that humans progress through: birth, adolescence, adulthood, middle age,

---

[4] Technology can change natural monopolies. We mentioned earlier how some firms are generating their own electrical power. Another example is that, currently, numerous states are allowing electric utilities to compete for customers.

old age. The number of stages in this **industry life cycle analysis** can vary based on how much detail you want. A five-stage model would include

1. Pioneering development

2. Rapid accelerating growth

3. Mature growth

4. Stabilization and market maturity

5. Deceleration of growth and decline

Exhibit 60-3 shows the growth path of sales during each stage. The vertical scale in logs reflects *rates* of growth, whereas the arithmetic horizontal scale has different widths representing different, unequal time periods. To estimate industry sales, you must predict the length of time for each stage. This requires answers to such questions as: How long will an industry grow at an accelerating rate (Stage 2)? How long will it be in a mature growth phase (Stage 3) before its sales growth stabilizes (Stage 4) and then declines (Stage 5)?

Besides being useful when estimating sales, this analysis of an industry's life cycle also can provide some insights into profit margins and earnings growth, although these profit measures do not necessarily parallel the sales growth. The profit margin series typically peaks very early in the total cycle and then levels off and declines as competition is attracted by the early success of the industry.

The following is a brief description of how these stages affect sales growth and profits:

1. *Pioneering development.* During this start-up stage, the industry experiences modest sales growth and very small or negative profit margins and profits.

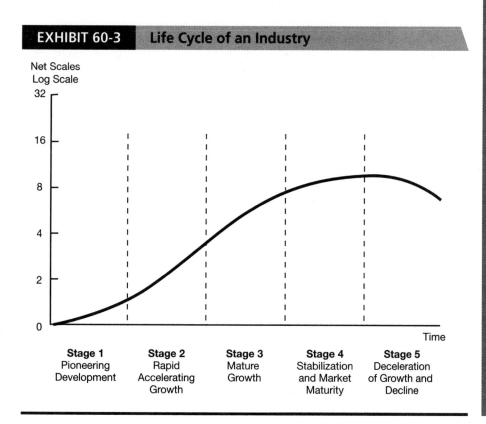

EXHIBIT 60-3 **Life Cycle of an Industry**

The market for the industry's product or service during this time period is small, and the firms involved incur major development costs.

2. *Rapid accelerating growth.* During this rapid growth stage, a market develops for the product or service and demand becomes substantial. The limited number of firms in the industry face little competition, and individual firms can experience substantial backlogs. The profit margins are very high. The industry builds its productive capacity as sales grow at an increasing rate as the industry attempts to meet excess demand. High sales growth and high profit margins that increase as firms become more efficient cause industry and firm profits to explode. During this phase, profits can grow at over 100 percent a year as a result of the low earnings base and the rapid growth of sales and net profit margins.

3. *Mature growth.* The success in Stage 2 has satisfied most of the demand for the industry goods or service. Thus, future sales growth may be above normal but it no longer accelerates. For example, if the overall economy is growing at 8 percent, sales for this industry might grow at an above normal rate of 15 percent to 20 percent a year. Also, the rapid growth of sales and the high profit margins attract competitors to the industry, which causes an increase in supply and lower prices, which means that the profit margins begin to decline to normal levels.

4. *Stabilization and market maturity.* During this stage, which is probably the longest phase, the industry growth rate declines to the growth rate of the aggregate economy or its industry segment. During this stage, investors can estimate growth easily because sales correlate highly with an economic series. Although sales grow in line with the economy, profit growth varies by industry because the competitive structure varies by industry, and by individual firms within the industry because the ability to control costs differs among companies. Competition produces tight profit margins, and the rates of return on capital (e.g., return on assets, return on equity) eventually become equal to or slightly below the competitive level.

5. *Deceleration of growth and decline.* At this stage of maturity, the industry's sales growth declines because of shifts in demand or growth of substitutes. Profit margins continue to be squeezed, and some firms experience low profits or even losses. Firms that remain profitable may show very low rates of return on capital. Finally, investors begin thinking about alternative uses for the capital tied up in this industry.

Although these are general descriptions of the alternative life cycle stages, they should help you identify the stage your industry is in, which should help you estimate its potential sales growth. Obviously, everyone is looking for an industry in the early phases of Stage 2 and hopes to avoid industries in Stage 4 or Stage 5. Comparing the sales and earnings growth of an industry to similar growth in the economy should help you identify the industry's stage within the industrial life cycle.

ANALYSIS OF INDUSTRY COMPETITION

6

Similar to the sales forecast that can be enhanced by the analysis of the industrial life cycle, an industry earnings forecast should be preceded by the analyses of the competitive structure for the industry. Specifically, a critical factor affecting the profit potential of an industry is the intensity of competition in the industry, as Porter (1980a, b, 1985) has discussed.

Competition and Expected Industry Returns

Porter's concept of **competitive strategy** is described as the search by a firm for a favorable competitive position in an industry. To create a profitable competitive strategy, a firm must first examine the basic competitive structure of its industry because the potential profitability of a firm is heavily influenced by the profitability of its industry. After determining the competitive structure of the industry, you examine the factors that determine the relative competitive position of a firm within its industry. In this section, we consider the competitive forces that determine the competitive structure of the industry. Our discussion of company analysis will cover the factors that determine the relative competitive position of a firm within its industry.

Basic Competitive Forces   Porter believes that the **competitive environment** of an industry (the intensity of competition among the firms in that industry) determines the ability of the firms to sustain above-average rates of return on invested capital. As shown in Exhibit 60-4, he suggests that five competitive forces determine the intensity of competition and that the relative effect of each of these five factors can vary dramatically among industries.

1. *Rivalry among the existing competitors.* For each industry analyzed, you must judge if the rivalry among firms is currently intense and growing, or if it is polite and stable. Rivalry increases when many firms of relatively equal size compete in an industry. When estimating the number and size of firms, be sure to include foreign competitors. Further, *slow growth* causes competitors to fight for market share and increases competition. *High fixed costs* stimulate the desire to sell at the full capacity, which can lead to price cutting

---

EXHIBIT 60-4   Force Driving Industry Competition

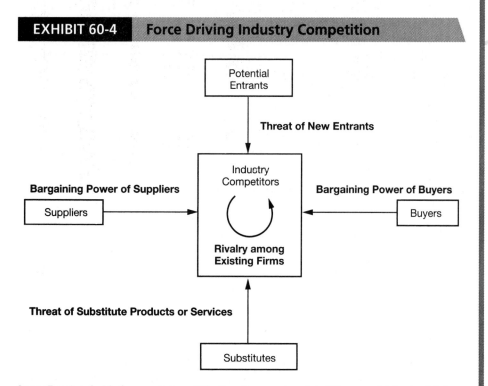

Source: Reprinted with the permission of The Free Press, an imprint of Simon and Schuster Adult Publishing Group, from *Competitive Strategy: Techniques for Analyzing Industries and Competitors* by Michael E. Porter. Copyright © 1980, 1998 by The Free Press.

and greater competition. Finally, look for *exit barriers,* such as specialized facilities or labor agreements. These can keep firms in the industry despite *below-average* or negative rates of return.

2. *Threat of new entrants.* Although an industry may have few competitors, you must determine the likelihood of firms entering the industry and increasing competition. *High barriers to entry,* such as low current prices relative to costs, keep the threat of new entrants low. Other barriers to entry include the need to invest large financial resources to compete and the availability of capital. Also, substantial economies of scale give a current industry member an advantage over a new firm. Further, entrants might be discouraged if success in the industry requires extensive distribution channels that are hard to build because of exclusive distribution contracts. Similarly, high costs of switching products or brands, such as those required to change a computer or telephone system, keep competition low. Finally, government policy can restrict entry by imposing licensing requirements or limiting access to materials (lumber, coal). Without some of these barriers, it might be very easy for competitors to enter an industry, increasing the competition and driving down potential rates of return.

3. *Threat of substitute products.* Substitute products limit the profit potential of an industry because they limit the prices firms in an industry can charge. Although almost everything has a substitute, you must determine how close the substitute is in price and function to the product in your industry. As an example, the threat of substitute glass containers hurts the metal container industry. Glass containers kept declining in price, forcing metal container prices and profits down. In the food industry, consumers constantly substitute between beef, pork, chicken, and fish. The more commoditylike the product, the greater the competition and the lower the profit margins.

4. *Bargaining power of buyers.* Buyers can influence the profitability of an industry because they can bid down prices or demand higher quality or more services by bargaining among competitors. Buyers become powerful when they purchase a large volume relative to the sales of a supplier (e.g., Wal-Mart, Home Depot). The most vulnerable firm is a one-customer firm that supplies a single large manufacturer, as is common for auto parts manufacturers or software developers. Buyers will be more conscious of the costs of items that represent a significant percentage of the firm's total costs. This consciousness increases if the buying firm is feeling cost pressure from its customers. Also, buyers who know a lot about the costs of supplying an industry will bargain more intensely—for example, when the buying firm supplies some of its own needs and buys from the outside.

5. *Bargaining power of suppliers.* Suppliers can alter future industry returns if they increase prices or reduce the quality of the product or the services they provide. The suppliers are more powerful if they are few and if they are more concentrated than the industry to which they sell and if they supply critical inputs to several industries for which few, if any, substitutes exist. In this instance, the suppliers are free to change prices and services they supply to the firms in an industry. When analyzing supplier bargaining power, be sure to consider labor's power within each industry.

An investor needs to analyze these competitive forces to determine the intensity of the competition in an industry and assess the effect of this competition on the industry's long-run profit potential. You should examine each of these factors and develop a relative competitive profile for each industry. You need to update this analysis of an industry's competitive environment over time, because an industry's competitive structure can and will change over time.

ESTIMATING INDUSTRY RATES OF RETURN

At this point, we have determined that industry analysis helps an investor select profitable investment opportunities and we have completed a thorough macroanalysis of the industry. Our next question is, How do we go about valuing an industry? Again, we consider the two equity valuation approaches introduced in Reading 59—the present value of cash flows and the relative valuation ratios. Beginning with the present value of cash flow models, we demonstrate the DDM with the two-stage growth assumption and then assume constant growth for the retailing industry. Following this, we consider the present value of free cash flow (FCF) model. Subsequently, we will analyze the alternative relative valuation techniques with the price/earnings ratio and analysis of the *P/BV*, *P/CF*, and *P/S* ratios compared to relative valuation ratios for the market.

Although our investment decision is always the same, the form of the comparison depends on which valuation approach is being used. In the case of the present value of cash flow techniques, we derive a present value for the industry using our required rate of return for the industry—that is, we compare the present value of the specified cash flow versus the prevailing value of the index. If our estimated present value exceeds the prevailing index value, we should overweight the industry. Alternatively, if the *PV* of cash flows is less than the market price of the industry index, it implies that the industry is overvalued (i.e., the industry will not provide our required rate of return if acquired at the prevailing market price) and we should underweight this industry in our portfolio.

Similarly, if we use the two-step *P/E* ratio approach, we compute a current intrinsic value for the industry and compare it to the current market price. If this estimated intrinsic value exceeds the prevailing market price for the industry, you should overweight the industry; if the intrinsic value is below the market price, you should underweight the industry.

To demonstrate industry analysis, we use Standard and Poor's retailing index to represent industrywide data. This retailing index (hereinafter referred to as the RET industry) contains about 30 individual companies from several retailing sectors including two drug stores. Therefore, it should be reasonably familiar to most observers, and it is consistent with the subsequent company analysis of Walgreens.

Valuation Using the Reduced Form DDM

Recall that the reduced form DDM is

$$P_i = \frac{D_1}{k - g}$$

(60-1)

where:

P_i = the price of Industry i at Time t
D_1 = expected dividend for Industry i in Period 1 equal to $D_0 (1 + g)$
k = the required rate of return on the equity for Industry i
g = the expected long-run growth rate of earnings and dividend for Industry i

As always, *the two major estimates for any valuation model are k and g.* We will discuss each of these at this point in the chapter with the understanding that we will also use these estimates subsequently when applying the two-step, price/earnings ratio technique for valuation.

Estimating the Required Rate of Return *(k)*   Because the required rate of return *(k)* on all investments is influenced by the risk-free rate and the expected inflation rate, the differentiating factor in this case is the risk premium for the retailing industry versus the market. In turn, we discussed the risk premium in terms of fundamental factors, including business risk *(BR)*, financial risk *(FR)*, liquidity risk *(LR)*, exchange rate risk *(ERR)*, and country (political) risk *(CR)*. Alternatively, you can estimate the risk premium based on the CAPM, which implies that the risk premium is a function of the systematic risk (beta) of the asset. Therefore, to derive an estimate of the industry's risk premium, you should examine the *BR, FR, LR, ERR,* and *CR* for the industry and compare these industry risk factors to those of the aggregate market. Alternatively, you can compute the systematic risk (beta) for the industry and compare this to the market beta of 1.0. Prior to calculating a beta for the industry, we briefly discuss the fundamental risk factors for the industry.

Business risk is a function of relative sales volatility and operating leverage. As we will see when we examine the sales and earnings for the industry, the annual percentage changes in retailing sales were less volatile than aggregate sales as represented by PCE. Also, the OPM (operating profit margin) for retail stores was less volatile than the S&P Industrials Index OPM. Therefore, because both sales and the OPM for the retailing industry have been less volatile than the market, operating profits are substantially less volatile. This implies that the business risk for the retailing industry is *below average.*

The *financial risk* for this industry is difficult to judge because of widespread use of building leases in the industry that are not included on the balance sheet. As a result, the reported data on debt to total capital or interest coverage ratios indicate that the *FR* for this industry is substantially below the market. Assuming substantial use of long-term lease contracts, when these are capitalized, the retailing industry probably has financial risk *about equal* to the market.

To evaluate the market *liquidity risk* for an industry, it is necessary to estimate the liquidity risk for all the firms in the industry and derive a composite view. The fact is, there is substantial variation in market liquidity among the firms in this industry. Firms such as Walgreens and Wal-Mart are fairly liquid, whereas small specialty retail chains are relatively illiquid. A conservative view is that the composite retailing industry probably has *above-average* liquidity risk.

Exchange rate risk (ERR) is the uncertainty of earnings due to changes in exchange rates faced by firms in this industry that sell outside the United States. The amount of *ERR* is determined by what proportion of sales is non-U.S., how these sales are distributed among countries, and the exchange rate volatility for these countries. This risk could range from an industry with very limited international sales (e.g., a service industry that is not involved overseas) to an industry that is clearly worldwide (e.g., the chemical or pharmaceutical industry). For a truly global industry, you need to examine the distribution of sales among specific countries because we know that the exchange rate risk varies among countries based on the volatility of exchange rates with the U.S. dollar. The *ERR* for the retailing industry would be relatively *low* because sales and earnings for the majority of retailing firms are mainly attributable to activity within the United States.

The existence of *country risk (CR)* is likewise a function of the proportion of foreign sales, the specific foreign countries involved, and the stability of the political/economic system in these countries. As noted, there is very little *CR* in the United Kingdom and Japan, but there can be substantial *CR* in China, Russia, or South Africa. Again, for the retailing industry, country risk would be relatively low because of limited foreign sales.

In summary, for the retailing industry, business risk is definitely below average, financial risk is at best equal to the market, liquidity risk is above average, and exchange rate risk and country risk are fairly low. The consensus is that the overall fundamental risk for the RET industry should be lower than for the aggregate market.

The *systematic risk* for the retailing (RET) industry is computed using the market model as follows:

$$\% \Delta RET_t = \alpha_i + \beta_i (\% \Delta S\&P\ 500_t) \qquad \text{(60-2)}$$

where:

$\% \Delta RET_t$ = the percentage price change in the retailing (RET) index during month t

α_i = the regression intercept for the RET industry

β_i = the systematic risk measure for the RET industry equal to $Cov_{i,m}/\sigma^2_m$

To derive an estimate for the RET industry, the model specified was run with monthly data for the five-year period 2000 to 2004. The results for this regression are as follows:

$\alpha_i = 0.003$	$R^2 = 0.62$
$\beta_t = 0.82$	$DW = 1.83$
t-value = 7.40	$F = 68.37$

The systematic risk ($\beta = 0.82$) for the RET industry is clearly below unity, indicating a low-risk industry (i.e., risk less than the market). These results are quite consistent with the prior analysis of fundamental risk factors *(BR, FR, LR, ERR, CR)*.

Translating this systematic risk into a required rate of return estimate *(k)* calls for using the security market line model as follows:

$$k_i = RFR + \beta_i (R_m - RFR) \qquad \text{(60-3)}$$

We can derive three estimates for the required market rate of return based on alternative risk premiums (0.048 − 0.085 − 0.108). For our purposes here, it seems like the midpoint is reasonable—that is, a nominal *RFR* of 0.045 and an R_m of 0.085. This, combined with a beta for the industry at 0.82, indicates the following:

$$
\begin{aligned}
k &= 0.045 + 0.82(0.085 - 0.045) \\
&= 0.045 + 0.82(0.04) \\
&= 0.045 + 0.0328 \\
&= 0.0778 = 7.78\%
\end{aligned}
$$

For ease of computation, we will use a k of 8.0% A microestimate of fundamental risk below average and a risk estimate using the CAPM likewise below average implies an industry earnings multiple *above* the market multiple, all other factors being equal.

Estimating the Expected Growth Rate *(g)* Recall that earnings and dividend growth are determined by the retention rate and the return on equity.

$$g = f(\text{Retention Rate and Return on Equity})$$

We have consistently broken down return on equity into the following three components:

$$\frac{\text{Net Profit}}{\text{Equity}} = \frac{\text{Net Income}}{\text{Sales}} \times \frac{\text{Sales}}{\text{Total Assets}} \times \frac{\text{Total Assets}}{\text{Equity}}$$

$$= \frac{\text{Profit}}{\text{Margin}} \times \frac{\text{Total Asset}}{\text{Turnover}} \times \frac{\text{Financial}}{\text{Leverage}}$$

Therefore, we need to examine each of these variables in Exhibit 60-5 to determine if they imply a difference in the expected growth rate for RET as compared to the aggregate market (S&P Industrials Index).

Earnings Retention Rate   The retention rate data in Exhibit 60-5 indicate that the RET industry has a higher retention rate (79 percent versus 67 percent). This means that the RET industry would have a potentially *higher* growth rate, all else being the same (i.e., equal *ROE*).

Return on Equity   Because the return on equity is a function of the net profit margin, total asset turnover, and a measure of financial leverage, these three variables are examined individually.

Historically, the net profit margin for the S&P Industrials Index series has been consistently higher than the margin for the RET industry. This is not surprising because retail firms typically have lower profit margins but higher turnover.

As noted, one would normally expect the total asset turnover *(TAT)* for a retail firm to be higher than the average industrial company. This expectation was confirmed because, as shown in Exhibit 60-6, the average *TAT* for the S&P Industrials Index was 0.86 versus 1.73 for the RET industry. Beyond the overall difference, the spread between the two series increased over the period. This change occurred because the *TAT* for the S&P Industrials Index series declined steadily over the period while the *TAT* for the RET industry experienced an overall increase, as shown in Exhibits 60-5, and 60-6. Multiplying these two ratios indicates the industry's return on total assets *(ROTA)*.

$$\frac{\text{Net Income}}{\text{Sales}} \times \frac{\text{Sales}}{\text{Total Assets}} = \frac{\text{Net Income}}{\text{Total Assets}}$$

When we do this for the two series, the results in Exhibit 60-5 indicate that the return on total assets *(ROTA)* for the S&P Industrials Index series went from 3.27 percent in 1993 to 4.29 percent in 2003 and averaged 4.35 percent, whereas the *ROTA* for the RET industry went from 4.14 percent to 7.28 percent and averaged 5.58 percent. Clearly, the industry *ROTA* results were superior on average.

The final component is the financial leverage multiplier (total assets/ equity). As shown in Exhibit 60-5 and Exhibit 60-7, the leverage multiplier for the S&P Industrials Index experienced a small increase to 3.38, whereas the leverage multiplier for the RET industry declined, it went from 3.54 to 2.27. Although the higher financial leverage multiplier implies greater financial risk for the S&P Industrials Index series, recall that the RET industry financial leverage is understated because the leases are not capitalized.

This brings us to the final value of *ROE*, which is the product of the three ratios. The data in Exhibit 60-5 and the plot in Exhibit 60-8 indicate that the *ROE*

EXHIBIT 60-5 — Earnings Multiplier for the S&P Industrials Index and the Retail Industry, and Influential Variables: 1993–2003

Year	EARNINGS MULTIPLIER (t+1)		RETENTION RATE		NET PROFIT MARGIN		TOTAL ASSET TURNOVER		RETURN ON TOTAL ASSETS		TOTAL ASSETS/ EQUITY		RETURN ON EQUITY	
	S&P Ind	Retail	S&P Ind	Retail	S&P Ind	Retail	S&P Ind	Retail	S&P Ind	Retail	S&P Ind	Retail	S&P Ind	Retail
1993	13.21	20.85	62.80	71.19	5.40	3.19	0.87	1.30	3.27	4.14	3.13	3.54	14.82	14.66
1994	11.78	23.48	66.97	72.42	6.03	3.14	0.89	1.40	4.91	4.40	3.42	3.47	18.41	15.30
1995	13.34	18.45	69.35	66.60	6.45	2.43	0.94	1.70	5.19	4.14	3.21	2.82	19.39	11.70
1996	15.40	17.66	67.47	78.26	6.58	2.87	0.95	1.77	5.62	5.06	3.32	2.81	20.84	14.27
1997	20.86	15.85	67.62	78.97	6.88	3.01	0.95	1.80	5.33	5.40	3.24	2.71	21.09	14.63
1998	24.00	21.65	64.18	82.98	6.43	3.45	0.88	1.94	4.90	6.69	3.27	2.66	18.37	17.84
1999	28.15	35.32	67.52	84.07	6.60	3.61	0.84	1.92	5.22	6.92	3.29	2.59	18.34	17.99
2000	39.72	32.53	71.73	82.31	6.90	2.86	0.86	1.96	5.45	5.61	3.41	2.57	20.15	14.42
2001	27.98	22.86	62.81	81.19	5.25	2.57	0.79	1.92	1.79	4.92	3.24	2.60	13.38	12.81
2002	22.70	16.18	66.79	86.22	6.23	3.71	0.76	1.84	1.92	6.82	3.17	2.49	15.06	16.99
2003	NA	NA	66.06	85.23	5.99	5.02	0.76	1.45	4.29	7.28	3.38	2.27	15.46	16.55
Mean	21.71	22.48	66.66	79.04	6.25	3.26	0.88	1.73	4.35	5.58	3.28	2.78	17.76	15.20

Source: Analyst's Handbook (New York: Standard & Poor's, 2004). Reprinted with permission.

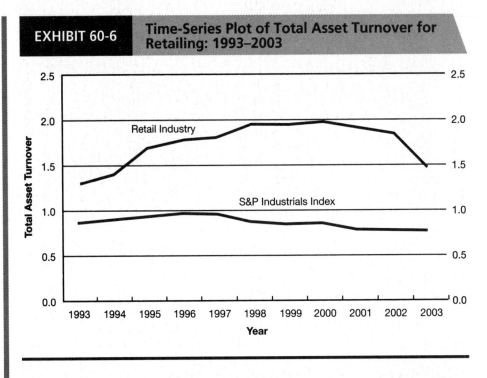

EXHIBIT 60-6 | **Time-Series Plot of Total Asset Turnover for Retailing: 1993–2003**

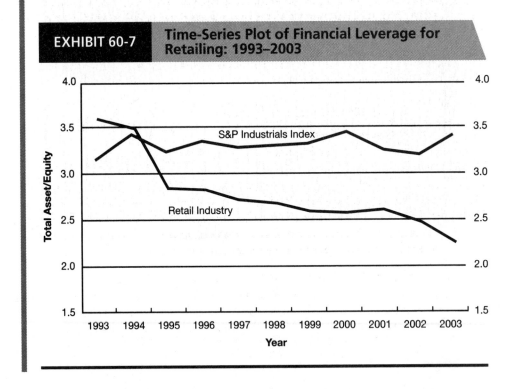

EXHIBIT 60-7 | **Time-Series Plot of Financial Leverage for Retailing: 1993–2003**

EXHIBIT 60-8	Time-Series Plot of Return on Equity for the S&P Industrials Index and the Retail Industry: 1993–2003

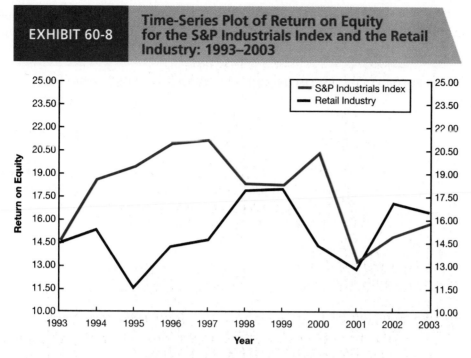

Source: Analyst's Handbook (New York: Standard & Poor's, 2004). Reprinted with permission.

for the RET industry was consistently lower than the market until the last two years. The average annual *ROE* was 15.20 percent for the RET industry versus 17.76 percent for the S&P Industrials Index series.

These average percentages are quite consistent with what would be derived from multiplying the averages of the components from Exhibit 60-5 as follows:

ROE ESTIMATE BASED ON TOTAL PERIOD AVERAGES (1993–2003)

	Profit Margin		Total Asset Turnover		Total Assets/ Equity		ROE
S&P Industrials Index	6.25	×	0.86	×	3.28	=	17.63
RET Industry	3.26	×	1.73	×	2.78	=	15.68

Although examining the historical trends and the averages for each of the components is important, you should not forget that expectations of *future* performance will determine the *ROE* value for the industry. In the current case, this analysis of expectations is very important because of the positive change in relative *ROE* during the last two years (2002, 2003). As an analyst, it is necessary to determine whether the change during this period is a permanent change in the relative performance of this industry versus the market. In this case, you should be encouraged because of the strong performance of the RET industry during 2002–2003. Specifically, if you use the results for the recent five-year period (1999–2003), the *ROE* results are:

ROE ESTIMATE BASED ON RECENT FIVE-YEAR AVERAGES (1999–2003)

	Profit Margin		Total Asset Turnover		Total Assets/ Equity		ROE
S&P Industrials Index	6.19	×	0.80	×	3.30	=	16.34
RET Industry	3.55	×	1.82	×	2.50	=	16.15

Notably, using the recent results, the *ROE* results are virtually the same. Combining these recent *ROE* results with alternative retention rates provides interesting growth estimates:

GROWTH ESTIMATES BASED ON RECENT *ROE* WITH HISTORICAL AND RECENT RETENTION RATES

	Recent* ROE	Historical** RR	Estimated g	Recent* ROE	Recent* RR	Estimated g
S&P Industrials Index	16.34	0.67	10.95	16.34	0.67	10.95
RET Industry	16.15	0.79	12.76	16.15	0.84	13.57

---

* Recent five-year average.

** Total period average.

The point is, using full-period retention results indicates a higher *g* for the RET industry. Similarly, using the retention rates for the recent five-year period indicates an even higher *g* for the industry. Given the increase in *g* for the industry when we consider the recent results, it is probably appropriate to use a growth estimate for the RET industry that is above the long-run historical estimate—that is, we will assume a near-term growth rate of 13 percent. Obviously, the best estimate of *g* would be based on an *estimate* of the three components of *ROE* for the *future* five years.

Combining the Estimates   At this point, we have the following estimates:

$$k = 0.080$$
$$g = 0.130$$
$$D_0 = \$3.10 \text{ (Estimated 2004 Dividends)}$$
$$D_1 = \$3.10 \times 1.13 = \$3.50 \text{ (Estimated Dividend for 2005)}$$

Because of the inequality between *k* and *g* (this *g* is above *k* and above the long-run market norm of about 7 percent and probably cannot be sustained), we need to evaluate this industry using the temporary growth company model. We will assume the following growth pattern:

2005–2007	0.130
2008–2010	0.110
2011–2013	0.090
2014–onward	0.070

Using these estimates of k and this growth pattern, the computation of value for the industry using the DDM is contained in Exhibit 60-9.

These computations imply a value of $490.48 compared to a price for the industry index of about $465.00 in mid-2005. Therefore, according to this valuation model and these k and g estimates, this industry is about 5 percent undervalued at this time. As will be shown, a fairly small change in the $k - g$ spread can have a large effect on the estimated value.

If we assumed a constant growth rate of 7 percent from the beginning and a D_1 of $3.96 the value would be as follows:

$$P = \frac{3.96}{(0.080 - 0.070)} = \frac{3.96}{0.010} = 396.00$$

While this valuation implies the industry is overvalued, it is clearly a low estimate of value since it assumes the base growth rate of 7 percent from the beginning. The point is, the industry is undervalued assuming strong growth in the next few years, but overvalued if one estimates only market growth. Clearly, the valuation is heavily dependent on the growth estimate.

EXHIBIT 60-9   Dividend Discount Calculations

Year	Estimated Dividend	Discount Factor @ 8.0%	Present Value of Dividend
2005	3.50	—	—
2006	3.96	.9259	3.67
2007	4.47	.8573	3.83
2008	4.97	.7938	3.95
2009	5.51	.7350	4.05
2010	6.12	.6806	4.17
2011	6.67	.6302	4.20
2012	7.27	.5835	4.24
2013	7.92	.5402	4.28
Continuing Value[a]	848.00	.5402	$458.09
		Total Value	$490.48

[a] Constant Growth Rate = 7%

Continuing Value: $\dfrac{D_1}{k - g} = \dfrac{\$7.92(1.07)}{0.080 - 0.070} = \dfrac{\$8.48}{0.010} = \$848.00$

Industry Valuation Using the Free Cash Flow to Equity (FCFE) Model

Similar to the presentation in Reading 59, we initially define the FCFE series and present the series for the recent 11-year period, including an estimate for 2004 in Exhibit 60-10. Given these data, we will consider the historical growth rates for the components and for the final FCFE series as inputs to estimating future growth for the valuation models. You will recall that FCFE is defined (measured) as follows:

> *Net Income*
> \+ Depreciation expense
> − Capital expenditures
> − Δ in working capital
> − Principal debt repayments
> \+ New debt issues

As noted, the FCFE data inputs and final annual value of FCFE for the RET industry for the period 1993–2004 is contained in Exhibit 60-10 along with 5-year and 10-year growth rates of the components. Using this data, we derive an estimate using the FCFE model under two scenarios: (1) a constant growth rate from the present, and (2) a two-stage growth rate assumption.

The Constant Growth Rate FCFE Model   We know that the constant growth rate model requires that the growth rate *(g)* be lower than the required rate of return *(k)*, which we have specified as 8.00 percent. In the current case, this is difficult because the 10-year growth rate exceeds this. Still, in order to use the model, we assume a 10 percent growth in 2005 and 7 percent long run growth in subsequent years. The result is as follows:

$g = 0.07$ (Long-Run Growth Beginning in 2006)
$k = 0.080$
FCFE (2004) = \$9.71
FCFE (2005) = \$9.71 (1.10) = \$10.68 = FCFE_0

$$V = \frac{\text{FCFE}_1}{k - g}$$
$$= \frac{10.68(1.07)}{0.080 - 0.070} = \frac{11.43}{0.01}$$
$$= 1,143$$

This \$1,143 value exceeds the industry price of about \$465 that prevailed in mid-2005. This implies that the industry is undervalued and should be **overweighted** in the portfolio. Notably, even if the long-run growth rate was only 6 percent, the estimated value would be \$571 which would also imply undervaluation.

The Two-Stage Growth FCFE Model   As before, we assume a period of above-average growth for several years followed by a second period of constant growth at 7 percent. The period of above-average growth will be as follows based on an estimated initial 10 percent growth rate of FCFE, which is lower than what was used for dividends because the FCFE series has been fairly erratic over the past 11 years including several years when the FCFE was negative.

EXHIBIT 60-10   Components of Free Cash Flow to Equity for the Retail Industry

Year	Net Income	Depreciation Expense	Capital Expenditures	Working Capital	Change In Working Capital	Principal Repayment	New Debt Issues	Total FCFE
1993	5.45	2.76	7.37	23.18	23.18	–	–	–22.34
1994	6.20	3.05	8.51	25.52	2.34	0.69	1.42	–1.60
1995	5.06	3.77	8.93	30.50	4.98	–0.21	7.62	–5.08
1996	6.67	4.27	8.28	29.54	–0.96	0.37	–0.01	3.62
1997	7.56	4.80	9.06	29.99	0.45	–0.75	1.92	2.85
1998	9.52	5.24	10.51	28.02	–1.97	–1.75	0.11	6.22
1999	10.92	6.01	12.93	24.67	–3.35	1.76	1.50	7.35
2000	9.44	6.52	15.60	23.24	–1.43	1.86	0.84	1.79
2001	9.04	7.25	15.76	33.66	10.42	–2.46	6.55	–9.89
2002	13.21	7.00	14.23	33.21	–0.45	2.11	1.42	6.43
2003	19.29	9.11	15.70	51.11	17.90	0.77	2.80	–5.20
2004E	20.00	9.60	16.50	54.00	2.89	1.50	2.00	9.71
5-Year Growth Rate*	17.81%	12.21%	9.06%	NM	NM	NM	NM	NM
10-Year Growth Rate*	15.55%	13.00%	8.39%	NM	NM	NM	NM	NM

* The growth rates do not include the 2004 estimates.

E = estimate

NM = not meaningful

2005	10%
2006	10%
2007	9%
2008	9%
2009	8%
2010	8%
2011–onward	7%

Assuming a k of 8.0 percent and an FCFE of $9.71 in 2004, $10.68 in 2005, and $11.75 in 2006, the value for the industry is as shown in Exhibit 60-11. These results are very encouraging for the industry because the computed value of $1,241 is substantially above the recent market price of about $465. This apparent undervaluation would indicate that the industry should be overweighted in the portfolio.

Notably, the alternative present value of cash flow models have generated a fairly wide range of intrinsic values as follows:

Model	Computed Value
Constant growth DDM	$490
Two-stage growth DDM	$396
Constant growth FCFE	$1,143
Two-stage growth FCFE	$1,241

Because of this wide range of estimated values compared to the recent market price of $465, one indicates overvaluation and three indicate undervaluation, it is clear that a critical variable is the $k - g$ spread.

EXHIBIT 60-11	Computation of RET Industry Value Using the FCFE Model and Two-Stage Growth

Year	FCFE	Discount Factor @ 0.080	Present Value
2006	11.75	.9259	10.88
2007	12.81	.8573	10.98
2008	13.96	.7938	11.08
2009	15.07	.7350	11.08
2010	16.28	.6806	11.08
Continuing Value[a]	1,742	.6806	1,185.61
		Total Present Value	$1,240.71

[a] $\dfrac{16.28(1.07)}{0.080 - 0.070} = \dfrac{17.42}{0.01} = 1,742$

INDUSTRY ANALYSIS USING THE RELATIVE VALUATION APPROACH

This section contains a discussion and demonstration of the relative valuation ratio techniques: (1) price/earnings ratios (*P/E*), (2) the price to book value ratios (*P/BV*), (3) price to cash flow ratios (*P/CF*), and (4) price to sales ratios (*P/S*). Again, we will begin with the detailed demonstration of the *P/E* ratio approach, which provides a specific valuation and an estimated rate of return for the industry based upon its intrinsic value that equals an estimate of future earnings per share and an industry multiple.

The analysis of the other relative valuation ratios is also more meaningful because we can compare the industry valuation ratios to the market valuation ratios while considering what factors affect the specific valuation ratios.

The Earnings Multiple Technique

You will recall that the earnings multiple technique is a two-step process that involves (1) a detailed estimation of future earnings per share, and (2) an estimate of an appropriate earnings multiplier (*P/E* ratio) based on a consideration of *P/E* determinants derived from the DDM.

Estimating Earnings per Share To estimate earnings per share, you must start by estimating sales per share. The first part of this section describes three techniques that provide help and insights for the sales estimate. Next, we derive an estimate of earnings per share, which implies a net profit margin for the industry. We begin with the operating profit margin, which leads to an estimate of operating profits. Then we subtract estimates of depreciation expense and interest expense and apply a tax rate to arrive at an estimate of earnings per share.

Forecasting Sales per Share Assuming an analyst has completed the macroanalysis of the industry that included (1) considering how the industry is impacted by the business cycle, (2) what structural changes have occurred within the industry, and (3) where the industry is in its life cycle, the analyst would have a strong start regarding a sales estimate for the industry. At this point, we would make suggestions regarding two minor estimation techniques (time series and input-output analysis) and one major technique that should be considered for almost all industries (a specific analysis of the industry-economy relationship).

Time-Series Analysis A simple time-series plot of the sales for an industry versus time can be very informative regarding the pattern and the rate of growth for industry sales. Analyzing this series along with designations of business cycle periods (expansions and recessions) and notations regarding major events will provide further insights. Finally, for many industries, it is possible to extrapolate the time series to derive an estimate of sales. For industries that have experienced consistent growth, this can be a very useful estimate, especially if it is a new industry that has not developed a history with the economy. If the sales growth has been at a constant rate, you should do the time-series plot on semi-log paper where the constant growth shows as a straight line.

Input-Output Analysis Input-output analysis is another way to gain insights regarding the outlook for an industry by separating industries that supply the input for a specific industry from those that get its output. In other words, we want to identify an industry's suppliers and customers. This will help us identify (1) the future demand from customers and (2) the ability of suppliers to provide the goods and services required by the industry. The goal is to determine the long-run sales outlook for the industry's suppliers and its major customers. To extend this analysis to global industries, we must include worldwide suppliers and customers.

Industry-Economy Relationships   The most rigorous and useful analysis involves comparing sales for an industry with one or several aggregate economic series that are related to the goods and services produced by the industry. The specific question is, What economic variables influence the demand for this industry? Notably, you should be thinking of numerous factors that will have an impact on industry sales, *how* these economic variables will impact demand, and how the factors might interact. In the following example, we will demonstrate this industry-economy technique for the retailing industry (RET).

Demonstrating a Sales Forecast   The RET industry includes retailers of basic necessities, including pharmaceuticals and medical supplies and nonmedical products, such as food, and clothing. Therefore, we want a series that (1) reflects broad consumption expenditures and (2) gives weight to food and clothing. The economic series we consider are personal consumption expenditures (PCE) and PCE food, clothing, and shoes. Exhibit 60-12 contains the aggregate and per-capita values for the two series.

A casual analysis of these time series indicates that although personal consumption expenditures (PCE) have experienced reasonably steady growth of about 5.7 percent a year during this period, PCE food and clothes has grown at a slower rate of about 4 percent. As a result, as shown in the exhibit's last column, food and clothes as a percentage of all PCE has declined from 20.6 percent in 1993 to only 17.7 percent in 2003. Obviously, as an analyst, you would be pleased because even though sales of food and clothing have grown slower than over-all PCE, retailing sales have grown faster than both of them at about 8.5 percent.

The scatterplot in Exhibit 60-13 indicates a strong linear relationship between retail sales per share and sales of food, clothing, and shoes. Although not shown, there also is a good relationship with PCE. Therefore, if you can accurately estimate changes in these economic series, you should be able to estimate expected sales for RET.

As the industry being analyzed becomes more specialized, you need a more individualized economic series that reflects the demand for the industry's product. The selection of an appropriate economic series is one place where an analyst can demonstrate knowledge and innovation. There also can be instances where industry sales are dependent on several components of the economy, in which case you should probably consider a multivariate model that would include two or more economic series. For example, if you were dealing with the tire industry, you might want to consider new-car production, new-truck production, and a series that would reflect the replacement tire demand.

You also should consider *per-capita* personal consumption expenditures. Although aggregate PCE increases each year, there also is an increase in the aggregate population, so the increase in PCE per capita (the average PCE for each adult and child) will be less than the increase in the aggregate series. As an example, during 2003, aggregate PCE increased about 5.2 percent, but per-capita PCE increased only 4.2 percent. Finally, an analysis of the relationship between changes in an economic variable and changes in industry sales will indicate how the two series move together and would be sensitive to any changes in the relationship. Using annual percentage changes provides the following regression model:

$$\% \ \Delta \ \text{Industry Sales} = \alpha_i + \beta_i (\% \ \Delta \ \text{in Economic Series}) \qquad \textbf{(60-4)}$$

EXHIBIT 60-12	S&P Retail Sales and Various Economic Series: 1993–2003					
				PER CAPITA		
Year	Retail Sales ($/Share)	Personal Consumption Expenditures ($ Billions)	PCE Food, Clothes, and Shoes ($ Billions)	Personal Consumption Expenditures (Dollars)	PCE Food, Clothes, and Shoes (Dollars)	Food, Clothing, and Shoes as a Percentage of PCE
1993	170.86	4,477.90	921.80	17,204.00	3,541.91	20.59
1994	197.21	4,743.30	958.70	18,004.00	3,639.21	20.21
1995	208.11	4,975.80	982.60	18,665.00	3,686.27	19.75
1996	232.78	5,256.80	1,018.90	19,490.00	3,778.36	19.39
1997	251.33	5,547.40	1,054.30	20,323.00	3,863.15	19.01
1998	276.12	5,879.50	1,100.70	21,291.00	3,986.38	18.72
1999	302.62	6,282.50	1,159.40	22,491.00	4,151.17	18.46
2000	329.76	6,739.40	1,222.90	23,862.00	4,330.57	18.15
2001	352.27	7,055.00	1,265.60	24,723.00	4,435.71	17.94
2002	355.62	7,376.10	1,307.90	25,592.00	4,538.09	17.73
2003	383.89	7,760.90	1,371.70	26,663.00	4,712.95	17.68
Mean Annual Growth	8.49%	5.66%	4.06%	4.48%	2.90%	−1.51%

Source: Analyst's Handbook (New York: Standard & Poor's, 2004); and *Economic Report of the President* (Washington, DC: U.S. Government Printing Office, 2003).

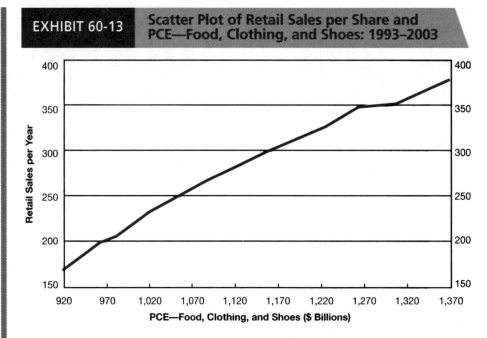

EXHIBIT 60-13 | Scatter Plot of Retail Sales per Share and PCE—Food, Clothing, and Shoes: 1993–2003

Source: Financial Analyst's Handbook (New York: Standard & Poor's, 2004); and *Economic Report of the President* (Washington, DC: U.S. Government Printing Office, 2003).

The size of the β_i coefficient should indicate how closely the two series move together. Assuming the intercept (α_i) is close to zero, a slope (β_i) value of 1.00 would indicate relatively equal percentages of change (e.g., this would indicate that a 10 percent increase in PCE typically is associated with a 10 percent increase in industry sales). A β_i of less than unity would imply that industry sales are not as volatile annually as the economy is. This analysis and the levels relationship reflected in Exhibit 60-13 would help you find an economic series that closely reflects the demand for the industry's products; it also would indicate the form of the relationship.

As indicated, there was a good relationship between retailing sales and PCE—Food, Clothing, and Shoes. The specific relationship as indicated by the regression was:

$$\% \Delta \text{ Retail Stores Sales} = 4.40 \; + \; 0.55 \; (\%\Delta \text{ PCE} - \text{Food, Clothing, and Shoes})$$

(t values)   (2.17)   (1.92)
$r^2 = 0.34$

(60-5)

Given the results for this regression, the specific sales forecast begins with an estimate of aggregate PCE growth for the years in question (i.e., 2004 and 2005). Because of the importance of PCE as a component of the economy, several estimates are available. The next step is to estimate the proportion of PCE spent on food, clothing, and shoes. As noted, this proportion has declined from 20.6 percent to 17.7 percent. You apply this proportion estimate to the PCE estimate and derive an estimate of the percent change in PCE—Food, Clothing, and Shoes that is used in the regression model to derive a sales estimate for Retail Store Sales.

To demonstrate this process, we examined several economic sources which indicated that nominal PCE increased by 6.1 percent in 2004 (to $8,231 billion) and the projection was for an increase in 2005 of 5.6 percent to $8,694 billion. Regarding the percent of PCE spent on food, clothing, and shoes, we expect this proportion to continue to decline to 17.55 percent in 2004 and 17.40 in 2005. This implies values for PCE—Food, Clothing, and Shoes of $1,444.5 billion in 2004 and $1,512.8 billion in 2005, which implies growth of 5.3 percent in 2004 and 4.7 percent in 2005. Using these percentages in the Equation 60-5 regression provides retail stores sales growth estimates of 7.3 percent for 2004 ($411.91) and 7.0 percent for 2005 ($440.74). These sales growth rates are somewhat conservative relative to the long-run results for this industry.

Forecasting Earnings per Share   After the sales forecast, it is necessary to estimate the industry's profitability based on an analysis of the industry income statement. An analyst should also benefit from the prior macroanalysis that considered where the industry is in its life cycle, which impacts its profitability. How does this industry relate to the business cycle and what does this imply regarding profit margins at this point in the cycle? Most important, what did you conclude regarding the competitive environment in the industry and what does this mean for pricing and profitability of sales?

Industry Profit Margin Forecast   Similar to the aggregate market, the net profit margin is the most volatile and the hardest margin to estimate directly. Alternatively, it is suggested that you begin with the operating profit margin (EBITDA/Sales) and then estimate depreciation expense, interest expense, and the tax rate.

The Industry's Operating Profit Margin   Recall that in the market analysis, we analyzed the factors that should influence the economy's operating profit margin, including capacity utilization, unit labor cost, inflation, and net exports. The most important variables were capacity utilization and unit labor cost. We cannot do such an analysis for most industries because the relevant variables typically are not available for individual industries. As an alternative, we can assume that movements in these industry profit margin variables are related to movements in similar economic variables. For example, when an increase in capacity utilization for the aggregate economy exists, there is probably a comparable increase in utilization for the auto industry or the chemical industry. The same could be true for unit labor cost. If there is a stable relationship between these variables for the industry and the economy, you would expect a relationship to exist between the profit margins for the industry and the economy. Although it is not necessary that the relationship be completely linear, it is important for the relationship (whatever it is) to be generally stable.

The operating profit margin (*OPM*) for the S&P Industrials Index and the retail (RET) index is presented in Exhibit 60-14. The time-series plot in Exhibit 60-15 indicates that the S&P Industrials Index *OPM* experienced a steady increase from 1993 through 2000, followed by a strong decline during the recession year 2001. The margin was flat in 2002 and had a small recovery in 2003. The *RET OPM* likewise experienced a fairly steady increase that peaked in 1999, followed by small declines in 2000 and 2001, a clear recovery in 2002 and a record high in 2003. The analysis of the relationship between the *OPM* for the market and industry using regression analysis was not useful, so it is not discussed. These results indicate that the best estimate for the RET industry can be derived from the *OPM* time-series plot using what we know about the changing competitive environment and profit trends in the retail business. It is a matter of judgment for each specific industry whether you use regression analysis and/or the time-series analysis. The point is, any such mathematical analysis should be considered a supplement to the economic analysis of the competitive environment for the industry.

EXHIBIT 60-14   Profit Margins and Component Expenses for the S&P Industrials Index and the Retail Industry

YEAR	EBITDA ($)		EBITDA MARGIN (%)		DEPRECIATION EXPENSE ($)		INTEREST EXPENSE ($)		TAX RATE (%)		NET PROFIT MARGIN (%)	
	S&P Ind	Retail	S&P Ind	Retail	S&P Ind	Retail	S&P Ind	Retail	S&P Ind	Retail	S&P Ind	Retail
1993	94.02	10.87	14.70	6.36	31.39	2.76	14.74	2.43	29.78	33.29	5.40	3.19
1994	106.91	13.11	15.91	6.65	32.61	3.05	14.56	1.9 0	34.06	35.62	6.03	3.14
1995	119.18	14.11	16.66	6.78	35.62	3.77	15.25	2.81	33.32	39.26	6.45	2.43
1996	124.27	16.85	16.87	7.24	36.90	4.27	14.17	3.01	34.59	37.84	6.58	2.87
1997	128.18	18.65	17.29	7.42	38.10	4.80	13.46	2.60	32.63	38.18	6.88	3.01
1998	125.93	21.58	17.04	7.82	40.40	5.24	14.21	2.99	32.37	36.36	6.43	3.45
1999	139.85	25.45	17.45	8.41	42.20	6.01	14.97	2.76	35.24	38.27	6.60	3.61
2000	151.98	25.46	18.12	7.72	43.80	6.52	16.59	3.09	35.90	39.45	6.90	2.86
2001	122.68	26.77	15.44	7.60	46.40	7.25	15.96	3.18	29.34	40.88	5.25	2.57
2002	121.61	29.53	15.38	8.30	36.80	7.00	15.18	2.72	30.08	36.91	6.23	3.71
2003	136.6	40.07	16.12	10.44	43.50	9.11	15.00	3.33	34.99	36.82	5.99	5.02

Source: Analyst's Handbook (New York: Standard & Poor's, 2004). Reprinted with permission.

| EXHIBIT 60-15 | Time-Series Plot of the Operating Profit Margins for the S&P Industrials Index and the Retail Stores Industry: 1993–2003 |

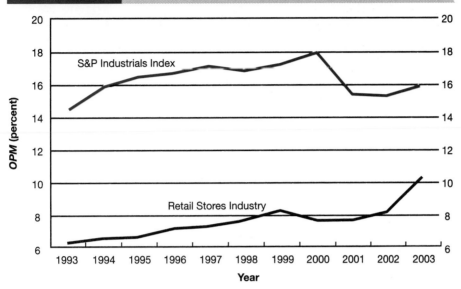

Source: Analyst's Handbook (New York: Standard & Poor's, 2004). Reprinted with permission.

Either regression analysis or time-series techniques can be useful tools, but *neither technique should be applied mechanically.* You should be aware of any unique factors affecting the specific industry, such as price wars, contract negotiations, building plans, or foreign competition. An analysis of these unique events is critical when estimating the final gross profit margin or when estimating a range of industry profit margins (optimistic, pessimistic, most likely).

Beyond this discussion, which is primarily concerned with an estimate of the near-term *OPM,* it also is important to consider the long-term profitability of the industry based on the competitive structure of the industry as discussed previously.

Industry Depreciation The next step is estimating industry depreciation, which typically is easier because the series generally is increasing; typically the only question is by how much. As shown in Exhibit 60-14, the depreciation series for RET increased every year since 1993. The time-series plots in Exhibit 60-16 relate depreciation for the S&P Industrials Index and the RET industry. To estimate depreciation expense, one can consider the two techniques used in the market analysis reading (i.e., the time-series analysis and the specific estimate technique using the depreciation expense/*PPE* ratio) or an industry-market relationship.

An analysis of the graph, as well as regression analysis of levels and annual percentage changes, indicates that the relationship between this industry and the market is not good enough to use for an estimate. Although the depreciation expense series increased at a fairly steady rate before 2002, the erratic changes in 2002, 2003 call into question the use of time-series estimates.

Exhibit 60-17 contains the components needed to derive a specific depreciation expense estimate similar to what we did for the S&P Industrials Index using the following four steps:

1. Calculate the annual *PPE* turnover for the RET industry.

2. Based upon your sales estimate and your expected *PPE* turnover ratio, estimate the expected *PPE* for next year.

| EXHIBIT 60-16 | Time-Series Plot of Depreciation Expense for the S&P Industrials Index and the Retail Stores Industry: 1993–2003 |

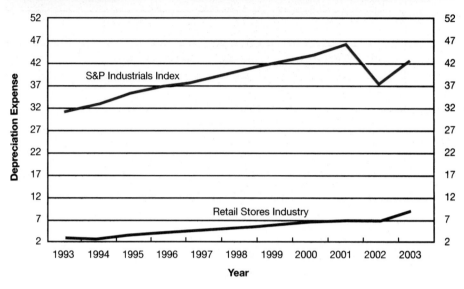

Source: Analyst's Handbook (New York: Standard & Poor's, 2004). Reprinted with permission.

3. Estimate the annual depreciation expense as a percent of *PPE* for the RET industry.

4. Estimate depreciation expense as follows:

$$(\text{Estimated } PPE) \times \text{Estimated} \left(\frac{\text{Depreciation Expense}}{PPE}\right) \text{Ratio}$$

For example, the *PPE* turnover has consistently declined since 1998. A conservative estimate would be a *PPE* turnover of 3.60. This turnover value combined with a per share sales estimate for 2005 of $441.00 implies a *PPE* estimate of $122.50. In turn, the depreciation expense/*PPE* ratio has been in the 9 percent range with the recent five-year average equal to 8.98. Therefore, we will use 9.0 percent. Applying this estimated percent to the *PPE* estimate of $122.50 implies a depreciation expense estimate of $11.02 ($122.50 × 0.09).

Subtracting an estimate of depreciation expense from the operating profit figure indicates the industry's net income before interest and taxes (EBIT).

Industry Interest Expense   An industry's interest expense will be a function of its financial leverage and interest rates. As shown in Exhibit 60-18, interest expense for the RET industry always has been relatively low when compared to the S&P Industrials Index and did not increase at the same rate during the 1980s. Therefore, looking for a relationship between the two interest expense series would not be fruitful. Your estimate for the future should be based on two separate estimates: (1) changes in the amount of debt outstanding for this industry during the year, and (2) an estimate of the level of interest rates (will they increase or decline?).

Estimating Interest Expense   The historical data needed to derive a specific estimate of interest expense are also in Exhibit 60-19. These are the steps:

1. Calculate the annual total asset turnover (*TAT*) for the RET industry.

EXHIBIT 60-17	Components for Deriving Specific Estimates for Depreciation Expense and Interest Expense for the Retail Industry											
Year	Net Sales	Net PPE	PPE Turnover	Depreciation Expense	Depr. Exp./PPE	Total Assets	Total Asset Turnover	L-T Debt	L-T Debt/ Total Assets	Interest Expense	Interest Exp L-T Debt
1993	170.86	34.34	4.98	2.76	8.04	131.72	1.30	23.59	17.91	2.43	10.30
1994	197.21	38.40	5.14	3.05	7.94	140.71	1.40	25.01	17.77	1.90	7.60
1995	208.11	46.40	4.49	3.77	8.13	122.07	1.70	32.63	26.73	2.81	8.61
1996	232.78	50.66	4.59	4.27	8.43	131.46	1.77	32.62	24.81	3.01	9.23
1997	251.33	54.83	4.58	4.80	8.75	139.75	1.80	34.54	24.72	2.60	7.53
1998	276.12	57.03	4.84	5.24	9.19	141.99	1.94	34.65	24.40	2.99	8.63
1999	302.62	65.12	4.65	6.01	9.23	157.36	1.92	36.15	22.97	2.76	7.63
2000	329.76	72.87	4.53	6.52	8.95	168.00	1.96	36.99	22.02	3.09	8.35
2001	352.27	79.78	4.42	7.25	9.09	183.22	1.92	43.54	23.76	3.18	7.30
2002	355.62	80.82	4.40	7.00	8.66	193.45	1.84	44.96	23.24	2.72	6.05
2003	383.89	101.39	3.79	9.11	8.99	264.83	1.45	47.76	18.03	3.33	6.97

Source: Analyst's Handbook (New York: Standard & Poor's, 2004). Reprinted with permission.

OPTIONAL SEGMENT

| EXHIBIT 60-18 | Time-Series Plot of Interest Expense for the S&P Industrials Index and the Retail Stores Industry: 1993–2003 |

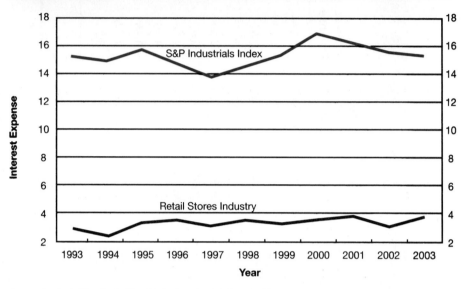

Source: Analyst's Handbook (New York: Standard & Poor's, 2004). Reprinted with permission.

| EXHIBIT 60-19 | Time-Series Plot of Tax Rates for the S&P Industrials Index and the Retail Stores Industry: 1993–2003 |

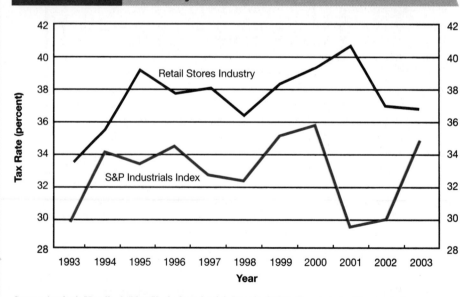

Source: Analyst's Handbook (New York: Standard & Poor's, 2004). Reprinted with permission.

2. Use your 2005 sales estimate and an estimate of *TAT* to estimate total assets next year.

3. Based on historical trends, estimate the long-term (interest-bearing) debt as a percentage of total assets ratio for the RET industry.

4. Use your estimate of total assets and the ratio of long-term debt as a percentage of total assets to estimate long-term debt for the next year.

5. Calculate the annual interest cost as a percentage of long-term debt and analyze the trend of this series.

6. Estimate next year's interest cost of debt for this industry based upon your prior estimate of market yields.

7. Estimate interest expense based on the following:

(Estimated Interest Cost of Debt) $\times$ (Estimated Long-Term Debt)

For example, our sales estimate of \$441.00 and a *TAT* that has averaged about 1.70 over the recent years including a decline in 2003 imply total assets of \$259.00 next year. Long-term, interest-bearing debt has averaged about 22–23 percent of total assets for the RET industry except for 2003. If we adjust this to 20 percent for 2005, the estimate for debt is about \$52.00 (.20 $\times$ \$259). In turn, interest expense as a percentage of long-term debt during the recent period has averaged about 7.00 percent for this industry. Based on the expectation of a small increase in market interest rates during 2005, we would estimate this interest rate to be 7.20 percent in 2005. This interest rate estimate combined with our long-term debt estimate of \$52.00 implies interest expense of \$3.74 (0.072 $\times$ \$52.00).

Industry Tax Rate   As you might expect, tax rates differ between industries. An extreme example would be the oil industry where heavy depletion allowances cause lower taxes. In some instances, however, you can assume that tax law changes have similar impacts on all industries. To see if this is valid, you need to examine the relationship of tax rates over time for your industry and the aggregate market to determine if you can use regression analysis in your estimation process. Alternatively, a time-series plot could provide a useful estimate.

As shown in Exhibit 60-19, except for 2001, the RET tax rate has been about 38 percent. Therefore, the time-series plot is fairly informative, although you still need to consider pending national legislation and unique industry tax factors. Once you have estimated the tax rate, you multiply the *EBT* per share value by (1 − tax rate) to get your estimate of earnings per share *(EPS)*.

In addition to estimating *EPS*, you also should examine the industry's net profit margin as a check on your *EPS* estimate. A time-series plot of the net profit margin series for the industry and the S&P Industrials Index is contained in Exhibit 60-20. Two important characteristics are notable. There was one significant difference between the two series. First, the S&P Industrials Index net profit margin series is much more volatile than that for RET. Second, although both profit margin series declined during the 2001 recession, the S&P Industrials Index recovered in 2002 but declined in 2003. While the RET margin experienced a nice recovery in 2002 and an increase to a record level in 2003, the result is a significant decline in the margin difference.

An Industry Earnings Estimate Example   Now that we have described how to estimate each variable in the equation, to help you understand the procedure, the following is an estimate of earnings per share for the RET industry using economic forecasts and the relationship between the RET industry and the market. Our results are not as exact as those of a practicing analyst who would use this example as an *initial* estimate that would be modified based on his or her industry knowledge, current events, and expectations of unique factors.

EXHIBIT 60-20	Time-Series Plot of Net Profit Margin for the S&P Industrials Index and the Retail Stores Industry: 1993–2003

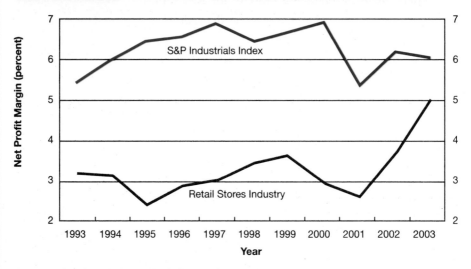

Source: Analyst's Handbook (New York: Standard & Poor's, 2004). Reprinted with permission.

The regressions and the plots in Exhibit 60-13 indicated that the best relationship was between RET sales and PCE Food, Clothing, and Shoes. Earlier in the reading, we demonstrated that using that relationship along with estimates of PCE and PCE—Food, Clothing, and Shoes as a percent of PCE we derived an RET sales estimate of $441.00 per share.

As noted earlier in connection with the analysis of Exhibit 60-15, the OPM for the RET industry recovered from the recession in 2002 and then experienced a record performance in 2003 with a 10.44 percent margin. While we can envision that the industry can maintain this level of profit, we do not think it can get much higher under current conditions. Thus, we estimate an *OPM* during 2005 of 10.50 percent, which implies operating profits of $46.31 (0.1050 × $441.00).

Earlier we derived a specific estimate for industry depreciation expense of $11.02 for 2005. Therefore, earnings before interest and taxes would be $35.29 ($46.31 − $11.02).

Given the flat yields during 2004 and the small increase in rates envisioned during 2005, our prior specific estimate of interest expense was $3.74 in 2005. Thus, *EBT* would be $31.55 ($35.29 − $3.74).

The tax rate for the RET industry has been consistently higher than the aggregate during the last seven years. The aggregate tax rate was expected to be relatively stable in 2004 and 2005. Therefore, a rate of about 38 percent seems appropriate for the RET industry. This implies taxes of $11.99 ($31.55 × 0.38) and net income (earnings per share) of $19.56 ($31.55 − $11.99). This indicates a net profit margin for the RET industry of 4.44 percent ($19.56/$441.00), which is below the record margin in 2003, but higher than all prior years.

Given an estimate of the industry's net income per share (for simplicity, we will round off the *EPS* estimate to $20 per share), your next step is to estimate the earnings multiplier for this industry. Together, the earnings per share and the earnings multiplier provide an estimate of the intrinsic value for the industry index.

Estimating an Industry Earnings Multiplier   This section discusses how to estimate an industry earnings multiplier using two alternative techniques: macroanalysis and microanalysis. In macroanalysis, you examine the relationship between the multiplier for the industry and the market. In microanalysis, you estimate the industry earnings multiplier by examining the specific variables that influence it: (1) the dividend-payout ratio, (2) the required rate of return for the industry *(k)*, and (3) the expected growth rate of earnings and dividends for the industry *(g)*.

Macroanalysis of an Industry Multiplier: Why a Relationship?   Given that this subsection considers the relationship between the earnings multiplier (*P/E* ratio) for an industry to the *P/E* for the aggregate market, a natural question is, Why do we *expect* a relationship? The reasons are based on the variables that influence the multiplier—the required rate of return, the expected growth rate of earnings and dividends, and the dividend-payout ratio. Specifically, as you know, the required rate of return *(k)* is a function of the nominal risk-free rate plus a risk premium. The fact is, the nominal risk-free rate is the same for all investment assets and is the major reason for changes in *k*. Also, though the level of the risk premium may differ between the market and an industry, any *changes* in the risk premium are probably related.

Although the rate of growth *(g)* for an industry may differ from that of the market, and this difference in *g* is a major reason for the difference in the level of the *P/E* ratio, *changes* in the growth expectations for many industries will be related to changes in *g* for the market and for other industries because they are driven by macroeconomic growth factors that affect the overall market and most industries. Therefore, since the major factor causing a change in the *P/E* ratio for the aggregate market and alternative industries is a change in the $k - g$ spread and these two variables have several components that move together, it is not unreasonable to look for an overall (macro) relationship between changes in an industry's *P/E* and the market *P/E* ratio.

An examination of the relationship between the *P/E* ratios for 71 S&P industries and the S&P Industrials Index by Reilly and Zeller (1974) during four partially overlapping 21-year periods indicated a significant positive relationship between percentage changes in *P/E* ratios for most industries examined. Notably, because there was a difference in the significance of the relationship between alternative industries and the market, it is necessary to evaluate the quality of the relationship between the *P/E* ratios for a specific industry and the market before using this technique.

The results in Exhibit 60-5 and Exhibit 60-21 for the RET industry during the period 1993 to 2003 indicate a relatively close relationship between the market and the RET industry. The *P/Es* for the market and RET industry have generally moved together, but the relationship between them has changed four times, with the market *P/E* larger since 1999. Given the recent differences in *P/E* ratios a crucial question that the analyst must consider is, Why is the RET multiplier smaller and will this differential continue?

Microanalysis of an Industry Multiplier   We estimate the specific future earnings multiplier for the stock market series by estimating a range of values for the three variables (i.e., dividend payout *k,* and *g*) that determine the multiplier and derived a range of *P/E* ratio estimates. This approach provided several multiplier estimates that were used with our EPS estimate to compute a range of estimated intrinsic values for the market index.

Our microanalysis of the industry multiplier could use the same approach. Although this is reasonable, it would not take advantage of the prior work on the stock market multiplier. Because the variables that affect the stock market multiplier and the industry multiplier are similar we can compare the two sets of variables.

EXHIBIT 60-21	Time-Series Plot of Annual Average Future Earnings Multipliers for the S&P Industrials Index and the Retail Stores Industry: 1993–2003

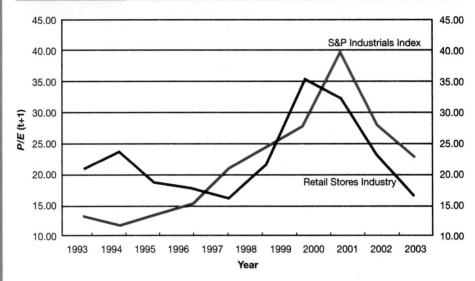

Source: Analyst's Handbook (New York: Standard & Poor's, 2004). Reprinted with permission.

Therefore, in our microanalysis, we estimate the three variables that determine the industry earnings multiplier and compare them to the comparable values for the market *P/E*. This allows us to determine whether the industry earnings multiplier *should* be above, below, or equal to the market multiplier. Once we feel confident about this relationship, it is easier to derive a specific estimate for the industry *P/E* ratio. First, we need to recall the long-run relationship between the industry and market *P/E* ratios.

Industry Multiplier versus the Market Multiplier   Recall from Exhibit 60-5 and Exhibit 60-21 that the *P/E* ratios for the RET industry and the market generally moved together but the relationship changed four times between 1993 and 2003. Notably, the market *P/E* has consistently been larger than the RET industry *P/E* since 1999. A comparative analysis of the factors that determine the earnings multiplier should help us determine if it is appropriate for the RET industry multiple to be smaller than the market multiple.

Comparing Dividend-Payout Ratios   We can discuss the dividend-payout ratio directly or in terms of the retention rate because the retention rate is one minus the dividend-payout ratio. Analyzing the data in Exhibit 60-5 indicates that the retention rates of retail stores have consistently been higher than the retention rates for the market (79 percent versus 67 percent). This indicates a higher dividend payout for the S&P Industrial Index, and this variable alone implies a higher multiplier for the S&P Industrials Index, holding all other variables constant.

Estimating the Required Rate of Return   Recall that we estimated the required rate of return *(k)* earlier in the chapter in connection with the present value of cash flow valuation models. The final estimate indicated a beta of 0.82 for the RET industry, which was generally consistent with the fundamental risk characteristics of the industry. In turn, this beta in the prevailing SML implied a *k* of 8.00 percent. This 8.00 percent compares to the *k* for the aggregate stock market derived in Reading ?? of 8.50 percent, which implies that all else the same, the industry *P/E* should be higher than the market *P/E*.

Estimating the Expected Growth Rate (g)   You will recall that we likewise estimated a growth rate for the industry early in this reading in connection with the present value of cash flow models. Using the relationship

$$g = \text{Retention Rate } (b) \times \text{Return on Equity } (ROE)$$
$$= (b) \times (ROE)$$

we estimated a *g* of over 12 percent based on long-run historical results, and a *g* of about 13 percent using the results for the recent five-year period 1999–2003.

This 13 percent growth rate estimate compares to the growth rates for the S&P Industrials Index of between 10 and 11 percent (using the long-run retention rate or the recent five-year retention rate). Notably, the growth rates implied for both the industry (13 percent) and the market (10–11 percent) appear too high for any long-term period—that is, we typically use continuing growth rates of 6–7 percent. Therefore, while we would not use the higher growth rates for long-run estimates, the comparison appears valid for our purposes here—the industry has a higher *g* than the market. This implies that based on the growth factor, the industry multiple would be higher than the market multiple.

In summary, a comparison of the dividend-payout ratios indicates that the market *P/E* ratio should be higher; the required rate of return comparison indicates that the industry multiple should be higher; while the growth rate comparison favors the industry multiple. The consensus tends to favor a higher industry multiple. Earlier it was discussed that the forward market multiple is currently about 18 times. This implies an industry multiplier in the low 20s.

Industry Estimated Value and Rate of Return   At this point, we have an estimate of the industry earnings per share ($20.00) and an estimate for an industry earnings multiple in the low 20s based on a comparison of the industry and market components. It is not possible to derive a specific estimate using the DDM formula because the *k* and *g* for the industry are roughly equal—that is, both *k* and *g* are about 8.50 percent. Because the multiple estimate is necessarily not specific, it seems appropriate to consider an optimistic and a pessimistic estimate, with the initial estimate of intrinsic value as follows:

Optimistic Multiple:	24 × $20.00 = $480
Expected Multiple:	22 × $20.00 = $440
Pessimistic Multiple:	20 × $20.00 = $400

Given a current market price for the industry index of about $465, these results indicate that the industry is slightly overpriced based upon general expectations and the pessimistic estimate, but it is slightly underpriced if one favors the optimistic multiple.

9

OTHER RELATIVE VALUATION RATIOS

Similar to the market analysis, we need to consider the other three relative valuation ratios (*P/BV; P/CF;* and *P/S*) and compare their performance over time relative to similar ratios for the aggregate stock market as represented by the S&P Industrials Index.

Again, the calculations will employ the average annual price and *future* book value, cash flow, and sales. The input data derived for the industry and the S&P Industrials Index with 10-year growth rates for each of these variables are contained in Exhibit 60-22. An important point to note for the subsequent comparison is that the compound growth rate for every RET industry variable is higher than the growth rate for the same market variable.

Exhibit 60-23 contains the four relative valuation ratios for the RET industry and for the S&P Industrials Index along with the ratio of the annual industry valuation ratio divided by the market valuation ratio. The idea is to determine for each valuation ratio the long-run relationship between the industry and the market, including any changes in this relationship. Subsequently, the goal is to explain the overall relationship and consider any changes that have occurred and whether these changes can be explained based upon the factors that should affect the particular relative valuation ratio. The comparative *P/E* ratios will not be discussed again.

The Price/Book Value Ratio

The time-series plot in Exhibit 60-24 shows the overall increase in the price/book value ratio experienced by both the aggregate stock market and the RET industry to a peak of almost five times in 1999 followed by declines in 2000, 2001, and 2002. Notably, the relationship between the industry and the market has been quite consistent with the market *P/BV* ratio almost always larger than the RET industry ratio.

The reason for this relationship is difficult to explain because the *P/BV* ratio should reflect the ability of the market, an industry, or a company to earn a return on equity capital that exceeds its cost of equity. In turn, this return on equity capital is the *ROE,* and we know from our earlier analysis that during the last decade, the *ROE* for the market and the RET industry has been very similar while the cost of equity for the industry is lower ($B = 0.82$), so there is a larger return spread for the industry that should lead to a higher *P/BV* ratio.

The Price/Cash Flow Ratio

As shown in Exhibit 60-23 and Exhibit 60-25, the *P/CF* ratio increased for both the market and the RET industry and the industry ratio has consistently been larger. The reason for the difference in the *P/CF* ratios is akin to the *P/E* ratio—that is, a difference in the growth rate of *CF* per share and the risk (volatility) of the *CF* series over time. As shown in Exhibit 60-22, the growth rate of the industry *CF* has been consistently higher than the growth of the market *CF* (i.e., 13 percent versus about 5 percent) and the industry *CF* series has also been more consistent in its growth. An important question is whether the industry *P/CF* ratio should be about 30 percent higher than the *P/CF* ratio for the market—that is, does the difference in consistent growth of *CF* justify the fairly large difference in the *P/CF* ratios?

EXHIBIT 60-22   Inputs for Relative Valuation Ratios: The Retail Stores Industry and the S&P Industrials Index: 1993–2003

RETAIL STORES INDUSTRY

Year	Mean Price	EPS	Cash Flow P/S	Book Value P/S	Net Sales P/S	Dividend P/S
1993	115.94	4.97	8.21	37.18	170.86	1.57
1994	109.67	5.56	9.26	40.53	197.21	1.71
1995	108.85	4.67	8.84	43.25	208.11	1.69
1996	117.46	5.90	10.94	46.75	232.78	1.45
1997	152.50	6.65	12.36	51.66	251.33	1.59
1998	230.78	9.62	14.76	53.34	276.12	1.62
1999	335.22	10.66	16.93	60.72	302.62	1.74
2000	320.07	9.49	15.97	65.48	329.76	1.67
2001	301.48	9.84	16.29	70.54	352.27	1.70
2002	309.90	13.19	20.21	77.76	355.62	1.82
2003	317.61	19.15	28.40	116.53	383.89	2.85
10-yr G	10.5%	14.3%	13.0%	12.7%	8.5%	6.4%

S&P INDUSTRIALS INDEX

Year	Mean Price	EPS	Cash Flow P/S	Book Value P/S	Net Sales P/S	Dividend P/S
1993	523.83	21.96	58.00	191.82	639.77	12.51
1994	543.85	33.12	72.39	210.98	672.04	13.01
1995	634.35	36.01	79.27	227.12	715.38	13.96
1996	795.58	41.15	82.89	238.76	736.65	15.58
1997	995.68	42.13	83.73	247.83	741.52	16.72
1998	1,300.27	38.37	87.38	264.63	738.82	17.28
1999	1,660.54	50.25	97.73	302.08	801.29	17.40
2000	1,684.89	53.85	105.09	337.51	838.78	16.59
2001	1,430.90	19.82	68.58	348.38	794.48	15.85
2002	1,169.97	22.57	61.59	310.61	790.86	16.18
2003	1,138.53	47.12	90.88	363.74	847.38	17.23
10-yr G	8.1%	8.0%	4.5%	6.7%	2.9%	3.1%

Source: Analyst's Handbook (New York: Standard & Poor's, 2004). Reprinted with permission.

OPTIONAL SEGMENT

EXHIBIT 60-23   Relative Valuation Ratios for the Retailing Industry Versus S&P Industrials: 1993–2002

Year	PRICE EARNINGS (t + 1)			PRICE CASH FLOW (t + 1)			PRICE BOOK VALUE (t + 1)			PRICE SALES (t + 1)		
	Retail	S&P Ind	Ratio Ind/Mkt	Retail	S&P Ind	Ratio Ind/Mkt	Retail	S&P Ind	Ratio Ind/Mkt	Retail	S&P Ind	Ratio Ind/Mkt
1993	20.85	13.21	1.58	12.52	4.87	2.57	2.86	2.47	1.16	0.59	0.77	0.76
1994	23.48	11.78	1.99	12.41	4.50	2.76	2.54	2.36	1.07	0.53	0.75	0.70
1995	18.45	13.34	1.38	9.95	5.14	1.94	2.33	2.68	0.87	0.47	0.87	0.54
1996	17.66	15.40	1.15	9.50	6.20	1.53	2.27	3.21	0.71	0.47	1.07	0.44
1997	15.85	20.86	0.76	10.33	7.99	1.29	2.86	3.80	0.75	0.55	1.36	0.41
1998	21.65	24.00	0.90	13.63	9.19	1.48	3.80	4.26	0.89	0.76	1.60	0.48
1999	35.32	28.15	1.25	20.99	10.87	1.93	5.12	4.89	1.05	1.02	1.97	0.52
2000	32.53	39.72	0.82	19.65	13.80	1.42	4.54	4.86	0.93	0.91	2.13	0.43
2001	22.86	27.98	0.82	14.92	11.21	1.33	3.88	4.39	0.88	0.85	1.72	0.49
2002	16.18	22.70	0.71	10.91	8.29	1.32	2.66	3.11	0.86	0.81	1.34	0.60

Source: Analyst's Handbook (New York: Standard & Poor's, 2004). Reprinted with permission.

EXHIBIT 60-24	Time-Series Plot of Price/Book Value Ratios for the S&P Industrials Index and the Retail Stores Industry: 1993–2002

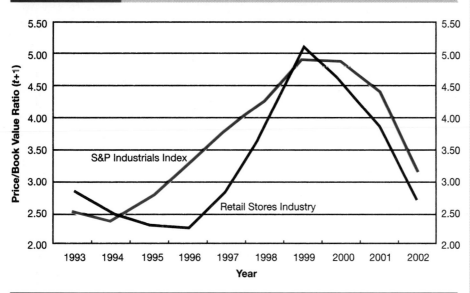

EXHIBIT 60-25	Time-Series Plot of Price/Cash Flow Ratios for the S&P Industrials Index and the Retail Stores Industry: 1993–2002

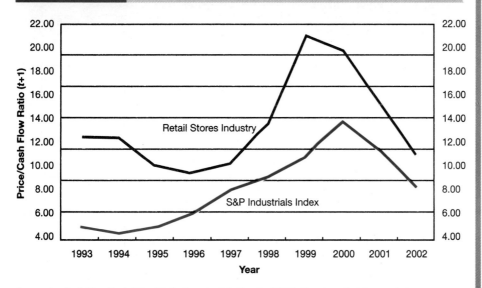

Source: Analyst's Handbook (New York: Standard & Poor's, 2004). Reprinted with permission.

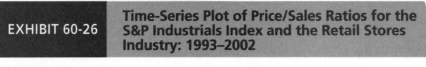

EXHIBIT 60-26	Time-Series Plot of Price/Sales Ratios for the S&P Industrials Index and the Retail Stores Industry: 1993–2002

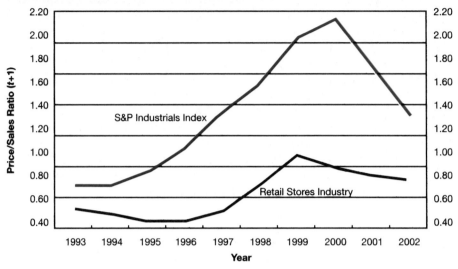

Source: Analyst's Handbook (New York: Standard & Poor's, 2004). Reprinted with permission.

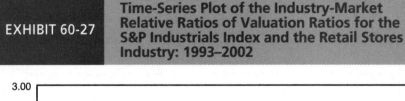

EXHIBIT 60-27	Time-Series Plot of the Industry-Market Relative Ratios of Valuation Ratios for the S&P Industrials Index and the Retail Stores Industry: 1993–2002

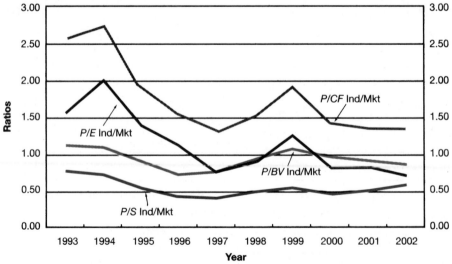

Source: Analyst's Handbook (New York: Standard & Poor's, 2004). Reprinted with permission.

The Price/Sales Ratio

As shown in Exhibit 60-23 and Exhibit 60-26, the *P/S* ratio for the market has always been higher and typically by a large amount (1.4 versus 0.8 at the end of the period). In terms of what should affect the *P/S* ratio, one can think of three factors: (1) sales growth rate, (2) the uncertainty (risk) of sales growth, and (3) the profitability of sales (i.e., the net profit margin). Because the industry experienced a *higher* rate of growth for sales during the 10-year period, it is not the rate of growth. Both have likewise experienced less volatility in sales growth. In contrast, the profit margin *(PM)* has always been higher for the market, but the difference declined in 2002 and 2003. Thus, the difference is questionable.

Exhibit 60-27 is a summary of the four industry-market ratios for each of the valuation ratios. In general, the results indicate that investors' assessment of this industry relative to the market has declined during this time period, as shown by the fact that all the industry-market relative ratios declined during this period. Only the price/CF ratio for the industry is above the market. Given the higher growth rates for these variables, this could indicate a valuation opportunity.

GLOBAL INDUSTRY ANALYSIS | 10

Because so many firms are active in foreign markets and because the proportion of foreign sales is growing for so many firms, it is necessary to consider the effects of foreign firms on industry returns. To see why this is so, consider the auto industry. Besides Ford and General Motors, the auto industry for a global investor includes numerous firms from Japan, Germany, Italy, and Korea, among others. Thus, we must extend the analysis described earlier to include global factors.

While space does not permit a complete example, the following major factors need to be analyzed in this context:

- ► The macroenvironment in the major producing and consuming countries for this industry. This will impact demand from these countries.

- ► An overall analysis of the significant global companies in the industry, the products they produce, and how successful they are in terms of the DuPont three-component analysis.

- ► As part of the company analysis, what are the accounting differences by country and how do these differences impact the relative valuation ratios? Because of the accounting differences, it is typically not possible to directly compare such ratios across countries but only examine them over time within a country. This problem should be reduced as the use of international accounting standards grows.

- ► What is the effect of currency exchange rate trends for the major countries? Significant changes can affect the demand for U.S. chemicals from specific countries and also costs assuming U.S. firms receive inputs from foreign firms.

This global industry analysis is growing in importance as documented in a study by Cavaglia, Brightman, and Aked (2000), which documents that, historically, research showed that country factors dominated industry factors in terms of explaining equity returns. The Cavaglia et al. (2000) study presented evidence that industry factors have been growing in importance and currently dominate country factors. In summary, it is important to carry out industry analysis on a global scale.

THE INTERNET

Investments Online

The Web can help researchers find information about an industry, but many industry analyses and studies are available online only to registered and paying clients of research firms, investment banks, and brokerage houses. You probably will not find up-to-date Porter analyses free on the Internet, at least not for a wide variety of industries. Web searches for industry information can focus on exploring Web sites of competitors in the industry. You may find trade group Web sites through key word searches using terms and phrases relevant to the industry you wish to study.

Because this reading focuses on the retail industry and our company analysis is a retail drugstore chain, a little investigation brought forth the sites described below; many more exist for your perusal.

www.lf.com The home page for Lebhar-Friedman, Inc., a publisher and provider of information about retailers.

www.nacds.org This page is sponsored by the National Association of Chain Drug Stores. It contains data relevant to chain drugstores. It offers news and links to related sites.

www.healthcaredistribution.org This is a site of the Healthcare Distribution Management Association. This page features links to managed-care issues, public policy issues, information for pharmacies, consumers, the press, manufacturers, analysts, and investors. Contains links to a number of related Web sites.

Retailindustry.about.com A part of the about.com Web site, this site contains a number of links to other Web sites that deal with the retail industry and the analysis of the retail industry.

www.valuationresources.com This site contains links to industry information sources and **economic information** sources. Industry report information is segmented by SIC code.

OPTIONAL SEGMENT ENDS

SUMMARY

► Several studies have examined industry performance and risk. They have found wide dispersion in the performance of alternative industries during specified time periods, implying that industry analysis can help identify superior investments. They also showed inconsistent industry performance over time, implying that looking at only past performance of an industry has little value in projecting future performance. Also, the performance by firms within industries typically is not very consistent, so you must analyze individual companies in an industry following the industry analysis.

► The analysis of industry risk indicated wide dispersion in the measures of risk for different industries but a fair amount of consistency in the risk measure over time for individual industries. These results imply that risk analysis and measurement are useful and necessary. The good news is that past risk measures may be of some value when estimating future risk.

► We discussed and demonstrated both approaches to the valuation of the RET industry. The present value of cash flow models indicated a fairly wide range of values.

► The four relative valuation ratio techniques also provided a range of results, including the two-step earnings multiple technique where the multiple results surrounded the current market price. All of the relative valuation ratios declined over time relative to the market.

► Industry analysis needs to be carried out on a global scale and must evaluate the effects not only of world supply, demand, and cost components for an industry but also different valuation levels due to accounting conventions and, finally, the impact of exchange rates on the total industry and the firms within it.

	4⅝	4¹¹/₁₆	⅜	
	5½	5½ −		
5½	20⅝	2¹³/₁₆ − ¼		
2¾	17⅜	18⅛ + ⅞		
18½	6½	6½ − ½		
7¼	15/16	3¹/₃₂ − ⅛		
1		⅝		
	9/16	9/16		
1³/₃₂	7¹³/₁₆	7¹⁵/₁₆		
7¹⁵/₁₆	2⅝	2¹¹/₃₂ 2½ +		
546	2¾	2¼ 2¼		
327	12¹/₁₆	11⅜ 11¾ +		
87	33¾	33 33¼ −		
602	25⅝	24⁹/₁₆ 25⅜ +		
833	12	11⅝ 11⅞ +		
16	10½	10½ 10½ −		
78	15⅞	15¹³/₁₆ 15⅞ −		
4608	9⁹/₁₆	8¼ 8⅜ +		
430	11¼	10⅛ 10⅛		

EQUITY: CONCEPTS AND TECHNIQUES
by Bruno Solnik and Dennis McLeavey

LEARNING OUTCOMES

The candidate should be able to:

a. classify business cycle stages and identify, for each stage, attractive investment opportunities;

b. discuss, with respect to global industry analysis, the key elements related to return expectations;

c. describe the industry life cycle and identify an industry's stage in its life cycle;

d. interpret and explain the significance of a concentration ratio and a Herfindahl index;

e. discuss, with respect to global industry analysis, the elements related to risk, and describe the basic forces that determine industry competition.

INTRODUCTION 1

Investing in foreign stocks poses at least two types of problems: First, the portfolio manager must gain sufficient familiarity with the operations, trading mechanisms, costs, and constraints of foreign markets. Second, the portfolio manager's investment approach must be global; that is, his method of analyzing and selecting stocks should be part of an optimal worldwide investment strategy. The conceptual and technical aspects of this analysis are discussed in this reading.

To structure their analysis of expected return and risk of stocks, investors must start from a view of the world. What are the worldwide factors affecting stock prices? In an open-economy world, companies should be valued relative to their global competitors; hence, global industry analysis is of primary importance. Before conducting such an analysis, it is important to understand the differences in national accounting standards that affect the raw information used. Then the important aspects of global industry analysis can be studied with data adjusted for comparability across countries. Global industry analysis of expected returns and risks leads naturally to a discussion of risk factor models used to structure global portfolios and manage their risk.

2   APPROACHING INTERNATIONAL ANALYSIS

There is nothing unique to financial analysis in an international context. Analysts must already take foreign variables into account in evaluating domestic firms. After all, product markets in which many domestic industrial companies compete are international.

Concepts in Action

Toyota Eclipses its U.S. Rivals

Japanese Carmaker Delivers Record Half-Year Results with a 90% Surge in Profits

Toyota Motor yesterday reinforced the Japanese car industry's ranking as the most profitable in the world when it produced record half-year results.

The 90 percent jump in consolidated net profits to ¥553bn ($4.5bn) put it on track to top Ford's profits of $7.2bn in 1999, the record by any carmaker excluding one-off gains.

In the six months to September the world's third-biggest carmaker made more than the combined profits of its U.S. rivals, General Motors, Ford and Chrysler, part of the German-U.S. group DaimlerChrysler. Its automotive operating margins of 10.1 percent were more than five times the average of Detroit's big three.

The ability of Toyota and domestic competitors Nissan Motor and Honda Motor to make record profits while America's big three are struggling with restructuring plans reflects the popularity of their vehicles in the U.S., which has driven strong growth in sales.

"The biggest reason why Japanese have suddenly started to make supernormal profits is not what is going on in their domestic market but what is happening in their export markets," said Mark Little, motor industry analyst at Deutsche Bank.

American carmakers blame their loss of market share on the weakness of the yen against the dollar. Bill Ford, chairman of Ford, told shareholders this week: "It really, competitively, puts us at a disadvantage."

Even Europe's BMW, which operates exclusively in the high-margin luxury sector, cannot match the operating margins of the Japanese.

Unlike their U.S. counterparts, Japan's leading manufacturers have implemented cost-cutting measures while simultaneously increasing sales in their core markets—especially the U.S. . . .

All three carmakers have drawn attention to the fact that they increased sales without relying on discounts.

Toyota also reported rising sales in its three remaining markets. In Europe, where Toyota has struggled in the past, sales rose 21 percent to ¥746.2bn, while sales in Japan where it has a dominant market share of

42 percent, were up 9.5 percent at ¥5,388bn. Sales to the rest of the world rose 61.9 percent to ¥823bn.

It announced an interim dividend of ¥16 per share, an increase of ¥3 per share on the same period last year.

Source: Financial Times, October 31, 2002, p. 1.

Large domestic firms tend to export extensively and head a network of foreign subsidiaries. These companies must be analyzed as global firms, not purely domestic ones. In many sectors, the competition is fully global. The methods and data required to analyze international manufacturers are quite similar. In brief, research on a company should produce two pieces of information:

▶ *Expected return.* The expected return on an investment can be measured by a rate of return, including potential price appreciation, over some time period, or by some other quantified form of buy-or-sell recommendation.

▶ *Risk exposure.* Risk sensitivity, or risk exposure, measures how much a company's value responds to certain key factors, such as economic activity, energy costs, interest rates, currency volatility, and general market conditions. Risk analysis enables a manager or investment policy committee to simulate the performance of an investment in different scenarios. It also helps the manager to design more diversified portfolios.

The overall purpose of analysis is to find securities with superior expected returns given current (or foreseeable) domestic and international risks.

Quantifying the analysis facilitates a consistent global approach to international investment. This is all the more desirable when the parameters that must be considered are numerous and their interrelationships are complex. Although qualitative analysis seems easier to conduct in some institutions than in others, it must be carefully structured so that it is consistent for every security, and provides an estimation of the reaction of security prices to various risk factors.

The Information Problem

Information on foreign firms is often difficult to obtain; once obtained, it is often difficult to interpret and analyze using domestic methods. It is no wonder, then, that comparisons of similar figures for foreign firms are often misleading.

In the United States, companies publish their quarterly earnings, which are publicly available within just a couple of weeks after the close of the quarter. The 10-K reports are particularly useful for trend analysis and intercompany comparisons. Moreover, these reports are available on computerized databases. In contrast, certain European and Far Eastern firms publish their earnings only once a year and with a considerable reporting time lag. French companies, for example, follow this pattern and don't actually publish their official earnings until two to six months after the end of their fiscal years. As a result, official earnings figures are outdated before they become public. To remedy this lack of information, most corporations with significant foreign ownership have begun announcing quarterly or semiannual earnings estimates a short time after the close of the quarter. This is true worldwide for large international corporations. These corporations also follow the American practice of issuing "warnings" as soon as some bad news is likely to affect earnings. The format and reliability of these announcements vary from firm to firm, but overall, they help investors to get better financial information more quickly. As do U.S. firms, British firms publish detailed financial information frequently. Similarly, Japanese firms have begun publishing U.S.-style financial statements, though sometimes only once a year.

Other problems arise from the language and presentation of the financial reports. Many reports are available only in a company's domestic language. Whereas multinational firms tend to publish both in their domestic language and in English, many smaller but nevertheless attractive firms do not. In general, financial reports vary widely from country to country in format, degree of detail, and reliability of the information disclosed. Therefore, additional information must sometimes be obtained directly from the company. Differences in national accounting standards are discussed later in this chapter.

As international investment has grown, brokers, banks, and information services have, fortunately, started to provide more financial data to meet investors' needs. In fact, today, many large international brokerage houses and banks provide analysts' guides covering companies from a large number of countries. The guides include information ranging from summary balance sheet and income statement information to growth forecasts, expected returns on equity investments, and risk measures, such as betas, which are discussed later. The reports are usually available in both the domestic language and English. Similarly, several data services, such as Bloomberg, Reuters, Thomson Financial, Factset, and Moody's, are extending their international coverage on companies and currently feature summary financial information on an increasing number of international corporations. Some financial firms, such as Thomson First Call, have specialized in collecting earnings forecasts from financial analysts worldwide. They provide a service giving the individual analyst's forecast for most large companies listed on the major stock exchanges of the world. They also calculate a consensus forecast, as well as various other global statistics.

Despite these developments, to get the most timely information possible, financial analysts may have to visit international corporations. This, of course, is a time-consuming and expensive process. Moreover, the information obtained is often not homogeneous across companies and countries. The next section reviews differences in international accounting standards.

A Vision of the World

A major challenge faced by all investment organizations is structuring their international research efforts. Their choice of method depends on what they believe are the major factors influencing stock returns. The objective of security analysis is to detect relative misvaluation, that is, investments that are preferable to other *comparable* investments. That is why sectoral analysis is so important. A financial analyst should be assigned the study of securities that belong to the same sector, that is, that are influenced by the *same* common factors and that can therefore be directly compared. The first task, though, is defining these sectors, or common factors. For example, one can reasonably claim that all dollar **Eurobonds** with fixed coupons belong to the same sector. Another sector would be French common stocks, which are all influenced by national factors. An alternative would be all high-technology companies across the world, which should be influenced by similar worldwide industrial factors. In a homogeneous sector, research should detect securities that are underpriced or overpriced relative to the others.

A first step for an organization to structure its global equity investment requires that it adhere to some vision of the world regarding the dominant factors affecting stock returns. Traditionally, investment organizations use one of three major approaches to international research, depending on their vision of the world:

▶ If a portfolio manager believes that the value of companies worldwide is affected primarily by global industrial factors, her research effort should be structured according to industrial sectors. This means that companies are valued relative to others within the same industry, for example, the chemical industry. Naturally, financial analysts who use this approach are specialists in particular industrial sectors.

▶ If a portfolio manager believes that all securities in a national stock market are influenced primarily by domestic factors, her research effort should be structured on a country-by-country basis. The most important investment decision in this approach is how to allocate assets among countries. Thereafter, securities are given a relative valuation within each national market.

▶ If a portfolio manager believes that some particular attributes of firms are valued worldwide, she will engage in *style* investing. For example, *value stocks* (corporations with a low stock market price compared with their book value) could be preferred to *growth stocks* (corporations with a high stock market price compared with their book value).

In general, an organization must structure its investment process based on some vision of the major common factors influencing stock returns worldwide.

DIFFERENCES IN NATIONAL ACCOUNTING STANDARDS

3

In this reading, we develop a top-down approach to global equity investing. We examine country and industry analysis before moving to equity security analysis. Global industry financial analysis examines each company in the industry against the industry average. Plots of one financial ratio against another can show the relative location of individual companies within the industry. To carry out such analysis, we must first know something about the differences in national accounting standards so that we can adjust ratios to make them comparable. For example, discounted cash flow analysis (DCF) and compound annual growth rates (CAGR) in cash flows must be based on comparable data to be meaningful.

In global industry financial analysis, the pattern is to contrast the financial ratios of individual firms against the same ratios for industry averages. The analyst will encounter and possibly need to adjust such ratios as: enterprise value (EV) to earnings before interest, taxes, depreciation, and amortization (EBIDTA), return on equity (ROE), and the book value multiple of price to book value per share (BV). In practice, one also sees such ratios as price to net asset value (NAV), EV to capital employed (CE), return on capital employed (ROCE), and value added margin. *Capital employed* is usually defined[1] as equity plus long-term debt. *Net asset value* is usually defined on a per-share basis as equity minus goodwill. *Value added margin* is ROCE minus the weighted average cost of capital (WACC).

With an understanding of differences in national accounting standards, the analyst will be prepared to evaluate companies from around the world within the context of global industry. After discussing these differences, we will return to global industry analysis.

---

[1] See Temple (2002) for definitions.

Today all companies compete globally. Capital markets of developed countries are well integrated, and international capital flows react quickly to any perceived mispricing. Hence, companies tend to be priced relative to their global competitors, and it is for this reason that this chapter focuses on global industry analysis.

Companies and investors have become more global. Mergers and acquisitions often occur on a global basis. Further, it is not unusual for a company to have its shares listed on multiple exchanges. Similarly, investors often seek to diversify their holdings and take advantage of opportunities across national borders. This globalization of financial markets creates challenges for investors, creditors, and other users of financial statements. Comparing financial statements of companies located in different countries is a difficult task. Different countries may employ different accounting principles, and even where the same accounting methods are used, currency, cultural, institutional, political, and tax differences can make between-country comparisons of accounting numbers hazardous and misleading.

For example, the treatment of depreciation and extraordinary items varies greatly among countries, such that net income of a company located in one country might be half that of a similarly performing company located in another country, even after adjustment for differences in currency. This disparity is partly the result of different national tax incentives and the creation of "secret" reserves (provisions) in certain countries. German and Swiss firms (among others), for example, have been known to stretch the definition of a liability; that is, they tend to overestimate contingent liabilities and future uncertainties when compared with other firms. The provisions for these liabilities reduce income in the current year, but increase income in later years when the provisions are reduced. This can have a smoothing impact on earnings and mask the underlying variability or riskiness of business operations.

Similarly, German and Swiss firms allow goodwill resulting from acquisitions to be deducted from equity immediately, bypassing the income statement and resulting in reporting the balance sheet based on book value, not on actual transaction prices. Similar idiosyncrasies often make comparisons of Japanese and U.S. earnings figures or accounting ratios meaningless. As a result, many large Japanese companies publish secondary financial statements in English that conform to the U.S. generally accepted accounting principles (GAAP). But even when we examine these statements, we find that financial ratios differ markedly between the two countries. For example, financial leverage is high in Japan compared with the United States, and coverage ratios are poor. But this does not necessarily mean that Japanese firms are more risky than their U.S. counterparts, only that the relationship between banks and their client corporations is different than in the United States.

With increasing globalization there has been a movement toward convergence of accounting standards internationally. In spite of this movement, there are still substantial differences in existing accounting standards that must be considered by investors.

Historical Setting

Each country follows a set of accounting principles that are usually prepared by the accounting profession and the national authorities. These sets of accounting principles are sometimes called national GAAP. Two distinct models can describe the preparation of these national accounting principles:

► In the Anglo-American model, accounting rules have historically been set in standards prepared by a well-established, influential accounting profession.

▶ In the Continental model, used by countries in Continental Europe and Japan, accounting rules have been set in a codified law system; governmental bodies write the law, and the accounting profession is less influential than in the Anglo-American model.

Anglo-American countries typically report financial statements intended to give a true and fair view of the firm's financial position. Hence, there can be large differences between accounting statements, the intent of which is to give a fair representation of the firm's financial position, and tax statements, the intent of which is to reflect the various tax provisions used to calculate the amount of income tax owed. Many other countries (France, Germany, Italy, and Japan, for example) have a tradition that the reported financial statements and earnings conform to the method used to determine taxable income. This implies that financial statements are geared to satisfy legal and tax provisions and may not give a true and fair view of the firm. This confusion between tax and book accounting is slowly disappearing under the pressure of international harmonization, as noted in the next section.

International Harmonization of Accounting Practices

Investors, creditors, and other users of financial statements have exerted pressure to harmonize national accounting principles. The *International Accounting Standards Committee (IASC)* was set up in 1973 by leading professional accounting organizations in nine countries: Australia, Canada, France, Germany, Japan, Mexico, the Netherlands, the United Kingdom and Ireland, and the United States. Over time additional countries became members of the IASC. The IASC issued its first international accounting standard (IAS) in 1974, entitled Disclosure of Accounting Policies. In 2001, the IASC was renamed the *International Accounting Standards Board (IASB)*, and we will use this name hereafter.

Although the IASB is able to propose international accounting standards, it does not have the authority to require companies to follow these standards. Without a mechanism to compel companies to use IAS and enforce the standards, harmonization is not easily achievable. In 1995, the *International Organization of Securities Commissions (IOSCO)* stated that it would consider adopting the international accounting standards once the IASB had prepared a comprehensive set of standards covering all the major areas of importance to general business. IOSCO is an important organization whose members are the agencies regulating securities markets in all countries.[2] IOSCO's objectives are to promote high standards of regulation in order to maintain just, efficient, and sound markets. IOSCO has two important committees: The Emerging Markets Committee endeavors to promote the development and improvement of efficiency of emerging securities and futures markets. The Technical Committee is made up of sixteen agencies that currently regulate the world's larger, more developed and internationalized markets in fourteen countries: Australia, France, Germany, Hong Kong, Italy, Japan, Mexico, the Netherlands, Canada, Spain, Sweden, Switzerland, the United Kingdom, and the United States.

"Multinational disclosure and accounting" is a major subject before this committee, and has led to the cooperation with the IASB. At the start of 1999, the IASB prepared a core set of standards and submitted them to IOSCO for review and endorsement. After deliberation, in May 2000 the Technical Committee of IOSCO recommended that IOSCO members use 30 selected IASB standards for cross-border listings and offerings by multinational companies. These 30 selected standards, referred to as IASB 2000 Standards by IOSCO, are listed in

---

[2] One hundred seventy members as of 31 December 2001, according to IOSCO Annual Report 2001.

EXHIBIT 61-1	IOSOCO Selected Standards for Cross-Border Listings

IAS	Description
IAS 1	Presentation of Financial Statements (revised 1997)
IAS 2	Inventories (revised 1993)
IAS 4	Depreciation Accounting (reformatted 1994)
IAS 7	Cash Flow Statements (revised 1992)
IAS 8	Net Profit or Loss for the Period, Fundamental Errors and Changes in Accounting Policies (revised 1993)
IAS 10	Events after the Balance Sheet Date (revised 1999)
IAS 11	Construction Contracts (revised 1993)
IAS 12	Income Taxes (revised 1996)
IAS 14	Segment Reporting (revised 1997)
IAS 16	Property, Plant and Equipment (revised 1998)
IAS 17	Leases (revised 1997)
IAS 18	Revenue (revised 1993)
IAS 19	Employee Benefits (revised 1998)
IAS 20	Accounting for Government Grants and Disclosure of Governmental Assistance (reformatted 1994)
IAS 21	The Effects of Changes in Foreign Exchange Rates (revised 1993)
IAS 22	Business Combinations (revised 1998)
IAS 23	Borrowing Costs (revised 1993)
IAS 24	Related Party Disclosures (reformatted 1994)
IAS 27	Consolidated Financial Statements and Accounting for Investments in Subsidiaries (reformatted 1994)
IAS 28	Accounting for Investments in Associates (revised 1998)
IAS 29	Financial Reporting in Hyperinflationary Economies (reformatted 1994)
IAS 31	Financial Reporting of Interests in Joint Ventures (revised 1998)
IAS 32	Financial Instruments: Disclosure and Presentation (revised 1998)
IAS 33	Earnings Per Share (1997)
IAS 34	Interim Financial Reporting (1998)
IAS 35	Discontinuing Operations (1998)
IAS 36	Impairment of Assets (1998)
IAS 37	Provisions, Contingent Liabilities and Contingent Assets (1998)
IAS 38	Intangible Assets (1998)
IAS 39	Financial Instruments: Recognition and Measurement (1998)

Source: IASB Standards—Assessment Report, Report of the Technical Committee of the International Organization of Securities Commissions, May 2000.

Exhibit 61-1. Due to concerns with some standards, the Technical Committee recommends that supplemental information be required for some standards in the form of reconciliations to national standards, additional disclosure, or specification of which alternative treatment in IAS must be used.

These two international organizations, one representative of the accounting profession (private sector) and the other of government regulators, play an important role in moving toward global harmonization of disclosure requirements and accounting practices. This is all the more important for multinational corporations that wish to raise capital globally. They need to be able to present their accounts in a single format, wherever they want to be listed or raise capital. Of particular importance is the attitude of the United States toward IAS. Convergence of the U.S. GAAP and IAS is a desirable but difficult goal. A topic under discussion is to allow foreign firms listed on a U.S. stock exchange to publish accounts according to IAS, rather than asking them to provide earnings statements calculated according to the U.S. GAAP.

The IASB also received the support of the *World Bank*. A large number of emerging countries, as well as Hong Kong, have adopted the IAS as a basis for their accounting standards. Corporations from many developed countries also use the IAS in their financial reporting. For example, most of the leading industrial companies in Switzerland voluntarily report their accounts according to international accounting standards.

In countries where accounting rules are governed by law, specific legislation is required to allow for the use of other accounting standards. The European Union (EU) is supporting the use of IAS. The harmonization of European accounting principles has come mostly through *Directives* published by the EU. These EU Directives are drafted by the EU Commission, and member states' parliaments must adapt the national law to conform to these Directives. The EU also issues *Regulations,* which have the force of law without requiring formal transposition into national legislation. In 2002, the EU issued a Regulation requiring listed companies to prepare their consolidated financial statements in accordance with IAS from 2005 onward.[3] The road to global cooperation is never easy, and it will be a long time before full harmonization of financial reporting is achieved.

Differences in Global Standards

A complete presentation of International Accounting Standards is beyond the scope of this book. The full text of standards can be obtained from the International Accounting Standards Board (www.iasb.org.uk).[4] We focus here on areas of differences among IAS and various national GAAP. A group of international accounting firms prepared a comparison of IAS and national GAAP for 62 countries.[5] The study found that there remains a lack of convergence globally particularly with regard to the following:

▶ The recognition and measurement of
  ▶ Financial assets and derivative financial instruments

---

[3] Regulation (EC) No. 1606/2002 of the European Parliament and of the Council of the European Union on the application of international accounting standards, 19 July 2002.

[4] Various summaries of IAS are also available. For example, *IAS In Your Pocket*, Deloitte Touche Tohmatsu, April 2002, and *GAAP Differences in Your Pocket: IAS and US GAAP*, Deloitte Touche Tohmatsu. Both are available at www.iasplus.com.

[5] GAAP 2001: *A Survey of National Accounting Rules Benchmarked against International Accounting Standards*, Anderson, BDO, Deloitte Touche Tohmatsu, Ernst & Young, Grant Thornton, KPMG, Pricewaterhouse-Coopers: Editor, Christopher W. Nobes. Available at www.ifad.net.

> ▶ Impairment losses
> ▶ Provisions
> ▶ Employee benefit liabilities
> ▶ Income taxes
▶ Accounting for business combinations
▶ Disclosure of
> ▶ Related party transactions
> ▶ Segment information

Several inconsistencies in accounting standards require that the analyst take particular care in making cross-border comparisons. For example, one question to ask is whether all assets and/or liabilities are properly reflected on the balance sheet. If not, these off-balance-sheet assets and liabilities must be analyzed and appropriate adjustments made in any valuation exercise.

Business Combinations

Under IAS 22 the *purchase method* of accounting is generally used (recording acquired assets and liabilities at fair value at the acquisition date), although the *uniting of interest method* (recording acquired assets and liabilities at historical book value) is used when the acquirer cannot be identified (i.e., which one is the acquirer?). Until recently, the United States permitted use of the *pooling method* (substantially equivalent to uniting of interest) for many acquisitions. Now all new acquisitions in the United States must be accounted for by using the purchase method. Previous acquisitions under the pooling method continue to be reported by using the pooling method. Australia prohibits the pooling/uniting of interest method. In France, Germany, and Italy (at least until 2005), there is a more liberal use of uniting of interests than under IAS. Japan and Switzerland do not have specific rules related to the classification of business combinations.

Concepts In Action

Rules Set for Big Change

Millions of Dollars of Debt Could Be Brought Back on to Companies' Balance Sheets

Among the many consequences of the collapse of Enron has been a new focus by regulators on how companies account for off-balance-sheet transactions.

Enron's swift demise raised questions over its complex web of off-balance-sheet transactions, leading the U.S.'s Financial Standards Accounting Board to consider new rules governing special purpose entities (SPEs). The changes could result in millions of dollars of debt being brought back on to corporate balance sheets, and represent a significant challenge for the rapidly developing structured finance market. SPEs are used for a wide range of financial transactions because they isolate assets from the financial fortunes of companies that own them.

SPEs can be organized in a variety of forms, such as trusts or corporations, but usually have no full-time employees or operating business. They can be used for different activities, including acquiring financial assets, property or equipment, and as a vehicle for raising funds from investors by issuing stock or other securities.

Depending on the type of SPE, its assets and liabilities may not appear in the financial statements of the entity that created it. . . .

Source: Jenny Wiggins, "Special Purpose Entities," *Financial Times,* October 7, 2002, p. 4.

Consolidation

In most countries, corporations publish financial statements that consolidate, to some extent, the accounts of their subsidiaries and affiliates. A full range of consolidation practices exists. In all countries, majority interests in domestic subsidiaries are typically consolidated. This is not always the case when dealing with foreign subsidiaries or with minority interests. In Italy and Japan, certain dissimilar subsidiaries can be excluded. In France, there is considerable leeway in the method used for consolidation. Japanese companies, like many German firms, tend to publish separately the (nonconsolidated) financial statements of the various companies belonging to the same group. This can be partly explained by the extent of cross-holdings in these countries. The perimeter of consolidation is often difficult to establish in Japan because of the extent of cross-holding. The practice of publishing (partly) nonconsolidated statements renders the valuation of a company a difficult exercise. IAS 27 imposes consolidation for all subsidiaries with uniform accounting policies. In addition to subsidiaries, there is also the question of nonoperating entities created to carry out a special purpose, such as leasing assets or securitizing receivables.

Concepts In Action

Enron Collapse Is IAS Weapon

Enron's multibillion dollar collapse is set to become the weapon the global accounting standard-setter has been looking for in its battle to convince the US to adopt international accounting rules.

Sir David Tweedie, International Accounting Standards Board chairman, and Allan Cook, UK Accounting Standards Board technical director, have indicated Enron's collapse could not have happened under existing UK or global rules. UK standards are the closest in the world to international rules.

Tweedie is now likely to reapply pressure to US watchdog the Securities and Exchange Commission to allow American companies to use global rules. Both UK and global rules on off-balance sheet reporting, which brought Enron to its knees, are much tougher.

But FASB, the US standard setter, has consistently resisted attempts to push through an updated standard. Highlighting Enron's off-balance sheet reporting, Cook said: "The IASB would probably have got it on the balance sheet. It's very tough."

As if to show the US its determination, the IASB could issue an even tougher rule on off-balance-sheet reporting, or derecognition, as early as next year.

> The ASB is compiling research into off-balance-sheet reporting to submit to the IASB in January.
>
> Sir David Tweedie, IASB chairman, said: "This wakes people up to the fact that accounting matters. They are looking across at us. The UK is well ahead of the rest of the world on this."
>
> A letter to the *Wall Street Journal* last week by Joe Berardino, chief executive of Andersen, Enron's auditor, also showed him in favour of a change in rules.
>
> ───────────
>
> *Source:* Michelle Perry, "Enron Collapse Is IAS Weapon," *Financial Director,* December 13, 2001.

Under IAS 27, special purpose entities (SPEs) are consolidated if controlled. This is also the case in the United Kingdom. In the United States, SPEs are consolidated if certain criteria are met (or not met); this leaves considerable leeway. Germany, Spain, and Switzerland have no requirement regarding SPEs. France requires holding at least one share of an SPE to consolidate. The ability of firms to avoid consolidation of SPEs has often enabled them to keep large amounts of liabilities off the balance sheet to the detriment of investors and creditors alike. National standards setters, such as the U.S. Financial Accounting Standards Board, are reconsidering standards in this area.

Joint Ventures

Joint ventures are increasingly used in international business. Most European countries consolidate joint ventures using *proportional consolidation,* as provided under IAS. In this method, assets, liabilities, and earnings are consolidated line by line, proportional to the percentage of ownership in the subsidiary U.K. and U.S. corporations use the *equity method.* A share of the subsidiary profits is consolidated on a one-line basis, proportional to the share of equity owned by the parent. The value of the investment in the subsidiary is adjusted to reflect the change in the subsidiary's equity. The two methods lead to marked differences in the corporation's balance sheet. IAS 31 states that the benchmark treatment should be proportional consolidation, although jointly controlled entities can alternatively be accounted for by using equity consolidation.

Goodwill

Goodwill can appear in various ways. Most commonly, goodwill is created when a company engages in an acquisition or merger at a market value different from the book value. Under IAS, goodwill is capitalized and amortized, usually over 20 years or less, and is subject to an impairment ("loss of value") test. In Switzerland and Germany, goodwill can be written off against equity immediately and does not affect the income statement. In the United Kingdom, goodwill need not be amortized. In the United States, until recently goodwill was capitalized as an asset and amortized. Now in the United States, goodwill and other intangibles without a determinable useful life are no longer amortized, but are subject to impairment tests.

Financial Leases

Financial leases are an indirect way to own an asset and provide the financing for it. In some countries, they are simply carried as off-balance-sheet items. In other countries, these leases are capitalized both as assets and liabilities. This was not common in countries in which accounting systems are driven by tax considerations (e.g., France, Germany, and Italy), but it is progressively implemented in most countries. IAS 17 requires capitalization of financial leases.

Asset Revaluation

Revaluation of assets is generally not permitted except when the market value declines, with the exception of financial assets discussed below. Investment properties can be revalued in Switzerland and Sweden. In Japan, land can be revalued. In Switzerland, Canada, and France, there is no requirement for recognizing impairment. Special laws have permitted periodic revaluation in France, Italy, and Spain in order to compensate for inflation, but the tax implications of these revaluations have sometimes been negative, making revaluation unpopular. Countries with higher inflation, such as Brazil, tend to have systems for automatic inflation indexing.

Provisions

A provision is an estimate of a likely future loss or expense. It appears as a liability on the balance sheet and is deducted from current reported earnings when initially taken. In many countries, such as the United States, United Kingdom, Italy, and Spain, provisions can be taken only for specific and likely future events. In Germany and Switzerland, generous provisions can be taken for all types of general risks. In the Netherlands, certain provisions can be made where there may not be a current obligation. In good times, German firms will build provisions to reduce earnings growth; in bad times, they will draw on these provisions to boost reported earnings. These provisions are called "hidden reserves" because they do not appear as equity reserves on the balance sheet, but rather as general liability (debt). However, they can be used to boost profits in bad times. IAS 37 supports a strong limitation on the creation of provisions, and when created, requires discounting. In the United States, provisions are not discounted.

Pensions

The accounting for pensions and retirement liabilities differs widely across countries, in part because of the national differences in pension systems. One difference is whether pension liabilities are accrued, that is, whether there is an actuarial evaluation of future pension expenses (and on what basis). Another difference is whether the pensions are funded off-balance sheets or whether pension assets and liabilities remain on a company's balance sheet. Some countries, for example, France and Italy, have primarily a national pay-as-you-go pension system, whereby current workers pay for the pensions of retired workers; companies contribute to pensions, but future pension liabilities are neither accrued nor funded, and current pension costs are expensed as incurred. In the United States, the Netherlands, Switzerland, the United Kingdom, and, to some extent, Japan, pensions are accrued and funded off-balance sheets; a separate entity, called a "pension fund," manages the pension assets and liabilities. In Germany or Spain, pensions are accrued but not funded, so pension liabilities do not appear on the company's balance sheet. The assumptions used to estimate accrued pension liabilities also vary among countries and firms.

Financial Assets and Derivatives

Under IAS and U.S. standards, trading and available-for-sale securities are recorded at fair value. Similarly, derivatives are reported at fair value, except certain hedging activities. In Switzerland, the United Kingdom, Spain, Canada, and Germany, trading securities, available-for-sale securities, and derivatives are not reported at fair value. Similarly, trading and derivative liabilities are not reported at fair value, and hedging treatment is applied more liberally.

Employee Stock Options

Employee stock options represent potential earnings dilution to existing shareholders. As a form of employee compensation, these stock options should be treated as expenses from an economic perspective. The fair value of this compensation paid to employees is treated as an expense, a deduction to pretax earnings recorded at the time the options are granted. The fair value is computed by using a standard option pricing model.

Currently IAS, as well as most national GAAP including the U.S. GAAP, does not require that an expense be recorded for the value of options granted to employees. In the United States, footnote disclosures are required, but recording of an expense is optional for most stock options. IAS requires some disclosures regarding options. In July 2000, the IASB in conjunction with some national standard-setters, issued a discussion paper proposing, among other things, that share based payments be expensed. The IASB added this project to their agenda and issued an exposure draft in November 2002. This matter is getting wide attention, and some U.S. firms have recently decided to voluntarily begin recording an expense for such stock options allocation.

Example 61-1

Employee Stock Options

A company has 100,000 shares outstanding at $100 per share. To its senior management, the company granted employee stock options on 5,000 shares. The options can be exercised at a price of $105 any time during the next five years. For five years, the employees thus have the right but not the obligation to purchase shares at the $105 price, regardless of the prevailing market price of the stock. Using price volatility estimates for the stock, a standard Black–Scholes valuation model gives an estimated value of $20 per share option. Without expensing the options, the company's pretax earnings per share are reported as $1 million/100,000 = $10 per share. What would they have been if they had been expensed?

Solution

The expense is 5000 × $20 = $100,000

The pretax income per share would be ($1,000,000 − $100,000) / 100,000 = $9 per share.

Concepts in Action

So Many Options

Have Accounting Regulators Chosen the Best Way of Expensing Share Options?

Several features of the wild bull market of the 1990s have since been branded as evil. Perhaps none more so than the billions of dollars of share options awarded to bosses and other employees. Once praised for their incentivizing power, share options are now blamed for encouraging bosses to do all manner of bad things to prop up their company's share price and so keep their lucrative options packages in the money, as the jargon has it. In this, it is now generally agreed, executives have been abetted by accounting standards that did not require the cost of awarding options to be treated as compensation and lopped off a company's reported profits.

This week, to right this wrong, the International Accounting Standards Board (IASB) unveiled proposals for expensing options, i.e., deducting their cost from a company's profits. In doing so, however, not only was the IASB declaring war on some powerful political opponents of expensing. It also took sides in a lively economic dispute.

Among economists, the debate is largely about how to value options and when to expense them, not about whether they should be expensed at all. (Only a few "renegades" disagree with expensing, declares Robert Merton, who won a Nobel prize in economics for his work on options pricing.) Economists mostly agree that options should be expensed using a so-called fair value method, one that broadly reflects what the options would cost to buy in the market, were they available.

In this, the economists agree with the IASB, which has chosen fair value accounting of options, ruling out several other methods. These include, for instance, intrinsic value: the difference between the market price of the underlying shares that the option confers the right to buy and the exercise price at which the underlying shares may be bought. If, when an option is issued, the exercise price equals the market price (and it often does), the intrinsic value is zero—which is nonsensical. Also ruled out is the minimum-value method, which is what somebody would willingly pay for an option if they knew that the firm's share price would be fixed for the life of the option. This ignores a big part of an option's value, namely the ability to cash in should the share price rise.

The IASB does not, though, specify exactly which method of fair value option pricing should be used. And here academics dispute vigorously. Mr. Merton helped to devise the Black–Scholes model for pricing options, named after Myron Scholes (who shared Mr. Merton's Nobel prize) and Fisher Black (who would have done, had he lived a little longer). The main alternative is what is called the binomial pricing model, developed by John Cox, Stephen Ross, and Mark Rubinstein.

Both models were devised to price simple options traded on an exchange. So, as the IASB acknowledges, each needs to be modified to reflect several peculiarities of employee share options—such as longer lifespan or term (a typical executive option lasts ten years, against a few months to two years for an exchange-traded option), restrictions on when options may be exercised, and even the fact that they may not be sold. How these adjustments are made—and the IASB allows wide discretion—can make a big difference to the size of the expense.

The binomial method is much more complex than Black–Scholes, but if done properly, the price it produces is likely to be accurate more often. Of course, the very complexity may make it easier for the price to be manipulated by a company wanting to massage its profits. On the other hand, plenty of scope for creativity exists with the Black–Scholes method, even given the few simple assumptions that are used. These assumptions, in essence, are expected volatility (how much a share price is likely to fluctuate), term, the expected dividend yield, the risk-free interest rate, and the exercise price.

Some critics reckon that these vagaries of valuation undermine the entire case for expensing. Few economists agree, however. Whatever uncertainties there are in fair value option pricing, goes the argument, they are smaller than the uncertainty in the value of other items already routinely expensed, such as depreciation and pension fund gains or losses.

Ask Not Whether, but When

The biggest philosophical dispute among economists concerns when options should be expensed. The IASB wants it done once and for all from the date they are awarded to employees (in other words, the grant date). Mr. Scholes, the Nobel laureate, agrees. But others, such as Mr. Rubinstein, one of the creators of binomial pricing, do not. He argues for full expensing at the time options are exercised, i.e., when the holder trades in the options for underlying shares. Under this approach, options would still initially be expensed on the grant date; but in subsequent public filings this estimate would be adjusted to take into account changes in their value. Upon exercise, the company would take a final extraordinary gain or loss to match up with the option's actual value when exercised. Mr. Rubinstein argues that, under this method, there would be less incentive to manipulate option valuations, because any divergence from an option's final true value would, in the end, result in an extraordinary charge.

The issue boils down to this: Is the granting of an option a once-only expense for the company, the equivalent of paying the employee in cash? Or is it a contingent liability, the potential cost of which to shareholders changes with the market price of the company's shares, and with the true cost becoming clear only when the option is either exercised or it expires? A once-only expense or a contingent liability: these are matters over which reasonable people can agree to differ. What is important is that share options are to be expensed at all.

The Effects of Accounting Principles on Earnings and Stock Prices

The same company using different national accounting standards could report different earnings. Some accounting standards are more conservative than others, in the sense that they lead to smaller reported earnings. Several comparative studies have attempted to measure the relative conservativeness of national standards. For example, Radebaugh and Gray (1997) conclude that U.S. accounting principles are significantly more conservative than U.K. accounting principles but significantly less conservative than Japanese and Continental European accounting principles. If the United States' earnings are arbitrarily scaled at 100, Japanese earnings would scale at 66, German earnings at 87, French earnings at 97, and British earnings at 125. Various studies come up with somewhat different adjustments, so these figures should be interpreted with some caution. Also, recent changes, particularly in the United States and Europe, will impact this assessment in the future.

These national accounting principles also affect the reported book value of equity. Speidell and Bavishi (1992) report the adjustment that should be made to the book value of foreign shareholders' equity if the U.S. GAAP were used. They find that the book value of equity would be increased by 41 percent in Germany and 14 percent in Japan, and would be reduced by 14 percent in the United Kingdom and 28 percent in France.

Price–earnings (P/E) ratios are of great interest to international investors, who tend to compare the P/E ratios of companies in the same industrial sector across the world. The P/E ratio divides the market price of a share by its current or estimated annual earnings. As of November 30, 1998, P/E ratios in the markets ranged from a low of 18.1 in Hong Kong to a high of 191.0 in Japan (at this time, the U.S. market P/E was 28.5).[6] Japanese companies have traditionally traded at very high P/E ratios in comparison with those of U.S. companies. For comparison purposes, these P/E ratios should be adjusted because of the accounting differences in reporting earnings. They also should be adjusted to reflect the fact that Japanese firms tend to report nonconsolidated statements despite the extent of cross-holding. For example, if Company A owns 20 percent of the shares of Company B, it will include in its own earnings only the dividend paid by Company B, not a proportion of Company B's earnings. In the P/E ratio of Company A, the stock price reflects the value of the holding of shares of Company B, but the earnings do not reflect the earnings of Company B. For all these reasons, French and Poterba (1991) claim that the average 1989 Japanese P/E ratio should be adjusted from 53.7 to 32.6. Other authors come up with an even bigger reduction in Japanese P/E ratios.

The Information Content of International Differences in GAAP

Investors request that companies disclose accurate information on a timely basis. The national GAAP dictates the format in which the information is disclosed. Investors would like companies to use accounting principles that provide the most informative presentation of the accounting numbers. It is difficult to tell whether an optimal accounting standard exists that would apply equally to all nations. The U.S. Securities and Exchange Commission (SEC) requests that all foreign firms listed on a public stock exchange in the United States, including Nasdaq, provide financial reports according to the U.S. GAAP (Form 10-K) or provide all necessary reconciliation information (Form 20-F). This is a controversial policy, as many foreign firms, especially medium-sized ones, do not wish to carry the burden and costs of presenting all their financial statements under two different accounting standards.

A major question for investors is determining which GAAP provides the best information. This is a difficult question to answer. Some insights can be gained by looking at the reaction of stock prices to earnings reported according to

---

[6] Schieneman (2000).

different national standards. Studies have focused on foreign firms that are dual-listed in the United States, which must also provide earnings statements calculated according to the U.S. GAAP. If the U.S. GAAP provides incremental information relative to the foreign GAAP, stock prices should show some reaction to the difference between the two reported earnings. Preliminary evidence seems to suggest that "the GAAP earnings adjustments add marginally to the ability of earnings to explain returns" (Pope and Rees, 1992, p. 190).

Another approach has been to survey international money managers to see whether they find added value in obtaining financial statements under different national GAAP. Choi and Levich (1991) surveyed a variety of capital market participants (institutional investment managers, corporate issuers, and regulators) and found that roughly half of them feel that their capital market decisions are affected by accounting diversity. However, most of them find ways to cope with this diversity. Some translate all financial statements to a common, more familiar accounting framework; others have become familiarized with foreign accounting practices and adopt a local perspective when analyzing foreign statements; others simply do not use accounting numbers in their investment decisions. Bhushan and Lessard (1992) surveyed 49 U.S.-based international money managers. All of them regard accounting harmonization as a good thing but do not find that providing reconciled accounting information is crucial; they tend to focus on valuing firms within their own markets and stress the importance of the quality and timeliness of the information disclosed.

Indeed the quality and speed of information disclosure are of paramount importance to investors. Restating the same information in a different accounting standard does not address the issue of the quality of the information disclosed or the firm's future prospects. Investment managers deciding to include a specific stock in a portfolio need to do more than simply look at past accounting data.

4   GLOBAL INDUSTRY ANALYSIS

The valuation of a common stock is usually conducted in several steps. A company belongs to a global industry and is based in a country. Hence, country and industry analysis is necessary. Companies compete against global players within their industry. Studying a company within its global industry is the primary approach to stock valuation.

With the knowledge that financial ratios from different international companies are difficult to compare, the analyst still faces the task of looking forward. What conditions in the industry prevail, and how are companies likely to compete in the future?

Within the framework of industrial organization, this section outlines the most important elements that should be looked at when conducting a company analysis in a global setting. Because a company is based in a country, we begin with a general introduction to country analysis to provide a starting point for the analysis of the company and industry.

Country Analysis

Companies tend to favor some countries in their business activities. They target some countries for their sales and base their production in only a few countries. Hence, country analysis is of importance in studying a company. In each country, economists try to monitor a large number of economic, social, and political variables, such as

▶ anticipated real growth,

▶ monetary policy,

▶ fiscal policy (including fiscal incentives for investments),

▶ wage and employment rigidities,

▶ competitiveness,

▶ social and political situations, and

▶ investment climate.

In the long run, real economic growth is probably the major influence on a national stock market. Economists focus on economic growth at two horizons:

▶ Business cycle

▶ Long-term sustainable growth

What are favorable country conditions for equity investment? There can be favorable business cycle conditions as well as favorable long-term sustainable growth conditions. If the favorable conditions are a consensus view, however, they will already be priced in the equity markets. The analyst must find a way of discerning these conditions before others do.

A high long-term sustainable growth rate in gross domestic product (GDP) is favorable, because this translates into high long-term profits and stock returns. In creating GDP and productivity growth rate expectations, the analyst will undoubtedly examine the country's savings rate, investment rate, and total factor productivity (TFP). TFP measures the efficiency with which the economy converts capital and labor into goods and services. Increased investment rates due to technical progress will increase rates of return; but the savings and investment rates themselves must be closely analyzed. A country's investments reflect replacement and capacity expansion, and influences future productivity gains. If the ratio of investment to GDP is low, then the investments are largely replacement investments; whereas a high rate suggests that capacity expansion is under way.[7] Further, a positive correlation between investment rates and subsequent GDP growth rates cannot be taken for granted, because there are other factors to consider.

The main factors that interact with the country's investment rate to affect GDP growth are the rate of growth in employment, work hours, educational levels, technological improvement, business climate, political stability, and the public or private nature of the investment. A higher long-term growth in the work force will lead to higher GDP growth just as a reduction in work hours will lead to less GDP growth. Increasing skills in the work force complement technological advances as they will both lead to higher GDP growth. A business climate of more privatization and reduced regulation is conducive to more investment. Attractive investment opportunities will also lead to more investment, although an increased propensity to invest can depress rates of return. Political stability will reduce the risk and hence increase the attractiveness of investments. Finally, private investments are more likely to be made with maximal return-on-invested capital as the objective and hence lead to higher GDP growth.

In the short term, business cycle conditions can be favorable for investments, but business cycle turning points are so difficult to predict that such predictions should only cause the analyst to make investment recommendations to slightly adjust portfolio. Business cycles represent a complex control system with many causes and interacting private and governmental decisions. For example, com-

---

[7] See Calverley (2003, p. 11).

panies invest in plant and equipment and build inventories based on expected demand but face the reality that actual demand does not continuously meet expectations. Although an investor would benefit from buying stocks at the trough of a business cycle and bonds at the peak, such perfect market timing is virtually impossible, and one might better take the approach of ignoring the country's business cycle and concentrate rather on its long-term sustainable growth rate in GDP. Nevertheless, even limited prescient ability can lead to informed adjustments to portfolio holdings. Calverley (2003, pp. 15–19) classifies the business cycle stages and attractive investment opportunities as:

▶ *Recovery:* The economy picks up from its slowdown or recession. Good investments to have are the country's cyclical stocks and commodities, followed by riskier assets as the recovery takes hold.

▶ *Early Upswing:* Confidence is up and the economy is gaining some momentum. Good investments to have are the country's stocks and also commercial and residential property.

▶ *Late Upswing:* Boom mentality has taken hold. This is not usually a good time to buy the country's stocks. The country's commodity and property prices will also be peaking. This is the time to purchase the country's bonds (yields are high) and interest rate sensitive stocks.

▶ *Economy Slows or Goes into Recession:* The economy is declining. Good investments to have are the country's bonds, which will rally (because of a drop in market interest rates), and its interest-rate-sensitive stocks.

▶ *Recession:* Monetary policy will be eased but there will be a lag before recovery. Particularly toward the end of the recession, good investments to make are the country's stocks and commodities.

Inflation is generally associated with the late upswing, and deflation is possible in a recession. Inflation effects on equity valuation are analyzed later in this reading.

Concepts in Action

Irish Central Bank Sees Uncertainty, Modest Growth Ahead

The Central Bank of Ireland said Thursday that a high degree of uncertainty and modest growth lie ahead for the Irish economy next year.

In its quarterly bulletin for autumn 2002, the bank sees gross national product growth of about 3.0% this year and 4.25% in 2003, which depends on whether the international economy picks up.

"This growth would be good by international standards and would be close to the medium-term sustainable rate for the economy," it said.

But, both the U.S. and U.K. economies, which take about four-fifths of Irish exports, are registering growth around 1.0%.

It is unlikely, therefore, that there will be an appreciable increase in Irish export demand in the short-run, the central bank said.

It said foreign direct investment is also likely to be adversely affected by the decline in stock markets and uncertainty regarding the true profitability of major multinationals.

The bank also cautioned the Irish government to ensure that the country's heady rate of inflation falls back as quickly as possible in-line with the rest of the euro zone.

Irish inflation, currently forecast at about 4.75% this year, continues to run above the European Central Bank's upper limit of 2.0% for euro-zone countries.

This, plus a stronger euro, has reduced Ireland's competitiveness and will subsequently impede employment growth in the future, the bank warned.

The European Union harmonized index of consumer prices, or HICP, forecasts Irish consumer price inflation to average about 4.25% next year owing to lower mortgage rates.

Adding more gloom to the central bank's report, Wednesday's data on third-quarter exchequer returns showed the Irish budget is back in the red for the first time since 1997.

The Irish government said it will now face a 2002 deficit of EUR750 million, compared with the EUR170 million surplus forecast nearly a year ago.

Many analysts, however, predict matters are even worse. Bloxham Stockbrokers forecasts a 2002 deficit of closer to EUR800 million, citing 20% annual growth in day-to-day spending in September.

Similarly, IIB Bank expects the government 2002 deficit to hit more than EUR1.0 billion owing to the government's high day-to-day spending.

Source: Quentin Fottrel, Dow Jones Newswires, October 3, 2002.

Business Cycle Synchronization

Stock market performance is clearly related to the business cycle and economic growth.[8] National business cycles are not fully synchronized. This lack of synchronization makes country analysis all the more important. For example, the United States witnessed a strong economic recovery in 1992, Britain started to enjoy strong economic growth in 1993, and the European continent only started to recover in 1995, but Japan's economy was still stagnant.

However, economies are becoming increasingly integrated. Growth of major economies is, in part, exported abroad. For example, growth in the United States can sustain the activity of an exporting European firm even if demand by European consumers is stagnant. But rigidities in a national economy can prevent it from quickly joining growth in a world business cycle. Studies of rigidities are important here.

What are the business cycle synchronization implications for equity valuation? Although national economies are becoming increasingly integrated with a world economy, there are so many economic variables involved that the chances of full synchronization are extremely remote. For example, within the European Union, tensions arise because governments are not free to pursue domestic and fiscal economic policies to deal with their own domestic business cycles. The experience of the 1990s and early 2000s is that the economies of Continental

---

[8] See Canova and De Nicolo (1995). An analysis of the business cycle is provided in Reilly and Brown (2003).

Europe, Japan, the United Kingdom, and the United States had markedly different GDP growth rates and entered various stages of the business cycle at different times. Recalling that any correlation less than unity supports diversification benefits, the lack of perfect business cycle synchronization is an a priori argument in favor of international diversification. If long-term GDP growth and business cycles were perfectly synchronized among countries, then one would expect a high degree of correlation between markets, especially in periods of crisis. In making investment asset-allocation decisions, one must always consider long-term expected returns, variances, and correlations. In the long term, international diversification will always be advantageous until national economies are expected to be perfectly synchronized around the world. It is difficult to imagine such a possibility. Expected returns and expected standard deviations will differ among countries with unsynchronized short-term business cycles and long-term GDP growth rates, even though investors may follow the crowd in their short term reactions to crises.

Further considerations in the divergence between countries come from a consideration of growth clubs. Baumol (1986) examined three convergence growth clubs (clubs converging to a similar steady state in terms of income per capita): western industrialized countries, centrally planned economies, and less developed countries. Regardless of the number of growth clubs, one can expect within-group convergence but inter-group divergence in TFP and income per capita. The degree of business cycle synchronicity also varies over time depending on the pattern of regional shocks and changes in economies' propagation mechanisms.

Growth Theory

Growth theory is a branch of economics that examines the role of countries in value creation. The output of a country is measured by gross domestic product (GDP), and growth theory attempts to explain the rate of GDP growth in different countries. For two countries with equal risk, portfolio managers will want to overweight the country with sustainable expected long-term GDP growth. The inputs considered are labor, capital, and productivity. In addition to labor and capital, there are also human capital and natural resources. Increases in educational levels can lead to an increase in labor skills, and discoveries of natural resources can lead to resource-based growth. Two competing economic theories attempt to shed light on the sustainable long-term growth rate of a nation.

Neoclassical growth theory assumes that the marginal productivity of capital declines as more capital is added. This is the traditional case in economics with diminishing marginal returns to input factors. *Endogenous growth theory* assumes that the marginal productivity of capital does not necessarily decline as capital is added. Technological advances and improved education of the labor force can lead to efficiency gains. Any one firm faces diminishing returns, but endogenous growth theory assumes that externalities arise when a firm develops a new technology. Thus, one firm's technical breakthrough, begets another's breakthrough, perhaps through imitation. In this case, the marginal product of capital does not decline with increasing capital per capita.

In growth theory, *steady state* is defined as the condition of no change in capital per capita. This comes about when the savings rate times GDP per capita just matches the investment required to maintain the amount of capital per capita. The rate of growth in the population plus the yearly depreciation in equipment gives a replacement rate to be multiplied by the amount of capital per capita, and this multiplication yields the investment required to maintain the amount of capital per capita.

Neoclassical growth theory predicts that the long-term level of GDP depends on the country's savings rate, but the long-term growth rate in GDP does not depend on the savings rate. This is because a steady state is reached, and this steady state is reached, because additions to the capital stock provide smaller and smaller increases to GDP and consequently to savings (the savings rate times GDP). In the context of endogenous growth theory, steady state may never be reached, because the ability to avoid a decline in the marginal product of capital means there is no necessary decline in savings as capital is increased. Thus, endogenous growth theory predicts that the long-term growth rate in GDP depends on the savings rate.

Equity valuation implications are different for countries experiencing neoclassical versus endogenous growth. If a country is experiencing neoclassical growth and its savings rate increases, there would be an increase in dividends as the new level of GDP is reached, but not an increase in the dividend growth rate. For a country experiencing endogenous growth with cascading breakthroughs, however, there would be an increase in both dividends and the dividend growth rate.

In an open world economy, it is important to ascertain whether growth is caused by an increased mobilization of inputs or by efficiency gains. Input-driven growth is necessarily limited. For example, many developing countries have witnessed high growth rates because of capital flows from abroad, but face diminishing returns in the absence of productivity gains. National sustainable growth rates require careful examination.

Concepts in Action

Nearly 30 Transnational Corporations Richer than Many Nations, UN Study Finds

Twenty-nine of the world's 100 largest economic entities are transnational corporations, according to a new list produced by the United Nations Conference on Trade and Development (UNCTAD) ranking both states and corporations.

Exxon Mobile, with a "value added" worth of $63 billion, is bigger in economic size than Pakistan, while General Motors, worth $56 billion, outpaces both Peru and New Zealand, according to the list.

UNCTAD also reports that Ford Motor and DaimlerChrysler, with value added of over $42 billion, are both larger than Nigeria, which is worth just $41 billion. Kuwait, at $38 billion, is outranked by General Electric. And Honda, Nissan, and Toshiba all have more value than Syria.

The rising importance of transnational corporations in the global economy is revealed in other statistics compiled by UNCTAD. The agency reports that the 100 largest companies accounted for 3.5 percent of global gross domestic product in 1990—a figure that jumped to 4.3 percent in 2000. There were 24 corporations in the 1990 combined top 100 list of companies and countries, compared with 29 in 2000.

Source: UN News Centre, August 13, 2002.

The Limitation of the Country Concept in Financial Analysis

The distinction between countries and companies is misleading in some respects. Both types of economic entities produce and market a portfolio of products. Indeed, some companies are bigger in economic size than some countries.

Many companies compete globally. The national location of their headquarters is not a determinant variable. Many multinational corporations realize most of their sales and profits in foreign countries. So, an analysis of the economic situation of the country of their headquarters is not of great importance. In Reading 5, we showed that many national stock markets are dominated by a few multinationals. For example, Nokia market capitalization is larger than the sum of that of all other Finnish firms. The top ten Swiss multinational firms account for more than 70 percent of the Swiss stock exchange. But these companies do most of their business outside of their home country, so their valuation should be based on the global competition they face in their industry, not on the state of their home economy.

Industry Analysis: Return Expectation Elements

To achieve excess equity returns on a risk-adjusted basis, an investor must find companies that can earn return on equity (ROE) above the required rate of return and do this on a sustained basis. For this reason, global industry analysis centers on an examination of sources of growth and sustainability of competitive advantage. Growth must be distinguished from level. A high profit level may yield high current cash flows for valuation purposes, but there is also the question of how these cash flows will grow. Continued reinvestment opportunities in positive net present value investment opportunities will create growth. Curtailment of research and development expenditures may yield high current cash flows at the expense of future growth.

An analyst valuing a company within its global industry should study several key elements. Following are some important conceptual issues.

Demand Analysis

Value analysis begins with an examination of demand conditions. The concepts of complements and substitutes help, but demand analysis is quite complex. Usually, surveys of demand as well as explanatory regressions are used to try to estimate demand. Demand is the target for all capacity, location, inventory, and production decisions. Often, the analyst tries to find a leading indicator to help give some forecast of demand.

In the global context, *demand* means *worldwide demand*. One cannot simply define the automobile market as a domestic market. A starting point, then, is a set of forecasts of global and country-specific GDP figures. The analyst will want to estimate the sensitivity of sales to global and national GDP changes.

Country analysis is important for demand analysis, because most companies tend to focus on specific regions. Most European car manufacturers tend to sell and produce outside of Europe, but the European car market is their primary market. An increase in demand for cars in Europe will affect them more than it will affect Japanese car producers.

Value Creation

Sources of value come from using inputs to produce outputs in the value chain. The *value chain* is the set of transformations in moving from raw materials to product or service delivery. This chain can involve many companies and countries, some providing raw materials, some producing intermediate goods, some producing finished consumer goods, and some delivering finished goods to the consumer. From the point of view of an intermediate goods producer, basic raw materials are considered to be *upstream* in the value chain, and transformations closer to the consumer are considered *downstream*.

Within the value chain, each transformation adds value. Value chain analysis can be used to determine how much value is added at each step. Indeed, some countries have a value-added tax. The value added at each transformation stage is partly a function of four major factors:

▶ *The learning (experience) curve:* As companies produce more output, they gain experience, so that the cost per unit produced declines.

▶ *Economies of scale:* As a company expands, its fixed costs may be spread over a larger output, and average costs decline over a range of output.

▶ *Economies of scope:* As a company produces related products, experience and reputation with one product may spill over to another product.

▶ *Network externalities:* Some products and services gain value as more consumers use them, so that they are able to share something popular.

Equity valuation implications come from an analysis of the industry's value chain and each company's strategy to exploit current and future profit opportunities within the chain. For company managers, Christensen, Raynor, and Verlinden (2001) recommend a strategy of predicting profit migration within the industry's value chain. For example, they break the computer industry down into value chain stages: equipment, materials, components, product design, assembly, operating system, application software, sales and distribution, and field service. In the early days of the computer industry, vertically integrated manufacturers delivered the entire value chain. The advent of the personal computer led to specialization within each stage and profits migrated to stages such as components and operating systems. For the analyst also, the strategy of predicting dividends and dividend growth rates must be based on profit migration in the value chain. The risk can be gauged from the degree of competition within the stage—the more the competition, the more the risk. The ability of companies to compete at each stage will be enhanced by their learning curve progress, economies of scale or scope, and network externalities.

Christensen et al. also point out that industries often evolve from vertical integration to disintegration. If an industry becomes too fragmented, however, consolidation pressures will come from resource bottlenecks as well as the continuing search for economies of scale. During the industry's life cycle, tension between disintegration and consolidation will require the company and the analyst to constantly monitor company positions in the profit migration cycle.

Industry Life Cycle

Traditionally, the industry life cycle is broken down into stages from pioneering development to decline. Of course, one must be careful in industry definition. If railroads were defined as an *industry*, we would see a global industry life cycle. Defining the industry as transportation provides a different picture. In any case, industry life cycles are normally categorized by rates of growth in sales. The stages of growth can clearly vary in length.

1. Pioneering development is the first stage and has a low but slowly increasing industry sales growth rate. Substantial development costs and acceptance by only early adopters can lead to low profit margins.

2. Rapid accelerating growth is the second stage, and the industry sales growth rate is still modest but is rapidly increasing. High profit margins are possible because firms from outside the new industry may face barriers to entering the newly established markets.

3. Mature growth is the third stage and has a high but more modestly increasing industry sales growth rate. The entry of competitors lowers profit margins, but the return on equity is high.

One would expect that somewhere in stage 2 or 3 the industry sales growth rate would move above the GDP growth rate in the economy.

4. Stabilization and market maturity is the fourth stage and has a high but only slowly increasing sales growth rate. The sales growth rate has not yet begun to decline, but increasing capacity and competition may cause returns on equity to decline to the level of average returns on equity in the economy.

5. Deceleration of growth and decline is the fifth stage with a decreasing sales growth rate. At this stage, the industry may experience overcapacity, and profit margins may be completely eroded.

One would expect that somewhere in stage 5, the industry sales growth rate would fall back to the GDP growth rate and then decline below it. (This cannot happen in stage 4 where the sales growth is still increasing.) The position of an industry in its life cycle should be judged on a global basis.

Competition Structure

One of the first steps in analyzing an industry is the determination of the amount of industry concentration. If the industry is fragmented, many firms compete, and the theories of competition and product differentiation are most applicable. With more concentration and fewer firms in the industry, oligopolistic competition and game theories become more important. Finally, the case of one firm is the case in which the theory of monopoly applies.

In analyzing industry concentration, two methods are normally used. One method is the N firm concentration ratio: the combined market share of the largest N firms in the industry. For example, a market in which the three largest firms have a combined share of 80 percent would indicate largely oligopolistic competition. A related but more precise measure is the Herfindahl index, the sum of the squared market shares of the firms in the industry. Letting M_i be the market share of an individual firm, the index is $H = M_1^2 + M_2^2 + \ldots + M_N^2$.

If two firms have a 15 percent market share each and one has a 70 percent market share, $H = 0.15^2 + 0.15^2 + 0.7^2 = 0.535$.

The Herfindahl index has a value that is always smaller than one. A small index indicates a competitive industry with no dominant players. If all firms have an equal share, $H = N(1/N^2) = 1/N$, and the reciprocal of the index shows the number of firms in the industry. When the firms have unequal shares, the reciprocal of the index indicates the "equivalent" number of firms in the industry. Using our example above, we find that the market structure is equivalent to having 1.87 firms of the same size:

$$\frac{1}{H} = \frac{1}{(0.15^2 + 0.15^2 + 0.70^2)} = \frac{1}{0.535} = 1.87$$

One can classify the competition structure of the industry according to this ratio.

In practice, the equity analyst will see both the N firm concentration ratio and the Herfindahl index. The analyst is searching for indicators of the likely degree of cooperation versus competition within the industry. Although the balance between cooperation and competition is dynamic and changing, the higher the N firm concentration ratio and the higher the Herfindahl index, the less likely it is that there is cut-throat competition and the more likely it is that companies will cooperate.

The advantage of the N firm concentration ratio is that it provides an intuitive sense of industry competition. If the analyst knows that the seven largest firms have a combined share of less than 15 percent, he or she immediately knows that the industry is extremely fragmented and thus more risky because of competitive pressures and the likely lack of cooperation.

The Herfindahl index (H) has the advantage of greater discrimination because it reflects all firms in the industry and it gives greater weight to the companies with larger market shares. An H below 0.1 indicates an unconcentrated industry, an H of 0.1 to 0.18 indicates moderate concentration, and an H above 0.18 indicates high concentration. A high Herfindahl index can also indicate the presence of a market leader with a higher share than others, another indication of likely coordination as the leader might impose discipline on the industry.

Suppose the analyst is comparing two industries:

Market Shares in Industry A	Market Shares in Industry B
One firm has 45%	Four firms have 15% each
Three firms have 5% each	Four firms have 10% each
Ten firms have 4% each	
Four firm concentration ratio is 60%	Four firm concentration ratio is 60%
Herfindahl index is 0.23	Herfindahl index is 0.13

Even though the four firm concentration ratios are the same for both industries, the Herfindahl index indicates that industry A is highly concentrated, but industry B is only moderately concentrated.

Competitive Advantage

In his book, *The Competitive Advantage of Nations*,[9] Michael Porter used the notions of economic geography that different locations have different competitive advantages. National factors that can lead to a competitive advantage are

- ▶ factor conditions such as human capital, perhaps measured by years of schooling;
- ▶ demand conditions such as the size and growth of the domestic market;
- ▶ related supplier and support industries such as the computer software industry to support the hardware industry; and
- ▶ strategy, structure, and rivalry such as the corporate governance, management practices, and the financial climate.

---

[9] Porter (1990).

Competitive Strategies

A competitive strategy is a set of actions that a firm is taking to optimize its future competitive position. In *Competitive Advantage,*[10] Porter distinguishes three generic competitive strategies:

▶ *Cost leadership:* The firm seeks to be the low-cost producer in its industry.

▶ *Differentiation:* The firm seeks to provide product benefits that other firms do not provide.

▶ *Focus:* The firm targets a niche with either a cost or a benefit (differentiation) focus.

Equity valuation analysis in large part is analysis of the probability of success of company strategies. Analysts will consider the company's commitment to a strategy as well as the likely responses of its competitors. Is the company a tough competitor that is likely to survive a war of attrition? Is it likely that a Nash equilibrium will hold, in which each company adopts a strategy to leave itself with the best outcome regardless of the competitor's strategy and, by doing this, causes a reduction in the size of the total reward to both?

Co-opetition and the Value Net

Co-opetition refers to cooperation along the value chain and is an application of game theory. Brandenberger and Nalebuff[11] developed the concept of the value net as the set of participants involved in producing value along the value chain: the suppliers, customers, competitors, and firms producing complementary goods and services. Although these participants compete with each other, they can also cooperate to produce mutually beneficial outcomes. In this respect, co-opetition is an application of cooperative game theory.

In the context of equity valuation, co-opetition analysis is an important element of risk analysis. Cooperating participants in a good economy may become staunch competitors in a poor economy. If a company's abnormal profits depend on co-opetition, those profits are riskier than if they are the result of a purely competitive environment. In a good economy, a company may outsource some of its production to cooperating value net participants who may build capabilities based on lucrative long-term contracts. In a poor economy, however, no new contracts may be forthcoming.

Sector Rotation

Many commercial providers sell reports on the relative performance of industries or sectors over the business cycle, and sector rotation is a popular investment-timing strategy. Some investors put more weight on industries entering a profitable portion of their role in the business cycle. Certainly industries behave differently over the business cycle. Because consumer cyclical industries (durables and nondurables) correlate highly with the economy as a whole, these industries do well in the early and middle growth portion of the business cycle. Defensive consumer staples (necessities) maintain their profitability during recessions. Nevertheless, a successful **sector rotation strategy** depends on an intensive analysis of

---

[10] Porter (1985).

[11] Brandenberger and Nalebuff (1996).

the industry and faces many pitfalls. An upturn in the economy and the demand for industry products do not automatically mean an increase in profits, because factors such as the status of industry capacity, the competitive structure, the lead time to increase capacity, and the general supply/demand conditions in the industry also have an impact on profits.

Indicators of the various stages of the business cycle are complex. We have already seen that different sectors, for example, cyclical sectors, will do well at various stages of the business cycle and that the five stages are:

▶ *Recovery:* The economy picks up from its slowdown or recession.

▶ *Early Upswing:* Confidence is up and the economy is gaining some momentum.

▶ *Late Upswing:* Boom mentality has taken hold.

▶ *Economy Slows or Goes into Recession:* The economy is declining.

▶ *Recession:* Monetary policy will be eased but there will be a lag before recovery.

Industry Analysis: Risk Elements

To achieve excess equity returns on a risk-adjusted basis, investors must be able to distinguish sources of risk in the investments they make. For example, an increase in ROE may be attributable solely to an increase in leverage (gearing). This increased leverage raises the financial risk and hence the required rate of return; the increased ROE then does not yield an excess risk-adjusted return. Although return expectations can be established by evaluating firm strategies within the industry, the analyst must always examine the risk that the strategy may be flawed or that assumptions about competition and co-opetition may hold only in good economic environment. What seems to be an attractive strategy in good times, can turn into a very dangerous one in bad times. The risks can differ widely, not only between firms in the same industry, but also across industries. Some industries are more sensitive to technological change and the business cycle than are others. So, the outlined growth factors that affect return expectations should also be taken into account to assess industry risk.

Ultimately, firms that follow high-risk strategies in an industry that is also risky will have a higher ex ante stock market risk, and this should be incorporated in expected risk measures. Ex post, this stock market risk will eventually be measured by looking at volatility and covariance measures.

Market Competition

Microeconomics[12] examines the various types of competition in markets. The question is always to look at price versus average cost. Particularly with oligopolies and monopolies, game theory helps to discern the likely success or failure of corporate strategies. Preservation of competitive position and competitive advantage often involves entry-deterring or exit-promoting strategies. *Limit pricing* is pricing below average cost to deter entry. Similarly, *holding excess capacity* can deter entry. **Predatory pricing** is pricing below average cost to drive others out of the industry. Any valuation of an individual company must examine the strategy contest in which companies in the industry are engaged. Risks are always present that the company's strategy will not sustain its competitive advantage.

---

[12] See Besanko, Dranove, and Shanley (2000).

Value Chain Competition

In producing goods and services of value, companies compete not just in markets, but also along the value chain. Suppliers can choose to compete rather than simply cooperate with the intermediate company. Labor, for example, may want some of the profit that a company is earning. In lean times, labor may make concessions, but in good times labor may want a larger share of the profits. Buyers may organize to wrest some of the profit from the company.

A major issue in value chain analysis is whether labor is unionized. Japanese automobile companies producing in the United States face lower production costs because of their ability to employ non-unionized workers. Union relations are a major factor in valuing airline companies worldwide.

Suppliers of commodity raw materials have less ability to squeeze profits out of a downstream company than do suppliers of differentiated intermediate products. Companies may manage their value chain competition by vertically integrating (buying upstream or downstream) or, for example, by including labor in their ownership structure.

Co-opetition risks are presented by the possibility that the company's supply may be held up or that its distributors may find other sources of products and services. Suppose a firm acts as a broker between producers and distributors and outsources its distribution services by selling long-term distribution contracts to producers, thus also keeping distributors happy. Because of the low fixed costs involved in brokering, this business strategy should make the firm less sensitive to recession than a distribution company with heavy fixed costs. But what if producers are unwilling to enter long-term distribution contracts during a recession?

In his book, Porter (1985) discussed five industry forces, as well as the generic competitive strategies mentioned earlier. Porter's so-called five forces analysis can be seen as an examination of the risks involved in the value chain. Oster (1999) provides a useful analysis of the five forces, and we show her insights as bulleted points below. In some cases, we slightly modify or extend them.

Rivalry Intensity

This is the degree of competition among companies in the industry. For example, airline competition is more intense now with more carriers and open skies agreements between countries than in the days of heavier regulation with fewer carriers limited to domestic companies. Coordination can make rivalry much less intense. The analyst must be alert for possible changes in coordination and rivalry intensity that are not yet reflected in equity prices.

► Intense rivalry among firms in an industry reduces average profitability.

► In an industry in which coordination yields excess profits (prices exceed marginal costs), there are market share incentives for individual companies to shade (slightly cut) prices as they weigh the benefits and costs of coordination versus shading.

► Large numbers of companies in a market reduce coordination opportunities.

► Rivalry is generally more intense when the major companies are all similarly sized, and no one large company can impose discipline on the industry.

► Generally, coordination is easier if companies in the market are similar. All gravitate to a mutually agreeable focal point, the solution that similar companies will naturally discern.

► Industries which have substantial specific (cannot be used for other purposes) assets exhibit high barriers to exit and intensified rivalry.

▶ Variability in demand creates more rivalry within an industry. For example, high fixed costs and cyclical demand creates capacity mismatches and price cutting from excess capacity.

Substitutes

This is the threat of products or services that are substitutes for the products or services of the industry. For example, teleconferencing is a substitute for travel. The analyst must be alert for possible changes in substitutes that are not yet reflected in equity prices.

▶ Substitute products constrain the ability of firms in the industry to raise their prices substantially.

▶ Industries without excess capacity or intense rivalry can present attractive investment opportunities; but substitute products can reduce the attraction by constraining the ability of firms in the industry to substantially raise their prices.

Buyer Power

This is the bargaining power of buyers of the producer's products or services. For example, car rental agencies have more bargaining power with automobile manufacturers than have individual consumers. The analyst must be alert for possible changes in buyer power that are not yet reflected in equity prices.

▶ The larger the number of buyers and the smaller their individual purchases, the less the bargaining power.

▶ Standardization of products increases buyer power because consumers can easily switch between suppliers.

▶ If buyers can integrate backwards, this increases their bargaining power because they would cut out the supplier if they choose to integrate.

▶ Greater buyer power makes an equity investment in the producer less attractive because of lower profit margins.

Supplier Power

This is the bargaining power of suppliers to the producers. For example, traditional aircraft manufacturers lost supplier power when niche players entered the market and began producing short-haul jets. The analyst must be alert for possible changes in supplier power that are not yet reflected in equity prices.

▶ The more suppliers there are for the industry, the less is the supplier power.

▶ Standardized raw materials (commodities) reduce supplier power because the supplier has no differentiation or quality advantage.

▶ If buyers can integrate backwards, this reduces supplier power because the buyer would cut out the supplier if it chooses to integrate.

▶ Greater supplier power makes an equity investment in the producer less attractive because of the possibility of a squeeze on profits.

New Entrants

This is the threat of new entrants into the industry. For example, a European consortium entered the aircraft manufacturing industry and has become a major company now competing globally. In addition, a Brazilian and a Canadian company have entered the short-haul aircraft market. The analyst must be alert for possible changes in new entrant threats that are not yet reflected in equity prices.

▶ The higher the payoffs the more likely will be the entry, all else equal.

▶ Barriers to entry are industry characteristics which reduce the rate of entry below that needed to remove excess profits.

▶ Expectations of incumbent reactions influence entry.

▶ Exit costs influence the rate of entry.

▶ All else equal, the larger the volume needed to reach minimal unit costs, the greater the difference between pre- and post-entry price (the increase in industry capacity would drive down prices), and thus the less likely entry is to occur.

▶ The steeper the cost curve, the less likely is entry at a smaller volume than the minimal unit cost volume.

▶ Long-term survival at a smaller than minimal unit cost volume requires an offsetting factor to permit a company to charge a price premium. Product differentiation and a monopoly in location are two possible offsets.

▶ Excess capacity deters entry by increasing the credibility of price cutting as an entry response by incumbents.

▶ Occasional actions that are unprofitable in the short run can increase a company's credibility for price cutting to deter entry, giving an entry deterring reputation as a tough incumbent.

▶ An incumbent contract to meet the price of any responsible rival can deter entry.

▶ Patents and licenses can prevent free entry from eliminating excess profits in an industry. They deter entry.

▶ Learning curve effects can deter entry unless new entrants can appropriate the experience of the incumbents. For example, Boeing learned about metal fatigue from the British experience of accidents with the Comet, the first commercial jet airliner.

▶ Pioneering brands can dominate the industry and deter entry when network externalities exist and when consumers find it costly to make product mistakes.

▶ High exit costs discourage entry. A primary determinant of high exit costs is asset specificity and the irreversibility of capital investments.

After presenting the insights above, Oster follows up with an excellent presentation of many related topics: strategic groups within industries, competition in global markets, issues of organizational structure and design, competitive advantage, corporate diversification, and the effect of rival behavior. Indeed, industry analysis is a complex subject as the analyst attempts to deduce the valuation implications of corporate strategies.

Government Participation

Government subsidies to companies can seed companies in the early stages and can also give companies an unfair advantage in steady state. There is extra uncertainty for a company competing head to head with one subsidized by its home country. Governments also participate by supporting their domestic country stock prices in one way or another. This creates uncertainty about future policy in addition to the normal risk associated with cash flows.

Governments participate indirectly by their involvement in the social contract. In the United States, automobile companies bear the costs of defined benefit pension funds. Japanese automobile companies do not bear these costs because of government-sponsored pension schemes. Some European governments dealt with the possibility of increased unemployment by shortening the work week to keep employment spread out. Such government policy may make a European company less competitive.

Governments control competition. Open-skies laws allow foreign airlines to operate between domestic cities. Closed-skies laws in the past prevented Canadian carriers from operating between U.S. cities. Closed-skies laws have also been a factor in the Eurozone. Risks are presented by the uncertainty involved in trying to predict government policy.

Risks and Covariance

Investors care about stock market risk, that is, the uncertainty about future stock prices. Risk is usually viewed at two levels. The total risk of a company or an industry is the first level of risk, and it is usually measured by the standard deviation of stock returns of that company or industry. But part of this risk can be diversified away in a portfolio. So, the second level of risk is measured by the covariance with the aggregate economy, which tells how the returns of a company vary with global market indexes. Although this risk is usually measured by the beta from regressions of company returns against market returns, it is useful to note those beta changes over time as a function of business cycle conditions and shifting competition within the industry.

When analyzing an industry, the analyst is faced with a continuing challenge of determining diversifiable versus nondiversifiable risk. Because future cash flow and return covariance must be predicted in order to estimate the firm and industry's beta, simple reliance on past regressions is not sufficient. Part of the risk from a strategy failure or a change from co-opetition to competition may be firm-specific and diversifiable. At the same time, part of the risk may be nondiversifiable, because it involves fundamental shifts in industry structure.

In order to manage a global equity portfolio, the risk of a company is usually summarized by its exposure to various risk factors. The last section of this reading is devoted to global risk factor models.

Global Industry Analysis in Practice: An Example

In the following analysis of the transportation and logistics industry, several global industry analysis factors are considered. Indeed, such analyses usually include a discussion of the competitive structure of the industry, the strategies of the players, and a comparative ratio analysis of companies within the industry.

Concepts In Action

Transportation and Logistics

Logistics remains a growth market . . . . the Asian logistics market should be a growth driver. For the individual logistics segments, we expect the following compound annual growth rates for the period 2002 to 2010: air freight: +5.9%; sea freight: +5.6%; overland transport: +3.3%; and value-added services/logistics outsourcing: 11%–12%.

Average 2003e price/earnings ratios of just below 10 and a price/book ratio of around 1.2 indicate attractive valuation levels for the sector. DCF and an economic profit analysis support this thesis. Higher valuation levels are strongly dependent on macroeconomic expectations. We will see ongoing dynamic changes in industry structures that are driven by positioning and repositioning questions. Related to this is the continuing consolidation process in the highly fragmented logistics market.

Attractive Sector Growth
Air freight: business is expected to grow until 2010 by 5.9% (CAGR)

In the period between 1981 and 2001, transport traffic in cross-border air freight increased at an average multiple of 2.5 times global GDP growth. In the last five years, the average multiple was much lower at 1.2 (3.4% p.a.[13]), because there were two slumps in a short period with the economic crisis in Asia and the terrorist attacks in the U.S. It is noticeable that the growth trend has been slowing since the mid-1980s and that the top peaks have declined steadily since 1985.

For the period 2002 to 2010, 5.9% compound annual growth amounts to a multiple of 2.1. This is lower than the 1981–2001 average multiple. The declining growth trend in air freight traffic is extrapolated in the long-term projection and growth dips were perpetuated with a weaker annual growth dynamic. In the event of economic crisis and open hostilities, the multiples are expected to be sharply lower in the corresponding years.

Sea freight: expect a volume growth of 5.6% (CAGR)

That translates into an average multiple of 2.0 times global GDP. In the past, the growth of container handling has significantly exceeded GDP growth. This outperformance is due, on the one hand, to a rising use of containers in total sea freight tonnage—in eight years it has doubled from 5% to 10%—and, on the other, to more frequent turnover per container.

Land transport: up to 2010 overland transport in Europe is expected to increase by 3.3% p.a.

The reluctance of many companies to penetrate this market is understandable given the competitive pressure and especially the resources needed to create a Europe-wide network. Compared with sea and air freight as well as value-added services, historical growth is more modest: between 1970 and 1998, ton kilometers transported by road (in the EU) increased by an average of 4% per year with a falling trend.

Continental Europe still has ground to make up on outsourcing

In the field of value-added services (VAS), we expect further potential to catch up in outsourcing value-added services in Continental Europe. A

---

[13] The abbreviation p.a. means per annum, or annually.

comparison of the different outsourcing levels in the UK (currently 37%) and the states of Continental Europe (29%) suggests that the latter has a lot of ground to make up. We expect the overall European outsourcing ratio to come close to approaching the UK level by 2005. For the UK market, we project no significant increase in the outsourcing ratio.

Consolidation momentum driven by an extremely fragmented market

The logistics market is one of the most fragmented markets and the structure of the market will change over the coming years. Besides the search for economies of scale, resource bottlenecks are resulting in acquisition pressure. This relates to management, employees, warehousing capacities and other operating structures. In air freight, the 10 largest forwarding companies have a combined share of less than 40%. The seafreight market is even more fragmented: the seven largest transportation companies have a combined market share of less than 15%.

The most fragmented market is European overland transport. Danzas and Schenker are the leading providers, each with a market share of 2.2%. Apart from the French company Geodis (1.5%) and the unlisted Dachser (1.0%), the market shares of the other providers are less than one-tenth of a percent. In a market undergoing dynamic change, the big players and the innovative niche players are expected to win additional market share. The companies "stuck in the middle" will run into problems.

Furthermore, state-owned or formerly state-owned companies (Deutsche Post, TPG, SNCF, La Poste, Deutsche Bahn, etc.) are driving the consolidation process. They are looking into portfolio changes in order to improve their core business. We assume the sale of Stinnes will rekindle the consolidation pressure.

Trend towards consolidation accompanied by difficult questions of positioning

The consolidation trend and the following market pressure force companies to continuously monitor their positioning. Within the European sample, we think Exel is the strategy leader. But the UK company cannot rest on its laurels because some competitors are in close pursuit. When looking at the positioning of companies, there are four major issues:

▶ The high-volume players are attempting to achieve the optimal mix by filling in the network gaps and upgrading their portfolio of services;

▶ the outsourcing-driven business models are expanding their range of services in order to become more deeply involved in the customer's value chain within the framework of outsourcing;

▶ companies caught between these areas must take care not to be backed into a corner; and

▶ regional providers have little prospect of closing the gap to the big players; because they lack the financial strength to close the gap, they must rely on cooperation agreements or they will be purchased.

Valuation multiples in line with economic projections

The performance of logistics stocks hinges to a great extent on the market's expectations for the economy. Such a statement is underpinned by correlating the performance of our HVB logistics index (excluding postal service companies), HVB-Logidexx, with the economic indicator provided by the price of copper, which trades every day. The susceptibility of the individual companies to cyclical fluctuation should be assessed on the basis of their cost and contract-business structures, outsourcing focus, the cyclical resistance of the sector in general, as well as their diversification by segment, customer and regional breakdown.

A look at these parameters indicates that Tibbett & Britten and Kuehne & Nagel have defensive capabilities within this pan-European sampling, while UK-based Exel is highly susceptible to cyclical fluctuation because of its exposure to the high tech and U.S. markets. We believe that a recovery by Exel is for the most part already factored into the price of its stock. We favor the stock of Tibbett & Britten and Kuehne & Nagel at present, both of which are likely to show more gains in market share.

A turnaround in the relative performance of the HVB-Logidexx and the Euro STOXX 50 index set in after September 11. Sentiment turned around: multiples of asset value—enterprise value/capital employed and price/book ratio—in some cases of well over one were exaggerated and did not correspond to either medium-term projections of earnings or forecast added-value margins. Upbeat guidance issued by Kuehne & Nagel, T&B, and Stinnes, among others, resulted in the Logidexx's outperformance of the Euro STOXX.

Opinions differ at present over the logistics business. We still expect to see a macroeconomic turnaround in the second half of the year. The uptrend in cargo volume in both Asia and Europe, which has been gathering speed since April, underpins this view. The risk lies in the fact that the brightening picture in terms of cargo volume, driven partly by companies restocking, might be a mere flash in the pan.

First up in the clouds, then down in the dumps

D.Logistics and Thiel, Europe's former high flyers, have seen both their operating profits and stock prices plunge. This has had a negative impact on sentiment vis-à-vis the sector. The capital market is increasingly coming to the realization that the majority of their problems are specific to these companies. They proved incapable of adjusting their internal structures to the pace of acquisition. The assumption that their business models, which are focused on logistics outsourcing, are resistant to cyclical fluctuation proved to be erroneous. What emerged was rather that customers are not prepared in tough times to enter into major contracts to outsource.

Adding value: looking at the margin alone is being too short-sighted

When looking at the returns on capital employed (2003), we find significant differences within the industry. Comparing Exel and Kuehne & Nagel makes it clear that looking at the margin alone does not provide guidance, because capital turnover can vary substantially due to the different business models. Kuehne & Nagel, for example, leads the ocean freight market but does not own a single vessel.

Compared with Exel, K&N's proportion of brokerage business is much greater, meaning that capital turnover on a low base of capital employed is substantially higher. A higher ROCE in particular reflects this. We think that Exel will grow at a stronger pace in the future and that it will boost its value driver of capital employed—without diluting its value-added margin—more quickly than K&N.

An attractive sector valuation

In our opinion, the European logistics stocks are favorably valued in fundamental terms. We would like to focus on the NAV multiples. We think Stinnes will be acquired without a valuation premium; one indication of this is the 2003 price/book ratio of 1.2x. On the basis of EV/capital employed, including goodwill, we calculate a multiple of 0.7x for the sample; even if all of the goodwill is subtracted, this value comes to 1.0x. A value of 1.0x means that the company will not create value in the future (value-added margin equals zero). But in fact, the value-added margins (ROCE minus WACC) are on average roughly three percentage points above the capital costs.

Things will remain exciting

Additional expected IPOs, such as that of Panalpina's, Deutsche Bahn's potential either full or partial access to the capital market, UPS' full war chest, and Kuehne & Nagel's major scope for investment will keep the sector on the edge. Deregulation of postal markets, moreover, will provide a further source of conjecture, change and speculative appeal. A favorably priced growth market is just waiting for the economy to turn up.

Source: Markus Hesse and Christian Cohrs, *The Euromoney: International Equity Capital Markets Handbook* (Adrian Hornbrook: Colchester, Essex, U.K.), 2003, pp. 15–21. (For further information about *Euromoney Handbooks,* visit www.euromoney-yearbooks.com.)

EQUITY ANALYSIS   5

Because it should be forward looking, equity analysis needs to be carried out within the context of the country and the industry. Reasonable prediction of cash flows and risk is required to provide useful inputs to the valuation process.

Industry Valuation or Country Valuation

A frequently asked question is whether a company should primarily be valued relative to the global industry to which it belongs or relative to other national companies listed on its home stock market. Indeed, many corporations are now very active abroad and, even at home, face worldwide competition. So, there are really two aspects to this question:

▶ Should the *financial analysis* of a company be conducted within its global industry?

▶ Do the stock prices of companies within the same global industry move together worldwide, so that the *relative valuation* of a company's equity should be conducted within the global industry rather than within its home stock market?

The answer to the first question is a clear yes. Prospective earnings of a company should be estimated taking into account the competition it is facing. In most cases, this competition is international as well as domestic. Most large corporations derive a significant amount of their cash flows from foreign sales and operations, so their competition is truly global.

The answer to the second question raised is less obvious. At a given point in time, different industries face different growth prospects, and that is true worldwide. Furthermore, different industries exhibit different sensitivities to unexpected changes in worldwide economic conditions. This implies that the stock market valuation should differ across industries. Some industries, such as "electronic components" or "health and personal care," have large P/E and P/BV ratios while other industries, such as "energy" and "materials," have low P/E and P/BV ratios. The major question related to the importance of industry factors in stock prices, however, is whether a company has more in common with other companies in the same global industry than with other companies in the same country. By "more in common," we mean that its stock price tends to move together with that of other companies, and to be influenced by similar events. Before presenting some empirical evidence on the relative importance of country and industry factor in stock pricing, let's stress some caveats:

▶ Any industry classification is open to questions. MSCI, S&P, FTSE, and Dow Jones produce global industry indexes with different industry classification systems. The number of industry groups identified differs. It is not easy to assign each company to a single industry group. Some industry activities are clearly identified (e.g., producing automobiles), but others are not so clearcut. It is not unusual to see the same company assigned to different industry groups by different classification systems. Some large corporations have diversified activities that cut across industry groups. Standard and Poor's and Morgan Stanley Capital International have recently designed a common Global Industry Classification Standard (GICS). The GICS system consists of four levels of detail: 10 sectors, 23 industry groupings, 59 industries, and 122 subindustries. At the most specific level of detail, an individual company is assigned to a single GICS subindustry, according to the definition of its principal business activity determined by S&P and MSCI. The hierarchical nature of the GICS structure will automatically assign the company's industry, industry group, and sector. There are currently over 25,000 companies globally that have been classified.

▶ The answer could be industry-specific. Some industries are truly global (e.g., oil companies), while others are less so (e.g., leisure and tourism). However, competition is becoming global in most, if not all, industries. For example, travel agencies have become regional, if not global, through a wave of mergers and acquisitions. Supermarket chains now cover many continents, and many retailers capitalize on their brand names globally.

▶ The answer could be period-specific. There could be periods in which global industry factors dominate, and other periods in which national factors are more important (desynchronized business cycles).

► The answer could be company-specific. Some companies in an industry group have truly international activities with extensive global competition, while others are mostly domestic in all respects. Small Swiss commercial banks with offices located only in one province (canton) of Switzerland have little in common with large global banks (even Crédit Suisse or UBS).

► Even if industry factors dominate, two opposing forces could be at play.[14] A worldwide growth in the demand for goods produced could benefit all players within the industry. However, competition also means that if one major player is highly successful, it will be at the expense of other major players in the industry. For example, Japanese car manufacturers could grow by extensively exporting to the United States, but it will be at the expense of U.S. car manufacturers. The stock price of Nissan would therefore be negatively correlated with that of GM or Ford.

Despite these caveats, all empirical studies find that industry factors have grown in importance in stock price valuation.[15] Global industry factors tend now to dominate country factors, but country factors are still of significant importance. Companies should be valued relative to their industry, but country factors should not be neglected, particularly when conducting a risk analysis.

Two industry valuation approaches are traditionally used: ratio analysis and discounted cash flow models.

Global Financial Ratio Analysis

As already mentioned, global industry financial analysis examines each company in the industry against the industry average. One well-accepted approach to this type of analysis is the DuPont model. (It may be better to think of this as an *approach* of decomposing return ratios, but this approach is usually called the DuPont model.) The basic technique of the DuPont model is to explain ROE or return on assets (ROA) in terms of its contributing elements. For example, we will see that ROA can be explained in terms of net profit margin and asset turnover. The analysis begins with five contributing elements, and these elements appear in several variations, depending on what most interests the analyst. The five elements reflect the financial and operating portions of the income statement as linked to the assets on the balance sheet and the equity supporting those assets. In the analysis here, past performance is being examined. Because income is a flow earned over a period of time, but the balance sheet reflects a balance (stock) at only one point in time, economists would calculate the flow (e.g., net income) over an average (e.g., the average of beginning and ending assets). The typical decomposition of ROE is given by:

$$\frac{NI}{EBT} \times \frac{EBT}{EBIT} \times \frac{EBIT}{Sales} \times \frac{Sales}{Assets} \times \frac{Assets}{Equity} = \frac{NI}{Equity}$$

where

NI   is net income

EBT   is earnings before taxes

NI/EBT   is one minus the tax rate, or the tax retention rate with a maximum value of 1.0 if there were no taxes (lower values imply higher tax burden)

---

[14] See Griffin and Stulz (2001).

[15] See, for example, Cavaglia, Brightman, and Aked (2000) and Hopkins and Miller (2001).

EBIT is earnings before interest and taxes, or operating income

EBT/EBIT is interest burden, with a maximum value of 1.0 if there are no interest payments (lower values imply greater debt burden)

EBIT/Sales is operating margin

Sales/Assets is asset turnover ratio (a measure of efficiency in the use of assets)

Assets/Equity is leverage (higher values imply greater use of debt)

NI/Equity is return on equity (ROE)

The analyst would then compare each firm ratio with the comparable ratio for the industry. Does the firm have a higher operating margin than the industry's? If the company has a higher ROE than the industry ROE, is this higher-than-average ROE due to leverage, or is it due to more operations management-oriented ratios, such as operating margin or asset turnover?

Depending on the analyst's focus, the ratios can be combined in different ways. What is essential in DuPont analysis is the specification of the question of interest rather than the question of whether the model has five, three, or two factors.

One can collapse the first three ratios into the net profit margin (NI/sales) to leave

$$\text{ROE} = \text{Net profit margin} \times \text{Asset turnover} \times \text{Leverage}$$

One could also combine the first three ratios and include the fourth ratio to yield a return on assets breakdown:

$$\text{ROA} = \frac{\text{NI}}{\text{Assets}} = \text{Net profit margin} \times \text{Asset turnover}$$

Without combining the first three ratios, one could also have a four ratio ROA breakdown (tax retention rate × interest burden × operating margin × asset turnover). Also, one could explore a two-ratio ROE explanation by using ROA × leverage.

In all of this analysis, a global comparison of ratios of different companies in the same industry should take into account national valuation specificities. Due to national accounting differences detailed previously, earnings figures should sometimes be reconciled to make comparisons meaningful.

In global financial analysis, the methods of debt analysis can inform and supplement those of equity analysis. The Concepts in Action feature in this reading provides a look at capital structure and industry analysis concerns resulting from debt burden and production capacity analysis.

Example 61-2

DuPont Analysis of General Motors and Toyota

A comparison of Toyota Motor Corporation (NYSE: TM) with General Motors Corporation (NYSE: GM) reveals Toyota's superior net profit margin but inferior ROE as of late 2002. Is this a recent development? Has an ROE comparison been in General Motors' favor, historically, and how have differences in operating margin and other factors explained differences in ROE? In making an international comparison, differences in accounting must be considered. Toyota prepares its original financials according to Japanese GAAP. However, because Toyota trades on the NYSE as ADRs, Toyota also reports financial results according to U.S. GAAP, the basis for General Motors' accounting. Thus, the analyst's task is eased. Exhibit 61-2 presents a side-by-side DuPont analysis for General Motors and Toyota using Toyota's U.S. GAAP prepared financial results.

EXHIBIT 61-2	DuPont Analysis of ROE *GM* and *Toyota*								
	FY 1998		FY 1999		FY 2000		FY 2001		Average	
	GM	TM	GM	TM	GM	TM	GM	TM	GM	TM
(1) NI/EBT	0.682	0.514	0.655	0.520	0.666	0.527	0.494	0.525	0.624	0.522
(2) EBT/EBIT	0.209	0.536	0.279	0.609	0.221	0.806	0.047	0.903	0.189	0.714
(3) EBIT/Sales	0.161	0.127	0.175	0.120	0.163	0.120	0.130	0.097	0.157	0.116
(4) Net profit margin = (1) × (2) × (3)	0.023	0.035	0.032	0.038	0.024	0.051	0.003	0.046	0.019	0.043
(5) Sales/Assets	0.627	0.805	0.643	0.773	0.609	0.772	0.547	0.742	0.607	0.773
(6) Assets/Equity	17.18	2.380	13.31	2.379	10.04	2.405	16.44	2.658	14.24	2.456
(7) ROE = (4) × (5) × (6)	0.248	0.067	0.274	0.070	0.147	0.095	0.027	0.091	0.164	0.082

Source: Company reports, Thomson Financial, *The Value Line Investment Survey*, September 2002.

Note: Fiscal year end is 31 March (of the following calendar year) for Toyota, and 31 December for General Motors.

Exhibit 61-2 shows that in each year from 1998 through 2001, General Motors has had a higher operating margin than Toyota: Toyota's operating margin averaged 11.6 percent compared with 15.7 percent for General Motors, and was lower in each individual year. Despite General Motors' advantages in operating margin and generally lower tax rates, Toyota's much lower interest burden translated into a consistent advantage in net profit margin. Nevertheless, a raw comparison of ROE is dramatically in General Motors' favor. GM's average ROE was 16.4 percent, compared with 8.2 percent for Toyota. Toyota held the advantage in net profit margin and efficiency in the use of assets (as shown by a higher asset turnover ratio) but had consistently lower ROE. However, General Motors' highly levered its operating results using debt, while Toyota employed a conservative level of debt. General Motors' average assets–equity ratio was about 14.2 versus only about 2.5 for Toyota. Because of its leverage, the stream of returns to GM shareholders as reflected by ROE was much more volatile than for Toyota. What does this mean in practice? ROE must be evaluated in relation to risk. According to valuation theory, the benchmark for risk in evaluating a company's ROE would be the required rate of return on its equity. If the analyst were pursuing the implications of the differences in ROE on valuation, a next step would be to estimate these required rates of return.

Concepts in Action

Ford and GM's Bonds Looking Less Roadworthy

Gyrations of the Carmakers' Securities Cause Concern

Corporate bond investors once thought of Ford and General Motors as bulletproof. Their strong balance sheets and well-established positions in the automotive industry meant that their paper was eagerly snapped up by investors looking for safe, liquid investments. They were also active issuers of debt, making them easy credits to buy and sell.

But times have changed. Wearied by the unprecedented numbers of bond defaults and shocked by how quickly corporate creditworthiness can deteriorate, investors are re-evaluating how much they are prepared to invest in any one company.

"It used to be that a 2 percent position in Ford was fine," said Lee Crabbe, head of the corporate bond group at Credit Suisse Asset Management.

"Now a 2 percent position in any name isn't fine."

Meanwhile, concern has grown over the U.S. manufacturers' ability to compete with European rivals and to fund their pension liabilities.

More recently, worries have surfaced over the continuing strength of U.S. consumer demand. In July, Ford Credit's 10-year bonds started to diverge from those of similarly rated mid-investment grade companies. They have since widened some 300 basis points to trade at 570 basis points over U.S. Treasuries—in other words, like "junk" bonds.

General Motors Acceptance Corp's 10-year bonds have also widened and now trade at 455 basis points over Treasuries. Both companies recently had their long-term debt ratings lowered one notch by Standard & Poor's.

The widening in spreads does not reflect fears that the vehicle makers will go bankrupt—most investors say they believe Ford's fundamentals are sound. However, it does show that investors are no longer prepared simply to follow the index.

The vehicle manufacturers are among the largest issuers of debt in the U.S. corporate bond market, with Ford, GM, and Daimler-Chrysler accounting for 6.5 percent of Lehman's Credit Index, or some $128bn in debt.

Ford, with $61bn in debt outstanding, has the biggest weighting in the index, accounting for 3 percent.

The group has issued an increasing amount of debt over the past decade to fund the growing activities of Ford Motor Credit, its financial services business. In 1992 it sold about $12bn of debt in the U.S., but last year sold more than $40bn, according to Thomson Financial.

As the amount of debt Ford has issued has risen, so has its weight in market indices, which in turn has encouraged investors to buy its securities, because most investment funds gauge their performance against market indices.

This, however, leaves funds with a conundrum. Those that hold the bonds as spreads widen may take losses if the securities do not recover. Many investors were burnt earlier this year on investments in energy and telecommunications companies.

"Anything that smacks of excess capacity and a high debt burden has been a disaster this year," says Steven Zamsky, corporate bond strategist at Morgan Stanley.

> However, funds that sell the vehicle makers' securities run the risk of missing a rally if the bonds tighten, and having their performance look bad in comparison with their peers.
>
> Ford and GM's bonds have been extraordinarily volatile this year—in part because of increased activity by short sellers and hedge funds—so any rally could be quite substantial.
>
> "When investors get nervous, they sell at any price," says Mark Kiesel, portfolio manager at bond fund Pimco. "But if the market bounces, they've lost both ways."

Source: Jenny Wiggins. "Ford and GM's Bonds Looking Less Roadworthy," *Financial Times,* Thursday, October 31, 2002, p. 15.

The Role of Market Efficiency in Individual Stock Valuation

The notion of an efficient market is central to finance theory and is important for valuing securities. Generally, the question in company analysis is whether a security is priced correctly, and if it is not, for how long will it be mispriced. In an efficient market, any new information would be immediately and fully reflected in prices. Because all current information is already impounded in the asset price, only news (unanticipated information) could cause a change in price in the future.

An efficient financial market quickly, if not instantaneously, discounts all available information. Any new information will immediately be used by some privileged investors, who will take positions to capitalize on it, thereby making the asset price adjust (almost) instantaneously to this piece of information. For example, a new balance of payments statistic would immediately be used by foreign exchange traders to buy or sell a currency until the foreign exchange rate reached a level considered consistent with the new information. Similarly, investors might use surprise information about a company, such as a new contract or changes in forecasted income, to reap a profit until the stock price reached a level consistent with the news. The adjustment in price would be so rapid it would not pay to buy information that has already been available to other investors. Hundreds of thousands of expert financial analysts and professional investors throughout the world search for information and make the world markets close to fully efficient.

In a perfectly efficient market, the typical investor could consider an asset price to reflect its true *fundamental value* at all times. The notion of fundamental value is somewhat philosophical; it means that at each point in time, each asset has an intrinsic value that all investors try to discover. Nevertheless, the analyst tries to find mispriced securities by choosing from a variety of valuation models and by carefully researching the inputs for the model. In this research, forecasting cash flows and risk is critical.

Valuation Models

Investors often rely on some form of a discounted cash flow analysis (DCF) for estimating the "intrinsic" value of a stock investment. This is simply a "present value" model, where the intrinsic value of an asset at time zero, P_0, is determined by the stream of cash flows it generates for the investor. This price is also called the "justified" price because it is the value that is "justified" by the forecasted cash flows. In a dividend discount model (DDM), the stock market price is set equal to the stream of forecasted dividends, D, discounted at the required rate of return, r:

$$P_0 = \frac{D_1}{1+r} + \frac{D_2}{(1+r)^2} + \frac{D_3}{(1+r)^3} \cdots$$ **(61-1)**

Financial analysts take great care in forecasting future earnings, and hence, dividends.

A simple version of the DDM assumes that dividends will grow indefinitely at a constant compounded annual growth rate (CAGR), g. Hence, Equation 61.1 becomes

$$P_0 = \frac{D_1}{1+r} + \frac{D_1(1+g)}{(1+r)^2} + \frac{D_1(1+g)^2}{(1+r)^3} \cdots$$

or

$$P_0 = \frac{D_1}{r-g}$$ **(61-2)**

Analysts forecast earnings, and a payout ratio is applied to transform earnings into dividends. Under the assumption of a constant earnings payout ratio, we find

$$P_0 = \frac{E_1(1-b)}{r-g}$$ **(61-3)**

where

P_0 is the justified or intrinsic price at time 0 (now)

E_1 is next year's earnings

b is the earnings retention ratio

$1-b$ is the earnings payout ratio

r is the required rate of return on the stock

g is the growth rate of earnings

Note that Equation 61-3 requires that the growth rate g remain constant infinitely and that it must be less than the required rate of return r. Take the example of a German corporation whose next annual earnings are expected to be €20 per share, with a constant growth rate of 5 percent per year, and with a 50 percent payout ratio. Hence, the next-year dividend is expected to be €10. Let's further assume that the required rate of return for an investment in such a corporation is 10 percent, which can be decomposed into a 6 percent risk-free rate plus a 4 percent risk premium. Then the firm's value is equal to

$$P_0 = \frac{10}{0.10 - 0.05} = €200$$

The intrinsic price-to-earnings ratio (P/E) is defined as P_0/E_1. The intrinsic P/E of this corporation, using prospective earnings, is equal to

$$P/E = \frac{1 - b}{r - g} = \frac{0.50}{0.10 - 0.05} = 10$$

A drop in the risk-free interest rate would lead to an increase in the P/E and in the stock price. For example, if the risk-free rate drops to 5 percent, and everything else remains unchanged, a direct application of the formula indicates that the P/E will move up to 12.5 and the stock price to €250.

A more realistic DDM approach is to decompose the future in three phases. In the near future (e.g., the next two years), earnings are forecasted individually. In the second phase (e.g., years 3 to 5), a general growth rate of the company's earnings is estimated. In the final stage, the growth rate in earnings is assumed to revert to some sustainable growth rate.[16]

A final step required by this approach is to estimate the normal rate of return required on such an investment. This rate is equal to the risk-free interest rate plus a risk premium that reflects the relevant risks of this investment. Relevant risks refer to risks that should be priced by the market.

Franchise Value and the Growth Process

Given the risk of the company's forecasted cash flows, the other key determinant of value is the growth rate in cash flows. The growth rate depends on relevant country GDP growth rates, industry growth rates, and the company's sustainable competitive advantage within the industry. Regardless of the valuation model used, some analysis of the growth-rate input is useful. Using the DDM as a representative model, Leibowitz and Kogelman (2000) developed the *franchise value* method and separated the intrinsic P/E value of a corporation into a tangible P/E value (the no-growth or zero-earnings retention P/E value of existing business) and the franchise P/E value (derived from prospective new investments). The franchise P/E value is related to the *present value of growth opportunities* (PVGO) in the traditional breakdown of intrinsic value into the no-growth value per share and the present value of growth opportunities. In that breakdown, the no-growth value per share is the value of the company if it were to distribute all its earnings in dividends, creating a perpetuity valued at E_1/r, where E_1 is next year's earnings and r is the required rate of return on the company's equity. Using the DDM and the company's actual payout ratio to generate an intrinsic value per share, P_0, the present value of growth opportunities must be the difference between intrinsic value and the no-growth value per share, $P_0 - E_1/r$.

The franchise value approach focuses on the intrinsic P/E rather than on the intrinsic value P_0; thus, the franchise value P/E is $PVGO/E_1$. In the franchise value approach, however, the franchise value P/E is further broken down into the *franchise factor* and the *growth factor*. The growth factor captures the present value of the opportunities for productive new investments, and the franchise factor is meant to capture the return levels associated with those new investments. The *Sales-Driven Franchise Value* has been developed to deal with multinational corporations that do business globally (see Leibowitz, 1997, 1998).

The separation of franchise P/E value into a franchise factor and a growth factor permits a direct examination of the response of the intrinsic P/E to ROE.[17] This factor helps an investor determine the response of the P/E to the ROE expected to be achieved by the company. It focuses on the sustainable

---

[16] A detailed analysis of the use of DDM in companies' valuation is provided in Stowe et al. (2002).

[17] The model is derived here under the assumptions of a constant growth rate g, a constant earnings retention rate b, and a constant ROE. It can accommodate more complex assumptions about the pattern of growth.

growth rate of earnings per share. Earnings per share will grow from one period to the next because reinvested earnings will earn the rate of ROE. So the company's sustainable growth rate is equal to the retention rate (b) multiplied by ROE: $g = b \times \text{ROE}$. Substituting into Equation 61-3 the sustainable growth rate calculation for g, we get the intrinsic price:

$$P_0 = \frac{E_1(1 - b)}{r - b \times \text{ROE}}$$

and converting to an intrinsic P/E ratio,

$$\frac{P_0}{E_1} = \frac{(1 - b)}{r - b \times \text{ROE}}$$

Now, multiplying through by r/r yields

$$\frac{P_0}{E_1} = \frac{1}{r}\left[\frac{r(1 - b)}{r - b \times \text{ROE}}\right]$$

$$= \frac{1}{r}\left[\frac{r - r \times b}{r - \text{ROE} \times b}\right]$$

and arbitrarily adding and subtracting $\text{ROE} \times b$ in the numerator,

$$\frac{P_0}{E_1} = \frac{1}{r}\left[\frac{r - r \times b + \text{ROE} \times b - \text{ROE} \times b}{r - \text{ROE} \times b}\right]$$

$$= \frac{1}{r}\left[\frac{r - \text{ROE} \times b + \text{ROE} \times b - r \times b}{r - \text{ROE} \times b}\right]$$

or

$$\frac{P_0}{E_1} = \frac{1}{r}\left[1 + \frac{b(\text{ROE} - r)}{r - \text{ROE} \times b}\right]$$

(61-4)

This P_0/E_1 equation is extremely useful because one can use it to examine the effects of different values of b and of the difference between ROE and r; that is, $\text{ROE} - r$. Two interesting results can be found. First, if $\text{ROE} = r$, the intrinsic P_0/E_1 equals $1/r$ regardless of b, the earnings retention ratio. Second, if $b = 0$, the intrinsic P_0/E_1 equals $1/r$ regardless of whether ROE is greater than r. These two results have an intuitive explanation.

▶ When the return on equity is exactly equal to the required rate of return ($\text{ROE} = r$), there is no *added* value in retaining earnings for additional investments, rather than distributing them to shareholders. A company with $\text{ROE} = r$ has no franchise value potential because its return on equity is just what the market requires, but no more.

▶ An earnings retention ratio of zero ($b = 0$) means that the company distributes all its earnings. So equity per share stays constant. There is no growth of equity and the stream of future earnings will be a perpetuity because the rate of return on equity (ROE) remains constant. The value of a share is given by discounting a perpetuity of E_1 at a rate r, hence the $P_0/E_1 = 1/r$ result. Of course, the total equity of the company could grow by issuing new shares, but there will be no growth of earnings per existing share. There is potential franchise value in the company with ROE $> r$, but because the company does not reinvest earnings at this superior rate of return, existing shareholders do not capture this potential.

In general, there is a franchise value created for existing shareholders, if the company can reinvest past earnings ($b > 0$) at a rate of return (ROE) higher than the market-required rate (r).

Examining Equation 61-4 further, we return to the intrinsic value version of the equation. We can transform Equation 61-4 by multiplying and dividing by ROE and replacing $b \times$ ROE by g:

$$\frac{P_0}{E_1} = \frac{1}{r}\left[1 + \frac{\text{ROE} \times b \times (\text{ROE} - r)}{\text{ROE} \times (r - \text{ROE} \times b)}\right] = \frac{1}{r} + \frac{g \times (\text{ROE} - r)}{r \times \text{ROE} \times (r - g)}$$

and simplify it as

$$\frac{P_0}{E_1} = \frac{1}{r} + \left(\frac{\text{ROE} - r}{\text{ROE} \times r}\right)\left(\frac{g}{r - g}\right)$$

$$\frac{P_0}{E_1} = \frac{1}{r} + \text{FF} \times \text{G} \qquad\qquad \textbf{(61-5)}$$

where the franchise factor is FF $= (\text{ROE} - r)/(\text{ROE} \times r)$ or $1/r - 1/\text{ROE}$, and the growth factor is G $= g/(r - g)$.

The growth factor is the ratio of the present value of future increases in the book value (BV) of equity to the current BV of equity. If the current BV of equity is B_0, then next year's increment to BV is gB_0. With a constant growth rate in BV increments, these increments can be treated as a growing perpetuity with a present value of $gB_0/(r - g)$. Because the present value of the BV increments is to be given as a ratio to the most recent BV, the growth factor is then given as $g/(r - g)$.

The franchise factor stems from the fact that a firm has a competitive advantage allowing it to generate a rate of return (ROE) greater than the rate of return normally required by investors for this type of risk (r). If the franchise factor is positive, it gives the rate of response of the intrinsic P_0/E_1 ratio to in the growth factor. The growth factor G will be high if the firm can sustain a growth rate that is high relative to r.

Consider a pharmaceutical firm with some attractive new drugs with large commercial interest. Its ROE will be high relative to the rate of return required by investors for pharmaceutical stocks. Hence, it has a large positive franchise factor FF. If it continues to make productive new investments (G positive), such a firm can continue to generate a return on equity well above the rate of return required by the stock market, and thus has a large positive franchise value. On the other hand, if the pharmaceutical company's sustainable growth rate is small because of a low earnings retention rate b, then G will be small and so will the franchise value, even though the franchise factor is large. For a firm with less franchise potential and ROE possibilities only equal to the company's required rate of return ($r = \text{ROE}$) the franchise factor is zero and the intrinsic P_0/E_1 is simply $1/r$, regardless of the earnings retention ratio.

Example 61-3

Franchise Value

A company can generate an ROE of 15 percent and has an earnings retention ratio of 0.60. Next year's earnings are projected at $100 million. If the required rate of return for the company is 12 percent, what is the company's tangible P/E value, franchise factor, growth factor, and franchise P/E value?

Solution

The company's tangible P/E value is $1/r = 1/0.12 = 8.33$.

The company's franchise factor is $1/r - 1/\text{ROE} = 1/0.12 - 1/0.15 = 1.67$.

Because the company's sustainable growth rate is $0.6 \times 0.15 = 0.09$, the company's growth factor is $g/(r - g) = 0.09/(0.12 - 0.09) = 3$.

The company's franchise P/E value is the franchise factor times the growth factor, $1.67 \times 3 = 5.01$.

Because its tangible P/E value is 8.33 and its franchise P/E value is 5.01, the company's intrinsic P/E is 13.34. Note that the intrinsic P/E calculated directly is $\text{P/E} = (1 - b)/(r - g) = 0.4/(0.12 - 0.09) = 13.33$. Thus, the franchise value method breaks this P/E into its basic components.

The Effects of Inflation on Stock Prices

Because inflation rates vary around the world and over time, it is important to consider the effects of inflation on stock prices. To do this, we begin at the obvious place—earnings. After examining the effects of inflation on reported earnings, we discuss an inflation flow-through model.[18]

Because historical costs are used in accounting, inflation has a distorting effect on reported earnings. These effects show up primarily in replacement, inventories, and borrowing costs. Replacement must be made at inflated costs, but depreciation is recorded at historical cost—hence, reported earnings based on depreciation as an estimate of replacement costs gives an overstatement of earnings. Similarly, a first-in, first-out inventory accounting system leads to an understatement of inventory costs and an overstatement of reported earnings. Unlike replacement and inventory distortions, borrowing costs at historical rates cause an understatement of reported earnings. Inflation causes borrowing costs to increase, but nominal interest costs do not reflect the increase. Finally, capital gains taxes reflect an inflation tax, because the base for the capital gains tax is historical cost.

To analyze the effects of inflation on the valuation process, analysts try to determine what part of inflation flows through to a firm's earnings. A full-flow-through firm has earnings that fully reflect inflation. Thus, any inflation cost increases must be getting passed along to consumers.

In an inflationary environment, consider a firm that would otherwise have no growth in earnings, a zero earnings retention ratio and full-inflation flow-through.

---

[18] For example, see Leibowitz and Kogelman (2000).

So, earnings only grow because of the inflation rate I, assumed constant over time. For example, we have

$$E_1 = E_0 \times (1 + I)$$

By discounting this stream of inflation-growing earnings at the required rate r, we find that the intrinsic value of such a firm would then be

$$P_0 = \frac{E_1}{r - I} = E_0 \left(\frac{1 + I}{r - I} \right) \qquad \textbf{(61-6)}$$

where

P_0 is the intrinsic value

E_0 is the initial earnings level

I is the annual inflation rate

r is the nominal required rate of return

Let's now consider a company with a partial inflation flow-through of λ percent, so that earnings are only inflated at a rate λI:

$$E_1 = E_0 (1 + \lambda I)$$

By discounting this stream of earnings at the nominal required rate r, we find

$$P_0 = E_0 \times \frac{1 + \lambda I}{r - \lambda I} \qquad \textbf{(61-7)}$$

If we introduce the real required rate of return $\rho = r - I$, we get

$$P_0 = E_0 \times \frac{1 + \lambda I}{\rho + (1 - \lambda)I} = \frac{E_1}{\rho + (1 - \lambda)I}$$

The intrinsic P/E using prospective earnings is now equal to

$$P_0/E_1 = \frac{1}{\rho + (1 - \lambda)I} \qquad \textbf{(61-8)}$$

From Equation 61-8 we can see that the higher the inflation flow-through rate, the higher the price of the company. Indeed, a company that cannot pass inflation through its earnings is penalized. Thus, the P/E ratio ranges from a high of $1/\rho$ to a low of $1/r$. For example, assume a real required rate of return of 6 percent and an inflation rate of 4 percent. Exhibit 61-3 shows the P/E of the

EXHIBIT 61-3   Inflation Effects on P/E

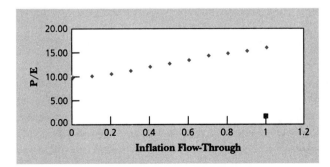

company with different flow-through rates. With a full-flow-through rate (λ = 100 percent), the P/E is equal to P/E = $1/\rho$ = $1/0.06$ = 16.67. The ratio drops to 12.5 if the company can only pass 50 percent of inflation through its earnings. If the company cannot pass through any inflation (λ = 0), its earnings remain constant, and the P/E ratio is equal to P/E = $1/(\rho + I)$ = $1/r$ = 10. The higher the inflation rate, the more negative the influence on the stock price if full inflation pass-through cannot be achieved.

This observation is important if we compare similar companies in different countries experiencing different inflation rates. A company operating in a high-inflation environment will be penalized if it cannot pass through inflation.

Example 61-4

Inflation

Consider two companies in the same line of business, but with mostly domestic operations. Company A is based in a country with no inflation. Company B is based in a country with a 4 percent inflation rate. There is no real growth in earnings for both companies. The real rate of return required by global investors for this type of stock investment is 6 percent. Company B can only pass 80 percent of inflation through its earnings. What should be the P/E of the two companies?

Solution

The nominal required rate of return for Company A is equal to the real rate because there is no inflation: $r = \rho = 6\%$. Earnings are constant and the P/E is equal to

$$P/E(A) = 1/\rho = 1/0.06 = 16.67$$

There is a 4 percent inflation rate in the country of Company B. Its earnings will only be inflated at a rate of $\lambda I = 80\% \times 4\% = 3.2\%$. The P/E of Company B will be

$$P/E(B) = \frac{1}{6\% + (20\%) \times 4\%} = \frac{1}{6.8\%} = 14.71$$

In the inflationary environment, Company B's earnings cannot grow as fast as inflation. Penalized by inflation and its inability to pass along inflation, Company B's P/E ratio is below that of Company A.

The Inflation-like Effects of Currency Movements on Stock Prices

A currency movement is a monetary variable that affects stock valuation in a fashion similar to the inflation variable. Just as some companies cannot fully pass inflation through their earnings, they cannot fully pass exchange rate movements either. Consider an importing firm faced with a sudden depreciation of the home currency. The products it imports suddenly become more expensive in terms of the home currency. If this price increase can be passed through to customers, earnings will not suffer from the currency adjustment. But this is often not the case. First, the price increase will tend to reduce demand for these imported products. Second, locally produced goods will become more attractive than imported goods, and some substitution will take place.

Currency exposure depends on such factors as each particular company's production cycle, the competitive structure of its product market, and the company's financing structure.

GLOBAL RISK FACTORS IN SECURITY RETURNS   6

The analysis of an individual company can require a detailed review of various strategic risk elements that are difficult to quantify precisely. However, a portfolio manager needs to summarize the information on a large number of securities into a few statistics that help construct a portfolio and manage its risk. To structure a portfolio properly, a manager must have a clear understanding of the main factors influencing the return on a security and of the risk exposures of each seurity.

The risk premium of a security should be proportional to the covariance (or beta) of the security's return with the world market return; this is the world market risk of a security. However, the world market risk of a security is the result of the exposure to many sources of risk that can be detailed in factor models. Factor models allow a better understanding of the risks that affect stock returns in the short run and allow the risk management of a portfolio.

Risk-Factor Model: Industry and Country Factors

A factor model, where R is the rate of return on the security, may be written mathematically as

$$R = \alpha + \beta_1 f_1 + \beta_2 f_2 + \ \ldots \ + \beta_k f_k + \varepsilon \qquad \textbf{(61-9)}$$

where

R is the rate of return on a security

α is a constant

$f_1 \ldots f_k$ are the k factors common to all securities

$\beta_1 \ldots \beta_k$ represent the sensitivity, or risk exposure, of this security to each factor

ε is a random term specific to this security

The ε is the source of idiosyncratic or diversifiable risk for the security, and $\beta_1 \ldots \beta_k$ represent the risk exposure of this security to each factor. The betas vary among securities. Some stocks may be highly sensitive to certain factors and much less sensitive to others, and vice versa.

A global risk-factor model would use industry and country as factors. The degree of granularity can be adapted; for example, one could use global sector factors, global industry factors, or regional industry factors. The geographical factors could be a list of regions (e.g., Europe) or of individual countries.

The factors are measured as the return on some index portfolio representative of the factor ("mimicking portfolios"). For example, the oil industry factor could be proxied by the return on a global stock index of oil firms. Various statistical techniques can be used to optimize the factor structure.

The determination of the risk-factor exposures can follow one of two techniques or a combination of the two:

► The exposure can be assessed a priori by using information on the company studied. This usually leads to a 0/1 exposure. For example, TotalFinaElf would have a unitary exposure to the oil industry factor and zero exposures to all other industry factors, because it is an oil company.

► The exposure can be estimated using a multiple regression approach. The exposures would then be the estimated betas in a time-series regression.

The question of currency should be addressed. A global risk-factor model can be written in some arbitrary currency (e.g., the U.S. dollar). It also can be written in currency-hedged terms. If companies are reacting differently to currency movements, currencies could be added as risk factors. For example, an exporting firm could be influenced negatively by an appreciation of its currency, while the reverse would be true for an importing firm. These currency exposures could be cancelled if the company adopts a currency-hedging policy in its business operations.

Other Risk Factors: Styles

Other factors influence the stock price behavior of companies worldwide. As mentioned, many researchers believe that the future performance of a stock also depends on other attributes of a company that have not been discussed so far. Among many others, three attributes have been researched extensively:

► *Value* stocks do not behave like *growth* **stocks**. A value stock is a company whose stock price is "cheap" in relation to its book value, or in relation to the cash flows it generates (low stock price compared with its earnings, cash flows, or dividends). A growth stock has the opposite attribute, implying that the stock price capitalizes growth in future earnings. This is known as the *value effect*.

► *Small* firms do not exhibit the same stock price behavior as *large* firms. The size of a firm is measured by its stock market capitalization. This is known as the *size effect*.

► In the short run, winners tend to repeat. In other words, stocks that have performed well (or badly) in the recent past, say in the past six months, will tend to be winners (or losers) in the next six months. This is known as the *momentum, success,* or *relative strength effect*.

The observation of these effects, or factors, has led to the development of *style investing,* in which portfolios are structured to favor some of these attributes (e.g., value stocks).

Risk-factor models often incorporate style factors in which the factors are proxied by some mimicking portfolio (e.g., long in value stocks and short in growth stocks). A security's exposure is either measured *a priori* by using some information on the company or by a regression technique, or by a combination of the two techniques.

Although this style approach has been extensively used in the United States, there is some practical difficulty in applying it in a global setting. This is best illustrated by looking at the size factor. An Austrian company that is regarded as "large" in Austria would be regarded as "medium-sized" in Europe and probably as "small" according to U.S. standards. To construct a global size factor, one must make assumptions on how to measure relative size. Different risk-factor models use different criteria.

Other Risk Factors: Macroeconomic

Factors are postulated *a priori* as sources of risk that are common to all companies. This clearly leads us to some macroeconomic variables that affect the economics of all firms, as well as the behavior of stock market participants who price those firms.

Selecting a set of *macroeconomic factors* is as much an art as a science. These factors must be logical choices, easy to interpret, robust over time, and able to explain a significant percentage of variation in stock returns. Some macroeconomic variables are logical candidates as factors but suffer from serious measurement error or long publication lags. For example, the evolution in industrial production is a logical candidate, but it is difficult to get timely, good-quality, reliable data. The technique is to use as factor proxies the returns on mimicking portfolios that are most strongly correlated with the economic variable.

Burmeister, Roll, and Ross (1994) propose a set of five factors.[19] These five factors, listed here, apply to domestic U.S. stocks:

▶ *Confidence factor* (f_1). This factor is measured by the difference in return on risky corporate bonds and on government bonds. The default-risk premium required by the market to compensate for the risk of default on corporate bonds is measured as the spread between the yields on risky corporate bonds and government bonds. A decrease in the default-risk spread will give a higher return on corporate bonds and implies an improvement in the investors' confidence level. Hence, confidence risk focuses on the willingness of investors to undertake risky investments. Most stocks have a positive exposure to the confidence factor ($\beta_1 > 0$), so their prices tend to rise when the confidence factor is positive ($f_1 > 0$). The underlying idea is that in periods when investors are becoming more sensitive to risks (less confident with $f_1 < 0$), they require a higher premium on risky corporate bonds, compared with government bonds. They also require a higher risk premium on risky stocks and will bid their prices down, inducing a negative stock-price movement.

▶ *Time horizon factor* (f_2). This factor is measured as the difference between the return on a 20-year government bond and a 1-month Treasury bill. A positive difference in return is caused by a decrease in the term spread (long minus short interest rates). This is a signal that investors require a lesser premium to hold long-term investments. Growth stocks are more exposed (higher β_2) to time horizon risk than income stocks. The underlying idea is to view the stock price as the discounted stream of its future cash flows. The present value of growth stocks is determined by the long-term prospects of growing earnings while current earnings are relatively weak (high P/E ratio). An increase in the market-required discount rate will penalize the price of growth stocks more than the price of value stocks.

▶ *Inflation factor* (f_3). This factor is measured as the difference between the actual inflation for a month and its expected value, computed the month before, using an econometric inflation model. An unexpected increase in inflation tends to be bad for most stocks ($\beta_3 < 0$), so they have a negative exposure to this inflation surprise ($f_3 > 0$). Luxury goods stocks tend to be

---

[19] Earlier, Chen, Roll, and Ross (1986) had identified four factors for the U.S. equity market as (1) growth rate in industrial production, (2) unexpected inflation, (3) slope of the yield curve (the difference between long- and short-term interest rates), and (4) changes in the attitude toward risk as proxied by changes in the pricing of default risk implicit in the difference between yields on Aaa and Baa corporate bonds.

most sensitive to inflation risk, whereas firms in the sectors of foods, cosmetics, or tires are less sensitive to inflation risk. Real estate holdings typically benefit from increased inflation.

▶ *Business-cycle factor* (f_4). This factor is measured by the monthly variation in a business activity index. Business-cycle risk comes from unanticipated changes in the level of real activity. The business-cycle factor is positive ($f_4 > 0$) when the expected real growth rate of the economy has increased. Most firms have a positive exposure to business-cycle risk ($\beta_4 > 0$). Retail stores are more exposed to business-cycle risk than are utility companies, because their business activity (sales) is much more sensitive to recession or expansion.

▶ *Market-timing factor* (f_5). This factor is measured by the part of the S&P 500 total return that is not explained by the first four factors. It captures the global movements in the market that are not explained by the four macroeconomic factors. The inclusion of this market-timing factor makes the capital asset pricing model (CAPM) a special case of this approach. If all relevant macroeconomic factors had been included, it would not be necessary to add this market-timing factor.

A common criticism of this approach is that the risk exposures (betas) have to be estimated statistically from past data and may not be stable over time. Even the factor proxies (mimicking portfolios) have to be constructed using statistical optimization, and the procedure could yield unstable proxies.

Practical Use of Factor Models

Risk-factor models are used in risk management and in selecting stocks. A major application is the analysis of the risk profile of portfolios. The exposure of the portfolio to the various factors is the weighted average of the exposures of the stocks making up the portfolio. A manager can estimate the risks taken and the exposure of the portfolio to the various sources of risk. If some specific stock index is assigned as a benchmark to measure performance, the manager can analyze the risks of deviations from the benchmark. This helps the manager identify and quantify the bets and risks that are taken in the portfolio.

Managers can also use factor models to tilt the portfolio along some factor bets. Assume, for example, that a manager believes that the economy is going to grow at a faster rate than generally forecasted, leading to some inflationary pressure. The manager will tend to increase the portfolio exposure to business risk but reduce its exposure to inflation risk. This could also lead the manager to take some industry bets and invest in small companies.

SUMMARY

▶ The major differences in accounting standards around the world appear in the treatment of business combinations, consolidation of subsidiary and affiliate information, goodwill, financial leases, asset revaluation, provisions for likely future losses or expenses, pensions, financial assets and derivatives, and employee stock options.

▶ Off-balance-sheet assets and liabilities are those assets and liabilities not properly reflected in the balance sheet. Examples are special purpose entities and financial leases.

▶ From an economic perspective, employee stock option compensation should be treated as an expense, with the options valued by an option-pricing model.

▶ Neoclassical growth theory predicts that the long-term level of GDP depends on the country's savings rate, but the long-term growth rate in GDP does not depend on the savings rate. Endogenous growth theory predicts that the longterm growth rate in GDP depends on the savings rate.

▶ A global industry analysis should examine return potential evidenced by demand analysis, value creation, industry life cycle, competition structure, competitive advantage, competitive strategies, co-opetition and the value net, and sector rotation. The analysis also should examine risk elements evidenced by market competition, value chain competition, government participation, and cash flow covariance.

▶ Global financial analysis involves comparing company ratios with global industry averages. In this context, DuPont analysis uses various combinations of the tax retention, debt burden, operating margin, asset turnover, and leverage ratios.

▶ The role of market efficiency in individual asset valuation is to equate fundamental value with asset valuation so that the analyst searches for mispricing or market inefficiency.

▶ Franchise value is the present value of growth opportunities divided by next year's earnings. The intrinsic P_0/E_1 ratio equals $1/r$ plus the franchise value, where r is the nominal required return on the stock. The franchise value is further divided into a franchise factor (FF) and a growth factor (G) to give $P_0/E_1 = 1/r + \text{FF} \times \text{G}$.

▶ To analyze the effects of inflation for valuation purposes, the analyst must recognize the distorting effects of historical inventory and borrowing costs on reported earnings, as well as recognize the inflation tax reflected in capital gains taxes. Further, the analyst must estimate the degree of inflation flow-through, λ.

▶ With earnings that are constant except for inflation, I as the inflation rate, r as the required nominal return on the stock, and ρ as the required real return on the stock, the P/E ratio can be estimated as $P_0/E_1 = 1/(\rho + (1 - \lambda)I)$.

▶ Multifactor models can be used in the analysis of the risk profile of portfolios. The exposure of a portfolio to the various factors is the weighted average of the exposures of the stocks making up the portfolio.

PROBLEMS FOR READING 61

1. The annual revenues (in billion dollars) in financial year 2001 for the top five players in the global media and entertainment industry are given in the following table. The top five corporations in this industry include three U.S.-based corporations (AOL Time Warner, Walt Disney, and Viacom), one French corporation (Vivendi Universal), and one Australian corporation (News Corporation). The revenue indicated for Vivendi Universal does not include the revenue from its environmental business. Assume that the total worldwide revenue of all firms in this industry was $250 billion.

Company	Revenue
AOL Time Warner	38
Walt Disney	25
Vivendi Universal	25
Viacom	23
News Corporation	13

A. Compute the three-firm and five-firm concentration ratios.

B. Compute the three-firm and five-firm Herfindahl indexes.

C. Make a simplistic assumption that in addition to the five corporations mentioned in the table, there are 40 other companies in this industry with an equal share of the remaining market. Compute the Herfindahl index for the overall industry.

D. Suppose there were not 40, but only 10 other companies in the industry with an equal share of the remaining market. Compute the Herfindahl index for the overall industry.

E. Interpret your answers to parts C and D in terms of the competition structure of the industry.

COMPANY ANALYSIS AND STOCK VALUATION*

by Frank K. Reilly and Keith C. Brown

LEARNING OUTCOMES

The candidate should be able to:

a. differentiate between 1) a growth company and a growth stock, 2) a defensive company and a defensive stock, 3) a cyclical company and a cyclical stock, 4) a speculative company and a speculative stock and 5) a value stock and a growth stock;

b. describe and estimate the expected earnings per share (EPS) and earnings multiplier for a company;

c. calculate and compare the expected rate of return (based on the estimate of intrinsic value) to the required rate of return.

INTRODUCTION　　　1

At this point, you have made two decisions about your investment in equity markets. First, after analyzing the economy and stock markets for several countries, you have decided what percent of your portfolio should be invested in common stocks. Second, after analyzing various industries, you have identified those that appear to offer above-average risk-adjusted performance over your investment horizon. The final questions in the fundamental analysis procedure are (1) which are the best companies within these desirable industries? and (2) are their stocks underpriced? Specifically, is the intrinsic value of the stock above its market value, or is the expected rate of return on the stock equal to or greater than its required rate of return?

---

* The authors acknowledge comments and suggestions on this chapter by Professor Edgar Norton of Illinois State University.

This reading begins with a discussion of the difference between company analysis and stock valuation. Company analysis should occur in the context of the prevailing economic and industry conditions. We discuss some competitive strategies that can help firms maximize returns in an industry's competitive environment. We demonstrate cash flow models and relative valuation ratios that can be used to determine a stock's intrinsic value and identify undervalued stocks. We also review factors that will help you determine when to sell a stock that you currently own and discuss the pressures and influences that affect professional stock analysts. We conclude with a discussion of important factors to consider when analyzing foreign stocks.

2   COMPANY ANALYSIS VERSUS THE VALUATION OF STOCK

This reading is titled "Company Analysis and Stock Valuation" to convey the idea that the common stocks of good companies are not necessarily good investments. The point is, after analyzing a company and deriving an understanding of its strengths and risks, you need to compute the fundamental intrinsic value of the firms's stock and compare the intrinsic value of a stock to its market value to determine if the company's stock should be purchased. The stock of a wonderful firm with superior management and strong performance measured by sales and earnings growth can be priced so high that the intrinsic value of the stock is below its current market price and should not be acquired. In contrast, the stock of a company with less success based on its sales and earnings growth may have a stock market price that is below its intrinsic value. In this case, although the company is not as good, its stock could be the better investment.

The classic confusion in this regard concerns growth companies versus growth stocks. The stock of a growth company is not necessarily a growth stock. Recognition of this difference is absolutely essential for successful investing.

Growth Companies and Growth Stocks

Observers have historically defined growth companies as those that consistently experience above-average increases in sales and earnings. This definition has some limitations because many firms could qualify due to certain accounting procedures, mergers, or other external events.

In contrast, financial theorists such as Salomon (1963) and Miller and Modigliani (1961) define a **growth company** as a firm with the management ability and the opportunities to make investments that yield rates of return greater than the firm's required rate of return. This required rate of return is the firm's weighted average cost of capital (WACC). As an example, a growth company might be able to acquire capital at an average cost of 10 percent and yet have the management ability and the opportunity to invest those funds at rates of return of 15 to 20 percent. As a result of these superior investment opportunities, the firm's sales and earnings grow faster than those of similar risk firms and the overall economy. In addition, a growth company that has above-average investment opportunities should, and typically does, retain a large portion of its earnings to fund these superior investment projects (i.e., they have low dividend-payout ratios).

Growth stocks are *not* necessarily shares in growth companies. A growth stock is a stock with a higher rate of return than other stocks in the market with similar risk characteristics. The stock achieves this superior risk-adjusted rate of return because at some point in time the market undervalued it compared to other stocks. Although the stock market adjusts stock prices relatively quickly and accurately to reflect new information, available information is not always perfect or complete. Therefore, imperfect or incomplete information may cause a given stock to be undervalued or overvalued at a point in time.[1]

If the stock is undervalued, its price should eventually increase to reflect its true fundamental value when the correct information becomes available. During this period of price adjustment, the stock's realized return will exceed the required return for a stock with its risk, and, during this period of adjustment, it will be considered a growth stock. Growth stocks are not necessarily limited to growth companies. A future growth stock can be the stock of any type of company; the stock need only be undervalued by the market.

The fact is, if investors recognize a growth company and discount its future earnings stream properly, the current market price of the growth company's stock will reflect its future earnings stream. Those who acquire the stock of a growth company at this correct market price will receive a rate of return consistent with the risk of the stock, even when the superior earnings growth is attained. In many instances, overeager investors tend to overestimate the expected growth rate of earnings and cash flows for the growth company and, therefore, inflate the price of a growth company's stock. Investors who pay the inflated stock price will earn a rate of return below the risk-adjusted required rate of return, despite the fact that the growth company experiences above-average growth of sales and earnings. Several studies, including those by Solt and Statman (1989), Shefrin and Statman (1995), and Clayman (1987), have examined the stock price performance for samples of growth companies and found that their stocks performed poorly—that is, the stocks of growth companies have generally *not* been growth stocks.

Defensive Companies and Stocks

Defensive companies are those whose future earnings are likely to withstand an economic downturn. One would expect them to have relatively low business risk and not excessive financial risk. Typical examples are public utilities or grocery chains—firms that supply basic consumer necessities.

There are two closely related concepts of a **defensive stock**. First, a defensive stock's rate of return is not expected to decline during an overall market decline, or decline less than the overall market. Second, our CAPM discussion indicated that an asset's relevant risk is its covariance with the market portfolio of risky assets—that is, an asset's systematic risk. A stock with low or negative systematic risk (a small positive or negative beta) may be considered a defensive stock according to this theory because its returns are unlikely to be harmed significantly in a bear market.

Cyclical Companies and Stocks

A **cyclical company's** sales and earnings will be heavily influenced by aggregate business activity. Examples would be firms in the steel, auto, or heavy machinery industries. Such companies will do well during economic expansions and poorly during economic contractions. This volatile earnings pattern is typically a function of the firm's business risk (both sales volatility and operating leverage) and can be compounded by financial risk.

---

[1] An analyst is more likely to find such stocks outside the top tier of companies that are scrutinized by numerous analysts; in other words, look for neglected stocks.

A **cyclical stock** will experience changes in its rates of return greater than changes in overall market rates of return. In terms of the CAPM, these would be stocks that have high betas. The stock of a cyclical company, however, is not necessarily cyclical. A cyclical stock is the stock of any company that has returns that are more volatile than the overall market—that is, high-beta stocks that have high correlation with the aggregate market and greater volatility.

Speculative Companies and Stocks

A **speculative company** is one whose assets involve great risk but that also has a possibility of great gain. A good example of a speculative firm is one involved in oil exploration.

A **speculative stock** possesses a high probability of low or negative rates of return and a low probability of normal or high rates of return. Specifically, a speculative stock is one that is overpriced, leading to a high probability that during the future period when the market adjusts the stock price to its true value, it will experience either low or possibly negative rates of return. Such an expectation might be the case for an excellent growth company whose stock is selling at an extremely high price/earnings ratio—that is, it is substantially overvalued.

Value versus Growth Investing

Some analysts also divide stocks into growth stocks and value stocks. As we have discussed, growth stocks are companies that will have positive earnings surprises and above-average risk-adjusted rates of return because the stocks are undervalued. If the analyst does a good job in identifying such companies, investors in these stocks will reap the benefits of seeing their stock prices rise after other investors identify their earnings growth potential. **Value stocks** are those that appear to be undervalued for reasons other than earnings growth potential. Value stocks are usually identified by analysts as having low price-earning or price-book value ratios. Notably, in these comparisons between growth and value stocks, the specification of a growth stock is *not* consistent with our preceding discussion. In these discussions, a growth stock is generally specified as a stock of a company that is experiencing rapid growth of sales and earnings (e.g., Intel and Microsoft). As a result of this company performance, the stock typically has a high *P/E* and price-book-value ratio. Unfortunately, the specification does not consider the critical comparison between intrinsic value and market price. Therefore, these specifications will not be used in subsequent discussions of valuation.

The major point of this section is that you must initially examine a company to determine its characteristics and use this information to derive an estimate of the intrinsic value of its stock. When you compare this intrinsic value of the stock to its current market price you decide whether you should acquire it—that is, will it be a growth stock that provides a rate of return equal to or greater than what is consistent with its risk?

3

ECONOMIC, INDUSTRY, AND STRUCTURAL LINKS TO COMPANY ANALYSIS

The analysis of companies and their stocks is the final step in the top-down approach to investing. Rather than selecting stocks on the basis of company-specific factors (as with bottom-up analysis), top-down analysts review the current state and future outlook for domestic and international sectors of the economy.

On the basis of this macroeconomic analysis, they identify industries that are expected to offer attractive returns in the expected future environment. Following this macroanalysis, we value the firms in the selected industries. Our analysis concentrates on the two significant determinants of a stock's intrinsic value: (1) growth of the firm's expected earnings and cash flows and (2) its risk and the appropriate discount rate.

Economic and Industry Influences

If economic trends are favorable for an industry, the company analysis should focus on firms in that industry that are well positioned to benefit from the economic trends. Research analysts should become familiar with the cash flow and risk attributes of the firms they are studying. In times of economic or industry growth, the most attractive candidates may be the firms in the industry with high levels of operating and financial leverage. A modest percentage increase in revenue can be magnified into a much larger percentage rise in earnings and cash flow for the highly leveraged firm. The point is, firms in an industry will have varying sensitivities to economic variables, such as economic growth, interest rates, input costs, and exchange rates. Because each firm is different, an investor must determine the best candidates for purchase under expected economic conditions.

Structural Influences

In addition to economic variables, other factors, such as social trends, technology, and political and regulatory influences, can have a major effect on some firms in an industry. Some firms in the industry can try to take advantage of demographic changes or shifts in consumer tastes and lifestyles, or invest in technology to lower costs and better serve their customers. Such firms may be able to grow and succeed despite unfavorable industry or economic conditions. For example, Wal-Mart became the nation's leading retailer because it benefited from several smart management decisions. The geographic location of many of its stores allowed it to benefit from rising regional population and lower labor costs. Its competitive strategy, which emphasized everyday low prices, was appealing to consumers who had become concerned about the price and value of purchases. Finally, its technologically advanced inventory and ordering systems and the logistics of its distribution system gave Wal-Mart a clear competitive (cost) advantage.

During the initial stage of an industry's life cycle, the original firms in the industry can refine their technologies and move down the learning curve. Subsequent followers may benefit from these initial actions and can learn from the leaders' mistakes and take the market lead away from them. Investors need to be aware of such strategies so they can evaluate companies and their stocks accordingly.

Political and regulatory events can create opportunities in an industry even during weak economic periods. Deregulation in trucking, airlines, and the financial services industries in the 1980s led to the creation of new companies and innovative strategies. As a result, sharp price declines following bad industry news may be a good buying opportunity for astute investors. Some stocks in an industry may deserve lower prices following some political or regulatory events; but, if the market also punishes the stock prices of good companies with smaller exposures to the bad news, then an alert analyst will identify buying opportunities of underpriced stocks within an industry.

The bottom line is that, although the economy plays a major role in determining overall market trends and industry groups display sensitivity to economic variables, other structural changes may counterbalance the economic effects, or company management may be able to minimize the impact of economic or industry events on a company. Analysts who are familiar with industry trends and company strategies can issue well-reasoned buy-and-sell recommendations irrespective of the economic forecast.

4   COMPANY ANALYSIS

This section groups various analysis components for discussion. The first subsection continues the Porter discussion of an industry's competitive environment. The basic **SWOT analysis** is intended to articulate a firm's strengths, weaknesses, opportunities, and threats. These two analyses should provide a complete understanding of a firm's overall *strategic* approach. Given this background, we review and demonstrate the two valuation approaches: (1) the present value of cash flows, and (2) relative valuation ratio techniques. Following this, we discuss the significance of site visits to companies, how to prepare for an interview with management, and suggestions on when an investor should consider selling an asset. This is followed by a discussion of unique considerations regarding evaluation of international companies and their stocks. The final section of the reading discusses the unique features of true growth companies and presents and demonstrates several models that can be used to value growth companies.

Firm Competitive Strategies

In describing competition within industries, we discussed the five competitive forces that could affect the competitive structure and profit potential of an industry. After you have determined the competitive structure of an industry, you should attempt to identify the specific competitive strategy employed by each firm in the industry.

A company's competitive strategy can either be *defensive* or *offensive.* A **defensive competitive strategy** involves positioning the firm to deflect the effect of the competitive forces in the industry. Examples may include investing in fixed assets and technology to lower production costs or creating a strong brand image with increased advertising expenditures.

An **offensive competitive strategy** is one in which the firm attempts to use its strengths to affect the competitive forces in the industry. For example, Wal-Mart used its buying power to obtain price concessions from its suppliers. This cost advantage, coupled with a superior delivery system to its stores, allowed Wal-Mart to grow against larger competitors and eventually become the leading U.S. retailer.

As an investor, you must understand the alternative competitive strategies available, determine each firm's strategy, judge whether the firm's strategy is reasonable for its industry, and, finally, evaluate how successful the firm is in implementing its strategy.

In the following sections, we discuss analyzing a firm's competitive position and strategy. The analyst must decide whether the firm's management is correctly positioning the firm to take advantage of industry and economic conditions. The analyst's opinion about management's decisions should ultimately be reflected in, and be the basis for the analyst's estimates of the firm's growth of cash flow and earnings.

Porter (1980a, 1985) suggests two major competitive strategies: low-cost leadership and differentiation. These two competitive strategies dictate how a firm has decided to cope with the five competitive conditions that define an industry's environment. The strategies available and the ways of implementing them differ within each industry.

Low-Cost Strategy   The firm that pursues the low-cost strategy is determined to become *the* low-cost producer and, hence, the cost leader in its industry. Cost advantages vary by industry and might include economies of scale, proprietary technology, or preferential access to raw materials. In order to benefit from cost leadership, the firm must command prices near the industry average, which means that it must differentiate itself about as well as other firms. If the firm discounts price too much, it could erode the superior rates of return available because of its low cost. During the past decade, Wal-Mart was considered a low-cost source. The firm achieved this by volume purchasing of merchandise and lower-cost operations. As a result, the firm charged less but still enjoyed higher profit margins and returns on capital than many of its competitors.

Differentiation Strategy With the differentiation strategy, a firm seeks to identify itself as unique in its industry in an area that is important to buyers. Again, the possibilities for differentiation vary widely by industry. A company can attempt to differentiate itself based on its distribution system (selling in stores, by mail order, or door-to-door) or some unique marketing approach. A firm employing the differentiation strategy will enjoy above-average rates of return only if the price premium attributable to its differentiation exceeds the extra cost of being unique. Therefore, when you analyze a firm using this strategy, you must determine whether the differentiating factor is truly unique, whether it is sustainable, its cost, and if the price premium derived from the uniqueness is greater than its cost (is the firm experiencing above-average rates of return?).

Focusing a Strategy

Whichever strategy it selects, a firm must determine where it will focus this strategy. Specifically, a firm must select segments in the industry and tailor its strategy to serve these specific groups. For example, a low-cost strategy would typically exploit cost advantages for certain segments of the industry, such as being the low-cost producer for the expensive segment of the market. Similarly, a differentiation focus would target the special needs of buyers in specific segments. For example, in the athletic shoe market, companies have attempted to develop shoes for unique sport segments, such as tennis, basketball, aerobics, or walkers and hikers, rather than offering only shoes for runners. Firms thought that participants in these activities needed shoes with characteristics different from those desired by joggers. Equally important, they believed that these athletes would be willing to pay a premium for these special shoes. Again, you must ascertain if special possibilities exist, if they are being served by another firm, and if they can be priced to generate abnormal returns to the firm. Exhibit 62-1 details some of Porter's ideas for the skills, resources, and company organizational requirements needed to successfully develop a cost leadership or a differentiation strategy.

Next, you must determine which strategy the firm is pursuing and its success. Also, can the strategy be sustained? Further, you should evaluate a firm's competitive strategy over time, because strategies need to change as an industry evolves; different strategies work during different phases of an industry's life cycle. For example, differentiation strategies may work for firms in an industry during the early growth stages. Subsequently, when the industry is in the mature stage, firms may try to lower their costs.

Through the analysis process, the analyst identifies what the company does well, what it doesn't do well, and where the firm is vulnerable to the five competitive forces. Some call this process developing a company's "story." This evaluation enables the analyst to determine the outlook and risks facing the firm. In summary, understanding the industry's competitive forces and the firm's strategy for dealing with them is the key to understanding how a company makes money and deriving an accurate estimate of the firm's long-run cash flows and its risks.

EXHIBIT 62-1	Skills, Resources, and Organizational Requirements Needed to Successfully Apply Cost Leadership and Differentiation Strategies

Generic Strategy	Commonly Required Skills and Resources	Common Organizational Requirements
Overall cost leadership	Sustained capital investment and access to capital Process engineering skills Intense supervision of labor Products designed for ease in manufacture Low-cost distribution system	Tight cost control Frequent, detailed control reports Structured organization and responsibilites Incentives based on meeting strict quantitative targets
Differentiation	Strong marketing abilities Product engineering Creative flair Strong capability in basic research Corporate reputation for quality or technological leadership Long tradition in the industry or unique combination of skills drawn from other businesses Strong cooperation from channels	Strong coordination among functions in R&D, product development, and marketing Subjective measurement and incentives instead of quantitative measures Amenities to attract highly skilled labor, scientists, or creative people

Source: Adapted from *Competitive Strategy: Techniques for Analyzing Industries and Competitors* by Michael E. Porter.

Another framework for examining and understanding a firm's competitive position and its strategy is the following SWOT analysis.

SWOT Analysis

SWOT analysis involves an examination of a firm's *S*trengths, *W*eaknesses, *O*pportunities, and *T*hreats. It should help you evaluate a firm's strategies to exploit its competitive advantages or defend against its weaknesses. Strengths and weaknesses involve identifying the firm's *internal* abilities or lack thereof. Opportunities and threats include *external* situations, such as competitive forces, discovery and development of new technologies, government regulations, and domestic and international economic trends.

The *strengths* of a company give the firm a comparative advantage in the marketplace. Perceived strengths can include good customer service, high-quality products, strong brand image, customer loyalty, innovative R&D, market leadership, or strong financial resources. To remain strengths, they must continue to be developed, maintained, and defended through prudent capital investment policies.

Weaknesses result when competitors have potentially exploitable advantages over the firm. Once weaknesses are identified, the firm can select strategies to mitigate or correct the weaknesses. For example, a firm that is only a domestic producer in a global market can make investments that will allow it to export or produce its product overseas. Another example would be a firm with poor financial resources that would form joint ventures with financially stronger firms.

Opportunities, or environmental factors that favor the firm, can include a growing market for the firm's products (domestic and international), shrinking competition, favorable exchange rate shifts, or identification of a new market or product segment.

Threats are environmental factors that can hinder the firm in achieving its goals. Examples would include a slowing domestic economy (or sluggish overseas economies for exporters), additional government regulation, an increase in industry competition, threats of entry, buyers or suppliers seeking to increase their bargaining power, or new technology that can obsolete the industry's product. By recognizing and understanding opportunities and threats, an investor can make informed decisions about how the firm can exploit opportunities and mitigate threats.

Some Lessons from Lynch

Peter Lynch (1989, 1993), the former portfolio manager of Fidelity Investments' highly successful Magellan Fund, looks for the following attributes when he analyzes firms.

Favorable Attributes of Firms   The following attributes of firms may result in favorable stock market performance:

1. The firm's product is not faddish; it is one that consumers will continue to purchase over time.

2. The company has a sustainable comparative competitive advantage over its rivals.

3. The firm's industry or product has market stability. Therefore, it has little need to innovate or create product improvements or fear that it may lose a technological advantage. Market stability means less potential for entry.

4. The firm can benefit from cost reductions (for example, a computer manufacturer that uses technology provided by suppliers to deliver a faster and less-expensive product).

5. The firm buys back its shares or management purchases shares which indicates that its insiders are putting their money into the firm.

Tenets of Warren Buffett

The following tenets are from Robert Hagstrom (2001). The parenthetical comments are based on discussions in the book and Berkshire Hathaway annual report letters.

Business Tenets

▶ Is the business simple and understandable?
(This makes it easier to estimate future cash flows with a high degree of confidence.)

▶ Does the business have a consistent operating history?
(Again, cash flow estimates can be made with more confidence.)

▶ Does the business have favorable long-term prospects?
(Does the business have a franchise product or service that is needed or desired, has no close substitute, and is not regulated? This implies that the firm has pricing flexibility.)

Management Tenets

▶ Is management rational?
(Is the allocation of capital to projects that provide returns above the cost of capital? If not, does management pay capital to stockholders through dividends or the repurchase of stock?)

▶ Is management candid with its shareholders?
(Does management tell owners everything you would want to know?)

▶ Does management resist the institutional imperative?
(Does management not attempt to imitate the behavior of other managers?)

Financial Tenets

▶ Focus on return on equity, not earnings per share.
(Look for strong *ROE* with little or no debt.)

▶ Calculate owner earnings.
(Owner earnings are basically equal to free cash flow after capital expenditures.)

▶ Look for a company with relatively high profit margins for its industry.

▶ Make sure the company has created at least one dollar of market value for every dollar retained.

Market Tenets

▶ What is the intrinsic value of the business?
(Value is equal to future free cash flows discounted at a government bond rate. Using this low discount rate is considered appropriate because Warren Buffett is very confident of his cash flow estimates due to extensive analysis, and this confidence implies low risk.)

▶ Can the business be purchased at a significant discount to its fundamental intrinsic value?

The point is to make use of research on the competitive forces in an industry, a firm's responses to those forces, SWOT analysis, Lynch's suggestions, and Buffett's tenets.

5 ESTIMATING INTRINSIC VALUE

Now that the analysis of the economy, structural forces, the industry, the company, and its competitors is completed, it is time to estimate the intrinsic value of the firm's common stock. If the intrinsic value estimate exceeds the stock's current market price, the stock should be purchased. In contrast, if the current market price exceeds our intrinsic value estimate, we should avoid the stock.

As noted in Reading 59, analysts use two general approaches to valuation and the following techniques.

Present Value of Cash Flows (PVCF)

1. Present value of dividends (DDM)

2. Present value of free cash flow to equity (FCFE)

3. Present value of free operating cash flow to the firm (FCFF)

Relative Valuation Techniques

1. Price/earnings ratio (*P/E*)

2. Price/cash flow ratio (*P/CF*)

3. Price/book value ratio (*P/BV*)

4. Price/sales ratio (*P/S*)

This section contains a brief presentation for each of these techniques as applied to Walgreens, the largest retail drugstore (RDS) chain in the United States. It operates 4,582 drugstores in 44 states and Puerto Rico. Its pharmacy operation generates 63.2 percent of sales.

Although we limit our demonstration to Walgreens (whose ticker symbol is WAG), your complete company analysis would cover all the firms in the RDS industry to determine which stocks should perform the best. The objective is to estimate the expected return and risk for all the individual firms in the industry over your investment horizon. The initial presentation considers the present value of cash flow (PVCF) models. Exhibit 62-2 contains historical data for Walgreens related to variables required for the PVCF models.

Present Value of Dividends

As noted in Reading 59, determining the present value of all future dividends is a difficult task. Therefore, analysts apply simplifying assumptions when employing the dividend discount models. The typical assumption is that the stock's dividends will grow at a constant rate over time. Although unrealistic for fast-growing or cyclical firms, this assumption may be appropriate for some mature firms. More complex DDMs exist for more complicated growth forecasts including two-stage growth models (a period of fast growth followed by a period of constant growth) and three-stage growth models (a period of fast growth followed by a period of diminishing growth rates followed by a period of constant growth).[2]

We initially discuss the constant growth DDM which implies that when dividends grow at a constant rate, a stock's price should equal next year's dividend, D_1, divided by investors' required rate of return on the stock (*k*) minus the dividend growth rate (*g*):

$$\text{Intrinsic Value} = D_1/(k - g) \qquad \textbf{(62-1)}$$

With constant dividend growth, next year's dividend (D_1) should equal the current dividend, D_0, increased by the constant dividend growth rate: $D_1 = D_0 (1 + g)$. Because the current dividend is known, to estimate intrinsic value we need only estimate the dividend growth rate and investors' required rate of return.

Growth Rate Estimates   If the stock has had fairly constant dividend growth over the past 5 to 10 years, one estimate of the constant growth rate is to use the actual growth of dividends over this period. The average compound rate of growth is found by computing

$$\text{Average Dividend Growth Rate} = \sqrt[n]{\frac{D_n}{D_0}} - 1 \qquad \textbf{(62-2)}$$

---

[2] These were discussed in Reading 59.

EXHIBIT 62-2 Walgreen Co.'s Input Data for Alternative Present Value of Cash Flow Models (Dollars in Millions, except per Share Data)

Year	Dividend per Share	Net Income	Depreciation Expense	Capital Spending	Change in Working Capital	Principal Repayment	New Debt Issued	FCFE	EBIT	Tax Rate	FCFF	100% Tax Rate	Time
1983	0.02	70	25	-71	-15	-3	0	6	147	45	19.9	55	1
1984	0.03	85	29	-68	-56	-3	0	-13	181	45	4.6	55	2
1985	0.03	94	34	-97	-61	-3	20	-33	209	46	-11.1	54	3
1986	0.03	103	44	-156	-72	-5	92	-86	229	45	-58.1	55	4
1987	0.04	104	54	-122	-118	-4	5	-86	243	46	-54.8	54	5
1988	0.04	129	59	-114	49	-4	31	119	263	38	157.1	62	6
1989	0.05	154	64	-121	-97	-4	0	-4	301	37	35.6	63	7
1990	0.05	175	70	-192	-69	-4	0	-20	344	38	22.3	62	8
1991	0.06	195	84	-202	-129	-24	0	-76	381	38	-10.8	62	9
1992	0.07	221	92	-145	-32	-6	0	130	429	37	185.3	63	10
1993	0.08	245	105	-185	-28	-112	0	25	483	39	186.6	61	11
1994	0.09	282	118	-290	-58	-6	0	46	550	38	111.0	62	12
1995	0.10	321	132	-310	-104	-7	0	32	629	39	101.7	61	13
1996	0.11	372	147	-364	-116	0	2	39	725	39	109.3	61	14
1997	0.12	436	164	-485	34	-1	0	148	842	39	226.6	61	15
1998	0.13	511	189	-641	-143	0	0	-84	878	39	-59.4	61	16
1999	0.13	624	210	-696	-206	0	0	-68	1028	39	-64.9	61	17
2000	0.14	777	230	-1119	-140	0	0	-252	1264	39	-258.0	61	18
2001	0.14	886	269	-1237	-569	0	0	-651	1426	38	-652.9	62	19
2002	0.15	1019	307	-934	-830	0	0	-438	1637	38	-442.5	62	20
2003	0.16	1176	346	-795	-726	0	0	1	1889	38	-3.8	62	21
2004	0.18	1360	403	-940	-748	0	0	75	2176	38	64.1	62	22

Source: Information calculated using publicly available data of Walgreen Co. Reprinted with the permission of Walgreen Co.

In the case of Walgreens, the 1983 dividend (D_0) was \$0.02 a share and the 2004 dividend (D_{21}) was \$0.18 a share. The average dividend growth rate was

$$\sqrt[21]{\frac{\$0.18}{0.02}} - 1 = \sqrt[21]{9.00} - 1 = 0.1103$$

or 11.03 percent. Clearly, it is inappropriate to blindly plug historical growth rates into our formulas because if we do, we've wasted our time analyzing economic, structural, industry, and company influences. Our analysis may have indicated that growth is expected to increase or decrease due to such factors as changes in government programs, demographic shifts, or changes in product mix. The historical growth rate may need to be raised or lowered to incorporate our findings.

There are other ways to estimate future growth. The sustainable growth rate

$$g = RR \times ROE \qquad \qquad \textbf{(62-3)}$$

assumes the firm will maintain a constant debt-equity ratio as it finances asset growth. As we know, ROE is the product of the net profit margin, total asset turnover, and the financial leverage multiplier. Thus, a firm's future growth rate and its components of ROE can be compared to those of its competitors, its industry, and the market. For Walgreens, the sustainable growth rate calculation using 2004 data is[3]

$$g = RR \times ROE = 0.86 \times .176$$
$$= 0.1514 = 15.14\%$$

The dividend growth rate will be influenced by the age of the industry life cycle, structural changes, and economic trends. Economic-industry-firm analysis provides valuable information regarding future trends in dividend growth. Information derived about management's plans to expand the firm, diversify into new areas, or change dividend policy can provide useful information about the firm's dividend policy. Averaging the historical growth rate of dividends (11.03 percent) and the implied sustainable growth estimate of 15.14 percent indicates a value of 13.08 percent. Although we feel that a firm's ROE is the critical growth factor and give this estimate more weight, we will use a conservative 13 percent for Walgreen Co.'s estimated g (this is also close to the firm's earning's growth rate).

Required Rate of Return Estimate   We know an investor's required rate of return has two basic components: the nominal risk-free interest rate and a risk premium. If the market is efficient, over time the return earned by investors should compensate them for the risk of the investment.

Notably, we must estimate *future* risk premiums to determine the stock's current intrinsic value. Estimates of the nominal risk-free interest rate are available from the initial analysis of the economy during the top-down approach. The risk premium of the firm must rely on other information including evaluation of the financial statements and capital market relationships.

We have ratios that measure business risk, financial risk, liquidity risk, exchange rate risk, and country risk. These measures can be compared against the firm's major competitors, its industry, and the overall market. This fundamental comparison should indicate if the firm deserves a higher or lower risk premium than the overall market, other firms in the industry, or the firm's

---

[3] This sustainable growth rate value uses year-end values for ROE, whereas the equity value is an average of the beginning and ending values.

historical risk premium. Accounting-based risk measures use historical data, whereas investment analysis requires an estimate of the future, including any information uncovered during the top-down process that would lead to higher or lower risk estimates.

For a market-based risk estimate, the firm's characteristic line is estimated by regressing market returns on the stock's returns. The slope of this regression line is the stock's measure of systematic risk. Estimates of the economy's risk-free rate, the future long-run market return, and an estimate of the stock's beta help estimate next year's required rate of return:

$$E(R_{\text{stock}}) = E(RFR) + \beta_{\text{stock}}[E(R_{\text{market}}) - E(RFR)] \qquad \textbf{(62-4)}$$

Again, this estimate of beta begins with historical market information. Because beta is affected by changes in a firm's business and financial risks, as well as other influences, an investor should increase or lower the historical beta estimate based on his or her analysis of the firm's *future* risk characteristics.

To demonstrate the estimate of the required rate of return equation for Walgreens, we make several assumptions regarding components of the security market line (SML). First, the prevailing nominal risk-free rate *(RFR)* is estimated at about 4.5 percent—the current yield to maturity for the intermediate-term (10 year) government bond. The expected equity market rate of return (R_{M}) depends on the expected market risk premium on stocks. As noted earlier, this is a very controversial topic wherein the estimates range from a high of about 8 percent to a low of about 3 percent. The authors reject both of these extreme values and will use a 4.0 percent risk premium (0.040). The final estimate is the firm's systematic risk value (beta), based upon the following regression model (the characteristic line):

$$R_{\text{WAG}} = \alpha + \beta_{\text{WAG}} R_{\text{M}} \qquad \textbf{(62-5)}$$

where:

R_{WAG} = monthly rate of return for Walgreens
α = constant term
β_{WAG} = beta coefficient for Walgreens
$\qquad$ equal to $\dfrac{\text{Cov}_{\text{W,M}}}{\sigma_{\text{M}}^2}$
R_{M} = monthly rates of return for a market proxy—typically the S&P 500 Index

When this regression was run using monthly rates of return during the five-year period 2000–2004 (60 observations), the beta coefficient was estimated at 0.90.

We put together the *RFR* of 0.045 and the market risk premium of 0.040, which implies an expected market return (R_{M}) of 0.085. This, combined with the Walgreen Co.'s beta of 0.90, indicates the following expected rate of return for Walgreens:

$$
\begin{aligned}
E(R) &= RFR + \beta_i(R_{\text{M}} - RFR) \\
&= 0.045 + 0.90(0.085 - 0.045) \\
&= 0.045 + 0.90(0.04) \\
&= 0.045 + 0.036 \\
&= 0.081 = 8.1\%
\end{aligned}
$$

We will round this to 8 percent.

Present Value of Dividends Model (DDM)

At this point, the analyst would face a problem: the intent was to use the basic DDM, which assumed a constant growth rate for an infinite period. You will recall that the model also required that $k > g$ (the required rate of return is larger than the expected growth rate), which is not true in this case because $k = 8$ percent and $g = 13$ percent (as computed earlier). Therefore, the analyst must employ a two- or three-stage growth model. Because of the fairly large difference between the current growth rate of 13 percent and the long-run constant growth rate of 7 percent, it seems reasonable to use a three-stage growth model, which includes a gradual transition period. We assume that the growth periods are as follows:

$g_1 = 7$ years (growing at 13 percent a year)
$g_2 = 6$ years (during this period it is assumed that the growth rate
    declines 1 percent per year for 6 years)
$g_3 = $ constant perpetual growth of 7 percent

Therefore, beginning with 2005 when dividends were expected to be \$0.21, the future dividend payments will be as follows (the growth rates are in parentheses):

	HIGH-GROWTH PERIOD					**DECLINING-GROWTH PERIOD**			
Year	**Gr Rate**	**Div.**	**8% PV Factor**	**PV**	**Year**	**Gr Rate**	**Div.**	**8% PV Factor**	**PV**
2006	(13%)	0.24	0.855	0.20	2013	(12%)	0.55	.500	0.28
2007	(13%)	0.27	0.794	0.21	2014	(11%)	0.61	.463	0.28
2008	(13%)	0.30	0.735	0.22	2015	(10%)	0.68	.429	0.29
2009	(13%)	0.34	0.680	0.23	2016	(9%)	0.74	.397	0.29
2010	(13%)	0.39	0.629	0.24	2017	(8%)	0.80	.368	0.29
2011	(13%)	0.44	0.585	0.26	2018	(7%)	0.85	.340	0.29
2012	(13%)	0.49	0.341	0.27					
			Sum	\$1.64				Sum	1.72

Constant Growth Period:

$$P_{2018} = \frac{0.85(1.07)}{0.08 - 0.07} - \frac{0.91}{0.08 - 0.07} = \frac{0.91}{0.01} = \$91.00 \times 0.340 = \$30.94$$

The total value of the stock is the sum of the three present-value streams discounted at 8 percent:

1. Present value of high-growth period dividends	\$1.64
2. Present value of declining-growth period dividends	1.72
3. Present value of constant-growth period dividends	30.94
Total present value of dividends	**\$34.30**

The estimated value based on the DDM (\$34.30) is substantially lower than the market price in mid-2005 of about \$42.00. This estimated value also implies a *P/E* ratio based on expected earnings in 2005 of about \$1.50 per share (that is, about 22.9 times earnings) compared to the prevailing market *P/E* of about 18 times 2005 earnings. In a subsequent section on relative valuation techniques, we compare Walgreen Co.'s *P/E* ratio to that of its industry and the market.

Present Value of Free Cash Flow to Equity

As noted in Reading 59, this technique resembles a present value of earnings concept except that it considers the capital expenditures required to maintain and grow the firm and the change in working capital required for a growing firm (that is, an increase in accounts receivable and inventory). The specific definition of free cash flow to equity (FCFE) is:

Net Income + Depreciation Expense − Capital Expenditures − Δ in Working Capital − Principal Debt Repayments + New Debt Issues

This technique attempts to determine the free cash flow that is available to the stockholders after payments to all other capital suppliers and after providing for the continued growth of the firm. As noted in Reading 59, given the current FCFE values, the alternative forms of the model are similar to those available for the DDM, which in turn depends on the firm's growth prospects. Specifically, if the firm is in its mature, constant-growth phase, it is possible to use a model similar to the reduced form DDM:

$$\text{Value} = \frac{\text{FCFE}_1}{k - g_{\text{FCFE}}} \qquad \text{(62-6)}$$

where:

FCFE = the expected free cash flow to equity in Period 1
k = the required rate of return on equity for the firm
g_{FCFE} = the expected constant growth rate of free cash flow to equity for the firm

We already know from the prior dividend model that the firm's net income has grown at a rate (about 13 percent) that exceeds the required rate of return. In the case of FCFE, it is necessary to consider the effect of capital expenditures relative to depreciation and changes in working capital as well as debt repayments and new debt issues. The historical data in Exhibit 62.2 shows a growth rate that exceeded 20 percent during some periods since 1983, in contrast to the negative values in 1998–2002. The reason for the dramatic change is evident—it is the very heavy capital expenditures and the significant negative working capital items. The firm has reduced the growth rate of stores—from a net increase (new stores minus closings) of about 475 stores per year. Based on discussions with management, it appears that this slowdown in growth is due to the prevailing shortage of pharmacists. While Walgreens will continue adding stores, the slower rate of growth and a reduction in the growth of inventory will allow the firm to build on the positive cash flows in 2004. Specifically, it is estimated that in 2005 the FCFE will be about $220 million and the FCFF (free cash flow to the firm) will be about $260 million. Such volatility makes it appropriate to use the conservative 13 percent growth rate going forward after 2005. Therefore, the following example again uses a three-stage growth model with characteristics similar to the dividend growth model.

g_1 = 13 percent for the six years after 2005
g_2 = a constantly declining growth rate to 7 percent over six years
k = 8 percent cost of equity

The specific estimates of annual FCFE, beginning with the actual estimated value of $220 million in 2005, are as follows:

HIGH-GROWTH PERIOD				DECLINING-GROWTH PERIOD			
Year	Growth	$ Million	PV @ 8%	Year	Growth	$ Million	PV @ 8%
2005	—	220	204	2012	(12%)	513	277
2006	(13%)	249	213	2013	(11%)	569	285
2007	(13%)	281	223	2014	(10%)	626	290
2008	(13%)	317	233	2015	(9%)	683	293
2009	(13%)	359	244	2016	(8%)	737	293
2010	(13%)	405	255	2017	(7%)	789	290
2011	(13%)	458	267				
	Total	$1,640			Total	$1,728	

$$\text{Constant Growth Period Value} = \frac{789(1.07)}{0.08 - 0.07} = \frac{844}{0.01} = \$84,400$$

$$\text{PV @ 8\%} = \$31,034$$

The total value of the stock is the sum of the three present-value streams discounted at 8 percent:

	$ Million
1. Present value of high-growth cash flows	1,640
2. Present value of declining-growth cash flows	1,728
3. Present value of constant-growth cash flows	31,034
Total present value of FCFE	34,402

The outstanding shares in 2004 were approximately 1,032 million. Therefore, the per share value, based on the present value of FCFE is $33.34 ($34,402/ 1,032). Again, this estimated value is lower than the prevailing market price of about $42.00. This estimated value implies a *P/E* ratio of about 22.2 times estimated 2005 earnings of $1.50 per share.

Present Value of Operating Free Cash Flow

This is also referred to as *free cash flow to the firm* (FCFF) by Damodaran (1994) and *the entity DCF model* by Copeland, Koller, and Murrin (2001). The object is to determine a value for the total firm and subtract the value of the firm's debt obligations to arrive at a value for the firm's equity. Notably, in this valuation technique, we discount the firm's operating free cash flow to the firm (FCFF) at the firm's weighted average cost of capital (WACC) rather than its cost of equity.

Operating free cash flow or *free cash flow to the firm* is equal to

EBIT (1 − Tax Rate) + Depreciation Expense
     − Capital Expenditures − Δ in Working Capital
     − Δ in other assets

This is the cash flow generated by a company's operations and available to all who have provided capital to the firm—both equity and debt. As noted, because it is the cash flow available to *all capital suppliers,* it is discounted at the firm's WACC.

Again, the alternative specifications of this operating FCF model are similar to the DDM—that is, the specification depends upon the firm's growth prospects. Assuming an expectation of constant growth, you can use the reduced form model:

$$\text{Firm Value} = \frac{\text{FCFF}_1}{\text{WACC} - g_{\text{FCFF}}} \text{ or } \frac{\text{OFCF}_1}{\text{WACC} - g_{\text{OFCF}}} \qquad \textbf{(62-7)}$$

where:

FCFF_1 = the free cash flow for the firm in Period 1
OFCF_1 = the firm's operating free cash flow in Period 1
WACC = the firm's weighted average cost of capital
g_{FCFF} = the constant infinite growth rate of free cash flow for the firm
g_{OFCF} = the constant infinite growth rate of operating free cash flow

As noted in Exhibit 62-3, the compound annual growth rate for operating free cash flow (free cash flow to the firm) during the 21-year period was very low and was negative between 1998 and 2003. It became positive in 2004, and it is estimated it will be $260 million in 2005. An alternative measure of long-run growth is the growth implied by the equation:

$$g = (RR)(ROIC) \qquad \textbf{(62-8)}$$

where:

RR = the average retention rate
$ROIC$ = EBIT $(1 -$ Tax Rate$)$/Total Capital

For Walgreens, the recent retention rate is about 82 percent and

$$ROIC = \frac{\text{EBIT}(1 - \text{Tax Rate})}{\text{Total Capital}} = \frac{2,176 \times (0.62)}{(7,985 + 9,264)/2} = \frac{1,349}{8,624} = 0.1564$$
$$= 15.64\%$$

Therefore,

$$g = (0.82)(0.1564)$$
$$= 0.1282 = 12.82\%$$

We will round this and begin with a growth estimate for OFCF/FCFF of 13 percent.

EXHIBIT 62-3 Inputs for Relative Valuation Technique: Walgreens, Retail Drugstore Industry, and S&P Industrials Index: 1993–2003

	WALGREENS					RETAIL DRUGSTORE INDUSTRY					S&P INDUSTRIALS INDEX				
Year	Mean Price	EPS	CF per Share	BV per Share	Sales per Share	Mean Price	EPS	CF per Share	BV per Share	Sales per Share	Mean Price	EPS	CF per Share	BV per Share	Sales per Share
1993	4.96	0.23	0.44	1.40	8.37	91.00	4.45	21.34	36.84	186.63	520.21	21.96	58.00	191.82	622.12
1994	5.06	0.29	0.50	1.60	9.32	91.27	4.55	22.41	38.68	202.90	536.52	33.12	72.39	210.98	653.75
1995	6.64	0.33	0.57	1.82	10.49	120.77	5.76	26.88	42.76	233.78	638.97	26.01	79.27	227.12	706.13
1996	9.10	0.38	0.65	2.08	11.85	158.78	9.06	17.05	44.27	265.93	795.01	41.15	82.89	238.76	727.40
1997	13.22	0.44	0.61	2.40	13.57	231.01	5.12	17.19	60.87	308.29	1006.12	42.13	83.73	247.83	750.71
1998	22.50	0.54	0.73	2.86	15.43	368.62	7.85	20.94	68.07	343.11	1285.73	38.37	87.38	264.63	750.48
1999	28.31	0.62	0.83	3.47	17.83	403.33	10.59	18.58	61.88	396.21	1651.82	50.25	97.73	302.08	812.00
2000	33.91	0.76	1.00	4.19	21.05	385.22	9.38	13.80	69.34	385.86	1692.85	53.85	105.09	337.51	853.86
2001	37.08	0.86	0.71	5.11	24.15	416.50	9.71	18.35	72.68	369.64	1363.30	19.82	68.58	348.38	811.04
2002	35.25	0.99	1.47	6.08	27.98	348.15	12.96	20.69	85.74	400.23	1133.05	22.57	61.59	310.61	781.65
2003	31.63	1.14	1.47	7.02	31.72	335.69	21.12	23.36	98.79	635.62	1097.27	47.12	90.88	363.74	847.38

OPTIONAL SEGMENT

Calculation of WACC   We calculate the discount rate (i.e., the firm's WACC) using the following formula:

$$\text{WACC} = W_E k + W_D i \tag{62-9}$$

where:

W_E = the proportion of equity in total capital
k = the after-tax cost of equity (from the SML)
W_D = the proportion of debt in total capital[4]
i = the after-tax cost of debt[5]

Recall from corporate finance courses that there are differences of opinion regarding how one should estimate the debt and equity weights—that is, using proportions based upon relative book values or based on relative market value weights. Without getting into the reasons for each choice, it is important to recognize that the use of market value weights will almost always result in a higher WACC because it will imply more equity financing since most firms have a *P/BV* ratio greater than one (for Walgreens the *P/BV* ratio is currently in excess of 5.0). To demonstrate this, we compute a WACC using both weightings. The cost of debt and cost of equity will be the same for both sets.

WACC Using Book Value Weights

k_e = 0.080 (from prior SML calculation)

k_d = 0.043 (current interest rate of 7% and recent tax rate of 38% for WAG)
   $0.07 \times (1 - 0.38) = 0.043$

W_d = 0.30 (including leases)

W_e = 0.70

$$
\begin{aligned}
\text{WACC} &= (W_d \times k_d) + (W_e \times k_e) \\
&= (0.30 \times 0.043) + (0.70 \times 0.080) \\
&= 0.013 + 0.056 = 0.069 = 6.90\%
\end{aligned}
$$

WACC Using Market Value Weights

k_e = 0.080 W_e = 0.90

k_d = 0.043 W_d = 0.10

$$
\begin{aligned}
\text{WACC} &= (W_d \times k_d) + (W_e \times k_e) \\
&= (0.10 \times 0.043) + (0.90 \times 0.080) \\
&= 0.0043 + 0.072 = 0.0763 = 7.63\%
\end{aligned}
$$

---

[4] The proportions of debt and equity capital used in the WACC estimate will be computed using both book value weights that consider the value of capitalized lease payments as debt, and market value weights.

[5] For this estimate, we use the prevailing interest rate on corporate A-rated bonds (7 percent), and Walgreen Co.'s (ticker symbol WAG) recent tax rate of 38 percent.

Therefore, we have a range of 6.90 percent to 7.63 percent and an average of 7.27 percent. We will use a WACC of 7 percent in the demonstration.

Again, because the expected growth rate of operating free cash flow (13 percent) is greater than the firm's WACC, we cannot use the reduced form model that assumes constant growth at this relatively high rate for an infinite period. Therefore, the following demonstration will employ the three-stage growth model with growth duration assumptions similar to the prior examples.

Given these inputs for recent growth and the firm's WACC, the growth estimates for a three-stage growth model are

g_1 = 13 percent for five years
g_2 = a constantly declining rate to 6 percent over seven years.[6]

The specific estimates for future OFCF (or FCFF) are as follows, beginning from the 2005 value of $260 million.

	HIGH-GROWTH PERIOD				DECLINING-GROWTH PERIOD		
Year	Growth Rate	FCFF	PV @ 7%	Year	Growth Rate	FCFF	PV @ 7%
2005	—	260	243	2011	(12%)	537	334
2006	(13%)	294	257	2012	(11%)	596	347
2007	(13%)	332	271	2013	(10%)	655	356
2008	(13%)	375	286	2014	(9%)	714	363
2009	(13%)	424	302	2015	(8%)	771	366
2010	(13%)	479	319	2016	(7%)	825	366
				2017	(6%)	874	363
		Total	$1,678			Total	$2,496

$$\text{Constant Growth Period Value} = \frac{874(1.06)}{0.07 - 0.06} = \frac{926}{0.07 - 0.06} = \$92,600$$

$$\text{PV @ 7\%} = \$38,426$$

Thus, the total value of the firm is:

	$ Million
1. Present value of high-growth cash flows	$1,678
2. Present value of declining-growth cash flows	2,496
3. Present value of constant-growth cash flows	38,426
Total present value of operating FCF (FCFF)	$42,600

---

[6] This 6 percent long-run growth rate assumption implies that we do not believe that FCFF can grow as long at 13 percent and as fast in the long run as FCFE. Given a beginning growth rate of 13 percent for only five years and a long-run rate of 6 percent means that the growth rate will decline by 0.01 per year as shown in the following example.

Recall that the value of equity is the total value of the firm (PV of OFCF) minus the current market value of debt, which is the present value of debt payments at the firm's cost of debt (0.07). The values are as follows:

Total present value of operating FCF	$ 42,600
Minus: Value of debt[7]	12,681
Value of equity	$ 29,909
Number of common shares	1,032 million
Value of equity per share	$ 28.98

Again, this estimated value compares to the recent market value of about $42.00. The $28.98 value implies a *P/E* of about 19 times estimated 2005 earnings of $1.50 per share.

To summarize, the valuations derived from the present value of cash flow techniques are as follows:

Present value of dividends	$34.30
Present value of FCFE	$33.34
Present value of OFCF	$28.98
(or the PV of FCFF)	

All of these prices must be compared to the prevailing market price of $42.00 to determine the investment decision.

Relative Valuation Ratio Techniques

In this section, we present the data required to compute the several relative valuation ratios and demonstrate the use of these relative valuation ratio techniques for Walgreens compared to the RDS industry and the S&P Industrials Index.

Exhibit 62-3 contains the basic data required to compute the relative valuation ratios, and Exhibit 62-4 contains the four sets of relative valuation ratios for Walgreens, its industry, and the aggregate market. This exhibit also contains a comparison of the company ratios to similar ratios for the company's industry and the market. Such a comparison helps the analyst determine changes in the relative valuation ratios over time and consider if the current valuation ratio for the company (Walgreens) is reasonable based on the financial characteristics of the firm versus its industry and the market. To aid in the analysis, four graphs contain the time series of the relative valuation ratios for the company, its industry, and the market. Four additional graphs show the relationship between the relative valuation ratios: for the company compared to its industry and for the company compared to the stock market. We begin with the *P/E* ratio approach where we derive an intrinsic value for the stock based upon an estimate of future EPS and an earnings multiple (*P/E*) for the stock that reflects future expectations.

6   ESTIMATING COMPANY EARNINGS PER SHARE

An estimate of the earnings per share for the company is a function of the sales forecast and the estimated profit margin. The sales forecast includes an analysis of the relationship of company sales to various relevant economic series and to

---

[7] This long-term debt value includes the present value of minimum lease payments discounted at the firm's cost of debt (7 percent).

EXHIBIT 62-4   Relative Valuation Variables: Walgreens, Retail Drugstore Industry, and S&P Industrials Index: 1993–2003

PRICE/EARNINGS RATIO

Year	Walgreens	Retail Drug	Ratio Co/Ind	S&P Ind.	Ratio Co/Mkt
1993	22.02	20.45	1.08	23.69	0.93
1994	17.75	20.06	0.88	16.20	1.10
1995	20.42	20.97	0.97	24.57	0.83
1996	24.25	17.53	1.38	19.32	1.26
1997	30.03	45.12	0.67	23.88	1.26
1998	41.66	46.96	0.89	33.51	1.24
1999	45.65	38.09	1.20	32.87	1.39
2000	44.81	41.07	1.09	31.44	1.43
2001	43.12	42.89	1.01	68.78	0.63
2002	35.61	26.86	1.33	50.20	0.71
2003	27.75	15.89	1.75	23.29	1.19
Mean	32.10	30.53	1.11	31.61	1.09

PRICE/CASH FLOW RATIO

Year	Walgreens	Retail Drug	Ratio Co/Ind	S&P Ind.	Ratio Co/Mkt
1993	11.27	4.26	2.64	8.97	1.26
1994	10.12	4.07	2.48	7.41	1.37
1995	11.65	4.49	2.59	8.06	1.45
1996	14.00	9.31	1.50	9.59	1.46
1997	21.67	13.44	1.61	12.02	1.80
1998	30.82	17.60	1.75	14.71	2.09
1999	34.11	21.71	1.57	16.90	2.02
2000	33.91	27.91	1.21	16.11	2.11
2001	52.23	22.70	2.30	19.38	2.63
2002	24.03	16.83	1.43	18.40	1.31
2003	21.55	14.37	1.50	12.07	1.79
Mean	24.12	14.25	1.87	13.10	1.75

PRICE/BOOK VALUE RATIO

Year	Walgreens	Retail Drug	Ratio Co/Ind	S&P Ind.	Ratio Co/Mkt
1993	3.54	2.47	1.43	2.71	1.31
1994	3.16	2.36	1.34	2.54	1.24
1995	3.65	2.82	1.29	2.81	1.30
1996	4.38	3.59	1.22	3.33	1.31
1997	5.51	3.80	1.45	4.06	1.36
1998	7.87	5.42	1.45	4.86	1.62
1999	8.16	6.52	1.25	5.47	1.49
2000	8.09	5.56	1.46	5.02	1.61
2001	7.26	5.73	1.27	3.91	1.85
2002	5.80	4.06	1.43	3.65	1.59
2003	4.51	3.40	1.33	3.02	1.49
Mean	5.63	4.16	1.36	3.76	1.47

PRICE/SALES RATIO

Year	Walgreens	Retail Drug	Ratio Co/Ind	S&P Ind.	Ratio Co/Mkt
1993	0.59	0.49	1.22	0.84	0.71
1994	0.54	0.45	1.21	0.82	0.66
1995	0.63	0.52	1.23	0.90	0.70
1996	0.77	0.60	1.29	1.09	0.70
1997	0.97	0.75	1.30	1.34	0.73
1998	1.46	1.07	1.36	1.71	0.85
1999	1.59	1.02	1.56	2.03	0.78
2000	1.61	1.00	1.61	1.98	0.81
2001	1.54	1.13	1.36	1.63	0.91
2002	1.26	0.87	1.45	1.45	0.87
2003	1.00	0.53	1.89	1.29	0.77
Mean	1.09	0.77	1.41	1.38	0.77

EXHIBIT 62-5	Walgreens, S&P Retail Drugstore Sales, and Various Economic Series: 1993–2003

Year	Sales Walgreen Co. ($ Millions)	Retail Drugstores (Sales/Share)	Personal Consumption Expenditures (PCE) ($ Billions)	PCE Medical Care ($ Billions)	Medical Care as a Percentage of PCE
1993	8,295	186.63	4,454.7	700.6	15.73%
1994	9,235	202.90	4,716.4	737.3	15.63%
1995	10,395	233.78	4,969.0	780.7	15.71%
1996	11,778	265.93	5,237.5	814.4	15.55%
1997	13,363	308.29	5,529.3	854.6	15.46%
1998	15,307	343.11	5,856.0	899.0	15.35%
1999	17,839	396.21	6,250.2	939.9	15.04%
2000	21,207	385.86	6,728.4	1,026.8	15.26%
2001	24,623	369.64	7,055.0	1,113.8	15.79%
2002	28,681	400.23	7,385.3	1,210.3	16.39%
2003	32,505	635.62	7,760.9	1,301.1	16.76%
CGR	13.22	11.78	5.18	5.79	0.58

CGR = compound annual growth rate

Source: Financial Analyst's Handbook (New York: Standard & Poor's, 2004) and *Economic Report of the President* (Washington, DC: U.S. Government Printing Office, 2005).

the RDS industry series. These comparisons tell us how the company is performing relative to the economy and to its closest competition.

Company Sales Forecast

Besides providing background on the company, these relationships can help us develop specific sales forecasts for Walgreens.

Exhibit 62-5 contains data on sales for Walgreens from its annual report, sales per share for the RDS industry, and several personal consumption expenditure (PCE) series for the period 1993 to 2003.

To examine the relationship of Walgreen Co.'s sales to the economy, we considered several alternative series. The series that had the strongest relationship was personal consumption expenditure for medicine (PCE medical care).[8] The scatterplot of Walgreen Co.'s sales and the PCE medical care expenditures contained in Exhibit 62-6 indicates a strong linear relationship, including the fact that Walgreen Co.'s sales grew faster than PCE medical care (i.e., 13.22 percent versus 5.79 percent). As a result, Walgreen Co.'s sales have gone from about 1.2 percent of PCE medical care to 2.50 percent.

---

[8] The relationship between Walgreen Co.'s sales and total PCE or per capital PCE was significant but not as strong as PCE medical care.

We also compared Walgreen Co.'s sales and sales per share for the RDS industry. Unfortunately, it did not reflect as strong a relationship and is not used subsequently.

The figures in the last column of Exhibit 62-5 indicate that during this period, the proportion of PCE allocated to medical care went from 15.7 percent in 1993 to 16.8 percent in 2003. The increasing proportion of PCE spent on medical care is a function of the growing proportion of the population over 65 and the rising cost of medical care. Because Walgreen Co.'s sales are growing faster than medical expenditures, these increases should continue to be beneficial for Walgreens because over 62 percent of its sales are prescriptions. Notably, these increases in medical care expenditures continued during the economic recession in 2001–2002.

As shown in Exhibit 62-7, the internal sales growth for Walgreens going back to 1977, resulted from an increase in the number of stores (from 626 in 1977 to 4,582 in 2004) and an increase in the annual sales per store because of the upgrading of stores. The net increase in stores includes numerous new, large stores and the closing of many smaller stores. As a result, the average size of stores has increased. More important, the firm has continued to increase its sales per thousand square feet at almost 4.4 percent a year. This is a critical statistic in the retailing industry, and the fact that Walgreens has been able to experience consistent growth in this metric is significant evidence of strong management.

Sample Estimate of Walgreen Co.'s Sales   The foregoing analysis indicates that you should use the Walgreens-PCE medical care graph. To estimate PCE medical care, you should initially project total PCE and then determine how much would be included in the medical care component. As noted in Reading 60 in connection with the industry analysis, economists were forecasting an increase in PCE of 3.6 percent during 2005, which implied a 2005 estimate of $8,694 billion. In addition, it was estimated that the percentage of PCE spent on medical care in 2005 would be almost 17.0 percent. This implies an estimate for PCE medical care of $1,475 billion, which is about a 6.5 percent increase from 2004. Based on the graph in Exhibit 62-6, which shows the historical relationship between PCE medical care and Walgreen co.'s sales, this would imply a 14 percent increase in Walgreen Co.'s sales to about $42.75 billion ($37.508 billion × 1.14).

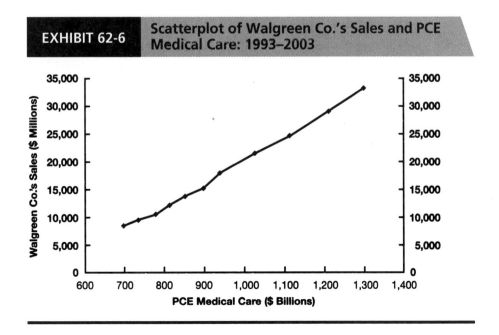

| EXHIBIT 62-6 | Scatterplot of Walgreen Co.'s Sales and PCE Medical Care: 1993–2003 |

EXHIBIT 62-7	Sales, Number of Stores, and Sales Area for Walgreens: 1977–2004					
Year	Sales Walgreens ($ Millions)	Number of Stores	Annual Sales per Store ($ Millions)	Store Area (000 Sq. Ft.)	Area per Store (000 Sq. Ft.)	Avg. Sales per Thousand Sq. Ft.
1977	1,223.2	626	1.95	5,188	8.29	235.77
1978	1,192.9	641	1.86	5,390	8.41	221.32
1979	1,334.5	688	1.94	5,851	8.50	228.08
1980	1,530.7	739	2.07	6,305	8.53	242.78
1981	1,743.5	821	2.12	7,209	8.78	241.85
1982	2,039.5	883	2.31	7,815	8.85	260.97
1983	2,360.6	941	2.51	8,402	8.93	280.96
1984	2,744.6	1,002	2.74	9,002	8.98	304.89
1985	3,161.9	1,095	2.89	10,010	9.14	315.87
1986	3,660.6	1,273	2.88	11,895	9.34	307.74
1987	4,281.6	1,356	3.16	12,844	9.47	333.35
1988	4,883.5	1,416	3.45	13,549	9.57	360.43
1989	5,380.1	1,484	3.63	14,272	9.62	376.97
1990	6,047.5	1,564	3.87	15,105	9.66	400.36
1991	6,733.0	1,646	4.09	15,877	9.65	424.08
1992	7,475.0	1,736	4.31	16,811	9.68	444.65
1993	8,294.8	1,836	4.52	17,950	9.78	462.11
1994	9,235.0	1,968	4.69	19,342	9.83	477.46
1995	10,395.1	2,085	4.99	20,731	9.94	501.43
1996	11,778.4	2,193	5.37	22,124	10.09	532.38
1997	13,363.0	2,358	5.67	23,935	10.15	558.30
1998	15,307.0	2,549	6.01	26,024	10.21	588.19
1999	17,838.8	2,821	6.32	29,230	10.36	610.29
2000	21,206.9	3,165	6.70	33,684	10.64	629.58
2001	24,623.0	3,520	7.00	38,226	10.86	644.14
2002	28,681.1	3,883	7.39	42,672	10.99	672.13
2003	32,505.4	4,227	7.69	46,734	11.06	695.54
2004	37,508.2	4,582	8.19	50,927	11.11	736.51
Average annual rate of growth (%)	13.59%	7.69%	5.50%	8.88%	1.09%	4.36%

Source: Information calculated using publicly available data of Walgreen Co. Reprinted with the permission of Walgreen Co.

Because Walgreens provides data on square footage and the number of stores, it allows us to compute an alternative sales estimate using the company data in Exhibit 62-7 to support the prior estimate. If we assume an increase in store area during 2005 of about 4.1 million square feet (which is less than in most years), the firm's total sales area would be about 55 million square feet. As noted, sales per square foot have likewise increased. Assuming a conservative increase to $750 of sales per thousand square feet implies a sales forecast of about $41.25 billion for 2005, a 10 percent increase over 2004 sales of $37.51 billion.

Another internal estimate is made possible by using the number of stores and sales per store. Walgreens is expected to open 450 stores during 2005. Assuming that it closes 85 stores as expected, this would be a net addition of 365 stores, resulting in 4,947 stores at the end of 2005. Assuming sales per store likewise continue to increase from $8.19 million to $8.50 million implies an estimate of $42.00 billion (4,947 × $8.50 million), an increase of 12 percent over 2004.

Given the three estimates, the preference is for the mid-range estimate of 12 percent, which is somewhat conservative, because we are in the fourth year of the economic expansion and recent increases have been in the 13–15 percent range. This implies a final sales forecast for 2005 of $42 billion.

Estimating the Company Profit Margin

The next step in projecting earnings per share is to estimate the firm's net profit margin, which should include three considerations: (1) identification and evaluation of the firm's specific competitive strategy—that is, either low-cost or differentiation; (2) the firm's internal performance, including general company trends and consideration of any problems that might affect its future performance; and (3) the firm's relationship with its industry, which should indicate whether the company's past performance is attributable to its industry or if it is unique to the firm. These examinations should help us understand the firm's past performance but should also provide the background to make a meaningful estimate for the future. In this analysis, we do not consider the company-economy relationship because the significant economywide profit factors are reflected in the industry results. Since we have already discussed these strategies in general, we concentrate on how they affect Walgreens.

WALGREEN CO.'S COMPETITIVE STRATEGIES   7

Over the years, has Walgreens pursued a low-cost strategy or has the firm attempted to differentiate itself from its competitors in some unique way? Based on its annual reports, Walgreens has pursued both strategies with different segments of its business. The firm's size and buying power allow it to be a cost leader for some of its nonprescription products, such as liquor, ice cream, candy, and soft drinks. These items are advertised heavily to attract customer traffic and to build consumer loyalty. At the same time, Walgreens has attempted to build a very strong franchise in the medical prescription business based on differentiation in service. Computer technology in the prescription area makes it possible for the firm to distinguish itself by providing outstanding service to its prescription customers. Specifically, the firm refers to itself as the nation's prescription druggist based on the number of prescriptions it fills and a nationwide computer system that allows customers to have their prescriptions filled at any of the 4,582 Walgreen Co.'s drugstores in the country. This service leadership in the growing medical field is a major goal.

EXHIBIT 62-8	Profit Margins and Component Expenses for Walgreens and the Retail Drugstore Industry: 1993–2003

	WALGREEN CO.			RETAIL DRUGSTORES		
Year	Operating Margin (%)	NBT Margin (%)	Net Profit Margin (%)	Operating Margin (%)	NBT Margin (%)	Net Profit Margin (%)
1993	4.90	4.82	2.96	29.96	4.55	2.78
1994	4.93	4.96	3.05	30.04	3.80	2.33
1995	5.00	5.04	3.09	31.41	4.65	2.84
1996	5.13	5.15	3.16	15.49	5.37	3.28
1997	5.30	5.33	3.84	13.29	3.54	2.02
1998	5.46	5.49	3.34	14.54	4.42	2.61
1999	5.69	5.69	3.43	10.70	3.97	2.27
2000	5.77	5.77	3.48	7.70	3.16	0.96
2001	5.68	5.67	3.48	9.60	4.42	2.69
2002	5.66	5.71	3.55	9.04	5.33	3.31
2003	5.69	5.81	3.62	6.64	3.85	2.39

The Internal Performance

Profit margin figures for Walgreens and the RDS industry are in Exhibit 62-8. The profit margins for Walgreens increased overall from 2.96 percent to 3.62 percent. In contrast, the margins for the RDS industry experienced an overall decline. Overall, Walgreens experienced a positive trend in its operating and net profit margins over the past 10 years. To predict future values, you need to determine the reason for the overall decline in the industry profit margin and, more important, what factors have contributed to Walgreen Co.'s strong positive performance.

Industry Factors Industry profit margins have declined over the past two decades due to price discounting by aggressive regional drug chains.[9] The discussion in Reading 60 suggested this as one of the competitive structure conditions that affect long-run profitability. Industry analysts have observed, however, that price cutting has subsided, and they foresee relative price stability following a period of consolidation in which CVS has acquired several of the smaller, less profitable chains. In addition, drugstores have tended toward a more profitable product mix featuring high-profit-margin items, such as cosmetics, which has had a positive influence on profit margins.

Company Performance The Walgreen Co.'s profit margin has shown consistent improvement, and a major reason has been the change in corporate structure and sales mix. The outlook for profit margins is good because the firm has developed a strong position in the pharmacy business and has invested in service (including

---

[9] For a more complete discussion, see "Retailing—Drug Stores" in *Standard & Poor's Industry Surveys* (New York: Standard & Poor's, 2004).

EXHIBIT 62-9	Time-Series Plot of Net Profit Margin for Walgreens and the Retail Drugstore Industry: 1993–2003

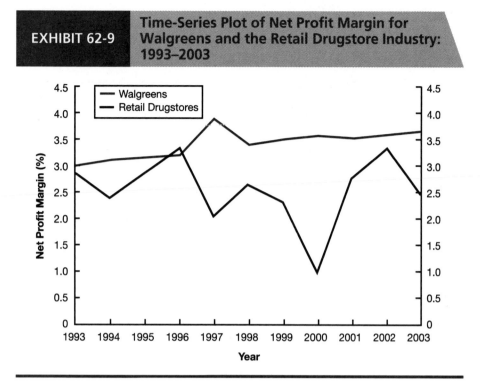

mail-order prescriptions) and inventory-control technology that will help the firm experience strong margins on this business. The firm also has emphasized high-profit-margin items, such as greeting cards, photofinishing, and cosmetics.

Specific estimates for Walgreen Co.'s future margins typically would begin with an analysis of the firm's relationship with drugstore industry margins using time-series plots, such as those in Exhibit 62-9.[10] This time-series plot for the period 1993–2003 showed good results for Walgreens versus its industry. You should consider any unique factors that would influence this long-run relationship, such as price wars or an abnormal number of store openings or closings by the firm.

Following the analysis of the company-industry profit margin relationship, you should analyze the firm's common-size income statement. Exhibit 62-10 shows a common-size income statement for Walgreens during the period 2001–2004. An analysis of the main items of interest—cost of goods sold and SG&A expense—was encouraging. The cost-of-sales percentage declined slightly (less than 1 percent) while there was a partially offsetting increase in the percentage of SG&A expense. As a result, the operating profit margin experienced a minimal increase from 5.68 percent to 5.71 percent. Finally, the tax rate was stable at 38 percent.

Net Profit Margin Estimate   The overall industry outlook is encouraging because of stable prices, an increase in mechanization within the industry, and the inclusion of more high-profit-margin items. Because of Walgreen Co.'s strong performance relative to its industry profit margin and a small increase in

---

[10] Both the operating margin and the net before tax margin were analyzed; the results indicated that the net profit margins yielded the best relationships. The long-run relationship cannot be very good because over the total period the industry margin was declining while Walgreens experienced fairly steady increases as shown in Exhibits 62-8 and 62-9.

EXHIBIT 62-10	Walgreen Co. and Subsidiaries Consolidated Statement of Income (Dollars in Millions, Except per Share Data): Years Ended August 31, 2001, 2002, 2003, and 2004							
	2004		**2003**		**2002**		**2001**	
Net sales	37,508	100.00%	32,505	100.00%	28.681	100.00%	24,623	100.00%
Cost of sales	27,310	72.81%	23,706	72.93%	21,076	73.48%	18,049	73.30%
Gross profit	10,198	27.19%	8.799	27.07%	7,605	26.52%	6,574	26.70%
Selling, occupancy, and administrative expense	8,055	21.48%	6,951	21.38%	5,981	20.85%	5,176	21.02%
Operating profit (EBIT)	2,143	5.71%	1,848	5.69%	1,624	5.66%	1,398	5.68%
Interest income	17	0.05%	11	0.03%	7	0.02%	5	0.02%
Interest expense	—	0.00%	—	0.00%	—	0.00%	(3)	−0.01%
Other Income	16	0.04%	30	0.09%	6	0.02%	22	0.09%
Operating income before income taxes	2,176	5.80%	1,889	5.81%	1,637	5.71%	1,422	5.78%
Provision for income taxes	816	2.18%	713	2.19%	618	2.15%	537	2.18%
Reported net income	1,360	3.63%	1,176	3.62%	1,019	3.55%	885	3.60%
Reported net income available for common shares	1,360	3.63%	1,176	3.62%	1,019	3.55%	885	3.60%

Source: These statements were created by the authors based upon financial statements supplied by Walgreen Co.'s

its margin as shown in Exhibit 62-10, it is estimated that the firm will show a slight increase to 3.66 in 2005.

Computing Earnings per Share   This margin estimate, combined with the prior sales estimate of $42 billion, indicates net income of $1,537 million. Assuming about 1,030 million common shares outstanding, earnings should be about $1.50 per share for 2005, which is an increase of almost 14 percent over the earnings of $1.32 per share in 2004. To find the value of Walgreen Co. stock, our next step is to estimate its earnings multiplier.

Importance of Quarterly Estimates

Once we have derived an estimate of next year's sales and net earnings, it is essential that we also derive an estimate of each of the quarterly results for two important reasons. First, this is a way to confirm our annual estimate—that is, do the quarterly estimates required to arrive at the annual estimate seem reasonable? If not, we need to reevaluate the annual forecast. Second, unless we have quarterly forecasts that confirm our annual forecast, we will not be in a position to determine whether the subsequent *actual* results are a positive surprise, negative surprise, or no surprise. Further, if the actual results are a surprise relative to our estimate, we will want to understand the reason for the surprise—for example, did we under- or overestimate sales growth and/or was it due to differences in the profit margin from our estimates? This understanding is needed for an estimated *earnings revision* that reflects the new information from the company—we would probably revise each of our future quarterly estimates to arrive at a new annual estimate.

ESTIMATING COMPANY EARNINGS MULTIPLIERS   8

As in our analysis of industry multipliers in Reading 60, we use two approaches to estimate a company multiplier. First, we estimate the *P/E* ratio from the relationships between Walgreens, its industry, and the market. This is the macroanalysis. Second, we estimate a multiplier based on its three components: the dividend-payout ratio, the required rate of return, and the rate of growth. We then resolve the estimates derived from each approach and settle on one estimate.

Macroanalysis of the Earnings Multiplier

Exhibit 62-11 shows the mean earnings multiple for the company, the RDS industry, and the aggregate market for the period 1993–2003. Notably, all these earnings multipliers are computed using future earnings. The Walgreen Co.'s multiplier has generally followed the industry multiplier with a company/industry ratio between 1.00 and 1.15. The Walgreen Co.'s earnings multiplier has been consistently higher than the market multiplier except during 2001–2002.

This pattern raises the question: Is the higher value for the Walgreens *P/E* relative to both its industry and the market justified? The microanalyses should provide some insights regarding this question.

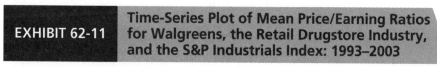

EXHIBIT 62-11 Time-Series Plot of Mean Price/Earning Ratios for Walgreens, the Retail Drugstore Industry, and the S&P Industrials Index: 1993–2003

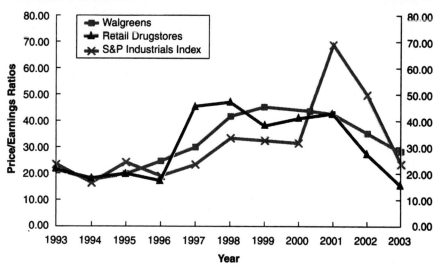

Microanalysis of the Earnings Multiplier

This historical data for the relevant series are contained in Exhibit 62-12.[11] The relevant question is, Why has the earnings multiplier for Walgreens been generally higher than the market and industry earnings multiplier? As before, we are looking for estimates of D/E, k, and g to find an earnings multiplier. We will use the historical data in Exhibit 62-12 to determine patterns for the data and to develop future projections.

Comparing Dividend-Payout Ratios   The dividend-payout ratio for Walgreens typically has been lower than its industry in recent years. The Walgreens-market comparison shows that Walgreens almost always had a lower payout, which by itself would imply a lower P/E ratio for Walgreens than for its industry and the market.

Estimating the Required Rate of Return   To find Walgreen Co.'s required rate of return (k), we need to analyze the firm's fundamental risk characteristics (BR, FR, LR, ERR, and CR) and also derive an estimate based on the SML and a measure of Walgreen Co.'s systematic risk (i.e., its beta).

Walgreens should have relatively low business risk due to its stable sales growth compared to its industry and the aggregate economy. For a growth company like Walgreens it is necessary to adjust for both the growth and size factor by measuring variability around the growth trend and relating this volatility to the mean as in Exhibit 62-13. After adjusting for size and trend, the results indicated that Walgreen Co.'s sales and EBIT experienced very stable growth, which indicates lower business risk.

Several financial risk variables for Walgreens, its industry, and the aggregate market are shown in Exhibit 62-14. Notably, these do not consider fairly large leases of stores. Without considering these financial leases, these financial risk ratios indicate that Walgreens has comparable financial risk to its industry and substantially lower financial risk than the aggregate stock market. In contrast, when the leases are considered as they should be, the firm's financial risk is equal to, or somewhat higher than the market.

The firm's liquidity risk is quite low compared to its industry and the average firm in the market. Indicators of market liquidity are (1) the number of stockholders, (2) the number and market value of shares outstanding, (3) the number of shares traded, and (4) institutional interest in the stock. As of January 1, 2005, Walgreens had 30,000 holders of common stock—a relatively large number. At mid-2005, there were over one billion common shares outstanding with a market value of over $35 billion. Clearly, Walgreens would qualify as an investment for institutions that require firms with large market value. Walgreen Co.'s stock has an annual trading turnover of 75 percent, which is below average. Financial institutions own about 460 million shares of Walgreens, which is about 45 percent of the outstanding shares. Therefore, Walgreen Co.'s large number of stockholders, very large market capitalization, fairly active trading of its stock, and strong institutional interest indicate that Walgreens has very little liquidity risk.

The exchange rate risk for companies depends on what proportion of sales and earnings are generated outside the United States and the volatility of the exchange rates in the specific countries. Walgreens has very little exchange rate risk or country risk because the firm has virtually no non-U.S. sales.

---

[11] Although some prior tables included data through 2003 using estimates for specific ratios, it is not possible to do this for all the variables in Exhibit 62-12 as of mid-2005.

EXHIBIT 62-12   Variables that Influence the Earnings Multiplier for Walgreens, the Retail Drugstore Industry, and the S&P Industrials: 1993–2004

Year	WALGREENS						RETAIL DRUGSTORES						S&P INDUSTRIALS					
	D/E	NPM	TAT	ROA	TAE	ROE	D/E	NPM	TAT	ROA	TAE	ROE	D/E	NPM	TAT	ROA	TAE	ROE
1993	33.52	2.67	3.27	8.73	1.84	16.08	35.71	2.78	2.73	7.59	1.85	14.06	45.79	5.26	0.90	3.27	3.59	16.97
1994	29.82	3.05	3.17	9.67	1.85	17.92	41.53	2.33	2.68	6.25	1.95	12.21	38.11	5.86	0.92	4.91	3.37	18.14
1995	30.77	3.09	3.20	9.87	1.81	19.10	32.98	2.84	2.61	7.41	2.10	15.53	35.02	6.37	0.95	5.19	3.25	19.63
1996	28.95	3.16	3.24	10.24	1.78	19.40	39.61	3.28	2.75	8.90	2.18	19.68	34.75	6.50	0.97	5.62	3.14	19.72
1997	26.97	3.26	3.18	10.36	1.77	19.80	40.85	2.02	2.19	4.34	2.24	9.88	32.24	6.96	0.93	5.33	3.14	20.40
1998	24.27	3.51	3.12	10.95	1.72	19.60	29.91	2.61	2.21	5.71	2.21	12.78	37.04	6.53	0.86	4.90	3.16	17.77
1999	20.97	3.50	3.02	10.57	1.70	17.91	31.00	2.27	2.10	4.69	2.85	13.58	33.36	6.69	0.83	5.22	3.11	17.31
2000	18.18	3.66	2.99	10.94	1.68	18.35	54.29	0.96	3.04	2.75	1.83	5.34	28.32	7.00	0.84	5.45	2.89	17.06
2001	16.09	3.60	2.79	10.03	1.70	17.01	19.37	2.69	2.70	7.20	1.83	13.35	38.36	5.36	0.77	4.13	3.64	15.05
2002	15.15	3.55	3.07	10.32	1.59	16.36	14.31	3.31	2.69	8.84	1.73	15.38	32.64	6.16	0.77	4.74	3.26	15.50
2003	14.04	3.62	3.02	10.31	1.59	16.34	13.00	2.39	3.78	8.98	1.69	15.29	31.51	5.89	0.76	4.29	3.02	13.57
2004	13.01	3.63	3.00	10.20	1.62	16.52	N/A	N/A	N/A	N/A	N/A	N/A	N/A	N/A	N/A	N/A	N/A	N/A
Mean	22.65	3.36	3.09	10.18	1.72	17.87	32.05	2.50	2.68	6.61	2.04	13.37	32.35	6.23	0.86	4.82	3.23	17.37

D/E = Dividend payout, equal to dividends/earnings.
NPM = Net profit margin, equal to net income/sales.
TAT = Total asset turnover, equal to sales/total assets.
ROA = Return on assets.

TAE = Leverage ratio, equal to total assets/equity.
ROE = Return on equity, equal to net income/equity.
N/A = Data not available.

Source: Adapted from data in *Financial Analyst's Handbook* (New York: Standard & Poor's, 2004).

In summary, Walgreens has below-average business risk, financial risk higher than the market when we consider leases, low liquidity risk, and virtually no exchange rate and country risk. This implies that—based on fundamental factors—the overall risk for Walgreens should be lower than the market.

Analysts should also consider market-determined risk (beta) based on the CAPM. As noted in connection with the cash flow models, the stock's beta derived from five years of monthly data relative to the S&P Industrials for the period 2000–2004 indicated a beta of 0.90.

These results are consistent with those derived from an analysis of the fundamental factors—both indicate that Walgreen Co.'s risk is below the aggregate market. This means that the required rate of return *(k)* for Walgreen Co.'s stock estimated earlier using the CAPM is reasonable—that is, 8 percent. By itself, this lower *k* would suggest an earnings multiplier above the market multiplier.

Estimating the Expected Growth Rate   Recall that the expected growth rate *(g)* is determined by the firm's retention rate and its expected return on equity *(ROE)*. We have already noted Walgreen Co.'s low dividend payout compared to the industry and the aggregate market, which implies a higher retention rate.

As discussed using the DuPont model, a firm's *ROE* can be estimated in terms of the three ratios: (1) net profit margin (NPM), (2) total asset turnover (TAT), and (3) the financial leverage multiplier. We also know that NPM × TAT = Return on Assets *(ROA)*. It is important to examine the relative impact of these two ratios and to compare the *ROA* of alternative firms as a measure of operating performance—that is, profitability and asset efficiency. Walgreens has experienced a small decline in TAT, but this has been offset by an increase in NPM, causing the firm's *ROA* to be relatively stable and substantially above its industry and the market.

EXHIBIT 62-13	Time-Series Plot of Walgreen Co.'s Sales Used in Calculation of Sales Volatility for Walgreens from Arithmetic Mean, from Linear Growth Curve, and from Compound Growth Curve

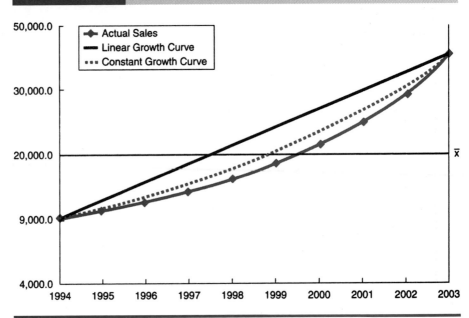

EXHIBIT 62-14   Financial Risk Ratios for Walgreens, the Retail Drugstore Industry, and the S&P Industrials: 1993–2003

	WALGREENS*				RETAIL DRUGSTORES				S&P INDUSTRIALS			
Year	Total Assets/ Equity	Interest Coverage	Cash Flow/ Long-Term Debt	Cash Flow/ Total Debt	Total Assets/ Equity	Interest Coverage	Cash Flow/ Long-Term Debt	Cash Flow/ Total Debt	Total Assets/ Equity	Interest Coverage	Cash Flow/ Long-Term Debt	Cash Flow/ Total Debt
1993	1.84	6.92	0.162	0.110	1.85	22.22	2.307	0.740	3.59	4.25	0.412	0.164
1994	1.85	6.53	0.150	0.108	1.95	16.73	1.952	0.661	3.37	5.10	0.424	0.192
1995	1.94	6.46	0.128	0.092	2.10	14.59	1.741	0.614	3.25	5.48	0.431	0.196
1996	1.90	6.43	0.133	0.096	2.18	14.11	0.897	0.346	3.14	6.17	0.452	0.205
1997	1.91	6.62	0.189	0.133	2.24	7.73	0.700	0.235	3.14	6.69	0.440	0.195
1998	1.72	6.38	0.130	0.096	2.21	9.71	0.796	0.275	3.16	6.02	0.422	0.191
1999	1.70	6.14	0.118	0.087	2.85	6.54	0.351	0.165	3.11	6.53	0.417	0.191
2000	1.68	5.91	0.144	0.107	1.83	4.92	2.150	0.261	2.89	6.52	0.444	0.199
2001	1.68	5.75	0.092	0.066	1.83	25.37	2.480	0.320	3.64	4.78	0.252	0.123
2002	1.59	5.69	0.166	0.125	1.73	50.58	2.203	0.365	3.26	5.59	0.213	0.109
2003	1.62	5.26	0.131	0.100	1.69	60.73	3.054	0.375	3.02	6.21	0.302	0.154

* All Walgreen Co.'s ratios are computed with leases capitalized and include consideration of implied interest on this lease debt

Source: Adapted from data in *Financial Analyst's Handbook* (New York: Standard & Poor's, 2004).

Finally, the firm's *ROE* equals the *ROA* times the financial leverage multiplier (total assets/equity). Notably, since 1993, Walgreens has reduced its leverage multiplier from 1.84 to 1.62 while the industry and market have experienced similar declines.

As a result, the *ROE*s are similar but the financial risk is different—that is, Walgreens has a higher *ROE* but equal financial risk relative to the industry and lower risk compared to the market using the ratios in Exhibit 62-14.

Using the results for the last three years (2001–2003), the *ROE*s would be approximately as follows:

	NPM	TAT	ROA	Total Assets/ Equity	ROE
Walgreens	3.59	2.96	10.63	1.63	17.33
Retail drugstores	2.80	3.06	8.57	1.75	15.00
S&P Industrials	5.80	0.77	4.47	3.31	14.80

The foregoing is meant to highlight the difference among the three units based on recent history. An analyst would need to *estimate* future components and derive an expected *ROE* that reflects the firm's expected *future* performance.

The demonstration can be extended by combining the average annual *ROE*s derived in the preceding table and the average of recent retention rates from Exhibit 62-15 to derive expected growth rates:

	Retention Rate	ROE	Expected Growth Rate
Walgreens	0.85	17.33	0.1473
Retail drugstores	0.84	15.00	0.1260
S&P Industrials	0.77	14.80	0.1140

Taken alone, these higher expected growth rates for Walgreens would indicate that it should definitely have a higher multiple than its industry and the market.

Computing the Earnings Multiplier   Comparing our estimates of *D/E*, *k*, and *g* to comparable values for the industry and the market, we find that the Walgreen Co.'s earnings multiplier based on the microanalysis should be greater than the multiplier for its industry and the market. Specifically, the dividend-payout ratio points toward a lower multiplier for Walgreens, whereas both the lower risk analysis and the higher expected growth rate would indicate a multiplier for Walgreens above that of its industry and the market.

The macroanalysis indicated that the Walgreen Co.'s multiplier typically has been above its industry and the market, and the microanalysis supported this relationship. Assuming a market multiple of about 18 and a retail drugstore multiplier of about 20 times, the multiplier for Walgreens should be between 22 and 26, with a tendency toward the upper end of the range and beyond (22–24–26 times). Alternatively, if we inserted some earlier estimated values for *D/E*, *k*, and *g* into the *P/E* ratio formula, we would not be able to derive an estimated multiplier for Walgreens because *g* is greater than *k*. As noted in Reading 59, because Walgreens is a true growth company, we cannot

EXHIBIT 62-15	Expected Growth Rate Components for Walgreens, the Retail Drugstore Industry, and the S&P Industrials: 1993–2003								
	WALGREENS			**RETAIL DRUGSTORES**			**S&P INDUSTRIALS**		
Year	Retention Rate	*ROE*	Expected Growth Rate	Retention Rate	*ROE*	Expected Growth Rate	Retention Rate	*ROE*	Expected Growth Rate
1993	0.66	16.08	10.69	0.64	14.06	9.04	0.68	16.97	11.51
1994	0.70	17.92	12.58	0.58	12.21	7.14	0.75	18.14	13.58
1995	0.69	19.10	13.22	0.67	15.53	10.41	0.77	19.63	15.04
1996	0.71	19.40	13.78	0.61	19.68	11.98	0.77	19.72	15.24
1997	0.73	19.80	14.46	0.60	9.88	5.92	0.78	20.40	15.97
1998	0.76	19.60	14.84	0.70	12.78	9.00	0.75	17.77	13.32
1999	0.79	17.91	14.16	0.69	13.58	9.43	0.78	17.31	13.57
2000	0.82	18.35	15.01	0.49	5.34	2.60	0.82	17.06	13.96
2001	0.84	17.01	14.29	0.81	13.35	10.79	0.73	15.05	10.97
2002	0.85	16.36	13.91	0.86	15.38	13.20	0.77	15.50	11.96
2003	0.86	16.34	14.05	0.87	15.29	13.31	0.80	13.57	10.79

Source: Adapted from data in *Financial Analyst's Handbook* (New York: Standard & Poor's, 2004).

use the standard DDM formula to estimate a specific multiple. We would need to estimate a value based on the direction of change and the macroanalysis estimates of 22–24–26 times.

Estimate of the Future Value for Walgreens   Earlier, we estimated 2005 earnings per share for Walgreens of about $1.50 per share. Assuming multipliers of 22–24–26 implies the following estimated future values:

22 × $1.50 = $33.00
24 × $1.50 = $36.00
26 × $1.50 = $39.00

Making the Investment Decision

In our prior discussions of valuation, we set forth the following investment decision rule: compute the estimated intrinsic value for an investment using your required rate of return as the discount rate. If this intrinsic value is equal to or greater than the current market price of the investment, buy it. If the estimated intrinsic value is less than the market price, do not buy it, and if you own it, sell it.

Therefore, the required comparisons are the estimated values derived using the present value of cash flow models and the values estimated using the earnings multiple model to the current market price of Walgreens of about $42.00 a share. The following is a summary of these estimated values. Recall that we could not calculate constant-growth models because Walgreens has consistently experienced growth rates above its required rates of return (it is a true growth company).

Present Value of Cash Flow Models	
Three-stage DDM	$34.30
Three-stage FCFE	$33.34
Three-stage FCFF (OFCF)	$28.98

Earnings Multiple Models	
22 times estimated earnings	$33.00
24 times estimated earnings	$36.00
26 times estimated earnings	$39.00

Because none of the computed values is equal to or larger than the current market price of $42.00, you would not recommend a purchase of the stock although Walgreens is clearly an outstanding firm. Stated in terms of our earlier discussion. Walgreens is obviously a true growth company, but based on the valuations the firm's stock is not expected to be a growth stock at its current price.

9 ADDITIONAL MEASURES OF RELATIVE VALUE

The best-known measure of relative value for common stock is the price/earnings ratio. Analysts have also begun to calculate three additional measures of relative value for common stocks—the price/book value ratio, the price/cash flow ratio, and the price/sales ratio, which were discussed in Reading 59.

Price/Book Value (P/BV) Ratio

The price-to-book-value ratio (P/BV) has gained prominence because of the studies by Fama and French (1992); Rosenberg, Reid, and Lanstein (1985); and Fairfield (1994). Book value is a reasonable measure of value for firms that have consistent accounting practice (for example, firms in the same industry) and can apply to firms with negative earnings or cash flows. You should not attempt to use this ratio to compare firms with different levels of hard assets—for example, a heavy industrial firm and a service firm.

The annual P/BV ratios for Walgreens, its industry, and the market are in Exhibit 62-4, along with the ratio of the company P/BV ratio relative to its industry and relative to the market ratio. In this instance, the major variable that should cause a difference in the P/BV ratio is the firm's return on investment (ROI) relative to its cost of capital (its WACC). Assuming that most firms in an industry have comparable WACCs, the major differential should be the firm's ROI because the larger the ROI-WACC difference, the greater the justified P/BV ratio. We will consider this in the subsequent section on EVA.

As shown in Exhibit 62-16, the P/BV ratios for the company, industry, and market components have increased from about 2.5–3.5 to a peak of 5–8 and ended at 3.0–4.5. As shown in Exhibit 62-17, which contains a plot of relative valuation ratios, Walgreens has experienced a smaller increase in its P/BV ratio

| EXHIBIT 62-16 | Time-Series Plot of Mean Price/Book Value Ratios for Walgreens, the Retail Drugstore Industry, and S&P Industrials: 1993–2003 |

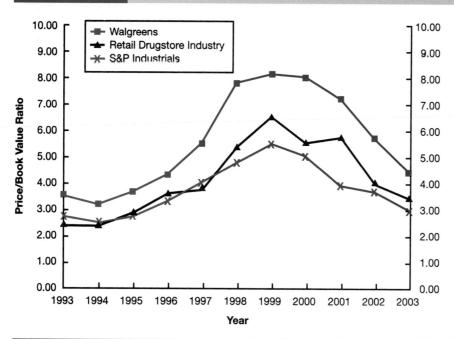

| EXHIBIT 62-17 | Time-Series Plot of Relative Price/Book Value Ratios for Walgreens/Industry and Walgreens/Market: 1993–2003 |

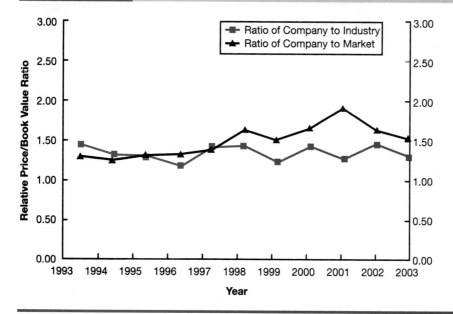

than its industry as indicated by its company/industry ratio that has gone from about 1.43 to 1.33. In contrast, the company-to-market ratio for Walgreens has increased from about 1.30 to about 1.50 at the end of the period. This latter trend is consistent with expectations because the *ROE* for Walgreens has consistently been greater than for the S&P Industrials.

Price/Cash Flow (*P/CF*) Ratio

The price/cash flow ratio has grown in prominence and use because many observers contend that a firm's cash flow is less subject to manipulation than its earnings per share and because cash flows are widely used in the present value of cash flow models discussed earlier. An important question is, which of the several cash flow specifications should an analyst employ? In this analysis, we use the EBITDA cash flow measure equal to net income plus interest, depreciation, and taxes because this cash flow measure can be derived for both the RDS industry and the market. Although it is certainly legitimate to have a preference for one of the other cash flow measures discussed, a demonstration using this measure should provide a valid comparison for learning purposes.

The time-series graph of the *P/CF* ratios in Exhibit 62-18 shows a general increase for Walgreens and its industry from about 10 times in 1993 to about 20 for WAG. The industry went from 5 to 15, the market *P/CF* ratio went from 9 times to 11 times. Notably, not only did the absolute value of the ratios increase, the graphs in Exhibit 62-19 show that Walgreen Co.'s *P/CF* ratios relative to its industry experienced a significant decline from a ratio of 2.64 in 1993 to a ratio of 1.50 in 2003. The company-to-market comparison experienced its low ratio of 1.26 in 1993 and experienced a rapid increase and decrease to an ending ratio of 1.79. This indicates an overall increase in the

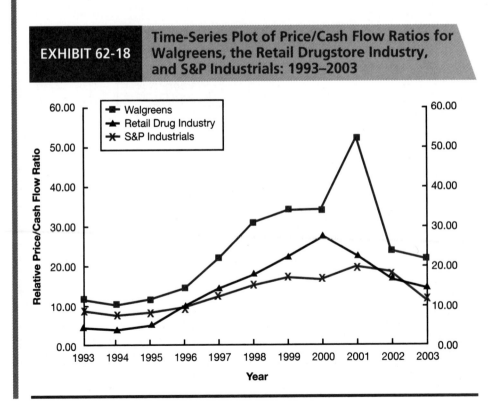

| EXHIBIT 62-18 | Time-Series Plot of Price/Cash Flow Ratios for Walgreens, the Retail Drugstore Industry, and S&P Industrials: 1993–2003 |

EXHIBIT 62-19	Time-Series Plot of Relative Price/Cash Flow Ratios for Walgreens/Industry and Walgreens/Market: 1993–2003

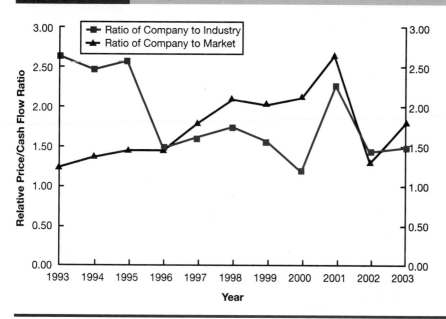

P/CF ratio and an increase since 1993 in the *P/CF* ratio relative to the overall market. The question becomes, what has happened to the firm's growth rate of cash flow and the risk of these cash flows that would justify this overall increase in the *P/CF* ratio relative to the market, in contrast to a decline relative to its industry?

Price/Sales (*P/S*) Ratio

The price-to-sales ratio (*P/S*) has had a long but generally neglected existence followed by a recent reawakening. Phillip Fisher (1958), in his classic book, suggested this ratio as a valuable tool when considering investments, including growth stocks. Subsequently, his son Kenneth Fisher (1984) used the ratio as a major stock selection variable in his book. In the late 1990s, *P/S* was suggested as a valuable tool by Leibowitz (1997), and this ratio was espoused by O'Shaughnessy (1997), in his book that compared several stock selection techniques. Leibowitz makes the point that sales growth drives the growth of all subsequent earnings and cash flow. Those who are concerned with accounting manipulation point out that sales is one of the purest numbers available. Notably, this ratio is equal to the *P/E* ratio times the net profit margin (earnings/sales), which implies that it is heavily influenced by the profit margin of the entity being analyzed in addition to sales growth and sales volatility (risk).

As shown in Exhibit 62-4 and Exhibit 62-20, the *P/S* ratio for Walgreens has experienced a significant overall increase from 0.59 to 1.00, compared to almost no overall increase by its industry (0.49 to 0.53) and a healthy increase by the market (from 0.84 to 1.29). This substantial relative performance by Walgreens is reflected in Exhibit 62-21, which shows the plot of relative ratios wherein the company-to-industry ratio increased notably from 1.22 to 1.89 while the

| EXHIBIT 62-20 | Time-Series Plot of Price/Sales Ratios for Walgreens, the Retail Drugstore Industry, and S&P Industrials: 1993–2003 |

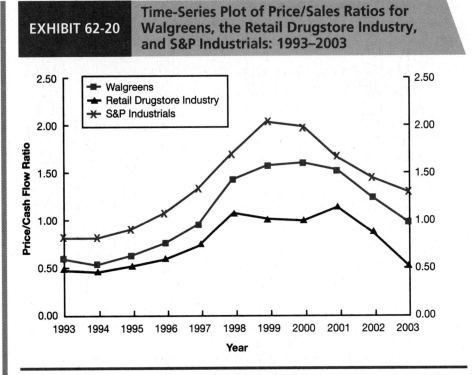

company-to-market ratio went from 0.71 to 0.77. As before, the analyst must ask whether the growth of sales, the risk related to the sales growth, and the profit margin of Walgreens can justify a much higher *P/S* ratio than its industry. The positive news is that Walgreens Co.'s sales have experienced strong consistent growth relative to its industry and Walgreens has also experienced an increase in its profit margin.

| EXHIBIT 62-21 | Time-Series Plot of Relative Price/Sales Ratios for Walgreens/Industry and Walgreens/Market: 1993–2003 |

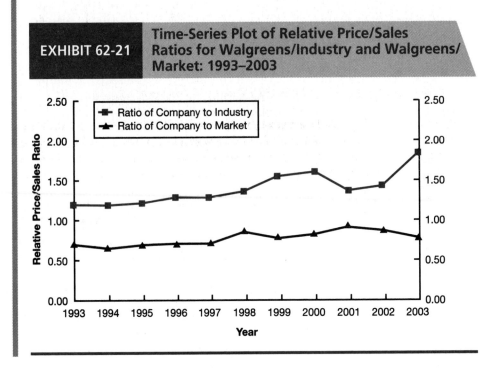

Summary of Relative Valuation Ratios

Notably, the four individual, relative valuation variables increased across the board—all four relative valuation ratios increased during the 11-year period for the firm, its industry, and the aggregate stock market. The widespread increases suggest changes in some aggregate economic variables, such as economic growth and risk factors. Interestingly, Dudley and McKelvey (1997) from Goldman, Sachs, & Co. argued that the U.S. economy has experienced several significant changes that have changed the nature and length of our economic expansions and contractions.

In addition to these overall increases, Walgreens experienced a larger increase than its industry in terms of its *P/E* ratio, and its *P/S* ratio, while lagging in terms of its *P/CF* ratio. Compared to the market, all the firm's relative valuation ratios increased more than the market. An investor who wants to use these ratios to determine relative value or to make an investment decision needs to explain the differences by analyzing the basic valuation factors that affect the ratios.

The following section considers some techniques used to analyze and derive values for growth companies.

ANALYSIS OF GROWTH COMPANIES

10

Investment literature contains numerous accounts of the rapid growth of such companies as Wal-Mart, Cisco Systems, Intel, Pfizer, and Microsoft, along with stories about investors who became wealthy because of the timely acquisition of these stocks. These very high rates of return indicate that the early and proper valuation of true growth companies can be extremely rewarding. At the same time, for every successful Wal-Mart or Microsoft, numerous firms did not survive. In addition, there are many instances where the stock price of a true growth company overcompensated for the firm's expected growth, and subsequent returns on the company's stock were below expectations. As noted in Solt and Statman (1989), the common stock of a growth company is *not* always a growth stock.

You are familiar with the DDM assumptions—that is, that dividends are expected to grow at a *constant rate* for an *infinite time period*. As explained in Reading 59, although these assumptions are reasonable when evaluating the aggregate market and some large industries, they can be very tenuous when analyzing individual securities. *These assumptions are extremely questionable for a growth company.*

Growth Company Defined

Recall that a growth company has the opportunities and ability to invest capital in projects that generate rates of return greater than the firm's cost of capital. Such a condition is considered to be *temporary* because, in a competitive economy, if the rates of return for a given industry exceed the rates of return expected based on the risk involved, other companies will enter the industry, increase the supply, and eventually drive prices down until the rates of return earned on capital invested are consistent with the risk involved.

Actual Returns above Required Returns

The notion of a firm consistently earning rates of return above its required rate of return needs elaboration. Firms are engaged in business ventures that offer opportunities for investment of corporate capital, and these investments entail some risk. Investors determine their required return for owning a firm based on the risk of its investments compared to the risk of other firms. This required rate of return is referred to as the firm's *cost of equity*. In a state of equilibrium, the rates of return earned on risky investments by the firm should equal the rates of return required by investors. Rates of return above those required for the risk involved are referred to as *pure profits* or *excess profits*.

Excess profits are possible only in a noncompetitive environment. Assume that a medical equipment firm is able to earn 20 percent on its capital, while investors require only 15 percent from the firm because of its risk. The extra 5 percent is defined as pure profit, and numerous companies would enter the medical equipment field to enjoy these excess profits. These competitors would increase the supply of equipment and reduce the price that producers could charge for the equipment until the marginal returns equaled the required return due to risk.

Because many firms have derived excess profits for a number of years, these excess returns are probably not due to a temporary disequilibrium but rather because of some non-competitive factors that exist, such as patents or copyrights that provide monopoly rights to a process or a manuscript for a specified period. During this period of protection from competition, the firm can derive above-normal returns. Also, a firm could possess strategies, discussed by Porter, that provide added profits (e.g., a unique marketing technique or other organizational characteristics). Finally, there may be significant barriers to entry, such as capital requirements.

In a purely competitive economy, true growth companies would not exist because competition would not allow continuing excess return investments. The fact is, our economy is not perfectly competitive (although this typically is the best model to use) because there are a number of frictions that restrict competition. Therefore, it is possible for *temporary* true growth companies to exist in our economy. The question is, How long can these growth companies earn these excess profits?

Growth Companies and Growth Stocks

Recall that a growth stock is expected to experience above-average risk-adjusted rates of return during some future period. This means that any undervalued stock can be a growth stock, regardless of the type of company. Alternatively, the stock of a growth company that is substantially overvalued could be a speculative stock because the probability of below-normal returns on the stock would be very high even if the company fulfilled expectations.

In this section, we discuss models that are meant to help you evaluate the unique earnings stream of a growth company. As a result, you should derive a better estimate of the firm's value and be able to judge whether the stock of a growth company is (1) a growth stock, (2) a properly valued stock, or (3) a speculative overvalued stock.

Alternative Growth Models[12]

In this section, we consider the full range of growth models, from no growth and negative growth to dynamic true growth. Knowledge of the full range will help

_____

[12] The discussion in this section draws heavily from Salomon (1963), and Miller and Modigliani (1961).

you understand the life cycle of true growth companies. We assume the company is an all-equity firm to simplify the computations.

No-Growth Firm

The no-growth firm is a mythical company that is established with a specified portfolio of investments that generate a constant stream of earnings (E) equal to r times the value of assets. Earnings are calculated after allowing for depreciation expense used to maintain the assets at their original value. Therefore,

$$E = r \times \text{Assets} \qquad\qquad\qquad \textbf{(62-10)}$$

It also is assumed that all earnings of the firm are paid out in dividends; if b is the rate of retention, $b = 0$. Hence,

$$E = r \times \text{Assets} = \text{Dividends} \qquad\qquad \textbf{(62-11)}$$

Under these assumptions, the value of the firm is the discounted value of the perpetual stream of earnings (E). The discount rate (the required rate of return) is specified as k. In this case, it is assumed that $r = k$. The firm's rate of return on assets equals its required rate of return. Therefore, the value of the firm is

$$V = \frac{E}{k} = \frac{(1 - b)E}{k} \qquad\qquad\qquad \textbf{(62-12)}$$

In the no-growth case, the earnings stream never changes because the asset base never changes, and the rate of return (r) on the assets never changes. Therefore, the value of the firm never changes, and investors continue to receive k on their investment.

$$k = E/V \qquad\qquad\qquad\qquad \textbf{(62-13)}$$

Long-Run Growth Models

Long-run models differ from the no-growth models because *they assume some of the earnings are reinvested.* In all cases, it is postulated that the market value (V) of an all-equity firm is the capitalized value of three component forms of returns discounted at the rate k.

▶ E = the level of (constant) net earnings expected from existing assets, without further net investments.

▶ G = the growth component that equals the present value of capital gains expected from reinvested funds. The return on reinvested funds is equal to r, which equals mk (m is the relative rate of return operator). If m is equal to 1, then $r = k$. If m is greater than 1, the projects that generate these returns are considered true growth investments $(r > k)$. If m is less than 1, the investments are generating returns (r) below the cost of capital $(r < k)$.

▶ R = the reinvestment of net earnings (E) and is equal to bE, where b is a percent of retention between zero (no reinvestment) and unity (total reinvestment; no dividends).

Simple Growth Model   This model assumes the firm has growth investment opportunities that provide rates of return equal to r, where r is greater than k (m is above 1). Further, it is assumed that the firm can invest R dollars a year at these rates and that $R = bE$; R is a *constant dollar amount* because E is the constant earnings at the beginning of the period.

The value of G, the capital gain component, is computed as follows: the first investment of bE dollars yields a stream of earnings equal to bEr dollars, and this is repeated every year. Each of these earnings streams has a present value, as of the year it begins, of bEr/k, which is the present value of a constant perpetual stream discounted at a rate consistent with the risk involved. Assuming the firm does this every year, it has a series of investments, each of which has a present value of bEr/k. The present value of all these series is $(bEr/k)/k$, which equals bEr/k^2. But because $r = mk$, this becomes

$$\frac{bEmk}{k^2} = \frac{bEm}{k} \text{ (Gross Present Value of Growth Investments)} \qquad \textbf{(62-14)}$$

To derive these flows, the firm must invest bE dollars each year. The present value of these annual investments is equal to bE/k. Therefore, the *net* present value of growth investments is equal to

$$\frac{bEm}{k} - \frac{bE}{k} \text{ (Net Present Value of Growth Investments)} \qquad \textbf{(62-15)}$$

The important variable is the value of m, which indicates the relationship of r to k. Combining this growth component with the capitalized value of the constant earnings stream indicates that the value of the firm is

$$V = \frac{E}{k} + \left[\frac{bEm}{k} - \frac{bE}{k} \right] \qquad \textbf{(62-16)}$$

This equation indicates that the value of the firm is equal to the capitalized value of the constant earnings stream plus a growth component equal to the *net* present value of reinvestment in growth projects. By combining the first and third terms in Equation 62-16, it becomes

$$V = \frac{E(1 - b)}{k} + \frac{bEm}{k} \qquad \textbf{(62-17)}$$

Because $E(1 - b)$ is the dividend (D), this model becomes

$$V = \frac{D}{k} + \frac{bEm}{k} \quad \text{(Present Value of Constant Dividend plus Present Value of Growth Investments)} \qquad \textbf{(62-18)}$$

It can be stated as earnings only by rearranging Equation 62-16:

$$V = \frac{E}{k} + \frac{bE(m - 1)}{k} \quad \text{(Present Value of Constant Earnings plus the Present Value of Excess Earnings Growth Investments)} \qquad \textbf{(62-19)}$$

Expansion Model   The expansion model assumes a firm retains earnings to reinvest but receives a rate of return on its investments that is equal to its cost of capital ($m = 1$, so $r = k$). The effect of such a change can be seen in Equation

62-15, where the net present value of growth investments would be zero. Therefore, Equation 62-16 would become

$$V = \frac{E}{k}$$

(62-20)

Equation 62-17 would become

$$V = \frac{E(1 - b)}{k} + \frac{bE}{k} = \frac{E}{k}$$

(62-21)

Equation 62-18 is still valid, but the present value of the growth investment component would be smaller because m would be equal to 1. Finally, the last term in Equation 62-19 would disappear.

This discussion indicates that simply because a firm retains earnings and reinvests them, it is not necessarily beneficial to the stockholder *unless the reinvestment rate is above the required rate* $(r > k)$. Otherwise, the investor in a tax-free world would be as well off with all earnings paid out in dividends. Either way, your return is k.

Negative Growth Model The negative growth model applies to a firm that retains earnings $(b > 0)$ and reinvests these funds in projects that generate rates of return *below* the firm's cost of capital $(r < k$ or $m < 1)$. The impact of this on the value of the firm can be seen from Equation 62-15, which indicates that with $m < 1$, the net present value of the growth investments would be *negative*. Therefore, the value of the firm in Equation 62-16 would be *less* than the value of a no-growth firm or an expansion firm. This also can be seen by examining the effect of $m < 1$ in Equation 62-19. The firm is withholding funds from the investor and investing them in projects that generate returns less than those available from comparable risk investments.

Such poor performance may be difficult to uncover because the firm's asset base will grow since it is retaining earnings and acquiring assets. Notably, the earnings of the firm will increase if it earns *any* positive rate of return on the new assets. The important point is, *the earnings will not grow by as much as they should*, so the value of the firm will decline over time when investors discount the cash flows from this reinvestment stream at the firm's cost of capital.

What Determines the Capital Gain Component? These equations highlight the factors that influence the capital gain component. Beginning with Equation 62-14, all the equations suggest that the gross present value of the growth investments is equal to

bEm/k

Therefore, three factors influence the size of this capital gain term. The first is b, the percentage of earnings retained for reinvestment. The greater the proportion of earnings retained, the larger the capital gain component. The second factor is m, which is critical because it indicates the relationship between the firm's rate of return on investments and the firm's required rate of return (i.e., its cost of capital). A value of 1 indicates the firm is earning only its required return. A firm with an m greater than 1 is a true growth company. The important question is, how much greater than k is the return? The final factor is the time period for the superior investments. How long can the firm make these superior return investments? This critical time factor often is overlooked because we have assumed an infinite horizon to simplify the computations. However, *when analyzing growth companies, this time estimate is clearly a major consideration.* In summary, the three factors that influence the capital gain component are

1. The amount of capital invested in growth investments *(b)*

2. The relative rate of return earned on the funds retained *(m)*

3. The time period for these growth investments

Dynamic True Growth Model   A dynamic true growth model applies to a firm that invests a constant *percentage of current* earnings in projects that generate rates of return above the firm's required rate ($r > k$, $m > 1$). In contrast to the simple growth model where the firm invests a *constant* dollar amount each year, in this model the amount invested is *growing* each year as earnings increase. As a result, the firm's earnings and dividends will grow at a *constant rate* that is equal to *br* (the percentage of earnings retained times the return on investments). In the current model, this would equal *bmk*, where *m* is greater than 1.

$$V = \frac{D_1}{k - g}$$

(62-22)

Applying this model to a true growth company means that earnings and dividends are growing at a constant rate and *the firm is investing larger and larger dollar amounts in projects that generate returns greater than* k. Moreover, the DDM model implicitly assumes that the firm can continue to do this for *an infinite time period.* If the growth rate *(g)* is greater than *k*, the model blows up and indicates that the firm should have an infinite value. Durand (1957) considered this possibility and concluded that, although many firms had current growth rates above the normal required rates of return, very few of their stocks were selling for infinite values. He explained this by contending that investors expected the reinvestment rate to decline or they felt that the investment opportunities would not be available for an infinite time period. Exhibit 62-22 contains a summary of the alternative company characteristics.

The Real World

Because these models are simplified to allow us to develop a range of alternatives, several of them are extremely unrealistic. In the real world, companies generally would combine these models. Unfortunately, most firms have made some investments where $r < k$, and many firms invest in projects that generate returns about equal to their cost of capital. Finally, most firms invest in *some* projects that provide rates of return above the firm's cost of capital ($r > k$). The crucial questions are (1) how much is invested in these true growth projects? and (2) how long do these true growth opportunities last?

Given this understanding of growth companies and what creates their value, the rest of the reading considers various models that help you understand how to identify a true growth company and estimate specific values for these growth companies. We begin with models that are intended to identify growth companies in terms of providing excess economic value, which some contend is due to

EXHIBIT 62-22	Summary of Company Descriptions	
	Retention	**Return on Investments**
No-growth company	$b = 0$	$r = k$
Long-run growth (assumes reinvestment)		
Negative growth	$b > 0$	$r < k$
Expansion	$b > 0$	$r = k$
Simple long-run growth	$b > 0$	
	(constant $)	$r > k$
Dynamic long-run growth	$b > 0$	
	(constant %)	$r > k$

franchise value. Subsequently, we consider several models that are intended to provide a valuation of these companies by concentrating on how long the superior growth can continue and, alternatively, the extent and length of the superior growth. This final model has some similarities to the three-stage cash flow models.

MEASURES OF VALUE ADDED[13]

11

In addition to the DDM, which feeds into the *P/E* ratio valuation technique and the supplementary *P/BV* and *P/CF*, ratios, there has been growing interest in a set of performance measures referred to as "value added" measures. Notably, these value-added measures of performance are directly related to the capital budgeting techniques used in corporation finance. Specifically, they consider *economic profit*, which is analogous to the net present value (NPV) technique used in corporate capital budgeting. These value-added measures examine management performance based on the ability of managers to add value to the firm. They are also being used by security analysts as possible indicators of future equity returns, based on the logic that superior management performance should be reflected in a company's stock returns. In the subsequent discussion, we concentrate on three measures of value added: **economic value added (EVA)** and **market value added (MVA),** pioneered by Stern and Stewart, and discussed in Stewart (1991), and the **franchise factor** developed by Leibowitz and Kogelman (1994).

Economic Value Added (EVA)[14]

As noted, EVA is closely related to the net present value (NPV) technique wherein you evaluate the expected performance of an investment by discounting

---

[13] This section benefited from Peterson and Peterson (1996).

[14] EVA is a registered trademark of Stern, Stewart, & Co.

its future cash flows at the firm's weighted average cost of capital (WACC) and compare this sum of discounted future cash flows to the cost of the project. If the discounted cash flows are greater than its cost, the project is expected to generate a positive NPV, which implies that it will add to the value of the firm and, therefore, it should be undertaken. In the case of EVA, you evaluate the annual performance of management by comparing the firm's net operating profit less adjusted taxes (NOPLAT) to the firm's total cost of capital in dollar terms, including the cost of equity. In this analysis, if the firm's NOPLAT during a specific year exceeds its dollar cost of capital, it has a positive EVA for the year and has added value for its stockholders. In contrast, if the EVA is negative, the firm has not earned enough during the year to cover its total cost of capital and the value of the firm has declined. Notably, NOPLAT indicates what the firm has earned for all capital suppliers and the dollar cost of capital is what all the capital suppliers required—including the firm's equity holders. The following summarizes the major calculations:[15]

EVA =

      (A) Adjusted Operating Profits before Taxes

      Minus (B) Cash Operating Taxes

      Equals (C) Net Operating Profits Less Adjusted Taxes (NOPLAT)

      Minus (D) The Dollar Cost of Capital

      Equals (E) Economic Value Added (EVA)

In turn, these items are calculated as follows:

Operating Profit (After Depreciation and Amortization)

Add:	Implied Interest on Operating Leases
Add:	An Increase in the LIFO Reserve
Add:	Goodwill Amortization
Equals:	*(A) Adjusted Operating Profits before Taxes*

Income Tax Expense

Add:	Decrease in Deferred Taxes
Add:	Tax Benefit from Interest Expenses
Add:	Tax Benefit from Interest on Leases
Less:	Taxes on Nonoperating Income
Equals:	*(B) Cash Operating Taxes*

(A) minus (B) equals: (C) Net Operating Profits Less Adjusted Taxes (NOPLAT)

---

[15] For a detailed discussion, see Stewart (1991), or Peterson and Peterson (1996). For summary discussions, see Jones (1995).

Capital =

    Net Working Capital (current assets less non-interest-bearing liabilities)

Add: LIFO Reserve

Add: Net Plant, Property, and Equipment

Add: Other Assets

Add: Goodwill

Add: Accumulated Goodwill Amortized

Add: Present Value of Operating Leases

Equals: *Capital*

Weighted Average Cost of Capital (WACC) =

    (Book Value of Debt/Total Book Value) × (the Market Cost of Debt)

    (1 − Tax Rate)

    (Book Value of Equity/Total Book Value) × (Cost of Equity)

    (Cost of equity is based on the CAPM using the prevailing 10-year Treasury bond as the *RFR*, a calculated beta, and a market risk premium between 3 and 6 percent.)

(D)   Dollar Cost of Capital = Capital × WACC

(E)   Economic Value Added (EVA) =

(C)   Net Operating Profits Less Adjusted Taxes (NOPLAT)

    Minus (D) Dollar Cost of Capital

EVA Return on Capital   The preceding calculations provide a positive or negative dollar value, which indicates whether the firm earned an excess above its cost of capital during the year analyzed. There are two problems with this annual dollar value for EVA. First, how does one judge over time if the firm is prospering relative to its past performance? Although you would want the absolute EVA to grow over time, the question is whether the rate of growth of EVA is adequate for the additional capital provided. Second, how does one compare alternative firms of different sizes? Both of these concerns can be met by calculating an *EVA return on capital* equal to

    EVA Return on Capital = EVA/Capital

You would want this EVA rate of return on capital for a firm to remain constant over time, or, ideally, to grow. Using this ratio you can compare firms of different sizes and determine which firm has the largest *economic profit per dollar of capital.*

An Alternative Measure of EVA   An alternative but equal way to measure and think about EVA is to compare directly the firm's return on capital employed to the firm's average cost of capital (i.e., its WACC). As noted previously, it is this difference in the actual rate of return earned compared to the firm's required rate of return that identifies a company as a true growth company. Another way to measure EVA is to multiply this EVA spread (return on capital minus WACC) by the amount of capital employed. The appeal of this EVA spread approach is that it concentrates on the factors that create a growth company. Also, it helps the management and analysts recognize that true growth can be created by either (1) increasing the firm's return on capital, or (2) reducing its cost of capital.

Market Value Added (MVA)

In contrast to EVA, which generally is an evaluation of internal performance, MVA is a measure of external performance—how the market has evaluated the firm's performance in terms of the market value of debt and market value of equity compared to the capital invested in the firm.

$$
\begin{aligned}
\text{Market Value Added (MVA)} = {} & (\text{Market Value of Firm}) - \text{Capital} \\
& - \text{Market Value of Debt} \\
& - \text{Market Value of Equity}
\end{aligned}
$$

Again, to properly analyze this performance, it is necessary to look for positive changes over time—that is, the percent change each year. Subsequently, you need to compare these annual changes in MVA with those for the aggregate stock and bond markets, because these market values can be impacted by interest rate changes and general economic conditions.

Relationships between EVA and MVA

Although EVA is used primarily for evaluating management performance, it also is being used by external analysts to evaluate management with the belief that superior internal performance should be reflected in a company's stock performance. Several studies have attempted to determine the relationship between the two variables (EVA and MVA), and the results have not been encouraging. Although the stock of firms with positive EVAs has tended to outperform the stocks of negative EVA firms, the differences are typically insignificant and the relationship does not occur every year. This poor relationship may be due to the timing of the analysis (how fast EVA is reflected in stocks) or because the market values (MVAs) are affected by factors other than EVA—for example, MVA can be impacted by market interest rates and by changes in *future* expectations for a firm not considered by EVA. The point is, EVA does an outstanding job of evaluating management's *past* performance in terms of adding value. While one would certainly hope that superior past performance will continue, there is nothing certain about this relationship.

The Franchise Factor

The franchise factor concept is similar to EVA since it recognizes that, to add value to a firm, it is necessary to invest in projects that provide excess NPV—that is, the firm must generate rates of return above its WACC. This technique is directly related to the valuation approach we have been using since the franchise value approach breaks a firm's observed *P/E* ratio down into two components: (1) the *P/E* that is based on the company's ongoing business (its base *P/E*), plus (2) a franchise *P/E* that the market assigns to *the expected value of new and profitable business opportunities*. This can be visualized as:

$$\text{Franchise } P/E = \text{Observed } P/E - \text{Base } P/E \qquad \text{(62-23)}$$

The base *P/E* is the reciprocal of the market discount rate *k* (it is $1/k$). For example, if the stock's market discount rate is 8 percent, the base *P/E* would be about 12.5 times.

What determines the franchise *P/E*? Not surprising, it is a function of the relative rate of return on new business opportunities compared to the firm's cost of equity (the franchise factor) and the size of the superior return opportunities (the growth factor).

Incremental Franchise P/E = Franchise Factor $\times$ Growth Factor

$$= \frac{R - k}{rk} \times G \qquad \text{(62-24)}$$

where:

> R = the expected return on the new opportunities
> k = the current cost of equity
> r = the current *ROE* on investment
> G = the present value of the new growth projects relative to the current value of the firm

The critical factors determining the franchise *P/E* are the difference between *R* and *k* and the size of these growth opportunities relative to the firm's current size (i.e., *G*).[16]

Growth Duration Model

The purpose of the growth duration model is to help you *evaluate* the high *P/E* ratio for the stock of a growth company by relating its *P/E* ratio to the firm's *rate* of growth and *duration* of growth. As discussed previously, a stock's *P/E* ratio is a function of (1) the firm's expected rate of growth of earnings per share, (2) the stock's required rate of return, and (3) the firm's dividend-payout ratio. Assuming equal risk and no significant difference in the payout ratio for different firms, the principal variable affecting differences in the earnings multiple for two firms *is the difference in expected growth.* It has been noted earlier that the growth estimate must consider both the *rate* of growth and how long this growth rate can be sustained— that is, the *duration* of expected growth. As noted earlier, no company can grow indefinitely at a rate substantially above normal. For example, Wal-Mart cannot continue to grow at 20 percent a year for an extended period, or it will eventually become the entire economy. In fact, Wal-Mart or any similar growth firm will eventually run out of excess profit investment projects. Recall that continued growth at a constant rate requires that larger amounts of money be invested in high-return projects because it requires that you invest a constant percentage of current earnings. Eventually, competition will encroach on these high-return investments and the firm's growth rate will decline to a rate consistent with the rate for the overall economy. Therefore, a reasonable and accurate estimate of the implied duration of a firm's high-growth period becomes significant.

Computation of Growth Duration   The growth duration concept was suggested by Holt (1962), who showed that if you assume equal risk between a given security and a market security, such as the S&P Industrials (i.e., a beta close to one), you can concentrate on the differential expected growth rates for the market

---

[16] For further detail and examples of the application, see Leibowitz and Kogelman (1994).

and the growth firm as a factor causing the alternative *P/E* ratios. This allows you to compute the market's *implied growth duration* for the growth firm.

If $E'(0)$ is the firm's current earnings, then $E'(t)$ is earnings in Period t according to the expression

$$E'(t) = E(0)(1 + G)^t \tag{62-25}$$

where G is the expected annual percentage growth rate for earnings. To adjust for dividend payments, it was assumed that all such payments are used to purchase further shares of the stock. This means the number of shares (N) will grow at the dividend rate (D). Therefore

$$N(t) = N(0)(1 + D)^t \tag{62-26}$$

To derive the total earnings for a firm, $E(t)$, the growth rate in per-share earnings and the growth rate in shares are combined as follows:

$$E(t) = E'(t)N(t) = E'(0)\big[(1 + G)(1 + D)\big]^t \tag{62-27}$$

Because G and D are small, this expression can be approximated by

$$E(t) \simeq E'(0)(1 + G + D)^t \tag{62-28}$$

Assuming the growth stock (g) and the nongrowth stock (a) have similar risk and payout, the market should value the two stocks in direct proportion to their earnings in year T (i.e., they will have the same *P/E* ratio), where T is the time when the growth company will begin to grow at the same rate as the market (i.e., the non-growth stock). Put another way, T is the number of years the growth stock is expected to grow at the high rate. In other words, *current prices should be in direct proportion to the expected future earnings ratio that will prevail in year T.* This relationship can be stated

$$\left(\frac{P_g(0)}{P_a(0)}\right) \simeq \left(\frac{E_g(0)(1 + G_g + D_g)^T}{E_a(0)(1 + G_a + D_a)^T}\right) \tag{62-29}$$

or

$$\left(\frac{P_g(0)/E_g(0)}{P_a(0)/E_a(0)}\right) \simeq \left(\frac{1 + G_g + D_g}{1 + G_a + D_a}\right)^T \tag{62-30}$$

As a result, *the P/E ratios of the two stocks are in direct proportion to the ratio of composite growth rates raised to the Tth power.* You can solve for T by taking the log of both sides as follows:

$$\ln\left(\frac{P_g(0)/E_g(0)}{P_a(0)/E_a(0)}\right) \simeq T\ln\left(\frac{1 + G_g + D_g}{1 + G_a + D_a}\right) \tag{62-31}$$

The growth duration model answers the question: How long must the earnings of the growth stock grow at this expected high rate, relative to the nongrowth stock, to justify its prevailing above-average *P/E* ratio? You must then determine whether this *implied* growth duration estimate is reasonable in terms of the company's potential.

Consider the following example. The stock of Walgreens is selling for $42 a share with expected per-share earnings of $1.50 (its future earnings multiple is

28.0 times). The expected EPS growth rate for Walgreens is estimated to be 13 percent a year, and its dividend yield has been 1 percent and is expected to remain at this level. In contrast, the S&P Industrials Index has a future P/E ratio of about 18, an average dividend yield of 2 percent, and an expected growth rate of 6 percent. Therefore, the comparison is as follows:

	S&P Industrials	Walgreens
P/E ratio	18.00	28.00
Expected growth rate	0.06	0.13
Dividend yield	0.02	0.01

Inserting these values into Equation 62-31 yields the following:

$$\ln\left(\frac{28.00}{18.00}\right) = T\ln\left(\frac{1 + 0.13 + 0.01}{1 + 0.06 + 0.02}\right)$$

$$\ln(1.56) = T\ln\left(\frac{1.14}{1.08}\right)$$

$$\ln(1.56) = T\ln(1.055)$$

$$T = \ln(1.56)/\ln(1.055)(\text{log base } 10)$$
$$= 0.1931/0.02325$$
$$= 8.31 \text{ Years}$$

These results indicate the market is implicitly assuming that Walgreens can continue to grow at this composite rate (14 percent) for about 8 more years, after which it is assumed Walgreens will grow at the same total rate (8 percent) as the aggregate market (i.e., the S&P Industrials). You must now ask, can this superior growth rate be sustained by Walgreens for at least this period? If the implied growth duration is greater than you believe is reasonable, you would advise against buying Walgreens stock. If the implied duration is below your expectations, you would recommend buying the stock.

Intraindustry Analysis Besides comparing a company to a market series, you can directly compare two firms. For an intercompany analysis, you should compare firms in the same industry because the equal risk assumptions of this model are probably more reasonable.

Consider the following example from the computer software industry:

	Company A	Company B
P/E ratios	31.00	25.00
Expected annual growth rate	0.1700	0.1200
Dividend yield	0.0100	0.0150
Growth rate plus dividend yield	0.1800	0.1350
Estimate of T[a]		5.53 years

[a] Readers should check to see that they get the same answer.

These results imply that the market expects Company A to grow at an annual total rate of 18 percent for about 5.5 years, after which it will grow at Company B's rate of 13.5 percent. If you believe the implied duration for growth at 18 percent is too long, you will prefer Company B; if you believe it is reasonable or low, you will recommend Company A.

An Alternative Use of T   Instead of solving for *T* and then deciding whether the figure derived is reasonable, you can use this formulation to compute a reasonable *P/E* ratio for a security relative to the aggregate market (or another stock) if the implicit assumptions are reasonable for the stock involved. Again, using Walgreens as an example, you estimate its expected composite growth to be 14 percent a year compared to the expected total market growth of 8 percent. Further, you believe that Walgreens can continue to grow at this above-normal rate for about five years. Using Equation 62-31, this becomes

$$
\begin{aligned}
\ln(X) &= 5 \times \ln\frac{1.14}{1.08} \\
&= 5 \times \ln(1.055) \\
&= 5 \times (0.02325) \\
&= 0.11625
\end{aligned}
$$

To determine what the *P/E* ratio should be given these assumptions, you must derive the antilog of 0.11625, which is approximately 1.3069. Therefore, assuming the market multiple is 18, the earnings multiple for Walgreens should be about 1.3069 times the market *P/E* ratio, or about 24.

Alternatively, if you estimate that Walgreens can maintain a lower growth rate of .12 for a long time period of 10 years, you would derive the antilog for 1.5794 (10 × 0.01579). The answer is 1.4386, which implies a *P/E* ratio of about 26 times for Walgreen Co.'s stock. Notably, both of these estimates are below the current forward *P/E* for Walgreens of 28 times.

Factors to Consider   When using the growth duration technique, remember the following factors: First, the technique assumes equal risk, which may be acceptable when comparing two large, well-established firms in the same industry (e.g., Merck and Pfizer) to each other. It is also reasonable for a large conglomerate, like General Electric, with a beta close to one. In the case of Walgreens, which has a beta of about 0.90, the result is conservative, meaning that the duration would be lower than the estimated 8 years. It is probably *not* a valid assumption when comparing a small firm with a beta of 1.50 to the aggregate market. In this case, the duration generated would be an underestimate of what should be required.

Second, which growth estimate should be used? We prefer to use the *expected* rate of growth based on the factors that affect *g* (i.e., the retention rate and the components of *ROE*).

Third, the growth duration technique assumes that stocks with higher *P/E* ratios have the higher growth rates. However, there are cases in which the stock with the higher *P/E* ratio does not have a higher expected growth rate or the stock with a higher expected growth rate has a lower *P/E* ratio. Either of the cases generates a useless negative growth duration value. Inconsistency between the expected growth and the *P/E* ratio could be attributed to one of four factors:

1. A major difference in the risk involved.

2. Inaccurate growth rate estimates. You may want to reexamine your growth rate estimate for the firm with the higher *P/E* ratio, that is, could it be higher or should the growth estimate for the low *P/E* stock be lower?

3. The stock with a low *P/E* ratio relative to its expected growth rate is undervalued. (Before you accept this possibility, consider the first two factors.)

4. The stock with a high *P/E* and a low expected growth rate is overvalued. (Before this is accepted, consider both its risk and your estimated growth rate.)

The growth duration concept is valid, *given the assumptions made,* and can help you evaluate growth investments. It is not universally valid, though, because its answers are only as good as the data inputs (expected growth rates) and the applicability of the assumptions. The answer must be evaluated based on the analyst's knowledge.

The technique probably is most useful for helping spot overvalued growth companies with very high multiples. In such a case, the technique will highlight that the company must continue to grow at some very high rate for an extended period of time to justify its high *P/E* ratio (e.g., 15 to 20 years). Also, it can help you decide between two growth companies in the same industry by comparing each to the market, the industry, or directly to each other. Such a comparison has provided interesting insights wherein the new firms in an industry were growing faster than the large competitor but their *P/E* ratios were *substantially* higher and implied that these new firms had to maintain this large growth rate superiority for over *10 years* to justify the much higher *P/E* ratio.

SITE VISITS AND THE ART OF THE INTERVIEW

Brokerage house analysts and portfolio managers have access to persons that the typical small investor does not. Analysts frequently have contact with corporate personnel by telephone (conference calls), at formal presentations, or during plant site visits. Though insider trading laws restrict the analyst's ability to obtain material nonpublic information, these visits facilitate dialog between the corporation and the investor community. The analyst can gather information about the firm's plans and strategies, which helps the analyst understand the firm's prospects as an investment.

Interviewing is an art. The analyst wants information about the firm, and top management wants to put the firm in the best light possible. Thus, the analyst must be prepared to focus the interview on management's plans, strategies, and concerns. Analysts try to gauge the sensitivity of the firm's revenues, costs, and earnings to different scenarios by asking "what if" questions.

Analysts have frequent telephone contact with the firm's investor relations (IR) department regarding company pronouncements. The chief financial officer and chief executive officer of the firm also meet with security analysts and discuss the firm's planning process and major issues confronting the industry.

The analyst should talk with people other than top managers. Talking with middle managers or factory workers during a plant tour, visiting stores, and talking with customers provide insights beyond those of management. The firm's major customers can provide information regarding product quality and customer satisfaction. The firm's suppliers can furnish information about rising or falling supply orders and the timeliness of payments. Finally, an outstanding source of information is the firm's competitors who will be happy to point out the firm's weaknesses or possible problems. They may even be willing to admit which firm is its toughest competitor.

The idea was always that analysts were able to create a mosaic regarding future expectations for the firm from numerous sources (including the company) and transmit this information to the market by sending research reports to brokerage clients and portfolio managers of pensions and mutual funds. This traditional way of doing research was changed by the SEC in 2000 when they issued the Fair Disclosure (FD) guidelines that required all disclosure of "material information" to be made public to all interested parties at the same time. The intent was to level the playing field by ensuring that professional analysts did not have a competitive advantage over nonprofessional investors. The result of this law is that many firms will not agree to interviews with analysts and will only provide information during large public presentations over the Internet.

The long-run impact of this FD requirement is not clear in terms of how firms will relate to the professional analyst community. One benefit is that analysts will spend more time with information sources beyond the firm such as trade shows, customers, suppliers, and competitors to build the mosaic.

13 WHEN TO SELL

Our analysis has focused on determining if a stock should be purchased. In fact, when we make a purchase, a subsequent question gains prominence: When should the stock be sold? Many times holding on to a stock too long leads to a return below expectations or less than what was available earlier. When stocks decline in value immediately following a portfolio manager's purchase, is this a further buying opportunity, or does the decline indicate that the stock analysis was incorrect?

The answer to the question of when to sell a stock is contained in the research that convinced the analyst to purchase the stock in the first place. The analyst should have identified the key assumptions and variables driving the expectations for the stock. Analysis of the stock doesn't end when intrinsic value is computed and the research report is written. Once the key value drivers are identified, the analyst must continually monitor and update his or her knowledge base about the firm. Notably, if the key value drivers appear to have weakened or there is a major change in management, it is time to reevaluate, and possibly sell, the stock.

The stock should also be closely evaluated when the current price approaches the intrinsic value estimate. When the stock becomes fairly priced (the undervaluation has been corrected), it may be time to sell it and reinvest the funds in other underpriced stocks. In short, if the "story" for buying the stock still appears to be true, continue to hold it if it has not become fully priced (i.e., market price equal to intrinsic value). If the "story" changes, it may be time to sell the stock. If you know why you bought the stock, you'll be able to recognize when to sell it.

14 INFLUENCES ON ANALYSTS

Stock analysts and portfolio managers are, for the most part, highly trained individuals who possess expertise in financial analysis and background in their industry. A computer hardware analyst knows as much about industry trends and new product offerings as any industry insider. A pharmaceutical analyst is able to independently determine the market potential of drugs undergoing testing and the FDA approval process. So why don't more brokerage house customers and portfolio managers who receive the analysts' expert advice achieve investment success? The following subsections discuss several factors that make it difficult to "beat the market."

Efficient Markets

As noted in Reading 57 the efficient market is difficult to outsmart, especially if you are considering actively traded and frequently analyzed companies. Information about the economy, a firm's industry, and the firm itself is reviewed by numerous bright analysts, investors, and portfolio managers. Because of the market's ability to review and absorb information, stock prices generally approximate fair market value. Investors look for situations where stocks may not be fairly valued. Notably, because there are numerous bright, hardworking analysts, it is difficult to successfully, frequently, and consistently find undervalued shares. Put another way, in most instances, the value estimated for a stock will be very close to its market price, which indicates that it is properly valued. The analyst's best place to seek attractive stocks is not among well known companies and actively traded stocks, because they are analyzed by dozens of Wall Street analysts. Stocks with smaller market capitalizations, those not covered by many analysts, or those whose shares are mainly held by individual investors may be the best places to search for inefficiencies. Smaller capitalization stocks sometimes are too small for time-constrained analysts or too small for purchase by institutional investors.[17] The price of stocks not researched by many analysts ("neglected stocks") may not reflect all relevant information.[18]

Paralysis of Analysis

Analysts spend most of their time in a relentless search for one more contact or one more piece of information that will ensure the correct stock recommendation. Analysts need to develop a systematic approach for gathering, monitoring, and reviewing relevant information about economic trends, industry competitive forces, and company strategy. Analysts must evaluate the information as a whole to discern patterns that indicate the intrinsic value of the stock rather than searching for one more piece of information.

Because markets are generally efficient, the consensus view about the firm is already reflected in its stock price. As noted previously, to earn above-average returns, there are two requirements; (1) the analyst must have expectations that differ from the consensus, *and* (2) the analyst must be correct. Thus, the analyst should concentrate on identifying what is wrong with the market consensus (i.e., why do you differ from the consensus?), or what surprises may upset the market consensus—that is, work at *estimating earning surprises.*

Analyst Conflicts of Interest

A potential conflict can arise if communication occurs between a firm's investment banking and equity research division. If the investment bankers assist a firm in a stock or bond offering, it will be difficult for an analyst to issue a negative evaluation of the company. Advisory fees have been lost because of a negative stock recommendation. Despite attempts to ensure the independence of stock analysts, firm politics may get in the way.

The analyst is in frequent contact with the top officers of the company he or she analyzes. Although there are guidelines about receiving gifts and favors, it is

---

[17] According to SEC regulations, mutual funds cannot own more than 10 percent of a firm's shares. For some large funds, this constraint will make the resulting investment too small to have any significant impact on fund returns, so analysts do not bother to consider such stocks for purchase.

[18] Information on the number of analysts covering a stock is available from research firms, such as IBES and Zacks.

sometimes difficult to separate personal friendship and impersonal corporate relationships. Corporate officials may try to convince the analyst that his or her pessimistic report is in error or suggest that it glosses over recent positive developments. To mitigate these problems, an analyst should call the company's investor relations department immediately *after* changing a recommendation to explain his or her perspective. The analyst needs to maintain independence and be objective in his or her analysis.

15 GLOBAL COMPANY AND STOCK ANALYSIS

As indicated on numerous occasions, a major goal of this text is to demonstrate investment technique that can be applied globally to markets, industries, and companies around the world. This chapter has been heavily concerned with presenting and demonstrating these techniques to U.S. firms. While space constraints do not allow a full demonstration to international firms, it is important to point out some of the major factors and constraints that analysts and portfolio managers need to acknowledge and adjust for when investing globally.

Availability of Data

In the United States, we suffer from information (data) overload, which is a blessing and a curse since we have more information than anywhere else in the world (which is good), but, as a result, there is a lot of information to digest and analyze. When you start analyzing international markets, industries, and stocks and cannot get the necessary data for valuation, you come to appreciate what is available in the United States. Beyond the limited amount of information, there is also the problem of timeliness (how long before you get the data?) and the reliability. (Can you believe and depend upon the data published in some countries and by some global industries?)

Differential Accounting Conventions

Even when the financial data for an industry and a firm are timely and reliable, it is necessary to recognize that the accounting rules and practices differ dramatically around the world. Not only are the financial statements very different in general presentation, but the accounting practices differ related to sales and expense recognition. The fact is, identical transactions in different countries can generate significant differences in income and cash flow. As a result, stocks in different countries will have very different *P/E* and *P/CF* ratios, not because investors differ in valuation but because the accounting numbers used are not the same. Notably, it is because of these accounting problems that many investors advocate using the price-to-sales ratio in valuations across countries since sales revenue is the least contaminated accounting figure. The good news in this regard is the movement toward the use of global accounting standards. For an overview of this transition, see Sandagaran (2001).

Currency Differences (Exchange Rate Risk)

It is widely recognized that a significant factor that must be considered by global investors is currency risk caused by changes in exchange rates among countries. While these changes can work for or against you, the point is that it creates a major uncertainty that must be considered in your evaluation of the company and its stock.

Political (Country) Risk

Again, in the United States, we are blessed with the most stable political and economic environment in the world. Therefore, by definition, every other country will have greater political/country risk, which in some cases (e.g., Russia, Indonesia, North Korea) can be substantial. Therefore, it is necessary to acknowledge this factor and estimate its effect on the cost of equity for firms in these countries.

Transaction Costs

Higher transaction costs result from less-liquid markets—where it takes longer to trade and there is more price volatility connected to a trade—or from a trade that costs more (e.g., higher commissions). Again, these costs vary dramatically among countries.

Valuation Differences

The point is, these individual differences among countries combine to cause a clear differential in the stock valuation for an international stock. Specifically, the earnings or cash flow numbers will differ and the required rate of return (the discount rate) for a non-U.S. stock will differ substantially because the nominal rate is different and there are additional risks that must be added such as exchange rate risk, political risk, and higher liquidity costs.

Summary

In summary, when investing globally, the *valuation process* is the same around the world, and the investment decision in terms of the ultimate comparison of intrinsic value and price is similar—the difference is in the *practice* of valuation that requires attention to these additional factors that must be considered by the global investor when valuing an international stock. Therefore, everything you have learned is relevant, but it must be applied differently (i.e., the inputs differ), depending on the country.

THE INTERNET

Investments Online

Many helpful sites have been reviewed in prior chapters, for example, examining individual firm sites and the SEC's EDGAR database for firm-specific information. Investment bank and brokerage house sites may also prove valuable, though they may expect payment for access to their published research on different firms. Still, many sites exist that allow users to examine free information and investing tips:

www.better-investing.org/ The home page for the National Association of Investment Clubs offers company information and investing ideas in addition to resources for those interested in setting up their own investment club.

(continued)

THE INTERNET *(continued)*

www.fool.com This is the home page for the Motley Fool; despite its name, it is a well-known and popular site for investors to visit. It is chock full of data, articles, educational resources, news, and investing ideas.

www.cfonews.com Corporate Financials Online provides links to news about selected publicly traded firms.

www.zacks.com This is the Web site for Zacks Investment Research. When the user types in a ticker symbol, Zacks provides links to a company profile, financials, analysts' current stock ratings, consensus earnings estimates, and the number of analysts recommending strong buy, moderate buy, hold, moderate sell, and strong sell. Links allow the user to order brokerage reports.

moneycentral.msn.com/investor/home.asp offers stock screens, price charts, and links to earnings estimates and analyst reports.

www.iaschicago.org/ The home page of the Investment Analysts Society of Chicago includes many financial web links and sources of market and company information.

www.valueline.com This site was mentioned in an earlier reading The Value Line Investment Survey is a favorite source of information for many investors.

OPTIONAL SEGMENT
ENDS

SUMMARY

▶ This reading demonstrates how to complete the fundamental analysis process by analyzing a company and deciding whether you should buy its stock. This requires a separate analysis of a company and its stock. A wonderful company can have an overpriced stock, or a mediocre firm can have an underpriced stock.

▶ Although the reading is mainly concerned with discussing and demonstrating several alternative valuation techniques, the initial section contained a discussion of the strategic alternatives available to firms in response to different competitive pressures in their industries. The alternative corporate strategies include low-cost leadership or differentiation which if properly implemented, should help the company attain above-average rates of return. In addition, we discussed SWOT analysis, which helps an analyst assess a firm's strengths and weaknesses as well as its external opportunities and threats. This strategic analysis of the firm's goals, objectives, and strategy should put you in a position to properly estimate the intrinsic value of the stock.

▶ When estimating a stock's intrinsic value, we can follow one or both of two approaches (the present value of cash flow, or the analysis of relative valuation ratios). We reviewed how to estimate the major inputs to the techniques and demonstrated results when these techniques are applied to Walgreens.

▶ We derived several estimated values for Walgreens based on the present value of cash flow techniques and applied the relative valuation ratios beginning with P/E ratios and the other relative valuation ratios, including the price/book value ratio, the price/cash flow ratio, and the price/sales ratio, and compared these relative valuation ratios for the company to comparable ratios for both the retail drugstore industry and the aggregate market.

▶ The investment decision is based on the critical comparisons of a stock's intrinsic value to the prevailing market price. If the stock's intrinsic value exceeds the market price, we would buy the stock. If the intrinsic value is less than the market price, we would not buy it and would sell it if we owned it. The estimation of the intrinsic value can be done by using the techniques demonstrated in this chapter.

▶ Because of the difficulty in estimating the intrinsic value of growth firms, we considered alternative specifications for growth companies and several techniques that provide insights on the valuation of these firms. These techniques include economic value added, the franchise factor models, and a growth duration model that emphasizes the importance of estimating how long superior growth is expected to last. These models help the analyst concentrate attention on the relevant factors that determine true growth, which determines the intrinsic value of these growth companies. The critical question is, is the stock of the growth company going to be a growth stock?

▶ We concluded the reading with a discussion of several unique considerations an analyst must consider when analyzing and valuing global industries or firms. The importance of different accounting conventions and the impact of exchange rate differences were highlighted.

TECHNICAL ANALYSIS*

by Frank K. Reilly and Keith C. Brown

READING

63

LEARNING OUTCOMES

The candidate should be able to:

a. explain the underlying assumptions of technical analysis and explain how technical analysis differs from fundamental analysis;

b. discuss the advantages and challenges of technical analysis;

c. identify examples of each of the major categories of technical indicators.

INTRODUCTION   1

▶ The market reacted yesterday to the report of a large increase in the short interest on the NYSE.

▶ Although the market declined today, it was not considered bearish because of the light volume.

▶ The market declined today after three days of increases due to profit taking by investors.

These and similar statements appear daily in the financial news. All of them have as their rationale one of numerous technical trading rules. *Technical analysts,* or *technicians,* develop technical trading rules from observations of past price movements of the stock market and individual stocks. The philosophy behind technical analysis is in sharp contrast to the efficient market hypothesis that we studied, which contends that past performance has no influence on future performance or market values. It also differs from what we learned about

---

* Richard T. McCabe, Chief Market Analyst at Merrill Lynch Capital Markets, provided helpful comments and material for this reading.

Investment Analysis and Portfolio Management, Eighth Edition, by Frank K. Reilly and Keith C. Brown, Copyright © 2005. Reprinted with permission of South-Western, a division of Thomson Learning.

fundamental analysis, which involves making investment decisions based on the examination of the economy, an industry, and company variables that lead to an estimate of intrinsic value for an investment, which is then compared to its prevailing market price. In contrast to the efficient market hypothesis or fundamental analysis, **technical analysis** involves the examination of past market data such as prices and the volume of trading, which leads to an estimate of future price trends and, therefore, an investment decision. Whereas fundamental analysts use economic data that are usually separate from the stock or bond market, the technical analyst uses data *from the market itself* because the market is its own best predictor. Therefore, technical analysis is an alternative method of making the investment decision and answering the questions: What securities should an investor buy or sell? When should these investments be made?

Technical analysts see no need to study the multitude of economic, industry, and company variables to arrive at an estimate of future value because they believe that past price movements will signal future price movements. Technicians also believe that a change in the price trend may predict a forthcoming change in the fundamental variables such as earnings and risk before the change is perceived by most fundamental analysis. Are technicians correct? Many investors using these techniques claim to have experienced superior rates of return on many investments. In addition, many newsletter writers base their recommendations on technical analysis. Finally, even the major investment firms that employ many fundamental analysis also employ technical analysts to provide investment advice. Numerous investment professionals and individual investors believe in and use technical trading rules to make their investment decisions. Therefore, whether a fan of technical analysis or an advocate of the efficient market hypothesis, investors should still have an understanding of the basic philosophy and reasoning behind technical approaches. Thus, we begin this reading with an examination of the basic philosophy underlying technical analysis. Subsequently, we consider the advantages and potential problems with the technical approach. Finally, we present alternative technical trading rules applicable to both the U.S. and foreign securities markets.

2   UNDERLYING ASSUMPTIONS OF TECHNICAL ANALYSIS

Technical analysts base trading decisions on examinations of prior price and volume data to determine past market trends from which they predict future behavior for the market as a whole and for individual securities. Several assumptions summarized in Levy (1966) lead to this view of price movements. Certain aspects of these assumptions are controversial, leading fundamental analysts and advocates of efficient markets to question their validity. We have italicized those aspects in our list.

1. The market value of any good or service is determined solely by the interaction of supply and demand.

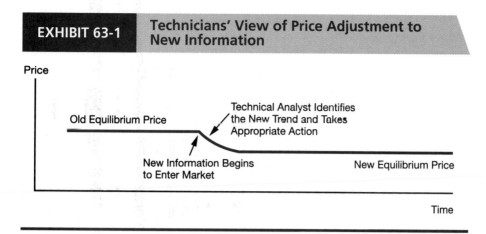

2. Supply and demand are governed by numerous rational and irrational factors. Included in these factors are those economic variables relied on by the fundamental analyst as well as opinions, moods, and guesses. The market weighs all these factors continually and automatically.

3. Disregarding minor fluctuations, *the prices for individual securities and the overall value of the market tend to move in trends, which persist for appreciable lengths of time.*

4. Prevailing trends change in reaction to shifts in supply and demand relationships. These shifts, no matter why they occur, *can be detected sooner or later in the action of the market itself.*

The first two assumptions are almost universally accepted by technicians and nontechnicians alike. Almost anyone who has had a basic course in economics would agree that, at any point in time, the price of a security (or any good or service) is determined by the interaction of supply and demand. In addition, most observers would acknowledge that supply and demand are governed by many variables. The only difference in opinion might concern the influence of the irrational factors. Certainly, everyone would agree that the market continually weighs all these factors.

In contrast, there is a significant difference of opinion regarding the assumption about the *speed of adjustment* of stock prices to changes in supply and demand. Technical analysts expect stock prices to move in trends that persist for long periods because they believe that new information does *not* come to the market at one point in time but rather enters the market *over a period of time*. This pattern of information access occurs because of different sources of information or because certain investors receive the information or perceive fundamental changes earlier than others. As various groups—ranging from insiders to well-informed professionals to the average investor—receive the information and buy or sell a security accordingly, its price moves gradually toward the new equilibrium. Therefore, technicians do not expect the price adjustment to be as abrupt as fundamental analysts and efficient market supporters do; rather, they expect a *gradual price adjustment* to reflect the gradual flow of information.

Exhibit 63-1 shows this process wherein new information causes a decrease in the equilibrium price for a security but the price adjustment is not rapid. It occurs as a trend that persists until the stock reaches its new equilibrium. Technical analysts look for the beginning of a movement from one equilibrium value to a new equilibrium value but do not attempt to predict the new equilibrium value. They look for the start of a change so that they can get on the bandwagon early and benefit from the move to the new equilibrium price by buying if the trend is up or selling if the trend is down. Obviously, if there is a rapid adjustment of prices to the new information (as expected by those who espouse an efficient market), the ride on the bandwagon would be so short that investors could not benefit.

3 ADVANTAGES OF TECHNICAL ANALYSIS

Although technicians understand the logic of fundamental analysis, they see several benefits in their approach. Most technical analysts admit that a fundamental analyst with good information, good analytical ability, and a keen sense of information's impact on the market should achieve above-average returns. However, this statement requires qualification. According to technical analysts, it is important to recognize that the fundamental analysts can experience superior returns *only* if they obtain new information before other investors and process it *correctly* and *quickly*. Technical analysts do not believe the majority of investors can consistently get new information before other investors and consistently process it correctly and quickly.

In addition, technical analysts claim that a major advantage of their method is that *it is not heavily dependent on financial accounting statements*—the major source of information about the past performance of a firm or industry. As we know from Readings 60 and 62, the fundamental analyst evaluates such statements to help project future return and risk characteristics for industries and individual securities. The technician contends that there are several major problems with accounting statements:

1. They lack a great deal of information needed by security analysts, such as information related to sales, earnings, and capital utilized by product line and customers.

2. According to GAAP (Generally Accepted Accounting Principles), corporations may choose among several procedures for reporting expenses, assets, or liabilities. Notably, these alternative procedures can produce vastly different values for expenses, income, return on assets, and return on equity, depending on whether the firm is conservative or aggressive. As a result, an investor can have trouble comparing the statements of two firms within the same industry, much less firms across industries.

3. Many psychological factors and other nonquantifiable variables do not appear in financial statements. Examples include employee training and loyalty, customer goodwill, and general investor attitude toward an industry. Investor attitudes could be important when investors become concerned about the risk from restrictions or taxes on products such as tobacco or alcohol or when firms do business in countries that have significant political risk.

Therefore, because technicians are suspicious of financial statements, they consider it advantageous not to depend on them. As we will show, most of the data used by technicians, such as security prices, volume of trading, and other trading information, are derived from the stock market itself.

Also, a fundamental analyst must process new information correctly and *quickly* to derive a new intrinsic value for the stock or bond before the other investors can. Technicians, on the other hand, only need to quickly recognize a movement to a new equilibrium value *for whatever reason*—that is, they do not need to know about a specific event and determine the effect of the event on the value of the firm and its stock.

Finally, assume a fundamental analyst determines that a given security is under- or overvalued a long time before other investors. He or she still must determine when to make the purchase or sale. Ideally, the highest rate of return would come from making the transaction just before the change in market value occurs. For example, assume that based on your analysis in February, you expect a firm to report substantially higher earnings in June. Although you could buy the stock in February, you would be better off waiting until about May to buy the stock so your funds would not be tied up for an extra three months, but you may be reticent to wait that long. Because most technicians do not invest until the move to the new equilibrium is under way, they contend that they are more likely than a fundamental analyst to experience ideal timing.

CHALLENGES TO TECHNICAL ANALYSIS 4

Those who doubt the value of technical analysis for investment decisions question the usefulness of this technique in two areas. First, they challenge some of its basic assumptions. Second, they challenge some specific technical trading rules and their long-run usefulness. In this section we consider these challenges.

Challenges to Technical Analysis Assumptions

The major challenge to technical analysis is based on the results of empirical tests of the efficient market hypothesis (EMH). As discussed in Reading 57, for technical trading rules to generate superior risk-adjusted returns after taking account of transaction costs, the market would have to be slow to adjust prices to the arrival of new information; that is, it would have to be inefficient. This is referred to as the **weak-form efficient market hypothesis**. The two sets of tests of the weak-form EMH are (1) the statistical analysis of prices to determine if prices moved in trends or were a random walk, and (2) the analysis of specific trading rules to determine if their use could beat a buy-and-hold policy after considering transactions costs and risk. Almost all the studies testing the weak-form EMH using statistical analysis have found that prices do not move in trends based on statistical tests of auto-correlation and runs. These results support the EMH.

Regarding the analysis of specific trading rules, as discussed in Reading 57, numerous technical trading rules exist that have not been or cannot be tested. Still, the vast majority of the results for the trading rules that have been tested support the EMH.

Challenges to Technical Trading Rules

An obvious challenge to technical analysis is that the past price patterns or relationships between specific market variables and stock prices may not be repeated. As a result, a technique that previously worked might miss subsequent market turns. This possibility leads most technicians to follow several trading rules and to seek a consensus of all of them to predict the future market pattern.

Other critics contend that many price patterns become self-fulfilling prophecies. For example, assume that many analysts expect a stock selling at $40 a share to go to $50 or more if it should rise above its current pattern and break through its channel at $45. As soon as it reaches $45, enough technicians will buy to cause the price to rise to $50, exactly as predicted. In fact, some technicians may place a limit order to buy the stock at such a breakout point. Under such conditions, the increase will probably be only temporary and the price will return to its true equilibrium.

Another problem with technical analysis is that the success of a particular trading rule will encourage many investors to adopt it. It is contended that this popularity and the resulting competition will eventually neutralize the technique. If numerous investors focus on a specific technical trading rule, some of them will attempt to anticipate the price pattern and either ruin the expected historical price pattern or eliminate profits for most traders by causing the price to change faster than expected. For example, suppose it becomes known that technicians who employ short-selling data have been enjoying high rates of return. Based on this knowledge, other technicians will likely start using these data and thus accelerate the stock price pattern following changes in short selling. As a result, this profitable trading rule may no longer be profitable after the first few investors react.

Further, as we will see when we examine specific trading rules, *they all require a great deal of subjective judgment.* Two technical analysts looking at the same price pattern may arrive at widely different interpretations of what has happened and, therefore, will come to different investment decisions. This implies that the use of various techniques is neither completely mechanical nor obvious. Finally, as we will discuss in connection with several trading rules, *the standard values that signal investment decisions can change over time.* Therefore, in some instances technical analysts adjust the specified values that trigger investment decisions to conform to the new environment. In other cases, trading rules have been abandoned because they no longer work.

5   TECHNICAL TRADING RULES AND INDICATORS

To illustrate the specific technical trading rules, Exhibit 63-2 shows a typical stock price cycle that could be an example for the overall stock market or for an individual stock. The graph shows a peak and trough, along with a rising trend channel, a flat trend channel, a declining trend channel, and indications of when a technical analyst would ideally want to trade.

The graph begins with the end of a declining (bear) market that finishes in a **trough**, followed by an upward trend that breaks through the **declining trend channel**. Confirmation that the declining trend has reversed would be a buy signal. The technical analyst would buy stocks that showed this pattern.

EXHIBIT 63-2   Typical Stock-Market Cycle

TYPICAL STOCK MARKET CYCLE

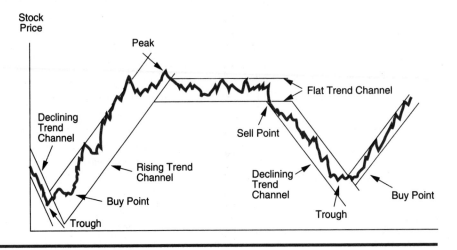

The analyst would then expect the development of a **rising trend channel**. As long as the stock price stayed in this rising channel, the technician would hold the stock(s). Ideally, they want to sell at the **peak** of the cycle, but they cannot identify a peak until after the trend changes.

If the stock (or the market) begins trading in a flat pattern, it will necessarily break out of its rising trend channel. At this point, some technical analysts would sell, but most would hold to see if the stock experiences a period of consolidation and then breaks out of the **flat trend channel** on the upside and begins rising again. Alternatively, if the stock were to break out of the channel on the downside, the technician would take this as a sell signal and would expect a declining trend channel. The next buy signal would come after the trough when the price breaks out of the declining channel and establishes a rising trend. We will consider strategies to detect these changes in trend and the importance of volume in this analysis shortly.

There are numerous technical trading rules and a range of interpretations for each of them. Almost all technical analysts watch many alternative rules and decide on a buy or sell decision based on a *consensus* of the signals because complete agreement of all the rules is rare. In the following discussion of several well-known techniques, we have divided the rules into four groups based on the attitudes of technical analysts. The first group includes trading rules used by analysts who like to trade against the crowd using contrary-opinion signals. The second group attempts to emulate astute investors, that is, the smart money. The third group includes popular technical indicators that are not easily classified. Finally, the fourth group includes pure price and volume techniques, including the famous Dow Theory.

Contrary-Opinion Rules

Many technical analysts rely on technical trading rules that assume that the majority of investors are wrong as the market approaches peaks and troughs. Therefore, these technicians try to determine when the majority of investors is either strongly bullish or bearish and then trade in the opposite direction.

Mutual Fund Cash Positions   Mutual funds hold some part of their portfolio in cash for one of several reasons. One is that they need cash to liquidate shares submitted by fundholders. Another is that new investments in the mutual fund may not have been invested. Third, the portfolio manager might be bearish on the market and want to increase the fund's defensive cash position.

Mutual funds' ratios of cash as a percentage of the total assets in their portfolios (the *cash ratio* or *liquid asset ratio*) are reported in the press, including monthly figures in *Barron's*.[1] This percentage of cash has varied in recent years from a low point of about 4 percent to a high point near 11 percent, although there appears to be a declining trend to the series.

Contrary-opinion technicians believe that mutual funds usually are wrong at peaks and troughs. Thus, they expect mutual funds to have a high percentage of cash near a market trough—the time when they should be fully invested to take advantage of the impending market rise. At the market peak, these technicians expect mutual funds to be almost fully invested with a low percentage of cash when they should be selling stocks and realizing gains. Therefore, contrary-opinion technicians watch for the mutual fund cash position to approach one of the extremes and act contrary to the mutual funds. Specifically, they would tend to buy when the cash ratio approaches 11 percent and to sell when the cash ratio approaches 4 percent.

---

[1] *Barron's* is a prime source for numerous technical indicators. For a readable discussion of relevant data and their use, see Martin E. Zweig (1987).

An alternative rationale is that a high cash position is a bullish indicator because of potential buying power. Irrespective of the reason for a large cash balance, these technicians believe the cash funds held will eventually be invested and will cause stock prices to increase. Alternatively, a low cash ratio would mean that the institutions have bought heavily and are left with little potential buying power.

Credit Balances in Brokerage Accounts   Credit balances result when investors sell stocks and leave the proceeds with their brokers, expecting to reinvest them shortly. The amounts are reported by the SEC and the NYSE in *Barron's*. Because technical analysts view these credit balances as potential purchasing power, a decline in these balances is considered bearish because it indicates lower purchasing power as the market approaches a peak. Alternatively, a buildup of credit balances indicates an increase in buying power and is a bullish signal.

Investment Advisory Opinions   Many technicians believe that if a large proportion of investment advisory services are bearish, this signals the approach of a market trough and the onset of a bull market. Because most advisory services tend to be trend followers, the number of bears usually is greatest when market bottoms are approaching. This trading rule is specified in terms of the percent of advisory services that are bearish/bullish given the number of services expressing an opinion.[2] A 60 percent bearish or 20 percent bullish reading indicates a major market bottom (a bullish indicator), while a 60 percent bullish or 20 percent bearish reading suggests a major market top (a bearish signal). Exhibit 63-3 shows a time-series plot of the DJIA and both the bearish sentiment index and the bullish sentiment index. As of mid-2005, both indexes are near the bearish boundary values.

OTC versus NYSE Volume   This ratio of trading volume is considered a measure of speculative activity. Speculative trading typically peaks at market peaks. Notably, the interpretation of the ratio has changed—that is, the decision rules have changed. Specifically, during the mid-1990s, the decision rule was in terms of specific percentages—112 percent was considered heavy speculative trading and an overbought market while 87 percent was considered low speculative trading and an oversold market. The problem was that the percentages kept increasing because of faster growth in OTC trading volume and dominance of the OTC market by a few large-cap stocks. It was subsequently decided to detect excess speculative activity by using the *direction* of the volume ratio as a guide. For example, if this ratio is increasing, it would indicate a bearish speculative environment.

Chicago Board Options Exchange (CBOE) Put-Call Ratio   Contrary-opinion technicians use put options, which give the holder the right to sell stock at a specified price for a given time period, as signals of a bearish attitude. A higher put-call ratio indicates a pervasive bearish attitude for investors, which technicians consider a bullish indicator.

This ratio fluctuates between 0.60 and 0.40 and has typically been substantially less than 1 because investors tend to be bullish and avoid selling short or buying puts. The current decision rule states that a put-call ratio above 0.60—that is, sixty puts are traded for every one hundred calls—indicates that investors are generally bearish, so it is considered bullish, while a relatively low put-call ratio of 0.40 or less is considered bearish.

Futures Traders Bullish on Stock-Index Futures   Another relatively new contrary-opinion measure is the percentage of speculators in stock-index futures who

---

[2] This ratio is compiled by Investors Intelligence, Larchmont, NY 10538. Richard McCabe at Merrill Lynch uses this series as one of his "Investor Sentiment Indicators."

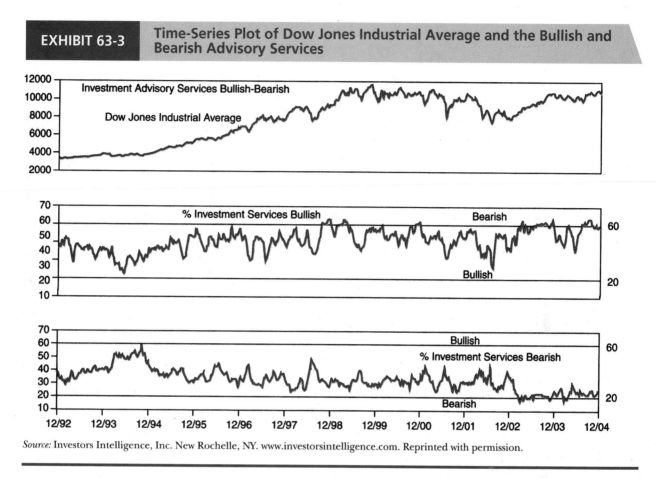

EXHIBIT 63-3 Time-Series Plot of Dow Jones Industrial Average and the Bullish and Bearish Advisory Services

Source: Investors Intelligence, Inc. New Rochelle, NY. www.investorsintelligence.com. Reprinted with permission.

are bullish regarding stocks based on a survey of individual futures traders. These technicians would consider it a bearish sign when more than 70 percent of the speculators are bullish, and a bullish sign when this ratio declines to 30 percent or lower. The plot in Exhibit 63-4 shows that as of mid-2005 this indicator was slightly less than 70 percent, so it is officially neutral but toward a bearish zone.

As we have shown, contrary-opinion technicians have several measures of how the majority of investors are investing that prompt them to take the opposite action. They generally employ several of these series to provide a consensus regarding investors' attitudes.

Follow the Smart Money

Some technical analysts have created a set of indicators and corresponding rules that they believe indicate the behavior of smart, sophisticated investors. We discuss three such indicators in this section.

Confidence Index   Published by *Barron's,* the Confidence Index is the ratio of *Barron's* average yield on 10 top-grade corporate bonds to the yield on the Dow Jones average of forty bonds.[3] This index measures the difference in yield spread between high-grade bonds and a large cross section of bonds. Because the yields

---

[3] Historical data for this index are contained in the *Dow Jones Investor's Handbook,* Princeton, NJ (Dow Jones Books, annual). Current figures appear in *Barron's.*

EXHIBIT 63-4	Time-Series Plot of Dow Jones Industrial Average and the Market Vane Percentage of Futures Traders Bullish and Bearish on Stock-Index Futures

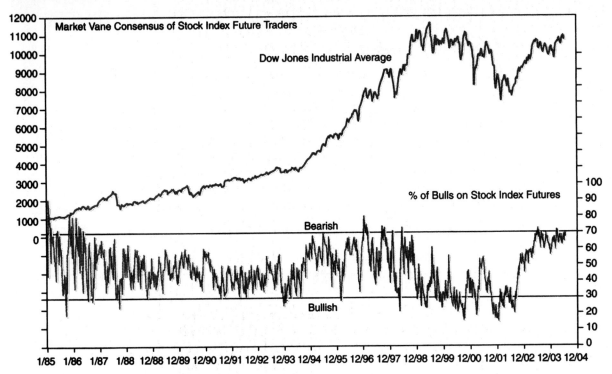

Source: Data Courtesy of Market Vane, http://www.marketvane.net.

on high-grade bonds always should be lower than those on a large cross section of bonds, this ratio should approach 100 as the spread between the two sets of bonds gets smaller.

Technicians believe the ratio is a bullish indicator because, during periods of high confidence, investors are willing to invest in lower-quality bonds for the added yield, which causes a decrease in the average yield for the large cross section of bonds relative to the yield on high-grade bonds. Therefore, this ratio of yields—the Confidence Index—will increase. In contrast, when investors are pessimistic, they avoid investing in low-quality bonds, which increases the yield spread between high-grade and average bonds, which in turn causes the Confidence Index to decline.

Unfortunately, this interpretation assumes that changes in the yield spread are caused almost exclusively by changes in investor demand for different quality bonds. In fact, the yield differences have frequently changed because of changes in the supply of bonds. For example, a large issue of high-grade AT&T bonds could cause a temporary increase in yields on all high-grade bonds, which would reduce the yield spread, and increase the Confidence Index without any change in investors' attitudes. Such a change can generate a false signal of a change in confidence.

T-Bill-Eurodollar Yield Spread   A popular measure of investor attitude or confidence on a global basis is the spread between T-bill yields and Eurodollar rates. It is reasoned that, at times of international crisis, this spread widens as the smart money flows to safe-haven U.S. T-bills, which causes a decline in this ratio. It is contended that the stock market typically experiences a trough shortly thereafter.

Debit Balances in Brokerage Accounts (Margin Debt)   Debit balances in brokerage accounts represent borrowing (margin debt) by knowledgeable investors from their brokers. Hence, these balances indicate the attitude of sophisticated investors who engage in margin transactions. Therefore, an increase in debit balances implies buying by these sophisticated investors and is considered a bullish sign, while a decline in debit balances would indicate selling and would be a bearish indicator.

Monthly data on margin debt is reported in *Barron's*. Unfortunately, this index does not include borrowing by investors from other sources such as banks. Also, because it is an absolute value, technicians would look for changes in the trend of borrowing—that is, increases are bullish, declines are bearish.

Momentum Indicators

In addition to contrary-opinion and smart money signals, several indicators of overall market momentum are used to make aggregate market decisions.

Breadth of Market   Breadth of market measures the number of issues that have increased each day and the number of issues that have declined. It helps explain the cause of a change of direction in a composite market index such as the S&P 500 Index. As we discussed in Reading 56, most stock-market indexes are heavily influenced by the stocks of large firms because they are value weighted. Therefore, a stock-market index can experience an increase while the majority of the individual issues do not, which means that most stocks are not participating in the rising market. Such a divergence can be detected by examining the advance-decline figures for all stocks on the exchange, along with the overall market index.

The advance–decline index is typically a cumulative index of net advances or net declines. Specifically, each day major newspapers publish figures on the number of issues on the NYSE that advanced, declined, or were unchanged. The figures for a five-day sample, as would be reported in *Barron's*, are shown in Exhibit 63-5. These figures, along with changes in the DJIA at the bottom of the table, indicate a strong market advance because the DJIA was increasing and the net advance figure was strong, indicating that the market increase was broadly

EXHIBIT 63-5	Daily Advances and Declines on the New York Stock Exchange				
Day	**1**	**2**	**3**	**4**	**5**
Issues traded	3,608	3,641	3,659	3,651	3,612
Advances	2,310	2,350	1,558	2,261	2,325
Declines	909	912	1,649	933	894
Unchanged	389	379	452	457	393
Net advances (advances minus declines)	+1,401	+1,438	−91	+1,328	+1,431
Cumulative net advances	+1,401	+2,839	+2,748	+4,076	+5,507
Changes in DJIA	+40.47	+95.75	−15.25	+108.42	+140.63

Sources: New York Stock Exchange and *Barron's*.

based. Even the results on Day 3, when the market declined 15 points, were encouraging since it was a small overall decline and the individual stock issues were split just about 50-50, which points toward a fairly even environment.

Stocks above Their 200-Day Moving Average Technicians often compute moving averages of an index to determine its general trend. To examine individual stocks, the 200-day **moving average** of prices has been fairly popular. From these moving-average indexes for numerous stocks, Media General Financial Services calculates how many stocks currently are trading above their 200-day moving-average index, and this is used as an indicator of general investor sentiment. The market is considered to be *overbought* and subject to a negative correction when more than 80 percent of the stocks are trading above their 200-day moving average. In contrast, if less than 20 percent of the stocks are selling above their 200-day moving average, the market is considered to be *oversold*, which means investors should expect a positive correction. As shown in Exhibit 63-6, as of mid-2005 the percent of stocks selling above their 200-day moving average has been above 80 percent, which indicates an overbought, bearish signal, but recently went below the 80 percent line.

Stock Price and Volume Techniques

In the introduction to this reading, we examined a hypothetical stock price chart that demonstrated market peaks and troughs along with rising and declining trend channels and breakouts from channels that signal new price trends or reversals of the price trends. While price patterns alone are important, most technical trading rules consider both stock price and corresponding volume movements.

Dow Theory Any discussion of technical analysis using price and volume data should begin with a consideration of the Dow Theory because it was among the earliest work on this topic and remains the basis for many technical indicators.[4] Dow described stock prices as moving in trends analogous to the movement of water. He postulated three types of price movements over time: (1) major trends that are like tides in the ocean, (2) intermediate trends that resemble waves, and (3) short-run movements that are like ripples. Followers of the Dow Theory attempt to detect the direction of the major price trend (tide), recognizing that

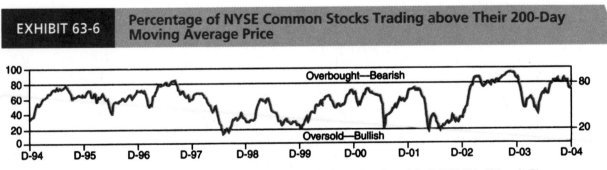

| EXHIBIT 63-6 | Percentage of NYSE Common Stocks Trading above Their 200-Day Moving Average Price |

Source: Walter G. Murphy, Research Analyst, Merrill Lynch. Reprinted by permission. Copyright © 2005 Merrill Lynch, Pierce, Fenner & Smith Incorporated. Further reproduction or distribution is strictly prohibited.

---

[4] A study that discusses and provides support for the Dow Theory is David A. Glickstein and Rolf E. Wubbels (1983).

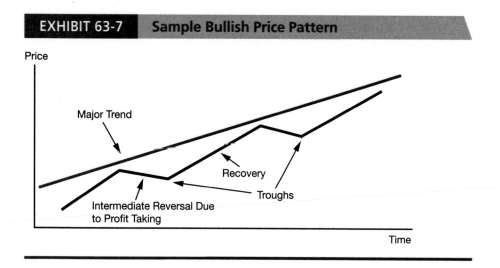

EXHIBIT 63-7   **Sample Bullish Price Pattern**

Price

Major Trend

Recovery

Troughs

Intermediate Reversal Due
to Profit Taking

Time

intermediate movements (waves) may occasionally move in the opposite direction. They recognize that a major market advance does not go straight up, but rather includes small price declines as some investors decide to take profits.

Exhibit 63-7 shows the typical bullish pattern. The technician would look for every recovery to reach a new peak above the prior peak, and this price rise should be accompanied by heavy trading volume. Alternatively, each profit-taking reversal that follows an increase to a new peak should have a trough above the prior trough, with relatively light trading volume during the profit-taking reversals. When this pattern of price and volume movements changes, the major trend may be entering a period of consolidation (a flat trend) or a major reversal.

Importance of Volume   As noted, technicians watch volume changes along with price movements as an indicator of changes in supply and demand. A price movement in one direction means that the net effect on price is in that direction, but the price change alone does not indicate the breadth of the excess demand or supply. Therefore, the technician looks for a price increase on heavy volume relative to the stock's normal trading volume as an indication of bullish activity. Conversely, a price decline with heavy volume is considered bearish. A generally bullish pattern would be when price increases are accompanied by heavy volume and small price reversals occur with light trading volume.

Technicians also use a ratio of upside-downside volume as an indicator of short-term momentum for the aggregate stock market. Each day the stock exchanges announce the volume of trading in stocks that experienced an increase divided by the volume of trading in stocks that declined. These data are reported daily in *The Wall Street Journal* and weekly in *Barron's*. This ratio is used as an indicator of market momentum. Specifically, technicians believe that an upside-downside volume value of 1.75 or more indicates an overbought position that is bearish. Alternatively, a value of 0.75 and lower supposedly reflects an oversold position and is considered bullish.

Support and Resistance Levels   A **support level** is the price range at which the technician would expect a substantial increase in the demand for a stock. Generally, a support level will develop after a stock has enjoyed a meaningful price increase and the stock experiences profit taking. Technicians reason that at some price below the recent peak other investors who did not buy during the first price increase (waiting for a small reversal) will get into the stock. When the price reaches this support price, demand surges and price and volume begin to increase again.

A **resistance level** is the price range at which the technician would expect an increase in the supply of stock and a price reversal. A resistance level develops after a significant decline from a higher price level. After the decline, the stock begins to recover, but the prior decline in price leads some investors who acquired the stock at a higher price to look for an opportunity to sell it near their breakeven points. Therefore, the supply of stock owned by these nervous investors is *overhanging* the market. When the price rebounds to the target price set by these investors, this overhanging supply of stock comes to the market and there is a price decline on heavy volume. It is also possible to envision a rising trend of support and resistance levels for a stock. For example, the rising support prices would be a set of higher prices where investors over time would see the price increase and would take the opportunity to buy when there is profit taking. In this latter case, there would be a succession of higher support levels over time.

Exhibit 63-8 contains the daily stock prices for Gillette (G), with support and resistance lines. The graphs show a rising pattern since Gillette has experienced strong price increases during this period. At present, the resistance level is at about $44 and is rising, while the support level is about $40 and is also rising. The bullish technician would look for future prices to rise in line with this channel. If prices fell significantly below the support line on strong volume, it would be considered a bearish signal, while an increase above the $44 resistance price would be bullish.

Moving-Average Lines   Earlier, we discussed how technicians use a moving average of past stock prices as an indicator of the long-run trend and how they examine current prices relative to this trend for signals of a change. We also noted that a 200-day moving average is a relatively popular measure for individual stocks and the aggregate market. In this discussion, we add a 50-day moving-average price line (short-term trend) and consider large volume.

Exhibit 63-9 is a daily stock price chart from Yahoo! Inc. for Pfizer, Inc. (PFE) for the year ending June 4, 2004. It also contains 50-day and 200-day moving-average (MA) lines. As noted, MA lines are meant to reflect the overall trend for the price series with the shorter MA line (the 50-day versus 200-day) reflecting shorter trends. Two comparisons involving the MA lines are considered

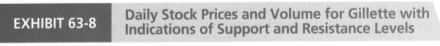

| **EXHIBIT 63-8** | **Daily Stock Prices and Volume for Gillette with Indications of Support and Resistance Levels** |

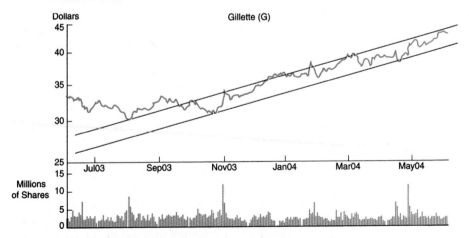

Source: Yahoo! Inc., finance.yahoo.com. Reproduced with permission of Yahoo! Inc. © 2005 by Yahoo! Inc. YAHOO! and the YAHOO! logo are trademarks of Yahoo! Inc.

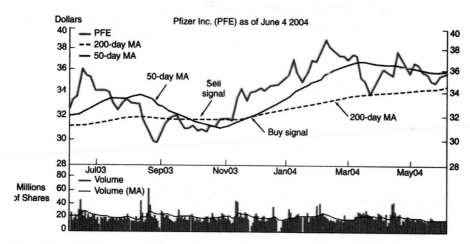

| EXHIBIT 63-9 | Daily Stock Prices for Pfizer, Inc. with 50-Day and 200-Day Moving-Average Lines |

Source: Yahoo! Inc., finance.yahoo.com. Reproduced with permission of Yahoo! Inc. © 2005 by Yahoo! Inc. YAHOO! and the YAHOO! logo are trademarks of YAHOO! Inc.

important. The first comparison is the specific prices to the shorter-run 50-day MA line. If the overall price trend of a stock or the market has been down, the moving-average price line generally would lie above current prices. If prices reverse and break through the moving-average line *from below* accompanied by heavy trading volume, most technicians would consider this a *positive* change and speculate that this breakthrough could signal a reversal of the declining trend. In contrast, if the price of a stock had been rising, the moving-average line would also be rising, but it would be below current prices. If current prices declined and broke through the moving-average line *from above* accompanied by heavy trading volume, this would be considered a bearish pattern that would possibly signal a reversal of the long-run rising trend.

The second comparison is between the 50- and 200-day MA lines. Specifically, when these two lines cross, it signals a change in the overall trend. Specifically, if the 50-day MA line crosses the 200-day MA line from below on good volume, this would be a bullish indicator (buy signal) because it confirms a reversal in trend from negative to positive. In contrast, when the 50-day line crosses the 200-day line from above, it confirms a change to a negative trend and would be a sell signal. As shown in Exhibit 63-9, in the case of Pfizer (PFE) there was a bearish crossing in late September 2003, but it was reversed in December 2003 when there was a bullish crossing. Following this bullish crossing, the 50-day line has been consistently above the 200-day line as prices reached a peak of about $38 and were at about $36 at the end of the period. There is a cautionary signal to this chart, since the price line has broken through the 50-day line from above several times and is slightly below this MA line at the end of the graph.

Overall, for a *bullish* trend the 50-day MA line should be above the 200-day MA line, as it has been for Pfizer since December 2003. Notably, if this positive gap between the 50-day and 200-day lines gets too large (which happens with a fast run-up in price), a technician might consider this an indication that the stock is temporarily overbought, which is bearish in the short run. A *bearish* trend is when the 50-day MA line is always below the 200-day MA line. Still, if the gap gets large on the downside, it might be considered a signal of an oversold stock, which is bullish for the short run.

Relative Strength   Technicians believe that once a trend begins, it will continue until some major event causes a change in direction. They believe this is also true of *relative* performance. If an individual stock or an industry group is outperforming the market, technicians believe it will continue to do so.

Therefore, technicians compute weekly or monthly **relative-strength (RS) ratios** for individual stocks and industry groups. The RS ratio is equal to the price of a stock or an industry index divided by the value for some stock-market index such as the S&P 500. If this ratio increases over time, it shows that the stock or industry is outperforming the overall stock market, and a technician would expect this superior performance to continue. Relative-strength ratios work during declining as well as rising markets. In a declining market, if a stock's price declines less than the market does, the stock's relative-strength ratio will continue to rise. Technicians believe that if this ratio is stable or increases during a bear market, the stock should do well during the subsequent bull market.

Merrill Lynch publishes relative-strength charts for industry groups. Exhibit 63-10 describes how to read the charts. Further, some technicians construct graphs of stocks relative to the stock's industry index in addition to the comparison relative to the market.

EXHIBIT 63-10   How to Read Industry Group Charts

HOW TO READ INDUSTRY GROUP CHARTS

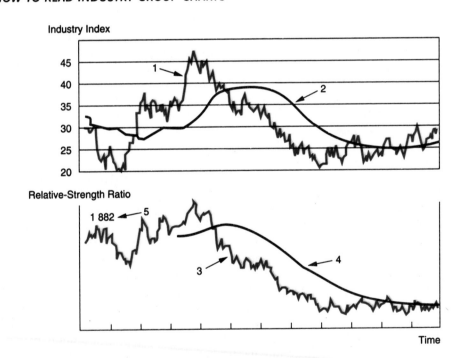

The industry group charts in this report display the following elements:

1. A line chart of the weekly close of the Standard & Poor's Industry Group Index for the past nine and one-half years, with the index range indicated to the left.
2. A line of the seventy-five-week moving average of the Standard & Poor's Industry Group Index.
3. A relative-strength line of the Standard & Poor's Industry Group Index compared with the New York Stock Exchange Composite Index.
4. A seventy-five-week moving average of relative strength.

(Exhibit continued on next page …)

EXHIBIT 63-10   **How to Read Industry Group Charts (continued)**

5. A volatility reading that measures the maximum amount by which the index has out-performed (or underperformed) the NYSE Composite Index during the time period displayed.

Source: Walter G. Murphy, Research Analyst, Merrill Lynch. Reprinted by permission. Copyright © 2002 Merrill Lynch, Pierce, Fenner & Smith Incorporated. Further reproduction or distribution is strictly prohibited.

Bar Charting   Technicians use charts that show daily, weekly, or monthly time series of stock prices. For a given interval, the technical analyst plots the high and low prices and connects the two points vertically to form a bar. Typically, he or she will also draw a small horizontal line across this vertical bar to indicate the closing price. Finally, almost all bar charts include the volume of trading at the bottom of the chart so that the technical analyst can relate the price and volume movements. A typical bar chart in Exhibit 63-11 shows data for the DJIA from *The Wall Street Journal* along with volume figures for the NYSE.

Multiple-Indicator Charts   Thus far we have presented charts that deal with only one trading technique such as moving-average lines or relative-strength rules. In the real world, it is fairly typical for technical charts to contain several indicators that can be used together like the two MA lines (50- and 200-day) and the RS

EXHIBIT 63-11   **A Typical Bar Chart**

Daily High, Low, and Close for Dow Jones Industrial Average and Volume on the NYSE, Year Ending June 10, 2004

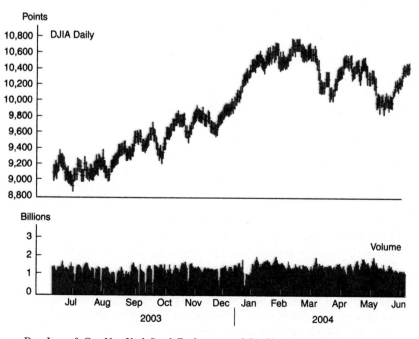

Sources: Dow Jones & Co., New York Stock Exchange, and *Big Charts* (www.BigCharts.com).

| EXHIBIT 63-12 | Sample Point-and-Figure Chart |

```
50  |       |   |   |   |   |   |   |   |
48  |       |   |   |   |   |   |   |   |
46  |       |   | X |   |   |   |   |   |
44  |       |   | X |   |   |   |   |   |
42  |     X | X | X |   |   |   |   |   |
40  |     X | X | X |   |   |   |   |   |
38  |       | X | X |   |   |   |   |   |
36  |       | X | X |   |   |   |   |   |
34  |       | X | X |   |   |   |   |   |
32  |       |   |   |   |   |   |   |   |
30  |       |   |   |   |   |   |   |   |
```

line, because they can provide added support to the analysis. Technicians include as many price and volume indicators as are reasonable on one chart and then, based on the performance of *several* technical indicators, try to arrive at a consensus about the future movement for the stock.

Point-and-Figure Charts   Another graph that is popular with technicians is the point-and-figure chart. Unlike the bar chart, which typically includes all ending prices and volumes to show a trend, the point-and-figure chart includes only significant price changes, regardless of their timing. The technician determines what price interval to record as significant (one point, two points, and so on) and when to note price reversals.

To demonstrate how a technical analyst would use such a chart, suppose we want to chart a volatile stock that is currently selling for $40 a share. Because of its volatility, we believe that anything less than a two-point price change is not significant. Also, we consider anything less than a four-point reversal, meaning a movement in the opposite direction, quite minor. Therefore, we would set up a chart similar to the one in Exhibit 63-12, but our new chart would start at 40; it would also progress in two-point increments. If the stock moved to $42, we would place an X in the box above 40 and do nothing else until the stock rose to $44 or dropped to $38 (a four-point reversal from its high of $42). If it dropped to $38, we would move a column to the right, which indicates a reversal in direction, and begin again at 38 (fill in boxes at 42 and 40). If the stock price dropped to $34, we would enter an X at 36 and another at 34. If the stock then rose to $38 (another four-point reversal), we would move to the next column and begin at 38, going up (fill in 34 and 36). If the stock then went to $46, we would fill in more Xs as shown and wait for further increases or a reversal.

Depending on how fast the prices rise and fall, this process might take anywhere from two to six months. Given these figures, the technician would attempt to determine trends just as with the bar chart. As always, the technician would look for breakouts to either higher or lower price levels. A long horizontal movement with many reversals but no major trends up or down would be considered a *period of consolidation* wherein the stock is moving from buyers to sellers and back again with no strong consensus about its direction. Once the stock breaks out and moves up or down after a period of consolidation, technical analysts anticipate a major move because previous trading set the stage for it. In other words, the longer the period of consolidation, the larger the subsequent move when there is finally a breakout.

Point-and-figure charts provide a compact record of movements because they only consider significant price changes for the stock being analyzed. Therefore, some technicians contend they are easier to work with and give more vivid pictures of price movements.

TECHNICAL ANALYSIS OF FOREIGN MARKETS

6

Our discussion thus far has concentrated on U.S. markets, but analysts have discovered that these techniques apply to foreign markets as well. Merrill Lynch, for instance, prepares separate technical analysis publications for individual countries such as Japan, Germany, and the United Kingdom as well as a summary of all world markets. The examples that follow show that when analyzing non-U.S. markets, many techniques are limited to price and volume data rather than the more detailed U.S. market information. The reason is that the detailed information available on the U.S. market through the SEC, the stock exchanges, the Nasdaq system, and various investment services is not always available for other countries.

Foreign Stock-Market Indexes

Exhibit 63-13 contains the daily time-series plot for the Japanese Nikkei Index. This chart shows the generally declining trend by the Japanese stock market during the period from May 2000 to April 2003, followed by rising stock prices through May 2004 and generally flat performance into May 2005. In the written analysis, the market analyst at Merrill Lynch estimated support and resistance levels for the Japanese Stock Exchange index and commented on the medium-term outlook for this market. Merrill Lynch publishes similar charts for 10 other countries and compares the countries and ranks them by stock and currency performance.

EXHIBIT 63-13   Graph and Summary Comments on the Japanese Stock Market

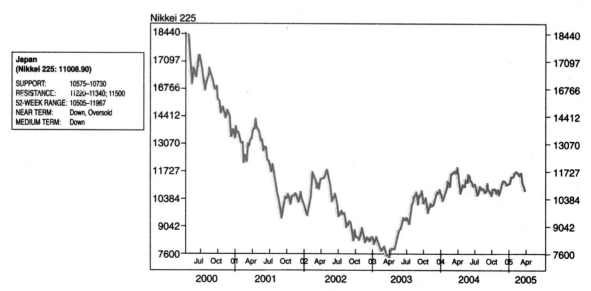

Source: Walter G. Murphy, Research Analyst, Merrill Lynch. Reprinted by permission. Copyright © 2005 Merrill Lynch, Pierce, Fenner & Smith Incorporated. Further reproduction or distribution is strictly prohibited.

Technical Analysis of Foreign Exchange Rates

On numerous occasions, we have discussed the importance of changes in foreign exchange rates on the rates of return on foreign securities. Because of the importance of these relationships, bond-and-stock traders in world markets examine the time-series data of various currencies such as the British pound and the Euro. They also analyze the spread between currencies, such as the difference between the Japanese yen and the British pound. Finally, they would typically examine the time series for the U.S. dollar trade-weighted exchange rate that experienced significant weakness during 2003–2005.

7   TECHNICAL ANALYSIS OF BOND MARKETS

Thus far, we have emphasized the use of technical analysis in stock markets. These techniques can also be applied to the bond market. The theory and rationale for technical analysis of bonds is the same as for stocks, and many of the same trading rules are used. A major difference is that it was generally not possible to consider the volume of trading of bonds because most bonds are traded OTC, where volume was not reported until 2004.

Exhibit 63-14 demonstrates the use of technical analysis techniques applied to bond-yield series. Specifically, the graph contains a time-series plot of world bond yields based on a seven-country composite. As shown, yields declined steadily until a trough in June 2003, followed by a sharp recovery and a roller-coaster pattern between late 2003 and mid-2005. Notably, the outlook by the analyst is for lower yields medium and longer term. Such a technical graph provides important insights to a global bond-portfolio manager interested in adjusting his or her bond portfolio.

EXHIBIT 63-14   Time-Series Plot of Global Bond Yields (Seven-Country Composite)

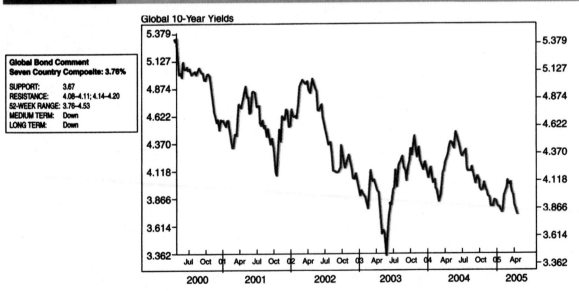

Source: Walter G. Murphy, Research Analyst, Merrill Lynch. Reprinted by permission. Copyright © 2005 Merrill Lynch, Pierce, Fenner & Smith Incorporated. Further reproduction or distribution is strictly prohibited.

THE INTERNET

Investments Online

By its nature, technical analysis uses charts and graphs, and many Web sites offer them for use by investors and analysts; some are free, but some of the sites for more sophisticated users require payment for access. Here are several interesting sites:

www.mta.org/ The home page of the Market Technicians Association, a professional group of chartists whose goal is to enhance technical analysis and educate investors about its role. The group sponsors the Chartered Market Technician (CMT) designation. This site features news groups, investment links, training and education sources, a journal, and a variety of technical analysis charts. Its "members" tab includes links to Web sites of its members' firms.

www.bigcharts.marketwatch.com/ This site offers free intraday and historical charts and price quotes. Its database includes stocks, mutual funds, and indexes. Users can learn which stocks have the largest percentage gain (loss) in price and volume and which stocks are hitting new 52-week highs (lows). Other features include momentum charts, stocks with the largest short interest, and a variety of other items of interest to technicians.

stockcharts.com/ This site offers a variety of charting options, including point-and-figure charts. It offers a "chart school," which offers summaries of different charting techniques and uses.

SUMMARY

► Numerous investors believe in and use the principles of technical analysis. The fact is, the large investment houses provide extensive support for technical analysis, and a large proportion of the discussion related to securities markets in the media is based on a technical view of the market.

► Their answers to two main questions separate technical analysts and efficient market advocates. First, in the information dissemination process does everybody get the information at about the same time? Second, how quickly do investors adjust security prices to reflect new information? Technical analysts believe that news takes time to travel from the insider and expert to the individual investor. They also believe that price adjustments are not instantaneous. As a result, they contend that security prices move in trends that persist and, therefore, they can use past price trends and volume information along with other market indicators to determine future price trends.

► Technical trading rules fall into four general categories: contrary-opinion rules, follow-the-smart-money tactics, momentum indicators, and stock price and volume techniques. These techniques and trading rules can be applied to both domestic and foreign markets. They can also be used to analyze currency exchange rates and determine the prevailing sentiment in the bond market.

► Most technicians employ several indicators and attempt to derive a consensus to guide their decision to buy, sell, or do nothing.[5]

---

[5] An analysis using numerous indicators is the study by Jerome Baesel, George Shows, and Edward Thorp (1982).

INTRODUCTION TO PRICE MULTIPLES

John D. Stowe, Thomas R. Robinson,
Jerald E. Pinto, and Dennis W. McLeavey

LEARNING OUTCOMES

The candidate should be able to:

a. discuss the rationales for the use of price to earnings (P/E), price to book value (P/BV), price to sales (P/S), and price to cash flow (P/CF) in equity valuation and discuss the possible drawbacks to the use of each price multiple;

b. calculate and interpret P/E, P/BV, P/S, and P/CF.

INTRODUCTION   1

All investors are concerned with the question of the value of common stock. The return an investor can expect from buying a stock depends on whether the stock is fairly valued, overvalued, or undervalued at the price at which it is purchased. Among the most familiar and widely used tools used in addressing questions of value are price multiples. **Price multiples** are ratios of a stock's market price to some measure of value per share. The intuition behind price multiples is that what a share represents in terms of assets, earnings, or some other measure of value is important for estimating its value. Price multiples have the appealing qualities of simplicity in use and ease in communication. From newspaper columns to research reports, the investor constantly sees them in action.

This presentation introduces four commonly used price multiples: price to earnings, price to book value, price to sales, and price to cash flow. The reader may observe multiples applied in various ways to select stocks as he reads the research of other analysts.

One approach is based on the idea that if two securities are very similar (if they have similar risk, profit margins, and growth prospects, for example) the security with the lower multiple is relatively undervalued compared to the other security. The reader may also observe other comparisons, for example, to an industry mean or median value of the multiple. This approach is valuation based on comparables (meaning similar assets).

Another approach relates the value of the multiple directly to fundamentals to estimate a fair value for the multiple; the value of the multiple might be related to the company's growth prospects, for example. This fair value (justified) multiple is then compared to the actual, market value of the multiple to reach a value judgment.

In this introduction to price multiples, we have two focuses:

▶ What are the reasons or rationales for selecting a particular price multiple? What are the possible drawbacks to using a particular multiple?
▶ How is a price multiple defined and calculated?

We now address these issues for each of the four multiples.

2   PRICE TO EARNINGS

In the first edition of *Security Analysis*, Benjamin Graham and David L. Dodd (1934, p. 351) described common stock valuation based on price-to-earnings (P/E) ratios as the standard method of that era, and the P/E ratio is doubtless still the most familiar valuation measure today.

We begin our discussion of the P/E with rationales offered by analysts for its use, as well as possible drawbacks. We then define the two chief variations of the P/E ratio: the **trailing P/E** and the **leading P/E**. As in other price multiples, the multiple's numerator, market price, is readily determinable; it presents no special problems of interpretation. But the denominator, EPS, is based on the complex rules of accrual accounting and presents important interpretation issues. We discuss those issues and the adjustments analysts can make to obtain more-meaningful P/Es.

2.1 Rationales for Using Price to Earnings Ratios

Analysts have offered several rationales for using P/Es:

▶ Earning power is a chief driver of investment value, and EPS is perhaps the chief focus of security analysts' attention. In Block's 1999 survey of AIMR members, earnings ranked first among four variables—earnings, cash flow, book value, and dividends—as an input in valuation.
▶ P/E is widely recognized and used by investors.

▶ Differences in P/Es may be related to differences in long-run average returns, according to empirical research.[1]

Drawbacks to using P/Es derive from the characteristics of EPS:

▶ EPS can be negative, and the P/E does not make economic sense with a negative denominator.

▶ The ongoing or recurring components of earnings are the most important in determining intrinsic value. Earnings often have volatile, transient components, however, making the analyst's task difficult.

▶ Within allowable accounting practices, management can exercise its discretion to distort EPS as an accurate reflection of economic performance. Distortions can affect the comparability of P/Es across companies.

Analysts have developed methods to attempt to address these potential drawbacks, and we will discuss these methods later. In the next section, we discuss the definition and calculation of EPS for use in P/Es.

2.2 Determining Earnings

In calculating a P/E, the current price for publicly traded companies is generally easily obtained and unambiguous. Determining the earnings figure to be used in the denominator, however, is not as straightforward. The following two issues must be considered:

▶ The time horizon over which earnings are measured, which results in two chief alternative definitions of the P/E, and

▶ The adjustments to accounting earnings that the analyst may make, so that P/Es can be compared across companies.

The two chief alternative definitions of P/E are trailing P/E and leading P/E. A stock's **trailing P/E** (sometimes referred to as a **current P/E**) is its current market price divided by the most recent four quarters' EPS. In such calculations, EPS is sometimes referred to as trailing 12 months (TTM) EPS. Trailing P/E is the P/E published in financial newspapers' stock listings. The **leading P/E** (also called the **forward P/E** or **prospective P/E**) is a stock's current price divided by next year's expected earnings. Other names and time horizon definitions also exist: First Call/Thomson Financial reports as the "current P/E" a stock's market price divided by the last reported annual EPS; Value Line reports as the "P/E" a stock's market price divided by the sum of the preceding two quarters' trailing earnings and the next two quarters' expected earnings.

In using P/Es, the same definition should be applied to all companies and time periods under examination. Otherwise the P/Es are not comparable, either for a given company over time or for different companies at a specific point in time. The differences in P/E calculated using different methods could be systematic (as opposed to random). For example, for companies with rising earnings, the leading P/E will be smaller than the trailing P/E because the denominator in the leading P/E calculation will be larger.

Logic sometimes indicates that a particular definition of the P/E is not relevant. For example, a major acquisition or divestiture may change the nature of a

---

[1] Block (1999) documented a belief among AIMR members that low-P/E stocks tend to outperform the market. See Bodie, Kane, and Marcus (2001) for a brief summary of the related academic research, which has wide ramifications and is the subject of continuing active debate.

business so that the trailing P/E based on past EPS is not informative about the future and thus not relevant to a valuation. In such a case, the leading P/E is the appropriate measure. Valuation is a forward-looking process and the analyst, when she has earnings forecasts, usually features the leading P/E in analyses. If a company's earnings are not readily predictable, however, then a trailing P/E (or alternative valuation metric) may be more appropriate. In the following section, we address issues that arise in calculating trailing P/Es.

2.2.1 Calculating the Trailing P/E

When calculating a P/E using trailing earnings, care must be taken in determining the EPS used in the denominator. An analyst must consider the following:

▶ transitory, nonrecurring components of earnings that are company specific,

▶ transitory components of earnings due to cyclicality (business or industry cyclicality),

▶ differences in accounting methods, and

▶ potential dilution of EPS.

Example 64-1 illustrates the first bullet point. Items in earnings that are not expected to recur in the future (nonrecurring earnings) are generally removed by analysts. Such items are not expected to reappear in future earnings, and valuation looks to the future as concerns cash flows. The analyst focuses on estimating **underlying earnings**: earnings excluding nonrecurring components.[2] An increase in underlying earnings reflects an increase in earnings that the analyst expects to persist into the future.

Example 64-1

Adjusting EPS for Nonrecurring Items

You are calculating a trailing P/E for American Electric Power (NYSE: AEP) as of 9 November 2001, when the share price closed at $44.50. In its fiscal year ended 31 December 2000, AEP recorded EPS of $0.83 that included an extraordinary loss of $0.11. Additionally, AEP took an expense of $203 million for merger costs during that calendar year, which are not expected to recur, and had unusual deficits in two out of four quarters. As of November 2001, the trailing twelve months' EPS was $2.16, including three quarters in 2001 and one quarter in 2000. The fourth quarter of calendar year 2000, however, had several nonrecurring items. Without making an adjustment for nonrecurring items, the trailing P/E was $44.50/$2.16 = 20.6. Adjusting for these items, you arrive at a figure for trailing EPS of $2.85 using an underlying earnings concept, and a trailing P/E of $44.50/$2.85 = 15.6. Which P/E would you use: 20.6 or 15.6?

Answer: 15.6. This number is the P/E an analyst would use in valuation, being consistent in the treatment of earnings for all stocks under review. In the course of this introduction, we will illustrate adjustments to earnings in many examples.

---

[2] Other names for underlying earnings include **persistent earnings**, **continuing earnings**, and **core earnings**.

The identification of nonrecurring items often requires detailed work, in particular the examination of the income statement, the footnotes to the income statement, and management discussion and analysis. The analyst cannot rely only on income statement classifications in identifying the nonrecurring components of earnings. Nonrecurring items (for example, gains and losses from the sale of assets, asset write-downs, provisions for future losses, and changes in accounting estimates) often appear in the income from continuing operations portion of a business's income statement.[3] An analyst taking the income statement classification at face value could draw incorrect conclusions in a valuation.

Besides company-specific effects such as restructuring costs, transitory effects on earnings can come from business-cycle or industry-cycle influences, as stated in the second bullet point on page 349. These effects are somewhat different in nature. Because business cycles repeat, such effects (although transitory) can be expected to recur over subsequent cycles.

Because of cyclic effects, the most recent four quarters of earnings may not accurately reflect the average or long-term earnings power of a business, particularly for **cyclical businesses**—businesses with high sensitivity to business- or industry-cycle influences. Analysts address this problem by calculating the level of EPS that the business could achieve currently under mid-cyclical conditions: **normal (business-cycle-adjusted) EPS**. In the discussion to follow, we use the term "normal" to mean business-cycle-adjusted EPS.[4] Two of several available methods to calculate normal EPS are as follows:

- ► *The method of historical average EPS*. Normal EPS is calculated as average EPS over the most recent full cycle.

- ► *The method of average return on equity*. Normal EPS is calculated as the average return on equity (ROE) from the most recent full cycle, multiplied by current book value per share.

The first method is one of several possible statistical approaches to the problem of cyclical earnings; however, this method does not account for changes in the company's size. The second alternative, by using recent book value per share, reflects more accurately the effect on EPS of growth or shrinkage in the company's size. For that reason, the method of average ROE is sometimes preferred. When reported current book value does not adequately reflect company size in relation to past values (because of items such as large write-downs), the analyst can make the appropriate adjustment. The analyst can also estimate normal earnings by multiplying total assets by an estimate of the long-run return on total assets.[5]

---

[3] An asset **write-down** is a reduction in the value of an asset as stated in the balance sheet. The timing and amount of write-downs often are at least in part discretionary. **Accounting estimates** include the useful lives of assets (depreciable lives), warranty costs, and the amount of uncollectible receivables.

[4] See Kisor and Whitbeck (1963, p. 57). Some writers describe the removal of any one-time or nonrecurring items from earnings as normalizing earnings as well. For example, White, Sondhi, and Fried (2003), pages 631–636, use the term *normalization* to refer to adjustments for nonrecurring items as well as for business cycle effects.

[5] An example of the application of this method is Lee, Myers, and Swaminathan (1999), who used 6 percent of total assets as an estimate of normal earnings levels when current earnings for a company were negative, in their study of the intrinsic value of the Dow Jones Industrial Average, a U.S. equity index. According to the authors, the long-run return on total assets in the United States is approximately 6 percent.

Example 64-2

Normalizing EPS for Business-Cycle Effects

You are researching the valuation of Koninklijke Philips Electronics N.V. (NYSE: PHG), Europe's largest electronics company, as of the beginning of November 2001. On 8 November 2001, PHG stock closed at $25.72. PHG experienced a severe cyclical contraction in its Consumer Electronics division in 2001, resulting in a loss of $1.94 per share; you thus decide to normalize earnings. You believe the 1995–2000 period (which excludes 2001) reasonably captures average profitability over a business cycle. Table 64-1 supplies data on EPS, book value per share (BVPS), and return on equity (ROE).[6]

TABLE 64-1   Koninklijke Philips (EPS and BVPS in US Dollars)

	2001	2002	1999	1998	1997	1996	1995
EPS	(1.94)	2.11	1.15	0.87	1.16	0.55	1.14
BVPS	13.87	16.62	9.97	11.68	6.57	6.43	6.32
ROE	NM	0.129	0.104	0.072	0.168	0.083	0.179

NM = not meaningful
Sources: www.philips.com for 2001 data; *The Value Line Investment Survey* for other data.

Using the data in Table 64-1,

1. Calculate a normal EPS for PHG based on the method of historical average EPS, and then calculate the P/E based on that estimate of normal EPS.

2. Calculate a normal EPS for PHG based on the method of average ROE and the P/E based on that estimate of normal EPS.

3. Explain the source of the differences in the normal EPS calculated by the two methods, and contrast the impact on the estimate of a normal P/E.

▶ **Solution to 1.** Averaging EPS over the 1995–2000 period, we find that ($1.14 + $0.55 + $1.16 + $0.87 + $1.15 + $2.11)/6 = $1.16. According to the method of historical average EPS, PHG's normal EPS is $1.16. The P/E based on this estimate is $25.72/1.16 = 22.2.

▶ **Solution to 2.** Averaging ROE over the 1995–2000 period, we find that (0.179 + 0.083 + 0.168 + 0.072 + 0.104 + 0.129)/6 = 0.1225, or 12.25%. For current BVPS, we use the 2001 value of $13.87. According to the method of average ROE, we have 0.1225 × $13.87 = $1.70 as normal EPS. The P/E based on this estimate is $25.72/$1.70 = 15.1.

---

[6] EPS and BVPS are based on EUR/USD translation rates for 2001 and 2000 and on Dutch guilder/USD translation rates for earlier years, as given by Value Line.

> ▶ **Solution to 3.** From 1995 to 2001, BVPS increased from $6.32 to $13.87, an increase of about 219 percent. The estimate of $1.70 from the average ROE method compared with $1.16 from the historical average EPS method reflects the use of information on the current size of the company. Because of that difference, PHG appears more conservatively valued (as indicated by a lower P/E) using the method based on average ROE.

We also need to adjust EPS for differences in accounting methods between different companies so that the P/Es are comparable.

Example 64-3

Adjusting for Differences in Accounting Methods

In late October 1999, Coachmen Industries (NYSE: COA) was trading at a price of $16 per share and had trailing twelve months EPS of $1.99. COA's P/E was thus 8.04. At the same time, Winnebago Industries (NYSE: WGO) was trading at a price of $17 per share and had trailing twelve months EPS of $1.99 for a P/E of 8.54. COA uses the first-in, first-out (FIFO) method of accounting for its inventory. WGO uses the last-in, first-out (LIFO) method of accounting for its inventory. Adjusting WGO's results for differences between the LIFO and FIFO methods produces an adjusted EPS of $2.02 and an adjusted P/E of 8.42. Adjusting EPS for WGO for consistency with COA's inventory accounting method narrows the difference between the two companies' P/Es.

In addition to adjustments for nonrecurring items and accounting methods, the analyst should consider the impact of potential dilution on EPS.[7] Companies are required to present both basic EPS and diluted EPS. **Basic earnings per share** reflects total earnings divided by the weighted-average number of shares actually outstanding during the period. **Diluted earnings per share** reflects division by the number of shares that would be outstanding if holders of securities such as executive stock options, equity warrants, and convertible bonds exercised their options to obtain common stock.

Example 64-4

Basic versus Diluted Earnings per share

For the fiscal year ended 31 June 2001, Microsoft (Nasdaq NMS: MSFT) had basic EPS of $1.38 and diluted EPS of $1.32. Based on a stock price of $60 shortly after the release of the annual report, Microsoft's trailing P/E is 43.5 using basic EPS and 45.5 using diluted EPS.

---

[7] Dilution refers to the reduction in the proportional ownership interests as a result of the issuance of new shares.

TABLE 64-2	P/E and E/P for Four Personal Computer Manufacturers (as of 13 November 2001; in US Dollars)			
	Current Price	Trailing EPS	Trailing P/E	E/P
Dell Computer Corporation (Nasdaq NMS: DELL)	26.00	0.49	52.41	1.9%
Apple Computer (Nasdaq NMS: AAPL)	19.20	−0.11	NM	−0.6%
Compaq Computer Corporation (NYSE: CPQ)	8.59	−0.40	NM	−4.7%
Gateway (NYSE: GTW)	8.07	−3.15	NM	−39.0%

Source: Morningstar, Inc.

How can the analyst using P/Es deal with negative earnings? Suppose she calculated P/Es without regard to whether earnings were positive or negative, and then ranked the stocks from highest value to lowest value of P/E. The security with the lowest positive P/E has the lowest purchase cost per currency unit of earnings among the securities ranked. Negative earnings, however, result in a negative P/E. A negative-P/E security will rank below the lowest positive-P/E security but, because earnings are negative, the negative-P/E security is actually the most costly in terms of earnings purchased.[8]

Thus negative P/Es are not meaningful. In some cases, an analyst might handle negative EPS by using normal EPS in its place. Also, when trailing EPS is negative, year-ahead EPS and thus the leading P/E may be positive. If the analyst is interested in a ranking, an available solution is to calculate a new ratio for all the stocks, with EPS in the numerator and with price in the denominator. This is E/P, the **earnings yield** ratio.[9] Ranked by earnings yields from highest to lowest, the securities are correctly ranked from cheapest to most costly in terms of the amount of earnings one unit of currency buys.

Table 64-2 illustrates the above points for a group of personal computer manufacturers, three of which have negative EPS. When reporting a P/E based on negative earnings, analysts should report such P/Es as NM (not meaningful).

3   PRICE TO BOOK VALUE

The ratio of market price per share to book value per share (P/B), like P/E, has a long history of use in valuation practice (as discussed in Graham and Dodd 1934). In Block's 1999 survey of AIMR members, book value ranked distinctly

---

[8] Some research indicates that stocks with negative P/Es have special risk–return characteristics (see Fama and French 1992), so care should be exercised in interpreting such rankings.

[9] Earnings yield can also be based on normal EPS and expected next-year EPS as well as on trailing EPS. In these cases too, earnings yield provides a consistent ranking.

behind earnings and cash flow, but ahead of dividends.[10] According to the *Merrill Lynch Institutional Factor Survey,* in the years 1989 to 2001, P/B has been only slightly less popular than P/E as a factor consistently used among institutional investors.[11]

In the P/E ratio, the measure of value (EPS) in the denominator is a flow variable (earnings over a period) relating to the income statement. In contrast, the measure of value in the P/B's denominator (book value per share) is a stock or level (one point in time) variable coming from the balance sheet. Intuitively, book value per share attempts to represent the investment that common shareholders have made in the company, on a per-share basis. (*Book* refers to the fact that the measurement of value comes from accounting records or books, in contrast to market value.) To define book value per share more precisely, we first find **shareholders' equity** (total assets minus total liabilities). Because our purpose is to value common stock, we subtract from shareholders' equity any value attributable to preferred stock; we thus obtain common shareholders' equity or the **book value of equity** (often called simply **book value**).[12] Dividing book value by the number of common stock shares outstanding, we obtain **book value per share**, the denominator in the P/B ratio.

In the balance of this section, we present the reasons analysts have offered for using P/B as well as possible drawbacks to its use. We then illustrate the calculation of P/B and discuss the fundamental factors that drive P/B. We end the section by showing the use of P/B based on the method of comparables.

3.1 Rationales for Using Price to Book Value Ratios

Analysts have offered several rationales for the use of the P/B ratio:

- ▶ Because book value is a cumulative balance sheet amount, book value is generally positive even when EPS is negative. We can generally use P/B when EPS is negative, whereas P/E based on a negative EPS is not meaningful.

- ▶ Because book value per share is more stable than EPS, P/B may be more meaningful than P/E when EPS is abnormally high or low, or is highly variable.

- ▶ As a measure of net asset value per share, book value per share has been viewed as appropriate for valuing companies composed chiefly of liquid assets, such as finance, investment, insurance, and banking institutions (Wild, Bernstein, and Subramanyam 2001, p. 233). For such companies, book values of assets may approximate market values.

- ▶ Book value has also been used in valuation of companies that are not expected to continue as a going concern (Martin 1998, p. 22).

- ▶ Differences in P/Bs may be related to differences in long-run average returns, according to empirical research.[13]

---

[10] Earnings received a ranking of 1.55, cash flow a ranking of 1.65, book value a ranking of 3.29, and dividends a ranking of 3.51, where 1, 2, 3, and 4 were assigned to inputs ranked first, second, third, and last in importance in averaging responses.

[11] From 1989 to 2001, an average of 37.3 percent of respondents reported consistently using P/B in valuation, compared with 40.4 percent for earnings yield (the reciprocal of P/E rather than P/E was the actual variable surveyed by Merrill Lynch).

[12] If we were to value a company as a whole, rather than just the common stock, we would not exclude the value of preferred stock from the computation.

[13] See Bodie, Kane, and Marcus (2001) for a brief summary of the empirical research.

Possible drawbacks of P/Bs in practice include the following:

▶ Other assets besides those recognized in accounting may be critical operating factors. For example, in many service companies, **human capital**—the value of skills and knowledge possessed by the workforce—is more important than physical capital as an operating factor.

▶ P/B can be misleading as a valuation indicator when significant differences exist among companies examined in terms of the level of assets used. Such differences may reflect differences in business models, for example.

▶ Accounting effects on book value may compromise book value as a measure of shareholders' investment in the company. As one example, book value can understate shareholders' investment as a result of the expensing of investment in research and development (R&D). Such expenditures often positively affect income over many periods and in principle create assets. Accounting effects such as these can impair comparability of P/B across companies and countries.[14]

▶ In the accounting of most countries, including the United States, book value largely reflects the historical purchase costs of assets, as well as accumulated accounting depreciation expenses. Inflation as well as technological change eventually drive a wedge between the book value and the market value of assets. As a result, book value per share often poorly reflects the value of shareholders' investments. Such effects can impair the comparability of P/Bs across companies, for example when significant differences exist in the average age of assets among companies being compared.

Example 64-5 illustrates one possible disadvantage to using P/B in valuation.

Example 64-5

Differences in Business Models Reflected in Differences in P/Bs

Dell Computer Corporation (Nasdaq NMS: DELL), Apple Computer (Nasdaq NMS: AAPL), Gateway (NYSE: GTW), and Compaq Computer Corporation (NYSE: CPQ) compete with each other in the personal computer industry. Table 64-3 gives valuation data for these companies according to P/B, as of the end of 2001.

TABLE 64-3 P/Bs for Four Peer Companies

Company	P/B
Dell	14.42
Apple	1.76
Gateway	1.83
Compaq	1.23

Source: Morningstar, Inc.

---

[14] For example, in some countries the values of brand name assets created by advertising are recognized on the balance sheet; in the United States, they are not.

Dell is an assembler rather than a manufacturer, uses a just-in-time inventory system for parts needed in assembly, and sells built-to-order computers directly to the end consumer. Just-in-time inventory systems attempt to minimize the inventory holding times of parts needed for building computers. How can these practices explain the much higher P/B of Dell compared with the P/Bs of peer group stocks?

Because Dell assembles parts manufactured elsewhere, it requires smaller investments in fixed assets than it would if it were a manufacturer; this translates into a smaller book value per share. The just-in-time inventory system reduces Dell's required investment in working capital. Because Dell does not need to respond to the inventory needs of large resellers, its need to invest in working capital is reduced. The overall effect of this business model is that Dell generates its sales on a comparatively small base of assets. As a result, Dell's P/B is not comparable with those of its peer group, and the question of relative valuation is not resolved by the comparison in Table 64-3. Because lower P/B ratios are considered more attractive, using P/B as a valuation indicator effectively penalizes Dell's efficient business model.[15]

3.2 Determining Book Value

In this section, we illustrate the calculation of book value and how analysts may adjust book value to improve the comparability of the P/B ratio across companies. To compute book value per share, we need to refer to the company's balance sheet, which has a shareholders' (or stockholders') equity section. The computation of book value is as follows:

► (Shareholders' equity) − (Total value of equity claims that are senior to common stock) = Common shareholders' equity

► (Common shareholders' equity)/(Number of common stock shares outstanding) = Book value per share

Possible senior claims to common stock include the value of preferred stock and dividends in arrears on preferred stock.[16] Example 64-6 illustrates the calculation.

Example 64-6

Computing Book Value per Share

Ennis Business Forms (NYSE: EBF), a wholesale manufacturer of custom business forms and other printed business products, reported the balance sheet given in Table 64-4 for its fiscal year ending 28 February 2001.

---

[15] There may be a second reason for Dell's relatively high P/B; Dell's substantial share repurchases have reduced its book value per share.

[16] Some preferred stock issues have the right to premiums (liquidation premiums) if they are liquidated. If present, these premiums should be deducted as well.

TABLE 64-4 Ennis Business Forms Balance Sheet
(in thousands, except per-share amounts)

	28 Feb 2001
Assets	
Current Assets:	
Cash and cash equivalents	$ 8,964
Short term investments	980
Net receivables	29.957
Inventory	13,088
Unbilled contract revenue	364
Other current assets	4,910
Total Current Assets	58,263
Noncurrent Assets:	
Investment securities	2,170
Net property, plant, and equipment	57,781
Goodwill	23,615
Other assets	1,025
Total Assets	**$142,854**
Liabilities and Shareholders' Equity	
Current Liabilities:	
Current installments of long-term debt	$ 4,176
Accounts payable	6,067
Accrued expenses	7,665
Total Current Liabilities	17,908
Noncurrent Liabilities:	
Long-term debt	23,555
Deferred credits	9,851
Total Liabilities	51,314
Shareholders' Equity:	
Common stock ($2.50 par value. Authorized 40,000,000; issued 21,249,860)	53,125
Additional paid-in capital	1,040
Retained earnings	127,817
Treasury stock (cost of 4,979,095 shares repurchased in 2001)	(90,442)
Total Shareholders' Equity	91,540
Total Liabilities and Shareholders' Equity	**$142,854**

The entries in the balance sheet should be familiar. Treasury stock results from share repurchases (or buybacks) and is a deduction (recorded at cost above) to reach shareholders' equity. For the number of shares to be used in the denominator, we take 21,249,860 shares issued (under Common stock) and subtract 4,979,095 shares repurchased in 2001 to get 16,270,765 shares outstanding.

1. Using the data in Table 64-4, calculate book value per share as of 28 February 2001.
2. Given a closing price per share for EBF of $8.42 as of 4 June 2001, and your answer to Problem 1, calculate EBF's P/B as of 4 June 2001.

▶ Solution to 1. (Common shareholders' equity)/(Number of common stock shares outstanding) = $91,540,000/16,270,765 = $5.63.

▶ Solution to 2. P/B = $8.42/$5.63 = 1.5.

Example 64-6 illustrated the calculation of book value per share without any adjustments. Adjusting P/B has two purposes: (1) to make P/B more accurately reflect the value of shareholders' investment and (2) to make P/B more useful for comparisons among different stocks.

▶ Some services and analysts report a tangible book value per share. Computing tangible book value per share involves subtracting reported intangible assets from common shareholders' equity. From the viewpoint of financial theory, however, the general exclusion of all intangibles may not be warranted. In the case of individual intangible assets such as patents, which can be separated from the entity and sold, exclusion may not be justified. Exclusion may be appropriate, however, for goodwill from acquisitions. Goodwill represents the excess of the purchase price of an acquisition over the net asset value of tangible assets and specifically identifiable intangibles. Many analysts feel that goodwill does not represent an asset, because it is not separable and may reflect overpayment for an acquisition.

▶ For book value per share to most accurately reflect current values, the balance sheet should be adjusted for significant off-balance-sheet assets and liabilities and for differences in the fair value of these assets/liabilities from recorded accounting amounts.[17] Internationally, accounting methods currently report some assets/liabilities at historical cost (with some adjustments) and others at fair value.[18] For example, assets such as land or

[17] An item is an off-balance-sheet asset if, when a specified event occurs, the off-balance sheet item moves to the asset side of the balance sheet. An item is an off-balance-sheet liability if, when a specified event occurs, the off-balance sheet item moves to the liability side of the balance sheet. An example of an off-balance sheet liability is a guarantee to pay a debt of another company in the event of that company's default.

[18] Fair value has been defined as the price at which an asset or liability would change hands between a willing buyer and a willing seller when the former is not under any compulsion to buy and the latter is not under any compulsion to sell.

equipment are reported at their historical acquisition cost, and in the case of equipment are being depreciated over their useful lives. These assets may have appreciated over time, or they may have declined in value more than is reflected in the depreciation computation. Other assets such as investments in marketable securities are reported at fair market value. Reporting assets at fair value would make P/B more relevant for valuation (including comparisons among companies).

▶ Certain adjustments may be appropriate for comparability. For example, one company may use FIFO and a peer company may use LIFO, which in an inflationary environment will generally understate inventory values. To more accurately assess the relative valuation of the two companies, the analyst should restate the book value of the company using LIFO to what it would be on a FIFO basis. Example 64-7 illustrates this and other adjustments to book value.[19]

Regarding the second bullet point, over the last few years, there has been a trend among accounting standard setters toward a fair value model—more assets/liabilities are stated at fair value. If this trend continues, the need for adjustments will be reduced (but not eliminated).

Example 64-7

Adjusting Book Value

Edward Stavros is a junior analyst at a major U.S. pension fund. Stavros is researching Harley Davidson (NYSE: HDI) for the fund's Consumer Cyclical portfolio. Stavros is particularly interested in determining Harley Davidson's relative P/B. He obtains the condensed balance sheet for Harley Davidson from Edgar Online (a computerized database of U.S. SEC filings); his data are shown in Table 64-5.

Stavros computes book value per share initially by dividing total shareholders' equity ($1,405,655,000) by the number of shares outstanding at 31 December 2000 (302,070,745). The resulting book value per share is $4.65. Stavros then realizes that he must examine the full set of financial statements to assess the impact of accounting methods on balance sheet data. Harley Davidson's footnotes indicate that the company uses the LIFO inventory method. Inventories on a FIFO basis are presented in the company's footnotes at $210,756,000. Additionally, an examination of Harley's pension footnotes indicates that the pension plan is currently overfunded but that accounting rules require the recognition of a net liability of $21,705,000. This overstatement of a liability is somewhat offset by an underfunded post-retirement health care plan that understates liabilities by $15,400,000.

---

[19] For a complete discussion of balance sheet adjustments, see Chapter 17, "Analysis of Financial Statements: A Synthesis," in White, Sondhi, and Fried (2003).

TABLE 64-5 Harley Davidson
Condensed Consolidated Balance Sheet
(in thousands)

	31 Dec 2000
Assets	
Current Assets:	
Cash and cash equivalents	$ 419,736
Accounts receivable, net	98,311
Finance receivables, net	530,859
Inventories	191,931
Other current assets	56,427
Total Current Assets	1,297,264
Noncurrent Assets:	
Finance receivables, net	234,091
Property, plant, and equipment, net	754,115
Goodwill	54,331
Other assets	96,603
Total Assets	**$2,436,404**
Liabilities and Shareholders' Equity	
Current Liabilities:	
Accounts payable	$ 169,844
Accrued and other liabilities	238,390
Current portion of finance debt	89,509
Total Current Liabilities	497,743
Noncurrent Liabilities:	
Finance debt	355,000
Other long-term liabilities	97,340
Postretirement health care benefits	80,666
Contingencies	
Shareholders' Equity:	1,405,655
Total Liabilities and Shareholders' Equity	**$2,436,404**

Stavros makes the following adjustments on an after-tax basis (HDI's average tax rate is 37 percent) to his book value computation (in dollars):

Total Shareholders' Equity		$1,405,655,000
Plus Inventory Adjustment	18,825,000 × 0.63 = 11,859,750	
Plus Pension Adjustment	21,705,000 × 0.63 = 13,674,150	
Less Post-Retirement Adjustment	15,400,000 × 0.63 = (9,702,000)	
Adjusted Book Value		$1,421,486,900
Adjusted Book Value per Share		$4.71

In the above calculations, the after-tax amount is found by multiplying the pretax amount by $(1 - 0.37) = 0.63$. Stavros is putting all the company's inventory valuation on a FIFO basis for comparability. Using after-tax amounts is necessary because if Harley Davidson were to change its inventory method to FIFO, the change would result in higher taxes as HDI liquidates old inventory. Although inventory on the balance sheet would increase by \$18,825,000, taxes payable would also increase (or cash would decrease). As a result, the net effect on book value equals the change in inventory less the associated tax increase.

In conclusion, adjusted book value per share is \$4.71.[20] Based on a price of \$42.00 shortly after year-end, HDI has a P/B (adjusted basis) of \$42/\$4.71 = 8.9. Outstanding stock options could dilute both book value per share figures by \$0.07, which would have a small impact on these ratios.

4   PRICE TO SALES

Certain types of privately held companies, including investment management companies and companies in partnership form, have long been valued as a multiple of annual revenues. In recent decades, the ratio of price to sales has become well known as a valuation indicator for publicly traded companies as well. According to the *Merrill Lynch Institutional Factor Survey*, from 1989 to 2001, on average, slightly more than one-quarter of respondents consistently used the P/S ratio in their investment process.

4.1 Rationales for Using Price to Sales Ratios

Analysts have offered the following rationales for using the P/S ratio:

▶ Sales are generally less subject to distortion or manipulation than are other fundamentals, such as EPS or book value. Through discretionary accounting decisions concerning expenses, for example, management can distort EPS as a reflection of economic performance. In contrast, total sales, as the top line in the income statement, comes prior to any expenses and thus is not affected by any distortion of expenses.

▶ Sales are positive even when EPS is negative. Therefore, analysts can use P/S when EPS is negative, whereas the P/E based on a negative EPS is not meaningful.

▶ Because sales are generally more stable than EPS, which reflects operating and financial leverage, P/S is generally more stable than P/E. Thus, P/S may be more meaningful than P/E when EPS is abnormally high or low.

---

[20] The calculation of tangible book value per share (adjusted basis for inventory accounting method) is as follows:

Adjusted Book Value	\$1,421,486,900
Less Goodwill	(54,331,000)
Tangible Adjusted Book Value	\$1,367,155,900
Tangible Adjusted Book Value per Share	\$4.53

and price to tangible book value is 9.3.

► P/S has been viewed as appropriate for valuing the stock of mature, cyclical, and zero-income companies (Martin 1998).

► Differences in P/S ratios may be related to differences in long-run average returns, according to empirical research.[21]

Possible drawbacks of using P/S in practice include the following:

► A business may show high growth in sales even when it is not operating profitably as judged by earnings and cash flow from operations. To have value as a going concern, a business must ultimately generate earnings and cash.

► Because the P/S ratio does not reflect a company's expenses (cost structure), differences in P/S among different companies may be explained by differences in cost structure. For example, a company may trade at a relatively low P/S ratio because its expenses are relatively high as a proportion of sales. Investors should pay more for each dollar or euro of sales when more of it flows through to earnings and cash flow.

► Although relatively robust with respect to manipulation, revenue recognition practices offer the potential to distort P/S.

4.2 Determining Sales

P/S is calculated as price per share divided by annual net sales per share (net sales is total sales less returns and customer discounts). Analysts usually use annual sales from the company's most recent fiscal year in the calculation, as illustrated in Example 64-8. Because valuation is forward-looking in principle, the analyst may also develop and use P/Ss based on forecasts of next year's sales.

Example 64-8

Calculating P/S

In 2001, Abitibi-Consolidated (Toronto Stock Exchange: A.TO), a manufacturer of newsprint and groundwood papers, reported 2001 net sales of CAD6,032,000,000 with 440 million shares outstanding. Calculate the P/S for Abitibi based on a closing price of CAD13.38 on 14 February 2002.

Sales per share = CAD6,032,000,000/440,000,000 = CAD13.71

So, P/S = CAD13.38/CAD13.71 = 0.9759.

Although the determination of sales is more straightforward than the determination of earnings, the analyst should evaluate a company's revenue recognition practices, in particular those tending to speed up the recognition of revenues. An analyst using a P/S approach who does not also assess the quality of accounting for sales may be led to place too high a value on such companies' shares. Example 64-9 illustrates the problem.

---

[21] See Nathan, Sivakumar, and Vijayakumar (2001), O'Shaughnessy (1997), and Senchack and Martin (1987).

Example 64-9

Revenue Recognition Practices (1)

Analysts label stock markets as *bubbles* when market prices appear to lose contact with intrinsic value. In the view of many, the run-up of the prices of Internet stocks in U.S. markets in the 1998–2000 period represented a bubble. During this period, many analysts adopted P/S as a metric for valuing Internet stocks with negative earnings and cash flow. Perhaps at least partly as a result of this practice, some Internet companies engaged in questionable revenue recognition practices to justify their high valuations. To increase sales, some companies engaged in activities such as bartering website advertising with other Internet companies. For example, InternetRiches.com might barter $1,000,000 worth of banner advertising with RevenueIsUs.com. Each would show $1,000,000 of revenue and $1,000,000 of expense. Although neither had any net income or cash flow, each company's revenue growth and market valuation was enhanced (at least temporarily). The value placed on the advertising was also questionable. As a result of these and other questionable activities, the U.S. SEC issued a stern warning to companies. International accounting standard setters have begun a study to define revenue recognition principles. The analyst should review footnote disclosures to assess whether the company may be recognizing revenue prematurely or otherwise aggressively.

Example 64-10 illustrates another instance in which an analyst would need to look behind the accounting numbers.

Example 64-10

Revenue Recognition Practices (2)

Sales on a **bill-and-hold basis** involve selling products but not delivering those products until a later date.[22] Sales on this basis have the effect of accelerating sales into an earlier reporting period. The following is a case in point. In its Form 10K filed 6 March 1998, for fiscal year ended 28 December 1997, Sunbeam Corporation listed the following footnote:

1. OPERATIONS AND SIGNIFICANT ACCOUNTING POLICIES
REVENUE RECOGNITION
The Company recognizes revenues from product sales principally at the time of shipment to customers. In limited circumstances, at the customer's request the Company may sell seasonal product on a bill and hold basis provided that the goods are completed, packaged and ready for shipment, such goods are segregated and the risks of ownership and legal title have passed to the customer. The amount of such bill and hold sales at 29 December 1997 was approximately 3 percent of consolidated revenues.

---

[22] For companies whose reports must conform to U.S. SEC accounting regulations, revenue from bill-and-hold sales cannot be reported unless the risk of loss on the products transfers to the buyer and additional criteria are met (see SEC Staff Accounting Bulletin 101 for criteria).

> Net sales are comprised of gross sales less provisions for expected customer returns, discounts, promotional allowances and cooperative advertising.
>
> After internal and SEC investigations, the company restated its financial results, including a restated revenue recognition policy:
>
> REVENUE RECOGNITION
> The Company recognizes sales and related cost of goods sold from product sales when title passes to the customers which is generally at the time of shipment. Net sales is comprised of gross sales less provisions for estimated customer returns, discounts, promotional allowances, cooperative advertising allowances and costs incurred by the Company to ship product to customers. Reserves for estimated returns are established by the Company concurrently with the recognition of revenue. Reserves are established based on a variety of factors, including historical return rates, estimates of customer inventory levels, the market for the product and projected economic conditions. The Company monitors these reserves and makes adjustment to them when management believes that actual returns or costs to be incurred differ from amounts recorded. In some situations, the Company has shipped product with the right of return where the Company is unable to reasonably estimate the level of returns and/or the sale is contingent upon the resale of the product. In these situations, the Company does not recognize revenue upon product shipment, but rather when it is reasonably expected the product will not be returned.
>
> The company had originally reported revenue of $1,168,182,000 for the fiscal year ended 31 December 1997. After restatement, the company reported revenue of $1,073,000,000 for the same period—a more than 8 percent reduction in revenue. The analyst reading the footnote in the original report would have noted the bill-and-hold practices and reduced revenue by 3 percent. At the time, this company engaged in other accounting practices tending to inflate revenue, which did not come to light until the investigation.

Sometimes, as in Example 64-10, it is not possible to determine precisely by how much sales may be overstated. If a company is engaged in questionable revenue recognition practices of an unknown amount, the analyst may well suggest avoiding that security. At the very least, the analyst should be skeptical and assess a higher risk premium, which would result in a lower justified P/S.

PRICE TO CASH FLOW   5

Price to cash flow is a widely reported valuation indicator. In Block's 1999 survey of AIMR members, cash flow ranked only behind earnings in importance. According to the *Merrill Lynch Institutional Factor Survey,* price to cash flow on average saw wider use in investment practice than P/E, P/B, P/S, or dividend yield in the 1989–2001 period, among the institutional investors surveyed.[23]

---

[23] On average, 46.1 percent of respondents reported consistently using P/CF over this period. In one year, 2001, P/CF ranked first among the 23 factors surveyed.

In this section, we present price to cash flow, based on alternative major cash flow concepts. With the wide variety of cash flow concepts in use, the analyst should be especially careful that she understands (and communicates, as a writer) the exact definition of *cash flow* that is the basis for the analysis.

5.1 Rationales for Using Price to Cash Flow Ratios

Analysts have offered the following rationales for the use of price to cash flow:

► Cash flow is less subject to manipulation by management than earnings.[24]

► Because cash flow is generally more stable than earnings, price to cash flow is generally more stable than P/E.

► Using price to cash flow rather than P/E addresses the issue of differences in accounting conservatism between companies (differences in the quality of earnings).

► Differences in price to cash flow may be related to differences in long-run average returns, according to empirical research.[25]

Possible drawbacks to the use of price to cash flow include the following:

► When the EPS plus noncash charges approximation to cash flow from operations is used, items affecting actual cash flow from operations, such as noncash revenue and net changes in working capital, are ignored.[26]

► Theory views free cash flow rather than cash flow (CF) as the appropriate variable for valuation. We can use price to free cash flow to equity (P/FCFE) ratios but FCFE does have the possible drawback of being more volatile compared to CF, for many businesses. FCFE is also more frequently negative than CF.

Example 64-11

Accounting Methods and Cash Flow

One approximation of cash flow in practical use is EPS plus per-share depreciation, amortization, and depletion. Even this simple approximation can point to issues of interest to the analyst in valuation, as this stylized illustration shows. Hypothetical companies A and B have constant cash revenues and cash expenses (as well as a constant number of shares outstanding) in 2000, 2001, and 2002. Company A incurs total depreciation of $15.00 per share during the three-year period, which it spreads out evenly (straight-line depreciation, SLD). Because revenues, expenses, and depreciation are constant over the period, EPS for Business A is also

---

[24] Cash flow from operations, precisely defined, can be manipulated only through "real" activities, such as the sale of receivables.

[25] See, for example, O'Shaughnessy (1997), who examined P/CF, and Hackel, Livnat, and Rai (1994) and Hackel and Livnat (1991), who examined price to average free cash flow.

[26] For example, aggressive recognition (front-end loading) of revenue would not be captured in the earnings-plus-noncash-charges definition.

constant, say at $10, as given in Column 1 in Table 64-6. Business B is identical to Business A except that it uses accelerated depreciation: Depreciation is 150 percent of SLD in 2000, declining to 50 percent of SLD in 2002, as given in Column 5. (We assume both A and B use the same depreciation method for tax purposes.)

TABLE 64-6 Earning Growth Rates and Cash Flow
(all amounts per share)

	Company A			Company B		
Year	Earnings (1)	Depreciation (2)	Cash Flow (3)	Earnings (4)	Depreciation (5)	Cash Flow (6)
2000	$10.00	$5.00	$15.00	$7.50	$7.50	$15.00
2001	$10.00	$5.00	$15.00	$10.00	$5.00	$15.00
2002	$10.00	$5.00	$15.00	$12.50	$2.50	$15.00
	Sum	$15.00		Sum	$15.00	

Because of different choices in how Companies A and B depreciate for financial reporting purposes, Company A's EPS is flat at $10.00 (Column 1) whereas Company B's shows 29 percent compound growth, $(\$12.50/\$7.50)^{1/2} - 1.00 = 0.29$ (Column 4). Company B shows apparent positive earnings momentum. As analysts comparing Companies A and B, we might be misled using EPS numbers as reported (without putting EPS on a comparable basis). For both companies, however, cash flow per share is level at $15. Thus, P/CF is more reliable here than P/E. Depreciation may be the simplest noncash charge to understand; write-offs and other noncash charges may offer more latitude for the management of earnings. Hawkins (1998) summarizes many corporate accounting issues for analysts, including how accounting choices can create the effect of **earnings momentum.**

SUMMARY

In this reading, we have defined and illustrated the use of price multiples.

▶ Price multiples are ratios of a stock's price to some measure of value per share.

▶ The key idea behind the use of P/Es is that earning power is a chief driver of investment value and EPS is probably the primary focus of security analysts' attention. EPS, however, is frequently subject to distortion, often volatile, and sometimes negative.

▶ The two alternative definitions of P/E are trailing P/E, based on the most recent four quarters of EPS, and leading P/E, based on next year's expected earnings.

▶ Analysts address the problem of cyclicality by normalizing EPS—that is, calculating the level of EPS that the business could achieve currently under mid-cyclical conditions (normal EPS).

▶ Two methods to normalize EPS are the method of historical average EPS (over the most recent full cycle) and the method of average ROE (average ROE multiplied by current book value per share).

▶ Earnings yield (E/P) is the reciprocal of the P/E. When stocks have negative EPS, a ranking by earnings yield is meaningful whereas a ranking by P/E is not.

▶ Book value per share attempts to represent the investment that common shareholders have made in the company, on a per-share basis. Inflation, technological change, and accounting distortions, however, can impair book value for this purpose.

▶ Book value is calculated as common shareholders' equity divided by the number of shares outstanding. Analysts adjust book value to more accurately reflect the value of shareholders' investment and to make P/B more useful for comparing different stocks.

▶ An important rationale for the price-to-sales ratio (P/S) is that sales, as the top line in an income statement, are generally less subject to distortion or manipulation than other fundamentals such as EPS or book value. Sales are also more stable than earnings and never negative.

▶ P/S fails to take into account differences in cost structure between businesses, may not properly reflect the situation of companies losing money, and can be subject to manipulation through revenue recognition practices.

▶ A key idea behind the use of price-to-cash-flow ratios is that cash flow is less subject to manipulation than are earnings. Price to cash flow ratios are often more stable than P/Es. Some common approximations to cash flow from operations have limitations, however, because they ignore items that may be subject to manipulation.

PROBLEMS FOR READING 64

For Problems 1 through 4, use the following data:
For four companies' stock, the following table gives current stock price (P), per-share sales (S), per-share cash flow (CF) using an earnings plus noncash charges definition, earnings for the most recent four quarters (EPS), forecasted EPS for the next year (FEPS), and the most recently reported book value per share (BVPS). The relationship between current and next year's earnings in the table reflects the predicted earnings growth trends for the companies.

	Price	S	CF	EPS	FEPS	BVPS
Abell Inc.	$36	$28.80	$2.88	$2.50	$3.00	$9
BluSedge Inc.	$40	$25.00	$0.25	−$0.50	$2.50	$50
Camdeem Inc.	$50	$25.00	$5.00	$2.50	$2.00	$40
Durnell Inc.	$69	$30.00	$3.00	$2.76	$3.45	$10

1. Calculate P/S, P/CF, trailing P/E, leading P/E, and P/B for Abell Inc., BluSedge Inc., Camdeem Inc., and Durnell Inc.

2. Suppose an analyst is comparing Abell Inc. to Camdeem Inc. on the basis of the price to earnings ratio. If he makes the comparison using a leading P/E for Abell and a trailing P/E for Camdeem how might his analysis be misleading?

3. **A.** In using a P/E approach, how might an analyst deal with the problem of negative EPS of −$0.50?

 B. Still within the context of a multiples approach to valuation, what alternatives to a price to earnings approach might an analyst consider?

4. Suppose that Camdeem is a financial institution and Durnell is a consulting company. How would these facts affect your interpretation of a comparison of the price to book ratio for these companies? For which company is P/B more appropriate?

5. As an energy analyst, as of mid-April 2002 you are researching Halliburton Company (NYSE: HAL), an oil field services company subject to cyclical demand for its services. You believe the 1997–2000 period reasonably captures average profitability. HAL closed at $17.10 on 15 April 2002.

	2001	2000	1999	1998	1997
EPS	$1.28	$0.58	$0.67	$1.65	$1.75
BVPS	10.95	9.20	9.70	9.23	9.85
ROE	11.6%	6.6%	7.0%	18.0%	17.6%

Source: The Value Line Investment Survey.

A. Define normal EPS.

B. Calculate a normal EPS for HAL based on the method of historical average EPS, and then calculate the P/E based on that estimate of normal EPS.

C. Calculate a normal EPS for HAL based on the method of average ROE and the P/E based on that estimate of normal EPS.

6. Melvin Stewart, CFA, a telecommunications analyst, is performing a P/E-based comparison of two telecom companies as of early 2003. He has the following data for HallWire (HLLW) and RuffWire (RFFW) for 2002.

▶ HLLW is priced at $44 with basic EPS of $2.00. RFFW is priced at $22 with basic EPS of $1.50.

▶ HLLW has not issued stock options or other instruments with dilutive effects. RFFW does have substantial stock option issuance; RFFW has not expensed the cost of stock options. If the stock options were exercised, RFFW's shares outstanding would increase by 10 percent.

▶ RFFW's 2002 EPS of $1.50 includes $0.50 of earnings that Stewart believes will not recur in the future. Stewart believes that all of HLLW's earnings reflect items that will contribute to future earnings.

A. Calculate P/E for HLLW and RFFW without making any EPS adjustments.

B. Calculate the price to earnings ratio for HLLW and RFFW based on estimated underlying earnings, making no other EPS adjustments.

C. Contrast the conclusions an analyst might draw from the calculations in A and B, and select the calculation that would be preferred in practice.

D. Calculate the P/E of HLLW and RFFW taking account of only underlying earnings, and reflecting the effects, if any, of possible share dilution.

For Problems 7 through 9, use the following data:
Abitibi-Consolidated Inc. (TSX: A) is a Montréal, Canada-headquartered manufacturer of newsprint, groundwood papers, and lumber. In 2001, Abitibi reported the following results:

From the Income Statement (and footnotes):

▶ net sales was CAD6,032 million

▶ net income was CAD289 million

▶ net interest expense was CAD470 million

▶ the effective income tax rate was 29 percent

▶ 440 million common shares were outstanding

From the Balance Sheet (and footnotes):

▶ total assets were CAD11,707 million (including CAD1,420 million of goodwill and approximately CAD379 million of deferred charges)

▶ total liabilities (claims senior to common equity) were CAD8,442 million

From the Statement of Cash Flows:

▶ depreciation and amortization was CAD707 million

▶ other noncash expenses netted to CAD91 million

▶ net investment in working capital (excluding cash and short-term debt) was CAD50 million

▶ net investment in fixed capital approximated CAD425 million

▶ net borrowing was −CAD20 million (debt repayments exceeded new issuance)

Other:

▶ the closing share price on 15 April 2002 was CAD13.89

7. A. Calculate P/E and P/S.

B. Identify and explain one possible advantage and drawback of P/S compared to P/E.

C. Identify and calculate one financial ratio that is relevant for evaluating the cost structure of Abitibi. Explain how that ratio relates to P/S.

8. A. Calculate P/B.

B. Identify and explain one possible advantage and drawback of P/B compared to P/E.

C. Calculate tangible book value per share and the price to tangible book value ratio.

9. A. Calculate P/CF using the CF approximation with EPS, depreciation, and amortization.

B. Identify and explain one possible advantage and drawback of P/CF compared to P/E.

10. Discuss three types of stocks or investment problems for which an analyst could appropriately use P/B in valuation.

4⅝ 4¹¹⁄₁₆ — ⅜
5½ 5½ —
5½ 2¹³⁄₁₆ — ¹⁄₁₆
20⅝ 21¹³⁄₁₆
17⅜ 18⅛ + ⅞
6½ 6½ — ½
7¼ 6½ 31⁄₃₂ — ⅛
15⁄₁₆ 9⁄₁₆
9⁄₁₆
1¹⁄₃₂ 7¹³⁄₁₆ 7¹⁵⁄₁₆
7¹⁵⁄₁₆ 2⁵⁄₈ 2¹¹⁄₃₂ 2½ +
2¾ 2¼ 2¼
6⅛ 12¹⁄₁₆ 11⅜ 11¾ +
87 33¾ 33 33¼ —
502 25⅝ 24⁹⁄₁₆ 25⅝ +
833 12 11⅝ 11⅝ +
16 10½ 10½ 10½ —
78 15⅞ 15¹³⁄₁₆ 15⅞
508 9¹⁄₁₆ 8¼ 8⅞ +
430 11¼ 10⅛ 10⅛
4⅝

ANALYSIS OF FIXED INCOME INVESTMENTS

STUDY SESSIONS

Study Session 15   Basic Concepts
Study Session 16   Analysis and Valuation

TOPIC LEVEL LEARNING OUTCOME

The candidate should be able to demonstrate a working knowledge of the analysis of fixed income investments, including basic characteristics of bonds in alternative sectors, valuation tools, and factors that influence bond yields.

STUDY SESSION 15
ANALYSIS OF FIXED INCOME INVESTMENTS:
Basic Concepts

READING ASSIGNMENTS

Reading 65 Features of Debt Securities
Reading 66 Risks Associated with Investing in Bonds
Reading 67 Overview of Bond Sectors and Instruments
Reading 68 Understanding Yield Spreads
Reading 69 Monetary Policy in an Environment of Global Financial Markets

This study session presents the basic concepts for fixed income investments. It begins with an introduction to the basic features and characteristics of fixed income securities and the associated risks. The session then builds by describing the primary issuers, sectors, and types of bonds. Finally, the study session concludes with an introduction to yields and spreads and the effect of monetary policy on financial markets. These readings combined are the primary building blocks for mastering the analysis, valuation, and management of fixed income securities.

LEARNING OUTCOMES

Reading 65: Features of Debt Securities
The candidate should be able to:

a. explain the purposes of a bond's indenture, and describe affirmative and negative covenants;

b. describe the basic features of a bond (e.g., maturity, par value, coupon rate), the various coupon rate structures (e.g., zero-coupon bonds, step-up notes, deferred coupon bonds, floating-rate securities), the structure of floating-rate securities (i.e., the coupon formula, caps and floors), and interest payment and price definitions (e.g., accrued interest, full price, and clean price);

c. describe the provisions for redeeming bonds, including the distinction between a nonamortizing bond and an amortizing bond;

d. explain the provisions for early retirement of debt (e.g., call and refunding provisions, prepayment options, and sinking fund provisions) and differentiate between a regular redemption price and a special redemption price;

e. identify the various options embedded in a bond issue (call option, prepayment option, accelerated sinking fund option, put option and conversion option), the importance of understanding embedded options, and whether such options benefit the issuer or the bondholder;

f. describe methods used by institutional investors in the bond market to finance the purchase of a security (i.e., margin buying and repurchase agreements).

Reading 66: Risks Associated with Investing in Bonds
The candidate should be able to:

a. explain the risks associated with investing in bonds (e.g., interest rate risk, yield curve risk, call and prepayment risk, reinvestment risk, credit risk, liquidity risk, exchange-rate risk, inflation risk, volatility risk, event risk, and sovereign risk);

b. identify the relationships among a bond's coupon rate, the yield required by the market, and the bond's price relative to par value (i.e., discount, premium, or equal to par);

c. explain how features of a bond (e.g., maturity, coupon, and embedded options) and the level of a bond's yield affect the bond's interest rate risk;

d. identify the relationship among the price of a callable bond, the price of an option-free bond, and the price of the embedded call option;

e. explain the interest rate risk of a floating-rate security and why such a security's price may differ from par value;

f. compute and interpret the duration of a bond, given the bond's change in price when interest rates change, and compute the approximate percentage price change of a bond and new price of a bond, given the duration and change in yield;

g. describe yield curve risk and explain why duration does not account for yield curve risk for a portfolio of bonds;

h. explain the disadvantages of a callable or prepayable security to an investor;

i. identify the factors that affect the reinvestment risk of a security and explain why prepayable amortizing securities expose investors to greater reinvestment risk than nonamortizing securities;

j. describe the various forms of credit risk (i.e., default risk, credit spread risk, downgrade risk) and describe the meaning and role of credit ratings;

k. explain why liquidity risk might be important to investors even if they expect to hold a security to the maturity date;

l. describe the exchange rate risk an investor faces when a bond makes payments in a foreign currency;

m. explain inflation risk;

n. explain how yield volatility affects the price of a bond with an embedded option and how changes in volatility affect the value of a callable bond and a putable bond;

o. describe the various forms of event risk (e.g., natural catastrophe, corporate takeover/restructuring and regulatory risk).

Reading 67: Overview of Bond Sectors and Instruments

The candidate should be able to:

a. explain how a country's bond market sectors are classified, including the distinguishing characteristics of internal and external bonds;

b. describe the features, credit risk characteristics and distribution methods for government securities;

c. describe the types of securities issued by the U.S. Department of the Treasury (e.g., bills, notes, bonds, and inflation protection securities), and distinguish between on-the-run and off-the-run Treasury securities;

d. describe how stripped Treasury securities are created and distinguish between coupon strips and principal strips;

e. describe the types and characteristics of securities issued by U.S. federal agencies;

f. describe mortgage-backed securities (including mortgage passthrough securities, collateralized mortgage obligations, and stripped MBS), and explain the cash flows, prepayments and prepayment risk for each;

g. state the motivation for creating a collateralized mortgage obligation;

h. describe the types of securities issued by municipalities in the United States, and distinguish between tax-backed debt and revenue bonds;

i. describe the characteristics and motivation for the various types of debt used by corporations (including corporate bonds, medium-term notes, structured notes, commercial paper, negotiable CDs and bankers acceptances);

j. define an asset-backed security, describe the role of a special purpose vehicle in an asset-backed securities transaction, state the motivation for a corporation to issue an asset-backed security, and describe the types of external credit enhancements for asset-backed securities;

k. describe collateralized debt obligations;

l. describe the structures of the primary and secondary markets in bonds.

Reading 68: Understanding Yield Spreads

The candidate should be able to:

a. identify the interest rate policy tools available to the U.S. Federal Reserve Board;

b. describe the Treasury yield curve and the various shapes of the yield curve;

c. explain the basic theories of the term structure of interest rates (i.e., pure expectations theory, liquidity preference theory, and market segmentation theory) and describe the implications of each theory for the shape of the yield curve;

d. define a Treasury spot rate;

e. explain the different types of yield spread measures (e.g., absolute yield spread, relative yield spread, yield ratio), compute yield spread measures given the yields for two securities, and explain why investors may find a relative yield spread to be a better measure of yield spread than the absolute yield spread;

f. describe a credit spread and discuss the suggested relationship between credit spreads and the economic well being of the economy;

g. identify how embedded options affect yield spreads;

h. explain how the liquidity or issue-size of a bond affects its yield spread relative to risk-free securities and relative to other issues that are comparable in all other ways except for liquidity;

i. compute the after-tax yield of a taxable security and the tax-equivalent yield of a tax-exempt security;

j. define LIBOR and explain why it is an important measure to funded investors who borrow short-term.

Reading 69: Monetary Policy in an Environment of Global Financial Markets

The candidate should be able to:

a. identify how central bank behavior affects financial markets, including the role of short-term interest rates, systemic liquidity and market expectations;

b. describe the importance of communication between a central bank and the financial markets;

c. discuss the importance of predictability, credibility, and transparency of monetary policy, measures of predictability, and the problem of information asymmetry.

FEATURES OF DEBT SECURITIES

by Frank J. Fabozzi

LEARNING OUTCOMES

The candidate should be able to:

a. explain the purposes of a bond's indenture, and describe affirmative and negative covenants;

b. describe the basic features of a bond (e.g., maturity, par value, coupon rate), the various coupon rate structures (e.g., zero-coupon bonds, step-up notes, deferred coupon bonds, floating-rate securities), the structure of floating-rate securities (i.e., the coupon formula, caps and floors), and interest payment and price definitions (e.g., accrued interest, full price, and clean price);

c. describe the provisions for redeeming bonds, including the distinction between a nonamortizing bond and an amortizing bond;

d. explain the provisions for early retirement of debt (e.g., call and refunding provisions, prepayment options, and sinking fund provisions) and differentiate between a regular redemption price and a special redemption price;

e. identify the various options embedded in a bond issue (call option, prepayment option, accelerated sinking fund option, put option and conversion option), the importance of understanding embedded options, and whether such options benefit the issuer or the bondholder;

f. describe methods used by institutional investors in the bond market to finance the purchase of a security (i.e., margin buying and repurchase agreements).

INTRODUCTION   1

In investment management, the most important decision made is the allocation of funds among asset classes. The two major asset classes are equities and fixed income securities. Other asset classes such as real estate, private equity, hedge funds, and commodities are referred to as "alternative asset classes." Our focus in this reading is on one of the two major asset classes: fixed income securities.

Fixed Income Analysis for the Chartered Financial Analyst® Program, Second Edition, edited by Frank J. Fabozzi, Copyright © 2005 by CFA Institute. Reprinted with permission.

While many people are intrigued by the exciting stories sometimes found with equities—who has not heard of someone who invested in the common stock of a small company and earned enough to retire at a young age?—we will find in our study of fixed income securities that the multitude of possible structures opens a fascinating field of study. While frequently overshadowed by the media prominence of the equity market, fixed income securities play a critical role in the portfolios of individual and institutional investors.

In its simplest form, a fixed income security is a financial obligation of an entity that promises to pay a specified sum of money at specified future dates. The entity that promises to make the payment is called the **issuer** of the security. Some examples of issuers are central governments such as the U.S. government and the French government, government-related agencies of a central government such as Fannie Mae and Freddie Mac in the United States, a municipal government such as the state of New York in the United States and the city of Rio de Janeiro in Brazil, a corporation such as Coca-Cola in the United States and Yorkshire Water in the United Kingdom, and supranational governments such as the World Bank.

Fixed income securities fall into two general categories: debt obligations and preferred stock. In the case of a debt obligation, the issuer is called the **borrower**. The investor who purchases such a fixed income security is said to be the **lender** or **creditor**. The promised payments that the issuer agrees to make at the specified dates consist of two components: interest and principal (principal represents repayment of funds borrowed) payments. Fixed income securities that are debt obligations include **bonds, mortgage-backed securities, asset-backed securities**, and **bank loans**.

In contrast to a fixed income security that represents a debt obligation, **preferred stock** represents an ownership interest in a corporation. Dividend payments are made to the preferred stockholder and represent a distribution of the corporation's profit. Unlike investors who own a corporation's common stock, investors who own the preferred stock can only realize a contractually fixed dividend payment. Moreover, the payments that must be made to preferred stockholders have priority over the payments that a corporation pays to common stockholders. In the case of the bankruptcy of a corporation, preferred stockholders are given preference over common stockholders. Consequently, preferred stock is a form of equity that has characteristics similar to bonds.

Prior to the 1980s, fixed income securities were simple investment products. Holding aside default by the issuer, the investor knew how long interest would be received and when the amount borrowed would be repaid. Moreover, most investors purchased these securities with the intent of holding them to their maturity date. Beginning in the 1980s, the fixed income world changed. First, fixed income securities became more complex. There are features in many fixed income securities that make it difficult to determine when the amount borrowed will be repaid and for how long interest will be received. For some securities it is difficult to determine the amount of interest that will be received. Second, the hold-to-maturity investor has been replaced by institutional investors who actively trade fixed income securities.

We will frequently use the terms "fixed income securities" and "bonds" interchangeably. In addition, we will use the term bonds generically at times to refer collectively to mortgage-backed securities, asset-backed securities, and bank loans.

In this reading we will look at the various features of fixed income securities and in the next reading we explain how those features affect the risks associated with investing in fixed income securities. The majority of our illustrations throughout this book use fixed income securities issued in the United States. While the U.S. fixed income market is the largest fixed income market in the world with a diversity of issuers and features, in recent years there has been significant growth in the fixed income markets of other countries as borrowers have shifted from funding via bank loans to the issuance of fixed income securities. This is a trend that is expected to continue.

INDENTURE AND COVENANTS   2

The promises of the issuer and the rights of the bondholders are set forth in great detail in a bond's indenture. Bondholders would have great difficulty in determining from time to time whether the issuer was keeping all the promises made in the indenture. This problem is resolved for the most part by bringing in a trustee as a third party to the bond or debt contract. The indenture identifies the trustee as a representative of the interests of the bondholders.

As part of the indenture, there are **affirmative covenants** and **negative covenants**. Affirmative covenants set forth activities that the borrower promises to do. The most common affirmative covenants are (1) to pay interest and principal on a timely basis, (2) to pay all taxes and other claims when due, (3) to maintain all properties used and useful in the borrower's business in good condition and working order, and (4) to submit periodic reports to a trustee stating that the borrower is in compliance with the loan agreement. Negative covenants set forth certain limitations and restrictions on the borrower's activities. The more common restrictive covenants are those that impose limitations on the borrower's ability to incur additional debt unless certain tests are satisfied.

MATURITY   3

The term to maturity of a bond is the number of years the debt is outstanding or the number of years remaining prior to final principal payment. The **maturity date** of a bond refers to the date that the debt will cease to exist, at which time the issuer will redeem the bond by paying the outstanding balance. The maturity date of a bond is always identified when describing a bond. For example, a description of a bond might state "due 12/1/2020."

The practice in the bond market is to refer to the "term to maturity" of a bond as simply its "maturity" or "term." As we explain below, there may be provisions in the indenture that allow either the issuer or bondholder to alter a bond's term to maturity.

Some market participants view bonds with a maturity between 1 and 5 years as "short-term." Bonds with a maturity between 5 and 12 years are viewed as "intermediate-term," and "long-term" bonds are those with a maturity of more than 12 years.

There are bonds of every maturity. Typically, the longest maturity is 30 years. However, Walt Disney Co. issued bonds in July 1993 with a maturity date of 7/15/2093, making them 100-year bonds at the time of issuance. In December 1993, the Tennessee Valley Authority issued bonds that mature on 12/15/2043, making them 50-year bonds at the time of issuance.

There are three reasons why the term to maturity of a bond is important:

Reason 1: Term to maturity indicates the time period over which the bondholder can expect to receive interest payments and the number of years before the principal will be paid in full.

Reason 2: The yield offered on a bond depends on the term to maturity. The relationship between the yield on a bond and maturity is called the **yield curve** and will be discussed in Reading 68.

Reason 3: The price of a bond will fluctuate over its life as interest rates in the market change. The price volatility of a bond is a function of its maturity (among other variables). More specifically, as explained in Reading 72, all other factors constant, the longer the maturity of a bond, the greater the price volatility resulting from a change in interest rates.

4   PAR VALUE

The **par value** of a bond is the amount that the issuer agrees to repay the bondholder at or by the maturity date. This amount is also referred to as the **principal value, face value, redemption value,** and **maturity value.** Bonds can have any par value.

Because bonds can have a different par value, the practice is to quote the price of a bond as a percentage of its par value. A value of "100" means 100% of par value. So, for example, if a bond has a par value of $1,000 and the issue is selling for $900, this bond would be said to be selling at 90. If a bond with a par value of $5,000 is selling for $5,500, the bond is said to be selling for 110.

When computing the dollar price of a bond in the United States, the bond must first be converted into a price per US$1 of par value. Then the price per $1 of par value is multiplied by the par value to get the dollar price. Here are examples of what the dollar price of a bond is, given the price quoted for the bond in the market, and the par amount involved in the transaction:[1]

---

[1] You may not be able to precisely reproduce some of the results in these readings. Rounding practices vary depending on the spreadsheet or calculator, and differences may be particularly noticeable in examples involving several interim calculations.

Quoted Price	Price per $1 of Par Value (rounded)	Par Value	Dollar Price
90½	0.9050	$1,000	905.00
102¾	1.0275	$5,000	5,137.50
70⅝	0.7063	$10,000	7,062.50
113¹¹/₃₂	1.1334	$100,000	113,343.75

Notice that a bond may trade below or above its par value. When a bond trades below its par value, it is said to be **trading at a discount**. When a bond trades above its par value, it is said to be **trading at a premium**. The reason why a bond sells above or below its par value will be explained in Reading 66.

Practice Question 1

Given the information in the first and third columns for a U.S. investor, complete the information in the second and fourth columns:

Quoted Price	Price per $1 of Par Value	Par Value	Dollar Price
103¼		$1,000	
70⅛		$5,000	
87⁵/₁₆		$10,000	
117³/₃₂		$100,000	

COUPON RATE 5

The **coupon rate**, also called the **nominal rate**, is the interest rate that the issuer agrees to pay each year. The annual amount of the interest payment made to bondholders during the term of the bond is called the **coupon**. The coupon is determined by multiplying the coupon rate by the par value of the bond. That is,

coupon = coupon rate × par value

For example, a bond with an 8% coupon rate and a par value of $1,000 will pay annual interest of $80 (= $1,000 × 0.08).

When describing a bond of an issuer, the coupon rate is indicated along with the maturity date. For example, the expression "6s of 12/1/2020" means a bond with a 6% coupon rate maturing on 12/1/2020. The "s" after the coupon rate indicates "coupon series." In our example, it means the "6% coupon series."

In the United States, the usual practice is for the issuer to pay the coupon in two semiannual installments. Mortgage-backed securities and asset-backed securities typically pay interest monthly. For bonds issued in some markets outside the United States, coupon payments are made only once per year.

The coupon rate also affects the bond's price sensitivity to changes in market interest rates. As illustrated in Reading 66, all other factors constant, the higher the coupon rate, the less the price will change in response to a change in market interest rates.

5.1 Zero-Coupon Bonds

Not all bonds make periodic coupon payments. Bonds that are not contracted to make periodic coupon payments are called **zero-coupon bonds**. The holder of a zero-coupon bond realizes interest by buying the bond substantially below its par value (i.e., buying the bond at a discount). Interest is then paid at the maturity date, with the interest being the difference between the par value and the price paid for the bond. So, for example, if an investor purchases a zero-coupon bond for 70, the interest is 30. This is the difference between the par value (100) and the price paid (70). The reason behind the issuance of zero-coupon bonds is explained in Reading 66.

5.2 Step-Up Notes

There are securities that have a coupon rate that increases over time. These securities are called **step-up notes** because the coupon rate "steps up" over time. For example, a 5-year step-up note might have a coupon rate that is 5% for the first two years and 6% for the last three years. Or, the step-up note could call for a 5% coupon rate for the first two years, 5.5% for the third and fourth years, and 6% for the fifth year. When there is only one change (or step up), as in our first example, the issue is referred to as a **single step-up note**. When there is more than one change, as in our second example, the issue is referred to as a **multiple step-up note**.

An example of an actual multiple step-up note is a 5-year issue of the Student Loan Marketing Association (Sallie Mae) issued in May 1994. The coupon schedule is as follows:

6.05%	from	5/3/94	to	5/2/95
6.50%	from	5/3/95	to	5/2/96
7.00%	from	5/3/96	to	5/2/97
7.75%	from	5/3/97	to	5/2/98
8.50%	from	5/3/98	to	5/2/99

5.3 Deferred Coupon Bonds

There are bonds whose interest payments are deferred for a specified number of years. That is, there are no interest payments during for the deferred period. At the end of the deferred period, the issuer makes periodic interest payments until the bond matures. The interest payments that are made after the deferred period are higher than the interest payments that would have been made if the issuer had paid interest from the time the bond was issued. The higher interest payments after the deferred period are to compensate the bondholder for the lack of interest payments during the deferred period. These bonds are called **deferred coupon bonds**.

5.4 Floating-Rate Securities

The coupon rate on a bond need not be fixed over the bond's life. **Floating-rate securities**, sometimes called **variable-rate securities**, have coupon payments that reset periodically according to some reference rate. The typical formula (called the **coupon formula**) on certain determination dates when the coupon rate is reset is as follows:

coupon rate = reference rate × quoted margin

The **quoted margin** is the additional amount that the issuer agrees to pay above the reference rate. For example, suppose that the reference rate is the 1-month London interbank offered rate (LIBOR).[2] Suppose that the quoted margin is 100 basis points.[3] Then the coupon formula is:

coupon rate = 1-month LIBOR + 100 basis points

So, if 1-month LIBOR on the coupon reset date is 5%, the coupon rate is reset for that period at 6% (5% plus 100 basis points).

The quoted margin need not be a positive value. The quoted margin could be subtracted from the reference rate. For example, the reference rate could be the yield on a 5-year Treasury security and the coupon rate could reset every six months based on the following coupon formula:

coupon rate = 5-year Treasury yield − 90 basis points

So, if the 5-year Treasury yield is 7% on the coupon reset date, the coupon rate is 6.1% (7% minus 90 basis points).

It is important to understand the mechanics for the payment and the setting of the coupon rate. Suppose that a floater pays interest semiannually and further assume that the coupon reset date is today. Then, the coupon rate is determined via the coupon formula and this is the interest rate that the issuer agrees to pay at the next interest payment date six months from now.

A floater may have a restriction on the maximum coupon rate that will be paid at any reset date. The maximum coupon rate is called a **cap**. For example, suppose for a floater whose coupon formula is the 3-month Treasury bill rate plus 50 basis points, there is a cap of 9%. If the 3-month Treasury bill rate is 9% at a coupon reset date, then the coupon formula would give a coupon rate of 9.5%. However, the cap restricts the coupon rate to 9%. Thus, for our hypothetical floater, once the 3-month Treasury bill rate exceeds 8.5%, the coupon rate is capped at 9%. Because a cap restricts the coupon rate from increasing, a cap is an unattractive feature for the investor. In contrast, there could be a minimum coupon rate specified for a floater. The minimum coupon rate is called a **floor**. If the coupon formula produces a coupon rate that is below the floor, the floor rate is paid instead. Thus, a floor is an attractive feature for the investor. As we explain in Section 10, caps and floors are effectively embedded options.

While the reference rate for most floaters is an interest rate or an interest rate index, a wide variety of reference rates appear in coupon formulas. The coupon for a floater could be indexed to movements in foreign exchange rates, the price of a commodity (e.g., crude oil), the return on an equity index (e.g., the S&P 500), or movements in a bond index. In fact, through financial engineering,

---

[2] LIBOR is the interest rate which major international banks offer each other on Eurodollar certificates of deposit.

[3] In the fixed income market, market participants refer to changes in interest rates or differences in interest rates in terms of basis points. A basis point is defined as 0.0001, or equivalently, 0.01%. Consequently, 100 basis points are equal to 1%. (In our example the coupon formula can be expressed as 1-month LIBOR + 1%.) A change in interest rates from, say, 5.0% to 6.2% means that there is a 1.2% change in rates or 120 basis points.

Practice Question 2

A floating-rate issue has the following coupon formula:

6-month Treasury rate + 50 basis points with a cap of 7%

The coupon rate is set every six months. Suppose that at the reset date the 6-month Treasury rate is as shown below. Compute the coupon rate for the next 6-month period:

	6-Month Treasury Rate	Coupon Rate
First reset date	5.5%	?
Second reset date	5.8%	?
Third reset date	6.3%	?
Fourth reset date	6.8%	?
Fifth reset date	7.3%	?
Sixth reset date	6.1%	?

---

issuers have been able to structure floaters with almost any reference rate. In several countries, there are government bonds whose coupon formula is tied to an inflation index.

The U.S. Department of the Treasury in January 1997 began issuing inflation-adjusted securities. These issues are referred to as **Treasury Inflation Protection Securities** (TIPS). The reference rate for the coupon formula is the rate of inflation as measured by the Consumer Price Index for All Urban Consumers (i.e., CPI-U). (The mechanics of the payment of the coupon will be explained in Reading 64 where these securities are discussed.) Corporations and agencies in the United States issue **inflation-linked** (or **inflation-indexed**) **bonds**. For example, in February 1997, J.P. Morgan & Company issued a 15-year bond that pays the CPI plus 400 basis points. In the same month, the Federal Home Loan Bank issued a 5-year bond with a coupon rate equal to the CPI plus 315 basis points and a 10-year bond with a coupon rate equal to the CPI plus 337 basis points.

Typically, the coupon formula for a floater is such that the coupon rate increases when the reference rate increases, and decreases when the reference rate decreases. There are issues whose coupon rate moves in the opposite direction from the change in the reference rate. Such issues are called **inverse floaters** or **reverse floaters**.[4] It is not too difficult to understand why an investor would be interested in an inverse floater. It gives an investor who believes interest rates will decline the opportunity to obtain a higher coupon interest rate. The issuer isn't necessarily taking the opposite view because it can hedge the risk that interest rates will decline.[5]

---

[4] In the agency, corporate, and municipal markets, inverse floaters are created as structured notes. We discuss structured notes in Reading 67. Inverse floaters in the mortgage-backed securities market are common and are created through a process that will be discussed at Level II.

[5] The issuer hedges by using financial instruments known as derivatives, which we cover at Level II.

The coupon formula for an inverse floater is:

$$\text{coupon rate} = K - L \times (\text{reference rate})$$

where K and L are values specified in the prospectus for the issue.

For example, suppose that for a particular inverse floater, K is 20% and L is 2. Then the coupon reset formula would be:

$$\text{coupon rate} = 20\% - 2 \times (\text{reference rate})$$

Suppose that the reference rate is the 3-month Treasury bill rate, then the coupon formula would be:

$$\text{coupon rate} = 20\% - 2 \times (\text{3-month Treasury bill rate})$$

If at the coupon reset date the 3-month Treasury bill rate is 6%, the coupon rate for the next period is:

$$\text{coupon rate} = 20\% - 2 \times 6\% = 8\%$$

If at the next reset date the 3-month Treasury bill rate declines to 5%, the coupon rate increases to:

$$\text{coupon rate} = 20\% - 2 \times 5\% = 10\%$$

Notice that if the 3-month Treasury bill rate exceeds 10%, then the coupon formula would produce a negative coupon rate. To prevent this, there is a floor imposed on the coupon rate. There is also a cap on the inverse floater. This occurs if the 3-month Treasury bill rate is zero. In that unlikely event, the maximum coupon rate is 20% for our hypothetical inverse floater.

There is a wide range of coupon formulas that we will encounter in our study of fixed income securities.[6] These are discussed below. The reason why issuers have been able to create floating-rate securities with offbeat coupon formulas is due to derivative instruments. It is too early in our study of fixed income analysis and portfolio management to appreciate why some of these offbeat coupon formulas exist in the bond market. Suffice it to say that some of these offbeat coupon formulas allow the investor to take a view on either the movement of some interest rate (i.e., for speculating on an interest rate movement) or to reduce exposure to the risk of some interest rate movement (i.e., for interest rate risk management). The advantage to the issuer is that it can lower its cost of borrowing by creating offbeat coupon formulas for investors.[7] While it may seem that the issuer is taking the opposite position to the investor, this is not the case. What in fact happens is that the issuer can hedge its risk exposure by using derivative instruments so as to obtain the type of financing it seeks (i.e., fixed rate borrowing or floating rate borrowing). These offbeat coupon formulas are typically found in "structured notes," a form of medium-term note that will be discussed in Reading 67.

---

[6] In Reading 67, we will describe other types of floating-rate securities.

[7] These offbeat coupon bond formulas are actually created as a result of inquiries from clients of dealer firms. That is, a salesperson will be approached by fixed income portfolio managers requesting a structure be created that provides the exposure sought. The dealer firm will then notify the investment banking group of the dealer firm to contact potential issuers.

Practice Question 3

Identify the following types of bonds based on their coupon structures:

A. Coupon formula:

coupon rate = 32% − 2 × (5-year Treasury rate)

B. Coupon structure:

Years 1-3	5.1%
Years 4-9	5.7%
Years 10-20	6.2%

C. Coupon formula:

coupon rate = change in the consumer price index + 3.1%

5.5 Accrued Interest

Bond issuers do not disburse coupon interest payments every day. Instead, typically in the United States coupon interest is paid every six months. In some countries, interest is paid annually. For mortgage-backed and asset-backed securities, interest is usually paid monthly. The coupon payment is made to the bondholder of record. Thus, if an investor sells a bond between coupon payments and the buyer holds it until the next coupon payment, then the entire coupon interest earned for the period will be paid to the buyer of the bond since the buyer will be the holder of record. The seller of the bond gives up the interest from the time of the last coupon payment to the time until the bond is sold. The amount of interest over this period that will be received by the buyer even though it was earned by the seller is called accrued interest. We will see how to calculate **accrued interest** in Reading 69.

In the United States and in many countries, the bond buyer must pay the bond seller the accrued interest. The amount that the buyer pays the seller is the agreed upon price for the bond plus accrued interest. This amount is called the **full price**. (Some market participants refer to this as the **dirty price**.) The agreed upon bond price without accrued interest is simply referred to as the **price**. (Some refer to it as the **clean price**.)

A bond in which the buyer must pay the seller accrued interest is said to be trading *cum-coupon* ("with coupon"). If the buyer forgoes the next coupon payment, the bond is said to be trading *ex-coupon* ("without coupon"). In the United States, bonds are always traded *cum-coupon*. There are bond markets outside the United States where bonds are traded *ex-coupon* for a certain period before the coupon payment date.

There are exceptions to the rule that the bond buyer must pay the bond seller accrued interest. The most important exception is when the issuer has not fulfilled its promise to make the periodic interest payments. In this case, the issuer is said to be in default. In such instances, the bond is sold without accrued interest and is said to be **traded flat**.

PROVISIONS FOR PAYING OFF BONDS   6

The issuer of a bond agrees to pay the principal by the stated maturity date. The issuer can agree to pay the entire amount borrowed in one lump sum payment at the maturity date. That is, the issuer is not required to make any principal repayments prior to the maturity date. Such bonds are said to have a **bullet maturity**. The bullet maturity structure has become the most common structure in the United States and Europe for both corporate and government issuers.

Fixed income securities backed by pools of loans (mortgage-backed securities and asset-backed securities) often have a schedule of partial principal payments. Such fixed income securities are said to be **amortizing securities**. For many loans, the payments are structured so that when the last loan payment is made, the entire amount owed is fully paid.

Another example of an amortizing feature is a bond that has a **sinking fund provision**. This provision for repayment of a bond may be designed to pay all of an issue by the maturity date, or it may be arranged to repay only a part of the total by the maturity date. We discuss this provision later in this section.

An issue may have a **call provision** granting the issuer an option to retire all or part of the issue prior to the stated maturity date. Some issues specify that the issuer must retire a predetermined amount of the issue periodically. Various types of call provisions are discussed below.

6.1 Call and Refunding Provisions

An issuer generally wants the right to retire a bond issue prior to the stated maturity date. The issuer recognizes that at some time in the future interest rates may fall sufficiently below the issue's coupon rate so that redeeming the issue and replacing it with another lower coupon rate issue would be economically beneficial. This right is a disadvantage to the bondholder since proceeds received must be reinvested in the lower interest rate issue. As a result, an issuer who wants to include this right as part of a bond offering must compensate the bondholder when the issue is sold by offering a higher coupon rate, or equivalently, accepting a lower price than if the right is not included.

The right of the issuer to retire the issue prior to the stated maturity date is referred to as a **call provision**. If an issuer exercises this right, the issuer is said to "call the bond." The price which the issuer must pay to retire the issue is referred to as the **call price** or **redemption price**.

When a bond is issued, typically the issuer may not call the bond for a number of years. That is, the issue is said to have a **deferred call**. The date at which the bond may first be called is referred to as the **first call date**. The first call date for the Walt Disney 7.55s due 7/15/2093 (the 100-year bonds) is 7/15/2023. For the 50-year Tennessee Valley Authority 6⅞s due 12/15/2043, the first call date is 12/15/2003.

Bonds can be called in whole (the entire issue) or in part (only a portion). When less than the entire issue is called, the certificates to be called are either selected randomly or on a **pro rata basis**. When bonds are selected randomly, a computer program is used to select the serial number of the bond certificates called. The serial numbers are then published in *The Wall Street Journal* and major metropolitan dailies. Pro rata redemption means that all bondholders of the issue will have the same percentage of their holdings redeemed (subject to the restrictions imposed on minimum denominations). Pro rata redemption is rare for publicly issued debt but is common for debt issues directly or privately placed with borrowers.

A bond issue that permits the issuer to call an issue prior to the stated maturity date is referred to as a **callable bond**. At one time, the callable bond structure was common for corporate bonds issued in the United States. However, since the mid-1990s, there has been significantly less issuance of callable bonds by corporate issuers of high credit quality. Instead, as noted above, the most popular structure is the bullet bond. In contrast, corporate issuers of low credit quality continue to issue callable bonds.[8] In Europe, historically the callable bond structure has not been as popular as in the United States.

6.1.1 Call (Redemption) Price

When the issuer exercises an option to call an issue, the call price can be either (1) fixed regardless of the call date, (2) based on a price specified in the call schedule, or (3) based on a make-whole premium provision. We will use various debt issues of Anheuser-Busch Companies to illustrate these three ways by which the call price is specified.

6.1.1.1 Single Call Price Regardless of Call Date

On 6/10/97, Anheuser-Busch Companies issued $250 million of notes with a coupon rate of 7.1% due June 15, 2007. The prospectus stated that:

> . . . The Notes will be redeemable at the option of the Company at any time on or after June 15, 2004, as set forth herein.
>
> The Notes will be redeemable at the option of the Company at any time on or after June 15, 2004, in whole or in part, upon not fewer than 30 days' nor more than 60 days' notice, at a Redemption Price equal to 100% of the principal amount thereof, together with accrued interest to the date fixed for redemption.

This issue had a deferred call of seven years at issuance and a first call date of June 15, 2004. Regardless of the call date, the call price is par plus accrued interest.

6.1.1.2 Call Price Based on Call Schedule

With a **call schedule**, the call price depends on when the issuer calls the issue. As an example of an issue with a call schedule, in July 1997 Anheuser-Busch Companies issued $250 million of debentures with a coupon rate of $7\frac{1}{8}$ due July 1, 2017. (We will see what a debt instrument referred to as a "debenture" is in Reading 67.) The provision dealing with the call feature of this issue states:

> The Debentures will be redeemable at the option of the Company at any time on or after July 1, 2007, in whole or in part, upon not fewer than 30 days' nor more than 60 days' notice, at Redemption Prices equal to the percentages set forth below of the principal amount to be redeemed for the respective 12-month periods beginning July 1 of the years indicated, together in each case with accrued interest to the Redemption Date:

---

[8] As explained in Reading 66, high credit quality issuers are referred to as "investment grade" issuers and low credit quality issuers are referred to as "non-investment grade" issuers. The reason why high credit quality issuers have reduced their issuance of callable bonds while it is still the more popular structure for low credit quality issuers is explained at Level III.

12 Months Beginning July 1	Redemption Price	12 Months Beginning July 1	Redemption Price
2007	103.026%	2012	101.513%
2008	102.723%	2013	101.210%
2009	102.421%	2014	100.908%
2010	102.118%	2015	100.605%
2011	101.816%	2016	100.303%

This issue had a deferred call of 10 years from the date of issuance, and the call price begins at a premium above par value and declines over time toward par value. Notice that regardless of when the issue is called, the issuer pays a premium above par value.

A second example of a call schedule is provided by the $150 million Anheuser-Busch Companies 8⅝s due 12/1/2016 issued November 20, 1986. This issue had a 10-year deferred call (the first call date was December 1, 1996) and the following call schedule:

If Redeemed During the 12 Months Beginning December 1:	Call Price	If Redeemed During the 12 Months Beginning December 1:	Call Price
1996	104.313	2002	101.725
1997	103.881	2003	101.294
1998	103.450	2004	100.863
1999	103.019	2005	100.431
2000	102.588	2006 and thereafter	100.000
2001	102.156		

Notice that for this issue the call price begins at a premium but after 2006 the call price declines to par value. The first date at which an issue can be called at par value is the **first par call date**.

6.1.1.3 Call Price Based on Make-Whole Premium

A **make-whole premium provision,** also called a **yield-maintenance premium provision,** provides a formula for determining the premium that an issuer must pay to call an issue. The purpose of the make-whole premium is to protect the yield of those investors who purchased the issue at issuance. A make-whole premium does so by setting an amount for the premium, such that when added to the principal amount and reinvested at the redemption date in U.S. Treasury securities having the same remaining life, it would provide a yield equal to the original issue's yield. The premium plus the principal at which the issue is called is referred to as the **make-whole redemption price.**

We can use an Anheuser-Busch Companies issue to illustrate a make-whole premium provision—the $250 million 6% debentures due 11/1/2041 issued on 1/5/2001. The prospectus for this issue states:

> We may redeem the Debentures, in whole or in part, at our option at any time at a redemption price equal to the greater of (i) 100% of the principal amount of such Debentures and (ii) as determined by a

Quotation Agent (as defined below), the sum of the present values of the remaining scheduled payments of principal and interest thereon (not including any portion of such payments of interest accrued as of the date of redemption) discounted to the date of redemption on a semi-annual basis (assuming a 360-day year consisting of twelve 30-day months) at the Adjusted Treasury Rate (as defined below) plus 25 basis points plus, in each case, accrued interest thereon to the date of redemption.

The prospectus defined what is meant by a "Quotation Agent" and the "Adjusted Treasury Rate." For our purposes here, it is not necessary to go into the definitions, only that there is some mechanism for determining a call price that reflects current market conditions as measured by the yield on Treasury securities. (Treasury securities are explained in Reading 67.)

6.1.2 Noncallable versus Nonrefundable Bonds

If a bond issue does not have any protection against early call, then it is said to be a **currently callable** issue. But most new bond issues, even if currently callable, usually have some restrictions against certain types of early redemption. The most common restriction is that of prohibiting the refunding of the bonds for a certain number of years or for the issue's life. Bonds that are noncallable for the issue's life are more common than bonds which are nonrefundable for life but otherwise callable.

Many investors are confused by the terms **noncallable** and **nonrefundable**. Call protection is much more robust than refunding protection. While there may be certain exceptions to absolute or complete call protection in some cases (such as sinking funds and the redemption of debt under certain mandatory provisions discussed later), call protection still provides greater assurance against premature and unwanted redemption than refunding protection. Refunding protection merely prevents redemption from certain sources, namely the proceeds of other debt issues sold at a lower cost of money. The holder is protected only if interest rates decline and the borrower can obtain lower-cost money to pay off the debt.

For example, Anheuser-Busch Companies issued on 6/23/88 10% coupon bonds due 7/1/2018. The issue was immediately callable. However, the prospectus specified in the call schedule that

prior to July 1, 1998, the Company may not redeem any of the Debentures pursuant to such option, directly or indirectly, from or in anticipation of the proceeds of the issuance of any indebtedness for money borrowed having an interest cost of less than 10% per annum.

Thus, this Anheuser Busch bond issue could not be redeemed prior to July 2, 1998 if the company raised the money from a new issue with an interest cost lower than 10%. There is nothing to prevent the company from calling the bonds within the 10-year refunding protected period from debt sold at a higher rate (although the company normally wouldn't do so) or from money obtained through other means. And that is exactly what Anheuser Busch did. Between December 1993 and June 1994, it called $68.8 million of these relatively high-coupon bonds at 107.5% of par value (the call price) with funds from its general operations. This was permitted because funds from the company's general operations are viewed as more expensive than the interest cost of indebtedness. Thus, Anheuser-Busch was allowed to call this issue prior to July 1, 1998.

6.1.3 Regular versus Special Redemption Prices

The call prices for the various issues cited above are called the **regular redemption prices** or **general redemption prices**. Notice that the regular redemption prices are above par until the first par call date. There are also **special redemption prices** for bonds redeemed through the sinking fund and through other provisions, and the proceeds from the confiscation of property through the right of eminent domain or the forced sale or transfer of assets due to deregulation. The special redemption price is usually par value. Thus, there is an advantage to the issuer of being able to redeem an issue prior to the first par call date at the special redemption price (usually par) rather than at the regular redemption price.

A concern of an investor is that an issuer will use all means possible to maneuver a call so that the special redemption price applies. This is referred to as the **par call problem**. There have been ample examples, and subsequent litigation, where corporations have used the special redemption price and bondholders have challenged the use by the issuer.

6.2 Prepayments

For amortizing securities that are backed by loans that have a schedule of principal payments, individual borrowers typically have the option to pay off all or part of their loan prior to a scheduled principal payment date. Any principal payment prior to a scheduled principal payment date is called a **prepayment**. The right of borrowers to prepay principal is called a **prepayment option**.

Basically, the prepayment option is the same as a call option. However, unlike a call option, there is not a call price that depends on when the borrower pays off the issue. Typically, the price at which a loan is prepaid is par value. Prepayments will be discussed when mortgage-backed and asset-backed securities are discussed at Level II.

6.3 Sinking Fund Provision

An indenture may require the issuer to retire a specified portion of the issue each year. This is referred to as a **sinking fund requirement**. The alleged purpose of the sinking fund provision is to reduce credit risk (discussed in the next reading). This kind of provision for debt payment may be designed to retire all of a bond issue by the maturity date, or it may be designed to pay only a portion of the total indebtedness by the end of the term. If only a portion is paid, the remaining principal is called a **balloon maturity**.

An example of an issue with a sinking fund requirement that pays the entire principal by the maturity date is the $150 million Ingersoll Rand 7.20s issue due 6/1/2025. This bond, issued on 6/5/1995, has a sinking fund schedule that begins on 6/1/2006. Each year the issuer must retire $7.5 million.

Generally, the issuer may satisfy the sinking fund requirement by either (1) making a cash payment to the trustee equal to the par value of the bonds to be retired; the trustee then calls the bonds for redemption using a lottery, or (2) delivering to the trustee bonds purchased in the open market that have a total par value equal to the amount to be retired. If the bonds are retired using the first method, interest payments stop at the redemption date.

Usually, the periodic payments required for a sinking fund requirement are the same for each period. Selected issues may permit variable periodic payments, where payments change according to certain prescribed conditions set forth in the indenture. Many bond issue indentures include a provision that grants the issuer the option to retire more than the sinking fund requirement. This is referred to as an **accelerated sinking fund provision**. For example, the Anheuser Busch 8⅝s due 12/1/2016, whose call schedule was presented earlier, has a sinking fund requirement of $7.5 million each year beginning on 12/01/1997. The issuer is permitted to retire up to $15 million each year.

Usually the sinking fund call price is the par value if the bonds were originally sold at par. When issued at a premium, the call price generally starts at the issuance price and scales down to par as the issue approaches maturity.

7   CONVERSION PRIVILEGE

A **convertible bond** is an issue that grants the bondholder the right to convert the bond for a specified number of shares of common stock. Such a feature allows the bondholder to take advantage of favorable movements in the price of the issuer's common stock. An **exchangeable bond** allows the bondholder to exchange the issue for a specified number of shares of common stock of a corporation different from the issuer of the bond. These bonds are discussed at Level II where a framework for analyzing them is also provided.

8   PUT PROVISION

An issue with a **put provision** included in the indenture grants the bondholder the right to sell the issue back to the issuer at a specified price on designated dates. The specified price is called the **put price**. Typically, a bond is putable at par if it is issued at or close to par value. For a zero-coupon bond, the put price is below par.

The advantage of a put provision to the bondholder is that if, after the issuance date, market rates rise above the issue's coupon rate, the bondholder can force the issuer to redeem the bond at the put price and then reinvest the put bond proceeds at the prevailing higher rate.

9   CURRENCY DENOMINATION

The payments that the issuer makes to the bondholder can be in any currency. For bonds issued in the United States, the issuer typically makes coupon payments and principal repayments in U.S. dollars. However, there is nothing that forces the issuer to make payments in U.S. dollars. The indenture can specify that the issuer may make payments in some other specified currency.

An issue in which payments to bondholders are in U.S. dollars is called a **dollar-denominated issue**. A **nondollar-denominated issue** is one in which payments are not denominated in U.S. dollars. There are some issues whose coupon payments are in one currency and whose principal payment is in another currency. An issue with this characteristic is called a **dual-currency issue**.

10   EMBEDDED OPTIONS

As we have seen, it is common for a bond issue to include a provision in the indenture that gives the issuer and/or the bondholder an option to take some action against the other party. These options are referred to as **embedded options** to distinguish them from stand alone options (i.e., options that can be purchased on an exchange or in the over-the-counter market). They are referred to as embedded options because the option is embedded in the issue. In fact, there may be more than one embedded option in an issue.

10.1 Embedded Options Granted to Issuers

The most common embedded options that are granted to issuers or borrowers discussed in the previous section include:

▶ the right to call the issue
▶ the right of the underlying borrowers in a pool of loans to prepay principal above the scheduled principal payment
▶ the accelerated sinking fund provision
▶ the cap on a floater

The accelerated sinking fund provision is an embedded option because the issuer can call more than is necessary to meet the sinking fund requirement. An issuer usually takes this action when interest rates decline below the issue's coupon rate even if there are other restrictions in the issue that prevent the issue from being called.

The cap of a floater can be thought of as an option requiring no action by the issuer to take advantage of a rise in interest rates. Effectively, the bondholder has granted to the issuer the right not to pay more than the cap.

Notice that whether or not the first three options are exercised by the issuer or borrower depends on the level of interest rates prevailing in the market relative to the issue's coupon rate or the borrowing rate of the underlying loans (in the case of mortgage-backed and asset-backed securities). These options become more valuable when interest rates fall. The cap of a floater also depends on the prevailing level of rates. But here the option becomes more valuable when interest rates rise.

10.2 Embedded Options Granted to Bondholders

The most common embedded options granted to bondholders are:

▶ conversion privilege
▶ the right to put the issue
▶ floor on a floater

The value of the conversion privilege depends on the market price of the stock relative to the embedded purchase price held by the bondholder when exercising the conversion option. The put privilege benefits the bondholder if interest rates rise above the issue's coupon rate. While a cap on a floater benefits the issuer if interest rates rise, a floor benefits the bondholder if interest rates fall since it fixes a minimum coupon rate payable.

10.3 Importance of Understanding Embedded Options

At the outset of this reading, we stated that fixed income securities have become more complex. One reason for this increased complexity is that embedded options make it more difficult to project the cash flows of a security. The cash flow for a fixed income security is defined as its interest and the principal payments.

To value a fixed income security with embedded options, it is necessary to:

1. model the factors that determine whether or not an embedded option will be exercised over the life of the security, and

2. in the case of options granted to the issuer/borrower, model the behavior of issuers and borrowers to determine the conditions necessary for them to exercise an embedded option.

For example, consider a callable bond issued by a corporation. Projecting the cash flow requires (1) modeling interest rates (over the life of the security) at which the issuer can refund an issue and (2) developing a rule for determining the economic conditions necessary for the issuer to benefit from calling the issue. In the case of mortgage-backed or asset-backed securities, again it is necessary to model how interest rates will influence borrowers to refinance their loan over the life of the security. Models for valuing bonds with embedded options will be covered at Level II.

It cannot be overemphasized that embedded options affect not only the value of a bond but also the total return of a bond. In the next reading, the risks associated with the presence of an embedded option will be explained. What is critical to understand is that due to the presence of embedded options it is necessary to develop models of interest rate movements and rules for exercising embedded options. Any analysis of securities with embedded options exposes an investor to **modeling risk**. Modeling risk is the risk that the model analyzing embedded options produces the wrong value because the assumptions are not correct or the assumptions were not realized. This risk will become clearer at Level II when we describe models for valuing bonds with embedded options.

11 BORROWING FUNDS TO PURCHASE BONDS

At Level II, we will discuss investment strategies an investor uses to borrow funds to purchase securities. The expectation of the investor is that the return earned by investing in the securities purchased with the borrowed funds will exceed the borrowing cost. There are several sources of funds available to an investor when borrowing funds. When securities are purchased with borrowed funds, the most common practice is to use the securities as collateral for the loan. In such instances, the transaction is referred to as a **collateralized loan**. Two collateralized borrowing arrangements are used by investors—margin buying and repurchase agreements.

11.1 Margin Buying

In a **margin buying arrangement**, the funds borrowed to buy the securities are provided by the broker and the broker gets the money from a bank. The interest rate banks charge brokers for these transactions is called the call money rate (or broker loan rate). The broker charges the investor the call money rate plus a service charge. The broker is not free to lend as much as it wishes to the investor to buy securities. In the United States, the Securities and Exchange Act of 1934 prohibits brokers from lending more than a specified percentage of the market value of the securities. The 1934 Act gives the Board of Governors of the Federal Reserve the responsibility to set initial margin requirements, which it does under

Regulations T and U. While margin buying is the most common collateralized borrowing arrangement for common stock investors (both retail investors and institutional investors) and retail bond investors (i.e., individual investors), it is not the common for institutional bond investors.

11.2 Repurchase Agreement

The collateralized borrowing arrangement used by institutional investors in the bond market is the repurchase agreement. We will discuss this arrangement in more detail at Level III. However, it is important to understand the basics of the repurchase agreement because it affects how some bonds in the market are valued.

A **repurchase agreement** is the sale of a security with a commitment by the seller to buy the same security back from the purchaser at a specified price at a designated future date. The **repurchase price** is the price at which the seller and the buyer agree that the seller will repurchase the security on a specified future date called the repurchase date. The difference between the repurchase price and the sale price is the dollar interest cost of the loan; based on the dollar interest cost, the sales price, and the length of the repurchase agreement, an implied interest rate can be computed. This implied interest rate is called the **repo rate**. The advantage to the investor of using this borrowing arrangement is that the interest rate is less than the cost of bank financing. When the term of the loan is one day, it is called an **overnight repo** (or overnight RP); a loan for more than one day is called a **term repo** (or term RP). As will be explained at Level III, there is not one repo rate. The rate varies from transaction to transaction depending on a variety of factors.

SUMMARY

▶ A fixed income security is a financial obligation of an entity (the issuer) who promises to pay a specified sum of money at specified future dates.

▶ Fixed income securities fall into two general categories: debt obligations and preferred stock.

▶ The promises of the issuer and the rights of the bondholders are set forth in the indenture.

▶ The par value (principal, face value, redemption value, or maturity value) of a bond is the amount that the issuer agrees to repay the bondholder at or by the maturity date.

▶ Bond prices are quoted as a percentage of par value, with par value equal to 100.

▶ The interest rate that the issuer agrees to pay each year is called the coupon rate; the coupon is the annual amount of the interest payment and is found by multiplying the par value by the coupon rate.

▶ Zero-coupon bonds do not make periodic coupon payments; the bondholder realizes interest at the maturity date equal to the difference between the maturity value and the price paid for the bond.

▶ A floating-rate security is an issue whose coupon rate resets periodically based on some formula; the typical coupon formula is some reference rate plus a quoted margin.

▶ A floating-rate security may have a cap, which sets the maximum coupon rate that will be paid, and/or a floor, which sets the minimum coupon rate that will be paid.

▶ A cap is a disadvantage to the bondholder while a floor is an advantage to the bondholder.

▶ A step-up note is a security whose coupon rate increases over time.

▶ Accrued interest is the amount of interest accrued since the last coupon payment; in the United States (as well as in many countries), the bond buyer must pay the bond seller the accrued interest.

▶ The full price (or dirty price) of a security is the agreed upon price plus accrued interest; the price (or clean price) is the agreed upon price without accrued interest.

▶ An amortizing security is a security for which there is a schedule for the repayment of principal.

▶ Many issues have a call provision granting the issuer an option to retire all or part of the issue prior to the stated maturity date.

▶ A call provision is an advantage to the issuer and a disadvantage to the bondholder.

▶ When a callable bond is issued, if the issuer cannot call the bond for a number of years, the bond is said to have a deferred call.

▶ The call or redemption price can be either fixed regardless of the call date or based on a call schedule or based on a make-whole premium provision.

▶ With a call schedule, the call price depends on when the issuer calls the issue.

▶ A make-whole premium provision sets forth a formula for determining the premium that the issuer must pay to call an issue, with the premium designed to protect the yield of those investors who purchased the issue.

► The call prices are regular or general redemption prices; there are special redemption prices for debt redeemed through the sinking fund and through other provisions.

► A currently callable bond is an issue that does not have any protection against early call.

► Most new bond issues, even if currently callable, usually have some restrictions against refunding.

► Call protection is much more absolute than refunding protection.

► For an amortizing security backed by a pool of loans, the underlying borrowers typically have the right to prepay the outstanding principal balance in whole or in part prior to the scheduled principal payment dates; this provision is called a prepayment option.

► A sinking fund provision requires that the issuer retire a specified portion of an issue each year.

► An accelerated sinking fund provision allows the issuer to retire more than the amount stipulated to satisfy the periodic sinking fund requirement.

► A putable bond is one in which the bondholder has the right to sell the issue back to the issuer at a specified price on designated dates.

► A convertible bond is an issue giving the bondholder the right to exchange the bond for a specified number of shares of common stock at a specified price.

► The presence of embedded options makes the valuation of fixed income securities complex and requires the modeling of interest rates and issuer/borrower behavior in order to project cash flows.

► An investor can borrow funds to purchase a security by using the security itself as collateral.

► There are two types of collateralized borrowing arrangements for purchasing securities: margin buying and repurchase agreements.

► Typically, institutional investors in the bond market do not finance the purchase of a security by buying on margin; rather, they use repurchase agreements.

► A repurchase agreement is the sale of a security with a commitment by the seller to repurchase the security from the buyer at the repurchase price on the repurchase date.

► The borrowing rate for a repurchase agreement is called the repo rate and while this rate is less than the cost of bank borrowing, it varies from transaction to transaction based on several factors.

PROBLEMS FOR READING 65

1. Consider the following two bond issues.

   Bond A: 5% 15-year bond
   Bond B: 5% 30-year bond
   Neither bond has an embedded option. Both bonds are trading in the market at the same yield.

   Which bond will fluctuate *more* in price when interest rates change? Why?

2. Given the information in the first and third columns, complete the table in the second and fourth columns:

Quoted Price	Price per $1 of Par Value	Par Value	Dollar Price
96¼		$1,000	
102⅞		$5,000	
109⁹⁄₁₆		$10,000	
68¹¹⁄₃₂		$100,000	

3. A floating-rate issue has the following coupon formula:

   1-year Treasury rate + 30 basis points with a cap of 7% and a floor of 4.5%

   The coupon rate is reset every year. Suppose that at the reset date the 1-year Treasury rate is as shown below. Compute the coupon rate for the next year:

	1-Year Treasury Rate	Coupon Rate
First reset date	6.1%	?
Second reset date	6.5%	?
Third reset date	6.9%	?
Fourth reset date	6.8%	?
Fifth reset date	5.7%	?
Sixth reset date	5.0%	?
Seventh reset date	4.1%	?
Eighth reset date	3.9%	?
Ninth reset date	3.2%	?
Tenth reset date	4.4%	?

4. An excerpt from the prospectus of a $200 million issue by Becton, Dickinson and Company 7.15% Notes due October 1, 2009:

   OPTIONAL REDEMPTION We may, at our option, redeem all or any part of the notes. If we choose to do so, we will mail a notice of redemption to you not less than 30 days and not more than 60 days before this redemption occurs. The redemption price will be equal to the greater of: (1) 100% of the principal amount of the notes to be redeemed; and (2) the sum of the present values of the Remaining Scheduled Payments on the notes, discounted to the redemption date on a semiannual basis, assuming a 360-day year consisting of twelve 30-day months, at the Treasury Rate plus 15 basis points.

A. What type of call provision is this?

B. What is the purpose of this type of call provision?

5. An excerpt from Cincinnati Gas & Electric Company's prospectus for the 10⅛% First Mortgage Bonds due in 2020 states,

> The Offered Bonds are redeemable (though CG&E does not contemplate doing so) prior to May 1, 1995 through the use of earnings, proceeds from the sale of equity securities and cash accumulations other than those resulting from a refunding operation such as hereinafter described. The Offered Bonds are not redeemable prior to May 1, 1995 as a part of, or in anticipation of, any refunding operation involving the incurring of indebtedness by CG&E having an effective interest cost (calculated to the second decimal place in accordance with generally accepted financial practice) of less than the effective interest cost of the Offered Bonds (similarly calculated) or through the operation of the Maintenance and Replacement Fund.

What does this excerpt tell the investor about provisions of this issuer to pay off this issue prior to the stated maturity date?

6. An assistant portfolio manager reviewed the prospectus of a bond that will be issued next week on January 1 of 2000. The call schedule for this $200 million, 7.75% coupon 20-year issue specifies the following:

> The Bonds will be redeemable at the option of the Company at any time in whole or in part, upon not fewer than 30 nor more than 60 days' notice, at the following redemption prices (which are expressed in percentages of principal amount) in each case together with accrued interest to the date fixed for redemption:
> If redeemed during the 12 months beginning January 1,

2000 through 2005	104.00%
2006 through 2010	103.00%
2011 through 2012	101.00%
from 2013 on	100.00%

> provided, however, that prior to January 1, 2006, the Company may not redeem any of the Bonds pursuant to such option, directly or indirectly, from or in anticipation of the proceeds of the issuance of any indebtedness for money borrowed having an interest cost of less than 7.75% per annum.

The prospectus further specifies that

> The Company will provide for the retirement by redemption of $10 million of the principal amount of the Bonds each of the years 2010 to and including 2019 at the principal amount thereof, together with accrued interest to the date of redemption. The Company may also provide for the redemption of up to an additional $10 million principal amount . . . annually, . . . such optional right being non-cumulative.

The assistant portfolio manager made the following statements to a client after reviewing this bond issue. Comment on each statement. *(When answering this question, remember that the assistant portfolio manager is responding to statements just before the bond is issued in 2000.)*

A. "My major concern is that if rates decline significantly in the next few years, this issue will be called by the Company in order to replace it with a bond issue with a coupon rate less than 7.75%."

B. "One major advantage of this issue is that if the Company redeems it *for any reason* in the first five years, investors are guaranteed receiving a price of 104, a premium over the initial offering price of 100."

C. "A beneficial feature of this issue is that it has a sinking fund provision that reduces the risk that the Company won't have enough funds to pay off the issue at the maturity date."

D. "A further attractive feature of this issue is that the Company can accelerate the payoff of the issue via the sinking fund provision, reducing the risk that funds will not be available at the maturity date."

E. In response to a client question about what will be the interest and principal that the client can depend on if $5 million par value of the issue is purchased, the assistant portfolio manager responded: "I can construct a schedule that shows every six months for the next 20 years the dollar amount of the interest and the principal repayment. It is quite simple to compute—basically it is just multiplying two numbers."

7. There are some securities that are backed by a pool of loans. These loans have a schedule of interest and principal payments every month and give each borrower whose loan is in the pool the right to payoff their respective loan at any time at par. Suppose that a portfolio manager purchased one of these securities. Can the portfolio manager rely on the schedule of interest and principal payments in determining the cash flow that will be generated by such securities (assuming no borrowers default)? Why or why not?

8. A. What is an accelerated sinking fund provision?

B. Why can an accelerated sinking fund provision be viewed as an embedded call option granted to the issuer?

9. The importance of knowing the terms of bond issues, especially those relating to redemption, cannot be emphasized. Yet there have appeared numerous instances of investors, professional and others, who acknowledge that they don't read the documentation. For example, in an Augusts 14, 1983 article published in *The New York Times* titled "The Lessons of a Bond Failure," the following statements were attributed to some stockbrokers: "But brokers in the field say they often don't spend much time reading these [official] statements," "I can be honest and say I never look at the prospectus . . . . Generally, you don't have time to do that," and "There are some clients who really don't know what they buy . . . . They just say, 'That's a good interest rate.'" Why it is important to understand the redemption features of a bond issue?

10. What is meant by an embedded option?

11. A. What is the typical arrangement used by institutional investors in the bond market: bank financing, margin buying, or repurchase agreement?

B. What is the difference between a term repo and an overnight repo?

RISKS ASSOCIATED WITH INVESTING IN BONDS

by Frank J. Fabozzi

LEARNING OUTCOMES

The candidate should be able to:

a. explain the risks associated with investing in bonds (e.g., interest rate risk, yield curve risk, call and prepayment risk, reinvestment risk, credit risk, liquidity risk, exchange-rate risk, inflation risk, volatility risk, event risk, and sovereign risk);

b. identify the relationships among a bond's coupon rate, the yield required by the market, and the bond's price relative to par value (i.e., discount, premium, or equal to par);

c. explain how features of a bond (e.g., maturity, coupon, and embedded options) and the level of a bond's yield affect the bond's interest rate risk;

d. identify the relationship among the price of a callable bond, the price of an option-free bond, and the price of the embedded call option;

e. explain the interest rate risk of a floating-rate security and why such a security's price may differ from par value;

f. compute and interpret the duration of a bond, given the bond's change in price when interest rates change, and compute the approximate percentage price change of a bond and new price of a bond, given the duration and change in yield;

g. describe yield curve risk and explain why duration does not account for yield curve risk for a portfolio of bonds;

h. explain the disadvantages of a callable or prepayable security to an investor;

i. identify the factors that affect the reinvestment risk of a security and explain why prepayable amortizing securities expose investors to greater reinvestment risk than nonamortizing securities;

j. describe the various forms of credit risk (i.e., default risk, credit spread risk, downgrade risk) and describe the meaning and role of credit ratings;

k. explain why liquidity risk might be important to investors even if they expect to hold a security to the maturity date;

l. describe the exchange rate risk an investor faces when a bond makes payments in a foreign currency;

Fixed Income Analysis for the Chartered Financial Analyst® Program, Second Edition, edited by Frank J. Fabozzi, Copyright © 2005 by CFA Institute. Reprinted with permission.

> **m.** explain inflation risk;
> ....
> **n.** explain how yield volatility affects the price of a bond with an embedded option and how changes in volatility affect the value of a callable bond and a putable bond;
> ....
> **o.** describe the various forms of event risk (e.g., natural catastrophe, corporate takeover/restructuring and regulatory risk).

1 INTRODUCTION

Armed with an understanding of the basic features of bonds, we now turn to the risks associated with investing in bonds. These risks include:

- ▶ interest rate risk
- ▶ call and prepayment risk
- ▶ yield curve risk
- ▶ reinvestment risk
- ▶ credit risk
- ▶ liquidity risk
- ▶ exchange-rate risk
- ▶ volatility risk
- ▶ inflation or purchasing power risk
- ▶ event risk
- ▶ sovereign risk

We will see how features of a bond that we described in Reading 65—coupon rate, maturity, embedded options, and currency denomination—affect several of these risks.

2 INTEREST RATE RISK

As we will demonstrate in Reading 70, the price of a typical bond will change in the opposite direction to the change in interest rates or yields.[1] That is, when interest rates rise, a bond's price will fall; when interest rates fall, a bond's price will rise. For example, consider a 6% 20-year bond. If the yield investors require to buy this bond is 6%, the price of this bond would be $100. However, if the required yield increased to 6.5%, the price of this bond would decline to $94.4479. Thus, for a 50 basis point increase in yield, the bond's price declines by 5.55%. If, instead, the yield declines from 6% to 5.5%, the bond's price will rise by 6.02% to $106.0195.

Since the price of a bond fluctuates with market interest rates, the risk that an investor faces is that the price of a bond held in a portfolio will decline if market interest rates rise. This risk is referred to as **interest rate risk** and is the major risk faced by investors in the bond market.

---

[1] At this stage, we will use the terms interest rate and yield interchangeably. We'll see in Reading 71 how to compute a bond's yield.

2.1 Reason for the Inverse Relationship between Changes in Interest Rates and Price

The reason for this inverse relationship between a bond's price change and the change in interest rates (or change in market yields) is as follows. Suppose investor X purchases our hypothetical 6% coupon 20-year bond at a price equal to par (100). As explained in Reading 71, the yield for this bond is 6%. Suppose that immediately after the purchase of this bond two things happen. First, market interest rates rise to 6.50% so that if a bond issuer wishes to sell a bond priced at par, it will require a 6.50% coupon rate to attract investors to purchase the bond. Second, suppose investor X wants to sell the bond with a 6% coupon rate. In attempting to sell the bond, investor X would not find an investor who would be willing to pay par value for a bond with a coupon rate of 6%. The reason is that any investor who wanted to purchase this bond could obtain a similar 20-year bond with a coupon rate 50 basis points higher, 6.5%.

What can the investor do? The investor cannot force the issuer to change the coupon rate to 6.5%. Nor can the investor force the issuer to shorten the maturity of the bond to a point where a new investor might be willing to accept a 6% coupon rate. The only thing that the investor can do is adjust the price of the bond to a new price where a buyer would realize a yield of 6.5%. This means that the price would have to be adjusted down to a price below par. It turns out, the new price must be 94.4479.[2] While we assumed in our illustration an initial price of par value, the principle holds for any purchase price. Regardless of the price that an investor pays for a bond, an instantaneous increase in market interest rates will result in a decline in a bond's price.

Suppose that instead of a rise in market interest rates to 6.5%, interest rates decline to 5.5%. Investors would be more than happy to purchase the 6% coupon 20-year bond at par. However, investor X realizes that the market is only offering investors the opportunity to buy a similar bond at par with a coupon rate of 5.5%. Consequently, investor X will increase the price of the bond until it offers a yield of 5.5%. That price turns out to be 106.0195.

Let's summarize the important relationships suggested by our example.

1. A bond will trade at a price equal to par when the coupon rate is equal to the yield required by market. That is,[3]

   coupon rate = yield required by market → price = par value

2. A bond will trade at a price below par (sell at a discount) or above par (sell at a premium) if the coupon rate is different from the yield required by the market. Specifically,

   coupon rate < yield required by market → price < par value (discount)
   coupon rate > yield required by market → price > par value (premium)

3. The price of a bond changes in the opposite direction to the change in interest rates. So, for an instantaneous change in interest rates the following relationship holds:

   if interest rates increase → price of a bond decreases
   if interest rates decrease → price of a bond increases

---

[2] We'll see how to compute the price of a bond in Reading 71.

[3] The arrow symbol in the expressions means "therefore."

Practice Question 1

The following information is reported in the business section of a newspaper:

Issue	Coupon	Maturity	Yield Required by Market	Price
A	7³⁄₈%	16 years	6.00%	114.02
B	6³⁄₄%	4 years	7.00%	99.14
C	0%	10 years	5.00%	102.10
D	5¹⁄₂%	20 years	5.90%	104.15
E	8¹⁄₂%	18 years	8.50%	100.00
F	4¹⁄₂%	6 years	4.00%	96.50
G	6¹⁄₄%	25 years	6.25%	103.45

Which issues have an error in their reported price? (No calculations are required.)

2.2 Bond Features that Affect Interest Rate Risk

A bond's price sensitivity to changes in market interest rates (i.e., a bond's interest rate risk) depends on various features of the issue, such as maturity, coupon rate, and embedded options.[4] While we discuss these features in more detail in Reading 72, we provide a brief discussion below.

2.2.1 The Impact of Maturity

All other factors constant, *the longer the bond's maturity, the greater the bond's price sensitivity to changes in interest rates.* For example, we know that for a 6% 20-year bond selling to yield 6%, a rise in the yield required by investors to 6.5% will cause the bond's price to decline from 100 to 94.4479, a 5.55% price decline. Similarly for a 6% 5-year bond selling to yield 6%, the price is 100. A rise in the yield required by investors from 6% to 6.5% would decrease the price to 97.8944. The decline in the bond's price is only 2.11%.

2.2.2 The Impact of Coupon Rate

A property of a bond is that all other factors constant, *the lower the coupon rate, the greater the bond's price sensitivity to changes in interest rates.* For example, consider a 9% 20-year bond selling to yield 6%. The price of this bond would be 134.6722. If the yield required by investors increases by 50 basis points to 6.5%, the price of this bond would fall by 5.13% to 127.7605. This decline is less than the 5.55% decline for the 6% 20-year bond selling to yield 6% discussed above.

An implication is that zero-coupon bonds have greater price sensitivity to interest rate changes than same-maturity bonds bearing a coupon rate and trading at the same yield.

---

[4] Recall from Reading 65 that an embedded option is the feature in a bond issue that grants either the issuer or the investor an option. Examples include call option, put option, and conversion option.

2.2.3 *The Impact of Embedded Options*

In Reading 65, we discussed the various embedded options that may be included in a bond issue. As we continue our study of fixed income analysis, we will see that the value of a bond with embedded options will change depending on how the value of the embedded options changes when interest rates change. For example, we will see that as interest rates decline, the price of a callable bond may not increase as much as an otherwise option-free bond (that is, a bond with no embedded options).

For now, to understand why, let's decompose the price of a callable bond into two components, as shown below:

price of callable bond = price of option-free bond − price of embedded call option

The reason for subtracting the price of the embedded call option from the price of the option-free bond is that the call option is a benefit to the issuer and a disadvantage to the bondholder. This reduces the price of a callable bond relative to an option-free bond.

Now, when interest rates decline, the price of an option-free bond increases. However, the price of the embedded call option in a callable bond also increases because the call option becomes more valuable to the issuer. So, when interest rates decline both price components increase in value, *but* the change in the price of the callable bond depends on the relative price change between the two components. Typically, a decline in interest rates will result in an increase in the price of the callable bond but not by as much as the price change of an otherwise comparable option-free bond.

Similarly, when interest rates rise, the price of a callable bond will not fall as much as an otherwise option-free bond. The reason is that the price of the embedded call option declines. So, when interest rates rise, the price of the option-free bond declines but this is partially offset by the decrease in the price of the embedded call option component.

Practice Question 2

All of the issues below are option-free bonds and the yield required by the market for each bond is the same. Which issue has the greatest interest rate risk and which has the least interest rate risk?

Issue	Coupon Rate	Maturity
1	5¼%	15 years
2	6½%	12 years
3	4¾%	20 years
4	8½%	10 years

(No calculations are required.)

2.3 The Impact of the Yield Level

Because of credit risk (discussed later), different bonds trade at different yields, even if they have the same coupon rate, maturity, and embedded options. How, then, holding other factors constant, does the level of interest rates affect a bond's price sensitivity to changes in interest rates? As it turns out, the higher a bond's yield, the lower the price sensitivity.

To see this, we compare a 6% 20-year bond initially selling at a yield of 6%, and a 6% 20-year bond initially selling at a yield of 10%. The former is initially at a price of 100, and the latter 65.68. Now, if the yield for both bonds increases by 100 basis points, the first bond trades down by 10.68 points (10.68%) to a price of 89.32. The second bond will trade down to a price of 59.88, for a price decline of only 5.80 points (or 8.83%). Thus, we see that the bond that trades at a lower yield is more volatile in both percentage price change and absolute price change, as long as the other bond characteristics are the same. An implication of this is that, for a given change in interest rates, price sensitivity is lower when the level of interest rates in the market is high, and price sensitivity is higher when the level of interest rates is low.

Practice Question 3

The following four issues are all option-free bonds; which has the greatest interest rate risk?

Issue	Coupon Rate	Maturity	Required Yield by the Market
4	6½%	12 years	7.00%
5	7¼%	12 years	7.40%
6	6½%	12 years	7.20%
7	7½%	11 years	8.00%

(No calculations are required.)

2.4 Interest Rate Risk for Floating-Rate Securities

The change in the price of a fixed-rate coupon bond when market interest rates change is due to the fact that the bond's coupon rate differs from the prevailing market interest rate. For a floating-rate security, the coupon rate is reset periodically based on the prevailing market interest rate used as the reference rate plus a quoted margin. The quoted margin is set for the life of the security. The price of a floating-rate security will fluctuate depending on three factors.

First, the longer the time to the next coupon reset date, the greater the potential price fluctuation.[5] For example, consider a floating-rate security whose coupon resets every six months and suppose the coupon formula is the 6-month Treasury rate plus 20 basis points. Suppose that on the coupon reset date the 6-month Treasury rate is 5.8%. If on the day after the coupon reset date, the 6-month Treasury rate rises to 6.1%, this security is paying a 6-month coupon rate that is less than the prevailing 6-month rate for the next six months. The price of the security must decline to reflect this lower coupon rate. Suppose instead that the coupon resets every month at the 1-month Treasury rate and that this rate rises immediately after the coupon rate is reset. In this case, while the investor would be realizing a sub-

---

[5] As explained in Reading 65, the coupon reset formula is set at the reset date at the beginning of the period but is not paid until the end of the period.

market 1-month coupon rate, it is only for one month. The one month coupon bond's price decline will be less than the six month coupon bond's price decline.

The second reason why a floating-rate security's price will fluctuate is that the required margin that investors demand in the market changes. For example, consider once again the security whose coupon formula is the 6-month Treasury rate plus 20 basis points. If market conditions change such that investors want a margin of 30 basis points rather than 20 basis points, this security would be offering a coupon rate that is 10 basis points below the market rate. As a result, the security's price will decline.

Finally, a floating-rate security will typically have a cap. Once the coupon rate as specified by the coupon reset formula rises above the cap rate, the coupon will be set at the cap rate and the security will then offer a below-market coupon rate and its price will decline. In fact, once the cap is reached, the security's price will react much the same way to changes in market interest rates as that of a fixed-rate coupon security. This risk for a floating-rate security is called **cap risk**.

Practice Question 4

A floating-rate issue of NotReal.com has the following coupon formula that is reset every six months:

> coupon rate = 6-month Treasury rate + 120 basis points with a cap of 8.5%

a. Assume that subsequent to the issuance of this floater, the market wants a higher margin than 120 basis points for purchasing a similar issue to NotReal.com. What will happen to the price of this issue?

b. Assume that the 6-month Treasury rate was 4% when this issue was purchased by an investor but today the 6-month Treasury rate is 7%. What risk has increased since the time the NotReal.com issue was purchased?

2.5 Measuring Interest Rate Risk

Investors are interested in estimating the price sensitivity of a bond to changes in market interest rates. We will spend a good deal of time looking at how to quantify a bond's interest rate risk in Reading 72, as well as other readings. For now, let's see how we can get a rough idea of how to quantify the interest rate risk of a bond.

What we are interested in is a first approximation of how a bond's price will change when interest rates change. We can look at the price change in terms of (1) the percentage price change from the initial price or (2) the dollar price change from the initial price.

2.5.1 Approximate Percentage Price Change

The most straightforward way to calculate the percentage price change is to average the percentage price change resulting from an increase and a decrease in interest rates of the same number of basis points. For example, suppose that we are trying to estimate the sensitivity of the price of bond ABC that is currently selling for 90 to yield 6%. Now, suppose that interest rates increase by 25 basis points from 6% to 6.25%. The change in yield of 25 basis points is referred to as the "rate shock." The question is, how much will the price of bond ABC change due to this rate shock? To determine what the new price will be if the yield increases to 6.25%, *it is necessary to have a valuation model.* A valuation model provides an estimate of what the value of a bond will be for a given yield level. We will discuss the various models for valuing simple bonds and complex bonds with embedded options in later readings.

For now, we will assume that the valuation model tells us that the price of bond ABC will be 88 if the yield is 6.25%. This means that the price will decline by 2 points or 2.22% of the initial price of 90. If we divide the 2.22% by 25 basis points, the resulting number tells us that the price will decline by 0.0889% per 1 basis point change in yield.

Now suppose that the valuation model tells us that if yields decline from 6% to 5.75%, the price will increase to 92.7. This means that the price increases by 2.7 points or 3.00% of the initial price of 90. Dividing the 3.00% by 25 basis points indicates that the price will change by 0.1200% per 1 basis point change in yield.

We can average the two percentage price changes for a 1 basis point change in yield up and down. The average percentage price change is 0.1044% [= (0.0889% + 0.1200%)/2]. This means that for a 100 basis point change in yield, the average percentage price change is 10.44% (100 times 0.1044%).

A formula for estimating the *approximate percentage price change for a 100 basis point change in yield is:*

$$\frac{\text{price if yields decline} - \text{price if yields rise}}{2 \times (\text{initial price}) \times (\text{change in yield in decimal})}$$

In our illustration,

> price if yields decline by 25 basis points = 92.7
> price if yields rise by 25 basis points = 88.0
> initial price = 90
> change in yield in decimal = 0.0025

Substituting these values into the formula we obtain the approximate percentage price change for a 100 basis point change in yield to be:

$$\frac{92.7 - 88.0}{2 \times (90) \times (0.0025)} = 10.44$$

There is a special name given to this estimate of the percentage price change for a 100 basis point change in yield. It is called **duration**. As can be seen, duration is a measure of the price sensitivity of a bond to a change in yield. So, for example, if the duration of a bond is 10.44, this means that the approximate percentage price change if yields change by 100 basis points is 10.44%. For a 50 basis point change in yields, the approximate percentage price change is 5.22% (10.44% divided by 2). For a 25 basis point change in yield, the approximate percentage price change is 2.61% (10.44% divided by 4).

Notice that the approximate percentage is assumed to be the same for a rise and decline in yield. When we discuss the properties of the price volatility of a bond to changes in yield in Reading 72, we will see that the percentage price change is not symmetric and we will discuss the implication for using duration as a measure of interest rate risk. *It is important to note that the computed duration of a bond is only as good as the valuation model used to get the prices when the yield is shocked up and down. If the valuation model is unreliable, then the duration is a poor measure of the bond's price sensitivity to changes in yield.*

2.5.2 *Approximating the Dollar Price Change*

It is simple to move from duration, which measures the approximate percentage price change, to the approximate dollar price change of a position in a bond given the market value of the position and its duration. For example, consider again bond ABC with a duration of 10.44. Suppose that the market value of this bond is $5 million. Then for a 100 basis point change in yield, the approximate dollar price change is equal to 10.44% times $5 million, or $522,000. For a 50 basis point change in yield, the approximate dollar price change is $261,000; for a 25 basis point change in yield the approximate dollar price change is $130,500.

The approximate dollar price change for a 100 basis point change in yield is sometimes referred to as the **dollar duration**.

Practice Question 5

A. A portfolio manager wants to estimate the interest rate risk of a bond using duration. The current price of the bond is 106. A valuation model employed by the manager found that if interest rates decline by 25 basis points, the price will increase to 108.5 and if interest rates increase by the same number of basis points, the price will decline to 104. What is the duration of this bond?

B. If the portfolio manager purchased $10 million in market value of this bond, using duration to estimate the percentage price change, how much will the value of the bond change if interest rates change by 50 basis points?

YIELD CURVE RISK

3

We know that if interest rates or yields in the market change, the price of a bond will change. One of the factors that will affect how sensitive a bond's price is to changes in yield is the bond's maturity. A portfolio of bonds is a collection of bond issues typically with different maturities. So, when interest rates change, the price of each bond issue in the portfolio will change and the portfolio's value will change.

As you will see in Reading 68, there is not one interest rate or yield in the economy. There is a structure of interest rates. One important structure is the relationship between yield and maturity. The graphical depiction of this relationship is called the **yield curve**. As we will see in Reading 68, when interest rates change, they typically do not change by an equal number of basis points for all maturities.

For example, suppose that a $65 million portfolio contains the four bonds shown in Exhibit 66-1. All bonds are trading at a price equal to par value.

If we want to know how much the value of the portfolio changes if interest rates change, typically it is assumed that all yields change by the same number of basis points. Thus, if we wanted to know how sensitive the portfolio's value is to a 25 basis point change in yields, we would increase the yield of the four bond issues by 25 basis points, determine the new price of each bond, the market value of each bond, and the new value of the portfolio. Panel (a) of Exhibit 66-2 illustrates the 25 basis point increase in yield. For our hypothetical portfolio, the value of each bond issue changes as shown in panel (a) of Exhibit 66-1. The portfolio's value decreases by $1,759,003 from $65 million to $63,240,997.

Suppose that, instead of an equal basis point change in the yield for all maturities, the 20-year yield changes by 25 basis points, but the yields for the other maturities change as follows: (1) 2-year maturity changes by 10 basis points (from 5% to 5.1%), (2) 5-year maturity changes by 20 basis points (from 5.25% to 5.45%), and (3) 30-year maturity changes by 45 basis points (from 5.75% to 6.2%). Panel (b) of Exhibit 66-2 illustrates these yield changes. We will see at Level II that this type of movement (or shift) in the yield curve is referred to as a "steepening of the yield curve." For this type of yield curve shift, the portfolio's value is shown in panel (b) of Exhibit 66-1. The decline in the portfolio's value is $2,514,375 (from $65 million to $62,485,625).

EXHIBIT 66-1   **Illustration of Yield Curve Risk Composition of the Portfolio**

Bond	Coupon (%)	Maturity (years)	Yield (%)	Par Value ($)
A	5.00	2	5.00	5,000,000
B	5.25	5	5.25	10,000,000
C	5.50	20	5.50	20,000,000
D	5.75	30	5.75	30,000,000
Total				65,000,000

A. Parallel Shift in Yield Curve of +25 Basis Points

Bond	Coupon (%)	Maturity (years)	Original Yield (%)	Par Value ($)	New Yield (%)	New Bond Price	Value
A	5.00	2	5.00	5,000,000	5.25	99.5312	4,976,558
B	5.25	5	5.25	10,000,000	5.50	98.9200	9,891,999
C	5.50	20	5.50	20,000,000	5.75	97.0514	19,410,274
D	5.75	30	5.75	30,000,000	6.00	96.5406	28,962,166
Total				65,000,000			63,240,997

B. Nonparallel Shift of the Yield Curve

Bond	Coupon (%)	Maturity (years)	Original Yield (%)	Par Value ($)	New Yield (%)	New Bond Price	Value
A	5.00	2	5.00	5,000,000	5.10	99.8121	4,990,606
B	5.25	5	5.25	10,000,000	5.45	99.1349	9,913,488
C	5.50	20	5.50	20,000,000	5.75	97.0514	19,410,274
D	5.75	30	5.75	30,000,000	6.20	93.9042	28,171,257
Total				65,000,000			62,485,625

(Exhibit continued on next page ...)

EXHIBIT 66-1   (continued)

C. Nonparallel Shift of the Yield Curve

Bond	Coupon (%)	Maturity (years)	Original Yield (%)	Par Value ($)	New Yield (%)	New Bond Price	Value
A	5.00	2	5.00	5,000,000	5.05	99.9060	4,995,300
B	5.25	5	5.25	10,000,000	5.40	99.3503	9,935,033
C	5.50	20	5.50	20,000,000	5.75	97.0514	19,410,274
D	5.75	30	5.75	30,000,000	6.10	95.2082	28,562,467
Total				65,000,000			62,903,074

Suppose, instead, that if the 20-year yield changes by 25 basis points, the yields for the other three maturities change as follows: (1) 2-year maturity changes by 5 basis points (from 5% to 5.05%), (2) 5-year maturity changes by 15 basis points (from 5.25% to 5.40%), and (3) 30-year maturity changes by 35 basis points (from 5.75% to 6.1%). Panel (c) of Exhibit 66-2 illustrates this shift in yields. The new value for the portfolio based on this yield curve shift is shown in panel (c) of Exhibit 66-1. The decline in the portfolio's value is $2,096,926 (from $65 million to $62,903,074). The yield curve shift in the third illustration does not steepen as much as in the second, when the yield curve steepens considerably.

The point here is that portfolios have different exposures to how the yield curve shifts. This risk exposure is called **yield curve risk**. The implication is that

EXHIBIT 66-2   A. Parallel Shift in Yield Curve of +25 Basis Points

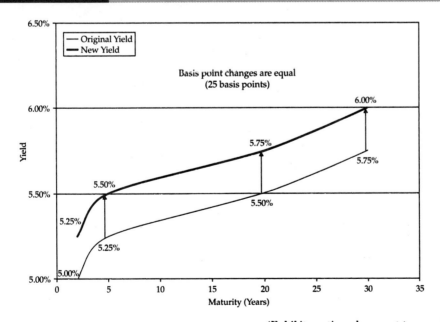

(Exhibit continued on next page ...)

EXHIBIT 66-2   (continued)

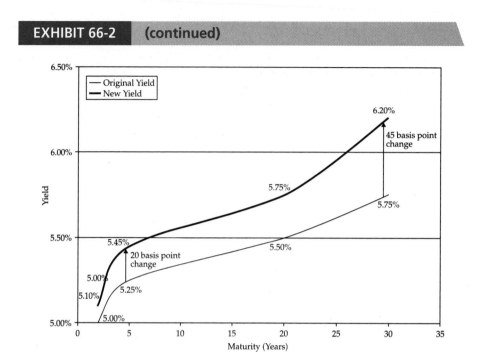

C. Another Nonparallel Shift of the Yield Curve

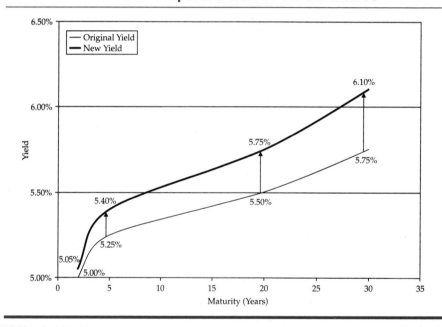

any measure of interest rate risk that assumes that the interest rates changes by an equal number of basis points for all maturities (referred to as a "parallel yield curve shift") is only an approximation.

This applies to the duration concept that we discussed above. We stated that the duration for an individual bond is the approximate percentage change in price for a 100 basis point change in yield. A duration for a portfolio has the same meaning: it is the approximate percentage change in the portfolio's value for a 100 basis point change in the yield *for all maturities*.

Because of the importance of yield curve risk, a good number of measures have been formulated to try to estimate the exposure of a portfolio to a non-parallel shift in the yield curve. We defer a discussion of these measures until Reading 72. However, we introduce one basic but popular approach here. In the next reading, we will see that the yield curve is a series of yields, one for each maturity. It is possible to determine the percentage change in the value of a portfolio if only one maturity's yield changes while the yield for all other maturities is unchanged. This is a form of duration called **rate duration**, where the word "rate" means the interest rate of a particular maturity. So, for example, suppose a portfolio consists of 40 bonds with different maturities. A "5-year rate duration" of 2 would mean that the portfolio's value will change by approximately 2% for a 100 basis point change in the 5-year yield, assuming all other rates do not change.

Practice Question 6

Suppose that an $85 million portfolio consists of the following five issues:

Issue	Maturity	Market value
1	2 years	$20 million
2	5 years	$15 million
3	10 years	$30 million
4	15 years	$5 million
5	28 years	$15 million

A. The portfolio manager computed a duration for the portfolio of 5. Approximately how much will the value of the portfolio decline if interest rates increase by 50 basis points?

B. In your calculation in part A, what is the assumption made in using the duration of 5 to compute the decline in the portfolio's value?

C. Suppose that the portfolio manager computes a 5-year rate duration of 1.5. What does that mean?

Consequently, in theory, there is not one rate duration but a rate duration for each maturity. In practice, a rate duration is not computed for all maturities. Instead, the rate duration is computed for several key maturities on the yield curve and this is referred to as **key rate duration**. Key rate duration is therefore simply the rate duration with respect to a change in a "key" maturity sector. Vendors of analytical systems report key rate durations for the maturities that in their view are the key maturity sectors. Key rate duration will be discussed further at Level II.

CALL AND PREPAYMENT RISK   4

As explained in Reading 65, a bond may include a provision that allows the issuer to retire, or call, all or part of the issue before the maturity date. From the investor's perspective, there are three disadvantages to call provisions:

Disadvantage 1: The cash flow pattern of a callable bond is not known with certainty because it is not known when the bond will be called.

Disadvantage 2: Because the issuer is likely to call the bonds when interest rates have declined below the bond's coupon rate, the investor is exposed to reinvestment risk, i.e., the investor will have to reinvest the proceeds when the bond is called at interest rates lower than the bond's coupon rate.

Disadvantage 3: The price appreciation potential of the bond will be reduced relative to an otherwise comparable option-free bond. (This is called **price compression**.)

We explained the third disadvantage in Section 2 when we discussed how the price of a callable bond may not rise as much as an otherwise comparable option-free bond when interest rates decline.

Because of these three disadvantages faced by the investor, a callable bond is said to expose the investor to **call risk**. The same disadvantages apply to mortgage-backed and asset-backed securities where the borrower can prepay principal prior to scheduled principal payment dates. This risk is referred to as **prepayment risk**.

5   REINVESTMENT RISK

Reinvestment risk is the risk that the proceeds received from the payment of interest and principal (i.e., scheduled payments, called proceeds, and principal prepayments) that are available for reinvestment must be reinvested at a lower interest rate than the security that generated the proceeds. We already saw how reinvestment risk is present when an investor purchases a callable or principal prepayable bond. When the issuer calls a bond, it is typically done to lower the issuer's interest expense because interest rates have declined after the bond is issued. The investor faces the problem of having to reinvest the called bond proceeds received from the issuer in a lower interest rate environment.

Reinvestment risk also occurs when an investor purchases a bond and relies on the yield of that bond as a measure of return. We have not yet explained how to compute the "yield" for a bond. When we do, it will be demonstrated that for the yield computed at the time of purchase to be realized, the investor must be able to reinvest any coupon payments at the computed yield. So, for example, if an investor purchases a 20-year bond with a yield of 6%, to realize the yield of 6%, every time a coupon interest payment is made, it is necessary to reinvest the payment at an interest rate of at 6% until maturity. So, it is assumed that the first coupon payment can be reinvested for the next 19.5 years at 6%; the second coupon payment can be reinvested for the next 19 years at 6%, and so on. The risk that the coupon payments will be reinvested at less than 6% is also reinvestment risk.

When dealing with amortizing securities (i.e., securities that repay principal periodically), reinvestment risk is even greater. Typically, amortizing securities pay interest and principal monthly and permit the borrower to prepay principal prior to schedule payment dates. Now the investor is more concerned with reinvestment risk due to principal prepayments usually resulting from a decline in interest rates, just as in the case of a callable bond. However, since payments are monthly, the investor has to make sure that the interest and principal can be reinvested at no less than the computed yield every month as opposed to semiannually.

This reinvestment risk for an amortizing security is important to understand. Too often it is said by some market participants that securities that pay both interest and principal monthly are advantageous because the investor has the opportunity to reinvest more frequently and to reinvest a larger amount (because principal is received) relative to a bond that pays only semiannual coupon payments. This is not the case in a declining interest rate environment, which will cause borrowers to accelerate their principal prepayments and force the investor to reinvest at lower interest rates.

With an understanding of reinvestment risk, we can now appreciate why zero-coupon bonds may be attractive to certain investors. Because there are no coupon payments to reinvest, there is no reinvestment risk. That is, zero-coupon bonds eliminate reinvestment risk. Elimination of reinvestment risk is important to some investors. That's the plus side of the risk equation. The minus side is that, as explained in Section 2, the lower the coupon rate the greater the interest rate risk for two bonds with the same maturity. Thus, zero-coupon bonds of a given maturity expose investors to the greatest interest rate risk.

Once we cover our basic analytical tools in later readings, we will see how to quantify a bond issue's reinvestment risk.

CREDIT RISK 6

An investor who lends funds by purchasing a bond issue is exposed to **credit risk**. There are three types of credit risk:

1. default risk
2. credit spread risk
3. downgrade risk

We discuss each type below.

6.1 Default Risk

Default risk is defined as the risk that the issuer will fail to satisfy the terms of the obligation with respect to the timely payment of interest and principal.

Studies have examined the probability of issuers defaulting. The percentage of a population of bonds that is expected to default is called the **default rate**. If a default occurs, this does not mean the investor loses the entire amount invested. An investor can expect to recover a certain percentage of the investment. This is called the **recovery rate**. Given the default rate and the recovery rate, the estimated expected loss due to a default can be computed. We will explain the findings of studies on default rates and recovery rates in Reading 67.

6.2 Credit Spread Risk

Even in the absence of default, an investor is concerned that the market value of a bond will decline and/or the price performance of a bond will be worse than that of other bonds. To understand this, recall that the price of a bond changes in the opposite direction to the change in the yield required by the market. Thus, if yields in the economy increase, the price of a bond declines, and vice versa.

As we will see in Reading 67, the yield on a bond is made up of two components: (1) the yield on a similar default-free bond issue and (2) a premium above the yield on a default-free bond issue necessary to compensate for the risks associated with the bond. The risk premium is referred to as a **yield spread**. In the

United States, Treasury issues are the benchmark yields because they are believed to be default free, they are highly liquid, and they are not callable (with the exception of some old issues). The part of the risk premium or yield spread attributable to default risk is called the **credit spread**.

The price performance of a non-Treasury bond issue and the return over some time period will depend on how the credit spread changes. If the credit spread increases, investors say that the spread has "widened" and the market price of the bond issue will decline (assuming U.S. Treasury rates have not changed). The risk that an issuer's debt obligation will decline due to an increase in the credit spread is called **credit spread risk**.

This risk exists for an individual issue, for issues in a particular industry or economic sector, and for all non-Treasury issues in the economy. For example, in general during economic recessions, investors are concerned that issuers will face a decline in cash flows that would be used to service their bond obligations. As a result, the credit spread tends to widen for U.S. non-Treasury issuers and the prices of all such issues throughout the economy will decline.

6.3 Downgrade Risk

While portfolio managers seek to allocate funds among different sectors of the bond market to capitalize on anticipated changes in credit spreads, an analyst investigating the credit quality of an individual issue is concerned with the prospects of the credit spread increasing for that particular issue. But how does the analyst assess whether he or she believes the market will change the credit spread associated with an individual issue?

One tool investors use to gauge the default risk of an issue is the credit ratings assigned to issues by rating companies, popularly referred to as **rating agencies**. There are three rating agencies in the United States: Moody's Investors Service, Inc., Standard & Poor's Corporation, and Fitch Ratings.

A **credit rating** is an indicator of the potential default risk associated with a particular bond issue or issuer. It represents in a simplistic way the credit rating agency's assessment of an issuer's ability to meet the payment of principal and interest in accordance with the terms of the indenture. Credit rating symbols or characters are uncomplicated representations of more complex ideas. In effect, they are summary opinions. Exhibit 66-3 identifies the ratings assigned by Moody's, S&P, and Fitch for bonds and the meaning of each rating.

In all systems, the term **high grade** means low credit risk, or conversely, a high probability of receiving future payments is promised by the issuer. The highest-grade bonds are designated by Moody's by the symbol Aaa, and by S&P and Fitch by the symbol AAA. The next highest grade is denoted by the symbol Aa (Moody's) or AA (S&P and Fitch); for the third grade, all three rating companies use A. The next three grades are Baa or BBB, Ba or BB, and B, respectively. There are also C grades. Moody's uses 1, 2, or 3 to provide a narrower credit quality breakdown within each class, and S&P and Fitch use plus and minus signs for the same purpose.

Bonds rated triple A (AAA or Aaa) are said to be **prime grade**; double A (AA or Aa) are of **high quality grade**; single A issues are called **upper medium grade**, and triple B are **lower medium grade**. Lower-rated bonds are said to have **speculative grade** elements or to be **distinctly speculative grade**.

Bond issues that are assigned a rating in the top four categories (that is, AAA, AA, A, and BBB) are referred to as **investment-grade bonds**. Issues that carry a rating below the top four categories are referred to as **non-investment-**

grade bonds or **speculative bonds**, or more popularly as **high yield bonds** or **junk bonds**. Thus, the bond market can be divided into two sectors: the investment grade and non-investment grade markets as summarized below:

Investment grade bonds　　　　　　　　　　　AAA, AA, A, and BBB
Non-investment grade bonds (speculative/high yield)　Below BBB

Once a credit rating is assigned to a debt obligation, a rating agency monitors the credit quality of the issuer and can reassign a different credit rating. An improvement in the credit quality of an issue or issuer is rewarded with a better credit rating, referred to as an **upgrade**; a deterioration in the credit rating of an issue or issuer is penalized by the assignment of an inferior credit rating, referred to as a **downgrade**. An unanticipated downgrading of an issue or issuer increases the credit spread and results in a decline in the price of the issue or the issuer's bonds. This risk is referred to as **downgrade risk** and is closely related to credit spread risk.

As we have explained, the credit rating is a measure of potential default risk. An analyst must be aware of how rating agencies gauge default risk for purposes of assigning ratings in order to understand the other aspects of credit risk. The agencies' assessment of potential default drives downgrade risk, and in turn, both default potential and credit rating changes drive credit spread risk.

A popular tool used by managers to gauge the prospects of an issue being downgraded or upgraded is a **rating transition matrix**. This is simply a table constructed by the rating agencies that shows the percentage of issues that were downgraded or upgraded in a given time period. So, the table can be used to approximate downgrade risk and default risk.

EXHIBIT 66-3			Bond Rating Symbols and Summary Description
Moody's	**S&P**	**Fitch**	**Summary Description**
		Investment Grade—High Credit Worthiness	
Aaa	AAA	AAA	Gilt edge, prime, maximum safety
Aa1	AA+	AA+	
Aa2	AA	AA	High-grade, high-credit quality
Aa3	AA−	AA−	
A1	A+	A+	
A2	A	A	Upper-medium grade
A3	A−	A−	
Baa1	BBB+	BBB+	
Baa2	BBB	BBB	Lower-medium grade
Baa3	BBB−	BBB−	

(Exhibit continued on next page ...)

EXHIBIT 66-3		(continued)	
Moody's	**S&P**	**Fitch**	**Summary Description**
		Speculative—Lower Credit Worthiness	
Ba1	BB+	BB+	
Ba2	BB	BB	Low grade, speculative
Ba3	BB−	BB−	
B1		B+	
B2	B	B	Highly speculative
B3		B−	
	Predominantly Speculative, Substantial Risk, or in Default		
	CCC+	CCC+	
Caa	CCC	CCC	Substantial risk, in poor standing
Ca	CC	CC	May be in default, very speculative
C	C	C	Extremely speculative
	CI		Income bonds—no interest being paid
		DDD	
		DD	Default
	D	D	

Exhibit 66-4 shows a hypothetical rating transition matrix for a 1-year period. The first column shows the ratings at the start of the year and the top row shows the rating at the end of the year. Let's interpret one of the numbers. Look at the cell where the rating at the beginning of the year is AA and the rating at the end of the year is AA. This cell represents the percentage of issues rated AA at the beginning of the year that did not change their rating over the year. That is, there were no downgrades or upgrades. As can be seen, 92.75% of the issues rated AA at the start of the year were rated AA at the end of the year. Now look at the cell where the rating at the beginning of the year is AA and at the end of the year

EXHIBIT 66-4	**Hypothetical 1-Year Rating Transition Matrix**							
Rating at Start of Year	**Rating at End of Year**							
	AAA	**AA**	**A**	**BBB**	**BB**	**B**	**CCC**	**D**	**Total**
AAA	93.20	6.00	0.60	0.12	0.08	0.00	0.00	0.00	100
AA	1.60	92.75	5.07	0.36	0.11	0.07	0.03	0.01	100
A	0.18	2.65	91.91	4.80	0.37	0.02	0.02	0.05	100
BBB	0.04	0.30	5.20	87.70	5.70	0.70	0.16	0.20	100
BB	0.03	0.11	0.61	6.80	81.65	7.10	2.60	1.10	100
B	0.01	0.09	0.55	0.88	7.90	75.67	8.70	6.20	100
CCC	0.00	0.01	0.31	0.84	2.30	8.10	62.54	25.90	100

is A. This shows the percentage of issues rated AA at the beginning of the year that were downgraded to A by the end of the year. In our hypothetical 1-year rating transition matrix, this percentage is 5.07%. One can view these percentages as probabilities. There is a probability that an issue rated AA will be downgraded to A by the end of the year and it is 5.07%. One can estimate total downgrade risk as well. Look at the row that shows issues rated AA at the beginning of the year. The cells in the columns A, BBB, BB, B, CCC, and D all represent downgrades from AA. Thus, if we add all of these columns in this row (5.07%, 0.36%, 0.11%, 0.07%, 0.03%, and 0.01%), we get 5.65% which is an estimate of the probability of an issue being downgraded from AA in one year. Thus, 5.65% can be viewed as an estimate of downgrade risk.

A rating transition matrix also shows the potential for upgrades. Again, using Exhibit 66-4 look at the row that shows issues rated AA at the beginning of the year. Looking at the cell shown in the column AAA rating at the end of the year, one finds 1.60%. This is the percentage of issues rated AA at the beginning of the year that were upgraded to AAA by the end of the year.

Finally, look at the D rating category. These are issues that go into default. We can use the information in the column with the D rating at the end of the year to estimate the probability that an issue with a particular rating will go into default at the end of the year. Hence, this would be an estimate of default risk. So, for example, the probability that an issue rated AA at the beginning of the year will go into default by the end of the year is 0.01%. In contrast, the probability of an issue rated CCC at the beginning of the year will go into default by the end of the year is 25.9%.

LIQUIDITY RISK　　　　7

When an investor wants to sell a bond prior to the maturity date, he or she is concerned with whether or not the bid price from broker/dealers is close to the indicated value of the issue. For example, if recent trades in the market for a particular issue have been between $90 and $90.5 and market conditions have not changed, an investor would expect to sell the bond somewhere in the $90 to $90.5 range.

Liquidity risk is the risk that the investor will have to sell a bond below its indicated value, where the indication is revealed by a recent transaction. The primary measure of liquidity is the size of the spread between the bid price (the price at which a dealer is willing to buy a security) and the ask price (the price at which a dealer is willing to sell a security). The wider the bid-ask spread, the greater the liquidity risk.

A liquid market can generally be defined by "small bid-ask spreads which do not materially increase for large transactions."[6] How to define the bid-ask spread in a multiple dealer market is subject to interpretation. For example, consider the bid-ask prices for four dealers. Each quote is for $92 plus the number of 32nds shown in Exhibit 66-5. The bid-ask spread shown in the exhibit is measured relative to a specific dealer. The best bid-ask spread is for $2/_{32}$ Dealers 2 and 3.

From the perspective of the overall market, the bid-ask spread can be computed by looking at the best bid price (high price at which a broker/dealer is willing to buy a security) and the lowest ask price (lowest offer price at which a broker/dealer is willing to sell the same security). This liquidity measure is called the **market bid-ask spread**. For the four dealers, the highest bid price is $92 {}^2/_{32}$ and the lowest ask price is $92 {}^3/_{32}$. Thus, the market bid-ask spread is $^1/_{32}$.

---

[6] Robert I. Gerber, "A User's Guide to Buy-Side Bond Trading," Chapter 16 in Frank J. Fabozzi (ed.), *Managing Fixed Income Portfolios* (New Hope, PA: Frank J. Fabozzi Associates, 1997), p. 278.

EXHIBIT 66-5	Broker/Dealer Bid-Ask Spreads for a Specific Security

	Dealer			
	1	**2**	**3**	**4**
Bid price	1	1	2	2
Ask price	4	3	4	5

Bid-ask spread for each dealer (in 32nds):

	Dealer			
	1	**2**	**3**	**4**
Bid-ask spread	3	2	2	3

7.1 Liquidity Risk and Marking Positions to Market

For investors who plan to hold a bond until maturity and need *not* mark the position to market, liquidity risk is not a major concern. An institutional investor who plans to hold an issue to maturity but is periodically marked to market is concerned with liquidity risk. By marking a position to market, the security is revalued in the portfolio based on its current market price. For example, mutual funds are required to mark to market at the end of each day the investments in their portfolio in order to compute the mutual fund's net asset value (NAV). While other institutional investors may not mark to market as frequently as mutual funds, they are marked to market when reports are periodically sent to clients or the board of directors or trustees.

Where are the prices obtained to mark a position to market? Typically, a portfolio manager will solicit bids from several broker/dealers and then use some process to determine the bid price used to mark (i.e., value) the position. The less liquid the issue, the greater the variation there will be in the bid prices obtained from broker/dealers. With an issue that has little liquidity, the price may have to be determined from a pricing service (i.e., a service company that employs models to determine the fair value of a security) rather than from dealer bid prices.

In Reading 65 we discussed the use of repurchase agreements as a form of borrowing funds to purchase bonds. The bonds purchased are used as collateral. The bonds purchased are marked to market periodically in order to determine whether or not the collateral provides adequate protection to the lender for funds borrowed (i.e., the dealer providing the financing). When liquidity in the market declines, a portfolio manager who has borrowed funds must rely solely on the bid prices determined by the dealer lending the funds.

7.2 Changes in Liquidity Risk

Bid-ask spreads, and therefore liquidity risk, change over time. Changing market liquidity is a concern to portfolio managers who are contemplating investing in new complex bond structures. Situations such as an unexpected change in interest rates might cause a widening of the bid-ask spread, as investors and dealers are reluctant to take new positions until they have had a chance to assess the new market level of interest rates.

Here is another example of where market liquidity may change. While there are opportunities for those who invest in a new type of bond structure, there are typically few dealers making a market when the structure is so new. If subsequently the new structure becomes popular, more dealers will enter the market and liquidity improves. In contrast, if the new bond structure turns out to be unappealing, the initial buyers face a market with less liquidity because some dealers exit the market and others offer bids that are unattractive because they do not want to hold the bonds for a potential new purchaser.

Thus, we see that the liquidity risk of an issue changes over time. An actual example of a change in market liquidity occurred during the Spring of 1994. One sector of the mortgage-backed securities market, called the derivative mortgage market, saw the collapse of an important investor (a hedge fund) and the resulting exit from the market of several dealers. As a result, liquidity in the market substantially declined and bid-ask spreads widened dramatically.

EXCHANGE RATE OR CURRENCY RISK   8

A bond whose payments are not in the domestic currency of the portfolio manager has unknown cash flows in his or her domestic currency. The cash flows in the manager's domestic currency are dependent on the exchange rate at the time the payments are received from the issuer. For example, suppose a portfolio manager's domestic currency is the U.S. dollar and that manager purchases a bond whose payments are in Japanese yen. If the yen depreciates relative to the U.S. dollar at the time a payment is made, then fewer U.S. dollars can be exchanged.

As another example, consider a portfolio manager in the United Kingdom. This manager's domestic currency is the pound. If that manager purchases a U.S. dollar denominated bond, then the manager is concerned that the U.S. dollar will depreciate relative to the British pound when the issuer makes a payment. If the U.S. dollar does depreciate, then fewer British pounds will be received on the foreign exchange market.

The risk of receiving less of the domestic currency when investing in a bond issue that makes payments in a currency other than the manager's domestic currency is called **exchange rate risk** or **currency risk**.

INFLATION OR PURCHASING POWER RISK   9

Inflation risk or **purchasing power risk** arises from the decline in the value of a security's cash flows due to inflation, which is measured in terms of purchasing power. For example, if an investor purchases a bond with a coupon rate of 5%, but the inflation rate is 3%, the purchasing power of the investor has not increased by 5%. Instead, the investor's purchasing power has increased by only about 2%.

For all but inflation protection bonds, an investor is exposed to inflation risk because the interest rate the issuer promises to make is fixed for the life of the issue.

10   VOLATILITY RISK

In our discussion of the impact of embedded options on the interest rate risk of a bond in Section 2, we said that a change in the factors that affect the value of the embedded options will affect how the bond's price will change. Earlier, we looked at how a change in the level of interest rates will affect the price of a bond with an embedded option. But there are other factors that will affect the price of an embedded option.

While we discuss these other factors at Level II, we can get an appreciation of one important factor from a general understanding of option pricing. A major factor affecting the value of an option is "expected volatility." In the case of an option on common stock, expected volatility refers to "expected price volatility." The relationship is as follows: the greater the expected price volatility, the greater the value of the option. The same relationship holds for options on bonds. However, instead of expected price volatility, for bonds it is the "expected yield volatility." The greater the expected yield volatility, the greater the value (price) of an option. The interpretation of yield volatility and how it is estimated are explained at Level II.

Now let us tie this into the pricing of a callable bond. We repeat the formula for the components of a callable bond below:

> Price of callable bond = Price of option-free bond − Price of embedded call option

If expected yield volatility increases, holding all other factors constant, the price of the embedded call option will increase. As a result, the price of a callable bond will decrease (because the former is subtracted from the price of the option-free bond).

To see how a change in expected yield volatility affects the price of a putable bond, we can write the price of a putable bond as follows:

> Price of putable bond = Price of option-free bond + Price of embedded put option

A decrease in expected yield volatility reduces the price of the embedded put option and therefore will decrease the price of a putable bond. Thus, the volatility risk of a putable bond is that expected yield volatility will decrease.

This risk that the price of a bond with an embedded option will decline when expected yield volatility changes is called **volatility risk**. Below is a summary of the effect of changes in expected yield volatility on the price of callable and putable bonds:

Type of Embedded Option	Volatility Risk due to
Callable bonds	an increase in expected yield volatility
Putable bonds	a decrease in expected yield volatility

11   EVENT RISK

Occasionally the ability of an issuer to make interest and principal payments changes dramatically and unexpectedly because of factors including the following:

1. a natural disaster (such as an earthquake or hurricane) or an industrial accident that impairs an issuer's ability to meet its obligations

2. a takeover or corporate restructuring that impairs an issuer's ability to meet its obligations

3. a regulatory change

These factors are commonly referred to as **event risk**.

11.1 Corporate Takeover/Restructurings

The first type of event risk results in a credit rating downgrade of an issuer by rating agencies and is therefore a form of downgrade risk. However, downgrade risk is typically confined to the particular issuer whereas event risk from a natural disaster usually affects more than one issuer.

The second type of event risk also results in a downgrade and can also impact other issuers. An excellent example occurred in the fall of 1988 with the leveraged buyout (LBO) of RJR Nabisco, Inc. The entire industrial sector of the bond market suffered as bond market participants withdrew from the market, new issues were postponed, and secondary market activity came to a standstill as a result of the initial LBO bid announcement. The yield that investors wanted on Nabisco's bonds increased by about 250 basis points. Moreover, because the RJR LBO demonstrated that size was not an obstacle for an LBO, other large industrial firms that market participants previously thought were unlikely candidates for an LBO were fair game. The spillover effect to other industrial companies of the RJR LBO resulted in required yields' increasing dramatically.

11.2 Regulatory Risk

The third type of risk listed above is **regulatory risk**. This risk comes in a variety of forms. Regulated entities include investment companies, depository institutions, and insurance companies. Pension funds are regulated by ERISA. Regulation of these entities is in terms of the acceptable securities in which they may invest and/or the treatment of the securities for regulatory accounting purposes.

Changes in regulations may require a regulated entity to divest itself from certain types of investments. A flood of the divested securities on the market will adversely impact the price of similar securities.

SOVEREIGN RISK   12

When an investor acquires a bond issued by a foreign entity (e.g., a French investor acquiring a Brazilian government bond), the investor faces **sovereign risk**. This is the risk that, as a result of actions of the foreign government, there may be either a default or an adverse price change even in the absence of a default. This is analogous to the forms of credit risk described in Section 6—credit risk spread and downgrade risk. That is, even if a foreign government does not default, actions by a foreign government can increase the credit risk spread sought by investors or increase the likelihood of a downgrade. Both of these will have an adverse impact on a bond's price.

Sovereign risk consists of two parts. First is the unwillingness of a foreign government to pay. A foreign government may simply repudiate its debt. The second is the inability to pay due to unfavorable economic conditions in the country. Historically, most foreign government defaults have been due to a government's inability to pay rather than unwillingness to pay.

SUMMARY

▶ The price of a bond changes inversely with a change in market interest rates.

▶ Interest rate risk refers to the adverse price movement of a bond as a result of a change in market interest rates; for the bond investor typically it is the risk that interest rates will rise.

▶ A bond's interest rate risk depends on the features of the bond—maturity, coupon rate, yield, and embedded options.

▶ All other factors constant, the longer the bond's maturity, the greater is the bond's price sensitivity to changes in interest rates.

▶ All other factors constant, the lower the coupon rate, the greater the bond's price sensitivity to changes in interest rates.

▶ The price of a callable bond is equal to the price of an option-free bond minus the price of any embedded call option.

▶ When interest rates rise, the price of a callable bond will not fall by as much as an otherwise comparable option-free bond because the price of the embedded call option decreases.

▶ The price of a putable bond is equal to the price of an option-free bond plus the price of the embedded put option.

▶ All other factors constant, the higher the level of interest rate at which a bond trades, the lower is the price sensitivity when interest rates change.

▶ The price sensitivity of a bond to changes in interest rates can be measured in terms of (1) the percentage price change from initial price or (2) the dollar price change from initial price.

▶ The most straightforward way to calculate the percentage price change is to average the percentage price change due to the same increase and decrease in interest rates.

▶ Duration is a measure of interest rate risk; it measures the price sensitivity of a bond to interest rate changes.

▶ Duration can be interpreted as the approximate percentage price change of a bond for a 100 basis point change in interest rates.

▶ The computed duration is only as good as the valuation model used to obtain the prices when interest rates are shocked up and down by the same number of basis points.

▶ There can be substantial differences in the duration of complex bonds because valuation models used to obtain prices can vary.

▶ Given the duration of a bond and its market value, the dollar price change can be computed for a given change in interest rates.

▶ Yield curve risk for a portfolio occurs when, if interest rates increase by different amounts at different maturities, the portfolio's value will be different than if interest rates had increased by the same amount.

▶ A portfolio's duration measures the sensitivity of the portfolio's value to changes in interest rates assuming the interest rates for all maturities change by the same amount.

▶ Any measure of interest rate risk that assumes interest rates change by the same amount for all maturities (referred to as a "parallel yield curve shift") is only an approximation.

▶ One measure of yield curve risk is rate duration, which is the approximate percentage price change for a 100 basis point change in the interest rate for one maturity, holding all other maturity interest rates constant.

▶ Call risk and prepayment risk refer to the risk that a security will be paid prior to the scheduled principal payment dates.

▶ Reinvestment risk is the risk that interest and principal payments (scheduled payments, called proceeds, or prepayments) available for reinvestment must be reinvested at a lower interest rate than the security that generated the proceeds.

▶ From an investor's perspective, the disadvantages to call and prepayment provisions are (1) the cash flow pattern is uncertain, (2) reinvestment risk increases because proceeds received will have to be reinvested at a relatively lower interest rate, and (3) the capital appreciation potential of a bond is reduced.

▶ Reinvestment risk for an amortizing security can be significant because of the right to prepay principal and the fact that interest and principal are repaid monthly.

▶ A zero-coupon bond has no reinvestment risk but has greater interest rate risk than a coupon bond of the same maturity.

▶ There are three forms of credit risk: default risk, credit spread risk, and downgrade risk.

▶ Default risk is the risk that the issuer will fail to satisfy the terms of indebtedness with respect to the timely payment of interest and principal.

▶ Credit spread risk is the risk that the price of an issuer's bond will decline due to an increase in the credit spread.

▶ Downgrade risk is the risk that one or more of the rating agencies will reduce the credit rating of an issue or issuer.

▶ There are three rating agencies in the United States: Standard & Poor's Corporation, Moody's Investors Service, Inc., and Fitch.

▶ A credit rating is an indicator of the potential default risk associated with a particular bond issue that represents in a simplistic way the credit rater's assessment of an issuer's ability to pay principal and interest in accordance with the terms of the debt contract.

▶ A rating transition matrix is prepared by rating agencies to show the change in credit ratings over some time period.

▶ A rating transition matrix can be used to estimate downgrade risk and default risk.

▶ Liquidity risk is the risk that the investor will have to sell a bond below its indicated value.

▶ The primary measure of liquidity is the size of the spread between the bid and ask price quoted by dealers.

▶ A market bid-ask spread is the difference between the highest bid price and the lowest ask price from among dealers.

▶ The liquidity risk of an issue changes over time.

▶ Exchange rate risk arises when interest and principal payments of a bond are not denominated in the domestic currency of the investor.

▶ Exchange rate risk is the risk that the currency in which the interest and principal payments are denominated will decline relative to the domestic currency of the investor.

► Inflation risk or purchasing power risk arises from the decline in value of a security's cash flows due to inflation, which is measured in terms of purchasing power.

► Volatility risk is the risk that the price of a bond with an embedded option will decline when expected yield volatility changes.

► For a callable bond, volatility risk is the risk that expected yield volatility will increase; for a putable bond, volatility risk is the risk that expected yield volatility will decrease.

► Event risk is the risk that the ability of an issuer to make interest and principal payments changes dramatically and unexpectedly because of certain events such as a natural catastrophe, corporate takeover, or regulatory changes.

► Sovereign risk is the risk that a foreign government's actions cause a default or an adverse price decline on its bond issue.

PROBLEMS FOR READING 66

1. For each of the following issues, indicate whether the price of the issue should be par value, above par value, or below par value:

	Issue	Coupon Rate	Yield Required by Market
A.	A	5¼%	7.25%
B.	B	6⅝%	7.15%
C.	C	0%	6.20%
D.	D	5⅞%	5.00%
E.	E	4½%	4.50%

2. Explain why a callable bond's price would be expected to decline less than an otherwise comparable option-free bond when interest rates rise.

3. **A.** Short-term investors such as money market mutual funds invest in floating-rate securities having maturities greater than 1 year. Suppose that the coupon rate is reset everyday. Why is the interest rate risk small for such issues?

   B. Why would it be improper to say that a floating-rate security whose coupon rate resets every day has no interest rate risk?

4. John Smith and Jane Brody are assistant portfolio managers. The senior portfolio manager has asked them to consider the acquisition of one of two option-free bond issues with the following characteristics:

   Issue 1 has a lower coupon rate than Issue 2
   Issue 1 has a shorter maturity than Issue 2

   Both issues have the same credit rating.
   Smith and Brody are discussing the interest rate risk of the two issues. Smith argues that Issue 1 has greater interest rate risk than Issue 2 because of its lower coupon rate. Brody counters by arguing that Issue 2 has greater interest rate risk because it has a longer maturity than Issue 1.

   A. Which assistant portfolio manager is correct with respect to their selection to the issue with the greater interest rate risk?

   B. Suppose that you are the senior portfolio manager. How would you suggest that Smith and Brody determine which issue has the greater interest rate risk?

5. A portfolio manager wants to estimate the interest rate risk of a bond using duration. The current price of the bond is 82. A valuation model found that if interest rates decline by 30 basis points, the price will increase to 83.50 and if interest rates increase by 30 basis points, the price will decline to 80.75. What is the duration of this bond?

6. A portfolio manager purchased $8 million in market value of a bond with a duration of 5. For this bond, determine the estimated change in its market value for the change in interest rates shown below:

   A. 100 basis points

   B. 50 basis points

   C. 25 basis points

   D. 10 basis points

7. A portfolio manager of a bond fund is considering the acquisition of an extremely complex bond issue. It is complex because it has multiple embedded options. The manager wants to estimate the interest rate risk of the bond issue so that he can determine the impact of including it in his current portfolio. The portfolio manager contacts the dealer who created the bond issue to obtain an estimate for the issue's duration. The dealer estimates the duration to be 7. The portfolio manager solicited his firm's in-house quantitative analyst and asked her to estimate the issue's duration. She estimated the duration to be 10. Explain why there is such a dramatic difference in the issue's duration as estimated by the dealer's analysts and the firm's in-house analyst.

8. Duration is commonly used as a measure of interest rate risk. However, duration does not consider yield curve risk. Why?

9. What measure can a portfolio manager use to assess the interest rate risk of a portfolio to a change in the 5-year yield?

10. For the investor in a callable bond, what are the two forms of reinvestment risk?

11. Investors are exposed to credit risk when they purchase a bond. However, even if an issuer does not default on its obligation prior to its maturity date, there is still a concern about how credit risk can adversely impact the performance of a bond. Why?

12. Using the hypothetical rating transition matrix shown in Exhibit 66-4 of the reading, answer the following questions:

   A. What is the probability that a bond rated BBB will be downgraded?

   B. What is the probability that a bond rated BBB will go into default?

   C. What is the probability that a bond rated BBB will be upgraded?

   D. What is the probability that a bond rated B will be upgraded to investment grade?

   E. What is the probability that a bond rated A will be downgraded to non-investment grade?

   F. What is the probability that a AAA rated bond will *not* be downgraded at the end of one year?

13. Suppose that the bid and ask prices of five dealers for Issue XYX is 96 plus the number of 32nds shown:

	Dealer				
	1	2	3	4	5
Bid price	14	14	15	15	13
Ask price	18	17	18	20	19

What is the market bid-ask spread for Issue XYX?

14. A portfolio manager is considering the purchase of a new type of bond. The bond is extremely complex in terms of its embedded options. Currently, there is only one dealer making a market in this type of bond. In addition, the manager plans to finance the purchase of this bond by using the bond as collateral. The bond matures in five years and the manager plans to hold the bond for five years. Because the manager plans to hold the bond to its maturity, he has indicated that he is not concerned with liquidity risk. Explain why you agree or disagree with the manager's view that he is not concerned with liquidity risk.

15. Identify the difference in the major risks associated with the following investment alternatives:

   A. For an investor who plans to hold a security for one year, purchasing a Treasury security that matures in one year versus purchasing a Treasury security that matures in 30 years.

   B. For an investor who plans to hold an investment for 10 years, purchasing a Treasury security that matures in 10 years versus purchasing an AAA corporate security that matures in 10 years.

   C. For an investor who plans to hold an investment for two years, purchasing a zero-coupon Treasury security that matures in one year versus purchasing a zero-coupon Treasury security that matures in two years.

   D. For an investor who plans to hold an investment for five years, purchasing an AA sovereign bond (with dollar denominated cash flow payments) versus purchasing a U.S. corporate bond with a B rating.

   E. For an investor who plans to hold an investment for four years, purchasing a less actively traded 10-year AA rated bond versus purchasing a 10-year AA rated bond that is actively traded.

   F. For a U.S. investor who plans to hold an investment for six years, purchasing a Treasury security that matures in six years versus purchasing an Italian government security that matures in six years and is denominated in lira.

16. Sam Stevens is the trustee for the Hole Punchers Labor Union (HPLU). He has approached the investment management firm of IM Associates (IMA) to manage its $200 million bond portfolio. IMA assigned Carol Peters as the portfolio manager for the HPLU account. In their first meeting, Mr. Stevens told Ms. Peters:

   "We are an extremely conservative pension fund. We believe in investing in only investment grade bonds so that there will be minimal risk that the principal invested will be lost. We want at least 40% of the portfolio to be held in bonds that will mature within the next three years. I would like your thoughts on this proposed structure for the portfolio."

   How should Ms. Peters respond?

17. A. A treasurer of a municipality with a municipal pension fund has required that its in-house portfolio manager invest all funds in the highest investment grade securities that mature in one month or less. The treasurer believes that this is a safe policy. Comment on this investment policy.

   B. The same treasurer requires that the in-house portfolio municipality's operating fund (i.e., fund needed for day-to-day operations of the municipality) follow the same investment policy. Comment on the appropriateness of this investment policy for managing the municipality's operating fund.

18. In January 1994, General Electric Capital Corporation (GECC) had outstanding $500 million of Reset Notes due March 15, 2018. The reset notes were floating-rate securities. In January 1994, the bonds had an 8% coupon rate for three years that ended March 15, 1997. On January 26, 1994, GECC notified the noteholders that it would redeem the issue on March 15th at par value. This was within the required 30 to 60 day prior notice period. Investors who sought investments with very short-term instruments (e.g., money market investors) bought the notes after GECC's planned redemption announcement. The notes were viewed as short-term because they

would be redeemed in six weeks or so. In early February, the Federal Reserve started to boost interest rates and on February 15th, GECC canceled the proposed redemption. Instead, it decided to reset the new interest rate based on the indenture at 108% of the three-year Treasury rate in effect on the tenth day preceding the date of the new interest period of March 15th. *The Wall Street Journal* reported that the notes dropped from par to 98 ($1,000 to $980 per note) after the cancellation of the proposed redemption.*

Why did the price decline?

19. A British portfolio manager is considering investing in Japanese government bonds denominated in yen. What are the major risks associated with this investment?

20. Explain how certain types of event risk can result in downgrade risk.

21. Comment on the following statement: "Sovereign risk is the risk that a foreign government defaults on its obligation."

---

* To complete this story, investors were infuriated and they protested to GECC. On March 8th the new interest rate of 5.61% was announced in the financial press. On the very next day GECC announced a tender offer for the notes commencing March 17th. It would buy them back at par plus accrued interest on April 15th. This bailed out many investors who had faith in GECC's original redemption announcement.

OVERVIEW OF BOND SECTORS AND INSTRUMENTS

by Frank J. Fabozzi

LEARNING OUTCOMES

The candidate should be able to:

a. explain how a country's bond market sectors are classified, including the distinguishing characteristics of internal and external bonds;

b. describe the features, credit risk characteristics and distribution methods for government securities;

c. describe the types of securities issued by the U.S. Department of the Treasury (e.g. bills, notes, bonds, and inflation protection securities), and distinguish between on-the-run and off-the-run Treasury securities;

d. describe how stripped Treasury securities are created and distinguish between coupon strips and principal strips;

e. describe the types and characteristics of securities issued by U.S. federal agencies;

f. describe mortgage-backed securities (including mortgage passthrough securities, collateralized mortgage obligations, and stripped MBS), and explain the cash flows, prepayments and prepayment risk for each;

g. state the motivation for creating a collateralized mortgage obligation;

h. describe the types of securities issued by municipalities in the United States, and distinguish between tax-backed debt and revenue bonds;

i. describe the characteristics and motivation for the various types of debt used by corporations (including corporate bonds, medium-term notes, structured notes, commercial paper, negotiable CDs and bankers acceptances);

j. define an asset-backed security, describe the role of a special purpose vehicle in an asset-backed securities transaction, state the motivation for a corporation to issue an asset-backed security, and describe the types of external credit enhancements for asset-backed securities;

k. describe collateralized debt obligations;

l. describe the structures of the primary and secondary markets in bonds.

1   INTRODUCTION

Thus far we have covered the general features of bonds and the risks associated with investing in bonds. In this reading, we will review the major sectors of a country's bond market and the securities issued. This includes sovereign bonds, semi-government bonds, municipal or province securities, corporate debt securities, mortgage-backed securities, asset-backed securities, and collateralized debt obligations. Our coverage in this reading is to describe the instruments found in these sectors.

2   SECTORS OF THE BOND MARKET

While there is no uniform system for classifying the sectors of the bond markets throughout the world, we will use the classification shown in Exhibit 67-1. From the perspective of a given country, the bond market can be classified into two markets: an **internal bond market** and an **external bond market**.

2.1 Internal Bond Market

The internal bond market of a country is also called the **national bond market**. It is divided into two parts: the **domestic bond market** and the **foreign bond market**. The domestic bond market is where issuers domiciled in the country issue bonds and where those bonds are subsequently traded.

The foreign bond market of a country is where bonds of issuers not domiciled in the country are issued and traded. For example, in the United States, the foreign bond market is the market where bonds are issued by non–U.S. entities and then subsequently traded in the United States. In the U.K., a sterling-denominated bond issued by a Japanese corporation and subsequently traded in the U.K. bond market is part of the U.K. foreign bond market. Bonds in the foreign sector of a bond market have nicknames. For example, foreign bonds in the

---

EXHIBIT 67-1   **Overview of the Sectors of the Bond Market**

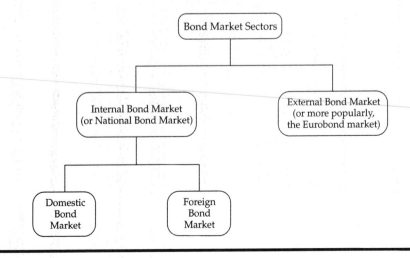

U.S. market are nicknamed "**Yankee bonds**" and sterling-denominated bonds in the U.K. foreign bond market are nicknamed "Bulldog bonds." Foreign bonds can be denominated in any currency. For example, a foreign bond issued by an Australian corporation in the United States can be denominated in U.S. dollars, Australian dollars, or euros.

Issuers of foreign bonds include central governments and their subdivisions, corporations, and supranationals. A **supranational** is an entity that is formed by two or more central governments through international treaties. Supranationals promote economic development for the member countries. Two examples of supranationals are the International Bank for Reconstruction and Development, popularly referred to as the World Bank, and the Inter-American Development Bank.

2.2 External Bond Market

The external bond market includes bonds with the following distinguishing features:

- they are underwritten by an international syndicate
- at issuance, they are offered simultaneously to investors in a number of countries
- they are issued outside the jurisdiction of any single country
- they are in unregistered form.

The external bond market is referred to as the **international bond market**, the **offshore bond market**, or, more popularly, the **Eurobond market**.[1] Throughout this book we will use the term Eurobond market to describe this sector of the bond market.

Eurobonds are classified based on the currency in which the issue is denominated. For example, when Eurobonds are denominated in U.S. dollars, they are referred to as Eurodollar bonds. Eurobonds denominated in Japanese yen are referred to as Euroyen bonds.

A **global bond** is a debt obligation that is issued and traded in the foreign bond market of one or more countries and the Eurobond market.

SOVEREIGN BONDS ◼ 3 ◢

In many countries that have a bond market, the largest sector is often bonds issued by a country's central government. These bonds are referred to as **sovereign bonds**. A government can issue securities in its national bond market which are subsequently traded within that market. A government can also issue bonds in the Eurobond market or the foreign sector of another country's bond market. While the currency denomination of a government security is typically the currency of the issuing country, a government can issue bonds denominated in any currency.

3.1 Credit Risk

An investor in any bond is exposed to credit risk. The perception throughout the world is that the credit risk of bonds issued by the U.S. government are virtually

---

[1] It should be noted that the classification used here is by no means universally accepted. Some market observers refer to the external bond market as consisting of the foreign bond market and the Eurobond market.

free of credit risk. Consequently, the market views these bonds as default-free bonds. Sovereign bonds of non-U.S. central governments are rated by the credit rating agencies. These ratings are referred to as **sovereign ratings**. Standard & Poor's and Moody's rate sovereign debt. We will discuss the factors considered in rating sovereign bonds at Level II.

The rating agencies assign two types of ratings to sovereign debt. One is a **local currency debt rating** and the other a **foreign currency debt rating**. The reason for assigning two ratings is, historically, the default frequency differs by the currency denomination of the debt. Specifically, defaults have been greater on foreign currency denominated debt. The reason for the difference in default rates for local currency debt and foreign currency debt is that if a government is willing to raise taxes and control its domestic financial system, it can generate sufficient local currency to meet its local currency debt obligation. This is not the case with foreign currency denominated debt. A central government must purchase foreign currency to meet a debt obligation in that foreign currency and therefore has less control with respect to its exchange rate. Thus, a significant depreciation of the local currency relative to a foreign currency denominated debt obligation will impair a central government's ability to satisfy that obligation.

3.2 Methods of Distributing New Government Securities

Four methods have been used by central governments to distribute new bonds that they issue: (1) regular auction cycle/multiple-price method, (2) regular auction cycle/single-price method, (3) ad hoc auction method, and (4) tap method.

With the **regular auction cycle/multiple-price method**, there is a regular auction cycle and winning bidders are allocated securities at the yield (price) they bid. For the **regular auction cycle/single-price method**, there is a regular auction cycle and all winning bidders are awarded securities at the highest yield accepted by the government. For example, if the highest yield for a single-price auction is 7.14% and someone bid 7.12%, that bidder would be awarded the securities at 7.14%. In contrast, with a multiple-price auction that bidder would be awarded securities at 7.12%. U.S. government bonds are currently issued using a regular auction cycle/single-price method.

In the **ad hoc auction system**, governments announce auctions when prevailing market conditions appear favorable. It is only at the time of the auction that the amount to be auctioned and the maturity of the security to be offered is announced. This is one of the methods used by the Bank of England in distributing British government bonds. In a **tap system**, additional bonds of a previously outstanding bond issue are auctioned. The government announces periodically that it is adding this new supply. The tap system has been used in the United Kingdom, the United States, and the Netherlands.

3.2.1 United States Treasury Securities

U.S. Treasury securities are issued by the U.S. Department of the Treasury and are backed by the full faith and credit of the U.S. government. As noted above, market participants throughout the world view U.S. Treasury securities as having no credit risk. Because of the importance of the U.S. government securities market, we will take a close look at this market.

Treasury securities are sold in the primary market through sealed-bid auctions on a regular cycle using a single-price method. Each auction is announced several days in advance by means of a Treasury Department press release or press conference. The auction for Treasury securities is conducted on a competitive bid basis.

The secondary market for Treasury securities is an over-the-counter market where a group of U.S. government securities dealers offer continuous bid and ask prices on outstanding Treasuries. There is virtually 24-hour trading of Treasury securities. The most recently auctioned issue for a maturity is referred to as the **on-the-run issue** or the **current issue**. Securities that are replaced by the on-the-run issue are called **off-the-run issues**.

Exhibit 67-2 provides a summary of the securities issued by the U.S. Department of the Treasury. U.S. Treasury securities are categorized as **fixed-principal securities** or **inflation-indexed securities**.

3.2.1.1 Fixed-Principal Treasury Securities

Fixed principal securities include Treasury bills, Treasury notes, and Treasury bonds. **Treasury bills** are issued at a discount to par value, have no coupon rate, mature at par value, and have a maturity date of less than 12 months. As discount securities, Treasury bills do not pay coupon interest; the return to the investor is the difference between the maturity value and the purchase price. We will explain how the price and the yield for a Treasury bill are computed in Reading 71.

Treasury coupon securities issued with original maturities of more than one year and no more than 10 years are called **Treasury notes**. Coupon securities are issued at approximately par value and mature at par value. Treasury coupon securities with original maturities greater than 10 years are called **Treasury bonds**. While a few issues of the outstanding bonds are callable, the U.S. Treasury has not issued callable Treasury securities since 1984. As of this writing, the U.S. Department of the Treasury has stopped issuing Treasury bonds.

3.2.1.2 Inflation-Indexed Treasury Securities

The U.S. Department of the Treasury issues Treasury notes and bonds that provide protection against inflation. These securities are popularly referred to as **Treasury inflation protection securities** or TIPS. (The Treasury refers to these securities as **Treasury inflation indexed securities**, TIIS.)

TIPS work as follows. The coupon rate on an issue is set at a fixed rate. That rate is determined via the auction process described later in this section. The

EXHIBIT 67-2   Overview of U.S. Treasury Debt Instruments

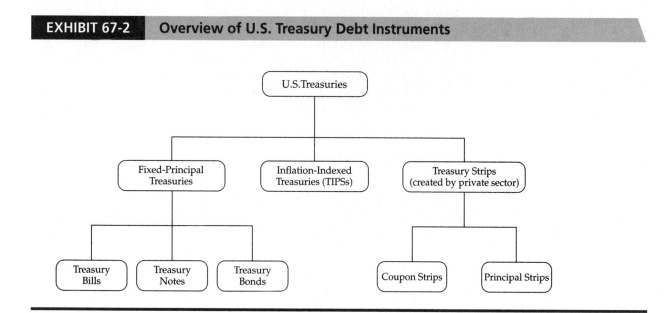

coupon rate is called the "real rate" because it is the rate that the investor ultimately earns above the inflation rate. The inflation index that the government uses for the inflation adjustment is the non-seasonally adjusted U.S. City Average All Items Consumer Price Index for All Urban Consumers (CPI-U).

The principal that the Treasury Department will base both the dollar amount of the coupon payment and the maturity value on is adjusted semiannually. This is called the **inflation-adjusted principal**. The adjustment for inflation is as follows. Suppose that the coupon rate for a TIPS is 3.5% and the annual inflation rate is 3%. Suppose further that an investor purchases on January 1, $100,000 of par value (principal) of this issue. The semiannual inflation rate is 1.5% (3% divided by 2). The inflation-adjusted principal at the end of the first six-month period is found by multiplying the original par value by (1 + the semiannual inflation rate). In our example, the inflation-adjusted principal at the end of the first six-month period is $101,500. It is this inflation-adjusted principal that is the basis for computing the coupon interest for the first six-month period. The coupon payment is then 1.75% (one half the real rate of 3.5%) multiplied by the inflation-adjusted principal at the coupon payment date ($101,500). The coupon payment is therefore $1,776.25.

Let's look at the next six months. The inflation-adjusted principal at the beginning of the period is $101,500. Suppose that the semiannual inflation rate for the second six-month period is 1%. Then the inflation-adjusted principal at the end of the second six-month period is the inflation-adjusted principal at the beginning of the six-month period ($101,500) increased by the semiannual inflation rate (1%). The adjustment to the principal is $1,015 (1% times $101,500). So, the inflation-adjusted principal at the end of the second six-month period (December 31 in our example) is $102,515 ($101,500 + $1,015). The coupon interest that will be paid to the investor at the second coupon payment date is found by multiplying the inflation-adjusted principal on the coupon payment date ($102,515) by one half the real rate (i.e., one half of 3.5%). That is, the coupon payment will be $1,794.01.

Practice Question 1

Suppose an investor purchases $10,000 of par value of a Treasury inflation protection security. The real rate (determined at the auction) is 3.8%.

A. Assume that at the end of the first six months the CPI-U is 2.4% (annual rate). Compute the (i) inflation adjustment to principal at the end of the first six months, (ii) the inflation-adjusted principal at the end of the first six months, and (iii) the coupon payment made to the investor at the end of the first six months.

B. Assume that at the end of the second six months the CPI-U is 2.8% (annual rate). Compute the (i) inflation adjustment to principal at the end of the second six months, (ii) the inflation-adjusted principal at the end of the second six months, and (iii) the coupon payment made to the investor at the end of the second six months.

As can be seen, part of the adjustment for inflation comes in the coupon payment since it is based on the inflation-adjusted principal. However, the U.S. government taxes the adjustment each year. This feature reduces the attractiveness of TIPS as investments for tax-paying entities.

Because of the possibility of disinflation (i.e., price declines), the inflation-adjusted principal at maturity may turn out to be less than the initial par value. However, the Treasury has structured TIPS so that they are redeemed at the greater of the inflation-adjusted principal and the initial par value.

An inflation-adjusted principal must be calculated for a **settlement date.** The inflation-adjusted principal is defined in terms of an index ratio, which is the ratio of the reference CPI for the settlement date to the reference CPI for the issue date. The reference CPI is calculated with a 3-month lag. For example, the reference CPI for May 1 is the CPI-U reported in February. The U.S. Department of the Treasury publishes and makes available on its website (www.publicdebt.treas.gov) a daily index ratio for an issue.

3.2.1.3 Treasury STRIPs

The Treasury does not issue zero-coupon notes or bonds. However, because of the demand for zero-coupon instruments with no credit risk and a maturity greater than one year, the private sector has created such securities.

To illustrate the process, suppose $100 million of a Treasury note with a 10-year maturity and a coupon rate of 10% is purchased to create zero-coupon Treasury securities (see Exhibit 67-3). The cash flows from this Treasury note are 20 semiannual payments of $5 million each ($100 million times 10% divided by 2) and the repayment of principal ("corpus") of $100 million 10 years from now. As there are 21 different payments to be made by the Treasury, a receipt representing a single payment claim on each payment is issued at a discount, creating 21 zero-coupon instruments. The amount of the maturity value for a receipt on a particular payment, whether coupon or principal, depends on the amount of the payment to be made by the Treasury on the underlying Treasury note. In our example, 20 coupon receipts each have a maturity value of $5 million, and one receipt, the principal, has a maturity value of $100 million. The maturity dates for the receipts coincide with the corresponding payment dates for the Treasury security.

Zero-coupon instruments are issued through the Treasury's Separate Trading of Registered Interest and Principal Securities (STRIPS) program, a program designed to facilitate the stripping of Treasury securities. The zero-coupon Treasury securities created under the STRIPS program are direct obligations of the U.S. government.

Stripped Treasury securities are simply referred to as **Treasury strips.** Strips created from coupon payments are called **coupon strips** and those created from the principal payment are called **principal strips.** The reason why a distinction is made between coupon strips and the principal strips has to do with the tax treatment by non-U.S. entities as discussed below.

A disadvantage of a taxable entity investing in Treasury coupon strips is that accrued interest is taxed each year even though interest is not paid until maturity. Thus, these instruments have negative cash flows until the maturity date because tax payments must be made on interest earned but not received in cash must be made. One reason for distinguishing between strips created from the principal and coupon is that some foreign buyers have a preference for the strips created from the principal (i.e., the principal strips). This preference is due to the tax treatment of the interest in their home country. Some countrie's tax laws treat the interest as a capital gain if the principal strip is purchased. The capital gain receives a preferential tax treatment (i.e., lower tax rate) compared to ordinary income.

| EXHIBIT 67-3 | Coupon Stripping: Creating Zero-Coupon Treasury Securities |

Security

| Par: $100 million
Coupon: 10%, semiannual
Maturity: 10 years |

Security

| Coupon:
$5 million
Receipt in:
6 months | Coupon:
$5 million
Receipt in:
1 year | Coupon:
$5 million
Receipt in:
1.5 years | .... | Coupon:
$5 million
Receipt in:
10 years | Principal:
$100 million
Receipt in:
10 years |

Zero-coupon securities created

| Maturity value:
$5 million
Maturity:
6 months | Maturity value:
$5 million
Maturity:
1 year | Maturity value:
$5 million
Maturity:
1.5 years | .... | Maturity value:
$5 million
Maturity:
10 years | Maturity value:
$100 million
Maturity:
10 years |

3.2.2 Non-U.S. Sovereign Bond Issuers

It is not possible to discuss the bonds/notes of all governments in the world. Instead, we will take a brief look at a few major sovereign issuers.

The German government issues bonds (called *Bunds*) with maturities from 8–30 years and notes (*Bundesobligationen*, Bobls) with a maturity of five years. Ten-year Bunds are the largest sector of the German government securities market in terms of amount outstanding and secondary market turnover. Bunds and Bobls have a fixed-rate coupons and are bullet structures.

The bonds issued by the United Kingdom are called "gilt-edged stocks" or simply *gilts*. There are more types of gilts than there are types of issues in other government bond markets. The largest sector of the gilt market is straight fixed-rate coupon bonds. The second major sector of the gilt market is index-linked issues, referred to as "linkers." There are a few issues of outstanding gilts called "irredeemables." These are issues with no maturity date and are therefore called "undated gilts." Government designated gilt issues may be stripped to create gilt strips, a process that began in December 1997.

The French Treasury issues long-dated bonds, *Obligation Assimilable du Trésor* (OATS), with maturities up to 30 years and notes, *Bons du Trésor á Taux Fixe et á Intérét Annuel* (BTANs), with maturities between 2 and 5 years. OATs are not callable. While most OAT issues have a fixed-rate coupon, there are some special issues with a floating-rate coupon. Long-dated OATs can be stripped to create OAT strips. The French government was one of the first countries after the United States to allow stripping.

The Italian government issues (1) bonds, *Buoni del Tresoro Poliennali* (BTPs), with a fixed-rate coupon that are issued with original maturities of 5, 10, and 30 years, (2) floating-rate notes, *Certificati di Credito del Tresoro* (CCTs), typically with a 7-year maturity and referenced to the Italian Treasury bill rate, (3) 2-year zero-coupon notes, *Certificati di Tresoro a Zero Coupon* (CTZs), and (4) bonds with **put options**, *Certificati del Tresoro con Opzione* (CTOs). The putable bonds are issued with the same maturities as the BTPs. The investor has the right to put the bond to the Italian government halfway through its stated maturity date. The Italian government has not issued CTOs since 1992.

The Canadian government bond market has been closely related to the U.S. government bond market and has a similar structure, including types of issues. Bonds have a fixed coupon rate except for the inflation protection bonds (called "real return bonds"). All new Canadian bonds are in "bullet" form; that is, they are not callable or putable.

About three quarters of the Australian government securities market consists of fixed-rate bonds and inflation protections bonds called "Treasury indexed bonds." Treasury indexed bonds have either interest payments or capital linked to the Australian Consumer Price Index. The balance of the market consists of floating-rate issues, referred to as "Treasury adjustable bonds," that have a maturity between 3 to 5 years and the reference rate is the Australian Bank Bill Index.

There are two types of Japanese government securities (referred to as JGBs) issued publicly: (1) medium-term bonds and (2) long-dated bonds. There are two types of medium-term bonds: bonds with coupons and zero-coupon bonds. Bonds with coupons have maturities of 2, 3, and 4 years. The other type of medium-term bond is the 5-year zero-coupon bond. Long-dated bonds are interest bearing.

The financial markets of Latin America, Asia with the exception of Japan, and Eastern Europe are viewed as "emerging markets." Investing in the government bonds of emerging market countries entails considerably more credit risk than investing in the government bonds of major industrialized countries. A good amount of secondary trading of government debt of emerging markets is in **Brady bonds** which represent a restructuring of nonperforming bank loans to emerging market governments into marketable securities. There are two types of Brady bonds. The first type covers the interest due on these loans ("past-due interest bonds"). The second type covers the principal amount owed on the bank loans ("principal bonds").

SEMI-GOVERNMENT/AGENCY BONDS   4

A central government can establish an agency or organization that issues bonds. The bonds of such entities are not issued directly by the central government but may have either a direct or implied government guarantee. These bonds are generically referred to as **semi-government bonds** or **government agency bonds**. In some countries, semi-government bonds include bonds issued by regions of the country.

Here are a few examples of semi-government bonds. In Australia, there are the bonds issued by Telstra or a State electric power supplier such as Pacific Power. These bonds are guaranteed by the full faith and credit of the Commonwealth of Australia. Government agency bonds are issued by Germany's Federal Railway (*Bundesbahn*) and the Post Office (*Bundespost*) with the full faith and credit of the central government.

In the United States, semi-government bonds are referred to as **federal agency securities**. They are further classified by the types of issuer—those issued by **federally related institutions** and those issued by **government-sponsored enterprises**. Our focus in the remainder of this section is on U.S. federal agency securities. Exhibit 67-4 provides an overview of the U.S. federal agency securities market.

Federally related institutions are arms of the federal government. They include the Export-Import Bank of the United States, the Tennessee Valley Authority (TVA), the Commodity Credit Corporation, the Farmers Housing Administration, the General Services Administration, the Government National Mortgage Association (Ginnie Mae), the Maritime Administration, the Private

Export Funding Corporation, the Rural Electrification Administration, the Rural Telephone Bank, the Small Business Administration, and the Washington Metropolitan Area Transit Authority. With the exception of securities of the TVA and the Private Export Funding Corporation, the securities are backed by the full faith and credit of the U.S. government. In recent years, the TVA has been the only issuer of securities directly into the marketplace.

Government-sponsored enterprises (GSEs) are privately owned, publicly chartered entities. They were created by Congress to reduce the cost of capital for certain borrowing sectors of the economy deemed to be important enough to warrant assistance. The entities in these sectors include farmers, homeowners, and students. The enabling legislation dealing with a GSE is reviewed periodically. GSEs issue securities directly in the marketplace. The market for these securities, while smaller than that of Treasury securities, has in recent years become an active and important sector of the bond market.

Today there are six GSEs that currently issue securities: Federal National Mortgage Association (Fannie Mae), Federal Home Loan Mortgage Corporation (Freddie Mac), Federal Agricultural Mortgage Corporation (Farmer Mac), Federal Farm Credit System, Federal Home Loan Bank System, and Student Loan Marketing Association (Sallie Mae). Fannie Mae, Freddie Mac, and the Federal Home Loan Bank are responsible for providing credit to the residential housing sector. Farmer Mac provides the same function for farm properties. The Federal Farm Credit Bank System is responsible for the credit market in the agricultural sector of the economy. Sallie Mae provides funds to support higher education.

EXHIBIT 67-4   Overview of U.S. Federal Agency Securities

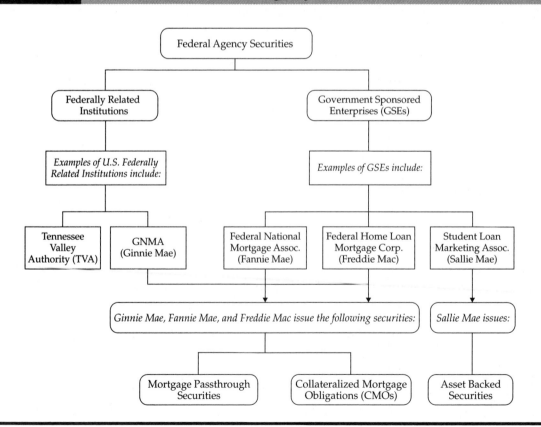

4.1 U.S. Agency Debentures and Discount Notes

Generally, GSEs issue two types of debt: debentures and discount notes. Debentures and discount notes do not have any specific collateral backing the debt obligation. The ability to pay debtholders depends on the ability of the issuing GSE to generate sufficient cash flows to satisfy the obligation.

Debentures can be either notes or bonds. GSE issued notes, with minor exceptions, have 1 to 20 year maturities and bonds have maturities longer than 20 years. **Discount notes** are short-term obligations, with maturities ranging from overnight to 360 days.

Several GSEs are frequent issuers and therefore have developed regular programs for the securities that they issue. For example, let's look at the debentures issued by Federal National Mortgage Association (Fannie Mae) and Freddie Mac (Federal Home Loan Mortgage Corporation). Fannie Mae issues **Benchmark Notes, Benchmark Bonds, Callable Benchmark Notes**, medium-term notes, and global bonds. The debentures issued by Freddie Mac are **Reference Notes, Reference Bonds, Callable Reference Notes**, medium-term notes, and global bonds. (We will discuss medium-term notes and global bonds in Section 6 and Section 8, respectively.) Callable Reference Notes have maturities of 2 to 10 years. Both Benchmark Notes and Bonds and Reference Notes and Bonds are eligible for stripping to create zero-coupon bonds.

4.2 U.S. Agency Mortgage-Backed Securities

The two GSEs charged with providing liquidity to the mortgage market—Fannie Mae and Freddie Mac—also issue securities backed by the mortgage loans that they purchase. That is, they use the mortgage loans they underwrite or purchase as collateral for the securities they issue. These securities are called **agency mortgage-backed securities** and include mortgage passthrough securities, collateralized mortgage obligations (CMOs), and stripped mortgage-backed securities. The latter two mortgage-backed securities are referred to as derivative mortgage-backed securities because they are created from mortgage passthrough securities.

While we confine our discussion to the U.S. mortgage-backed securities market, most developed countries have similar mortgage products.

4.2.1 Mortgage Loans

A mortgage loan is a loan secured by the collateral of some specified real estate property which obliges the borrower to make a predetermined series of payments. The mortgage gives the lender the right, if the borrower defaults, to "foreclose" on the loan and seize the property in order to ensure that the debt is paid off. The interest rate on the mortgage loan is called the **mortgage rate** or **contract rate**.

There are many types of mortgage designs available in the United States. A mortgage design is a specification of the mortgage rate, term of the mortgage, and the manner in which the borrowed funds are repaid. For now, we will use the most common mortgage design to explain the characteristics of a mortgage-backed security: a fixed-rate, level-payment, fully amortizing mortgage.

The basic idea behind this mortgage design is that each monthly mortgage payment is the same dollar amount and includes interest and principal payment. The monthly payments are such that at the end of the loan's term, the loan has been fully amortized (i.e., there is no mortgage principal balance outstanding).

Each monthly mortgage payment for this mortgage design is due on the first of each month and consists of:

1. interest of $1/12$ of the fixed annual interest rate times the amount of the outstanding mortgage balance at the end of the previous month, and

2. a payment of a portion of the outstanding mortgage principal balance.

The difference between the monthly mortgage payment and the portion of the payment that represents interest equals the amount that is applied to reduce the outstanding mortgage principal balance. This amount is referred to as the **amortization**. We shall also refer to it as the **scheduled principal payment**.

To illustrate this mortgage design, consider a 30-year (360-month), $100,000 mortgage with an 8.125% mortgage rate. The monthly mortgage payment would be $742.50.[2] Exhibit 67-5 shows for selected months how each monthly mortgage payment is divided between interest and scheduled principal payment. At the beginning of month 1, the mortgage balance is $100,000, the amount of the original loan. The mortgage payment for month 1 includes interest on the $100,000 borrowed for the month. Since the interest rate is 8.125%, the monthly interest rate is 0.0067708 (0.08125 divided by 12). Interest for month 1 is therefore $677.08 ($100,000 times 0.0067708). The $65.41 difference between the monthly mortgage payment of $742.50[2] and the interest of $677.08 is the portion of the monthly mortgage payment that represents the scheduled principal payment (i.e., amortization). This $65.41 in month 1 reduces the mortgage balance.

The mortgage balance at the end of month 1 (beginning of month 2) is then $99,934.59 ($100,000 minus $65.41). The interest for the second monthly mortgage payment is $676.64, the monthly interest rate (0.0066708) times the mortgage balance at the beginning of month 2 ($99,934.59). The difference between the $742.50 monthly mortgage payment and the $676.64 interest is $65.86, representing the amount of the mortgage balance paid off with that monthly mortgage payment. Notice that the mortgage payment in month 360—the final payment—is sufficient to pay off the remaining mortgage principal balance.

As Exhibit 67-5 clearly shows, the portion of the monthly mortgage payment applied to interest declines each month and the portion applied to principal repayment increases. The reason for this is that as the mortgage balance is reduced with each monthly mortgage payment, the interest on the mortgage balance declines. Since the monthly mortgage payment is a fixed dollar amount, an increasingly larger portion of the monthly payment is applied to reduce the mortgage principal balance outstanding in each subsequent month.

---

[2] The calculation of the monthly mortgage payment is simply an application of the present value of an annuity. The formula as applied to mortgage payments is as follows:

$$MP = B\left[\frac{r(1+r)^n}{(1+r)^n - 1}\right]$$

where

    MP = monthly mortgage payment

    B = amount borrowed (i.e., original loan balance)

    r = monthly mortgage rate (annual rate divided by 12)

    n = number of months of the mortgage loan

    In our example,

    B = $100,000 $r = 0.0067708$ (0.08125/12) $n = 360$

Then

$$MP = \$100{,}000\left[\frac{0.0067708(1.0067708)^{360}}{(1.0067708)^{360} - 1}\right] = \$742.50$$

EXHIBIT 67-5	Amortization Schedule for a Level-Payment, Fixed-Rate, Fully Amortized Mortgage (Selected Months)

Mortgage loan: $100,000   Monthly payment: $742.50
Mortgage rate: 8.125%   Term of loan: 30 years (360 months)

(1)	(2)	(3)	(4)	(5)	(6)
Month	Beginning of Month Mortgage Balance	Mortgage Payment	Interest	Scheduled Principal Repayment	End of Month Mortgage Balance
1	$100,000.00	$742.50	$677.08	$65.41	$99,934.59
2	99,934.59	742.50	676.64	65.86	99,868.73
3	99,868.73	742.50	676.19	66.30	99,802.43
4	99,802.43	742.50	675.75	66.75	99,735.68
. . .	. . .	. . .	. . .	. . .	. . .
25	98,301.53	742.50	665.58	76.91	98,224.62
26	98,224.62	742.50	665.06	77.43	98,147.19
27	98,147.19	742.50	664.54	77.96	98,069.23
. . .	. . .	. . .	. . .	. . .	. . .
184	76,446.29	742.50	517.61	224.89	76,221.40
185	76,221.40	742.50	516.08	226.41	75,994.99
186	75,994.99	742.50	514.55	227.95	75,767.04
. . .	. . .	. . .	. . .	. . .	. . .
289	42,200.92	742.50	285.74	456.76	41,744.15
290	41,744.15	742.50	282.64	459.85	41,284.30
291	41,284.30	742.50	279.53	462.97	40,821.33
. . .	. . .	. . .	. . .	. . .	. . .
358	2,197.66	742.50	14.88	727.62	1,470.05
359	1,470.05	742.50	9.95	732.54	737.50
360	737.50	742.50	4.99	737.50	0.00

To an investor in a mortgage loan (or a pool of mortgage loans), the monthly mortgage payments as described above do not equal an investor's cash flow. There are two reasons for this: (1) servicing fees and (2) prepayments.

Every mortgage loan must be serviced. Servicing of a mortgage loan involves collecting monthly payments and forwarding proceeds to owners of the loan; sending payment notices to mortgagors; reminding mortgagors when payments are overdue; maintaining records of principal balances; administering an escrow balance for real estate taxes and insurance; initiating foreclosure proceedings if necessary; and, furnishing tax information to mortgagors when applicable. The servicing fee is a portion of the mortgage rate. If the mortgage rate is 8.125% and the servicing fee is 50 basis points, then the investor receives interest of 7.625%. The interest rate that the investor receives is said to be the **net interest**.

Our illustration of the cash flow for a level-payment, fixed-rate, fully amortized mortgage assumes that the homeowner does not pay off any portion of the mortgage principal balance prior to the scheduled payment date. But homeowners do pay off all or part of their mortgage balance prior to the scheduled payment date. A payment made in excess of the monthly mortgage payment is called a

prepayment. The prepayment may be for the entire principal outstanding principal balance or a partial additional payment of the mortgage principal balance. When a prepayment is not for the entire amount, it is called a **curtailment**. Typically, there is no penalty for prepaying a mortgage loan.

Thus, the cash flows for a mortgage loan are monthly and consist of three components: (1) net interest, (2) scheduled principal payment, and (3) prepayments. The effect of prepayments is that the amount and timing of the cash flow from a mortgage is not known with certainty. This is the risk that we referred to as **prepayment risk** in Reading 66.[3]

For example, all that the investor in a $100,000, 8.125% 30-year mortgage knows is that as long as the loan is outstanding and the borrower does not default, interest will be received and the principal will be repaid at the scheduled date each month; then at the end of the 30 years, the investor would have received $100,000 in principal payments. What the investor does not know—the uncertainty—is for how long the loan will be outstanding, and therefore what the timing of the principal payments will be. This is true for all mortgage loans, not just the level-payment, fixed-rate, fully amortized mortgage.

Practice Question 2

Suppose that a mortgage loan for $100,000 is obtained for 30 years. The mortgage is a level-payment, fixed-rate, fully amortized mortgage. The mortgage rate is 7.5% and the monthly mortgage payment is $699.21. Compute an amortization schedule as shown in Exhibit 67-5 for the first six months.

4.2.2 Mortgage Passthrough Securities

A **mortgage passthrough security**, or simply passthrough, is a security created when one or more holders of mortgages form a collection (pool) of mortgages and sell shares or participation certificates in the pool. A pool may consist of several thousand or only a few mortgages. When a mortgage is included in a pool of mortgages that is used as collateral for a passthrough, the mortgage is said to be **securitized**.

The cash flow of a passthrough depends on the cash flow of the underlying pool of mortgages. As we just explained, the cash flow consists of monthly mortgage payments representing net interest, the scheduled principal payment, and any principal prepayments. Payments are made to security holders each month. Because of prepayments, the amount of the cash flow is uncertain in terms of the timing of the principal receipt.

To illustrate the creation of a passthrough look at Exhibits 67-6 and 67-7. Exhibit 67-6 shows 2,000 mortgage loans and the cash flows from these loans. For the sake of simplicity, we assume that the amount of each loan is $100,000 so that the aggregate value of all 2,000 loans is $200 million.

An investor who owns any one of the individual mortgage loans shown in Exhibit 67-6 faces prepayment risk. In the case of an individual loan, it is particularly difficult to predict prepayments. If an individual investor were to purchase all 2,000 loans, however, prepayments might become more predictable based on historical prepayment experience. However, that would call for an investment of $200 million to buy all 2,000 loans.

---

[3] Factors affecting prepayments will be discussed at Level II.

EXHIBIT 67-6   Mortgage Loans

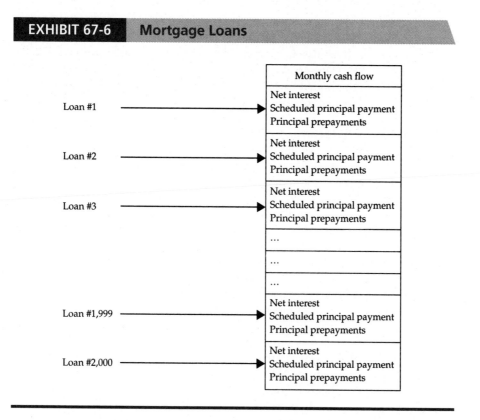

EXHIBIT 67-7   Creation of a Passthrough Security

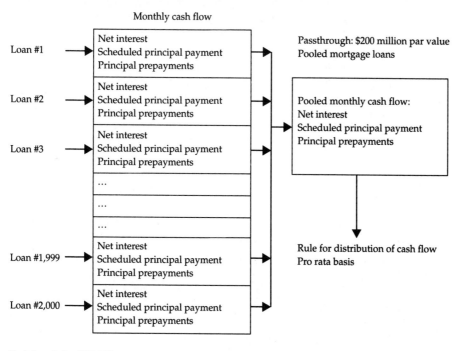

Each loan is for $100,000.
Total loans: $200 million.

Suppose, instead, that some entity purchases all 2,000 loans in Exhibit 67-6 and pools them. The 2,000 loans can be used as collateral to issue a security whose cash flow is based on the cash flow from the 2,000 loans, as depicted in Exhibit 67-7. Suppose that 200,000 certificates are issued. Thus, each certificate is initially worth $1,000 ($200 million divided by 200,000). Each certificate holder would be entitled to 0.0005% (1/200,000) of the cash flow. The security created is a mortgage passthrough security.

Let's see what has been accomplished by creating the passthrough. The total amount of prepayment risk has not changed. Yet, the investor is now exposed to the prepayment risk spread over 2,000 loans rather than one individual mortgage loan and for an investment of less than $200 million.

Let's compare the cash flow for a mortgage passthrough security (an amortizing security) to that of a noncallable coupon bond (a nonamortizing security). For a standard coupon bond, there are no principal payments prior to maturity while for a mortgage passthrough security the principal is paid over time. Unlike a standard coupon bond that pays interest semiannually, a mortgage passthrough makes monthly interest and principal payments. Mortgage pass-through securities are similar to coupon bonds that are callable in that there is uncertainty about the cash flows due to uncertainty about when the entire principal will be paid.

Passthrough securities are issued by Ginnie Mae, Fannie Mae, and Freddie Mac. They are guaranteed with respect to the timely payment of interest and principal.[4] The loans that are permitted to be included in the pool of mortgage loans issued by Ginnie Mae, Fannie Mae, and Freddie Mac must meet the underwriting standards that have been established by these entities. Loans that satisfy the underwriting requirements are referred to as **conforming loans**. Mortgage-backed securities not issued by agencies are backed by pools of nonconforming loans.

4.2.3 Collateralized Mortgage Obligations

Now we will show how one type of agency mortgage **derivative security** is created—a **collateralized mortgage obligation** (CMO). The motivation for creation of a CMO is to distribute prepayment risk among different classes of bonds.

The investor in our passthrough in Exhibit 67-7 remains exposed to the total prepayment risk associated with the underlying pool of mortgage loans, regardless of how many loans there are. Securities can be created, however, where investors do not share prepayment risk equally. Suppose that instead of distributing the monthly cash flow on a pro rata basis, as in the case of a passthrough, the distribution of the principal (both scheduled principal and prepayments) is carried out on some prioritized basis. How this is done is illustrated in Exhibit 67-8.

The exhibit shows the cash flow of our original 2,000 mortgage loans and the passthrough. Also shown are three classes of bonds, commonly referred to as **tranches**,[5] the par value of each tranche, and a set of payment rules indicating how the principal from the passthrough is to be distributed to each tranche. Note that the sum of the par value of the three tranches is equal to $200 million. Although it is not shown in the exhibit, for each of the three tranches, there will be certificates representing a proportionate interest in a tranche. For example, suppose that for Tranche A, which has a par value of $80 million, there are 80,000 certificates issued. Each certificate would receive a proportionate share (0.00125%) of payments received by Tranche A.

---

[4] Freddie Mac previously issued passthrough securities that guaranteed the timely payment of interest but guaranteed only the eventual payment of principal (when it is collected or within one year).

[5] "Tranche" is from an old French word meaning "slice." (The pronunciation of tranche rhymes with the English word "launch," as in launch a ship or a rocket.)

EXHIBIT 67-8	Creation of a Collateralized Mortgage Obligation

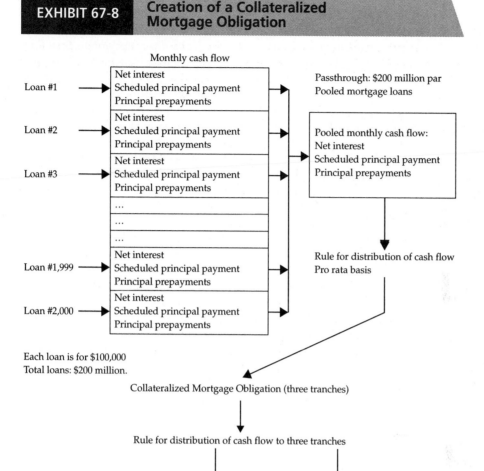

Each loan is for $100,000
Total loans: $200 million.

Tranche (par value)	Net interest	Principal
A ($80 million)	Pay each month based on par amount outstanding	Receives all monthly principal until completely paid off
B ($70 million)	Pay each month based on par amount outstanding	After Tranche A paid off, receives all monthly principal
C ($50 million)	Pay each month based on par amount outstanding	After Tranche B paid off, receives all monthly principal

The rule for the distribution of principal shown in Exhibit 67-8 is that Tranche A will receive all principal (both scheduled and prepayments) until that tranche's remaining principal balance is zero. Then, Tranche B receives all principal payments until its remaining principal balance is zero. After Tranche B is completely paid, Tranche C receives principal payments. The rule for the distribution of the cash flows in Exhibit 67-8 indicates that each of the three tranches receives interest on the basis of the amount of the par value outstanding.

The mortgage-backed security that has been created is called a CMO. The collateral for a CMO issued by the agencies is a pool of passthrough securities which is placed in a trust. The ultimate source for the CMO's cash flow is the pool of mortgage loans.

Let's look now at what has been accomplished. Once again, the total prepayment risk for the CMO is the same as the total prepayment risk for the 2,000 mortgage loans. However, the prepayment risk has been distributed differently across the three tranches of the CMO. Tranche A absorbs prepayments first, then Tranche B, and then Tranche C. The result of this is that Tranche A effectively is a shorter term security than the other two tranches; Tranche C will have the longest maturity. Different institutional investors will be attracted to the different tranches, depending on the nature of their liabilities and the effective maturity of the CMO tranche. Moreover, there is less uncertainty about the maturity of each tranche of the CMO than there is about the maturity of the pool of pass-throughs from which the CMO is created. Thus, redirection of the cash flow from the underlying mortgage pool creates tranches that satisfy the asset/liability objectives of certain institutional investors better than a passthrough. Stated differently, the rule for distributing principal repayments redistributes prepayment risk among the tranches.

The CMO we describe in Exhibit 67-8 has a simple set of rules for the distribution of the cash flow. Today, much more complicated CMO structures exist. The basic objective is to provide certain CMO tranches with less uncertainty about prepayment risk. Note, of course, that this can occur only if the reduction in prepayment risk for some tranches is absorbed by other tranches in the CMO structure. A good example is one type of CMO tranche called a **planned amortization class tranche** or PAC tranche. This is a tranche that has a schedule for the repayment of principal (hence the name "planned amortization") if prepayments are realized at a certain prepayment rate.[6] As a result, the prepayment risk is reduced (not eliminated) for this type of CMO tranche. The tranche that realizes greater prepayment risk in order for the PAC tranche to have greater prepayment protection is called the **support tranche**.

We will describe in much more detail PAC tranches and supports tranches, as well as other types of CMO tranches at Level II.

5   STATE AND LOCAL GOVERNMENTS

Non-central government entities also issue bonds. In the United States, this includes state and local governments and entities that they create. These securities are referred to as **municipal securities** or **municipal bonds**. Because the U.S. bond market has the largest and most developed market for non-central government bonds, we will focus on municipal securities in this market.

In the United States, there are both tax-exempt and taxable municipal securities. "Tax-exempt" means that interest on a municipal security is exempt from federal income taxation. The tax-exemption of municipal securities applies to interest income, not capital gains. The exemption may or may not extend to taxation at the state and local levels. Each state has its own rules as to how interest on municipal securities is taxed. Most municipal securities that have been issued are tax-exempt. Municipal securities are commonly referred to as **tax-exempt securities** despite the fact that there are taxable municipal securities that have been issued and are traded in the market. Municipal bonds are traded in the over-the-counter market supported by municipal bond dealers across the country.

Like other non-Treasury fixed income securities, municipal securities expose investors to credit risk. The nationally recognized rating organizations rate municipal securities according to their credit risk. In Level II, we look at the factors rating agencies consider in assessing credit risk.

---

[6] We will explain what is meant by "prepayment rate" at Level II.

There are basically two types of municipal security structures: **tax-backed debt** and **revenue bonds**. We describe each below, as well as some variants.

5.1 Tax-Backed Debt

Tax-backed debt obligations are instruments issued by states, counties, special districts, cities, towns, and school districts that are secured by some form of tax revenue. Exhibit 67-9 provides an overview of the types of tax-backed debt issued in the U.S. municipal securities market. Tax-backed debt includes **general obligation debt**, **appropriation-backed obligations**, and **debt obligations supported by public credit enhancement programs**. We discuss each below.

5.1.1 General Obligation Debt

The broadest type of tax-backed debt is general obligation debt. There are two types of general obligation pledges: unlimited and limited. An **unlimited tax general obligation debt** is the stronger form of general obligation pledge because it is secured by the issuer's unlimited taxing power. The tax revenue sources include corporate and individual income taxes, sales taxes, and property taxes. Unlimited tax general obligation debt is said to be secured by the full faith and credit of the issuer. A **limited tax general obligation debt** is a limited tax pledge because, for such debt, there is a statutory limit on tax rates that the issuer may levy to service the debt.

Certain general obligation bonds are secured not only by the issuer's general taxing powers to create revenues accumulated in a general fund, but also by certain identified fees, grants, and special charges, which provide additional

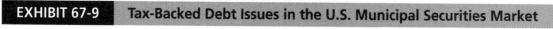

EXHIBIT 67-9   **Tax-Backed Debt Issues in the U.S. Municipal Securities Market**

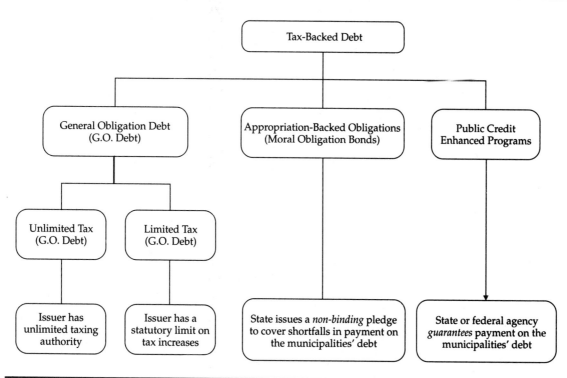

revenues from outside the general fund. Such bonds are known as **double-barreled in security** because of the dual nature of the revenue sources. For example, the debt obligations issued by special purpose service systems may be secured by a pledge of property taxes, a pledge of special fees/operating revenue from the service provided, or a pledge of both property taxes and special fees/operating revenues. In the last case, they are double-barreled.

5.1.2 Appropriation-Backed Obligations

Agencies or authorities of several states have issued bonds that carry a potential state liability for making up shortfalls in the issuing entity's obligation. The appropriation of funds from the state's general tax revenue must be approved by the state legislature. However, the state's pledge is not binding. Debt obligations with this nonbinding pledge of tax revenue are called **moral obligation bonds**. Because a moral obligation bond requires legislative approval to appropriate the funds, it is classified as an appropriation-backed obligation. The purpose of the moral obligation pledge is to enhance the credit worthiness of the issuing entity. However, the investor must rely on the best-efforts of the state to approve the appropriation.

5.1.3 Debt Obligations Supported by Public Credit Enhancement Programs

While a moral obligation is a form of credit enhancement provided by a state, it is not a legally enforceable or legally binding obligation of the state. There are entities that have issued debt that carries some form of public credit enhancement that is legally enforceable. This occurs when there is a guarantee by the state or a federal agency or when there is an obligation to automatically withhold and deploy state aid to pay any defaulted debt service by the issuing entity. Typically, the latter form of public credit enhancement is used for debt obligations of a state's school systems.

Some examples of state credit enhancement programs include Virginia's bond guarantee program that authorizes the governor to withhold state aid payments to a municipality and divert those funds to pay principal and interest to a municipality's general obligation holders in the event of a default. South Carolina's constitution requires mandatory withholding of state aid by the state treasurer if a school district is not capable of meeting its general obligation debt. Texas created the Permanent School Fund to guarantee the timely payment of principal and interest of the debt obligations of qualified school districts. The fund's income is obtained from land and mineral rights owned by the state of Texas.

More recently, states and local governments have issued increasing amounts of bonds where the debt service is to be paid from so-called "dedicated" revenues such as sales taxes, tobacco settlement payments, fees, and penalty payments. Many are structured to mimic the asset-backed bonds that are discussed later in this reading (Section 7).

5.2 Revenue Bonds

The second basic type of security structure is found in a revenue bond. **Revenue bonds** are issued for enterprise financings that are secured by the revenues generated by the completed projects themselves, or for general public-purpose financings in which the issuers pledge to the bondholders the tax and revenue resources that were previously part of the general fund. This latter type of revenue bond is usually created to allow issuers to raise debt outside general obligation debt limits and without voter approval.

Revenue bonds can be classified by the type of financing. These include utility revenue bonds, transportation revenue bonds, housing revenue bonds, higher education revenue bonds, health care revenue bonds, sports complex and convention center revenue bonds, seaport revenue bonds, and industrial revenue bonds.

5.3 Special Bond Structures

Some municipal securities have special security structures. These include **insured bonds** and **prerefunded bonds**.

5.3.1 Insured Bonds

Insured bonds, in addition to being secured by the issuer's revenue, are also backed by insurance policies written by commercial insurance companies. Insurance on a municipal bond is an agreement by an insurance company to pay the bondholder principal and/or coupon interest that is due on a stated maturity date but that has not been paid by the bond issuer. Once issued, this municipal bond insurance usually extends for the term of the bond issue and cannot be canceled by the insurance company.

5.3.2 Prerefunded Bonds

Although originally issued as either revenue or general obligation bonds, municipals are sometimes prerefunded and thus called **prerefunded municipal bonds**. A prerefunding usually occurs when the original bonds are escrowed or collateralized by direct obligations guaranteed by the U.S. government. By this, it is meant that a portfolio of securities guaranteed by the U.S. government is placed in a trust. The portfolio of securities is assembled such that the cash flows from the securities match the obligations that the issuer must pay. For example, suppose that a municipality has a 7% $100 million issue with 12 years remaining to maturity. The municipality's obligation is to make payments of $3.5 million every six months for the next 12 years and $100 million 12 years from now. If the issuer wants to prerefund this issue, a portfolio of U.S. government obligations can be purchased that has a cash flow of $3.5 million every six months for the next 12 years and $100 million 12 years from now.

Once this portfolio of securities whose cash flows match those of the municipality's obligation is in place, the prerefunded bonds are no longer secured as either general obligation or revenue bonds. The bonds are now supported by cash flows from the portfolio of securities held in an escrow fund. Such bonds, if escrowed with securities guaranteed by the U.S. government, have little, if any, credit risk. They are the safest municipal bonds available.

The escrow fund for a prerefunded municipal bond can be structured so that the bonds to be refunded are to be called at the first possible call date or a subsequent call date established in the original bond indenture. While prerefunded bonds are usually retired at their first or subsequent call date, some are structured to match the debt obligation to the maturity date. Such bonds are known as **escrowed-to-maturity bonds**.

6   CORPORATE DEBT SECURITIES

Corporations throughout the world that seek to borrow funds can do so through either bank borrowing or the issuance of debt securities. The securities issued include bonds (called corporate bonds), medium term notes, asset-backed securities, and commercial paper. Exhibit 67-10 provides an overview of the structures found in the corporate debt market. In many countries throughout the world, the principal form of borrowing is via bank borrowing and, as a result, a well-developed market for non-bank borrowing has not developed or is still in its infancy stage. However, even in countries where the market for corporate debt securities is small, large corporations can borrow outside of their country's domestic market.

Because in the United States there is a well developed market for corporations to borrow via the public issuance of debt obligations, we will look at this market. Before we describe the features of corporate bonds in the United States, we will discuss the rights of bondholders in a bankruptcy and the factors considered by rating agencies in assigning a credit rating.

6.1 Bankruptcy and Bondholder Rights in the United States

Every country has securities laws and contract laws that govern the rights of bondholders and a bankruptcy code that covers the treatment of bondholders in the case of a bankruptcy. There are principles that are common in the legal arrangements throughout the world. Below we discuss the features of the U.S. system.

EXHIBIT 67-10   Overview of Corporate Debt Securities

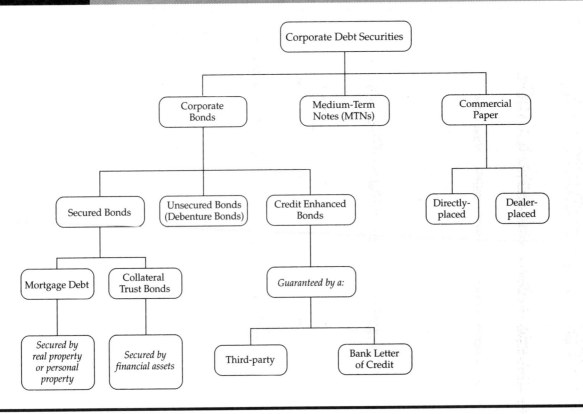

The holder of a U.S. corporate debt instrument has priority over the equity owners in a bankruptcy proceeding. Moreover, there are creditors who have priority over other creditors. The law governing bankruptcy in the United States is the Bankruptcy Reform Act of 1978 as amended from time to time. One purpose of the act is to set forth the rules for a corporation to be either liquidated or reorganized when filing bankruptcy.

The **liquidation** of a corporation means that all the assets will be distributed to the claim holders of the corporation and no corporate entity will survive. In a **reorganization**, a new corporate entity will emerge at the end of the bankruptcy proceedings. Some security holders of the bankrupt corporation will receive cash in exchange for their claims, others may receive new securities in the corporation that results from the reorganization, and others may receive a combination of both cash and new securities in the resulting corporation.

Another purpose of the bankruptcy act is to give a corporation time to decide whether to reorganize or liquidate and then the necessary time to formulate a plan to accomplish either a reorganization or liquidation. This is achieved because when a corporation files for bankruptcy, the act grants the corporation protection from creditors who seek to collect their claims. The petition for bankruptcy can be filed either by the company itself, in which case it is called a **voluntary bankruptcy**, or be filed by its creditors, in which case it is called an **involuntary bankruptcy**. A company that files for protection under the bankruptcy act generally becomes a "debtor-in-possession" and continues to operate its business under the supervision of the court.

The bankruptcy act is comprised of 15 chapters, each chapter covering a particular type of bankruptcy. Chapter 7 deals with the liquidation of a company; Chapter 11 deals with the reorganization of a company.

When a company is liquidated, creditors receive distributions based on the **absolute priority rule** to the extent assets are available. The absolute priority rule is the principle that senior creditors are paid in full before junior creditors are paid anything. For secured and unsecured creditors, the absolute priority rule guarantees their seniority to equity holders. In liquidations, the absolute priority rule generally holds. In contrast, there is a good body of literature that argues that strict absolute priority typically has not been upheld by the courts or the SEC in reorganizations.

6.2 Factors Considered in Assigning a Credit Rating

In the previous reading, we explained that there are companies that assign credit ratings to corporate issues based on the prospects of default. These companies are called rating agencies. In conducting a credit examination, each rating agency, as well as credit analysts employed by investment management companies, consider the four C's of credit—**character**, **capacity**, **collateral**, and **covenants**.

It is important to understand that a credit analysis can be for an entire company or a particular debt obligation of that company. Consequently, a rating agency may assign a different rating to the various issues of the same corporation depending on the level of seniority of the bondholders of each issue in the case of bankruptcy. For example, we will explain below that there is senior debt and subordinated debt. Senior debtholders have a better position relative to subordinated debtholders in the case of a bankruptcy for a given issuer. So, a rating agency, for example, may assign a rating of "A" to the senior debt of a corporation and a lower rating, "BBB," to the subordinated debt of the same corporation.

Character analysis involves the analysis of the quality of management. In discussing the factors it considers in assigning a credit rating, Moody's Investors Service notes the following regarding the quality of management:

Although difficult to quantify, management quality is one of the most important factors supporting an issuer's credit strength. When the unexpected occurs, it is a management's ability to react appropriately that will sustain the company's performance.[7]

In assessing management quality, the analysts at Moody's, for example, try to understand the business strategies and policies formulated by management. Moody's considers the following factors: (1) strategic direction, (2) financial philosophy, (3) conservatism, (4) track record, (5) succession planning, and (6) control systems.[8]

In assessing the ability of an issuer to pay (i.e., capacity), the analysts conduct financial statement analysis as discussed at Level II. In addition to financial statement analysis, the factors examined by analysts at Moody's are (1) industry trends, (2) the regulatory environment, (3) basic operating and competitive position, (4) financial position and sources of liquidity, (5) company structure (including structural subordination and priority of claim), (6) parent company support agreements, and (7) special event risk.[9]

The third C, collateral, is looked at not only in the traditional sense of assets pledged to secure the debt, but also to the quality and value of those unpledged assets controlled by the issuer. Unpledged collateral is capable of supplying additional sources of funds to support payment of debt. Assets form the basis for generating cash flow which services the debt in good times as well as bad. We discuss later the various types of collateral used for a corporate debt issue and features that analysts should be cognizant of when evaluating an investor's secured position.

Covenants deal with limitations and restrictions on the borrower's activities. **Affirmative covenants** call upon the debtor to make promises to do certain things. **Negative covenants** are those which require the borrower not to take certain actions. Negative covenants are usually negotiated between the borrower and the lender or their agents. Borrowers want the least restrictive loan agreement available, while lenders should want the most restrictive, consistent with sound business practices. But lenders should not try to restrain borrowers from accepted business activities and conduct. A borrower might be willing to include additional restrictions (up to a point) if it can get a lower interest rate on the debt obligation. When borrowers seek to weaken restrictions in their favor, they are often willing to pay more interest or give other consideration. We will see examples of positive and negative covenants later in this reading.

6.3 Corporate Bonds

In Reading 65, we discussed the features of bonds including the wide range of coupon types, the provisions for principal payments, provisions for early retirement, and other embedded options. Also, in Reading 66, we reviewed the various forms of credit risk and the ratings assigned by rating agencies. In our discussion of corporate bonds here, we will discuss secured and unsecured debt and information about default and recovery rates.

6.3.1 Secured Debt, Unsecured Debt, and Credit Enhancements

A corporate debt obligation may be secured or unsecured. **Secured debt** means that there is some form of collateral pledged to ensure payment of the debt. Remove the pledged collateral and we have **unsecured debt**.

---

[7] "Industrial Company Rating Methodology," *Moody's Investors Service: Global Credit Research* (July 1998), p. 6.

[8] "Industrial Company Rating Methodology," p. 7.

[9] "Industrial Company Rating Methodology," p. 3.

It is important to recognize that while a superior legal status will strengthen a bondholder's chance of recovery in case of default, it will not absolutely prevent bondholders from suffering financial loss when the issuer's ability to generate sufficient cash flow to pay its obligations is seriously eroded. Claims against a weak borrower are often satisfied for less than par value.

6.3.1.1 Secured Debt

Either **real property** or **personal property** may be pledged as security for secured debt. With **mortgage debt**, the issuer grants the bondholders a lien against pledged assets. A lien is a legal right to sell mortgaged property to satisfy unpaid obligations to bondholders. In practice, foreclosure and sale of mortgaged property is unusual. If a default occurs, there is usually a financial reorganization of the issuer in which provision is made for settlement of the debt to bondholders. The mortgage lien is important, though, because it gives the mortgage bondholders a strong bargaining position relative to other creditors in determining the terms of a reorganization.

Some companies do not own fixed assets or other real property and so have nothing on which they can give a mortgage lien to secure bondholders. Instead, they own securities of other companies; they are holding companies and the other companies are subsidiaries. To satisfy the desire of bondholders for security, the issuer grants investors a lien on stocks, notes, bonds or other kind of financial asset they own. Bonds secured by such assets are called **collateral trust bonds**. The eligible collateral is periodically marked to market by the trustee to ensure that the market value has a liquidation value in excess of the amount needed to repay the entire outstanding bonds and accrued interest. If the collateral is insufficient, the issuer must, within a certain period, bring the value of the collateral up to the required amount. If the issuer is unable to do so, the trustee would then sell collateral and redeem bonds.

Mortgage bonds have many different names. The following names have been used: **first mortgage bonds** (most common name), **first and general mortgage bonds**, **first refunding mortgage bonds**, and **first mortgage and collateral trusts**. There are instances (excluding prior lien bonds as mentioned above) when a company might have two or more layers of mortgage debt outstanding with different priorities. This situation usually occurs because companies cannot issue additional first mortgage debt (or the equivalent) under the existing indentures. Often this secondary debt level is called **general and refunding mortgage bonds** (G&R). In reality, this is mostly second mortgage debt. Some issuers may have third mortgage bonds.

Although an indenture may not limit the total amount of bonds that may be issued with the same lien, there are certain **issuance tests** that usually have to be satisfied before the company may sell more bonds. Typically there is an **earnings test** that must be satisfied before additional bonds may be issued with the same lien.

6.3.1.2 Unsecured Debt

Unsecured debt is commonly referred to as **debenture bonds**. Although a debenture bond is not secured by a specific pledge of property, that does not mean that bondholders have no claim on property of issuers or on their earnings. Debenture bondholders have the claim of general creditors on all assets of the issuer not pledged specifically to secure other debt. And they even have a claim on pledged assets to the extent that these assets generate proceeds in liquidation that are greater than necessary to satisfy secured creditors. **Subordinated debenture bonds** are issues that rank after secured debt, after debenture bonds, and often after some general creditors in their claim on assets and earnings.

One of the important protective provisions for unsecured debt holders is the **negative pledge clause**. This provision, found in most senior unsecured debt issues and a few subordinated issues, prohibits a company from creating or assuming any lien to secure a debt issue without equally securing the subject debt issue(s) (with certain exceptions).

6.3.1.3 Credit Enhancements

Some debt issuers have other companies guarantee their loans. This is normally done when a subsidiary issues debt and the investors want the added protection of a **third-party guarantee**. The use of guarantees makes it easier and more convenient to finance special projects and affiliates, although guarantees are also extended to operating company debt.

An example of a third-party (but related) guarantee was US West Capital Funding, Inc. 8% Guaranteed Notes that were due October 15, 1996 (guaranteed by US West, Inc.). The principal purpose of Capital Funding was to provide financing to US West and its affiliates through the issuance of debt guaranteed by US West. PepsiCo, Inc. has guaranteed the debt of its financing affiliate, PepsiCo Capital Resources, Inc., and The Standard Oil Company (an Ohio Corporation) has unconditionally guaranteed the debt of Sohio Pipe Line Company.

Another credit enhancing feature is the **letter of credit** (LOC) issued by a bank. A LOC requires the bank make payments to the trustee when requested so that monies will be available for the bond issuer to meet its interest and principal payments when due. Thus the credit of the bank under the LOC is substituted for that of the debt issuer. Specialized insurance companies also lend their credit standing to corporate debt, both new issues and outstanding secondary market issues. In such cases, the credit rating of the bond is usually no better than the credit rating of the guarantor.

While a guarantee or other type of credit enhancement may add some measure of protection to a debtholder, caution should not be thrown to the wind. In effect, one's job may even become more complex as an analysis of both the issuer and the guarantor should be performed. In many cases, only the latter is needed if the issuer is merely a financing conduit without any operations of its own. However, if both concerns are operating companies, it may very well be necessary to analyze both, as the timely payment of principal and interest ultimately will depend on the stronger party. Generally, a downgrade of the credit enhancer's claims-paying ability reduces the value of the credit-enhanced bonds.

6.3.2 Default Rates and Recovery Rates

Now we turn our attention to the various aspects of the historical performance of corporate issuers with respect to fulfilling their obligations to bondholders. Specifically, we will review two aspects of this performance. First, we will review the default rate of corporate borrowers. Second, we will review the default loss rate of corporate borrowers. From an investment perspective, default rates by themselves are not of paramount significance: it is perfectly possible for a portfolio of bonds to suffer defaults and to outperform Treasuries at the same time, provided the yield spread of the portfolio is sufficiently high to offset the losses from default. Furthermore, because holders of defaulted bonds typically recover some percentage of the face amount of their investment, the **default loss rate** is substantially lower than the default rate. Therefore, it is important to look at default loss rates or, equivalently, **recovery rates**.

6.3.2.1 Default Rates

A default rate can be measured in different ways. A simple way to define a default rate is to use the issuer as the unit of study. A default rate is then measured as the number of issuers that default divided by the total number of issuers at the beginning of the year. This measure—referred to as the **issuer default rate**—gives no recognition to the amount defaulted nor the total amount of issuance. Moody's, for example, uses this default rate statistic in its study of default rates. The rationale for ignoring dollar amounts is that the credit decision of an investor does not increase with the size of the issuer. The second measure—called the **dollar default rate**—defines the default rate as the par value of all bonds that defaulted in a given calendar year, divided by the total par value of all bonds outstanding during the year. With either default rate statistic, one can measure the default for a given year or an average annual default rate over a certain number of years.

There have been several excellent studies of corporate bond default rates. All of the studies found that the lower the credit rating, the greater the probability of a corporate issuer defaulting.

There have been extensive studies focusing on default rates for non-investment grade corporate bonds (i.e., speculative-grade issuer or high yield bonds). Studies by Edward Altman suggest that the annual default rate for speculative-grade corporate debt has been between 2.15% and 2.4% per year.[10] Asquith, Mullins, and Wolff, however, found that nearly one out of every three speculative-grade bonds defaults.[11] The large discrepancy arises because researchers use three different definitions of "default rate"; even if applied to the same universe of bonds (which they are not), the results of these studies could be valid simultaneously.[12]

Altman defines the default rate as the dollar default rate. His estimates (2.15% and 2.40%) are simple averages of the annual dollar default rates over a number of years. Asquith, Mullins, and Wolff use a cumulative dollar default rate statistic. While both measures are useful indicators of bond default propensity, they are not directly comparable. Even when restated on an annualized basis, they do not all measure the same quantity. The default statistics reported in both studies, however, are surprisingly similar once cumulative rates have been annualized. A majority of studies place the annual dollar default rates for all original issue high-yield bonds between 3% and 4%.

6.3.1.2 Recovery Rates

There have been several studies that have focused on recovery rates or default loss rates for corporate debt. Measuring the amount recovered is not a simple task. The final distribution to claimants when a default occurs may consist of cash and securities. Often it is difficult to track what was received and then determine the present value of any non-cash payments received.

Here we review recovery information as reported in a study by Moody's which uses the trading price at the time of default as a proxy for the amount recovered.[13] The recovery rate is the trading price at that time divided by the par

---

[10] Edward I. Altman and Scott A. Nammacher, *Investing in Junk Bonds* (New York: John Wiley, 1987) and Edward I. Altman, "Research Update: Mortality Rates and Losses, Bond Rating Drift," unpublished study prepared for a workshop sponsored by Merrill Lynch Merchant Banking Group, High Yield Sales and Trading, 1989.

[11] Paul Asquith, David W. Mullins, Jr., and Eric D. Wolff, "Original Issue High Yield Bonds: Aging Analysis of Defaults, Exchanges, and Calls," *Journal of Finance* (September 1989), pp. 923-952.

[12] As a parallel, we know that the mortality rate in the United States is currently less than 1% per year, but we also know that 100% of all humans (eventually) die.

[13] Moody's Investors Service, *Corporate Bond Defaults and Default Rates: 1970-1994*, Moody's Special Report, January 1995, p. 13.

value. Moody's found that the recovery rate was 38% for all bonds. Moreover, the study found that the higher the level of seniority, the greater the recovery rate.

6.4 Medium-Term Notes

A **medium-term note** (MTN) is a debt instrument, with the unique characteristic that notes are offered continuously to investors by an agent of the issuer. Investors can select from several maturity ranges: 9 months to 1 year, more than 1 year to 18 months, more than 18 months to 2 years, and so on up to 30 years. Medium-term notes are registered with the Securities and Exchange Commission under Rule 415 (the shelf registration rule) which gives a borrower (corporation, agency, sovereign, or supranational) the maximum flexibility for issuing securities on a continuous basis. As with corporate bonds, MTNs are rated by the nationally recognized statistical rating organizations.

The term "medium-term note" used to describe this debt instrument is misleading. Traditionally, the term "note" or "medium-term" was used to refer to debt issues with a maturity greater than one year but less than 15 years. Certainly this is not a characteristic of MTNs since they have been sold with maturities from nine months to 30 years, and even longer. For example, in July 1993, Walt Disney Corporation issued a security with a 100-year maturity off its medium-term note shelf registration. From the perspective of the borrower, the initial purpose of the MTN was to fill the funding gap between commercial paper and long-term bonds. It is for this reason that they are referred to as "medium term."

Borrowers have flexibility in designing MTNs to satisfy their own needs. They can issue fixed- or floating-rate debt. The coupon payments can be denominated in U.S. dollars or in a foreign currency. MTNs have been designed with the same features as corporate bonds.

6.4.1 The Primary Market

Medium-term notes differ from bonds in the manner in which they are distributed to investors when they are initially sold. Although some corporate bond issues are sold on a "best-efforts basis" (i.e., the underwriter does not purchase the securities from the issuer but only agrees to sell them),[14] typically corporate bonds are underwritten by investment bankers. When "underwritten," the investment banker purchases the bonds from the issuer at an agreed upon price and yield and then attempts to sell them to investors. This is discussed further in Section 9. MTNs have been traditionally distributed on a best-efforts basis by either an investment banking firm or other broker/dealers acting as agents. Another difference between bonds and MTNs is that when offered, MTNs are usually sold in relatively small amounts on either a continuous or an intermittent basis, while bonds are sold in large, discrete offerings.

An entity that wants to initiate a MTN program will file a shelf registration[15] with the SEC for the offering of securities. While the SEC registration for MTN

---

[14] The primary market for bonds is described in Section 9.1.

[15] SEC Rule 415 permits certain issuers to file a single registration document indicating that it intends to sell a certain amount of a certain class of securities at one or more times within the next two years. Rule 415 is popularly referred to as the "shelf registration rule" because the securities can be viewed as sitting on the issuer's "shelf" and can be taken off that shelf and sold to the public without obtaining additional SEC approval. In essence, the filing of a single registration document allows the issuer to come to market quickly because the sale of the security has been preapproved by the SEC. Prior to establishment of Rule 415, there was a lengthy period required before a security could be sold to the public. As a result, in a fast-moving market, issuers could not come to market quickly with an offering to take advantage of what it perceived to be attractive financing opportunities.

offerings are between $100 million and $1 billion, once completely sold, the issuer can file another shelf registration for a new MTN offering. The registration will include a list of the investment banking firms, usually two to four, that the borrower has arranged to act as agents to distribute the MTNs.

The issuer then posts rates over a range of maturities: for example, nine months to one year, one year to 18 months, 18 months to two years, and annually thereafter. In an offering rate schedule, an issuer will post rates as a spread over a Treasury security of comparable maturity. Rates will not be posted for maturity ranges that the issuer does not desire to sell.

The agents will then make the offering rate schedule available to their investor base interested in MTNs. An investor who is interested in the offering will contact the agent. In turn, the agent contacts the issuer to confirm the terms of the transaction. Since the maturity range in an offering rate schedule does not specify a specific maturity date, the investor can chose the final maturity subject to approval by the issuer.

The rate offering schedule can be changed at any time by the issuer either in response to changing market conditions or because the issuer has raised the desired amount of funds at a given maturity. In the latter case, the issuer can either not post a rate for that maturity range or lower the rate.

6.4.2 Structured MTNs

At one time, the typical MTN was a fixed-rate debenture that was noncallable. It is common today for issuers of MTNs to couple their offerings with transactions in the derivative markets (options, futures/forwards, swaps, caps, and floors) so they may create debt obligations with more complex risk/return features than are available in the corporate bond market. Specifically, an issue can have a floating-rate over all or part of the life of the security and the coupon formula can be based on a benchmark interest rate, equity index, individual stock price, foreign exchange rate, or commodity index. There are MTNs with inverse floating coupon rates and can include various embedded options.

MTNs created when the issuer simultaneously transacts in the derivative markets are called **structured notes**. The most common derivative instrument used in creating structured notes is a swap, an instrument described at Level II. By using the derivative markets in combination with an offering, issuers are able to create investment vehicles that are more customized for institutional investors to satisfy their investment objectives, but who are forbidden from using swaps for hedging or speculating. Moreover, it allows institutional investors who are restricted to investing in investment grade debt issues the opportunity to participate in other asset classes such as the equity market. Hence, structured notes are sometimes referred to as "rule busters." For example, an investor who buys an MTN whose coupon rate is tied to the performance of the S&P 500 (the reference rate) is participating in the equity market without owning common stock. If the coupon rate is tied to a foreign stock index, the investor is participating in the equity market of a foreign country without owning foreign common stock. In exchange for creating a structured note product, issuers can reduce their funding costs.

Common structured notes include: step-up notes, inverse floaters, deleveraged floaters, dual-indexed floaters, range notes, and index amortizing notes.

6.4.2.1 Deleveraged Floaters

A **deleveraged floater** is a floater that has a coupon formula where the coupon rate is computed as a fraction of the reference rate plus a quoted margin. The general formula for a deleveraged floater is:

$$\text{coupon rate} = b \times (\text{reference rate}) + \text{quoted margin}$$

where b is a value between zero and one.

6.4.2.2 Dual-Indexed Floaters

The coupon rate for a **dual-indexed floater** is typically a fixed percentage plus the difference between two reference rates. For example, the Federal Home Loan Bank System issued a floater whose coupon rate (reset quarterly) as follows:

$$(\text{10-year Constant Maturity Treasury rate}) - (\text{3-month LIBOR}) + 160 \text{ basis points}$$

6.4.2.3 Range Notes

A **range note** is a type of floater whose coupon rate is equal to the reference rate as long as the reference rate is within a certain range at the reset date. If the reference rate is outside of the range, the coupon rate is zero for that period. For example, a 3-year range note might specify that the reference rate is the 1-year Treasury rate and that the coupon rate resets every year. The coupon rate for the year is the Treasury rate as long as the Treasury rate at the coupon reset date falls within the range as specified below:

	Year 1	Year 2	Year 3
Lower limit of range	4.5%	5.25%	6.00%
Upper limit of range	6.5%	7.25%	8.00%

If the 1-year Treasury rate is outside of the range, the coupon rate is zero. For example, if in Year 1 the 1-year Treasury rate is 5% at the coupon reset date, the coupon rate for the year is 5%. However, if the 1-year Treasury rate is 7%, the coupon rate for the year is zero since the 1-year Treasury rate is greater than the upper limit for Year 1 of 6.5%.

6.4.2.4 Index Amortizing Notes

An **index amortizing note** (IAN) is a structured note with a fixed coupon rate but whose principal payments are made prior to the stated maturity date based on the prevailing value for some reference interest rate. The principal payments are structured so that the time to maturity of an IAN increases when the reference interest rate increases and the maturity decreases when the reference interest rate decreases.

From our understanding of reinvestment risks, we can see the risks associated with investing in an IAN. Since the coupon rate is fixed, when interest rates rise, an investor would prefer to receive principal back faster in order to reinvest the proceeds received at the prevailing higher rate. However, with an IAN, the rate of principal repayment is decreased. In contrast, when interest rates decline, an investor does not want principal repaid quickly because the investor would then be forced to reinvest the proceeds received at the prevailing lower interest rate. With an IAN, when interest rates decline, the investor will, in fact, receive principal back faster.

6.5 Commercial Paper

Commercial paper is a short-term unsecured promissory note that is issued in the open market and represents the obligation of the issuing corporation. Typically, commercial paper is issued as a zero-coupon instrument. In the United States, the maturity of commercial paper is typically less than 270 days and the most common maturity is 50 days or less.

To pay off holders of maturing paper, issuers generally use the proceeds obtained from selling new commercial paper. This process is often described as "rolling over" short-term paper. The risk that the investor in commercial paper faces is that the issuer will be unable to issue new paper at maturity. As a safeguard against this "roll-over risk," commercial paper is typically backed by unused bank credit lines.

There is very little secondary trading of commercial paper. Typically, an investor in commercial paper is an entity that plans to hold it until maturity. This is understandable since an investor can purchase commercial paper in a direct transaction with the issuer which will issue paper with the specific maturity the investor desires.

Corporate issuers of commercial paper can be divided into financial companies and nonfinancial companies. There has been significantly greater use of commercial paper by financial companies compared to nonfinancial companies. There are three types of financial companies: captive finance companies, bank-related finance companies, and independent finance companies. Captive finance companies are subsidiaries of manufacturing companies. Their primary purpose is to secure financing for the customers of the parent company. For example, U.S. automobile manufacturers have captive finance companies. Furthermore, a bank holding company may have a subsidiary that is a finance company, providing loans to enable individuals and businesses to acquire a wide range of products. Independent finance companies are those that are not subsidiaries of equipment manufacturing firms or bank holding companies.

Commercial paper is classified as either directly placed paper or dealer-placed paper. **Directly placed paper** is sold by the issuing firm to investors without the help of an agent or an intermediary. A large majority of the issuers of directly placed paper are financial companies. These entities require continuous funds in order to provide loans to customers. As a result, they find it cost effective to establish a sales force to sell their commercial paper directly to investors. General Electric Capital Corporation (GE Capital)—the principal financial services arm of General Electric Company—is the largest and most active direct issuer of commercial paper in the United States. **Dealer-placed commercial paper** requires the services of an agent to sell an issuer's paper.

The three nationally recognized statistical rating organizations that rate corporate bonds and medium-term notes also rate commercial paper. The ratings are shown in Exhibit 67-11. Commercial paper ratings, as with the ratings on other securities, are categorized as either investment grade or noninvestment grade.

6.6 Bank Obligations

Commercial banks are special types of corporations. Larger banks will raise funds using the various debt obligations described earlier. In this section, we describe two other debt obligations of banks—negotiable certificates of deposit and bankers acceptances—that are used by banks to raise funds.

EXHIBIT 67-11	Commercial Paper Ratings		
	Commercial rating company		
Category	**Fitch**	**Moody's**	**S&P**
Investment grade	F-1+		A-1+
	F-1	P-1	A-1
	F-2	P-2	A-2
	F-3	P-3	A-3
Noninvestment grade	F-S	NP(Not Prime)	B
			C
In default	D		D

6.6.1 Negotiable CDs

A **certificate of deposit** (CD) is a financial asset issued by a bank (or other deposit-accepting entity) that indicates a specified sum of money has been deposited at the issuing depository institution. A CD bears a maturity date and a specified interest rate; it can be issued in any denomination. In the United States, CDs issued by most banks are insured by the Federal Deposit Insurance Corporation (FDIC), but only for amounts up to $100,000. There is no limit on the maximum maturity. A CD may be nonnegotiable or negotiable. In the former case, the initial depositor must wait until the maturity date of the CD to obtain the funds. If the depositor chooses to withdraw funds prior to the maturity date, an early withdrawal penalty is imposed. In contrast, a **negotiable CD** allows the initial depositor (or any subsequent owner of the CD) to sell the CD in the open market prior to the maturity date. Negotiable CDs are usually issued in denominations of $1 million or more. Hence, an investor in a negotiable CD issued by an FDIC insured bank is exposed to the credit risk for any amount in excess of $100,000.

An important type of negotiable CD is the **Eurodollar CD**, which is a U.S. dollar-denominated CD issued primarily in London by U.S., European, Canadian, and Japanese banks. The interest rates paid on Eurodollar CDs play an important role in the world financial markets because they are viewed globally as the cost of bank borrowing. This is due to the fact that these interest rates represent the rates at which major international banks offer to pay each other to borrow money by issuing a Eurodollar CD with given maturities. The interest rate paid is called the **London interbank offered rate** (LIBOR). The maturities for the Eurodollar CD range from overnight to five years. So, references to "3-month LIBOR" indicate the interest rate that major international banks are offering to pay to other such banks on a Eurodollar CD that matures in three months. During the 1990s, LIBOR has increasingly become the reference rate of choice for borrowing arrangements—loans and floating-rate securities.

6.6.2 Bankers Acceptances

Simply put, a **bankers acceptance** is a vehicle created to facilitate commercial trade transactions. The instrument is called a bankers acceptance because a bank accepts the ultimate responsibility to repay a loan to its holder. The use of bankers acceptances to finance a commercial transaction is referred to as "acceptance financing." In the United States, the transactions in which bankers acceptances are created include (1) the importing of goods; (2) the exporting of goods to foreign entities; (3) the storing and shipping of goods between two foreign countries where neither the importer nor the exporter is a U.S. firm; and (4) the storing and shipping of goods between two U.S. entities in the United States. Bankers acceptances are sold on a discounted basis just as Treasury bills and commercial paper.

The best way to explain the creation of a bankers acceptance is by an illustration. Several entities are involved in our hypothetical transaction:

- Luxury Cars USA (Luxury Cars), a firm in Pennsylvania that sells automobiles
- Italian Fast Autos Inc. (IFA), a manufacturer of automobiles in Italy
- First Doylestown Bank (Doylestown Bank), a commercial bank in Doylestown, Pennsylvania
- *Banco di Francesco*, a bank in Naples, Italy
- The Izzabof Money Market Fund, a U.S. mutual fund

Luxury Cars and IFA are considering a commercial transaction. Luxury Cars wants to import 45 cars manufactured by IFA. IFA is concerned with the ability of Luxury Cars to make payment on the 45 cars when they are received.

Acceptance financing is suggested as a means for facilitating the transaction. Luxury Cars offers $900,000 for the 45 cars. The terms of the sale stipulate payment to be made to IFA 60 days after it ships the 45 cars to Luxury Cars. IFA determines whether it is willing to accept the $900,000. In considering the offering price, IFA must calculate the present value of the $900,000, because it will not be receiving payment until 60 days after shipment. Suppose that IFA agrees to these terms.

Luxury Cars arranges with its bank, Doylestown Bank, to issue a letter of credit. The letter of credit indicates that Doylestown Bank will make good on the payment of $900,000 that Luxury Cars must make to IFA 60 days after shipment. The letter of credit, or time draft, will be sent by Doylestown Bank to IFA's bank, *Banco di Francesco*. Upon receipt of the letter of credit, *Banco di Francesco* will notify IFA, which will then ship the 45 cars. After the cars are shipped, IFA presents the shipping documents to *Banco di Francesco* and receives the present value of $900,000. IFA is now out of the picture.

Banco di Francesco presents the time draft and the shipping documents to Doylestown Bank. The latter will then stamp "accepted" on the time draft. By doing so, Doylestown Bank has created a bankers acceptance. This means that Doylestown Bank agrees to pay the holder of the bankers acceptance $900,000 at the maturity date. Luxury Cars will receive the shipping documents so that it can procure the 45 cars once it signs a note or some other type of financing arrangement with Doylestown Bank.

At this point, the holder of the bankers acceptance is *Banco di Francesco*. It has two choices. It can continue to hold the bankers acceptance as an investment in its loan portfolio, or it can request that Doylestown Bank make a payment of the present value of $900,000. Let's assume that *Banco di Francesco* requests payment of the present value of $900,000. Now the holder of the bankers acceptance is Doylestown Bank. It has two choices: retain the bankers acceptance as an investment as part of its loan portfolio or sell it to an investor. Suppose that Doylestown Bank chooses the latter, and that The Izzabof Money Market Fund is seeking a high-quality investment with the same maturity as that of the bankers acceptance. Doylestown Bank sells the bankers acceptance to the money market fund at the present value of $900,000. Rather than sell the instrument directly to an investor, Doylestown Bank could sell it to a dealer, who would then resell it to an investor such as a money market fund. In either case, at the maturity date, the money market fund presents the bankers acceptance to Doylestown Bank, receiving $900,000, which the bank in turn recovers from Luxury Cars.

Investing in bankers acceptances exposes the investor to credit risk and liquidity risk. Credit risk arises because neither the borrower nor the accepting bank may be able to pay the principal due at the maturity date. When the bankers acceptance market was growing in the early 1980s, there were over 25 dealers. By 1989, the decline in the amount of bankers acceptances issued drove many one-time major dealers out of the business. Today, there are only a few major dealers and therefore bankers acceptances are considered illiquid. Nevertheless, since bankers acceptances are typically purchased by investors who plan to hold them to maturity, liquidity risk is not a concern to such investors.

7 ASSET-BACKED SECURITIES

In Section 4.2 we described how residential mortgage loans have been securitized. While residential mortgage loans is by far the largest type of asset that has been securitized, the major types of assets that have been securitized in many countries have included the following:

▶ auto loans and leases
▶ consumer loans
▶ commercial assets (e.g., including aircraft, equipment leases, trade receivables)
▶ credit cards
▶ home equity loans
▶ manufactured housing loans

Asset-backed securities are securities backed by a pool of loans or receivables. Our objective in this section is to provide a brief introduction to asset-backed securities.

7.1 The Role of the Special Purpose Vehicle

The key question for investors first introduced to the asset-backed securities market is why doesn't a corporation simply issue a corporate bond or medium-term note rather than an asset-backed security? To understand why, consider a triple B rated corporation that manufactures construction equipment. We will refer to this corporation as XYZ Corp. Some of its sales are for cash and others are on an installment sales basis. The installment sales are assets on the balance sheet of XYZ Corp., shown as "installment sales receivables."

Suppose XYZ Corp. wants to raise $75 million. If it issues a corporate bond, for example, XYZ Corp.'s funding cost would be whatever the benchmark Treasury yield is plus a yield spread for BBB issuers. Suppose, instead, that XYZ Corp. has installment sales receivables that are more than $75 million. XYZ Corp. can use the installment sales receivables as collateral for a bond issue. What will its funding cost be? It will probably be the same as if it issued a corporate bond. The reason is if XYZ Corp. defaults on any of its obligations, the creditors will have claim on all of its assets, including the installment sales receivables to satisfy payment of their bonds.

However, suppose that XYZ Corp. can create another corporation or legal entity and sell the installment sales receivables to that entity. We'll refer to this entity as SPV Corp. If the transaction is done properly, SPV Corp. owns the installment sales receivables, not XYZ Corp. It is important to understand that SPV Corp. is *not* a subsidiary of XYZ Corp.; therefore, the assets in SPV Corp. (i.e., the installment sales receivables) are not owned by XYZ Corp. This means that if XYZ Corp. is forced into bankruptcy, its creditors cannot claim the installment sales receivables because they are owned by SPV Corp. What are the implications?

Suppose that SPV Corp. sells securities backed by the installment sales receivables. Now creditors will evaluate the credit risk associated with collecting the receivables independent of the credit rating of XYZ Corp. What credit rating will be received for the securities issued by SPV Corp.? Whatever SPV Corp. wants the rating to be! It may seem strange that the issuer (SPV Corp.) can get any rating it wants, but that is the case. The reason is that SPV Corp. will show the characteristics of the collateral for the security (i.e., the installment sales receivables) to a rating agency. In turn, the rating agency will evaluate the credit quality of the collateral and inform the issuer what must be done to obtain specific ratings.

More specifically, the issuer will be asked to "credit enhance" the securities. There are various forms of credit enhancement. Basically, the rating agencies will look at the potential losses from the pool of installment sales receivables and make a determination of how much credit enhancement is needed for it to issue a specific rating. The higher the credit rating sought by the issuer, the greater the credit enhancement. Thus, XYZ Corp. which is BBB rated can obtain funding using its installment sales receivables as collateral to obtain a better credit rating for the securities issued. In fact, with enough credit enhancement, it can issue a AAA-rated security.

The key to a corporation issuing a security with a higher credit rating than the corporation's own credit rating is using SPV Corp. as the issuer. Actually, this legal entity that a corporation sells the assets to is called a **special purpose vehicle** or **special purpose corporation**. It plays a critical role in the ability to create a security—an asset-backed security—that separates the assets used as collateral from the corporation that is seeking financing.

Why doesn't a corporation always seek the highest credit rating (AAA) for its securities backed by collateral? The answer is that credit enhancement does not come without a cost. Credit enhancement mechanisms increase the costs associated with a securitized borrowing via an asset-backed security. So, the corporation must monitor the trade-off when seeking a higher rating between the additional cost of credit enhancing the security versus the reduction in funding cost by issuing a security with a higher credit rating.

Additionally, if bankruptcy occurs, there is the risk that a bankruptcy judge may decide that the assets of the special purpose vehicle are assets that the creditors of the corporation seeking financing (XYZ Corp. in our example) may claim after all. This is an important but unresolved legal issue in the United States. Legal experts have argued that this is unlikely. In the prospectus of an asset-backed security, there will be a legal opinion addressing this issue. This is the reason why special purpose vehicles in the United States are referred to as "bankruptcy remote" entities.

7.2 Credit Enhancement Mechanisms

In Level II, we will review how rating agencies analyze collateral in order to assign ratings. What is important to understand is that the amount of credit enhancement will be determined relative to a particular rating. There are two general types of credit enhancement structures: external and internal.

External credit enhancements come in the form of third-party guarantees. The most common forms of external credit enhancements are (1) a corporate guarantee, (2) a letter of credit, and (3) bond insurance. A corporate guarantee could be from the issuing entity seeking the funding (XYZ Corp. in our illustration above) or its parent company. Bond insurance provides the same function as in municipal bond structures and is referred to as an insurance "wrap."

A disadvantage of an external credit enhancement is that it is subject to the credit risk of the third-party guarantor. Should the third-party guarantor be downgraded, the issue itself could be subject to downgrade even if the collateral is performing as expected. This is based on the "weak link" test followed by rating agencies. According to this test, when evaluating a proposed structure, the credit quality of the issue is only as good as the weakest link in credit enhancement regardless of the quality of the underlying loans. Basically, an external credit enhancement exposes the investor to event risk since the downgrading of one entity (the third-party guarantor) can result in a downgrade of the asset-backed security.

Internal credit enhancements come in more complicated forms than external credit enhancements. The most common forms of internal credit enhancements are reserve funds, over collateralization, and senior/subordinate structures. We discuss each of these at Level II.

8　COLLATERALIZED DEBT OBLIGATIONS

A fixed income product that is also classified as part of the asset-backed securities market is the **collateralized debt obligation** (CDO). CDOs deserve special attention because of their growth since 2000. Moreover, while a CDO is backed by various assets, it is managed in a way that is not typical in other asset-backed security transactions. CDOs have been issued in both developed and developing countries.

A CDO is a product backed by a diversified pool of one or more of the following types of debt obligations:

▶ U.S. domestic investment-grade and high-yield corporate bonds

▶ U.S. domestic bank loans

▶ emerging market bonds

▶ special situation loans and distressed debt

▶ foreign bank loans

▶ asset-backed securities

▶ residential and commercial mortgage-backed securities

▶ other CDOs

When the underlying pool of debt obligations consists of bond-type instruments (corporate and emerging market bonds), a CDO is referred to as a **collateralized bond obligation** (CBO). When the underlying pool of debt obligations are bank loans, a CDO is referred to as a **collateralized loan obligation** (CLO).

In a CDO structure, an asset manager is responsible for managing the portfolio of assets (i.e., the debt obligations in which it invests). The funds to purchase the underlying assets (i.e., the bonds and loans) are obtained from the issuance of a CDO. The CDO is structured into notes or *tranches* similar to a CMO issue. The tranches are assigned ratings by a rating agency. There are restrictions as to how the manager manages the CDO portfolio, usually in the form of specific tests that must be satisfied. If any of the restrictions are violated by the asset manager, the notes can be downgraded and it is possible that the trustee begin paying principal to the senior noteholders in the CDO structure.

CDOs are categorized based on the motivation of the sponsor of the transaction. If the motivation of the sponsor is to earn the spread between the yield offered on the fixed income products held in the portfolio of the underlying pool (i.e., the collateral) and the payments made to the noteholders in the structure, then the transaction is referred to as an **arbitrage transaction**. (Moreover, a CDO is a vehicle for a sponsor that is an investment management firm to gather additional assets to manage and thereby generate additional management fees.) If the motivation of the sponsor is to remove debt instruments (primarily loans) from its balance sheet, then the transaction is referred to as a **balance sheet transaction**. Sponsors of balance sheet transactions are typically financial institutions such as banks and insurance companies seeking to reduce their capital requirements by removing loans due to their higher risk-based capital requirements.

PRIMARY MARKET AND SECONDARY MARKET FOR BONDS

9

Financial markets can be categorized as those dealing with financial claims that are newly issued, called the primary market, and those for exchanging financial claims previously issued, called the secondary market.

9.1 Primary Market

The primary market for bonds involves the distribution to investors of newly issued securities by central governments, its agencies, municipal governments, and corporations. Investment bankers work with issuers to distribute newly issued securities. The traditional process for issuing new securities involves investment bankers performing one or more of the following three functions: (1) advising the issuer on the terms and the timing of the offering, (2) buying the securities from the issuer, and (3) distributing the issue to the public. The advisor role may require investment bankers to design a security structure that is more palatable to investors than a particular traditional instrument.

In the sale of new securities, investment bankers need not undertake the second function—buying the securities from the issuer. An investment banker may merely act as an advisor and/or distributor of the new security. The function of buying the securities from the issuer is called underwriting. When an investment banking firm buys the securities from the issuer and accepts the risk of selling the securities to investors at a lower price, it is referred to as an underwriter. When the investment banking firm agrees to buy the securities from the issuer at a set price, the underwriting arrangement is referred to as a firm commitment. In contrast, in a best efforts arrangement, the investment banking firm only agrees to use its expertise to sell the securities—it does not buy the entire issue from the issuer. The fee earned from the initial offering of a security is the difference between the price paid to the issuer and the price at which the investment bank reoffers the security to the public (called the reoffering price).

9.1.1 Bought Deal and Auction Process

Not all bond issues are underwritten using the traditional firm commitment or best effort process we just described. Variations in the United States, the Euromarkets, and foreign markets for bonds include the **bought deal** and the **auction**

process. The mechanics of a bought deal are as follows. The underwriting firm or group of underwriting firms offers a potential issuer of debt securities a firm bid to purchase a specified amount of securities with a certain coupon rate and maturity. The issuer is given a day or so (maybe even a few hours) to accept or reject the bid. If the bid is accepted, the underwriting firm has "bought the deal." It can, in turn, sell the securities to other investment banking firms for distribution to their clients and/or distribute the securities to its clients. Typically, the underwriting firm that buys the deal will have presold most of the issue to its institutional clients. Thus, the risk of capital loss for the underwriting firm in a bought deal may not be as great as it first appears. There are some deals that are so straightforward that a large underwriting firm may have enough institutional investor interest to keep the risks of distributing the issue at the reoffering price quite small. Moreover, hedging strategies using interest rate risk control tools can reduce or eliminate the risk of realizing a loss of selling the bonds at a price below the reoffering price.

In the auction process, the issuer announces the terms of the issue and interested parties submit bids for the entire issue. This process is more commonly referred to as a competitive bidding underwriting. For example, suppose that a public utility wishes to issue $400 million of bonds. Various underwriters will form syndicates and bid on the issue. The syndicate that bids the lowest yield (i.e., the lowest cost to the issuer) wins the entire $400 million bond issue and then reoffers it to the public.

9.1.2 Private Placement of Securities

Public and private offerings of securities differ in terms of the regulatory requirements that must be satisfied by the issuer. For example, in the United States, the Securities Act of 1933 and the Securities Exchange Act of 1934 require that all securities offered to the general public must be registered with the SEC, unless there is a specific exemption. The Securities Acts allow certain exemptions from federal registration. Section 4(2) of the 1933 Act exempts from registration "transactions by an issuer not involving any public offering."

The exemption of an offering does not mean that the issuer need not disclose information to potential investors. The issuer must still furnish the same information deemed material by the SEC. This is provided in a private placement memorandum, as opposed to a prospectus for a public offering. The distinction between the private placement memorandum and the prospectus is that the former does not include information deemed by the SEC as "non-material," whereas such information is required in a prospectus. Moreover, unlike a prospectus, the private placement memorandum is not subject to SEC review.

In the United States, one restriction that was imposed on buyers of privately placed securities is that they may not be sold for two years after acquisition. Thus, there was no liquidity in the market for that time period. Buyers of privately placed securities must be compensated for the lack of liquidity which raises the cost to the issuer of the securities. SEC Rule 144A, which became effective in 1990, eliminates the two-year holding period by permitting large institutions to trade securities acquired in a private placement among themselves without having to register these securities with the SEC. Private placements are therefore now classified as Rule 144A offerings or non-Rule 144A offerings. The latter are more commonly referred to as traditional private placements. Rule 144A offerings are underwritten by investment bankers.

9.2 Secondary Market

In the secondary market, an issuer of a bond—whether it is a corporation or a governmental unit—may obtain regular information about the bond's value. The periodic trading of a bond reveals to the issuer the consensus price that the bond commands in an open market. Thus, issuers can discover what value investors attach to their bonds and the implied interest rates investors expect and demand from them. Bond investors receive several benefits from a secondary market. The market obviously offers them liquidity for their bond holdings as well as information about fair or consensus values. Furthermore, secondary markets bring together many interested parties and thereby reduces the costs of searching for likely buyers and sellers of bonds.

A bond can trade on an exchange or in an over-the-counter market. Traditionally, bond trading has taken place predominately in the over-the-counter market where broker-dealer trading desks take principal positions to fill customer buy and sell orders. In recent years, however, there has been an evolution away from this form of traditional bond trading and toward electronic bond trading. This evolution toward electronic bond trading is likely to continue.

There are several related reasons for the transition to the electronic trading of bonds. First, because the bond business has been a principal business (where broker-dealer firms risk their own capital) rather than an agency business (where broker-dealer firms act merely as an agent or broker), the capital of the market makers is critical. The amount of capital available to institutional investors to invest throughout the world has placed significant demands on the capital of broker-dealer firms. As a result, making markets in bonds has become more risky for broker-dealer firms. Second, the increase in bond market volatility has increased the capital required of broker-dealer firms in the bond business. Finally, the profitability of bond market trading has declined since many of the products have become more commodity-like and their bid-offer spreads have decreased.

The combination of the increased risk and the decreased profitability of bond market trading has induced the major broker-dealer firms to deemphasize this business in the allocation of capital. Broker-dealer firms have determined that it is more efficient to employ their capital in other activities such as underwriting and asset management, rather than in principal-type market-making businesses. As a result, the liquidity of the traditionally principal-oriented bond markets has declined, and this decline in liquidity has opened the way for other market-making mechanisms. This retreat by traditional market-making firms opened the door for electronic trading. In fact, the major broker-dealer firms in bonds have supported electronic trading in bonds.

Electronic trading in bonds has helped fill this developing vacuum and provided liquidity to the bond markets. In addition to the overall advantages of electronic trading in providing liquidity to the markets and price discovery (particularly for less liquid markets) is the resulting trading and portfolio management efficiencies that have been realized. For example, portfolio managers can load their buy/sell orders into a web site, trade from these orders, and then clear these orders.

There are a variety of types of electronic trading systems for bonds. The two major types of electronic trading systems are **dealer-to-customer systems** and **exchange systems**. Dealer-to-customer systems can be a single-dealer system or multiple-dealer system. Single-dealer systems are based on a customer dealing with a single, identified dealer over the computer. The single-dealer system simply computerizes the traditional customer-dealer market-making mechanism. Multi-dealer systems provide some advancement over the single-dealer method. A customer can select from any of several identified dealers whose bids and offers are provided on a computer screen. The customer knows the identity of the dealer.

In an exchange system, dealer and customer bids and offers are entered into the system on an anonymous basis, and the clearing of the executed trades is done through a common process. Two different major types of exchange systems are those based on continuous trading and call auctions. Continuous trading permits trading at continuously changing market-determined prices throughout the day and is appropriate for liquid bonds, such as Treasury and agency securities. Call auctions provide for fixed price auctions (that is, all the transactions or exchanges occur at the same "fixed" price) at specific times during the day and are appropriate for less liquid bonds such as corporate bonds and municipal bonds.

SUMMARY

▶ The bond market of a country consists of an internal bond market (also called the national bond market) and an external bond market (also called the international bond market, the offshore bond market, or, more popularly, the Eurobond market).

▶ A country's national bond market consists of the domestic bond market and the foreign bond market.

▶ Eurobonds are bonds which generally have the following distinguishing features: (1) they are underwritten by an international syndicate, (2) at issuance they are offered simultaneously to investors in a number of countries, (3) they are issued outside the jurisdiction of any single country, and (4) they are in unregistered form.

▶ Sovereign debt is the obligation of a country's central government.

▶ Sovereign credits are rated by Standard & Poor's and Moody's.

▶ There are two ratings assigned to each central government: a local currency debt rating and a foreign currency debt rating.

▶ Historically, defaults have been greater on foreign currency denominated debt.

▶ There are various methods of distribution that have been used by central governments when issuing securities: regular auction cycle/single-price system; regular auction cycle/multiple-price system, ad hoc auction system, and the tap system.

▶ In the United States, government securities are issued by the Department of the Treasury and include fixed-principal securities and inflation-indexed securities.

▶ The most recently auctioned Treasury issue for a maturity is referred to as the on-the-run issue or current coupon issue; off-the-run issues are issues auctioned prior to the current coupon issue.

▶ Treasury discount securities are called bills and have a maturity of one year or less.

▶ A Treasury note is a coupon-bearing security which when issued has an original maturity between two and 10 years; a Treasury bond is a coupon-bearing security which when issued has an original maturity greater than 10 years.

▶ The Treasury issues inflation-protection securities (TIPS) whose principal and coupon payments are indexed to the Consumer Price Index.

▶ Zero-coupon Treasury instruments are created by dealers stripping the coupon payments and principal payment of a Treasury coupon security.

▶ Strips created from the coupon payments are called coupon strips; those created from the principal payment are called principal strips.

▶ A disadvantage for a taxable entity investing in Treasury strips is that accrued interest is taxed each year even though interest is not received.

▶ The bonds of an agency or organization established by a central government are called semi-government bonds or government agency bonds and may have either a direct or implied credit guarantee by the central government.

▶ In the U.S. bond market, federal agencies are categorized as either federally related institutions or government sponsored enterprises.

▶ Federally related institutions are arms of the U.S. government and, with the exception of securities of the Tennessee Valley Authority and the Private Export Funding Corporation, are backed by the full faith and credit of the U.S. government.

▶ Government sponsored enterprises (GSEs) are privately owned, publicly chartered entities that were created by Congress to reduce the cost of capital for certain borrowing sectors of the economy deemed to be important enough to warrant assistance.

▶ A mortgage loan is a loan secured by the collateral of some specified real estate property.

▶ Mortgage loan payments consist of interest, scheduled principal payment, and prepayments.

▶ Prepayments are any payments in excess of the required monthly mortgage payment.

▶ Prepayment risk is the uncertainty about the cash flows due to prepayments.

▶ Loans included in an agency issued mortgage-backed security are conforming loans—loans that meet the underwriting standards established by the issuing entity.

▶ For a mortgage passthrough security the monthly payments are passed through to the certificate holders on a pro rata basis.

▶ In a collateralized mortgage obligation (CMO), there are rules for the payment of interest and principal (scheduled and prepaid) to the bond classes (tranches) in the CMO.

▶ The payment rules in a CMO structure allow for the redistribution of prepayment risk to the tranches comprising the CMO.

▶ In the U.S. bond market, municipal securities are debt obligations issued by state governments, local governments, and entities created by state and local governments.

▶ There are both tax-exempt and taxable municipal securities, where "tax-exempt" means that interest is exempt from federal income taxation; most municipal securities that have been issued are tax-exempt.

▶ There are basically two types of municipal security structures: tax-backed debt and revenue bonds.

▶ Tax-backed debt obligations are instruments secured by some form of tax revenue.

▶ Tax-backed debt includes general obligation debt (the broadest type of tax-backed debt), appropriation-backed obligations, and debt obligations supported by public credit enhancement programs.

▶ Revenue bonds are issued for enterprise financings that are secured by the revenues generated by the completed projects themselves, or for general public-purpose financings in which the issuers pledge to the bondholders the tax and revenue resources that were previously part of the general fund.

▶ Insured bonds, in addition to being secured by the issuer's revenue, are backed by insurance policies written by commercial insurance companies.

▶ Prerefunded bonds are supported by a portfolio of Treasury securities held in an escrow fund.

▶ In the United States, the Bankruptcy Reform Act of 1978 as amended governs the bankruptcy process.

▶ Chapter 7 of the bankruptcy act deals with the liquidation of a company; Chapter 11 of the bankruptcy act deals with the reorganization of a company.

► In theory, creditors should receive distributions based on the absolute priority rule to the extent assets are available; this rule means that senior creditors are paid in full before junior creditors are paid anything.

► Generally, the absolute priority rule holds in the case of liquidations and is typically violated in reorganizations.

► In analyzing a corporate bond, a credit analyst must consider the four C's of credit—character, capacity, collateral, and covenants.

► Character relates to the ethical reputation as well as the business qualifications and operating record of the board of directors, management, and executives responsible for the use of the borrowed funds and their repayment.

► Capacity deals with the ability of an issuer to pay its obligations.

► Collateral involves not only the traditional pledging of assets to secure the debt, but also the quality and value of unpledged assets controlled by the issuer.

► Covenants impose restrictions on how management operates the company and conducts its financial affairs.

► A corporate debt issue is said to be secured debt if there is some form of collateral pledged to ensure payment of the debt.

► Mortgage debt is debt secured by real property such as land, buildings, plant, and equipment.

► Collateral trust debentures, bonds, and notes are secured by financial assets such as cash, receivables, other notes, debentures or bonds, and not by real property.

► Unsecured debt, like secured debt, comes in several different layers or levels of claim against the corporation's assets.

► Some debt issues are credit enhanced by having other companies guarantee their payment.

► One of the important protective provisions for unsecured debt holders is the negative pledge clause which prohibits a company from creating or assuming any lien to secure a debt issue without equally securing the subject debt issue(s) (with certain exceptions).

► Investors in corporate bonds are interested in default rates and, more importantly, default loss rates or recovery rates.

► There is ample evidence to suggest that the lower the credit rating, the higher the probability of a corporate issuer defaulting.

► Medium-term notes are corporate debt obligations offered on a continuous basis and are offered through agents.

► The rates posted for medium-term notes are for various maturity ranges, with maturities as short as nine months to as long as 30 years.

► MTNs have been issued simultaneously with transactions in the derivatives market to create structured MTNs allowing issuers greater flexibility in creating MTNs that are attractive to investors who seek to hedge or take a market position that they might otherwise be prohibited from doing.

► Common structured notes include: step-up notes, inverse floaters, deleveraged floaters, dual-indexed floaters, range notes, and index amortizing notes.

► Commercial paper is a short-term unsecured promissory note issued in the open market that is an obligation of the issuing entity.

► Commercial paper is sold on a discount basis and has a maturity less than 270 days.

► Bank obligations in addition to the traditional corporate debt instruments include certificates of deposits and bankers acceptances.

► Asset-backed securities are securities backed by a pool of loans or receivables.

► The motivation for issuers to issue an asset-backed security rather than a traditional debt obligation is that there is the opportunity to reduce funding cost by separating the credit rating of the issuer from the credit quality of the pool of loans or receivables.

► The separation of the pool of assets from the issuer is accomplished by means of a special purpose vehicle or special purpose corporation.

► In obtaining a credit rating for an asset-backed security, the rating agencies require that the issue be credit enhanced; the higher the credit rating sought, the greater the credit enhancement needed.

► There are two general types of credit enhancement structures: external and internal.

► A collateralized debt obligation is a product backed by a pool of one or more of the following types of fixed income securities: bonds, asset-backed securities, mortgage-backed securities, bank loans, and other CDOs.

► The asset manager in a collateralized debt obligation is responsible for managing the portfolio of assets (i.e., the debt obligations backing the transaction) and there are restrictions imposed on the activities of the asset manager.

► The funds to purchase the underlying assets in a collateral debt obligation are obtained from the CDO issuance with ratings assigned by a rating agency.

► Collateralized debt obligations are categorized as either arbitrage transactions or balance sheet transactions, the classification being based on the motivation of the sponsor of the transaction.

► Bonds have traditionally been issued via an underwriting as a firm commitment or on a best efforts basis; bonds are also underwritten via a bought deal or an auction process.

► A bond can be placed privately with an institutional investor rather than issued via a public offering.

► In the United States, private placements are now classified as Rule 144A offerings (underwritten by an investment bank) and non-Rule 144A offerings (a traditional private placement).

► Bonds typically trade in the over-the-counter market.

► The two major types of electronic trading systems for bonds are the dealer-to-customer systems and the exchange systems.

PROBLEMS FOR READING 67

1. Explain whether you agree or disagree with each of the following statements:

   A. "The foreign bond market sector of the Japanese bond market consists of bonds of Japanese entities that are issued outside of Japan."

   B. "Because bonds issued by central governments are backed by the full faith and credit of the issuing country, these bonds are not rated."

   C. "A country's semi-government bonds carry the full faith and credit of the central government."

   D. "In the United States, all federal agency bonds carry the full faith and credit of the U.S. government."

2. Why do rating agencies assign two types of ratings to the debt of a sovereign entity?

3. When issuing bonds, a central government can select from several distribution methods.

   A. What is the difference between a single-price auction and a multiple-price auction?

   B. What is a tap system?

4. Suppose a portfolio manager purchases $1 million of par value of a Treasury inflation protection security. The real rate (determined at the auction) is 3.2%.

   A. Assume that at the end of the first six months the CPI-U is 3.6% (annual rate). Compute the (i) inflation adjustment to principal at the end of the first six months, (ii) the inflation-adjusted principal at the end of the first six months, and (iii) the coupon payment made to the investor at the end of the first six months.

   B. Assume that at the end of the second six months the CPI-U is 4.0% (annual rate). Compute the (i) inflation adjustment to principal at the end of the second six months, (ii) the inflation-adjusted principal at the end of the second six months, and (iii) the coupon payment made to the investor at the end of the second six months.

5. **A.** What is the measure of the rate of inflation selected by the U.S. Treasury to determine the inflation adjustment for Treasury inflation protection securities?

   B. Suppose that there is deflation over the life of a Treasury inflation protection security resulting in an inflation-adjusted principal at the maturity date that is less than the initial par value. How much will the U.S. Treasury pay at the maturity date to redeem the principal?

   C. Why is it necessary for the U.S. Treasury to report a daily index ratio for each TIPS issue?

6. What is a U.S. federal agency debenture?

7. Suppose that a 15-year mortgage loan for $200,000 is obtained. The mortgage is a level-payment, fixed-rate, fully amortized mortgage. The mortgage rate is 7.0% and the monthly mortgage payment is $1,797.66.

   A. Compute an amortization schedule for the first six months.

   B. What will the mortgage balance be at the end of the 15th year?

   C. If an investor purchased this mortgage, what will the timing of the cash flow be assuming that the borrower does not default?

8. A. What is a prepayment?

   B. What do the monthly cash flows of a mortgage-backed security consist of?

   C. What is a curtailment?

9. What is prepayment risk?

10. A. What is the difference between a mortgage passthrough security and a collateralized mortgage obligation?

   B. Why is a collateralized mortgage obligation created?

11. Name two U.S. government-sponsored enterprises that issue mortgage-backed securities.

12. What is the difference between a limited and unlimited general obligation bond?

13. What is a moral obligation bond?

14. What is an insured municipal bond?

15. A. What is a prerefunded bond?

   B. Why does a properly structured prerefunded municipal bond have no credit risk?

16. A. What is the difference between a liquidation and a reorganization?

   B. What is the principle of absolute priority?

   C. Comment on the following statement: "An investor who purchases a mortgage bond issued by a corporation knows that should the corporation become bankrupt, mortgage bondholders will be paid in full before the stockholders receive any proceeds."

17. A. What is a subordinated debenture corporate bond?

   B. What is negative pledge clause?

18. A. Why is the default rate alone not an adequate measure of the potential performance of corporate bonds?

   B. One study of default rates for speculative grade corporate bonds has found that one-third of all such issues default. Other studies have found that the default rate is between 2.15% and 2.4% for speculative grade corporate bonds. Why is there such a difference in these findings for speculative grade corporate bonds?

   C. Comment on the following statement: "Most studies have found that recovery rates are less than 15% of the trading price at the time of default and the recovery rate does not vary with the level of seniority."

19. A. What is the difference between a medium-term note and a corporate bond?

   B. What is a structured note?

   C. What factor determines the principal payment for an index amortizing note and what is the risk of investing in this type of structured note?

20. A. What is the risk associated with investing in a negotiable certificate of deposit issued by a U.S. bank?

   B. What is meant by "1-month LIBOR"?

21. What are the risks associated with investing in a bankers acceptance?

22. A financial corporation with a BBB rating has a consumer loan portfolio. An investment banker has suggested that this corporation consider issuing an asset-backed security where the collateral for the security is the consumer loan portfolio. What would be the advantage of issuing an asset-backed security rather than a straight offering of corporate bonds?

23. What is the role played by a special purpose vehicle in an asset-backed security structure?

24. A. What are the various forms of external credit enhancement for an asset-backed security?

    B. What is the disadvantage of using an external credit enhancement in an asset-backed security structure?

25. A. What is a collateralized debt obligation?

    B. Explain whether you agree or disagree with the following statement: "The asset manager in a collateralized debt obligation is free to manage the portfolio as aggressively or passively as he or she deems appropriate."

    C. What distinguishes an arbitrage transaction from a balance sheet transaction?

26. What is a bought deal?

27. How are private placements classified?

28. Explain the two major types of electronic bond trading systems.

$4\frac{5}{8}$ $4^{11}/_{16}$ — $\frac{3}{8}$

$5\frac{1}{2}$ $5\frac{1}{2}$ —

$5\frac{1}{8}$ $5\frac{1}{2}$ $21^{3}/_{16}$ — $\frac{1}{16}$

$20\frac{5}{8}$ $21^{3}/_{16}$ — $\frac{1}{16}$

$2\frac{1}{8}$ $17\frac{3}{8}$ $18\frac{1}{8}$ + $\frac{7}{8}$

$18\frac{1}{2}$ $6\frac{1}{2}$ $6\frac{1}{2}$ — $\frac{1}{2}$

$7\frac{1}{4}$ $6\frac{1}{2}$ $31/_{32}$ — $\frac{1}{8}$

$15/_{16}$ $9/_{16}$

$9/_{16}$

$1^{1}/_{32}$ $7^{15}/_{16}$ $7^{15}/_{16}$

$7^{15}/_{16}$ $7^{13}/_{16}$ $7^{15}/_{16}$

$2\frac{5}{8}$ $2^{11}/_{32}$ $2\frac{1}{2}$ +

545 $2\frac{3}{4}$ $2\frac{1}{4}$ $2\frac{1}{4}$

$2\frac{3}{4}$ $2\frac{1}{4}$ $2\frac{1}{4}$

$12^{1}/_{16}$ $11\frac{3}{8}$ $11\frac{3}{4}$ +

$5\frac{1}{8}$ $12^{1}/_{16}$ $11\frac{3}{8}$ $11\frac{3}{4}$ +

87 $33\frac{3}{4}$ 33 $33^{1}/_{16}$ —

602 $25\frac{5}{8}$ $24^{9}/_{16}$ $25\frac{5}{8}$ +

833 12 $11\frac{5}{8}$ $11\frac{7}{8}$ +

16 $10\frac{1}{2}$ $10\frac{1}{2}$ $10\frac{1}{2}$ —

78 $15\frac{7}{8}$ $15^{13}/_{16}$ $15\frac{7}{8}$ —

608 $9^{1}/_{16}$ $8\frac{1}{4}$ $8\frac{5}{8}$ +

430 $11\frac{1}{4}$ $10\frac{5}{8}$

UNDERSTANDING YIELD SPREADS

by Frank J. Fabozzi

LEARNING OUTCOMES

The candidate should be able to:

a. identify the interest rate policy tools available to the U.S. Federal Reserve Board;

b. describe the Treasury yield curve and the various shapes of the yield curve;

c. explain the basic theories of the term structure of interest rates (i.e., pure expectations theory, liquidity preference theory, and market segmentation theory) and describe the implications of each theory for the shape of the yield curve;

d. define a Treasury spot rate;

e. explain the different types of yield spread measures (e.g., absolute yield spread, relative yield spread, yield ratio), compute yield spread measures given the yields for two securities, and explain why investors may find a relative yield spread to be a better measure of yield spread than the absolute yield spread;

f. describe a credit spread and discuss the suggested relationship between credit spreads and the economic well being of the economy;

g. identify how embedded options affect yield spreads;

h. explain how the liquidity or issue-size of a bond affects its yield spread relative to risk-free securities and relative to other issues that are comparable in all other ways except for liquidity;

i. compute the after-tax yield of a taxable security and the tax-equivalent yield of a tax-exempt security;

j. define LIBOR and explain why it is an important measure to funded investors who borrow short-term.

INTRODUCTION 1

The interest rate offered on a particular bond issue depends on the interest rate that can be earned on (1) risk-free instruments and (2) the perceived risks associated with the issue. We refer to the interest rates on risk-free instruments as

Fixed Income Analysis for the Chartered Financial Analyst® Program, Second Edition, edited by Frank J. Fabozzi, Copyright © 2005 by CFA Institute. Reprinted with permission.

the "level of interest rates." The actions of a country's central bank influence the level of interest rates as does the state of the country's economy. In the United States, the level of interest rates depends on the state of the economy, the interest rate policies implemented by the Board of Governors of the Federal Reserve Board, and the government's fiscal policies.

A casual examination of the financial press and dealer quote sheets shows a wide range of interest rates reported at any given point in time. Why are there differences in interest rates among debt instruments? We provided information on this topic in Reading 65 and 66. In Reading 65, we explained the various features of a bond while in Reading 66 we explained how those features affect the risk characteristics of a bond relative to bonds without that feature.

In this reading, we look more closely at the differences in yields offered by bonds in different sectors of the bond market and within a sector of the bond market. This information is used by investors in assessing the "relative value" of individual securities within a bond sector, or among sectors of the bond market. Relative value analysis is a process of ranking individual securities or sectors with respect to expected return potential. We will continue to use the terms "interest rate" and "yield" interchangeably.

2   INTEREST RATE DETERMINATION

Our focus in this reading is on (1) the relationship between interest rates offered on different bond issues at a point in time and (2) the relationships among interest rates offered in different sectors of the economy at a given point in time. We will provide a brief discussion of the role of the U.S. Federal Reserve (the Fed), the policy making body whose interest rate policy tools directly influence short-term interest rates and indirectly influence long-term interest rates.

Once the Fed makes a policy decision it immediately announces the policy in a statement issued at the close of its meeting. The Fed also communicates its future intentions via public speeches or its Chairman's testimony before Congress. Managers who pursue an active strategy of positioning a portfolio to take advantage of expected changes in interest rates watch closely the same key economic indicators that the Fed watches in order to anticipate a change in the Fed's monetary policy and to assess the expected impact on short-term interest rates. The indicators that are closely watched by the Fed include non-farm payrolls, industrial production, housing starts, motor vehicle sales, durable good orders, National Association of Purchasing Management supplier deliveries, and commodity prices.

In implementing monetary policy, the Fed uses the following interest rate policy tools:

1. open market operations
2. the discount rate
3. bank reserve requirements
4. verbal persuasion to influence how bankers supply credit to businesses and consumers

Engaging in open market operations and changing the discount rate are the tools most often employed. Together, these tools can raise or lower the cost of funds in the economy. Open market operations do this through the Fed's buying and selling of U.S. Treasury securities. This action either adds funds to the market (when Treasury securities are purchased) or withdraws funds from the market (when Treasury securities are sold). Fed open market operations influence the federal funds rate, the rate at which banks borrow and lend funds from each other. The discount rate is the interest rate at which banks can borrow on a collateralized basis at the Fed's discount window. Increasing the discount rate makes the cost of funds more expensive for banks; the cost of funds is reduced when the discount rate is lowered. Changing bank reserve requirements is a less frequently used policy, as is the use of verbal persuasion to influence the supply of credit.

U.S. TREASURY RATES 3

The securities issued by the U.S. Department of the Treasury are backed by the full faith and credit of the U.S. government. Consequently, market participants throughout the world view these securities as being "default risk-free" securities. However, there are risks associated with owning U.S. Treasury securities.

The Treasury issues the following securities:

Treasury bills: Zero-coupon securities with a maturity at issuance of one year or less. The Treasury currently issues 1-month, 3-month, and 6-month bills.

Treasury notes: Coupon securities with maturity at issuance greater than 1 year but not greater than 10 years. The Treasury currently issues 2-year, 5-year, and 10-year notes.

Treasury bonds: Coupon securities with maturity at issuance greater than 10 years. Although Treasury bonds have traditionally been issued with maturities up to 30 years, the Treasury suspended issuance of the 30-year bond in October 2001.

Inflation-protection securities: Coupon securities whose principal's reference rate is the Consumer Price Index.

The on-the-run issue or current issue is the most recently auctioned issue of Treasury notes and bonds of each maturity. The off-the-run issues are securities that were previously issued and are replaced by the on-the-run issue. Issues that have been replaced by several more recent issues are said to be "well off-the-run issues."

The secondary market for Treasury securities is an over-the-counter market where a group of U.S. government securities dealers provides continuous bids and offers on specific outstanding Treasuries. This secondary market is the most liquid financial market in the world. Off-the-run issues are less liquid than on-the-run issues.

3.1 Risks of Treasury Securities

With this brief review of Treasury securities, let's look at their risks. We listed the general risks in Reading 66 and repeat them here: (1) interest rate risk, (2) call and prepayment risk, (3) yield curve risk, (4) reinvestment risk, (5) credit risk,

(6) liquidity risk, (7) exchange-rate risk, (8) volatility risk, (9) inflation or purchasing power risk, and (10) event risk.

All fixed income securities, including Treasury securities, expose investors to interest rate risk.[1] However, the degree of interest rate risk is not the same for all securities. The reason is that maturity and coupon rate affect how much the price changes when interest rates change. One measure of a security's interest rate risk is its *duration*.[2] Since Treasury securities, like other fixed income securities, have different durations, they have different exposures to interest rate risk as measured by duration.

Technically, yield curve risk and volatility risk are risks associated with Treasury securities. However, at this early stage of our understanding of fixed income analysis, we will not attempt to explain these risks. It is not necessary to understand these risks at this point in order to appreciate the material that follows in this section.

Because Treasury securities are noncallable, there is no reinvestment risk due to an issue being called.[3] Treasury coupon securities carry reinvestment risk because in order to realize the yield offered on the security, the investor must reinvest the coupon payments received at an interest rate equal to the computed yield. So, all Treasury coupon securities are exposed to reinvestment risk. Treasury bills are not exposed to reinvestment risk because they are zero-coupon instruments.

As for credit risk, the perception in the global financial community is that Treasury securities have no credit risk. In fact, when market participants and the popular press state that Treasury securities are "risk free," they are referring to credit risk.

Treasury securities are highly liquid. However, on-the-run and off-the-run Treasury securities trade with different degrees of liquidity. Consequently, the yields offered by on-the-run and off-the-run issues reflect different degrees of liquidity.

Since U.S. Treasury securities are dollar denominated, there is no exchange-rate risk for an investor whose domestic currency is the U.S. dollar. However, non-U.S. investors whose domestic currency is not the U.S. dollar are exposed to exchange-rate risk.

Fixed-rate Treasury securities are exposed to inflation risk. Treasury inflation protection securities (TIPS) have a coupon rate that is effectively adjusted for the rate of inflation and therefore have protection against inflation risk.

Finally, the yield on Treasury securities is impacted by a myriad of events that can be classified as political risk, a form of event risk. The actions of monetary and fiscal policy in the United States, as well as the actions of other central banks and governments, can have an adverse or favorable impact on U.S. Treasury yields.

---

[1] Interest rate risk is the risk of an adverse movement in the price of a bond due to changes in interest rates.

[2] Duration is a measure of a bond's price sensitivity to a change in interest rates.

[3] The Treasury no longer issues callable bonds. The Treasury issued callable bonds in the early 1980s and all of these issues will mature no later than November 2014 (assuming that they are not called before then). Moreover, as of 2004, the longest maturity of these issues is 10 years. Consequently, while outstanding callable issues of the Treasury are referred to as "bonds," based on their current maturity these issues would not be compared to long-term bonds in any type of relative value analysis. Therefore, because the Treasury no longer issues callable bonds and the outstanding issues do not have the maturity characteristics of a long-term bond, we will ignore these callable issues and simply treat Treasury bonds as noncallable.

3.2 The Treasury Yield Curve

Given that Treasury securities do not expose investors to credit risk, market participants look at the yield offered on an on-the-run Treasury security as the minimum interest rate required on a non-Treasury security with the same maturity. The relationship between yield and maturity of on-the-run Treasury securities on February 8, 2002 is displayed in Exhibit 68-1 in tabular form. The relationship shown in Exhibit 68-1 is called the **Treasury yield curve**—even though the "curve" shown in the exhibit is presented in tabular form.

The information presented in Exhibit 68-1 indicates that the longer the maturity the higher the yield and is referred to as an **upward sloping yield** curve. Since this is the most typical shape for the Treasury yield curve, it is also referred to as a **normal yield curve**. Other relationships have been observed. An inverted yield curve indicates that the longer the maturity, the lower the yield. For a **flat yield curve** the yield is approximately the same regardless of maturity.

Exhibit 68-2 provides a graphic example of the variants of these shapes and also shows how a yield curve can change over time. In the exhibit, the yield curve at the beginning of 2001 was inverted up to the 5-year maturity but was upward sloping beyond the 5-year maturity. By December 2001, all interest rates had declined. As seen in the exhibit, interest rates less than the 10-year maturity dropped substantially more than longer-term rates resulting in an upward sloping yield curve.

The number of on-the-run securities available in constructing the yield curve has decreased over the last two decades. While the 1-year and 30-year yields are shown in the February 8, 2002 yield curve, as of this writing there is no 1-year Treasury bill and the maturity of the 30-year Treasury bond (the last one issued before suspension of the issuance of 30-year Treasury bonds) will decline over time. To get a yield for maturities where no on-the-run Treasury issue exists, it is necessary to interpolate from the yield of two on-the-run issues. Several methodologies are used in practice. (The simplest is just a linear interpolation.) Thus, when market participants talk about a yield on the Treasury yield curve that is not one of the available on-the-run maturities—for example, the 8-year yield—it is only an approximation.

EXHIBIT 68-1	Relationship Between Yield and Maturity for On-the-Run Treasury Issues on February 8, 2002

Issue (maturity)	Yield (%)
1 month	1.68
3 months	1.71
6 months	1.81
1 year[1]	2.09
2 years	2.91
5 years	4.18
10 years	4.88
30 years[2]	5.38

[1] The 1-year issue is based on the 2-year issue closest to maturing in one year.

[2] The 30-year issue shown is based on the last 30-year issue before the Treasury suspended issuance of Treasury bonds in October 2001.

Source: Global Relative Value, Lehman Brothers, Fixed Income Research, February 11, 2002, p. 128.

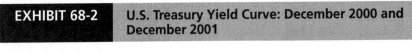

| EXHIBIT 68-2 | U.S. Treasury Yield Curve: December 2000 and December 2001 |

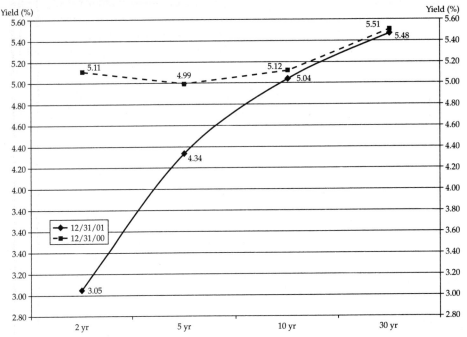

Source: Lehman Brothers Fixed Income Research, *Global Fixed Income Strategy "Playbook,"* January 2002.

It is critical to understand that any non-Treasury issue must offer a premium above the yield offered for the same maturity on-the-run Treasury issue. For example, if a corporation wanted to offer a 10-year noncallable issue on February 8, 2002, the issuer must offer a yield greater than 4.88% (the yield for the 10-year on-the-run Treasury issue). How much greater depends on the additional risks associated with investing in the 10-year corporate issue compared to investors in the 10-year on-the-run Treasury issue. Even off-the-run Treasury issues must offer a premium to reflect differences in liquidity.

Two factors complicate the relationship between maturity and yield as portrayed by the yield curve. The first is that the yield for on-the-run issues may be distorted by the fact that purchase of these securities can be financed at lower rates and as a result these issues offer artificially low yields. To clarify, some investors purchase securities with borrowed funds and use the securities purchased as collateral for the loan. This type of collateralized borrowing is called a repurchase agreement. Since dealers want to obtain use of these securities for their own trading activities, they are willing to lend funds to investors at a lower interest rate than is otherwise available for borrowing in the market. Consequently, incorporated into the price of an on-the-run Treasury security is the cheaper financing available, resulting in a lower yield for an on-the-run issue than would prevail in the absence of this financing advantage.

The second factor complicating the comparison of on-the-run and off-the-run Treasury issues (in addition to liquidity differences) is that they have different interest rate risks and different reinvestment risks. So, for example, if the coupon rate for the 5-year on-the-run Treasury issue in February 2002 is 4.18% and an off-the-run Treasury issue with just less than 5 years to maturity has a

5.25% coupon rate, the two bonds have different degrees of interest rate risk. Specifically, the on-the-run issue has greater interest rate risk (duration) because of the lower coupon rate. However, it has less reinvestment risk because the coupon rate is lower.

Because of this, when market participants talk about interest rates in the Treasury market and use these interest rates to value securities they look at another relationship in the Treasury market: the relationship between yield and maturity for zero-coupon Treasury securities. But wait, we said that the Treasury only issues three zero-coupon securities—1-month, 3-month, and 6-month Treasury bills. Where do we obtain the relationship between yield and maturity for zero-coupon Treasury securities? We discuss this next.

3.2.1 Theories of the Term Structure of Interest Rates

What information does the yield curve reveal? How can we explain and interpret changes in the yield curve? These questions are of great interest to anyone concerned with such tasks as the valuation of multiperiod securities, economic forecasting, and risk management. Theories of the term structure of interest rates[4] address these questions. Here we introduce the three main theories or explanations of the term structure. We shall present these theories intuitively.[5]

The three main term structure theories are:

► the pure expectations theory (unbiased expectations theory)
► the liquidity preference theory (or liquidity premium theory)
► the market segmentation theory

Each theory is explained below.

3.2.1.1 Pure Expectations Theory

The pure expectations theory makes the simplest and most direct link between the yield curve and investors' expectations about future interest rates, and, because long-term interest rates are plausibly linked to investor expectations about future inflation, it also opens the door to some interesting economic interpretations.

The **pure expectations theory** explains the term structure in terms of expected future short-term interest rates. According to the pure expectations theory, the market sets the yield on a two-year bond so that the return on the two-year bond is approximately equal to the return on a one-year bond plus the expected return on a one-year bond purchased one year from today.

Under this theory, a rising term structure indicates that the market expects short-term rates to rise in the future. For example, if the yield on the two-year bond is higher than the yield on the one-year bond, according to this theory, investors expect the one-year rate a year from now to be sufficiently higher than the one-year rate available now so that the two ways of investing for two years have the same expected return. Similarly, a flat term structure reflects an expectation that future short-term rates will be unchanged from today's short-term

---

[4] Term structure means the same as maturity—structure a description of how a bond's yield changes as the bond's maturity changes. In other words, term structure asks the question: Why do long-term bonds have a different yield than short-term bonds?

[5] At level II, we provide a more mathematical treatment of these theories in terms of forward rates that we will discuss in Reading 71.

rates, while a falling term structure reflects an expectation that future short-term rates will decline. This is summarized below:

Shape of Term Structure	Implication According to Pure Expectations Theory
upward sloping (normal)	rates expected to rise
downward sloping (inverted)	rates expected to decline
flat	rates not expected to change

The implications above are the broadest interpretation of the theory.

How does the pure expectations theory explain a humped yield curve? According to the theory, this can result when investors expect the returns on one-year securities to rise for a number of years, then fall for a number of years.

The relationships that the table above illustrates suggest that the shape of the yield curve contains information regarding investors' expectations about future inflation. A pioneer of the theory of interest rates (the economist Irving Fisher) asserted that interest rates reflect the sum of a relatively stable real rate of interest plus a premium for expected inflation. Under this hypothesis, if short-term rates are expected to rise, investors expect inflation to rise as well. An upward (downward) sloping term structure would mean that investors expected rising (declining) future inflation. Much economic discussion in the financial press and elsewhere is based on this interpretation of the yield curve.

The shortcoming of the pure expectations theory is that it assumes investors are indifferent to interest rate risk and any other risk factors associated with investing in bonds with different maturities.

3.2.1.2 Liquidity Preference Theory

The **liquidity preference theory** asserts that market participants want to be compensated for the interest rate risk associated with holding longer-term bonds. The longer the maturity, the greater the price volatility when interest rates change and investors want to be compensated for this risk. According to the liquidity preference theory, the term structure of interest rates is determined by (1) expectations about future interest rates and (2) a yield premium for interest rate risk.[6] Because interest rate risk increases with maturity, the liquidity preference theory asserts that the yield premium increases with maturity.

Consequently, based on this theory, an upward-sloping yield curve may reflect expectations that future interest rates either (1) will rise, or (2) will be unchanged or even fall, but with a yield premium increasing with maturity fast enough to produce an upward sloping yield curve. Thus, for an upward sloping yield curve (the most frequently observed type), the liquidity preference theory by itself has nothing to say about expected future short-term interest rates. For flat or downward sloping yield curves, the liquidity preference theory is consistent with a forecast of declining future short-term interest rates, given the theory's prediction that the yield premium for interest rate risk increases with maturity.

---

[6] In the liquidity preference theory, "liquidity" is measured in terms of interest rate risk. Specifically, the more interest rate risk, the less the liquidity.

Because the liquidity preference theory argues that the term structure is determined by both expectations regarding future interest rates and a yield premium for interest rate risk, it is referred to as **biased expectations theory**.

3.2.1.3 Market Segmentation Theory

Proponents of the **market segmentation theory** argue that within the different maturity sectors of the yield curve the supply and demand for funds determine the interest rate for that sector. That is, each maturity sector is an independent or segmented market for purposes of determining the interest rate in that maturity sector. Thus, positive sloping, inverted, and humped yield curves are all possible. In fact, the market segmentation theory can be used to explain any shape that one might observe for the yield curve.

Let's understand why proponents of this theory view each maturity sector as independent or segmented. In the bond market, investors can be divided into two groups based on their return needs: investors that manage funds versus a broad-based bond market index and those that manage funds versus their liabilities. The easiest case is for those that manage funds against liabilities. Investors managing funds where liabilities represent the benchmark will restrict their activities to the maturity sector that provides the best match with the maturity of their liabilities.[7] This is the basic principle of asset-liability management. If these investors invest funds outside of the maturity sector that provides the best match against liabilities, they are exposing themselves to the risks associated with an asset-liability mismatch. For example, consider the manager of a defined benefit pension fund. Since the liabilities of a defined benefit pension fund are long-term, the manager will invest in the long-term maturity sector of the bond market. Similarly, commercial banks whose liabilities are typically short-term focus on short-term fixed-income investments. Even if the rate on long-term bonds were considerably more attractive than that on short-term investments, according to the market segmentation theory commercial banks will restrict their activities to investments at the short end of the yield curve. Reinforcing this notion of a segmented market are restrictions imposed on financial institutions that prevent them from mismatching the maturity of assets and liabilities.

A variant of the market segmentation theory is the **preferred habitat theory**. This theory argues that investors prefer to invest in particular maturity sectors as dedicated by the nature of their liabilities. However, proponents of this theory do not assert that investors would be unwilling to shift out of their preferred maturity sector; instead, it is argued that if investors are given an inducement to do so in the form of a yield premium they will shift out of their preferred habitat. The implication of the preferred habitat theory for the shape of the yield curve is that any shape is possible.

3.3 Treasury Strips

Although the U.S. Department of the Treasury does not issue zero-coupon Treasury securities with maturity greater than one year, government dealers can synthetically create zero-coupon securities, which are effectively guaranteed by the full faith and credit of the U.S. government, with longer maturities. They create these securities by separating the coupon payments and the principal payment of a coupon-bearing

---

[7] One of the principles of finance is the "matching principle:" short-term assets should be financed with (or matched with) short-term liabilities; long-term assets should be financed with (or matched with) long-term sources of financing.

Treasury security and selling them off separately. The process, referred to as **stripping a Treasury security**, results in securities called **Treasury strips**. The Treasury strips created from coupon payments are called Treasury coupon strips and those created from the principal payment are called Treasury principal strips. We explained the process of creating Treasury strips in Reading 67.

Because zero-coupon instruments have no reinvestment risk, Treasury strips for different maturities provide a superior relationship between yield and maturity than do securities on the on-the-run Treasury yield curve. The lack of reinvestment risk eliminates the bias resulting from the difference in reinvestment risk for the securities being compared. Another advantage is that the duration of a zero-coupon security is approximately equal to its maturity. Consequently, when comparing bond issues against Treasury strips, we can compare them on the basis of duration.

The yield on a zero-coupon security has a special name: the **spot rate**. In the case of a Treasury security, the yield is called a **Treasury spot rate**. The relationship between maturity and Treasury spot rates is called **the term structure of interest rates**. Sometimes discussions of the term structure of interest rates in the Treasury market get confusing. The Treasury yield curve and the Treasury **term structure of interest rates** are often used interchangeably. While there is a technical difference between the two, the context in which these terms are used should be understood.

4   YIELDS ON NON-TREASURY SECURITIES

Despite the imperfections of the Treasury yield curve as a benchmark for the minimum interest rate that an investor requires for investing in a non-Treasury security, it is commonplace to refer to the additional yield over the benchmark Treasury issue of the same maturity as the **yield spread**. In fact, because non-Treasury sectors of the fixed income market offer a yield spread to Treasury securities, non-Treasury sectors are commonly referred to as **spread sectors** and non-Treasury securities in these sectors are referred to as **spread products**.

4.1 Measuring Yield Spreads

While it is common to talk about spreads relative to a Treasury security of the same maturity, a yield spread between any two bond issues can be easily computed. In general, the yield spread between any two bond issues, bond X and bond Y, is computed as follows:

yield spread = yield on bond X − yield on bond Y

where bond Y is considered the reference bond (or benchmark) against which bond X is measured.

When a yield spread is computed in this manner it is referred to as an **absolute yield spread** and it is measured in basis points. For example, on February 8, 2002, the yield on the 10-year on-the-run Treasury issue was 4.88% and the yield on a single A rated 10-year industrial bond was 6.24%. If bond X is the 10-year industrial bond and bond Y is the 10-year on-the-run Treasury issue, the absolute yield spread was:

yield spread = 6.24% − 4.88% = 1.36% or 136 basis points

Unless otherwise specified, yield spreads are typically measured in this way. Yield spreads can also be measured on a relative basis by taking the ratio of the yield spread to the yield of the reference bond. This is called a **relative yield spread** and is computed as shown below, assuming that the reference bond is bond Y:

$$\text{relative yield spread} = \frac{\text{yield on bond X} - \text{yield on bond Y}}{\text{yield on bond Y}}$$

Sometimes bonds are compared in terms of a **yield ratio**, the quotient of two bond yields, as shown below:

$$\text{yield ratio} = \frac{\text{yield on bond X}}{\text{yield on bond Y}}$$

Typically, in the U.S. bond market when these measures are computed, bond Y (the reference bond) is a Treasury issue. In that case, the equations for the yield spread measures are as follows:

$$\text{absolute yield spread} = \text{yield on bond X} - \text{yield of on-the-run Treasury}$$

$$\text{relative yield spread} = \frac{\text{yield on bond X} - \text{yield of on-the-run Treasury}}{\text{yield of on-the-run Treasury}}$$

$$\text{yield ratio} = \frac{\text{yield on bond X}}{\text{yield of on-the-run Treasury}}$$

For the above example comparing the yields on the 10-year single A rated industrial bond and the 10-year on-the-run Treasury, the relative yield spread and yield ratio are computed below:

$$\text{absolute yield spread} = 6.24\% - 4.88\% = 1.36\% = 136 \text{ basis points}$$

$$\text{relative yield spread} = \frac{6.24\% - 4.88\%}{4.88\%} = 0.279 = 27.9\%$$

$$\text{yield ratio} = \frac{6.24\%}{4.88\%} = 1.279$$

The reason for computing yield spreads in terms of a relative yield spread or a yield ratio is that the magnitude of the yield spread is affected by the level of interest rates. For example, in 1957 the yield on Treasuries was about 3%. At that time, the absolute yield spread between triple B rated utility bonds and Treasuries was 40 basis points. This was a relative yield spread of 13% (0.40% divided by 3%). However, when the yield on Treasuries exceeded 10% in 1985, an absolute yield spread of 40 basis points would have meant a relative yield spread of only 4% (0.40% divided by 10%). Consequently, in 1985 an absolute yield spread greater than 40 basis points would have been required in order to produce a similar relative yield spread.

In this reading, we will focus on the yield spread as most commonly measured, the absolute yield spread. So, when we refer to yield spread, we mean absolute yield spread.

Whether we measure the yield spread as an absolute yield spread, a relative yield spread, or a yield ratio, the question to answer is what causes the yield spread between two bond issues. Basically, active bond portfolio strategies involve assessing the factors that cause the yield spread, forecasting how that yield spread may change over an investment horizon, and taking a position to capitalize on that forecast.

Practice Question 1

The following table gives the yield for the 5-year Treasury and for two 5-year corporate bonds as of February 8, 2002.

Issue	Yield
5-year on-run-Treasury issue:	4.18%
5-year yield for GE (Aaa/AAA)	4.93%
5-year yield for Verizon Communications (A1/A+)	5.11%

A. Compute the following yield spread measures between the 5-year GE yield and the 5-year on-the-run Treasury yield: absolute yield spread, relative yield spread, and yield ratio.

B. Compute the following yield spread measures between the 5-year Verizon Communications yield and the 5-year on-the-run Treasury yield: absolute yield spread, relative yield spread, and yield ratio.

4.2 Intermarket Sector Spreads and Intramarket Spreads

The bond market is classified into sectors based on the type of issuer. In the United States, these sectors include the U.S. government sector, the U.S. government agencies sector, the municipal sector, the corporate sector, the mortgage-backed securities sector, the asset-backed securities sector, and the foreign (sovereign, supranational, and corporate) sector. Different sectors are generally perceived as offering different risks and rewards.

The major market sectors are further divided into sub-sectors reflecting common economic characteristics. For example, within the corporate sector, the sub-sectors are: (1) industrial companies, (2) utility companies, (3) finance companies, and (4) banks. In the market for asset-backed securities, the sub-sectors are based on the type of collateral backing the security. The major types are securities backed by pools of (1) credit card receivables, (2) home equity loans, (3) automobile loans, (4) manufactured housing loans, and (5) student loans. Excluding the Treasury market sector, the other market sectors have a wide range of issuers, each with different abilities to satisfy their contractual obligations. Therefore, a key feature of a debt obligation is the nature of the issuer.

The yield spread between the yields offered in two sectors of the bond market with the same maturity is referred to as an **intermarket sector spread**. The most common intermarket sector spread calculated by market participants is the yield spread between a non-Treasury sector and Treasury securities with the same maturity.

The yield spread between two issues within a market sector is called an **intramarket sector spread**. As with Treasury securities, a yield curve can be estimated for a given issuer. The yield spread typically increases with maturity. The yield spreads for a given issuer can be added to the yield for the corresponding maturity of the on-the-run Treasury issue. The resulting yield curve is then an **issuer's on-the-run yield curve**.

The factors other than maturity that affect the intermarket and intramarket yield spreads are (1) the relative credit risk of the two issues, (2) the presence of embedded options, (3) the liquidity of the two issues, and (4) the taxability of interest received by investors.

4.3 Credit Spreads

The yield spread between non-Treasury securities and Treasury securities that are identical in all respects except for credit rating is referred to as a **credit spread** or **quality spread**. "Identical in all respects except credit rating" means that the maturities are the same and that there are no embedded options.

For example, Exhibit 68-3 shows information on the yield spread within the corporate sector by credit rating and maturity, for the 90-day period ending February 8, 2002. The high, low, and average spreads for the 90-day period are reported. Note that the lower the credit rating, the higher the credit spread. Also note that, for a given sector of the corporate market and a given credit rating, the credit spread increases with maturity.

It is argued that credit spreads between corporates and Treasuries change systematically with changes in the economy. Credit spreads widen (i.e., become larger) in a declining or contracting economy and narrow (i.e., become smaller) during economic expansion. The economic rationale is that, in a declining or contracting economy, corporations experience declines in revenue and cash flow,

EXHIBIT 68-3	Credit Spreads (in Basis Points) in the Corporate Sector on February 8, 2002								
	AA–90-day			A–90-day			BBB–90-day		
Maturity (years)	High	Low	Avg	High	Low	Avg	High	Low	Avg
Industrials									
5	87	58	72	135	85	112	162	117	140
10	102	73	90	158	109	134	180	133	156
30	114	93	106	170	132	152	199	154	175
Utilities									
5	140	0	103	153	112	134	200	163	184
10	160	0	121	168	132	153	220	182	204
30	175	0	132	188	151	171	240	200	222
Finance									
5	103	55	86	233	177	198			
10	125	78	103	253	170	209			
30	148	100	130	253	207	228			
Banks									
5	97	60	81	113	83	100			
10	120	78	95	127	92	110			
30	138	105	121	170	127	145			

Source: Abstracted from *Global Relative Value*, Lehman Brothers, Fixed Income Research, February 11, 2002, p. 133.

making it more difficult for corporate issuers to service their contractual debt obligations. To induce investors to hold spread products as credit quality deteriorates, the credit spread widens. The widening occurs as investors sell off corporates and invest the proceeds in Treasury securities (popularly referred to as a "flight to quality"). The converse is that, during economic expansion and brisk economic activity, revenue and cash flow increase, increasing the likelihood that corporate issuers will have the capacity to service their contractual debt obligations.

Exhibit 68-4 provides evidence of the impact of the business cycle on credit spreads since 1919. The credit spread in the exhibit is the difference between Baa rated and Aaa rated corporate bonds; the shaded areas in the exhibit represent periods of economic recession as defined by the National Bureau of Economic Research (NBER). In general, corporate credit spreads tightened during the early stages of economic expansion, and spreads widened sharply during economic recessions. In fact, spreads typically begin to widen before the official beginning of an economic recession.[8]

Some market observers use the yield spread between issuers in cyclical and non-cyclical industry sectors as a proxy for yield spreads due to expected economic conditions. The rationale is as follows. While companies in both cyclical and non-cyclical industries are adversely affected by expectations of a recession, the impact is greater for cyclical industries. As a result, the yield spread between issuers in cyclical and non-cyclical industry sectors will widen with expectations of a contracting economy.

| EXHIBIT 68-4 | Credit Spreads Between Baa and Aaa Corporate Bonds Over the Business Cycle Since 1919 |

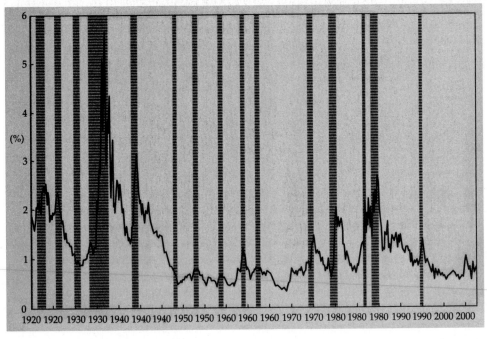

Shaded areas = economic recession as defined by the NBER

Source: Exhibit 1 in Leland E. Crabbe and Frank J. Fabozzi, *Managing a Corporate Portfolio* (Hoboken, NJ: John Wiley & Sons, 2002), p. 154.

[8] For a further discussion and evidence regarding business cycles and credit spreads, see Chapter 10 in Leland E. Crabbe and Frank J. Fabozzi, *Managing a Corporate Portfolio* (Hoboken, NJ: John Wiley & Sons, 2002).

4.4 Including Embedded Options

It is not uncommon for a bond issue to include a provision that gives either the issuer and/or the bondholder an option to take some action against the other party. The most common type of option in a bond issue is the call provision that grants the issuer the right to retire the debt, fully or partially, before the scheduled maturity date.

The presence of an embedded option has an effect on both the yield spread of an issue relative to a Treasury security and the yield spread relative to otherwise comparable issues that do not have an embedded option. In general, investors require a larger yield spread to a comparable Treasury security for an issue with an embedded option that is favorable to the issuer (e.g., a call option) than for an issue without such an option. In contrast, market participants require a smaller yield spread to a comparable Treasury security for an issue with an embedded option that is favorable to the investor (e.g., put option or conversion option). In fact, for a bond with an option favorable to an investor, the interest rate may be less than that on a comparable Treasury security.

Even for callable bonds, the yield spread depends on the type of call feature. For a callable bond with a deferred call, the longer the deferred call period, the greater the call protection provided to the investor. Thus, all other factors equal, the longer the deferred call period, the lower the yield spread attributable to the call feature.

A major part of the bond market is the mortgage-backed securities sector.[9] These securities expose an investor to prepayment risk and the yield spread between a mortgage-backed security and a comparable Treasury security reflects this prepayment risk. To see this, consider a basic mortgage-backed security called a Ginnie Mae passthrough security. This security is backed by the full faith and credit of the U.S. government. Consequently, the yield spread between a Ginnie Mae passthrough security and a comparable Treasury security is not due to credit risk. Rather, it is primarily due to prepayment risk. For example, Exhibit 68-5 reports the yield on 30-year Ginnie Mae passthrough securities with different coupon rates. The first issue to be addressed is the maturity of the comparable Treasury issue against which the Ginnie Mae should be benchmarked in order to calculate a yield spread. This is an issue because a mortgage passthrough security is an amortizing security that repays principal over time rather than just at the

EXHIBIT 68-5	Yield Spreads and Option-Adjusted Spread (OAS) for Ginnie Mae 30-year Passthrough Securities (February 8, 2002)					
Coupon Rate (%)	Yield Spread (bps)	Benchmark Treasury	OAS on 2/8/02 (bps)	90-Day OAS (bps)		
				High	Low	Avg.
6.5	203	5 year	52	75	46	59
7.0	212	5 year	57	83	54	65
7.5	155	3 year	63	94	62	74
8.0	105	3 year	73	108	73	88
9.0	244	2 year	131	160	124	139

Source: Abstracted from *Global Relative Value*, Lehman Brothers, Fixed Income Research, February 11, 2002, p.132.

---

[9] The mortgage-backed securities sector is often referred to as simply the "mortgage sector."

Practice Question 2

Below are the yield spreads estimated between 10-year federal agency securities and the 10-year on-the-run Treasury issue on June 30, 1998 as reported in the July 20, 1998 issue of *Spread Talk* published by Prudential Securities (p. 7):

Issue	Yield spread (bps)
noncallable	40
callable, 1 year deferred call	110
callable, 2 year deferred call	95
callable, 3 year deferred call	75

A. Why is the yield spread for the noncallable issue less than for the three callable issues?

B. Why is it that, for the callable issues, the longer the deferred call period, the smaller the yield spread?

---

stated maturity date (30 years in our illustration). Consequently, while the stated maturity of a Ginnie Mae passthrough is 30 years, its yield should not be compared to the yield on a 30-year Treasury issue. For now, you can see that the Treasury benchmark in Exhibit 68-5 depends on the coupon rate. The yield spread, shown in the second column, depends on the coupon rate.

In general, when a yield spread is cited for an issue that is callable, part of the spread reflects the risk associated with the embedded option. Reported yield spreads do not adjust for embedded options. The raw yield spreads are sometimes referred to as **nominal spreads**—nominal in the sense that the value of embedded options has not been removed in computing an adjusted yield spread. The yield spread that adjusts for the embedded option is OAS.

The last four columns in Exhibit 68-5 show Lehman Brothers' estimate of the option-adjusted spread for the 30-year Ginnie Mae passthroughs shown in the exhibit—the option-adjusted spread on February 8, 2002 and for the prior 90-day period (high, low, and average). The nominal spread is the yield spread shown in the second column. Notice that the option-adjusted spread is considerably less than the nominal spread. For example, for the 7.5% coupon issue the nominal spread is 155 basis points. After adjusting for the prepayment risk (i.e., the embedded option), the spread as measured by the option-adjusted spread is considerably less, 63 basis points.

4.5 Liquidity

Even within the Treasury market, a yield spread exists between off-the-run Treasury issues and on-the-run Treasury issues of similar maturity due to differences in liquidity and the effects of the repo market. Similarly, in the spread sectors, generic on-the-run yield curves can be estimated and the liquidity spread due to an off-the-run issue can be computed.

A Lehman Brother's study found that one factor that affects liquidity (and therefore the yield spread) is the size of an issue—the larger the issue, the greater the liquidity relative to a smaller issue, and the greater the liquidity, the lower the yield spread.[10]

4.6 Taxability of Interest Income

In the United States, unless exempted under the federal income tax code, interest income is taxable at the federal income tax level. In addition to federal income taxes, state and local taxes may apply to interest income.

The federal tax code specifically exempts interest income from qualified municipal bond issues from taxation.[11] Because of the tax-exempt feature of these municipal bonds, the yield on municipal bonds is less than that on Treasuries with the same maturity. Exhibit 68-6 shows this relationship on February 12, 2002, as reported by Bloomberg Financial Markets. The yield ratio shown for municipal bonds is the ratio of AAA general obligation bond yields to yields for the same maturity on-the-run Treasury issue.[12]

The difference in yield between tax-exempt securities and Treasury securities is typically measured not in terms of the absolute yield spread but as a yield ratio. More specifically, it is measured as the quotient of the yield on a tax-exempt security relative to the yield on a comparable Treasury security. This is reported in Exhibit 68-6. The yield ratio has changed over time due to changes in tax rates, as well as other factors. The higher the tax rate, the more attractive the tax-exempt feature and the lower the yield ratio.

The U.S. municipal bond market is divided into two bond sectors: general obligation bonds and revenue bonds. For the tax-exempt bond market, the benchmark

EXHIBIT 68-6	Yield Ratio for AAA General Obligation Municipal Bonds to U.S. Treasuries of the Same Maturity (February 12, 2002)		
Maturity	**Yield on AAA General Obligation (%)**	**Yield on U.S. Treasury (%)**	**Yield Ratio**
3 months	1.29	1.72	0.75
6 months	1.41	1.84	0.77
1 year	1.69	2.16	0.78
2 years	2.20	3.02	0.73
3 years	2.68	3.68	0.73
4 years	3.09	4.13	0.75
5 years	3.42	4.42	0.77
7 years	3.86	4.84	0.80
10 years	4.25	4.95	0.86
15 years	4.73	5.78	0.82
20 years	4.90	5.85	0.84
30 years	4.95	5.50	0.90

Source: Bloomberg Financial Markets

---

[10] *Global Relative Value*, Lehman Brothers, Fixed Income Research, June 28, 1999, COR-2 AND 3.

[11] As explained in Reading 67, some municipal bonds are taxable.

[12] Some maturities for Treasury securities shown in the exhibit are not on-the-run issues. These are estimates for the market yields.

for calculating yield spreads is not Treasury securities, but rather a generic AAA general obligation yield curve constructed by dealer firms active in the municipal bond market and by data/analytics vendors.

4.6.1 After-Tax Yield and Taxable-Equivalent Yield

The yield on a taxable bond issue after federal income taxes are paid is called the **after-tax yield** and is computed as follows:

$$\text{after-tax yield} = \text{pre-tax yield} \times (1 - \text{marginal tax rate})$$

Of course, the marginal tax rate[13] varies among investors. For example, suppose a taxable bond issue offers a yield of 5% and is acquired by an investor facing a marginal tax rate of 31%. The after-tax yield would then be:

$$\text{after-tax yield} = 0.05 \times (1 - 0.31) = 0.0345 = 3.45\%$$

Alternatively, we can determine the yield that must be offered on a taxable bond issue to give the same after-tax yield as a tax-exempt issue. This yield is called the **taxable-equivalent yield** or **tax-equivalent yield** and is computed as follows:

$$\text{taxable-equivalent yield} = \frac{\text{tax-exempt yield}}{(1 - \text{marginal tax rate})}$$

For example, consider an investor facing a 31% marginal tax rate who purchases a tax-exempt issue with a yield of 4%. The taxable-equivalent yield is then:

$$\text{taxable equivalent yield} = \frac{0.04}{(1 - 0.31)} = 0.058 = 5.80\%$$

Notice that the higher the marginal tax rate, the higher the taxable equivalent yield. For instance, in our last example if the marginal tax rate is 40% rather

---

Practice Question 3

Following is information about two investors, Ms. High and Mr. Low:

	Marginal Tax Bracket
Ms. High	40%
Mr. Low	15%

A. Suppose that these two investors are considering investing in a taxable bond that offers a yield of 6.8%. What is the after-tax yield for each investor?

B. Suppose that these two investors can purchase a tax-exempt security offering a yield of 4.8%. What is the taxable-equivalent yield for each investor?

---

[13] The marginal tax rate is the tax rate at which an additional dollar is taxed.

than 31%, the taxable-equivalent yield would be 6.67% rather than 5.80%, as shown below:

$$\text{taxable-equivalent yield} = \frac{0.04}{(1 - 0.40)} = 0.0667 = 6.67\%$$

Some state and local governments tax interest income from bond issues that are exempt from federal income taxes. Some municipalities exempt interest income from all municipal issues from taxation, while others do not. Some states exempt interest income from bonds issued by municipalities within the state but tax the interest income from bonds issued by municipalities outside of the state. The implication is that two municipal securities with the same credit rating and the same maturity may trade at different yield spreads because of the relative demand for bonds of municipalities in different states. For example, in a high income tax state such as New York, the demand for bonds of New York municipalities drives down their yields relative to bonds issued by municipalities in a zero income tax state such as Texas.

4.7 Technical Factors

At times, deviations from typical yield spreads are caused by temporary imbalances between supply and demand. For example, in the second quarter of 1999, issuers became concerned that the Fed would pursue a policy to increase interest rates. In response, a record issuance of corporate securities resulted in an increase in the yield spread between corporates and Treasuries.

In the municipal market, yield spreads are affected by the temporary oversupply of issues within a market sector. For example, a substantial new issue volume of high-grade state general obligation bonds may tend to decrease the yield spread between high-grade and low-grade revenue bonds. In a weak market environment, it is easier for high-grade municipal bonds to come to market than for weaker credits. So at times high grades flood weak markets even when there is a relative scarcity of medium- and low-grade municipal bond issues.

Since technical factors cause temporary misalignments of the yield spread relationship, some investors look at the forward calendar of planned offerings to project the impact on future yield spreads. Some corporate analysts identify the risk of yield spread changes due to the supply of new issues when evaluating issuers or sectors.

NON-U.S. INTEREST RATES   5

The same factors that affect yield spreads in the United States are responsible for yield spreads in other countries and between countries. Major non-U.S. bond markets have a government benchmark yield curve similar to that of the U.S. Treasury yield curve. Exhibit 68-7 shows the government yield curve as of the beginning and end of 2001 for Germany, Japan, the U.K., and France. These yield curves are presented to illustrate the different shapes and the way in which they can change. Notice that only the Japanese yield curve shifted in an almost parallel fashion (i.e., the rate for all maturities changed by approximately the same number of basis points).

The German bond market is the largest market for publicly issued bonds in Europe. The yields on German government bonds are viewed as benchmark interest rates in Europe. Because of the important role of the German bond

| EXHIBIT 68-7 | Yield Curves in Germany, Japan, the U.K., and France: 2001 |

(a) German Bund Yield Curve

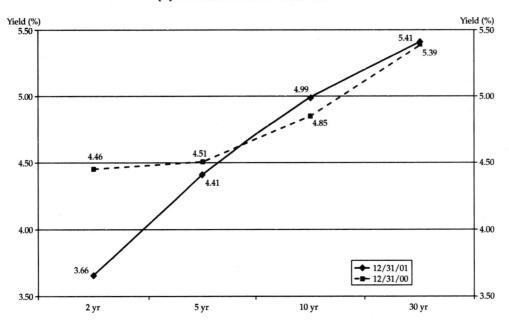

(b) Japanese Government Bond Yield Curve

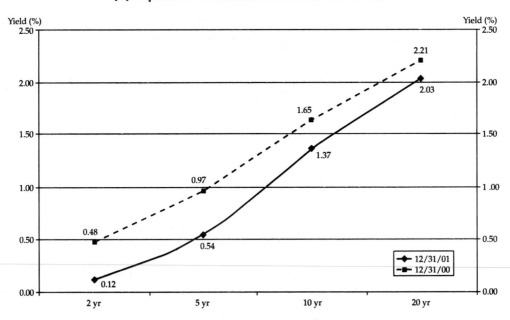

(Exhibit continued on next page …)

EXHIBIT 68-7 (continued)

(c) U.K. Gilt Yield Curve

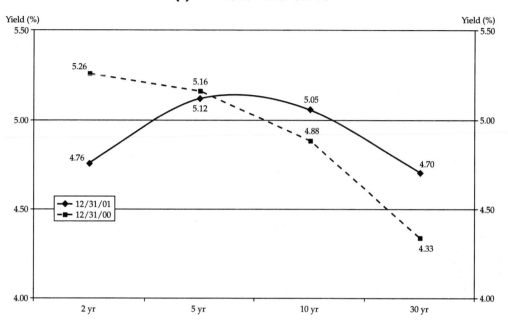

(d) French OAT Yield Curve

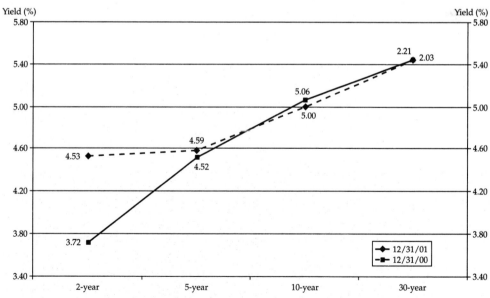

Source: Lehman Brothers Fixed Income Research, *Global Fixed Income Strategy "Playbook,"* January 2002.

market, nominal spreads are typically computed relative to German government bonds (German bunds).

Institutional investors who borrow funds on a short-term basis to invest (referred to as "funded investors") obviously desire to earn an amount in excess of their borrowing cost. The most popular borrowing cost reference rate is the **London interbank offered rate** (LIBOR). LIBOR is the interest rate at which banks pay to borrow funds from other banks in the London interbank market. The borrowing occurs via a cash deposit of one bank (the lender) into a certificate of deposit (CD) in another bank (the borrower). The maturity of the CD can be from overnight to five years. So, 3-month LIBOR represents the interest rate paid on a CD that matures in three months. The CD can be denominated in one of several currencies. The currencies for which LIBOR is reported are the U.S. dollar, the British pound, the Euro, the Canadian dollar, the Australian dollar, the Japanese yen, and Swiss francs. When it is denominated in U.S. dollars, it is referred to as a Eurodollar CD. LIBOR is determined for every London business day by the British Bank Association (BBA) by maturity and for each currency and is reported by various services.

Entities seeking to borrow funds pay a spread over LIBOR and seek to earn a spread over that funding cost when they invest the borrowed funds. So, for example, if the 3-month borrowing cost for a funded investor is 3-month LIBOR plus 25 basis points and the investor can earn 3-month LIBOR plus 125 basis points for three months, then the investor earns a spread of 100 basis points for three months (125 basis points − 25 basis points).

6   SWAP SPREADS

Another important spread measure is the **swap spread**.

6.1 Interest Rate Swap and the Swap Spread

In an interest rate swap, two parties (called **counterparties**) agree to exchange periodic interest payments. The dollar amount of the interest payments exchanged is based on a predetermined dollar principal, which is called the **notional principal** or **notional amount**. The dollar amount each counterparty pays to the other is the agreed-upon periodic interest rate times the notional principal. The only dollars exchanged between the parties are the interest payments, not the notional principal. In the most common type of swap, one party agrees to pay the other party fixed interest payments at designated dates for the life of the swap. This party is referred to as the **fixed-rate payer**. The fixed rate that the fixed-rate payer pays is called the **swap rate**. The other party, who agrees to make interest rate payments that float with some reference rate, is referred to as the **fixed-rate receiver**.

The reference rates used for the floating rate in an interest rate swap is one of various money market instruments: LIBOR (the most common reference rate used in swaps), Treasury bill rate, commercial paper rate, bankers' acceptance rate, federal funds rate, and prime rate.

The convention that has evolved for quoting a swap rate is that a dealer sets the floating rate equal to the reference rate and then quotes the fixed rate that will apply. The fixed rate has a specified "spread" above the yield for a Treasury with the same term to maturity as the swap. This specified spread is called the **swap spread**. The **swap rate** is the sum of the yield for a Treasury with the same maturity as the swap plus the swap spread.

To illustrate an interest rate swap in which one party pays fixed and receives floating, assume the following:

- ▶ term of swap: 5 years
- ▶ swap spread: 50 basis points
- ▶ reference rate: 3-month LIBOR
- ▶ notional amount: $50 million
- ▶ frequency of payments: every three months

Suppose also that the 5-year Treasury rate is 5.5% at the time the swap is entered into. Then the swap rate will be 6%, found by adding the swap spread of 50 basis points to the 5-year Treasury yield of 5.5%.

This means that the fixed-rate payer agrees to pay a 6% annual rate for the next five years with payments made quarterly and receive from the fixed-rate receiver 3-month LIBOR with the payments made quarterly. Since the notional amount is $50 million, this means that every three months, the fixed-rate payer pays $750,000 (6% times $50 million divided by 4). The fixed-rate receiver pays 3-month LIBOR times $50 million divided by 4. The table below shows the payment made by the fixed-rate receiver to the fixed-rate payer for different values of 3-month LIBOR:[14]

If 3-Month LIBOR Is	Annual Dollar Amount	Quarterly Payment
4%	$2,000,000	$500,000
5	2,500,000	625,000
6	3,000,000	750,000
7	3,500,000	875,000
8	4,000,000	1,000,000

In practice, the payments are netted out. For example, if 3-month LIBOR is 4%, the fixed-rate receiver would receive $750,000 and pay to the fixed-rate payer $500,000. Netting the two payments, the fixed-rate payer pays the fixed-rate receiver $250,000 ($750,000 − $500,000).

6.2 Role of Interest Rate Swaps

Interest rate swaps have many important applications in fixed income portfolio management and risk management. They tie together the fixed-rate and floating-rate sectors of the bond market. As a result, investors can convert a fixed-rate asset into a floating-rate asset with an interest rate swap.

Suppose a financial institution has invested in 5-year bonds with a $50 million par value and a coupon rate of 9% and that this bond is selling at par value. Moreover, this institution borrows $50 million on a quarterly basis (to fund the purchase of the bonds) and its cost of funds is 3-month LIBOR plus 50 basis points. The "income spread" between its assets (i.e., 5-year bonds) and its liabilities (its funding cost) for any 3-month period depends on 3-month LIBOR. The following table shows how the annual spread varies with 3-month LIBOR:

---

[14] The amount of the payment is found by dividing the annual dollar amount by four because payments are made quarterly. In a real world application, both the fixed-rate and floating-rate payments are adjusted for the number of days in a quarter, but it is unnecessary for us to deal with this adjustment here.

Asset Yield	3-Month LIBOR	Funding Cost	Annual Income Spread
9.00%	4.00%	4.50%	4.50%
9.00%	5.00%	5.50%	3.50%
9.00%	6.00%	6.50%	2.50%
9.00%	7.00%	7.50%	1.50%
9.00%	8.00%	8.50%	0.50%
9.00%	8.50%	9.00%	0.00%
9.00%	9.00%	9.50%	−0.50%
9.00%	10.00%	10.50%	−1.50%
9.00%	11.00%	11.50%	−2.50%

As 3-month LIBOR increases, the income spread decreases. If 3-month LIBOR exceeds 8.5%, the income spread is negative (i.e., it costs more to borrow than is earned on the bonds in which the borrowed funds are invested).

This financial institution has a mismatch between its assets and its liabilities. An interest rate swap can be used to hedge this mismatch. For example, suppose the manager of this financial institution enters into a 5-year swap with a $50 million notional amount in which it agrees to pay a fixed rate (i.e., to be the fixed-rate payer) in exchange for 3-month LIBOR. Suppose further that the swap rate is 6%. Then the annual income spread taking into account the swap payments is as follows for different values of 3-month LIBOR:

Asset Yield	3-Month LIBOR	Funding Cost	Fixed Rate Paid in Swap	3-Month LIBOR Rec. in Swap	Annual Income Spread
9.00%	4.00%	4.50%	6.00%	4.00%	2.50%
9.00%	5.00%	5.50%	6.00%	5.00%	2.50%
9.00%	6.00%	6.50%	6.00%	6.00%	2.50%
9.00%	7.00%	7.50%	6.00%	7.00%	2.50%
9.00%	8.00%	8.50%	6.00%	8.00%	2.50%
9.00%	8.50%	9.00%	6.00%	8.50%	2.50%
9.00%	9.00%	9.50%	6.00%	9.00%	2.50%
9.00%	10.00%	10.50%	6.00%	10.00%	2.50%
9.00%	11.00%	11.50%	6.00%	11.00%	2.50%

Assuming the bond does not default and is not called, the financial institution has locked in a spread of 250 basis points.

Effectively, the financial institution using this interest rate swap converted a fixed-rate asset into a floating-rate asset. The reference rate for the synthetic floaing-rate asset is 3-month LIBOR and the liabilities are in terms of 3-month LIBOR. Alternatively, the financial institution could have converted its liabilities to a fixed-rate by entering into a 5-year $50 million notional amount swap by being the fixed-rate payer and the results would have been the same.

This simple illustration shows the critical importance of an interest rate swap. Investors and issuers with a mismatch of assets and liabilities can use an interest rate swap to better match assets and liabilities, thereby reducing their risk.

Practice Question 4

Assume that the asset yield in the illustration is 8.6% instead of 9% and the funding cost is 3-month LIBOR plus 60 basis points. Demonstrate the spread that has been locked in by the interest rate swap (assuming the issuer of the assets does not default) by completing the following table:

Asset Yield	3-Month LIBOR	Funding Cost	Fixed Rate Paid in Swap	3-Month LIBOR Rec. in Swap	Annual Income Spread
	4.00%				
	5.00%				
	6.00%				
	7.00%				
	8.00%				
	8.50%				
	9.00%				
	10.00%				
	11.00%				

6.3 Determinants of the Swap Spread

Market participants throughout the world view the swap spread as the appropriate spread measure for valuation and relative value analysis. Here we discuss the determinants of the swap spread.

We know that

swap rate = Treasury rate + swap spread

where Treasury rate is equal to the yield on a Treasury with the same maturity as the swap. Since the parties are swapping the future reference rate for the swap rate, then:

reference rate = Treasury rate + swap spread

Solving for the swap spread we have:

swap spread = reference rate − Treasury rate

Since the most common reference rate is LIBOR, we can substitute this into the above formula getting:

swap spread = LIBOR − Treasury rate

Thus, the swap spread is a spread of the global cost of short-term borrowing over the Treasury rate.

Source: Lehman Brothers Fixed Income Research, *Global Fixed Income Strategy "Playbook,"* January 2002.

The swap spread primarily reflects the credit spreads in the corporate bond market.[15] Studies have found a high correlation between swap spreads and credit spreads in various sectors of the fixed income market. This can be seen in Exhibit 68-8 which shows the 3-year trailing correlation from June 1992 to December 2001 between swap spreads and AA, A, and BBB credit spreads. Note from the exhibit that the highest correlation is with AA credit spreads.

6.4 Swap Spread Curve

A **swap spread curve** shows the relationship between the swap rate and swap maturity. A swap spread curve is available by country. The swap spread is the amount added to the yield of the respective country's government bond with the same maturity as the maturity of the swap. Exhibit 68-9 shows the swap spread curves for Germany, Japan, the U.K., and the U.S. for January 2001 and December 2001. The swap spreads move together. For example, Exhibit 68-10 shows the daily 5-year swap spreads from December 2000 to December 2001 for the U.S. and Germany.

---

[15] We say primarily because there are also technical factors that affect the swap spread. For a discussion of these factors, see Richard Gordon, "The Truth about Swap Spreads," in Frank J. Fabozzi (ed.), *Professional Perspectives on Fixed Income Portfolio Management: Volume 1* (New Hope, PA: Frank J. Fabozzi Associates, 2000), pp. 97–104.

EXHIBIT 68-9	January and December 2001 Swap Spread Curves for Germany, Japan, U.K., and U.S.

	Germany				Japan				U.K.				U.S.			
	2-Year	5-Year	10-Year	30-Year	2-Year	5-Year	10-Year	30-Year	2-Year	5-Year	10-Year	30-Year	2-Year	5-Year	10-Year	30-Year
Jan-01	23	40	54	45	8	10	14	29	40	64	83	91	63	82	81	73
Dec-01	22	28	28	14	3	(2)	(1)	8	36	45	52	42	46	76	77	72

Source: Lehman Brothers Fixed Income Research, *Global Fixed Income Strategy "Playbook,"* January 2002.

EXHIBIT 68-10	Daily 5-Year Swap Spreads in Germany and the United States: 2001

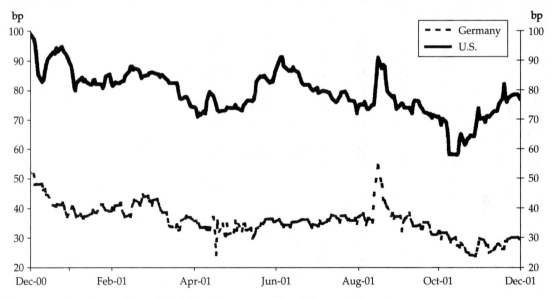

Source: Lehman Brothers Fixed Income Research, *Global Fixed Income Strategy "Playbook,"* January 2002.

SUMMARY

▶ The interest rate offered on a particular bond issue depends on the interest rate that can be earned on risk-free instruments and the perceived risks associated with the issue.

▶ The U.S. Federal Reserve Board is the policy making body whose interest rate policy tools directly influence short-term interest rates and indirectly influence long-term interest rates in the United States.

▶ The Fed's most frequently employed interest rate policy tools are open market operations and changing the discount rate; less frequently used tools are changing bank reserve requirements and verbal persuasion to influence how bankers supply credit to businesses and consumers.

▶ Because Treasury securities have no credit risk, market participants look at the interest rate or yield offered on an on-the-run Treasury security as the minimum interest rate required on a non-Treasury security with the same maturity.

▶ The Treasury yield curve shows the relationship between yield and maturity of on-the-run Treasury issues.

▶ The typical shape for the Treasury yield curve is upward sloping—yield increases with maturity—which is referred to as a normal yield curve.

▶ Inverted yield curves (yield decreasing with maturity) and flat yield curves (yield roughly the same regardless of maturity) have been observed for the yield curve.

▶ Two factors complicate the relationship between maturity and yield as indicated by the Treasury yield curve: (1) the yield for on-the-run issues is distorted since these securities can be financed at cheaper rates and, as a result, offer a lower yield than in the absence of this financing advantage and (2) on-the-run Treasury issues and off-the-run issues have different interest rate reinvestment risks.

▶ The yields on Treasury strips of different maturities provide a superior relationship between yield and maturity compared to the on-the-run Treasury yield curve.

▶ The yield on a zero-coupon or stripped Treasury security is called the Treasury spot rate.

▶ The term structure of interest rates is the relationship between maturity and Treasury spot rates.

▶ Three theories have been offered to explain the shape of the yield curve: pure expectations theory, liquidity preference theory, and market segmentation theory.

▶ The pure expectations theory asserts that the market sets yields based solely on expectations for future interest rates.

▶ According to the pure expectations theory: (1) a rising term structure reflects an expectation that future short-term rates will rise, (2) a flat term structure reflects an expectation that future short-term rates will be mostly constant, and (3) a falling term structure reflects an expectation that future short-term rates will decline.

▶ The liquidity preference theory asserts that market participants want to be compensated for the interest rate risk associated with holding longer-term bonds.

▶ The market segmentation theory asserts that there are different maturity sectors of the yield curve and that each maturity sector is independent or segmented from the other maturity sectors. Within each maturity sector, the interest rate is determined by the supply and demand for funds.

▶ According to the market segmentation theory, any shape is possible for the yield curve.

▶ Despite the imperfections of the Treasury yield curve as a benchmark for the minimum interest rate that an investor requires for investing in a non-Treasury security, it is common to refer to a non-Treasury security's additional yield over the nearest maturity on-the-run Treasury issue as the "yield spread."

▶ The yield spread can be computed in three ways: (1) the difference between the yield on two bonds or bond sectors (called the absolute yield spread), (2) the difference in yields as a percentage of the benchmark yield (called the relative yield spread), and (3) the ratio of the yield relative to the benchmark yield (called the yield ratio).

▶ An intermarket yield spread is the yield spread between two securities with the same maturity in two different sectors of the bond market.

▶ The most common intermarket sector spread calculated is the yield spread between the yield on a security in a non-Treasury market sector and a Treasury security with the same maturity.

▶ An intramarket sector spread is the yield spread between two issues within the same market sector.

▶ An issuer specific yield curve can be computed given the yield spread, by maturity, for an issuer and the yield for on-the-run Treasury securities.

▶ The factors other than maturity that affect the intermarket and intramarket yield spreads are (1) the relative credit risk of the two issues; (2) the presence of embedded options; (3) the relative liquidity of the two issues; and, (4) the taxability of the interest.

▶ A credit spread or quality spread is the yield spread between a non-Treasury security and a Treasury security that are "identical in all respects except for credit rating."

▶ Some market participants argue that credit spreads between corporates and Treasuries change systematically because of changes in economic prospects—widening in a declining economy ("flight to quality") and narrowing in an expanding economy.

▶ Generally investors require a larger spread to a comparable Treasury security for issues with an embedded option favorable to the issuer, and a smaller spread for an issue with an embedded option favorable to the investor.

▶ For mortgage-backed securities, one reason for the increased yield spread relative to a comparable Treasury security is exposure to prepayment risk.

▶ The option-adjusted spread of a security seeks to measure the yield spread after adjusting for embedded options.

▶ A yield spread exists due to the difference in the perceived liquidity of two issues.

▶ One factor that affects liquidity (and therefore the yield spread) is the size of an issue—the larger the issue, the greater the liquidity relative to a smaller issue, and the greater the liquidity, the lower the yield spread.

▶ Because of the tax-exempt feature of municipal bonds, the yield on municipal bonds is less than that on Treasuries with the same maturity.

▶ The difference in yield between tax-exempt securities and Treasury securities is typically measured in terms of a yield ratio—the yield on a tax-exempt security as a percentage of the yield on a comparable Treasury security.

▶ The after-tax yield is computed by multiplying the pre-tax yield by one minus the marginal tax rate.

▶ In the tax-exempt bond market, the benchmark for calculating yield spreads is a generic AAA general obligation bond with a specified maturity.

▶ Technical factors having to do with temporary imbalances between the supply of and demand for new issues affect yield spreads.

▶ The same factors that affect yield spreads in the United States affect yield spreads in other countries and between countries.

▶ Major non-U.S. bond markets have government benchmark yield curves similar to the U.S. Treasury yield curve.

▶ Because of the important role of the German bond market, nominal spreads in the European bond market are typically computed relative to German government bonds.

▶ Funded investors who borrow short term typically measure the relative value of a security using borrowing rates rather than the Treasury rate.

▶ The most popular borrowing cost reference rate is the London interbank offered rate (LIBOR), which is the interest rate banks pay to borrow funds from other banks in the London interbank market.

▶ Funded investors typically pay a spread over LIBOR and seek to earn a spread over that funding cost when they invest the borrowed funds.

▶ In an interest rate swap, two parties agree to exchange periodic interest payments with the dollar amount of the interest payments exchanged based on a notional principal (also called a notional amount).

▶ In a typical interest rate swap, one party (the fixed-rate payer) agrees to pay to the counterparty fixed interest payments at designated dates for the life of the contract and the counterparty (the fixed-rate receiver) agrees to make interest rate payments that float with some reference rate.

▶ In an interest rate swap, the fixed rate paid by the fixed-rate payer is called the swap rate.

▶ The most common reference rate used in a swap is LIBOR.

▶ The swap spread is the spread that the fixed-rate payer agrees to pay above the Treasury yield with the same term to maturity as the swap.

▶ The swap rate is the sum of the yield of a Treasury with the same maturity as the swap plus the swap spread.

▶ Institutional investors can use an interest rate swap to convert a fixed-rate asset (or liability) into a floating-rate asset (or liability) and vice versa.

▶ The swap spread is viewed by market participants throughout the world as the appropriate spread measure for valuation and relative value analysis.

▶ The swap spread is the spread of the global cost of short-term borrowing over the Treasury rate.

▶ There is a high correlation between swap spreads and credit spreads in various sectors of the bond market.

▶ A swap spread curve shows the relationship between the swap rate and swap maturity for a given country.

PROBLEMS FOR READING 68

1. The following statement appears on page 2 of the August 2, 1999 issue of Prudential Securities' *Spread Talk*.

   > The market appears to be focusing all of its energy on predicting whether or not the Fed will raise rates again at the August and/or October FOMC [Federal Open Market Committee] meetings.

   How do market observers try to predict "whether or not the Fed will raise rates"?

2. Ms. Peters is a financial advisor. One of her clients called and asked about a recent change in the shape of the yield curve from upward sloping to downward sloping. The client told Ms. Peters that she thought that the market was signaling that interest rates were expected to decline in the future. What should Ms. Peters' response be to her client?

3. How does the liquidity preference theory differ from the pure expectations theory?

4. According to the pure expectations theory, what does a humped yield curve suggest about the expectations of future interest rates?

5. Assume the following information pertaining to federal agency spreads was reported:

Agency Spreads versus Benchmark Treasury (basis points)

| | Last 12 Months | | | |
	Yield Spread	High	Low	Average
Noncallable				
3-year	70	70	28	44.1
5-year	80	80	32	55.4
10-year	95	95	45	71.2
Callable				
3-year (NC1)	107	107	50	80.2
5-year (NC1)	145	145	77	112.1
5-year (NC2)	132	132	65	96.9
5-year (NC3)	124	124	—	33.6
10-year (NC3)	178	178	99	132.9
10-year (NC5)	156	156	79	112.5

	Last 12 Months			
	Yield Spread	High	Low	Average
Callable OAS (volatility = 14%)				
3-year (NC1)	75	75	20	50.0
5-year (NC1)	100	100	20	63.8
5-year (NC2)	100	100	23	60.7
5-year (NC3)	100	100	29	59.6
10-year (NC3)	115	115	34	77.0
10-year (NC5)	115	115	36	77.4

Note: NCX = *X*-year deferred call;— = not available

A. Relative to the previous 12 months, what does the yield spread data above indicate about yield spreads?

B. Explain what causes the yield spread relationship between callable and noncallable issues for a given maturity?

C. Explain what causes the yield spread relationship among the different callable issues for a given maturity?

D. Why are the yield spreads shown in the second panel referred to as nominal spreads?

E. Explain what causes the yield spread relationship between the callable yield spread and the callable OAS for a given maturity and given deferred call?

6. Comment on the following statement by a representative of an investment management firm who is working with a client in selecting sectors in which the manager for the account will be permitted to invest:

> Mortgage-backed securities give our managers the opportunity to increase yield because these securities offer a higher yield than comparable Treasury securities. In particular, our managers prefer Ginnie Mae mortgage-backed securities because they have no credit risk since they are backed by the full faith and credit of the U.S. government. Therefore, our managers can pick up additional yield with no additional credit risk. While Ginnie Mae mortgage-backed securities may not be as liquid as U.S. Treasury securities, the yield spread is more than adequate to compensate for the lesser liquidity.

7. A. Why is the yield spread between a bond with an embedded option and an otherwise comparable Treasury security referred to as a "nominal spread"?

B. What is an option-adjusted spread and why is it superior to a nominal spread as a yield spread measure for a bond with an embedded option?

8. Suppose that the yield on a 10-year noncallable corporate bond is 7.25% and the yield for the on-the-run 10-year Treasury is 6.02%. Compute the following:

A. the absolute yield spread

B. the relative yield spread

C. the yield ratio

9. Following is a quote that appeared in the May 19, 1999 *Global Relative Value* by Lehman Brothers (COR-1):

> As we have written in the past, percent yield spreads (spread as a percent of Treasury yields) are still cheap on an historical basis. As an illustration, the average single A 10-year industrial percent yield spread was 17% on April 30 compared to a 10 year monthly average of 12%.

  A. What is another name for the yield spread measure cited in the quote?

  B. Why would the analysts at Lehman Brothers focus on "percent yield spreads" rather than absolute yield spread?

10. If proposals are being considered by Congress to reduce tax rates and the market views that passage of such legislation is likely, what would you expect to happen to municipal bond yields?

11. A. Why isn't the Treasury yield curve used as a benchmark in measuring yield spreads between different sectors of the municipal bond market?

  B. What benchmark is used?

12. A. What is the after-tax yield for an investor in the 40% tax bracket if the taxable yield is 5%?

  B. What is the taxable-equivalent yield for an investor in the 39% tax bracket if the tax-exempt yield on an investment is 3.1%?

13. Why are funded investors who borrow short term interested in a LIBOR yield curve rather than the Treasury yield curve?

14. If the swap spread for a 5-year interest rate swap is 120 basis points and the yield on the 5-year Treasury is 4.4%, what is the swap rate?

15. Why is the swap spread an important spread measure?

16. Suppose that an institutional investor has entered into an interest rate swap, as the fixed-rate payer, with the following terms:

Term of swap:	2 years
Frequency of payments:	quarterly
Notional amount:	$10 million
Reference rate:	3-month LIBOR
Swap spread:	100 basis points

At the time of the swap, the Treasury yield curve is as follows:

3-month rate:	4.0%	3-year rate:	6.5%
6-month rate:	4.4%	4-year rate:	7.1%
1-year rate:	4.9%	5-year rate:	7.8%
2-year rate:	5.8%		

  A. What is the swap rate?

  B. What is the dollar amount of the quarterly payment that will be made by the fixed-rate payer?

  C. Complete the following table showing the quarterly payment that will be received by the fixed-rate payer, based on 3-month LIBOR:

If 3-Month LIBOR Is	Annual Dollar Amount	Amount of Payment
5.00%		
5.50%		
6.00%		
6.50%		
7.00%		
7.50%		
8.00%		
8.50%		

D. Complete the following table showing the quarterly net payment that the fixed-rate payer must make, based on 3-month LIBOR:

If 3-Month LIBOR Is	Floating-Rate Received	Net Payment by Fixed-Rate Payer
5.00%		
5.50%		
6.00%		
6.50%		
7.00%		
7.50%		
8.00%		
8.50%		

17. An investor has purchased a floating-rate security with a 5-year maturity. The coupon formula for the floater is 6-month LIBOR plus 200 basis points and the interest payments are made *semiannually*. The floater is not callable. At the time of purchase, 6-month LIBOR is 7.5%. The investor borrowed the funds to purchase the floater by issuing a 5-year note at par value with a fixed coupon rate of 7%.

    A. Ignoring credit risk, what is the risk that this investor faces?

    B. Explain why an interest rate swap can be used to offset this risk?

    C. Suppose that the investor can enter into a 5-year interest rate swap in which the investor pays LIBOR (i.e., the investor is the fixed-rate receiver). The swap rate is 7.3% and the frequency of the payments is *semiannual*. What annual income spread can the investor lock in?

MONETARY POLICY IN AN ENVIRONMENT OF GLOBAL FINANCIAL MARKETS

by Otmar Issing

LEARNING OUTCOMES

The candidate should be able to:

a. identify how central bank behavior affects financial markets, including the role of short-term interest rates, systemic liquidity and market expectations;

b. describe the importance of communication between a central bank and the financial markets;

c. discuss the importance of predictability, credibility, and transparency of monetary policy, measures of predictability, and the problem of information asymmetry.

Address given at the Launching Workshop of the ECB-CFS Research Network on "Capital Markets and Financial Integration in Europe," Frankfurt am Main, 29 April 2002.

Let me first say that it is a great pleasure to open the launching workshop for the Research Network "Capital Markets and Financial Integration in Europe." Understanding global financial linkages is important, not least from the perspective of a central banker. Further integration of European financial markets is one of the expected benefits from monetary unification. By focusing on these issues, the Network will stimulate research on topics we as policymakers can benefit from.

In my remarks today, I would like to focus on the interaction between the central bank and financial markets. Specifically, I will first address the interdependence between monetary policy making and financial market expectations. Linked to this, I will then discuss some of our experiences of the first years of policy making at the ECB. I will conclude by briefly mentioning the recent changes that we have witnessed in the euro area financial landscape, and touch upon some areas where I believe more research is needed and where your contribution will be particularly valuable.

Let me start by elaborating on the issue of how central bank behaviour affects financial markets. In this respect, financial markets can be seen as a transmission channel of monetary policy. The central bank controls the short-term interest rate, but what matters for consumers' and firms' decisions are market interest rates beyond the direct control of the monetary authority. In this regard, the role of private banks in the transmission of monetary policy has traditionally been strong in the euro area and still plays a dominant role. Increases in liquidity are redistributed to end users through the banking system, at interest rates reflecting both current and expected future refinancing costs for the banks. Therefore, not only the actual situation of banks' balance sheets, but also market expectations about the future course of monetary policy and future inflation become important, since these expectations to a large extent determine those interest rates.

In this context, the monetary policy strategy is crucial. By a clear commitment to price stability, the ECB provides the markets with a reference against which new information can be consistently evaluated. If new information indicates risks to price stability, and markets understand the strategy, expectations will adjust in anticipation of the appropriate reaction of monetary policy. This fosters a smooth implementation of policy, where much of the actual work is done by the market's adjustment of the term structure of interest rates.

We have structured the strategy of the ECB around two pillars, which can be seen as a means of organising information concerning risks to price stability. The first pillar assigns a prominent role to money, and in this context monetary aggregates are carefully monitored to reveal such threats. Under the second pillar, other macroeconomic and financial variables that contain information about future price developments are analysed. Financial markets, by their inherent forward-looking nature, provide the central bank with valuable information about expected economic developments. Two key markets to be monitored in this context are bond markets and equity markets. The former gives an assessment of expected interest rates through the term structure of interest rates. Bond derivatives can provide important information of the prevailing uncertainty about future interest rate developments. Such information is especially useful when deciding on communication issues, should market expectations deviate too far from the central banks own evaluation of the current circumstances. Equity markets can convey information about future economic activity. They also have a direct role in the transmission of economic shocks, in that changes in consumer's wealth can impact consumption. Traditionally, this effect has been stronger in the US than in Europe. However, recent trends point to an increase in equity holdings by Europeans which might make this channel more important. Increasing globalisation and cross-border ownership seems to have resulted in faster transmission of shocks, perhaps also more oriented towards sectors rather than countries. For example, the recent IT bubble both gained momentum and collapsed simultaneously across a number of countries. This has major impact on our economies because the traditional mitigating effects of trade and diversification do not apply when similar events take place everywhere.

To conclude, under the second pillar the financial markets (as well as other markets such as those for labour and goods) provide the central bank with relevant information about risks to price stability. This, together with the monetary analysis under the first pillar, allows two complementary pictures of the threats to price stability to emerge. In turn, this facilitates cross-checking, stimulates internal discussion, and ultimately, I believe, leads to appropriate monetary policy decisions.

Traditionally, bank lending was the main source of financing economic activities in most countries of the euro area and banks were therefore the main "actors" in the monetary transmission process. However, market based financing has become more important during the last few years. An interesting questions for research is how the evolution of financial markets, for example the continuing expansion of corporate bond markets, will impact the transmission of monetary policy.

Let me turn to the issue of predictability of monetary policy. In the environment I have just described, deliberate attempts to surprise markets would be counterproductive. Rather, implementation of policy will be smoother the more predictable it is. Woodford e.g. emphasises[1] that developments in financial markets have increased the possibilities of the central bank to influence markets, to the extent that it may do so by signalling without actually moving interest rates:

"The more sophisticated markets become, the more scope there will be for communication about even subtle aspects of the bank's decision and reasoning, and it will be desirable for central banks to take advantage of this opportunity."

Communicating with sophisticated financial markets is indeed important. At the same time it is a tricky issue, since the central bank needs to ensure that it guides rather than follows the markets. An eloquent quote by Alan Blinder illustrates the danger of failing to do so:[2] "...Following the markets may be a nice way of unsettling financial surprises, which is a legitimate end in itself. But I fear that it may produce rather poor monetary policy for several reasons. One is that speculative markets tend to run in herds and to overreact to almost everything. Central bankers need to be more cautious and prudent. Another is that financial markets seem extremely susceptible to fads and speculative bubbles which sometimes stray far from fundamentals. Central bankers must innoculate themselves against whimsy and keep their eyes on the fundamentals."

It is of utmost importance that the financial markets believe the stated goals of policy and understand the monetary policy strategy. In time, markets can evaluate the track-record of the ECB relative to the goal of price stability. Adherence to the strategy should gradually enhance the credibility in that markets can interpret monetary policy decisions through the strategy. In this respect, communication with markets is essential to foster a proper understanding of the strategy, and to send clear signals about the central banks current assessment of economic conditions.

It is therefore interesting to study actual developments in market-based indicators in order to gain some insight into how market participants have perceived the predictability and credibility of the ECB. Concentrating initially on the issue of predictability, Gaspar et al. (2001) examine the behaviour of overnight interest rates between the start of 1999 and early 2001.[3] They find that the markets during that period did not appear to make systematic errors with respect to monetary policy announcements. Moreover, Hartmann et al. (2001) find that overnight rates on average moved by less than 5 basis points immediately following monetary policy announcements by the ECB.[4] Finally, if we take a look at the behaviour of implied short-term forward rates at the one-month horizon during the entire period since the introduction of the euro, we see that the majority of ECB interest rate moves have been in line with the expectations of financial market participants. In this regard, the track record of the ECB is comparable to

---

[1] Michael Woodford, "Monetary Policy in the Information Economy," in Economic Policy for the Information Economy, Kansas City Fed, 2001.

[2] Alan Blinder, "Central Banking in Theory and Practice," MIT Press, 1998, p. 61.

[3] Gaspar, Perez-Quiros & Sicilia (2001), "The ECB Monetary Policy Strategy and the Money Market," International Journal of Finance and Economics 6(4).

[4] Hartmann, Manna and Manzanares (2001), "The microstructure of the euro money market," Journal of International Money and Finance 20.

that of other major—and substantially older—central banks, such as the US Federal Reserve or the Bank of England. In my view, this performance is not bad for a young central bank like the ECB.

Of course, one could not claim that the money market has perfectly anticipated policy moves on every single occasion. Sometimes, rapidly changing economic conditions or extraordinary events, such as the September 11 terrorist attacks, require swift and decisive policy action that cannot be fully anticipated in advance. Furthermore, at times the monetary authority has access to information that market participants do not have. This information asymmetry may on rare occasions lead to policy moves that are unexpected by markets. This being said, I again repeat that there can be no interest in the monetary authority deliberately aiming to surprise the financial markets. Such a strategy would merely increase uncertainty in the markets and damage the credibility of the monetary authority.

Turning to this very aspect, taking due account of caveats such as liquidity and risk premia considerations, the market for French index-linked government bonds provides a useful measure of the credibility of monetary policy. The ten-year break-even inflation rate obtained from this market has consistently been in line with the ECB's quantitative definition of price stability, indicating a persistently high degree of credibility. Moreover, there is little evidence that monetary policy moves have generated any systematically higher volatility in the break even rate. This would seem to indicate that markets have perceived ECB monetary policy actions as transparent, in the sense that they do not appear to have induced investors to revise their beliefs about the objective of the ECB. Interestingly, in the last few months, the French treasury has issued new index-linked bonds linked to a measure of euro area HICP, which I am convinced will provide us with additional useful information in this respect.

Consistent with the notion that the monetary policy actions of the ECB have not resulted in increased market uncertainty, there is some evidence that bond market volatility has even declined since the introduction of the euro. For example, since 1999 the **implied volatility** on 10-year German Bund futures has— apart from a brief surge following September 11—declined to historically low levels. All these indications from prices of financial instruments, determined by market forces which continuously judge the actions of the ECB, lead me to conclude that our monetary policy has been credible and largely transparent to investors.

This being said, it is also clear to me that we still have much to learn about what determines financial asset prices. Moreover, the nature of financial markets, constantly changing and evolving, adds to the need of widening and deepening our understanding of these markets. This is particularly true for financial markets in the euro area, which arguably have seen the most remarkable pace of change among all developed financial markets over the last few years. For example, the euro area money market has undergone a substantial transformation, including the creation of completely new segments, such as the EONIA swap market. Similarly, the bond market has evolved considerably, with very rapid growth of the corporate bond market segment over the last few years and a sizeable expansion of the international issuance of euro-denominated bonds.

No doubt, the introduction of the single currency and a common monetary policy framework acted as a powerful catalyst in bringing about many of the changes to the euro area financial landscape that we have witnessed in recent years. However, we still need to better understand the exact mechanisms which brought about these developments. In addition, as markets evolve and new financial instruments are introduced, this will bring about new ways to extract market information which may be highly relevant for monetary policy purposes. The Research Network can make a very valuable contribution on these topics, and generally with respect to the increasing importance of finance research—both at the macro and at the micro level—for central banks. We should also learn more about international financial linkages as well as the role of global trends and other international factors in determining the evolution of financial markets in Europe. The ongoing financial integration process within the euro area should have beneficial effects for monetary policy, for example by facilitating policy signaling and transmission through enhanced market liquidity. Financial integration and international linkages are the core areas of the Research Network. All these issues which I have mentioned are key for policymakers since we need to correctly interpret the information coming from markets, and also understand how monetary policy is propagated to the real economy through financial markets.

I am convinced that the Research Network will contribute significantly to our understanding of these and other issues. I personally will follow the progress of your work with great interest. I would like to end by wishing you a very productive and fruitful workshop, and all the best in your future research work on these important topics.

4⅝ 4¹¹/₁₆ – ⅜

5½ 5½ –

20⅝ 21¹³/₁₆ – 1/₁₆

17⅜ 18⅛ + ⅞

6½ 6½ – ½

7¼ 6½ 31/32 – ⅛

15/16

9/16 9/16

7¹⁵/₁₆ 7¹³/₁₆ 7¹⁵/₁₆

2⅝ 2¹¹/₃₂ 2½ +

2¾ 2¼ 2¼

12¹/₁₆ 11⅜ 11¾ +

33¾ 33 33¹/₁₆ –

25⅝ 24⁹/₁₆ 25⅝ +

12 11⅝ 11⅞ +

10½ 10½ 10⅞ –

15⅞ 15¹³/₁₆ 15⅞ +

9¹/₁₆ 8¼ 8⅞

11¼ 10⅛

STUDY SESSION 16
ANALYSIS OF FIXED INCOME INVESTMENTS:
Analysis and Valuation

READING ASSIGNMENTS

Reading 70 Introduction to the Valuation of Debt Securities
Reading 71 Yield Measures, Spot Rates, and Forward Rates
Reading 72 Introduction to the Measurement of Interest Rate Risk

This study session describes the primary tools for valuation and analysis of fixed income securities and markets. It begins with a study of basic valuation theory and techniques for bonds and concludes with a more in-depth explanation of the primary tools for fixed income investment valuation, specifically, interest rate and yield valuation and interest rate risk measurement and analysis.

LEARNING OUTCOMES

Reading 70: Introduction to the Valuation of Debt Securities
The candidate should be able to:

a. explain the steps in the bond valuation process (i.e., estimate expected cash flows, determine an appropriate discount rate or rates, and compute the present value of the cash flows);

b. identify the types of bonds for which estimating the expected cash flows is difficult, and explain the problems encountered when estimating the cash flows for these bonds;

c. compute the value of a bond, given the expected annual or semiannual cash flows and the appropriate single (constant) discount rate, explain how the value of a bond changes if the discount rate increases or decreases, and compute the change in value that is attributable to the rate change;

d. explain how the price of a bond changes as the bond approaches its maturity date, and compute the change in value that is attributable to the passage of time;

e. compute the value of a zero-coupon bond;

f. explain the arbitrage-free valuation approach and the market process that forces the price of a bond toward its arbitrage-free value, and explain how a dealer could generate an arbitrage profit if a bond is mispriced.

Reading 71: Yield Measures, Spot Rates, and Forward Rates

The candidate should be able to:

a. explain the sources of return from investing in a bond (i.e., coupon interest payments, capital gain/loss, reinvestment income);

b. compute and interpret the traditional yield measures for fixed-rate bonds (e.g., current yield, yield to maturity, yield to first call, yield to first par call date, yield to refunding, yield to put, yield to worst, cash flow yield) and explain the assumptions underlying traditional yield measures and the limitations of the traditional yield measures;

c. explain the importance of reinvestment income in generating the yield computed at the time of purchase, calculate the amount of income required to generate that yield, and discuss the factors that affect reinvestment risk;

d. compute and interpret the bond equivalent yield of an annual-pay bond, and the annual-pay yield of a semiannual-pay bond;

e. describe the methodology for computing the theoretical Treasury spot rate curve and compute the value of a bond using spot rates;

f. distinguish between the nominal spread and the zero-volatility spread and explain the limitations of the nominal spread;

g. explain an option-adjusted spread for a bond with an embedded option and explain the option cost;

h. define a forward rate, and compute spot rates from forward rates and forward rates from spot rates;

i. compute the value of a bond using forward rates.

Reading 72: Introduction to the Measurement of Interest Rate Risk

The candidate should be able to:

a. distinguish between the full valuation approach (the scenario analysis approach) and the duration/convexity approach for measuring interest rate risk, and explain the advantage of using the full valuation approach;

b. describe the price volatility characteristics for option-free, callable, prepayable, and putable bonds when interest rates change (including the concepts of "positive convexity" and "negative convexity");

c. compute and interpret the effective duration of a bond, given information about how the bond's price will increase and decrease for given changes in interest rates, and compute the approximate percentage price change for a bond, given the bond's effective duration and a specified change in yield;

d. distinguish among the alternative definitions of duration (modified, effective or option-adjusted, and Macaulay), and explain why effective duration is the most appropriate measure of interest rate risk for bonds with embedded options;

e. compute the duration of a portfolio, given the duration of the bonds comprising the portfolio, and identify the limitations of portfolio duration;

f. describe the convexity measure of a bond and estimate a bond's percentage price change, given the bond's duration and convexity and a specified change in interest rates;

g. distinguish between modified convexity and effective convexity;

h. compute the price value of a basis point (PVBP), and explain its relationship to duration.

INTRODUCTION TO THE VALUATION OF DEBT SECURITIES

by Frank J. Fabozzi

LEARNING OUTCOMES

The candidate should be able to:

a. explain the steps in the bond valuation process (i.e., estimate expected cash flows, determine an appropriate discount rate or rates, and compute the present value of the cash flows);

b. identify the types of bonds for which estimating the expected cash flows is difficult, and explain the problems encountered when estimating the cash flows for these bonds;

c. compute the value of a bond, given the expected annual or semiannual cash flows and the appropriate single (constant) discount rate, explain how the value of a bond changes if the discount rate increases or decreases, and compute the change in value that is attributable to the rate change;

d. explain how the price of a bond changes as the bond approaches its maturity date, and compute the change in value that is attributable to the passage of time;

e. compute the value of a zero-coupon bond;

f. explain the arbitrage-free valuation approach and the market process that forces the price of a bond toward its arbitrage-free value, and explain how a dealer could generate an arbitrage profit if a bond is mispriced.

INTRODUCTION 1

Valuation is the process of determining the fair value of a financial asset. The process is also referred to as "valuing" or "pricing" a financial asset. In this reading, we will explain the general principles of fixed income security valuation. In this reading, we will limit our discussion to the valuation of option-free bonds.

Fixed Income Analysis for the Chartered Financial Analyst® Program, Second Edition, edited by Frank J. Fabozzi, Copyright © 2005 by CFA Institute. Reprinted with permission.

GENERAL PRINCIPLES OF VALUATION

The fundamental principle of financial asset valuation is that its value is equal to the present value of its expected cash flows. This principle applies regardless of the financial asset. Thus, the valuation of a financial asset involves the following three steps:

Step 1: Estimate the expected cash flows.

Step 2: Determine the appropriate interest rate or interest rates that should be used to discount the cash flows.

Step 3: Calculate the present value of the expected cash flows found in step 1 using the interest rate or interest rates determined in step 2.

2.1 Estimating Cash Flows

Cash flow is simply the cash that is expected to be received in the future from an investment. In the case of a fixed income security, it does not make any difference whether the cash flow is interest income or payment of principal. The **cash flows** of a security are the collection of each period's cash flow. Holding aside the risk of default, the cash flows for few fixed income securities are simple to project. Noncallable U.S. Treasury securities have known cash flows. For Treasury coupon securities, the cash flows are the coupon interest payments every six months up to and including the maturity date and the principal payment at the maturity date.

At times, investors will find it difficult to estimate the cash flows when they purchase a fixed income security. For example, if

1. the issuer or the investor has the option to change the contractual due date for the payment of the principal, or
2. the coupon payment is reset periodically by a formula based on some value or values of reference rates, prices, or exchange rates, or
3. the investor has the choice to convert or exchange the security into common stock.

Callable bonds, putable bonds, mortgage-backed securities, and asset-backed securities are examples of (1). Floating-rate securities are an example of (2). Convertible bonds and exchangeable bonds are examples of (3).

For securities that fall into the first category, future interest rate movements are the key factor to determine if the option will be exercised. Specifically, if interest rates fall far enough, the issuer can sell a new issue of bonds at the lower interest rate and use the proceeds to pay off (call) the older bonds that have the higher coupon rate. (This assumes that the interest savings are larger than the costs involved in refunding.) Similarly, for a loan, if rates fall enough that the interest savings outweigh the refinancing costs, the borrower has an incentive to refinance. For a putable bond, the investor will put the issue if interest rates rise enough to drive the market price below the put price (i.e., the price at which it must be repurchased by the issuer).

What this means is that to properly estimate the cash flows of a fixed income security, it is necessary to incorporate into the analysis how, in the future, changes in interest rates and other factors affecting the embedded option may affect cash flows.

2.2 Determining the Appropriate Rate or Rates

Once the cash flows for a fixed income security are estimated, the next step is to determine the appropriate interest rate to be used to discount the cash flows. As we did in the previous reading, we will use the terms *interest rate* and *yield* interchangeably. The minimum interest rate that an investor should require is the yield available in the marketplace on a default-free cash flow. In the United States, this is the yield on a U.S. Treasury security. This is *one* of the reasons that the Treasury market is closely watched. What is the *minimum* interest rate U.S. investors demand? At this point, we can assume that it is the yield on the on-the-run Treasury security with the same as the security being valued.[1] We will qualify this shortly.

For a security that is not issued by the U.S. government, investors will require a yield premium over the yield available on an on-the-run Treasury issue. This yield premium reflects the additional risks that the investor accepts.

For each cash flow estimated, the same interest rate can be used to calculate the present value. However, since each cash flow is unique, it is more appropriate to value each cash flow using an interest rate specific to that cash flow's maturity. In the traditional approach to valuation a single interest rate is used. In Section 4, we will see that the proper approach to valuation uses multiple interest rates each specific to a particular cash flow. In that section, we will also demonstrate why this must be the case.

2.3 Discounting the Expected Cash Flows

Given expected (estimated) cash flows and the appropriate interest rate or interest rates to be used to discount the cash flows, the final step in the valuation process is to value the cash flows.

What is the value of a single cash flow to be received in the future? It is the amount of money that must be invested today to generate that future value. The resulting value is called the **present value** of a cash flow. (It is also called the **discounted value**.) The present value of a cash flow will depend on (1) when a cash flow will be received (i.e., the **timing** of a cash flow) and (2) the interest rate used to calculate the present value. The interest rate used is called the **discount rate**.

First, we calculate the present value for each expected cash flow. Then, to determine the value of the security, we calculate the sum of the present values (i.e., for all of the security's expected cash flows).

If a discount rate i can be earned on any sum invested today, the present value of the expected cash flow to be received t years from now is:

$$\text{present value}_t = \frac{\text{expected cash flow in period } t}{(1 + i)^t}$$

The value of a financial asset is then the sum of the present value of all the expected cash flows. That is, assuming that there are N expected cash flows:

$$\text{value} = \text{present value}_1 + \text{present value}_2 + \dots + \text{present value}_N$$

To illustrate the present value formula, consider a simple bond that matures in four years, has a coupon rate of 10%, and has a maturity value of $100. For simplicity, let's assume the bond pays interest annually and a discount rate of 8%

---

[1] As explained in Reading 67, the on-the-run Treasury issues are the most recently auctioned Treasury issues.

should be used to calculate the present value of each cash flow. The cash flow for this bond is:

Year	Cash Flow
1	$10
2	10
3	10
4	110

The present value of each cash flow is:

Year 1: present value$_1 = \dfrac{\$10}{(1.08)^1} = \$9.2593$

Year 2: present value$_2 = \dfrac{\$10}{(1.08)^2} = \$8.5734$

Year 3: present value$_3 = \dfrac{\$10}{(1.08)^3} = \$7.9383$

Year 4: present value$_4 = \dfrac{\$110}{(1.08)^4} = \$80.8533$

The value of this security is then the sum of the present values of the four cash flows. That is, the present value is $106.6243 ($9.2593 + $8.5734 + $7.9383 + $80.8533).

Practice Question 1

A. What is the present value of a 5-year security with a coupon rate of 7% that pays annually assuming a discount rate of 5% and a par value of $100?

B. A 5-year amortizing security with a par value of $10,000 and a coupon rate of 5% has an expected cash flow of $2,309.75 per year, assuming there are no principal prepayments. The annual cash flow includes interest and principal payment. What is the present value of this amortizing security assuming a discount rate of 6%?

2.3.1 Present Value Properties

An important property about the present value can be seen from the above illustration. For the first three years, the cash flow is the same ($10) and the discount rate is the same (8%). The present value decreases as we go further into the future. *This is an important property of the present value: for a given discount rate, the further into the future a cash flow is received, the lower its present value.* This can be seen in the present value formula. As *t* increases, present value$_t$ decreases.

Suppose that instead of a discount rate of 8%, a 12% discount rate is used for each cash flow. Then, the present value of each cash flow is:

Year 1: present value$_1 = \dfrac{\$10}{(1.12)^1} = \$8.9286$

Year 2: present value$_2 = \dfrac{\$10}{(1.12)^2} = \$7.9719$

Year 3: present value$_3 = \dfrac{\$10}{(1.12)^3} = \$7.1178$

Year 4: present value$_4 = \dfrac{\$110}{(1.12)^4} = \$69.9070$

EXHIBIT 70-1	Price Discount Rate Relationship for an Option-Free Bond

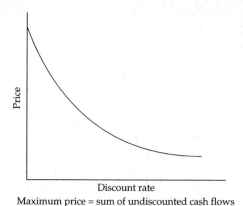

Maximum price = sum of undiscounted cash flows

The value of this security is then $93.9253 ($8.9286 + $7.9719 + $7.1178 + $69.9070). The security's value is lower if a 12% discount rate is used compared to an 8% discount rate ($93.9253 versus $106.6243). This is another general property of present value: *the higher the discount rate, the lower the present value.* Since the value of a security is the present value of the expected cash flows, this property carries over to the value of a security: *the higher the discount rate, the lower a security's value.* The reverse is also true: *the lower the discount rate, the higher a security's value.*

Exhibit 70-1 shows, for an option-free bond, this inverse relationship between a security's value and the discount rate. The shape of the curve in Exhibit 70-1 is referred to as **convex**. By convex, it is meant the curve is bowed in from the origin. As we will see in Reading 72, this **convexity** or bowed shape has implications for the price volatility of a bond when interest rates change. What is important to understand is that the relationship is not linear.

Practice Question 2

What is the present value of the cash flow of the 5-year 7% coupon security in Practice Question 1 assuming a discount rate of 4% rather than 5%?

2.3.2 Relationship between Coupon Rate, Discount Rate, and Price Relative to Par Value

In Reading 66, we described the relationship between a bond's coupon rate, required market yield, and price relative to its par value (i.e., premium, discount, or equal to par). The required yield is equivalent to the discount rate discussed above. We stated the following relationship:

coupon rate = yield required by market, *therefore* price = par value
coupon rate < yield required by market, *therefore* price < par value (discount)
coupon rate > yield required by market, *therefore* price > par value (premium)

Now that we know how to value a bond, we can demonstrate the relationship. The coupon rate on our hypothetical bond is 10%. When an 8% discount rate is used, the bond's value is $106.6243. That is, the price is greater than par value (premium). This is because the coupon rate (10%) is greater than the required yield (the 8% discount rate). We also showed that when the discount rate is 12% (i.e., greater than the coupon rate of 10%), the price of the bond is $93.9253. That is, the bond's value is less than par value when the coupon rate is less than the required yield (discount). When the discount rate is the same as the coupon rate, 10%, the bond's value is equal to par value as shown below:

Year	Cash Flow	Present Value at 10%
1	$10	$9.0909
2	10	8.2645
3	10	7.5131
4	110	75.1315
	Total	$100.0000

Practice Question 3

A. What is the value of a 5-year 7% coupon bond per $100 of par value when the discount rate is (i) 6%, (ii) 7%, and (iii) 8%?

B. Show that the results obtained in part A are consistent with the relationship between the coupon rate, discount rate, and price relative to par value given in the text.

2.3.3 Change in a Bond's Value as it Moves Toward Maturity

As a bond moves closer to its maturity date, its value changes. More specifically, assuming that the discount rate does not change, a bond's value:

1. decreases over time if the bond is selling at a premium

2. increases over time if the bond is selling at a discount

3. is unchanged if the bond is selling at par value

At the maturity date, the bond's value is equal to its par value. So, over time as the bond moves toward its maturity date, its price will move to its par value—a characteristic sometimes referred to as a "pull to par value."

To illustrate what happens to a bond selling at a premium, consider once again the 4-year 10% coupon bond. When the discount rate is 8%, the bond's price is 106.6243. Suppose that one year later, the discount rate is still 8%. There are only three cash flows remaining since the bond is now a 3-year security. The cash flow and the present value of the cash flows are given below:

Year	Cash Flow	Present Value at 8%
1	$10	$9.2593
2	10	8.5734
3	110	87.3215
	Total	$105.1542

The price has declined from $106.6243 to $105.1542.

Now suppose that the bond's price is initially below par value. For example, as stated earlier, if the discount rate is 12%, the 4-year 10% coupon bond's value is $93.9253. Assuming the discount rate remains at 12%, one year later the cash flow and the present value of the cash flow would be as shown below:

Year	Cash Flow	Present Value at 12%
1	$10	$8.9286
2	10	7.9719
3	110	78.2958
	Total	$95.1963

The bond's price increases from $93.9253 to $95.1963.

To understand how the price of a bond changes as it moves towards maturity, consider the following three 20-year bonds for which the yield required by the market is 8%: a premium bond (10% coupon), a discount bond (6% coupon), and a par bond (8% coupon). To simplify the example, it is assumed that each bond pays interest annually. Exhibit 70-2 shows the price of each bond as it moves toward maturity, assuming that the 8% yield required by the market does not change. The premium bond with an initial price of 119.6363 decreases in price until it reaches par value at the maturity date. The discount bond with an initial price of 80.3637 increases in price until it reaches par value at the maturity date.

In practice, over time the discount rate will change. So, the bond's value will change due to both the change in the discount rate and the change in the cash flow as the bond moves toward maturity. For example, again suppose that the discount rate for the 4-year 10% coupon is 8% so that the bond is selling for $106.6243. One year later, suppose that the discount rate appropriate for a 3-year 10% coupon bond increases from 8% to 9%. Then the cash flow and present value of the cash flows are shown on the following page:

Year	Cash Flow	Present Value at 9%
1	$10	$9.1743
2	10	8.4168
3	110	84.9402
	Total	$102.5313

The bond's price will decline from $106.6243 to $102.5313. As shown earlier, if the discount rate did not increase, the price would have declined to only $105.1542. The price decline of $4.0930 ($106.6243 − $102.5313) can be decomposed as follows:

Price change attributable to moving to
    maturity (no change in discount rate) $1.4701 (106.6243 − 105.1542)
Price change attributable to an increase in
    the discount rate from 8% to 9% $2.6229 (105.1542 − 102.5313)
Total price change $4.0930

EXHIBIT 70-2 **Movement of a Premium, Discount, and Par Bond as a Bond Moves Towards Maturity**

Information about the three bonds:

All bonds mature in 20 years and have a yield required by the market of 8%

Coupon payments are annual

Premium bond = 10% coupon selling for 119.6363

Discount bond = 6% coupon selling for 80.3637

Par bond = 8% coupon selling at par value

Assumption: The yield required by the market is unchanged over the life of the bond at 8%.

Time to Maturity in Years	Premium Bond	Discount Bond	Par Bond
20	119.6363	80.3637	100.0000
19	119.2072	80.7928	100.0000
18	118.7438	81.2562	100.0000
17	118.2433	81.7567	100.0000
16	117.7027	82.2973	100.0000
15	117.1190	82.8810	100.0000
14	116.4885	83.5115	100.0000
13	115.8076	84.1924	100.0000
12	115.0722	84.9278	100.0000
11	114.2779	85.7221	100.0000
10	113.4202	86.5798	100.0000
9	112.4938	87.5062	100.0000
8	111.4933	88.5067	100.0000
7	110.4127	89.5873	100.0000

(Exhibit continued on next page ...)

EXHIBIT 70-2	(continued)		
Time to Maturity in Years	Premium Bond	Discount Bond	Par Bond
6	109.2458	90.7542	100.0000
5	107.9854	92.0146	100.0000
4	106.6243	93.3757	100.0000
3	105.1542	94.8458	100.0000
2	103.5665	96.4335	100.0000
1	101.8519	98.1481	100.0000
0	100.0000	100.0000	100.0000

The Effect of Time on a Bond's Price

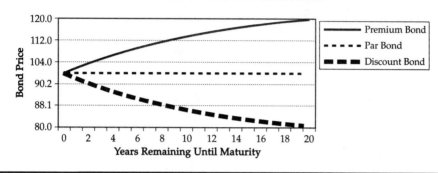

2.4 Valuation Using Multiple Discount Rates

Thus far, we have used one discount rate to compute the present value of each cash flow. As we will see shortly, the proper way to value the cash flows of a bond is to use a different discount rate that is unique to the time period in which a cash flow will be received. So, let's look at how we would value a security using a different discount rate for each cash flow.

Suppose that the appropriate discount rates are as follows:

year 1   6.8%
year 2   7.2%
year 3   7.6%
year 4   8.0%

Then, for the 4-year 10% coupon bond, the present value of each cash flow is:

$$\textit{Year 1: } \text{present value}_1 = \frac{\$10}{(1.068)^1} = \$9.3633$$

$$\textit{Year 2: } \text{present value}_2 = \frac{\$10}{(1.072)^2} = \$8.7018$$

$$\textit{Year 3: } \text{present value}_3 = \frac{\$10}{(1.076)^3} = \$8.0272$$

$$\textit{Year 4: } \text{present value}_4 = \frac{\$110}{(1.080)^4} = \$80.8533$$

The present value of this security, assuming the above set of discount rates, is $106.9456.

> **Practice Question 4**
>
> Compute the value per $100 of par value of a 5-year 7% coupon bond, assuming the payments are annual and the discount rate for each year is as follows:
>
> | Year | Discount rate (%) |
> |------|-------------------|
> | 1 | 3.5 |
> | 2 | 3.9 |
> | 3 | 4.2 |
> | 4 | 4.5 |
> | 5 | 5.0 |

2.5 Valuing Semiannual Cash Flows

In our illustrations, we assumed coupon payments are paid once per year. For most bonds, the coupon payments are semiannual. This does not introduce any complexities into the calculation. The procedure is to simply adjust the coupon payments by dividing the annual coupon payment by 2 and adjust the discount rate by dividing the annual discount rate by 2. The time period t in the present value formula is treated in terms of 6-month periods rather than years.

For example, consider once again the 4-year 10% coupon bond with a maturity value of $100. The cash flow for the first 3.5 years is equal to $5 ($10/2). The last cash flow is equal to the final coupon payment ($5) plus the maturity value ($100). So the last cash flow is $105.

Now the tricky part. If an annual discount rate of 8% is used, how do we obtain the semiannual discount rate? We will simply use one-half the annual rate, 4% (or 8%/2). The reader should have a problem with this: a 4% semiannual rate is not an 8% effective annual rate. That is correct. However, as we will see in the next reading, the *convention* in the bond market is to quote annual interest rates that are just double semiannual rates. This will be explained more fully in the next reading. Don't let this throw you off here. For now, just accept the fact that one-half an annual discount rate is used to obtain a semiannual discount rate in the balance of the reading.

Given the cash flows and the semiannual discount rate of 4%, the present value of each cash flow is shown below:

$$\textit{Period 1: } \text{present value}_1 = \frac{\$5}{(1.04)^1} = \$4.8077$$

$$\textit{Period 2: } \text{present value}_2 = \frac{\$5}{(1.04)^2} = \$4.6228$$

$$\textit{Period 3: } \text{present value}_3 = \frac{\$5}{(1.04)^3} = \$4.4450$$

$$\textit{Period 4: } \text{present value}_4 = \frac{\$5}{(1.04)^4} = \$4.2740$$

Period 5: present value$_5$ = $\dfrac{\$5}{(1.04)^5}$ = $4.1096

Period 6: present value$_6$ = $\dfrac{\$5}{(1.04)^6}$ = $3.9516

Period 7: present value$_7$ = $\dfrac{\$5}{(1.04)^7}$ = $3.7996

Period 8: present value$_8$ = $\dfrac{\$105}{(1.04)^8}$ = $76.7225

The security's value is equal to the sum of the present value of the eight cash flows, $106.7327. Notice that this price is greater than the price when coupon payments are annual ($106.6243). This is because one-half the annual coupon payment is received six months sooner than when payments are annual. This produces a higher present value for the semiannual coupon payments relative to the annual coupon payments.

The value of a non-amortizing bond can be divided into two components: (1) the present value of the coupon payments and (2) the present value of the maturity value. For a fixed-rate coupon bond, the coupon payments represent an annuity. A short-cut formula can be used to compute the value of a bond when using a single discount rate: compute the present value of the annuity and then add the present value of the maturity value.[2]

The present value of an annuity is equal to:

$$\text{annuity payment} \times \left[\dfrac{1 - \dfrac{1}{(1 + i)^{\text{no. of periods}}}}{i} \right]$$

For a bond with annual interest payments, i is the annual discount rate and the "no. of periods" is equal to the number of years.

Applying this formula to a semiannual-pay bond, the annuity payment is one-half the annual coupon payment and the number of periods is double the number of years to maturity. So, the present value of the coupon payments can be expressed as:

$$\text{semiannual coupon payment} \times \left[\dfrac{1 - \dfrac{1}{(1 + i)^{\text{no. of years} \times 2}}}{i} \right]$$

where i is the semiannual discount rate (annual rate/2). Notice that in the formula, we use the number of years multiplied by 2 since a period in our illustration is six months.

The present value of the maturity value is equal to

$$\text{present value of maturity value} = \dfrac{\$100}{(1 + i)^{\text{no. of years} \times 2}}$$

---

[2] Note that in our earlier illustration, we computed the present value of the semiannual coupon payments before the maturity date and then added the present value of the last cash flow (last semiannual coupon payment plus the maturity value). In the presentation of how to use the short-cut formula, we are computing the present value of all the semiannual coupon payments and then adding the present value of the maturity value. Both approaches will give the same answer for the value of a bond.

To illustrate this computation, consider once again the 4-year 10% coupon bond with an annual discount rate of 8% and a semiannual discount rate of one-half this rate (4%) for the reason cited earlier. Then:

semiannual coupon payment = $5
semiannual discount rate (i) = 4%
number of years   = 4

then the present value of the coupon payments is

$$\$5 \times \left[\frac{1 - \dfrac{1}{(1.04)^{4 \times 2}}}{0.04} \right] = \$33.6637$$

To determine the price, the present value of the maturity value must be added to the present value of the coupon payments. The present value of the maturity value is

$$\text{present value of maturity value} = \frac{\$100}{(1.04)^{4 \times 2}} = \$73.0690$$

The price is then $106.7327 ($33.6637 + $73.0690). This agrees with our previous calculation for the price of this bond.

Practice Question 5

What is the value of a 5-year 7% coupon bond that pays interest semi-annually assuming that the annual discount rate is 5%?

2.6 Valuing a Zero-Coupon Bond

For a zero-coupon bond, there is only one cash flow—the maturity value. The value of a zero-coupon bond that matures N years from now is

$$\frac{\text{maturity value}}{(1 + i)^{\text{no. of years} \times 2}}$$

where i is the semiannual discount rate.

It may seem surprising that the number of periods is double the number of years to maturity. In computing the value of a zero-coupon bond, the number of 6-month periods (i.e., "no. of years $\times$ 2") is used in the denominator of the formula. The rationale is that the pricing of a zero-coupon bond should be consistent with the pricing of a semiannual coupon bond. Therefore, the use of 6-month periods is required in order to have uniformity between the present value calculations.

To illustrate the application of the formula, the value of a 5-year zero-coupon bond with a maturity value of $100 discounted at an 8% interest rate is $67.5564, as shown below:

$i = 0.04 \ (= 0.08/2)$
$N = 5$

$$\frac{\$100}{(1.04)^{5 \times 2}} = \$67.5564$$

Practice Question 6

A. Complete the following table for a 10-year zero-coupon bond with a maturity value of $1,000 for each of the following *annual* discount rates.

Annual Rate	Semiannual Rate	Price
1%		
2%		
3%		
4%		
5%		
6%		
7%		
8%		
9%		
10%		
11%		
12%		
13%		
14%		

B. Given the prices for the bond in part A, draw a graph of the price/yield relationship. On the horizontal axis (*x*-axis) should be the annual rate and on the vertical axis (*y*-axis) should be the price.

2.7 Valuing a Bond Between Coupon Payments

For coupon-paying bonds, a complication arises when we try to price a bond between coupon payments. The amount that the buyer pays the seller in such cases is the present value of the cash flow. But one of the cash flows, the very next cash flow, encompasses two components as shown below:

1. interest earned by the seller
2. interest earned by the buyer

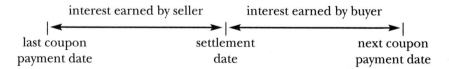

interest earned by seller	interest earned by buyer
last coupon payment date	settlement date	next coupon payment date

The interest earned by the seller is the interest that has accrued[3] between the last coupon payment date and the settlement date.[4] This interest is called **accrued interest**. At the time of purchase, the buyer must compensate the seller for the

---

[3] "Accrued" means that the interest is earned but not distributed to the bondholder.
[4] The settlement date is the date a transaction is completed.

accrued interest. The buyer recovers the accrued interest when the next coupon payment is received.

When the price of a bond is computed using the present value calculations described earlier, it is computed with accrued interest embodied in the price. This price is referred to as the **full price**. (Some market participants refer to it as the **dirty price**.) It is the full price that the buyer pays the seller. From the full price, the accrued interest must be deducted to determine the **price** of the bond, sometimes referred to as the **clean price**.

Below, we show how the present value formula is modified to compute the full price when a bond is purchased between coupon periods.

2.7.1 Computing the Full Price

To compute the full price, it is first necessary to determine the fractional periods between the settlement date and the next coupon payment date. This is determined as follows:

$$w \text{ periods} = \frac{\text{days between settlement date and next coupon payment date}}{\text{days in coupon period}}$$

Then the present value of the expected cash flow to be received t periods from now using a discount rate i assuming the first coupon payment is w periods from now is:

$$\text{present value}_t = \frac{\text{expected cash flow}}{(1 + i)^{t-1+w}}$$

This procedure for calculating the present value when a security is purchased between coupon payments is called the "Street method."

To illustrate the calculation, suppose that there are five semiannual coupon payments remaining for a 10% coupon bond. Also assume the following:

1. 78 days between the settlement date and the next coupon payment date

2. 182 days in the coupon period

Then w is 0.4286 periods (= 78/182). The present value of each cash flow assuming that each is discounted at 8% annual discount rate is

$$\textit{Period 1:} \ \text{present value}_1 = \frac{\$5}{(1.04)^{0.4286}} = \$4.9167$$

$$\textit{Period 2:} \ \text{present value}_2 = \frac{\$5}{(1.04)^{1.4286}} = \$4.7276$$

$$\textit{Period 3:} \ \text{present value}_3 = \frac{\$5}{(1.04)^{2.4286}} = \$4.5457$$

$$\textit{Period 4:} \ \text{present value}_4 = \frac{\$5}{(1.04)^{3.4286}} = \$4.3709$$

$$\textit{Period 5:} \ \text{present value}_5 = \frac{\$105}{(1.04)^{4.4286}} = \$88.2583$$

The full price is the sum of the present value of the cash flows, which is $106.8192. Remember that the full price includes the accrued interest that the buyer is paying the seller.

Practice Question 7

Suppose that a bond is purchased between coupon periods. The days between the settlement date and the next coupon period is 58. There are 183 days in the coupon period. Suppose that the bond purchased has a coupon rate of 7% and there are 10 semiannual coupon payments remaining. What is the full price for this bond if a 5% annual discount rate is used?

2.7.2 Computing the Accrued Interest and the Clean Price

To find the price without accrued interest, called the **clean price** or simply **price**, the accrued interest must be computed. To determine the accrued interest, it is first necessary to determine the number of days in the accrued interest period. The number of days in the accrued interest period is determined as follows:

days in accrued interest period =
    days in coupon period − days between settlement and next coupon payment

The percentage of the next semiannual coupon payment that the seller has earned as accrued interest is found as follows:

$$\frac{\text{days in accrued interest period}}{\text{days in coupon period}}$$

So, for example, returning to our illustration where the full price was computed, since there are 182 days in the coupon period and there are 78 days from the settlement date to the next coupon payment, the days in the accrued interest period is 182 minus 78, or 104 days. Therefore, the percentage of the coupon payment that is accrued interest is:

$$\frac{104}{182} = 0.5714 = 57.14\%$$

This is the same percentage found by simply subtracting w from 1. In our illustration, w was 0.4286. Then $1 - 0.4286 = 0.5714$.

Given the value of w, the amount of accrued interest (AI) is equal to:

AI = semiannual coupon payment × $(1 - w)$

So, for the 10% coupon bond whose full price we computed, since the semiannual coupon payment per $100 of par value is $5 and w is 0.4286, the accrued interest is:

$5 × (1 - 0.4286) = \$2.8570$

The clean price is then:

full price − accrued interest

In our illustration, the clean price is[5]

$$\$106.8192 - \$2.8570 = \$103.9622$$

Practice Question 8

What is the accrued interest and the clean price for the bond whose full price is computed in Practice Question 7?

2.7.3 Day Count Conventions

The practice for calculating the number of days between two dates depends on *day count conventions* used in the bond market. The convention differs by the type of security. Day count conventions are also used to calculate the number of days in the numerator and denominator of the ratio w.

The accrued interest (AI) assuming semiannual payments is calculated as follows:

$$AI = \frac{\text{annual coupon}}{2} \times \frac{\text{days in AI period}}{\text{days in coupon period}}$$

In calculating the number of days between two dates, the actual number of days is not always the same as the number of days that should be used in the accrued interest formula. The number of days used depends on the day count convention for the particular security. Specifically, day count conventions differ for Treasury securities and government agency securities, municipal bonds, and corporate bonds.

For coupon-bearing Treasury securities, the day count convention used is to determine the actual number of days between two dates. This is referred to as the "actual/actual" day count convention. For example, consider a coupon-bearing Treasury security whose previous coupon payment was March 1. The next coupon payment would be on September 1. Suppose this Treasury security is purchased with a settlement date of July 17th. The actual number of days between July 17 (the settlement date) and September 1 (the date of the next coupon payment) is 46 days, as shown below:

July 17 to July 31	14 days
August	31 days
September 1	1 day
	46 days

Note that the settlement date (July 17) is not counted. The number of days in the coupon period is the actual number of days between March 1 and September 1, which is 184 days. The number of days between the last coupon payment (March 1) through July 17 is therefore 138 days (184 days − 46 days).

For coupon-bearing agency, municipal, and corporate bonds, a different day count convention is used. It is assumed that every month has 30 days, that

---

[5] Notice that in computing the full price the present value of the next coupon payment is computed. However, the buyer pays the seller the accrued interest now despite the fact that it will be recovered at the next coupon payment date.

any 6-month period has 180 days, and that there are 360 days in a year. This day count convention is referred to as "30/360." For example, consider once again the Treasury security purchased with a settlement date of July 17, the previous coupon payment on March 1, and the next coupon payment on September 1. If the security is an agency, municipal, or corporate bond, the number of days until the next coupon payment is 44 days as shown below:

July 17 to July 31	13 days
August	30 days
September 1	1 day
	44 days

Note that the settlement date, July 17, is not counted. Since July is treated as having 30 days, there are 13 days (30 days minus the first 17 days in July). The number of days from March 1 to July 17 is 136, which is the number of days in the accrued interest period.

TRADITIONAL APPROACH TO VALUATION 3

The traditional approach to valuation has been to discount every cash flow of a fixed income security by the same interest rate (or discount rate). For example, consider the three hypothetical 10-year Treasury securities shown in Exhibit 70-3: a 12% coupon bond, an 8% coupon bond, and a zero-coupon bond. The cash flows for each bond are shown in the exhibit. Since the cash flows of all three bonds are viewed as default free, the traditional practice is to use the same discount rate to calculate the present value of all three bonds and use the same discount rate for the cash flow for each period. The discount rate used is the yield for the on-the-run issue obtained from the Treasury yield curve. For example, suppose that the yield for the 10-year on-the-run Treasury issue is 10%. Then, the practice is to discount each cash flow for each bond using a 10% discount rate.

For a non-Treasury security, a yield premium or yield spread is added to the on-the-run Treasury yield. The yield spread is the same regardless of when a cash flow is to be received in the traditional approach. For a 10-year non-Treasury security, suppose that 90 basis points is the appropriate yield spread. Then all cash flows would be discounted at the yield for the on-the-run 10-year Treasury issue of 10% plus 90 basis points.

EXHIBIT 70-3	Cash Flows for Three 10-Year Hypothetical Treasury Securities Per $100 of Par Value

Each Period Is Six Months

	Coupon Rate		
Period	12%	8%	0%
1-19	$6	$4	$0
20	106	104	100

4 THE ARBITRAGE-FREE VALUATION APPROACH

The fundamental flaw of the traditional approach is that it views each security as the same package of cash flows. For example, consider a 10-year U.S. Treasury issue with an 8% coupon rate. The cash flows per $100 of par value would be 19 payments of $4 every six months and $104 twenty 6-month periods from now. The traditional practice would discount each cash flow using the same discount rate.

The proper way to view the 10-year 8% coupon Treasury issue is as a package of zero-coupon bonds whose maturity value is equal to the amount of the cash flow and whose maturity date is equal to each cash flow's payment date. Thus, the 10-year 8% coupon Treasury issue should be viewed as 20 zero-coupon bonds. The reason this is the proper way to value a security is that it does not allow arbitrage profit by taking apart or "stripping" a security and selling off the stripped securities at a higher aggregate value than it would cost to purchase the security in the market. We'll illustrate this later. We refer to this approach to valuation as the **arbitrage-free valuation approach**.[6]

By viewing any financial asset as a package of zero-coupon bonds, a consistent valuation framework can be developed. Viewing a financial asset as a package of zero-coupon bonds means that any two bonds would be viewed as different packages of zero-coupon bonds and valued accordingly.

The difference between the traditional valuation approach and the arbitrage-free approach is illustrated in Exhibit 70-4, which shows how the three bonds whose cash flows are depicted in Exhibit 70-3 should be valued. With the traditional approach, the discount rate for all three bonds is the yield on a 10-year U.S. Treasury security. With the arbitrage-free approach, the discount rate for a cash flow is the theoretical rate that the U.S. Treasury would have to pay if it issued a zero-coupon bond with a maturity date equal to the maturity date of the cash flow.

Therefore, to implement the arbitrage-free approach, it is necessary to determine the theoretical rate that the U.S. Treasury would have to pay on a zero-coupon Treasury security for each maturity. As explained in the previous reading, the name given to the zero-coupon Treasury rate is the **Treasury spot rate**. In Reading 71, we will explain how the Treasury spot rate can be calculated. The spot rate for a Treasury security is the interest rate that should be used to discount a default-free cash flow with the same maturity. We call the value of a bond based on spot rates the **arbitrage-free value**.

4.1 Valuation Using Treasury Spot Rates

For the purposes of our discussion, we will take the Treasury spot rate for each maturity as given. To illustrate how Treasury spot rates are used to compute the arbitrage-free value of a Treasury security, we will use the hypothetical Treasury

---

[6] In its simple form, arbitrage is the simultaneous buying and selling of an asset at two different prices in two different markets. The arbitrageur profits without risk by buying cheap in one market and simultaneously selling at the higher price in the other market. Such opportunities for arbitrage are rare. Less obvious arbitrage opportunities exist in situations where a package of assets can produce a payoff (expected return) identical to an asset that is priced differently. This arbitrage relies on a fundamental principle of finance called the "law of one price" which states that a given asset must have the same price regardless of the means by which one goes about creating that asset. The law of one price implies that if the payoff of an asset can be synthetically created by a package of assets, the price of the package and the price of the asset whose payoff it replicates must be equal.

| EXHIBIT 70-4 | Comparison of Traditional Approach and Arbitrage-Free Approach in Valuing a Treasury Security |

Each Period Is Six Months

	Discount (Base Interest) Rate		Cash Flows For*		
Period	Traditional Approach	Arbitrage-Free Approach	12%	8%	0%
1	10-year Treasury rate	1-period Treasury spot rate	$6	$4	$0
2	10-year Treasury rate	2-period Treasury spot rate	6	4	0
3	10-year Treasury rate	3-period Treasury spot rate	6	4	0
4	10-year Treasury rate	4-period Treasury spot rate	6	4	0
5	10-year Treasury rate	5-period Treasury spot rate	6	4	0
6	10-year Treasury rate	6-period Treasury spot rate	6	4	0
7	10-year Treasury rate	7-period Treasury spot rate	6	4	0
8	10-year Treasury rate	8-period Treasury spot rate	6	4	0
9	10-year Treasury rate	9-period Treasury spot rate	6	4	0
10	10-year Treasury rate	10-period Treasury spot rate	6	4	0
11	10-year Treasury rate	11-period Treasury spot rate	6	4	0
12	10-year Treasury rate	12-period Treasury spot rate	6	4	0
13	10-year Treasury rate	13-period Treasury spot rate	6	4	0
14	10-year Treasury rate	14-period Treasury spot rate	6	4	0
15	10-year Treasury rate	15-period Treasury spot rate	6	4	0
16	10-year Treasury rate	16-period Treasury spot rate	6	4	0
17	10-year Treasury rate	17-period Treasury spot rate	6	4	0
18	10-year Treasury rate	18-period Treasury spot rate	6	4	0
19	10-year Treasury rate	19-period Treasury spot rate	6	4	0
20	10-year Treasury rate	20-period Treasury spot rate	106	104	100

* Per $100 of par value.

spot rates shown in the third column of Exhibit 70-5 to value an 8% 10-year Treasury security. The present value of each period's cash flow is shown in the last column. The sum of the present values is the arbitrage-free value for the Treasury security. For the 8% 10-year Treasury, it is $115.2619.

As a second illustration, suppose that a 4.8% coupon 10-year Treasury bond is being valued based on the Treasury spot rates shown in Exhibit 70-5. The arbitrage-free value of this bond is $90.8428 as shown in Exhibit 70-6.

In the next reading, we discuss yield measures. The yield to maturity is a measure that would be computed for this bond. We won't show how it is computed in this reading, but simply state the result. The yield for the 4.8% coupon 10-year Treasury bond is 6.033%. Notice that the spot rates are used to obtain the price and the price is then used to compute a conventional yield measure. *It is important to understand that there are an infinite number of spot rate curves that can generate the same price of $90.8428 and therefore the same yield.* (We return to this point in the next reading.)

EXHIBIT 70-5	Determination of the Arbitrage-Free Value of an 8% 10-Year Treasury			
Period	Years	Cash Flow ($)	Spot Rate (%)*	Present Value ($)**
1	0.5	4	3.0000	3.9409
2	1.0	4	3.3000	3.8712
3	1.5	4	3.5053	3.7968
4	2.0	4	3.9164	3.7014
5	2.5	4	4.4376	3.5843
6	3.0	4	4.7520	3.4743
7	3.5	4	4.9622	3.3694
8	4.0	4	5.0650	3.2747
9	4.5	4	5.1701	3.1791
10	5.0	4	5.2772	3.0829
11	5.5	4	5.3864	2.9861
12	6.0	4	5.4976	2.8889
13	6.5	4	5.6108	2.7916
14	7.0	4	5.6643	2.7055
15	7.5	4	5.7193	2.6205
16	8.0	4	5.7755	2.5365
17	8.5	4	5.8331	2.4536
18	9.0	4	5.9584	2.3581
19	9.5	4	6.0863	2.2631
20	10.0	104	6.2169	56.3830
			Total	$115.2621

* The spot rate is an annual discount rate. The convention to obtain a semiannual discount rate is to take one-half the annual discount rate. So, for period 6 (i.e., 3 years), the spot rate is 4.7520%. The semiannual discount rate is 2.376%.

** The present value for the cash flow is equal to:

$$\frac{\text{Cash flow}}{(1 + \text{Spot rate}/2)^{\text{period}}}$$

Practice Question 9

A. Using the Treasury spot rates shown in Exhibit 70-5, what is the arbitrage-free value of a 7.4% coupon 8-year Treasury security?

B. Using the Treasury spot rates shown in Exhibit 70-5, what is the arbitrage-free value of a 4% coupon 8-year Treasury security?

4.2 Reason for Using Treasury Spot Rates

Thus far, we simply asserted that the value of a Treasury security should be based on discounting each cash flow using the corresponding Treasury spot rate. But what if market participants value a security using the yield for the on-the-run Treasury with a maturity equal to the maturity of the Treasury security being valued? (In other words, what if participants use the yield on coupon-bearing securities rather than the yield on zero-coupon securities?) Let's see why a Treasury security will have to trade close to its arbitrage-free value.

4.2.1 Stripping and the Arbitrage-Free Valuation

The key in the process is the existence of the Treasury strips market. As explained in Reading 67, a dealer has the ability to take apart the cash flows of a Treasury coupon security (i.e., strip the security) and create zero-coupon securities. These zero-coupon securities, which we called Treasury strips, can be sold to investors.

EXHIBIT 70-6	Determination of the Arbitrage-Free Value of a 4.8% 10-Year Treasury			
Period	Years	Cash Flow ($)	Spot Rate (%)*	Present Value ($)**
1	0.5	2.4	3.0000	2.3645
2	1.0	2.4	3.3000	2.3227
3	1.5	2.4	3.5053	2.2781
4	2.0	2.4	3.9164	2.2209
5	2.5	2.4	4.4376	2.1506
6	3.0	2.4	4.7520	2.0846
7	3.5	2.4	4.9622	2.0216
8	4.0	2.4	5.0650	1.9648
9	4.5	2.4	5.1701	1.9075
10	5.0	2.4	5.2772	1.8497
11	5.5	2.4	5.3864	1.7916
12	6.0	2.4	5.4976	1.7334
13	6.5	2.4	5.6108	1.6750
14	7.0	2.4	5.6643	1.6233
15	7.5	2.4	5.7193	1.5723
16	8.0	2.4	5.7755	1.5219
17	8.5	2.4	5.8331	1.4722
18	9.0	2.4	5.9584	1.4149
19	9.5	2.4	6.0863	1.3578
20	10.0	102.4	6.2169	55.5156
			Total	90.8430

* The spot rate is an annual discount rate. The convention to obtain a semiannual discount rate is to take one-half the annual discount rate. So, for period 6 (i.e., 3 years), the spot rate is 4.7520%. The semiannual discount rate is 2.376%.

** The present value for the cash flow is equal to:

$$\frac{\text{Cash flow}}{(1 + \text{Spot rate}/2)^{\text{period}}}$$

EXHIBIT 70-7	Price of an 8% 10-Year Treasury Valued at a 6% Discount Rate			

Period	Years	Cash Flow ($)	Discount Rate (%)*	Present Value ($)**
1	0.5	4	6.0000	3.8835
2	1.0	4	6.0000	3.7704
3	1.5	4	6.0000	3.6606
4	2.0	4	6.0000	3.5539
5	2.5	4	6.0000	3.4504
6	3.0	4	6.0000	3.3499
7	3.5	4	6.0000	3.2524
8	4.0	4	6.0000	3.1576
9	4.5	4	6.0000	3.0657
10	5.0	4	6.0000	2.9764
11	5.5	4	6.0000	2.8897
12	6.0	4	6.0000	2.8055
13	6.5	4	6.0000	2.7238
14	7.0	4	6.0000	2.6445
15	7.5	4	6.0000	2.5674
16	8.0	4	6.0000	2.4927
17	8.5	4	6.0000	2.4201
18	9.0	4	6.0000	2.3496
19	9.5	4	6.0000	2.2811
20	10.0	104	6.0000	57.5823
			Total	$114.8775

* The spot rate is an annual discount rate. The convention to obtain a semiannual discount rate is to take one-half the annual discount rate. So, since the discount rate for each period is 6%. The semiannual discount rate is 3%.

** The present value for the cash flow is equal to:

$$\frac{\text{Cash flow}}{(1.03)^{\text{period}}}$$

At what interest rate or yield can these Treasury strips be sold to investors? They can be sold at the Treasury spot rates. If the market price of a Treasury security is less than its value using the arbitrage-free valuation approach, then a dealer can buy the Treasury security, strip it, and sell off the Treasury strips so as to generate greater proceeds than the cost of purchasing the Treasury security. The resulting profit is an arbitrage profit. Since, as we will see, the value determined by using the Treasury spot rates does not allow for the generation of an arbitrage profit, this is the reason why the approach is referred to as an "arbitrage-free" approach.

To illustrate this, suppose that the yield for the on-the-run 10-year Treasury issue is 6%. (We will see in Reading 71 that the Treasury spot rate curve in Exhibit 70-5 was generated from a yield curve where the on-the-run 10-year Treasury issue was 6%.) Suppose that the 8% coupon 10-year Treasury issue is valued using the traditional approach based on 6%. Exhibit 70-7 shows the value based on discounting all the cash flows at 6% is $114.8775.

		EXHIBIT 70-8	Arbitrage Profit from Stripping the 8% 10-Year Treasury	
Period	**Years**	**Sell for**	**Buy for**	**Arbitrage Profit**
1	0.5	3.9409	3.8835	0.0574
2	1.0	3.8712	3.7704	0.1008
3	1.5	3.7968	3.6606	0.1363
4	2.0	3.7014	3.5539	0.1475
5	2.5	3.5843	3.4504	0.1339
6	3.0	3.4743	3.3499	0.1244
7	3.5	3.3694	3.2524	0.1170
8	4.0	3.2747	3.1576	0.1170
9	4.5	3.1791	3.0657	0.1134
10	5.0	3.0829	2.9764	0.1065
11	5.5	2.9861	2.8897	0.0964
12	6.0	2.8889	2.8055	0.0834
13	6.5	2.7916	2.7238	0.0678
14	7.0	2.7055	2.6445	0.0611
15	7.5	2.6205	2.5674	0.0531
16	8.0	2.5365	2.4927	0.0439
17	8.5	2.4536	2.4201	0.0336
18	9.0	2.3581	2.3496	0.0086
19	9.5	2.2631	2.2811	−0.0181
20	10.0	56.3830	57.5823	−1.1993
		115.2621	114.8775	0.3846

Consider what would happen if the market priced the security at $114.8775. The value based on the Treasury spot rates (Exhibit 70-5) is $115.2621. What can the dealer do? The dealer can buy the 8% 10-year issue for $114.8775, strip it, and sell the Treasury strips at the spot rates shown in Exhibit 70-5. By doing so, the proceeds that will be received by the dealer are $115.2621. This results in an arbitrage profit of $0.3846 (= $115.2621 − $114.8775).[7] Dealers recognizing this arbitrage opportunity will bid up the price of the 8% 10-year Treasury issue in order to acquire it and strip it. At what point will the arbitrage profit disappear? When the security is priced at $115.2621, the value that we said is the arbitrage-free value.

To understand in more detail where this arbitrage profit is coming from, look at Exhibit 70-8. The third column shows how much each cash flow can be sold for by the dealer if it is stripped. The values in the third column are simply the present values in Exhibit 70-5 based on discounting the cash flows at the Treasury spot rates. The fourth column shows how much the dealer is effectively purchasing the cash flow if each cash flow is discounted at 6%. This is the last column in Exhibit 70-7. The sum of the arbitrage profit from each cash flow stripped is the total arbitrage profit.

---

[7] This may seem like a small amount, but remember that this is for a single $100 par value bond. Multiply this by thousands of bonds and you can see a dealer's profit potential.

4.2.2 Reconstitution and Arbitrage-Free Valuation

We have just demonstrated how coupon stripping of a Treasury issue will force its market value to be close to the value determined by arbitrage-free valuation when the market price is less than the arbitrage-free value. What happens when a Treasury issue's market price is greater than the arbitrage-free value? Obviously, a dealer will not want to strip the Treasury issue since the proceeds generated from stripping will be less than the cost of purchasing the issue.

When such situations occur, the dealer will follow a procedure called **reconstitution**.[8] Basically, the dealer can purchase a package of Treasury strips so as to create a synthetic (i.e., artificial) Treasury coupon security that is worth more than the same maturity and same coupon Treasury issue.

To illustrate this, consider the 4.8% 10-year Treasury issue whose arbitrage-free value was computed in Exhibit 70-6. The arbitrage-free value is $90.8430. Exhibit 70-9 shows the price assuming the traditional approach where all the cash flows are discounted at a 6% interest rate. The price is $91.0735. What the dealer can do is purchase the Treasury strip for each 6-month period at the prices shown in Exhibit 70-6 and sell short the 4.8% 10-year Treasury coupon issue whose cash flows are being replicated. By doing so, the dealer has the cash flow of a 4.8% coupon 10-year Treasury security at a cost of $90.8430, thereby generating an arbitrage profit of $0.2305 ($91.0735 − $90.8430). The cash flows from the package of Treasury strips purchased are used to make the payments for the Treasury coupon security shorted. Actually, in practice, this can be done in a more efficient manner using a procedure for reconstitution provided for by the Department of the Treasury.

What forces the market price to the arbitrage-free value of $90.8430? As dealers sell short the Treasury coupon issue (4.8% 10-year issue), the price of the issue decreases. When the price is driven down to $90.8430, the arbitrage profit no longer exists.

This process of stripping and reconstitution assures that the price of a Treasury issue will not depart materially from its arbitrage-free value. In other countries, as governments permit the stripping and reconstitution of their issues, the value of non-U.S. government issues have also moved toward their arbitrage-free value.

4.3 Credit Spreads and the Valuation of Non-Treasury Securities

The Treasury spot rates can be used to value any default-free security. For a non-Treasury security, the theoretical value is not as easy to determine. The value of a non-Treasury security is found by discounting the cash flows by the Treasury spot rates plus a yield spread to reflect the additional risks.

The spot rate used to discount the cash flow of a non-Treasury security can be the Treasury spot rate plus a constant credit spread. For example, suppose the 6-month Treasury spot rate is 3% and the 10-year Treasury spot rate is 6%. Also suppose that a suitable credit spread is 90 basis points. Then a 3.9% spot rate is used to discount a 6-month cash flow of a non-Treasury bond and a 6.9% discount rate to discount a 10-year cash flow. (Remember that when each semiannual cash flow is discounted, the discount rate used is one-half the spot rate—1.95% for the 6-month spot rate and 3.45% for the 10-year spot rate.)

The drawback of this approach is that there is no reason to expect the credit spread to be the same regardless of when the cash flow is received. We actually

---

[8] The definition of *reconstitute* is to provide with a new structure, often by assembling various parts into a whole. *Reconstitution* then, as used here, means to assemble the parts (the Treasury strips) in such a way that a new whole (a Treasury coupon bond) is created. That is, it is the opposite of *stripping* a coupon bond.

EXHIBIT 70-9	Price of a 4.8% 10-Year Treasury Valued at a 6% Discount Rate			

Period	Years	Cash Flow ($)	Discount Rate (%)	Present Value ($)
1	0.5	2.4	6.0000	2.3301
2	1.0	2.4	6.0000	2.2622
3	1.5	2.4	6.0000	2.1963
4	2.0	2.4	6.0000	2.1324
5	2.5	2.4	6.0000	2.0703
6	3.0	2.4	6.0000	2.0100
7	3.5	2.4	6.0000	1.9514
8	4.0	2.4	6.0000	1.8946
9	4.5	2.4	6.0000	1.8394
10	5.0	2.4	6.0000	1.7858
11	5.5	2.4	6.0000	1.7338
12	6.0	2.4	6.0000	1.6833
13	6.5	2.4	6.0000	1.6343
14	7.0	2.4	6.0000	1.5867
15	7.5	2.4	6.0000	1.5405
16	8.0	2.4	6.0000	1.4956
17	8.5	2.4	6.0000	1.4520
18	9.0	2.4	6.0000	1.4097
19	9.5	2.4	6.0000	1.3687
20	10.0	102.4	6.0000	56.6964
			Total	91.0735

observed this in the previous reading when we saw how credit spreads increase with maturity. Consequently, it might be expected that credit spreads increase with the maturity of the bond. That is, there is a **term structure of credit spreads**.

Dealer firms typically estimate a term structure for credit spreads for each credit rating and market sector. Generally, the credit spread increases with maturity. This is a typical shape for the term structure of credit spreads. In addition, the shape of the term structure is not the same for all credit ratings. Typically, the lower the credit rating, the steeper the term structure of credit spreads.

When the credit spreads for a given credit rating and market sector are added to the Treasury spot rates, the resulting term structure is used to value bonds with that credit rating in that market sector. This term structure is referred to as the **benchmark spot rate curve** or **benchmark zero-coupon rate curve**.

For example, Exhibit 70-10 reproduces the Treasury spot rate curve in Exhibit 70-5. Also shown in the exhibit is a hypothetical credit spread for a non-Treasury security. The resulting benchmark spot rate curve is in the next-to-the-last column. It is this spot rate curve that is used to value the securities that have the same credit rating and are in the same market sector. This is done in Exhibit 70-10 for a hypothetical 8% 10-year issue. The arbitrage-free value is $108.4616. Notice that the theoretical value is less than that for an otherwise comparable Treasury security. The arbitrage-free value for an 8% 10-year Treasury is $115.2621 (see Exhibit 70-5).

5 VALUATION MODELS

A **valuation model** provides the fair value of a security. Thus far, the two valuation approaches we have presented have dealt with valuing simple securities. By simple we mean that it assumes the securities do not have an embedded option. A Treasury security and an option-free non-Treasury security can be valued using the arbitrage-free valuation approach.

More general valuation models handle securities with embedded options. In the fixed income area, two common models used are the **binomial model** and the **Monte Carlo simulation model**. The former model is used to value callable bonds, putable bonds, floating-rate notes, and structured notes in which the coupon formula is based on an interest rate. The Monte Carlo simulation model is used to value mortgage-backed securities and certain types of asset-backed securities.[9]

In very general terms, the following five features are common to the binomial and Monte Carlo simulation valuation models:

EXHIBIT 70-10	Calculation of Arbitrage-Free Value of a Hypothetical 8% 10-Year Non-Treasury Security Using Benchmark Spot Rate Curve				
Period	Years	Cash Flow ($)	Treasury Spot Rate (%)	Credit Spread (%)	Benchmark Spot (%)	Present Value ($)
1	0.5	4	3.0000	0.20	3.2000	3.9370
2	1.0	4	3.3000	0.20	3.5000	3.8636
3	1.5	4	3.5053	0.25	3.7553	3.7829
4	2.0	4	3.9164	0.30	4.2164	3.6797
5	2.5	4	4.4376	0.35	4.7876	3.5538
6	3.0	4	4.7520	0.35	5.1020	3.4389
7	3.5	4	4.9622	0.40	5.3622	3.3237
8	4.0	4	5.0650	0.45	5.5150	3.2177
9	4.5	4	5.1701	0.45	5.6201	3.1170
10	5.0	4	5.2772	0.50	5.7772	3.0088
11	5.5	4	5.3864	0.55	5.9364	2.8995
12	6.0	4	5.4976	0.60	6.0976	2.7896
13	6.5	4	5.6108	0.65	6.2608	2.6794
14	7.0	4	5.6643	0.70	6.3643	2.5799
15	7.5	4	5.7193	0.75	6.4693	2.4813
16	8.0	4	5.7755	0.80	6.5755	2.3838
17	8.5	4	5.8331	0.85	6.6831	2.2876
18	9.0	4	5.9584	0.90	6.8584	2.1801
19	9.5	4	6.0863	0.95	7.0363	2.0737
20	10.0	104	6.2169	1.00	7.2169	51.1835
					Total	$108.4616

---

[9] A short summary reason is: mortgage-backed securities and certain asset-backed securities are interest rate path dependent securities and the binomial model cannot value such securities.

1. Each model begins with the yields on the on-the-run Treasury securities and generates Treasury spot rates.

2. Each model makes an assumption about the expected volatility of short-term interest rates. This is a critical assumption in both models since it can significantly affect the security's fair value.

3. Based on the volatility assumption, different "branches" of an interest rate tree (in the case of the binomial model) and interest rate "paths" (in the case of the Monte Carlo model) are generated.

4. The model is calibrated to the Treasury market. This means that if an "on-the-run" Treasury issue is valued using the model, the model will produce the observed market price.

5. Rules are developed to determine when an issuer/borrower will exercise embedded options—a call/put rule for callable/putable bonds and a prepayment model for mortgage-backed and certain asset-backed securities.

The user of any valuation model is exposed to **modeling risk**. This is the risk that the output of the model is incorrect because the assumptions upon which it is based are incorrect. Consequently, it is imperative the results of a valuation model be stress-tested for modeling risk by altering assumptions.

SUMMARY

- ▶ Valuation is the process of determining the fair value of a financial asset.

- ▶ The fundamental principle of valuation is that the value of any financial asset is the present value of the expected cash flows, where a cash flow is the amount of cash expected to be received at some future periods.

- ▶ The valuation process involves three steps: (1) estimating the expected cash flows, (2) determining the appropriate interest rate or interest rates to be used to discount the cash flows, and (3) calculating the present value of the expected cash flows.

- ▶ For any fixed income security which neither the issuer nor the investor can alter the payment of the principal before its contractual due date, the cash flows can easily be determined assuming that the issuer does not default.

- ▶ The difficulty in determining cash flows arises for securities where either the issuer or the investor can alter the cash flows, or the coupon rate is reset by a formula dependent on some reference rate, price, or exchange rate.

- ▶ On-the-run Treasury yields are viewed as the minimum interest rate an investor requires when investing in a bond.

- ▶ The risk premium or yield spread over the interest rate on a Treasury security investors require reflects the additional risks in a security that is not issued by the U.S. government.

- ▶ For a given discount rate, the present value of a single cash flow received in the future is the amount of money that must be invested today that will generate that future value.

- ▶ The present value of a cash flow will depend on when a cash flow will be received (i.e., the timing of a cash flow) and the discount rate (i.e., interest rate) used to calculate the present value.

- ▶ The sum of the present values for a security's expected cash flows is the value of the security.

- ▶ The present value is lower the further into the future the cash flow will be received.

- ▶ The higher the discount rate, the lower a cash flow's present value and since the value of a security is the sum of the present value of the cash flows, the higher the discount rate, the lower a security's value.

- ▶ The price/yield relationship for an option-free bond is convex.

- ▶ The value of a bond is equal to the present value of the coupon payments plus the present value of the maturity value.

- ▶ When a bond is purchased between coupon periods, the buyer pays a price that includes accrued interest, called the full price or dirty price.

- ▶ The clean price or simply price of a bond is the full price minus accrued interest.

- ▶ In computing accrued interest, day count conventions are used to determine the number of days in the coupon payment period and the number of days since the last coupon payment date.

- ▶ The traditional valuation methodology is to discount every cash flow of a security by the same interest rate (or discount rate), thereby incorrectly viewing each security as the same package of cash flows.

▶ The arbitrage-free approach values a bond as a package of cash flows, with each cash flow viewed as a zero-coupon bond and each cash flow discounted at its own unique discount rate.

▶ The Treasury zero-coupon rates are called Treasury spot rates.

▶ The Treasury spot rates are used to discount the cash flows in the arbitrage-free valuation approach.

▶ To value a security with credit risk, it is necessary to determine a term structure of credit rates.

▶ Adding a credit spread for an issuer to the Treasury spot rate curve gives the benchmark spot rate curve used to value that issuer's security.

▶ Valuation models seek to provide the fair value of a bond and accommodate securities with embedded options.

▶ The common valuation models used to value bonds with embedded options are the binomial model and the Monte Carlo simulation model.

▶ The binomial model is used to value callable bonds, putable bonds, floating-rate notes, and structured notes in which the coupon formula is based on an interest rate.

▶ The Monte Carlo simulation model is used to value mortgage-backed and certain asset-backed securities.

▶ The user of a valuation model is exposed to modeling risk and should test the sensitivity of the model to alternative assumptions.

PROBLEMS FOR READING 70

1. Compute the value of a 5-year 7.4% coupon bond that pays interest annually assuming that the appropriate discount rate is 5.6%.

2. A 5-year amortizing security with a par value of $100,000 and a coupon rate of 6.4% has an expected cash flow of $23,998.55 per year assuming no prepayments. The annual cash flow includes interest and principal payment. What is the value of this amortizing security assuming no principal prepayments and a discount rate of 7.8%?

3. **A.** Assuming annual interest payments, what is the value of a 5-year 6.2% coupon bond when the discount rate is (i) 4.5%, (ii) 6.2%, and (iii) 7.3%?

   B. Show that the results obtained in part A are consistent with the relationship between the coupon rate, discount rate, and price relative to par value.

4. A client is reviewing a year-end portfolio report. Since the beginning of the year, market yields have increased slightly. In comparing the beginning-of-the-year price for the bonds selling at a discount from par value to the end-of-year prices, the client observes that all the prices are higher. The client is perplexed since he expected that the price of all bonds should be lower since interest rates increased. Explain to the client why the prices of the bonds in the portfolio selling at discount have increased in value.

5. A 4-year 5.8% coupon bond is selling to yield 7%. The bond pays interest annually. One year later interest rates decrease from 7% to 6.2%.

   A. What is the price of the 4-year 5.8% coupon bond selling to yield 7%?

   B. What is the price of this bond one year later assuming the yield is unchanged at 7%?

   C. What is the price of this bond one year later if instead of the yield being unchanged the yield decreases to 6.2%?

   D. Complete the following:

   Price change attributable to moving to maturity
        (no change in discount rate)

   Price change attributable to an increase in the
        discount rate from 7% to 6.2%

   Total price change

6. What is the value of a 5-year 5.8% annual coupon bond if the appropriate discount rate for discounting each cash flow is as follows:

Year	Discount rate
1	5.90%
2	6.40%
3	6.60%
4	6.90%
5	7.30%

7. What is the value of a 5-year 7.4% coupon bond selling to yield 5.6% assuming the coupon payments are made semiannually?

8. What is the value of a zero-coupon bond paying semiannually that matures in 20 years, has a maturity of $1 million, and is selling to yield 7.6%?

9. Suppose that a bond is purchased between coupon periods. The days between the settlement date and the next coupon period are 115. There are 183 days in the coupon period. Suppose that the bond purchased has a coupon rate of 7.4% and there are 10 semiannual coupon payments remaining.

   A. What is the dirty price for this bond if a 5.6% discount rate is used?

   B. What is the accrued interest for this bond?

   C. What is the clean price?

10. Suppose that the prevailing Treasury spot rate curve is the one shown in Exhibit 70-5.

    A. What is the value of a 7.4% 8-year Treasury issue?

    B. Suppose that the 7.4% 8-year Treasury issue is priced in the market based on the on-the-run 8-year Treasury yield. Assume further that yield is 5.65%, so that each cash flow is discounted at 5.65% divided by 2. What is the price of the 7.4% 8-year Treasury issue based on a 5.65% discount rate?

    C. Given the arbitrage-free value found in part A and the price in part B, what action would a dealer take and what would the arbitrage profit be if the market priced the 7.4% 8-year Treasury issue at the price found in part B?

    D. What process assures that the market price will not differ materially from the arbitrage-free value?

11. Suppose that the prevailing Treasury spot rate curve is the one shown in Exhibit 70-5.

    A. What is the value of a 4% 8-year Treasury issue?

    B. Suppose that the 4% 8-year Treasury issue is priced in the market based on the on-the-run 8-year Treasury yield. Assume further that yield is 5.65%, so that each cash flow is discounted at 5.65% divided by 2. What is the price of the 4% 8-year Treasury issue based on a 5.65% discount rate?

    C. Given the arbitrage-free value found in part A and the price in part B, what action would a dealer take and what would the arbitrage profit be if the market priced the 4% 8-year Treasury issue at the price found in part B?

    D. What process assures that the market price will not differ materially from the arbitrage-free value?

4⅝ 4¹¹/₁₆ — ⅜

5½ 5½ —

5½ 5½ — ¹/₁₆

20⅝ 21³/₁₆ — ¼

17⅜ 18⅛ + ⅞

16½ 6½ 6½ — ½

7¼ 6½ 31/₃₂ — ⅛

15/₁₆

9/₁₆ 9/₁₆

9/₃₂ 9/₁₆

7⁵/₁₆ 7¹³/₁₆ 7¹⁵/₁₆

25⅝ 2¹¹/₃₂ 2½ +

546 23¾ 2¼ 2¼

616 12¹/₁₆ 11⅜ 11¼ +

87 33¾ 33 33¹/₁₆ —

612 25⅝ 24⁹/₁₆ 25⅜ +

833 12 11⅝ 11⅞ +

16 10½ 10½ 10½ —

78 15⅞ 15¹³/₁₆ 15¼ —

4608 9¹/₁₆ 8¼ 8½ +

430 11¼ 10⅛ 4⅞

YIELD MEASURES, SPOT RATES, AND FORWARD RATES

By Frank J. Fabozzi

The candidate should be able to:

a. explain the sources of return from investing in a bond (i.e., coupon interest payments, capital gain/loss, reinvestment income);

b. compute and interpret the traditional yield measures for fixed-rate bonds (e.g., current yield, yield to maturity, yield to first call, yield to first par call date, yield to refunding, yield to put, yield to worst, cash flow yield) and explain the assumptions underlying traditional yield measures and the limitations of the traditional yield measures;

c. explain the importance of reinvestment income in generating the yield computed at the time of purchase, calculate the amount of income required to generate that yield, and discuss the factors that affect reinvestment risk;

d. compute and interpret the bond equivalent yield of an annual-pay bond, and the annual-pay yield of a semiannual-pay bond;

e. describe the methodology for computing the theoretical Treasury spot rate curve and compute the value of a bond using spot rates;

f. distinguish between the nominal spread and the zero-volatility spread and explain the limitations of the nominal spread;

g. explain an option-adjusted spread for a bond with an embedded option and explain the option cost;

h. define a forward rate, and compute spot rates from forward rates and forward rates from spot rates;

i. compute the value of a bond using forward rates.

INTRODUCTION 1

Frequently, investors assess the relative value of a security by some yield or yield spread measure quoted in the market. These measures are based on assumptions that limit their use to gauge relative value. This reading explains the various yield and yield spread measures and their limitations.

In this reading, we will see a basic approach to computing the spot rates from the on-the-run Treasury issues. We will see the limitations of the nominal spread measure and explain two measures that overcome these limitations—zero-volatility spread and option-adjusted spread.

2   SOURCES OF RETURN

When an investor purchases a fixed income security, he or she can expect to receive a dollar return from one or more of the following sources:

1. the coupon interest payments made by the issuer
2. any capital gain (or capital loss—a negative dollar return) when the security matures, is called, or is sold
3. income from reinvestment of interim cash flows (interest and/or principal payments prior to stated maturity)

Any yield measure that purports to measure the potential return from a fixed income security should consider all three sources of return described above.

2.1 Coupon Interest Payments

The most obvious source of return on a bond is the periodic coupon interest payments. For zero-coupon instruments, the return from this source is zero. By purchasing a security below its par value and receiving the full par value at maturity, the investor in a zero-coupon instrument is effectively receiving interest in a lump sum.

2.2 Capital Gain or Loss

An investor receives cash when a bond matures, is called, or is sold. If these proceeds are greater than the purchase price, a capital gain results. For a bond held to maturity, there will be a capital gain if the bond is purchased below its par value. For example, a bond purchased for $94.17 with a par value of $100 will generate a capital gain of $5.83 ($100 − $94.17) if held to maturity. For a callable bond, a capital gain results if the price at which the bond is called (i.e., the call price) is greater than the purchase price. For example, if the bond in our previous example is callable and subsequently called at $100.50, a capital gain of $6.33 ($100.50 − $94.17) will be realized. If the same bond is sold prior to its maturity or before it is called, a capital gain will result if the proceeds exceed the purchase price. So, if our hypothetical bond is sold prior to the maturity date for $103, the capital gain would be $8.83 ($103 − $94.17).

Similarly, for all three outcomes, a capital loss is generated when the proceeds received are less than the purchase price. For a bond held to maturity, there will be a capital loss if the bond is purchased for more than its par value (i.e., purchased at a premium). For example, a bond purchased for $102.50 with a par value of $100 will generate a capital loss of $2.50 ($102.50 − $100) if held to maturity. For a callable bond, a capital loss results if the price at which the bond is called is less than the purchase price. For example, if the bond in our example is callable and subsequently called at $100.50, a capital loss of $2 ($102.50 − $100.50) will be realized. If the same bond is sold prior to its maturity or before it is called, a capital loss will result if the sale price is less than the purchase price. So, if our hypothetical bond is sold prior to the maturity date for $98.50, the capital loss would be $4 ($102.50 − $98.50).

2.3 Reinvestment Income

Prior to maturity, with the exception of zero-coupon instruments, fixed income securities make periodic interest payments that can be reinvested. Amortizing securities (such as mortgage-backed securities and asset-backed securities) make periodic principal payments that can be reinvested prior to final maturity. The interest earned from reinvesting the interim cash flows (interest and/or principal payments) prior to final or stated maturity is called **reinvestment income**.

TRADITIONAL YIELD MEASURES 3

Yield measures cited in the bond market include current yield, yield to maturity, yield to call, yield to put, yield to worst, and cash flow yield. These yield measures are expressed as a percent return rather than a dollar return. Below we explain how each measure is calculated and its limitations.

3.1 Current Yield

The **current yield** relates the annual dollar coupon interest to a bond's market price. The formula for the current yield is:

$$\text{current yield} = \frac{\text{annual dollar coupon interest}}{\text{price}}$$

For example, the current yield for a 7% 8-year bond whose price is $94.17 is 7.43% as shown below:

annual dollar coupon interest = 0.07 × $100 = $7
price = $94.17

$$\text{current yield} = \frac{\$7}{\$94.17} = 0.0743 \text{ or } 7.43\%$$

The current yield will be greater than the coupon rate when the bond sells at a discount; the reverse is true for a bond selling at a premium. For a bond selling at par, the current yield will be equal to the coupon rate.

The drawback of the current yield is that it considers only the coupon interest and no other source for an investor's return. No consideration is given to the capital gain an investor will realize when a bond purchased at a discount is held to maturity; nor is there any recognition of the capital loss an investor will realize if a bond purchased at a premium is held to maturity. No consideration is given to reinvestment income.

3.2 Yield to Maturity

The most popular measure of yield in the bond market is the **yield to maturity**. The yield to maturity is the interest rate that will make the present value of a bond's cash flows equal to its market price plus accrued interest. To find the yield to maturity, we first determine the expected cash flows and then search, by trial and error, for the interest rate that will make the present value of cash flows equal to the market price plus accrued interest. (This is simply a special case of an **internal rate of return** (IRR) calculation where the cash flows are those received if the bond is held to the maturity date.) In the illustrations presented in this reading, we assume that the next coupon payment will be six months from now so that there is no accrued interest.

To illustrate, consider a 7% 8-year bond selling for $94.17. The cash flows for this bond are (1) 16 payments every 6-months of $3.50 and (2) a payment sixteen 6-month periods from now of $100. The present value using various *semiannual* discount (interest) rates is:

Semiannual interest rate	3.5%	3.6%	3.7%	3.8%	3.9%	4.0%
Present value	100.00	98.80	97.62	96.45	95.30	94.17

When a 4.0% interest rate is used, the present value of the cash flows is equal to $94.17, which is the price of the bond. Hence, 4.0% is the *semiannual* yield to maturity.

The market convention adopted to annualize the semiannual yield to maturity is to double it and call that the yield to maturity. Thus, the yield to maturity for the above bond is 8% (2 times 4.0%). The yield to maturity computed using this convention—doubling the semiannual yield—is called a **bond-equivalent yield**.

The following relationships between the price of a bond, coupon rate, current yield, and yield to maturity hold:

Bond selling at	Relationship
par	coupon rate = current yield = yield to maturity
discount	coupon rate < current yield < yield to maturity
premium	coupon rate > current yield > yield to maturity

Practice Question 1

Determine whether the yield to maturity of a 6% 15-year bond selling for $84.25 is either 7.2%, 7.6%, or 7.8%.

3.2.1 The Bond-Equivalent Yield Convention

The *convention* developed in the bond market to move from a semiannual yield to an annual yield is to simply double the semiannual yield. As just noted, this is called the bond-equivalent yield. In general, when one doubles a semiannual yield (or a semiannual return) to obtain an annual measure, one is said to be computing the measure on a **bond-equivalent basis**.

Students of the bond market are troubled by this convention. The two questions most commonly asked are: First, why is the practice of simply doubling a semiannual yield followed? Second, wouldn't it be more appropriate to compute the effective annual yield by compounding the semiannual yield?[1]

The answer to the first question is that it is simply a convention. There is no danger with a convention unless you use it improperly. The fact is that market participants recognize that a yield (or return) is computed on a semiannual basis by convention and adjust accordingly when using the number. So, if the bond-equivalent yield on a security purchased by an investor is 6%, the investor knows the semiannual yield is 3%. Given that, the investor can use that semiannual yield to compute an effective annual yield or any other annualized measure desired. For a manager comparing the yield on a security as an asset purchased to a yield required on a liability to satisfy, the yield figure will be measured in a manner consistent with that of the yield required on the liability.

The answer to the second question is that it is true that computing an effective annual yield would be better. But so what? Once we discover the limitations of yield measures in general, we will question whether or not an investor should use a bond-equivalent yield measure or an effective annual yield measure in making investment decisions. That is, when we identify the major problems with yield measures, the doubling of a semiannual yield is the least of our problems.

So, don't lose any sleep over this convention. Just make sure that you use a bond-equivalent yield measure properly.

3.2.2 Limitations of Yield-to-Maturity Measure

The yield to maturity considers not only the coupon income but any capital gain or loss that the investor will realize by holding the bond to maturity. The yield to maturity also considers the timing of the cash flows. *It does consider reinvestment income; however, it assumes that the coupon payments can be reinvested at an interest rate equal to the yield to maturity.* So, if the yield to maturity for a bond is 8%, for example, to earn that yield the coupon payments must be reinvested at an interest rate equal to 8%.

The illustrations below clearly demonstrate this. In the illustrations, the analysis will be in terms of dollars. Be sure you keep in mind the difference between the **total future dollars**, which is equal to all the dollars an investor expects to receive (including the recovery of the principal), and the **total dollar return**, which is equal to the dollars an investor expects to realize from the three sources of return (coupon payments, capital gain/loss, and reinvestment income).

Suppose an investor has $94.17 and places the funds in a certificate of deposit (CD) that matures in 8 years. Let's suppose that the bank agrees to pay 4% interest every six months. This means that the bank is agreeing to pay 8% on a bond equivalent basis (i.e., doubling the semiannual yield). We can translate all of this into the total future dollars that will be generated by this investment at the end of 8 years. From the standard formula for the future value of an investment today, we can determine the total future dollars as:

$$\$94.17 \times (1.04)^{16} = \$176.38$$

---

[1] By compounding the semiannual yield it is meant that the annual yield is computed as follows:

$$\text{effective annual yield} = (1 + \text{semiannual yield})^2 - 1$$

So, to an investor who invests $94.17 for 8 years at an 8% yield on a bond equivalent basis and interest is paid semiannually, the investment will generate $176.38. Decomposing the total future dollars we see that:

Total future dollars	=	$176.38
Return of principal	=	$94.17
Total interest from CD	=	$82.21

Thus, any investment that promises a yield of 8% on a bond equivalent basis for 8 years on an investment of $94.17 must generate total future dollars of $176.38 or equivalently a return from all sources of $82.21. That is, if we look at the three sources of a bond return that offered an 8% yield with semiannual coupon payments and sold at a price of $94.17, the following would have to hold:

	Coupon interest
+	Capital gain
+	Reinvestment income
=	Total dollar return = Total interest from CD = $82.21

Now, instead of a certificate of deposit, suppose that an investor purchases a bond with a coupon rate of 7% that matures in 8 years. We know that the three sources of return are coupon income, capital gain/loss, and reinvestment income. Suppose that the price of this bond is $94.17. The yield to maturity for this bond (on a bond equivalent basis) is 8%. Notice that this is the same type of investment as the certificate of deposit—the bank offered an 8% yield on a bond equivalent basis for 8 years and made payments semiannually. So, what should the investor in this bond expect in terms of *total future dollars*? As we just demonstrated, an investment of $94.17 must generate $176.38 in order to say that it provided a yield of 8%. Or equivalently, the total dollar return that must be generated is $82.21. Let's look at what in fact is generated in terms of dollar return.

The coupon is $3.50 every six months. So the dollar return from the coupon interest is $3.50 for 16 six-month periods, or $56. When the bond matures, there is a capital gain of $5.83 ($100 − $94.17). Therefore, based on these two sources of return we have:

Coupon interest	=	$56.00
Capital gain	=	$ 5.83
Dollar return *without reinvestment income*	=	$61.83

Something's wrong here. Only $61.83 is generated from the bond whereas $82.21 is needed in order to say that this bond provided an 8% yield. That is, there is a dollar return shortfall of $20.38 ($82.21 − $61.83). How is this dollar return shortfall generated?

Recall that in the case of the certificate of deposit, the bank does the reinvesting of the principal and interest, and pays 4% every six months or 8% on a bond equivalent basis. In contrast, for the bond, the investor has to reinvest any coupon interest until the bond matures. It is the reinvestment income that must generate the dollar return shortfall of $20.38. But at what yield will the investor have to reinvest the coupon payments in order to generate the $20.38? The answer is: the yield to maturity.[2] That is, the reinvestment income will be $20.38 if each semiannual coupon payment of $3.50 can be reinvested at a semiannual yield of 4% (one half the yield to maturity). The reinvestment income earned on a given coupon payment of $3.50, if it is invested from the time of receipt in period t to the maturity date (16 periods in our example) at a 4% semiannual rate, is:

$$\$3.50 \ (1.04)^{16-t} - \$3.50$$

The first coupon payment ($t = 1$) can be reinvested for 15 periods. Applying the formula above we find the reinvestment income earned on the first coupon payment is:

$$\$3.50 \ (1.04)^{16-1} - \$3.50 = \$2.80$$

Similarly, the reinvestment income for all coupon payments is shown below:

Period	Periods reinvested	Coupon payment	Reinvestment income
1	15	$3.5	$2.80
2	14	3.5	2.56
3	13	3.5	2.33
4	12	3.5	2.10
5	11	3.5	1.89
6	10	3.5	1.68
7	9	3.5	1.48
8	8	3.5	1.29
9	7	3.5	1.11
10	6	3.5	0.93
11	5	3.5	0.76
12	4	3.5	0.59
13	3	3.5	0.44
14	2	3.5	0.29
15	1	3.5	0.14
16	0	3.5	0.00
		Total	$20.39

---

[2] This can be verified by using the future value of an annuity. The future of an annuity is given by the following formula:

$$\text{Annuity payment} = \left[\frac{(1 + i)^n - 1}{i} \right]$$

where i is the interest rate and n is the number of periods.

In our example, i is 4%, n is 16, and the amount of the annuity is the semiannual coupon of $3.50. Therefore, the future value of the coupon payment is

$$\$3.50 \left[\frac{(1.04)^{16} - 1}{0.04} \right] = \$76.38$$

Since the coupon payments are $56, the reinvestment income is $20.38 ($76.38 − $56). This is the amount that is necessary to produce the dollar return shortfall in our example.

The total reinvestment income is $20.39 (differing from $20.38 due to rounding).

So, with the reinvestment income of $20.38 at 4% semiannually (i.e., one half the yield to maturity on a bond-equivalent basis), the total dollar return is

Coupon interest	=	$56.00
Capital gain	=	$5.83
Reinvestment income	=	$20.38
Total dollar return	=	$82.21

In our illustration, we used an investment in a certificate of deposit to show what the total future dollars will have to be in order to obtain a yield of 8% on an investment of $94.17 for 8 years when interest payments are semiannual. However, this holds for any type of investment, not just a certificate of deposit. For example, if an investor is told that he or she can purchase a debt instrument for $94.17 that offers an 8% yield (on a bond-equivalent basis) for 8 years and makes interest payments semiannually, then the investor should translate this yield into the following:

I should be receiving total future dollars of $176.38
I should be receiving a total dollar return of $82.21

It is always important to think in terms of dollars (or pound sterling, yen, or other currency) because "yield measures" are misleading.

We can also see that the reinvestment income can be a significant portion of the total dollar return. In our example, the total dollar return is $82.21 and the total dollar return from reinvestment income to make up the shortfall is $20.38. This means that reinvestment income is about 25% of the total dollar return.

This is such an important point that we should go through this one more time for another bond. Suppose an investor purchases a 15-year 8% coupon bond at par value ($100). The yield for this bond is simple to determine since the bond is trading at par. The yield is equal to the coupon rate, 8%. Let's translate this into dollars. We know that if an investor makes an investment of $100 for 15 years that offers an 8% yield and the interest payments are semiannual, the total future dollars will be:

$$\$100 \times (1.04)^{30} = 324.34$$

Decomposing the total future dollars we see that:

Total future dollars	=	$324.34
Return of principal	=	$100.00
Total dollar return	=	$224.34

Without reinvestment income, the dollar return is:

Coupon interest	=	$120
Capital gain	=	$ 0
Dollar return *without reinvestment income*	=	$120

Note that the capital gain is $0 because the bond is purchased at par value.

The dollar return shortfall is therefore $104.34 ($224.34 − $120). This shortfall is made up if the coupon payments can be reinvested at a yield of 8% (the yield on the bond at the time of purchase). For this bond, the reinvestment income is 46.5% of the total dollar return needed to produce a yield of 8% ($104.34/$224.34).[3]

Clearly, the investor will only realize the yield to maturity stated at the time of purchase if the following two assumptions hold:

Assumption 1: the coupon payments can be reinvested at the yield to maturity

Assumption 2: the bond is held to maturity

With respect to the first assumption, the risk that an investor faces is that future interest rates will be less than the yield to maturity at the time the bond is purchased, known as **reinvestment risk**. If the bond is not held to maturity, the investor faces the risk that he may have to sell for less than the purchase price, resulting in a return that is less than the yield to maturity, known as **interest rate risk**.

Practice Question 2

A. Suppose that an investor purchases a 6% coupon bond with 20 years to maturity at a price of $89.32 per $100 par value. The yield to maturity for this bond is 7%. Determine the dollar return that must be generated from reinvestment income in order to generate a yield of 7% and the percentage of the reinvestment income relative to the total dollar return needed to generate a 7% yield.

B. Suppose that a zero-coupon bond that matures in 10 years is selling to yield 7%. Determine the dollar return that must be generated from reinvestment income in order to generate a yield of 7% and the percentage of the reinvestment income relative to the total dollar return needed to generate a 7% yield.

3.2.3 Factors Affecting Reinvestment Risk

There are two characteristics of a bond that affect the degree of reinvestment risk:

Characteristic 1. For a given yield to maturity and a given non-zero coupon rate, the longer the maturity, the more the bond's total dollar return depends on reinvestment income to realize the yield to maturity at the time of purchase. That is, the greater the reinvestment risk.

---

[3] The future value of the coupon payments of $4 for 30 six-month periods is:

$$\$4.00\left[\frac{(1.04)^{30} - 1}{0.04}\right] = \$224.34$$

Since the coupon payments are $120 and the capital gain is $0, the reinvestment income is $104.34. This is the amount that is necessary to produce the dollar return shortfall in our example.

The implication is the yield to maturity measure for long-term maturity coupon bonds tells little about the potential return that an investor may realize if the bond is held to maturity. For long-term bonds, in high interest rate environments, the reinvestment income component may be as high as 70% of the bond's total dollar return.

> *Characteristic 2.* For a coupon paying bond, for a given maturity and a given yield to maturity, the higher the coupon rate, the more dependent the bond's total dollar return will be on the reinvestment of the coupon payments in order to produce the yield to maturity at the time of purchase.

This means that holding maturity and yield to maturity constant, bonds selling at a premium will be more dependent on reinvestment income than bonds selling at par. This is because the reinvestment income has to make up the capital loss due to amortizing the price premium when holding the bond to maturity. In contrast, a bond selling at a discount will be less dependent on reinvestment income than a bond selling at par because a portion of the return is coming from the capital gain due to accrediting the price discount when holding the bond to maturity. For zero-coupon bonds, none of the bond's total dollar return is dependent on reinvestment income. So, a zero-coupon bond has no reinvestment risk if held to maturity.

The dependence of the total dollar return on reinvestment income for bonds with different coupon rates and maturities is shown in Exhibit 71-1.

EXHIBIT 71-1   **Percentage of Total Dollar Return from Reinvestment Income for a Bond to Generate an 8% Yield (BEY)**

	Years to maturity				
	2	**3**	**5**	**8**	**15**
Bond with a 7% coupon					
Price	98.19	97.38	95.94	94.17	91.35
% of total	5.2%	8.6%	15.2%	24.8%	44.5%
Bond with an 8% coupon					
Price	100.00	100.00	100.00	100.00	100.00
% of total	5.8%	9.5%	16.7%	26.7%	46.5%
Bond with a 12% coupon					
Price	107.26	110.48	116.22	122.30	134.58
% of total	8.1%	12.9%	21.6%	31.0%	51.8%

3.2.4 *Comparing Semiannual-Pay and Annual-Pay Bonds*

In our yield calculations, we have been dealing with bonds that pay interest semi-annually. A non-U.S. bond may pay interest annually rather than semiannually. This is the case for many government bonds in Europe and Eurobonds. In such instances, an adjustment is required to make a direct comparison between the yield to maturity on a U.S. fixed-rate bond and that on an annual-pay non-U.S. fixed-rate bond.

Given the yield to maturity on an annual-pay bond, its bond-equivalent yield is computed as follows:

bond-equivalent yield of an annual-pay bond $= 2[(1 +$ yield on annual-pay bond$)^{0.5} - 1]$

The term in the square brackets involves determining what semiannual yield, when compounded, produces the yield on an annual-pay bond. Doubling this semiannual yield (i.e., multiplying the term in the square brackets by 2) gives the bond-equivalent yield.

For example, suppose that the yield to maturity on an annual-pay bond is 6%. Then the bond-equivalent yield is:

$$2[(1.06)^{0.5} - 1] = 5.91\%$$

Notice that the bond-equivalent yield will always be less than the annual-pay bond's yield to maturity.

To convert the bond-equivalent yield of a U.S. bond issue to an annual-pay basis so that it can be compared to the yield on an annual-pay bond, the following formula can be used:

$$\text{yield on an annual-pay basis} = \left[\left(1 + \frac{\text{yield on a bond-equivalent basis}}{2}\right)^2 - 1\right]$$

By dividing the yield on a bond-equivalent basis by 2 in the above expression, the semiannual yield is computed. The semiannual yield is then compounded to get the yield on an annual-pay basis.

For example, suppose that the yield of a U.S. bond issue quoted on a bond-equivalent basis is 6%. The yield to maturity on an annual-pay basis would be:

$$[(1.03)^2 - 1] = 6.09\%$$

The yield on an annual-pay basis is always greater than the yield on a bond-equivalent basis because of compounding.

Practice Question 3

A. If the yield to maturity on an annual-pay bond is 4.8%, what is the bond-equivalent yield?

B. If the yield of a U.S. bond issue quoted on a bond-equivalent basis is 4.8%, what is the yield to maturity on an annual-pay basis?

3.3 Yield to Call

When a bond is callable, the practice has been to calculate a yield to call as well as a yield to maturity. A callable bond may have a call schedule.[4] The yield to call assumes the issuer will call a bond on some assumed call date and that the call price is the price specified in the call schedule. Typically, investors calculate a yield to first call or yield to next call, a yield to first par call, and a yield to refunding. The **yield to first call** is computed for an issue that is not currently callable, while the **yield to next call** is computed for an issue that is currently callable.

Yield to refunding is used when bonds are currently callable but have some restrictions on the source of funds used to buy back the debt when a call is exercised. Namely, if a debt issue contains some refunding protection, bonds cannot be called for a certain period of time with the proceeds of other debt issues sold at a lower cost of money. As a result, the bondholder is afforded some protection if interest rates decline and the issuer can obtain lower-cost funds to pay off the debt. It should be stressed that the bonds can be called with funds derived from other sources (e.g., cash on hand) during the refunded-protected period. The refunding date is the first date the bond can be called using lower-cost debt.

The procedure for calculating any yield to call measure is the same as for any yield to maturity calculation: determine the interest rate that will make the present value of the expected cash flows equal to the price plus accrued interest. In the case of yield to first call, the expected cash flows are the coupon payments to the first call date and the call price. For the **yield to first par call**, the expected cash flows are the coupon payments to the first date at which the issuer can call the bond at par and the par value. For the yield to refunding, the expected cash flows are the coupon payments to the first refunding date and the call price at the first refunding date.

To illustrate the computation, consider a 7% 8-year bond with a maturity value of $100 selling for $106.36. Suppose that the first call date is three years from now and the call price is $103. The cash flows for this bond if it is called in three years are (1) 6 coupon payments of $3.50 every six months and (2) $103 in six 6-month periods from now.

The present value for several semiannual interest rates is shown in Exhibit 71-2. Since a semiannual interest rate of 2.8% makes the present value of the cash flows equal to the price, 2.8% is the yield to first call. Therefore, the yield to first call on a bond-equivalent basis is 5.6%.

For our 7% 8-year callable bond, suppose that the first par call date is 5 years from now. The cash flows for computing the first par call are then: (1) a total 10 coupon payments of $3.50 each paid every six months and (2) $100 in ten 6-month periods. The yield to par call is 5.53%. Let's verify that this is the case. The semiannual yield is 2.765% (one half of 5.53%). The present value of the 10 coupon payments of $3.50 every six months when discounted at 2.765% is $30.22. The present value of $100 (the call price of par) at the end of five years (10 semiannual periods) is $76.13. The present value of the cash flow is then $106.35 (= $30.22 + $76.13). Since the price of the bond is $106.36 and since using a yield of 5.53% produces a value for this callable bond that differs from $106.36 by only 1 penny, 5.53% is the yield to first par call.

Let's take a closer look at the yield to call as a measure of the potential return of a security. The yield to call considers all three sources of potential return from owning a bond. However, as in the case of the yield to maturity, it

---

[4] A call schedule shows the call price that the issuer must pay based on the date when the issue is called. An example of a call schedule is provided in Reading 65.

EXHIBIT 71-2	Yield to Call for an 8-Year 7% Coupon Bond with a Maturity Value of $100, First Call Date is the End of Year 3, and Call Price of $103			
Annual interest rate (%)	Semiannual interest rate (%)	Present value of 6 payments of $3.5	Present value of $103 6 periods from now	Present value of cash flows
5.0	2.5	$19.28	$88.82	$108.10
5.2	2.6	19.21	88.30	107.51
5.4	2.7	19.15	87.78	106.93
5.6	2.8	19.09	87.27	106.36

assumes that all cash flows can be reinvested at the yield to call until the assumed call date. As we just demonstrated, this assumption may be inappropriate. Moreover, the yield to call assumes that

> *Assumption 1:* the investor will hold the bond to the assumed call date
> *Assumption 2:* the issuer will call the bond on that date

These assumptions underlying the yield to call are unrealistic. Moreover, comparison of different yields to call with the yield to maturity are meaningless because the cash flows stop at the assumed call date. For example, consider two bonds, M and N. Suppose that the yield to maturity for bond M, a 5-year non-callable bond, is 7.5% while for bond N the yield to call, assuming the bond will be called in three years, is 7.8%. Which bond is better for an investor with a 5-year investment horizon? It's not possible to tell from the yields cited. If the investor intends to hold the bond for five years and the issuer calls bond N after three years, the total dollar return that will be available at the end of five years will depend on the interest rate that can be earned from investing funds from the call date to the end of the investment horizon.

Practice Question 4

Suppose that a 9% 10-year bond has the following call structure:

> not callable for the next 5 years
> first callable at beginning of year 6 (i.e., at the end of the fifth year) at $104.50
> first par call date at beginning of year 9 (i.e., at the end of the eighth year)

The price of the bond is $123.04.

A. Is the yield to first call for this bond 4.4%, 4.6%, or 4.8%?

B. Is the yield to first par call for this bond 5.41%, 5.62%, or 5.75%?

3.4 Yield to Put

When a bond is putable, the yield to the first put date is calculated. The yield to put is the interest rate that will make the present value of the cash flows to the first put date equal to the price plus accrued interest. As with all yield measures (except the current yield), yield to put assumes that any interim coupon payments can be reinvested at the yield calculated. Moreover, the yield to put assumes that the bond will be put on the first put date.

For example, suppose that a 6.2% coupon bond maturing in 8 years is putable at par in 3 years. The price of this bond is $102.19. The cash flows for this bond if it is put in three years are: (1) a total of 6 coupon payments of $3.10 each paid every six months and (2) the $100 put price in six 6-month periods from now. The semiannual interest rate that will make the present value of the cash flows equal to the price of $102.19 is 2.7%. Therefore, 2.7% is the semiannual yield to put and 5.4% is the yield to put on a bond equivalent basis.

3.5 Yield to Worst

A yield can be calculated for every possible call date and put date. In addition, a yield to maturity can be calculated. The lowest of all these possible yields is called the **yield to worst**. For example, suppose that there are only four possible call dates for a callable bond, that the yield to call assuming each possible call date is 6%, 6.2%, 5.8%, and 5.7%, and that the yield to maturity is 7.5%. Then the yield to worst is the minimum of these yields, 5.7% in our example.

The yield to worst measure holds little meaning as a measure of potential return. It supposedly states that this is the worst possible yield that the investor will realize. However, as we have noted about any yield measure, it does not identify the potential return over some investment horizon. Moreover, the yield to worst does not recognize that each yield calculation used in determining the yield to worst has different exposures to reinvestment risk.

3.6 Cash Flow Yield

Mortgage-backed securities and asset-backed securities are backed by a pool of loans or receivables. The cash flows for these securities include principal payment as well as interest. The complication that arises is that the individual borrowers whose loans make up the pool typically can prepay their loan in whole or in part prior to the scheduled principal payment dates. Because of principal prepayments, in order to project cash flows it is necessary to make an assumption about the rate at which principal prepayments will occur. This rate is called the **prepayment rate** or **prepayment speed**.

Given cash flows based on an assumed prepayment rate, a yield can be calculated. The yield is the interest rate that will make the present value of the projected cash flows equal to the price plus accrued interest. The yield calculated is commonly referred to as a **cash flow yield**.[5]

3.6.1 Bond-Equivalent Yield

Typically, the cash flows for mortgage-backed and asset-backed securities are monthly. Therefore the interest rate that will make the present value of pro-

---

[5] Some firms such as Prudential Securities refer to this yield as yield to maturity rather than cash flow yield.

jected principal and interest payments equal to the market price plus accrued interest is a monthly rate. The monthly yield is then annualized as follows.

First, the semiannual effective yield is computed from the monthly yield by compounding it for six months as follows:

effective semiannual yield $= (1 + \text{monthly yield})^6 - 1$

Next, the effective semiannual yield is doubled to get the annual cash flow yield on a bond-equivalent basis. That is,

$$\text{cash flow yield} = 2 \times \text{effective semiannual yield}$$

$$= 2\big[(1 + monthly\ yield)^6 - 1\big]$$

For example, if the monthly yield is 0.5%, then:

cash flow yield on a bond-equivalent basis $= 2\big[(1.005)^6 + 1\big] = 6.08\%$

The calculation of the cash flow yield may seem strange because it first requires the computing of an effective semiannual yield given the monthly yield and then doubling. This is simply a market convention. Of course, the student of the bond market can always ask the same two questions as with the yield to maturity: Why it is done? Isn't it better to just compound the monthly yield to get an effective annual yield? The answers are the same as given earlier for the yield to maturity. Moreover, as we will see next, this is the least of our problems in using a cash flow yield measure for an asset-backed and mortgage-backed security.

3.6.2 *Limitations of Cash Flow Yield*

As we have noted, the yield to maturity has two shortcomings as a measure of a bond's potential return: (1) it is assumed that the coupon payments can be reinvested at a rate equal to the yield to maturity and (2) it is assumed that the bond is held to maturity. These shortcomings are equally present in application of the cash flow yield measure: (1) the projected cash flows are assumed to be reinvested at the cash flow yield and (2) the mortgage-backed or asset-backed security is assumed to be held until the final payoff of all the loans, based on some prepayment assumption. The significance of reinvestment risk, the risk that the cash flows will be reinvested at a rate less than the cash flow yield, is particularly important for mortgage-backed and asset-backed securities since payments are typically monthly and include principal payments (scheduled and prepaid), and interest. Moreover, the cash flow yield is dependent on realizing of the projected cash flows according to some prepayment rate. If actual prepayments differ significantly from the prepayment rate assumed, the cash flow yield will not be realized.

3.7 Spread/Margin Measures for Floating-Rate Securities

The coupon rate for a floating-rate security (or floater) changes periodically according to a reference rate (such as LIBOR or a Treasury rate). Since the future value for the reference rate is unknown, it is not possible to determine the cash flows. This means that a yield to maturity cannot be calculated. Instead, "margin" measures are computed. Margin is simply some spread above the floater's reference rate.

Several spread or margin measures are routinely used to evaluate floaters. Two margin measures commonly used are spread for life and discount margin.[6]

3.7.1 Spread for Life

When a floater is selling at a premium/discount to par, investors consider the premium or discount as an additional source of dollar return. **Spread for life** (also called **simple margin**) is a measure of potential return that accounts for the accretion (amortization) of the discount (premium) as well as the constant quoted margin over the security's remaining life. Spread for life (in basis points) is calculated using the following formula:

$$\text{Spread for life} = \left[\frac{100\left(100 - \text{Price}\right)}{\text{Maturity}} + \text{Quoted margin} \right] \times \left(\frac{100}{\text{Price}} \right)$$

where

Price	=	market price per \$100 of par value
Maturity	=	number of years to maturity
Quoted margin	=	quoted margin in the coupon reset formula measured in basis points

For example, suppose that a floater with a quoted margin of 80 basis points is selling for 99.3098 and matures in 6 years. Then,

Price	=	99.3098
Maturity	=	6
Quoted margin	=	80

$$\text{Spread for life} = \left[\frac{100(100 - 99.3098)}{6} + 80 \right] \times \left(\frac{100}{99.3098} \right)$$

$$= 92.14 \text{ Basis points}$$

The limitations of the spread for life are that it considers only the accretion/amortization of the discount/premium over the floater's remaining term to maturity and does not consider the level of the coupon rate or the time value of money.

3.7.2 Discount Margin

Discount margin estimates the average margin over the reference rate that the investor can expect to earn over the life of the security. The procedure for calculating the discount margin is as follows:

Step 1. Determine the cash flows assuming that the reference rate does *not* change over the life of the security.

Step 2. Select a margin.

---

[6] For a discussion of other traditional measures, see Chapter 3 in Frank J. Fabozzi and Steven V. Mann, *Floating Rate Securities* (New Hope, PA; Frank J. Fabozzi Associates, 2000).

Step 3. Discount the cash flows found in Step 1 by the current value of
the reference rate plus the margin selected in Step 2.

Step 4. Compare the present value of the cash flows as calculated in Step
3 to the price plus accrued interest. If the present value is equal
to the security's price plus accrued interest, the discount margin
is the margin assumed in Step 2. If the present value is not equal
to the security's price plus accrued interest, go back to Step 2
and try a different margin.

For a security selling at par, the discount margin is simply the quoted margin
in the coupon reset formula.

To illustrate the calculation, suppose that the coupon reset formula for a 6-
year floating-rate security selling for $99.3098 is 6-month LIBOR plus 80 basis
points. The coupon rate is reset every 6 months. Assume that the current value
for the reference rate is 10%.

Exhibit 71-3 shows the calculation of the discount margin for this security.
The second column shows the current value for 6-month LIBOR. The third column sets forth the cash flows for the security. The cash flow for the first 11 periods

EXHIBIT 71-3	Calculation of the Discount Margin for a Floating-Rate Security

Floating rate security:

Maturity	=	6 years
Price	=	99.3098
Coupon formula	=	LIBOR + 80 basis points
		Reset every six months

Period	LIBOR (%)	Cash flow ($)*	Present value ($) at assumed margin of**				
			80 bp	84 bp	88 bp	96 bp	100 bp
1	10	5.4	5.1233	5.1224	5.1214	5.1195	5.1185
2	10	5.4	4.8609	4.8590	4.8572	4.8535	4.8516
3	10	5.4	4.6118	4.6092	4.6066	4.6013	4.5987
4	10	5.4	4.3755	4.3722	4.3689	4.3623	4.3590
5	10	5.4	4.1514	4.1474	4.1435	4.1356	4.1317
6	10	5.4	3.9387	3.9342	3.9297	3.9208	3.9163
7	10	5.4	3.7369	3.7319	3.7270	3.7171	3.7122
8	10	5.4	3.5454	3.5401	3.5347	3.5240	3.5186
9	10	5.4	3.3638	3.3580	3.3523	3.3409	3.3352
10	10	5.4	3.1914	3.1854	3.1794	3.1673	3.1613
11	10	5.4	3.0279	3.0216	3.0153	3.0028	2.9965
12	10	105.4	56.0729	55.9454	55.8182	55.5647	55.4385
		Present value	100.0000	99.8269	99.6541	99.3098	99.1381

* For periods 1-11: cash flow = $100 (0.5) (LIBOR + assumed margin)
  For period 12: cash flow = $100 (0.5) (LIBOR + assumed margin) + $100
** The discount rate is found as follows. To LIBOR of 10%, the assumed margin is added. Thus, for an 80 basis point assumed margin, the discount rate
  is 10.80%. This is an annual discount rate on a bond-equivalent basis. The semiannual discount rate is then half this amount, 5.4%. It is this discount
  rate that is used to compute the present value of the cash flows for an assumed margin of 80 basis points.

is equal to one-half the current 6-month LIBOR (5%) plus the semiannual quoted margin of 40 basis points multiplied by $100. At the maturity date (i.e., period 12), the cash flow is $5.4 plus the maturity value of $100. The column headings of the last five columns show the assumed margin. The rows below the assumed margin show the present value of each cash flow. The last row gives the total present value of the cash flows.

For the five assumed margins, the present value is equal to the price of the floating-rate security ($99.3098) when the assumed margin is 96 basis points. Therefore, the discount margin is 96 basis points. Notice that the discount margin is 80 basis points, the same as the quoted margin, when this security is selling at par.

There are two drawbacks of the discount margin as a measure of the potential return from investing in a floating-rate security. First, the measure assumes that the reference rate will not change over the life of the security. Second, if the floating-rate security has a cap or floor, this is not taken into consideration.

Practice Question 5

Suppose that the price of the floater in our illustration was 99.8269 rather than 99.3098. Without doing any calculation, determine what the discount margin would be.

3.8 Yield on Treasury Bills

Treasury bills are zero-coupon instruments with a maturity of one year or less. The convention in the Treasury bill market is to calculate a bill's **yield on a discount basis**. This yield is determined by two variables:

1. the **settlement price** per $1 of maturity value (denoted by p)
2. the number of days to maturity which is calculated as the number of days between the settlement date and the maturity date (denoted by N_{SM})

The yield on a discount basis (denoted by d) is calculated as follows:

$$d = (1 - p)\left(\frac{360}{N_{SM}}\right)$$

We will use two actual Treasury bills to illustrate the calculation of the yield on a discount basis assuming a settlement date in both cases of 8/6/97. The first bill has a maturity date of 1/8/98 and a price of 0.97769722. For this bill, the number of days from the settlement date to the maturity date, N_{SM}, is 155. Therefore, the yield on a discount basis is

$$d = (1 - 0.97769722)\left(\frac{360}{155}\right) = 5.18\%$$

For our second bill, the maturity date is 7/23/98 and the price is 0.9490075. Assuming a settlement date of 8/6/97, the number of days from the settlement date to the maturity date is 351. The yield on a discount basis for this bill is

$$d = (1 - 0.9490075)\left(\frac{360}{351}\right) = 5.23\%$$

Given the yield on a discount basis, the price of a bill (per \$1 of maturity value) is computed as follows:

$$p = 1 - d(N_{SM}/360)$$

For the 155-day bill selling for a yield on a discount basis of 5.18%, the price per \$1 of maturity value is

$$p = 1 - 0.0518 \, (155/360) = 0.97769722$$

For the 351-day bill selling for a yield on a discount basis of 5.23%, the price per \$1 of maturity value is

$$p = 1 - 0.0523 \, (351/360) = 0.9490075$$

The quoted yield on a discount basis is not a meaningful measure of the return from holding a Treasury bill for two reasons. First, the measure is based on a maturity value investment rather than on the actual dollar amount invested. Second, the yield is annualized according to a 360-day year rather than a 365-day year, making it difficult to compare yields on Treasury bills with Treasury notes and bonds which pay interest based on the actual number of days in a year. The use of 360 days for a year is a convention for money market instruments. Despite its shortcomings as a measure of return, this is the method dealers have adopted to quote Treasury bills.

Market participants recognize this limitation of yield on a discount basis and consequently make adjustments to make the yield quoted on a Treasury bill comparable to that on a Treasury coupon security. For investors who want to compare the yield on Treasury bills to that of other money market instruments (i.e., debt obligations with a maturity that does not exceed one year), there is a formula to convert the yield on a discount basis to that of a money market yield. The key point is that while the convention is to quote the yield on a Treasury bill in terms of a yield on a discount basis, no one uses that yield measure other than to compute the price given the quoted yield.

Practice Question 6

A. A Treasury bill with 115 days from settlement to maturity is selling for \$0.9825 per \$1 of maturity value. What is the yield on a discount basis?

B. A Treasury bill with 162 days from settlement to maturity is quoted as having a yield on a discount basis of 5.9%. What is the price of this Treasury bill?

THEORETICAL SPOT RATES

The theoretical spot rates for Treasury securities represent the appropriate set of interest rates that should be used to value default-free cash flows. A default-free theoretical spot rate curve can be constructed from the observed Treasury yield curve. There are several approaches that are used in practice. The approach that we describe below for creating a theoretical spot rate curve is called **bootstrapping**. (The bootstrapping method described here is also used in constructing a theoretical spot rate curve for LIBOR.)

4.1 Bootstrapping

Bootstrapping begins with the yield for the on-the-run Treasury issues because there is no credit risk and no liquidity risk. In practice, however, there is a problem of obtaining a sufficient number of data points for constructing the U.S. Treasury yield curve. In the United States, the U.S. Department of the Treasury currently issues 3-month and 6-month Treasury bills and 2-year, 5-year, and 10-year Treasury notes. Treasury bills are zero-coupon instruments and Treasury notes are coupon-paying instruments. Hence, there are not many data points from which to construct a Treasury yield curve, particularly after two years. At one time, the U.S. Treasury issued 30-year Treasury bonds. Since the Treasury no longer issues 30-year bonds, market participants currently use the last issued Treasury bond (which has a maturity less than 30 years) to estimate the 30-year yield. The 2-year, 5-year, and 10-year Treasury notes and an estimate of the 30-year Treasury bond are used to construct the Treasury yield curve.

On September 5, 2003, Lehman Brothers reported the following values for these four yields:

2 year	1.71%
5 year	3.25%
10 year	4.35%
30 year	5.21%

To fill in the yield for the 25 missing whole year maturities (3 year, 4 year, 6 year, 7 year, 8 year, 9 year, 11 year, and so on to the 29-year maturity), the yield for the 25 whole year maturities are interpolated from the yield on the surrounding maturities. The simplest interpolation, and the one most commonly used in practice, is simple linear interpolation.

For example, suppose that we want to fill in the gap for each one year of maturity. To determine the amount to add to the on-the-run Treasury yield as we go from the lower maturity to the higher maturity, the following formula is used:

$$\frac{\text{Yield at higher maturity} - \text{Yield at lower maturity}}{\text{Number of years between two observed maturity points}}$$

The estimated on-the-run yield for all intermediate whole-year maturities is found by adding the amount computed from the above formula to the yield at the lower maturity.

For example, using the September 5, 2003 yields, the 5-year yield of 3.25% and the 10-year yield of 4.35% are used to obtain the interpolated 6-year, 7-year, 8-year, and 9-year yields by first calculating:

$$\frac{4.35\% - 3.25\%}{5} = 0.22\%$$

Then,

$$
\begin{aligned}
\text{interpolated 6-year yield} &= 3.25\% + 0.22\% = 3.47\% \\
\text{interpolated 7-year yield} &= 3.47\% + 0.22\% = 3.69\% \\
\text{interpolated 8-year yield} &= 3.69\% + 0.22\% = 3.91\% \\
\text{interpolated 9-year yield} &= 3.91\% + 0.22\% = 4.13\%
\end{aligned}
$$

Thus, when market participants talk about a yield on the Treasury yield curve that is not one of the on-the-run maturities—for example, the 8-year yield—it is only an approximation. Notice that there is a large gap between maturity points. This may result in misleading yields for the interim maturity points when estimated using the linear interpolation method, a point that we return to later in this reading.

To illustrate bootstrapping, we will use the Treasury yields shown in Exhibit 71-4 for maturities up to 10 years using 6-month periods.[7] Thus, there are 20 Treasury yields shown. The yields shown are assumed to have been interpolated

EXHIBIT 71-4	Hypothetical Treasury Yields (Interpolated)			
Period	**Years**	**Annual Par Yield to Maturity (BEY) (%)***	**Price**	**Spot Rate (BEY) (%)***
1	0.5	3.00	—	3.0000
2	1.0	3.30	—	3.3000
3	1.5	3.50	100.00	3.5053
4	2.0	3.90	100.00	3.9164
5	2.5	4.40	100.00	4.4376
6	3.0	4.70	100.00	4.7520
7	3.5	4.90	100.00	4.9622
8	4.0	5.00	100.00	5.0650
9	4.5	5.10	100.00	5.1701
10	5.0	5.20	100.00	5.2772
11	5.5	5.30	100.00	5.3864
12	6.0	5.40	100.00	5.4976
13	6.5	5.50	100.00	5.6108
14	7.0	5.55	100.00	5.6643
15	7.5	5.60	100.00	5.7193
16	8.0	5.65	100.00	5.7755
17	8.5	5.70	100.00	5.8331
18	9.0	5.80	100.00	5.9584
19	9.5	5.90	100.00	6.0863
20	10.0	6.00	100.00	6.2169

* The yield to maturity and the spot rate are annual rates. They are reported as bond-equivalent yields. To obtain the semiannual yield or rate, one half the annual yield or annual rate is used

---

[7] Two points should be noted abut the yields reported in Exhibit 71-4. First, the yields are unrelated to our earlier Treasury yields on September 5, 2003 that we used to show how to calculate the yield on interim maturities using linear interpolation. Second, the Treasury yields in our illustration after the first year are all shown at par value. Hence the Treasury yield curve in Exhibit 71-4 is called a *par yield curve*.

| EXHIBIT 71-5 | Treasury Par Yield Curve |

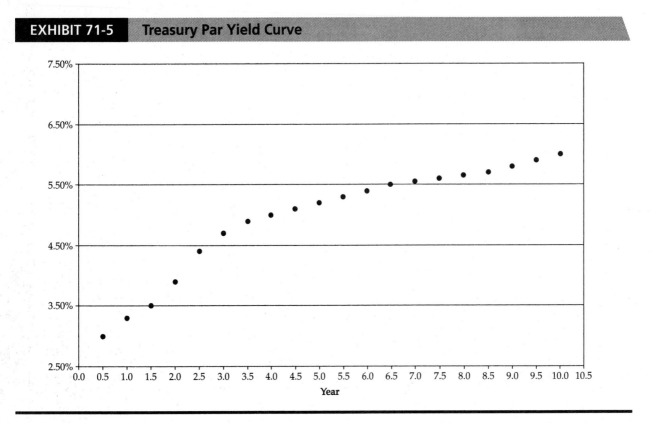

from the on-the-run Treasury issues. Exhibit 71-5 shows the Treasury yield curve based on the yields shown in Exhibit 71-4. Our objective is to show how the values in the last column of Exhibit 71-4 (labeled "Spot Rate") are obtained.

Throughout the analysis and illustrations to come, it is important to remember that the basic principle is the value of the Treasury coupon security should be equal to the value of the package of zero-coupon Treasury securities that duplicates the coupon bond's cash flows. We saw this in Reading 70 when we discussed arbitrage-free valuation.

Consider the 6-month and 1-year Treasury securities in Exhibit 71-4. As we explained in Reading 70, these two securities are called Treasury bills and they are issued as zero-coupon instruments. Therefore, the annualized yield (not the discount yield) of 3.00% for the 6-month Treasury security is equal to the 6-month spot rate.[8] Similarly, for the 1-year Treasury security, the cited yield of 3.30% is the 1-year spot rate. Given these two spot rates, we can compute the spot rate for a theoretical 1.5-year zero-coupon Treasury. The value of a theoretical 1.5-year Treasury should equal the present value of the three cash flows from the 1.5-year coupon Treasury, where the yield used for discounting is the spot rate corresponding to the time of receipt of each six-month cash flow. Since all the coupon bonds are selling at par, as explained in the previous section, the yield to maturity for each bond is the coupon rate. Using $100 par, the cash flows for the 1.5-year coupon Treasury are:

---

[8] We will assume that the annualized yield for the Treasury bill is computed on a bond-equivalent basis. Earlier in this reading, we saw how the yield on a Treasury bill is quoted. The quoted yield can be converted into a bond-equivalent yield; we assume this has already been done in Exhibit 71-4.

0.5 year	0.035	×	\$100	×	0.5		=	\$1.75
1.0 year	0.035	×	\$100	×	0.5		=	\$1.75
1.5 years	0.035	×	\$100	×	0.5	+ 100	=	\$101.75

The present value of the cash flows is then:

$$\frac{1.75}{(1 + z_1)^1} + \frac{1.75}{(1 + z_2)^2} + \frac{101.75}{(1 + z_3)^3}$$

where

z_1 = one-half the annualized 6-month theoretical spot rate
z_2 = one-half the 1-year theoretical spot rate
z_3 = one-half the 1.5-year theoretical spot rate

Since the 6-month spot rate is 3% and the 1-year spot rate is 3.30%, we know that:

$$z_1 = 0.0150 \text{ and } z_2 = 0.0165$$

We can compute the present value of the 1.5-year coupon Treasury security as:

$$\frac{1.75}{(1 + z_1)^1} + \frac{1.75}{(1 + z_2)^2} + \frac{101.75}{(1 + z_3)^3} = \frac{1.75}{(1.015)^1} + \frac{1.75}{(1.0165)^2} + \frac{101.75}{(1 + z_3)^3}$$

Since the price of the 1.5-year coupon Treasury security is par value (see Exhibit 71-4), the following relationship must hold:[9]

$$\frac{1.75}{(1.015)^1} + \frac{1.75}{(1.0165)^2} + \frac{101.75}{(1 + z_3)^3} = 100$$

We can solve for the theoretical 1.5-year spot rate as follows:

$$1.7241 + 1.6936 + \frac{101.75}{(1 + z_3)^3} = 100$$

$$\frac{101.75}{(1 + z_3)^3} = 96.5822$$

$$(1 + z_3)^3 = \frac{101.75}{96.5822}$$

$$z_3 = 0.0175265 = 1.7527\%$$

Doubling this yield, we obtain the bond-equivalent yield of 3.5053%, which is the theoretical 1.5-year spot rate. That rate is the rate that the market would apply to a 1.5-year zero-coupon Treasury security if, in fact, such a security existed. In other words, all Treasury cash flows to be received 1.5 years from now should be valued (i.e., discounted) at 3.5053%.

Given the theoretical 1.5-year spot rate, we can obtain the theoretical 2-year

---

[9] If we had not been working with a par yield curve, the equation would have been set equal to whatever the market price for the 1.5-year issue is.

spot rate. The cash flows for the 2-year coupon Treasury in Exhibit 71-3 are:

0.5 year	$0.039 \times \$100 \times 0.5$	$= \$1.95$
1.0 year	$0.039 \times \$100 \times 0.5$	$= \$1.95$
1.5 years	$0.039 \times \$100 \times 0.5$	$= \$1.95$
2.0 years	$0.039 \times \$100 \times 0.5 + 100$	$= \$101.95$

The present value of the cash flows is then:

$$\frac{1.95}{(1 + z_1)^1} + \frac{1.95}{(1 + z_2)^2} + \frac{1.95}{(1 + z_3)^3} + \frac{101.95}{(1 + z_4)^4}$$

where z_4 = one-half the 2-year theoretical spot rate.

Since the 6-month spot rate, 1-year spot rate, and 1.5-year spot rate are 3.00%, 3.30%, and 3.5053%, respectively, then:

$$z_1 = 0.0150 \quad z_2 = 0.0165 \quad z_3 = 0.017527$$

Therefore, the present value of the 2-year coupon Treasury security is:

$$\frac{1.95}{(1.0150)^1} + \frac{1.95}{(1.0165)^2} + \frac{1.95}{(1.017527)^3} + \frac{101.95}{(1 + z_4)^4}$$

Since the price of the 2-year coupon Treasury security is par, the following relationship must hold:

$$\frac{1.95}{(1.0150)^1} + \frac{1.95}{(1.0165)^2} + \frac{1.95}{(1.017527)^3} + \frac{101.95}{(1 + z_4)^4} = 100$$

We can solve for the theoretical 2-year spot rate as follows:

$$\frac{101.95}{(1 + z_4)^4} = 94.3407$$

$$(1 + z_4)^4 = \frac{101.95}{94.3407}$$

$$z_4 = 0.019582 = 1.9582\%$$

Doubling this yield, we obtain the theoretical 2-year spot rate bond-equivalent yield of 3.9164%.

One can follow this approach sequentially to derive the theoretical 2.5-year spot rate from the calculated values of z_1, z_2, z_3, and z_4 (the 6-month, 1-year, 1.5-year, and 2-year rates), and the price and coupon of the 2.5-year bond in Exhibit 71-4. Further, one could derive theoretical spot rates for the remaining 15 half-yearly rates.

The spot rates thus obtained are shown in the last column of Exhibit 71-4. They represent the term structure of default-free spot rate for maturities up to 10 years at the particular time to which the bond price quotations refer. In fact, it is the default-free spot rates shown in Exhibit 71-4 that were used in our illustrations in the previous reading.

Exhibit 71-6 shows a plot of the spot rates. The graph is called the **theoretical spot rate curve**. Also shown on Exhibit 71-6 is a plot of the par yield curve from Exhibit 71-5. Notice that the theoretical spot rate curve lies above the par yield

EXHIBIT 71-6   Theoretical Spot Rate Curve and Treasury Yield Curve

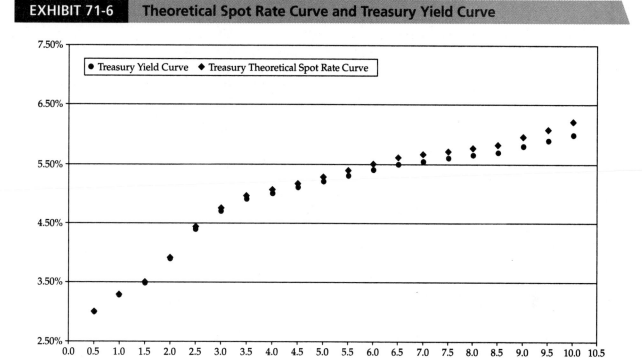

curve. This will always be the case when the par yield curve is upward sloping. When the par yield curve is downward sloping, the theoretical spot rate curve will lie below the par yield curve.

Practice Question 7

Show how the 2.5-year spot rate reported in Exhibit 71-4 is obtained.

4.2 Yield Spread Measures Relative to a Spot Rate Curve

Traditional analysis of the yield spread for a non-Treasury bond involves calculating the difference between the bond's yield and the yield to maturity of a benchmark Treasury coupon security. The latter is obtained from the Treasury yield curve. For example, consider the following 10-year bonds:

Issue	Coupon	Price	Yield to maturity
Treasury	6%	100.00	6.00%
Non-Treasury	8%	104.19	7.40%

The yield spread for these two bonds as traditionally computed is 140 basis points (7.4% minus 6%). We have referred to this traditional yield spread as the **nominal spread.**

Exhibit 71-7 shows the Treasury yield curve from Exhibit 71-5. The nominal spread of 140 basis points is the difference between the 7.4% yield to maturity for the 10-year non-Treasury security and the yield on the 10-year Treasury, 6%.

What is the nominal spread measuring? It is measuring the compensation for the additional credit risk, option risk (i.e., the risk associated with embedded options),[10] and liquidity risk an investor is exposed to by investing in a non-Treasury security rather than a Treasury security with the same maturity.

The drawbacks of the nominal spread measure are

1. for both bonds, the yield fails to take into consideration the term structure of spot rates and
2. in the case of callable and/or putable bonds, expected interest rate volatility may alter the cash flows of the non-Treasury bond.

Let's examine each of the drawbacks and alternative spread measures for handling them.

4.2.1 Zero-Volatility Spread

The **zero-volatility spread** or **Z-spread** is a measure of the spread that the investor would realize over the entire Treasury spot rate curve if the bond is held to maturity. It is not a spread off one point on the Treasury yield curve, as

EXHIBIT 71-7   Illustration of the Nominal Spread

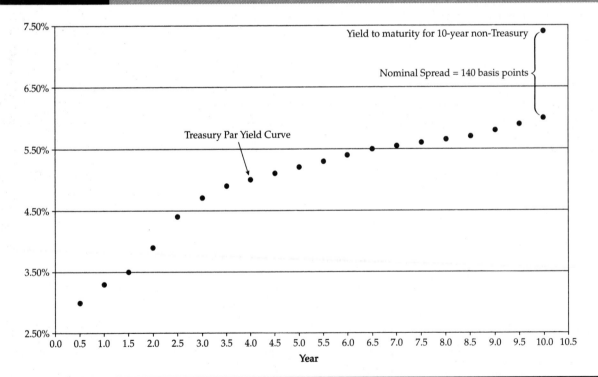

| EXHIBIT 71-8 | Determining Z-Spread for an 8% Coupon, 10-Year Non-Treasury Issue Selling at $104.19 to Yield 7.4% | | | | | |

Period	Years	Cash flow ($)	Spot rate (%)*	Present value ($) assuming a spread of**		
				100 bp	125 bp	146 bp
1	0.5	4.00	3.0000	3.9216	3.9168	3.9127
2	1.0	4.00	3.3000	3.8334	3.8240	3.8162
3	1.5	4.00	3.5053	3.7414	3.7277	3.7163
4	2.0	4.00	3.9164	3.6297	3.6121	3.5973
5	2.5	4.00	4.4376	3.4979	3.4767	3.4590
6	3.0	4.00	4.7520	3.3742	3.3497	3.3293
7	3.5	4.00	4.9622	3.2565	3.2290	3.2061
8	4.0	4.00	5.0650	3.1497	3.1193	3.0940
9	4.5	4.00	5.1701	3.0430	3.0100	2.9825
10	5.0	4.00	5.2772	2.9366	2.9013	2.8719
11	5.5	4.00	5.3864	2.8307	2.7933	2.7622
12	6.0	4.00	5.4976	2.7255	2.6862	2.6536
13	6.5	4.00	5.6108	2.6210	2.5801	2.5463
14	7.0	4.00	5.6643	2.5279	2.4855	2.4504
15	7.5	4.00	5.7193	2.4367	2.3929	2.3568
16	8.0	4.00	5.7755	2.3472	2.3023	2.2652
17	8.5	4.00	5.8331	2.2596	2.2137	2.1758
18	9.0	4.00	5.9584	2.1612	2.1148	2.0766
19	9.5	4.00	6.0863	2.0642	2.0174	1.9790
20	10.0	104.00	6.2169	51.1835	49.9638	48.9632
			Total	107.5416	105.7165	104.2146

* The spot rate is an annual rate.
** The discount rate used to compute the present value of each cash flow in the third column is found by adding the assumed spread to the spot rate and then dividing by 2. For example, for period 4 the spot rate is 3.9164%. If the assumed spread is 100 basis points, then 100 basis points is added to 3.9164% to give 4.9164%. Dividing this rate by 2 gives the semiannual rate of 2.4582%. The present value is then

$$\frac{\text{cash flow in period } t}{(1.024582)^t}$$

is the nominal spread. The Z-spread, also called the **static spread,** is calculated as the spread that will make the present value of the cash flows from the non-Treasury bond, when discounted at the Treasury spot rate plus the spread, equal to the non-Treasury bond's price. A trial-and-error procedure is required to determine the Z-spread.

To illustrate how this is done, let's use the non-Treasury bond in our previous illustration and the Treasury spot rates in Exhibit 71-4. These spot rates are repeated in Exhibit 71-8. The third column in Exhibit 71-8 shows the cash flows for the 8% 10-year non-Treasury issue. The goal is to determine the spread that, when added to all the Treasury spot rates, will produce a present value for the cash flows of the non-Treasury bond equal to its market price of $104.19.

Suppose we select a spread of 100 basis points. To each Treasury spot rate shown in the fourth column of Exhibit 71-8, 100 basis points is added. So, for example, the 5-year (period 10) spot rate is 6.2772% (5.2772% plus 1%). The spot rate plus 100 basis points is then used to calculate the present values as shown in the fifth column. The total present value of the fifth column is $107.5414. Because the present value is not equal to the non-Treasury issue's price ($104.19), the Z-spread is not 100 basis points. If a spread of 125 basis points is tried, it can be seen from the next-to-the-last column of Exhibit 71-8 that the present value is $105.7165; again, because this is not equal to the non-Treasury issue's price, 125 basis points is not the Z-spread. The last column of Exhibit 71-8 shows the present value when a 146 basis point spread is tried. The present value is equal to the non-Treasury issue's price. Therefore 146 basis points is the Z-spread, compared to the nominal spread of 140 basis points.

A graphical presentation of the Z-spread is shown in Exhibit 71-9. Since the benchmark for computing the Z-spread is the theoretical spot rate curve, that curve is shown in the exhibit. Above each yield at each maturity on the theoretical spot rate curve is a yield that is 146 basis points higher. This is the Z-spread. It is a spread over the entire spot rate curve.

What should be clear is that the difference between the nominal spread and the Z-spread is the benchmark that is being used: the nominal spread is a spread off of one point on the Treasury yield curve (see Exhibit 71-7) while the Z-spread is a spread over the entire theoretical Treasury spot rate curve.

What does the Z-spread represent for this non-Treasury security? Since the Z-spread is measured relative to the Treasury spot rate curve, it represents a spread to compensate for the non-Treasury security's credit risk, liquidity risk, and any option risk (i.e., the risks associated with any embedded options).

EXHIBIT 71-9   Illustration of the Z-Spread

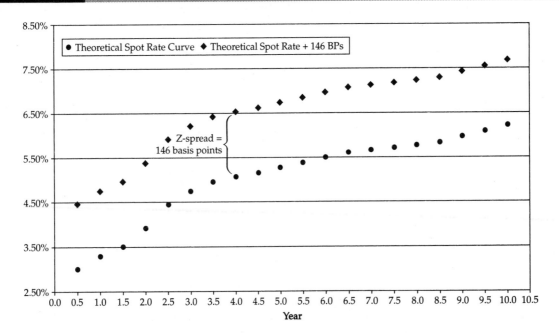

Practice Question 8

Suppose the price of the non-Treasury issue in our example is 105.7165 instead of 104.2145. Without doing computations, what would the Z-spread be?

4.2.1.1 Divergence Between Z-Spread and Nominal Spread

Typically, for standard coupon-paying bonds with a bullet maturity (i.e., a single payment of principal) the Z-spread and the nominal spread will not differ significantly. In our example, it is only 6 basis points. In general terms, the divergence (i.e., amount of difference) is a function of (1) the shape of the term structure of interest rates and (2) the characteristics of the security (i.e., coupon rate, time to maturity, and type of principal payment provision—non-amortizing versus amortizing).

For short-term issues, there is little divergence. The main factor causing any difference is the shape of the Treasury spot rate curve. The steeper the spot rate curve, the greater the difference. To illustrate this, consider the two spot rate curves shown in Exhibit 71-10. The yield for the longest maturity of both spot rate curves is 6%. The first curve is steeper than the one used in Exhibit 71-8; the

EXHIBIT 71-10	Two Hypothetical Spot Rate Curves		
Period	**Years**	**Steep curve (%)**	**Flat curve (%)**
1	0.5	2.00	6.00
2	1.0	2.40	6.00
3	1.5	2.80	6.00
4	2.0	2.90	6.00
5	2.5	3.00	6.00
6	3.0	3.10	6.00
7	3.5	3.30	6.00
8	4.0	3.80	6.00
9	4.5	3.90	6.00
10	5.0	4.20	6.00
11	5.5	4.40	6.00
12	6.0	4.50	6.00
13	6.5	4.60	6.00
14	7.0	4.70	6.00
15	7.5	4.90	6.00
16	8.0	5.00	6.00
17	8.5	5.30	6.00
18	9.0	5.70	6.00
19	9.5	5.80	6.00
20	10.0	6.00	6.00

second curve is flat, with the yield for all maturities equal to 6%. For our 8% 10-year non-Treasury issue, it can be shown that for the first spot rate curve in Exhibit 71-10 the Z-spread is 192 basis points. Thus, with this steeper spot rate curve, the difference between the Z-spread and the nominal spread is 52 basis points. For the flat curve the Z-spread is 140 basis points, the same as the nominal spread. This will always be the case because the nominal spread assumes that the same yield is used to discount each cash flow and, with a flat yield curve, the same yield is being used to discount each flow. Thus, the **nominal yield** spread and the Z-spread will produce the same value for this security.

The difference between the Z-spread and the nominal spread is greater for issues in which the principal is repaid over time rather than only at maturity. Thus the difference between the nominal spread and the Z-spread will be considerably greater for mortgage-backed and asset-backed securities in a steep yield curve environment. We can see this intuitively if we think in terms of a 10-year zero-coupon bond and a 10-year amortizing security with equal semiannual cash flows (that includes interest and principal payment). The Z-spread for the zero-coupon bond will not be affected by the shape of the term structure but the amortizing security will be.

4.2.1.2 Z-Spread Relative to Any Benchmark

In the same way that a Z-spread relative to a Treasury spot rate curve can be calculated, a Z-spread to any benchmark spot rate curve can be calculated. To illustrate, suppose that a hypothetical non-Treasury security with a coupon rate of 8% and a 10-year maturity is trading at $105.5423. Assume that the *benchmark spot rate curve for this issuer* is the one given in Exhibit 70-10 of the previous reading. The Z-spread relative to that issuer's benchmark spot rate curve is the spread that must be added to the spot rates shown in the next-to-last column of that exhibit that will make the present value of the cash flows equal to the market price. In our illustration, the Z-spread relative to this benchmark is 40 basis points.

What does the Z--spread mean when the benchmark is not the Treasury spot rate curve (i.e., default-free spot rate curve)? When the Treasury spot rate curve is the benchmark, we said that the Z-spread for a non-Treasury issue embodies credit risk, liquidity risk, and any option risk. When the benchmark is the spot rate curve for the issuer, the Z-spread is measuring the spread attributable to the liquidity risk of the issue and any option risk.

Thus, when a Z-spread is cited, it must be cited relative to some benchmark spot rate curve. This is necessary because it indicates the credit and sector risks that are being considered when the Z-spread was calculated. While Z-spreads are typically calculated using Treasury securities as the benchmark interest rates, this need not be the case. Vendors of analytical systems commonly allow the user to select a benchmark spot rate curve. Moreover, in non-U.S. markets, Treasury securities are typically not the benchmark. The key point is that an investor should always ask what benchmark was used to compute the Z-spread.

4.2.2 Option-Adjusted Spread

The Z-spread seeks to measure the spread over a spot rate curve thus overcoming the first problem of the nominal spread that we cited earlier. Now let's look at the second shortcoming—failure to take future interest rate volatility into account which could change the cash flows for bonds with embedded options.

4.2.2.1 Valuation Models

What investors seek to do is to buy undervalued securities (securities whose value is greater than their price). Before they can do this though, they need to know what the security is worth (i.e., a fair price to pay). A valuation model is designed to provide precisely this. If a model determines the fair price of a share of common stock is $36 and the market price is currently $24, then the stock is considered to be undervalued. If a bond is selling for less than its fair value, then it too is considered undervalued.

A valuation model need not stop here, however. Market participants find it more convenient to think about yield spread than about price differences. A valuation model can take this difference between the fair price and the market price and convert it into a yield spread measure. Instead of asking, "How much is this security undervalued?", the model can ask, "How much return will I earn in exchange for taking on these risks?"

The **option-adjusted spread** (OAS) was developed as a way of doing just this: taking the dollar difference between the fair price and market price and converting it into a yield spread measure. Thus, the OAS is used to reconcile the fair price (or value) to the market price by finding a return (spread) that will equate the two (using a trial and error procedure). This is somewhat similar to what we did earlier when calculating yield to maturity, yield to call, etc., only in this case, we are calculating a spread (measured in basis points) rather than a percentage rate of return as we did then.

The OAS is model dependent. That is, the OAS computed depends on the valuation model used. In particular, OAS models differ considerably in how they forecast interest rate changes, leading to variations in the level of OAS. What are two of these key modeling differences?

▶ Interest rate volatility is a critical assumption. Specifically, when the issuer/borrower has the option (e.g., callable bonds and mortgage pass-through securities), the higher the interest rate volatility assumed, the lower the OAS. In the case of a putable bond, the higher the interest rate volatility assumed, the higher the OAS. In comparing OAS of dealer firms, it is important to check on the volatility assumption made.

▶ The OAS is a spread, but what is it a "spread" over? The OAS is a spread over the Treasury spot rate curve or the issuer's benchmark used in the analysis. In the model, the spot rate curve is actually the result of a series of assumptions that allow for changes in interest rates. Again, different models yield different results.

Why is the spread referred to as "option adjusted"? Because the security's embedded option can change the cash flows; the value of the security should take this change of cash flow into account. Note that the Z-spread doesn't do this—it ignores the fact that interest rate changes can affect the cash flows. In essence, it assumes that interest rate volatility is zero. This is why the Z-spread is also referred to as the **zero-volatility OAS.**

4.2.2.2 Option Cost

The implied cost of the option embedded in any security can be obtained by calculating the difference between the OAS at the assumed interest rate or yield volatility and the Z-spread. That is, since the Z-spread is just the sum of the OAS and option cost, i.e.,

Z-spread = OAS + option cost

it follows that:

$$\text{option cost} = \text{Z-spread} - \text{OAS}$$

The reason that the option cost is measured in this way is as follows. In an environment in which interest rates are assumed not to change, the investor would earn the Z-spread. When future interest rates are uncertain, the spread is different because of the embedded option(s); the OAS reflects the spread after adjusting for this option. Therefore, the option cost is the difference between the spread that would be earned in a static interest rate environment (the Z-spread, or equivalently, the zero-volatility OAS) and the spread after adjusting for the option (the OAS).

For callable bonds and most mortgage-backed and asset-backed securities, the option cost is positive. This is because the issuer's ability to alter the cash flows will result in an OAS that is less than the Z-spread. In the case of a putable bond, the OAS is greater than the Z-spread so that the option cost is negative. This occurs because of the investor's ability to alter the cash flows.

In general, when the option cost is positive, this means that the investor has sold an option to the issuer or borrower. This is true for callable bonds and most mortgage-backed and asset-backed securities. A negative value for the option cost means that the investor has purchased an option from the issuer or borrower. A putable bond is an example of this negative option cost. There are certain securities in the mortgage-backed securities market that also have an option cost that is negative.

4.2.2.3 Highlighting the Pitfalls of the Nominal Spread

We can use the concepts presented in this reading to highlight the pitfalls of the nominal spread. First, we can recast the relationship between the option cost, Z-spread, and OAS as follows:

$$\text{Z-spread} = \text{OAS} + \text{option cost}$$

Next, recall that the nominal spread and the Z-spread may not diverge significantly. Suppose that the nominal spread is approximately equal to the Z-spread. Then, we can substitute nominal spread for Z-spread in the previous relationship giving:

$$\text{nominal spread} \approx \text{OAS} + \text{option cost}$$

This relationship tells us that a high nominal spread could be hiding a high option cost. The option cost represents the portion of the spread that the investor has given to the issuer or borrower. Thus, while the nominal spread for a security that can be called or prepaid might be, say 200 basis points, the option cost may be 190 and the OAS only 10 basis points. But, an investor is only compensated for the OAS. An investor that relies on the nominal spread may not be adequately compensated for taking on the option risk associated with a security with an embedded option.

4.2.3 Summary of Spread Measures

We have just described three spread measures:

▶ nominal spread
▶ zero-volatility spread
▶ option-adjusted spread

To understand different spread measures we ask two questions:

1. What is the benchmark for computing the spread? That is, what is the spread measured relative to?

2. What is the spread measuring?

The table below provides a summary showing for each of the three spread measures the benchmark and the risks for which the spread is compensating.

Spread measure	Benchmark	Reflects compensation for:
Nominal	Treasury yield curve	Credit risk, option risk, liquidity risk
Zero-volatility	Treasury spot rate curve	Credit risk, option risk, liquidity risk
Option-adjusted	Treasury spot rate curve	Credit risk, liquidity risk

FORWARD RATES   5

We have seen how a default-free theoretical spot rate curve can be extrapolated from the Treasury yield curve. Additional information useful to market participants can be extrapolated from the default-free theoretical spot rate curve: **forward rates**. Under certain assumptions described later, these rates can be viewed as the market's consensus of future interest rates.

Examples of forward rates that can be calculated from the default-free theoretical spot rate curve are the:

▶ 6-month forward rate six months from now

▶ 6-month forward rate three years from now

▶ 1-year forward rate one year from now

▶ 3-year forward rate two years from now

▶ 5-year forward rates three years from now

Since the forward rates are implicitly extrapolated from the default-free theoretical spot rate curve, these rates are sometimes referred to as **implied forward rates**. We begin by showing how to compute the 6-month forward rates. Then we explain how to compute any forward rate.

While we continue to use the Treasury yield curve in our illustrations, as noted earlier, a LIBOR spot rate curve can also be constructed using the bootstrapping methodology and forward rates for LIBOR can be obtained in the same manner as described below.

5.1 Deriving 6-Month Forward Rates

To illustrate the process of extrapolating 6-month forward rates, we will use the yield curve and corresponding spot rate curve from Exhibit 71-4. We will use a very simple arbitrage principle as we did earlier in this reading to derive the spot rates. Specifically, if two investments have the same cash flows and have the same risk, they should have the same value.

Consider an investor who has a 1-year investment horizon and is faced with the following two alternatives:

▶ buy a 1-year Treasury bill, or
▶ buy a 6-month Treasury bill and, when it matures in six months, buy another 6-month Treasury bill.

The investor will be indifferent toward the two alternatives if they produce the same return over the 1-year investment horizon. The investor knows the spot rate on the 6-month Treasury bill and the 1-year Treasury bill. However, he does not know what yield will be on a 6-month Treasury bill purchased six months from now. That is, he does not know the 6-month forward rate six months from now. Given the spot rates for the 6-month Treasury bill and the 1-year Treasury bill, the forward rate on a 6-month Treasury bill is the rate that equalizes the dollar return between the two alternatives.

To see how that rate can be determined, suppose that an investor purchased a 6-month Treasury bill for $X. At the end of six months, the value of this investment would be:

$$X(1 + z_1)$$

where z_1 is one-half the bond-equivalent yield (BEY) of the theoretical 6-month spot rate.

Let f represent one-half the forward rate (expressed as a BEY) on a 6-month Treasury bill available six months from now. If the investor were to rollover his investment by purchasing that bill at that time, then the future dollars available at the end of one year from the $X investment would be:

$$X(1 + z_1)(1 + f)$$

Now consider the alternative of investing in a 1-year Treasury bill. If we let z_2 represent one-half the BEY of the theoretical 1-year spot rate, then the future dollars available at the end of one year from the $X investment would be:

$$X(1 + z_2)^2$$

The reason that the squared term appears is that the amount invested is being compounded for two periods. (Recall that each period is six months.)

The two choices are depicted in Exhibit 71-11. Now we are prepared to analyze the investor's choices and what this says about forward rates. The investor will be indifferent toward the two alternatives confronting him if he makes the same dollar investment ($X) and receives the same future dollars from both alternatives at the end of one year. That is, the investor will be indifferent if:

$$X(1 + z_1)(1 + f) = X(1 + z_2)^2$$

Solving for f, we get:

$$f = \frac{(1 + z_2)^2}{(1 + z_1)} - 1$$

Doubling f gives the BEY for the 6-month forward rate six months from now.

EXHIBIT 71-11	Graphical Depiction of the Six-Month Forward Rate Six Months from Now

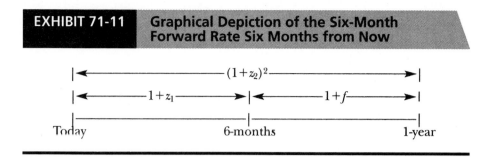

We can illustrate the use of this formula with the theoretical spot rates shown in Exhibit 71-4. From that exhibit, we know that:

6-month bill spot rate = 0.030, therefore z_1 = 0.0150
1-year bill spot rate = 0.033, therefore z_2 = 0.0165

Substituting into the formula, we have:

$$f = \frac{(1.0165)^2}{(1.0150)} - 1 = 0.0180 = 1.8\%$$

Therefore, the 6-month forward rate six months from now is 3.6% (1.8% × 2) BEY.

Let's confirm our results. If \$$X$ is invested in the 6-month Treasury bill at 1.5% and the proceeds then reinvested for six months at the 6-month forward rate of 1.8%, the total proceeds from this alternative would be:

$$X(1.015)(1.018) = 1.03327\,X$$

Investment of \$$X$ in the 1-year Treasury bill at one-half the 1-year rate, 1.0165%, would produce the following proceeds at the end of one year:

$$X(1.0165)^2 = 1.03327\,X$$

Both alternatives have the same payoff if the 6-month Treasury bill yield six months from now is 1.8% (3.6% on a BEY). This means that, if an investor is guaranteed a 1.8% yield (3.6% BEY) on a 6-month Treasury bill six months from now, he will be indifferent toward the two alternatives.

The same line of reasoning can be used to obtain the 6-month forward rate beginning at any time period in the future. For example, the following can be determined:

▶ the 6-month forward rate three years from now
▶ the 6-month forward rate five years from now

The notation that we use to indicate 6-month forward rates is $_1f_m$ where the subscript 1 indicates a 1-period (6-month) rate and the subscript m indicates the period beginning m periods from now. When m is equal to zero, this means the current rate. Thus, the first 6-month forward rate is simply the current 6-month spot rate. That is, $_1f_0 = z_1$.

The general formula for determining a 6-month forward rate is:

$$_1f_m = \frac{(1 + z_{m+1})^{m+1}}{(1 + z_m)^m} - 1$$

For example, suppose that the 6-month forward rate four years (eight 6-month periods) from now is sought. In terms of our notation, m is 8 and we seek $_1f_8$. The formula is then:

$$_1f_8 = \frac{(1 + z_9)^9}{(1 + z_8)^8} - 1$$

From Exhibit 71-4, since the 4-year spot rate is 5.065% and the 4.5-year spot rate is 5.1701%, z_8 is 2.5325% and z_9 is 2.58505%. Then,

$$_1f_8 = \frac{(1.0258505)^9}{(1.025325)^8} - 1 = 3.0064\%$$

Doubling this rate gives a 6-month forward rate four years from now of 6.01%.

Exhibit 71-12 shows all of the 6-month forward rates for the Treasury yield curve shown in Exhibit 71-4. The forward rates reported in Exhibit 71-12 are the annualized rates on a bond-equivalent basis. In Exhibit 71-13, the short-term for-

EXHIBIT 71-12	Six-Month Forward Rates (Annualized Rates on a Bond-Equivalent Basis)

Notation	Forward Rate
$_1f_0$	3.00
$_1f_1$	3.60
$_1f_2$	3.92
$_1f_3$	5.15
$_1f_4$	6.54
$_1f_5$	6.33
$_1f_6$	6.23
$_1f_7$	5.79
$_1f_8$	6.01
$_1f_9$	6.24
$_1f_{10}$	6.48
$_1f_{11}$	6.72
$_1f_{12}$	6.97
$_1f_{13}$	6.36
$_1f_{14}$	6.49
$_1f_{15}$	6.62
$_1f_{16}$	6.76
$_1f_{17}$	8.10
$_1f_{18}$	8.40
$_1f_{19}$	8.71

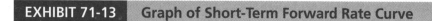

EXHIBIT 71-13   **Graph of Short-Term Forward Rate Curve**

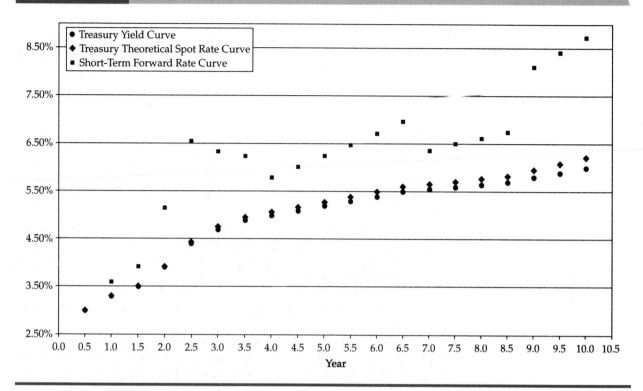

ward rates are plotted along with the Treasury par yield curve and theoretical spot rate curve. The graph of the short-term forward rates is called the **short-term forward-rate curve**. Notice that the short-term forward rate curve lies above the other two curves. This will always be the case if the par yield curve is upward sloping. If the par yield curve is downward sloping, the short-term forward rate curve will be the lowest curve. Notice the unusual shape for the short-term forward rate curve. There is a mathematical reason for this shape. In practice, analysts will use statistical techniques to create a smooth short-term forward rate curve.

Practice Question 9

Show how the 6-month forward rate 6.5 years (13 periods from now) reported in Exhibit 71-12 is computed.

5.2 Relationship between Spot Rates and Short-Term Forward Rates

Suppose an investor invests $X in a 3-year zero-coupon Treasury security. The total proceeds three years (six periods) from now would be:

$$X(1 + z_6)^6$$

The investor could instead buy a 6-month Treasury bill and reinvest the proceeds every six months for three years. The future dollars or dollar return will depend on the 6-month forward rates. Suppose that the investor can actually reinvest the proceeds maturing every six months at the calculated 6-month forward rates shown in Exhibit 71-12. At the end of three years, an investment of $\$X$ would generate the following proceeds:

$$X (1 + z_1) (1 + {}_1f_1) (1 + {}_1f_2) (1 + {}_1f_3) (1 + {}_1f_4) (1 + {}_1f_5)$$

Since the two investments must generate the same proceeds at the end of three years, the two previous equations can be equated:

$$X (1 + z_6)^6 = X (1 + z_1) (1 + {}_1f_1) (1 + {}_1f_2) (1 + {}_1f_3) (1 + {}_1f_4) (1 + {}_1f_5)$$

Solving for the 3-year (6-period) spot rate, we have:

$$z_6 = [(1 + z_1) (1 + {}_1f_1) (1 + {}_1f_2) (1 + {}_1f_3) (1 + {}_1f_4) (1 + {}_1f_5)]^{1/6} - 1$$

This equation tells us that the 3-year spot rate depends on the current 6-month spot rate and the five 6-month forward rates. In fact, the right-hand side of this equation is a geometric average of the current 6-month spot rate and the five 6-month forward rates.

Let's use the values in Exhibits 71-4 and 71-12 to confirm this result. Since the 6-month spot rate in Exhibit 71-4 is 3%, z_1 is 1.5% and therefore[11]

$$z_6 = [(1.015) (1.018) (1.0196) (1.0257) (1.0327) (1.03165)]^{1/6} - 1$$
$$= 0.023761 = 2.3761\%$$

Doubling this rate gives 4.7522%. This agrees with the spot rate shown in Exhibit 71-4.

In general, the relationship between a T-period spot rate, the current 6-month spot rate, and the 6-month forward rates is as follows:

$$z_T = [(1 + z_1) (1 + {}_1f_1) (1 + {}_1f_2) \dots (1 + {}_1f_{T-1})]^{1/T} - 1$$

Therefore, discounting at the forward rates will give the same present value as discounting at spot rates.

5.3 Valuation Using Forward Rates

Since a spot rate is simply a package of short-term forward rates, it will not make any difference whether we discount cash flows using spot rates or forward rates. That is, suppose that the cash flow in period T is $\$1$. Then the present value of the cash flow can be found using the spot rate for period T as follows:

$$\text{PV of \$1 in } T \text{ periods} = \frac{1}{(1 + z_T)^T}$$

---

[11] Actually, the semiannual forward rates are based on annual rates calculated to more decimal places. For example, $f_{1,3}$ is 5.15% in Exhibit 71-12 but based on the more precise value, the semiannual rate is 2.577%.

Alternatively, since we know that

$$z_T = [(1+z_1)\,(1+{}_1f_1)\,(1+{}_1f_2)\cdots(1+{}_1f_{T-1})]^{1/T} - 1$$

then, adding 1 to both sides of the equation,

$$(1+z_T) = [(1+z_1)\,(1+{}_1f_1)\,(1+{}_1f_2)\cdots(1+{}_1f_{T-1})]^{1/T}$$

Raising both sides of the equation to the T-th power we get:

$$(1+z_T)^T = (1+z_1)\,(1+{}_1f_1)\,(1+{}_1f_2)\cdots(1+{}_1f_{T-1})$$

Substituting the right-hand side of the above equation into the present value formula we get:

$$\text{PV of \$1 in } T \text{ periods} = \frac{1}{(1+z_1)(1+{}_1f_1)(1+{}_1f_2)\cdots(1+{}_1f_{T-1})}$$

In practice, the present value of $1 in T periods is called the **forward discount factor for period T.**

For example, consider the forward rates shown in Exhibit 71-12. The forward discount rate for period 4 is found as follows:

$$z_1 = 3\%/2 = 1.5\% \qquad {}_1f_1 = 3.6\%/2 = 1.8\%$$
$$_1f_2 = 3.92\%/2 = 1.958\% \qquad {}_1f_3 = 5.15\%/2 = 2.577\%$$

$$\text{forward discount factor of \$1 in 4 periods} = \frac{\$1}{(1.015)(1.018)(1.01958)(1.02577)}$$
$$= 0.925369$$

To see that this is the same present value that would be obtained using the spot rates, note from Exhibit 71-4 that the 2-year spot rate is 3.9164%. Using that spot rate, we find:

$$z_4 = 3.9164\%/2 = 1.9582\%$$
$$\text{PV of \$1 in 4 periods} = \frac{\$1}{(1.019582)^4} = 0.925361$$

The answer is the same as the forward discount factor (the slight difference is due to rounding).

Exhibit 71-14 shows the computation of the forward discount factor for each period based on the forward rates in Exhibit 71-12. Let's show how both the forward rates and the spot rates can be used to value a 2-year 6% coupon Treasury bond. The present value for each cash flow is found as follows using spot rates:

$$\frac{\text{cash flow for period } t}{(1+z_t)^t}$$

The following table uses the spot rates in Exhibit 71-4 to value this bond:

Spot rate Period	Semiannual BEY (%)	spot rate (%)	PV of $1	PV of Cash flow	cash flow
1	3.0000	1.50000	0.9852217	3	2.955665
2	3.3000	1.65000	0.9677991	3	2.903397
3	3.5053	1.75266	0.9492109	3	2.847633
4	3.9164	1.95818	0.9253619	103	95.312278
				Total	104.018973

EXHIBIT 71-14   Calculation of the Forward Discount Factor for Each Period

Periods	Years	Notation	Forward Rate*	0.5 ×Forward Rate**	1 + Forward Rate	Forward Discount Factor
1	0.5	$_1f_0$	3.00%	1.5000%	1.01500	0.985222
2	1.0	$_1f_1$	3.60%	1.8002%	1.01800	0.967799
3	1.5	$_1f_2$	3.92%	1.9583%	1.01958	0.949211
4	2.0	$_1f_3$	5.15%	2.5773%	1.02577	0.925362
5	2.5	$_1f_4$	6.54%	3.2679%	1.03268	0.896079
6	3.0	$_1f_5$	6.33%	3.1656%	1.03166	0.868582
7	3.5	$_1f_6$	6.23%	3.1139%	1.03114	0.842352
8	4.0	$_1f_7$	5.79%	2.8930%	1.02893	0.818668
9	4.5	$_1f_8$	6.01%	3.0063%	1.03006	0.794775
10	5.0	$_1f_9$	6.24%	3.1221%	1.03122	0.770712
11	5.5	$_1f_{10}$	6.48%	3.2407%	1.03241	0.746520
12	6.0	$_1f_{11}$	6.72%	3.3622%	1.03362	0.722237
13	6.5	$_1f_{12}$	6.97%	3.4870%	1.03487	0.697901
14	7.0	$_1f_{13}$	6.36%	3.1810%	1.03181	0.676385
15	7.5	$_1f_{14}$	6.49%	3.2450%	1.03245	0.655126
16	8.0	$_1f_{15}$	6.62%	3.3106%	1.03310	0.634132
17	8.5	$_1f_{16}$	6.76%	3.3778%	1.03378	0.613412
18	9.0	$_1f_{17}$	8.10%	4.0504%	1.04050	0.589534
19	9.5	$_1f_{18}$	8.40%	4.2009%	1.04201	0.565767
20	10.0	$_1f_{19}$	8.72%	4.3576%	1.04357	0.542142

* The rates in this column are rounded to two decimal places.
** The rates in this column used the forward rates in the previous column carried to four decimal places.

Based on the spot rates, the value of this bond is $104.0190.

Using forward rates and the forward discount factors, the present value of the cash flow in period *t* is found as follows:

cash flow in period *t* × discount factor for period *t*

The following table uses the forward rates and the forward discount factors in Exhibit 71-14 to value this bond:

Period	Semiannual forward rate	Forward discount factor	Cash flow	PV of cash flow
1	1.5000%	0.985222	3	2.955665
2	1.8002%	0.967799	3	2.903397
3	1.9583%	0.949211	3	2.847633
4	2.5773%	0.925362	103	95.312278
			Total	104.018973

The present value of this bond using forward rates is $104.0190.

So, it does not matter whether one discounts cash flows by spot rates or forward rates, the value is the same.

Practice Question 10

Compute the value of a 10% coupon 3-year bond using the forward rates in Exhibit 71-12.

5.4 Computing Any Forward Rate

Using spot rates, we can compute any forward rate. Using the same arbitrage arguments as used above to derive the 6-month forward rates, any forward rate can be obtained.

There are two elements to the forward rate. The first is when in the future the rate begins. The second is the length of time for the rate. For example, the 2-year forward rate 3 years from now means a rate three years from now for a length of two years. The notation used for a forward rate, f, will have two subscripts—one before f and one after f as shown below:

$$_t f_m$$

The subscript before f is t and is the length of time that the rate applies. The subscript after f is m and is when the forward rate begins. That is,

the length of time of the forward rate f when the forward rate begins

Remember our time periods are still 6-month periods. Given the above notation, here is what the following mean:

Notation	Interpretation for the forward rate
$_1 f_{12}$	6-month (1-period) forward rate beginning 6 years (12 periods) from now
$_2 f_8$	1-year (2-period) forward rate beginning 4 years (8 periods) from now
$_6 f_4$	3-year (6-period) forward rate beginning 2 years (4 periods) from now
$_8 f_{10}$	4-year (8-period) forward rate beginning 5 years (10 periods) from now

To see how the formula for the forward rate is derived, consider the following two alternatives for an investor who wants to invest for $m + t$ periods:

▶ buy a zero-coupon Treasury bond that matures in $m + t$ periods, or
▶ buy a zero-coupon Treasury bond that matures in m periods and invest the proceeds at the maturity date in a zero-coupon Treasury bond that matures in t periods.

The investor will be indifferent between the two alternatives if they produce the same return over the $m + t$ investment horizon.

For $100 invested in the first alternative, the proceeds for this investment at the horizon date assuming that the semiannual rate is z_{m+t} is

$$\$100 \, (1 + z_{m+t})^{m+t}$$

For the second alternative, the proceeds for this investment at the end of m periods assuming that the semiannual rate is z_m is

$$\$100 \, (1 + z_m)^m$$

When the proceeds are received in m periods, they are reinvested at the forward rate, $_t f_m$, producing a value for the investment at the end of $m + t$ periods of

$$\$100 \, (1 + z_m)^m \, (1 + {_t f_m})^t$$

For the investor to be indifferent to the two alternatives, the following relationship must hold:

$$\$100 \, (1 + z_{m+t})^{m+t} = \$100 \, (1 + z_m)^m \, (1 + {_t f_m})^t$$

Solving for $_t f_m$ we get:

$$_t f_m = \left[\frac{(1 + z_{m+t})^{m+t}}{(1 + z_m)^m} \right]^{1/t} - 1$$

Notice that if t is equal to 1, the formula reduces to the 1-period (6-month) forward rate.

To illustrate, for the spot rates shown in Exhibit 71-4, suppose that an investor wants to know the 2-year forward rate three years from now. In terms of the notation, t is equal to 4 and m is equal to 6. Substituting for t and m into the equation for the forward rate we have:

$$_4 f_6 = \left[\frac{(1 + z_{10})^{10}}{(1 + z_6)^6} \right]^{1/4} - 1$$

This means that the following two spot rates are needed: z_6 (the 3-year spot rate) and z_{10} (the 5-year spot rate). From Exhibit 71-4 we know

z_6 (the 3-year spot rate) = 4.752%/2 = 0.02376
z_{10} (the 5-year spot rate) = 5.2772%/2 = 0.026386

then

$$_4 f_6 = \left[\frac{(1.026386)^{10}}{(1.02376)^6} \right]^{1/4} - 1 = 0.030338$$

Therefore, $_4f_6$ is equal to 3.0338% and doubling this rate gives 6.0675% the forward rate on a bond-equivalent basis.

We can verify this result. Investing $100 for 10 periods at the spot rate of 2.6386% will produce the following value:

$$\$100 \, (1.026386)^{10} = \$129.7499$$

By investing $100 for 6 periods at 2.376% and reinvesting the proceeds for 4 periods at the forward rate of 3.030338% gives the same value

$$\$100 \, (1.02376)^6 \, (1.030338)^4 = \$129.75012$$

Practice Question 11

A. Given the spot rates in Exhibit 71-4, compute the 6-year forward rate 4 years from now.

B. Demonstrate that the forward rate computed in part A is correct.

SUMMARY

▶ The sources of return from holding a bond to maturity are the coupon interest payments, any capital gain or loss, and reinvestment income.

▶ Reinvestment income is the interest income generated by reinvesting coupon interest payments and any principal payments from the time of receipt to the bond's maturity.

▶ The current yield relates the annual dollar coupon interest to the market price and fails to recognize any capital gain or loss and reinvestment income.

▶ The yield to maturity is the interest rate that will make the present value of the cash flows from a bond equal to the price plus accrued interest.

▶ The market convention to annualize a semiannual yield is to double it and the resulting annual yield is referred to as a bond-equivalent yield.

▶ When market participants refer to a yield or return measure as computed on a bond-equivalent basis it means that a semiannual yield or return is doubled.

▶ The yield to maturity takes into account all three sources of return but assumes that the coupon payments and any principal repayments can be reinvested at an interest rate equal to the yield to maturity.

▶ The yield to maturity will only be realized if the interim cash flows can be reinvested at the yield to maturity and the bond is held to maturity.

▶ Reinvestment risk is the risk an investor faces that future reinvestment rates will be less than the yield to maturity at the time a bond is purchased.

▶ Interest rate risk is the risk that if a bond is not held to maturity, an investor may have to sell it for less than the purchase price.

▶ The longer the maturity and the higher the coupon rate, the more a bond's return is dependent on reinvestment income to realize the yield to maturity at the time of purchase.

▶ The yield to call is the interest rate that will make the present value of the expected cash flows to the assumed call date equal to the price plus accrued interest.

▶ Yield measures for callable bonds include yield to first call, yield to next call, yield to first par call, and yield to refunding.

▶ The yield to call considers all three sources of potential return but assumes that all cash flows can be reinvested at the yield to call until the assumed call date, the investor will hold the bond to the assumed call date, and the issuer will call the bond on the assumed call date.

▶ For a putable bond a yield to put is computed assuming that the issue will be put on the first put date.

▶ The yield to worst is the lowest yield from among all possible yield to calls, yield to puts, and the yield to maturity.

▶ For mortgage-backed and asset-backed securities, the cash flow yield based on some prepayment rate is the interest rate that equates the present value of the projected principal and interest payments to the price plus accrued interest.

▶ The cash flow yield assumes that all cash flows (principal and interest payments) can be reinvested at the calculated yield and that the assumed prepayment rate will be realized over the security's life.

▶ For amortizing securities, reinvestment risk is greater than for standard coupon nonamortizing securities because payments are typically made monthly and include principal as well as interest payments.

▶ For floating-rate securities, instead of a yield measure, margin measures (i.e., spread above the reference rate) are computed.

▶ Two margin measures commonly used are spread for life and discount margin.

▶ The discount margin assumes that the reference rate will not change over the life of the security and that there is no cap or floor restriction on the coupon rate.

▶ The theoretical spot rate is the interest rate that should be used to discount a default-free cash flow.

▶ Because there are a limited number of on-the-run Treasury securities traded in the market, interpolation is required to obtain the yield for interim maturities; hence, the yield for most maturities used to construct the Treasury yield curve are interpolated yields rather than observed yields.

▶ Default-free spot rates can be derived from the Treasury yield curve by a method called bootstrapping.

▶ The basic principle underlying the bootstrapping method is that the value of a Treasury coupon security is equal to the value of the package of zero-coupon Treasury securities that duplicates the coupon bond's cash flows.

▶ The nominal spread is the difference between the yield for a non-Treasury bond and a comparable-maturity Treasury coupon security.

▶ The nominal spread fails to consider the term structure of the spot rates and the fact that, for bonds with embedded options, future interest rate volatility may alter its cash flows.

▶ The zero-volatility spread or Z-spread is a measure of the spread that the investor will realize over the entire Treasury spot rate curve if the bond is held to maturity, thereby recognizing the term structure of interest rates.

▶ Unlike the nominal spread, the Z-spread is not a spread off one point on the Treasury yield curve but is a spread over the entire spot rate curve.

▶ For bullet bonds, unless the yield curve is very steep, the nominal spread will not differ significantly from the Z-spread; for securities where principal is paid over time rather than just at maturity there can be a significant difference, particularly in a steep yield curve environment.

▶ The option-adjusted spread (OAS) converts the cheapness or richness of a bond into a spread over the future possible spot rate curves.

▶ An OAS is said to be option adjusted because it allows for future interest rate volatility to affect the cash flows.

▶ The OAS is a product of a valuation model and, when comparing the OAS of dealer firms, it is critical to check on the volatility assumption (and other assumptions) employed in the valuation model.

▶ The cost of the embedded option is measured as the difference between the Z-spread and the OAS.

▶ Investors should not rely on the nominal spread for bonds with embedded options since it hides how the spread is split between the OAS and the option cost.

▶ OAS is used as a relative value measure to assist in the selection of bonds with embedded options.

▶ Using arbitrage arguments, forward rates can be extrapolated from the Treasury yield curve or the Treasury spot rate curve.

▶ The spot rate for a given period is related to the forward rates; specifically, the spot rate is a geometric average of the current 6-month spot rate and the subsequent 6-month forward rates.

PROBLEMS FOR READING 71

1. What are the sources of return any yield measure should incorporate?

2. A. Suppose a 10-year 9% coupon bond is selling for $112 with a par value of $100. What is the current yield for the bond?

B. What is the limitation of the current yield measure?

3. Determine whether the yield to maturity of a 6.5% 20-year bond that pays interest semiannually and is selling for $90.68 is 7.2%, 7.4%, or 7.8%.

4. The following yields and prices were reported in the financial press. Are any of them incorrect assuming that the reported price and coupon rate are correct? If so, explain why. (No calculations are needed to answer this question.)

Bond	Price	Coupon rate	Current Yield	Yield to Maturity
A	100	6.0%	5.0%	6.0%
B	110	7.0%	6.4%	6.1%
C	114	7.5%	7.1%	7.7%
D	95	4.7%	5.2%	5.9%
E	75	5.6%	5.1%	4.1%

5. Comment on the following statement: "The yield to maturity measure is a useless measure because it doubles a semiannual yield (calling the annual yield a bond-equivalent yield) rather than computing an effective annual yield. This is the major shortcoming of the yield-to-maturity measure."

6. A. Suppose that an investor invests $108.32 in a 5-year certificate of deposit that pays 7% annually (on a bond-equivalent basis) or 3.5% semiannually and the interest payments are semiannual. What are the total future dollars of this investment at the end of 5 years (i.e., ten 6-month periods)?

B. How much total interest is generated from the investment in this certificate of deposit?

C. Suppose an investor can purchase any investment for $108.32 that offers a 7% yield on a bond-equivalent basis and pays interest semi-annually. What is the total future dollars and the total dollar return from this investment?

D. Suppose an investor can purchase a 5-year 9% coupon bond that pays interest semiannually and the price of this bond is $108.32. The yield to maturity for this bond is 7% on a bond-equivalent basis. What is the total future dollars and the total dollar return that will be generated from this bond if it is to yield 7%?

E. Complete the following for this bond:

    coupon interest   =

    capital gain/loss   =

    reinvestment income =
    _____

    total dollar return   =

F. What percentage of the total dollar return is dependent on reinvestment income?

G. How is the reinvestment income in part E realized?

7. A. Which of the following three bonds has the greatest dependence on reinvestment income to generate the computed yield? Assume that each bond is offering the same yield to maturity. (No calculations are needed to answer this question.)

Bond	Maturity	Coupon rate
X	25 years	0%
Y	20 years	7%
Z	20 years	8%

B. Which of the three bonds in part A has the least dependence on reinvestment income to generate the computed yield? Assume that each bond is offering the same yield to maturity. (No calculations are needed to answer this question.)

8. What is the reinvestment risk and interest rate risk associated with a yield to maturity measure?

9. A. If the yield to maturity on an annual-pay bond is 5.6%, what is the bond-equivalent yield?

B. If the yield of a U.S. bond issue quoted on a bond-equivalent basis is 5.6%, what is the yield to maturity on an annual-pay basis?

10. Suppose that a 10% 15-year bond has the following call structure:

not callable for the next 5 years
first callable in 5 years at $105
first par call date is in 10 years
The price of the bond is $127.5880.

A. Is the yield to maturity for this bond 7.0%, 7.4%, or 7.8%?

B. Is the yield to first call for this bond 4.55%, 4.65%, or 4.85%?

C. Is the yield to first par call for this bond 6.25%, 6.55%, or 6.75%?

11. Suppose a 5% coupon 6-year bond is selling for $105.2877 and is putable in four years at par value. The yield to maturity for this bond is 4%. Determine whether the yield to put is 3.38%, 3.44% or 3.57%.

12. Suppose that an amortizing security pays interest monthly. Based on the projected principal payments and interest, suppose that the monthly interest rate that makes the present value of the cash flows equal to the price of the security is 0.41%. What is the cash flow yield on a bond-equivalent basis?

13. Two portfolio managers are discussing the investment characteristics of amortizing securities. Manager A believes that the advantage of these securities relative to nonamortizing securities is that since the periodic cash flows include principal payments as well as coupon payments, the manager can generate greater reinvestment income. In addition, the payments are typically monthly so even greater reinvestment income can be generated.

Manager B believes that the need to reinvest monthly and the need to invest larger amounts than just coupon interest payments make amortizing securities less attractive. Who do you agree with and why?

14. An investor is considering the purchase of a 5-year floating-rate note that pays interest semiannually. The coupon formula is equal to 6-month LIBOR plus 30 basis points. The current value for 6-month LIBOR is 5% (annual rate). The price of this note is 99.1360. Is the discount margin 40 basis points, 50 basis points, or 55 basis points?

15. How does the discount margin handle any cap on a floater and the fact that the reference rate may change over time?

16. A. A Treasury bill with 105 days from settlement to maturity is selling for $0.989 per $1 of maturity value. What is the yield on a discount basis?

B. A Treasury bill with 275 days from settlement to maturity is quoted as having a yield on a discount basis of 3.68%. What is the price of this Treasury bill?

C. What are the problems with using the yield on a discount basis as measure of a Treasury bill's yield?

17. Explain how a Treasury yield curve is constructed even though there are only a limited number of on-the-run Treasury issues available in the market.

18. Suppose that the annual yield to maturity for the 6-month and 1-year Treasury bill is 4.6% and 5.0%, respectively. These yields represent the 6-month and 1-year spot rates. Also assume the following Treasury yield curve (i.e., the price for each issue is $100) has been estimated for 6-month periods out to a maturity of 3 years:

Years to maturity	Annual yield to maturity (BEY)
1.5	5.4%
2.0	5.8%
2.5	6.4%
3.0	7.0%

Compute the 1.5-year, 2-year, 2.5-year, and 3-year spot rates.

19. Given the spot rates computed in the previous question and the 6-month and 1-year spot rates, compute the arbitrage-free value of a 3-year Treasury security with a coupon rate of 8%.

20. What are the two limitations of the nominal spread as a measure of relative value of two bonds?

21. Suppose that the Treasury spot rate curve is as follows:

Period	Years to maturity	Spot rate
1	0.5	5.0%
2	1.0	5.4
3	1.5	5.8
4	2.0	6.4
5	2.5	7.0
6	3.0	7.2
7	3.5	7.4
8	4.0	7.8

Suppose that the market price of a 4-year 6% coupon non-Treasury issue is $91.4083. Determine whether the zero-volatility spread (Z-spread) relative to the Treasury spot rate curve for this issue is 80 basis points, 90 basis points, or 100 basis points.

22. The Prestige Investment Management Company sent a report to its pension client. In the report, Prestige indicated that the yield curve is currently flat (i.e., the yield to maturity for each maturity is the same) and then discussed the nominal spread for the corporate bonds held in the client's portfolio. A trustee of the pension fund was concerned that Prestige focused on the nominal spread rather than the zero-volatility spread or option-adjusted spread for these bond issues. Joan Thomas is Prestige's employee who is the contact person for this account. She received a phone call from the trustee regarding his concern. How should she respond regarding the use of nominal spread rather than zero-volatility spread and option-adjusted spread as a spread measure for corporate bonds?

23. John Tinker is a junior portfolio manager assigned to work for Laura Sykes, the manager of the corporate bond portfolio of a public pension fund. Ms. Sykes asked Mr. Tinker to construct a portfolio profile that she could use in her presentation to the trustees. One of the measures Ms. Sykes insisted that Mr. Tinker include was the option-adjusted spread of each issue. In preparing the portfolio profile, Mr. Tinker encountered the following situations that he did not understand. Provide Mr. Tinker with an explanation.

    A. Mr. Tinker checked with several dealer firms to determine the option-adjusted spread for each issue. For several of the issues, there were substantially different option-adjusted spreads reported. For example, for one callable issue one dealer reported an OAS of 100 basis points, one dealer reported 170 basis points, and a third dealer 200 basis points. Mr. Tinker could not understand how the dealers could have substantially different OAS values when in fact the yield to maturity and nominal spread values for each of the issues did not differ from dealer to dealer.

    B. The dealers that Mr. Tinker checked with furnished him with the nominal spread and the Z-spread for each issue in addition to the OAS. For all the bond issues where there were no embedded options, each dealer reported that the Z-spread was equal to the OAS. Mr. Tinker could not understand why.

C. One dealer firm reported an option cost for each issue. There were positive, negative, and zero values reported. Mr. Tinker observed that for all the bond issues that were putable, the option cost was negative. For all the option-free bond issues, the reported value was zero.

24. Max Dumas is considering the purchase of a callable corporate bond. He has available to him two analytical systems to value the bond. In one system, System A, the vendor uses the on-the-run Treasury issues to construct the theoretical spot rate that is used to construct a model to compute the OAS. The other analytical system, System B, uses the on-the-run issue for the particular issuer in constructing a model to compute the OAS.

   A. Suppose that using System A, Mr. Dumas finds that the OAS for the callable corporate he is considering is 50 basis points. How should he interpret this OAS value?

   B. Suppose that using System B, Mr. Dumas finds that the OAS computed is 15 basis points. How should he interpret this OAS value?

   C. Suppose that a dealer firm shows Mr. Dumas another callable corporate bond of the same credit quality and duration with an OAS of 40 basis points. Should Mr. Dumas view that this bond is more attractive or less attractive than the issue he is considering for acquisition?

25. Assume the following Treasury spot rates:

Period	Years to maturity	Spot rate
1	0.5	5.0%
2	1.0	5.4
3	1.5	5.8
4	2.0	6.4
5	2.5	7.0
6	3.0	7.2
7	3.5	7.4
8	4.0	7.8

Compute the following forward rates:

   A. the 6-month forward rate six months from now.

   B. the 6-month forward rate one year from now.

   C. the 6-month forward rate three years from now.

   D. the 2-year forward rate one year from now.

   E. the 1-year forward rate two years from now.

26. For the previous question, demonstrate that the 6-month forward rate six months from now is the rate that will produce at the end of one year the same future dollars as investing either (1) at the current 1-year spot rate of 5.4% or (2) at the 6-month spot rate of 5.0% and reinvesting at the 6-month forward rate six months from now.

27. Two sales people of analytical systems are making a presentation to you about the merits of their respective systems. One sales person states that in valuing bonds the system first constructs the theoretical spot rates and then discounts cash flows using these rates. The other sales person interjects that his firm takes a different approach. Rather than using spot rates, forward rates are used to value the cash flows and he believes this is a better approach to valuing bonds compared to using spot rates. How would you respond to the second sales person's comment about his firm's approach?

28. A. Given the following 6-month forward rates, compute the forward discount factor for each period.

Period	Annual forward rate (BEY)
1	4.00%
2	4.40
3	5.00
4	5.60
5	6.00
6	6.40

B. Compute the value of a 3-year 8% coupon bond using the forward rates.

4⅝ 4¹¹/₁₆ ⅜
5½ 5½ — ⅜
5½ 21³/₁₆ — ¼₆
20⅝ 21³/₁₆ + ⅞
17⅜ 18⅛ +
13½ 6½ — ½
7¼ 6½ 6½ —
15/₁₆ 3¹/₃₂ — ⅛
9/₁₆ ⅜
1¹/₃₂ 7¹³/₁₆ 7¹⁵/₁₆
7¹⁵/₁₆ 2¹¹/₃₂ 2½ +
545 2⅝ 2¼ 2¼
327 2¾ 2¼
6⅛ 12¹/₁₆ 11⅜ 11¾ +
87 33¾ 33 33¹/₁₆ —
602 25⅝ 24⁹/₁₆ 25⅜ +
833 12 11⅝ 11⅞ +
16 10½ 10½ 10½ —
78 15⅞ 15¹³/₁₆ 15⅞ —
4808 9¹/₁₆ 8¼ 8
430 11¼ 10⅛

INTRODUCTION TO THE MEASUREMENT OF INTEREST RATE RISK

by Frank J. Fabozzi

LEARNING OUTCOMES

The candidate should be able to:

a. distinguish between the full valuation approach (the scenario analysis approach) and the duration/convexity approach for measuring interest rate risk, and explain the advantage of using the full valuation approach;

b. describe the price volatility characteristics for option-free, callable, prepayable, and putable bonds when interest rates change (including the concepts of "positive convexity" and "negative convexity");

c. compute and interpret the effective duration of a bond, given information about how the bond's price will increase and decrease for given changes in interest rates, and compute the approximate percentage price change for a bond, given the bond's effective duration and a specified change in yield;

d. distinguish among the alternative definitions of duration (modified, effective or option-adjusted, and Macaulay), and explain why effective duration is the most appropriate measure of interest rate risk for bonds with embedded options;

e. compute the duration of a portfolio, given the duration of the bonds comprising the portfolio, and identify the limitations of portfolio duration;

f. describe the convexity measure of a bond and estimate a bond's percentage price change, given the bond's duration and convexity and a specified change in interest rates;

g. distinguish between modified convexity and effective convexity;

h. compute the price value of a basis point (PVBP), and explain its relationship to duration.

Fixed Income Analysis for the Chartered Financial Analyst® Program, Second Edition, edited by Frank J. Fabozzi, Copyright © 2005 by CFA Institute. Reprinted with permission.

1

INTRODUCTION

In Reading 66, we discussed the interest rate risk associated with investing in bonds. We know that the value of a bond moves in the opposite direction to a change in interest rates. If interest rates increase, the price of a bond will decrease. For a short bond position, a loss is generated if interest rates fall. However, a manager wants to know more than simply when a position generates a loss. To control interest rate risk, a manager must be able to quantify that result.

What is the key to measuring the interest rate risk? It is the accuracy in estimating the value of the position after an adverse interest rate change. A valuation model determines the value of a position after an adverse interest rate move. Consequently, if a reliable valuation model is not used, there is no way to properly measure interest rate risk exposure.

There are two approaches to measuring interest rate risk—the full valuation approach and the duration/convexity approach.

THE FULL VALUATION APPROACH

The most obvious way to measure the interest rate risk exposure of a bond position or a portfolio is to re-value it when interest rates change. The analysis is performed for different scenarios with respect to interest rate changes. For example, a manager may want to measure the interest rate exposure to a 50 basis point, 100 basis point, and 200 basis point instantaneous change in interest rates. This approach requires the re-valuation of a bond or bond portfolio for a given interest rate change scenario and is referred to as the **full valuation approach**. It is sometimes referred to as **scenario analysis** because it involves assessing the exposure to interest rate change scenarios.

To illustrate this approach, suppose that a manager has a $10 million par value position in a 9% coupon 20-year bond. The bond is option-free. The current price is 134.6722 for a yield (i.e., yield to maturity) of 6%. The market value of the position is $13,467,220 (134.6722% × $10 million). Since the manager owns the bond, she is concerned with a rise in yield since this will decrease the market value of the position. To assess the exposure to a rise in market yields, the manager decides to look at how the value of the bond will change if yields change instantaneously for the following three scenarios: (1) 50 basis point increase, (2) 100 basis point increase, and (3) 200 basis point increase. This means that the manager wants to assess what will happen to the bond position if the yield on the bond increases from 6% to (1) 6.5%, (2) 7%, and (3) 8%. Because this is an option-free bond, valuation is straightforward. In the examples that follow, we will use one yield to discount each of the cash flows. In other words, to simplify the calculations, we will assume a flat yield curve (even though that assumption doesn't fit the examples perfectly). The price of this bond per $100 par value and the market value of the $10 million par position is shown in Exhibit 72-1. Also shown is the new market value and the percentage change in market value.

| EXHIBIT 72-1 | Illustration of Full Valuation Approach to Assess the Interest Rate Risk of a Bond Position for Three Scenarios |

Current bond position: 9% coupon 20-year bond (option-free)
Price: 134.6722
Yield to maturity: 6%
Par value owned: $10 million
Market value of position: $13,467,220.00

Scenario	Yield change (bp)	New yield	New price	New market value ($)	Percentage change in market value (%)
1	50	6.5%	127.7606	12,776,050	–5.13%
2	100	7.0%	121.3551	12,135,510	–9.89%
3	200	8.0%	109.8964	10,989,640	–18.40%

In the case of a portfolio, each bond is valued for a given scenario and then the total value of the portfolio is computed for a given scenario. For example, suppose that a manager has a portfolio with the following two option-free bonds: (1) 6% coupon 5-year bond and (2) 9% coupon 20-year bond. For the shorter term bond, $5 million of par value is owned and the price is 104.3760 for a yield of 5%. For the longer term bond, $10 million of par value is owned and the price is 134.6722 for a yield of 6%. Suppose that the manager wants to assess the interest rate risk of this portfolio for a 50, 100, and 200 basis point increase in interest rates assuming both the 5-year yield and 20-year yield change by the same number of basis points. Exhibit 72-2 shows the interest rate risk exposure. Panel a of the exhibit shows the market value of the 5-year bond for the three scenarios. Panel b does the same for the 20-year bond. Panel c shows the total market value of the two-bond portfolio and the percentage change in the market value for the three scenarios.

In the illustration in Exhibit 72-2, it is assumed that both the 5-year and the 20-year yields changed by the same number of basis points. The full valuation approach can also handle scenarios where the yield curve does not change in a parallel fashion. Exhibit 72-3 illustrates this for our portfolio that includes the 5-year and 20-year bonds. The scenario analyzed is a yield curve shift combined with shifts in the level of yields. In the illustration in Exhibit 72-3, the following yield changes for the 5-year and 20-year yields are assumed:

Scenario	Change in 5-year rate (bp)	Change in 20-year rate (bp)
1	50	10
2	100	50
3	200	100

The last panel in Exhibit 72-3 shows how the market value of the portfolio changes for each scenario.

EXHIBIT 72-2	Illustration of Full Valuation Approach to Assess the Interest Rate Risk of a Two Bond Portfolio (Option-Free) for Three Scenarios Assuming a Parallel Shift in the Yield Curve

Panel a

Bond 1:   6% coupon 5-year bond   Par value: $5,000,000
Initial price: 104.3760   Initial market value: $5,218,800
Yield: 5%

Scenario	Yield change (bp)	New yield	New price	New market value ($)
1	50	5.5%	102.1600	5,108,000
2	100	6.0%	100.0000	5,000,000
3	200	7.0%	95.8417	4,792,085

Panel b

Bond 2:   9% coupon 20-year bond   Par value: $10,000,000
Initial price: 134.6722   Initial market value: $13,467,220
Yield: 6%

Scenario	Yield change (bp)	New yield	New price	New market value ($)
1	50	6.5%	127.7605	12,776,050
2	100	7.0%	121.3551	12,135,510
3	200	8.0%	109.8964	10,989,640

Panel c

Initial Portfolio Market value: $18,686,020.00

Scenario	Yield change (bp)	Market Value of Bond 1 ($)	Market Value of Bond 2 ($)	Market Value of Portfolio ($)	Percentage change in market value (%)
1	50	5,108,000	12,776,050	17,884,020	−4.29%
2	100	5,000,000	12,135,510	17,135,510	−8.30%
3	200	4,792,085	10,989,640	15,781,725	−15.54%

The full valuation approach seems straightforward. If one has a good valuation model, assessing how the value of a portfolio or individual bond will change for different scenarios for parallel and nonparallel yield curve shifts measures the interest rate risk of a portfolio.

A common question that often arises when using the full valuation approach is which scenarios should be evaluated to assess interest rate risk exposure. For some regulated entities, there are specified scenarios established by regulators. For example, it is common for regulators of depository institutions to require entities to determine the impact on the value of their bond portfolio for a 100, 200, and 300 basis point instantaneous change in interest rates (up and down). (Regulators tend to refer to this as "simulating" interest rate scenarios rather than scenario analysis.) Risk managers and highly leveraged investors such as

EXHIBIT 72-3	Illustration of Full Valuation Approach to Assess the Interest Rate Risk of a Two Bond Portfolio (Option-Free) for Three Scenarios Assuming a Nonparallel Shift in the Yield Curve

Panel a

Bond 1:	6% coupon 5-year bond	Par value:	$5,000,000
Initial price:	104.3760	Initial market value:	$5,218,800
Yield:	5%		

Scenario	Yield change (bp)	New yield	New price	New market value ($)
1	50	5.5%	102.1600	5,108,000
2	100	6.0%	100.0000	5,000,000
3	200	7.0%	95.8417	4,792,085

Panel b

Bond 2:	9% coupon 20-year bond	Par value:	$10,000,000
Initial price:	134.6722	Initial market value:	$13,467,220
Yield:	6%		

Scenario	Yield change (bp)	New yield	New price	New market value ($)
1	10	6.1%	133.2472	13,324,720
2	50	6.5%	127.7605	12,776,050
3	100	7.0%	121.3551	12,135,510

Panel c

Initial Portfolio Market value: $18,686,020.00

	Market Value of			
Scenario	Bond 1 ($)	Bond 2 ($)	Portfolio ($)	Percentage change in market value (%)
1	5,108,000	13,324,720	18,432,720	−1.36%
2	5,000,000	12,776,050	17,776,050	−4.87%
3	4,792,085	12,135,510	16,927,595	−9.41%

hedge funds tend to look at extreme scenarios to assess exposure to interest rate changes. This practice is referred to as **stress testing**.

Of course, in assessing how changes in the yield curve can affect the exposure of a portfolio, there are an infinite number of scenarios that can be evaluated. The state-of-the-art technology involves using a complex statistical procedure[1] to determine a likely set of yield curve shift scenarios from historical data.

It seems like the reading should end right here. We can use the full valuation approach to assess the exposure of a bond or portfolio to interest rate changes to evaluate any scenario, assuming—and this must be repeated continuously—*that the manager has a good valuation model to estimate what the price of the bonds will be in each interest rate scenario.* However, we are not stopping here. In fact, the balance of this reading is considerably longer than this section. Why? The reason is that

---

[1] The procedure used is principal component analysis.

the full valuation process can be very time consuming. This is particularly true if the portfolio has a large number of bonds, even if a minority of those bonds are complex (i.e., have embedded options). While the full valuation approach is the recommended method, managers want one simple measure that they can use to get an idea of how bond prices will change if rates change in a parallel fashion, rather than having to revalue an entire portfolio. In Reading 66, such a measure was introduced—duration. We will discuss this measure as well as a supplementary measure (convexity) in Sections 4 and 5, respectively. To build a foundation to understand the limitations of these measures, we describe the basic price volatility characteristics of bonds in Section 3. The fact that there are limitations of using one or two measures to describe the interest rate exposure of a position or portfolio should not be surprising. These measures provide a starting point for assessing interest rate risk.

3 PRICE VOLATILITY CHARACTERISTICS OF BONDS

In Reading 66, we described the characteristics of a bond that affect its price volatility: (1) maturity, (2) coupon rate, and (3) presence of embedded options. We also explained how the level of yields affects price volatility. In this section, we will take a closer look at the price volatility of bonds.

3.1 Price Volatility Characteristics of Option-Free Bonds

Let's begin by focusing on option-free bonds (i.e., bonds that do not have embedded options). A fundamental characteristic of an option-free bond is that the price of the bond changes in the opposite direction to a change in the bond's yield. Exhibit 72-4 illustrates this property for four hypothetical bonds assuming a par value of $100.

EXHIBIT 72-4	Price/Yield Relationship for Four Hypothetical Option-Free Bonds			
	Price ($)			
Yield (%)	**6%/5 year**	**6%/20 year**	**9%/5 year**	**9%/20 year**
4.00	108.9826	127.3555	122.4565	168.3887
5.00	104.3760	112.5514	117.5041	150.2056
5.50	102.1600	106.0195	115.1201	142.1367
5.90	100.4276	101.1651	113.2556	136.1193
5.99	100.0427	100.1157	112.8412	134.8159
6.00	100.0000	100.0000	112.7953	134.6722
6.01	99.9574	99.8845	112.7494	134.5287
6.10	99.5746	98.8535	112.3373	133.2472
6.50	97.8944	94.4479	110.5280	127.7605
7.00	95.8417	89.3225	108.3166	121.3551
8.00	91.8891	80.2072	104.0554	109.8964

EXHIBIT 72-5	**Price/Yield Relationship for a Hypothetical Option-Free Bond**

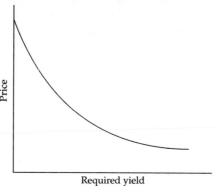

Maximum price = sum of undiscounted cash flows

When the price/yield relationship for any option-free bond is graphed, it exhibits the shape shown in Exhibit 72-5. Notice that as the yield increases, the price of an option-free bond declines. However, this relationship is not linear (i.e., not a straight line relationship). The shape of the price/yield relationship for any option-free bond is referred to as **convex**. This price/yield relationship reflects an instantaneous change in the required yield.

The price sensitivity of a bond to changes in the yield can be measured in terms of the dollar price change or the percentage price change. Exhibit 72-6 uses the four hypothetical bonds in Exhibit 72-4 to show the percentage change in each bond's price for various changes in yield, assuming that the initial yield for all four bonds is 6%. An examination of Exhibit 72-6 reveals the following properties concerning the price volatility of an option-free bond:

Property 1: Although the price moves in the opposite direction from the change in yield, the percentage price change is not the same for all bonds.

EXHIBIT 72-6	**Instantaneous Percentage Price Change for Four Hypothetical Bonds (Initial yield for all four bonds is 6%)**

	Percentage Price Change			
New Yield (%)	**6%/5 year**	**6%/20 year**	**9%/5 year**	**9%/20 year**
4.00	8.98	27.36	8.57	25.04
5.00	4.38	12.55	4.17	11.53
5.50	2.16	6.02	2.06	5.54
5.90	0.43	1.17	0.41	1.07
5.99	0.04	0.12	0.04	0.11
6.01	−0.04	−0.12	−0.04	−0.11
6.10	−0.43	−1.15	−0.41	−1.06
6.50	−2.11	−5.55	−2.01	−5.13
7.00	−4.16	−10.68	−3.97	−9.89
8.00	−8.11	−19.79	−7.75	−18.40

Property 2: For small changes in the yield, the percentage price change for a given bond is roughly the same, whether the yield increases or decreases.

Property 3: For large changes in yield, the percentage price change is not the same for an increase in yield as it is for a decrease in yield.

Property 4: For a given large change in yield, the percentage price increase is greater than the percentage price decrease.

While the properties are expressed in terms of percentage price change, they also hold for dollar price changes.

An explanation for these last two properties of bond price volatility lies in the convex shape of the price/yield relationship. Exhibit 72-7 illustrates this. The following notation is used in the exhibit

$$
\begin{aligned}
Y &= \text{initial yield} \\
Y_1 &= \text{lower yield} \\
Y_2 &= \text{higher yield} \\
P &= \text{initial price} \\
P_1 &= \text{price at lower yield } Y_1 \\
P_2 &= \text{price at higher yield } Y_2
\end{aligned}
$$

What was done in the exhibit was to change the initial yield (Y) up and down by the same number of basis points. That is, in Exhibit 72–7, the yield is decreased from Y to Y_1 and increased from Y to Y_2 such that the change is the same:

$$Y - Y_1 = Y_2 - Y$$

Also, the change in yield is a large number of basis points.

The vertical distance from the horizontal axis (the yield) to the intercept on the graph shows the price. The change in the initial price (P) when the yield declines from Y to Y_1 is equal to the difference between the new price (P_1) and the initial price (P). That is,

| **EXHIBIT 72-7** | **Graphical Illustration of Properties 3 and 4 for an Option-Free Bond** |

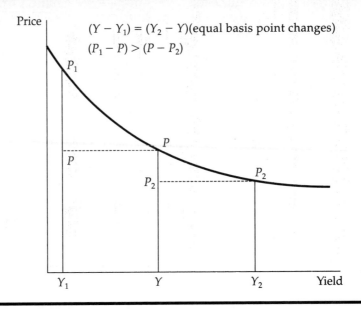

change in price when yield decreases $= P_1 - P$

The change in the initial price (P) when the yield increases from Y to Y_2 is equal to the difference between the new price (P_2) and the initial price (P). That is,

change in price when yield increases $= P_2 - P$

As can be seen in the exhibit, the change in price when yield decreases is not equal to the change in price when yield increases by the same number of basis points. That is,

$P_1 - P \neq P_2 - P$

This is what Property 3 states.

A comparison of the price change shows that the change in price when yield decreases is greater than the change in price when yield increases. That is,

$P_1 - P > P_2 - P$

This is Property 4.

The implication of Property 4 is that if an investor owns a bond, the capital gain that will be realized if the yield decreases is greater than the capital loss that will be realized if the yield increases by the same number of basis points. For an investor who is short a bond (i.e., sold a bond not owned), the reverse is true: the potential capital loss is greater than the potential capital gain if the yield changes by a given number of basis points.

The convexity of the price/yield relationship impacts Property 4. Exhibit 72-8 shows a less convex price/yield relationship than Exhibit 72-7. That is, the price/yield relationship in Exhibit 72-8 is less bowed than the price/yield relationship in Exhibit 72-7. Because of the difference in the convexities, look at what happens

EXHIBIT 72-8	Impact of Convexity on Property 4: Less Convex Bond

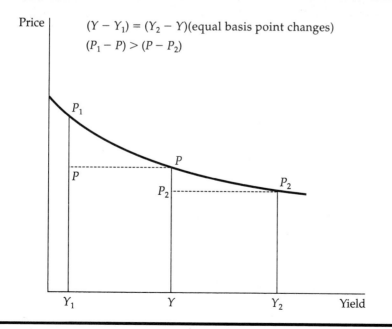

$(Y - Y_1) = (Y_2 - Y)$(equal basis point changes)
$(P_1 - P) > (P - P_2)$

| EXHIBIT 72-9 | Impact of Convexity on Property 4: Highly Convex Bond |

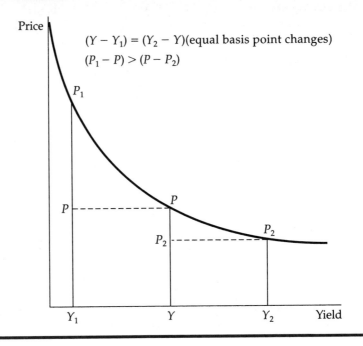

$(Y - Y_1) = (Y_2 - Y)$(equal basis point changes)

$(P_1 - P) > (P - P_2)$

when the yield increases and decreases by the same number of basis points and the yield change is a large number of basis points. We use the same notation in Exhibits 72-8 and 72-9 as in Exhibit 72-7. Notice that while the price gain when the yield decreases is greater than the price decline when the yield increases, the gain is not much greater than the loss. In contrast, Exhibit 72-9 has much greater convexity than the bonds in Exhibits 72-7 and 72-8 and the price gain is significantly greater than the loss for the bonds depicted in Exhibits 72-7 and 72-8.

3.2 Price Volatility of Bonds with Embedded Options

Now let's turn to the price volatility of bonds with embedded options. As explained in previous readings, the price of a bond with an embedded option is comprised of two components. The first is the value of the same bond if it had no embedded option (that is, the price if the bond is option free). The second component is the value of the embedded option. In other words, the value of a bond with embedded options is equal to the value of an option-free bond plus or minus the value of embedded options.

The two most common types of embedded options are call (or prepay) options and put options. As interest rates in the market decline, the issuer may call or prepay the debt obligation prior to the scheduled principal payment date. The other type of option is a put option. This option gives the investor the right to require the issuer to purchase the bond at a specified price. Below we will examine the price/yield relationship for bonds with both types of embedded options (calls and puts) and implications for price volatility.

3.2.1 Bonds with Call and Prepay Options

In the discussion below, we will refer to a bond that may be called or is prepayable as a callable bond. Exhibit 72-10 shows the price/yield relationship for an option-

EXHIBIT 72-10	Price/Yield Relationship for a Callable Bond and an Option-Free Bond

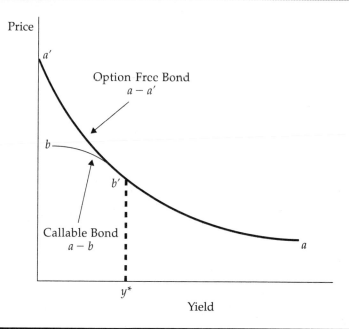

free bond and a callable bond. The convex curve given by a-a' is the price/yield relationship for an option-free bond. The unusual shaped curve denoted by a–b in the exhibit is the price/yield relationship for the callable bond.

The reason for the price/yield relationship for a callable bond is as follows. When the prevailing market yield for comparable bonds is higher than the coupon rate on the callable bond, it is unlikely that the issuer will call the issue. For example, if the coupon rate on a bond is 7% and the prevailing market yield on comparable bonds is 12%, it is highly unlikely that the issuer will call a 7% coupon bond so that it can issue a 12% coupon bond. Since the bond is unlikely to be called, the callable bond will have a similar price/yield relationship to an otherwise comparable option-free bond. Consequently, the callable bond will be valued as if it is an option-free bond. However, since there is still some value to the call option,[2] the bond won't trade exactly like an option-free bond.

As yields in the market decline, the concern is that the issuer will call the bond. The issuer won't necessarily exercise the call option as soon as the market yield drops below the coupon rate. Yet, the value of the embedded call option increases as yields approach the coupon rate from higher yield levels. For example, if the coupon rate on a bond is 7% and the market yield declines to 7.5%, the issuer will most likely not call the issue. However, market yields are now at a level at which the investor is concerned that the issue may eventually be called if market yields decline further. Cast in terms of the value of the embedded call option, that option becomes more valuable to the issuer and therefore it reduces the price relative to an otherwise comparable option-free bond[3]. In Exhibit 72-10, the value of the

---

[2] This is because there is still some chance that interest rates will decline in the future and the issue will be called.

[3] For readers who are already familiar with option theory, this characteristic can be restated as follows: When the coupon rate for the issue is below the market yield, the embedded call option is said to be "out-of-the-money." When the coupon rate for the issue is above the market yield, the embedded call option is said to be "in-the-money."

EXHIBIT 72-11	Negative Convexity Region of the Price/Yield Relationship for a Callable Bond

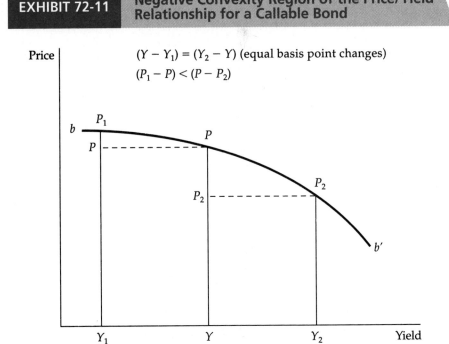

$(Y - Y_1) = (Y_2 - Y)$ (equal basis point changes)

$(P_1 - P) < (P - P_2)$

embedded call option at a given yield can be measured by the difference between the price of an option-free bond (the price shown on the curve a-a') and the price on the curve a-b. Notice that at low yield levels (below y^* on the horizontal axis), the value of the embedded call option is high.

Using the information in Exhibit 72-10, let's compare the price volatility of a callable bond to that of an option-free bond. Exhibit 72-11 focuses on the portion of the price/yield relationship for the callable bond where the two curves in Exhibit 72-10 depart (segment b'-b in Exhibit 72-10). We know from our earlier discussion that for a large change in yield, the price of an option-free bond increases by more than it decreases (Property 4). Is that what happens for a callable bond in the region of the price/yield relationship shown in Exhibit 72-11? No, it is not. In fact, as can be seen in the exhibit, the opposite is true! That is, for a given large change in yield, the price appreciation is less than the price decline.

This very important characteristic of a callable bond—that its price appreciation is less than its price decline when rates change by a large number of basis points—is referred to as **negative convexity**.[4] But notice from Exhibit 72-10 that callable bonds don't exhibit this characteristic at every yield level. When yields are high (relative to the issue's coupon rate), the bond exhibits the same price/yield relationship as an option-free bond; therefore at high yield levels it also has the characteristic that the gain is greater than the loss. Because market participants have referred to the shape of the price/yield relationship shown in Exhibit 72-11 as negative convexity, market participants refer to the relationship for an option-free bond as **positive convexity**. Consequently, a callable bond exhibits negative convexity at low yield levels and positive convexity at high yield levels. This is depicted in Exhibit 72-12.

As can be seen from the exhibits, when a bond exhibits negative convexity, the bond compresses in price as rates decline. That is, at a certain yield level

---

[4] Mathematicians refer to this shape as being "concave."

EXHIBIT 72-12 Negative and Positive Convexity Exhibited by a Callable Bond

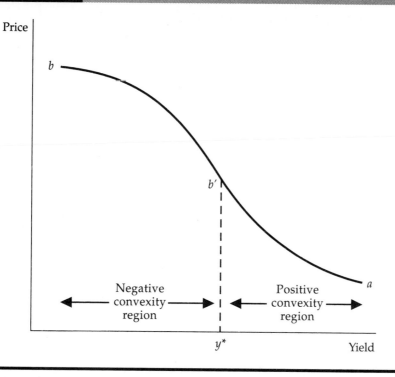

EXHIBIT 72-13 Price/Yield Relationship for a Putable Bond and an Option-Free Bond

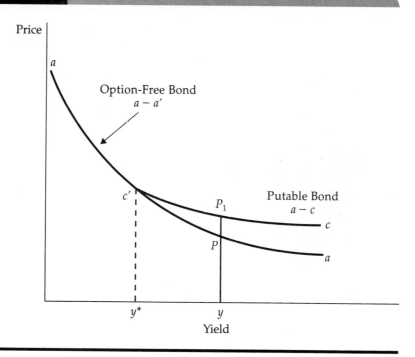

there is very little price appreciation when rates decline. When a bond enters this region, the bond is said to exhibit "price compression."

3.2.2 Bonds with Embedded Put Options

Putable bonds may be redeemed by the bondholder on the dates and at the put price specified in the indenture. Typically, the put price is par value. The advantage to the investor is that if yields rise such that the bond's value falls below the put price, the investor will exercise the put option. If the put price is par value, this means that if market yields rise above the coupon rate, the bond's value will fall below par and the investor will then exercise the put option.

The value of a putable bond is equal to the value of an option-free bond plus the value of the put option. Thus, the difference between the value of a putable bond and the value of an otherwise comparable option-free bond is the value of the embedded put option. This can be seen in Exhibit 72-13 which shows the price/yield relationship for a putable bond is the curve *a-c* and for an option-free bond is the curve *a-a′*.

At low yield levels (low relative to the issue's coupon rate), the price of the putable bond is basically the same as the price of the option-free bond because the value of the put option is small. As rates rise, the price of the putable bond declines, but the price decline is less than that for an option-free bond. The divergence in the price of the putable bond and an otherwise comparable option-free bond at a given yield level (y) is the value of the put option ($P_1 - P$). When yields rise to a level where the bond's price would fall below the put price, the price at these levels is the put price.

4   DURATION

With the background about the price volatility characteristics of a bond, we can now turn to an alternate approach to full valuation: the duration/convexity approach. As explained in Reading 66, *duration is a measure of the approximate price sensitivity of a bond to interest rate changes.* More specifically, *it is the approximate percentage change in price for a 100 basis point change in rates.* We will see in this section that duration is the first (linear) approximation of the percentage price change. To improve the approximation provided by duration, an adjustment for "convexity" can be made. Hence, using duration combined with convexity to estimate the percentage price change of a bond caused by changes in interest rates is called the **duration/convexity approach**.

4.1 Calculating Duration

In Reading 66, we explained that the duration of a bond is estimated as follows:

$$\frac{\text{price if yields decline} - \text{price if yields rise}}{2(\text{initial price})(\text{change in yield in decimal})}$$

If we let

$$\Delta y = \text{change in yield in decimal}$$
$$V_0 = \text{initial price}$$
$$V_- = \text{price if yields decline by } \Delta y$$
$$V_+ = \text{price if yields increase by } \Delta y$$

then duration can be expressed as

$$duration = \frac{V_- - V_+}{2\,(V_0)\,(\Delta y)}$$

(72-1)

For example, consider a 9% coupon 20-year option-free bond selling at 134.6722 to yield 6% (see Exhibit 72-4). Let's change (i.e., shock) the yield down and up by 20 basis points and determine what the new prices will be for the numerator. If the yield is decreased by 20 basis points from 6.0% to 5.8%, the price would increase to 137.5888. If the yield increases by 20 basis points, the price would decrease to 131.8439. Thus,

$$
\begin{aligned}
\Delta y &= 0.002 \\
V_0 &= 134.6722 \\
V_- &= 137.5888 \\
V_+ &= 131.8439
\end{aligned}
$$

Then,

$$duration = \frac{137.5888 - 131.8439}{2 \times (134.6722) \times (0.002)} = 10.66$$

As explained in Reading 66, duration is interpreted as the approximate percentage change in price for a 100 basis point change in rates. Consequently, a duration of 10.66 means that the approximate change in price for this bond is 10.66% for a 100 basis point change in rates.

A common question asked about this interpretation of duration is the consistency between the yield change that is used to compute duration using equation (72-1) and the interpretation of duration. For example, recall that in computing the duration of the 9% coupon 20-year bond, we used a 20 basis point yield change to obtain the two prices to use in the numerator of equation (72-1). Yet, we interpret the duration computed as the approximate percentage price change for a 100 basis point change in yield. The reason is that regardless of the yield change used to estimate duration in equation (72-1), the interpretation is the same. If we used a 25 basis point change in yield to compute the prices used in the numerator of equation (72-1), the resulting duration is interpreted as the approximate percentage price change for a 100 basis point change in yield. Later we will use different changes in yield to illustrate the sensitivity of the computed duration.

Practice Question 1

A. Compute the duration of the 9% coupon 20-year option-free bond by changing the yield down and up by 10 basis points. (The relevant values can be found in Exhibit 72-4.)

B. Suppose a 6% coupon 20-year option-free bond is selling at par value and therefore offering a yield of 6%. Compute the duration by changing the yield down and up by 10 basis points. (The relevant values can be found in Exhibit 72-4.)

4.2 Approximating the Percentage Price Change Using Duration

In Reading 66, we explained how to approximate the percentage price change for a given change in yield and a given duration. Here we will express the process using the following formula:

$$\text{approximate percentage price change} = -\text{duration} \times \Delta y* \times 100 \quad \textbf{(72-2)}$$

where $\Delta y*$ is the yield change (in decimal) for which the estimated percentage price change is sought.[5] The reason for the negative sign on the right-hand side of equation (72-2) is due to the inverse relationship between price change and yield change (e.g., as yields increase, bond prices decrease). The following two examples illustrate how to use duration to estimate a bond's price change.

Example #1: small change in basis point yield. For example, consider the 9% 20-year bond trading at 134.6722 whose duration we just showed is 10.66. The approximate percentage price change for a 10 basis point increase in yield (i.e., $\Delta y* = +0.001$) is:

$$\text{approximate percentage price change} = -10.66 \times (+0.001) \times 100 = -1.066\%$$

How good is this approximation? The actual percentage price change is -1.06% (as shown in Exhibit 72-6 when yield increases to 6.10%). Duration, in this case, did an excellent job in estimating the percentage price change.

We would come to the same conclusion if we used duration to estimate the percentage price change if the yield declined by 10 basis points (i.e., $\Delta y = -0.001$). In this case, the approximate percentage price change would be +1.066% (i.e., the direction of the estimated price change is the reverse but the magnitude of the change is the same). Exhibit 72-6 shows that the actual percentage price change is +1.07%.

In terms of estimating the new price, let's see how duration performed. The initial price is 134.6722. For a 10 basis point increase in yield, duration estimates that the price will decline by 1.066%. Thus, the price will decline to 133.2366 (found by multiplying 134.6722 by one minus 0.01066). The actual price from Exhibit 72-4 if the yield increases by 10 basis points is 133.2472. Thus, the price estimated using duration is close to the actual price.

For a 10 basis point decrease in yield, the actual price from Exhibit 72-4 is 136.1193 and the estimated price using duration is 136.1078 (a price increase of 1.066%). Consequently, the new price estimated by duration is close to the actual price for a 10 basis point change in yield.

Example #2: large change in basis point yield. Let's look at how well duration does in estimating the percentage price change if the yield increases by 200 basis points instead of 10 basis points. In this case, Δy is equal to +0.02. Substituting into equation (72-2), we have

$$\text{approximate percentage price change} = -10.66 \times (+0.02) \times 100 = -21.32\%$$

---

[5] The difference between Δy in the duration formula given by equation (72-1) and $\Delta y*$ in equation (72-2) to get the approximate percentage change is as follows. In the duration formula, the Δy is used to estimate duration and, as explained later, for reasonably small changes in yield the resulting value for duration will be the same. We refer to this change as the "rate shock." Given the duration, the next step is to estimate the percentage price change for any change in yield. The $\Delta y*$ in equation (72-2) is the specific change in yield for which the approximate percentage price change is sought.

How good is this estimate? From Exhibit 72-6, we see that the actual percentage price change when the yield increases by 200 basis points to 8% is −18.40%. Thus, the estimate is not as accurate as when we used duration to approximate the percentage price change for a change in yield of only 10 basis points. If we use duration to approximate the percentage price change when the yield decreases by 200 basis points, the approximate percentage price change in this scenario is +21.32%. The actual percentage price change as shown in Exhibit 72-6 is +25.04%.

Let's look at the use of duration in terms of estimating the new price. Since the initial price is 134.6722 and a 200 basis point increase in yield will decrease the price by 21.32%, the estimated new price using duration is 105.9601 (found by multiplying 134.6722 by one minus 0.2132). From Exhibit 72-4, the actual price if the yield is 8% is 109.8964. Consequently, the estimate is not as accurate as the estimate for a 10 basis point change in yield. The estimated new price using duration for a 200 basis point decrease in yield is 163.3843 compared to the actual price (from Exhibit 72-4) of 168.3887. Once again, the estimation of the price using duration is not as accurate as for a 10 basis point change. *Notice that whether the yield is increased or decreased by 200 basis points, duration underestimates what the new price will be. We will see why shortly.*

Summary. Let's summarize what we found in our application of duration to approximate the percentage price change:

Yield change (bp)	Initial price	New price		Percent price change		Comment
		Based on duration	Actual	Based on duration	Actual	
+10	134.6722	133.2366	133.2472	−1.066	−1.06	estimated price close to new price
−10	134.6722	136.1078	136.1193	+1.066	+1.07	estimated price close to new price
+200	134.6722	105.9601	109.8964	−21.320	−18.40	underestimates new price
−200	134.6722	163.3843	168.3887	+21.320	+25.04	underestimates new price

Should any of this be a surprise to you? No, not after reading Section 3 of this reading and evaluating equation (72-2) in terms of the properties for the price/yield relationship discussed in that section. Look again at equation (72-2). Notice that whether the change in yield is an increase or a decrease, the approximate percentage price change will be the same except that the sign is reversed. This violates Property 3 and Property 4 with respect to the price volatility of option-free bonds when yields change. Recall that Property 3 states that the percentage price change will not be the same for a large increase and decrease in yield by the same number of basis points. Property 4 states the percentage price increase is greater than the percentage price decrease. These are two reasons why the estimate is inaccurate for a 200 basis point yield change.

Why did the duration estimate of the price change do a good job for a small change in yield of 10 basis points? Recall from Property 2 that the percentage price change will be approximately the same whether there is an increase or decrease in yield by a small number of basis points. We can also explain these results in terms of the graph of the price/yield relationship.

Practice Question 2

Using the duration for the 6% coupon 20-year bond found in part B of Practice Question 1, answer the following questions.

1. What is the approximate percentage price change if interest rates increase by 10 basis points?
2. Comment on the approximation compared to the actual price change as given in Exhibit 72-6.
3. What is the approximate percentage price change if interest rates decrease by 10 basis points?
4. Comment on the approximation compared to the actual price change as given in Exhibit 72-6.
5. What is the approximate percentage price change if interest rates increase by 200 basis points?
6. Comment on the approximation compared to the actual price change as given in Exhibit 72-6.
7. What is the approximate percentage price change if interest rates decrease by 200 basis points?
8. Comment on the approximation compared to the actual price change as given in Exhibit 72-6.

4.3 Graphical Depiction of Using Duration to Estimate Price Changes

In Section 3, we used the graph of the price/yield relationship to demonstrate the price volatility properties of bonds. We can also use graphs to illustrate what we observed in our examples about how duration estimates the percentage price change, as well as some other noteworthy points.

The shape of the price/yield relationship for an option-free bond is convex. Exhibit 72-14 shows this relationship. In the exhibit, a tangent line is drawn to the price/yield relationship at yield y^*. (For those unfamiliar with the concept of a tangent line, it is a straight line that just touches a curve at one point within a relevant (local) range. In Exhibit 72-14, the tangent line touches the curve at the point where the yield is equal to y^* and the price is equal to p^*.) The tangent line is used to *estimate* the new price if the yield changes. If we draw a vertical line from any yield (on the horizontal axis), as in Exhibit 72-14, the distance between the horizontal axis and the tangent line represents the price approximated by using duration starting with the initial yield y^*.

Now how is the tangent line related to duration? Given an initial price and a specific yield change, the tangent line tells us the approximate new price of a bond. The approximate percentage price change can then be computed for this change in yield. But this is precisely what duration [using equation (72-2)] gives us: the approximate percentage price change for a given change in yield. Thus, using the tangent line, one obtains the same approximate percentage price change as using equation (72-2).

This helps us understand why duration did an effective job of estimating the percentage price change, or equivalently the new price, when the yield changes by a small number of basis points. Look at Exhibit 72-15. Notice that for a small change in yield, the tangent line does not depart much from the price/yield relationship. Hence, when the yield changes up or down by 10 basis points, the

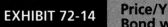

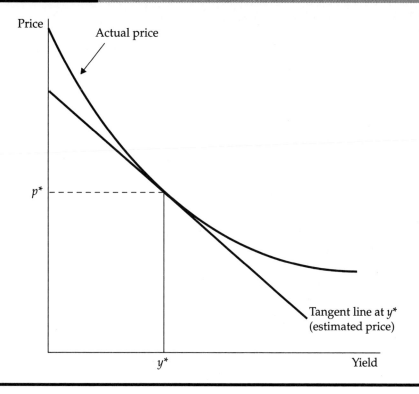

EXHIBIT 72-14   **Price/Yield Relationship for an Option-Free Bond with a Tangent Line**

tangent line does a good job of estimating the new price, as we found in our earlier numerical illustration.

Exhibit 72-15 shows what happens to the estimate using the tangent line when the yield changes by a large number of basis points. Notice that the error in the estimate gets larger the further one moves from the initial yield. The estimate is less accurate the more convex the bond as illustrated in Exhibit 72-16.

Also note that, regardless of the magnitude of the yield change, the tangent line always underestimates what the new price will be for an option-free bond because the tangent line is below the price/yield relationship. This explains why we found in our illustration that when using duration, we underestimated what the actual price will be.

The results reported in Exhibit 72-17 are for option-free bonds. When we deal with more complicated securities, small rate shocks that do not reflect the types of rate changes that may occur in the market do not permit the determination of how prices can change. This is because expected cash flows may change when dealing with bonds with embedded options. In comparison, if large rate shocks are used, we encounter the asymmetry caused by convexity. Moreover, large rate shocks may cause dramatic changes in the expected cash flows for bonds with embedded options that may be far different from how the expected cash flows will change for smaller rate shocks.

There is another potential problem with using small rate shocks for complicated securities. The prices that are inserted into the duration formula as given by equation (72-1) are derived from a valuation model. The duration measure depends crucially on the valuation model. If the rate shock is small and the valuation model used to obtain the prices for equation (72-1) is poor, dividing poor price estimates by a small shock in rates (in the denominator) will have a significant effect on the duration estimate.

EXHIBIT 72-15   **Estimating The New Price Using A Tangent Line**

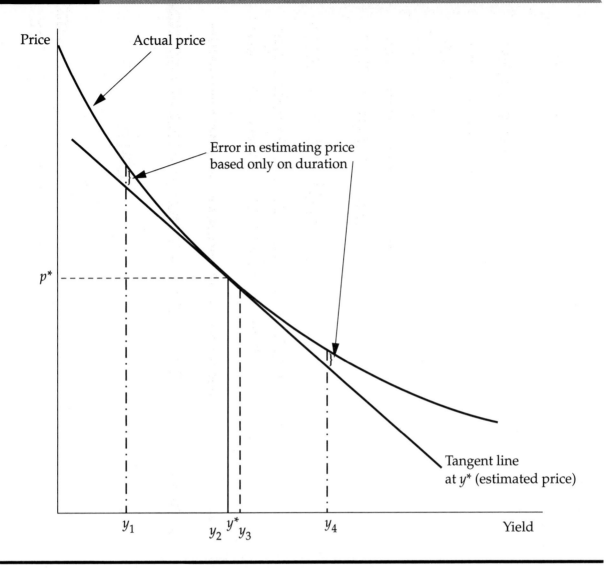

4.4 Rate Shocks and Duration Estimate

In calculating duration using equation (72-1), it is necessary to shock interest rates (yields) up and down by the same number of basis points to obtain the values for V_- and V_+. In our illustration, 20 basis points was arbitrarily selected. But how large should the shock be? That is, how many basis points should be used to shock the rate?

In Exhibit 72-17, the duration estimates for our four hypothetical bonds using equation (72-1) for rate shocks of 1 basis point to 200 basis points are reported. The duration estimates for the two 5-year bonds are not affected by the size of the shock. The two 5-year bonds are less convex than the two 20-year bonds. But even for the two 20-year bonds, for the size of the shocks reported in Exhibit 72-17, the duration estimates are not materially affected by the greater convexity.

What is done in practice by dealers and vendors of analytical systems? Each system developer uses rate shocks that they have found to be realistic based on historical rate changes.

EXHIBIT 72-16 Estimating the New Price for a Large Yield Change for Bonds with Different Convexities

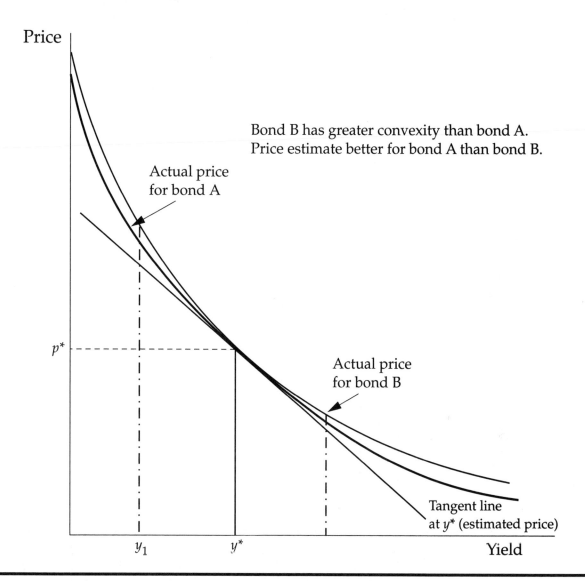

Bond B has greater convexity than bond A. Price estimate better for bond A than bond B.

Actual price for bond A

Actual price for bond B

Tangent line at y^* (estimated price)

EXHIBIT 72-17 Duration Estimates for Different Rate Shocks

Assumption: Initial yield is 6%

Bond	1 bp	10 bps	20 bps	50 bps	100 bps	150 bps	200 bps
6% 5 year	4.27	4.27	4.27	4.27	4.27	4.27	4.27
6% 20 year	11.56	11.56	11.56	11.57	11.61	11.69	11.79
9% 5 year	4.07	4.07	4.07	4.07	4.07	4.08	4.08
9% 20 year	10.66	10.66	10.66	10.67	10.71	10.77	10.86

EXHIBIT 72-18	Modified Duration versus Effective Duration

Duration
Interpretation: Generic description of the sensitivity of a bond's price (as a percentage of initial price) to a change in yield

Modified Duration	*Effective Duration*
Duration measure in which it is assumed that yield changes do not change the expected cash flows	Duration measure in which recognition is given to the fact that yield changes may change the expected cash flows

4.5 Modified Duration versus Effective Duration

One form of duration that is cited by practitioners is **modified duration**. Modified duration is the approximate percentage change in a bond's price for a 100 basis point change in yield *assuming that the bond's expected cash flows do not change when the yield changes*. What this means is that in calculating the values of V_- and V_+ in equation (72-1), the same cash flows used to calculate V_0 are used. Therefore, the change in the bond's price when the yield is changed is due solely to discounting cash flows at the new yield level.

The assumption that the cash flows will not change when the yield is changed makes sense for option-free bonds such as noncallable Treasury securities. This is because the payments made by the U.S. Department of the Treasury to holders of its obligations do not change when interest rates change. However, the same cannot be said for bonds with embedded options (i.e., callable and putable bonds and mortgage-backed securities). For these securities, a change in yield may significantly alter the expected cash flows.

In Section 3, we showed the price/yield relationship for callable and prepayable bonds. Failure to recognize how changes in yield can alter the expected cash flows will produce two values used in the numerator of equation (72-1) that are not good estimates of how the price will actually change. The duration is then not a good number to use to estimate how the price will change.

Some valuation models for bonds with embedded options take into account how changes in yield will affect the expected cash flows. Thus, when V_- and V_+ are the values produced from these valuation models, the resulting duration takes into account both the discounting at different interest rates and how the expected cash flows may change. When duration is calculated in this manner, it is referred to as **effective duration** or **option-adjusted duration**. (Lehman Brothers refers to this measure in some of its publications as **adjusted duration**.) Exhibit 72-18 summarizes the distinction between modified duration and effective duration.

The difference between modified duration and effective duration for bonds with embedded options can be quite dramatic. For example, a callable bond could have a modified duration of 5 but an effective duration of only 3. For certain collateralized mortgage obligations, the modified duration could be 7 and the effective duration 20! Thus, using modified duration as a measure of the price sensitivity for a security with embedded options to changes in yield would be misleading. Effective duration is the more appropriate measure for any bond with an embedded option.

4.6 Macaulay Duration and Modified Duration

It is worth comparing the relationship between modified duration to the another duration measure, **Macaulay duration**. Modified duration can be written as:[6]

$$\frac{1}{(1 + \text{yield}/k)} \left[\frac{1 \times \text{PVCF}_1 + 2 \times \text{PVCF}_2 + \ldots + n \times \text{PVCF}_n}{k \times \text{Price}} \right] \quad \textbf{(72-3)}$$

where

k	= number of periods, or payments, per year (e.g., $k = 2$ for semiannual-pay bonds and $k = 12$ for monthly-pay bonds)
n	= number of periods until maturity (i.e., number of years to maturity times k)
yield	= yield to maturity of the bond
PVCF_t	= present value of the cash flow in period t discounted at the yield to maturity where $t = 1, 2, \ldots, n$

We know that duration tells us the approximate percentage price change for a bond if the yield changes.

The expression in the brackets of the modified duration formula given by equation (72-3) is a measure formulated in 1938 by Frederick Macaulay.[7] This measure is popularly referred to as Macaulay duration. Thus, modified duration is commonly expressed as:

$$\text{Modified duration} = \frac{\text{Macaulay duration}}{(1 + \text{yield}/k)}$$

The general formulation for duration as given by equation (72-1) provides a short-cut procedure for determining a bond's modified duration. Because it is easier to calculate the modified duration using the short-cut procedure, most vendors of analytical software will use equation (72-1) rather than equation (72-3) to reduce computation time.

However, *modified duration is a flawed measure of a bond's price sensitivity to interest rate changes for a bond with embedded options and therefore so is Macaulay duration.* The duration formula given by equation (72-3) misleads the user because it masks the fact that changes in the expected cash flows must be recognized for bonds with embedded options. Although equation (72-3) will give the same estimate of percent price change for an option-free bond as equation (72-1), equation (72-1) is still better because it acknowledges cash flows and thus value can change due to yield changes.

4.7 Interpretations of Duration

Throughout this book, the definition provided for duration is: the approximate percentage price change for a 100 basis point change in rates. That definition is the most relevant for how a manager or investor uses duration. In fact, if you understand this definition, you can easily calculate the change in a bond's value.

---

[6] More specifically, this is the formula for the modified duration of a bond on a coupon anniversary date.

[7] Frederick Macaulay, *Some Theoretical Problems Suggested by the Movement of Interest Rates, Bond Yields, and Stock Prices in the U.S. Since 1856* (New York: National Bureau of Economic Research, 1938).

For example, suppose we want to know the approximate percentage change in price for a 50 basis point change in yield for our hypothetical 9% coupon 20-year bond selling for 134.6722. Since the duration is 10.66, a 100 basis point change in yield would change the price by about 10.66%. For a 50 basis point change in yield, the price will change by approximately 5.33% (= 10.66%/2). So, if the yield increases by 50 basis points, the price will decrease by about 5.33% from 134.6722 to 127.4942.

Now let's look at some other duration definitions or interpretations that appear in publications and are cited by managers in discussions with their clients.

4.7.1 Duration Is the "First Derivative"

Sometimes a market participant will refer to duration as the "first derivative of the price/yield function" or simply the "first derivative." Wow! Sounds impressive. First, "derivative" here has nothing to do with "derivative instruments" (i.e., futures, swaps, options, etc.). A derivative as used in this context is obtained by differentiating a mathematical function using calculus. There are first derivatives, second derivatives, and so on. When market participants say that duration is the first derivative, here is what they mean. The first derivative calculates the slope of a line—in this case, the slope of the tangent line in Exhibit 72-14. If it were possible to write a mathematical equation for a bond in closed form, the first derivative would be the result of differentiating that equation the first time. Even if you don't know how to do the process of differentiation to get the first derivative, it sounds like you are really smart since it suggests you understand calculus! While it is a correct interpretation of duration, it is an interpretation that in no way helps us understand what the interest rate risk is of a bond. That is, it is an operationally meaningless interpretation.

Why is it an operationally meaningless interpretation? Go back to the $10 million bond position with a duration of 6. Suppose a client is concerned with the exposure of the bond to changes in interest rates. Now, tell that client the duration is 6 and that it is the first derivative of the price function for that bond. What have you told the client? Not much. In contrast, tell that client that the duration is 6 and that duration is the approximate price sensitivity of a bond to a 100 basis point change in rates and you have told the client more relevant information with respect to the bond's interest rate risk.

4.7.2 Duration Is Some Measure of Time

When the concept of duration was originally introduced by Macaulay in 1938, he used it as a gauge of the time that the bond was outstanding. More specifically, Macaulay defined duration as the weighted average of the time to each coupon and principal payment of a bond. Subsequently, duration has too often been thought of in temporal terms, i.e., years. This is most unfortunate for two reasons.

First, in terms of dimensions, there is nothing wrong with expressing duration in terms of years because that is the proper dimension of this value. But the proper interpretation is that duration is the price volatility of a zero-coupon bond with that number of years to maturity. So, when a manager says a bond has a duration of 4 years, it is not useful to think of this measure in terms of time, but that the bond has the price sensitivity to rate changes of a 4-year zero-coupon bond.

Second, thinking of duration in terms of years makes it difficult for managers and their clients to understand the duration of some complex securities. Here are a few examples. For a mortgage-backed security that is an interest-only security (i.e., receives coupons but not principal repayment) discussed at Level II, the duration is negative. What does a negative number, say, −4 mean? In terms of our interpretation as a percentage price change, it means that when rates change by 100 basis points, the price of the bond changes by about 4% but the change is in the same direction as the change in rates.

As a second example, consider an inverse floater created in the collateralized mortgage obligation (CMO) market. The underlying collateral for such a security might be loans with 25 years to final maturity. However, an inverse floater can have a duration that easily exceeds 25. This does not make sense to a manager or client who uses a measure of time as a definition for duration.

As a final example, consider derivative instruments, such as an option that expires in one year. Suppose that it is reported that its duration is 60. What does that mean? To someone who interprets duration in terms of time, does that mean 60 years, 60 days, 60 seconds? It doesn't mean any of these. It simply means that the option tends to have the price sensitivity to rate changes of a 60-year zero-coupon bond.

4.7.3 Forget First Derivatives and Temporal Definitions

The bottom line is that one should not care if it is technically correct to think of duration in terms of years (volatility of a zero-coupon bond) or in terms of first derivatives. There are even some who interpret duration in terms of the "half life" of a security.[8] Subject to the limitations that we will describe as we proceed in this book, duration is the measure of a security's price sensitivity to changes in yield. We will fine tune this definition as we move along.

Users of this interest rate risk measure are interested in what it tells them about the price sensitivity of a bond (or a portfolio) to changes in interest rates. Duration provides the investor with a feel for the dollar price exposure or the percentage price exposure to potential interest rate changes. Try the following definitions on a client who has a portfolio with a duration of 4 and see which one the client finds most useful for understanding the interest rate risk of the portfolio when rates change:

Definition 1: The duration of 4 for your portfolio indicates that the portfolio's value will change by approximately 4% if rates change by 100 basis points.

Definition 2: The duration of 4 for your portfolio is the first derivative of the price function for the bonds in the portfolio.

Definition 3: The duration of 4 for your portfolio is the weighted average number of years to receive the present value of the portfolio's cash flows.

Definition 1 is clearly preferable. It would be ridiculous to expect clients to understand the last two definitions better than the first.

Moreover, interpreting duration in terms of a measure of price sensitivity to interest rate changes allows a manager to make comparisons between bonds regarding their interest rate risk under certain assumptions.

4.8 Portfolio Duration

A portfolio's duration can be obtained by calculating the weighted average of the duration of the bonds in the portfolio. The weight is the proportion of the portfolio that a security comprises. Mathematically, a portfolio's duration can be calculated as follows:

$$w_1 D_1 + w_2 D_2 + w_3 D_3 + \ldots w_K D_K$$

---

[8] "Half-life" is the time required for an element to be reduced to half its initial value.

where

w_i = market value of bond i/market value of the portfolio
D_i = duration of bond i
K = number of bonds in the portfolio

To illustrate this calculation, consider the following 3-bond portfolio in which all three bonds are option free:

Bond	Price ($)	Yield (%)	Par amount owned	Market value	Duration
10% 5-year	100.0000	10	$4 million	$4,000,000	3.861
8% 15-year	84.6275	10	5 million	4,231,375	8.047
14% 30-year	137.8586	10	1 million	1,378,586	9.168

In this illustration, it is assumed that the next coupon payment for each bond is exactly six months from now (i.e., there is no accrued interest). The market value for the portfolio is $9,609,961. Since each bond is option free, modified duration can be used. The market price per $100 par value of each bond, its yield, and its duration are given below:
In this illustration, K is equal to 3 and:

w_1 = $4,000,000/$9,609,961 = 0.416 D_1 = 3.861
w_2 = $4,231,375/$9,609,961 = 0.440 D_2 = 8.047
w_3 = $1,378,586/$9,609,961 = 0.144 D_3 = 9.168

The portfolio's duration is:

0.416 (3.861) + 0.440 (8.047) + 0.144 (9.168) = 6.47

A portfolio duration of 6.47 means that for a 100 basis point change in the yield for each of the three bonds, the market value of the portfolio will change by approximately 6.47%. But keep in mind, the yield for each of the three bonds must change by 100 basis points for the duration measure to be useful. (In other words, there must be a parallel shift in the yield curve.) This is a *critical assumption* and its importance cannot be overemphasized.

An alternative procedure for calculating the duration of a portfolio is to calculate the dollar price change for a given number of basis points for each security in the portfolio and then add up all the price changes. Dividing the total of the price changes by the initial market value of the portfolio produces a percentage price change that can be adjusted to obtain the portfolio's duration.

For example, consider the 3-bond portfolio shown above. Suppose that we calculate the dollar price change for each bond in the portfolio based on its respective duration for a 50 basis point change in yield. We would then have:

Bond	Market value	Duration	Change in value for 50 bp yield change
10% 5-year	$4,000,000	3.861	$77,220
8% 15-year	4,231,375	8.047	170,249
14% 30-year	1,378,586	9.168	63,194
		Total	$310,663

Thus, a 50 basis point change in all rates changes the market value of the 3-bond portfolio by $310,663. Since the market value of the portfolio is $9,609,961, a 50 basis point change produced a change in value of 3.23% ($310,663 divided by $9,609,961). Since duration is the approximate percentage change for a 100 basis point change in rates, this means that the portfolio duration is 6.46 (found by doubling 3.23). This is essentially the same value for the portfolio's duration as found earlier.

CONVEXITY ADJUSTMENT   5

The duration measure indicates that regardless of whether interest rates increase or decrease, the approximate percentage price change is the same. However, as we noted earlier, this is not consistent with Property 3 of a bond's price volatility. Specifically, while for small changes in yield the percentage price change will be the same for an increase or decrease in yield, for large changes in yield this is not true. This suggests that duration is only a good approximation of the percentage price change for small changes in yield.

We demonstrated this property earlier using a 9% 20-year bond selling to yield 6% with a duration of 10.66. For a 10 basis point change in yield, the estimate was accurate for both an increase or decrease in yield. However, for a 200 basis point change in yield, the approximate percentage price change was off *considerably*.

The reason for this result is that duration is in fact a first (linear) approximation for a small change in yield.[9] The approximation can be improved by using a second approximation. This approximation is referred to as the "convexity adjustment." It is used to approximate the change in price that is not explained by duration.

The formula for the convexity adjustment to the percentage price change is

Convexity adjustment to the percentage price change =
$C \times (\Delta y*)^2 \times 100$ **(72-4)**

where $\Delta y* =$ the change in yield for which the percentage price change is sought and

$$C = \frac{V_+ + V_- - 2V_0}{2V_0(\Delta y)^2}$$ **(72-5)**

The notation is the same as used in equation (72-1) for duration.[10]

---

[9] The reason it is a linear approximation can be seen in Exhibit 72-15 where the tangent line is used to estimate the new price. That is, a straight line is being used to approximate a non-linear (i.e., convex) relationship.

[10] See **footnote 5** for the difference between Δy in the formula for C and $\Delta y*$ in equation (72-4).

For example, for our hypothetical 9% 20-year bond selling to yield 6%, we know from Section 4.1 that for a 20 basis point change in yield ($\Delta y = 0.002$):

$$V_0 = 134.6722, \ V_- = 137.5888, \ \text{and} \ V_+ = 131.8439$$

Substituting these values into the formula for C:

$$C = \frac{131.8439 + 137.5888 - 2(134.6722)}{2(134.6722)(0.002)^2} = 81.95$$

Suppose that a convexity adjustment is sought for the approximate percentage price change for our hypothetical 9% 20-year bond for a change in yield of 200 basis points. That is, in equation (72-4), Δy_* is 0.02. Then the convexity adjustment is

$$81.95 \times (0.02)^2 \times 100 = 3.28\%$$

If the yield decreases from 6% to 4%, the convexity adjustment to the percentage price change based on duration would also be 3.28%.

The approximate percentage price change based on duration and the convexity adjustment is found by adding the two estimates. So, for example, if yields change from 6% to 8%, the estimated percentage price change would be:

Estimated change using duration	= −21.32%
Convexity adjustment	= +3.28%
Total estimated percentage price change	= −18.04%

The actual percentage price change is −18.40%.

For a decrease of 200 basis points, from 6% to 4%, the approximate percentage price change would be as follows:

Estimated change using duration	= −21.32%
Convexity adjustment	= +3.28%
Total estimated percentage price change	= +24.60%

The actual percentage price change is +125.04%. Thus, duration *combined* with the convexity adjustment does a better job of estimating the sensitivity of a bond's price change to large changes in yield (i.e., better than using duration alone).

5.1 Positive and Negative Convexity Adjustment

Notice that when the convexity adjustment is positive, we have the situation described earlier that the gain is greater than the loss for a given large change in rates. That is, the bond exhibits positive convexity. We can see this in the example above. However, if the convexity adjustment is negative, we have the situation where the loss will be greater than the gain. For example, suppose that a callable bond has an effective duration of 4 and a convexity adjustment for a 200 basis point change of −1.2%.

The bond then exhibits the negative convexity property illustrated in Exhibit 72-11. The approximate percentage price change after adjusting for convexity is:

Estimated change using duration	= −8.0%
Convexity adjustment	= −1.2%
Total estimated percentage price change	= −9.2%

For a decrease of 200 basis points, the approximate percentage price change would be as follows:

Estimated change using duration	=	+8.0%
Convexity adjustment	=	−1.2%
Total estimated percentage price change	=	+6.8%

Notice that the loss is greater than the gain—a property called negative convexity that we discussed in Section 3 and illustrated in Exhibit 72-11.

Practice Question 3

A. What is the value for C in equation (72-4) for a 6% 20-year option-free bond selling at par to yield 6% using an interest rate shock of 10 basis points (i.e., $\Delta y_* = 0.001$)? (The relevant values can be found in Exhibit 72-4.)

B. Using the convexity adjustment for the 6% coupon 20-year option-free bond selling at 100 to yield 6% found in part A, complete the following:

    i. For a 10 basis point increase in interest rates (i.e., $\Delta y_* = 0.001$):

Estimated change using duration	=	_____ %
Convexity adjustment	=	_____ %
Total estimated percentage price change	=	_____ %
Actual percentage price change*	=	_____ %

    ii. For a 10 basis point decrease in interest rates (i.e., $\Delta y_* = -0.001$):

Estimated change using duration	=	_____ %
Convexity adjustment	=	_____ %
Total estimated percentage price change	=	_____ %
Actual percentage price change*	=	_____ %

    iii. For a 200 basis point decrease in interest rates (i.e., $\Delta y_* = 0.02$):

Estimated change using duration	=	_____ %
Convexity adjustment	=	_____ %
Total estimated percentage price change	=	_____ %
Actual percentage price change*	=	_____ %

    iv. For a 200 basis point decrease in interest rates (i.e., $\Delta y_* = -0.02$):

Estimated change using duration	=	_____ %
Convexity adjustment	=	_____ %
Total estimated percentage price change	=	_____ %
Actual percentage price change*	=	_____ %

* See Exhibit 72-6.

5.2 Modified and Effective Convexity Adjustment

The prices used in computing C in equation (72-4) to calculate the convexity adjustment can be obtained by assuming that, when the yield changes, the expected cash flows either do not change or they do change. In the former case, the resulting convexity is referred to as **modified convexity adjustment**. (Actually, in the industry, convexity adjustment is not qualified by the adjective "modified.") In contrast, **effective convexity adjustment** assumes that the cash flows change when yields change. This is the same distinction made for duration.

As with duration, there is little difference between a modified convexity adjustment and an effective convexity adjustment for option-free bonds. However, for bonds with embedded options, there can be quite a difference between the calculated modified convexity adjustment and an effective convexity adjustment. In fact, for all option-free bonds, either convexity adjustment will have a positive value. For bonds with embedded options, the calculated effective convexity adjustment can be negative when the calculated modified convexity adjustment is positive.

6   PRICE VALUE OF A BASIS POINT

Some managers use another measure of the price volatility of a bond to quantify interest rate risk—the **price value of a basis point** (PVBP). This measure, also called the **dollar value of an 01** (DV01), is the absolute value of the change in the price of a bond for a 1 basis point change in yield. That is,

PVBP = | initial price − price if yield is changed by 1 basis point |

Does it make a difference if the yield is increased or decreased by 1 basis point? It does not because of Property 2—the change will be about the same for a small change in basis points.

To illustrate the computation, let's use the values in Exhibit 72-4. If the initial yield is 6%, we can compute the PVBP by using the prices for either the yield at 5.99% or 6.01%. The PVBP for both for each bond is shown below:

Coupon	6.0%	6.0%	9.0%	9.0%
Maturity	5	20	5	20
Initial price	$100.0000	$100.0000	$112.7953	$134.6722
Price at 5.99%	100.0427	100.1157	112.8412	134.8159
PVBP at 5.99%	$0.0427	$0.1157	$0.0459	$0.1437
Price at 6.01%	99.9574	99.8845	112.7494	134.5287
PVBP at 6.01%	$0.0426	$0.1155	$0.0459	$0.1435

The PVBP is related to duration. In fact, PVBP is simply a special case of dollar duration described in Reading 66. We know that the duration of a bond is the approximate percentage price change for a 100 basis point change in interest rates. We also know how to compute the approximate percentage price change for any number of basis points given a bond's duration using equation (72-2). Given the initial price and the approximate percentage price change for 1 basis point, we can compute the change in price for a 1 basis point change in rates.

For example, consider the 9% 20-year bond. The duration for this bond is 10.66. Using equation (72-2), the approximate percentage price change for a 1 basis point increase in interest rates (i.e., $\Delta y = 0.0001$), ignoring the negative sign in equation (72-2), is:

$$10.66 \times (0.0001) \times 100 = 0.1066\%$$

Given the initial price of 134.6722, the dollar price change estimated using duration is

$$0.1066\% \times 134.6722 = \$0.1435$$

This is the same price change as shown above for a PVBP for this bond. Below is (1) the PVBP based on a 1 basis point increase for each bond and (2) the estimated price change using duration for a 1 basis point increase for each bond:

Coupon	6.0%	6.0%	9.0%	9.0%
Maturity	5	20	5	20
PVBP for 1 bp increase	$0.0426	$0.1155	$0.0459	$0.1435
Duration of bond	4.2700	11.5600	4.0700	10.6600
Duration estimate	$0.0427	$0.1156	$0.0459	$0.1436

THE IMPORTANCE OF YIELD VOLATILITY   7

What we have not considered thus far is the volatility of interest rates. For example, as we explained in Reading 66, all other factors equal, the higher the coupon rate, the lower the price volatility of a bond to changes in interest rates. In addition, the higher the level of yields, the lower the price volatility of a bond to changes in interest rates. This is illustrated in Exhibit 72-19 which shows the price/yield relationship for an option-free bond. When the yield level is high (Y_H, for example, in the exhibit), a change in interest rates does not produce a large change in the initial price. For example, as yields change from Y_H to Y_H'', the price changes a *small* amount from P_H to P_H''. However, when the yield level is low and changes (Y_L to Y_L', for example, in the exhibit), a change in interest rates of the same number of basis points as Y_H to Y_H'' produces a *large* change in the initial price (P_L to P_L').

This can also be cast in terms of duration properties: the higher the coupon, the lower the duration; the higher the yield level, the lower the duration. Given these two properties, a 10-year non-investment grade bond has a lower duration than a current coupon 10-year Treasury note since the former has a higher coupon rate and trades at a higher yield level. Does this mean that a 10-year non-investment grade bond has less interest rate risk than a current coupon 10-year Treasury note? Consider also that a 10-year Swiss government bond has a lower coupon rate than a current coupon 10-year U.S. Treasury note and trades at a lower yield level. Therefore, a 10-year Swiss government bond will have a higher duration than a current coupon 10-year Treasury note. Does this mean that a 10-year Swiss government bond has greater interest rate risk than a current coupon 10-year U.S. Treasury note? The missing link is the relative volatility of rates, which we shall refer to as **yield volatility** or **interest rate volatility**.

EXHIBIT 72-19	The Effect of Yield Level on Price Volatility— Option-Free Bond

$$(Y_H' - Y_H) = (Y_H - Y_H'') = (Y_L' - Y_L) = (Y_L - Y_L'')$$
$$(P_H - P_H') < (P_L - P_L') \text{ and}$$
$$(P_H - P_H'') < (P_L - P_L'')$$

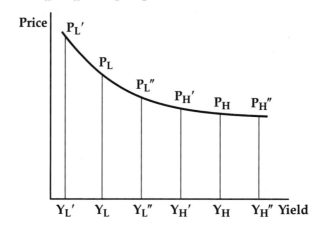

The greater the expected yield volatility, the greater the interest rate risk for a given duration and current value of a position. In the case of non-investment grade bonds, while their durations are less than current coupon Treasuries of the same maturity, the yield volatility of non-investment grade bonds is greater than that of current coupon Treasuries. For the 10-year Swiss government bond, while the duration is greater than for a current coupon 10-year U.S. Treasury note, the yield volatility of 10-year Swiss bonds is considerably less than that of 10-year U.S. Treasury notes.

Consequently, to measure the exposure of a portfolio or position to interest rate changes, it is necessary to measure yield volatility. This requires an understanding of the fundamental principles of probability distributions. The measure of yield volatility is the standard deviation of yield changes. As we will see, depending on the underlying assumptions, there could be a wide range for the yield volatility estimates.

A framework that ties together the price sensitivity of a bond position to interest rate changes and yield volatility is the **value-at-risk (VaR) framework**. Risk in this framework is defined as the maximum estimated loss in market value of a given position that is expected to occur with a specified probability.

SUMMARY

▶ To control interest rate risk, a manager must be able to quantify what will occur from an adverse change in interest rates.

▶ A valuation model is used to determine the value of a position after an interest rate movement and therefore, if a reliable valuation model is not used, there is no way to measure interest rate risk exposure.

▶ There are two approaches to measure interest rate risk: full valuation approach and duration/convexity approach.

▶ The full valuation approach involves revaluing a bond position (every position in the case of a portfolio) for a scenario of interest rate changes.

▶ The advantage of the full valuation approach is its accuracy with respect to interest rate exposure for a given interest rate change scenario—accurate relative to the valuation model used—but its disadvantage for a large portfolio is having to revalue each bond for each scenario.

▶ The characteristics of a bond that affect its price volatility are (1) maturity, (2) coupon rate, and (3) presence of any embedded options.

▶ The shape of the price/yield relationship for an option-free bond is convex.

▶ The price sensitivity of a bond to changes in the required yield can be measured in terms of the dollar price change or percentage price change.

▶ One property of an option-free bond is that although its price moves in the opposite direction of a change in yield, the percentage price change is not the same for all bonds.

▶ A second property of an option-free bond is that for small changes in the required yield, the percentage price change for a given bond is roughly the same whether the yield increases or decreases.

▶ A third property of an option-free bond is that for a large change in yield, the percentage price change for an increase in yield is not the same for a decrease in yield.

▶ A fourth property of an option-free bond is that for a large change in yield, the price of an option-free bond increases more than it decreases.

▶ "Negative convexity" means that for a large change in interest rates, the amount of the price appreciation is less than the amount of the price depreciation.

▶ Option-free bonds exhibit positive convexity.

▶ "Positive convexity" means that for a large change in interest rates, the amount of the price appreciation is greater than the amount of the price depreciation.

▶ A callable bond exhibits positive convexity at high yield levels and negative convexity at low yield levels where "high" and "low" yield levels are relative to the issue's coupon rate.

▶ At low yield levels (low relative to the issue's coupon rate), the price of a putable bond is basically the same as the price of an option-free bond because the value of the put option is small; as rates rise, the price of a putable bond declines, but the price decline is less than that for an option-free bond.

▶ Duration is a first approximation of a bond's price or a portfolio's value to interest rate changes.

▶ To improve the estimate provided by duration, a convexity adjustment can be used.

▶ Using duration combined with a convexity adjustment to estimate the percentage price change of a bond to changes in interest rates is called the duration/convexity approach to interest rate risk measurement.

▶ Duration does a good job of estimating the percentage price change for a small change in interest rates but the estimation becomes poorer the larger the change in interest rates.

▶ In calculating duration, it is necessary to shock interest rates (yields) up and down by the same number of basis points to obtain the values when rates change.

▶ In calculating duration for option-free bonds, the size of the interest rate shock is unimportant for reasonable changes in yield.

▶ For bonds with embedded options, the problem with using a small shock to estimate duration is that divergences between actual and estimated price changes are magnified by dividing by a small change in rate in the denominator of the duration formula; in addition, small rate shocks that do not reflect the types of rate changes that may occur in the market do not permit the determination of how prices can change because expected cash flows may change.

▶ For bonds with embedded options, if large rate shocks are used the asymmetry caused by convexity is encountered; in addition, large rate shocks may cause dramatic changes in the expected cash flows for bonds with embedded options that may be far different from how the expected cash flows will change for smaller rate shocks.

▶ Modified duration is the approximate percentage change in a bond's price for a 100 basis point change in yield assuming that the bond's expected cash flows do not change when the yield changes.

▶ In calculating the values to be used in the numerator of the duration formula, for modified duration the cash flows are not assumed to change and therefore, the change in the bond's price when the yield is changed is due solely to discounting at the new yield levels.

▶ Effective duration is the approximate percentage change in a bond's price for a 100 basis point change in yield assuming that the bond's expected cash flows do change when the yield changes.

▶ Modified duration is appropriate for option-free bonds; effective duration should be used for bonds with embedded options.

▶ The difference between modified duration and effective duration for bonds with an embedded option can be quite dramatic.

▶ Macaulay duration is mathematically related to modified duration and is therefore a flawed measure of the duration of a bond with an embedded option.

▶ Interpretations of duration in temporal terms (i.e., some measure of time) or calculus terms (i.e., first derivative of the price/yield relationship) are operationally meaningless and should be avoided.

▶ The duration for a portfolio is equal to the market-value weighted duration of each bond in the portfolio.

▶ In applying portfolio duration to estimate the sensitivity of a portfolio to changes in interest rates, it is assumed that the yield for all bonds in the portfolio change by the same amount.

- ► The duration measure indicates that regardless of whether interest rates increase or decrease, the approximate percentage price change is the same; however, this is not a property of a bond's price volatility for large changes in yield.

- ► A convexity adjustment can be used to improve the estimate of the percentage price change obtained using duration, particularly for a large change in yield.

- ► The convexity adjustment is the amount that should be added to the duration estimate for the percentage price change in order to obtain a better estimate for the percentage price change.

- ► The same distinction made between modified duration and effective duration applies to modified convexity adjustment and effective convexity adjustment.

- ► For a bond with an embedded option that exhibits negative convexity at some yield level, the convexity adjustment will be negative.

- ► The price value of a basis point (or dollar value of an 01) is the change in the price of a bond for a 1 basis point change in yield.

- ► The price value of a basis point is the same as the estimated dollar price change using duration for a 1 basis point change in yield.

- ► Yield volatility must be recognized in estimating the interest rate risk of a bond and a portfolio.

- ► Value-at-risk is a measure that ties together the duration of a bond and yield volatility.

PROBLEMS FOR READING 72

1. Explain why you agree or disagree with the following statement:

   The disadvantage of the full valuation approach to measuring interest rate risk is that it requires a revaluation of each bond in the portfolio for each interest rate scenario. Consequently, you need a valuation model. In contrast, for the duration/convexity approach there is no need for a valuation model because the duration and convexity adjustment can be obtained without a valuation model.

2. Explain why you agree or disagree with the following statement:

   The problem with both the full valuation approach and the duration/convexity approach is that they fail to take into account how the change in the yield curve can affect a portfolio's value.

3. Explain why you agree or disagree with the following statement:

   If two bonds have the same duration, then the percentage change in price of the two bonds will be the same for a given change in interest rates.

4. James Smith and Donald Robertson are assistant portfolio managers for Micro Management Partners. In a review of the interest rate risk of a portfolio, Smith and Robertson discussed the riskiness of two Treasury securities. Following is the information about these two Treasuries:

Bond	Price	Modified duration
A	90	4
B	50	6

   Smith noted that Treasury bond B has more price volatility because of its higher modified duration. Robertson disagreed noting that Treasury bond A has more price volatility despite its lower modified duration. Which manager is correct?

5. At its quarterly meeting, the trustees of the National Baggage Handlers Pension Fund reviewed the status of its bond portfolio. The portfolio is managed by William Renfro of Wiser and Wiser Management Company. The portfolio consists of 20% Treasury bonds, 10% corporate bonds that are noncallable for the life of the bonds, 30% callable corporate bonds, and 40% mortgage-backed securities. The report provided by Wiser and Wiser includes the following information for each bond in the portfolio: (1) modified duration and (2) effective duration. The portfolio's modified duration and effective duration were reported to be 5 and 3, respectively. Renfro attended the board meeting to answer any questions that the trustees might have. Nancy Weston, one of the trustees for the fund, prepared the following list of questions:

   A. What does the duration of a bond mean and how should the board interpret the portfolio duration?

B. Why is the modified duration and effective duration for each Treasury bond and noncallable corporate bond the same?

C. What is the appropriate duration measure, effective duration or modified duration?

D. How were the effective duration measures obtained?

E. What are the limitations in using duration?

The minutes of the board meeting indicated the following response by Mr. Renfro to each of these questions:

A. Duration is a measure of the approximate weighted average life of a bond or a bond portfolio. For example, a portfolio duration of 5 means that the fund will realize the return of the amount invested (in present value terms) in about 5 years.

B. Because the Treasury bonds in the portfolio are noncallable, modified duration is the same as effective duration. The same is true for the corporate bonds that are noncallable for life.

C. The appropriate measure is the effective duration since it takes into account the option embedded in the bonds held in the portfolio.

D. We obtained the effective duration from various sources—dealers firms and commercial vendors. There is a standard formula that all of these sources use to obtain the effective duration. Sometimes, a source may provide an effective duration that is not logical and we override the value by using the modified duration. For example, for some of the collateralized mortgage obligations, one vendor reported an effective duration of 40. This value was obviously wrong since the underlying collateral is 30-year loans; therefore, the duration cannot exceed 30. Moreover, for some of the CMOs, the duration is negative and this is obviously wrong. Again, in such instances we use the modified duration.

E. Duration is only a good measure for small changes in yield and assumes that the yield curve will shift in a parallel fashion. However, if these assumptions are satisfied, two portfolios with the same duration will perform in exactly the same way.

You are employed by Pension Consultants, a consultant to the labor union. You have been given the minutes of the meeting of the board of trustees with the responses of Mr. Renfro to the questions of Ms. Weston. Prepare a report indicating whether you agree or disagree with Mr. Renfro's responses.

6. Lewis Marlo, an assistant portfolio manager, was reviewing a potential buy list of corporate bonds. The list provided information on the effective duration and effective convexity adjustment assuming a 200 basis point change in interest rates for each corporate bond on the list. The senior portfolio manager, Jane Zorick, noticed that Mr. Marlo crossed out each bond with a negative convexity adjustment. When Ms. Zorick asked Mr. Marlo why, he responded that a negative value meant that the particular corporate bond was unattractive. How do you think Ms. Zorick should respond?

7. A client is reviewing information about the portfolio. For one of the issues in the portfolio the client sees the following:

Issue	Maturity	Duration
X	10 years	13

The client has questioned you as to whether or not the reported duration of 13 is correct. The client's concern is that he has heard that duration is some measure of time for a bond and as such cannot exceed the maturity of the security. Yet, the duration of Issue X exceeds its maturity. What explanation do you give to the client?

8. Suppose that you are given the following information about two callable bonds of the same issuer that can be called immediately:

	Estimated percentage change in price if interest rates change by:	
	−50 basis points	**+50 basis points**
Bond ABC	+2%	−5%
Bond XYZ	+11%	−8%

You are told that both bonds have about the same maturity and the coupon rate of one bond is 7% and the other 13%. Suppose that the yield curve for this issuer is flat at 8%. Based on this information, which bond is the lower coupon bond and which is the higher coupon bond? Explain why.

9. A. Why is modified duration an inappropriate measure for a high-coupon callable bond?

   B. What would be a better measure than modified duration?

10. Suppose that a 7% coupon corporate bond is immediately callable. Also suppose that if this issuer issued new bonds the coupon rate would be 12%. Why would the modified duration be a good approximation of the effective duration for this bond?

Questions 11–15 are based on the following price information for four bonds and assuming that all four bonds are trading to yield 5%:

	Coupon	**5.0%**	**5.0%**	**8.0%**	**8.0%**
Yield	**Maturity**	**4**	**25**	**4**	**25**
3.00%		107.4859	134.9997	118.7148	187.4992
4.00%		103.6627	115.7118	114.6510	162.8472
4.50%		101.8118	107.4586	112.6826	152.2102
4.75%		100.9011	103.6355	111.7138	147.2621
4.90%		100.3593	101.4324	111.1374	144.4042
5.00%		100.0000	100.0000	110.7552	142.5435
5.10%		99.6423	98.5959	110.3746	140.7175
5.25%		99.1085	96.5416	109.8066	138.0421
5.50%		98.2264	93.2507	108.8679	133.7465
6.00%		96.4902	87.1351	107.0197	125.7298
7.00%		93.1260	76.5444	103.4370	111.7278

Percentage price change based on an initial yield of 5%

Yield	Coupon Maturity	5.0% 4	5.0% 25	8.0% 4	8.0% 25
3.00%		7.49%	35.00%	7.19%	31.54%
4.00%		3.66%	15.71%	3.52%	14.24%
4.50%		1.81%	7.46%	1.74%	6.78%
4.75%		0.90%	3.64%	0.87%	3.31%
4.90%		0.36%	1.43%	0.35%	1.31%
5.00%		0.00%	0.00%	0.00%	0.00%
5.10%		−0.36%	−1.40%	−0.34%	−1.28%
5.25%		−0.89%	−3.46%	−0.86%	−3.16%
5.50%		−1.77%	−6.75%	−1.70%	−6.17%
6.00%		−3.51%	−12.86%	−3.37%	−11.80%
7.00%		−6.87%	−23.46%	−6.61%	−21.62%

11. Assuming all four bonds are selling to yield 5%, compute the following for each bond:

  A. duration based on a 25 basis point rate shock ($\Delta y = 0.0025$)

  B. duration based on a 50 basis point rate shock ($\Delta y = 0.0050$)

12. Assuming all four bonds are selling to yield 5%, compute the value for C in the convexity equation for each bond using a 25 basis point rate shock ($\Delta y = 0.0025$).

13. A. Using the duration computed in question 11A, compute the approximate percentage price change using duration for the two 8% coupon bonds assuming that the yield changes by 10 basis points ($\Delta y_* = 0.0010$).

  B. How does the estimated percentage price change compare to the actual percentage price change?

14. A. Using the duration computed in question 11A, compute the approximate percentage price change using duration for the two 8% coupon bonds assuming that the yield changes by 200 basis points ($\Delta y_* = 0.02$).

  B. How does the estimated percentage price change compare to the actual percentage price change?

15. A. Using the value for C computed in question 12, compute the convexity adjustment for the two 25-year bonds assuming that the yield changes by 200 basis points ($\Delta y_* = 0.02$).

  B. Compute the estimated percentage price change using duration (as computed in question 11A) and convexity adjustment if yield changes by 200 basis points.

  C. How does the estimated percentage price change using duration and convexity adjustment compare to the actual percentage price change for a 200 basis point change in yield?

16. A. Given the information below for a 6.2% 18-year bond compute the price value of a basis point:

  price = 114.1338   yield = 5%   price if yield is 5.01% = 114.0051

    B. If the duration of the 6.2% 18-year bond is 11.28, what is the estimated price change for a 1 basis point change in yield.

17. Why is information about a bond's duration and convexity adjustment insufficient to quantify interest rate risk exposure?

APPENDIX

Appendix A Solutions to End-of-Reading Problems and Practice Questions

SOLUTIONS FOR READING 55

1. A. Since the margin is 40 percent and Lauren currently has $50,000 on deposit in her margin account, if Lauren uses the maximum allowable margin her $50,000 deposit must represent 40% of her total investment. Thus, if $50,000 = .4x then x = $125,000. Since the shares are priced at $35 each, Lauren can purchase $125,000 − $35 = 3,571 shares (rounded).

B. Total Profit = Total Return − Total Investment

    1. If stock rises to $45/share, Lauren's total return is:
3,571 shares × $45 = $160,695.
Total profit = $160,695 − $125,000 = $35,695

    2. If stock falls to $25/share, Lauren's total return is:
3,571 shares × $25 = $89,275.
Total loss = $89,275 − $125,000 = −$35,725.

C. $$\text{Margin} = \frac{\text{Market Value} - \text{Debit Balance}}{\text{Market Value}}$$

where Market Value = Price per share × Number of shares.

Initial Loan Value   = Total Investment − Initial Margin.
                     = $125,000 − $50,000 = $75,000

Therefore, if maintenance margin is 30 percent:

$$.30 = \frac{(3,571 \text{ shares} \times \text{Price}) - \$75,000}{(3,571 \text{ shares} \times \text{Price})}$$

.30 (3,571 × Price = (3,571 × Price) − $75,000.
1,071.3 × Price   = (3,571 × Price) − $75,000
−2,499.7 × Price = $75,000
Price   = $30.00

2. Profit = Ending Value − Beginning Value + Dividends − Transaction Costs − Interest

Beginning Value of Investment = $20 × 100 shares = $2,000

Your Investment = margin requirement + commission.
                   = (.55 × $2,000) + (.03 × $2,000)
                   = $1,100 + $60
                   = $1,160

Ending Value of Investment = $27 × 100 shares
                         = $2,700

Dividends = $.50 × 100 shares = $50.00

Transaction Costs = (.03 × $2,000) + (.03 × $2,700)
(Commission)   = $60 + $81
                  = $141

Interest = .10 × (.45 × $2,000) = $90.00

Therefore:

Profit = $2,700 − $2,000 + $50 − $141 − $90
        = $519

The rate of return on your investment of $1,160 is:
    $519/$1,160 = 44.74%

3. Profit on a Short Sale = Begin. Value − Ending Value − Dividends − Trans. Costs − Interest

Beginning Value of Investment = $56.00 × 100 shares = $5,600
(sold under a short sale arrangement)

Your investment = margin requirement + commission
              = (.45 × $5,600) + $155
              = $2,520 + $155
              = $2,675

Ending Value of Investment = $45.00 × 100 = $4,500
(Cost of closing out position)

Dividends = $2.50 × 100 shares = $250.00

Transaction Costs = $155 + $145 = $300.00

Interest = .08 × (.55 × $5,600) = $246.40
Therefore:

Profit = $5,600 − $4,500 − $250 − $300 − $246.40
        = $303.60

The rate of return on your investment of $2,675 is:

    $303.60/$2,675 = 11.35%

SOLUTIONS FOR READING 56

1. A. Given a three security series and a price change from period t to t+1, the percentage change in the series would be 42.85 percent.

	Period t	**Period t+1**
A	$60	$ 80
B	20	35
C	18	25
Sum	$98	$140
Divisor	3	3
Average	32.67	46.67

$$\text{Percentage change} = \frac{46.67 - 32.67}{32.67} = \frac{14.00}{32.67} = 42.85\%$$

B.

Stock	**Period t** Price/Share	# of Shares	**Market Value**
A	$60	1,000,000	$ 60,000,000
B	20	10,000,000	200,000,000
C	18	30,000,000	540,000,000
Total			$800,000,000

Stock	**Period t+1** Price/Share	# of Shares	**Market Value**
A	$80	1,000,000	$ 80,000,000
B	35	10,000,000	350,000,000
C	25	30,000,000	750,000,000
Total			$1,180,000,000

$$\text{Percentage change} = \frac{1,180 - 800}{800} = \frac{380}{800} = 47.50\%$$

C. The percentage change for the price-weighted series is a simple average of the differences in price from one period to the next. Equal weights are applied to each price change.

The percentage change for the value-weighted series is a weighted average of the differences in price from one period t to t+1. These weights are the relative market values for each stock. Thus, Stock C carries the greatest weight followed by B and then A. Because Stock C had the greatest percentage increase and the largest weight, it is easy to see that the percentage change would be larger for this series than the price-weighted series.

2. A.

Stock	Price/Share	Period t # of Shares	Market Value
A	$60	16.67	$ 1,000,000
B	20	50.00	1,000,000
C	18	55.56	1,000,000
Total			$3,000,000

Stock	Price/Share	Period t+1 # of Shares	Market Value
A	$80	16.67	$ 1,333.60
B	35	50.00	1,750.00
C	25	55.56	1,389.00
Total			$4,470.60

$$\text{Percentage change} = \frac{4,472.60 - 3,000}{3,000} = \frac{1,472.60}{3,000} = 49.09\%$$

B.

$$A = \frac{80 - 60}{60} = \frac{20}{60} = 33.33\%$$

$$B = \frac{35 - 20}{20} = \frac{15}{20} = 75.00\%$$

$$C = \frac{25 - 18}{18} = \frac{7}{18} = 38.89\%$$

$$\text{Arithmetic average} = \frac{33.33\% + 75.00\% + 38.89\%}{3}$$

$$= \frac{147.22\%}{3} = 49.07\%$$

The answers are the same (slight difference due to rounding). This is what you would expect since Part A represents the percentage change of an equal-weighted series and Part B applies an equal weight to the separate stocks in calculating the arithmetic average.

C. Geometric average is the nth root of the product of n items.

$$\begin{aligned}\text{Geometric average} &= [(1.3333)(1.75)(1.3889)]^{1/3} - 1 \\ &= [3.2407]^{1/3} - 1 \\ &= 1.4798 - 1 \\ &= .4798 \text{ or } 47.98\%\end{aligned}$$

The geometric average is less than the arithmetic average. This is because variability of return has a greater affect on the arithmetic average than the geometric average.

SOLUTIONS FOR READING 57

1. There are several reasons why one would expect capital markets to be efficient, the foremost being that there are a large number of independent, profit-maximizing investors engaged in the analysis and valuation of securities. A second assumption is that new information comes to the market in a random fashion. The third assumption is that the numerous profit-maximizing investors will adjust security prices rapidly to reflect this new information. Thus, price changes would be independent and random. Finally, because stock prices reflect all information, one would expect prevailing prices to reflect "true" current value.

   Capital markets as a whole are generally expected to be efficient, but the markets for some securities might not be as efficient as others. Recall that markets are expected to be efficient because there are a large number of investors who receive new information and analyze its effect on security values. If there is a difference in the number of analysts following a stock and the volume of trading, one could conceive of differences in the efficiency of the markets. For example, new information regarding actively traded stocks such as IBM and Exxon is well publicized and numerous analysts evaluate the effect. Therefore, one should expect the prices for these stocks to adjust rapidly and fully reflect the new information. On the other hand, new information regarding a stock with a small number of stockholders and low trading volume will not be as well publicized and few analysts follow such firms. Therefore, prices may not adjust as rapidly to new information and the possibility of finding a temporarily undervalued stock are also greater. Some also argue that the size of the firms is another factor to differentiate the efficiency of stocks. Specifically, it is believed that the markets for stocks of small firms are less efficient than that of large firms.

2. The weak-form efficient market hypothesis contends that current stock prices reflect all available security-market information including the historical sequence of prices, price changes, and any volume information. The implication is that there should be no relationship between past price changes and future price changes. Therefore, any trading rule that uses past market data alone should be of little value.

   The two groups of tests of the weak-form EMH are (1) statistical tests of independence and (2) tests of trading rules. Statistical tests of independence can be divided further into two groups: the autocorrelation tests and the runs tests. The autocorrelation tests are used to test the existence of significant correlation, whether positive or negative, of price changes on a particular day with a series of consecutive previous days. The runs tests examine the sequence of positive and negative changes in a series and attempt to determine the existence of a pattern. For a random series one would expect $1/3(2n - 1)$ runs, where n is the number of observations. If there are too few runs (i.e., long sequences of positive changes or long sequences of negative changes), the series is not random, i.e., you would not expect a positive change to consistently follow a positive change and a negative change consistently after a negative change. Alternatively, if there are too many runs $(+-+-+-$ etc.$)$, again the series is not random since you would not expect a negative change to consistently follow a positive change.

   In the trading rule studies, the second major set of tests, investigators attempted to examine alternative technical trading rules through simulation. The trading rule studies compared the risk-return results derived from the simulations, including transaction costs, to results obtained from a simple buy-and-hold policy.

3. The semistrong-form efficient market hypothesis contends that security prices adjust rapidly to the release of all new public information and that stock prices reflect all public information. The semistrong-form goes beyond the weak-form because it includes all market and also all nonmarket public information such as stock splits, economic news, political news, etc.

   Using the organization developed by Fama, studies of the semistrong-form EMH can be divided into two groups: (1) Studies that attempt to predict futures rates of return using publicly available information (goes beyond weak-form EMH). These studies involve either time-series analysis of returns or the cross-section distribution of returns. (2) Event studies that examine abnormal rates of return surrounding a specific event or item of public information. These studies determine whether it is possible to make average risk-adjusted profits by acting after the information is made public.

4. The strong-form efficient market hypothesis asserts that stock prices fully reflect all information, whether public or private. It goes beyond the semistrong-form because it requires that no group of investors have a monopolistic access to any information. Thus, the strong-form efficient market hypothesis calls for perfect markets in which all information is available to everyone at the same time.

5. CFA Examination II (1995)

   A. Efficient market hypothesis (EMH) states that a market is efficient if security prices immediately and fully reflect all available relevant information. Efficient means informationally efficient, not operationally efficient. Operational efficiency deals with the cost of transferring funds. If the market fully reflects information, the knowledge that information would not allow anyone to profit from it because stock prices already incorporate the information.

      1. **Weak** form asserts that stock prices already reflect all information that can be derived by examining market trading data such as the history of past prices and trading volume.

         ### Empirical evidence supports the weak-form.

         A strong body of evidence supports weak-form efficiency in the major U.S. securities markets. For example, test results suggest that technical trading rules do not produce superior returns after adjusting for transaction costs and taxes.

      2. **Semi-strong** form says that a firm's stock price already reflects all publicly available information about a firm's prospects. Examples of publicly available information are annual reports of companies and investment data.

         ### Empirical evidence mostly supports the semi-strong form.

         Evidence strongly supports the notion of semi-strong efficiency, but occasional studies (e.g., those identifying market anomalies including the small-firm effect and the January effect) and events (e.g., stock market crash of October 1987) are inconsistent with this form of market efficiency. Black suggests that most so-called "anomalies" result from data mining.

3. Strong form of EMH holds that current market prices reflect all information, whether publicly available or privately held, that is relevant to the firm.

Empirical evidence does not support the strong form.

Empirical evidence suggests that strong-form efficiency does not hold. If this form were correct, prices would fully reflect all information, although a corporate insider might exclusively hold such information. Therefore, insiders could not earn excess returns. Research evidence shows that corporate officers have access to pertinent information long enough before public release to enable them to profit from trading on this information.

B. Technical analysis in the form of charting involves the search for recurrent and predictable patterns in stock prices to enhance returns. The EMH implies that this type of technical analysis is without value. If past prices contain no useful information for predicting future prices, there is no point in following any technical trading rule for timing the purchases and sales of securities. According to weak-form efficiency, no investor can earn excess returns by developing trading rules based on historical price and return information. A simple policy of buying and holding will be at least as good as any technical procedure. Tests generally show that technical trading rules do not produce superior returns after making adjustments for transactions costs and taxes.

Fundamental analysis uses earnings and dividend prospects of the firm, expectations of future interest rates, and risk evaluation of the firm to determine proper stock prices. The EMH predicts that most fundamental analysis is doomed to failure. According to semi-strong form efficiency, no investor can earn excess returns from trading rules based on any publicly available information. Only analysts with unique insight receive superior returns. Fundamental analysis is no better than technical analysis in enabling investors to capture above-average returns. However, the presence of many analysts contributes to market efficiency.

In summary, the EMH holds that the market appears to adjust so quickly to information about individual stocks and the economy as a whole that no technique of selecting a portfolio—using either technical or fundamental analysis—can consistently outperform a strategy of simply buying and holding a diversified group of securities, such as those making up the popular market averages.

C. Portfolio managers have several roles or responsibilities even in perfectly efficient markets. The most important responsibility is to:

1. Identify the risk/return objectives for the portfolio given the investor's constraints. In an efficient market, portfolio managers are responsible for tailoring the portfolio to meet the investor's needs rather than requirements and risk tolerance. Rational portfolio management also requires examining the investor's constraints, such as liquidity, time horizon, laws and regulations, taxes, and such unique preferences and circumstances as age and employment.

Other roles and responsibilities include:

2. Developing a well-diversified portfolio with the selected risk level. Although an efficient market prices securities fairly, each security still has firm-specific risk that portfolio managers can eliminate through diversification. Therefore, rational security selection requires selecting a well-diversified portfolio that provides the level of systematic risk that matches the investor's risk tolerance.

3. Reducing transaction costs with a buy-and-hold strategy. Proponents of the EMH advocate a passive investment strategy that does not try to find under or-overvalued stocks. A buy-and-hold strategy is consistent with passive management. Because the efficient market theory suggests that securities are fairly priced, frequently buying and selling securities, which generate large brokerage fees without increasing expected performance, makes little sense. One common strategy for passive management is to create an index fund that is designed to replicate the performance of a broad-based index of stocks.

4. Developing capital market expectations. As part of the asset-allocation decision, portfolio managers need to consider their expectations for the relative returns of the various capital markets to choose an appropriate asset allocation.

5. Implement the chosen investment strategy and review it regularly for any needed adjustments. Under the EMH, portfolio managers have the responsibility of implementing and updating the previously determined investment strategy of each client.

D. Whether active asset allocation among countries could consistently outperform a world market index depends on the degree of international market efficiency and the skill of the portfolio manager. Investment professionals often view the basic issue of international market efficiency in terms of cross-border financial market integration or segmentation. An integrated world financial market would achieve international efficiency in the sense that arbitrage across markets would take advantage of any new information throughout the world. In an efficient integrated international market, prices of all assets would be in line with their relative investment values.

Some claim that international markets are not integrated, but segmented. Each national market might be efficient, but factors might prevent international capital flows from taking advantage of relative mispricing among countries. These factors include psychological barriers, legal restrictions, transaction costs, discriminatory taxation, political risks, and exchange risks.

Markets do not appear fully integrated or fully segmented. Markets may or may not become more correlated as they become more integrated since other factors help to determine correlation. Therefore, the degree of international market efficiency is an empirical question that has not yet been answered.

SOLUTIONS FOR READING 59

1. Annual dividend $9.00
Required return   11%

Therefore, the value of the preferred stock = $9.00/.11 = $81.82

At a market price of $96.00, the promised yield would be $9.00/$96.00 = 9.375%, which is less than your required rate of return of 11%. Therefore, you would decide against a purchase at this price. The maximum price you will be willing to pay is $81.82.

2. Earnings per share: last year $10.00
Dividends per share: last year $6.00
Estimated earnings per share: this year $11.00
Required rate of return   12%
Expected sales price at end of year $132.00

Since the last dividend payout ratio = $6.00/$10.00 = 60%, and assuming you maintain the same payout ratio, then dividends per share at the end of the year is:

EPS × Payout = $11.00 × 60% = $6.60.

Therefore, the present value of BBC's share is:

$$\text{Value} = \frac{\$6.60}{(1 + .12)} + \frac{\$132.00}{(1 + .12)} = \$5.89 + \$117.86 = \$123.75$$

Thus $123.75 is the maximum price you would be willing to pay for BBC's stock.

3. Earnings per share: last year $10.00
Dividends per share: last year $6.00
Required rate of return   8%
Expected sell price $110.00

$$\text{Value} = \frac{\$6.60}{(1 + .08)} + \frac{\$110.00}{(1 + .08)} = \$6.11 + \$101.85 = \$107.96$$

Thus $107.96 is the maximum price you would be willing to pay for BBC's stock.

4. Dividends at the end of this year: $6 × 1.08 = $6.48
Required rate of return   11%
Growth rate of dividends   8%

$$\text{Value} = \frac{\$6.48}{.11 - .08} = \$216.00$$

Thus, you would be willing to pay up to $216.00 for BBC's stock.

5. Estimated earnings per share $11.00
Dividend payout ratio   60%
Required rate of return   12%
Growth rate of dividends   9%

$$\text{P/E of BBC Company} = \frac{.60}{.12 - .09} = 20x$$

Thus, the maximum price you would be willing to pay for BBC's stock is:

$20 \times \$11 = \$220.00$

6. Dividend payout ratio   40%
Return on equity   16%

Growth rate = (Retention rate) × (Return on equity)
$\qquad$ = (1 − payout ratio) × (Return on equity)
$\qquad$ = (1 − .40) × (.16)
$\qquad$ = .60 × .16
$\qquad$ = 9.6%

7. Dividend payout ratio   40%
Dividend growth rate   9.6%
Required rate of return   13%

$$\text{P/E of SDC Company} = \frac{.40}{.13 - .096} = 11.76x$$

8. Dividend payout ratio   50%
Required rate of return   13%

Growth rate =   (1 − .50) × (.16)
(new)   =   .50 × .16
$\qquad$ =   .08

$$\text{P/E of SDC Company} = \frac{.50}{.13 - .08} = 10.00x$$
(new)

9. Required rate of return (k)   14%
Return on equity (ROE)   30%
Retention rate (RR)   90%
Earnings per share (EPS) $5.00

Then growth rate = RR × ROE
$\qquad$ = .90 × .30 = .27

$$\text{P/E} = \frac{\text{D/E}}{k - g} = \frac{.10}{.14 - .27}$$

Since the required rate of return (k) is less than the growth rate (g), the earnings multiplier cannot be used (the answer is meaningless).

However, if ROE = .19 and RR = .60,
then growth rate = .60 × .19 = .114

$$\text{P/E} = \frac{.40}{.14 - .114} = \frac{.40}{.026} = 15.38 = 15.38x$$

If next year's earnings are expected to be: $5.57 = $5.00 × (1 + .114)

Applying the P/E: Price = (15.38) × ($5.57) = $85.69

Thus, you would be willing to pay up to $85.69 for Maddy Computer Company stock.

10. A. Projected dividends next 3 years:

$$\text{Year 1 } (\$1.25 \times 1.08) = \$1.35$$
$$\text{Year 2 } (\$1.35 \times 1.08) = \$1.46$$
$$\text{Year 3 } (\$1.46 \times 1.08) = \$1.58$$

Required rate of return   12%

Growth rate of dividends   8%

The present value of the stock is:

$$V = \frac{1.35}{1.12} + \frac{1.46}{(1.12)^2} + \frac{1.58}{(1.12)^3} + \frac{40}{(1.12)^3}$$
$$= \frac{1.35}{1.12} + \frac{1.45}{1.2544} + \frac{1.58}{1.4049} + \frac{40}{1.4049}$$
$$= 1.21 + 1.16 + 1.12 + 28.47 = \$31.96$$

B. Growth rate   8%

Required rate of return   12%

$$V = \frac{1.35}{.12 - .08} = \frac{1.35}{.04} = \$33.75$$

C. Assuming all the above assumptions remain the same, the price at end of year 3 will be:

$$P_3 = \frac{D_4}{k - g} = \frac{1.25 \times (1.08)^4}{.12 - .08} = \frac{1.25 \times 1.3605}{.04} = \$42.52$$

SOLUTIONS FOR READING 61

1. Under the assumption that the total worldwide revenue of all firms in this industry was $250 billion, the market shares of the top five corporations are the following:

AOL Time Warner: $38 billion/$250 billion = 15.2%

Walt Disney: 25/250 = 10.0%

Vivendi Universal: 25/250 = 10.0%

Viacom: 23/250 = 9.2%

News Corporation: 13/250 = 5.2%

   A. The three-firm concentration ratio is the combined market share of the largest three firms in the industry = 15.2 + 10 + 10 = 35.2%.

   B. The three-firm Herfindahl index is the sum of the squared market shares of the largest three firms in the industry = $0.152^2 + 0.10^2 + 0.10^2$ = 0.043, or 430 percent squared. The five-firm Herfindahl index is the sum of the squared market shares of the largest five firms in the industry = $0.152^2 + 0.10^2 + 0.10^2 + 0.092^2 + 0.052^2 = 0.054$.

   C. The combined market share of the top five firms, as computed in part a, is 49.6 percent. Therefore, the combined market share of the 40 other firms is 100 − 49.6 = 50.4%. Assuming that each of them has the same share, the share of each is 50.4/40 = 1.26%. So, the Herfindahl index for the industry, which is the sum of the squared market shares of all the firms in the industry, is $0.152^2 + 0.10^2 + 0.10^2 + 0.092^2 + 0.052^2 + 0.0126^2 + \ldots + 0.0126^2 = 0.054 + 40 \times 0.0126^2 = 0.0603$.

   D. The combined market share of the 10 other firms is 100 − 49.6 = 50.4%. Assuming that each of them has the same share, the share of each is 50.4/10 = 5.04%. So, the Herfindahl index for the industry, which is the sum of the squared market shares of all the firms in the industry, is $0.152^2 + 0.10^2 + 0.10^2 + 0.092^2 + 0.052^2 + 0.0504^2 + \ldots + 0.0504^2 = 0.054 + 10 \times 0.0504^2 = 0.0794$.

   E. There is greater competition in the scenario in part C than in part D. The Herfindahl index in part C is smaller than that in part D, reflecting a more competitive industry structure in part C. Also, the reciprocal of the Herfindahl index is 16.6 in part C and 12.6 in part D. Thus, the market structure in part C is equivalent to having 16.6 firms of the same size, and the market structure in part D is equivalent to having 12.6 firms of the same size. This reflects that the market structure in part D is relatively more oligopolistic, or less competitive, than in part C.

SOLUTIONS FOR READING 64

1. The calculations for P/S, P/CF, P/E, leading P/E, and P/B are given in the following table:

	P/S	P/CF	P/E	Leading P/E	P/B
Abell Inc.	$36/$28.80 = 1.25	$36/$2.88 = 12.5	$36/$2.50 = 14.4	$36/$3.00 = 12	$36/$9 = 4
BluSedge Inc.	$40/$25 = 1.6	$40/$0.25 = 160	NM ($40/−0.50 = −80)	$40/$2.50 = 16	$40/$50 = 0.8
Camdeem Inc.	$50/$25 = 2.0	$50/$5.00 = 10	$50/$2.50 = 20.0	$50/$2.00 = 25	$50/$40 = 1.25
Durnell Inc	$69/$30 = 2.3	$69/$3.00 = 23	$69/$2.76 = 25	$69/$3.45 = 20	$69/$10 = 6.9

Note: NM is not meaningful.

2. Using the leading P/E of 12 for Abell and the trailing P/E of 20 misrepresents differences in valuation for the two companies. For a company with rising earnings, such as Abell, leading P/Es will be systematically smaller than trailing P/Es. For a company with declining earnings, the trailing P/E will be systematically smaller. Although the comparison chose the smaller P/E for each stock, it is still a comparison of unlike quantities. More appropriate is a comparison of similar quantities: trailing P/Es (14.4 for Abell versus 20 for Camdeem), or of leading P/Es (12 for Abell versus 25 for Camdeem).

3. A. BluSedge's trailing P/E is not meaningful because EPS is negative. Using P/Es, the two broad alternatives would be

▶ Calculate a P/E based on normal (business-cycle-adjusted) earnings per share, reflecting the average earning power of the company. This approach is often appropriate for cyclical companies.

▶ Use a leading P/E ratio, because next year's expected EPS is positive.

To note also is that the inverse of P/E, earnings yield or E/P, is meaningful with either negative or positive earnings. Ranked from highest to lowest by earnings yield, stocks are correctly ordered from cheapest to most costly in terms of the amount of earnings one unit of currency buys.

B. Three multiples that might be used instead of trailing earnings are price to sales, price to book value, and price to cash flow. The price to sales ratio is always positive. Because book value is a cumulative balance sheet amount, the price to book value is generally positive even earnings are negative, as here for BluSedge. Because cash flow for BluSedge is positive, P/CF is another possible choice in this instance.

4. Finance, investment, insurance, and banking institutions such as Camdeem are often composed largely of liquid assets, and book values of assets may approximate market values of the company's assets. A consulting company such as Durnell may have few physical assets, however; its chief asset may be human capital (the consultants), which is not recognized in accounting.

Analysis of Equity Investments: Valuation, by John D. Stowe, Thomas R. Robinson, Jerald E. Pinto, and Dennis W. McLeavey, Copyright © 2002 by Association for Investment Management and Research. Reprinted with permission.

Thus the much higher P/B for Durnell (a consultancy) compared to Camdeem (a financial institution) may simply reflect how well the assets of these companies are captured by the book value concept. In general, P/B would be a more appropriate tool for Camdeem.

5. A. Normal EPS is the level of earnings per share that the company could currently achieve under mid-cyclical conditions.

  B. Averaging EPS over the 1997–2000 period, we find that ($1.75 + $1.65 + $0.67 + $0.58)/4 = $1.16. According to the method of historical average EPS, HAL's normal EPS is $1.16. The P/E based on this estimate is $17.10/1.16 = 14.7.

  C. Averaging ROE over the 1997–2000 period, we find that (0.176 + 0.18 + 0.07 + 0.066)/4 = 0.123. The most recent BVPS is $10.95. According to the method of average ROE, we have 0.123 × $10.95 = $1.35 as normal EPS. The P/E based on this estimate is $17.10/$1.35 = 12.7.

6. A. For HLLW: P/E = $44/$2 = 22;

  For RFFW: P/E = $22/$1.50 = 14.7.

  B. For HLLW, all of EPS of $2.00 represents underlying earnings. For RFFW, $1.50 − $0.50 = $1.00 represents underlying earnings. Therefore, with a focus on underlying earnings, the P/E of HLLW would still be 22, but RFFW's P/E would increase from 14.7 (not taking account of nonrecurring earnings components) to $22/$1 = 22.

  C. Holding all else equal, RFFW might appear to be undervalued using P/E without any earnings adjustments because its P/E is smaller. With the specified adjustment the apparent valuation difference disappears.

  Because valuation looks toward the future, and nonrecurring earnings are not expected to reappear in future earnings, the calculation of P/E focusing on underlying earnings affords a more accurate comparison of the valuation of HLLW and RFFW.

  D. HLLW's P/E remains at 22. For RFFW, with potential 10 percent dilution, dividing underlying earnings by 1.10 yields $1.00/1.10 = $0.91 and the P/E would be 24.2, contrasting to 14.7 calculated in Part A and 22 calculated in Part B.

7. A. P/E: EPS equals net income divided by the number of shares outstanding or CAD289/CAD440 = CAD0.66. P/E = CAD13.89/CAD0.66 = 21.

  P/S: per-share sales equals net sales divided by the number of shares outstanding or CAD6,032/CAD440 = CAD13.71. P/S = CAD13.89/CAD13.71 = 1.

  B. One advantage of P/S over P/E is that companies' accounting decisions can have a much greater impact upon reported earnings than they are likely to have on reported sales. Although companies are able to make a number of legitimate business and accounting decisions that affect earnings, their discretion over reported sales (revenue recognition) is more limited. Other possible advantages include:

  ▶ Analysts can use P/S when EPS is negative, whereas the P/E ratio based upon negative EPS is not meaningful.

  ▶ The P/S ratio is relatively more stable than P/E and P/S may be more meaningful than P/E when EPS is abnormally high or low.

  C. The net profit margin, calculated as net income/net sales, is a financial ratio, calculable using the information given, which reflects the company's cost structure. For Abitibi, the profit margin equals CAD289/CAD6,032 = 0.048 or 4.8 percent. Sales is the top line in the income statement: It does not reflect costs. Thus differences in P/S ratios may reflect differences in cost structure; the net profit margin, reflect cost structures, is relevant to determining whether this possible explanation for different P/S ratios may be valid in a given instance.

8. A. Book value per share = [(Shareholders' equity) − (Total value of equity claims that are senior to common stock)]/(Number of common stock shares outstanding) = (CAD11,707 − CAD8,442)/440 = CAD3,265/440 = CAD7.42. P/B = CAD13.89/CAD7.42 = 1.9.

B. One advantage of P/B over P/E is that book value is more stable than EPS and P/B may be more meaningful than P/E when EPS is abnormally high or low.

One possible disadvantage is that book value ignores assets such as human capital that are important for some companies. Another is that differences in P/B may just reflect differences in the business model of companies as it pertains to asset use.

C. Recognizing that both goodwill and deferred charges are intangible assets, Tangible book value = book value − intangible assets = CAD3,265 − (CAD1,420 + CAD379) = CAD3,265 − CAD1,799 = CAD1,466. Then, on a per-share basis, CAD1,466/440 = CAD3.33. Thus price to tangible book value is CAD13.89/CAD3.33 = 4.2.

Such a large fraction of Abitibi's assets were composed of intangibles that the price to tangible book value ratio is much larger than the P/B ratio.

9. A. Per-share CF = EPS plus per-share depreciation, amortization, and depletion. CF = net income of CAD289 + depreciation and amortization of CAD707 = CAD996 million. So per-share CF = CAD996/440 = CAD2.26. P/CF = CAD13.89/CAD2.26 = 6.1.

Note that "other noncash expenses" of CAD91 were not added back to net income in computing CF.

B. *Advantage:* P/CF is generally more stable than P/E. Note too that cash flow is generally less subject to manipulation by management than earnings, although CF may be more vulnerable in this respect than CFO which can only be affected by real activities such as the sale of receivables. *Limitation:* CF ignores changes in working capital and noncash revenue. CF is not a free cash flow concept.

10. Although the measurement of book value has a number of widely recognized shortcomings, it can still be applied fruitfully in several categories of circumstances:

▶ The company is not expected to continue as a going concern. When a company is likely to be liquidated (so that ongoing earnings and cash flow are not relevant) the value of its assets less its liabilities is of utmost importance. Naturally, the analyst must establish the fair value of these assets.

▶ The company is composed mainly of liquid assets, such as finance, investment, insurance, and banking institutions.

▶ The company's EPS is highly variable or negative.

SOLUTIONS FOR READING 65

1. All other factors constant, the longer the maturity, the greater the price change when interest rates change. So, Bond B is the answer.

2.

Quoted Price	Price per $1 Par Value (rounded)	Par Value	Dollar Price
96 1/4	0.9625	$1,000	962.50
102 7/8	1.0288	$5,000	5,143.75
109 9/16	1.0956	$10,000	10,956.25
68 11/32	0.6834	$100,000	68,343.75

3.

	1-Year Treasury Rate	Coupon Rate
First reset date	6.1%	6.4%
Second reset date	6.5%	6.8%
Third reset date	6.9%	7.0%
Fourth reset date	6.8%	7.0%
Fifth reset date	5.7%	6.0%
Sixth reset date	5.0%	5.3%
Seventh reset date	4.1%	4.5%
Eighth reset date	3.9%	4.5%
Ninth reset date	3.2%	4.5%
Tenth reset date	4.4%	4.7%

4. **A.** This provision is a make-whole redemption provision (also called a yield maintenance premium provision).

   B. A make-whole premium provision provides a formula for determining the redemption price, called the make-whole redemption price. The purpose of the provision is to protect the yield of those investors who purchased the issue at its original offering.

5. For this bond the excerpt tells us that the issue may be redeemed prior to May 1, 1995 but they may not be refunded—that is, they cannot be called using a lower cost of funds than the issue itself. After May 1, 1995, the issue may be redeemed via a refunding. The issue can be called using any source of funds such as a new bond issue with a lower coupon rate than the issue itself.

6. **A.** While it may be true that the Company can call the issue if rates decline, there is a nonrefunding restriction prior to January 1, 2006. The Company may not refund the issue with a source of funds that costs less than 7.75% until after that date.

B. This is only true if the issuer redeems the issue as permitted by the call schedule. In that case the premium is paid. However, there is a sinking fund provision. If the issuer calls in the particular certificates of the issue held by the investor in order to satisfy the sinking fund provision, the issue is called at par value. So, there is no guarantee that the issue will be paid off at a premium at any time if the issue is called to satisfy the sinking fund provision.

C. It is commonly thought that the presence of a sinking fund provision reduces the risk that the issuer will not have sufficient funds to pay off the amount due at the maturity date. But this must be balanced against the fact that a bondholder might have his or her bonds taken away at par value when the issuer calls a part of the issue to satisfy the sinking fund provision. If the issue is trading above par value, the bondholder only receives par. So, for example, if the issue is trading at 115 and it is called by the Company to satisfy the sinking fund provision, the investor receives par value (100), realizing a loss of 15.

D. As in part C, while it may seem that the right of the issuer to make additional payments beyond the required amount of the sinking fund will reduce the likelihood that the issuer will have insufficient funds to pay off the issue at the maturity date, there is still the potential loss if the issue is called at par. Moreover, the issuer is likely to make additional payments permitted to retire the issue via the sinking fund special call price of 100 when the bond is trading at a premium, because that is when interest rates in the market are less than the coupon rate on the issue.

E. The assistant portfolio manager cannot know for certain how long the bond issue will be outstanding because it can be called per the call schedule. Moreover, because of the sinking fund provision, a portion of their particular bonds might be called to satisfy the sinking fund requirement. (One of the major topics in fixed income analysis is that because of the uncertainty about the cash flow of a bond due to the right to call an issue, sophisticated analytical techniques and valuation models are needed.)

7. The borrowers whose loans are included in the pool can at lower interest rates refinance their loans if interest rates decline below the rate on their loans. Consequently, the security holder cannot rely on the schedule of principal and interest payments of the pool of loans to determine with certainty future cash flow.

8. A. An accelerated sinking fund provision grants the issuer the right to redeem more than the minimum amount necessary to satisfy the sinking fund requirement.

B. An accelerated sinking fund provision is an embedded option granted to an issuer because it allows the issuer to retire the issue at par value when interest rates have declined. The issuer can do this even if the issue is nonrefundable or noncallable at that time.

9. When an investor is considering the purchase of a bond, he or she should evaluate any provision granted to the issuer that may affect their expected return over their desired time horizon. Moreover, when a bond is purchased in the secondary market at a price above par value, the concern is that the issue may be paid off prior to the maturity date. The result would be the loss of the premium. So, for example, if an investor believes that a bond is noncallable but the issue has a sinking fund requirement, it is possible that the issue held by an investor can be called at the special redemption price of 100 when the issue is trading at a premium.

10. An investor can purchase a stand alone option on an exchange or in the over-the-counter market. When an investor purchases a bond, there are choices or "options" provided for in the indenture that grants either the bondholder or the issuer the right or option to do something. These choices are commonly referred to as embedded options.

11. **A.** Institutional investors typically use a repurchase agreement to finance the purchase of a bond.

    B. A term repo is a repurchase agreement where the borrowing is for more than one day; an overnight repo involves borrowing for only one day.

SOLUTIONS FOR READING 65

Solutions are for Practice Questions found in Reading.

1.

Quoted Price	Price per $1 Par Value (rounded)	Par Value	Dollar Price
103 1/4	1.0325	$1,000	1,032.50
70 1/8	0.7013	$5,000	3,506.25
87 5/16	0.8731	$10,000	8,731.25
117 3/32	1.1709	$100,000	117,093.75

2.

	6-Month Treasury Rate	Coupon Rate
First reset date	5.5%	6.0%
Second reset date	5.8%	6.3%
Third reset date	6.3%	6.8%
Fourth reset date	6.8%	7.0%
Fifth reset date	7.3%	7.0%
Sixth reset date	6.1%	6.6%

3. A. Inverse floater

   B. Step-up note (or multiple step-up note)

   C. Inflation-linked bond

SOLUTIONS FOR READING 66

1. **A.** Below par value since the coupon rate is less than the yield required by the market.

   B. Below par value since the coupon rate is less than the yield required by the market.

   C. Below par value since the coupon rate is less than the yield required by the market.

   D. Above par value since the coupon rate is greater than the yield required by the market.

   E. Par value since the coupon rate is equal to the yield required by the market.

	Issue	Coupon Rate	Yield Required by the Market	Price
A.	A	5¼%	7.25%	Below par
B.	B	6⅝%	7.15%	Below par
C.	C	0%	6.20%	Below par
D.	D	5⅞%	5.00%	Above par
E.	E	4½%	4.50%	Par

2. The price of a callable bond can be expressed as follows:

   price of callable bond = price of option-free bond − price of embedded call option

   An increase in interest rates will reduce the price of the option-free bond. However, to partially offset that price decline of the option-free bond, the price of the embedded call option will decrease. This is because as interest rates rise the value of the embedded call option to the issuer is worth less. Since a lower price for the embedded call option is subtracted from the lower price of the option-free bond, the price of the callable bond does not fall as much as that of an option-free bond.

3. **A.** A floating-rate security's exposure to interest rate risk is affected by the time to the next reset date. The shorter the time, the less likely the issue will offer a below-market interest rate until the next reset date. So, a daily reset will not expose the investor of this floater to interest rate risk due to this factor. However, there is interest rate risk which we will see in part B.

   B. The reason there is still interest rate risk with a daily reset floating-rate security is that the margin required by the market may change. And, if there is a cap on the floater, there is cap risk.

4. **A.** While both assistant portfolio managers are correct in that they have identified two features of an issue that will impact interest rate risk, it is the interaction of the two that will affect an issue's interest rate risk. From the information provided in the question, it cannot be determined which has the greater interest rate risk.

B. You, as the senior portfolio manager, might want to suggest that the two assistant portfolio managers compute the duration of the two issues.

5. The information for computing duration:

price if yields decline by 30 basis points = 83.50
price if yields rise by 30 basis points = 80.75
initial price = 82.00
change in yield in decimal = 0.0030

Then,

$$\text{duration} = \frac{83.50 - 80.75}{2(82.00)(0.0030)} = 5.59$$

6. Since the duration is the approximate percentage price change for a 100 basis point change in interest rates, a bond with a duration of 5 will change by approximately 5% for a 100 basis point change in interest rates. Since the market value of the bond is $8 million, the change in the market value for a 100 basis point change in interest rates is found by multiplying 5% by $8 million. Therefore, the change in market value per 100 basis point change in interest rates is $400,000. To get an estimate of the change in the market value for any other change in interest rates, it is only necessary to scale the change in market value accordingly.

A. for 100 basis points = $400,000

B. for 50 basis points = $200,000 (=$400,000/2)

C. for 25 basis points = $100,000 ($400,000/4)

D. for 10 basis points = $40,000 ($400,000/10)

7. To calculate duration, the price must be estimated for an increase and decrease (i.e., a rate shock) of the same number of basis points. A valuation model must be employed to obtain the two prices. With an extremely complex bond issue, the valuation models by different analysts can produce substantially different prices when rates are shocked. This will result in differences in estimates of duration.

8. For an individual bond, duration is an estimate of the price sensitivity of a bond to changes in interest rates. A portfolio duration can be estimated from the duration of the individual bond holdings in the portfolio. To use the portfolio's duration as an estimate of interest rate risk it is assumed that when interest rates change, the interest rate for all maturities change by the same number of basis points. That is, it does not consider non-parallel changes of the yield curve.

9. The approach briefly discussed in this reading for doing so is *rate duration*. Specifically, the 5-year rate duration indicates the approximate percentage change in the value of the portfolio if the yield on all maturities are unchanged but the yield for the 5-year maturity changes by 100 basis points.

10. The first form of reinvestment risk is due to the likelihood the proceeds from the called issue will be reinvested at a lower interest rate. The second form of reinvestment risk is the typical risk faced by an investor when purchasing a bond with a coupon. It is necessary to reinvest all the coupon payments at the computed yield in order to realize the yield at the time the bond is purchased.

11. Credit risk includes default risk, credit spread risk, and downgrade risk. While an investor holds a bond in his or her portfolio, if the issuer does not default there is still (1) the risk that credit spreads in the market will increase (credit spread risk) causing the price of the bond to decline and (2) the risk that the issue will be downgraded by the rating agencies causing the price to decline or not perform as well as other issues (downgrade risk).

12. A. The probability that a bond rated BBB will be downgraded is equal to the sum of the probabilities of a downgrade to BB, B, CCC or D. From the corresponding cells in the exhibit: 5.70% + 0.70% + 0.16% + 0.20% = 6.76%. Therefore, the probability of a downgrade is 6.76%.

B. The probability that a bond rated BBB will go into default is the probability that it will fall into the D rating. From the exhibit we see that the probability is 0.20%.

C. The probability that a bond rated BBB will be upgraded is equal to the sum of the probabilities of an upgrade to AAA, AA, or A. From the corresponding cells in the exhibit: 0.04% + 0.30% + 5.20% = 5.54%. Therefore, the probability of an upgrade is 5.54%.

D. The probability that a bond rated B will be upgraded to investment grade is the sum of the probabilities that the bond will be rated AAA, AA, A or BBB at the end of the year. (Remember that the first four rating categories are investment grade.) From the exhibit: 0.01% + 0.09% + 0.55% + 0.88% = 1.53%. Therefore, the probability that a bond rated B will be upgraded to investment grade is 1.53%.

E. The probability that a bond rated A will be downgraded to noninvestment grade is the sum of the probabilities that the bond will be downgraded to below BBB. From the exhibit: 0.37% + 0.02% + 0.02% + 0.05% = 0.46%, therefore, the probability that a bond rated A will be downgraded to noninvestment grade is 0.46%.

F. The probability that a bond rated AAA will not be downgraded is 93.2%.

13. The market bid-ask spread is the difference between the highest bid price and the lowest ask price. Dealers 3 and 4 have the best bid price (96 15/32). Dealer 2 has the lowest ask price (96 17/32). The market bid-ask spread is therefore 2/32.

14. If this manager's portfolio is marked-to-market, the manager must be concerned with the bid prices provided to mark the position to market. With only one dealer, there is concern that if this dealer decides to discontinue making a market in this issue, bids must be obtained from a different source. Finally, this manager intends to finance the purchase. The lender of the funds (the dealer financing the purchase) will mark the position to market based on the price it determines and this price will reflect the liquidity risk. Consequently, this manager should be concerned with the liquidity risk even if the manager intends to hold the security to the maturity date.

15. A. The purchase of a 30-year Treasury exposes the investor to interest rate risk since at the end of one year, the security is a 29-year instrument. Its price at the end of one year depends on what happens to interest rates one year later.

B. The major difference in risk is with respect to credit risk. Specifically, the AAA issue exposes the investor to credit risk.

C. There is reinvestment risk for the 1-year zero-coupon Treasury issue because the principal must be reinvested at the end of one year.

D. The major difference is the quantity of credit risk exposure of both issues. The U.S. corporate bond issue has greater credit risk. (Note that the sovereign issue is dollar denominated so that there is no exchange rate risk.)

E. The less actively traded issue will have greater liquidity risk.

F. There are two differences in risk. First, there is the greater credit risk of investing in Italian government bonds relative to U.S. Treasury bonds. Second, investing in the Italian government bonds denominated in lira exposes a U.S. investor to exchange rate risk.

16. Probably the first thing that Ms. Peters should ask is what the investment objectives are of HPLU. Addressing directly the two statements Mr. Stevens made, consider the first. Mr. Stevens believes that by buying investment grade bonds the portfolio will not be exposed to a loss of principal. However, all bonds—investment grade and non-investment grade—are exposed to the potential loss of principal if interest rates rise (i.e., interest rate risk) if an issue must be sold prior to its maturity date. If a callable bond is purchased, there can be a loss of principal if the call price is less than the purchase price (i.e., call risk). The issue can also be downgraded (i.e., downgrade risk) or the market can require a higher spread (i.e., credit spread risk), both resulting in a decline in the price of an issue. This will result in a loss of principal if the issue must be sold prior to the maturity date.

The request that the bond portfolio have 40% in issues that mature within three years will reduce the interest rate risk of the portfolio. However, it will expose the HPLU to reinvestment risk (assuming the investment horizon for HPLU is greater than three years) since when the bonds mature there is the risk that the proceeds received may have to be reinvested at a lower interest rate than the coupon rate of the maturing issues.

17. A. It is reasonable to assume that the municipality will not need to redeem proceeds from the pension fund to make current payments to beneficiaries. Instead, the investment objective is to have the fund grow in order to meet future payments that must be made to retiring employees. Investing in just high investment grade securities that mature in one month or less exposes the pension fund to substantial reinvestment risk. So, while the fund reduces its interest rate risk by investing in such securities, it increases exposure to reinvestment risk. In the case of a pension fund, it would be expected that it can absorb some level of interest rate risk but would not want to be exposed to substantial reinvestment risk. So, this investment strategy may not make sense for the municipality's pension fund.

B. The opposite is true for the operating fund. The municipality can be expected to need proceeds on a shorter term basis. It should be less willing to expose the operating fund to interest rate risk but willing to sacrifice investment income (i.e., willing to accept reinvestment risk).

18. When the proposed redemption was announced, the securities were treated as short-term investments with a maturity of about six weeks—from the announcement date of January 26th to the redemption date of March 15th. When GECC canceled the proposed redemption issue and set the coupon rate as allowed by the indenture, the price of the issue declined because the new coupon rate was not competitive with market rates for issues with GECC's rating with the same time to the next reset date in three years.

19. A major risk is foreign exchange risk. This is the risk that the Japanese yen will depreciate relative to the British pound when a coupon payment or principal repayment is received. There is still the interest rate risk associated with the Japanese government bond that results from a rise in Japanese interest rates. There is reinvestment risk. There is also credit risk, although this risk is minimal. Sovereign risk is also a minimal concern.

20. Certain events can impair the ability of an issue or issuer to repay its debt obligations. For example, a corporate takeover that increases the issuer's debt can result in a downgrade. Regulatory changes that reduce revenues or increase expenses of a regulated company or a company serving a market that is adversely affected by the regulation will be downgraded if it is viewed by the rating agency that the ability to satisfy obligations has been impaired.

21. This statement about sovereign risk is incomplete. There are actions that can be taken by a foreign government other than a default that can have an adverse impact on a bond's price. These actions can result in an increase in the credit spread risk or an increase in downgrade risk.

SOLUTIONS FOR READING 66

Solutions are for Practice Questions found in Reading.

1. ► The price for Issue A should be a premium since the coupon rate is greater than the yield required by the market. So, there is no error for Issue A.

   ► The price for Issue B should be a discount since the coupon rate is less than the yield required by the market. So, there is no error for Issue B.

   ► Issue C's coupon rate (0%) is less than the yield required by the market (5%). So, Issue C should be selling at a discount but the reported price is above par value. Hence, the reported price for Issue C is wrong.

   ► Issue D's coupon rate (5.5%) is less than the yield required by the market (5.9%). So, Issue D should be selling at a discount but the reported price is above par value. Hence, the reported price for Issue D is wrong.

   ► The price for Issue E should be par value since the coupon rate is equal to the yield required by the market. So, there is no error for Issue E.

   ► Issue F's coupon rate (4½%) is greater than the yield required by the market (4.0%). So, Issue F should be selling at a premium but the reported price is below par value. Hence, the reported price for Issue F is wrong.

   ► The coupon rate for Issue G and the yield required by the market are equal. So, the price should be par value. Since the reported price is above par value, Issue G's reported price is wrong.

2. Interest rate risk is the exposure of an issue to a change in the yield required by the market or to a change in interest rates. For option-free bonds selling at the same yield, maturity and coupon rate determine the interest rate risk of an issue. Since Issue 3 has both the longest maturity and the lowest coupon, it will have the greatest price sensitivity to changes in interest rates. The issue with the least interest rate risk is Issue 4 since it has the shortest maturity and the highest coupon rate.

3. Issues 5 and 7 have a higher coupon rate and a maturity less than or equal to Issues 4 and 6 and are trading at a higher yield. Thus, Issues 5 and 7 must have less interest rate risk. Issues 4 and 6 have the same maturity and coupon rate. However, Issue 4 is trading at a lower yield relative to issue 6 (7.00% versus 7.20%). Consequently, Issue 4 has the greatest interest rate risk.

4. **A.** If the market wants a higher margin than 120 basis points for similar issues to NotReal.com after issuance, the price will decline because the quoted margin for the issue (120 basis points) is a below-market margin. Even when the coupon rate is reset it will be less than the market required rate for similar issues.

   B. At the time NotReal.com was purchased by an investor, the coupon rate based on the 6-month Treasury rate of 4% was 5.2% (4% plus 120 basis points) considerably below the cap of 8.5%. With the assumed 6-month Treasury rate at 7.0%, the coupon rate is 8.2% (7% plus 120 basis points). Obviously, this is much closer to the cap of 8.5%. While cap risk was present at the time of purchase of this issue, the cap risk was low. With the rise in the 6-month Treasury rate to 7%, cap risk is considerably greater.

5. **A.** In our illustration,

> price if yields decline by 25 basis points = 108.50
> price if yields rise by 25 basis points = 104.00
> initial price = 106.00
> change in yield in decimal = 0.0025

$$\text{duration} = \frac{108.50 - 104.00}{2(106.00)(0.0025)} = 8.49$$

B. For a 100 basis point change and a duration of 8.49, the price will change by approximately 8.49%. For a 50 basis point change it would change by approximately 4.245%. Since the current market value is $10 million, the market value will change by approximately $10 million times 4.245% or $424,500.

6. **A.** The portfolio will change by approximately 5% for a 100 basis point change in interest rates and 2.5% for a 50 basis point change. Since the current market value is $85 million, the portfolio's value will change by approximately 2.5% times $85 million, or $2,125,000.

B. The five bonds in the portfolio have different maturities, ranging from 2 years to 28 years. The assumption when using duration is that if interest rates change, the interest rate for all the maturities changes by the same number of basis points.

C. A 5-year rate duration of 1.5 means that if all other key rates are unchanged but the 5-year rate increases by 100 basis points, the value of the portfolio will change by approximately 1.5%.

SOLUTIONS FOR READING 67

1. None of the statements is correct and therefore one must disagree with each statement for the following reasons.

   A. The foreign bond market sector of the Japanese bond market consists of non-Japanese entities that issue bonds in Japan.

   B. All but U.S. government bonds are rated.

   C. The guarantee of semi-government bonds varies from country to country. Some may carry the full faith and credit of the central government while others may have an implied or indirect guarantee.

   D. In the United States, federally related agency securities (with some exceptions) carry the full faith and credit of the U.S. government. Government sponsored enterprises (with some exceptions) have an implied guarantee.

2. The reason for assigning two types of ratings is that historically the default frequency for government issues denominated in a foreign currency is different from that of government issues denominated in the local currency.

3. A. In a single-price auction, all winning bidders are awarded securities at the highest yield bid. In a multiple-price auction, all winning bidders are awarded securities at the yield they bid.

   B. In a tap system, a government issues additional bonds of a previously outstanding bond issue via an auction.

4. A. Since the inflation rate (as measured by the CPI-U) is 3.6%, the semiannual inflation rate for adjusting the principal is 1.8%.

   i. The inflation adjustment to the principal is

   $$\$1,000,000 \times 0.018\% = \$18,000$$

   ii. The inflation-adjusted principal is

   $$\$1,000,000 + \text{the inflation adjustment to the principal}$$
   $$= \$1,000,000 + \$18,000 = \$1,018,000$$

   iii. The coupon payment is equal to

   $$\text{inflation-adjusted principal} \times (\text{real rate}/2)$$
   $$= \$1,018,000 \times (0.032/2) = \$16,288.00$$

   B. Since the inflation rate is 4.0%, the semiannual inflation rate for adjusting the principal is 2.0%.

   i. The inflation adjustment to the principal is

   $$\$1,018,000 \times 0.02\% = \$20,360$$

   ii. The inflation-adjusted principal is

   $$\$1,018,000 + \text{the inflation adjustment to the principal}$$
   $$= \$1,018,000 + \$20,360 = \$1,038,360$$

    iii. The coupon payment is equal to

$$\text{inflation-adjusted principal} \times (\text{real rate}/2)$$
$$= \$1,038,360 \times (0.032/2) = \$16,613.76$$

5. A. The inflation rate selected is the non-seasonally adjusted U.S. City Average All Items Consumer Price Index for All Urban Consumers (denoted CPI-U).

   B. The Treasury has agreed that if the inflation-adjusted principal is less than the initial par value, the par value will be paid at maturity.

   C. When a TIPS issue is purchased between coupon payments, the price paid by the buyer has to be adjusted for the inflation up to the settlement date. That is why the Treasury reports a daily index ratio for an issue.

6. Agency debentures are securities issued by government sponsored enterprises that do not have any specific collateral securing the bond. The ability to pay bondholders depends on the ability of the issuing GSE to generate sufficient cash flow to satisfy the obligation.

7. A. Monthly mortgage payment = \$1,797.66
Monthly mortgage rate = 0.00583333 (0.07/12)

Month	Beginning of Month Mortgage Balance	Mortgage Payment	Interest	Scheduled Principal Repayment	End of Month Mortgage Balance
1	200,000.00	1,797.66	1,166.67	630.99	199,369.01
2	199,369.01	1,797.66	1,162.99	634.67	198,734.34
3	198,734.34	1,797.66	1,159.28	638.37	198,095.97
4	198,095.97	1,797.66	1,155.56	642.10	197,453.87
5	197,453.87	1,797.66	1,151.81	645.84	196,808.03
6	196,808.03	1,797.66	1,148.05	649.61	196,158.42

   B. In the last month (month 180), after the final monthly mortgage payment is made, the ending mortgage balance will be zero. That is, the mortgage will be fully paid.

   C. The cash flow is unknown even if the borrower does not default. This is because the borrower has the right to prepay in whole or in part the mortgage balance at any time.

8. A. A prepayment is additional principal paid by the borrower in excess of the monthly mortgage payment.

   B. The monthly cash flow of a mortgage-backed security is made up of three elements: (1) net interest (i.e., interest less servicing and other fees), (2) scheduled principal repayments (amortization), and (3) prepayments.

   C. A curtailment is a form of prepayment. Rather than prepaying the entire outstanding mortgage balance, a curtailment is a pay off of only part of the outstanding balance—it shortens (or "curtails") the life of the loan.

9. Prepayment risk is the uncertainty regarding the receipt of cash flows due to prepayments. Because of prepayments the investor does not know when principal payments will be received even if borrowers do not default on their mortgage loan.

10. **A.** In a mortgage passthrough security, the monthly cash flow from the underlying pool of mortgages is distributed on a pro rata basis to all the certificate holders. In contrast, for a collateralized mortgage obligation, there are rules for the distribution of the interest (net interest) and the principal (scheduled and prepaid) to different tranches.

    B. The rules for the distribution of interest and rules for the distribution of principal to the different tranches in a CMO structure effectively redistributes prepayment risk among the tranches.

11. Two government-sponsored enterprises that issue mortgage-backed securities are Fannie Mae and Freddie Mac.

12. An unlimited tax general obligation bond is a stronger form of a general obligation bond than a limited tax general obligation bond. The former is secured by the issuer's unlimited taxing power. The latter is a limited tax pledge because for such debt there is a statutory limit on tax rates that the issuer may levy to service the debt.

13. A moral obligation bond is a municipal bond that in the case of default of an issuer allows the state where the issuer is located to appropriate funds that are scheduled to be paid to the defaulted issuer and use those funds to meet the defaulted issuer's obligation. This is a nonbinding obligation that depends on the best efforts of the state to appropriate the funds to satisfy the defaulted issuer's obligation.

14. An insured municipal bond is an issue that is backed by an insurance policy written by a commercial insurance company such that the insurer agrees to pay bondholders any principal and/or coupon interest that the municipal issuer fails to pay.

15. **A.** A prerefunded bond is a municipal bond that may have originally been a general obligation bond or a revenue bond that is effectively refunded by creating a portfolio of Treasury securities that generates a cash flow equal to the debt service payments on the issue.

    B. Regardless of the credit rating of the issue prior to prerefunding, after prerefunding the issue is effectively collateralized by a portfolio of Treasury obligations such that the cash flow of the Treasury portfolio matches the payments on the issue when they are due. Hence, a prerefunded issue has no credit risk if properly structured.

16. **A.** In a liquidation, all the assets of a corporation will be distributed to the holders of claims and no corporate entity will survive. In a reorganization, a new corporate entity will be created and some security holders will receive in exchange for their claims cash and/or new securities in the new corporation.

    B. The absolute priority principle is that senior creditors are paid in full before junior creditors are paid anything.

    C. The statement is true in a liquidation; however, this is not necessarily the case in a reorganization. In fact, studies suggest that the principle of absolute priority is the exception rather than the rule in a reorganization.

17. **A.** An unsecured bond is called a debenture. Subordinated debenture bonds are issues that rank after secured debt, after debenture bonds, and often after some general creditors in their claim on assets and earnings.

    B. A negative pledge clause prohibits a corporation from creating or assuming any lien to secure a debt issue at the expense of existing creditors. This is an important provision for unsecured creditors.

18. **A.** The performance of corporate bonds will depend not only on the default rate, but the recovery rate as well as the spread over Treasury securities.

B. The reason for the discrepancy is that these studies are measuring defaults over different periods. Studies that find that one-third default look at cumulative default rates over a period of time. The 2.15% to 2.4% figure is an annual default rate.

C. The comment is wrong for two reasons. First, studies have found that the recovery rate is about 38% of the trading price at the time of default. Second, studies have found that the higher the level of seniority, the greater the recovery rate.

19. **A.** A medium-term note and corporate bond differ as to how they are distributed to investors when they are initially sold. For a MTN, an issuer offers securities on a continuous basis via an investment banking firm or a broker/dealer acting as an agent by posting rates daily as to the rate it is willing to pay for specific maturities. In contrast, a corporate bond is issued on a discrete basis—it is issued at a given point in time by an investment banker.

B. An issuer can couple a medium-term note offering with one or more positions in derivative instruments to create an instrument that has a coupon rate customized with respect to risk-return characteristics for an institutional investor. Such medium-term notes are called structured notes.

C. With an index amortizing note (IAN), the coupon rate is fixed and the principal payments are made prior to the stated maturity date based on the prevailing value for some reference interest rate. Specifically, the principal payments decrease when the reference interest rate increases (hence the maturity increases) and increases when the reference interest rate decreases (hence the maturity decreases). The risk faced by the investor is that an IAN will be outstanding for a longer period when interest rates rise, just when the investor would like proceeds to reinvest at a higher interest rate; there is reinvestment risk when interest rates fall because more principal is paid as rates decline, just when the investor would not want to receive principal.

20. **A.** Since negotiable certificates of deposit issued by U.S. banks typically exceed the federally insured amount of $100,000, there is credit risk for the amount invested in excess of $100,000.

B. LIBOR refers to the London interbank offered rate and it is the interest rate paid on Eurodollar certificates of deposit. "1-month LIBOR" is the interest rate that major international banks are offering to pay to each other on a Eurodollar CD that matures in one month.

21. Investing in bankers acceptances exposes the investor to the risk that neither the borrower nor the accepting bank will be able to pay the principal due at the maturity date; that is, the investor faces credit risk. On the surface, there is liquidity risk because there are few dealers who make a market in bankers acceptances. However, investors typically purchase bankers acceptances with the intent of holding them to maturity. Consequently, in practice, liquidity risk is not a concern to such investors.

22. The advantage is that depending on the quality of the consumer loan portfolio, this BBB rated issuer may be able to issue an asset-backed security with a higher rating than BBB and thereby reduce its borrowing costs, net of the cost of credit enhancement.

23. A special purpose vehicle allows a corporation seeking funds to issue a security backed by collateral such that the security will be rated based on the credit quality of the collateral rather than the entity seeking funds.

Effectively, the special purpose vehicle is the owner of the collateral so that the creditors of the entity seeking funds cannot claim the collateral should the entity default.

24. **A.** External credit enhancement includes corporate guarantees, a letter of credit, and bond insurance.

    B. A disadvantage of an external credit enhancement is that it exposes the asset-backed security structure to a credit downgrading should the third-party guarantor be downgraded.

25. **A.** A collateralized debt obligation is a structure backed by a portfolio of one or more fixed income products—corporate bonds, asset-backed securities, mortgage-backed securities, bank loans, and other CDOs. Funds are raised to purchase the assets by the sale of the CDO. An asset manager manages the assets.

    B. The statement is incorrect. When a CDO is issued, the notes are rated. Restrictions are imposed on the asset manager in order to avoid a down-grading of the tranches or the possibility that the trustee must begin paying off the principal to the senior tranches.

    C. The distinction between an arbitrage transaction from a balance sheet transaction is based on the motivation of the sponsor of the CDO. Arbitrage transactions are motivated by the objective to capture the spread between the yield offered on the pool of assets underlying the CDO and the cost of borrowing which is the yield offered to sell the CDO. In balance sheet transactions, typically undertaken by financial institutions such as banks and insurance companies, the motivation is to remove assets from the balance sheet, thereby obtaining capital relief in the form of lower risk-based capital requirements.

26. A bought deal is a form of a bond underwriting. The underwriting firm or group of underwriting firms offers an issuer a firm bid to purchase a specified amount of the bonds with a certain coupon rate and maturity. The issuer is given a short time period to accept or reject the bid. If the bid is accepted, the underwriting firm has bought the deal.

27. In the United States, SEC Rule 144A eliminates the two-year holding period requirement for privately placed securities by permitting large institutions to trade securities acquired in a private placement among themselves without having to register these securities with the SEC. As a result, private placements are classified in two types. The first type are Rule 144A offerings which are underwritten securities. The second type are the traditional private placements which are referred to as non-Rule 144A offerings.

28. The two major types of electronic bond trading systems are the dealer-to-customer systems and exchange systems. The former are further divided into single-dealer systems and multiple-dealer systems. Single-dealer systems are based on a customer dealing with a single, identified dealer over the computer. In multi-dealer systems a customer can select from any of several identified dealers whose bids and offers are provided on a computer screen.

    The second type of electronic system for bonds is the exchange system. In this system, dealer and customer bids and offers are entered into the system on an anonymous basis, and the clearing of the executed trades is done through a common process. Exchange systems can be further divided into continuous trading and call auction systems. Continuous trading permits trading at continuously changing market determined prices throughout the day. Call auctions provide for fixed price auctions at specific times during the day.

SOLUTIONS FOR READING 67

Solutions are for Practice Questions found in Reading.

1. A. Since the inflation rate (as measured by the CPI-U) is 2.4%, the semiannual inflation rate for adjusting the principal is 1.2%.

   i. The inflation adjustment to the principal is

$$\$10,000 \times 0.012\% = \$120.00$$

   ii. The inflation-adjusted principal is

$$\$10,000 + \text{the inflation adjustment to the principal}$$
$$= \$10,000 + \$120 = \$10,120$$

   iii. The coupon payment is equal to

$$\text{inflation-adjusted principal} \times (\text{real rate}/2)$$
$$= \$10,120 \times (0.038/2) = \$192.28$$

B. Since the inflation rate is 2.8%, the semiannual inflation rate for adjusting the principal is 1.4%.

   i. The inflation adjustment to the principal is

$$\$10,120 \times 0.014\% = \$141.68$$

   ii. The inflation-adjusted principal is

$$\$10,120 + \text{the inflation adjustment to the principal}$$
$$= \$10,120 + \$141.68 = \$10,261.68$$

   iii. The coupon payment is equal to

$$\text{inflation-adjusted principal} \times (\text{real rate}/2)$$
$$= \$10,261.68 \times (0.038/2) = \$194.97$$

2. Monthly mortgage payment = $699.21
Monthly mortgage rate = 0.00625 (0.075/12)

Month	Beginning of Month Mortgage Balance	Mortgage Payment	Interest	Scheduled Principal Repayment	End of Month Mortgage Balance
1	100,000.00	699.21	625.00	74.21	99,925.79
2	99,925.79	699.21	624.54	74.68	99,851.11
3	99,851.11	699.21	624.07	75.15	99,775.96
4	99,775.96	699.21	623.60	75.61	99,700.35
5	99,700.35	699.21	623.13	76.09	99,624.26
6	99,624.26	699.21	622.65	76.56	99,547.70

SOLUTIONS FOR READING 68

1. Market participants look at the key indicators watched by the Fed in order to try to predict how the Fed will react to the movement in those indicators.

2. Ms. Peters should inform her client that under one theory of the term structure of interest rates, the pure expectations theory, a downward sloping yield curve does suggest that short-term interest rates in the future will decline. According to the liquidity preference theory a downward sloping yield curve suggests that rates are expected to decline. But it should be noted that the liquidity preference theory does not view a positive yield curve as one where rates may be expected to rise. This is because the yield premium for liquidity can be large enough so that even if expected future rates are expected to decline, the yield curve would be upward sloping. A downward sloping yield curve according to the market segmentation theory cannot be interpreted in terms of the market's expectations regarding future rates.

3. The pure expectations theory asserts that the only factor affecting the shape of the yield curve is expectations about future interest rates. The liquidity preference theory asserts that there are two factors that affect the shape of the yield curve: expectations about future interest rate and a yield premium to compensate for interest rate risk.

4. According to the pure expectations theory, a humped yield curve means that short-term interest rates are expected to rise for a time and then begin to fall.

5. **A.** The data clearly indicate that yield spreads are at their 12-month highs.

   B. A callable agency issue offers a higher yield spread than a noncallable agency issue because of the call risk faced by investors in the former.

   C. For a given maturity, the longer the deferred call period the lower the call risk. Hence, the yield spread for a callable issue is less the longer the deferred call period.

   D. Because yield spreads are not adjusted for call risk, they are referred to as nominal spreads.

   E. The compensation for credit risk, liquidity risk, and call risk are lumped together in the nominal spreads (i.e., yield spreads shown in the second panel). The OAS is an estimate of the yield spread after adjusting for the call (or option) risk. So, the OAS is less than the nominal yield spread.

6. While it is true that a Ginnie Mae mortgage-backed security has no credit risk and that part of the yield spread between a Ginnie Mae mortgage-backed security and a U.S. Treasury security is due to differences in liquidity, the major reason for the yield spread is the prepayment risk of a mortgage-backed security. This risk is ignored in the statement made by the representative of the investment management firm.

7. **A.** Part of the yield spread between a non-Treasury bond with an embedded option and a Treasury security (which is an option-free security) is due to the value of the embedded option. For example, for a callable non-Treasury bond, the yield spread relative to a Treasury security represents compensation for the following: (1) credit risk, (2) liquidity risk, and (3) call risk. When a spread measure includes all three forms of compensation, it is called a "nominal spread." However, investors want to know the yield spread after adjusting for the value of the embedded options (the call option in our illustration).

B. The option-adjusted spread seeks to measure the part of the yield spread between a non-Treasury security and a Treasury security once the portion attributed to the call risk is removed. So, the option-adjusted spread is less than the nominal spread. The option-adjusted spread allows an investor to better compare the yield spread on bonds with and without embedded options.

8. A. absolute yield spread $= 7.25\% - 6.02\% = 1.23\% = 123$ basis points

   B. relative yield spread $= \dfrac{7.25\% - 6.02\%}{6.02\%} = 0.204 = 20.4\%$

   C. yield ratio $= \dfrac{7.25\%}{6.02\%} = 1.204$

9. A. The percent yield spread is the relative yield spread.

   B. Analysts recognize that historical comparisons of the absolute yield spread for assessing how yield spreads are changing do not take into account the level of yields. For example, a 40 basis point absolute yield spread in a 5% interest rate environment is quite different from a 40 basis point absolute yield spread in a 10% yield environment.

10. Tax-exempt municipal securities offer a lower yield than Treasury securities because of the value of the tax-exempt feature. This feature is more attractive to high tax bracket investors than to low tax bracket investors. A reduction in marginal tax rates makes the tax-exempt feature less attractive to investors. This would require that tax-exempt municipals to offer higher yields compared to yields prior to the reduction.

   Anticipating a reduction in tax rates would affect municipal yields. The extent of this effect would depend on the market's assessment of the probability the proposal would be enacted.

11. A. Because municipals are tax-exempt, their return or yield spread depends on each investor's marginal tax rate. Treasuries are subject to federal income tax so comparing the two yields to calculate a yield spread would be different for various investors.

   B. The AAA rated municipal general obligation yield curve is used because it offers a similar tax-exempt status to compare its yield against when considering other tax-exempt municipal bonds.

12. A. The after-tax yield is

$$0.05 \times (1 - 0.40) = 0.03 = 3\%$$

   B. The taxable-equivalent yield is

$$\frac{0.031}{(1 - 0.39)} = 0.0508 = 5.08\%$$

13. A funded investor who borrows short term is interested in the spread above the borrowing cost. Since LIBOR is the global cost of borrowing, a LIBOR yield curve is a more appropriate measure for assessing the potential return than the Treasury yield curve.

14. The swap rate is the sum of the 5-year Treasury yield of 4.4% and the swap spread of 120 basis points. The swap rate is therefore 5.6%.

15. The swap spread is an important spread measure because it is related to credit spreads and therefore can be used in relative value analysis.

16. A. From the Treasury yield curve, the relevant rate is the 2-year rate because the swap has a two year term. The swap rate is 6.8%, computing by adding the 2-year rate of 5.8% and the swap spread of 100 basis points.

B. The annual payment made by the fixed-rate payer of a $10 million notional amount interest rate swap with a swap rate of 6.8% is: $10,000,000 × 0.068 = $680,000. Since the swap specifies quarterly payments, the quarterly payment is $170,000 (= $680,000/4).

C.

If 3-Month LIBOR Is	Annual Dollar Amount	Amount of Payment
5.00%	$500,000	$125,000
5.50%	550,000	137,500
6.00%	600,000	150,000
6.50%	650,000	162,500
7.00%	700,000	175,000
7.50%	750,000	187,500
8.00%	800,000	200,000
8.50%	850,000	212,500

D. The net payment is equal to the floating-rate payment received by the fixed-rate payer less the fixed-rate payment made by the fixed-rate payer. The quarterly fixed-rate payment is $170,000. In the table below, a negative sign means that the fixed-rate payer must make a payment.

If 3-Month LIBOR Is	Floating-Rate Received	Net Payment by Fixed-Rate Payer
5.00%	$125,000	−$45,000
5.50%	137,500	−32,500
6.00%	150,000	−20,000
6.50%	162,500	−7,500
7.00%	175,000	5,000
7.50%	187,500	17,500
8.00%	200,000	30,000
8.50%	212,500	42,500

17. A. The risk that the investor faces is that, if 6-month LIBOR falls below 5%, then the return from the floater for the 6-month period (on an annual basis) would be less than the 7% borrowing cost (the fixed coupon rate of 7%). Thus, the investor is exposed to the risk of a decline in 6-month LIBOR. In general terms, the investor is mismatched with respect to assets (which are floating) and liabilities (which are fixed).

B. When there is a mismatch of the assets and liabilities as this investor faces, an interest rate swap can be used to convert a floating-rate asset into a fixed-rate asset or a fixed-rate liability into a floating-rate liability.

C. Note that the payments for the floater, the fixed-rate liability, and the swap are semiannual. Here are the cash flows from the asset, the liability, and the swap:

Cash inflow from the floater	=	6-month LIBOR + 200 basis points
Cash inflow from the swap	=	7.3%
Total cash inflow	=	9.3% + 6-month LIBOR

Cash outflow for the note issued	=	7%
Cash outflow for the swap	=	6-month LIBOR
Total cash outflow	=	7% + 6-month LIBOR

Net cash flow = annual income spread = 2.3% = 230 basis points

SOLUTIONS FOR READING 68

Solutions are for Practice Questions found in Reading.

1. In the computation, we will treat the Treasury issue as bond B and the corporate issue as bond A.

   A. GE versus Treasury

   $$\text{absolute yield spread} = 4.93\% - 4.18\% = 0.75\% = 75 \text{ basis points}$$

   $$\text{relative yield spread} = \frac{4.93\% - 4.18\%}{4.18\%} = 0.179 = 17.9\%$$

   $$\text{yield ratio} = \frac{4.93\%}{4.18\%} = 1.179$$

   B. Verizon versus Treasury

   $$\text{absolute yield spread} = 5.11\% - 4.18\% = 0.93\% = 93 \text{ basis points}$$

   $$\text{relative yield spread} = \frac{5.11\% - 4.18\%}{4.18\%} = 0.222 = 22.2\%$$

   $$\text{yield ratio} = \frac{5.11\%}{4.18\%} = 1.222$$

2. **A.** Since the call feature is unattractive to an investor because it results in call risk, the callable issues must offer higher yield spreads.

   B. The longer the protection against the issue being called, the lower the call risk. Consequently, the longer the deferred call period, the lower the yield spread.

3. **A.**

   $$\text{after-tax yield for Ms. High} = 0.068(1 - 0.40) = 0.0408 = 4.08\%$$
   $$\text{after-tax yield for Mr. Low} = 0.068(1 - 0.15) = 0.0578 = 5.78\%$$

   B.

   $$\text{taxable equivalent yield for Ms. High} = \frac{0.048}{1 - 0.40} = 0.0800 = 8.00\%$$

   $$\text{taxable equivalent yield for Mr. Low} = \frac{0.048}{1 - 0.15} = 0.0565 = 5.65\%$$

4. The annual income spread locked in is 2% or 200 basis points.

Asset Yield	3-Month LIBOR	Funding Cost	Fixed Rate Paid in Swap	3-Month LIBOR Rec. in Swap	Annual Income Spread*
8.60%	4.00%	4.60%	6.00%	4.00%	2.00%
8.60%	5.00%	5.60%	6.00%	5.00%	2.00%
8.60%	6.00%	6.60%	6.00%	6.00%	2.00%
8.60%	7.00%	7.60%	6.00%	7.00%	2.00%
8.60%	8.00%	8.60%	6.00%	8.00%	2.00%
8.60%	8.50%	9.10%	6.00%	8.50%	2.00%
8.60%	9.00%	9.60%	6.00%	9.00%	2.00%
8.60%	10.00%	10.60%	6.00%	10.00%	2.00%
8.60%	11.00%	11.60%	6.00%	11.00%	2.00%

* Annual income spread = Asset yield − Funding cost − Fixed rate paid in swap + 3-month LIBOR received in swap

SOLUTIONS FOR READING 70

1. The value is $107.6655 as shown below:

Year	Cash Flow	PV at 5.6%
1	7.4	7.0076
2	7.4	6.6360
3	7.4	6.2841
4	7.4	5.9508
5	107.4	81.7871
	Total	107.6655

2. The value is $96,326.46 as shown below

Year	Cash Flow	PV at 7.8%
1	$23,998.55	$22,262.11
2	23,998.55	20,651.30
3	23,998.55	19,157.05
4	23,998.55	17,770.92
5	23,998.55	16,485.09
	Total	96,326.47

3. A. The present value of the cash flows for the three discount rates is provided below:

Year	Cash Flow	PV at 4.5%	Cash Flow	PV at 6.2%	Cash Flow	PV at 7.3%
1	$6.2	$5.9330	$6.2	$5.8380	$6.2	$5.7782
2	6.2	5.6775	6.2	5.4972	6.2	5.3851
3	6.2	5.4330	6.2	5.1763	6.2	5.0187
4	6.2	5.1991	6.2	4.8741	6.2	4.6773
5	106.2	85.2203	106.2	78.6144	106.2	74.6665
	Total	107.4630	Total	100.0000	Total	95.5258

B. The following relationship holds:

- ► When the coupon rate (6.2%) is greater than the discount rate (4.5%), the bond's value is a premium to par value ($107.4630).
- ► When the coupon rate is equal to the discount rate, the bond's value is par value.
- ► When the coupon rate (6.2%) is less than the discount rate (7.3%), the bond's value is a discount to par value ($95.5258).

4. A basic property of a discount bond is that its price increases as it moves toward maturity assuming that interest rates do not change. Over the one year that the portfolio is being reviewed, while market yields have increased slightly, the bonds selling at a discount at the beginning of the year can increase despite a slight increase in the market yield since the beginning of the year.

5. A. The price is $95.9353 as shown below:

Year	Cash Flow	PV at 7%
1	5.8	5.4206
2	5.8	5.0659
3	5.8	4.7345
4	105.8	80.7143
	Total	$95.9353

B. The price of the 3-year 5.8% coupon bond assuming the yield is unchanged at 7% is $96.8508, as shown below.

Year	Cash Flow	PV at 7%
1	5.8	5.4206
2	5.8	5.0659
3	105.8	86.3643
	Total	$96.8508

C. The price is $98.9347 as shown below:

Year	Cash Flow	PV at 6.2%
1	5.8	5.4614
2	5.8	5.1426
3	105.8	88.3308
	Total	$98.9347

D.

Price change attributable to moving to maturity
    (no change in discount rate) $0.9155 (96.8508 − 95.9353)
Price change attribute to an increase in the
    discount rate from 7% to 6.2% $2.0839 (98.9347 − 96.8508)
Total price change $2.9994

6. The value is $94.2148 as shown below:

Year	Discount Rate	Cash Flow	PV
1	5.90%	5.8	5.4769
2	6.40%	5.8	5.1232
3	6.60%	5.8	4.7880
4	6.90%	5.8	4.4414
5	7.30%	105.8	74.3853
		Total	$94.2148

7. The value is $107.7561 as shown below:

Period	Discount Rate	Cash Flow	PV at 2.8%
1	0.028	3.7	3.5992
2	0.028	3.7	3.5012
3	0.028	3.7	3.4058
4	0.028	3.7	3.3131
5	0.028	3.7	3.2228
6	0.028	3.7	3.1350
7	0.028	3.7	3.0496
8	0.028	3.7	2.9666
9	0.028	3.7	2.8858
10	0.028	103.7	78.6770
		Total	107.7561

Alternatively, the short-cut formula can be used.

    semiannual coupon payment = $3.70
    semiannual discount rate   = 2.8%
    number of years   = 5

then

$$\$3.70 \times \left[\frac{1 - \dfrac{1}{(1.028)^{5 \times 2}}}{0.028} \right] = \$31.8864$$

To determine the price, the present value of the maturity value must be added to the present value of the coupon payments. The present value of the maturity value is

$$\text{present value of maturity value} = \frac{\$100}{(1.028)^{5\times2}} = \$75.8698$$

The price is then $107.7561 ($31.8864 + $75.8698). This agrees with our previous calculation for the price of this bond.

8.

$$\frac{\$1,000,000}{(1.038)^{40}} = \$224,960.29$$

9. A. First, w must be calculated. We know that

Days between settlement date and next coupon payment   115
Days in the coupon period   183

Therefore,

$$w\text{ periods} = \frac{115}{183} = 0.6284$$

Since the discount rate is 5.6%, the semiannual rate is 2.8%. The present value of the cash flows is $108.8676 and is therefore the full price.

Period	Cash Flow	PV at 2.8%
1	3.7	3.6363
2	3.7	3.5373
3	3.7	3.4410
4	3.7	3.3472
5	3.7	3.2561
6	3.7	3.1674
7	3.7	3.0811
8	3.7	2.9972
9	3.7	2.9155
10	103.7	79.4885
	Total	108.8676

B. The accrued interest is

$$\text{AI} = \text{semiannual coupon payment} \times (1 - w)$$
$$\text{AI} = \$3.7 \times (1 - 0.6284) = 1.3749$$

C. The clean price is

$$\text{clean price} = \text{full price} - \text{accrued interest}$$
$$\$108.8676 - \$1.3749 = \$107.4927$$

10. A. The arbitrage-free value was found in Practice Question 9A to be $111.3324.

  B. The price based on single discount rate of 5.65% is $111.1395 as shown below:

Period	Years	Cash Flow	PV at 2.825%
1	0.5	3.7	3.5983
2	1.0	3.7	3.4995
3	1.5	3.7	3.4033
4	2.0	3.7	3.3098
5	2.5	3.7	3.2189
6	3.0	3.7	3.1305
7	3.5	3.7	3.0445
8	4.0	3.7	2.9608
9	4.5	3.7	2.8795
10	5.0	3.7	2.8004
11	5.5	3.7	2.7234
12	6.0	3.7	2.6486
13	6.5	3.7	2.5758
14	7.0	3.7	2.5051
15	7.5	3.7	2.4362
16	8.0	103.7	66.4048
		Total	111.1395

  C. Dealers would buy the 7.4% 8-year issue for $111.1395, strip it, and sell the Treasury strips for $111.3324. The arbitrage profit is $0.1929 ($111.3324 − $111.1395). The table below shows how that arbitrage profit is realized.

Period	Years	Sell For	Buy For	Arbitrage profit
1	0.5	3.6453	3.5983	0.0470
2	1.0	3.5809	3.4995	0.0814
3	1.5	3.5121	3.4033	0.1087
4	2.0	3.4238	3.3098	0.1140
5	2.5	3.3155	3.2189	0.0966
6	3.0	3.2138	3.1305	0.0833
7	3.5	3.1167	3.0445	0.0722
8	4.0	3.0291	2.9608	0.0683
9	4.5	2.9407	2.8795	0.0612
10	5.0	2.8516	2.8004	0.0513
11	5.5	2.7621	2.7234	0.0387
12	6.0	2.6723	2.6486	0.0237
13	6.5	2.5822	2.5758	0.0064
14	7.0	2.5026	2.5051	−0.0024
15	7.5	2.4240	2.4362	−0.0123
16	8.0	65.7597	66.4048	−0.6451
Total		111.3324	111.1395	0.1929

D. The process of bidding up the price of the 7.4% 8-year Treasury issue by dealers in order to strip it will increase the price until no material arbitrage profit is available—the arbitrage-free value of $111.3324.

11. A. The arbitrage-free value was found in Practice Question 9B to be $89.3155.44.

B. The price based on a single discount rate of 5.65% is as shown below to be $89.4971.

Period	Years	Cash Flow	Present Value 2.825%
1	0.5	2	1.9451
2	1.0	2	1.8916
3	1.5	2	1.8396
4	2.0	2	1.7891
5	2.5	2	1.7399
6	3.0	2	1.6921
7	3.5	2	1.6457
8	4.0	2	1.6004
9	4.5	2	1.5565
10	5.0	2	1.5137
11	5.5	2	1.4721
12	6.0	2	1.4317
13	6.5	2	1.3923
14	7.0	2	1.3541
15	7.5	2	1.3169
16	8.0	102	65.3162
		Total	89.4971

C. The dealer will buy a package of Treasury strips such that the cash flow from the package will replicate the cash flow of a 4% 8-year Treasury issue and sell the overvalued Treasury issue. The cost of buying the package of Treasury strips is $89.3155. The value of selling the Treasury issue or, if reconstituted, the value of the synthetic coupon Treasury created is $89.4971. The arbitrage profit is therefore $0.1816 ($89.4971 − $89.3155).

D. The process of dealers selling the Treasury issue will drive down its prices until the market price is close to the arbitrage-free value of $89.3154.

SOLUTIONS FOR READING 70

Solutions are for Practice Questions found in Reading.

1. A. The cash flow per $100 of par value for this security is:

Year	Cash Flow
1	$7
2	7
3	7
4	7
5	107

The present value for each cash flow assuming a discount rate of 5% is:

$$Year\ 1: \text{present value}_1 = \frac{\$7}{(1.05)^1} = \$6.6667$$

$$Year\ 2: \text{present value}_2 = \frac{\$7}{(1.05)^2} = \$6.3492$$

$$Year\ 3: \text{present value}_3 = \frac{\$7}{(1.05)^3} = \$6.0469$$

$$Year\ 4: \text{present value}_4 = \frac{\$7}{(1.05)^4} = \$5.7589$$

$$Year\ 5: \text{present value}_5 = \frac{\$107}{(1.05)^5} = \$83.8373$$

The present value is the sum of the five present values above, $108.6590.

B. The cash flow for this security is $2,309.75 for each year. The present value of each cash flow assuming a discount rate of 6% is:

$$Year\ 1: \text{present value}_1 = \frac{\$2,309.75}{(1.06)^1} = \$2,179.0094$$

$$Year\ 2: \text{present value}_2 = \frac{\$2,309.75}{(1.06)^2} = \$2,055.6693$$

$$Year\ 3: \text{present value}_3 = \frac{\$2,309.75}{(1.06)^3} = \$1,939.3106$$

$$Year\ 4: \text{present value}_4 = \frac{\$2,309.75}{(1.06)^4} = \$1,829.5383$$

$$Year\ 5: \text{present value}_5 = \frac{\$2,309.75}{(1.06)^5} = \$1,725.9796$$

The present value of the five cash flows is $9,729.5072.

2. The present value for each cash flow assuming a discount rate of 4% is:

$$Year\ 1: \text{present value}_1 = \frac{\$7}{(1.04)^1} = \$6.7308$$

$$Year\ 2: \text{present value}_2 = \frac{\$7}{(1.04)^2} = \$6.4719$$

$$\textit{Year 3: } \text{present value}_3 = \frac{\$7}{(1.04)^3} = \$6.2230$$

$$\textit{Year 4: } \text{present value}_4 = \frac{\$7}{(1.04)^4} = \$5.9836$$

$$\textit{Year 5: } \text{present value}_5 = \frac{\$107}{(1.04)^5} = \$87.9462$$

The present value is the sum of the five present values above, $113.3555. A 4% discount produced a present value of $113.3555 which is greater than the present value of $108.6590 when the higher discount rate of 5% is used.

3. A. The value of the bond for the three discount rates is provided below:

Year	Present Value at 6%	Present Value at 7%	Present Value at 8%
1	$6.6038	$6.5421	$6.4815
2	6.2300	6.1141	6.0014
3	5.8773	5.7141	5.5568
4	5.5447	5.3403	5.1452
5	79.9566	76.2895	72.8224
	$104.2124	$100.0000	$96.0073

B. The following relationship holds:

▶ When the coupon rate is greater than the discount rate (7% versus 6%), the bond's value is a premium to par value ($104.2124).

▶ When the coupon rate is equal to the discount rate, the bond's value is par value.

▶ When the coupon rate is less than the discount rate (7% versus 8%), the bond's value is a discount to par value ($96.0073).

4. The cash flow per $100 of par value for this security is:

Year	Cash Flow
1	$7
2	7
3	7
4	7
5	107

The present value of each cash flow is

$$\textit{Year 1: } \text{present value}_1 = \frac{\$7}{(1.035)^1} = \$6.7633$$

$$\textit{Year 2: } \text{present value}_2 = \frac{\$7}{(1.039)^2} = \$6.4844$$

$$\textit{Year 3: present value}_3 = \frac{\$7}{(1.042)^3} = \$6.1872$$

$$\textit{Year 4: present value}_4 = \frac{\$7}{(1.045)^4} = \$5.8699$$

$$\textit{Year 5: present value}_5 = \frac{\$107}{(1.050)^5} = \$83.8373$$

The sum of the present values is $109.1421.

5. The semiannual cash flows for the first 9 six-month periods per $100 of par value is $3.50. For the last period, the cash flow is $103.50. The semiannual discount rate is 2.5%. The present value of each cash flow discounted at 2.5% is shown below:

$$\textit{Year 1: present value}_1 = \frac{\$3.5}{(1.025)^1} = \$3.4146$$

$$\textit{Year 2: present value}_2 = \frac{\$3.5}{(1.025)^2} = \$3.3314$$

$$\textit{Year 3: present value}_3 = \frac{\$3.5}{(1.025)^3} = \$3.2501$$

$$\textit{Year 4: present value}_4 = \frac{\$3.5}{(1.025)^4} = \$3.1708$$

$$\textit{Year 5: present value}_5 = \frac{\$3.5}{(1.025)^5} = \$3.0935$$

$$\textit{Year 6: present value}_6 = \frac{\$3.5}{(1.025)^6} = \$3.0180$$

$$\textit{Year 7: present value}_7 = \frac{\$3.5}{(1.025)^7} = \$2.9444$$

$$\textit{Year 8: present value}_8 = \frac{\$3.5}{(1.025)^8} = \$2.8726$$

$$\textit{Year 9: present value}_9 = \frac{\$3.5}{(1.025)^9} = \$2.8025$$

$$\textit{Year 10: present value}_{10} = \frac{\$103.5}{(1.025)^{10}} = \$80.8540$$

The value of this bond is the sum of the present values, $108.7519.

Alternatively, the short-cut formula can be used. The present value of the coupon payments is:

$$\$3.5 \times \left[\frac{1 - \dfrac{1}{(1.025)^{5 \times 2}}}{0.025} \right] = \$30.6322$$

The present value of the maturity value is

$$\text{present value of maturity} = \frac{\$100}{(1.025)^{5 \times 2}} = \$78.1198$$

The price is then $108.7520 (= $30.6322 + $78.1198), the same value as computed above.

6. A. The value given the semiannual discount rate i (one-half the annual discount rate) is found by the following formula:

$$\frac{\$1,000}{(1 + i)^{20}}$$

The solutions follow:

Annual Discount Rate	Semiannual Discount Rate	Present Value
1%	0.5%	905.0629
2%	1.0%	819.5445
3%	1.5%	742.4704
4%	2.0%	672.9713
5%	2.5%	610.2709
6%	3.0%	553.6758
7%	3.5%	502.5659
8%	4.0%	456.3869
9%	4.5%	414.6429
10%	5.0%	376.8895
11%	5.5%	342.7290
12%	6.0%	311.8047
13%	6.5%	283.7970
14%	7.0%	258.4190

B.

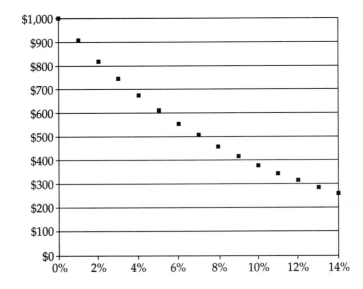

7. First, w must be calculated. We know that

Days between settlement date and next coupon payment   58
Days in the coupon period   183

Therefore,

$$w \text{ periods} = \frac{58}{183} = 0.3169$$

Since the discount rate is 5%, the semiannual rate is 2.5%. The present value of each cash flow is:

$$Year\ 1: \text{present value}_1 = \frac{\$3.5}{(1.025)^{0.3169}} = \$3.4727$$

$$Year\ 2: \text{present value}_2 = \frac{\$3.5}{(1.025)^{1.3169}} = \$3.3880$$

$$Year\ 3: \text{present value}_3 = \frac{\$3.5}{(1.025)^{2.3169}} = \$3.3054$$

$$Year\ 4: \text{present value}_4 = \frac{\$3.5}{(1.025)^{3.3169}} = \$3.2248$$

$$Year\ 5: \text{present value}_5 = \frac{\$3.5}{(1.025)^{4.3169}} = \$3.1461$$

$$Year\ 6: \text{present value}_6 = \frac{\$3.5}{(1.025)^{5.3169}} = \$3.0694$$

$$Year\ 7: \text{present value}_7 = \frac{\$3.5}{(1.025)^{6.3169}} = \$2.9945$$

$$Year\ 8: \text{present value}_8 = \frac{\$3.5}{(1.025)^{7.3169}} = \$2.9215$$

$$Year\ 9: \text{present value}_9 = \frac{\$3.5}{(1.025)^{8.3169}} = \$2.8502$$

$$Year\ 10: \text{present value}_{10} = \frac{\$103.5}{(1.025)^{9.3169}} = \$82.2293$$

The full price for this bond is the sum of the present values, \$110.6019.

8. The value of w is 0.3169 and the coupon interest for the period is \$3.50. Therefore, the accrued interest is:

$$AI = \$3.5 \times (1 - 0.3169) = \$2.3908$$

Since the full price is \$110.6019, the clean price is

$$\text{clean price} = \$110.6019 - \$2.3908 = \$108.2111$$

9. A. The value for the 7.4% coupon 8-year Treasury security is $111.3324 as shown below:

Period	Years	Cash Flow ($)	Spot Rate (%)	Present Value ($)
1	0.5	3.7	3.0000	3.6453
2	1.0	3.7	3.3000	3.5809
3	1.5	3.7	3.5053	3.5121
4	2.0	3.7	3.9164	3.4238
5	2.5	3.7	4.4376	3.3155
6	3.0	3.7	4.7520	3.2138
7	3.5	3.7	4.9622	3.1167
8	4.0	3.7	5.0650	3.0291
9	4.5	3.7	5.1701	2.9407
10	5.0	3.7	5.2772	2.8516
11	5.5	3.7	5.3864	2.7621
12	6.0	3.7	5.4976	2.6723
13	6.5	3.7	5.6108	2.5822
14	7.0	3.7	5.6643	2.5026
15	7.5	3.7	5.7193	2.4240
16	8.0	103.7	5.7755	65.7597
		Total		111.3324

B. The value for the 4% coupon 8-year Treasury security is $89.3155 as shown below:

Period	Years	Cash Flow ($)	Spot Rate (%)	Present Value ($)
1	0.5	2	3.0000	1.9704
2	1.0	2	3.3000	1.9356
3	1.5	2	3.5053	1.8984
4	2.0	2	3.9164	1.8507
5	2.5	2	4.4376	1.7922
6	3.0	2	4.7520	1.7372
7	3.5	2	4.9622	1.6847
8	4.0	2	5.0650	1.6373
9	4.5	2	5.1701	1.5895
10	5.0	2	5.2772	1.5414
11	5.5	2	5.3864	1.4930
12	6.0	2	5.4976	1.4445
13	6.5	2	5.6108	1.3958
14	7.0	2	5.6643	1.3528
15	7.5	2	5.7193	1.3103
16	8.0	102	5.7755	64.6817
		Total		89.3155

SOLUTIONS FOR READING 71

1. The three sources are (1) coupon interest, (2) any capital gain (or loss, a reduction in return), and (3) reinvestment income.

2. **A.** The current yield for the bond is

   annual coupon payment $= 0.09 \times \$100 = \$9$

   current yield $= \dfrac{\$9}{\$112} = 0.0804 = 8.04\%$

   B. The current yield measure only considers coupon interest and ignores any capital gain or loss (a capital loss of $12 for the bond in our example), and reinvestment income.

3. The present value of the cash flows of a 6.5% 20-year semiannual-pay bond using the three discount rates is shown below:

Discount Rate (annual BEY)	Semiannual Rate (half annual rate)	Present Value of Cash Flows
7.2%	3.6%	92.64
7.4	3.7	90.68
7.8	3.9	86.94

   Since 3.7% equates the present value of the cash flows to the price of 90.68, 3.7% is the semiannual yield to maturity. Doubling that rate gives a 7.4% yield to maturity on a bond-equivalent basis.

4. This question requires no calculations. (Note that the maturity of each bond is intentionally omitted.) The question tests for an understanding of the relationship between coupon rate, current yield, and yield to maturity for a bond trading at par, a discount, and a premium.

   ▶ Bond A's current yield is incorrect. The current yield should be equal to the coupon rate.

   ▶ Bond B is fine. That is, it has the expected relationship between coupon rate, current yield, and yield to maturity for a bond trading at a premium.

   ▶ Bond C's yield to maturity is incorrect. Since the bond is a premium bond, the yield to maturity should be less than the coupon rate.

   ▶ Bond D is fine. That is, it has the expected relationship between coupon rate, current yield, and yield to maturity for a bond trading at a discount.

   ▶ Bond E is incorrect. Both the current yield and the yield to maturity should be greater than the coupon rate since the bond is trading at a discount.

5. The statement is misleading in that while it is true that the yield to maturity computed on a bond-equivalent basis is flawed, it is not the reason why the yield to maturity is limited. The major reason is that it assumes that the

bond is held to maturity and the coupon payments are assumed to be reinvested at the computed yield to maturity.

6. A. The total future dollars are found as follows:

$$\$108.32(1.035)^{10} = \$152.80$$

B. Since the total future dollars are $152.80 and the investment is $108.32, the total interest from the CD is $44.48.

C. The answer is the same as for parts A and B. The total future dollars are $152.80. The total dollar return is the same as the total interest, $44.48.

D. The answer is the same as for part C:

total future dollars = $152.80
total dollar return   = $ 44.48

E.

coupon interest   = $ 45.00
capital gain/loss   = -$ 8.32
reinvestment income   = $ 7.80
total dollar return   = $ 44.48

F. The percentage of the total dollar return that must be generated from reinvestment income is 17.5% ($7.80/$44.48).

G. The $7.80 reinvestment income must be generated by reinvesting the semiannual coupon payments from the time of receipt to the maturity date at the semiannual yield to maturity, 3.5% in this example. The reinvestment income earned on a given coupon payment of $4.50 if it is invested from the time of receipt in period t to the maturity date (10 periods in our example) at a 3.5% semiannual rate is:

$$\$4.50(1.035)^{10-t} - \$4.50$$

The reinvestment income for each coupon payment is shown below:

Period	Periods Reinvested	Coupon Payment	Reinvestment Income at 3.5%
1	9	$4.5	$1.63
2	8	4.5	1.43
3	7	4.5	1.23
4	6	4.5	1.03
5	5	4.5	0.84
6	4	4.5	0.66
7	3	4.5	0.49
8	2	4.5	0.32
9	1	4.5	0.16
10	0	4.5	0.00
		Total	7.79

The reinvestment income totals $7.79 which differs from $7.80 due to rounding.

7. **A.** Bond X has no dependence on reinvestment income since it is a zero-coupon bond. So it is either Bond Y or Bond Z. The two bonds have the same maturity. Since they are both selling at the same yield, Bond Z, the one with the higher coupon rate, is more dependent on reinvestment income.

    B. As explained in part A, since Bond X is a zero-coupon bond, it has the least dependence (in fact, no dependence) on reinvestment income.

8. The reinvestment risk is that to realize the computed yield, it is necessary to reinvest the interim cash flows (i.e., coupon payments in the case of a non-amortizing security and principal plus coupon payments in the case of an amortizing security) at the computed yield. The interest rate risk comes into play because it is assumed the security will be held to the maturity date. If it is not, the yield no longer applies because there is the risk of having to sell the security below its purchase price.

9. **A.** The bond-equivalent yield is

$$2[(1.056)^{0.5} - 1] = 0.0552 = 5.52\%$$

    B. The annual yield is

$$[(1.028)^2 - 1] = 0.0568 = 5.68\%$$

10. **A.** The cash flows for this bond to the maturity date are (1) 30 coupon payments of $5 and (2) $100 at the maturity date. The table below shows the present values of the coupon payments and maturity value for the three interest rates in the question:

Annual Interest Rate (%)	Semiannual Interest Rate (%)	Present Value of 30 Payments of $5	Present Value of $100 30 Periods From Now	Present value of Cash Flows
7.0	3.5	91.9602	35.6278	127.5880
7.4	3.7	89.6986	33.6231	123.3217
7.8	3.9	87.5197	31.7346	119.2543

    Since a semiannual interest rate of 3.5% produces a present value equal to the price of the bond ($127.5880), the yield to maturity is 7% on a bond-equivalent basis.

    B. The cash flows for this bond up to the first call date are (1) 10 coupon payments of $5 and (2) $105 ten 6-month periods from now. The table below shows the present values of the coupon payments and maturity value for the three interest rates in the question:

Annual Interest Rate (%)	Semiannual Interest Rate (%)	Present Value of 10 Payments of $5	Present Value of $105 10 Periods From Now	Present Value of Cash Flows
4.55	2.275	44.2735	83.8483	128.1218
4.65	2.325	44.1587	83.4395	127.5982
4.85	2.425	43.9304	82.6284	126.5588

Since of the three interest rates in the question, a semiannual interest rate of 2.325% makes the present value of the cash flows closest to the price of $127.5880, the yield to the first call date is 4.65% on a bond-equivalent basis.

C. The cash flows for this bond up to the first par call date are (1) 20 coupon payments of $5 and (2) $100 twenty 6-month periods from now. The table below shows the present values of the coupon payments and maturity value for the three interest rates in the question:

Annual Interest Rate (%)	Semiannual Interest Rate (%)	Present Value of 20 Payments of $5	Present Value of $100 20 Periods From Now	Present Value of Cash Flows
6.25	3.125	73.5349	54.0407	127.5756
6.55	3.275	72.5308	52.4923	125.0231
6.75	3.375	71.8725	51.4860	123.3585

Since of the three interest rates in the question, a semiannual interest rate of 3.125% makes the present value of the cash flows closest to the price of $127.5880, the yield to the first par call date is 6.25% on a bond-equivalent basis.

11. The cash flows to the put date are (1) 8 coupon payments of $2.50 and (2) $100 (the put price) eight 6-month periods from now. The table below shows the present values of the coupon payments and maturity value for the three interest rates in the question:

Annual Interest Rate (%)	Semiannual Interest Rate (%)	Present Value of 8 Payments of $2.5	Present Value of $100 8 Periods From Now	Present Value of Cash Flows
3.38	1.690	18.5609	87.4529	106.0136
3.44	1.720	18.5367	87.2467	105.7834
3.57	1.785	18.4846	86.8020	105.2866

Since of the three interest rates in the question, a semiannual interest rate of 1.785% makes the present value of the cash flows closest to the price of $105.2877, the yield to the put date is 3.57% on a bond-equivalent basis.

12. First, the semiannual effective yield is computed from the monthly yield by compounding it for six months as follows:

$$\text{effective semiannual yield} = (1.0041)^6 - 1 = 0.024854 = 2.4854\%$$

Next, the effective semiannual yield is doubled to get the annual cash flow yield on a bond-equivalent basis. Thus, the cash flow yield on a bond-equivalent basis is 4.97% (2 times 2.4854%).

13. You should agree with Manager B. The cash flow yield, as with any other yield measure such as the yield to maturity or any yield to call date, requires that the investor be able to reinvest any interim cash flows in order to realize the computed yield. A cash flow yield is even more dependent on reinvestment income because the interim cash flows are monthly coupon and principal, rather than simply semiannual coupon for a standard coupon bond. Consequently, the reinvestment risk is greater with an amortizing security.

14. The table below shows the present value using the three discount margins:

5-year floater

current LIBOR   5.00%

quoted margin   30 basis points

				Present Value ($) at Assumed Margin of		
Period	LIBOR (annual rate) (%)	Coupon rate (%)	Cash Flow ($)	40 5.400%	50 5.500%	55 5.550%
1	5.00	5.300	2.65	2.5803	2.5791	2.5784
2	5.00	5.300	2.65	2.5125	2.5100	2.5088
3	5.00	5.300	2.65	2.4464	2.4429	2.4411
4	5.00	5.300	2.65	2.3821	2.3775	2.3752
5	5.00	5.300	2.65	2.3195	2.3139	2.3110
6	5.00	5.300	2.65	2.2585	2.2519	2.2486
7	5.00	5.300	2.65	2.1991	2.1917	2.1879
8	5.00	5.300	2.65	2.1413	2.1330	2.1289
9	5.00	5.300	2.65	2.0850	2.0759	2.0714
10	5.00	5.300	102.65	78.6420	78.2601	78.0700
			Total	99.5669	99.1360	98.9214

When a margin of 50 basis points is used, the present value of the cash flows is equal to the price ($99.1360).

15. The discount margin ignores both and hence is a limitation of this measure. The cap is not considered because the reference rate is assumed to be unchanged at the current value for the reference rate. The only way in which the cap is considered is in the special case where the current value for the reference rate is capped and in this case it assumes that the reference rate will not fall below the cap for the life of the floater.

16. A. The yield on a discount basis, d, is

$$(1 - 0.989)\left(\frac{360}{105}\right) = 0.0377 = 3.77\%$$

B. The price of this Treasury bill, p, per $1 dollar of maturity value is:

$$1 - 0.0368\ (275/360) = 0.971889$$

C. The yield on a discount basis has two major shortcomings. First, it relates the interest return to the maturity or face value rather than the amount invested. Second, it is based on a 360-day year rather than 365-day year as used for Treasury coupon securities.

17. Beyond the 1-year maturity, there are only a few on-the-run Treasury issues available: 2 year, 5 year, and 10 year. For the 30-year maturity, market participants estimate the yield based on the last 30-year Treasury bond that was issued by the U.S. Department of the Treasury. The yield for interim maturities is calculated using an interpolation methodology. The simplest is linear interpolation; however, more elaborate statistical methods can be used.

18. We will use the same notation as in the reading. One-half the annualized spot rate for a 6-month period will be denoted by z_t. We know that the 6-month Treasury bill yield is 4.6% and the 1-year Treasury yield is 5.0%, so

$$z_1 = 4.6\%/2 = 2.3\% \quad \text{and} \quad z_2 = 5.0\%/2 = 2.5\%$$

Now we use the bootstrapping methodology. The 1.5-year Treasury yield from the Treasury yield curve is selling to yield 5.4%. Since the price of the issue is its par value, the coupon rate is 5.4%. So, the cash flow for this issue is:

0.5 year	$0.054 \times \$100 \times 0.5$	$= \$2.70$
1.0 year	$0.054 \times \$100 \times 0.5$	$= \$2.70$
1.5 years	$0.054 \times \$100 \times 0.5 \ + \$100$	$= \$102.70$

The present value of the cash flows is then:

$$\frac{2.7}{(1 + z_1)^1} + \frac{2.7}{(1 + z_2)^2} + \frac{102.7}{(1 + z_3)^3}$$

Substituting the first two spot rates we have:

$$\frac{2.7}{(1.023)^1} + \frac{2.7}{(1.025)^2} + \frac{102.7}{(1 + z_3)^3}$$

The goal is to find z_3. Since the value of this cash flow must be equal to the price of the 1.5-year issue which is par value, we can set the previous equation equal to 100:

$$\frac{2.7}{(1.023)^1} + \frac{2.7}{(1.025)^2} + \frac{102.7}{(1 + z_3)^3} = 100$$

We then solve for z_3 as follows:

$$2.639296 + 2.569899 + \frac{102.7}{(1 + z_3)^3} = 100$$

$$\frac{102.7}{(1 + z_3)^3} = 94.7908$$

$$z_3 = 0.027073 = 2.7073\%$$

Doubling this yield we obtain the bond-equivalent yield of 5.4146%.

The equation for obtaining the 2-year, 2.5-year, and 3-year spot rates are given below.

For the 2-year spot rate, the coupon rate from the Treasury yield curve is 5.8%. So, the present value of the cash flow is:

$$\frac{2.9}{(1 + z_1)^1} + \frac{2.9}{(1 + z_2)^2} + \frac{2.9}{(1 + z_3)^3} + \frac{102.9}{(1 + z_4)^4}$$

Substituting: $z_1 = 2.3\%$ $z_2 = 2.5\%$ $z_3 = 2.7073\%$
and setting the present value equal to the price of the 2-year issue (100), we obtain:

$$\frac{2.9}{(1.023)^1} + \frac{2.9}{(1.025)^2} + \frac{2.9}{(1.027073)^3} + \frac{102.9}{(1 + z_4)^4} = 100$$

Solving the above equation we would find that z_4 is 2.9148%. Therefore, the 2- year spot rate on a bond-equivalent basis is 5.8297%.

For the 2.5-year spot rate, we use the 2.5-year issue from the par yield curve. The yield is 6.4% and therefore the coupon rate is 6.4%. The present value of the cash flow for this issue is then:

$$\frac{3.2}{(1 + z_1)^1} + \frac{3.2}{(1 + z_2)^2} + \frac{3.2}{(1 + z_3)^3} + \frac{3.2}{(1 + z_4)^4} + \frac{103.2}{(1 + z_5)^5}$$

Substituting: $z_1 = 2.3\%$ $z_2 = 2.5\%$ $z_3 = 2.7073\%$ $z_4 = 2.9148\%$
and setting the present value equal to the price of the 2.5-year issue (100), we obtain:

$$\frac{3.2}{(1.023)^1} + \frac{3.2}{(1.025)^2} + \frac{3.2}{(1.027073)^3} + \frac{3.2}{(1.029148)^4} + \frac{103.2}{(1 + z_5)^5} = 100$$

Solving the above equation we would find that z_5 is 3.2333%. Therefore, the 2.5-year spot rate on a bond-equivalent basis is 6.4665%.

For the 3-year spot rate, we use the 3-year issue from the par yield curve. The yield is 7.0% and therefore the coupon rate is 7.0%. The present value of the cash flow for this issue is then:

$$\frac{3.5}{(1 + z_1)^1} + \frac{3.5}{(1 + z_2)^2} + \frac{3.5}{(1 + z_3)^3} + \frac{3.5}{(1 + z_4)^4} + \frac{3.5}{(1 + z_5)^5} + \frac{103.5}{(1 + z_6)^6}$$

Substituting: $z_1 = 2.3\%$ $z_2 = 2.5\%$ $z_3 = 2.7073\%$ $z_4 = 2.9148\%$
$z_5 = 3.2333\%$ and setting the present value equal to the price of the 3-year issue (100), we obtain:

$$\frac{3.5}{(1.023)^1} + \frac{3.5}{(1.025)^2} + \frac{3.5}{(1.027073)^3} + \frac{3.5}{(1.029148)^4} + \frac{3.5}{(1.032333)^5} + \frac{103.5}{(1 + z_6)^6} = 100$$

Solving the above equation we would find that z_6 is 3.5586%. Therefore, the 3-year spot rate on a bond-equivalent basis is 7.1173%.

To summarize the findings for the spot rates:

Period	Year	Annualized Spot Rate (BEY)	z_t
1	0.5	4.6000%	2.3000%
2	1.0	5.0000	2.5000
3	1.5	5.4146	2.7073
4	2.0	5.8297	2.9148
5	2.5	6.4665	3.2333
6	3.0	7.1173	3.5586

19. To obtain the arbitrage-free value of an 8% coupon 3-year Treasury bond, the cash flows for the bond are discounted at the spot rates in the previous question as shown below:

Period	Annual Spot Rate (%)	Semiannual Spot Rate (%)	Cash Flow	PV of CF
1	4.6000	2.3000	$4.0	$3.9101
2	5.0000	2.5000	4.0	3.8073
3	5.4146	2.7073	4.0	3.6919
4	5.8297	2.9148	4.0	3.5657
5	6.4665	3.2333	4.0	3.4116
6	7.1173	3.5586	104.0	84.3171
			Total	$102.7037

The arbitrage-free value of this bond is $102.7037.

20. The nominal spread fails to take into consideration (1) the shape of the yield curve (and therefore spot rates) and (2) any option embedded in a bond.

21. The Z-spread relative to the Treasury spot rate curve is the spread that when added to all the Treasury spot rates will produce a present value for the cash flows equal to the market price. The present value using each of the three spreads in the question—80, 90, and 100 basis points—is shown below:

Period	Years to Maturity	Spot Rate (BEY) (%)	Semiannual Spot Rate (%)	Cash Flow	PV at Assumed Spread (bp) 80	90	100
1	0.5	5.0	2.50	$3	$2.9155	$2.9140	$2.9126
2	1.0	5.4	2.70	3	2.8223	2.8196	2.8168
3	1.5	5.8	2.90	3	2.7216	2.7176	2.7137
4	2.0	6.4	3.20	3	2.6042	2.5992	2.5942
5	2.5	7.0	3.50	3	2.4777	2.4717	2.4658
6	3.0	7.2	3.60	3	2.3709	2.3641	2.3573
7	3.5	7.4	3.70	3	2.2645	2.2569	2.2493
8	4.0	7.8	3.90	103	73.5466	73.2652	72.9849
				Total	91.7233	91.4083	91.0947

The last three columns in the table show the assumed spread. One-half of the spread is added to the column showing the semiannual spot rate. Then the cash flow is discounted used the semiannual spot rate plus one-half the assumed spread.

As can be seen, when a 90 basis point spread is used, the present value of the cash flow is equal to the price of the non-Treasury issue, $91.4083. Therefore, the Z-spread is 90 basis points.

22. When the yield curve is flat, all the cash flows are discounted at the same rate. Therefore, if Treasury securities are the benchmark, the nominal spread will be equal to the Z-spread. So, in the case of the corporate bond issues where there is no embedded option, using either measure is acceptable. In contrast, for corporate bonds issues in the portfolio with embedded options, the option-adjusted spread is more appropriate than either the nominal spread or the Z-spread regardless of the shape of the yield curve. Consequently, Joan Thomas would have to agree that the option-adjusted spread should be used for the corporate issues with embedded options.

23. **A.** There are several assumptions that are made in valuing bonds with embedded options. One important assumption is interest rate volatility. Because these assumptions differ from dealer to dealer, the OAS values may differ substantially.

   B. The relationship between the OAS, Z-spread, and option cost is as follows:

   $$\text{option cost} = \text{Z-spread} - \text{OAS}$$

   If a bond has no embedded option, then there is no option cost. That is, the option cost is zero. Substituting zero into the above equation, we have

   $$\text{Z-spread} = \text{OAS}$$

   That is, the Z-spread is equal to the OAS. This is the reason why Mr. Tinker observed that for the issues with no embedded options the OAS is the same as the Z-spread.

   C. A negative value for the option cost means that the investor has purchased an option from the issuer. A putable bond is an example of where the investor purchases an option. This explains why Mr. Tinker finds that a negative value for the option cost was reported for the putable bond issues. When there is no embedded option, the option cost is zero and that is why Mr. Tinker finds this value for issues with this characteristic. A positive value for the option cost means that the investor has sold an option to the issuer. This occurs for callable bond issues, as Mr. Tinker observes.

24. **A.** Because the Treasury securities are the benchmark, the OAS reflects a spread to compensate for credit risk and liquidity risk. (Remember that option risk has already been removed.)

   B. Since the benchmark is the issuer's on-the-run yield curve, the spread already reflects credit risk. So, basically the OAS reflects compensation for liquidity risk. (Remember that option risk has already been removed.)

C. The answer depends on the benchmark interest rates used by the dealer firm. If the benchmark interest rates are Treasury rates, then the OAS is better for the issue that Mr. Dumas is considering. If the benchmark is the issuer's on-the-run yield curve, then the issue that the dealer is offering to Mr. Dumas is more attractive. However, the qualifier is that the answer also depends on the interest rate volatility assumed by the dealer and the interest rate volatility assumed by Mr. Dumas when analyzing the issue using System A and System B. Without knowing the assumed interest rate volatilities, no statement can be made about the relative value of these two issues.

25. We will use these notations in the reading:

> f will denote the forward rate
> t will be the subscript before f and will indicate the length of time that the rate applies
> m will be the subscript after f and will indicate when the forward rate begins

All periods are equal to six months.

The forward rate is then found as follows:

$$_{t}f_{m} = \left[\frac{(1 + z_{m+t})^{m+t}}{(1 + z_{m})^{m}} \right]^{1/t} - 1$$

A. For the 6-month forward rate six months from now, $t = 1$ and $m = 1$. Therefore,

$$_{1}f_{1} = \left[\frac{(1 + z_{1+1})^{1+1}}{(1 + z_{1})^{1}} \right]^{1/1} - 1$$

or

$$_{1}f_{1} = \left[\frac{(1 + z_{2})^{2}}{(1 + z_{1})^{1}} \right]^{1} - 1$$

Since

$$z_{1} = 5.0\%/2 = 2.5\% \quad \text{and} \quad z_{2} = 5.4\%/2 = 2.7\%$$

then

$$_{1}f_{1} = \left[\frac{(1.027)^{2}}{(1.025)^{1}} \right]^{1} - 1 = 0.029004 = 2.9004\%$$

Then the annualized 6-month forward rate six months from now on a bond-equivalent basis is 5.8008%.

B. For the 6-month forward rate one year from now, $t = 1$ and $m = 2$. Therefore,

$$_{1}f_{2} = \left[\frac{(1 + z_{2+1})^{2+1}}{(1 + z_{2})^{2}} \right]^{1/1} - 1$$

or

$$_1f_2 = \left[\frac{(1 + z_3)^3}{(1 + z_2)^2}\right]^1 - 1$$

Since

$$z_2 = 5.4\%/2 = 2.7\% \quad \text{and} \quad z_3 = 5.8\%/2 = 2.9\%$$

then

$$_1f_2 = \left[\frac{(1.029)^3}{(1.027)^2}\right]^1 - 1 = 0.033012 = 3.3012\%$$

Then the annualized 6-month forward rate one year from now on a bond-equivalent basis is 6.6023%.

C. For the 6-month forward rate three years from now, $t = 1$ and $m = 6$. Therefore,

$$_1f_6 = \left[\frac{(1 + z_{6+1})^{6+1}}{(1 + z_6)^6}\right]^{1/1} - 1$$

or

$$_1f_6 = \left[\frac{(1 + z_7)^7}{(1 + z_6)^6}\right]^{1/1} - 1$$

Since

$$z_6 = 7.2\%/2 = 3.6\% \quad \text{and} \quad z_7 = 7.4\%/2 = 3.7\%$$

then

$$_1f_6 = \left[\frac{(1.037)^7}{(1.036)^6}\right]^{1/1} - 1 = 0.04302 = 4.302\%$$

Then the annualized 6-month forward rate three years from now on a bond-equivalent basis is 8.6041%.

D. For the 2-year forward rate one year from now, $t = 4$ and $m = 2$. Therefore,

$$_4f_2 = \left[\frac{(1 + z_{4+2})^{4+2}}{(1 + z_2)^2}\right]^{1/4} - 1$$

or

$$_4f_2 = \left[\frac{(1 + z_6)^6}{(1 + z_2)^2}\right]^{1/4} - 1$$

Since

$$z_2 = 5.4\%/2 = 2.7\% \quad \text{and} \quad z_6 = 7.2\%/2 = 3.6\%$$

then

$$_4f_2 = \left[\frac{(1.036)^6}{(1.027)^2}\right]^{1/4} - 1 = 0.04053 = 4.053\%$$

Then the annualized 2-year forward rate one year from now on a bond-equivalent basis is 8.1059%.

E. For the 1-year forward rate two years from now, $t = 2$ and $m = 4$. Therefore,

$$_2f_4 = \left[\frac{(1 + z_{2+4})^{2+4}}{(1 + z_4)^4}\right]^{1/2} - 1$$

or

$$_2f_4 = \left[\frac{(1 + z_6)^6}{(1 + z_4)^4}\right]^{1/2} - 1$$

Since

$$z_4 = 6.4\%/2 = 3.2\% \quad \text{and} \quad z_6 = 7.2\%/2 = 3.6\%$$

then

$$_2f_4 = \left[\frac{(1.036)^6}{(1.032)^4}\right]^{1/2} - 1 = 0.04405 = 4.405\%$$

Then the annualized 1-year forward rate two years from now on a bond-equivalent basis is 8.810%.

26. The 6-month forward rate six months from now as found in the previous question is 5.8008%. The two alternatives are:

Alternative 1: Invest $X at the 1-year spot rate of 5.4% for one year
Alternative 2: Invest $X today at the 6-month spot rate of 5.0% and reinvest at the end of six months the proceeds at the 6-month forward rate of 5.8008%

For Alternative 1, the amount at the end of one year will be:

$X (1 + 0.054/2)^2 = 1.054729 (\$X)$

For Alternative 2, the amount at the end of one year will be:

$X (1 + 0.05/2) (1 + 0.058008/2) = 1.054729 (\$X)$

Thus, the two alternatives produce the same future value if the 6-month forward rate six months from now is 5.8008%.

27. Discounting at spot rates and forward rates will produce the same value for a bond. This is because spot rates are nothing more than packages of short-term forward rates. So, the second sales person's comment is wrong about the superiority of forward rates for valuation compared to spot rates.

28. A. The forward discount factor for period T is computed as follows.

$$\frac{1}{(1 + z_1)(1 + {}_1f_1)(1 + {}_1f_2)...(1 + {}_1f_{T-1})}$$

Therefore,

Period	Annual Forward Rate (BEY)	Semiannual Rate	Forward Discount Factor
1	4.00%	2.00%	0.980392
2	4.40	2.20	0.959288
3	5.00	2.50	0.935891
4	5.60	2.80	0.910399
5	6.00	3.00	0.883883
6	6.40	3.20	0.856476

B. The value is found by multiplying each cash flow by the forward discount factor for the period as shown below:

Period	Forward Discount Factor	Cash Flow	PV of Cash Flow
1	0.980392	$4	$3.921569
2	0.959288	4	3.837151
3	0.935891	4	3.743562
4	0.910399	4	3.641598
5	0.883883	4	3.535532
6	0.856476	104	89.073470
		Total	$107.752881

The value of this bond is $107.752881.

SOLUTIONS FOR READING 71

Solutions are for Practice Questions found in Reading.

1. The cash flow for this bond is 30 payments of $3 plus a maturity value of $100 thirty 6-month periods from now. Below is the present value of the cash flow when discounted at one-half the yields of 7.2%, 7.6%, and 7.8%. The short-cut formula given in Reading 66 was used so the information is provided for the present value of the coupon payments and the present value of the maturity value.

Annual rate (BEY)	7.2%	7.6%	7.8%
Semiannual rate	3.6%	3.8%	3.9%
Present value of:			
Coupon payments	54.49	53.16	52.51
Maturity value	34.61	32.66	31.74
Total present value	89.10	85.82	84.25

Since the semiannual discount rate of 3.9% equates the present value of the cash flows to the price of $84.25, 3.9% is the semiannual yield to maturity. Doubling this yield gives a yield to maturity of 7.8% on a bond equivalent basis.

2. **A.** The total future dollars from an investment of $89.32 if the yield is 7% is:

$$\$89.32 \times (1.035)^{40} = \$353.64$$

Decomposing the total future dollars we see that:

Total future dollars	= $353.64
Return of principal	= $ 89.32
Total dollar return	= $264.32

Without reinvestment income, the dollar return is:

Coupon interest	= $120.00
Capital gain	= $ 10.68
Dollar return	= $130.68

The dollar return shortfall is therefore $133.64 ($264.32 − $130.68). This shortfall is made up if the coupon payments can be reinvested at a yield of 7% (the yield on the bond at the time of purchase). For this bond, the reinvestment income is 51% of the total dollar return needed to produce a yield of 7% ($133.64/$264.32).

   B. There are no coupon payments to reinvest because the coupon rate is 0%. Therefore, no portion of the dollar return of a zero-coupon bond comes from reinvestment income.

3. **A.** The bond-equivalent yield is

$$2[(1.048)^{0.5} - 1] = 4.74\%$$

B. The annual yield is

$$[(1.024)^2 - 1] = 4.86\%$$

4. A. The cash flows for this bond up to the first call date are (1) 10 coupon payments of $4.50 and (2) $104.50 ten 6-month periods from now. The table below shows the present values of the coupon payments and maturity value for the three interest rates in the question:

Annual Interest Rate (%)	Semiannual Interest Rate (%)	Present Value of 10 Payments of $4.5	Present Value of $104.5 10 Periods From Now	Present Value of Cash Flows
4.4	2.2	40.0019	84.0635	124.0654
4.6	2.3	39.7944	83.2453	123.0397
4.8	2.4	39.5886	82.4360	122.0246

Since a semiannual rate of 2.3% produces a present value for the cash flows of $123.0397 and the price is $123.04, 2.3% is the semiannual yield to call. Doubling this yield gives a 4.6% yield to call on a bond-equivalent basis.

b. The cash flows for this bond up to the first par call date are (1) 16 coupon payments of $4.50 and (2) $100 sixteen 6-month periods from now. The table below shows the present values of the coupon payments and maturity value for the three interest rates in the question:

Annual Interest Rate (%)	Semiannual Interest Rate (%)	Present Value of 16 Payments of $4.5	Present Value of $100 16 Periods From Now	Present Value of Cash Flows
5.41	2.705	57.8211	65.2431	123.0642
5.62	2.810	57.3548	64.1851	121.5399
5.75	2.875	57.0689	63.5393	120.6082

For the three semiannual interest rates used, the one that makes the present value of the cash flows to the first par call date closest to the price of $123.04 is 2.705%. Doubling this yield gives a 5.41% yield to first par call date on a bond-equivalent basis.

5. The discount margin is the margin that when added to LIBOR will make the present value of the cash flows (assuming LIBOR is unchanged over the life of the floater) equal to the price. When the price is 99.8269, it can be seen from Exhibit 71-3 that a margin of 84 basis points makes the present value of the cash flows equal to that price. Thus, if the floater's price is 99.8269, the discount margin is 84 basis points.

6. A. The yield on a discount basis, d, is

$$(1 - 0.9825)\left(\frac{360}{115}\right) = 0.0548 = 5.48\%$$

B. The price of this Treasury bill, p, per \$1 dollar of maturity value is:

$$1 - 0.059 \, (162/360) = 0.97345$$

7. From Exhibit 71-4, the coupon rate for the on-the-run issue is 4.4%. Thus, the semiannual coupon payment per \$100 of par value is \$2.20 (4.4%/2 times \$100). The present value of the cash flow is:

$$\frac{2.2}{(1 + z_1)^1} + \frac{2.2}{(1 + z_2)^2} + \frac{2.2}{(1 + z_3)^3} + \frac{2.2}{(1 + z_4)^4} + \frac{102.2}{(1 + z_5)^5}$$

where z_5 is one half of the 2.5-year theoretical spot rate.

Given the other four spot rates, we can write

$$\frac{2.2}{(1.0150)^1} + \frac{2.2}{(1.0165)^2} + \frac{2.2}{(1.017527)^3} + \frac{2.2}{(1.019582)^4} + \frac{102.2}{(1 + z_5)^5} = 100$$

Since the price of the 2.5-year coupon Treasury security is par, the present value must equal par. Therefore,

$$\frac{2.2}{(1.0150)^1} + \frac{2.2}{(1.0165)^2} + \frac{2.2}{(1.017527)^3} + \frac{2.2}{(1.019582)^4} + \frac{102.2}{(1 + z_5)^5} = 100$$

Solving the above equation:

$$2.167488 + 2.129158 + 2.088261 + 2.0355795 + \frac{102.20}{(1 + z_5)^5} = 100$$

$$8.420702 + \frac{102.20}{(1 + z_5)^5} = 100$$

$$\frac{102.20}{(1 + z_5)^5} = 91.5793$$

$$(1 + z_5)^5 = \frac{102.20}{91.5793}$$

$$z_5 = 0.022188 = 2.2188\%$$

Doubling the semiannual yield gives 4.4376% for the 2.5-year spot rate on a bond-equivalent basis. This rate agrees with the rate in Exhibit 71-4.

8. From Exhibit 71-5 it can be seen that if 125 basis points is added to each spot rate, the present value of the cash flow is 105.7165, the assumed price for the non-Treasury issue. Therefore, the Z-spread is 125 basis points.

9. $_1f_{13}$ is found as follows:

$$_1f_{13} = \frac{(1 + z_{14})^{14}}{(1 + z_{13})^{13}} - 1$$

From Exhibit 71-4, the annual spot rates for z_{13} and z_{14} are reported. They are 5.6108% and 5.6643%, respectively. Therefore,

$$z_{13} = 0.056108/2 = 0.028054$$
$$z_{14} = 0.056643/2 = 0.028322$$

Substituting we get

$$_1f_{13} = \frac{(1.028322)^{14}}{(1.028054)^{13}} - 1 = 0.0318 = 3.18\%$$

Doubling this rate gives the annualized rate for $_1f_{13}$ on a bond-equivalent basis of 6.36% reported in Exhibit 71-8.

10. The value is $114.8195 as shown below:

Period	Semiann. Forward Rate (%)	Forward Discount Factor	Cash Flow	PV of Cash Flow
1	1.500	0.985222	$5	$4.926108
2	1.800	0.967799	5	4.838996
3	1.958	0.949211	5	4.746055
4	2.577	0.925362	5	4.626810
5	3.268	0.896079	5	4.480396
6	3.166	0.868582	105	91.201111
		Total		$114.819476

11. A. The forward rate sought is $_{12}f_8$. The formula for this forward rate is therefore:

$$_{12}f_8 = \left[\frac{(1 + z_{20})^{20}}{(1 + z_8)^8}\right]^{1/12} - 1$$

The spot rates needed are z_8 (the 4-year spot rate) and z_{20} (the 10-year spot rate). From Exhibit 71-4 we know

z_8 (the 4-year spot rate) = 5.065%/2 = 0.025325
z_{20} (the 10-year spot rate) = 6.2169%/2 = 0.031085

then

$$_{12}f_8 = \left[\frac{(1.031085)^{20}}{(1.025325)^8}\right]^{1/12} - 1 = 0.035943$$

Therefore, $_{12}f_8$ is equal to 3.4943% and doubling this rate gives 6.9885% the forward rate on a bond-equivalent basis.

B. We can verify this result. Investing $100 for 20 periods at the spot rate of 3.1085% will produce the following value:

$$\$100(1.031085)^{20} = \$184.4545$$

By investing $100 for 8 periods at 2.5325% and reinvesting the proceeds for 12 periods at the forward rate of 3.4942% gives the same value

$$\$100\,(1.025325)^8\,(1.034942)^{12} = \$184.4545$$

SOLUTIONS FOR READING 72

1. While it is true that a disadvantage of the full valuation approach is that it requires revaluing the bonds in the portfolio, it is not true that the duration/convexity approach does not require a valuation model. A valuation model is required in order to obtain the prices when rates are shocked that are used in the duration and convexity adjustment formulas.

2. The duration/convexity approach does not take into consideration how the yield curve can shift. However, this is not correct for the full valuation approach since yield curve scenarios are part of the full valuation method. In addition, the two bonds may have different prices and coupons thus leading to different percentage price changes for the two bonds.

3. The statement is not correct. While two bonds may have the same duration, they can have different convexities.

4. The problem here is in the definition of price volatility. It can be measured in terms of dollar price change or percentage price change. Smith is correct that there is greater price volatility for bond B because of its higher modified duration—that is, a higher percentage price change. Robertson is correct that bond A has greater price volatility but in terms of dollar price change. Specifically, for a 100 basis point change in rates, bond A will change by $3.60 (4% times 90); for bond B the dollar price change will be $3 (6% times 50) for a 100 basis point rate change.

5. **A.** Mr. Renfro's definition is a temporal definition and it is best not to use such an interpretation. Duration is related to the percentage price change of a bond when interest rates change.

   B. Mr. Renfro's response is correct.

   C. Mr. Renfro's response is correct.

   D. The computation of effective duration requires a valuation model to determine what the new prices will be when interest rates change. These models are based on assumptions. When duration is taken from different sources, there is no consistency of assumptions. While it is true that there is a formula for computing duration once the new prices for the bond are determined from a valuation model when rates are shocked, there is no simple valuation formula for bonds with embedded options.

   Mr. Renfro incorrectly overrode duration measures. It is possible—and it does occur in practice—to have a duration for a bond that is greater than the maturity of the bond. A negative duration does occur for some securities as well. For example, certain mortgage-backed securities have a negative duration. A negative duration of −3, for example, would mean that if interest rates increased by 100 basis points, the price of the bond will increase by approximately 3%. That is, the price of the bond moves in the same direction as the change in rates. In fact, for the types of bonds that have a duration longer than maturity and a negative duration, modified duration is not what the manager would want to use.

   E. The first part of the statement is correct. However, the second part is not true. Two portfolios can have the same duration but perform differently when rates change because they have different convexities. Also, the portfolios may have different yield and coupon characteristics.

6. A negative convexity adjustment simply means that a bond's price appreciation will be less than its price decline for a large change in interest rates (200 basis points in the question). Whether or not a bond with negative convexity is attractive depends on its price and expectations about future interest rate changes.

7. If one interprets duration as some measure of time, it is difficult to understand why a bond will have a duration greater than its maturity. Duration is the approximate percentage price change of a bond for a 100 basis point change in interest rates. It is possible to have a security with a maturity of 10 years and a duration of 13.

8. Bond ABC exhibits negative convexity—for a 100 basis point change in rates, the gain is less than the loss; Bond XYZ exhibits positive convexity. A high coupon bond will exhibit negative convexity. A low coupon bond will exhibit positive convexity. Therefore, bond ABC is probably the high coupon bond while bond XYZ is probably the low coupon bond.

9 **A.** Modified duration is an inappropriate duration measure for a high coupon callable bond because it fails to recognize that as interest rates change, the expected cash flows will change.

   B. A better measure for a high-coupon callable bond is effective or option-adjusted duration.

10. Because the issue's coupon rate is substantially below the prevailing rate at which the issue can be refunded (500 basis points below), this issue is not likely to be called. Basically, if rates are shocked up and down, the expected cash flows are not likely to change because the coupon rate is so far below the market rate. Thus, modified duration—which assumes that the expected cash flow will not change when rates are changed—will be a good approximation for effective duration.

11. **A.** For a 25 basis point rate shock, the duration formula is:

$$\text{duration} = \frac{V_- - V_+}{2V_0(0.0025)}$$

		5%, 4 Year	5%, 25 Year	8%, 4 Year	8%, 25 Year
Initial value	V_0	100.0000	100.0000	110.7552	142.5435
Value at 4.75%	V_-	100.9011	103.6355	111.7138	147.2621
Value at 5.25%	V_+	99.1085	96.5416	109.8066	138.0421
Duration		3.59	14.19	3.44	12.94

B. For a 50 basis point rate shock, the duration formula is:

$$\text{duration} = \frac{V_- - V_+}{2V_0(0.0050)}$$

		5%, 4 Year	5%, 25 Year	8%, 4 Year	8%, 25 Year
Initial value	V_0	100.0000	100.0000	110.7552	142.5435
Value at 4.50%	V_-	101.8118	107.4586	112.6826	152.2102
Value at 5.50%	V_+	98.2264	93.2507	108.8679	133.7465
Duration		3.59	14.21	3.44	12.95

12. For a 25 basis point rate shock, the value for C is:

$$C = \frac{V_+ + V_- - 2V_0}{2V_0(0.0025)^2}$$

		5%, 4 Year	5%, 25 Year	8%, 4 Year	8%, 25 Year
Initial value	V_0	100.0000	100.0000	110.7552	142.5435
Value at 4.75%	V_-	100.9011	103.6355	111.7138	147.2621
Value at 5.25%	V_+	99.1085	96.5416	109.8066	138.0421
C		7.68	141.68	7.23	121.89

13. A. For a 10 basis point change:

duration for 8% 4-year bond   = 3.44
duration for 8% 25-year bond = 12.94
$\Delta y*$ = 0.0010

For the 8% 4-year bond: approximate percentage price change for 10 basis point change in yield ($\Delta y* = 0.0010$):

10 basis point increase:
approximate percentage price change = $-3.44 \times (0.0010) \times 100$
= -0.34%

10 basis point decrease:
approximate percentage price change = $-3.44 \times (-0.0010) \times 100$
= $+0.34\%$

For the 8% 25-year bond: approximate percentage price change for 10 basis point change in yield (0.0010):

10 basis point increase:
approximate percentage price change = $-12.94 \times (0.0010) \times 100$
= -1.29%

10 basis point decrease:
approximate percentage price change = $-12.94 \times (-0.0010) \times 100$
= $+1.29\%$

B. For the 4-year bond, the estimated percentage price change using duration is excellent for a 10 basis point change, as shown below:

	Duration Estimate	Actual Change
10 bp increase	-0.34%	-0.34%
10 bp decrease	$+0.34\%$	$+0.35\%$

For the 25-year bond, the estimated percentage price change using duration is excellent for a 10 basis point change, as shown below:

	Duration Estimate	Actual Change
10 bp increase	-1.29%	-1.28%
10 bp decrease	$+1.29\%$	$+1.31\%$

14. A. For a 200 basis point change:

duration for 8% 4-year bond = 3.44
duration for 8% 25-year bond = 12.94
$\Delta y* = 0.02$

For the 8% 4-year bond: approximate percentage price change for 200 basis point change in yield ($\Delta y* = 0.02$):

200 basis point increase:

approximate percentage price change $= -3.44 \times (0.02) \times 100$
$= -6.89\%$

200 basis point decrease:

approximate percentage price change $= -3.44 \times (-0.02) \times 100$
$= +6.89\%$

For the 8% 25-year bond: approximate percentage price change for 200 basis point shock:

200 basis point increase:

approximate percentage price change $= -12.94 \times (0.02) \times 100 =$
-25.88%

200 basis point decrease:

approximate percentage price change $= -12.94 \times (-0.02) \times 100$
$= +25.88\%$

B. For the 4-year bond, the estimated percentage price change using duration is very good despite a 200 basis point change, as shown below:

	Duration Estimate	Actual Change
200 bp increase	-6.88%	-6.61%
200 bp decrease	$+6.88\%$	$+7.19\%$

For the 25-year bond, the estimated percentage price change using duration is poor for a 200 basis point change, as shown on the next page:

	Duration Estimate	Actual Change
200 bp increase	−25.88%	−21.62%
200 bp decrease	+25.88%	+31.54%

15. A. The convexity adjustment for the two 25-year bonds is:
For the 5% 25-year bond:

$$C = 141.68$$
$$\Delta y* = 0.02$$

convexity adjustment to percentage price change $= 141.68 \times (0.02)^2 \times 100 = 5.67\%$

For the 8% 25-year bond:

$$C = 121.89$$

convexity adjustment to percentage price change $= 121.89 \times (0.02)^2 \times 100 = 4.88\%$

B. Estimated price change using duration and convexity adjustment.
For the 5% 25 year bond:

$$duration = 14.19$$
$$\Delta y* = 0.02$$

approximate percentage price change based on duration $= -14.19 \times 0.02 \times 100 = -28.38\%$

convexity adjustment $= 5.67\%$

Therefore,

Yield change ($\Delta y*$)	+200 bps
Estimated change using duration	−28.38%
Convexity adjustment	5.67%
Total estimated percentage price change	−22.71%

Yield change ($\Delta y*$)	−200 bps
Estimated change using duration	28.38%
Convexity adjustment	5.67%
Total estimated percentage price change	34.05%

For the 8% 25-year bond:

$$duration = 12.94$$
$$\Delta y* = 0.02$$

approximate percentage price change based on duration $= -12.94 \times 0.02 \times 100 = -25.88\%$

convexity adjustment = 4.88%

Yield change ($\Delta y*$)	+200 bps
Estimated change using duration	−25.88%
Convexity adjustment	4.88%
Total estimated percentage price change	−21.00%

Yield change ($\Delta y*$)	−200 bps
Estimated change using duration	25.88%
Convexity adjustment	4.88%
Total estimated percentage price change	30.76%

C. For a large change in rates of 200 basis points, duration with the convexity adjustment does a pretty good job of estimating the actual percentage price change, as shown below.

	Duration/Convexity Estimate	Actual Change
For 5% 25-year bond		
200 bp increase	−22.71%	−23.46%
200 bp decrease	+34.05%	+35.00%
For 8% 25-year bond		
200 bp increase	−21.00%	−21.62%
200 bp decrease	+30.76%	+31.54%

16. A. The price value of a basis point is

$114.1338 − $114.0051 = $0.1287

B. Using equation (72-2), the approximate percentage price change for a 1 basis point increase in interest rates (i.e., $\Delta y = 0.0001$), ignoring the negative sign in equation (72-2), is:

11.28 × (0.0001) × 100 = 0.1128%

Given the initial price of 114.1338, the dollar price change estimated using duration is

0.1128% × 114.1338 = $0.1287

17. Duration even after adjusting for convexity indicates what the exposure of a bond or bond portfolio will be if interest rates change. However, to capture fully the interest rate exposure, it is necessary to know how volatile interest rates are. For example, in comparing duration of government bonds in different countries, the duration only indicates the sensitivity of the price to changes in interest rates by a given number of basis points. It does not consider the volatility of rates. In a country with little volatility in rates but where the government bonds have a high duration, just looking at duration misleads the investor as to the interest rate risk exposure.

SOLUTIONS FOR READING 72

Solutions are for Practice Questions found in Reading.

1. A. From Exhibit 72-4 we know that

$$V_- \text{ (price at 5.9\% yield)} = 136.1193$$
$$V_+ \text{ (price at 6.1\% yield)} = 133.2472$$

and

$$\Delta y = 0.001$$
$$V_0 = 134.6722$$
$$\text{duration} = \frac{136.1193 - 133.2472}{2(134.6722)(0.001)} = 10.66$$

Note that this is the same value computed for duration when a 20 basis point rate shock was used. Duration is therefore the same for this bond regardless of whether the yield change used is 20 basis points or 10 basis points.

B. From Exhibit 72-4 we know that

$$V_- \text{ (price at 5.9\% yield)} = 101.1651$$
$$V_+ \text{ (price at 6.1\% yield)} = 98.8535$$

and

$$\Delta y = 0.001$$
$$V_0 = 100$$
$$\text{duration} = \frac{101.1651 - 98.8535}{2(100)(0.001)} = 11.56$$

2. A. The duration for this bond is 11.56. The approximate percentage price change for a 10 basis point increase in interest rates is

$$= -11.56 \times 0.0010 \times 100 = -1.156\%$$

B. The actual percentage price change from Exhibit 72-6 is -1.15%. Therefore the estimate is good.

C. The approximate percentage price change for a 10 basis point decrease in interest rates is

$$= -11.56 \times (-0.0010) \times 100 = 1.156\%$$

D. The actual percentage price change from Exhibit 72-6 is 1.17%. Therefore the estimate is good.

E. The approximate percentage price change for a 200 basis point increase in interest rates is

$$= -11.56 \times 0.02 \times 100 = -23.12\%$$

F. The actual percentage price change from Exhibit 72-6 is -19.79%. Therefore duration provides a poor estimate and underestimates the new price.

G. The approximate percentage price change for a 200 basis point decrease in interest rates is

$$= -11.56 \times (-0.02) \times 100 = 23.12\%$$

H. The actual percentage price change from Exhibit 72-6 is 27.36%. Therefore duration provides a poor estimate and underestimates the new price.

3. A. For a rate shock of 10 basis points ($\Delta y = 0.001$)

$$C = \frac{98.8535 + 101.1651 - 2(100)}{2(100)(0.001)^2} = 93.00$$

B.

i. For a 10 basis point increase in interest rates ($\Delta y* = 0.001$)

Estimated change using duration	-1.16%
Convexity adjustment	0.0093%
Total estimated percentage price change	-1.15%
Actual percentage price change	-1.15%

ii. For a 10 basis point decrease in interest rates ($\Delta y* = -0.001$)

Estimated change using duration	1.16%
Convexity adjustment	0.0093%
Total estimated percentage price change	1.17%
Actual percentage price change	1.17%

iii. For a 200 basis point increase in interest rates ($\Delta y* = 0.02$)

Estimated change using duration	-23.12%
Convexity adjustment	3.72%
Total estimated percentage price change	-19.40%
Actual percentage price change	-19.79%

iv. For a 200 basis point decrease in interest rates ($\Delta y* = -0.02$)

Estimated change using duration	23.12%
Convexity adjustment	3.72%
Total estimated percentage price change	26.84%
Actual percent price change	27.36%

4⅝ 4¹¹⁄₁₆ — ⅜
5½ 5½ — ⅜
20⅝ 21¹³⁄₁₆ — ¹⁄₁₆
17⅜ 18⅛ + ⅞
13½ 6½ 6½ — ½
7¼ 3¹⁄₃₂ — ⅛
15⁄16
9⁄16 9⁄8
1³⁄₃₂ 7¹³⁄₁₆ 7¹⁵⁄₁₆
7¹⁵⁄₁₆ 2½ +
2⅝ 2¹¹⁄₃₂ 2½ +
2¾ 2¼ 2¼
11⅜ 11¾ +
6⅛ 12¹⁄₁₆ 33¼ —
87 33¾ 33 33¼ —
502 25⅝ 24⁹⁄₁₆ 25⅜ +
833 12 11⅝ 11⅞ +
16 10½ 10½ 10½ —
78 15⅞ 15¹³⁄₁₆ 15⅞ —
4508 9¹⁄₁₆ 8¼ 8⅞ +
430 11¼ 10⅛ 10⅜
4⅞ 4⅞

GLOSSARY

Abnormal rate of return The amount by which a security's actual return differs from its expected rate of return which is based on the market's rate of return and the security's relationship with the market.

Above full-employment equilibrium A macroeconomic equilibrium in which real GDP exceeds potential GDP.

Absolute dispersion The amount of variability present without comparison to any reference point or benchmark.

Absolute frequency The number of observations in a given interval (for grouped data).

Accelerated method A method of depreciation that allocates relatively large amounts of the depreciable cost of an asset to earlier years and reduced amounts to later years.

Accrual accounting The system of recording financial transactions as they come into existence as a legally enforceable claim, rather than when they settle.

Accrued interest (1) Interest earned but not yet due and payable. This is equal to the next coupon to be paid on a bond multiplied by the time elapsed since the last payment date and divided by the total coupon period. Exact conventions differ across bond markets. (2) Interest earned but not yet paid.

Additional information Information that is required or recommended under the GIPS standards and is not considered as "supplemental information" for the purposes of compliance.

Addition rule for probabilities A principle stating that the probability that A or B occurs (both occur) equals the probability that A occurs, plus the probability that B occurs, minus the probability that both A and B occur.

Additions Enlargements to the physical layout of a plant asset.

Add-on interest A procedure for determining the interest on a bond or loan in which the interest is added onto the face value of a contract.

Administrative fees All fees other than the trading expenses and the investment management fee. Administrative fees include custody fees, accounting fees, consulting fees, legal fees, performance measurement fees, or other related fees. These administrative fees are typically outside the control of the investment management firm and are not included in either the gross-of-fees return or the net-of-fees return. However, there are some markets and investment vehicles where administrative fees are controlled by the firm. (See the term "bundled fee.")

Aggregate demand The relationship between the quantity of real GDP demanded and the price level.

Aggregate hours The total number of hours worked by all the people employed, both full time and part time, during a year.

Aggregate production function The relationship between the quantity of real GDP supplied and the quantities of labor and capital and the state of technology.

Allocative efficiency A situation in which we cannot produce more of any good without giving up some of another good that we value more highly.

Alpha A term commonly used to describe a manager's abnormal rate of return, which is the difference between the return the portfolio actually produced and the expected return given its risk level.

Alternative hypothesis The hypothesis accepted when the null hypothesis is rejected.

American Depository Receipts (ADRs) Certificates of ownership issued by a U.S. bank that represent indirect ownership of a certain number of shares of a specific foreign firm. Shares are held on deposit in a bank in the firm's home country.

American option An option contract that can be exercised at any time until its expiration date. (1) An option contract that can be exercised at any time until its expiration date. (2) An option that can be exercised on any day through the expiration day. Also referred to as American-style exercise.

American terms With reference to U.S. dollar exchange rate quotations, the U.S. dollar price of a unit of another currency.

Amortization The periodic allocation of the cost of an intangible asset to the periods it benefits.

Amortizing and accreting swaps A swap in which the notional principal changes according to a formula related to changes in the underlying.

Analysis of variance (ANOVA) The analysis of the total variability of a dataset (such as observations on the dependent variable in a regression) into components representing different sources of variation; with reference to regression, ANOVA provides the inputs for an F-test of the significance of the regression as a whole.

Annual percentage rate The cost of borrowing expressed as a yearly rate.

Annuity A finite set of level sequential cash flows.

Annuity due An annuity having a first cash flow that is paid immediately.

Anomalies Security price relationships that appear to contradict a well-regarded hypothesis; in this case, the efficient market hypothesis.

A priori probability A probability based on logical analysis rather than on observation or personal judgment.

Arbitrage (1) The simultaneous purchase of an undervalued asset or portfolio and sale of an overvalued but equivalent asset or portfolio, in order to obtain a riskless profit on the price differential. Taking advantage of a market inefficiency in a risk-free manner. (2) A trading strategy designed to generate a guaranteed profit from a transaction that requires no capital commitment or risk bearing on the part of the trader. A simple example of an arbitrage trade would be the simultaneous purchase and sale of the same security in different markets at different prices. (3) The condition in a financial market in which equivalent assets or combinations of assets sell for two different prices, creating an opportunity to profit at no risk with no commitment of money. In a well-functioning financial market, few arbitrage opportunities are possible. Equivalent to the law of one price. (4) A risk-free operation that earns an expected positive net profit but requires no net investment of money.

Arbitrage pricing theory (APT) A theory that posits that the expected return to a financial asset can be described by its relationship with several common risk factors. The multifactor APT can be contrasted with the single-factor CAPM.

Arithmetic mean (AM) The sum of the observations divided by the number of observations.

Arrears swap A type of interest rate swap in which the floating payment is set at the end of the period and the interest is paid at that same time.

Asian call option A European-style option with a value at maturity equal to the difference between the stock price at maturity and the average stock price during the life of the option, or $0, whichever is greater.

Asset allocation The process of deciding how to distribute an investor's wealth among different asset classes for investment purposes.

Asset class Securities that have similar characteristics, attributes, and risk/return relationships.

Asset impairment Loss of revenue-generating potential of a long-lived asset before the end of its useful life; the difference between an asset's carrying value and its fair value, as measured by the present value of the expected cash flows.

Assets under management (AUM) The total market value of the assets managed by an investment firm.

At-the-money option An option for which the strike (or exercise) price is close to (at) the current market price of the underlying asset.

Automatic fiscal policy A change in fiscal policy that is triggered by the state of the economy.

Automatic stabilizers Mechanisms that stabilize real GDP without explicit action by the government.

Autonomous expenditure The sum of those components of aggregate planned expenditure that are not influenced by real GDP. Autonomous expenditure equals investment, government purchases, exports, and the autonomous parts of consumption expenditure and imports.

Average cost pricing rule A rule that sets price to cover cost including normal profit, which means setting the price equal to average total cost.

Average fixed cost Total fixed cost per unit of output—total fixed cost divided by output.

Average product The average product of a resource. It equals total product divided by the quantity of the resource employed.

Average tax rate A person's total tax payment divided by his or her total income.

Average total cost Total cost per unit of output.

Average variable cost Total variable cost per unit of output.

Backwardation A condition in the futures markets in which the benefits of holding an asset exceed the costs, leaving the futures price less than the spot price.

Balance of payments (1) A summary of all economic transactions between a country and all other countries for a specific time period, usually a year. The balance-of-payments account reflects all payments and liabilities to foreigners (debits) and all payments and obligations received from foreigners (credits). (2) A record of all financial flows crossing the borders of a country during a given time period (a quarter or a year).

Balance of payments accounts A country's record of international trading, borrowing, and lending.

Balance of trade *See* Trade balance.

Balance sheet A financial statement that shows what assets the firm controls at a fixed point in time and how it has financed these assets.

Balanced budget A government budget in which tax revenues and expenditures are equal.

Balanced budget multiplier The magnification on aggregate demand of a *simultaneous* change in government purchases and taxes that leaves the budget balance unchanged.

Balanced fund A mutual fund with, generally, a three-part investment objective: (1) to conserve the investor's principal, (2) to pay current income, and (3) to increase both principal and income. The fund aims to achieve this by owning a mixture of bonds, preferred stocks, and common stocks.

Bank discount basis A quoting convention that annualizes, on a 360-day year, the discount as a percentage of face value.

Barriers to entry Legal or natural constraints that protect a firm from potential competitors.

Barter The direct exchange of one good or service for other goods and services.

Basic earnings per share Total earnings divided by the weighted average number of shares actually outstanding during the period.

Basis The difference between the spot price of the underlying asset and the futures contract price at any point in time (e.g., the *initial* basis at the time of contract origination, the *cover* basis at the time of contract termination).

Basis swap (1) An interest rate swap involving two floating rates. (2) A swap in which both parties pay a floating rate.

Bayes' formula A method for updating probabilities based on new information.

Bear spread An option strategy that involves selling a put with a lower exercise price and buying a put with a higher exercise price. It can also be executed with calls.

Behavioral finance Involves the analysis of various psychological traits of individuals and how these traits affect how they act as investors, analysts, and portfolio managers.

Below full-employment equilibrium A macroeconomic equilibrium in which potential GDP exceeds real GDP.

Benchmark An independent rate of return (or hurdle rate) forming an objective test of the effective implementation of an investment strategy.

Benchmark bond A bond representative of current market conditions and used for performance comparison.

Benchmark error Situation where an inappropriate or incorrect benchmark is used to compare and assess portfolio returns and management.

Benchmark portfolio A comparison standard of risk and assets included in the policy statement and similar to the investor's risk preference and investment needs, which can be used to evaluate the investment performance of the portfolio manager.

Bernoulli random variable A random variable having the outcomes 0 and 1.

Bernoulli trial An experiment that can produce one of two outcomes.

Beta A standardized measure of systematic risk based upon an asset's covariance with the market portfolio.

Betterments Improvements that do not add to the physical layout of a plant asset.

Bid-ask spread The difference between the quoted ask and the bid prices.

Big tradeoff A tradeoff between equity and efficiency.

Bill-and-hold basis Sales on a bill-and-hold basis involve selling products but not delivering those products until a later date.

Binomial model A model for pricing options in which the underlying price can move to only one of two possible new prices.

Binomial option pricing model A valuation equation that assumes the price of the underlying asset changes through a series of discrete upward or downward movements.

Binomial random variable The number of successes in n Bernoulli trials for which the probability of success is constant for all trials and the trials are independent.

Binomial tree (1) A diagram representing price movements of the underlying in a binomial model. (2) The graphical representation of a model of asset price dynamics in which, at each period, the asset moves up with probability p or down with probability $(1 - p)$.

Black market An illegal trading arrangement in which the price exceeds the legally imposed price ceiling.

Black-Scholes option pricing model A valuation equation that assumes the price of the underlying asset changes continuously through the option's expiration date by a statistical process known as *geometric Brownian motion.*

Bond A long-term debt security with contractual obligations regarding interest payments and redemption.

Bond-equivalent basis A basis for stating an annual yield that annualizes a semiannual yield by doubling it.

Bond-equivalent yield The yield to maturity on a basis that ignores compounding.

Bond option An option in which the underlying is a bond; primarily traded in over-the-counter markets.

Bond price volatility The percentage changes in bond prices over time.

Book value of equity (or book value) (1) Shareholders' equity (total assets minus total liabilities) minus the value of preferred stock; common shareholders' equity. (2) The accounting value of a firm.

Book value per share   Book value of equity divided by the number of common shares outstanding.

Box spread   An option strategy that combines a bull spread and a bear spread having two different exercise prices, which produces a risk-free payoff of the difference in the exercise prices.

Brady bonds   Bonds issued by emerging countries under a debt-reduction plan named after Mr. Brady, former U.S. Secretary of the Treasury.

Brand name   A registered name that can be used only by its owner to identify a product or service.

Broker   (1) An agent who executes orders to buy or sell securities on behalf of a client in exchange for a commission. (2) *See* Futures commission merchants.

Budget deficit   A government's budget balance that is negative—expenditures exceed tax revenues.

Budget surplus   A government's budget balance that is positive—tax revenues exceed expenditures.

Bull spread   An option strategy that involves buying a call with a lower exercise price and selling a call with a higher exercise price. It can also be executed with puts.

Bundled fee   A fee that combines multiple fees into one "bundled" fee. Bundled fees can include any combination of management, transaction, custody, and other administrative fees. Two specific examples of bundled fees are the wrap fee and the all-in fee.

All-in fee   Due to the universal banking system in some countries, asset management, brokerage, and custody are often part of the same company. This allows banks to offer a variety of choices to customers regarding how the fee will be charged. Customers are offered numerous fee models in which fees may be bundled together or charged separately. All-in fees can include any combination of investment management, trading expenses, custody, and other administrative fees.

Wrap fee   Wrap fees are specific to a particular investment product. The U.S. Securities and Exchange Commission (SEC) defines a wrap fee account (now more commonly known as a separately managed account or SMA) as "any advisory program under which a specified fee or fees not based upon transactions in a client's account is charged for investment advisory services (which may include portfolio management or advice concerning the selection of other investment advisers) and execution of client transactions." A typical separately managed account has a contract or contracts (and fee) involving a sponsor (usually a broker or independent provider) acting as the investment advisor, an investment management firm typically as the subadvisor, other services (custody, consulting, reporting, performance, manager selection, monitoring, and execution of trades), distributor, and the client (brokerage customer). Wrap fees can be all-inclusive, asset-based fees (which may include any combination of management, transaction, custody, and other administrative fees).

Business cycle   The periodic but irregular up-and-down movement in production.

Business risk   The variability of operating income arising from the characteristics of the firm's industry. Two sources of business risk are sales variability and operating leverage.

Butterfly spread   An option strategy that combines two bull or bear spreads and has three exercise prices.

Buy-and-hold strategy   A passive portfolio management strategy in which securities (bonds or stocks) are bought and held to maturity.

Call   An option that gives the holder the right to buy an underlying asset from another party at a fixed price over a specific period of time.

Call market   A market in which trading for individual stocks only takes place at specified times. All the bids and asks available at the time are combined and the market administrators specify a single price that will possibly clear the market at that time.

Call option   Option to buy an asset within a certain period at a specified price called the *exercise price*.

Call premium   Amount above par that an issuer must pay to a bondholder for retiring the bond before its stated maturity.

Call provisions   Specifies when and how a firm can issue a call for bonds outstanding prior to their maturity.

Cap   (1) A contract on an interest rate, whereby at periodic payment dates, the writer of the cap pays the difference between the market interest rate and a specified cap rate if, and only if, this difference is positive. This is equivalent to a stream of call options on the interest rate. (2) A combination of interest rate call options designed to hedge a borrower against rate increases on a floating-rate loan.

Capital   The tools, equipment, buildings, and other constructions that businesses now use to produce goods and services.

Capital account   (1) The record of transactions with foreigners that involve either (a) the exchange of ownership rights to real or financial assets or (b) the extension of loans. (2) A component of the balance of payments that reflects unrequited (or unilateral) transfers corresponding to capital flows entailing no compensation (in the form of goods, services, or assets). Examples include investment capital given (without future repayment) in favor of poor countries, debt forgiveness, and expropriation losses.

Capital accumulation The growth of capital resources.

Capital appreciation A return objective in which the investor seeks to increase the portfolio value, primarily through capital gains, over time to meet a future need rather than dividend yield.

Capital asset pricing model (CAPM) A theory concerned with deriving the expected or required rates of return on risky assets based on the assets' systematic risk relative to a market portfolio.

Capital budgeting The process of planning expenditures on assets whose cash flows are expected to extend beyond one year.

Capital Employed (Real Estate) The denominator of the return expressions, defined as the "weighted-average equity" (weighted-average capital) during the measurement period. Capital employed should not include any income or capital return accrued during the measurement period. Beginning capital is adjusted by weighting the cash flows (contributions and distributions) that occurred during the period. Cash flows are typically weighted based on the actual days the flows are in or out of the portfolio. Other weighting methods are acceptable; however, once a methodology is chosen, it should be consistently applied.

Capital expenditure An expenditure for the purchase or expansion of a long-term asset, recorded in an asset account.

Capital market line (CML) The line from the intercept point that represents the risk-free rate tangent to the original efficient frontier; it becomes the new efficient frontier since investments on this line dominate all the portfolios on the original Markowitz efficient frontier.

Capital preservation A return objective in which the investor seeks to minimize the risk of loss; generally a goal of the risk-averse investor.

Capital return (real estate) The change in the market value of the real estate investments and cash/cash equivalent assets held throughout the measurement period (ending market value less beginning market value) adjusted for all capital expenditures (subtracted) and the net proceeds from sales (added). The return is computed as a percentage of the capital employed through the measurement period. Synonyms: capital appreciation return, appreciation return.

Capital stock The total quantity of plant, equipment, buildings, and inventories.

Capital structure A company's specific mixture of long-term financing.

Caplet Each component call option in a cap.

Capped swap A swap in which the floating payments have an upper limit.

Carried interest (private equity) The profits that general partners earn from the profits of the investments made by the fund (generally 20–25%). Also known as "carry."

Carrying value The unexpired part of an asset's cost. Also called *book value*.

Cartel A group of firms that has entered into a collusive agreement to restrict output and increase prices and profits.

Carve-Out A single or multiple asset class segment of a multiple asset class portfolio.

Cash For purposes of the statement of cash flows, both cash and cash equivalents.

Cash equivalents Short-term (90 days or less), highly liquid investments, including money market accounts, commercial paper, and U.S. Treasury bills.

Cash flow additivity principle The principle that dollar amounts indexed at the same point in time are additive.

Cash-generating efficiency A company's ability to generate cash from its current or continuing operations.

Cash price or spot price The price for immediate purchase of the underlying asset.

Cash settlement (1) A procedure for settling futures contracts in which the cash difference between the futures price and the spot price is paid instead of physical delivery. (2) A procedure used in certain derivative transactions that specifies that the long and short parties engage in the equivalent cash value of a delivery transaction.

CD equivalent yield *See* Money market yield.

Central bank A bank's bank and a public authority that regulates a nation's depository institutions and controls the quantity of money.

Central limit theorem A result in statistics that states that the sample mean computed from large samples of size n from a population with finite variance will follow an approximate normal distribution with a mean equal to the population mean and a variance equal to the population variance divided by n.

Certificates of deposit (CDs) Instruments issued by banks and S&Ls that require minimum deposits for specified terms and that pay higher rates of interest than deposit accounts.

Ceteris paribus Other things being equal—all other relevant things remaining the same.

Change in demand   A change in buyers' plans that occurs when some influence on those plans other than the price of the good changes. It is illustrated by a shift of the demand curve.

Change in supply   A change in sellers' plans that occurs when some influence on those plans other than the price of the good changes. It is illustrated by a shift of the supply curve.

Change in the quantity demanded   A change in buyers' plans that occurs when the price of a good changes but all other influences on buyers' plans remain unchanged. It is illustrated by a movement along the demand curve.

Characteristic line   Regression line that indicates the systematic risk (beta) of a risky asset.

Cheapest to deliver   A bond in which the amount received for delivering the bond is largest compared with the amount paid in the market for the bond.

Classical   A macroeconomist who believes that the economy is self-regulating and that it is always at full employment.

Clean price   The price of a bond obtained as the total price of the bond minus accrued interest. Most bonds are traded on the basis of their clean price.

Closed-end fund (private equity)   A type of investment fund where the number of investors and the total committed capital is fixed and not open for subscriptions and/or redemptions.

Closed-end investment company   An investment company that issues only a limited number of shares, which it does not redeem (buy back). Instead, shares of a closed-end fund are traded in securities markets at prices determined by supply and demand.

Coefficient of variation (CV)   The ratio of a set of observations' standard deviation to the observations' mean value.

Collar   (1) A combination of a cap and a floor. (2) An option strategy involving the purchase of a put and sale of a call in which the holder of an asset gains protection below a certain level, the exercise price of the put, and pays for it by giving up gains above a certain level, the exercise price of the call. Collars also can be used to provide protection against rising interest rates on a floating-rate loan by giving up gains from lower interest rates.

Collateralized mortgage obligation (CMO)   A debt security based on a pool of mortgage loans that provides a relatively stable stream of payments for a relatively predictable term.

Collateral trust bonds   A mortgage bond wherein the assets backing the bond are financial assets like stocks and bonds.

Collusive agreement   An agreement between two (or more) producers to restrict output, raise the price, and increase profits.

Combination   A listing in which the order of the listed items does not matter.

Command system   A method of organizing production that uses a managerial hierarchy.

Commercial bank   A firm that is licensed by the Comptroller of the Currency in the U.S. Treasury or by a state agency to receive deposits and make loans.

Commercial paper   Unsecured short-term corporate debt that is characterized by a single payment at maturity.

Commission brokers   Employees of a member firm who buy or sell securities for the customers of the firm.

Committed capital (private equity)   Pledges of capital to a venture capital fund. This money is typically not received at once but drawn down over three to five years, starting in the year the fund is formed. Also known as "commitments."

Common stock   An equity investment that represents ownership of a firm, with full participation in its success or failure. The firm's directors must approve dividend payments.

Comparative advantage   A person or country has a comparative advantage in an activity if that person or country can perform the activity at a lower opportunity cost than anyone else or any other country.

Competitive bid   An underwriting alternative wherein an issuing entity (governmental body or a corporation) specifies the type of security to be offered (bonds or stocks) and the general characteristics of the issue, and the issuer solicits bids from competing investment banking firms with the understanding that the issuer will accept the highest bid from the bankers.

Competitive environment   The level of intensity of competition among firms in an industry, determined by an examination of five competitive forces.

Competitive market   A market that has many buyers and many sellers, so no single buyer or seller can influence the price.

Competitive strategy   The search by a firm for a favorable competitive position within an industry within the known competitive environment.

Complement   A good that is used in conjunction with another good.

Complement With reference to an event S, the event that S does not occur.

Completely diversified portfolio A portfolio in which all unsystematic risk has been eliminated by diversification.

Composite Aggregation of individual portfolios representing a similar investment mandate, objective, or strategy.

Composite creation date The date when the firm first groups the portfolios to create a composite. The composite creation date is not necessarily the earliest date for which performance is reported for the composite. (See composite inception date.)

Composite definition Detailed criteria that determine the allocation of portfolios to composites. Composite definitions must be documented in the firm's policies and procedures.

Composite description General information regarding the strategy of the composite. A description may be more abbreviated than the composite definition but includes all salient features of the composite.

Compounding The process of accumulating interest on interest.

Computer-Assisted Execution System (CAES) A service created by Nasdaq that automates order routing and execution for securities listed on domestic stock exchanges and involved on the Intermarket Trading System (ITS).

Conditional expected value (1) Expected value of a variable conditional on some available information set. The expected value changes over time with changes in the information set. (2) The expected value of a stated event given that another event has occurred.

Conditional probability The probability of an event given (conditioned on) another event.

Conditional variance (1) Variance of a variable conditional on some available information set. (2) The variance of one variable, given the outcome of another.

Confidence interval A range that has a given probability that it will contain the population parameter it is intended to estimate.

Consistency A desirable property of estimators; a consistent estimator is one for which the probability of estimates close to the value of the population parameter increases as sample size increases.

Consistent With reference to estimators, describes an estimator for which the probability of estimates close to the value of the population parameter increases as sample size increases.

Consolidated Quotation System (CQS) An electronic quotation service for issues listed on the NYSE, the AMEX, or regional exchanges and traded on the Nasdaq InterMarket.

Constant maturity swap or CMT swap A swap in which the floating rate is the rate on a security known as a constant maturity treasury or CMT security.

Constant maturity treasury or CMT A hypothetical U.S. Treasury note with a constant maturity. A CMT exists for various years in the range of 2 to 10.

Constant returns to scale Features of a firm's technology that leads to constant long-run average cost as output increases. When constant returns to scale are present, the *LRAC* curve is horizontal.

Consumer Price Index (CPI) An index that measures the average of the prices paid by urban consumers for a fixed "basket" of the consumer goods and services.

Consumer surplus The value of a good minus the price paid for it, summed over the quantity bought.

Consumption expenditure The total payment for consumer goods and services.

Contango A situation in a futures market where the current contract price is greater than the current spot price for the underlying asset.

Contestable market A market in which firms can enter and leave so easily that firms in the market face competition from potential entrants.

Continuously compounded return The natural logarithm of 1 plus the holding period return, or equivalently, the natural logarithm of the ending price over the beginning price.

Continuous market A market where stocks are priced and traded continuously by an auction process or by dealers when the market is open.

Continuous random variable A random variable for which the range of possible outcomes is the real line (all real numbers between $-$ and $+$) or some subset of the real line.

Continuous time Time thought of as advancing in extremely small increments.

Contract price The transaction price specified in a forward or futures contract.

Convenience yield (1) An adjustment made to the theoretical forward or futures contract delivery price to account for the preference that consumers have for holding spot positions in the underlying asset. (2) The nonmonetary return offered by an asset when the asset is in short supply, often associated with assets with seasonal production processes.

Conversion value The value of the convertible security if converted into common stock at the stock's current market price.

Convertible bonds A bond with the added feature that the bondholder has the option to turn the bond back to the firm in exchange for a specified number of common shares of the firm.

Convexity (1) A measure of the change in duration with respect to changes in interest rates. (2) A measure of the degree to which a bond's price-yield curve departs from a straight line. This characteristic affects estimates of a bond's price volatility for a given change in yields.

Cooperative equilibrium The outcome of a game in which the players make and share the monopoly profit.

Copyright A government-sanctioned exclusive right granted to the inventor of a good, service, or productive process to produce, use, and sell the invention for a given number of years.

Correlation A number between –1 and +1 that measures the co-movement (linear association) between two random variables.

Correlation analysis The analysis of the strength of the linear relationship between two data series.

Correlation coefficient A standardized measure of the relationship between two variables that ranges from − 1.00 to + 1.00.

Cost averaging The periodic investment of a fixed amount of money.

Cost of carry (1) The cost associated with holding some asset, including financing, storage, and insurance costs. Any yield received on the asset is treated as a negative carrying cost. (2) The net amount that would be required to store a commodity or security for future delivery, usually calculated as physical storage costs plus financial capital costs less dividends paid to the underlying asset. (3) The costs of holding an asset.

Cost of carry model A model for pricing futures contracts in which the futures price is determined by adding the cost of carry to the spot price.

Cost-push inflation An inflation that results from an initial increase in costs.

Council of Economic Advisers The President's council whose main work is to monitor the economy and keep the President and the public well informed about the current state of the economy and the best available forecasts of where it is heading.

Counterparty A participant to a derivative transaction.

Country risk Uncertainty due to the possibility of major political or economic change in the country where an investment is located. Also called *political risk*.

Coupon Indicates the interest payment on a debt security. It is the coupon rate times the par value that indicates the interest payments on a debt security.

Covariance (1) A measure of the degree to which two variables, such as rates of return for investment assets, move together over time relative to their individual mean returns. (2) A measure of

the extent to which the returns on two assets move together. (3) A measure of the co-movement (linear association) between two random variables.

Covariance matrix A matrix or square array whose entries are covariances; also known as a variance–covariance matrix.

Covered call An option strategy involving the holding of an asset and sale of a call on the asset.

Credit analysis An active bond portfolio management strategy designed to identify bonds that are expected to experience changes in rating. This strategy is critical when investing in high-yield bonds.

Credit risk or default risk The risk of loss due to nonpayment by a counterparty.

Credit union A depository institution owned by a social or economic group such as firm's employees that accepts savings deposits and makes mostly consumer loans.

Creditor nation A country that during its entire history has invested more in the rest of the world than other countries have invested in it.

Cross elasticity of demand The responsiveness of the demand for a good to the price of a substitute or complement, other things remaining the same. It is calculated as the percentage change in the quantity demanded of the good divided by the percentage change in the price of the substitute or complement.

Cross-sectional analysis An examination of a firm's performance in comparison to other firms in the industry with similar characteristics to the firm being studied.

Cross-sectional data Observations over individual units at a point in time, as opposed to time-series data.

Crowding-out effect The tendency for a government budget deficit to decrease in investment.

Cumulative distribution function A function giving the probability that a random variable is less than or equal to a specified value.

Cumulative relative frequency For data grouped into intervals, the fraction of total observations that are less than the value of the upper limit of a stated interval.

Currency The bills and coins that we use today.

Currency appreciation The rise in the value of one currency in terms of another currency.

Currency depreciation The fall in the value of one currency in terms of another currency.

Currency drain An increase in currency held outside the banks.

Currency option An option that allows the holder to buy (if a call) or sell (if a put) an underlying currency at a fixed exercise rate, expressed as an exchange rate.

Current account   A record of the payments for imports of goods and services, receipts from exports of goods and services, the interest income, and net transfers.

Current account   (1) The record of all transactions with foreign nations that involve the exchange of merchandise goods and services, current income derived from investments, and unilateral gifts. (2) A component of the balance of payments covering all current transactions that take place in the normal business of the residents of a country, such as exports and imports, services, income, and current transfers.

Current credit risk   The risk associated with the possibility that a payment currently due will not be made.

Current income   A return objective in which the investor seeks to generate income rather than capital gains; generally a goal of an investor who wants to supplement earnings with income to meet living expenses.

Current P/E   *See* Trailing P/E.

Current yield   A bond's yield as measured by its current income (coupon) as a percentage of its market price.

Customer list   A list of customers or subscribers.

Cyclical businesses   Businesses with high sensitivity to business- or industry-cycle influences.

Cyclical company   A firm whose earnings rise and fall with general economic activity.

Cyclical stock   A stock with a high beta; its gains typically exceed those of a rising market and its losses typically exceed those of a falling market.

Cyclical surplus or deficit   The actual surplus or deficit minus the structural surplus or deficit.

Cyclical unemployment   The fluctuations in unemployment over the business cycle.

Daily settlement   *See* Marking to market.

Data mining   The practice of determining a model by extensive searching through a dataset for statistically significant patterns.

Day trader   A trader holding a position open somewhat longer than a scalper but closing all positions at the end of the day.

Deadweight loss   A measure of inefficiency. It is equal to the decrease in consumer surplus and producer surplus that results from an inefficient level of production.

Debentures   Bonds that promise payments of interest and principal but pledge no specific assets. Holders have first claim on the issuer's income and unpledged assets. Also known as *unsecured bonds*.

Debtor nation   A country that during its entire history has borrowed more from the rest of the world than it has lent to it.

Deciles   Quantiles that divide a distribution into 10 equal parts.

Declining-balance method   An accelerated method of depreciation in which depreciation is computed by applying a fixed rate to the carrying value (the declining balance) of a tangible long-lived asset.

Declining trend channel   The range defined by security prices as they move progressively lower.

Deep in the money   Options that are far in-the-money.

Deep out of the money   Options that are far out-of-the-money.

Default risk   The risk that an issuer will be unable to make interest and principal payments on time.

Default risk premium   An extra return that compensates investors for the possibility that the borrower will fail to make a promised payment at the contracted time and in the contracted amount.

Defensive competitive strategy   Positioning the firm so that its capabilities provide the best means to deflect the effect of the competitive forces in the industry.

Defensive stock   A stock whose return is not expected to decline as much as that of the overall market during a bear market (a beta less than one).

Deflation   A process in which the price level falls—a negative inflation.

Degree of confidence   The probability that a confidence interval includes the unknown population parameter.

Degrees of freedom (df)   The number of independent observations used.

Delivery   A process used in a deliverable forward contract in which the long pays the agreed-upon price to the short, which in turn delivers the underlying asset to the long.

Delivery option   The feature of a futures contract giving the short the right to make decisions about what, when, and where to deliver.

Delta   The change in the price of the option with respect to a one dollar change in the price of the underlying asset; this is the option's *hedge ratio,* or the number of units of the underlying asset that can be hedged by a single option contract.

Delta hedge   (1) A dynamic hedging strategy using options with continuous adjustment of the number of options used, as a function of the delta of the option. (2) An option strategy in which a position in an asset is converted to a risk-free position with a position in a specific number of options.

The number of options per unit of the underlying changes through time, and the position must be revised to maintain the hedge.

Demand The relationship between the quantity of a good that consumers plan to buy and the price of the good when all other influences on buyers' plans remain the same. It is described by a demand schedule and illustrated by a demand curve.

Demand curve A curve that shows the relationship between the quantity demanded of a good and its price when all other influences on consumers' planned purchases remain the same.

Demand for labor The relationship between the quantity of labor demanded and the real wage rate when all other influences on firm's hiring plans remain the same.

Demand-pull inflation An inflation that results from an initial increase in aggregate demand.

Dependent With reference to events, the property that the probability of one event occurring depends on (is related to) the occurrence of another event.

Dependent variable The variable whose variation about its mean is to be explained by the regression; the left-hand-side variable in a regression equation.

Depletion The exhaustion of a natural resource through mining, cutting, pumping, or other extraction, and the way in which the cost is allocated.

Depository institution A firm that takes deposits from households and firms and makes loans to other households and firms.

Depreciable cost The cost of an asset less its residual value.

Depreciation The decrease in the capital stock that results from wear and tear and obsolescence.
The periodic allocation of the cost of a tangible long-lived asset (other than land and natural resources) over its estimated useful life.

Derivatives (1) Securities bearing a contractual relation to some underlying asset or rate. Options, futures, forward, and swap contracts, as well as many forms of bonds, are derivative securities. (2) A financial instrument that offers a return based on the return of some other underlying asset.

Derivatives dealers The commercial and investment banks that make markets in derivatives. Also referred to as market makers.

Derivative security An instrument whose market value ultimately depends upon, or derives from, the value of a more fundamental investment vehicle called the underlying asset or security.

Derived demand The demand for a productive resource, which is derived from the demand for the goods and services produced by the resource.

Descriptive statistics The study of how data can be summarized effectively.

Diff swaps A swap in which the payments are based on the difference between interest rates in two countries but payments are made in only a single currency.

Diluted earnings per share Total earnings divided by the number of shares that would be outstanding if holders of securities such as executive stock options and convertible bonds exercised their options to obtain common stock.

Diminishing marginal returns The tendency for the marginal product of an additional unit of a factor of production is less than the marginal product of the previous unit of the factor.

Diminishing marginal utility The decrease in marginal utility as the quantity consumed increases.

Direct method The procedure for converting the income statement from an accrual basis to a cash basis by adjusting each item on the income statement.

Discount (1) A bond selling at a price below par value due to capital market conditions. (2) To reduce the value of a future payment in allowance for how far away it is in time; to calculate the present value of some future amount. Also, the amount by which an instrument is priced below its face value.

Discounting The conversion of a future amount of money to its present value.

Discount interest A procedure for determining the interest on a loan or bond in which the interest is deducted from the face value in advance.

Discouraged workers People who are available and willing to work but have not made specific efforts to find a job within the previous four weeks.

Discrete random variable A random variable that can take on at most a countable number of possible values.

Discrete time Time thought of as advancing in distinct finite increments.

Discretionary fiscal policy A policy action that is initiated by an act of Congress.

Discretionary policy A policy that responds to the state of the economy in a possibly unique way that uses all the information available, including perceived lessons from past "mistakes."

Diseconomies of scale Features of a firm's technology that leads to rising long-run average cost as output increases.

Dispersion (1) The variability around the central tendency. (2) A measure of the spread of the annual returns of individual portfolios within a composite. Measures may include, but are not limited to, high/low, inter-quartile range, and standard deviation (asset weighted or equal weighted).

Disposable income Aggregate income minus taxes plus transfer payments.

Distinct business entity A unit, division, department, or office that is organizationally and functionally segregated from other units, divisions, departments, or offices and retains discretion over the assets it manages and autonomy over the investment decision-making process. Possible criteria that can be used to determine this include: (a) being a legal entity; (b) having a distinct market or client type (e.g., institutional, retail, private client, etc.); (c) using a separate and distinct investment process

Dividend discount model (DDM) A technique for estimating the value of a stock issue as the present value of all future dividends.

Dominant strategy equilibrium A Nash equilibrium in which the best strategy of each player is to cheat (deny) regardless of the strategy of the other player.

Double-declining-balance method An accelerated method of depreciation in which a fixed rate equal to twice the straight-line percentage is applied to the carrying value (the declining balance) of a tangible long-lived asset.

Down transition probability The probability that an asset's value moves down in a model of asset price dynamics.

Dumping The sale by a foreign firm of exports at a lower price that the cost of production.

Duopoly A market structure in which two producers of a good or service compete.

DuPont system A method of examining ROE by breaking it down into three component parts: (1) profit margin, (2) total asset turnover, and (3) financial leverage.

Duration (1) A measure of an option-free bond's average maturity. Specifically, the weighted average maturity of all future cash flows paid by a security, in which the weights are the present value of these cash flows as a fraction of the bond's price. More importantly, a measure of a bond's price sensitivity to interest rate movements (*see* Modified duration). (2) A measure of the interest rate sensitivity of a bond's market price taking into consideration its coupon and term to maturity. (3) A measure of the size and timing of the cash flows paid by a bond. It quantifies these factors by summarizing them in the form of a single number. For bonds without option features attached, duration is interpreted as a weighted average maturity of the bond.

Dutch Book Theorem A result in probability theory stating that inconsistent probabilities create profit opportunities.

Dynamic comparative advantage A comparative advantage that a person or country possesses as a result of having specialized in a particular activity and then, as a result of learning-by-doing, having become the producer with the lowest opportunity cost.

Earnings momentum A strategy in which portfolios are constructed of stocks of firms with rising earnings.

Earnings multiplier model A technique for estimating the value of a stock issue as a multiple of its earnings per share.

Earnings surprise A company announcement of earnings that differ from analysts' prevailing expectations.

Earnings yield Earnings per share divided by price; the reciprocal of the P/E ratio.

EBITDA Earnings before interest, taxes, depreciation, and amortization.

Economic depreciation The change in the market value of capital over a given period.

Economic efficiency A situation that occurs when the firm produces a given output at the least cost.

Economic growth The expansion of production possibilities that results from capital accumulation and technological change.

Economic information Data on prices, quantities, and qualities of goods and services and factors of production.

Economic model A description of some aspect of the economic world that includes only those features of the world that are needed for the purpose at hand.

Economic profit A firm's total revenue minus its opportunity cost.

Economic rent The income received by the owner of a factor of production over and above the amount required to induce that owner to offer the factor for use.

Economics The social science that studies the *choices* that individuals, businesses, governments, and entire societies make and how they cope with *scarcity* and the *incentives* that influence and reconcile those choices.

Economic theory A generalization that summarizes what we think we understand about the economic choices that people make and the performance of industries and entire economies.

Economic value added (EVA) Internal management performance measure that compares net operating profit to total cost of capital. Indicates how profitable company projects are as a sign of management performance.

Economies of scale Features of a firm's technology that leads to a falling long-run average cost as output increases.

Economies of scope Decreases in average total cost that occur when a firm uses specialized resources to produce a range of goods and services.

Effective annual rate The amount by which a unit of currency will grow in a year with interest on interest included.

Effective annual yield (EAY) An annualized return that accounts for the effect of interest on interest; EAY is computed by compounding 1 plus the holding period yield forward to one year, then subtracting 1.

Effective duration Direct measure of the interest rate sensitivity of a bond (or any financial instrument) based upon price changes derived from a pricing model.

Efficiency A desirable property of estimators; an efficient estimator is the unbiased estimator with the smallest variance among unbiased estimators of the same parameter.

Efficient capital market A market in which security prices rapidly reflect all information about securities.

Efficient frontier The set of portfolios that has the maximum rate of return for every given level of risk, or the minimum risk for every potential rate of return.

Efficient market A market in which the actual price embodies all currently available relevant information. Resources are sent to their highest valued use.

Elastic demand Demand with a price elasticity greater than 1; other things remaining the same, the percentage change in the quantity demanded exceeds the percentage change in price.

Elasticity of demand The responsiveness of the quantity demanded of a good to a change in its price, other things remaining the same.

Elasticity of supply The responsiveness of the quantity supplied of a good to a change in its price, other things remaining the same.

Empirical probability The probability of an event estimated as a relative frequency of occurrence.

Employment Act of 1946 A landmark Congressional act that recognized a role for government actions to keep unemployment, keep the economy expanding, and keep inflation in check.

Employment-to-population ratio The percentage of people of working age who have jobs.

Ending market value (private equity) The remaining equity that a limited partner has in a fund. Also referred to as net asset value or residual value.

Entrepreneurship The human resource that organizes labor, land, and capital. Entrepreneurs come up with new ideas about what and how to produce, make business decisions, and bear the risks that arise from their decisions.

Equation of exchange An equation that states that the quantity of money multiplied by the velocity of circulation equals GDP.

Equilibrium price The price at which the quantity demanded equals the quantity supplied.

Equilibrium quantity The quantity bought and sold at the equilibrium price.

Equity forward A contract calling for the purchase of an individual stock, a stock portfolio, or a stock index at a later date at an agreed-upon price.

Equity options Options on individual stocks; also known as stock options.

Equity swap A swap transaction in which one cash flow is tied to the return to an equity portfolio position, often an index such as the Standard and Poor's 500, while the other is based on a floating-rate index.

Error term The portion of the dependent variable that is not explained by the independent variable(s) in the regression.

Estimate The particular value calculated from sample observations using an estimator.

Estimated (or fitted) parameters With reference to regression analysis, the estimated values of the population intercept and population slope coefficient(s) in a regression.

Estimated rate of return The rate of return an investor anticipates earning from a specific investment over a particular future holding period.

Estimated useful life The total number of service units expected from a long-term asset.

Estimation With reference to statistical inference, the subdivision dealing with estimating the value of a population parameter.

Estimator An estimation formula; the formula used to compute the sample mean and other sample statistics are examples of estimators.

Eurobonds Bonds denominated in a currency not native to the country in which they are issued.

Eurodollar A dollar deposited outside the United States.

European option An option contract that can only be exercised on its expiration date.

European-style option or European option An option exercisable only at maturity.

European terms With reference to U.S. dollar exchange rate quotations, the price of a U.S. dollar in terms of another currency.

European Union (EU) A formal association of European countries founded by the Treaty of Rome in 1957. Formerly known as the EEC.

Event study Research that examines the reaction of a security's price to a specific company, world event, or news announcement.

Ex-ante Before the fact.

Excess kurtosis Degree of peakedness (fatness of tails) in excess of the peakedness of the normal distribution.

Excess reserves A bank's actual reserves minus its required reserves.

Exchange for physicals (EEP) A permissible delivery procedure used by futures market participants, in which the long and short arrange a delivery procedure other than the normal procedures stipulated by the futures exchange.

Exchange rate risk Uncertainty due to the denomination of an investment in a currency other than that of the investor's own country.

Exchange-traded fund (ETF) A tradable depository receipt that gives investors a pro rata claim to the returns associated with a portfolio of securities (often designed to mimic an index, such as the Standard & Poor's 500) held in trust by a financial institution.

Exercise (or exercising the option) The process of using an option to buy or sell the underlying.

Exercise price The transaction price specified in an option contract; also known as the *strike price.*

Exercise price (or strike price or striking price, or strike) (1) The transaction price specified in an option contract. *See also* Strike price. (2) The fixed price at which an option holder can buy or sell the underlying.

Exercise rate or strike rate The fixed rate at which the holder of an interest rate option can buy or sell the underlying.

Exhaustive Covering or containing all possible outcomes.

Expansion A business cycle phase between a trough and a peak—phase in which real GDP increases.

Expected rate of return The return that analysts' calculations suggest a security should provide, based on the market's rate of return during the period and the security's relationship to the market.

Expected return The rate of return that an investor expects to get on an investment.

Expected utility The average utility arising from all possible outcomes.

Expected value The probability-weighted average of the possible outcomes of a random variable.

Expenditure A payment or obligation to make future payment for an asset or a service.

Expiration date The date on which a derivative contract expires.

Expiry The expiration date of a derivative security.

Exports The goods and services that we sell to people in other countries.

Extended DuPont System A method of examining *ROE* by breaking it down into five component parts.

External benefits Benefits that accrue to people other than the buyer of the good.

External cash flow Cash, securities, or assets that enter or exit a portfolio.

External costs Costs that are not borne by the producer of the good but borne by someone else.

External diseconomies Factors outside the control of a firm that raise the firm's costs as the industry produces a larger output.

External economies Factors beyond the control of a firm that lower the firm's costs as the industry produces a larger output.

Externality A cost or a benefit that arises from production and falls on someone other than the producer of or cost of a benefit that arises from consumption and falls on someone other than the consumer.

External valuation (real estate) An external valuation is an assessment of market value performed by a third party who is a qualified, professionally designated, certified, or licensed commercial property valuer/appraiser. External valuations must be completed following the valuation standards of the local governing appraisal body.

Extraordinary repairs Repairs that affect the estimated residual value or estimated useful life of an asset thereby increasing its carrying value.

Face value (1) The amount paid on a bond at redemption and traditionally printed on the bond certificate. This face value excludes the final coupon payment. Sometimes referred to as par value. (2) The promised payment at maturity separate from any coupon payment.

Factors of production The productive resources that businesses use to produce goods and services.

Federal budget The annual statement of the expenditures and tax revenues of the government of the United States together with the laws and regulations that approve and support those expenditures and taxes.

Federal funds rate The interest rate that banks charge each other on overnight loans of reserves.

Federal Open Market Committee The main policy-making organ of the Federal Reserve System.

Federal Reserve System The central bank of the United States.

Feedback-rule policy   A rule that specifies how policy actions respond to changes in the state of the economy.

Fee Schedule   The firm's current investment management fees or bundled fees for a particular presentation. This schedule is typically listed by asset level ranges and should be appropriate to the particular prospective client.

Fiduciary   A person who supervises or oversees the investment portfolio of a third party, such as in a trust account, and makes investment decisions in accordance with the owner's wishes.

Fiduciary call   A combination of a European call and a risk-free bond that matures on the option expiration day and has a face value equal to the exercise price of the call.

Financial account   A component of the balance of payments covering investments by residents abroad and investments by nonresidents in the home country. Examples include direct investment made by companies, portfolio investments in equity and bonds, and other investments and liabilities.

Financial innovation   The development of new financial products—new ways of borrowing and lending.

Financial risk   (1) The variability of future income arising from the firm's fixed financing costs, for example, interest payments. The effect of fixed financial costs is to magnify the effect of changes in operating profit on net income or earnings per share. (2) Risk relating to asset prices and other financial variables.

Financing activities   Business activities that involve obtaining resources from stockholders and creditors and providing the former with a return on their investments and the latter with repayment.

Firm   (1) For purposes of the GIPS standards, the term "firm" refers to the entity defined for compliance with the GIPS standards. See the term "distinct business entity." (2) An economic unit that hires factors of production and organizes those factors to produce and sell goods and services.

Fiscal imbalance   The present value of the government's commitments to pay benefits minus the present value of its tax revenues.

Fiscal policy   The government's attempt to achieve macroeconomic objectives such as full employment, sustained economic growth, and price level stability by setting and changing taxes, making transfer payments, and purchasing goods and services.

Fixed exchange rate   An exchange rate that is set at a determined amount by government policy.

Fixed exchange rate regime   A system in which the exchange rate between two currencies remains fixed at a preset level, known as official parity.

Fixed-income forward   A forward contract in which the underlying is a bond.

Fixed-income investments   Loans with contractually mandated payment schedules from firms or governments to investors.

Fixed-rule policy   A rule that specifies an action to be pursued independently of the state of the economy.

Flat trend channel   The range defined by security prices as they maintain a relatively steady level.

Flexible exchange rates   Exchange rates that are determined by the market forces of supply and demand. They are sometimes called floating exchange rates.

Flexible exchange rate system   A system in which exchange rates are determined by supply and demand.

Floating-rate loan   A loan in which the interest rate is reset at least once after the starting date.

Floor   (1) A contract on an interest rate, whereby the writer of the floor periodically pays the difference between a specified floor rate and the market interest rate if, and only if, this difference is positive. This is equivalent to a stream of put options on the interest rate. (2) A combination of interest rate put options designed to hedge a lender against lower rates on a floating-rate loan.

Floor brokers   Independent members of an exchange who act as brokers for other members.

Floored swap   A swap in which the floating payments have a lower limit.

Floorlet   Each component put option in a floor.

Flow   A quantity per unit of time.

Foreign bond   A bond issued by a foreign company on the local market and in the local currency (e.g., Yankee bonds in the United States, Bulldog bonds in the United Kingdom, or Samurai bonds in Japan).

Foreign exchange expectation   A relation that states that the forward exchange rate, quoted at time 0 for delivery at time 1, is equal to the expected value of the spot exchange rate at time 1. When stated relative to the current spot exchange rate, the relation states that the forward discount (premium) is equal to the expected exchange rate movement.

Foreign exchange market   The market in which the currency of one country is exchanged for the currency of another.

Foreign exchange rate   The price at which one currency exchanges for another.

Forward contract An agreement between two parties in which one party, the buyer, agrees to buy from the other party, the seller, an underlying asset at a later date for a price established at the start of the contract.

Forward discount A situation where, from the perspective of the domestic country, the spot exchange rate is smaller than the forward exchange rate with a foreign country.

Forward P/E *See* Leading P/E.

Forward premium A situation where, from the perspective of the domestic country, the spot exchange rate is larger than the forward exchange rate with a foreign country.

Forward price or forward rate The fixed price or rate at which the transaction scheduled to occur at the expiration of a forward contract will take place. This price is agreed on at the initiation date of the contract.

Forward rate A short-term yield for a future holding period implied by the spot rates of two securities with different maturities.

Forward rate agreement (FRA) A forward contract calling for one party to make a fixed interest payment and the other to make an interest payment at a rate to be determined at the contract expiration.

Four-firm concentration ratio A measure of market power that is calculated as the percentage of the value of sales accounted for by the four largest firms in an industry.

Franchise The right or license to an exclusive territory or market.

Franchise factor A firm's unique competitive advantage that makes it possible for a firm to earn excess returns (rates of return above a firm's cost of capital) on its capital projects. In turn, these excess returns and the franchise factor cause the firm's stock price to have a *P/E* ratio above its base *P/E* ratio that is equal to $1/k$.

Free cash flow to equity This cash flow measure equals cash flow from operations minus capital expenditures and debt payments.

Free-rider problem The absence of an incentive for people to pay for what they consume.

Frequency distribution A tabular display of data summarized into a relatively small number of intervals.

Frequency polygon A graph of a frequency distribution obtained by drawing straight lines joining successive points representing the class frequencies.

Frictional unemployment The unemployment that arises from normal labor turnover—from people entering and leaving the labor force and from the ongoing creation and destruction of jobs.

Full-costing A method of accounting for the costs of exploring and developing oil and gas resources in which all costs are recorded as assets and depleted over the estimated life of the producing resources.

Full-costing method A method of accounting for the costs of exploring and developing oil and gas resources in which all costs are recorded as assets and depleted over the estimated life of the producing resources.

Full employment A situation in which the quantity of labor demanded equal the quantity supplied. At full employment, there is no cyclical unemployment—all unemployment is frictional and structural.

Full price (or dirty price) (1) The total price of a bond, including accrued interest. (2) The price of a security with accrued interest.

Futures commission merchants (FCMs) Individuals or companies that execute futures transactions for other parties off the exchange.

Futures contract A variation of a forward contract that has essentially the same basic definition but with some additional features, such as a clearinghouse guarantee against credit losses, a daily settlement of gains and losses, and an organized electronic or floor trading facility.

Future value (FV) The amount to which a payment or series of payments will grow by a stated future date.

Game theory A tool that economists use to analyze strategic behavior—behavior that takes into account the expected behavior of others and the mutual recognition of independence.

Gamma A numerical measure of how sensitive an option's delta is to a change in the underlying.

GDP deflator One measure of the price level, which is the average of current-year prices as a percentage of base-year prices.

General Agreement on Tariffs and Trade An international agreement signed in 1947 to reduce tariffs on international trade.

Generally accepted accounting principles (GAAP) Accounting principles formulated by the Financial Accounting Standards Board and used to construct financial statements.

Generational accounting An accounting system that measures the lifetime tax burden and benefits of each generation.

Generational imbalance The division of the fiscal imbalance between the current and future generations, assuming that the current generation will enjoy the existing levels of taxes and benefits

Generic *See* Plain-vanilla.

Geometric mean (GM) A measure of central tendency computed by taking the nth root of the product of n non-negative values.

Goods and services   The objects that people value and produce to satisfy their wants.

Goodwill   The excess of the cost of a group of assets (usually a business) over the fair market value of the assets if purchased individually.

Government budget deficit   The deficit that arises when federal government spends more than it collects in taxes.

Government budget surplus   The surplus that arises when the federal government collects more in taxes than it spends.

Government debt   The total amount of borrowing that the government has borrowed. It equals the sum of past budget deficits minus budget surpluses.

Government purchases   Goods and services bought by the government.

Government purchases multiplier   The magnification effect of a change in government purchases of goods and services on aggregate demand.

Government sector surplus or deficit   An amount equal to net taxes minus government purchases of goods and services.

Great Depression   A decade (1929–1939) of high unemployment and stagnant production throughout the world economy.

Gross domestic product (GDP)   The market value of all the final goods and services produced within a country during a given time period—usually a year.

Gross-Of-Fees Return   The return on assets reduced by any trading expenses incurred during the period.

Gross investment   The total amount spent on purchases of new capital and on replacing depreciated capital.

Group depreciation   The grouping of similar items to calculate depreciation.

Growth company   A company that consistently has the opportunities and ability to invest in projects that provide rates of return that exceed the firm's cost of capital. Because of these investment opportunities, it retains a high proportion of earnings, and its earnings grow faster than those of average firms.

Growth stock   A stock issue that generates a higher rate of return than other stocks in the market with similar risk characteristics.

Harmonic mean   A type of weighted mean computed by averaging the reciprocals of the observations, then taking the reciprocal of that average.

Hedge   A trading strategy in which derivative securities are used to reduce or completely offset a counterparty's risk exposure to an underlying asset.

Hedge fund   An investment vehicle designed to manage a private, unregistered portfolio of assets according to any of several strategies. The investment strategy often employs arbitrage trading and significant financial leverage (e.g., short selling, borrowing, derivatives) while the compensation arrangement for the manager typically specifies considerable profit participation.

Hedge ratio   The number of derivative contracts that must be transacted to offset the price volatility of an underlying commodity or security position.

Herfindahl-Hirschman Index   A measure of market power that is calculated as the square of the market share of each firm (as a percentage) summed over the largest 50 firms (or over all firms if there are fewer than 50) in a market.

High-yield bond   A bond rated below investment grade. Also referred to as *speculative-grade bonds* or *junk bonds.*

Histogram   A bar chart of data that have been grouped into a frequency distribution.

Holding period return (HPR)   The return that an investor earns during a specified holding period; a synonym for total return.

Holding period yield (HPY)   (1) The total return from an investment for a given period of time stated as a percentage. (2) The return that an investor earns during a specified holding period; holding period return with reference to a fixed-income instrument.

Human capital   The value of skills and knowledge possessed by the workforce.

Hurdle rate   The discount rate (cost of capital) which the IRR must exceed if a project is to be accepted.

Hypothesis   With reference to statistical inference, a statement about one or more populations.

Hypothesis testing   With reference to statistical inference, the subdivision dealing with the testing of hypotheses about one or more populations.

Implicit rental rate   The firm's opportunity cost of using its own capital.

Implied repo rate   The rate of return from a cash-and-carry transaction implied by the futures price relative to the spot price.

Implied volatility   The volatility that option traders use to price an option, implied by the price of the option and a particular option-pricing model.

Imports   The goods and services that we buy from people in other countries.

Incentive   A reward that encourages or a penalty that discourages an action.

Incentive system   A method of organizing production that uses a market-like mechanism inside the firm.

Income effect   The effect of a change in income on consumption, other things remaining the same.

Income elasticity of demand The responsiveness of demand to a change in income, other things remaining the same. It is calculated as the percentage change in the quantity demanded divided by the percentage change in income.

Income statement A financial statement that shows the flow of the firm's sales, expenses, and earnings over a period of time.

Incremental cash flows The changes or increments to cash flows resulting from a decision or action.

Indenture The legal agreement that lists the obligations of the issuer of a bond to the bondholder, including payment schedules, call provisions, and sinking funds.

Independent With reference to events, the property that the occurrence of one event does not affect the probability of another event occurring.

Independent variable A variable used to explain the dependent variable in a regression; a right-hand-side variable in a regression equation.

Index amortizing swap An interest rate swap in which the notional principal is indexed to the level of interest rates and declines with the level of interest rates according to a predefined schedule. This type of swap is frequently used to hedge securities that are prepaid as interest rates decline, such as mortgage-backed securities.

Indexing An investment strategy in which an investor constructs a portfolio to mirror the performance of a specified index.

Indirect method The procedure for converting the income statement from an accrual basis to a cash basis by adjusting net income for items that do not affect cash flows, including depreciation, amortization, depletion, gains, losses, and changes in current assets and current liabilities.

Individual transferable quota (ITQ) A production limit that is assigned to an individual who is free to transfer the quota to someone else.

Induced taxes Taxes that vary with real GDP.

Industry life cycle analysis An analysis that focuses on the industry's stage of development.

Inelastic demand A demand with a price elasticity between 0 and 1; the percentage change in the quantity demanded is less than the percentage change in price.

Infant-industry argument The argument that it is necessary to protect a new industry to enable it to grow into a mature industry that can compete in world markets.

Inferior good A good for which demand decreases as income increases.

Inflation A process in which the price level is rising and money is losing value.

Inflationary gap The amount by which real GDP exceeds potential GDP.

Inflation rate The percentage change in the price level from one year to the next.

Information An attribute of a good market that includes providing buyers and sellers with timely, accurate information on the volume and prices of past transactions and on all currently outstanding bids and offers.

Informationally efficient market A more technical term for an efficient capital market that emphasizes the role of information in setting the market price.

Information ratio Statistic used to measure a portfolio's average return in excess of a comparison, benchmark portfolio divided by the standard deviation of this excess return.

Initial margin requirement The margin requirement on the first day of a transaction as well as on any day in which additional margin funds must be deposited.

Initial public offering (IPO) A new issue by a firm that has no existing public market.

Intangible assets Long-term assets with no physical substance whose value is based on rights or advantages accruing to the owner.

Intellectual property rights Property rights for discoveries owned by the creators of knowledge.

Interest The income that capital earns.

Interest-on-interest Bond income from reinvestment of coupon payments.

Interest rate A rate of return that reflects the relationship between differently dated cash flows; a discount rate.

Interest rate call An option in which the holder has the right to make a known interest payment and receive an unknown interest payment.

Interest rate cap or cap A series of call options on an interest rate, with each option expiring at the date on which the floating loan rate will be reset, and with each option having the same exercise rate. A cap in general can have an underlying other than an interest rate.

Interest rate collar A combination of a long cap and a short floor, or a short cap and a long floor. A collar in general can have an underlying other than an interest rate.

Interest rate floor or floor A series of put options on an interest rate, with each option expiring at the date on which the floating loan rate will be reset, and with each option having the same exercise rate. A floor in general can have an underlying other than the interest rate.

Interest rate forward *See* Forward rate agreement.

Interest rate option An option in which the underlying is an interest rate.

Interest rate parity The relationship that must exist in an efficient market between the spot and forward foreign exchange rates between two countries and the interest rates in those countries.

Interest rate put An option in which the holder has the right to make an unknown interest payment and receive a known interest payment.

Interest rate risk The uncertainty of returns on an investment due to possible changes in interest rates over time.

Interest rate swap An agreement calling for the periodic exchange of cash flows, one based on an interest rate that remains fixed for the life of the contract and the other that is linked to a variable-rate index.

Intergenerational data mining A form of data mining that applies information developed by previous researchers using a dataset to guide current research using the same or a related dataset.

Intermarket Trading System (ITS) A computerized system that connects competing exchanges and dealers who trade stocks listed on an exchange. Its purpose is to help customers find the best market for these stocks at a point in time.

Internal liquidity (solvency) ratios Financial ratios that measure the ability of the firm to meet future short-term financial obligations.

Internal rate of return (IRR) The discount rate that makes net present value equal 0; the discount rate that makes the present value of an investment's costs (outflows) equal to the present value of the investment's benefits (inflows).

Internal Rate of Return (Private Equity) (IRR) IRR is the annualized implied discount rate (effective compounded rate) that equates the present value of all the appropriate cash inflows (paid-in capital, such as drawdowns for net investments) associated with an investment with the sum of the present value of all the appropriate cash outflows (such as distributions) accruing from it and the present value of the unrealized residual portfolio (unliquidated holdings). For an interim cumulative return measurement, any IRR depends on the valuation of the residual assets.

Internal Valuation (Real Estate) An internal valuation is an advisor's or underlying third-party manager's best estimate of market value based on the most current and accurate information available under the circumstances. An internal valuation could include industry practice techniques, such as discounted cash flow, sales comparison, replacement cost, or a review of all significant events (both general market and asset specific) that could have a material impact on the investment. Prudent assumptions and estimates must be used, and the process must be applied consistently from period to period, except where a change would result in better estimates of market value.

International Fisher relation The assertion that the interest rate differential between two countries should equal the expected inflation rate differential over the term of the interest rates.

Interval With reference to grouped data, a set of values within which an observation falls.

Interval scale A measurement scale that not only ranks data but also gives assurance that the differences between scale values are equal.

In the money An option that has positive intrinsic value.

In-the-money option (1) An option that has a positive value if exercised immediately. For example, a call when the strike price is below the current price of the underlying asset, or a put when the strike price is above the current price of the underlying asset. (2) An option that has positive intrinsic value. (3) Options that, if exercised, would result in the value received being worth more than the payment required to exercise.

Intrinsic value The portion of a call option's total value equal to the greater of either zero or the difference between the current value of the underlying asset and the exercise price; for a put option, intrinsic value is the greater of either zero or the exercise price less the underlying asset price. For a stock, it is the value derived from fundamental analysis of the stock's expected returns or cash flows.

Inverse floater A floating-rate note or bond in which the coupon is adjusted to move opposite to a benchmark interest rate.

Inverse relationship A relationship between variables that move in opposite directions.

Invested Capital (Private Equity) The amount of paid-in capital that has been invested in portfolio companies.

Investing activities Business activities that involve the acquisition and sale of marketable securities and long-term assets and the making and collecting of loans.

Investment The current commitment of dollars for a period of time in order to derive future payments that will compensate the investor for the time the funds are committed, the expected rate of inflation, and the uncertainty of future payments.

Investment The purchase of new plant, equipment, and buildings and additions to inventories.

Investment Advisor (Private Equity) Any individual or institution that supplies investment advice to clients on a per fee basis. The investment advisor inherently has no role in the management of the underlying portfolio companies of a partnership/fund.

Investment company A firm that sells shares of the company and uses the proceeds to buy portfolios of stock, bonds, or other financial instruments.

Investment decision process Estimation of intrinsic value for comparison with market price to determine whether or not to invest.

Investment demand The relationship between investment and real interest rate, other things remaining the same.

Investment horizon The time period used for planning and forecasting purposes or the future time at which the investor requires the invested funds.

Investment management company A company separate from the investment company that manages the portfolio and performs administrative functions.

Investment Management Fee The fee payable to the investment management firm for the on-going management of a portfolio. Investment management fees are typically asset based (percentage of assets), performance based (based on performance relative to a benchmark), or a combination of the two but may take different forms as well.

Investment Multiple (TVPI Multiple) (Private Equity) The ratio of total value to paid-in-capital. It represents the total return of the investment to the original investment not taking into consideration the time invested. Total value can be found by adding the residual value and distributed capital together.

Investment strategy A decision by a portfolio manager regarding how he or she will manage the portfolio to meet the goals and objectives of the client. This will include either active or passive management and, if active, what style in terms of top-down or buttom-up or fundamental versus technical.

IRR The discount rate which forces the PV of a project's inflows to equal the PV of its costs.

IRR rule An investment decision rule that accepts projects or investments for which the IRR is greater than the opportunity cost of capital.

January effect A frequent empirical anomaly where risk-adjusted stock returns in the month of January are significantly larger than those occurring in any other month of the year.

Job search The activity of looking for acceptable vacant jobs.

Joint probability The probability of the joint occurrence of stated events.

Keynesian An economist who believes that left alone, the economy would rarely operate at full employment and that to achieve full employment, active help from fiscal policy and monetary policy is required.

Kurtosis The statistical measure that indicates the peakedness of a distribution.

Labor The work time and work effort that people devote to producing goods and services.

Labor force The sum of the people who are employed and who are unemployed.

Labor force participation rate The percentage of the working-age population who are members of the labor force.

Labor productivity Real GDP per hour of work.

Labor union An organized group of workers whose purpose is to increase wages and to influence other job conditions.

Laffer curve The relationship between the tax rate and the amount of tax revenue collected.

Land The gifts of nature that we use to produce goods and services.

Law of demand Other things remaining the same, the higher the price of a good, the smaller is the quantity demanded of it.

Law of diminishing returns As a firm uses more of a variable input, with a given quantity of other inputs (fixed inputs), the marginal product of the variable input eventually diminishes.

Law of one price The condition in a financial market in which two financial instruments or combinations of financial instruments can sell for only one price. Equivalent to the principle that no arbitrage opportunities are possible.

Law of supply Other things remaining the same, the higher the price of a good, the greater is the quantity supplied of it.

Leading indicators A set of economic variables whose values reach peaks and troughs in advance of the aggregate economy.

Leading P/E (or forward P/E or prospective P/E) A stock's current price divided by next year's expected earnings.

Learning-by-doing People become more productive in an activity (learn) just by repeatedly producing a particular good or service (doing).

Leasehold A right to occupy land or buildings under a long-term rental contract.

Leasehold improvements Improvements to leased property that become the property of the lessor at the end of the lease.

Legal monopoly A market structure in which there is one firm and entry is restricted by the granting of a public franchise, government license, patent, or copyright.

Leptokurtic Describes a distribution that is more peaked than a normal distribution.

License The right to use a formula, technique, process, or design.

Likelihood The probability of an observation, given a particular set of conditions.

Limit down A limit move in the futures market in which the price at which a transaction would be made is at or below the lower limit.

Limited Partnership (Private Equity) The legal structure used by most venture and private equity funds. Usually fixed life investment vehicles. The general partner or management firm manages the partnership using the policy laid down in a partnership agreement. The agreement also covers terms, fees, structures, and other items agreed between the limited partners and the general partner.

Limit move A condition in the futures markets in which the price at which a transaction would be made is at or beyond the price limits.

Limit order An order that lasts for a specified time to buy or sell a security when and if it trades at a specified price.

Limit pricing The practice of setting the price at the highest level that inflicts a loss on an entrant.

Limit up A limit move in the futures market in which the price at which a transaction would be made is at or above the upper limit.

Linear association A straight-line relationship, as opposed to a relationship that cannot be graphed as a straight line.

Linear interpolation The estimation of an unknown value on the basis of two known values that bracket it, using a straight line between the two known values.

Linear regression Regression that models the straight-line relationship between the dependent and independent variable(s).

Linear relationship A relationship between two variables that is illustrated by a straight line.

Liquid Term used to describe an asset that can be quickly converted to cash at a price close to fair market value.

Liquidity premium A premium added to the equilibrium interest rate on a security if that security cannot be converted to cash on short notice and at close to "fair market value."

Liquidity risk Uncertainty due to the ability to buy or sell an investment in the secondary market.

Living wage An hourly wage rate that enables a person who works a 40-hour week to rent adequate housing for not more than 30 percent of the amount earned.

Locked limit A condition in the futures markets in which a transaction cannot take place because the price would be beyond the limits.

London InterBank Offer Rate (LIBOR) (1) The rate at which international banks lend on the Eurocurrency market. This is the rate quoted to a top-quality borrower. The most common maturities are one month, three months, and six months. There is a LIBOR for the U.S. dollar and a few other major currencies. LIBOR is determined by the British Banking Association in London. *See* also Euribor. (2) The Eurodollar rate at which London banks lend dollars to other London banks; considered to be the best representative rate on a dollar borrowed by a private, high-quality borrower.

Long The buyer of a derivative contract. Also refers to the position of owning a derivative.

Longitudinal data Observations on characteristic(s) of the same observational unit through time.

Long position The buyer of a commodity or security or, for a forward contract, the counterparty who will be the eventual buyer of the underlying asset.

Long run A period of time in which the quantities of all resources can be varied.

Long-run aggregate supply curve The relationship between the real GDP supplied and the price level in the long run when real GDP equals potential GDP.

Long-run average cost curve The relationship between the lowest attainable average total cost and output when both capital and labor are varied.

Long-run industry supply curve A curve that shows how the quantity supplied by an industry varies as the market price varies after all the possible adjustments have been made, including changes in plant size and the number of firms in the industry.

Long-run macroeconomic equilibrium A situation that occurs when real GDP equals potential GDP—the economy is on its long-run aggregate supply curve.

Long-run Phillips curve A curve that shows the relationship between inflation and unemployment when the actual inflation rate equals the expected inflation rate.

Long-term assets Assets that have a useful life of more than one year, are used in the operation of a business, and are not intended for resale. Less commonly called *fixed assets*.

Long-term equity anticipatory securities (LEAPS) Options originally created with expirations of several years.

Look-ahead bias A bias caused by using information that was unavailable on the test date.

Lower bound The lowest possible value of an option.

Lucas wedge The accumulated loss of output that results from a slowdown in the growth rate of real GDP per person.

M1 A measure of money that consists of currency and traveler's checks plus checking deposits owned by individuals and businesses.

M2 A measure of money that consists of M1 plus time deposits, savings deposits, and money market mutual funds and other deposits.

Macroeconomic long run. A time frame that is sufficiently long for real GDP to return to potential GDP so that full employment prevails.

Macaulay duration A measure of the time flow of cash from a bond where cash flows are weighted by present values discounted by the yield to maturity.

Macroeconomics The study of the performance of the national economy and the global economy.

Macroeconomic short run A period during which some money prices are sticky and real GDP might be below, above, or at potential GDP and unemployment might be above, below, or at the natural rate of unemployment.

Maintenance margin The required proportion that the investor's equity value must be to the total market value of the stock. If the proportion drops below this percent, the investor will receive a margin call.

Maintenance margin requirement The margin requirement on any day other than the first day of a transaction.

Management fee The compensation an investment company pays to the investment management company for its services. The average annual fee is about 0.5 percent of fund assets.

Margin (1) The percent of cost a buyer pays in cash for a security, borrowing the balance from the broker. This introduces leverage, which increases the risk of the transaction. (2) The amount of money that a trader deposits in a margin account. The term is derived from the stock market practice in which an investor borrows a portion of the money required to purchase a certain amount of stock. In futures markets, there is no borrowing so the margin is more of a down payment or performance bond.

Margin account The collateral posted with the futures exchange clearinghouse by an outside counterparty to insure its eventual performance; the *initial* margin is the deposit required at contract origination while the *maintenance* margin is the minimum collateral necessary at all times.

Marginal benefit The benefit that a person receives from consuming one more unit of a good or service. It is measured as the maximum amount that a person is willing to pay for one more unit of the good or service.

Marginal benefit curve A curve that shows the relationship between the marginal benefit of a good and the quantity of that good consumed.

Marginal cost The opportunity cost of producing one more unit of a good or service. It is the best alternative forgone. It is calculated as the increase in total cost divided by the increase in output.

Marginal cost pricing rule A rule that sets the price of a good or service equal to the marginal cost of producing it.

Marginal probability *See* Unconditional probability.

Marginal product The increase in total product that results from a one-unit increase in the variable input, with all other inputs remaining the same. It is calculated as the increase in total product divided by the increase in the variable input employed, when the quantities of all other inputs are constant.

Marginal product of labor The additional real GDP produced by an additional hour of labor when all other influences on production remain the same.

Marginal propensity to consume The fraction of a change in disposable income that is consumed. It is calculated as the change in consumption expenditure divided by the change in disposable income.

Marginal revenue The change in total revenue that results from a one-unit increase in the quantity sold. It is calculated as the change in total revenue divided by the change in quantity sold.

Marginal revenue product The change in total revenue that results from employing one more unit of a resource (labor) while the quantity of all other resources remains the same. It is calculated as the increase in total revenue divided by the increase in the quantity of the resource (labor).

Marginal social benefit The marginal benefit enjoyed by society—by the consumer of a good or service (marginal private benefit) plus the marginal benefit enjoyed by others (marginal external benefit).

Marginal social cost The marginal cost incurred by the entire society—by the producer and by everyone else on whom the cost falls—and is the sum of marginal private cost and the marginal external cost.

Marginal tax rate The part of each additional dollar in income that is paid as tax.

Margin call A request by an investor's broker for additional capital for a security bought on margin if the investor's equity value declines below the required maintenance margin.

Marked to market The settlement process used to adjust the margin account of a futures contract for daily changes in the price of the underlying asset.

Market demand The relationship between the total quantity demanded of a good and its price. It is illustrated by the market demand curve.

Market failure A state in which the market does not allocate resources efficiently.

Market order An order to buy or sell a security immediately at the best price available.

Market portfolio The portfolio that includes all risky assets with relative weights equal to their proportional market values.

Market power The ability to influence the market, and in particular the market price, by influencing the total quantity offered for sale.

Market risk The risk associated with interest rates, exchange rates, and equity prices.

Market risk premium The amount of return above the risk-free rate that investors expect from the market in general as compensation for systematic risk.

Market Value The current listed price at which investors buy or sell securities at a given time.

Market Value (Real Estate) The most probable price that a property should bring in a competitive and open market under all conditions requisite to a fair sale, the buyer and seller each acting prudently and knowledgeably, and assuming the price is not affected by undue stimulus. Implicit in this definition is the consummation of a sale as of a specified date and the passing of title from seller to buyer under conditions whereby: (a) Buyer and seller are typically motivated. (b) Both parties are well informed or well advised and each acting in what they consider their own best interests. (c) A reasonable time is allowed for exposure in the open market. (d) Payment is made in terms of currency or in terms of financial arrangements comparable thereto. (e) The price represents the normal consideration for the property sold unaffected by special or creative financing or sales concessions granted by anyone associated with the sale.

Market value added (MVA) External management performance measure to compare the market value of the company's debt and equity with the total capital invested in the firm.

Marking to market (1) Procedure whereby potential profits and losses on a futures position are realized daily. The daily futures price variation is debited (credited) in cash to the loser (winner) at the end of the day. (2) A procedure used primarily in futures markets in which the parties to a contract settle the amount owed daily. Also known as the daily settlement.

McCallum rule A rule that adjusts the growth rate of the monetary base to target the inflation rate but also to take into account changes in the trend productivity growth rate and fluctuations in aggregate demand.

Mean absolute deviation With reference to a sample, the mean of the absolute values of deviations from the sample mean.

Mean excess return The average rate of return in excess of the risk-free rate.

Means of payment A method of settling a debt.

Mean–variance analysis An approach to portfolio analysis using expected means, variances, and covariances of asset returns.

Measurement scales A scheme of measuring differences. The four types of measurement scales are nominal, ordinal, interval, and ratio.

Measure of central tendency A quantitative measure that specifies where data are centered.

Median The value of the middle item of a set of items that has been sorted into ascending or descending order; the 50th percentile.

Mesokurtic Describes a distribution with kurtosis identical to that of the normal distribution.

Microeconomics The study of the choices that individuals and businesses make, the way those choices interact, and the influence governments exert on them.

Minimum efficient scale The smallest quantity of output at which the long-run average cost curve reaches its lowest level.

Minimum wage A regulation that makes the hiring of labor below a specified wage rate illegal.

Modal interval With reference to grouped data, the most frequently occurring interval.

Mode The most frequently occurring value in a set of observations.

Modified duration (1) Measure of a bond's price sensitivity to interest rate movements. Equal to the duration of a bond divided by one plus its yield to maturity. (2) A measure of Macaulay duration divided by one plus the bond's periodic yield used to approximate the bond's price volatility. (3) An adjustment of the duration for the level of the yield. Contrast with Macaulay duration.

Monetarist An economist who believes that the economy is self regulating and that it will normally operate at full employment, provided that monetary policy is not erratic and that the pace of money growth is kept steady.

Monetary base The sum of the Federal Reserve notes, coins, and banks' deposits at the Fed.

Monetary policy The Fed conducts the nation's monetary policy by changing in interest rates and adjusting the quantity of money.

Money Any commodity or token that is generally acceptable as a means of payment.

Money market The market for short-term debt securities with maturities of less than one year.

Money market fund A fund that invests in short-term securities sold in the money market. (Large companies, banks, and other institutions also invest their surplus cash in the money market for short periods of time.) In the entire investment spectrum, these are generally the safest, most stable securities available. They include Treasury bills, certificates of deposit of large banks, and commercial paper (short-term IOUs of large corporations).

Money market mutual fund A fund operated by a financial institution that sells shares in the fund and holds liquid assets such as U.S. Treasury bills and short-term commercial bills.

Money market yield (or CD equivalent yield) A yield on a basis comparable to the quoted yield on an interest-bearing money market instrument that pays interest on a 360-day basis; the annualized holding period yield, assuming a 360-day year.

Money multiplier The amount by which a change in the monetary base is multiplied to determine the resulting change in the quantity of money.

Moneyness The relationship between the price of the underlying and an option's exercise price.

Money price The number of dollars that must be given up in exchange for a good or service.

Money wage rate The number of dollars that an hour of labor earns.

Monopolistic competition A market structure in which a large number of firms compete by making similar but slightly different products.

Monopoly A market structure in which there is one firm, which produces a good or service that has no close substitute and in which the firm is protected from competition by a barrier preventing the entry of new firms.

Monte Carlo simulation A risk analysis technique in which probable future events are simulated on a computer, generating estimated rates of return and risk indexes.

Mortgage bonds Bonds that pledge specific assets such as buildings and equipment. The proceeds from the sale of these assets are used to pay off bondholders in case of bankruptcy.

Moving average The continually recalculating average of security prices for a period, often 200 days, to serve as an indication of the general trend of prices and also as a benchmark price.

Multifactor model An empirical version of the APT where the investor chooses the exact number and identity of the common risk factors used to describe an asset's risk-return relationship. Risk factors are often designated as *macroeconomic* variables (e.g., inflation, changes in gross domestic product) or *microeconomic* variables (e.g., security-specific characteristics like firm size or book-to-market ratios).

Multiplication rule for probabilities The rule that the joint probability of events A and B equals the probability of A given B times the probability of B.

Multiplier The amount by which a change in autonomous expenditure is magnified or multiplied to determine the change in equilibrium expenditure and real GDP.

Multivariate distribution A probability distribution that specifies the probabilities for a group of related random variables.

Multivariate normal distribution A probability distribution for a group of random variables that is completely defined by the means and variances of the variables plus all the correlations between pairs of the variables.

Must A required provision for claiming compliance with the GIPS standards.

Mutual fund An investment company that pools money from shareholders and invests in a variety of securities, including stocks, bonds, and money market securities. A mutual fund ordinarily stands ready to buy back (redeem) its shares at their current net asset value, which depends on the market value of the fund's portfolio of securities at the time. Mutual funds generally continuously offer new shares to investors.

Mutually exclusive events Events such that only one can occur at a time.

Nasdaq InterMarket A trading system that includes Nasdaq market makers and ECNs that quote and trade stocks listed on the NYSE and the AMEX. It involves dealers from the Nasdaq market and the Intermarket Trading System (ITS). In many ways, this has become what had been labeled the third market.

Nash equilibrium The outcome of a game that occurs when player A takes the best possible action given the action of player B and player B takes the best possible action given the action of player A.

National saving The sum of private saving (saving by households and businesses) and government saving.

Natural monopoly A monopoly that occurs when one firm can supply the entire market at a lower price than two or more firms can.

Natural rate of unemployment The unemployment rate when the economy is at full employment. There is no cyclical unemployment; all unemployment is frictional and structural.

Natural resources Long-term assets purchased for the economic value that can be taken from the land and used up.

Near-term, high-priority goal A short-term financial investment goal of personal importance, such as accumulating funds for making a house down payment or buying a car.

Needs-tested spending Government spending on programs that pay benefits to suitably qualified people and businesses.

Negative relationship A relationship between variables that move in opposite directions.

Negotiated sales An underwriting arrangement wherein the sale of a security issue by an issuing entity (governmental body or a corporation) is done using an investment banking firm that maintains an ongoing relationship with the issuer. The characteristics of the security issue are determined by the issuer in consultation with the investment banker.

Neoclassical growth theory A theory of economic growth that proposes that real GDP grows because technological change induces a level of saving and investment that makes capital per hour of labor grow.

Net asset value The market value of the assets owned by a fund.

Net borrower A country that is borrowing more from the rest of the world than it is lending to it.

Net exports The value of exports minus the value of imports.

Net investment Net increase in the capital stock—gross investment minus depreciation.

Net lender A country that is lending more to the rest of the world than it is borrowing from it.

Net-of-Fees Return The gross-of-fees return reduced by the investment management fee.

Net present value The present value of the future flow of marginal revenue product generated by capital minus the cost of the capital.

Net present value (NPV) A measure of the excess cash flows expected from an investment proposal. It is equal to the present value of the cash *inflows* from an investment proposal, discounted at the required rate of return for the investment, minus the present value of the cash *outflows* required by the investment, also discounted at the investment's required rate of return. If the derived net present value is a positive value (i.e., there is an excess net present value), the investment should be acquired since it will provide a rate of return above its required returns.

Net taxes Taxes paid to governments minus transfer payments received from governments.

Netting When parties agree to exchange only the net amount owed from one party to the other.

New issue Common stocks or bonds offered by companies for public sale.

New Keynesian A Keynesian who holds the view that not only is the money wage rate sticky but that prices of goods and services are also sticky.

Node Each value on a binomial tree from which successive moves or outcomes branch.

No-load fund A mutual fund that sells its shares at net asset value without adding sales charges.

Nominal GDP The value of the final goods and services produced in a given year valued at the prices that prevailed in that same year. It is a more precise name for GDP.

Nominal risk-free interest rate The sum of the real risk-free interest rate and the inflation premium.

Nominal scale A measurement scale that categorizes data but does not rank them.

Nominal yield A bond's yield as measured by its coupon rate.

Noncash investing and financing transactions Significant investing and financing transactions involving only long-term assets, long-term liabilities, or stockholders' equity that do not affect current cash inflows or outflows.

Nonlinear relation An association or relationship between variables that cannot be graphed as a straight line.

Nonparametric test A test that is not concerned with a parameter, or that makes minimal assumptions about the population from which a sample comes.

Nonrenewable natural resources Natural resources that can be used only once and that cannot be replaced once they have been used.

Nontariff barrier Any action other than a tariff that restricts international trade.

Normal backwardation The condition in futures markets in which futures prices are lower than expected spot prices.

Normal contango The condition in futures markets in which futures prices are higher than expected spot prices.

Normal good A good for which demand increases as income increases.

Normal profit The expected return for supplying entrepreneurial ability.

North American Free Trade Agreement An agreement, which became effective on January 1, 1994, to eliminate all barriers to international trade between the United States, Canada, and Mexico after a 15-year phasing in period.

Notes Intermediate-term debt securities with maturities longer than 1 year but less than 10 years.

Notional principal The principal value of a swap transaction, which is not exchanged but is used as a scale factor to translate interest rate differentials into cash settlement payments.

NPV rule An investment decision rule that states that an investment should be undertaken if its NPV is positive but not undertaken if its NPV is negative.

Null hypothesis The hypothesis to be tested.

Objective probabilities Probabilities that generally do not vary from person to person; includes a priori and objective probabilities.

Objectives The investor's goals expressed in terms of risk and return and included in the policy statement.

Obsolescence The process of becoming out of date, which is a factor in the limited useful life of tangible assets.

Offensive competitive strategy A strategy whereby a firm attempts to use its strengths to affect the competitive forces in the industry and, in so doing, improves the firm's relative position in the industry.

Official reserves The amount of reserves owned by the central bank of a government in the form of gold, Special Drawing Rights, and foreign cash or marketable securities.

Official settlements account A record of the change in a country's official reserves.

Off-market FRA A contract in which the initial value is intentionally set at a value other than zero and therefore requires a cash payment at the start from one party to the other.

Offsetting A transaction in exchange-listed derivative markets in which a party re-enters the market to close out a position.

Okun gap The gap between real GDP and potential GDP, and so is another name for the output gap.

Oligopoly A market structure in which a small number of firms compete.

One-sided hypothesis test (or one-tailed hypothesis test) A test in which the null hypothesis is rejected only if the evidence indicates that the population parameter is greater than (smaller than) θ_0. The alternative hypothesis also has one side.

Open-End Fund (Private Equity) A type of investment fund where the number of investors and the total committed capital is not fixed (i.e., open for subscriptions and/or redemptions).

Open market operation The purchase or sale of government securities—U.S. Treasury bills and bonds—by the Federal Reserve System in the open market.

Operating activities Business activities that involve the cash effects of transactions and other events that enter into the determination of net income.

Operating efficiency ratios Financial ratios intended to indicate how efficiently management is utilizing the firm's assets in terms of dollar sales generated per dollar of assets. Primary examples would be: total asset turnover, fixed asset turnover, or equity turnover.

Operating leverage The use of fixed-production costs in the firm's operating cost structure. The effect of fixed costs is to magnify the effect of a change in sales on operating profits.

Operating profitability ratios Financial ratios intended to indicate how profitable the firm is in terms of the percent of profit generated from sales. Alternative measures would include: operating profit (EBIT)/net sales; pretax profit (EBT)/net sales; and net profit/sales.

Opportunity cost The highest-valued alternative that we give up to something.

Optimal portfolio The portfolio on the efficient frontier that has the highest utility for a given investor. It lies at the point of tangency between the efficient frontier and the curve with the investor's highest possible utility.

Option A financial instrument that gives one party the right, but not the obligation, to buy or sell an underlying asset from or to another party at a fixed price over a specific period of time. Also referred to as contingent claims.

Option-adjusted spread A type of yield spread that considers changes in the term structure and alternative estimates of the volatility of interest rates.

Option contract An agreement that grants the owner the right, but not the obligation, to make a future transaction in an underlying commodity or security at a fixed price and within a predetermined time in the future.

Option premium The initial price that the option buyer must pay to the option seller to acquire the contract.

Option premium (or option price or premium) (1) The price of an option. (2) The initial price that the option buyer must pay to the option seller to acquire the contract. (3) The amount of money a buyer pays and seller receives to engage in an option transaction.

Ordinal scale A measurement scale that sorts data into categories that are ordered (ranked) with respect to some characteristic.

Ordinary annuity An annuity with a first cash flow that is paid one period from the present.

OTC Electronic Bulletin Board (OTCBB) A regulated quotation service that displays real-time quotes, last-sale prices, and volume information for a specified set of over-the-counter (OTC) securities that are not traded on the formal Nasdaq market.

Outcome   A possible value of a random variable.

Out-of-sample test   A test of a strategy or model using a sample outside the time period on which the strategy or model was developed.

Out-of-the-money option   (1) An option that has no value if exercised immediately. For example, a call when the strike price is above the current price of the underlying asset, or a put when the strike price is below the current price of the underlying asset. (2) An option that has no intrinsic value. (3) Options that, if exercised, would require the payment of more money than the value received and therefore would not be currently exercised.

Overnight index swap (OIS)   A swap in which the floating rate is the cumulative value of a single unit of currency invested at an overnight rate during the settlement period.

Overweighted   A condition in which a portfolio, for whatever reason, includes more of a class of securities than the relative market value alone would justify.

Paid-In Capital (Private Equity)   The amount of committed capital a limited partner has actually transferred to a venture fund. Also known as the cumulative drawdown amount.

Paired comparisons test   A statistical test for differences based on paired observations drawn from samples that are dependent on each other.

Paired observations   Observations that are dependent on each other.

Pairs arbitrage trade   A trade in two closely related stocks involving the short sale of one and the purchase of the other.

Panel data   Observations through time on a single characteristic of multiple observational units.

Parameter   A descriptive measure computed from or used to describe a population of data, conventionally represented by Greek letters.

Parameter instability   The problem or issue of population regression parameters that have changed over time.

Parametric test   Any test (or procedure) concerned with parameters or whose validity depends on assumptions concerning the population generating the sample.

Par value   *See* Principal.
The principal amount repaid at maturity of a bond. Also called face value.

Patent   A government-sanctioned exclusive right granted to the inventor of a good, service, or productive process to produce, use, and sell the invention for a given number of years.

Patent   An exclusive right granted by the federal government for a period of 20 years to make a particular product or use a specific process.

Payback   The time required for the added income from the convertible security relative to the stock to offset the conversion premium.

Payer swaption   A swaption that allows the holder to enter into a swap as the fixed-rate payer and floating-rate receiver.

Payment date   The date on which a firm actually mails dividend checks.

Payoff   The value of an option at expiration.

Payoff matrix   A table that shows the payoffs for every possible action by each player for every possible action by each other player.

Pegged exchange rate regime   A system in which a country's exchange rate in relation to a major currency is set at a target value (the peg) but allowed to fluctuate within a small band around the target.

Percentiles   Quantiles that divide a distribution into 100 equal parts.

Perfect competition   A market in which there are many firms each selling an identical product; there are many buyers; there are no restrictions on entry into the industry; firms in the industry have no advantage over potential new entrants; and firms and buyers are well informed about the price of each firm's product.

Perfectly elastic demand   Demand with an infinite price elasticity; the quantity demanded changes by an infinitely large percentage in response to a tiny price change.

Perfectly inelastic demand   Demand with a price elasticity of zero; the quantity demanded remains constant when the price changes.

Perfect price discrimination   Price discrimination that extracts the entire consumer surplus.

Performance appraisal   (1) The assessment of an investment record for evidence of investment skill. (2) The evaluation of risk-adjusted performance; the evaluation of investment skill.

Performance measurement   The calculation of returns in a logical and consistent manner.

Permutation   An ordered listing.

Perpetuity   (1) An investment without any maturity date. It provides returns to its owner indefinitely. (2) A perpetual annuity, or a set of never-ending level sequential cash flows, with the first cash flow occurring one period from now.

Personal trust   An amount of money set aside by a grantor and often managed by a third party, the trustee. Often constructed so one party receives income from the trust's investments and another party receives the residual value of the trust after the income beneficiaries' death.

Phillips curve   A curve that shows a relationship between inflation and unemployment.

Physical deterioration   A decline in the useful life of a depreciable asset resulting from use and from exposure to the elements.

Plain-vanilla   Refers to a security, especially a bond or a swap, issued with standard features. Sometimes called generic.

Plain vanilla swap   An interest rate swap in which one party pays a fixed rate and the other pays a floating rate, with both sets of payments in the same currency.

Platykurtic   Describes a distribution that is less peaked than the normal distribution.

Point estimate   A single numerical estimate of an unknown quantity, such as a population parameter.

Policy statement   A statement in which the investor specifies investment goals, constraints, and risk preferences.

Pooled estimate   An estimate of a parameter that involves combining (pooling) observations from two or more samples.

Population   All members of a specified group.

Population mean   The arithmetic mean value of a population; the arithmetic mean of all the observations or values in the population.

Population standard deviation   A measure of dispersion relating to a population in the same unit of measurement as the observations, calculated as the positive square root of the population variance.

Population variance   A measure of dispersion relating to a population, calculated as the mean of the squared deviations around the population mean.

Portfolio   An individually managed pool of assets. A portfolio may be a subportfolio, account, or pooled fund.

Position trader   A trader who typically holds positions open overnight.

Positive relationship   A relationship between two variables that move in the same direction.

Potential GDP   The quantity of real GDP at full employment.

Posterior probability   An updated probability that reflects or comes after new information.

Potential credit risk   The risk associated with the possibility that a payment due at a later date will not be made.

Poverty   A situation in which a household's income is too low to be able to buy the quantities of food, shelter, and clothing that are deemed necessary.

Power of a test   The probability of correctly rejecting the null—that is, rejecting the null hypothesis when it is false.

Predatory pricing   Setting a low price to drive competitors out of business with the intention of setting a monopoly price when the competition has gone.

Preferences   A description of a person's likes and dislikes.

Preferred stock   An equity investment that stipulates the dividend payment either as a coupon or a stated dollar amount. The firm's directors may withhold payments.

Premium   A bond selling at a price above par value due to capital market conditions.

Present value   The amount of money that, if invested today, will grow to be as large as a given future amount when the interest that it will earn is taken into account.

Present value (PV)   (1) The current worth of future income after it is discounted to reflect the fact that revenues in the future are valued less highly than revenues now. (2) The current worth of a future cash flow. Obtained by discounting the future cash flow at the market-required rate of return. (3) The current (discounted) value of a future cash flow or flows.

Price ceiling   A regulation that makes it illegal to charge a price higher than a specified level.

Price continuity   A feature of a liquid market in which there are small price changes from one transaction to the next due to the depth of the market.

Price discovery   A feature of futures markets in which futures prices provide valuable information about the price of the underlying asset.

Price discrimination   The practice of selling different units of a good or service for different prices or of charging one customer different prices for different quantities bought.

Price/earnings (P/E) ratio   The number by which expected earnings per share is multiplied to estimate a stock's value; also called the *earnings multiplier*.

Price effect   The effect of a change in the price on the quantity of a good consumed, other things remaining the same.

Price elasticity of demand   A units-free measure of the responsiveness of the quantity demanded of a good to a change in its price, when all other influences on buyers' plans remain the same.

Price floor   A regulation that makes it illegal to charge a price lower than a specified level.

Price level   The average level of prices as measured by a price index.

Price limits   Limits imposed by a futures exchange on the price change that can occur from one day to the next.

Price momentum A portfolio strategy in which you acquire stocks that have enjoyed above-market stock price increases.

Price multiple The ratio of a stock's market price to some measure of value per share.

Price relative A ratio of an ending price over a beginning price; it is equal to 1 plus the holding period return on the asset.

Price risk The component of interest rate risk due to the uncertainty of the market price of a bond caused by changes in market interest rates.

Price taker A firm that cannot influence the price of the good or service it produces.

Price-weighted index An index calculated as an arithmetic mean of the current prices of the sampled securities.

Primary market The market in which newly issued securities are sold by their issuers, who receive the proceeds.

Principal-agent problem The problem of devising compensation rules that induce an agent to act in the best interest of a principal.

Prior probabilities Probabilities reflecting beliefs prior to the arrival of new information.

Private Equity Private equity includes, but is not limited to, organizations devoted to venture capital, leveraged buyouts, consolidations, mezzanine and distressed debt investments, and a variety of hybrids, such as venture leasing and venture factoring.

Private information Information that is available to one person but is too costly for anyone else to obtain.

Private placement A new issue sold directly to a small group of investors, usually institutions

Private sector surplus or deficit An amount equal to saving minus investment.

Probability A number between 0 and 1 describing the chance that a stated event will occur.

Probability density function A function with non-negative values such that probability can be described by areas under the curve graphing the function.

Probability distribution A distribution that specifies the probabilities of a random variable's possible outcomes.

Probability function A function that specifies the probability that the random variable takes on a specific value.

Producer surplus The price of a good minus the opportunity cost of producing it, summed over the quantity sold.

Product differentiation Making a product slightly different from the product of a competing firm.

Production efficiency A situation in which the economy cannot produce more of one good without producing less of some other good.

Production function The relationship between real GDP and the quantity of labor when all other influences on production remain the same.

Production method A method of depreciation that assumes depreciation is solely the result of use and that allocates depreciation based on the units of use or output during each period of an asset's useful life.

Production possibilities frontier The boundary between the combinations of goods and services that can be produced and the combinations that cannot.

Production quota An upper limit to the quantity of a good that may be produced in a specified period.

Productivity growth slowdown A slowdown in the growth rate of output per person.

Profit The income earned by entrepreneurship.

Property rights Social arrangements that govern the ownership, use, and disposal of resources or factors of production, goods, and services that are enforceable in the courts.

Prospective P/E *See* Leading P/E.

Protective put An option strategy in which a long position in an asset is combined with a long position in a put.

Public good A good or service that is both nonrival and nonexcludable—it can be consumed simultaneously by everyone and from which no one can be excluded.

Purchasing power parity The equal value of different monies.

Purchasing power parity (PPP) A theory stating that the exchange rate between two currencies will exactly reflect the purchasing power of the two currencies.

Pure discount instruments Instruments that pay interest as the difference between the amount borrowed and the amount paid back.

Put An option that gives the holder the right to sell an underlying asset to another party at a fixed price over a specific period of time.

Put option A contract giving the right to sell an asset at a specified price, on or before a specified date.

Put–call–forward parity The relationship among puts, calls, and forward contracts.

Put-call parity The relationship that must exist in an efficient market between the prices for put and call options having the same underlying asset, exercise price, and expiration date.

p-**Value**   The smallest level of significance at which the null hypothesis can be rejected; also called the marginal significance level.

Quality financial statements   Financial statements that most knowledgeable observers (analysts, portfolio managers) would consider conservatively prepared in terms of sales, expenses, earnings, and asset valuations. The results reported would reflect reasonable estimates and indicate what truly happened during the period and the legitimate value of assets and liabilities on the balance sheet.

Quantile (or fractile)   A value at or below which a stated fraction of the data lies.

Quantity demanded   The amount of a good or service that consumers plan to buy during a given time period at a particular price.

Quantity of labor demanded   The labor hours hired by the firms in the economy.

Quantity of labor supplied   The number of labor hours that all households in the economy plan to work.

Quantity supplied   The amount of a good or service that producers plan to sell during a given time period at a particular price.

Quantity theory of money   The proposition that in the long run, an increase in the quantity of money brings an equal percentage increase in the price level.

Quartiles   Quantiles that divide a distribution into four equal parts.

Quintiles   Quantiles that divide a distribution into five equal parts.

Quota   A quantitative restriction on the import of a particular good, which specifies the maximum amount that can be imported in a given time period.

Random number   An observation drawn from a uniform distribution.

Random number generator   An algorithm that produces uniformly distributed random numbers between 0 and 1.

Random variable   A quantity whose future outcomes are uncertain.

Random walk theory   (1) The theory that current stock prices already reflect known information about the future. Therefore, the future movement of stock prices will be determined by surprise occurrences. This will cause them to change in a random fashion. (2) A theory stating that all current information is reflected in current security prices and that future price movements are random because they are caused by unexpected news.

Range   The difference between the maximum and minimum values in a dataset.

Range forward   A trading strategy based on a variation of the put-call parity model where, for the same underlying asset but different exercise prices, a call option is purchased and a put option is sold (or vice versa).

Rational expectation   The most accurate forecast possible, a forecast that uses all the available information, including knowledge of the relevant economic forces that influence the variable being forecasted.

Ratio scales   A measurement scale that has all the characteristics of interval measurement scales as well as a true zero point as the origin.

Real business cycle theory   A theory that regards random fluctuations in productivity as the main source of economic fluctuations.

Real Estate   Real estate Investments include: (a) Wholly owned or partially owned properties, (b) Commingled funds, property unit trusts, and insurance company separate accounts, (c) Unlisted, private placement securities issued by private real estate investment trusts (REITs) and real estate operating companies (REOCs), and (d) Equity-oriented debt, such as participating mortgage loans or any private interest in a property where some portion of return to the investor at the time of investment is related to the performance of the underlying real estate.

Real estate investment trusts (REITs)   Investment funds that hold portfolios of real estate investments.

Real income   A household's income expressed as a quantity of goods that the household can afford to buy.

Real interest rate   The nominal interest rate adjusted for inflation; the nominal interest rate minus the inflation rate.

Realization Multiple (Private Equity)   The realization multiple (DPI) is calculated by dividing the cumulative distributions by the paid-in-capital.

Realized capital gains   Capital gains that result when an appreciated asset is sold; realized capital gains are taxable.

Real options   Options embedded in a firm's real assets that give managers valuable decision-making flexibility, such as the right to either undertake or abandon an investment project.

Real rate of interest   The money rate of interest minus the expected rate of inflation. The real rate of interest indicates the interest premium, in terms of real goods and services, that one must pay for earlier availability.

Real risk-free rate (RRFR) The basic interest rate with no accommodation for inflation or uncertainty. The pure time value of money.

Real wage rate The quantity of goods ands services that an hour's work can buy. It is equal to the money wage rate divided by the price level.

Receiver swaption A swaption that allows the holder to enter into a swap as the fixed-rate receiver and floating-rate payer.

Recession There are two common definitions of recession. They are (1) A business cycle phase in which real GDP decreases for at least two successive quarters. (2) A significant decline in activity spread across the economy, lasting for more than a few months, visible in industrial production, employment, real income, and wholesale-retail trade.

Recessionary gap The amount by which potential GDP exceeds real GDP.

Reference base period The period in which the CPI is defined to be 100.

Registered competitive market makers (RCMMs) Members of an exchange who are allowed to use their memberships to buy or sell for their own account within the specific trading obligations set down by the exchange.

Registered traders Members of the stock exchange who are allowed to use their memberships to buy and sell for their own account, which means they save commissions on their trading but they provide liquidity to the market, and they abide by exchange regulations on how they can trade.

Regression coefficients The intercept and slope coefficient(s) of a regression.

Regulation Rules administrated by a government agency to influence economic activity by determining prices, product standards and types, and conditions under which new firms may enter an industry.

Regulatory risk The risk associated with the uncertainty of how derivative transactions will be regulated or with changes in regulations.

Relative dispersion The amount of dispersion relative to a reference value or benchmark.

Relative frequency With reference to an interval of grouped data, the number of observations in the interval divided by the total number of observations in the sample.

Relative price The ratio of the price of one good or service to the price of another good or service. A relative price is an opportunity cost.

Renewable natural resources Natural resources that can be used repeatedly without depleting what is available for future use.

Rent The income that land earns.

Rent ceiling A regulation that makes it illegal to charge a rent higher than a specified level.

Rent seeking Any attempt to capture a consumer surplus, a producer surplus, or an economic profit.

Replacement value The market value of a swap.

Required rate of return The return that compensates investors for their time, the expected rate of inflation, and the uncertainty of the return.

Required reserve ratio The ratio of reserves to deposits that banks are required, by regulation, to hold.

Reserve ratio The fraction of a bank's total deposits that are held in reserves.

Reserves Cash in a bank's vault plus the bank's deposits at Federal Reserve banks.

Ricardo-Barro effect The equivalence of financing government purchases by taxes or by borrowing.

Residual value The estimated net scrap, salvage, or trade-in value of a tangible asset at the estimated date of its disposal. Also called *salvage value* or *disposal value*.

Resistance level A price at which a technician would expect a substantial increase in the supply of a stock to reverse a rising trend.

Return prediction studies Studies wherein investigations attempt to predict the time series of future rates of return using public information. An example would be predicting above-average returns for the stock market based on the aggregate dividend yield—e.g., high dividend yield indicates above average future market returns.

Revenue bond A bond that is serviced by the income generated from specific revenue-producing projects of the municipality.

Revenue expenditure An expenditure for ordinary repairs and maintenance of a long-term asset, which is recorded by a debit to an expense account.

Rising trend channel The range defined by security prices as they move progressively higher.

Risk averse The assumption about investors that they will choose the least risky alternative, all else being equal.

Risk-free asset An asset with returns that exhibit zero variance.

Risk management The process of identifying the level of risk an entity wants, measuring the level of risk the entity currently has, taking actions that bring the actual level of risk to the desired level of risk, and monitoring the new actual level of risk so that it continues to be aligned with the desired level of risk.

Risk-neutral probabilities Weights that are used to compute a binomial option price. They are the probabilities that would apply if a risk-neutral investor valued an option.

Risk-neutral valuation The process by which options and other derivatives are priced by treating investors as though they were risk neutral.

Risk premium (1) The difference between the expected return on an asset and the risk-free interest rate. (2) The increase over the nominal risk-free rate that investors demand as compensation for an investment's uncertainty. (3) The expected return on an investment minus the risk-free rate.

Risk premium (RP) The increase over the nominal risk-free rate that investors demand as compensation for an investment's uncertainty.

Risky asset An asset with uncertain future returns.

Rival A good or services or a resource is rival if its use by one person decreases the quantity available for someone else.

Robust The quality of being relatively unaffected by a violation of assumptions.

Runs test A test of the weak-form efficient market hypothesis that checks for trends that persist longer in terms of positive or negative price changes than one would expect for a random series.

Safety-first rules Rules for portfolio selection that focus on the risk that portfolio value will fall below some minimum acceptable level over some time horizon.

Sample A subset of a population.

Sample excess kurtosis A sample measure of the degree of a distribution's peakedness in excess of the normal distribution's peakedness.

Sample kurtosis A sample measure of the degree of a distribution's peakedness.

Sample mean The sum of the sample observations, divided by the sample size.

Sample selection bias Bias introduced by systematically excluding some members of the population according to a particular attribute—for example, the bias introduced when data availability leads to certain observations being excluded from the analysis.

Sample skewness A sample measure of degree of asymmetry of a distribution.

Sample standard deviation The positive square root of the sample variance.

Sample statistic or statistic A quantity computed from or used to describe a sample.

Sample variance A sample measure of the degree of dispersion of a distribution, calculated by dividing the sum of the squared deviations from the sample mean by the sample size (n) minus 1.

Sampling (1) A technique for constructing a passive index portfolio in which the portfolio manager buys a representative sample of stocks that comprise the benchmark index. (2) The process of obtaining a sample.

Sampling distribution The distribution of all distinct possible values that a statistic can assume when computed from samples of the same size randomly drawn from the same population.

Sampling error The difference between the observed value of a statistic and the quantity it is intended to estimate.

Sampling plan The set of rules used to select a sample.

Sandwich spread An option strategy that is equivalent to a short butterfly spread.

Saving The amount of income that households have left after they have paid their taxes and bought their consumption goods and services.

Savings and loan association (S&L) A depository institution that receives checking deposits and savings deposits and that makes personal, commercial, and home-purchase loans.

Savings bank A depository institution, owned by its depositors, that accepts savings deposits and makes mortgage loans.

Saving supply The relationship between saving and the real interest rate, other things remaining the same.

Scalper A trader who offers to buy or sell futures contracts, holding the position for only a brief period of time. Scalpers attempt to profit by buying at the bid price and selling at the higher ask price.

Scarcity Our inability to satisfy all our wants.

Scatter diagram A diagram that plots the value of one economic variable against the value of another.

Scatter plot A two-dimensional plot of pairs of observations on two data series.

Scenario analysis A risk management technique involving the examination of the performance of a portfolio under specified situations. Closely related to stress testing.

Search activity The time spent looking for someone with whom to do business.

Seasoned equity issues New equity shares offered by firms that already have stock outstanding.

Seats Memberships in a derivatives exchange.

Secondary market The market in which outstanding securities are bought and sold by owners other than the issuers. Purpose is to provide liquidity for investors.

Sector rotation strategy An active strategy that involves purchasing stocks in specific industries or stocks with specific characteristics (low *P/E*, growth, value) that are anticipated to rise in value more than the overall market.

Security market line (SML) The line that reflects the combination of risk and return of alternative investments. In CAPM, risk is measured by systematic risk (beta).

SelectNet An order-routing and trade-execution system for institutional investors (brokers and dealers) that allows communication through the Nasdaq system rather than by phone.

Self-interest The choices that you think are the best for you.

Semideviation The positive square root of semivariance (sometimes called semistandard deviation).

Semilogarithmic Describes a scale constructed so that equal intervals on the vertical scale represent equal rates of change, and equal intervals on the horizontal scale represent equal amounts of change.

Semivariance The average squared deviation below the mean.

Separation theorem The proposition that the investment decision, which involves investing in the market portfolio on the capital market line, is separate from the financing decision, which targets a specific point on the CML based on the investor's risk preference.

Settlement date or payment date The date on which the parties to a swap make payments.

Settlement period The time between settlement dates.

Settlement price The price determined by the exchange clearinghouse with which futures contract margin accounts are marked to market.

Settlement risk When settling a contract, the risk that one party could be in the process of paying the counterparty while the counterparty is declaring bankruptcy.

Shareholders' equity Total assets minus total liabilities.

Sharpe measure A relative measure of a portfolio's benefit-to-risk ratio, calculated as its average return in excess of the risk-free rate divided by the standard deviation of portfolio returns.

Sharpe ratio (1) The ratio of mean excess return (return minus the risk-free rate) to standard deviation of returns (or excess returns). (2) The average return in excess of the risk-free rate divided by the standard deviation of return; a measure of the average excess return earned per unit of standard deviation of return.

Shortfall risk The risk that portfolio value will fall below some minimum acceptable level over some time horizon.

Short hedge A short position in a forward or futures contract used to offset the price volatility of a long position in the underlying asset.

Short position The seller of a commodity or security or, for a forward contract, the counterparty who will be the eventual seller of the underlying asset.

Short run The short run in microeconomics has two meanings. For the firm, it is the period of time in which the quantity of at least one input is fixed and the quantities of the other inputs can be varied. The fixed input is usually capital—that is, the firm has a given plant size. For the industry, the short run is the period of time in which each firm has a given plant size and the number of firms in the industry is fixed.

Short-run aggregate supply curve A curve that shows the relationship between the quantity of real GDP supplied and the price level in the short run when the money wage rate, other resource prices, and potential GDP remain constant.

Short-run industry supply curve A curve that shows the quantity supplied by the industry at each price varies when the plant size of each firm and the number of firms in the industry remain the same.

Short-run macroeconomic equilibrium A situation that occurs when the quantity of real GDP demanded equals quantity of real GDP supplied—at the point of intersection of the *AD* curve and the *SAS* curve.

Short-run Phillips curve A curve that shows the tradeoff between inflation and unemployment, when the expected inflation rate and the natural rate of unemployment remain the same.

Short sale The sale of borrowed securities with the intention of repurchasing them later at a lower price and earning the difference.

Should Encouraged (recommended) to follow the recommendation of the GIPS standards but not required.

Shutdown point The output and price at which the firm just covers its total variable cost. In the short run, the firm is indifferent between producing the profit-maximizing output and shutting down temporarily.

Signal An action taken by an informed person (or firm) to send a message to uninformed people or an action taken outside a market that conveys information that can be used by that market.

Simple interest The interest earned each period on the original investment; interest calculated on the principal only.

Simple random sample A subset of a larger population created in such a way that each element of the population has an equal probability of being selected to the subset.

Simulation trial A complete pass through the steps of a simulation.

Single-price monopoly A monopoly that must sell each unit of its output for a same price to all its customers.

Sinking fund (1) Bond provision that requires the bond to be paid off progressively rather than in full at maturity. (2) Bond provision that requires the issuer to redeem some or all of the bond systematically over the term of the bond rather than in full at maturity.

Skewed Not symmetrical.

Skewness A quantitative measure of skew (lack of symmetry); a synonym of skew.

Slope The change in the value of the variable measured on the y-axis divided by the change in the value of the variable measured on the x-axis.

Small-firm effect A frequent empirical anomaly where risk-adjusted stock returns for companies with low market capitalization (i.e., share price multiplied by number of outstanding shares) are significantly larger than those generated by high market capitalization (large cap) firms.

Small-Order Execution System (SOES) A quotation and execution system for retail (nonprofessional) investors who place orders with brokers who must honor their prevailing bid-ask for automatic execution up to 1,000 shares.

Social interest Choices that are the best for society as a whole.

Soft dollars A form of compensation to a money manager generated when the manager commits the investor to paying higher brokerage fees in exchange for the manager receiving additional services (e.g., stock research) from the brokcr.

Software Capitalized costs associated with computer programs developed for sale, lease, or internal use and amortized over the estimated economic life of the programs.

Sovereign risk The risk that a government may default on its debt.

Spearman rank correlation coefficient A measure of correlation applied to ranked data.

Specialist The major market maker on U.S. stock exchanges who acts as a broker or dealer to ensure the liquidity and smooth functions of the secondary stock market.

Speculative company A firm with a great degree of business and/or financial risk, with commensurate high earnings potential.

Speculative stock A stock that appears to be highly overpriced compared to its intrinsic valuation.

Spending phase Phase in the investment life cycle during which individuals' earning years end as they retire. They pay for expenses with income from social security and returns from prior investments and invest to protect against inflation.

Spot price Current market price of an asset. Also called cash price.

Spot rate The required yield for a cash flow to be received at some specific date in the future—for example, the spot rate for a flow to be received in one year, for a cash flow in two years, and so on.

Spread An option strategy involving the purchase of one option and sale of another option that is identical to the first in all respects except either exercise price or expiration.

Spurious correlation A correlation that misleadingly points towards associations between variables.

Stagflation The combination of recession and inflation.

Standard deviation A measure of variability equal to the square root of the variance.

Standardizing A transformation that involves subtracting the mean and dividing the result by the standard deviation.

Standard normal distribution (or unit normal distribution) The normal density with mean (μ) equal to 0 and standard deviation (σ) equal to 1.

Stated annual interest rate or quoted interest rate A quoted interest rate that does not account for compounding within the year.

Statement of cash flows A financial statement that shows how a company's operating, investing, and financing activities have affected cash during an accounting period.

Statistic A quantity computed from or used to describe a sample of data.

Statistical inference Making forecasts, estimates, or judgments about a larger group from a smaller group actually observed; using a sample statistic to infer the value of an unknown population parameter.

Statistically significant A result indicating that the null hypothesis can be rejected; with reference to an estimated regression coefficient, frequently understood to mean a result indicating that the corresponding population regression coefficient is different from 0.

Statistics The science of describing, analyzing, and drawing conclusions from data; also, a collection of numerical data.

Stock A quantity that exists at a point in time.

Stock dividend A dividend paid in the form of additional shares rather than in cash.

Stock split An action taken by a firm to increase the number of shares outstanding, such as doubling the number of shares outstanding by giving each stockholder two new shares for each one formerly held.

Storage costs or carrying costs The costs of holding an asset, generally a function of the physical characteristics of the underlying asset.

Straddle An option strategy involving the purchase of a put and a call with the same exercise price. A straddle is based on the expectation of high volatility of the underlying.

Straight-line method A method of depreciation that assumes depreciation depends only on the passage of time and that allocates an equal amount of depreciation to each accounting period in an asset's useful life.

Strangle A variation of a straddle in which the put and call have different exercise prices.

Strap An option strategy involving the purchase of two calls and one put.

Strategies All the possible actions of each player in a game.

Stratified random sampling A procedure by which a population is divided into subpopulations (strata) based on one or more classification criteria. Simple random samples are then drawn from each stratum in sizes proportional to the relative size of each stratum in the population. These samples are then pooled.

Stress testing A risk management technique in which the risk manager examines the performance of the portfolio under market conditions involving high risk and usually high correlations across markets. Closely related to scenario analysis.

Stress testing/scenario analysis A set of techniques for estimating losses in extremely unfavorable combinations of events or scenarios.

Strike price Price at which an option can be exercised (same as exercise price).

Strip An option strategy involving the purchase of two puts and one call.

Structural change Economic trend occurring when the economy is undergoing a major change in organization or in how it functions.

Structural surplus or deficit The budget balance that would occur if the economy were at full employment and real GDP were equal to potential GDP.

Structural unemployment The unemployment that arises when changes in technology or international competition change the skills needed to perform jobs or change the locations of jobs.

Structured note (1) A bond or note issued with some unusual, often option-like, clause. (2) A bond with an embedded derivative designed to create a payoff distribution that satisfies the needs of a specific investor clientele. (3) A variation of a floating-rate note that has some type of unusual characteristic such as a leverage factor or in which the rate moves opposite to interest rates.

Style analysis An attempt to explain the variability in the observed returns to a security portfolio in terms of the movements in the returns to a series of benchmark portfolios designed to capture the essence of a particular security characteristic such as size, value, and growth.

Subjective probability A probability drawing on personal or subjective judgment.

Subsidy A payment that the government makes to a producer.

Substitute A good that can be used in place of another good.

Substitution effect The effect of a change in price of a good or service on the quantity bought when the consumer (hypothetically) remains indifferent between the original and the new consumption situations—that is, the consumer remains on the same indifference curve.

Successful efforts accounting A method of accounting for the costs of exploring and developing oil and gas resources in which successful exploration is recorded as an asset and depleted over the estimated life of the resource and all unsuccessful efforts are immediately written off as losses.

Sunk cost The past cost of buying a plant that has no resale value.

Supplemental Information Any performance-related information included as part of a compliant performance presentation that supplements or enhances the required and/or recommended disclosure and presentation provisions of the GIPS standards.

Supply The relationship between the quantity of a good that producers plan to sell and the price of the good when all other influences on sellers' plans remain the same. It is described by a supply schedule and illustrated by a supply curve.

Supply curve A curve that shows the relationship between the quantity supplied and the price of a good when all other influences on producers' planned sales remain the same.

Supply of labor The relationship between the quantity of labor supplied and the real wage rate when all other influences on work plans remain the same.

Supply-side effects The effects of fiscal policy on employment, potential GDP, and aggregate supply.

Support level A price at which a technician would expect a substantial increase in price and volume for a stock to reverse a declining trend that was due to profit taking.

Survivorship bias The bias resulting from a test design that fails to account for companies that have gone bankrupt, merged, or are otherwise no longer reported in a database.

Sustainable growth rate A measure of how fast a firm can grow using internal equity and debt financing and a constant capital structure. Equal to retention rate _ ROE.

Swap (1) A contract whereby two parties agree to a periodic exchange of cash flows. In certain types of swaps, only the net difference between the amounts owed is exchanged on each payment date. (2) An agreement between two parties to exchange a series of future cash flows.

Swap spread The difference between the fixed rate on an interest rate swap and the rate on a Treasury note with equivalent maturity; it reflects the general level of credit risk in the market.

Swaption (1) An option to enter into a swap contract at a later date. (2) An option to enter into a swap.

SWOT analysis An examination of a firm's Strengths, Weaknesses, Opportunities, and Threats. This analysis helps an analyst evaluate a firm's strategies to exploit its competitive advantages or defend against its weaknesses.

Symmetry principle A requirement that people in similar situations be treated similarly.

Synthetic call The combination of puts, the underlying, and risk-free bonds that replicates a call option.

Synthetic forward contract The combination of the underlying, puts, calls, and risk-free bonds that replicates a forward contract.

Synthetic put The combination of calls, the underlying, and risk-free bonds that replicates a put option.

Systematic risk The variability of returns that is due to macroeconomic factors that affect all risky assets. Because it affects all risky assets, it cannot be eliminated by diversification.

Systematic sampling A procedure of selecting every *k*th member until reaching a sample of the desired size. The sample that results from this procedure should be approximately random.

Tangible assets Long-term assets that have physical substance.

Tangible book value per share Common shareholders' equity minus intangible assets from the balance sheet, divided by the number of shares outstanding.

Tap Procedure by which a borrower can keep issuing additional amounts of an old bond at its current market value. This procedure is used for bond issues, notably by the British and French governments, as well as for some short-term debt instruments.

Target semideviation The positive square root of target semivariance.

Target semivariance The average squared deviation below a target value.

Tariff A tax that is imposed by the importing country when an imported good crosses its international boundary.

Tax incidence The division of the burden of a tax between the buyer and the seller.

Tax multiplier The magnification effect of a change in taxes on aggregate demand.

Tax wedge The gap between the before-tax and after-tax wage rates.

Taylor rule A rule that adjusts the federal funds rate to target the inflation rate and to take into account deviations of the inflation rate from its target and deviations of real GDP from potential GDP.

Technical analysis Estimation of future security price movements based on past price and volume movements.

Technological change The development of new goods and better ways of producing goods and services.

Technological efficiency A situation that occurs when the firm produces a given output by using the least amount of inputs.

Technology Any method of producing a good or service.

***t*-Distribution** A symmetrical distribution defined by a single parameter, degrees of freedom, that is largely used to make inferences concerning the mean of a normal distribution whose variance is unknown.

Temporary New Account A tool that firms can use to remove the effect of significant cash flows on a portfolio. When a significant cash flow occurs in a portfolio, the firm may treat this cash flow as a "temporary new account," allowing the firm to implement the mandate of the portfolio without the impact of the cash flow on the performance of the portfolio.

Termination date The date of the final payment on a swap; also, the swap's expiration date.

Terms of trade The quantity of goods and services that a country exports to pay for its imports of goods and services.

Term structure of interest rates The relationship between term to maturity and yield to maturity for a sample of comparable bonds at a given time. Popularly known as the *yield curve.*

Term to maturity Specifies the date or the number of years before a bond matures or expires.

Test statistic A quantity, calculated based on a sample, whose value is the basis for deciding whether or not to reject the null hypothesis.

Theta The rate at which an option's time value decays.

Third market Over-the-counter trading of securities listed on an exchange.

Thrift institutions Thrift institutions include savings and loan associations, savings banks, and credit unions.

Tick The minimum price movement for the asset underlying a forward or futures contract; for Treasury bonds, one tick equals 1/32 of 1 percent of par value.

Time-period bias The possibility that when we use a time-series sample, our statistical conclusion may be sensitive to the starting and ending dates of the sample.

Time-series analysis An examination of a firm's performance data over a period of time.

Time-series data Observations of a variable over time.

Time-series graph A graph that measures time (for example, months or years) on the *x*-axis and the variable or variables in which we are interested on the *y*-axis.

Time to expiration The time remaining in the life of a derivative, typically expressed in years.

Time value decay The loss in the value of an option resulting from movement of the option price toward its payoff value as the expiration day approaches.

Time-weighted rate of return (1) The compound rate of growth of one unit of currency invested in a portfolio during a stated measurement period; a measure of investment performance that is not sensitive to the timing and amount of withdrawals or additions to the portfolio. (2) Calculation that computes period-by-period returns on an investment and removes the effects of external cash flows, which are generally client-driven, and best reflects the firm's ability to manage assets according to a specified strategy or objective.

Total cost The cost of all the productive resources that a firm uses.

Total Firm Assets Total firm assets are all assets for which a firm has investment management responsibility. Total firm assets include assets managed outside the firm (e.g., by subadvisors) for which the firm has asset allocation authority.

Total fixed cost The cost of the firm's fixed inputs.

Total probability rule for expected value A rule explaining the expected value of a random variable in terms of expected values of the random variable conditional on mutually exclusive and exhaustive scenarios.

Total product The total output produced by a firm in a given period of time.

Total return A return objective in which the investor wants to increase the portfolio value to meet a future need by both capital gains and current income reinvestment.

Total revenue The value of a firm's sales. It is calculated as the price of the good multiplied by the quantity sold.

Total revenue test A method of estimating the price elasticity of demand by observing the change in total revenue that results from a change in the price, when all other influences on the quantity sold remain the same.

Total variable cost The cost of all the firm's variable inputs.

Tracking error (1) The standard deviation of the difference in returns between an active investment portfolio and its benchmark portfolio; also called tracking error volatility. (2) The condition in which the performance of a portfolio does not match the performance of an index that serves as the portfolio's benchmark. (3) A synonym for tracking risk and active risk; also, the total return on a portfolio (gross of fees) minus the total return on a benchmark.

Tracking risk The standard deviation of the differences between a portfolio's returns and its benchmark's returns; a synonym of active risk.

Trade balance The balance of a country's exports and imports; part of the current account.

Trade Date Accounting The transaction is reflected in the portfolio on the date of the purchase or sale, and not on the settlement date. Recognizing the asset or liability within at least 3 days of the date the transaction is entered into (Trade Date, T + 1, T + 2 or T + 3) all satisfy the trade date accounting requirement for purposes of the GIPS standards. (See settlement date accounting.)

Trademark A registered symbol that can be used only by its owner to identify a product or service.

Tradeoff An exchange—giving up one thing to get something else.

Trading effect The difference in performance of a bond portfolio from that of a chosen index due to short-run changes in the composition of the portfolio.

Trading Expenses The costs of buying or selling a security. These costs typically take the form of brokerage commissions or spreads from either internal or external brokers. Custody fees charged per transaction should be considered custody fees and not direct transaction costs. Estimated trading expenses are not permitted.

Trading rule A formula for deciding on current transactions based on historical data.

Trading turnover The percentage of outstanding shares traded during a period of time.

Trailing P/E (or current P/E) A stock's current market price divided by the most recent four quarters of earnings per share.

Tranche Refers to a portion of an issue that is designed for a specific category of investors. French for "slice."

Transaction cost The cost of executing a trade. Low costs characterize an operationally efficient market.

Transaction Expenses (Private Equity) Include all legal, financial, advisory, and investment banking fees related to buying, selling, restructuring, and recapitalizing portfolio companies.

Transactions costs The costs that arise from finding someone with whom to do business, of reaching an agreement about the price and other aspects of the exchange, and of ensuring that the terms of the agreement are fulfilled. The opportunity costs of conducting a transaction.

Treasury bill A negotiable U.S. government security with a maturity of less than one year that pays no periodic interest but yields the difference between its par value and its discounted purchase price.

Treasury bond A U.S. government security with a maturity of more than 10 years that pays interest periodically.

Treasury note A U.S. government security with maturities of 1 to 10 years that pays interest periodically.

Tree diagram A diagram with branches emanating from nodes representing either mutually exclusive chance events or mutually exclusive decisions.

Trend The general tendency for a variable to move in one direction.

Trimmed mean A mean computed after excluding a stated small percentage of the lowest and highest observations.

_t_-Test A hypothesis test using a statistic (_t_-statistic) that follows a _t_-distribution.

Two-sided hypothesis test (or two-tailed hypothesis test) A test in which the null hypothesis is rejected in favor of the alternative hypothesis if the evidence indicates that the population parameter is either smaller or larger than a hypothesized value.

Type I error The error of rejecting a true null hypothesis.

Type II error The error of not rejecting a false null hypothesis.

Unbiasedness Lack of bias. A desirable property of estimators, an unbiased estimator is one whose expected value (the mean of its sampling distribution) equals the parameter it is intended to estimate.

Uncertainty A situation in which more than one event might occur but it is not known which one.

Unconditional probability (or marginal probability) The probability of an event not conditioned on another event.

Uncovered interest rate parity The assertion that expected currency depreciation should offset the interest differential between two countries over the term of the interest rate.

Underlying (1) Refers to a security on which a derivative contract is written. (2) An asset that trades in a market in which buyers and sellers meet, decide on a price, and the seller then delivers the asset to the buyer and receives payment. The underlying is the asset or other derivative on which a particular derivative is based. The market for the underlying is also referred to as the spot market.

Underweighted A condition in which a portfolio, for whatever reason, includes less of a class of securities than the relative market value alone would justify.

Unemployment rate The percentage of the people in the labor force who are unemployed.

Unit elastic demand Demand with a price elasticity of 1; the percentage change in the quantity demanded equals the percentage change in price.

Unit normal distribution _See_ Standard normal distribution.

Univariate distribution A distribution that specifies the probabilities for a single random variable.

Unrealized capital gains Capital gains that reflect the price appreciation of currently held unsold assets.

Unsystematic risk Risk that is unique to an asset, derived from its particular characteristics. It can be eliminated in a diversified portfolio.

Unweighted index An indicator series affected equally by the performance of each security in the sample regardless of price or market value. Also referred to as an _equal-weighted series_.

Unwind The negotiated termination of a forward or futures position before contract maturity.

Up transition probability The probability that an asset's value moves up.

U.S. interest rate differential A gap equal to the U.S. interest rate minus the foreign interest rate.

U.S. Official reserves   The government's holdings of foreign currency.

Utilitarianism   A principle that states that we should strive to achieve "the greatest happiness for the greatest number of people."

Utility   The benefit or satisfaction that a person gets from the consumption of a good or service.

Utility of wealth   The amount of utility that a person attaches to a given amount of wealth.

Value   The maximum amount that a person is willing to pay for a good. The value of one more unit of the good or service is its marginal benefit.

Valuation   The process of determining the value of an asset or service.

Valuation analysis   An active bond portfolio management strategy designed to capitalize on expected price increases in temporarily undervalued issues.

Valuation process   Part of the investment decision process in which you estimate the value of a security.

Value at risk (VaR)   (1) A money measure of the minimum loss that is expected over a given period of time with a given probability. (2) A probability-based measure of loss potential for a company, a fund, a portfolio, a transaction, or a strategy over a specified period of time. (3) A money measure of the minimum value of losses expected during a specified time period at a given level of probability.

Value chain   The set of transformations to move from raw material to product or service delivery.

Value stocks   Stocks that appear to be undervalued for reasons besides earnings growth potential. These stocks are usually identified based on high dividend yields, low *P/E* ratios, or low price-to-book ratios.

Value-weighted index   An index calculated as the total market value of the securities in the sample. Market value is equal to the number of shares or bonds outstanding times the market price of the security.

Variance   The expected value (the probability-weighted average) of squared deviations from a random variable's expected value.

Variation margin   Profits or losses on open positions in futures and option contracts that are paid or collected daily.

Vega   The relationship between option price and volatility.

Velocity of circulation   The average number of times a dollar of money is used annually to buy the goods and services that make up GDP.

Venture Capital (Private Equity)   Risk capital in the form of equity and/or loan capital that is provided by an investment institution to back a business venture that is expected to grow in value.

Vintage Year (Private Equity)   The year that the venture capital or private equity fund or partnership first draws down or calls capital from its investors.

Volatility   (1) A measure of the uncertainty about the future price of an asset. Typically measured by the standard deviation of returns on the asset. (2) As used in option pricing, the standard deviation of the continuously compounded returns on the underlying asset.

Voluntary export restraint   An agreement between two governments in which the government of the exporting country agrees to restrain the volume of its own exports.

Wages   The income that labor earns.

Warrant   An instrument that allows the holder to purchase a specified number of shares of the firm's common stock from the firm at a specified price for a given period of time.

Weak-form efficient market hypothesis   The belief that security prices fully reflect all security market information.

Wealth   The market value of all the things that people own.

Weighted-average cost of capital   A weighted average of the after-tax required rates of return on a company's common stock, preferred stock, and long-term debt, where the weights are the fraction of each source of financing in the company's target capital structure.

Weighted mean   An average in which each observation is weighted by an index of its relative importance.

Winsorized mean   A mean computed after assigning a stated percent of the lowest values equal to one specified low value, and a stated percent of the highest values equal to one specified high value.

Working-age population   The total number of people aged 16 years and over who are not in jail, hospital, or some other form of institutional care.

Working capital management   The management of a company's short-term assets (such as inventory) and short-term liabilities (such as money owed to suppliers).

World Trade Organization   An international organization that places greater obligations on its member countries to observe the GATT rules.

Yankee bonds   Bonds sold in the United States and denominated in U.S. dollars but issued by a foreign firm or government.

Yield   The promised rate of return on an investment under certain assumptions.

Yield spread   The difference between the promised yields of alternative bond issues or market segments at a given time relative to yields on Treasury issues of equal maturity.

Yield to maturity The total yield on a bond obtained by equating the bond's current market value to the discounted cash flows promised by the bond. Also called actuarial yield.

Yield to worst Given a bond with multiple potential maturity dates and prices due to embedded call options, the practice is to calculate a yield to maturity for each of the call dates and prices and select the lowest yield (the most conservative possible yield) as yield to worst.

Zero-cost collar A transaction in which a position in the underlying is protected by buying a put and selling a call with the premium from the sale of the call offsetting the premium from the purchase of the put. It can also be used to protect a floating-rate borrower against interest rate increases with the premium on a long cap offsetting the premium on a short floor.

45/8 411/16 — 3/8
51/2 51/2 — 3/8
51/2 213/16 — 1/8
205/8 181/8 + 7/8
173/8 61/2 — 1/2
191/2 61/2 — 1/8
71/4 6 1/2 31/32 —
15/16 9/8
9/16
9/32 715/16
715/16 713/16 715/16
25/8 211/32 21/2 +
23/4 21/4 21/4
61/6 121/16 113/8 113/4 +
87 333/4 33 331/8 —
802 255/8 249/16 253/8 +
833 12 115/8 117/8 +
16 101/2 101/2 101/2 —
78 157/8 1513/16 157/8 —
308 91/16 81/4 87/8 —
130 111/4 101/8 101/8
47/8

INDEX

Page numbers followed by n refer to footnotes.